HCCA®
Health Care Compliance
Association

S0-DSB-225

COMPLETE
HEALTHCARE
COMPLIANCE
MANUAL

Volume 2

2023

Complete Healthcare Compliance Manual is published by Society of Corporate Compliance and Ethics & Health Care Compliance Association, Eden Prairie, MN.

Copyright © 2023 by Society of Corporate Compliance and Ethics & Health Care Compliance Association. Printed in the United States of America. All rights reserved. This book or parts thereof may not be reproduced in any form without express written permission of the publisher.

ISBN 979-8-9851272-2-5

Editor: Karen Latchana Kenney
Copy Editor: Kathleen Kimball-Baker
Designer: Craig Micke

This publication is designed to provide accurate, comprehensive, and authoritative information on the subject matter covered. However, the publisher does not warrant that information contained herein is complete or accurate. This book is published with the understanding that the publisher is not engaged in rendering legal or other professional services. If legal advice or other expert assistance is required, the services of a competent professional should be sought.

Society of Corporate Compliance and Ethics & Health Care Compliance Association
6462 City West Parkway
Eden Prairie, MN 55344
p+ 952.567.6210 or 888.277.4977
hcca-info.org | helpteam@hcca-info.org

Table of Contents

Volume 1

Chapter 4   Evaluation Processes, Investigations, and Noncompliance Response · 391

Volume 2

Chapter 5

Key Laws in Healthcare Compliance

Anti-Kickback Statute

By Gabriel Imperato,[1] Esq., CHC; Anne Novick Branan,[2] Esq., CHC; Richard Sena[3]; and Megan Speltz,[4] JD

Fast Facts

Title of law: The Anti-Kickback Statute, Criminal penalties for acts involving Federal health care programs

Categories:

- Fraud and abuse
- Medicare
- Medicaid

U.S. Code: 42 U.S.C. § 1320a-7b(b)

Year enacted: 1972

Major amendments: 1977, 1980, 1987 (safe harbors implemented), 1996, 1997, 2003, 2010, 2015, 2018

Enforcement agencies: U.S. Department of Justice (DOJ), U.S. Department of Health & Human Services (HHS), Office of Inspector General (OIG), Centers for Medicare & Medicaid Services (CMS)

Link to full text of law: https://www.govinfo.gov/content/pkg/USCODE-2018-title42/pdf/USCODE-2018-title42-chap7-subchapXI-partA-sec1320a-7b.pdf

Applies to: Any medical providers accepting payment through government health-care programs.

What Is the Anti-Kickback Statute?

The Anti-Kickback Statute (AKS) is a federal criminal statute prohibiting transactions intended to induce or reward referrals for items or services reimbursed by federal healthcare programs. It provides both criminal and civil penalties for violations of the statute. If "one purpose" of the transaction is to induce referrals, then the entire transaction is tainted. This statute is designed to protect federal healthcare program beneficiaries from referral decisions based on monetary influence.

The purposes of the statute include:

- To prevent inappropriate medical referrals by providers who may be unduly influenced by financial incentives.
- To prevent overutilization and increased federal healthcare program costs.
- To prevent unfair competition.
- To ensure the proper reporting of costs to the government.

Safe Harbors

The law includes safe harbors, which are forms of payment and business practices that may appear to violate the Anti-Kickback Statute but are protected if the party in question meets various tests to qualify. Examples of protected practices include:

- Space rental
- Equipment rental
- Electronic health records items and services
- Electronic prescribing items and services
- Discounts
- Health centers
- Payments made to bona fide employees
- Personal services and management contracts
- Warranties
- Investment interests
- Referral services
- Practitioner recruitment
- Ambulatory surgical centers[5]

History

The Anti-Kickback Statute was originally enacted as part of the Social Security Amendments of 1972. Before 1972, only one provision prohibited false claims and misrepresentation to the government, and the statute's language made it difficult to prosecute Medicare and Medicaid fraud. Despite the update to the AKS, Medicare and Medicaid abuse continued to rise, resulting in new amendments being added to further discourage fraudulent activity.

The original statute made the receipt of kickbacks, bribes, or rebates in connection with items or services covered by Medicare and Medicaid programs a misdemeanor punishable by a fine, imprisonment, or both. In 1977, the Medicare-Medicaid Anti-Fraud and Abuse Amendments increased the penalty for violating the AKS from a misdemeanor to a felony to discourage Medicare and Medicaid fraud. In 1980, the statute was updated to require proof that the defendant acted "knowingly and willfully."[6]

The Medicare and Medicaid Patient and Program Protection Act (MMPPPA) was passed in 1987, which also made two important changes to the AKS.[7] First, the OIG was granted authority to exclude violators of the AKS from participating in federal health care programs. Second, the legislation directed HHS to promulgate regulations that created additional exceptions to the AKS, which would become known as "safe harbors." The first series of "safe harbor" regulations were implemented in 1991. In 1996, Congress further amended the AKS through the Health Insurance Portability and Accountability Act (HIPAA), primarily by expanding the law to cover all federal health care programs rather than just Medicare and state health care programs, adding a new exception relating to certain risk-sharing organizations, and enhancing communication between the OIG and public about the applicability of the AKS to certain transactions. One year later, Congress added a civil monetary penalty. Finally, the Patient Protection and Affordable Care Act of 2010 amended the intent requirement to clarify that the government no longer had to prove that the defendant intended to violate the law.[8]

Related Laws

Cal. Bus. & Prof. Code § 650 (West 2019)—Unearned rebates, refunds, and discounts.

- Prohibits state medical professionals to offer, deliver, or receive compensation for referring healthcare services.

Cal. Welf. & Inst. Code § 14107.2(a)-(b) (West 2019)—Renumeration for healthcare services.

- Prohibits anyone from receiving or paying any remuneration for referrals of healthcare services covered by the state healthcare system.

Cal. Health & Safety Code § 445 (West 2019)—Patient referrals.

- Prohibits anyone from profiting from referring patients to a healthcare provider.

Fla. Stat. § 456.054(2)(3)(a)—Renumeration and solicitation of patient referrals.

- Prohibits healthcare providers to "pay, solicit, or receive a kickback" as money or other compensation for referring or soliciting patients.

- Persons or entities are prohibited from paying or receiving commissions, bonuses, kickbacks, or rebates, and from engaging in split-fee arrangements with certain healthcare providers for referrals to clinical laboratories.

N.Y. Soc. Serv. Law § 366-d(2) (McKinney 2019)—Renumeration and solicitation of patients, facilities, goods.

- Prohibits healthcare providers from soliciting, receiving, or agreeing to receive or accept payment from persons for Medicaid patients or for the purchase, lease, or order of any goods, facility, service, or item covered under Medicaid.

Texas Occ. Code Ann. § 102.001(a) (West 2019)—Renumeration for solicitation of patients.

- Prohibits persons from offering to pay or accept, or paying or receiving renumeration, for soliciting patients for healthcare providers.

Anti-Kickback Statute Compliance Risks

The Anti-Kickback Statute is important to compliance professionals because violations expose healthcare organizations to criminal liability, including prison time for persons directly involved in violations. Healthcare organizations found liable for illegal renumeration or illegal patient admittance and retention practices are subject to up to $100,000 in fines, and those involved may be imprisoned for up to 10 years. Additionally, the AKS includes liability for false claims, and healthcare organizations that violate the AKS are likely to have also violated the False Claims Act. The following are specific AKS risk areas that compliance professionals need to monitor closely.

Risk Area: Making False Statements or Representations

42 U.S.C. § 1320a-7b(a)(1)–(6)

Whoever—

1. knowingly and willfully makes or causes to be made any false statement or representation of a material fact in any application for any benefit or payment under a Federal health care program (as defined in subsection (f)),

2. at any time knowingly and willfully makes or causes to be made any false statement or representation of a material fact for use in determining rights to such benefit or payment,

3. having knowledge of the occurrence of any event affecting (A) his initial or continued right to any such benefit or payment, or (B) the initial or continued right to any such benefit or payment of any other individual in whose behalf he has

applied for or is receiving such benefit or payment, conceals or fails to disclose such event with an intent fraudulently to secure such benefit or payment either in a greater amount or quantity than is due or when no such benefit or payment is authorized,

4. having made application to receive any such benefit or payment for the use and benefit of another and having received it, knowingly and willfully converts such benefit or payment or any part thereof to a use other than for the use and benefit of such other person,

5. presents or causes to be presented a claim for a physician's service for which payment may be made under a Federal health care program and knows that the individual who furnished the service was not licensed as a physician, or

6. for a fee knowingly and willfully counsels or assists an individual to dispose of assets (including by any transfer in trust) in order for the individual to become eligible for medical assistance under a State plan under [Medicaid], if disposing the assets results in the imposition of a period of ineligibility for such assistance under [42 U.S.C. §] 1396p(c)],

shall (i) in the case of such a statement, representation, concealment, failure, or conversion by any person in connection with the furnishing (by that person) of items or services for which payment is or may be made under the program, be guilty of a felony and upon conviction thereof fined not more than $100,000 or imprisoned for not more than 10 years or both, or (ii) in the case of such a statement, representation, concealment, failure, conversion, or provision of counsel or assistance by any other person, be guilty of a misdemeanor and upon conviction thereof fined not more than $20,000 or imprisoned not more than one year, or both. In addition, in any case where an individual who is otherwise eligible for assistance under a Federal health care program is convicted of an offense under the preceding provisions of this subsection, the administrator of such program may at its option (notwithstanding any other provision of such program) limit, restrict, or suspend the eligibility of that individual for such period (not exceeding one year) as it deems appropriate; but the imposition of a limitation, restriction, or suspension with respect to the eligibility of any individual under this sentence shall not affect the eligibility of any other person for assistance under the plan, regardless of the relationship between that individual and such other person.[9]

Context: The AKS overlaps some with the False Claims Act. Both statutes prohibit knowing and willful false statements for the procurement of federal funds; however, the AKS explicitly prohibits false claims made in regards to benefits or payments under a federal health program. Additionally, the AKS includes liability for healthcare organizations that misappropriate federal health program funds, present a claim for services furnished by a nonphysician, or assist a patient with disposing assets in order to become eligible for certain hospice and long-term care services.

Risk Area: Illegal Remunerations

42 U.S.C. § 1320a–7b(b)(1)(2)

1. Whoever knowingly and willfully solicits or receives any remuneration (including any kickback, bribe, or rebate) directly or indirectly, overtly or covertly, in cash or in kind—

   A. in return for referring an individual to a person for the furnishing or arranging for the furnishing of any item or service for which payment may be made in whole or in party under a Federal health care program, or

   B. in return for purchasing, leasing, ordering, or arranging for or recommending purchasing, leasing, or ordering any good, facility, service, or item for which payment may be made in whole or in part under a Federal health care program,

   shall be guilty of a felony and upon conviction thereof, shall be fined not more than $100,000 or imprisoned for not more than 10 years, or both.

2. Whoever knowingly and willfully offers or pays any remuneration (including any kickback, bribe, or rebate) directly or indirectly, overtly or covertly, in cash or in kind to any person to induce such person—

   A. to refer an individual to a person for the furnishing or arranging for the furnishing of any item or service for which payment may be made in whole or in part under a Federal health care program, or

   B. to purchase, lease, order, or arrange for or recommend purchasing, leasing, or ordering any good, facility, service, or item for which payment may be made in whole or in part under a Federal health care program,

   shall be guilty of a felony and upon conviction thereof, shall be fined not more than $100,000 or imprisoned for not more than 10 years, or both.[10]

42 U.S.C. § 1320a-7b(b)(4)

4. Whoever without lawful authority knowingly and willfully purchases, sells or distributes, or arranges for the purchase, sale, or distribution of a beneficiary identification number or unique health identifier for a health care provider under [Medicare, Medicaid, or the State Children's Health Insurance Program (SCHIP)] shall be imprisoned for not more than 10 years or fined not more than $500,000 ($1,000,000 in the case of a corporation), or both.[11]

Context: The AKS expressly prohibits anyone from knowingly and willfully soliciting patients, goods, facilities, and services covered under a federal healthcare program for compensation. Further, everyone, including healthcare organizations, is prohibited from offering or paying compensation for referrals of patients, goods, facilities, and services covered under a federal healthcare program. Lastly, attempting to buy, sell, or distribute patient beneficiary identification numbers or providers' health identifier numbers given under Medicare, Medicaid, or SCHIP is strictly prohibited.

Risk Area: False Statements or Representations with Respect to Condition or Operation of Institutions

42 U.S.C. § 1320a-7b(c)

> Whoever knowingly and willfully makes or causes to be made, or induces or seeks to induce the making of, any false statement or representation of a material fact with respect to the conditions or operation of any institution, facility, or entity in order that such institution, facility, or entity may qualify (either upon initial certification or upon recertification) as a hospital, skilled nursing facility, nursing facility, intermediate care facility for the mentally retarded, home health agency, or other entity (including an eligible organization under [42 U.S.C. § 1395mm(b)]) for which certification is required under [Medicare] or a State health care program (as defined by [42 U.S.C. § 1320a-7(h)]), or with respect to information required to be provided under [42 U.S.C. § 1320a-3a], shall be guilty of a felony and upon conviction thereof shall be fined not more than $100,000 or imprisoned for not more than 10 years, or both.[12]

Context: Keeping with the AKS's prohibition of false claims, section 1320a-7b(c) of the statute prohibits the false claims relating to the operation of Medicare certified healthcare facilities.

Risk Area: Illegal Patient Admittance and Retention Practices

42 U.S.C. § 1320a-7b(d)(1)(2)(A)(B)

> Whoever knowingly and willfully—

1. charges, for any service provided to a patient under a State plan approved under [Medicaid], money or other consideration at a rate in excess of the rates established by the State (or, in the case of services provided to an individual enrolled with a medicaid managed care organization under [Medicaid] under a contract under [42 U.S.C. § 1396b(m)] or under a contractual, referral, or other arrangement under such contract, at a rate in excess of the rate permitted under such contract), or

2. charges, solicits, accepts, or receives, in addition to any amount otherwise required to be paid under a State plan approved under [Medicaid], any gift,

money, donation, or other consideration (other than charitable, religious, or philanthropic contribution from an organization or from a person unrelated to the patient)—

A.   as a precondition of admitting a patient to a hospital, nursing facility, or intermediate care facility for the mentally retarded, or

B.   as a requirement for the patient's continued stay in such a facility,

when the cost of the services provided therein to the patient is paid for (in whole or in part) under the State plan,

shall be guilty of a felony and upon conviction thereof shall be fined not more than $100,000 or imprisoned for not more than 10 years, or both.[13]

Context: Healthcare providers are prohibited from knowingly and willfully overcharging Medicaid patients under a state Medicaid plan or requiring a Medicaid patient to pay as a precondition to being admitted, or continuing to stay, at a hospital when the services are at least partially covered by a state Medicaid plan.

Risk Area: Violation of Assignment Terms

42 U.S.C. § 1320a-7b(e)

Whoever accepts assignments described in [42 U.S.C. § 1395u(b)(3)(B)(ii)] or agrees to be a participating physician or supplier under [42 U.S.C. § 1395u(h)(1)] and knowingly, willfully, and repeatedly violates the term of such assignments or agreement, shall be guilty of a misdemeanor and upon conviction thereof shall be fined not more than $4,000 or imprisoned for not more than six months, or both.[14]

Context: Healthcare providers agreeing to accept assignment of Medicare's reasonable charges must not intentionally and repeatedly violate the terms of the assignment.

Consequences for Noncompliance

Violations of false statements or representations, illegal remunerations, or illegal patient admittance and retention practices under the AKS result in a fine of up to $100,000 per violation and imprisonment of up to 10 years. Violations of the prohibition of the solicitation or distribution of beneficiary identification or unique health identifier numbers may result in a fine of up to $500,000 per violation and imprisonment of up to 10 years. Violations of false claims under the AKS may result in a fine of up to $100,000 per violation and imprisonment of up to 10 years. Violations of assignment of terms may result in a fine of up to $4,000 per violation and imprisonment of up to 6 months.

Administrative Proceedings

Penalties

- Criminal penalties per violation are up to $100,000 for a felony conviction and up to $20,000 for a misdemeanor conviction for making false statements or representations.
- Criminal penalties per violation are up to $100,000 for illegal remuneration and up to $1,000,000 for buying, selling, or distributing beneficiary IDs or unique health identifiers.
- Criminal penalties per violation are up to $100,000 for making false statements or representations with respect to condition or operation of a healthcare institution.
- Criminal penalties per violation are up to $100,000 for illegal patient admittance and retention practices.
- Criminal penalties per violation are up to $4,000 for violating assignment terms.
- Civil money penalties per violation of up to $20,000 and not more than three times the amount of remuneration offered, paid, solicited, or received.[15]
- Exclusion from participating in federal healthcare programs.
- Typical monetary penalties range from several hundred thousand to several million dollars. Extraordinary cases may range up to several hundred million to billions of dollars.

Corrective Actions

- Developing and implementing policies and practices to ensure compliance with the AKS.
- Making periodic internal compliance reports.
- Daily monitoring of compliance activities.
- Requiring employee training on federal healthcare program regulations.
- Conspicuous posting of the OIG hotline telephone number for patients to report fraud.
- Requiring eligibility screening of current and prospective employees ineligible to furnish services under a federal healthcare program.

Civil Litigation

Damages

Violations of the AKS involving illegal renumeration for items or services constitute a violation of the False Claims Act, which provides three times the damages the government sustains as a result of a false claims violation.

Criminal Proceedings

Sentencing

- Up to 10 years for a felony conviction of false statements or representations.

- Up to 10 years for illegal remuneration or for buying, selling, or distributing beneficiary IDs or unique health identifiers.

- Up to 10 years for making false statements or representations with respect to condition or operation of a healthcare institution.

- Up to 10 years for illegal patient admittance and retention practices.

- Up to 6 months for violating assignment terms.

Important Compliance Guidance and Tools

Department of Health and Human Services, Office of Inspector General

Compliance Guidance

HHS has set forth supplemental compliance program guidance for different segments of the healthcare industry in a series of publications on their website. They contain compliance recommendations and an expanded discussion of risk areas, enforcement priorities, and lessons learned in the area of corporate compliance. The guidance is intended to help healthcare systems and practices identify significant risk areas and refine ongoing compliance efforts.

https://oig.hhs.gov/compliance/compliance-guidance/index.asp

Comparison of Anti-Kickback Statute and Stark Law

This document compares two similar laws, the Anti-Kickback Statute and the Stark Law, and helps clarify the application of the laws and which areas to be mindful of when evaluating compliance programs.

https://oig.hhs.gov/compliance/provider-compliance-training/files/ StarkandAKSChartHandout508.pdf

Safe Harbor Regulations

Find links to *Federal Register* notices containing preambles to the safe harbor regulations on this site.

https://oig.hhs.gov/compliance/safe-harbor-regulations/index.asp

Relevant Anti-Kickback Statute Cases and Opinions

United States v. Hong, 938 F.3d 1040 (9th Cir. 2019)

Case summary: Seong Hong operated acupuncture and massage clinics and provided infrastructure, facilities, therapists, and other staff to physical therapy companies in exchange for Medicare provider numbers. Under the arrangement, patients would receive acupuncture and massage treatments not covered by Medicare and virtually no physical therapy covered by Medicare. The physical therapy companies would still submit claims to the government for payment, and Hong would receive 56% of the Medicare payments—amounting to more than $1.6 million over the course of more than five years. Hong would be charged with healthcare fraud, illegal renumerations under the Anti-Kickback Statute, and identity theft.

Opinion issued: September 12, 2019

Link to full text: https://www.leagle.com/decision/infco20190912125

On appeal, Hong raised three arguments against his illegal remuneration conviction. First, he argued the remunerations were not for patient referrals but for the maintenance of clinics. Second, he argued that because the patients found the clinics on their own, no referral took place. And third, he argued no illegal remuneration occurred because no services were furnished.

In response to Hong's first argument, the court explained that the Anti-Kickback Statute prohibits payment to induce future referrals, even if payment also includes compensation for professional services. Hong was the one providing the physical therapy companies the Medicare identifying information they needed to submit claims to Medicare. Thus, the court found sufficient evidence to determine the payments to Hong were, at least partially, for the patient's information (i.e., referrals).

To the second argument, the court determined how patients found the clinic was immaterial to the issue of illegal remuneration. Instead, the issue was how patients and their information reached the physical therapy companies. Citing the same facts as above, the court found there was sufficient evidence showing patients' information ended up in the physical therapy companies' hands because of the payments they made to Hong.

Lastly, the court cited the Anti-Kickback Statute itself to find that no actual furnishing of services is necessary for a violation to occur. The court explained the statute prohibits the "arranging for the furnishing of any item or service." Further, the court pointed to the statute's purpose: "to address 'the potential for unnecessary drain on the Medicare system.'" Thus, even though the physical therapy companies provided almost none of the physical therapy presented in the claims to Medicare, Hong still violated the statute. Accordingly, the court upheld Hong's conviction with respect to the illegal remunerations under the Anti-Kickback Statute.

United States v. Vernon, 723 F.3d 1234 (11th Cir. 2013)

Case summary: Chris and Jeff Vernon were executives of an Alabama specialty pharmacy, MedfusionRx LLC, which filled prescriptions for factor medication. Specialty pharmacies fill critical and expensive medications and provide limited healthcare services to their clients. Factor medication is a type of medication filled by specialty pharmacies and is used to treat chronic illnesses, like hemophilia.

Alabama Medicaid covered healthcare services, including the cost of factor medication, for low-income or disabled state residents. In order to get reimbursed by Medicaid for the factor medication, specialty pharmacies were required to provide hemophilia patients with a myriad of ancillary services to go along with filling their prescription. Complying pharmacies would be reimbursed by Medicaid the average sales price, plus 6%, and additional furnishing and dispensing fees for factor medication.

MedfusionRx, through Chris and Jeff, arranged with Hemophilia Management Specialties (HMS), through Lori Brill and Leroy Waters, to refer hemophilia patients to MedfusionRx in exchange for 45%–50% of the profits MedfusionRx received as a result of Alabama Medicaid's generous reimbursement calculation. Based on these arrangements, Chris and Jeff Vernon were convicted under the Anti-Kickback Statute for illegal remunerations for referral services; however, Chris Vernon successfully moved for a judgment of acquittal.

Opinion issued: July 26, 2013

Link to full text: https://casetext.com/case/united-states-v-vernon-2

On appeal, the government argued that enough evidence existed to show Chris Vernon knowingly and willfully paid money to Brill to induce her to refer patients to MedfusionRx to fill their factor medication.[16] First, the government established that payments were made between MedfusionRx and HMS as evidenced by checks Chris signed to Brill under his capacity as CFO. Regarding knowledge and willfulness, Chris was privy to communications between Jeff, in-house counsel, and outside counsel showing the defendants attempted, and failed, to bring their arrangement with HMS within the Anti-Kickback Statute's safe harbor.

The court rejected Chris's assertion that Brill, because she was a nonphysician, did not refer patients under the statute, explaining that the prohibition on illegal referrals was not limited to physicians under subsection 42 U.S.C. § 1320a-7b(b)(2)(A): "Whoever knowingly and willfully offers or pays any remuneration . . . to *induce such person* to refer an individual to a person" (emphasis added).[17] Further, Brill, as a "patient advocate," was in a position to have overwhelming influence over where her clients filled their factor prescriptions. Lastly, the court rejected Chris's argument that because the evidence of payment occurred after HMS's clients had already established a relationship with MedfusionRx, no referrals were taking place (i.e., the patients were existing clients of MedfusionRx). The court explained that adopting Chris's reasoning "would lead to the absurd result that the first kickback payment for a referral is unlawful, but future kickback payments for the same patient are lawful."[18]

In appealing his conviction, Jeff specifically argued that Waters was a bona fide employee of MedfusionRx and thus fell within the statute's safe harbor. Ample evidence existed, however, that Waters' employment agreement was a sham. Waters, who was a hemophiliac himself, brought himself and other patients to MedfusionRx. Although Waters had an employment contract, he almost never visited MedfusionRx's headquarters, had no interaction with other employees, and spent most of his time gambling. The employment contract was instead a furtive agreement meant to conceal illegal remunerations for patient referrals.

Lastly, Jeff argued that he relied in good faith on the advice of counsel when he entered and continued the illegal arrangement with HMS. The court found that Jeff had not fully disclosed all material facts to MedfusionRx's in-house counsel when attempting to draft a written agreement with HMS. Further, the arrangement with HMS was not disclosed to in-house counsel until after the illegal conduct had begun. Also, upon outside counsel's determination that MedfusionRx's arrangement with HMS was likely unlawful, the defendants failed to change their conduct.

Accordingly, the court affirmed the convictions of Jeff and reversed Chris's judgment of acquittal.

United States ex rel. Louis Longo v. Wheeling Hosp., Inc., No. 19-cv-192 (N.D.W. Va. 2020)

Case summary: Wheeling Hospital CEO Ronald Violi and his consulting company, R & V Associates Ltd., violated the Anti-Kickback Statute by paying physicians for patient referrals. Violi was hired as Wheeling Hospital's CEO to turn around the hospital's financial situation.

In doing so, Violi contracted with physicians who provided hefty revenue from patient referrals under federal healthcare plans. Physicians were compensated well above market value for their productivity, and compensation was computed considering the "downstream revenue" from their patient referrals. Wheeling Hospital would enter into a $50 million settlement agreement with the Department of Justice.

Opinion issued: September 9, 2020

Link to full text: https://www.justice.gov/opa/pr/ west-virginia-hospital-agrees-pay-50-million-settle-allegations-concerning-improper

In its corporate settlement press release, the Department of Justice cited the purpose of the Anti-Kickback Statute in preventing the type of behavior Wheeling Hospital engaged in. Assistant Attorney General Jeffrey Bossert Clark said, "'Improper financial arrangements between hospitals and physicians can influence the type and amount of health care that is provided.'"[19] Scott W. Brady, the U.S. Attorney for the Western District of Pennsylvania referred to the trust Medicare and Medicaid patients must have in their healthcare providers, and enforcement of the Anti-Kickback Statute helps ensure providers do not breach that trust.

Endnotes

1. **Gabriel Imperato** is managing partner at the Fort Lauderdale office of Nelson Mullins Riley & Scarborough. He is the team leader of the firm's Health Care Criminal and Civil Enforcement, Litigation and Compliance Practice. He has practiced healthcare law in both the public and private sectors for more than 40 years. He is board certified as a specialist in health law by The Florida Bar. Imperato recently served as the general counsel of the North Broward Hospital District, the tenth largest healthcare system in the United States. He has also served as deputy chief counsel for the U.S. Department of Health & Human Services' Office of the General Counsel. Imperato is also a longtime member of the board of directors of Society of Corporate Compliance and Ethics & the Health Care Compliance Association (SCCE & HCCA), where he was also a past president and interim CEO.

2. **Anne Novick Branan** is an of counsel attorney in the Fort Lauderdale office of Nelson Mullins Riley & Scarborough.She has been board certified in health law by The Florida Bar since 1995. Branan counsels healthcare providers about avoiding and responding to allegations of fraud under the Medicare and Medicaid programs. She helps her clients navigate the complex regulatory environment affecting acquisitions and contracting in the healthcare industry. Branan regularly assists healthcare companies in developing and assessing the effectiveness of corporate compliance and ethics programs. She was recognized in *The Best Lawyers in America* for healthcare law, 2015–2020, and selected as Fort Lauderdale Health Care Law "Lawyer of the Year" in 2017.

3. **Richard Sena** is an associate attorney at Nelson Mullins Riley & Scarborough in Fort Lauderdale. Sena conducted health law research under the guidance of attorneys Gabriel Imperato and Anne Novick Branan and helped author sections of the "Key Laws in Healthcare Compliance" chapter in the 2021 HCCA Complete Healthcare Compliance Manual. Sena also coauthored an article titled "Compliance Risks and Tips for Home Health Agencies" with Branan, appearing in the July 2021 edition of *Compliance Today* magazine.

4. **Megan Speltz** is a digital product owner at SCCE & HCCA, where she helps define and deliver new digital products to the COSMOS platform. She graduated from the University of St. Thomas School of Law in May 2020; she obtained her juris doctor with a concentration in organizational ethics and compliance. In addition to working at SCCE & HCCA, Speltz is a licensed attorney practicing in the state of Minnesota and represents small businesses and nonprofit organizations.

5. 42 C.F.R. § 1001.952.

6. Medicare-Medicaid Anti-Fraud and Abuse Amendments, Pub. L. 95-142, 91 Stat. 1175 (October 25, 2977).

7. Medicare and Medicaid Patient and Program Protection Act, Pub. L. 100-93, 101 Stat. 680 (August 18, 1987).

8. Thomas S. Crane et al., "What is the Anti-Kickback Statute?" American Bar Association, accessed September 16, 2020, https://www.americanbar.org/groups/young_lawyers/publications/tyl/topics/health-law/what-is-anti-kickback-statute/.

9. 42 U.S.C. § 1320a-7b(a)(1)–(6).

10. 42 U.S.C. § 1320a-7b(b)(3)(A)–(J).

11. 42 U.S.C. § 1320a-7b(b)(1)(2)(4).
12. 42 U.S.C. § 1320a-7b(c).
13. 42 U.S.C. § 1320a-7b(d)(1)(2)(A)(B).
14. 42 U.S.C. § 1320a-7b(e).
15. 42 U.S.C. § 1320a-7a(a)(7) (2018).
16. A judgment of acquittal is granted if the trial court determines the evidence presented was insufficient to support a guilty verdict. On appeal, the court views the evidence most favorably to the government to determine whether "a reasonable jury could have found the defendant guilty beyond a reasonable doubt." *United States v. Vernon*, 723 F.3d 1234 (11th Cir. 2013).
17. A judgment of acquittal is granted if the trial court determines the evidence presented was insufficient to support a guilty verdict. On appeal, the court views the evidence most favorably to the government to determine whether "a reasonable jury could have found the defendant guilty beyond a reasonable doubt." *United States v. Vernon*, 723 F.3d 1234 (11th Cir. 2013).
18. United States v. Vernon, 723 F.3d 1234 (11th Cir. 2013).
19. Department of Justice, "West Virginia Hospital Agrees to Pay $50 Million to Settle Allegations Concerning Improper Compensation to Referring Physicians," news release, September 9, 2020, http://www.justice.gov/opa/pr/west-virginia-hospital-agrees-pay-50-million-settle-allegations-concerning-improper.

Civil Monetary Penalties Law

By Gabriel Imperato, [1] Esq., CHC; Anne Novick Branan, [2] Esq., CHC; Richard Sena[3]; Zackary Weiss[4]; and Megan Speltz, [5] JD

Fast Facts

Title of law: The Civil Monetary Penalties Law (CMPL), exclusion of certain individuals and entities from participation in Medicare and state health care programs

Categories:

- Fraud and abuse
- Medicare
- Medicaid

U.S. Code: 42 U.S.C. § 1320a–7a

Year enacted: 1981

Major amendments: Not applicable.

Enforcement agencies: U.S. Department of Health & Human Services (HHS) Office of Inspector General (OIG), Centers for Medicare & Medicaid Services (CMS)

Link to full text of law: https://www.govinfo.gov/content/pkg/USCODE-2010-title42/pdf/USCODE-2010-title42-chap7-subchapXI-partA-sec1320a-7a.pdf

Applies to: Any person or entity that presents fraudulent Medicare or Medicaid claims to federal or state agencies; authorizes the secretary of the U.S. Department of Health & Human Services to impose civil monetary penalties, assessment, and Medicare and Medicaid program exclusion.

What Is the Civil Monetary Penalties Law?

The Civil Monetary Penalties Law (CMPL) authorizes the HHS to impose civil money penalties against any person or entity, including a laboratory, that presents fraudulent claims to a federal or state agency. The law also prohibits the following conduct:

- Offering something of value to a Medicare or other state or federal healthcare program beneficiary that the person knows or should know is likely to influence the beneficiary to obtain items or services billed to a state or federal healthcare program.
- Employing or contracting with an individual or entity that the provider knows or should know is excluded from participation in a federal healthcare program.
- Billing for services requested by an unlicensed physician or an excluded provider.
- Knowing of an overpayment and failing to return and report it in a timely fashion.
- Billing for medically unnecessary services.[6]

History

The CMPL was enacted in 1981 in response to widespread fraud and abuse involving the Medicare and Medicaid programs. It was designed to not only punish healthcare providers who knowingly committed fraud and abuse through their healthcare claims, but also providers who were unaware of the fraud and abuse they were committing. This law encourages providers to verify the accuracy of the Medicare, Medicaid, and state health claim forms submitted by in-house staff and billing services.[7]

Related Laws

Federal Anti-Kickback Statute, 42 U.S.C. 1320a-7b(b)

The federal Anti-Kickback Statute is a criminal law that prohibits the knowing and willful payment of "renumeration" to induce or reward patient referrals or the generation of business involving any item or service payable by federal healthcare programs (e.g., drugs, supplies, or healthcare services for Medicare or Medicaid patients). Renumeration includes anything of value, such as free rent, expensive hotel stays and meals, and excessive compensation for medical directorships or consultancies. Physicians are common targets for kickback schemes because they can be a source of referrals for fellow physicians or other healthcare providers and suppliers.[8]

Physician Self-Referral Law, 42 U.S.C. § 1395nn

The Physician Self-Referral Law, commonly referred to as the Stark Law, prohibits physicians from referring patients to receive "designated health services" payable by Medicare or Medicaid from entities with which the physician or an immediate family member has a financial relationship. Financial relationships include both ownership/investment interest and compensation arrangements. The Stark Law is a strict liability statute, which means proof of specific intent to violate the law is not required.[9]

Exclusion Statute, 42 U.S.C. § 1320a-7

The HHS OIG excludes healthcare providers in all federal healthcare programs who are convicted of the following types of criminal offenses: (1) Medicare or Medicaid fraud, as well as any other offenses related to the delivery of items or services under Medicare or Medicaid; (2) patient abuse or neglect; (3) felony convictions for other healthcare-related fraud, theft, or other financial misconduct; and (4) felony convictions for unlawful manufacture, distribution, prescription, or dispensing of controlled substance.[10]

False Claims Act, 31 U.S.C. §§ 3729-3733

The civil False Claims Act protects the government from being overcharged or sold faulty goods or services. It is illegal to submit claims for payment to Medicare or Medicaid that a provider knows or should know are false or fraudulent. The fact that a claim results from a kickback or is made in violation of the Stark Law also may render it as being false or fraudulent, creating liability under the civil False Claims Act as well as the Anti-Kickback Statute, Stark Law, or CMPL.[11]

Civil Monetary Penalties Law Compliance Risks

The CMPL is important to healthcare professionals because violations can expose organizations to a great deal of civil liability. Healthcare organizations and officials found liable are subject to large fines and potential exclusion from federal programs. The two main provisions of the act focus on improperly filed claims and payments to induce reduction or limitations of services.

Risk Area: Improperly Filed Claims

42 U.S.C. § 1320a-7a(a)(1)–(2)

a. Any person . . . that—

1. knowingly presents or causes to be presented to an officer, employee, or agent of the United States, or of any department or agency thereof, or of any State agency . . . a claim . . . that the Secretary determines—

   A. is for medical or other item or service that the person knows or should know was not provided as claimed, including any person who engages in a pattern or practice of presenting or causing to be presented a claim for an item or service that is based on a code that the person knows or should know will result in a greater payment to the person than the code the person knows or should know is applicable to the item actually provided,

   B. is for a medical or other item or service and the person knows or should know the claim is false or fraudulent,

    C. is presented for a physician's service (or an item or service incident to a physician's service) by a person who knows or should know that the individual who furnished (or supervised the furnishing of) the service—

        i. was not licensed as a physician,

        ii. was licensed as a physician, but such license had been obtained through a misrepresentation of material fact . . . , or

        iii. represented to the patient at the time the service was furnished that the physician was certified in a medical specialty by a medical specialty board when the individual was not so certified,

    D. is for a medical or other item or service furnished during a period in which the person was excluded from the Federal health care program . . . under which the claim was made pursuant to Federal law.

    E. is for a pattern of medical or other items or services that a person knows or should know are not medically necessary;

2. knowingly presents or causes to be presented to any person a request for payment which is in violation of the terms of (A) an assignment under section 1395u(b)(3)(B)(ii) of this title, or (B) an agreement with a State agency . . . not to charge a person for an item or service in excess of the amount permitted to be charged, or (C) an agreement to be a participating physician or supplier under section 1395u(h)(1) of this title, or (D) an agreement pursuant to section 1395cc(a)(1)(G) of this title.[12]

Context: Under this provision of the CMPL, a healthcare provider, owner, or operator can be held liable based on their own negligence or the negligence of employees. There is no requirement that intent to defraud be proven. Thus, if a healthcare provider improperly files a claim for a variety of reasons, they can be liable under this statute. Furthermore, sanctions imposed generally exceed the damages actually sustained by filing the improper claim.

Risk Area: Payments to Induce Reduction or Limitations of Services

42 U.S.C. § 1320a–7a(a)(5)

Offers to or transfers remuneration to any individual eligible for benefits under subchapter XVIII of this chapter, or under a State health care program (as defined in section 1320a-7(h) of this title) that such person knows or should know is likely to influence such individual to order or receive from a particular provider, practitioner, or supplier any item or service for which payment may be made, in whole or in part, under subchapter XVIII, or a State health care program (as so defined).[13]

42 U.S.C. § 1320a–7a(b)(1)–(3)(A)

1. If a hospital or a critical access hospital knowingly makes a payment, directly or indirectly, to a physician as an inducement to reduce or limit medically necessary services provided with respect to individuals who . . .

2. Any physician who knowingly accepts receipt of a payment described in paragraph (1) shall be subject, in addition to any other penalties that may be prescribed by law, to a civil money penalty of not more than $5,000 for each individual described in such paragraph with respect to whom the payment is made.

3.

   A. Any physician who executes a document described in subparagraph (B) with respect to an individual knowing that all of the requirements referred to in such subparagraph are not met with respect to the individual shall be subject to a civil monetary policy of not more than the greater of—

      i. $10,000, or

      ii. three times the amount of the payments under subchapter XVIII for home health services which are made pursuant to such certification.[14]

Context: The CMPL generally prohibits hospitals from paying physicians to reduce or limit services to Medicare or Medicaid beneficiaries. The law prohibits "gainsharing" arrangements whereby hospitals share cost savings with referring physicians unless the arrangement has been approved by the deferral government in an advisory opinion or the arrangement is structured to satisfy new exceptions applicable to accountable care organizations.

Risk Area: Violating Exclusion

42 U.S.C. § 1320a–7a(a)(6)

Arranges or contracts (by employment or otherwise) with an individual or entity that the person knows or should know is excluded from participation in a Federal health care program (as defined in section 1320a–7b(f) of this title), for the provision of items or services for which payment may be made under such a program.[15]

42 U.S.C. § 1320a–7a(a)(8)

Orders or prescribes a medical or other item or service during a period in which the person was excluded from a Federal health care program (as so defined), in the case where the person knows or should know that a claim for such medical or other item or service will be made under such a program.[16]

Context: Healthcare providers or owners can be held liable under the CMPL for not only practicing medicine while being excluded from federal programs but also for dealing with an excluded individual.

Risk Area: Knowing of Falsity, Omissions, Misrepresentations, and Overpayments and Not Acting

42 U.S.C. § 1320a–7a(a)(3)

> Knowingly gives or causes to be given to any person, with respect to coverage under subchapter XVIII of inpatient hospital services subject to the provisions of section 1395ww of this title, information that he knows or should know is false or misleading, and that could reasonably be expected to influence the decision when to discharge such person or another individual from the hospital.[17]

42 U.S.C. § 1320a–7a(a)(9)

> Knowingly makes or causes to be made any false statement, omission, or misrepresentation of a material fact in any application, bid, or contract to participate or enroll as a provider of services or a supplier under a Federal health care program (as so defined) . . . .[18]

42 U.S.C. § 1320a–7a(a)(10)

> Knows of an overpayment (as defined in paragraph (4) of section 1320a–7k(d) of this title) and does not report and return the overpayment in accordance with such section . . . [19]

Context: Healthcare providers or owners who partake in a variety of types of fraud can be held liable under the CMPL. Providers who knowingly misrepresent or omit key information will be held liable to civil penalties. Furthermore, intentionally retaining an overpayment can lead to penalties under the CMPL.

Consequences for Noncompliance

Administrative Proceedings

Penalties

> In determining the amount or scope of any penalty, assessment, or exclusion imposed pursuant to subsection (a) or (b), the Secretary shall take into account—

1. the nature of claims and the circumstances under which they were presented,

2. the degree of culpability, history of prior offenses, and financial condition of the person presenting the claims, and

3. such other matters as justice may require.[20]

Corrective Actions

- Exclusion from participating in federal healthcare programs.

Civil Litigation

Damages

- Penalties range from $10,000 to $100,000 per violation.[21]
- Civil monetary penalties also may include an assessment of up to three times the amount claimed for each item or service, or up to three times the amount of remuneration offered, paid, solicited, or received.[22]
- The maximum penalties under the CMPL for various improperly filed claims have increased to $20,000 (from $10,000), $30,000 (from $15,000), and $100,000 (from $50,000). Maximum penalties under the CMPL for various payments to induce reduction or limitation of services have increased to $5,000 (from $2,000) and $10,000 (from $5,000).[23]
- In addition to any other penalties that may be prescribed by law, to a civil money penalty of not more than:
  - $20,000 for each item or service,
    - "The term 'item or service' includes (A) any particular item, device, medical supply, or service claimed to have been provided to a patient and listed in an itemized claim for payment, and (B) in the case of a claim based on costs, any entry in the cost report, books of account or other documents supporting such claim."[24]
  - $30,000 for each individual with respect to whom false or misleading information was given that could reasonably be expected to influence the decision when to discharge such person or another individual from the hospital (in cases under paragraph 3 of the CMPL),
  - $20,000 for each day the prohibited relationship with an excluded healthcare provider occurs (in cases under paragraph 4 of the CMPL),
  - $100,000 for each such act (in cases under paragraph 7 of the CMPL),
  - $100,000 for each false record or statement relating to ordering or prescribing during a period in which the person was excluded from a federal health care program (in cases under paragraph 8 of the CMPL),
  - $15,000 for each day of the failure to grant timely access, upon reasonable request to the inspector general of the Department of Health & Human Services (in cases under paragraph 9 of the CMPL), and

- $100,000 for each false statement or misrepresentation of a material fact to participate or enroll as a provider of services or a supplier under a federal health care program (in cases under paragraph 9 of the CMPL).[25]
- The OIG may impose a penalty of up to $50,000 and assessments of up to three times the amount of funds at issue: (1) for each instance of knowingly making a false statement in a document required to be submitted in order to receive funds under an HHS contract, grant, or other agreement; (2) for knowingly making or using a false record or statement that is material to a false or fraudulent claim; and (3) for knowingly making or using a false record or statement material to an obligation to pay or transmit funds or property owed to HHS.[26]

Criminal Proceedings

Sentencing

Not applicable.

Important Compliance Guidance and Tools

Centers for Medicare & Medicaid Services

Provider Compliance

This site lists links to resources providers can use to stay in compliance with Medicare and Medicaid claims by reducing their coverage and billing and coding errors.

https://www.cms.gov/Outreach-and-Education/Medicare-Learning-Network-MLN/MLNProducts/ProviderCompliance

U.S. Department of Health & Human Services, Office of Inspector General

Civil Monetary Penalties and Affirmative Exclusions

The following link shows recently closed cases initiated by the OIG's Office of Counsel to the Inspector General. These cases may illustrate frequent charges and provide a guide to organizations on what charges may be likely for given violations.

https://oig.hhs.gov/fraud/enforcement/cmp/index.asp

Civil Monetary Penalties Background and CMP Navigation

This HHS page lists the OIG's commonly used CMP authorities and descriptions of why the OIG may seek monetary penalties or exclusions. These examples include drug price reporting; false and fraudulent claims; grants, contracts, and other agreements; kickbacks; physician self-referral; and other examples.

https://oig.hhs.gov/fraud/enforcement/about/

Exclusions

Providers may learn about the HHS OIG exclusion authority and activities on this site, and access a searchable list of currently excluded individuals and entities on the List of Excluded Individuals/Entities.

https://oig.hhs.gov/exclusions/

Relevant Civil Monetary Penalties Law Settlements

Friends Care Health Care Association, Inc. d/b/a Friends Extended Care Center

Settlement summary: The OIG alleged that Friends Care submitted claims for services provided by an unlicensed individual. The provider here self-disclosed the violation to the OIG. Friends Care agreed to pay $101,691.20 for allegedly violating the CMPL. [27]

Settlement reported: October 7, 2021

Link to full text: https://oig.hhs.gov/fraud/enforcement/friends-extended-care-center-agreed-to-pay-101000-for-allegedly-violating-the-civil-monetary-penalties-law-by-submitting-claims-for-services-by-an-unlicensed-individual/

Farah Rodefshalom Kohan

Settlement summary: On October 29, 2021, Farah Rodefshalom Kohan of Los Angeles, California, agreed to be excluded under 42 U.S.C. § 1320a-7(b)(7) for 20 years. The OIG alleged that Kohan offered and paid improper remuneration in the form of free nutritional shakes to bariatric patients to induce such patients to order—and/or arrange for the purchasing and/or ordering of—certain prescription drugs, namely scar creams and metabolic supplements, for which payment was made in whole or in part by the TRICARE program. Senior Counsel Matthew Westbrook represented the OIG.[28]

Settlement signed: October 29, 2021

Link to full text: https://oig.hhs.gov/fraud/enforcement/farah-rodefshalom-kohan-agreed-to-be-excluded-for-20-years-for-paying-remuneration-to-beneficiaries/

Washington State University

Settlement summary: The OIG brought allegations against Washington State University (WSU), located in Pullman, Washington, that WSU presented or caused to be presented requests for payment for direct salary expenses above the HHS salary cap limitation and indirect cost charges associated with those salary expenses to (1) the HHS Payment Management System and (2) HHS award recipients related to awards on which WSU was a subrecipient. On September 20, 2021, WSU entered into an $824,208.09 settlement agreement with the OIG. Senior Counsel Michael Torrisi and Associate Counsel Shawnda Atkins represented the OIG.[29]

Settlement signed: September 20, 2021

Link to full text: https://oig.hhs.gov/fraud/enforcement/washington-state-university-agreed-to-pay-824000-for-allegedly-violating-the-civil-monetary-penalties-law-by-overcharging-hhs-grants/

Rachel Paragas & DR Home Healthcare LLC

Settlement summary: On October 21, 2021, Raquel Paragas and DR Home Healthcare LLC of Lemont, Illinois, entered into a $112,000 settlement agreement with the OIG. The settlement agreement resolves allegations that Paragas offered and paid improper remuneration to a doctor in exchange for Medicare beneficiary referrals to her home health agency, DR Home Healthcare LLC. OIG's Office of Investigations and Office of Counsel to the Inspector General, represented by Senior Counsel Gregory Becker with the assistance of Chief Investigator Amber Mahmood, collaborated to achieve this settlement.[30]

Settlement signed: October 21, 2021

Link to full text: https://oig.hhs.gov/fraud/enforcement/raquel-paragas-and-dr-home-healthcare-agreed-to-pay-112000-for-allegedly-violating-the-civil-monetary-penalties-law-by-paying-improper-remuneration-in-exchange-for-referrals/

Carolina Behavioral Care PA

Settlement summary: The OIG alleged that Carolina Behavioral Care PA (CBC), located in Durham, North Carolina, submitted claims to Medicare specimen validity testing (SVT) in conjunction with claims for urine drug testing when SVT was a noncovered service. On October 27, 2021, CBC entered into a $23,816.94 settlement agreement with the OIG.[31]

Settlement signed: October 27, 2021

Link to full text: https://oig.hhs.gov/fraud/enforcement/carolina-behavioral-care-agreed-to-pay-23000-for-allegedly-violating-the-civil-monetary-penalties-law-by-submitting-claims-for-non-covered-services/

Endnotes

1. **Gabriel Imperato** is managing partner at the Fort Lauderdale office of Nelson Mullins Riley & Scarborough. He is the team leader of the firm's Health Care Criminal and Civil Enforcement, Litigation and Compliance Practice. He has practiced healthcare law in both the public and private sectors for more than 40 years. He is board certified as a specialist in health law by The Florida Bar. Imperato recently served as the general counsel of the North Broward Hospital District, the tenth largest healthcare system in the United States. He has also served as deputy chief counsel for the U.S. Department of Health & Human Services' Office of the General Counsel. Imperato is also a longtime member of the board of directors of the Society of Corporate Compliance and Ethics & Health Care Compliance Association (SCCE & HCCA), where he was also a past president and interim CEO.

2. **Anne Novick Branan** is an of counsel attorney in the Fort Lauderdale office of Nelson Mullins Riley & Scarborough. She has been board certified in health law by The Florida Bar since 1995. Branan counsels healthcare providers about avoiding and responding to allegations of fraud under the Medicare and Medicaid programs. She helps her clients navigate the complex regulatory environment affecting acquisitions and contracting in the healthcare industry. Branan regularly assists healthcare companies in developing and assessing the effectiveness of corporate compliance and ethics programs. She was recognized in *The Best Lawyers in America* for healthcare law, 2015–2020, and selected as Fort Lauderdale Health Care Law "Lawyer of the Year" in 2017.

3. **Richard Sena** is an associate attorney at Nelson Mullins Riley & Scarborough in Fort Lauderdale. Sena conducted health law research under the guidance of attorneys Gabriel Imperato and Anne Novick Branan and helped author sections of the "Key Laws in Healthcare Compliance" chapter in the 2021 HCCA *Complete Healthcare Compliance Manual*. Sena also coauthored an article titled "Compliance Risks and Tips for Home Health Agencies" with Branan, appearing in the July 2021 edition of *Compliance Today* magazine.

4. **Zackary Weiss** is a juris doctor candidate at the University of Miami School of Law. He is an editor for the *International & Comparative Law Review*, past judicial intern for United States Magistrate Judge Jonathan Goodman, and a law clerk at Nelson Mullins Riley & Scarborough in Fort Lauderdale since the summer of 2020. Weiss has conducted health law research under the guidance of attorneys Gabriel Imperato and Anne Novick Branan and helped author sections of the "Key Laws in Healthcare Compliance" chapter in the 2022 HCCA *Complete Healthcare Compliance Manual*. He is expected to graduate in May 2022 and plans to continue his career as an associate attorney at Nelson Mullins.

5. **Megan Speltz** is a digital product owner at SCCE & HCCA, where she helps define and deliver new digital products to the COSMOS platform. She graduated from the University of St. Thomas School of Law in May 2020; she obtained her juris doctor with a concentration in organizational ethics and compliance. In addition to working at SCCE & HCCA, Speltz is a licensed attorney practicing in the state of Minnesota and represents small businesses and nonprofit organizations.

6. "Federal Laws and Regulations—Civil Monetary Penalties Law," § 41:5, *Health Law Practice Guide*, Westlaw: 2020.

7. Richard P. Kusserow, "Civil Money Penalties Law of 1981: A New Effort to Confront Fraud and Abuse in Federal Health Care Programs," *Notre Dame Law Review* 58, no. 5, Art. 3 (June 1, 1983), 985–994, https://scholarship.law.nd.edu/cgi/viewcontent.cgi?referer=https://www.google.com/&httpsredir=1&article=2436&context=ndlr.

8. 42 U.S.C. § 1320a-7b(b).

9. 42 U.S.C. § 1395nn.

10. 42 U.S.C. § 1320a-7.

11. 31 U.S.C. §§ 3729-3733.

12. 42 U.S.C. § 1320a-7a(a)(1)–(2).

13. 42 U.S.C. § 1320a-7a(a)(5).

14. 42 U.S.C. § 1320a-7a(b)(1)–(3)(A).

15. 42 U.S.C. § 1320a-7a(a)(6).

16. 42 U.S.C. § 1320a-7a(a)(8).

17. 42 U.S.C. § 1320a-7a(a)(3).

18. 42 U.S.C. § 1320a-7a(a)(9).

19. 42 U.S.C. § 1320a-7a(a)(10).

20. 42 U.S.C. § 1320a-7a(d).

21. "Civil Monetary Penalties Law (CMPL)," University of Florida Office of Clinical Research, accessed November 23, 2021, https://clinicalresearch.ctsi.ufl.edu/resources/policies/civil-monetary-penalties-law-cmpl/.

22. 42 U.S.C. § 1320a-7a(a)(10). (penalty guidelines are listed underneath)

23. 42 U.S.C. § 1320a-7a(b)(1)–(2).

24. 42 U.S.C. § 1320a-7a(i)(3).

25. 42 U.S.C. § 1320a-7a(a)(10).

26. 42 U.S.C. § 1320(a)(o)(5).

27. U.S. Department of Health & Human Services Office of Inspector General, "Friends Extended Care Center Agreed to Pay $101,000 for Allegedly Violating the Civil Monetary Penalties Law by Submitting Claims for Services by an Unlicensed Individual," enforcement actions, October 7, 2021, https://oig.hhs.gov/fraud/enforcement/friends-extended-care-center-agreed-to-pay-101000-for-allegedly-violating-the-civil-monetary-penalties-law-by-submitting-claims-for-services-by-an-unlicensed-individual/.

28. U.S. Department of Health & Human Services Office of Inspector General, "Farah Rodefshalom Kohan Agreed to Be Excluded for 20 Years for Paying Remuneration to Beneficiaries," enforcement actions, October 29, 2021, https://oig.hhs.gov/fraud/enforcement/farah-rodefshalom-kohan-agreed-to-be-excluded-for-20-years-for-paying-remuneration-to-beneficiaries/.

29. U.S. Department of Health & Human Services Office of Inspector General, "Washington State University Agreed to Pay $824,000 for Allegedly Violating the Civil Monetary Penalties Law by Overcharging HHS Grants," September 20, 2021, https://oig.hhs.gov/fraud/enforcement/washington-state-university-agreed-to-pay-824000-for-allegedly-violating-the-civil-monetary-penalties-law-by-overcharging-hhs-grants/.

30. U.S. Department of Health & Human Services Office of Inspector General, "Raquel Paragas and DR Home Healthcare Agreed to Pay $112,000 for Allegedly Violating the Civil Monetary Penalties Law by Paying Improper Remuneration in Exchange for Referrals," enforcement actions, October 21, 2021, https://oig.hhs.gov/fraud/enforcement/raquel-paragas-and-dr-home-healthcare-agreed-to-pay-112000-for-allegedly-violating-the-civil-monetary-penalties-law-by-paying-improper-remuneration-in-exchange-for-referrals/.

31. U.S. Department of Health & Human Services Office of Inspector General, "Carolina Behavioral Care Agreed to Pay $23,000 for Allegedly Violating the Civil Monetary Penalties Law by Submitting Claims for Non-Covered Services," enforcement actions, October 27, 2021, https://oig.hhs.gov/fraud/enforcement/carolina-behavioral-care-agreed-to-pay-23000-for-allegedly-violating-the-civil-monetary-penalties-law-by-submitting-claims-for-non-covered-services/.

Emergency Medical Treatment and Labor Act

By Gabriel Imperato,[1] Esq., CHC; Anne Novick Branan,[2] Esq., CHC; Richard Sena[3] ; and Megan Speltz,[4] JD

Fast Facts

Title of law: Emergency Medical Treatment and Labor Act (EMTALA); Examination and treatment for emergency medical conditions and women in labor

CategoriEs:

- Discrimination in medical care
- Emergency medical services
- Health facilities
- Medicaid
- Medicare

U.S. Code: 42 U.S.C. § 1395dd

Year enacted: 1986

Major amendments: Not applicable.

Enforcement agency: U.S. Department of Health & Human Services (HHS) Centers for Medicare & Medicaid Services (CMS)

Link to full text of law: https://www.govinfo.gov/content/pkg/FR-2012-02-02/pdf/2012-2287.pdf

Applies to: Any hospital or health system that accepts payment from the Department of Health & Human Services Centers for Medicare & Medicaid Services under the Medicare program for services provided to beneficiaries of that program. Provisions of the act are applicable to all patients, not just Medicare patients. Hence, it applies to almost all hospitals in the United States, aside from some private hospitals and military hospitals.

What Is the Emergency Medical Treatment and Labor Act?

Emergency Medical Treatment and Labor Act (EMTALA) is a federal law that was enacted to prevent discrimination of patients in hospital emergency departments and ban "patient dumping" on public hospitals. The law ensures public access to emergency medical services regardless of ability to pay.

There are three main legal obligations created by EMTALA:

1. Any person who comes into the emergency department must be able to receive a medical screening examination to determine whether an emergency medical condition exists, regardless of their financial or insurance status. The exam and treatment may not be delayed in order to ask about methods of payment or insurance.

2. If an emergency medical condition exists, treatment must be provided until the condition is resolved or the patient is stabilized. If the hospital is unable to treat the emergency medical condition due to capacity or ability, an appropriate transfer to another hospital must be done in accordance with EMTALA provisions.

3. Hospitals with specialized capabilities must accept transfers from hospitals that lack the capacity to treat unstable emergency medical conditions.[5,6]

EMTALA was passed as part of the Consolidated Omnibus Budget Reconciliation Act (COBRA) of 1985.[7] Referred to as the "anti-dumping" law, it was designed to prevent hospitals from transferring uninsured or Medicaid patients without providing at least a medical screening examination to ensure they were stable for transfer. In 2000, Congress made EMTALA enforcement a priority and began issuing penalties for violations of the act of more than $1.17 million. A technical advisory group was convened in 2005 by the Centers for Medicare & Medicaid Services (CMS) to discuss improvements to EMTALA. Their purpose was to provide advice and recommendations regarding the application of the law to hospitals and physicians, as well as solicit comments and recommendations from hospitals, physicians, and the public to create incremental updates to the law.[8]

Related Laws

Fla. Stat. § 395.1041(3) (2019)—Access to emergency services and care

- Requires hospitals to provide emergency services and care.
- An unstabilized patient may only be transferred if:
  - Patient or legally responsible person, after being informed of the hospital's obligation, requests a transfer;
  - A physician, considering the risk to the patient at the time, signs a certificate effectuating a medically necessary transfer.

Cal. Health and Safety Code § 1317.3 (West 2019)—Policies and transfer protocols, discrimination, failure to adopt policies and protocols, submission for approval

- Prohibits hospitals from discrimination, including insurance status and ability to pay, in providing medical services.

Cal. Health and Safety Code § 1262.5 (West 2019)—Discharge planning policy and process, requirements, written homeless patient discharge plan, documentation

- Amended in 2019 (Sen. B. 1152) to include the arrangement of a post-discharge plan for homeless people.

Tex. Health and Safety Code Ann. § 241.027(b),(c) (2015); Tex. Health and Safety Code Ann. § 254.153(a) (2009) – Freestanding emergency centers

- Urgent care centers cannot transfer before stabilization unless:
  - The patient consents;
  - A licensed physician approves, or designates someone to approve, the transfer as medically appropriate.

Utah Code Ann. § R432-100-17(2)(c) (LexisNexis 2020)

- The evaluation and treatment of a patient who presents himself or is brought to the emergency care area shall be the responsibility of a licensed practitioner and shall include an appropriate medical screening examination, stabilizing treatment, and, if necessary for definitive treatment, an appropriate transfer to another medical facility that has agreed to accept the patient for care.[9]

N.Y. Public Health Law § 2805-b(2)(b) (McKinney 2019)

- Any licensed medical practitioner who refuses to treat a person arriving at a general hospital to receive emergency medical treatment who is in need of such treatment; or any person who in any manner excludes, obstructs or interferes with the ingress of another person into a general hospital who appears there for the purpose of being examined or diagnosed or treated; or any person who obstructs or prevents such other person from being examined or diagnosed or treated by an attending physician thereat shall be guilty of a misdemeanor and subject to a term of imprisonment not to exceed one year and a fine not to exceed one thousand dollars.[10]

Emergency Medical Treatment and Labor Act Compliance Risks

Compliance professionals need to pay special attention to EMTALA's provisions because violations expose healthcare providers to civil penalties and damages. While the breadth and purpose of the act is important for compliance professionals to understand, its specific provisions offer strict guidelines. For instance, the act requires written consent from either the patient or a physician before certain exceptions to compliance apply. Compliance professionals should be prudent in advising emergency medical staff on the exceptions to compliance and should err on the side of dutiful adherence to the act. The following are specific EMTALA risk areas that compliance professionals need to monitor closely.

Risk Area: Failure to Medically Screen

42 U.S.C. § 1395dd(a)

> [I]f any individual . . . comes to the emergency department and [requests] . . . examination or treatment for a medical condition, the hospital must provide for an appropriate medical screening examination within the capability of the hospital's emergency department, including ancillary services routinely available to the emergency department, to determine whether or not an emergency medical condition . . . exists.[11]

Context: Medical compliance professionals need to ensure their emergency medical staff are aware of the requirement to screen individuals with emergency medical conditions. EMTALA defines an emergency medical condition as one that "[manifests] itself by acute symptoms of sufficient severity (including severe pain) such that the absence of immediate medical attention could reasonably be expected to result in . . . placing the health of the individual . . . in serious jeopardy."[12]

Risk Area: Failure to Secure Consent for Refusal of Treatment or Medically Appropriate Transfer

42 U.S.C. § 1395dd(b)(2)–(3)

> A hospital is deemed to [have met the requirement of stabilizing the individual with an emergency medical condition] if the hospital offers the individual the further medical examination and treatment . . . and informs the individual . . . of the risks and benefits [of the treatment, or informs the individual of a medically appropriate transfer], but the individual . . . refuses to consent to the examination and treatment [or medically appropriate transfer]. The hospital shall take all reasonable steps to secure the individual's . . . written informed consent to refuse such examination and treatment [or medically appropriate transfer].[13]

Context: Compliance professionals may already be aware of the need to secure patient consent, and that awareness necessarily extends to a patient refusing to consent to the treatment or transfer requirements of EMTALA.

Risk Area: Failure to Get Consent or a Licensed Physician to Sign Off on a Medically Appropriate Transfer

42 U.S.C. § 1395dd(c)(1)(A)(i)–(iii)

> If an individual at a hospital has an emergency medical condition which has not been stabilized . . . the hospital may not transfer the individual unless . . . the individual . . . after being informed of the hospital's obligations under this section and of the risk of transfer, in writing requests transfer to another medical facility, [or] a physician [or qualified medical person authorized by a physician who has consulted with the qualified person if the physician is not present] has signed a certification that . . . based upon the information available at the time of transfer, the medical benefits reasonably expected from the provision of appropriate medical treatment at another medical facility outweigh the increased risks to the individual.[14]

Context: When a physician determines the benefits of a transfer outweighs the risk to the individual, it is imperative that the physician certifies the transfer to avoid a violation.

Risk Area: Transfer to an Inappropriate Medical Facility

42 U.S.C. § 1395dd(c)(2)(A)–(E)

> An appropriate transfer to a medical facility is a transfer . . . in which the transferring hospital provides the medical treatment within its capacity which minimizes the risks to the individual's health . . . in which the receiving facility . . . has available space and qualified personnel for the treatment of the individual, and . . . has agreed to accept transfer of the individual and to provide appropriate medical treatment . . . in which the transferring hospital sends to the receiving facility all medical records (or copies thereof), related to the emergency condition for which the individual has presented, available at the time of the transfer, including records related to the individual's emergency medical condition, observations of signs or symptoms, preliminary diagnosis, treatment provided, results of any tests and the informed written consent or certification (or copy thereof) . . . and the name and address of any on-call physician . . . who has refused or failed to appear within a reasonable time to provide necessary stabilizing treatment . . . in which the transfer is effected through qualified personnel and transportation equipment, as required including the use of necessary and medically appropriate life support measures during the transfer; and . . . which meets such other

requirements as the Secretary may find necessary in the interest of the health and safety of individuals transferred.[15]

Context: Although a transfer away from the admitting emergency department to a medically appropriate facility may be justified, transfer is not proper without consideration of the receiving medical facility. When a transfer is proper, the transferee medical facility must be able to receive the patient, have agreed to receive the patient, have received the appropriate paperwork to treat the patient, and the transfer is conducted with qualified personnel and equipment.

Consequences for Noncompliance

Compliance with EMTALA is especially important to compliance professionals because of the severe civil penalties and civil actions arising from compliance violations. Civil money penalties can reach up to $50,000 for large hospitals and $25,000 for hospitals with less than 100 beds, per violation. Concurrently, civil enforcement in the form of private personal injury claims and economic loss of other medical facilities because of a compliance violation are available.

Administrative Proceedings

Penalties

- Termination of the healthcare provider's Medicare agreement,

- Money penalties of up to $50,000 per violation, and

- Settlement with the Office of Inspector General or Department of Justice ranging from $100,000 to well over $1 million.

Corrective Actions

- Required training of hospital staff to better comply with EMTALA's provisions,

- Conspicuous posting of the availability of financial assistance in the hospital and on the hospital's website,

- Provision of free financial counseling to all patients,

- Prohibition from collecting fees of patients applying for financial assistance, and

- Required reasonable payment schedules to uninsured or underinsured patients.

Civil Litigation

Damages

Under EMTALA, hospitals are subject to damages arising from personal injury under applicable state law. Apart from patients asserting personal injury, the receiving facility who suffered economic loss from an EMTALA violation may recover damages from the violating hospital or physician.

Important Compliance Guidance and Tools

Centers for Medicare & Medicaid Services

Emergency Medical Treatment & Labor Act (EMTALA)

The following is a link to the CMS website with a brief overview of the law. The website has related links, including the text of the law and other CMS resources for guidance on the law.

https://www.cms.gov/Regulations-and-Guidance/Legislation/EMTALA/index?redirect=/EMTALA/

Health Care Compliance Association

EMTALA Compliance Checklist

This checklist on the Health Care Compliance Association's website is a tool to help evaluate whether your institution is EMTALA compliant. The checklist covers all areas of process, including entrances and registration, treatment, transfers, and general best practices.

https://assets.hcca-info.org/Portals/0/PDFs/Resources/Conference_Handouts/Compliance_Institute/2016/308handout2.pdf

Relevant EMTALA Cases and Opinions

Saint Joseph Healthcare, Inc. v. Thomas, 487 S.W.3d 864 (Ky. 2016)

Case summary: The Kentucky Supreme Court upheld a $1.45 million punitive damage award against a hospital for failing to stabilize a disabled indigent patient. The underlying facts occurred in 1999 and involved the patient arriving at the hospital's emergency room because of acute stomach pain. The patient was given "pain medication, an enema, and manual disimpaction of his colon" before being discharged more than four hours later.

Over the course of the same night, the patient would return to the hospital twice more. In each instance, the patient was not given screening treatment or stabilized before discharge. When he first returned to the hospital, instead of being readmitted, he was left alone without a wheelchair in a motel room. Upon his last visit to the emergency room, he was warned he would be arrested if he returned. After his final discharge, the patient would die from his untreated ailment. The jury found the hospital acted with "gross negligence" in its treatment of the patient, which was the basis for its punitive damage award.

Opinion issued: May 5, 2016

Link to full text: https://www.leagle.com/decision/inkyco20160505169

EMTALA's civil action provision is subject to state law. Kentucky's state law allows punitive damage awards for findings of "gross negligence" or "oppression, fraud or malice" toward the plaintiff. The court found the hospital acted to oppress the patient by imposing a "cruel and unjust hardship" by leaving the patent alone in a motel room in a wheelchair and threatening to arrest him if he returned for medical treatment.

The court also agreed with the trial court that the hospital's actions amounted to gross negligence, or "wanton or reckless disregard for the lives, safety, or property of others." While the hospital argued the patient wasn't mistreated because of the "extensive list of the medical services" the hospital provided him, the court reasoned that although the hospital did "some things right," it was not absolved of liability. Specifically, the court pointed to the nature of the patient: wheelchair bound, gravely ill, destitute, in great pain, and "[i]n that condition only hours away from death, he was twice ushered out the Hospital door."[16]

The court also rejected the hospital's argument that it did not "ratify" the actions against the patient. Kentucky law attaches punitive liability on an employer for the actions of employees when there is authorization, anticipation, or ratification by the employer. The court held the hospital ratified the conduct against the patient because the hospital's employees "went well beyond . . . idle neglect that might reasonably go unnoticed by supervising administrators."[17] Pointing to the deliberate actions over a 16-hour period against a patient who was conspicuously ill, the court determined the jury could, and did, legitimately make the inference of the hospital's intention to ratify its employees' actions.

In determining whether the punitive damage award against the hospital should be lowered, the court considered the degree of reprehensibility, the ratio between punitive and compensatory damages, and the possible civil or criminal penalties. Citing the facts in the above paragraphs, the court found the hospital's actions clearly reprehensible. The court determined the punitive to compensatory damages ratio (386 to 1) was proper because the hospital's egregious acts amounted only to $3,750 in damages for the plaintiff. Thus, a deviation from the usual rule that the ratio between damages should not exceed single digits was justified. Lastly, in considering the limitations on civil penalties under EMTALA ($100,000 in this case), the court determined the statutory penalties did not prevent the justification of the punitive award.

Romar v. Fresno Community Hosp. Medical Center, 583 F. Supp. 2d 1179 (E.D. Cal. 2008)

Case summary: In *Romar*, the court allowed a plaintiff to sidestep the state professional negligence cap of $250,000 under an EMTALA claim where a hospital failed to screen a patient in the same manner as it had other patients. This case involved a minor patient who was "disparately screened" compared to 30 other patients showing the same symptoms. Unlike a traditional failure to screen violation, a disparate screening violation under EMTALA involves a question of whether the patient's screening was compliant with the hospital's own screening standards.

Opinion issued: October 10, 2008

Link to full text: https://www.leagle.com/decision/20081762583cvfsupp2d117911663

Because EMTALA does not establish negligence claims, the plaintiff was able to seek damages outside of the purview of California's professional negligence cap. As the court put it, "It is … possible for a hospital with 'high standards' to violate EMTALA because it treated a plaintiff differently, but at the same time comply with state medical malpractice law because the care provided exceeded the professional standard of care."[18]

The court highlighted the key difference between EMTALA and professional liability violations: "[It is] whether Plaintiff was treated differently, [and] not whether [the hospital] breached the standard of professional medical care." In its analysis, the court considered the closeness of EMTALA (and similar state statutes) and professional negligence, however made a distinction in the context of disparate screening claims because "the professional standard of care is not incorporated into the duty to provide materially similar screenings."[19]

Thus, court ordered that the state's professional negligence cap does not apply to the plaintiff's EMTALA disparate screening claims.

Endnotes

1. **Gabriel Imperato** is managing partner at the Fort Lauderdale office of Nelson Mullins Riley & Scarborough. He is the team leader of the firm's Health Care Criminal and Civil Enforcement, Litigation and Compliance Practice. He has practiced healthcare law in both the public and private sectors for more than 40 years. He is board certified as a specialist in health law by The Florida Bar. Imperato recently served as the general counsel of the North Broward Hospital District, the tenth largest healthcare system in the United States. He has also served as deputy chief counsel for the U.S. Department of Health & Human Services' Office of the General Counsel. Imperato is also a longtime member of the board of directors of Society of Corporate Compliance and Ethics & the Health Care Compliance Association (SCCE & HCCA), where he was also a past president and interim CEO.

2. **Anne Novick Branan** is an of counsel attorney in the Fort Lauderdale office of Nelson Mullins Riley & Scarborough. She has been board certified in health law by The Florida Bar since 1995. Branan counsels healthcare providers about avoiding and responding to allegations of fraud under the Medicare and Medicaid programs. She helps her clients navigate the complex regulatory environment affecting acquisitions and contracting in the healthcare industry. Branan regularly assists healthcare companies in developing and assessing the effectiveness of corporate compliance and ethics programs. She was recognized in *The Best Lawyers in America* for healthcare law, 2015–2020, and selected as Fort Lauderdale Health Care Law "Lawyer of the Year" in 2017.

3. **Richard Sena** is a juris doctor candidate at the Nova Southeastern University Shepard Broad College of Law. He is the editor-in-chief of the *Nova Law Review* and a law clerk at Nelson Mullins Riley & Scarborough in Fort Lauderdale since the summer of 2020. Sena has conducted health law research under the guidance of attorneys Gabriel Imperato and Anne Novick Branan and helped author sections of the "Key Laws in Healthcare Compliance" chapter in the 2021 HCCA *Complete Healthcare Compliance Manual*. He is expected to graduate in May 2021 and plans to continue his career as an associate attorney at Nelson Mullins.

4. **Megan Speltz** is a digital product owner at SCCE & HCCA, where she helps define and deliver new digital products to the COSMOS platform. She graduated from the University of St. Thomas School of Law in May 2020; she obtained her juris doctor with a concentration in organizational ethics and compliance. In addition to working at SCCE & HCCA, Speltz is a licensed attorney practicing in the state of Minnesota and represents small businesses and nonprofit organizations.

5. "EMTALA Fact Sheet," American College of Emergency Physicians, accessed October 22, 2020, https://www.acep.org/life-as-a-physician/ethics--legal/emtala/emtala-fact-sheet/.

6. Joseph Zibulewsky, "The Emergency Medical Treatment and Active Labor Act (EMTALA): what it is and what it means for physicians," *Baylor University Medical Center Proceedings* 14, no. 4, 339–346 (October 2001), https://www.ncbi.nlm.nih.gov/pmc/articles/PMC1305897/.

7. "EMTALA Fact Sheet," American College of Emergency Physicians.

8. "Emergency Medical Treatment and Labor Act Technical Advisory Group (EMTALA TAG)," Centers for Medicare & Medicaid Services, last modified February 11, 2020, https://www.cms.gov/Regulations-and-Guidance/Legislation/EMTALA/emtalatag.

9. Utah Code Ann. § R432-100-17(2)(c) (LexisNexis 2020).

10. N.Y. Public Health Law § 2805-b(2)(b) (McKinney 2019).

11. 42 U.S.C. § 1395dd(a).

12. 42 U.S.C. § 1395dd(e).

13. 42 U.S.C. § 1395dd(b)(2),(3).

14. 42 U.S.C. § 1395dd(c)(1)(A)(i)–(iii).

15. 42 U.S.C. § 1395dd(c)(2)(A)–(E).

16. Saint Joseph Healthcare, Inc. v. Thomas, 487 S.W.3d 864 (Ky. 2016).

17. Saint Joseph Healthcare, Inc. v. Thomas, 487 S.W.3d 864 (Ky. 2016).

18. Romar v. Fresno Community Hosp. Medical Center, 583 F. Supp. 2d 1179 (E.D. Cal. 2008).

19. Romar v. Fresno Community Hosp. Medical Center, 583 F. Supp. 2d 1179 (E.D. Cal. 2008).

False Claims Act

By Gabriel Imperato,[1] Esq., CHC; Anne Novick Branan,[2] Esq., CHC;
Richard Sena[3] ; and Megan Speltz,[4] JD

Fast Facts

Title of law: False Claims Act, civil actions for false claims, false claims procedure, false claims jurisdiction, civil investigative demands

Categories:

- Fraud and abuse
- Medicare
- Medicaid

U.S. Code: 31 U.S.C. §§ 3729–3733

Year enacted: 1863

Major amendments: 1943, 1986, 2009, 2010

Enforcement agencies: U.S. Department of Health & Human Services (HHS) Office of Inspector General (OIG), U.S. Department of Justice (DOJ)

Links to full text of law:

- https://www.govinfo.gov/content/pkg/USCODE-2011-title31/pdf/USCODE-2011-title31-subtitleIII-chap37-subchapIII-sec3729.pdf
- https://www.govinfo.gov/content/pkg/USCODE-2010-title31/pdf/USCODE-2010-title31-subtitleIII-chap37-subchapIII-sec3730.pdf
- https://www.govinfo.gov/content/pkg/USCODE-2010-title31/pdf/USCODE-2010-title31-subtitleIII-chap37-subchapIII-sec3731.pdf
- https://www.govinfo.gov/content/pkg/USCODE-2010-title31/pdf/USCODE-2010-title31-subtitleIII-chap37-subchapIII-sec3732.pdf
- https://www.govinfo.gov/content/pkg/USCODE-2010-title31/pdf/USCODE-2010-title31-subtitleIII-chap37-subchapIII-sec3733.pdf

Applies to: Fraud involving any federally funded contract or program, with the exception of tax fraud. Concerns to healthcare include upcoding, off-label promotion, Medicaid rebates, failure to document patient care, deficient compliance, worthless services, and improperly retaining overpayment from a government healthcare program.[5]

What Is the False Claims Act?

The False Claims Act (FCA), also known as the "Lincoln Law," is a federal law that imposes liability on persons and companies who defraud governmental programs. It is one of the government's primary tools for combatting fraud. The FCA creates liability for any person who knowingly submits a false claim or makes a false claim to the government. The FCA also includes a qui tam provision, which allows private persons to file suit for violations of the FCA on behalf of the government. The FCA provides for up to treble damages and also provides awards of 15%–30% of recovery for those bringing cases.[6]

Healthcare fraud represents the largest and most profitable industry for qui tam false claims collections. In 2019, the healthcare industry accounted for 87% of all FCA judgments and settlements.[7] The FCA covers every claim for Medicare reimbursement. For example, if a practice group submits a Medicare claim for reimbursement for the examination of a patient that never took place, then this is a false claim. Other examples of false claims include upcoding procedures, unbundling procedures, filing multiple claims for the same procedure, and billing for medically unnecessary procedures, etc.[8]

History

The FCA was enacted in 1863 by Congress in response to concerns that suppliers of goods during the Civil War were defrauding the Union Army.[9] President Abraham Lincoln advocated for the passage of the FCA when war suppliers were shipping boxes of sawdust instead of guns and selling the same cavalry horses several times to the Union Army, amongst other fraudulent activities.[10] The law contained qui tam provisions that allowed private citizens to sue on the government's behalf. "Those who filed lawsuits . . . were entitled to receive 50 percent of the amount the government recovered as a result of their case."

In 1943, Congress changed the qui tam provisions, drastically reducing the reward amount for those bringing a claim on the government's behalf. This created less of an incentive for citizens to report fraud. A new provision also prevented whistleblowers from filing a lawsuit based on information already possessed by the government or a government employee, even if the whistleblower provided the information and the government chose not to investigate.

In the 1980s, the law was revised again after reports of widespread fraud against the government during the Cold War. There were many reports of outrageous billing practices by defense contractors against the military, and government enforcement agencies lacked resources to investigate. Congress amended the qui tam provisions to provide that whistleblowers who brought successful cases "were entitled to [15%–30%] of the government's recovery and attorneys' fees paid by the defendant."[11] They also removed the "government possession of information" bar against suits.

The FCA was amended again in 2009 and 2010 to clarify terms and expand its scope from the original law.[12]

Related Laws

Social Security Act: 42 U.S.C. § 1396h

Allows states to receive a 10% increase in their share of recovery in false claims related to Medicaid if the state enacts a qualifying state false claims law. As of early 2021, 21 states have a qualifying law and 8 states' laws have been denied approval after seeking review by the Office of Inspector General.[13] Alabama, Alaska, Arizona, Arkansas, Idaho, Kansas, Kentucky, Maine, Maryland, Mississippi, Missouri, Nebraska, North Dakota, Ohio, Oregon, Pennsylvania, South Carolina, South Dakota, Utah, West Virginia, and Wyoming do not have a qualifying law and have not sought approval. A qualifying law is required to include the following:

- Liability for false claims as defined by the FCA with respect to any federal healthcare plan,
- Provisions that reward qui tam actions as effectively as the FCA,
- Requirement that the action remains under seal for 60 days, and
- Civil penalty not less than the penalty under the FCA.

Examples of Qualifying State False Claims Laws

Cal. Gov't Code §§ 12650-12656 (West 2020)
- Prohibits knowingly making false claims for money, property, or services to the state.
- Rewards qui tam plaintiff 15%–33% of the proceeds from a successful action. If the state does not proceed with the action, plaintiff may receive 25%–50% of the proceeds.
- Action remains under seal for 60 days.
- Protects employee whistleblowers from retaliation.
- Provides for treble damages, court costs, and a civil penalty not less than $5,500 and not more than $11,000 for each violation.

Tex. Hum. Res. Code Ann. §§ 36.001–36.132 (West 2019)
- Prohibits knowingly making false claims under a Medicaid program to receive an unauthorized benefit or payment.
- Rewards qui tam plaintiff 15%–25% of the proceeds from a successful action. If the state does not proceed with the action, plaintiff may receive 25%–30% of the proceeds.
- Action remains under seal for 180 days.
- Provides for two-times damages, interest, and a civil penalty not less than $5,500 and not more than $11,000 for each violation. Limit increases to $15,000 if the false claim results in injury to an elderly person, person with a disability, or a person younger than 18 years old.

740 Ill. Comp. Stat. 175/3 (2020)

- Prohibits knowingly making false claim for payment or approval to the state.

- Rewards qui tam plaintiff 15%–25% of the proceeds from a successful action. If the state determines the claim is based primarily on information not from the qui tam plaintiff, plaintiff's award may be no less than 10%. If the state does not proceed with the action, plaintiff may receive 25%–30% of the proceeds.
- Action remains under seal for 60 days.
- Provides civil penalties equal to the federal False Claims Act plus treble damages. However, in qui tam actions where the state chooses not to intervene, the tax owed to the state equals or is under $50,000, and the violation relates to a tax from the state Department of Revenue, penalties include a $5,500–$11,000 civil penalty plus treble damages for each violation.

False Claims Act Compliance Risks

The False Claims Act is important to compliance professionals because violations expose healthcare organizations to sizeable civil penalties and damages. Although the text of the law provides for a civil penalty range between $5,000 and $10,000, these amounts are adjusted for inflation. Accordingly, healthcare organizations found to violate the statute may have to pay up to $23,331 per violation that occurs in 2020 and three times the damages the government sustains as a result of the violation. Additionally, violations of the Anti-Kickback Statute and Stark Law also trigger violations of the False Claims Act.[14] The following are specific False Claims Act risk areas that compliance professionals need to monitor closely.

Risk Area: Making False Claims

31 U.S.C. § 3729

1. [A]ny person who—

    A. knowingly presents, or causes to be presented, a false or fraudulent claim for payment or approval;

    B. knowingly makes, uses, or causes to be made or used, a false record or statement material to a false or fraudulent claim;

    C. conspires to commit a violation [under 31 U.S.C. § 3729(a)(1)];

    D. has possession, custody, or control of property or money used, or to be used, by the Government and knowingly delivers, or causes to be delivered, less than all of that money or property;

    E. is authorized to make or deliver a document certifying receipt of property used, or to be used, by the Government and, intending to defraud the

Government, makes or delivers the receipt without completely knowing that the information on the receipt is true;

F. knowingly buys, or receives as a pledge of an obligation or debt, public property from an officer or employee of the Government, or a member of the Armed Forces, who lawfully may not sell or pledge property; or

G. knowingly makes, uses, or causes to be made or used, a false record or statement material to an obligation to pay or transmit money or property to the Government, or knowingly conceals or knowingly and improperly avoids or decreases an obligation to pay or transmit money or property to the Government,

is liable to the United States Government for a civil penalty of not less than $5,000 and not more than $10,000, as adjusted by the Federal Civil Penalties Inflation Adjustment Act of 1990 (28 U.S.C. § 2461 note; Public Law 104–410), plus 3 times the amount of damages which the Government sustains because of the act of that person.

2. … If the court finds that—

A. the person committing the violation of this subsection furnished officials of the United States responsible for investigating false claims violations with all information known to such person about the violation within 30 days after the date on which the defendant first obtained the information;

B. such person fully cooperated with any Government investigation of such violation; and

C. at the time such person furnished the United States with the information about the violation, no criminal prosecution, civil action, or administrative action had commenced under this title with respect to such violation, and the person did not have actual knowledge of the existence of an investigation into such violation, the court may assess not less than 2 times the amount of damages which the Government sustains because of the act of that person.

3. … A person violating this subsection shall also be liable to the United States Government for the costs of a civil action brought to recover any such penalty or damages.[15]

Context: 31 U.S.C. § 3729(a)(1) bars several types of false claims. 31 U.S.C. § 3729(a)(1)(A) and (B) prohibit making or presenting a false claim for payment or approval. 31 U.S.C. § 3729(a)(1)(D) alludes to the bait and switch situation alluded to in the "History" section of this article, where suppliers would defraud the government by shipping sawdust instead of the guns. 31 U.S.C. § 3729(a)(1)(G) is commonly referred to as the "reverse false claims section."[16] Instead of prohibiting claims to receive payment or approval, 31 U.S.C. § 3729(a)(1)(G) prohibits a false record or statement in order to avoid a payment obligation to the government. Further, 31 U.S.C. § 3729(a)(2) provides for mitigation of the amount of damages a cooperative violating party would pay to the government. Lastly, violations of 31 U.S.C. § 3729 may trigger violations of the Anti-Kickback Statute and Stark Law.

Risk Area: Civil Actions for False Claims

31 U.S.C. § 3730

a. Responsibilities of the Attorney General.—The Attorney General diligently shall investigate a violation under section 3729. If the Attorney General finds that a person has violated or is violating section 3729, the Attorney General may bring a civil action under this section against the person.

b. Actions by Private Persons.—

1. A person may bring a civil action for a violation of section 3729 for the person and for the United States Government. The action shall be brought in the name of the Government. The action may be dismissed only if the court and the Attorney General give written consent to the dismissal and their reasons for consenting.

2. A copy of the complaint and written disclosure of substantially all material evidence and information the person possesses shall be served on the Government pursuant to Rule 4(d)(4) of the Federal Rules of Civil Procedure. The complaint shall be filed in camera, shall remain under seal for at least 60 days, and shall not be served on the defendant until the court so orders. The Government may elect to intervene and proceed with the action within 60 days after it receives both the complaint and the material evidence and information.

3. The Government may, for good cause shown, move the court for extensions of the time during which the complaint remains under seal under paragraph (2). Any such motions may be supported by affidavits or other submissions in camera. The defendant shall not be required to respond to any complaint filed under this section until 20 days after the complaint is unsealed and served upon the defendant pursuant to Rule 4 of the Federal Rules of Civil Procedure.

4. Before the expiration of the 60-day period or any extensions obtained under paragraph (3), the Government shall—

   A. proceed with the action, in which case the action shall be conducted by the Government; or

B. notify the court that it declines to take over the action, in which case the person bringing the action shall have the right to conduct the action.

5. When a person brings an action under this subsection, no person other than the Government may intervene or bring a related action based on the facts underlying the pending action.

c. Rights of the Parties to Qui Tam Actions.—

1. If the Government proceeds with the action, it shall have the primary responsibility for prosecuting the action, and shall not be bound by an act of the person bringing the action. Such person shall have the right to continue as a party to the action, subject to the limitations set forth in paragraph (2).

2.

A. The Government may dismiss the action notwithstanding the objections of the person initiating the action if the person has been notified by the Government of the filing of the motion and the court has provided the person with an opportunity for a hearing on the motion.

B. The Government may settle the action with the defendant notwithstanding the objections of the person initiating the action if the court determines, after a hearing, that the proposed settlement is fair, adequate, and reasonable under all the circumstances. Upon a showing of good cause, such hearing may be held in camera.

C. Upon a showing by the Government that unrestricted participation during the course of the litigation by the person initiating the action would interfere with or unduly delay the Government's prosecution of the case, or would be repetitious, irrelevant, or for purposes of harassment, the court may, in its discretion, impose limitations on the person's participation, such as—

   i. limiting the number of witnesses the person may call;

   ii. limiting the length of the testimony of such witnesses;

   iii. limiting the person's cross-examination of witnesses; or

   iv. otherwise limiting the participation by the person in the litigation.

D. Upon a showing by the defendant that unrestricted participation during the course of the litigation by the person initiating the action would be for purposes of harassment or would cause the defendant undue burden or unnecessary expense, the court may limit the participation by the person in the litigation.

3. If the Government elects not to proceed with the action, the person who initiated the action shall have the right to conduct the action. If the Government so requests, it shall be served with copies of all pleadings filed in the action and shall be supplied with copies of all deposition transcripts (at the Government's expense). When a person proceeds with the action, the court, without limiting the status and rights of the person initiating the action, may nevertheless permit the Government to intervene at a later date upon a showing of good cause.

4. Whether or not the Government proceeds with the action, upon a showing by the Government that certain actions of discovery by the person initiating the action would interfere with the Government's investigation or prosecution of a criminal or civil matter arising out of the same facts, the court may stay such discovery for a period of not more than 60 days. Such a showing shall be conducted in camera. The court may extend the 60-day period upon a further showing in camera that the Government has pursued the criminal or civil investigation or proceedings with reasonable diligence and any proposed discovery in the civil action will interfere with the ongoing criminal or civil investigation or proceedings.

5. Notwithstanding subsection (b), the Government may elect to pursue its claim through any alternate remedy available to the Government, including any administrative proceeding to determine a civil money penalty. If any such alternate remedy is pursued in another proceeding, the person initiating the action shall have the same rights in such proceeding as such person would have had if the action had continued under this section. Any finding of fact or conclusion of law made in such other proceeding that has become final shall be conclusive on all parties to an action under this section. For purposes of the preceding sentence, a finding or conclusion is final if it has been finally determined on appeal to the appropriate court of the United States, if all time for filing such an appeal with respect to the finding or conclusion has expired, or if the finding or conclusion is not subject to judicial review.

d. Award to Qui Tam Plaintiff.—

1. If the Government proceeds with an action brought by a person under subsection (b), such person shall, subject to the second sentence of this paragraph, receive at least 15 percent but not more than 25 percent of the proceeds of the action or settlement of the claim, depending upon the extent to which the person substantially contributed to the prosecution of the action. Where the action is one which the court finds to be based primarily on disclosures of specific information (other than information provided by

the person bringing the action) relating to allegations or transactions in a criminal, civil, or administrative hearing, in a congressional, administrative, or Government Accounting Office report, hearing, audit, or investigation, or from the news media, the court may award such sums as it considers appropriate, but in no case more than 10 percent of the proceeds, taking into account the significance of the information and the role of the person bringing the action in advancing the case to litigation. Any payment to a person under the first or second sentence of this paragraph shall be made from the proceeds. Any such person shall also receive an amount for reasonable expenses which the court finds to have been necessarily incurred, plus reasonable attorneys' fees and costs. All such expenses, fees, and costs shall be awarded against the defendant.

2. If the Government does not proceed with an action under this section, the person bringing the action or settling the claim shall receive an amount which the court decides is reasonable for collecting the civil penalty and damages. The amount shall be not less than 25 percent and not more than 30 percent of the proceeds of the action or settlement and shall be paid out of such proceeds. Such person shall also receive an amount for reasonable expenses which the court finds to have been necessarily incurred, plus reasonable attorneys' fees and costs. All such expenses, fees, and costs shall be awarded against the defendant.

3. Whether or not the Government proceeds with the action, if the court finds that the action was brought by a person who planned and initiated the violation of section 3729 upon which the action was brought, then the court may, to the extent the court considers appropriate, reduce the share of the proceeds of the action which the person would otherwise receive under paragraph (1) or (2) of this subsection, taking into account the role of that person in advancing the case to litigation and any relevant circumstances pertaining to the violation. If the person bringing the action is convicted of criminal conduct arising from his or her role in the violation of section 3729, that person shall be dismissed from the civil action and shall not receive any share of the proceeds of the action. Such dismissal shall not prejudice the right of the United States to continue the action, represented by the Department of Justice.

4. If the Government does not proceed with the action and the person bringing the action conducts the action, the court may award to the defendant its reasonable attorneys' fees and expenses if the defendant prevails in the action and the court finds that the claim of the person bringing the action was clearly frivolous, clearly vexatious, or brought primarily for purposes of harassment.

e. Certain Actions Barred.—

1. No court shall have jurisdiction over an action brought by a former or present member of the armed forces under subsection (b) of this section against a member of the armed forces arising out of such person's service in the armed forces.

2.

   A. No court shall have jurisdiction over an action brought under subsection (b) against a Member of Congress, a member of the judiciary, or a senior executive branch official if the action is based on evidence or information known to the Government when the action was brought.

   B. For purposes of this paragraph, 'senior executive branch official' means any officer or employee listed in paragraphs (1) through (8) of section 101(f) of the Ethics in Government Act of 1978 (5 U.S.C. App.)

3. In no event may a person bring an action under subsection (b) which is based upon allegations or transactions which are the subject of a civil suit or an administrative civil money penalty proceeding in which the Government is already a party.

4.

   A. The court shall dismiss an action or claim under this section, unless opposed by the Government, if substantially the same allegations or transactions as alleged in the action or claim were publicly disclosed—

      i. in a Federal criminal, civil, or administrative hearing in which the Government or its agent is a party;

      ii. in a congressional, Government Accountability Office, or other Federal report, hearing, audit, or investigation; or

      iii. from the news media, unless the action is brought by the Attorney General or the person bringing the action is an original source of the information.

   B. For purposes of this paragraph, 'original source' means an individual who either (i) prior to a public disclosure under subsection (e)(4)(a), has voluntarily disclosed to the Government the information on which allegations or transactions in a claim are based, or (2) who has knowledge that is independent of and materially adds to the publicly disclosed allegations or transactions, and who has voluntarily provided the information to the Government before filing an action under this section.

f. Government Not Liable for Certain Expenses.—The Government is not liable for expenses which a person incurs in bringing an action under this section.

g. Fees and Expenses to Prevailing Defendant.—In civil actions brought under this section by the United States, the provisions of section 2412(d) of title 28 shall apply.

h. Relief from Retaliatory Actions.—

  1. In General.—Any employee, contractor, or agent shall be entitled to all relief necessary to make that employee, contractor, or agent whole, if that employee, contractor, or agent is discharged, demoted, suspended, threatened, harassed, or in any other manner discriminated against in the terms and conditions of employment because of lawful acts done by the employee, contractor, agent or associated others in furtherance of an action under this section or other efforts to stop 1 or more violations of this subchapter.

  2. Relief.—Relief under paragraph (1) shall include reinstatement with the same seniority status that employee, contractor, or agent would have had but for the discrimination, 2 times the amount of back pay, interest on the back pay, and compensation for any special damages sustained as a result of the discrimination, including litigation costs and reasonable attorneys' fees. An action under this subsection may be brought in the appropriate district court of the United States for the relief provided in this subsection.

  3. Limitation on Bringing Civil Action.—A civil action under this subsection may not be brought more than 3 years after the date when the retaliation occurred.[17]

Context: False Claims Act lawsuits are often brought by private individuals who are often former or current employees of the alleged violator. The False Claims Act incentivizes individuals to bring suit, known as qui tam plaintiffs or relators, by awarding them a sizeable share of the proceeds from a successful suit or settlement. When an action is brought by a private individual, the complaint is sealed for 60 days while the government investigates and decides whether to take over the action. If the government declines, the private individual may still prosecute the action; however, the government may still choose to intervene. 31 U.S.C. § 3730(h) protects employee whistleblowers from employer retaliation.

Consequences for Noncompliance

Violations of the False Claims Act expose healthcare organizations to civil penalties up to the statutory limit, subject to adjustment for inflation, per violation. Violators are also liable for three times the damages the government sustains as a result of the false claim or reverse false claim.

Administrative Proceedings

Penalties

- Violations before August 1999 are subject to civil penalties from $5,000 to $10,000.

- Violations from September 29, 1999, to November 2, 2015, are subject to civil penalties from $5,500 to $11,000.

- Civil penalties for violations after August 2016 are calculated when the court awards the penalties. As of June 19, 2020, the penalty range is from $11,665 to $23,331 and is updated annually or biennially.[18]

Corrective Actions

- Appointment of a compliance officer.

- Development of a written training plan to ensure compliance with federal healthcare programs.

- Required hiring of an independent review organization to review claims for reimbursement by Medicare and Medicaid.

- Establishment of an internal disclosure program for employees to report possible compliance violations to the compliance officer without risk of retaliation.

Civil Litigation

Damages

Violators of the False Claims Act are liable for three times the damages the government sustains because of the violation. Violators who cooperate under section 31 U.S.C. § 3729(a)(2) may have damages reduced to two times the damages sustained by the government.

Important Compliance Guidance and Tools

Centers for Medicare & Medicaid Services

Medicare Fraud & Abuse: Prevent, Detect, Report

This booklet for Medicare fee-for-service providers details kinds of Medicare-related fraud and abuse, including information about the False Claims Act.

https://www.cms.gov/Outreach-and-Education/Medicare-Learning-Network-MLN/
MLNProducts/Downloads/Fraud-Abuse-MLN4649244.pdf

U.S. Department of Health & Human Services, Office of Inspector General

Fraud Risk Indicator

This article provides the different risk categories that organizations that violate the FCA may fall into.[19] Further, it includes a link to the published criteria that the department looks to when assessing future risk and placing parties to a settlement on the risk spectrum.

https://oig.hhs.gov/compliance/corporate-integrity-agreements/risk.asp

Compliance Guidance

The following link from the Office of Inspector General website includes a variety of compliance program guidance documents for various segments of the healthcare industry.[20] The guidance is meant to encourage the development and use of internal controls to monitor adherence to applicable statutes, regulations, and program requirements.

https://oig.hhs.gov/compliance/compliance-guidance/index.asp

U.S. Department of Justice, Civil Division, Commercial Litigation Branch, Fraud Section

The U.S. Department of Justice website includes a section on healthcare fraud that explains the types of cases handled by the department and how violators may be prosecuted.

https://www.justice.gov/civil/practice-areas-0#healthcare

Fraud Recovery Statistics

This chart shows the total number of fraud cases that have been reported, which ones have been acted on, and which ones have been settled.[21] The chart also shows how many cases are qui tam actions.

https://www.justice.gov/opa/press-release/file/1233201/download

Relevant False Claims Act Cases and Opinions

United States ex rel. Simon, et al. v. HealthSouth Corp., et al., No. 08-CV-236 (M.D. Fla.); United States ex rel. Higgins v. HealthSouth Corp., No.: 3:12 CV 2496 (N.D. Tex.); United States ex rel. Clarke et al. v. HealthSouth Corp., No.: 1:12 CV 853 (E.D. Va.)

Case summary: Three separate lawsuits were filed against Encompass Health Corporation (formerly HealthSouth Corporation) in Florida, Texas, and Virginia for providing inaccurate information to Medicare in order to maintain its status as an inpatient rehabilitation facility (IRF) and receive reimbursement for services that were not medically necessary. In order for a provider to maintain its IRF status and eligibility for increased Medicare reimbursement, the provider must meet a minimum threshold of patients with conditions qualifying for rehabilitative care.[22] Encompass Health allegedly provided false or unsupported patient diagnoses and admitted patients too sick or disabled to be eligible for IRF care in order to maintain its threshold for eligibility for increased reimbursement. Encompass Health Corporation entered into a $48 million settlement agreement with the Department of Justice.

Opinion issued: June 28, 2019

Link to full text: https://www.justice.gov/opa/pr/encompass-health-agrees-pay-48-million-resolve-false-claims-act-allegations-relating-its?utm_medium=email&utm_source=govdelivery

Commenting on the settlement, U.S. Attorney Maria Chapa Lopez said: "This important civil settlement concludes a lengthy, comprehensive investigation that brought to light a nationwide scheme that the government contends was intended to defraud our fragile public health programs."[23] The suits were all brought by the government on behalf of private plaintiffs, all of whom were either former Encompass Health Corporation employees or contractors. For their efforts, the whistleblowers collectively received $12.4 million from the $48 million settlement.

United States ex rel. Aldridge v. Corporate Management, Inc., et al., No.: 1:16cv369-HTW-LRA (S.D. Miss.)

Case summary: In a jury trial, Stone County Hospital, Corporate Management Inc. (CMI), and defendant officers Ted Cain, Julie Cain, and Tommy Kuluz were found guilty of violating the False Claims Act for submitting fraudulent Medicare cost reports. The complaint was brought by the former chief operating officer, James Aldridge, of Stone County Hospital in Mississippi, which operated as a Medicare provider and was designated as a rural critical access hospital entitled to special reimbursement rates. Aldridge was initially hired by CMI, the latter acting as Stone County Hospital's administrator.

The complaint alleged Stone County Hospital, through CMI, submitted cost reports to Medicare for nonreimbursable costs in the form of executive compensation for Ted Cain over an 11-year period despite no evidence he did any work for the hospital. The total reimbursement by Medicare for Ted Cain's compensation totaled nearly $11.8 million. Similarly, Julie Cain received more than $800,000 in reimbursed compensation by Medicare despite no evidence she worked at the hospital or provided any of the alleged consulting services. Additionally, a state Medicaid audit found discrepancies between CMI's cost reporting to Medicaid and Medicare despite both programs following the same guidelines.

Opinion issued: March 13, 2020

Link to full text: https://casetext.com/case/ aldridge-ex-rel-united-states-v-h-ted-cain-julie-cain-corporate-mgmt-inc-1

The jury ultimately found the defendants guilty and the judge ordered a recovery of nearly $11 million to Medicare. In commenting on the verdict, U.S. Attorney Mike Hurst stated: "This was one of the most egregious cases of Medicare fraud we have litigated in the State of Mississippi," adding that "[t]his verdict is a victory for the American taxpayer and all the beneficiaries of Medicare and other government programs."[24] In addition to the government's recovery, the defendants were also liable for monetary penalties of $5,500 to $11,000 for the cost reports between 2004 and 2014, and $11,181 to $22,363 for the cost report in 2015.

United States ex rel. Peters v. Hope Hospice and Cmty. Servs., No. 2:16-cv-6-FtM-99MRM (M.D. Fla. 2020)

Case summary: Hope Hospice, a hospice care facility in Fort Myers, allegedly violated the False Claims act by knowingly submitting false claims to Medicare, Medicaid, and TRICARE for patients who were not terminally ill. Medicare patients are considered terminally ill and eligible for hospice services when their life expectancy is six months or less. Hope Hospice's illegal actions allegedly occurred between the summers of 2012 and 2016, when Hope Hospice billed Medicare for hospice services for patients who stayed at the facility for more than four years without a terminal illness.

Hope Hospice also allegedly overbilled Medicare, Medicaid, and TRICARE for expensive general inpatient (GIP) services. GIP services are reserved for short-term specialized pain control and symptom management. However, Hope Hospice unnecessarily billed the federal healthcare programs for GIP services provided for multiweek stints during a five-year period. Hope Hospice entered into a $3.2 million settlement agreement with the Department of Justice.

Opinion issued: July 8, 2020

Link to full text: https://www.leagle.com/decision/infdco20200710a81

In its corporate settlement news release, the Department of Justice cited the alleged behavior of Hope Hospice and the potential strain it puts on seniors and all others who rely on state and federal healthcare programs. "This investigation and settlement demonstrates our continued commitment to combating health care fraud and protecting the financial solvency of this critical benefit," said United States Attorney Maria Chapa Lopez. Further, Special Agent in Charge Omar Pérez Aybar added, "Hospice care is designed to provide quality end-of-life care and is only medically appropriate—and reimbursable by Medicare—for terminally ill patients."[25]

As part of the settlement, Hope Hospice entered into a corporate integrity agreement with the Office of Inspector General. The terms of the agreement include requiring Hope Hospice to do the following: appoint a compliance officer, create a compliance committee consisting of senior management, develop policies to ensure compliance, develop training for employees subject to compliance rules, hire a third party to review claims to Medicare and Medicaid, and institute other institutional changes to ensure compliance with federal healthcare programs.[26]

This case was initially brought by a former employee of Hope Hospice, Margaret Peters. As a result of the settlement, Peters received 19% of the settlement proceeds.

Endnotes

1. **Gabriel Imperato** is managing partner at the Fort Lauderdale office of Nelson Mullins Riley & Scarborough. He is the team leader of the firm's Health Care Criminal and Civil Enforcement, Litigation and Compliance Practice. He has practiced healthcare law in both the public and private sectors for more than 40 years. He is board certified as a specialist in health law by The Florida Bar. Imperato recently served as the general counsel of the North Broward Hospital District, the tenth largest healthcare system in the United States. He has also served as deputy chief counsel for the U.S. Department of Health & Human Services' Office of the General Counsel. Imperato is also a longtime member of the board of directors of Society of Corporate Compliance and Ethics & the Health Care Compliance Association (SCCE & HCCA), where he was also a past president and interim CEO.

2. **Anne Novick Branan** is an of counsel attorney in the Fort Lauderdale office of Nelson Mullins Riley & Scarborough. She has been board certified in health law by The Florida Bar since 1995. Branan counsels healthcare providers about avoiding and responding to allegations of fraud under the Medicare and Medicaid programs. She helps her clients navigate the complex regulatory environment affecting acquisitions and contracting in the healthcare industry. Branan regularly assists healthcare companies in developing and assessing the effectiveness of corporate compliance and ethics programs. She was recognized in *The Best Lawyers in America* for healthcare law, 2015–2020, and selected as Fort Lauderdale Health Care Law "Lawyer of the Year" in 2017.

3. **Richard Sena** is a juris doctor candidate at the Nova Southeastern University Shepard Broad College of Law. He is the editor-in-chief of the *Nova Law Review* and

a law clerk at Nelson Mullins Riley & Scarborough in Fort Lauderdale since the summer of 2020. Sena has conducted health law research under the guidance of attorneys Gabriel Imperato and Anne Novick Branan and helped author sections of the "Key Laws in Healthcare Compliance" chapter in the 2021 HCCA *Complete Healthcare Compliance Manual*. He is expected to graduate in May 2021 and plans to continue his career as an associate attorney at Nelson Mullins.

4. **Megan Speltz** is a digital product owner at SCCE & HCCA, where she helps define and deliver new digital products to the COSMOS platform. She graduated from the University of St. Thomas School of Law in May 2020; she obtained her juris doctor with a concentration in organizational ethics and compliance. In addition to working at SCCE & HCCA, Speltz is a licensed attorney practicing in the state of Minnesota and represents small businesses and nonprofit organizations.

5. John T. Boese, *Recent Developments Under the Federal False Claims Act*, Health Care Compliance Association 2018 Compliance Institute, March 2018, https://assets. hcca-info.org/Portals/0/PDFs/Resources/Conference_ Handouts/Compliance_Institute/2018/P6_Handout1. pdf.

6. "The Federal False Claims Act Explained," Waters Kraus & Paul, July 20, 2015, http://www.waterskraus.com/the-federal-false-claims-act-explained/.

7. Epstein Becker & Green, "Health Care Continues to Drive False Claims Act Recoveries: Through Leaders in Health Law Video Series," JD Supra, January 28, 2020, http://www.jdsupra.com/legalnews/health-care-continu-es-to-drive-false-cla-95101/.

8. Sara Kropf, "Healthcare Fraud 101: The False Claims Act," *Physicians Practice*, March 10, 2017, http://www. physicianspractice.com/view/healthcare-fraud-101-false-claims-act.

9. U.S. Department of Justice, "The False Claims Act: A Primer," April 22, 2011, http://www.justice.gov/sites/ default/files/civil/legacy/2011/04/22/C-FRAUDS_FCA_ Primer.pdf.

10. "False Claims Act," Whistleblower Resources, Phillips & Cohen, accessed October 23, 2020, http://www. phillipsandcohen.com/false-claims-act-history/#:~:-text=The%20False%20Claims%20Act%20was,sup-plies%20to%20the%20Union%20Army.&text=It%20 contained%20%E2%80%9Cqui%20tam%E2%80%9D%20 provisions,that%20were%20defrauding%20the%20gov-ernment.

11. "The Federal False Claims Act Explained," Waters Kraus & Paul, July 26, 2015, http://www.waterskraus.com/the-federal-false-claims-act-explained/.

12. "2010 Mid-Year False Claims Act Update," Gibson Dunn, July 9, 2020, http://www.gibsondunn.com/2010-mid-year-false-claims-act-update/.

13. "State False Claims Act Reviews," Office of Inspector General, U.S. Department of Health & Human Services, accessed November 5, 2020, http://oig.hhs.gov/fraud/ state-false-claims-act-reviews/.

14. "A Roadmap for New Physicians: Fraud & Abuse Laws," Office of Inspector General, U.S. Department of Health & Human Services, accessed September 25, 2020, https://oig.hhs.gov/compliance/physician-educa-tion/01laws.asp.

15. 31 U.S.C. § 3729.

16. U.S. Department of Justice, "The False Claims Act: A Primer," April 22, 2011, http://www.justice.gov/sites/ default/files/civil/legacy/2011/04/22/C-FRAUDS_FCA_ Primer.pdf.

17. 31 U.S.C. § 3730.

18. David W.S. Lieberman, "2020 False Claims Act Penalties," Whistleblower Law Collabora-tive, July 1, 2020, http://www.whistleblowerllc. com/2020-false-claims-act-penalties/#:~:text=The%20 False%20Claims%20Act%2C%2031,does%20that%20 apply%20in%20practice%3F.

19. "Fraud Risk Indicator," Office of Inspector General, U.S. Department of Health & Human Services, last accessed November 24, 2020, https://oig.hhs.gov/compliance/ corporate-integrity-agreements/risk.asp.

20. "Compliance Guidance," Office of Inspector General, U.S. Department of Health & Human Services, last accessed November 24, 2020, https://oig.hhs.gov/com-pliance/compliance-guidance/index.asp.

21. U.S. Department of Justice, Civil Division, "Fraud Statistics - Overview: October 1, 1986 - September 30, 2019," September 30, 2019, https://www.justice.gov/opa/ press-release/file/1233201/download.

22. 42 C.F.R. § 412.23(b)(2)(ii).

23. U.S. Department of Justice, "Encompass Health Agrees to Pay $48 Million to Resolve False Claims Act Allega-tions Relating to its Inpatient Rehabilitation Facilities," news release, June 28, 2019, http://www.justice.gov/opa/ pr/encompass-health-agrees-pay-48-million-resolve-false-claims-act-allegations-relating-its?utm_medium=e-mail&utm_source=govdelivery.

24. U.S. Attorney's Office for the Southern District of Missis-sippi, "Federal Jury finds Defendants Guilty of Submit-ting False Claims to Medicare Under Civil False Claims Act," news release, March 13, 2020, http://www.justice. gov/usao-sdms/pr/federal-jury-finds-defendants-guilty-submitting-false-claims-medicare-under-civil-false.

25. U.S. Attorney's Office Middle District of Florida, "Hope Hospice Agrees to Pay $3.2 Million to Settle False Claims Act Liability," U.S. Department of Justice, July 8, 2020, http://www.justice.gov/usao-mdfl/pr/hope-hospice-agrees-pay-32-million-settle-false-claims-act-liability.

26. U.S. Department of Health & Human Services, Office of Inspector General, "Corporate Integrity Agree-ment between the Office of Inspector General of the Department of Health and Human Services and Hope Hospice and Community Services, Inc., D/B/A Hope Hospice," corporate integrity agreement, July 2, 2020, https://oig.hhs.gov/fraud/cia/agreements/Hope_Hos-pice_and_Community_Services_Inc_dba_Hope_Hos-pice_07022020.pdf.

Foreign Corrupt Practices Act

By Gabriel Imperato,[1] Esq., CHC; Anne Novick Branan,[2] Esq., CHC; Richard Sena[3]; Zackary Weiss[4]; and Megan Speltz, JD[5]

Fast Facts

Title of law: The Foreign Corrupt Practices Act (FCPA), Prohibited foreign trade practices by issuers

Categories:

- Accounting and financial reporting
- International law
- Fraud and abuse
- Political activity
- Trade regulation

U.S. Code: 15 U.S.C. § 78dd-1, et seq.

Year enacted: 1977

Major amendments:

- Foreign Corrupt Practices Act Amendments of 1988
- International Anti-Bribery and Fair Competition Act of 1998

Enforcement agencies: U.S. Department of Justice (DOJ), U.S. Securities and Exchange Commission (SEC)

Link to full text of law: https://www.govinfo.gov/content/pkg/USCODE-2010-title15/pdf/USCODE-2010-title15-chap2B-sec78dd-1.pdf

Applies to: US healthcare companies working with foreign government agencies, officials, and healthcare systems

What Is the Foreign Corrupt Practices Act?

The Foreign Corrupt Practices Act (FCPA) prohibits the payment of bribes to foreign officials to assist in obtaining or retaining business.[6] It requires publicly held corporations to keep accurate books and records and establish accounting controls to prevent activity that formerly disguised corporate bribes. The anti-bribery provision prohibits the willful use of mail or any other form of interstate commerce to deliver "any offer, payment, promise to pay, or authorization of the payment of money or anything of value to any person, while knowing that all or a portion of such money or thing of value will be offered, given or promised, directly or indirectly, to a foreign official to influence the foreign official in his or her official capacity, induce the foreign official to do or omit to do an act in violation of his or her lawful duty, or to secure any improper advantage in order to assist in obtaining or retaining business for or with, or directing business to, any person."[7]

The FCPA also requires that all companies whose securities are listed in the United States to meet its accounting provisions. The accounting provisions require corporations to maintain books and records that accurately and fairly reflect a corporation's transactions and create and maintain an adequate system of internal accounting controls.[8]

The FCPA was the first global law to criminalize the payment of bribes in foreign countries. The increased globalization of healthcare has created serious potential FCPA compliance risks. US healthcare organizations are at a particularly high risk of violating the FCPA because of an increase in government owned or controlled health systems, which may be instrumentalities of a foreign government.

History

The FCPA was enacted in 1977 as an amendment to the Securities Exchange Act of 1934. The FCPA legislation resulted from an SEC investigation into undisclosed payments to domestic and foreign officials triggered by the Watergate scandal, as well as the negative effects foreign bribery had on the United States during the Cold War. Investigations following the Watergate scandal revealed that corporations had made illegal political contributions to foreign officials that were concealed in secret slush funds. This raised concerns that companies were inaccurately reporting their financials in their SEC filings.[9]

Congressional hearings leading up to the passage of the FCPA focused on wanting to renew moral leadership and emphasized the United States' obligation to set integrity standards in domestic and foreign business relations.

In 1988, Congress amended the FCPA to add two affirmative defenses: the local law defense and the reasonable and bona fide promotional expense defense. They also requested that the president negotiate an international treaty with members of the Organisation for Economic Co-Operation and Development (OECD) to prohibit bribery in international business transactions by many major trading partners of the United States. In 1998, the law was amended by the International Anti-Bribery and Fair Competition Act to expand the FCPA's scope and conform to the requirements of the OECD Convention on Combating Bribery of Foreign Public Officials in International Business Transactions.

Related Laws

The Travel Act: 18 U.S.C. § 1952

Prohibits travel in interstate or foreign commerce or using the mail or any facility in interstate or foreign commerce with the intent to distribute the proceeds of any unlawful activity or to promote, manage, establish, or carry on any unlawful activities. "Unlawful activity" includes violations of not only the FCPA, but also state commercial bribery laws. Thus, bribery between private commercial enterprises may, in some circumstances, be covered by the Travel Act.[10]

Sarbanes-Oxley Act of 2002: Pub. L. 107–204, 116 Stat. 745

This act implemented new rules for corporations in response to a series of accounting scandals involving US companies. The act strengthened accounting requirements for issuers. All issuers must comply with Sarbanes-Oxley requirements, several of which have FCPA implications. Some requirements under this act include:

- Section 302 requiring every public company to file periodic financial reports with the SEC;
- Section 404 requiring all annual financial reports to include an internal control report;
- Section 409 requiring companies to disclose any material changes in financial condition or operations; and
- Section 802 imposing civil and criminal liability for falsifying records or documents.[11]

Bribery in the First Degree: New York Penal Code § 200.04

A person is guilty of bribery in the first degree when the person confers, or offers or agrees to confer, "any benefit upon a public servant upon an agreement or understanding that such public servant's vote, opinion, judgment, action, decision or exercise of discretion as a public servant will thereby be influenced in the investigation, arrest, detention, prosecution or incarceration of any person for the commission or alleged commission of a class A felony . . . ."[12]

Commercial Bribery: Texas Penal Code § 32.43

"A person who is a fiduciary commits an offense if, without the consent of his beneficiary, he intentionally or knowingly solicits, accepts, or agrees to accept any benefit from another person on agreement or understanding that the benefit will influence the conduct of the fiduciary in relation to the affairs of his beneficiary." Section 32.43(a)(2)(C) includes physicians as fiduciaries.[13]

Commercial Bribery: Fla. Stat. Ann § 838.16

"A person commits the crime of commercial bribery if, knowing that another is subject to a duty described in s. 838.15(1) and with intent to influence the other person to violate that duty, the person confers, offers to confer, or agrees to confer a benefit on the other."[14]

Foreign Corrupt Practices Act Compliance Risks

The FCPA is important to compliance professionals because violations expose healthcare organizations to both criminal and civil liability. Healthcare organizations and officials found liable are subject to large fines, remedial measures, and even criminal prosecution. There are several critical areas of risk that healthcare companies must address to comply with the FCPA. Besides the anti-bribery provisions of the act, healthcare providers should make sure their periodical and other reports (related to securities filings) are in compliance, and their sales and marketing techniques are in compliance. The following are specific FCPA risk areas that healthcare providers and officials need to monitor closely.

Risk Area: Anti-Bribery Provisions

15 U.S.C. §§ 78dd-1(a)(1)(A), 78dd-1(a)(2)(A), 78dd-1(a)(3)(A)

The FCPA applies only to payments, offers, or promises made for the purpose of:

- Influencing any act or decision of a foreign official in his official capacity,
- Inducing a foreign official to do or omit to do any act in violation of the Lawful duty of such official,
- Securing any improper advantage; or
- Inducing a foreign official to use his influence with a foreign government or instrumentality thereof to affect or influence any act or decision of such government or instrumentality.[15]

Context: The FCPA's anti-bribery provisions encompass both direct and indirect corrupt payments. Healthcare organizations' financial relationships with third-party agents, consultants, distributors, and joint-venture partners present risk under the FCPA. First, a third party may channel payments to a foreign official or US healthcare professional in an effort to drive sales. Second, recommendations for prescribing services or products covered by federal healthcare programs may be suspect. Finally, healthcare professionals who participate in research and development initiatives abroad may be linked to state-owned or -controlled entities, which can create liability under FCPA.

Risk Area: Accounting Requirements

15 U.S.C. § 78m(b)(2)(A)

2. Every issuer which has a class of securities registered pursuant to section 78l of this title and every issuer which is required to file reports pursuant to section 78o(d) of this title shall—

    A. make and keep books, records, and accounts, which, in reasonable detail, accurately and fairly reflect the transactions and dispositions of the assets of the issuer.[16]

Context: Bribes, both foreign and domestic, are often mischaracterized in companies' books and records. The "in reasonable" detail qualification was adopted by Congress "in light of the concern that such a standard, if unqualified, might connote a degree of exactitude and precision which is unrealistic . . . . In instances where all the elements of a violation of the anti-bribery provisions are not met—where, for example, there was no use of interstate commerce— companies nonetheless may be liable if the improper payments are inaccurately recorded." Briberies have been mischaracterized as consulting fees, sales and marketing expenses, scientific incentives, travel and entertainment expenses, rebates or discounts, miscellaneous expenses, etc.[17]

Risk Area: Internal Controls

15 U.S.C. § 78m(b)(2)(B)

    B. devise and maintain a system of internal accounting controls sufficient to provide reasonable assurances that—

        i. transactions are executed in accordance with management's general or specific authorization;

        ii. transactions are recorded as necessary (I) to permit preparation of financial statements in conformity with generally accepted accounting principles or any other criteria applicable to such statements, and (II) to maintain accountability for assets;

        iii. access to assets is permitted only in accordance with management's general or specific authorization; and

        iv. the recorded accountability for assets is compared with the existing assets at reasonable intervals and appropriate action is taken with respect to any differences.[18]

Context: Internal controls over financial reporting are used by companies to provide reasonable assurance regarding the reliability of financial reporting and the preparation of financial statements. Internal controls include a control environment that covers the tone set by the organization regarding integrity and ethics; risk assessments; control activities that cover policies and procedures designed to ensure that management directives are carried out (e.g., approvals, authorizations, reconciliations, and segregation of duties); and monitoring.

Consequences for Noncompliance

Administrative Proceedings

Penalties

For each violation of the law's anti-bribery provisions:

- Up to $2 million fine for corporations and other business entities
- Up to $250,000 fine and imprisonment up to five years for individuals[19]

For each violation of the law's accounting provisions:

- Up to $25 million fine for corporations and other business entities
- Up to $5 million fine and imprisonment up to 20 years for individuals[20]

Corrective Actions

- Appoint an independent corporate monitor who assesses and monitors a company's adherence to the compliance requirements of an agreement that is designed to reduce the risk of recurrence of the company's misconduct.
- Update internal controls and compliance programs and focus future training on such issues, as appropriate.
- Continuously review and improve compliance programs to meet DOJ and SEC evaluation requirements.

Civil Litigation

Damages

- For violations of the anti-bribery provisions, corporations and other business entities are subject to a civil penalty up to $21,410 per violation.[21]
- For violations of the anti-bribery provisions, individuals (including officers, directors, stockholders, and agents of companies) are subject to a civil penalty up $21,410 per violation.[22]
- For violating the FCPA's accounting provision, the SEC may impose "a civil penalty not to exceed the greater of (a) the gross amount of the pecuniary gain to the defendant as a result of the violations or (b) a specified dollar limitation." The specified dollar limitations are determined by the egregiousness of the violation and can range from $9,639 to $192,768 for an individual and from $96,384 to $963,837 for a company.[23]
- Both the DOJ and SEC have civil enforcement authority under the FCPA.

Criminal Proceedings

Sentencing

- Up to five years for violations of anti-bribery provisions.[24]
- Up to 20 years for violations of accounting provisions.[25]
- Only the DOJ has the authority to pursue criminal actions.
- The DOJ may agree to resolve criminal FCPA matters against companies either through a declination or, in appropriate cases, a negotiated resolution resulting in a plea agreement, deferred prosecution agreement, or non-prosecution agreement:
  - Generally, in a *plea agreement*, the defendant "admits to the facts supporting the charges, admits guilt, and is convicted of the charged crimes when the plea agreement is presented to and accepted by a court."[26]
  - Under a *deferred prosecution agreement* (DPA), the "DOJ files a charging document with the court, but it simultaneously requests that the prosecution be deferred ... allowing the company to demonstrate its good conduct. DPAs generally require a defendant to agree to pay a monetary penalty, waive the statute of limitation, cooperate with the government, admit the relevant facts, and enter into certain compliance and remediation commitments, potentially including a corporate compliance monitor."[27]
  - Under a *non-prosecution agreement* (NPA), the "DOJ maintains the right to file charges but refrains from doing so to allow the company to demonstrate its good conduct during the term of the NPA. Unlike a DPA, an NPA is not filed with a court but is instead maintained by the parties."[28]

Important Compliance Guidance and Tools

Stanford Law School

Foreign Corrupt Practices Act Clearinghouse

This site focuses on FCPA enforcement actions, providing datasets, analytics, and reports as resources. Readers will find legal opinions, articles about FCPA compliance, and data about FCPA investigations and enforcement actions.

http://fcpa.stanford.edu/index.html

U.S. Department of Justice

FCPA Resource Guide

This site has the downloadable resource guide, *FCPA: A Resource Guide to the U.S. Foreign Corrupt Practices Act, Second Edition,* released by the U.S. Securities and Exchange Commission and U.S. Department of Justice in 2020. It contains information and analysis of the FCPA and its enforcement, including factors considered by the DOJ and SEC when deciding to open an investigation or bring charges, such as full cooperation, voluntary self-disclosure, and remediation, including implementation of an effective compliance program.

https://www.justice.gov/criminal-fraud/fcpa-resource-guide

U.S. Securities and Exchange Commission

SEC Enforcement Actions: FCPA Cases

This SEC site lists FCPA enforcement actions by calendar year.

https://www.sec.gov/spotlight/fcpa/fcpa-cases.shtml

Relevant Foreign Corrupt Practices Act Cases and Opinions

United States v. Olympus Latin America, Inc.

Case summary: The United States' largest distributor of endoscopes and related equipment paid $22.8 million to resolve criminal charges relating to the FCPA in Latin America. The FCPA complaint, filed in the Newark federal court, against Olympus Corporation of the Americas' Miami-based subsidiary Olympus Latin America (OLA) alleged FCPA violations in connection with improper payments to health officials in Central and South America. According to the court documents, from 2006 until August 2011 OLA implemented a plan to increase medical equipment sales in Central and South America by providing payments to healthcare practitioners at government-owned healthcare facilities. These payments included cash, money transfers, personal grants, personal travel, and free or heavily discounted equipment. OLA and its partners paid nearly $3 million to practitioners to induce the purchase of Olympus products and recognized more than $7.5 million in profits as a result.

Opinion issued: February 29, 2016

Link to full text: https://www.justice.gov/criminal-fraud/file/831256/download

"Olympus Latin America admitted to bribing publicly employed health care providers and hospital officials across Central and South America so that it could illegally win business and sell its product," said David Bitkower, principal deputy assistant attorney general at the time.[29] OLA entered into a deferred prosecution agreement requiring payment of a $22.8 million criminal penalty and implementation of a number of compliance measures, including the retention of an independent compliance monitor; continued implementation of a compliance program; and conducting a review of existing internal controls, policies, and procedures regarding compliance with the FCPA. The department reached this resolution based on a number of factors, including that OLA did not voluntarily disclose the misconduct in a timely manner.

United States v. GlaxoSmithKline, PLC

Case summary: GlaxoSmithKline (GSK) agreed to pay $20 million to settle charges that it violated the FCPA when its China-based subsidiaries engaged in pay-to-prescribe schemes to increase sales. Between 2010 and 2013, GSK gave healthcare professionals and medical officials large amounts of gifts, improper travel, and entertainment that had little or no educational purpose. The costs associated with these payments were recorded in GSK's books and records as legitimate expenses.

GSK implemented a strategy to confer improper benefits on healthcare professionals and medical officials in order to increase sales of GSK products. The illegal program was supervised and operated by senior marketing and sales managers at GSK's China-based subsidiary, and it was condoned by regional and district managers.

Opinion issued: September 30, 2016

Link to full text: https://www.sec.gov/litigation/admin/2016/34-79005.pdf

The case was brought by the SEC, and the DOJ declined to prosecute this case. GSK entered into a civil settlement with the SEC. Additionally, in 2014, a Chinese court fined GSK $490 million for domestic bribery, GSK's former China executive was given a three-year suspended sentence and deported, and a number of Chinese nationals were given prison sentences between two and four years.[30]

Besides the monetary damages owed by GSK to the SEC, the settlement ordered GSK to make a number of changes to its global practices. They included the elimination of most payments to doctors, including speaker fees, and altering their compensation structure to eliminate sales incentives based on the number of prescriptions generated. GSK has also enhanced its global risk assessment process, strengthened its monitoring and risk assessment tools, and expanded its global compliance organization. The SEC required GSK to submit regular reports of the status of its remediation and implementation of compliance measures.

United States v. Teva Pharmaceutical Industries Ltd.

Case summary: The world's largest manufacturer of generic pharmaceutical products agreed to pay more than $519 million to resolve FCPA charges with the DOJ and SEC arising from corrupt payments made between 2002 and 2012 to high-ranking ministry of health officials in Russia and Ukraine. These payments were used to influence the approval of drug registrations and made to state-employed physicians in Mexico to influence the prescription of products.

Opinion issued: December 22, 2016

Link to full text:https://www.justice.gov/criminal-fraud/file/920436/download

Teva entered into a deferred prosecution agreement charging FCPA anti-bribery and internal controls violations, and its Russian subsidiary pleaded guilty to a one-count criminal information charge of conspiracy to violate the FCPA's anti-bribery provision, with a combined criminal penalty of $283.18 million.

On the civil side, Teva agreed to disgorge more than $236 million in profits and prejudgment interest to the SEC to resolve charges of FCPA anti-bribery, books-and-record, and internal controls violations. Teva was also ordered to retain a corporate compliance monitor with a three-year term.

Endnotes

1. **Gabriel Imperato** is managing partner at the Fort Lauderdale office of Nelson Mullins Riley & Scarborough. He is the team leader of the firm's Health Care Criminal and Civil Enforcement, Litigation and Compliance Practice. He has practiced healthcare law in both the public and private sectors for more than 40 years. He is board certified as a specialist in health law by The Florida Bar. Imperato recently served as the general counsel of the North Broward Hospital District, the tenth largest healthcare system in the United States. He has also served as deputy chief counsel for the U.S. Department of Health & Human Services' Office of the General Counsel. Imperato is also a longtime member of the board of directors of the Society of Corporate Compliance and Ethics & Health Care Compliance Association (SCCE & HCCA), where he was also a past president and interim CEO.

2. **Anne Novick Branan, Esq.** is an of counsel attorney in the Fort Lauderdale office of Nelson Mullins Riley & Scarborough. She has been board certified in health law by The Florida Bar since 1995. Branan counsels healthcare providers about avoiding and responding to allegations of fraud under the Medicare and Medicaid programs. She helps her clients navigate the complex regulatory environment affecting acquisitions and contracting in the healthcare industry. Branan regularly assists healthcare companies in developing and assessing the effectiveness of corporate compliance and ethics programs. She was recognized in *The Best Lawyers in America* for healthcare law, 2015–2020, and selected as Fort Lauderdale Health Care Law "Lawyer of the Year" in 2017.

3. **Richard Sena** is an associate attorney at Nelson Mullins Riley & Scarborough in Fort Lauderdale. Sena conducted health law research under the guidance of attorneys Gabriel Imperato and Anne Novick Branan and helped author sections of the "Key Laws in Healthcare Compliance" chapter in the 2021 HCCA *Complete Healthcare Compliance Manual*. Sena also coauthored an article titled "Compliance Risks and Tips for Home Health Agencies" with Branan, appearing in the July 2021 edition of *Compliance Today* magazine.

4. **Zackary Weiss** is a juris doctor candidate at the University of Miami School of Law. He is an editor for the *International & Comparative Law Review*, past judicial intern for United States Magistrate Judge Jonathan Goodman, and a law clerk at Nelson Mullins Riley & Scarborough in Fort Lauderdale since the summer of 2020. Weiss has conducted health law research under the guidance of attorneys Gabriel Imperato and Anne Novick Branan and helped author sections of the "Key Laws in Healthcare Compliance" chapter in the 2022 HCCA *Complete Healthcare Compliance Manual*. He is expected to graduate in May 2022 and plans to continue his career as an associate attorney at Nelson Mullins.

5. **Megan Speltz, JD** is a digital product owner at SCCE & HCCA, where she helps define and deliver new digital products to the COSMOS platform. She graduated from the University of St. Thomas School of Law in May 2020; she obtained her juris doctor with a concentration in organizational ethics and compliance. In addition to working at SCCE & HCCA, Speltz is a licensed attorney practicing in the state of Minnesota and represents small businesses and nonprofit organizations.

6. "Spotlight on Foreign Corrupt Practices Act," U.S. Securities and Exchange Commission, last modified February 2, 2017, https://www.sec.gov/spotlight/foreign-corrupt-practices-act.shtml.

7. "Foreign Corrupt Practices Act," U.S. Department of Justice, last modified February 3, 2017, https://www.justice.gov/criminal-fraud/foreign-corrupt-practices-act.

8. "Foreign Corrupt Practices Act," U.S. Department of Justice, last modified February 3, 2017, https://www.justice.gov/criminal-fraud/foreign-corrupt-practices-act.

9. Ann Eberhardt, "How the Foreign Corrupt Practices Act Came to Be," Corporate Compliance Insights, July 3, 2018, https://www.corporatecomplianceinsights.com/foreign-corrupt-practices-act-came/.

10. 18 U.S.C. § 1952.

11. Sarbanes-Oxley Act of 2002, Pub. L. No. 107-204, H.R. 3763, 107th Cong.

12. New York Penal Code § 200.04.

13. Texas Penal Code § 32.43.

14. Fla. Stat. Ann § 838.16.

15. 15 U.S.C. § 78dd-1(a)(1)(A); 15 U.S.C. § 78dd-1(a)(2)(A); 15 U.S.C. § 78dd-1(a)(3)(A).

16. 15 U.S.C. § 78m(b)(2)(A).

17. U.S. Department of Justice, Criminal Division; and U.S. Securities and Exchange Commission, Enforcement Division; *FCPA: A Resource Guide to the U.S. Foreign Corrupt Practice Act*, July, 2020, 39–40, https://www.justice.gov/criminal-fraud/file/1292051/download.

18. 15 U.S.C. § 78m(b)(2)(B).

19. U.S. Department of Justice, Criminal Division; and U.S. Securities and Exchange Commission, Enforcement Division; *FCPA: A Resource Guide to the U.S. Foreign Corrupt Practice Act*, 69.

20. U.S. Department of Justice, Criminal Division; and U.S. Securities and Exchange Commission, Enforcement Division; *FCPA: A Resource Guide to the U.S. Foreign Corrupt Practice Act*, 69.

21. U.S. Department of Justice, Criminal Division; and U.S. Securities and Exchange Commission, Enforcement Division; *FCPA: A Resource Guide to the U.S. Foreign Corrupt Practice Act*, 71.

22. U.S. Department of Justice, Criminal Division; and U.S. Securities and Exchange Commission, Enforcement Division; *FCPA: A Resource Guide to the U.S. Foreign Corrupt Practice Act*, 71.

23. U.S. Department of Justice, Criminal Division; and U.S. Securities and Exchange Commission, Enforcement Division; *FCPA: A Resource Guide to the U.S. Foreign Corrupt Practice Act*, 71.

24. U.S. Department of Justice, Criminal Division; and U.S. Securities and Exchange Commission, Enforcement Division; *FCPA: A Resource Guide to the U.S. Foreign Corrupt Practice Act*, 69.

25. U.S. Department of Justice, Criminal Division; and U.S. Securities and Exchange Commission, Enforcement Division; *FCPA:A Resource Guide to the U.S. Foreign Corrupt Practice Act*, 69.

26. U.S. Department of Justice, Criminal Division; and U.S. Securities and Exchange Commission, Enforcement Division; *FCPA:A Resource Guide to the U.S. Foreign Corrupt Practice Act*, 75.

27. U.S. Department of Justice, Criminal Division; and U.S. Securities and Exchange Commission, Enforcement Division; *FCPA:A Resource Guide to the U.S. Foreign Corrupt Practice Act*, 75.

28. U.S. Department of Justice, Criminal Division; and U.S. Securities and Exchange Commission, Enforcement Division; *FCPA:A Resource Guide to the U.S. Foreign Corrupt Practice Act*, 76.

29. U.S. Department of Justice, "Medical Equipment Company Will Pay $646 Million for Making Illegal Payments to Doctors and Hospitals in United States and Latin America," news release, March 1, 2016, https://www.justice.gov/opa/pr/medical-equipment-company-will-pay-646-million-making-illegal-payments-doctors-and-hospitals.

30. "GlaxoSmithKline fined $490m by China for bribery," BBC News, September 19, 2014, https://www.bbc.com/news/business-29274822.

Health Information Technology for Economic and Clinical Health Act

By Gabriel Imperato,[1] Esq., CHC; Anne Novick Branan,[2] Esq., CHC; Richard Sena[3] ; and Megan Speltz,[4] JD

Fast Facts

Title of law: Health Information Technology for Economic and Clinical Health (HITECH) Act

Categories:

- Medical records
- Privacy
- Cybersecurity
- Data protection

U.S. Code: 42 U.S.C. §§ 17937, 17953

Public law: Pub. L. No. 111-5, 123 Stat. 226

Year enacted: 2009

Major amendments: Not applicable.

Enforcement agency: U.S. Department of Health & Human Services' Office for Civil Rights (OCR)

Link to full text of law: https://www.hhs.gov/sites/default/files/ocr/privacy/hipaa/understanding/coveredentities/hitechact.pdf

Applies to: All health plans, healthcare clearinghouses, healthcare providers, and endorsed sponsors of the Medicare prescription drug discount card, including business associates that supply services and certain functions for covered entities and have access to personal health information.

What Is the Health Information Technology for Economic and Clinical Health Act?

The Health Information Technology for Economic and Clinical Health (HITECH) Act was created to motivate the implementation of electronic health records (EHRs) and supporting technology in the United States. The act implemented changes such as:[5]

- Increasing Health Insurance Portability and Accountability Act (HIPAA) enforcement and penalties;
- Requiring notification to patients of any unsecured data breaches related to protected health information (PHI), and notifying the U.S. Department of Health & Human Services (HHS) if the breach affected more than 500 patients;
- Giving patients and designated third parties access to their PHI in an electronic format; and
- Extending HIPAA requirements to apply to business associates.

History

The HITECH Act was signed into law by President Barack Obama on February 17, 2009, as part of the American Recovery and Reinvestment Act of 2009 (ARRA), an economic stimulus bill.[6] It was passed to promote the expansion of health information technology (IT) and the adoption of EHRs by healthcare organizations by providing incentives for organizations to migrate from paper to electronic records. Prior to the HITECH Act's adoption, only 10% of hospitals had adopted EHRs.[7] Since the act's passage, the EHR adoption rate dramatically increased, and, as of 2017, 86% of office-based physicians have moved to EHRs. Accordingly, the HITECH Act has caused a significant growth in healthcare technology fields, such as research informatics, IT, electronic medical records, and other related disciplines.[8]

The HITECH Act is split into four subtitles, with each focusing on either promotion and funding of health IT or strengthening privacy, security, and enforcement of existing HIPAA rules.[9] The act strengthened HIPAA's Privacy and Security rules by increasing enforcement penalties and expanding HIPAA compliance to business associates of covered entities. Further, the act imposed a data breach notification requirement and increased the protection of electronic protected health information (ePHI). The HITECH Act also gave the HHS Office of the National Coordinator for Health Information Technology (ONC) the authority to manage and set standards for promoting and expanding the adoption of health information technology.

Related Laws

Health Insurance Portability and Accountability Act of 1996, Pub. L. No. 104-191

The HITECH Act bolsters the scope, language, and enforcement penalties of the Health Insurance Portability and Accountability Act of 1996 (HIPAA). HIPAA established national standards to protect sensitive patient health information from being disclosed without the patient's consent or knowledge. It consists of a number of rules that lay out different requirements for HIPAA compliance.

HIPAA was enacted to:[10]

- Improve portability and continuity of health insurance coverage;
- Combat waste, fraud, and abuse in health insurance and healthcare delivery;
- Promote the use of medical savings accounts; and
- Improve access to long-term care services and coverage to simplify the administration of health insurance.

For more information on this law, please see the "HIPAA" article in this chapter.

Health Information Technology for Economic and Clinical Health Act Compliance Risks

The following are specific HITECH risk areas that compliance professionals need to monitor closely.

Risk Area: Individuals' Right to Access PHI in Electronic Format

42 U.S.C. § 17935(e)(1-3)

e. Access to certain information in electronic format

In applying section 164.524 of title 45, Code of Federal Regulations, in the case that a covered entity uses or maintains an electronic health record with respect to protected health information of an individual—

1. the individual shall have a right to obtain from such covered entity a copy of such information in an electronic format and, if the individual chooses, to direct the covered entity to transmit such copy directly to an entity or person designated by the individual, provided that any such choice is clear, conspicuous, and specific;

2. if the individual makes a request to a business associate for access to, or a copy of, protected health information about the individual, or if an individual makes a request to a business associate to grant such access to, or

transmit such copy directly to, a person or entity designated by the individual, a business associate may provide the individual with such access or copy, which may be in an electronic form, or grant or transmit such access or copy to such person or entity designated by the individual; and

3. notwithstanding paragraph (c)(4) of such section, any fee that the covered entity may impose for providing such individual with a copy of such information (or a summary or explanation of such information) if such copy (or summary or explanation) is in an electronic form shall not be greater than the entity's labor costs in responding to the request for the copy (or summary or explanation).[11]

Context: Considering the HITECH Act's promotion of ePHI, the act also imposed a requirement that such information may be transmitted in electronic format to an individual upon request. This includes a request made by an individual to transmit ePHI to another entity. Considering the complexity in providing ePHI while maintaining security and privacy standards, healthcare organizations are permitted to charge a fee commensurate with the cost of transmitting the ePHI.

Risk Area: Application of HIPAA Security and Privacy Rules on Business Associates

42 U.S.C. § 17934

a. Application of contract requirements

In the case of a business associate of a covered entity that obtains or creates protected health information pursuant to a written contract (or other written arrangement) described in section 164.502(e)(2) of title 45, Code of Federal Regulations, with such covered entity, the business associate may use and disclose such protected health information only if such use or disclosure, respectively, is in compliance with each applicable requirement of section 164.504(e) of such title. The additional requirements of this subchapter that relate to privacy and that are made applicable with respect to covered entities shall also be applicable to such a business associate and shall be incorporated into the business associate agreement between the business associate and the covered entity.

b. Application of knowledge elements associated with contracts

Section 164.504(e)(1)(ii) of title 45, Code of Federal Regulations, shall apply to a business associate described in subsection (a), with respect to compliance with such subsection, in the same manner that such section applies to a covered entity, with respect to compliance with the standards in sections 164.502(e) and 164.504(e) of such title, except that in applying such section 164.504(e)(1)

(ii) each reference to the business associate, with respect to a contract, shall be treated as a reference to the covered entity involved in such contract.

c. Application of civil and criminal penalties

In the case of a business associate that violates any provision of subsection (a) or (b), the provisions of sections 1176 and 1177 of the Social Security Act (42 U.S.C. §§ 1320d–5, 1320d–6) shall apply to the business associate with respect to such violation in the same manner as such provisions apply to a person who violates a provision of part C of title XI of such Act [42 U.S.C. § 1320d et seq.].[12]

Context: Various nonhealthcare provider or insurance provider organizations that have access to PHI were not subject to HIPAA's Privacy and Security rules prior to the HITECH Act's passage. The HITECH Act stretched HIPAA's umbrella over business associates, which include entities such as claims processors, accountants, law firms, consultants, or any other entity that routinely handles PHI to service a healthcare provider or another business associate.[13]

Risk Area: Required Notification of Breach

42 U.S.C. § 17932

a. In general

A covered entity that accesses, maintains, retains, modifies, records, stores, destroys, or otherwise holds, uses, or discloses unsecured protected health information (as defined in subsection (h)(1)) shall, in the case of a breach of such information that is discovered by the covered entity, notify each individual whose unsecured protected health information has been, or is reasonably believed by the covered entity to have been, accessed, acquired, or disclosed as a result of such breach.

b. Notification of covered entity by business associate

A business associate of a covered entity that accesses, maintains, retains, modifies, records, stores, destroys, or otherwise holds, uses, or discloses unsecured protected health information shall, following the discovery of a breach of such information, notify the covered entity of such breach. Such notice shall include the identification of each individual whose unsecured protected health information has been, or is reasonably believed by the business associate to have been, accessed, acquired, or disclosed during such breach.

c. Breaches treated as discovered

For purposes of this section, a breach shall be treated as discovered by a covered entity or by a business associate as of the first day on which such breach is known to such entity or associate, respectively, (including any person, other than the individual committing the breach, that is an employee, officer, or other agent of such entity or associate, respectively) or should reasonably have been known to such entity or associate (or person) to have occurred.

d. Timeliness of notification

1. In general

Subject to subsection (g), all notifications required under this section shall be made without unreasonable delay and in no case later than 60 calendar days after the discovery of a breach by the covered entity involved (or business associate involved in the case of a notification required under subsection (b)).

2. Burden of proof

The covered entity involved (or business associate involved in the case of a notification required under subsection (b)), shall have the burden of demonstrating that all notifications were made as required under this part, including evidence demonstrating the necessity of any delay.

e. Methods of notice

1. Individual notice

Notice required under this section to be provided to an individual, with respect to a breach, shall be provided promptly and in the following form:

A. Written notification by first-class mail to the individual (or the next of kin of the individual if the individual is deceased) at the last known address of the individual or the next of kin, respectively, or, if specified as a preference by the individual, by electronic mail. The notification may be provided in one or more mailings as information is available.

B. In the case in which there is insufficient, or out-of-date contact information (including a phone number, email address, or any other form of appropriate communication) that precludes direct written (or, if specified by the individual under subparagraph (A), electronic) notification to the individual, a substitute form of notice shall be provided, including, in the case that there are 10 or more individuals for which there is insufficient or out-of-date contact information, a conspicuous posting for a period determined by the Secretary on the home page of the Web site of the covered entity involved or notice in major print or broadcast media, including major media in geographic areas where the individuals affected by the breach likely reside. Such a notice in media or web posting will include a toll-free phone number where an individual can learn whether or not the individual's unsecured protected health information is possibly included in the breach.

C. In any case deemed by the covered entity involved to require urgency because of possible imminent misuse of unsecured protected health information, the covered entity, in addition to notice provided under subparagraph (A), may provide information to individuals by telephone or other means, as appropriate.

2. Media notice

Notice shall be provided to prominent media outlets serving a State or jurisdiction, following the discovery of a breach described in subsection (a), if the unsecured protected health information of more than 500 residents of such State or jurisdiction is, or is reasonably believed to have been, accessed, acquired, or disclosed during such breach.

3. Notice to Secretary

Notice shall be provided to the Secretary by covered entities of unsecured protected health information that has been acquired or disclosed in a breach. If the breach was with respect to 500 or more individuals than such notice must be provided immediately. If the breach was with respect to less than 500 individuals, the covered entity may maintain a log of any such breach occurring and annually submit such a log to the Secretary documenting such breaches occurring during the year involved.

4. Posting on HHS public website

The Secretary shall make available to the public on the Internet website of the Department of Health and Human Services a list that identifies each covered entity involved in a breach described in subsection (a) in which the unsecured protected health information of more than 500 individuals is acquired or disclosed.

f. Content of notification

Regardless of the method by which notice is provided to individuals under this section, notice of a breach shall include, to the extent possible, the following:

1. A brief description of what happened, including the date of the breach and the date of the discovery of the breach, if known.

2. A description of the types of unsecured protected health information that were involved in the breach (such as full name, Social Security number, date of birth, home address, account number, or disability code).

3. The steps individuals should take to protect themselves from potential harm resulting from the breach.

4. A brief description of what the covered entity involved is doing to investigate the breach, to mitigate losses, and to protect against any further breaches.

5. Contact procedures for individuals to ask questions or learn additional information, which shall include a toll-free telephone number, an e-mail address, Web site, or postal address.

g. Delay of notification authorized for law enforcement purposes

If a law enforcement official determines that a notification, notice, or posting required under this section would impede a criminal investigation or cause damage to national security, such notification, notice, or posting shall be delayed in the same manner as provided under section 164.528(a)(2) of title 45, Code of Federal Regulations, in the case of a disclosure covered under such section.

h. Unsecured protected health information

1. Definition

A. In general

Subject to subparagraph (B), for purposes of this section, the term "unsecured protected health information" means protected health information that is not secured through the use of a technology or methodology specified by the Secretary in the guidance issued under paragraph (2).

B. Exception in case timely guidance not issued

In the case that the Secretary does not issue guidance under paragraph (2) by the date specified in such paragraph, for purposes of this section, the term "unsecured protected health information" shall mean protected health information that is not secured by a technology standard that renders protected health information unusable, unreadable, or indecipherable to unauthorized individuals and is developed or endorsed by a standards developing organization that is accredited by the American National Standards Institute.

2. Guidance

For purposes of paragraph (1) and section 17937(f)(3) of this title, not later than the date that is 60 days after February 17, 2009, the Secretary shall, after consultation with stakeholders, issue (and annually update) guidance specifying the technologies and methodologies that render protected health information unusable, unreadable, or indecipherable to unauthorized individuals, including the use of standards developed under section 300jj–12(b)(2)(B)(vi) of this title, as added by section 13101 of this Act.

i. Report to Congress on breaches

1. In general

Not later than 12 months after February 17, 2009, and annually thereafter, the Secretary shall prepare and submit to the Committee on Finance and the Committee on Health, Education, Labor, and Pensions of the Senate and the Committee on Ways and Means and the Committee on Energy and Commerce of the House of Representatives a report containing the information described in paragraph (2) regarding breaches for which notice was provided to the Secretary under subsection (e)(3).

2. Information

The information described in this paragraph regarding breaches specified in paragraph (1) shall include—

A. the number and nature of such breaches; and

B. actions taken in response to such breaches.

j. Regulations; effective date

To carry out this section, the Secretary of Health and Human Services shall promulgate interim final regulations by not later than the date that is 180 days after February 17, 2009. The provisions of this section shall apply to breaches that are discovered on or after the date that is 30 days after the date of publication of such interim final regulations.[14]

Context: Breach notification is an important aspect of HIPAA imposed by the HITECH Act, prompting covered entities and business associates to self-report breaches of PHI. The Breach Notification Rule, which is codified under HIPAA at 45 C.F.R. §§ 164.404, 164.406, and 164.408, requires that covered entities and business associates report breaches to individuals. If the breach exceeds 500 individuals, then the covered entity or business associate must notify the Secretary of the U.S. Department of Health & Human Services. If the breach exceeds 500 individuals in a particular state or jurisdiction, then the covered entity or business associate must notify local media outlets in that location of the breach.

Risk Area: Tougher Enforcement Penalties Under HIPAA

42 U.S.C. § 1320d-5

a. General penalty

1. In general

    Except as provided in subsection (b), the Secretary shall impose on any person who violates a provision of this part—

    A. in the case of a violation of such provision in which it is established that the person did not know (and by exercising reasonable diligence would not have known) that such person violated such provision, a penalty for each such violation of an amount that is at least the amount described in paragraph (3)(A) but not to exceed the amount described in paragraph (3)(D);

    B. in the case of a violation of such provision in which it is established that the violation was due to reasonable cause and not to willful neglect, a penalty for each such violation of an amount that is at least the amount described in paragraph (3)(B) but not to exceed the amount described in paragraph (3)(D); and

    C. in the case of a violation of such provision in which it is established that the violation was due to willful neglect—

        i.   if the violation is corrected as described in subsection (b)(3)(A), a penalty in an amount that is at least the amount described in paragraph (3)(C) but not to exceed the amount described in paragraph (3)(D); and

        ii. if the violation is not corrected as described in such subsection, a penalty in an amount that is at least the amount described in paragraph (3)(D).

        In determining the amount of a penalty under this section for a violation, the Secretary shall base such determination on the nature and extent of the violation and the nature and extent of the harm resulting from such violation.

2. Procedures

   The provisions of section 1320a–7a of this title (other than subsections (a) and (b) and the second sentence of subsection (f)) shall apply to the imposition of a civil money penalty under this subsection in the same manner as such provisions apply to the imposition of a penalty under such section 1320a–7a of this title.

3. Tiers of penalties described

   For purposes of paragraph (1), with respect to a violation by a person of a provision of this part—

   A. the amount described in this subparagraph is $100 for each such violation, except that the total amount imposed on the person for all such violations of an identical requirement or prohibition during a calendar year may not exceed $25,000;

   B. the amount described in this subparagraph is $1,000 for each such violation, except that the total amount imposed on the person for all such violations of an identical requirement or prohibition during a calendar year may not exceed $100,000;

   C. the amount described in this subparagraph is $10,000 for each such violation, except that the total amount imposed on the person for all such violations of an identical requirement or prohibition during a calendar year may not exceed $250,000; and

   D. the amount described in this subparagraph is $50,000 for each such violation, except that the total amount imposed on the person for all such violations of an identical requirement or prohibition during a calendar year may not exceed $1,500,000.

b. Limitations

1. Offenses otherwise punishable

   No penalty may be imposed under subsection (a) and no damages obtained under subsection (d) with respect to an act if a penalty has been imposed under section 1320d–6 of this title with respect to such act.

2. Failures due to reasonable cause

   A. In general

      Except as provided in subparagraph (B) or subsection (a)(1)(C), no penalty may be imposed under subsection (a) and no damages obtained under subsection (d) if the failure to comply is corrected during the 30-day period beginning on the first date the person liable for the penalty or damages knew, or by exercising reasonable diligence would have known, that the failure to comply occurred.

B. Extension of period

    i. No penalty

        With respect to the imposition of a penalty by the Secretary under subsection (a), the period referred to in subparagraph (A) may be extended as determined appropriate by the Secretary based on the nature and extent of the failure to comply.

    ii. Assistance

        If the Secretary determines that a person failed to comply because the person was unable to comply, the Secretary may provide technical assistance to the person during the period described in subparagraph (A). Such assistance shall be provided in any manner determined appropriate by the Secretary.

3. Reduction

In the case of a failure to comply which is due to reasonable cause and not to willful neglect, any penalty under subsection (a) and any damages under subsection (d) that is [2] not entirely waived under paragraph (3) may be waived to the extent that the payment of such penalty would be excessive relative to the compliance failure involved.

c. Noncompliance due to willful neglect

1. In general

A violation of a provision of this part due to willful neglect is a violation for which the Secretary is required to impose a penalty under subsection (a)(1).

2. Required investigation

For purposes of paragraph (1), the Secretary shall formally investigate any complaint of a violation of a provision of this part if a preliminary investigation of the facts of the complaint indicate such a possible violation due to willful neglect.

d. Enforcement by State attorneys general

1. Civil action

Except as provided in subsection (b), in any case in which the attorney general of a State has reason to believe that an interest of one or more of the residents of that State has been or is threatened or adversely affected by any person who violates a provision of this part, the attorney general of the State, as parens patriae, may bring a civil action on behalf of such residents of the State in a district court of the United States of appropriate jurisdiction—

A. to enjoin further such violation by the defendant; or

B. to obtain damages on behalf of such residents of the State, in an amount equal to the amount determined under paragraph (2).

2. Statutory damages

A. In general

For purposes of paragraph (1)(B), the amount determined under this paragraph is the amount calculated by multiplying the number of violations by up to $100. For purposes of the preceding sentence, in the case of a continuing violation, the number of violations shall be determined consistent with the HIPAA privacy regulations (as defined in section 1320d–9(b)(3) of this title) for violations of subsection (a).

B. Limitation

The total amount of damages imposed on the person for all violations of an identical requirement or prohibition during a calendar year may not exceed $25,000.

C. Reduction of damages

In assessing damages under subparagraph (A), the court may consider the factors the Secretary may consider in determining the amount of a civil money penalty under subsection (a) under the HIPAA privacy regulations.

3. Attorney fees

In the case of any successful action under paragraph (1), the court, in its discretion, may award the costs of the action and reasonable attorney fees to the State.

4. Notice to Secretary

    The State shall serve prior written notice of any action under paragraph (1) upon the Secretary and provide the Secretary with a copy of its complaint, except in any case in which such prior notice is not feasible, in which case the State shall serve such notice immediately upon instituting such action. The Secretary shall have the right—

    A. to intervene in the action;

    B. upon so intervening, to be heard on all matters arising therein; and

    C. to file petitions for appeal.

5. Construction

    For purposes of bringing any civil action under paragraph (1), nothing in this section shall be construed to prevent an attorney general of a State from exercising the powers conferred on the attorney general by the laws of that State.

6. Venue; service of process

    A. Venue

        Any action brought under paragraph (1) may be brought in the district court of the United States that meets applicable requirements relating to venue under section 1391 of title 28.

    B. Service of process

        In an action brought under paragraph (1), process may be served in any district in which the defendant—

        i.   is an inhabitant; or

        ii. maintains a physical place of business.

7. Limitation on State action while Federal action is pending

    If the Secretary has instituted an action against a person under subsection (a) with respect to a specific violation of this part, no State attorney general may bring an action under this subsection against the person with respect to such violation during the pendency of that action.

8. Application of CMP statute of limitation

    A civil action may not be instituted with respect to a violation of this part unless an action to impose a civil money penalty may be instituted under subsection (a) with respect to such violation consistent with the second sentence of section 1320a–7a(c)(1) of this title.

e. Allowing continued use of corrective action

    Nothing in this section shall be construed as preventing the Office for Civil Rights of the Department of Health and Human Services from continuing, in its discretion, to use corrective action without a penalty in cases where the person did not know (and by exercising reasonable diligence would not have known) of the violation involved.[15]

Context: Before the HITECH Act, HIPAA violations were relatively mild, with each violation limited to $100 and totaling no more than $25,000 per calendar year. The HITECH Act imposed a more complex penalty scheme with much tougher potential penalties. Penalties for violations occurring after the HITECH Act's passage may range from $100 to $10,000 per violation with the total aggregate limit of $1.5 million per calendar year. Further, the penalties are subject to yearly adjustments according to inflation. Current penalty amounts are found at 45 C.F.R. § 102.3.

Consequences for Noncompliance

The HITECH Act significantly increases the civil money penalty amount per violation and the cumulative amount per calendar year under HIPAA. Noncompliance and violations of HIPAA expose healthcare organizations to not only civil money penalties and civil litigation, but also corrective actions imposed by corrective action plans should a healthcare organization choose to settle potential violations with the Office for Civil Rights (OCR).

Administrative Proceedings

Penalties

- Violations that occurred before February 18, 2019, are subject to civil penalties no more than $100 per violation and no more than $25,000 per calendar year.

- Violations occurring on or after February 18, 2019, are subject to civil penalty limits dependent on the nature of the violation.

- If unaware of violation and would not have known by exercising reasonable due diligence of the violation: $100–$50,000 per violation or up to $1.5 million per year for identical violations.

- Violations due to reasonable cause and not willful neglect: $1,000–$50,000 per violation or up to $1,500,000 per year for identical violations.

- Violations due to willful neglect but corrected within 30 days: $10,000–$50,000 per violation or up to $1.5 million per year for identical violations.

- Violations due to willful neglect and not corrected within 30 days: No less than $50,000 per violation or up to $1.5 million per year for identical violations.

- Civil penalties are adjusted for inflation on a yearly basis, and updated amounts are published at 45 C.F.R. § 102.3.

Corrective actions

- Required risk analysis submission to HHS.

- Required implementation of a risk management plan.

- Revision of policies and procedures to ensure compliance with HIPAA rules.

- Instituting procedures ensuring proper contracting between covered entities and business associates.

- Required training on revised policies and procedures ensuring HIPAA compliance.

Civil Litigation

Damages

A person who was financially harmed by a HIPAA violation may sue a covered entity or business associate for damages under state law.[16]

Important Compliance Guidance and Tools

U.S. Department of Health & Human Services

Health Information Technology

This site has information about cloud computing, processing, and storing electronic health information, and links to guidance documents from the Privacy and Security Toolkit.

https://www.hhs.gov/hipaa/for-professionals/special-topics/health-information-technology/index.html

HIPAA Guidance Materials

This web page includes links to important HIPAA guidance resources for small providers, small health plans, and other small businesses; health plan care coordination and continuity of care; and covered entities.

https://www.hhs.gov/hipaa/for-professionals/privacy/guidance/index.html

U.S. Department of Health & Human Services,
Office of the National Coordinator for Health Information Technology

Privacy, Security, and HIPAA

Find educational videos, articles, model privacy notice, and other tools related to privacy, security, and the use of health information technology.

https://www.healthit.gov/topic/privacy-security-and-hipaa

Relevant HITECH Cases and Opinions

Premera Blue Cross

Case summary: Premera Blue Cross (Premera), the largest health plan in the Pacific Northwest, had its IT system breached by hackers who were able to access patient PHI for nearly nine months between May 2014 and January 2015. Hackers used a phishing email to install malware into Premera's IT system. Premera self-reported the breach to the Office for Civil Rights in March 2015, but by then the hackers were able to access the PHI of more than 10.4 million individuals. The PHI breach included improper disclosure of names, addresses, dates of birth, Social Security numbers, bank account information, and other information.

Opinion issued: September 25, 2020

Link to full text: https://www.hhs.gov/sites/default/files/premera-ra-cap.pdf

OCR's investigation revealed a failure by Premera to conduct a thorough risk analysis and failures to implement risk management and audit controls as required under HIPAA. Commenting on the breach, then-OCR Director Roger Severino said, "If large health insurance entities don't invest the time and effort to identify their security vulnerabilities, be they technical or human, hackers surely will. This case vividly demonstrates the damage that results when hackers are allowed to roam undetected in a computer system for nearly nine months."[17] Premera agreed to settle with the OCR for $6.85 million and enter a corrective action plan. The corrective action plan included a requirement that Premera conduct a risk analysis and implement a risk management plan—which would be reviewed and approved by the HHS—and develop and distribute revised policies and procedures to its employees to ensure HIPAA compliance.

Athens Orthopedic Clinic PA

Case summary: Athens Orthopedic Clinic PA (Athens), an orthopedic service provider to more than 130,000 patients annually, located in Georgia, was notified by a journalist from DataBreaches.net that a database of its patient records may have been published online for sale.[18] Two days later, the hacker group named "The Dark Overlord" purportedly responsible for the breach contacted Athens demanding payment for the stolen database. It was later determined that the hacker used a third-party vendor's credentials to access Athens' medical records system to siphon ePHI. For more than a month, the hacker had access to the records of Athens' 208,557 patients, which included improper disclosure of sensitive information such as names, Social Security numbers, medical procedures, test results, and health insurance information.

Opinion issued: September 21, 2020

Link to full text: https://www.hhs.gov/sites/default/files/athens-orthopedic-ra-cap.pdf

In finding that Athens failed to conduct a thorough risk analysis, implement risk management and audit controls, maintain HIPAA policies and procedures, secure business associate agreements with certain business associates, and provide HIPAA Privacy Rule training to its employees, OCR Director Roger Severine commented that "[h]ealth care providers that fail to follow the HIPAA Security Rule make their patients' health data a tempting target for hackers."[19]

Athens agreed to pay OCR $1.5 million and enter a corrective action plan to settle the potential violations. Because the Athens breach was effectuated by a hacker stealing the credentials of a third party, the corrective action plan required Athens review and account its relationships with its vendors and business associates, including its business associate agreements, and report to HHS. Additionally, Athens had to conduct a thorough risk analysis and implement a risk management plan that includes all electronic equipment, data systems, programs, and applications controlled, owned, or managed by Athens.

Athens was also required to review and revise its policies to address technical access controls, technical mechanisms, password policies, user account termination, employee training, and other procedures related to the protection of ePHI in Athens' care. Athens had to amend its business associate policies and procedures to ensure that Athens drafts HIPAA-compliant business associate contracts prior to providing an entity access to PHI. With respect to business associate relationships, Athens had to increase its standards for determining business associates, improve contract negotiation procedures, and create a standard contract template. Lastly, Athens was required to implement its updated policies and procedures through employee training within 30 days of HHS approving the updated policies or 14 days of hiring a new employee.

Lifespan Health System Affiliated Covered Entity

Case summary: Lifespan Corporation reported a breach involving its subsidiary, Lifespan Health System Affiliated Covered Entity (Lifespan), a Rhode Island-based nonprofit health system. The breach occurred when a Rhode Island hospital (a hospital affiliated with Lifespan) employee's car was broken into and the employee's work laptop was stolen. Although the laptop was never recovered, Lifespan determined that the employee's work emails may have been preserved on the laptop's unencrypted hard drive, allowing the thieves to have access to patient names, medical records, demographic information, and various medical information. In sum, the breach affected 20,431 individuals.

Opinion issued: July 27, 2020

Link to full text: https://www.hhs.gov/sites/default/files/lifespan-ra-cap-signed.pdf

OCR's investigation revealed systemic noncompliance with HIPAA, including a failure to encrypt ePHI on laptops after Lifespan determined it should have. The investigation also revealed a lack of device and media controls, and a failure to have a business associate agreement with Lifespan's parent company, Lifespan Corporation. "Laptops, cellphones, and other mobile devices are stolen every day," remarked OCR Director Roger Severino, adding, that "[c]overed entities can best protect their patients' data by encrypting mobile devices to thwart identity thieves."[20]

Lifespan settled with OCR by agreeing to pay $1,040,000 and enter a corrective action plan. The plan requires Lifespan to report to HHS proof of encryption and access controls of Lifespan's devices. The report must include an accounting of all of Lifespan's electronic devices that could be used to access, store, download, or transmit ePHI; which devices are encrypted; Lifespan's plan to encrypt unprotected devices or alternatives to protect those devices if encryption is not reasonable; and an update on how Lifespan is controlling access to its network. Further, Lifespan must follow up with HHS and provide an updated report on the encryption status of its devices and periodically test the effectiveness of its encryption solution.

Endnotes

1. **Gabriel Imperato** is managing partner at the Fort Lauderdale office of Nelson Mullins Riley & Scarborough. He is the team leader of the firm's Health Care Criminal and Civil Enforcement, Litigation and Compliance Practice. He has practiced healthcare law in both the public and private sectors for more than 40 years. He is board certified as a specialist in health law by The Florida Bar. Imperato recently served as the general counsel of the North Broward Hospital District, the tenth largest healthcare system in the United States. He has also served as deputy chief counsel for the U.S. Department of Health & Human Services' Office of the General Counsel. Imperato is also a longtime member of the board of directors of Society of Corporate Compliance and Ethics & the Health Care Compliance Association (SCCE & HCCA), where he was also a past president and interim CEO.

2. **Anne Novick Branan** is an of counsel attorney in the Fort Lauderdale office of Nelson Mullins Riley & Scarborough. She has been board certified in health law by The Florida Bar since 1995. Branan counsels healthcare providers about avoiding and responding to allegations of fraud under the Medicare and Medicaid programs. She helps her clients navigate the complex regulatory environment affecting acquisitions and contracting in the healthcare industry. Branan regularly assists healthcare companies in developing and assessing the effectiveness of corporate compliance and ethics programs. She was recognized in *The Best Lawyers in America* for healthcare law, 2015–2020, and selected as Fort Lauderdale Health Care Law "Lawyer of the Year" in 2017.

3. **Richard Sena** is a juris doctor candidate at the Nova Southeastern University Shepard Broad College of Law. He is the editor-in-chief of the *Nova Law Review* and a law clerk at Nelson Mullins Riley & Scarborough in Fort Lauderdale since the summer of 2020. Sena has conducted health law research under the guidance of attorneys Gabriel Imperato and Anne Novick Branan and helped author sections of the "Key Laws in Healthcare Compliance" chapter in the 2021 HCCA *Complete Healthcare Compliance Manual*. He is expected to graduate in May 2021 and plans to continue his career as an associate attorney at Nelson Mullins.

4. **Megan Speltz** is a digital product owner at SCCE & HCCA, where she helps define and deliver new digital products to the COSMOS platform. She graduated from the University of St. Thomas School of Law in May 2020; she obtained her juris doctor with a concentration in organizational ethics and compliance. In addition to working at SCCE & HCCA, Speltz is a licensed attorney practicing in the state of Minnesota and represents small businesses and nonprofit organizations.

5. "HITECH Act Summary," University of South Florida Health Morsani College of Medicine, accessed January 20, 2021, http://www.usfhealthonline.com/resources/key-concepts/hitech-act-summary/.

6. "What is the HITECH Act?" Compliancy Group, accessed January 20, 2021, http://compliancy-group.com/what-is-the-hitech-act/.

7. "What is the HITECH Act?" *HIPAA Journal*, accessed January 20, 2021, http://www.hipaajournal.com/what-is-the-hitech-act/.

8. "HITECH Act Summary," University of South Florida Health Morsani College of Medicine.

9. "What is the HITECH Act?" *HIPAA Journal*.

10. Health Insurance Portability and Accountability Act of 1996, Pub. L. No. 104-191, 110 Stat. 1936 (1996).

11. 42 U.S.C. § 17935.

12. 42 U.S.C. § 17934.

13. "Business Associates," Office for Civil Rights, U.S. Department of Health & Human Services, last reviewed May 24, 2019, http://www.hhs.gov/hipaa/for-professionals/privacy/guidance/business-associates/index.html.

14. 42 U.S.C. § 17932.

15. 42 U.S.C. § 1320d-5.

16. Steve Alder, "Can a Patient Sue for A HIPAA Violation?" *HIPAA Journal*, November 7, 2017, http://www.hipaa-journal.com/sue-for-hipaa-violation/.

17. U.S. Department of Health & Human Services, "Health Insurer Pays $6.85 Million to Settle Data Breach Affecting Over 10.4 Million People," news release, September 25, 2020, http://www.hhs.gov/about/news/2020/09/25/health-insurer-pays-6-85-million-settle-data-breach-affecting-over-10-4-million-people.html.

18. Theresa Defino, "Settlement Involves 'Dark Overlord' Hack, Tip by Breach-Tracking Journalist," *Report on Patient Privacy* 20, no 10 (October 08, 2020), https://compliancecosmos.org/settlement-involves-dark-overlord-hack-tip-breach-tracking-journalist.

19. U.S. Department of Health & Human Services, "Orthopedic Clinic Pays $1.5 Million to Settle Systemic Noncompliance with HIPAA Rules," news release, September 21, 2020, http://www.hhs.gov/about/news/2020/09/21/orthopedic-clinic-pays-1.5-million-to-settle-systemic-noncompliance-with-hipaa-rules.html.

20. U.S. Department of Health & Human Services, "Lifespan Pays $1,040,000 to OCR to Settle Unencrypted Stolen Laptop Breach," news release, July 27, 2020, https://www.hhs.gov/about/news/2020/07/27/lifespan-pays-1040000-ocr-settle-unencrypted-stolen-laptop-breach.html.

Health Insurance Portability and Accountability Act of 1996

By Gabriel Imperato,[1] Esq., CHC; Anne Novick Branan,[2] Esq., CHC; Richard Sena[3] ; and Megan Speltz,[4] JD

Fast Facts

Title of law: Health Insurance Portability and Accountability Act of 1996 (HIPAA)

Category: Privacy

Public law: Pub. L. 104–191

Year enacted: 1996

Major amendments: HIPAA Privacy Rule (2003); HIPAA Security Rule (2005); Enforcement Rule (2006); Health Information Technology for Economic and Clinical Health Act (2009); Omnibus Final Rule (2013)

Enforcement agency: U.S. Department of Health & Human Services' Office for Civil Rights (OCR)

Link to full text of law:https://www.govinfo.gov/content/pkg/PLAW-104publ191/pdf/PLAW-104publ191.pdf

Applies to: All health plans, healthcare clearinghouses, healthcare providers, and endorsed sponsors of the Medicare prescription drug discount card, including business associations that supply services and certain functions for covered entities that have access to personal health information.

What Is the Health Insurance Portability and Accountability Act of 1996?

The Health Insurance Portability and Accountability Act of 1996 (HIPAA) establishes national standards to protect sensitive patient health information from being disclosed without the patient's consent or knowledge. It consists of a number of rules that lay out different requirements for HIPAA compliance. The Privacy Rule[5] dictates how, when, and under what circumstances personal health information (PHI) can be used and disclosed. The Security Rule[6] sets the minimum standards to safeguard electronic PHI (ePHI). The Breach Notification Rule[7] requires covered entities to provide notification to affected individuals, the Department of Health & Human Services (HHS) Secretary, and the media (under specific circumstances) if there is a breach of unsecured PHI; and business associates must notify covered entities if a breach occurs at or by the associates.[8] The Omnibus Rule made clarifications to the HIPAA Privacy and Security rules and improved the ability of the Office for Civil Rights (OCR) to enforce HIPAA, while also implementing the mandates of the Health Information Technology for Economic and Clinical Health (HITECH) Act.[9] The Enforcement Rule[10] established how OCR can determine liability and impose civil monetary penalties for HIPAA violations.[11]

HIPAA was enacted to:

- Improve portability and continuity of health insurance coverage
- Combat waste, fraud, and abuse in health insurance and healthcare delivery
- Promote the use of medical savings accounts
- Improve access to long-term care services and coverage to simplify the administration of health insurance[12]

The act consists of five titles. Title I protects health insurance coverage for workers and their families when they change or lose their jobs. Title II, known as the Administrative Simplification provisions, requires the establishment of national standards for electronic healthcare transactions and national identifiers for providers, health insurance plans, and employers. This title is also known as the Privacy rule. Title III sets guidelines for pretax medical spending accounts. Titles IV and V set guidelines for group health plans and company-owned insurance policies.

Violations of HIPAA generally result from the following:

- Lack of adequate risk analyses
- Lack of comprehensive employee training
- Inadequate business associate agreements
- Inappropriate disclosures of PHI
- Ignorance of the minimum necessary rule
- Failure to report breaches within the prescribed time frame

History

HIPAA was enacted by the 104th Congress and signed into law by President Bill Clinton in 1996. When the act was originally passed, it only required the Secretary of HHS to propose standards that would protect individually identifiable health information. The initial proposed "Code Set" standards were not published until 1999, with the first proposals for the Privacy Rule being established in 2000.

Since its original passage, HIPAA legislation has evolved significantly. The language of the act has been modified to address changes in technology, and the scope has shifted to include third-party service providers (business associates) that perform a function on behalf of a HIPAA-covered entity that involves the use or disclosure of PHI. Each of the major rules were passed throughout the early 2000s and build out various requirements of HIPAA compliance.

Related Laws

Preemption of State Law, 45 C.F.R. § 160, Subpart B

HIPAA provides a minimum set of requirements states must follow in protecting individuals' PHI. With respect to these minimums, states cannot pass laws contrary to the HIPAA rules, unless one of the following exceptions apply:

- The law relates to the privacy of PHI and provides greater privacy protection or rights.
- The law provides for the reporting of disease or injury; child abuse; birth or death; or public health surveillance, investigation, or intervention.
- The law requires certain health plan reporting (e.g., financial audits). However, a covered entity is not required to comply with parts of the law that are contrary to HIPAA.[13]

Examples of State Laws Not Preempted by HIPAA

Cal. Health & Safety Code § 123110 (West 2020)
- Healthcare providers must allow patients to inspect their medical records within five business days from the request (as opposed to 30 days under HIPAA).
- A copy of the medical record must be sent to the patient within 15 days from the request.

Fla. Stat. § 501.171 (West 2020)
- Decreases the outer time limit for individual notification of a breach from 60 days to 30 days.

N.Y. Pub. Health § 18 (McKinney 2020)
- Healthcare providers must allow patients to inspect their medical records within 10 business days from the request (as opposed to 30 days under HIPAA).
- A copy of the medical record must be sent to the patient within a reasonable time of the request.

Health Insurance Portability and Accountability Act Compliance Risks

The following are specific HIPAA risk areas that compliance professionals need to monitor closely.

Risk Area: Lack of Adequate Risk Analysis, Policies and Procedures, and Employee Training

45 C.F.R. § 164.308(a)

a. A covered entity or business associate must, in accordance with § 164.306:

   1.

      i. Standard: Security management process. Implement policies and procedures to prevent, detect, contain, and correct security violations.

      ii. Implementation specifications:

         A. Risk analysis (Required). Conduct an accurate and thorough assessment of the potential risks and vulnerabilities to the confidentiality, integrity, and availability of electronic protected health information held by the covered entity or business associate.

         B. Risk management (Required). Implement security measures sufficient to reduce risks and vulnerabilities to a reasonable and appropriate level to comply with § 164.306(a).

         C. Sanction policy (Required). Apply appropriate sanctions against workforce members who fail to comply with the security policies and procedures of the covered entity or business associate.

         D. Information system activity review (Required). Implement procedures to regularly review records of information system activity, such as audit logs, access reports, and security incident tracking reports.

2. Standard: Assigned security responsibility. Identify the security official who is responsible for the development and implementation of the policies and procedures required by this subpart for the covered entity or business associate.

3.

   i. Standard: Workforce security. Implement policies and procedures to ensure that all members of its workforce have appropriate access to electronic protected health information, as provided under paragraph (a)(4) of this section, and to prevent those workforce members who do not have access under paragraph (a)(4) of this section from obtaining access to electronic protected health information.

   ii. Implementation specifications:

      A. Authorization and/or supervision (Addressable). Implement procedures for the authorization and/or supervision of workforce members who work with electronic protected health information or in locations where it might be accessed.

      B. Workforce clearance procedure (Addressable). Implement procedures to determine that the access of a workforce member to electronic protected health information is appropriate.

      C. Termination procedures (Addressable). Implement procedures for terminating access to electronic protected health information when the employment of, or other arrangement with, a workforce member ends or as required by determinations made as specified in paragraph (a)(3)(ii)(B) of this section.

4.

   i. Standard: Information access management. Implement policies and procedures for authorizing access to electronic protected health information that are consistent with the applicable requirements of subpart E of this part.

   ii. Implementation specifications:

      A. Isolating health care clearinghouse functions (Required). If a health care clearinghouse is part of a larger organization, the clearinghouse must implement policies and procedures that protect the electronic protected health information of the clearinghouse from unauthorized access by the larger organization.

B. Access authorization (Addressable). Implement policies and procedures for granting access to electronic protected health information, for example, through access to a workstation, transaction, program, process, or other mechanism.

C. Access establishment and modification (Addressable). Implement policies and procedures that, based upon the covered entity's or the business associate's access authorization policies, establish, document, review, and modify a user's right of access to a workstation, transaction, program, or process.

5.

i. Standard: Security awareness and training. Implement a security awareness and training program for all members of its workforce (including management).

ii. Implementation specifications. Implement:

A. Security reminders (Addressable). Periodic security updates.

B. Protection from malicious software (Addressable). Procedures for guarding against, detecting, and reporting malicious software.

C. Log-in monitoring (Addressable). Procedures for monitoring log-in attempts and reporting discrepancies.

D. Password management (Addressable). Procedures for creating, changing, and safeguarding passwords.

6.

i. Standard: Security incident procedures. Implement policies and procedures to address security incidents.

ii. Implementation specification: Response and reporting (Required). Identify and respond to suspected or known security incidents; mitigate, to the extent practicable, harmful effects of security incidents that are known to the covered entity or business associate; and document security incidents and their outcomes.

7.

i. Standard: Contingency plan. Establish (and implement as needed) policies and procedures for responding to an emergency or other occurrence (for example, fire, vandalism, system failure, and natural disaster) that damages systems that contain electronic protected health information.

    ii.   Implementation specifications:

        A.   Data backup plan (Required). Establish and implement procedures to create and maintain retrievable exact copies of electronic protected health information.

        B.   Disaster recovery plan (Required). Establish (and implement as needed) procedures to restore any loss of data.

        C.   Emergency mode operation plan (Required). Establish (and implement as needed) procedures to enable continuation of critical business processes for protection of the security of electronic protected health information while operating in emergency mode.

        D.   Testing and revision procedures (Addressable). Implement procedures for periodic testing and revision of contingency plans.

        E.   Applications and data criticality analysis (Addressable). Assess the relative criticality of specific applications and data in support of other contingency plan components.

8.   Standard: Evaluation. Perform a periodic technical and nontechnical evaluation, based initially upon the standards implemented under this rule and, subsequently, in response to environmental or operational changes affecting the security of electronic protected health information, that establishes the extent to which a covered entity's or business associate's security policies and procedures meet the requirements of this subpart.[14]

Context: Central to HIPAA compliance is the preemption of inappropriate access to PHI. HIPAA requires that healthcare organizations conduct a risk analysis, implement policies to curb risk, and implement disciplinary measures against employees who fail to adhere to those policies. Training is also an essential part of HIPAA's breach preemption rules. Healthcare organizations must implement policies that make employees aware of the need to maintain security and what to do in the event a security incident occurs. Additionally, healthcare organizations must be prepared in the event that data centers containing PHI are compromised by properly backing up and protecting data. Lastly, keeping PHI secure is an ongoing process for healthcare organizations, and they must conduct routine evaluations to comply with HIPAA and changes in the organizational and security environment.

Risk Area: Inadequate Business Associate Agreements

45 C.F.R. § 164.308(b)

b.

1. Business associate contracts and other arrangements. A covered entity may permit a business associate to create, receive, maintain, or transmit electronic protected health information on the covered entity's behalf only if the covered entity obtains satisfactory assurances, in accordance with § 164.314(a), that the business associate will appropriately safeguard the information. A covered entity is not required to obtain such satisfactory assurances from a business associate that is a subcontractor.

2. A business associate may permit a business associate that is a subcontractor to create, receive, maintain, or transmit electronic protected health information on its behalf only if the business associate obtains satisfactory assurances, in accordance with § 164.314(a), that the subcontractor will appropriately safeguard the information.

3. Implementation specifications: Written contract or other arrangement (Required). Document the satisfactory assurances required by paragraph (b)(1) or (b)(2) of this section through a written contract or other arrangement with the business associate that meets the applicable requirements of § 164.314(a).[15]

45 C.F.R. § 164.314(a)

a.

1. Standard: Business associate contracts or other arrangements. The contract or other arrangement required by § 164.308(b)(3) must meet the requirements of paragraph (a)(2)(i), (a)(2)(ii), or (a)(2)(iii) of this section, as applicable.

2. Implementation specifications (Required) -

   i. Business associate contracts. The contract must provide that the business associate will -

   A. Comply with the applicable requirements of this subpart;

   B. In accordance with § 164.308(b)(2), ensure that any subcontractors that create, receive, maintain, or transmit electronic protected health information on behalf of the business associate agree to comply with the applicable requirements of this subpart by entering into a contract or other arrangement that complies with this section; and

  C. Report to the covered entity any security incident of which it becomes aware, including breaches of unsecured protected health information as required by § 164.410.

 ii. Other arrangements. The covered entity is in compliance with paragraph (a)(1) of this section if it has another arrangement in place that meets the requirements of § 164.504(e)(3).

 iii. Business associate contracts with subcontractors. The requirements of paragraphs (a)(2)(i) and (a)(2)(ii) of this section apply to the contract or other arrangement between a business associate and a subcontractor required by § 164.308(b)(4) in the same manner as such requirements apply to contracts or other arrangements between a covered entity and business associate.[16]

Context: HIPAA generally applies to two types of entities: (1) covered entities and (2) business associates.[17] Covered entities include healthcare providers, healthcare clearinghouses, and health plans. Business associates include organizations or persons, and their subcontractors, that transmit PHI to or from covered entities. Because PHI often needs to be transmitted, covered entities contract with business associates to provide these services, and both entities are bound by HIPAA's various rules. In order for these contracts to comply with HIPAA, they must include "satisfactory assurances" that the business associate will protect the PHI. These assurances extend to subcontractors of the business associates, and they include a requirement to report "security incidents" to the covered entity if they arise.

Risk Area: Unauthorized Disclosure

45 C.F.R. § 164.508

 a. Standard: Authorizations for uses and disclosures -

  1. Authorization required: General rule. Except as otherwise permitted or required by this subchapter, a covered entity may not use or disclose protected health information without an authorization that is valid under this section. When a covered entity obtains or receives a valid authorization for its use or disclosure of protected health information, such use or disclosure must be consistent with such authorization.

  2. Authorization required: Psychotherapy notes. Notwithstanding any provision of this subpart, other than the transition provisions in § 164.532, a covered entity must obtain an authorization for any use or disclosure of psychotherapy notes, except:

         i.   To carry out the following treatment, payment, or health care operations:

              A. Use by the originator of the psychotherapy notes for treatment;

              B. Use or disclosure by the covered entity for its own training programs in which students, trainees, or practitioners in mental health learn under supervision to practice or improve their skills in group, joint, family, or individual counseling; or

              C. Use or disclosure by the covered entity to defend itself in a legal action or other proceeding brought by the individual; and

        ii.   A use or disclosure that is required by § 164.502(a)(2)(ii) or permitted by § 164.512(a); § 164.512(d) with respect to the oversight of the originator of the psychotherapy notes; § 164.512(g)(1); or § 164.512(j)(1)(i).

    3.   Authorization required: Marketing.

         i.   Notwithstanding any provision of this subpart, other than the transition provisions in § 164.532, a covered entity must obtain an authorization for any use or disclosure of protected health information for marketing, except if the communication is in the form of:

              A. A face-to-face communication made by a covered entity to an individual; or

              B. A promotional gift of nominal value provided by the covered entity.

        ii.   If the marketing involves financial remuneration, as defined in paragraph (3) of the definition of marketing at § 164.501, to the covered entity from a third party, the authorization must state that such remuneration is involved.

    4.   Authorization required: Sale of protected health information.

         i.   Notwithstanding any provision of this subpart, other than the transition provisions in § 164.532, a covered entity must obtain an authorization for any disclosure of protected health information which is a sale of protected health information, as defined in § 164.501 of this subpart. (ii) Such authorization must state that the disclosure will result in remuneration to the covered entity.

  b.   Implementation specifications: General requirements -

    1.   Valid authorizations.

i.   A valid authorization is a document that meets the requirements in paragraphs (a)(3)(ii), (a)(4)(ii), (c)(1), and (c)(2) of this section, as applicable.

ii.   A valid authorization may contain elements or information in addition to the elements required by this section, provided that such additional elements or information are not inconsistent with the elements required by this section.

2.   Defective authorizations. An authorization is not valid, if the document submitted has any of the following defects:

i.   The expiration date has passed or the expiration event is known by the covered entity to have occurred;

ii.   The authorization has not been filled out completely, with respect to an element described by paragraph (c) of this section, if applicable;

iii.   The authorization is known by the covered entity to have been revoked;

iv.   The authorization violates paragraph (b)(3) or (4) of this section, if applicable;

v.   Any material information in the authorization is known by the covered entity to be false.

3.   Compound authorizations. An authorization for use or disclosure of protected health information may not be combined with any other document to create a compound authorization, except as follows:

i.   An authorization for the use or disclosure of protected health information for a research study may be combined with any other type of written permission for the same or another research study. This exception includes combining an authorization for the use or disclosure of protected health information for a research study with another authorization for the same research study, with an authorization for the creation or maintenance of a research database or repository, or with a consent to participate in research. Where a covered health care provider has conditioned the provision of research-related treatment on the provision of one of the authorizations, as permitted under paragraph (b)(4)(i) of this section, any compound authorization created under this paragraph must clearly differentiate between the conditioned and unconditioned components and provide the individual with an opportunity to opt in to the research activities described in the unconditioned authorization.

ii. An authorization for a use or disclosure of psychotherapy notes may only be combined with another authorization for a use or disclosure of psychotherapy notes.

iii. An authorization under this section, other than an authorization for a use or disclosure of psychotherapy notes, may be combined with any other such authorization under this section, except when a covered entity has conditioned the provision of treatment, payment, enrollment in the health plan, or eligibility for benefits under paragraph (b)(4) of this section on the provision of one of the authorizations. The prohibition in this paragraph on combining authorizations where one authorization conditions the provision of treatment, payment, enrollment in a health plan, or eligibility for benefits under paragraph (b)(4) of this section does not apply to a compound authorization created in accordance with paragraph (b)(3)(i) of this section.

4. Prohibition on conditioning of authorizations. A covered entity may not condition the provision to an individual of treatment, payment, enrollment in the health plan, or eligibility for benefits on the provision of an authorization, except:

   i. A covered health care provider may condition the provision of research-related treatment on provision of an authorization for the use or disclosure of protected health information for such research under this section;

   ii. A health plan may condition enrollment in the health plan or eligibility for benefits on provision of an authorization requested by the health plan prior to an individual's enrollment in the health plan, if:

      A. The authorization sought is for the health plan's eligibility or enrollment determinations relating to the individual or for its underwriting or risk rating determinations; and

      B. The authorization is not for a use or disclosure of psychotherapy notes under paragraph (a)(2) of this section; and

   iii. A covered entity may condition the provision of health care that is solely for the purpose of creating protected health information for disclosure to a third party on provision of an authorization for the disclosure of the protected health information to such third party.

5. Revocation of authorizations. An individual may revoke an authorization provided under this section at any time, provided that the revocation is in writing, except to the extent that:

      i.   The covered entity has taken action in reliance thereon; or

      ii.   If the authorization was obtained as a condition of obtaining insurance coverage, other law provides the insurer with the right to contest a claim under the policy or the policy itself.

6.   Documentation. A covered entity must document and retain any signed authorization under this section as required by § 164.530(j).

c.   Implementation specifications: Core elements and requirements -

   1.   Core elements. A valid authorization under this section must contain at least the following elements:

      i.   A description of the information to be used or disclosed that identifies the information in a specific and meaningful fashion.

      ii.   The name or other specific identification of the person(s), or class of persons, authorized to make the requested use or disclosure.

      iii.   The name or other specific identification of the person(s), or class of persons, to whom the covered entity may make the requested use or disclosure.

      iv.   A description of each purpose of the requested use or disclosure. The statement "at the request of the individual" is a sufficient description of the purpose when an individual initiates the authorization and does not, or elects not to, provide a statement of the purpose.

      v.   An expiration date or an expiration event that relates to the individual or the purpose of the use or disclosure. The statement "end of the research study," "none," or similar language is sufficient if the authorization is for a use or disclosure of protected health information for research, including for the creation and maintenance of a research database or research repository.

      vi.   Signature of the individual and date. If the authorization is signed by a personal representative of the individual, a description of such representative's authority to act for the individual must also be provided.

   2.   Required statements. In addition to the core elements, the authorization must contain statements adequate to place the individual on notice of all of the following:

      i.   The individual's right to revoke the authorization in writing, and either:

      A. The exceptions to the right to revoke and a description of how the individual may revoke the authorization; or

      B. To the extent that the information in paragraph (c)(2)(i)(A) of this section is included in the notice required by § 164.520, a reference to the covered entity's notice.

  ii. The ability or inability to condition treatment, payment, enrollment or eligibility for benefits on the authorization, by stating either:

      A. The covered entity may not condition treatment, payment, enrollment or eligibility for benefits on whether the individual signs the authorization when the prohibition on conditioning of authorizations in paragraph (b)(4) of this section applies; or

      B. The consequences to the individual of a refusal to sign the authorization when, in accordance with paragraph (b)(4) of this section, the covered entity can condition treatment, enrollment in the health plan, or eligibility for benefits on failure to obtain such authorization.

  iii. The potential for information disclosed pursuant to the authorization to be subject to redisclosure by the recipient and no longer be protected by this subpart.

3. Plain language requirement. The authorization must be written in plain language.

4. Copy to the individual. If a covered entity seeks an authorization from an individual for a use or disclosure of protected health information, the covered entity must provide the individual with a copy of the signed authorization.[18]

Context: The default rule under HIPAA is that healthcare providers may not use or disclose a patient's PHI without authorization. This rule also governs what makes an effective authorization, which includes a description of the information, names of those authorized to transmit and those authorized to receive the information, a purpose for the authorization, a date or event of expiration, and the individual's signature. Authorizations must also include certain adequate notices to the authorizing individual, and a signed copy must be supplied to the individual.

Risk Area: Minimum Necessary Disclosure Rule

45 C.F.R. § 164.502(b)

    b.   Standard: Minimum necessary -

        1.   Minimum necessary applies. When using or disclosing protected health information or when requesting protected health information from another covered entity or business associate, a covered entity or business associate must make reasonable efforts to limit protected health information to the minimum necessary to accomplish the intended purpose of the use, disclosure, or request.

        2.   Minimum necessary does not apply. This requirement does not apply to:

            i.   Disclosures to or requests by a health care provider for treatment;

            ii.   Uses or disclosures made to the individual, as permitted under paragraph (a)(1)(i) of this section or as required by paragraph (a)(2)(i) of this section;

            iii.   Uses or disclosures made pursuant to an authorization under § 164.508;

            iv.   Disclosures made to the Secretary in accordance with subpart C of part 160 of this subchapter;

            v.   Uses or disclosures that are required by law, as described by § 164.512(a); and

            vi.   Uses or disclosures that are required for compliance with applicable requirements of this subchapter.[19]

Context: An important subpart of section 164.502 is subsection (b), which is known as the Minimum Necessary Rule. When authorized, a healthcare provider or its business associate may disclose PHI, but only to the extent necessary. The rule does have exceptions for disclosures or requests by a healthcare provider for treatment, disclosures to patients of their own PHI, certain authorized disclosures, compliance investigations, and disclosures required by law (e.g., court orders or subpoenas) or for compliance.

Risk Area: PHI Security Requirements

45 C.F.R. § 164.306

a. General requirements. Covered entities and business associates must do the following:

    1. Ensure the confidentiality, integrity, and availability of all electronic protected health information the covered entity or business associate creates, receives, maintains, or transmits.

    2. Protect against any reasonably anticipated threats or hazards to the security or integrity of such information.

    3. Protect against any reasonably anticipated uses or disclosures of such information that are not permitted or required under subpart E of this part.

    4. Ensure compliance with this subpart by its workforce.

b. Flexibility of approach.

    1. Covered entities and business associates may use any security measures that allow the covered entity or business associate to reasonably and appropriately implement the standards and implementation specifications as specified in this subpart.

    2. In deciding which security measures to use, a covered entity or business associate must take into account the following factors:

        i. The size, complexity, and capabilities of the covered entity or business associate.

        ii. The covered entity's or the business associate's technical infrastructure, hardware, and software security capabilities.

        iii. The costs of security measures.

        iv. The probability and criticality of potential risks to electronic protected health information.

c. Standards. A covered entity or business associate must comply with the applicable standards as provided in this section and in §§ 164.308, 164.310, 164.312, 164.314 and 164.316 with respect to all electronic protected health information.

d. Implementation specifications. In this subpart:

1. Implementation specifications are required or addressable. If an implementation specification is required, the word "Required" appears in parentheses after the title of the implementation specification. If an implementation specification is addressable, the word "Addressable" appears in parentheses after the title of the implementation specification.

2. When a standard adopted in § 164.308, § 164.310, § 164.312, § 164.314, or § 164.316 includes required implementation specifications, a covered entity or business associate must implement the implementation specifications.

3. When a standard adopted in § 164.308, § 164.310, § 164.312, § 164.314, or § 164.316 includes addressable implementation specifications, a covered entity or business associate must –

    i. Assess whether each implementation specification is a reasonable and appropriate safeguard in its environment, when analyzed with reference to the likely contribution to protecting electronic protected health information; and

    ii. As applicable to the covered entity or business associate -

        A. Implement the implementation specification if reasonable and appropriate; or

        B. If implementing the implementation specification is not reasonable and appropriate -

            1. Document why it would not be reasonable and appropriate to implement the implementation specification; and

            2. Implement an equivalent alternative measure if reasonable and appropriate.

e. Maintenance. A covered entity or business associate must review and modify the security measures implemented under this subpart as needed to continue provision of reasonable and appropriate protection of electronic protected health information, and update documentation of such security measures in accordance with § 164.316(b)(2)(iii).[20]

Context: Covered entities and business associates are required to implement security measures to protect PHI. These measures must ensure employees are adequately trained in PHI security and must protect against reasonably anticipated threats, unauthorized uses, and unauthorized disclosures. Although HIPAA does not prescribe specific measures and implementation of PHI security, covered entities and business associates must consider their size and security capabilities, infrastructure, cost, and potential risks of their chosen security method.

Risk Area: Required Notification of Breach

45 C.F.R. § 164.404

    a.   Standard -

        1.   General rule. A covered entity shall, following the discovery of a breach of unsecured protected health information, notify each individual whose unsecured protected health information has been, or is reasonably believed by the covered entity to have been, accessed, acquired, used, or disclosed as a result of such breach.

        2.   Breaches treated as discovered. For purposes of paragraph (a)(1) of this section, §§ 164.406(a), and 164.408(a), a breach shall be treated as discovered by a covered entity as of the first day on which such breach is known to the covered entity, or, by exercising reasonable diligence would have been known to the covered entity. A covered entity shall be deemed to have knowledge of a breach if such breach is known, or by exercising reasonable diligence would have been known, to any person, other than the person committing the breach, who is a workforce member or agent of the covered entity (determined in accordance with the federal common law of agency).

    b.   Implementation specification: Timeliness of notification. Except as provided in § 164.412, a covered entity shall provide the notification required by paragraph (a) of this section without unreasonable delay and in no case later than 60 calendar days after discovery of a breach.

    c.   Implementation specifications: Content of notification -

        1.   Elements. The notification required by paragraph (a) of this section shall include, to the extent possible:

            A.   A brief description of what happened, including the date of the breach and the date of the discovery of the breach, if known;

            B.   A description of the types of unsecured protected health information that were involved in the breach (such as whether full name, social security number, date of birth, home address, account number, diagnosis, disability code, or other types of information were involved);

            C.   Any steps individuals should take to protect themselves from potential harm resulting from the breach;

            D.   A brief description of what the covered entity involved is doing to investigate the breach, to mitigate harm to individuals, and to protect against any further breaches; and

E. Contact procedures for individuals to ask questions or learn additional information, which shall include a toll-free telephone number, an e-mail address, Web site, or postal address.

2. Plain language requirement. The notification required by paragraph (a) of this section shall be written in plain language.

d. Implementation specifications: Methods of individual notification. The notification required by paragraph (a) of this section shall be provided in the following form:

1. Written notice.

    i. Written notification by first-class mail to the individual at the last known address of the individual or, if the individual agrees to electronic notice and such agreement has not been withdrawn, by electronic mail. The notification may be provided in one or more mailings as information is available.

    ii. If the covered entity knows the individual is deceased and has the address of the next of kin or personal representative of the individual (as specified under § 164.502(g)(4) of subpart E), written notification by first-class mail to either the next of kin or personal representative of the individual. The notification may be provided in one or more mailings as information is available.

2. Substitute notice. In the case in which there is insufficient or out-of-date contact information that precludes written notification to the individual under paragraph (d)(1)(i) of this section, a substitute form of notice reasonably calculated to reach the individual shall be provided. Substitute notice need not be provided in the case in which there is insufficient or out-of-date contact information that precludes written notification to the next of kin or personal representative of the individual under paragraph (d)(1)(ii).

    i. In the case in which there is insufficient or out-of-date contact information for fewer than 10 individuals, then such substitute notice may be provided by an alternative form of written notice, telephone, or other means.

    ii. In the case in which there is insufficient or out-of-date contact information for 10 or more individuals, then such substitute notice shall:

        A. Be in the form of either a conspicuous posting for a period of 90 days on the home page of the Web site of the covered entity involved, or conspicuous notice in major print or broadcast media in geographic areas where the individuals affected by the breach likely reside; and

    B.   Include a toll-free phone number that remains active for at least 90 days where an individual can learn whether the individual's unsecured protected health information may be included in the breach.

    3.   Additional notice in urgent situations. In any case deemed by the covered entity to require urgency because of possible imminent misuse of unsecured protected health information, the covered entity may provide information to individuals by telephone or other means, as appropriate, in addition to notice provided under paragraph (d)(1) of this section.[21]

45 C.F.R. § 164.406

a.   Standard. For a breach of unsecured protected health information involving more than 500 residents of a State or jurisdiction, a covered entity shall, following the discovery of the breach as provided in § 164.404(a)(2), notify prominent media outlets serving the State or jurisdiction.

b.   Implementation specification: Timeliness of notification. Except as provided in § 164.412, a covered entity shall provide the notification required by paragraph (a) of this section without unreasonable delay and in no case later than 60 calendar days after discovery of a breach.

c.   Implementation specifications: Content of notification. The notification required by paragraph (a) of this section shall meet the requirements of § 164.404(c).[22]

45 C.F.R. § 164.408

a.   Standard. A covered entity shall, following the discovery of a breach of unsecured protected health information as provided in § 164.404(a)(2), notify the Secretary.

b.   Implementation specifications: Breaches involving 500 or more individuals. For breaches of unsecured protected health information involving 500 or more individuals, a covered entity shall, except as provided in § 164.412, provide the notification required by paragraph (a) of this section contemporaneously with the notice required by § 164.404(a) and in the manner specified on the HHS Web site.

c.   Implementation specifications: Breaches involving less than 500 individuals. For breaches of unsecured protected health information involving less than 500 individuals, a covered entity shall maintain a log or other documentation of such breaches and, not later than 60 days after the end of each calendar year, provide the notification required by paragraph (a) of this section for breaches discovered during the preceding calendar year, in the manner specified on the HHS web site.[23]

Context: In the event of a breach, covered entities are required to notify individuals within 60 days of discovering the breach. A breach is considered to be known when any employee or agent of the covered entity discovers the breach or should have discovered the breach had the entity conducted "reasonable diligence." Once discovered, the covered entity must contact the individual via first-class mail and disclose what happened, what information was compromised, and self-protecting steps the individual can take. The rule also requires covered entities to disclose to the affected individual what the entity is doing to investigate the breach, mitigate harm, and protect against further breaches. For breaches affecting more than 500 people, the covered entity must contact prominent media outlets where the affected individuals are located.

Risk Area: Civil Money Penalties

45 C.F.R. § 160.404

a. The amount of a civil money penalty will be determined in accordance with paragraph (b) of this section, and §§ 160.406, 160.408, and 160.412. These amounts were adjusted in accordance with the Federal Civil Monetary Penalty Inflation Adjustment Act of 1990, (Pub. L. 101-140), as amended by the Federal Civil Penalties Inflation Adjustment Act Improvements Act of 2015, (section 701 of Pub. L. 114-74), and appear at 45 CFR part 102. These amounts will be updated annually and published at 45 CFR part 102.

b. The amount of a civil money penalty that may be imposed is subject to the following limitations:

    1. For violations occurring prior to February 18, 2009, the Secretary may not impose a civil money penalty -

        i. In the amount of more than $100 for each violation; or

        ii. In excess of $25,000 for identical violations during a calendar year (January 1 through the following December 31);

    2. For violations occurring on or after February 18, 2009, the Secretary may not impose a civil money penalty -

        i. For a violation in which it is established that the covered entity or business associate did not know and, by exercising reasonable diligence, would not have known that the covered entity or business associate violated such provision,

      A. In the amount of less than $100 or more than $50,000 for each violation; or

      B. In excess of $1,500,000 for identical violations during a calendar year (January 1 through the following December 31);

ii. For a violation in which it is established that the violation was due to reasonable cause and not to willful neglect,

      A. In the amount of less than $1,000 or more than $50,000 for each violation; or

      B. In excess of $1,500,000 for identical violations during a calendar year (January 1 through the following December 31);

iii. For a violation in which it is established that the violation was due to willful neglect and was corrected during the 30-day period beginning on the first date the covered entity or business associate liable for the penalty knew, or, by exercising reasonable diligence, would have known that the violation occurred,

      A. In the amount of less than $10,000 or more than $50,000 for each violation; or

      B. In excess of $1,500,000 for identical violations during a calendar year (January 1 through the following December 31);

iv. For a violation in which it is established that the violation was due to willful neglect and was not corrected during the 30-day period beginning on the first date the covered entity or business associate liable for the penalty knew, or, by exercising reasonable diligence, would have known that the violation occurred,

      A. In the amount of less than $50,000 for each violation; or

      B. In excess of $1,500,000 for identical violations during a calendar year (January 1 through the following December 31).

3. If a requirement or prohibition in one administrative simplification provision is repeated in a more general form in another administrative simplification provision in the same subpart, a civil money penalty may be imposed for a violation of only one of these administrative simplification provisions.[24]

Context: Civil penalties for HIPAA violations depend on both when the violations occurred and the nature of the violation. Violations prior to February 18, 2009, are limited to civil penalties of no more than $100 per violation and no more than $25,000 for the calendar year. Violations on or after February 18, 2009, may range from no less than $100 to no less than $10,000 per violation depending on the nature of the violation. However, the calendar year limit is uniformly set at $1,500,000. The amounts are subject to yearly adjustments in accordance with inflation, and adjusted civil penalty amounts may be found at 45 C.F.R. § 102.3.

Risk Area: Criminal Penalties

42 U.S.C. § 1320d–6

a. Offense:

A person who knowingly and in violation of this part—

1. uses or causes to be used a unique health identifier;

2. obtains individually identifiable health information relating to an individual; or

3. discloses individually identifiable health information to another person,

shall be punished as provided in subsection (b). For purposes of the previous sentence, a person (including an employee or other individual) shall be considered to have obtained or disclosed individually identifiable health information in violation of this part if the information is maintained by a covered entity (as defined in the HIPAA privacy regulation described in section 1320d–9(b)(3) of this title) and the individual obtained or disclosed such information without authorization.

b. Penalties:

A person described in subsection (a) shall—

1. be fined not more than $50,000, imprisoned not more than 1 year, or both;

2. if the offense is committed under false pretenses, be fined not more than $100,000, imprisoned not more than 5 years, or both; and

3. if the offense is committed with intent to sell, transfer, or use individually identifiable health information for commercial advantage, personal gain, or malicious harm, be fined not more than $250,000, imprisoned not more than 10 years, or both.[25]

Context: Criminal liability under HIPAA is appropriate for individuals without authorization who knowingly use, cause to be used, obtain, or disclose individually identifiable health information maintained by a covered entity. Criminal penalties depend on the nature of the offense and the intent of the violator. Maximum limits for the most egregious violations range up to a $250,000 fine and 10 years in prison.

Consequences for Noncompliance

Noncompliance and violations of HIPAA expose healthcare organizations to civil money penalties within a defined statutory range, subject to adjustment for inflation, and dependent on the nature of the violation.

Administrative Proceedings

Penalties

- Violations before February 18, 2019, are subject to civil penalties no more than $100 per violation and no more than $25,000 per calendar year.

- Violations occurring on or after February 18, 2019, are subject to civil penalty limits dependent on the nature of the violation.

- If unaware of the violation and would not have known by exercising reasonable due diligence of the violation: $100–$50,000 per violation or up to $1.5 million per year for identical violations.

- Violations due to reasonable cause and not willful neglect: $1,000–$50,000 per violation or up to $1.5 million per year for identical violations.

- Violations due to willful neglect but corrected within 30 days: $10,000–$50,000 per violation, or up to $1.5 million per year for identical violations.

- Violations due to willful neglect and not corrected within 30 days: No less than $50,000 per violation or up to $1.5 million per year for identical violations.

- Civil penalties are adjusted for inflation on a yearly basis, and updated amounts are published at 45 C.F.R. § 102.3.

Corrective Actions

- Required risk analysis submission to HHS.

- Required implementation of a risk management plan.

- Revision of policies and procedures to ensure compliance with HIPAA rules.

- Instituting procedures ensuring proper contracting between covered entity and business associate.

- Required training on revised policies and procedures ensuring HIPAA compliance.

Civil Litigation

Damages

A person who was financially harmed by a HIPAA violation may sue a covered entity or business associate for damages under state law.[26]

Criminal Proceedings

Sentencing

- Knowing violation: Up to $50,000 fine and/or up to one-year imprisonment.

- Knowing violation committed under false pretenses: Up to $100,000 and/or up to five-year imprisonment.

- Knowing violation committed with intent to sell, transfer, or use individual identifiable health information for commercial advantage, personal gain, or malicious harm: Up to $250,000 and/or up to 10-year imprisonment.

Important Compliance Guidance and Tools

Centers for Medicare & Medicaid Services

Medicare Learning Network

The *HIPAA Basics for Providers: Privacy, Security, and Breach Notification Rules* booklet for Medicare fee-for-service providers details the basics of HIPAA rules.

https://www.cms.gov/outreach-and-education/medicare-learning-network-mln/mlnproducts/downloads/hipaaprivacyandsecurity.pdf

National Institutes of Health

OCR Privacy and Security Email Lists

These email lists regularly inform the public about health information privacy and security frequently asked questions, guidance, and technical assistance materials.

Privacy: https://list.nih.gov/cgi-bin/wa.exe?A0=OCR-PRIVACY-LIST

Security: https://list.nih.gov/cgi-bin/wa.exe?A0=ocr-security-list

U.S. Department of Health & Human Services

HIPAA Guidance Materials

This web page includes links to important HIPAA guidance resources for small providers, small health plans, and other small businesses; health plan care coordination and continuity of care; and covered entities.

https://www.hhs.gov/hipaa/for-professionals/privacy/guidance/index.html

Security Rule Guidance Material

Educational materials on the HIPAA Security Rule and safeguarding standards for ePHI can be accessed through links on this site. These materials include National Institute of Standards and Technology special publications, Federal Trade Commission guidance, OCR cybersecurity newsletters, and HHS educational papers and security guidance materials.

https://www.hhs.gov/hipaa/for-professionals/security/guidance/index.html

Relevant HIPAA Cases and Opinions

Elite Dental Associates—Dallas, P.C.

Case summary: Elite Dental Associates (Elite), a privately owned dental practice, impermissibly disclosed the PHI of its patients when responding to patients' reviews on Yelp.[27] The Yelp response that prompted a complaint to HHS included the patient's last name, details of the treatment plan, insurance, and cost information. The OCR investigation revealed Elite had disclosed the PHI of other patients in the same or similar manner by responding to reviews on Yelp.

Opinion issued: October 2, 2019

Link to full text: https://www.hhs.gov/about/news/2019/10/02/dental-practice-pays-10000-settle-social-media-disclosures-of-patients-phi.html

OCR's investigation revealed Elite lacked any policies or procedures governing the protection of PHI and lacked the minimum content required in its Notice of Privacy Practices. The HIPAA Privacy Rule ensures individually identifiable health information remains private. In reconciling the Privacy Rule and the proliferation of business use of social media, then-OCR Director Roger Severino said, "Social media is not the place for providers to discuss a patient's care." He added, "Doctors and dentists must think carefully about patient privacy before responding to online reviews."

Elite settled the potential violation for $10,000, which was reduced due to the size, financial circumstances, and Elite's cooperation with the OCR investigation. Elite, however, also was required to conduct corrective actions to ensure its compliance with HIPAA, including developing policies and procedures to ensure HIPAA compliance, updating its Notice of Privacy Practices, and training its employees on the updated policies and procedures.

Aetna Life Insurance Company

Case summary: Between June 2017 and November 2017, Aetna Life Insurance Company (Aetna) reported three breaches of PHI to HHS, affecting more than 18,000 people.[28] In June 2017, Aetna reported that certain web services it used to display plan information online to patients allowed the information to be accessed without login credentials. In August 2017, Aetna reported that certain notices to patients used window envelopes that allowed the words "HIV medication" to be seen underneath the recipient's name and address. Lastly, in November 2017, Aetna sent research study mailers to participating members that contained the name and logo of the research study on the face of the envelope.

Opinion issued: October 28, 2020

Link to full text: https://www.hhs.gov/about/news/2020/10/28/aetna-pays-one-million-to-settle-three-hipaa-breaches.html

Along with the impermissible disclosures of PHI, OCR's investigation revealed that Aetna failed to perform "periodic technical and nontechnical evaluations of operational changes"affecting the security of PHI as required by 45 C.F.R. § 164.308(a)(8). The June report was a violation of the required implementation of procedures to verify a person's identity when seeking access to PHI under 45 C.F.R. § 164.312(d). The August windowed notices and the November mailers violated the minimum necessary rule, because Aetna disclosed more information than necessary "to accomplish the purpose of the use or disclosure." Lastly, OCR found that Aetna violated 45 C.F.R. § 164.530(c) by not having the appropriate administrative, technical, and physical safeguards in order to prevent breaches of PHI.

Commenting on the breaches, Severino said members of health plans "expect plans to keep their medical information safe from public exposure."[29] Ultimately, Aetna would settle the three breach instances for $1 million, as well as adopt a corrective action plan to prevent further violations of the breached HIPAA rules.

South Broward Hospital District d/b/a Memorial Healthcare System

Case summary: On April 12 and July 11, 2012, Memorial Healthcare System (MHS) reported to HHS that its employees had inappropriately accessed and disclosed the PHI of 115,143 people.[30] The breach involved MHS employees accessing the names, dates of birth, and Social Security numbers of people, and impermissibly disclosing the information to affiliated physician's offices. Additionally, the login credentials of a former employee of an affiliated physician's office was used to impermissibly access PHI maintained by MHS.

Opinion issued: February 16, 2017

Link to full text: https://www.hhs.gov/about/news/2017/02/16/hipaa-settlement-shines-light-on-the-importance-of-audit-controls.html

OCR found that MHS violated HIPAA's Security Rule when its employees disclosed PHI to affiliated physician's offices. Further, MHS failed to implement policies and procedures to regularly review records of information system activity under 45 C.F.R. § 164.308(a)(1)(ii)(D). With respect to the use of a former employee's credentials to access PHI, OCR found that MHS failed to implement policies and procedures to review and modify a user's right of access to PHI under 45 C.F.R. § 164.308(a)(4)(ii)(C). Compounding these violations, MHS was made aware these potential breaches in its internal risk analyses conducted from 2007 to 2012.

Robinsue Frohboese, then-acting director of OCR, commented on the violations, noting "a lack of access controls and regular review of audit logs helps hackers or malevolent insiders to cover their electronic tracks, making it difficult for covered entities and business associates to not only recover from breaches, but to prevent them before they happen."[31] MHS settled with HHS for $5.5 million, including implementing a corrective action plan (CAP). Central to the CAP is MHS's creation of an internal monitoring plan and contracting with an external assessor to ensure compliance with the CAP.

Shands Jacksonville Med. Ctr. v. Pusha, 254 So. 3d 1076 (Fla. Dist. Ct. App. 2018)

Case summary: Eartha Pusha brought a claim under Florida's Medical Malpractice Act (MMA) against Shands Jacksonville Medical Center (Shands) for the alleged negligent treatment of Pusha's mother, Regina Freeman, resulting in Freeman's death. The MMA requires a presuit investigation before a claim can be brought, which includes the disclosure of requested medical records by a defendant hospital. If a defendant hospital fails to timely comply with a request for medical records, the plaintiff's requirement to include a verified written medical expert opinion accompanying the malpractice complaint is waived.

On April 6, 2011, Pusha's counsel sent Shands a request for Freeman's medical records that identified Pusha as the client and personal representative of Freeman's estate. However, it did not disclose the relationship between Pusha and Freeman. An authorization form was attached to the request and signed by Takara Teague, identified as Freeman's personal representative and daughter; however, there was no indication that Pusha and Teague were related to one another. A representative from Shands testified that the hospital did not immediately disclose medical records and responded to Pusha informing her that the request lacked proper authorization or valid power of attorney.

When the complaint was ultimately filed, Shands would move to dismiss because Pusha failed to obtain a verified written medical expert opinion, as is required by the MMA. In response, Pusha argued that Shands's failure to respond with Freeman's medical records within 10 business days—as is required under the MAA—waived the requirement to include an expert opinion with the complaint. The trial court ruled in Pusha's favor and denied Shands's motion to dismiss.

Opinion issued: August 24, 2018

Link to full text: https://www.leagle.com/decision/inflco20180824204

On appeal, the Florida's First District Court of Appeal considered whether during a presuit investigation required under the MMA, "may a hospital seek verification that a person requesting confidential medical records is legally authorized to obtain those records?"[32] The court answered this question in the affirmative. First, the court did not consider Shands's response an outright refusal to disclose Freeman's medical records, but a reasonable request for more information to ensure disclosure was proper. The court explained that the April 6 request "did not clearly identify Pusha or Teague as claimants or as persons legally authorized to receive Freeman's medical records" and instead "only served to confuse the issue."[33]

Next, the court considered Pusha's argument that the MMA requires disclosure of medical records upon request, without consideration of patient privacy laws. In rebuffing this argument, the court pointed to both state law and HIPAA. In consideration of section 395.3025(4), Florida Statutes, which provides that valid authorization of confidential medical records may only be disclosed by the patient or a legal representative, the court found that the letter was not valid authorization, because neither Pusha nor Teague were demonstrated as legal representatives. Under this statute, patient privacy extends even after death, and without a death certificate, the letter provided no indication Teague was Freeman's next of kin authorized to request medical records on her behalf. Further confusing the matter, the request was made on behalf of the law firm's client, Pusha, but the authorization form to release the records was signed by Teague.

Under HIPAA, the disclosure of medical records is prohibited without valid authorization under 45 C.F.R. § 164.508(a)(1). HIPAA requires that authorization to disclose medical records "must be completed by someone legally authorized to receive the records."[34] The April 6 letter failed to meet this requirement, because neither Pusha nor Teague were identified as persons legally authorized to receive Freeman's records. There was no power of attorney attached authorizing Teague to receive the records, Freeman was not identified as being deceased, and neither Pusha nor Teague were appointed as personal representatives of Freeman's estate. Ultimately, the court held it would be improper for the MMA's presuit requirements to pave over patient privacy mandates, because it would require hospitals to decide whether to comply with the presuit requirements or state and federal patient privacy laws. Thus, the court quashed the trial court's denial of Shands's motion to dismiss and instructed that Pusha's complaint be dismissed with prejudice for failure to comply with the expert opinion requirement and for now falling outside the statute of limitations for medical malpractice suits in the state.

Endnotes

1. **Gabriel Imperato** is managing partner at the Fort Lauderdale office of Nelson Mullins Riley & Scarborough. He is the team leader of the firm's Health Care Criminal and Civil Enforcement, Litigation and Compliance Practice. He has practiced healthcare law in both the public and private sectors for more than 40 years. He is board certified as a specialist in health law by The Florida Bar. Imperato recently served as the general counsel of the North Broward Hospital District, the tenth largest healthcare system in the United States. He has also served as deputy chief counsel for the U.S. Department of Health & Human Services' Office of the General Counsel. Imperato is also a longtime member of the board of directors of Society of Corporate Compliance and Ethics & the Health Care Compliance Association (SCCE & HCCA), where he was also a past president and interim CEO.

2. **Anne Novick Branan** is an of counsel attorney in the Fort Lauderdale office of Nelson Mullins Riley & Scarborough. She has been board certified in health law by The Florida Bar since 1995. Branan counsels healthcare providers about avoiding and responding to allegations of fraud under the Medicare and Medicaid programs. She helps her clients navigate the complex regulatory environment affecting acquisitions and contracting in the healthcare industry. Branan regularly assists healthcare companies in developing and assessing the effectiveness of corporate compliance and ethics programs. She was recognized in *The Best Lawyers in America* for healthcare law, 2015–2020, and selected as Fort Lauderdale Health Care Law "Lawyer of the Year" in 2017.

3. **Richard Sena** is a juris doctor candidate at the Nova Southeastern University Shepard Broad College of Law. He is the editor-in-chief of the *Nova Law Review* and a law clerk at Nelson Mullins Riley & Scarborough in Fort Lauderdale since the summer of 2020. Sena has conducted health law research under the guidance of attorneys Gabriel Imperato and Anne Novick Branan and helped author sections of the "Key Laws in Healthcare Compliance" chapter in the 2021 HCCA *Complete Healthcare Compliance Manual.* He is expected to graduate in May 2021 and plans to continue his career as an associate attorney at Nelson Mullins.

4. **Megan Speltz** is a digital product owner at SCCE &

HCCA, where she helps define and deliver new digital products to the COSMOS platform. She graduated from the University of St. Thomas School of Law in May 2020; she obtained her juris doctor with a concentration in organizational ethics and compliance. In addition to working at SCCE & HCCA, Speltz is a licensed attorney practicing in the state of Minnesota and represents small businesses and nonprofit organizations.

5. 45 C.F.R. §§ 160, 164.102, 164.500.

6. 45 C.F.R. §§ 160, 164.102, 164.302.

7. 45 C.F.R. §§ 164.400–164.414.

8. Office for Civil Rights, "Breach Notification Rule," U.S. Department of Health & Human Services, last reviewed July 26, 2013, http://www.hhs.gov/hipaa/for-professionals/breach-notification/index.html.

9. Carol Stryker, "Two Essentials for HIPAA Omnibus Final Rule Compliance," Physicians Practice, September 18, 2013, http://www.physicianspractice.com/view/two-essentials-hipaa-omnibus-final-rule-compliance.

10. 45 C.F.R. § 160.

11. Office for Civil Rights, "The HIPAA Enforcement Rule," HHS.gov, U.S. Department of Health & Human Services, August 31, 2020, http://www.hhs.gov/hipaa/for-professionals/special-topics/enforcement-rule/index.html.

12. Health Insurance Portability and Accountability Act of 1996, Pub. L. No. 104–191, 110 Stat. 1936 (August 21, 1996).

13. Office for Civil Rights, "Does the HIPAA Privacy Rule Preempt State Laws?" U.S. Department of Health & Human Services, last reviewed July 26, 2013, http://www.hhs.gov/hipaa/for-professionals/faq/399/does-hipaa-preempt-state-laws/index.html.

14. 45 C.F.R. § 164.308(a).

15. 45 C.F.R. § 164.308(b).

16. 45 C.F.R. § 164.314(a).

17. 45 C.F.R. § 160.103.

18. 45 C.F.R. § 164.508.

19. 45 C.F.R. § 164.502.

20. 45 C.F.R. § 164.306.

21. 45 C.F.R. § 164.404.

22. 45 C.F.R. § 164.406.

23. 45 C.F.R. § 164.408.

24. 45 C.F.R. § 160.404.

25. 42 U.S.C. § 1320d–6.

26. Steve Adler, "Can a Patient Sue for A HIPAA Violation?," *HIPAA Journal*, November 7, 2017, http://www.hipaajournal.com/sue-for-hipaa-violation/.

27. U.S. Department of Health & Human Services, "Dental Practice Pays $10,000 to Settle Social Media Disclosures of Patients' Protected Health Information," news release, October 2, 2019, http://www.hhs.gov/about/news/2019/10/02/dental-practice-pays-10000-settle-social-media-disclosures-of-patients-phi.html.

28. U.S. Department of Health & Human Services, "Aetna Pays $1,000,000 to Settle Three HIPAA Breaches," news release, October 28, 2020, http://www.hhs.gov/about/news/2020/10/28/aetna-pays-one-million-to-settle-three-hipaa-breaches.html.

29. U.S. Department of Health & Human Services, "Aetna Pays $1,000,000 to Settle Three HIPAA Breaches," news release, October 28, 2020, http://www.hhs.gov/about/news/2020/10/28/aetna-pays-one-million-to-settle-three-hipaa-breaches.html.

30. U.S. Department of Health & Human Services, "$5.5 million HIPAA settlement shines light on the importance of audit controls," news release, February 16, 2017, http://www.hhs.gov/about/news/2017/02/16/hipaa-settlement-shines-light-on-the-importance-of-audit-controls.html.

31. U.S. Department of Health & Human Services, "$5.5 Million HIPAA Settlement Shines Light on the Importance of Audit Controls," news release, February 16, 2017, http://www.hhs.gov/about/news/2017/02/16/hipaa-settlement-shines-light-on-the-importance-of-audit-controls.html.

32. Shands Jacksonville Med. Ctr. v. Pusha, 254 So. 3d 1076 (Fla. Dist. Ct. App. 2018).

33. Shands Jacksonville Med. Ctr. v. Pusha, 254 So. 3d 1076 (Fla. Dist. Ct. App. 2018).

34. Shands Jacksonville Med. Ctr. v. Pusha, 254 So. 3d 1076 (Fla. Dist. Ct. App. 2018).

Physician Payments Sunshine Act (Affordable Care Act)

By Gabriel Imperato,[1] Esq., CHC; Anne Novick Branan,[2] Esq., CHC;
Richard Sena[3]; Zackary Weiss[4]; and Megan Speltz,[5] JD

Fast Facts

Title of law: Physician Payments Sunshine Act (PPSA), Transparency reports and reporting of physician ownership or investment interests

Categories:

- Accounting and financial reporting
- Antitrust
- Fraud and abuse

U.S. Code: 42 U.S.C. § 1320a–7h

Year enacted: 2013

Major amendments: Not applicable.

Enforcement agency: Centers for Medicare & Medicaid Services (CMS)

Link to full text of law: https://www.govinfo.gov/content/pkg/USCODE-2011-title42/pdf/USCODE-2011-title42-chap7-subchapXI-partA-sec1320a-7h.pdf

Applies to: Manufacturers of drugs, medical devices, and biologics.

What Is the Physician Payments Sunshine Act?

The Physician Payments Sunshine Act (PPSA), which is section 6002 of the Affordable Care Act (ACA) of 2010, requires manufacturers of drugs, medical devices, and biologics to report to the Centers for Medicare & Medicaid Services (CMS) any payments or other transfers of value made to physicians or teaching hospitals. The PPSA also requires certain manufacturers and group purchasing organizations (GPOs) to disclose physician ownership or investment interests held in those companies.[6] This call for transparency within the physician-industry relationship is predicated on the idea that the requirement of industry to track, report, and publicly release financial data will encourage stronger ethical collaborations that will ultimately help achieve better patient care while lowering health insurance costs for covered recipients.

History

The PPSA was introduced in the U.S. Congress on September 6, 2007, by Senators Chuck Grassley and Herb Kohl. The goal of the bill was to "shed light" on the nature and extent of financial relationships between physicians and teaching hospitals and applicable manufacturers and GPOs with whom they interact. The expectations were that the bill would reveal the potential overall effect that these relationships have on patient care and rising healthcare costs. The PPSA failed as an independent bill but was signed into law as section 6002 of the ACA in 2010. The PPSA's final rule was proposed in December 2011, and, after a public comment period, went into effect on August 1, 2013.

Related Laws

Nevada Revised Statutes § 639.570, Duty of wholesalers or manufacturers who employ person to sell or market drug, medicine, chemical, device or appliance; submission of information annually to Board; Board to report certain information to Governor and Legislature; duties of Board.
Under Nevada's Business Practices statutes, a wholesaler or manufacturer that employs a person to sell or market a drug, medicine, chemical, device or appliance in Nevada must submit to the board annually:

- The marketing code of conduct
- Description of training program
- Description of its investigation policies
- Name of its compliance officer, and more[7]

Federal Anti-Kickback Statute, 42 U.S.C. § 1320a-7b(b)

The federal Anti-Kickback Statute is a criminal law that prohibits the knowing and willful payment of "renumeration" to induce or reward patient referrals or the generation of business involving any item or service payable by federal healthcare programs (e.g., drugs, supplies, or healthcare services for Medicare or Medicaid patients). Renumeration includes anything of value, such as free rent, expensive hotel stays and meals, and excessive compensation for medical directorships or consultancies. Physicians are common targets for kickback schemes because they can be a source of referrals for fellow physicians or other healthcare providers and suppliers.[8]

Civil Monetary Penalties Law, 42 U.S.C. § 1320a–7a

The Civil Monetary Penalties Law (CMPL) is important to healthcare professionals because violations can expose organizations to a great deal of civil liability. Healthcare organizations and officials found liable are subject to large fines and potential exclusion from federal programs. The two main provisions of the act focus on improperly filed claims and payments to induce reduction or limitations of services.

Physician Payments Sunshine Act Compliance Risks

The PPSA (or "Sunshine Act") is important to compliance professionals because violations expose healthcare organizations to civil liability. The U.S. Department of Justice (DOJ) has recently increased PPSA enforcement. Several critical risk areas exist which healthcare organizations must report in order to be in compliance with the PPSA. Healthcare organizations must report a variety of payments to any applicable manufacturer. Furthermore, the PPSA requires drug, biological, and medical manufacturers and GPOs to annually disclose direct and indirect ownership and investment interests held by physicians and their immediate family members. To prevent liability under the PPSA, healthcare companies should update and enforce their compliance plans, monitor their employees, and audit their payment data. The following are specific PPSA risk areas that healthcare providers and officials need to monitor closely.

Risk Area: General Payments or Transfers of Value Such As Meals, Travel Reimbursement, and Consulting Fees

42 U.S.C. § 1320a–7h(a)(1)(A)

1. Payments or other transfers of value

A. In general

> On March 31, 2013, and on the 90th day of each calendar year beginning thereafter, any applicable manufacturer that provides a payment or other transfer of value to a covered recipient (or to an entity or individual at the request of or designated on behalf of a covered recipient), shall submit to the Secretary, in such electronic form as the Secretary shall require, the following information with respect to the preceding calendar year:

   i. The name of the covered recipient.

   ii. The business address of the covered recipient and, in the case of a covered recipient who is a physician, the specialty and National Provider Identifier of the covered recipient.

   iii. The amount of the payment or other transfer of value.

   iv. The dates on which the payment or other transfer of value was provided to the covered recipient.

   v. A description of the form of the payment or other transfer of value, indicated (as appropriate for all that apply) as—

      I. cash or a cash equivalent;

      II. in-kind items or services;

      III. stock, a stock option, or any other ownership interest, dividend, profit, or other return on investment; or

      IV. any other form of payment or other transfer of value (as defined by the Secretary).

   vi. A description of the nature of the payment or other transfer of value, indicated (as appropriate for all that apply) as—

      I. consulting fees;

      II. compensation for services other than consulting;

      III. honoraria;

      IV. gift;

      V. entertainment;

      VI. food;

      VII.   travel (including the specified destinations);

      VIII. education;

      IX.   research;

      X.   charitable contribution;

      XI.   royalty or license;

      XII.   current or prospective ownership or investment interest;

      XIII. direct compensation for serving as faculty or as a speaker for a continuing medical education program;

      XIV. grant; or

      XV.   any other nature of the payment or other transfer of value (as defined by the Secretary).

   vii. If the payment or other transfer of value is related to marketing, education, or research specific to a covered drug, device, biological, or medical supply, the name of that covered drug, device, biological, or medical supply.

   viii. Any other categories of information regarding the payment or other transfer of value the Secretary determines appropriate.[9]

Context: Under the PPSA, manufacturers of drugs, devices, biologics, and medical supplies covered by Medicare, Medicaid, or the Children's Health Insurance Program are required to report to CMS any payment. Furthermore, any payment made for participation in pre-clinical research, clinical trials, or other product development activities must be reported. To qualify as research under the final rule, it must be subject to a written agreement or a research protocol.

Risk Area: Ownership and Investment Interests in Manufacturers Held by Physicians as Well as Their Immediate Family Members

42 U.S.C. § 1320a–7h(2)(A-D)

  2. Physician ownership
In addition to the requirement under paragraph (1)(A), on March 31, 2013, and on the 90th day of each calendar year beginning thereafter, any applicable manufacturer or applicable group purchasing organization shall submit to the Secretary, in such electronic form as the Secretary shall require, the following information regarding any ownership or investment interest (other than an

ownership or investment interest in a publicly traded security and mutual fund, as described in section 1395nn(c)) held by a physician (or an immediate family member of such physician (as defined for purposes of section 1395nn(c)) in the applicable manufacturer or applicable group purchasing organization during the preceding year:

A. The dollar amount invested by each physician holding such an ownership or investment interest.

B. The value and terms of each such ownership or investment interest.

C. Any payment or other transfer of value provided to a physician holding such an ownership or investment interest (or to an entity or individual at the request of or designated on behalf of a physician holding such an ownership or investment interest), including the information described in clauses (i) through (viii) of paragraph (1)(A), except that in applying such clauses, "physician" shall be substituted for "covered recipient" each place it appears.

D. Any other information regarding the ownership or investment interest the Secretary determines appropriate.[10]

Context: The PPSA requires drug, biological, and medical manufacturers (Applicable Manufacturers), and GPOs to annually disclose direct and indirect ownership and investment interests held by physician and their immediate family members. Ownership or investment interest includes, but is not limited to, stock, partnership shares, limited liability company memberships, and loans, bonds, or other financial instruments.

Consequences for Noncompliance

Administrative Proceedings

- Penalties: Not applicable.
- Corrective Actions: Not applicable.

Civil Litigation

Damages

- Any applicable manufacturer or applicable group purchasing organization that fails to submit information required under subsection (a) in a timely manner in accordance with rules or regulations promulgated to carry out such subsection, shall be subject to a civil money penalty of not less than \$1,000, but not more than \$10,000, for each payment or other transfer of value or ownership or investment interest not reported as required under such subsection.[11]

- Any applicable manufacturer or applicable group purchasing organization that **knowingly** fails to submit information required under subsection (a) in a timely manner in accordance with rules or regulations promulgated to carry out such subsection, shall be subject to a civil money penalty of not less than \$10,000, but not more than \$100,000, for each payment or other transfer of value or ownership or investment interest not reported as required under such subsection.[12]

Criminal Proceedings

Not applicable.

Important Compliance Guidance and Tools

U.S. Department of Health & Human Services, Centers for Medicare & Medicaid Services

What Is Open Payments?

The Open Payments database is the national disclosure system used by reporting entities to disclose payments made to covered recipients, such as physicians. This site provides an overview of that system.

https://www.cms.gov/OpenPayments

Open Payments Annual Report to Congress FY2020

This report summarizes the information reported to the Open Payments system.

https://www.cms.gov/files/document/open-payments-2020-annual-report-congress.pdf

Open Payments: General Resources

Find information about the Open Payments system for general users, reporting entities, and covered recipients on this site.

https://www.cms.gov/OpenPayments/Resources#general-resources

Relevant Physician Payments Sunshine Act Settlements

Medtronic Settlement of $9.2 Million Regarding Allegations of Improper Payments to South Dakota Neurosurgeon

Settlement summary: Medtronic is a Minnesota corporation that sells medical devices and other products throughout the United States. The DOJ brought civil claims against Medtronic arising from conduct throughout 2010 to 2019. Medtronic paid $1.1 million to settle PPSA claims, as well as an additional $8.1 million to resolve the related AKS and False Claims Act (FCA) allegations.

According to the DOJ, Medtronic paid for social events at Carnaval Brazilian Grill (Carnaval) for the benefit of South Dakota neurosurgeon, Wilson Asfora, MD, at his request. Knowing that Asfora's restaurant was struggling, a Medtronic sales representatives agreed to host events at Carnaval, allegedly to induce Asfora to use Medtronic's SynchroMed II intrathecal infusion pumps.

From 2010 to 2019, Medtronic hosted more than 130 events at Carnaval, paying more than $87,000 to the restaurant. Seventy-four of these events were held after the PPSA went into effect. Medtronic sales personnel allegedly falsely stated that these events served educational purposes, when there was little to no discussion surrounding Medtronic products during the dinners. Further, Asfora allegedly personally selected the guests for these events—inviting his friends, partners, favored colleagues, and other social acquaintances, as well as their significant others. Medtronic only reported the total amount of food and drinks that individuals consumed during these dinners, but did not report the total amount paid to Asfora through Carnaval. The government claims that this underreporting violated the PPSA and that the events themselves amounted to kickbacks under the AKS.

Settlement signed: October 29, 2020

Link to full text: https://www.justice.gov/opa/press-release/file/1332261/download

Neurosurgeon and Two Affiliated Companies Settle for $4.4 Million Regarding Healthcare Fraud Allegations

Settlement summary: The second Wilson Asfora-related settlement involved government claims that between 2010 and 2019, Asfora solicited and received improper remunerations for using spinal devices made by Medical Designs LLC (Medical Designs) and Sicage LLC (Sicage). The companies allegedly violated the PPSA by failing to disclose Asfora's ownership interests in Medical Designs and Sicage.

Asfora and two medical device distributorships that he owns, Medical Designs and Sicage, agreed to pay $4.4 million to resolve FCA allegations relating to illegal payments made to Asfora to induce the use of certain medical devices, in violation of the AKS, as well as claims for medically unnecessary surgeries.

Asfora received profit distributions from companies in exchange for using Medical Designs and Sicage's spinal devices. Medical Designs also allegedly acted as a distributor for Asfora, reselling other manufacturer's spinal devices to Asfora and splitting the profits with the neurosurgeon when he used those devices in surgery. Furthermore, Asfora would sometimes use these devices to perform medically unnecessary procedures and then submit false claims to government entities.

To settle the matter, Asfora, along with Medical Designs and Sicage, agreed to pay $100,000 to resolve the PPSA claims and an additional $4.4 million to resolve the FCA and AKS allegations. Under the terms of the settlement agreement, Asfora, Medical Designs, and Sicage will each be excluded from participating in federal healthcare programs for a period of six years.

Settlement signed: May 3, 2021

Link to full text: https://www.justice.gov/usao-sd/pr/
neurosurgeon-and-two-affiliated-companies-agree-pay-44-million-settle-healthcare-fraud

French Medical Device Manufacturer Agrees to Pay $2 Million Settlement Regarding Alleged Physician Kickbacks and Related Medicare Open Payments Program Violations

Settlement summary: Medicrea International, a French medical device manufacturer, and its American affiliate Medicrea USA Inc., agreed to pay $1 million to the United States to resolve allegations that the companies violated the PPSA by failing to fully report physician-entertainment expenses to the Centers for Medicare & Medicaid Services (CMS). These claims were brought in addition to civil whistleblower allegations, violations of the AKS and, resulting claims to federal healthcare programs, the FCA, and similar state statutes, which Medicrea agreed to pay an additional $1 million to settle.

This settlement resolved Medicrea's liability under CMS's Open Payments Program. The government alleged that Medicrea provided US-based physicians with meals, alcoholic beverages, entertainment, and travel-related expenses for attending the Scoliosis Research Society's September 2013 congress in France. Medicrea covered the value of travel for the physicians as well as their family members. Medicrea allegedly offered these benefits in an attempt to get the physicians to purchase Medicrea spinal devices. Following this event and from a period between April 2014 and March 2018, Medicrea failed to report the full value of the benefit payments made to the physician attendees.

Settlement signed: May 19, 2021

Link to full text: https://www.justice.gov/usao-edpa/pr/
french-medical-device-manufacturer-pay-2-million-resolve-alleged-kickbacks-physicians

Endnotes

1. **Gabriel Imperato** is managing partner at the Fort Lauderdale office of Nelson Mullins Riley & Scarborough. He is the team leader of the firm's Health Care Criminal and Civil Enforcement, Litigation and Compliance Practice. He has practiced healthcare law in both the public and private sectors for more than 40 years. He is board certified as a specialist in health law by The Florida Bar. Imperato recently served as the general counsel of the North Broward Hospital District, the tenth largest healthcare system in the United States. He has also served as deputy chief counsel for the U.S. Department of Health & Human Services' Office of the General Counsel. Imperato is also a longtime member of the board of directors of the Society of Corporate Compliance and Ethics & Health Care Compliance Association (SCCE & HCCA), where he was also a past president and interim CEO.

2. **Anne Novick Branan** is an of counsel attorney in the Fort Lauderdale office of Nelson Mullins Riley & Scarborough. She has been board certified in health law by The Florida Bar since 1995. Branan counsels healthcare providers about avoiding and responding to allegations of fraud under the Medicare and Medicaid programs. She helps her clients navigate the complex regulatory environment affecting acquisitions and contracting in the healthcare industry. Branan regularly assists healthcare companies in developing and assessing the effectiveness of corporate compliance and ethics programs. She was recognized in *The Best Lawyers in America* for healthcare law, 2015–2020, and selected as Fort Lauderdale Health Care Law "Lawyer of the Year" in 2017.

3. **Richard Sena** is an associate attorney at Nelson Mullins Riley & Scarborough in Fort Lauderdale. Sena conducted health law research under the guidance of attorneys Gabriel Imperato and Anne Novick Branan and helped author sections of the "Key Laws in Healthcare Compliance" chapter in the 2021 HCCA *Complete Healthcare Compliance Manual*. Sena also coauthored an article titled "Compliance Risks and Tips for Home Health Agencies" with Branan, appearing in the July 2021 edition of *Compliance Today* magazine.

4. **Zackary Weiss** is a juris doctor candidate at the University of Miami School of Law. He is an editor for the *International & Comparative Law Review*, past judicial intern for United States Magistrate Judge Jonathan Goodman, and a law clerk at Nelson Mullins Riley & Scarborough in Fort Lauderdale since the summer of 2020. Weiss has conducted health law research under the guidance of attorneys Gabriel Imperato and Anne Novick Branan and helped author sections of the "Key Laws in Healthcare Compliance" chapter in the 2022 HCCA *Complete Healthcare Compliance Manual*. He is expected to graduate in May 2022 and plans to continue his career as an associate attorney at Nelson Mullins.

5. **Megan Speltz** is a digital product owner at SCCE & HCCA, where she helps define and deliver new digital products to the COSMOS platform. She graduated from the University of St. Thomas School of Law in May 2020; she obtained her juris doctor with a concentration in organizational ethics and compliance. In addition to working at SCCE & HCCA, Speltz is a licensed attorney practicing in the state of Minnesota and represents small businesses and nonprofit organizations.

6. Elizabeth Richardson, "The Physician Payments Sunshine Act," *Health Affairs* blog, October 2, 2014, https://www.healthaffairs.org/do/10.1377/hpb20141002.272302/full/.

7. Nev. Rev. Stat. § 639.570 (2007).

8. 42 U.S.C. § 1320a-7b(b).

9. 42 U.S.C. § 1320a-7h(a)(1)(A).

10. 42 U.S.C. § 1320a-7h(2)(A-D).

11. 42 U.S.C. § 1320a-7h(b)(1)(A).

12. 42 U.S.C. § 1320a-7h(b)(2)(A).

Physician Self-Referral Law (Stark Law)

By Gabriel Imperato,[1] Esq., CHC; Anne Novick Branan,[2] Esq., CHC; Richard Sena[3]; and Megan Speltz,[4] JD

Fast Facts

Title of law: Limitation on certain physician referrals (commonly called the Stark Law or Physician Self-Referral Law)

Categories:

- Medicare
- Medicaid
- Fraud and abuse

U.S. Code: 42 U.S.C. § 1395nn

Year enacted: 1989

Major amendments:

- Omnibus Budget Reconciliation Act of 1990 (Stark I)
- Omnibus Budget Reconciliation Act of 1993 (Stark II)
- Medicare Program; Modernizing and Clarifying the Physician Self-Referral Regulations, 85 Fed. Reg. 77,492 (December 2, 2020)

Enforcement agencies: U.S. Department of Justice (DOJ), Centers for Medicare & Medicaid Services (CMS), U.S. Department of Health & Human Services (HHS)

Link to full text of law: https://www.govinfo.gov/content/pkg/USCODE-2010-title42/pdf/USCODE-2010-title42-chap7-subchapXVIII-partE-sec1395nn.pdf

Applies to: Physician referrals for health services in which the referring physician has some financial relationship with the referred entity.

What Is the Physician Self-Referral Law (Stark Law)?

The Physician Self-Referral Law/Stark Law (referred to as Stark Law in this article) prohibits a physician from making referrals for certain designated health services payable by Medicare to an entity with which they (or an immediate family member) have a financial relationship, unless an exception applies. It also prohibits the entity from presenting (or causing to be presented) claims to Medicare for those referred services. There are a number of specific exceptions and grants to the law, and the U.S. Department of Health & Human Services (HHS) secretary has the authority to create regulatory exceptions for financial relationships that do not pose a risk of program or patient abuse. The exceptions include:

- **Physician services**: Permits physicians to refer to other physicians who are members of the same group practice or under the supervision of a physician in the same group practice.
- **In-office ancillary services**: Permits a group medical practice to make referrals for in-office ancillary services, such as laboratory or radiology services.
- **Services furnished by an organization to enrollees**: Physicians can refer patients to organizations that provide prepaid health services to enrollees, including approved health maintenance organizations (HMOs) and competitive medical plans (CMPs), plans approved by the Centers for Medicare & Medicaid Services (CMS), and other plans identified by the Stark Law.
- **Academic medical centers**: Physicians can refer patients to academic medical centers the physician has a financial relationship with, if the physician:
  - Is a "bona fide" employee of the medical center,
  - Is licensed in the state where the medical center is located,
  - Is a faculty member of the facility,
  - Provides paid clinical teaching services at the center, and
  - Refers the patient to an academic medical center that is approved under the Stark Law.
- **Implants furnished by an ambulatory surgery center (ASC)**: Physicians can refer patients to have certain implant procedures done at an ASC by a physician who belongs to the same medical group.
- **Eyeglasses and contact lenses after the patient has cataract surgery**: Applies when Medicare approved the eyeglasses or contact lenses.
- **Erythropoietin (EPO) and other prescription drugs for dialysis patients who need outpatient treatment**: Applies to referrals for specified drugs (preapproved) that are given in an end-stage renal disease (ERSD) facility.
- **Preventive services**: Vaccines, immunizations, and screening tests covered by Medicare are generally allowed if they are given prudently.
- **Intra-family rural referrals**: Some referrals in rural areas are permitted if the services are for an immediate family member and there are no nearby facilities or people that can provide the same service.

- **Fair market compensation**: Applies when a compensation arrangement is in writing, specifies a timeframe and the compensation to be provided, involves a commercially reasonable transaction, and meets the safe harbors under the Anti-Kickback Statute.
- **Indirect compensation**: Permits indirect compensation arrangements between a physician and an entity if the compensation received by the referring physician is of fair market value, does not take into account the value or volume of referrals, and is set out in writing and signed by the parties.
- **Nonmonetary exemptions**: Applies to the payment of nonmonetary compensation to a physician of up to $300 per year if the physician did not solicit the compensation and it does not take into account the volume or value of referrals.
- **Rental of office space and/or equipment**: Physicians can rent out office space and equipment if the lease is in writing, the term is at least for one year, the lease is commercially reasonable, and other conditions are met.
- **Bona fide employee relationship**: An employer can pay a physician or family member if the physician/family member is a true bona fide employee with the employer, the compensation is fair, it's clear what services the physician/family member is providing, and other factors are met.
- **Physician incentive plan**: Incentive plants are permitted if they do not limit necessary medical services to eligible patients.
- **Physician recruitment**: Hospitals can pay physicians to persuade them to work for the hospital if the agreement is in writing and does not require the physician to refer patients to the hospital, the amount of the payment is not related to the value or volume of referrals, and the physician can obtain staff privileges at other hospitals.
- **Charity**: A physician may donate to an approved Internal Revenue Service tax-exempt charity as long as the donation is not based on the value or volume of referrals.
- **Medical staff incidental benefits**: Hospitals can provide noncash benefits to medical staff as long as the value of the benefit is less than $25, is provided at the hospital to all members of the medical staff, is comparable to benefits given by other hospitals, and all other conditions are met.[5]

History

The Stark Law—named after its sponsor Congressman Pete Stark—was enacted by Congress in 1989 as the Ethics in Patient Referrals Act. The original intent of the law was to prohibit physicians from referring Medicare patients to clinical labs that a physician had a financial or ownership interest in. In 1993 and 1994, Congress expanded the prohibition to include aspects of physician self-referral to the Medicaid program. In 1997, Congress added a provision that permitted the HHS secretary to issue written advisory opinions as to whether a referral other than clinical laboratory services is prohibited by the act. In late 2020, HHS published two new rules in order to reduce regulatory burdens without increasing the risk of abuse of the federal healthcare system and to promote coordinated and value-based care for patients. "Coordinated care" refers to patient care spanning across care settings in both the federal healthcare programs and the commercial sector.

Related Laws

Like its sister laws, the Anti-Kickback Statute (AKS) and the False Claims Act (FCA), the Stark Law was enacted to preserve federal healthcare programs from undue waste by bad actors who look to leverage public funds for personal gain. Thus, there is significant overlap between the three laws.

Anti-Kickback Statute, 42 U.S.C. § 1320a-7b(b)

The AKS provides for criminal and civil liability for "knowing and willful" renumeration for the purpose of rewarding patient referrals for services provided by a federal healthcare program. Both the AKS and the Stark Law prohibit renumeration for patient referrals; however, the Stark Law only provides for civil liability and does provide for strict liability (i.e., no knowing or willful requirement) for sanctions (i.e., denial of payment or requirement of refunds).[6]

For more information on this law, please see the "Anti-Kickback Statute" article in this chapter.

False Claims Act, 31 U.S.C. §§ 3729–3733

The FCA makes it illegal for a person or entity to submit claims for payment to the government that the claimant knows are false or fraudulent. Similarly, the Stark Law makes it illegal for physicians to "present or cause to be presented" claims that constitute as self-referrals under the law and do not fall under any exception. Although the FCA does not specifically apply to healthcare and does include a "knowing" requirement, violations under the Stark Law do expose healthcare organizations to dual liability under the statutes if the FCA's conditions are met.[7]

For more information on this law, please see the "False Claims Act" article in this chapter.

Physician Self-Referral Law (Stark Law) Compliance Risks

The following are specific Stark Law risk areas that compliance professionals need to monitor closely.

Risk Area: General Prohibition on Physician Self-Referrals

42 U.S.C. § 1395nn(a)

a. Prohibition of certain referrals

1. In general

Except as provided in subsection (b) ... if a physician (or an immediate family member of such physician) has a financial relationship with an entity specified in paragraph (2), then—

A. the physician may not make a referral to the entity for the furnishing of designated health services for which payment otherwise may be made under this subchapter, and

B. the entity may not present or cause to be presented a claim under this subchapter or bill to any individual, third party payor, or other entity for designated health services furnished pursuant to a referral prohibited under subparagraph (A).

2. Financial relationship specified

For purposes of this section, a financial relationship of a physician (or an immediate family member of such physician) with an entity specified in this paragraph is—

A. except as provided in subsections (c) and (d) . . . , an ownership or investment interest in the entity, or

B. except as provided in subsection (d) . . . , a compensation arrangement (as defined in subsection (h)(1) . . .) between the physician (or an immediate family member of such physician) and the entity.

An ownership or investment interest described in subparagraph (A) may be through equity, debt, or other means and includes an interest in an entity that holds an ownership or investment interest in any entity providing the designated health service.[8]

Context: The Stark Law provides a general prohibition against physicians referring Medicare or Medicaid patients to an entity to provide designated health services if the physician or the physician's immediate family members have a financial stake in the referred entity. Designated health services include the following:[9]

- Clinical laboratory services;
- Physical therapy;
- Occupational therapy;
- Radiology services;
- Radiation therapy services and supplies;
- Durable medical equipment and supplies;
- Parenteral and enteral nutrients, equipment, and supplies;
- Prosthetics, orthotics, and prosthetic devices and supplies;
- Home health services;
- Outpatient prescription drugs;
- Inpatient and outpatient hospital services; and
- Outpatient speed-language pathology services.

42 U.S.C. § 1395nn(a)(2) describes a "financial relationship" as either ownership or an investment interest, or a compensation arrangement between the physician and the entity. However, the law does provide for exceptions discussed in later sections of the law.

Risk Area: Reporting Requirements

42 U.S.C. § 1395nn(f)

f.   Reporting requirements

Each entity providing covered items or services for which payment may be made under this subchapter shall provide the Secretary with the information concerning the entity's ownership, investment, and compensation arrangements, including—

1.   the covered items and services provided by the entity, and

2.   the names and unique physician identification numbers of all physicians with an ownership or investment interest (as described in subsection (a)(2) (A)), or with a compensation arrangement (as described in subsection (a) (2)(B)), in the entity, or whose immediate relatives have such an ownership or investment interest or who have such a compensation relationship with the entity.

Such information shall be provided in such form, manner, and at such times as the Secretary shall specify. The requirement of this subsection shall not apply to designated health services provided outside the United States or to entities which the Secretary determines provides services for which payment may be made under this subchapter very infrequently[10]

Context: The Stark Law requires facilities providing designated healthcare services to disclose to the HHS secretary their ownership and investment information, as well as any compensation agreements they have with other entities or physicians.

Risk Area: Sanctions and Penalties for Noncompliance

42 U.S.C. § 1395nn(g)

g.   Sanctions

1.   Denial of payment

No payment may be made under this subchapter for a designated health service which is provided in violation of subsection (a)(1).

2. Requiring refunds for certain claims

   If a person collects any amounts that were billed in violation of subsection (a)(1) the person shall be liable to the individual for, and shall refund on a timely basis to the individual, any amounts so collected.

3. Civil money penalty and exclusion for improper claims

   Any person that presents or causes to be presented a bill or a claim for a service that such person knows or should know is for a service for which payment may not be made under paragraph (1) or for which a refund has not been made under paragraph (2) shall be subject to a civil money penalty of not more than $15,000 for each such service. The provisions of section 1320a–7a of this title (other than the first sentence of subsection (a) and other than subsection (b)) shall apply to a civil money penalty under the previous sentence in the same manner as such provisions apply to a penalty or proceeding under section 1320a–7a(a) of this title.

4. Civil money penalty and exclusion for circumvention schemes

   Any physician or other entity that enters into an arrangement or scheme (such as a cross-referral arrangement) which the physician or entity knows or should know has a principal purpose of assuring referrals by the physician to a particular entity which, if the physician directly made referrals to such entity, would be in violation of this section, shall be subject to a civil money penalty of not more than $100,000 for each such arrangement or scheme. The provisions of section 1320a–7a of this title (other than the first sentence of subsection (a) and other than subsection (b)) shall apply to a civil money penalty under the previous sentence in the same manner as such provisions apply to a penalty or proceeding under section 1320a–7a(a) of this title.

5. Failure to report information

   Any person who is required, but fails, to meet a reporting requirement of subsection (f) is subject to a civil money penalty of not more than $10,000 for each day for which reporting is required to have been made. The provisions of section 1320a–7a of this title (other than the first sentence of subsection (a) and other than subsection (b)) shall apply to a civil money penalty under the previous sentence in the same manner as such provisions apply to a penalty or proceeding under section 1320a–7a(a) of this title.

6. Advisory opinions

    A. In general

        The Secretary shall issue written advisory opinions concerning whether a referral relating to designated health services (other than clinical laboratory services) is prohibited under this section. Each advisory opinion issued by the Secretary shall be binding as to the Secretary and the party or parties requesting the opinion.

    B. Application of certain rules

        The Secretary shall, to the extent practicable, apply the rules under subsections (b)(3) and (b)(4) . . . and take into account the regulations promulgated under subsection (b)(5) of section 1320a–7d of this title in the issuance of advisory opinions under this paragraph.

    C. Regulations

        In order to implement this paragraph in a timely manner, the Secretary may promulgate regulations that take effect on an interim basis, after notice and pending opportunity for public comment.

    D. Applicability

        This paragraph shall apply to requests for advisory opinions made after the date which is 90 days after August 5, 1997, and before the close of the period described in section 1320a–7d(b)(6) of this title.[11]

Context: Stark Law violations may result in certain prohibitions, sanctions, and civil penalties. Violating physicians may be prohibited from being reimbursed by Medicare or Medicaid, or from billing patients or other providers for services. A physician may also be banned from participating in Medicare and Medicaid entirely. Civil penalties include up to $15,000 per isolated violation, and up to $100,000 for violations considered as "circumvention schemes," which are often illegal referral arrangements resulting in multiple individual violations. Lastly, entities that fail to report their ownership, investment, and compensation arrangements under 42 U.S.C. § 1395nn(f) are subject to fines up to $10,000.

Exceptions to the Stark Law

Risk Area: General Exceptions to Compensation Arrangement Prohibitions

42 U.S.C. §§ 1395nn(b),(e)

b. General exceptions to both ownership and compensation arrangement prohibitions

Subsection (a)(1) shall not apply in the following cases:

1. Physicians' services

    In the case of physicians' services (as defined in section 1395x(q) of this title) provided personally by (or under the personal supervision of) another physician in the same group practice (as defined in subsection (h)(4)) as the referring physician.

2. In-office ancillary services

    In the case of services (other than durable medical equipment (excluding infusion pumps) and parenteral and enteral nutrients, equipment, and supplies)—

    A. that are furnished—

        i. personally by the referring physician, personally by a physician who is a member of the same group practice as the referring physician, or personally by individuals who are directly supervised by the physician or by another physician in the group practice, and

        ii.

            I. in a building in which the referring physician (or another physician who is a member of the same group practice) furnishes physicians' services unrelated to the furnishing of designated health services, or

            II. in the case of a referring physician who is a member of a group practice, in another building which is used by the group practice—

                aa. for the provision of some or all of the group's clinical laboratory services, or

                bb. for the centralized provision of the group's designated health services (other than clinical laboratory services),

                    unless the Secretary determines other terms and conditions under which the provision of such services does not present a risk of program or patient abuse, and

    B. that are billed by the physician performing or supervising the services, by a group practice of which such physician is a member under a billing number assigned to the group practice, or by an entity that is wholly owned by such physician or such group practice,

if the ownership or investment interest in such services meets such other requirements as the Secretary may impose by regulation as needed to protect against program or patient abuse. Such requirements shall, with respect to magnetic resonance imaging, computed tomography, positron emission tomography, and any other designated health services specified under subsection (h)(6)(D) that the Secretary determines appropriate, include a requirement that the referring physician inform the individual in writing at the time of the referral that the individual may obtain the services for which the individual is being referred from a person other than a person described in subparagraph (A)(i) and provide such individual with a written list of suppliers (as defined in section 1395x(d) of this title) who furnish such services in the area in which such individual resides.

3. Prepaid plans

In the case of services furnished by an organization—

A. with a contract under section 1395mm of this title to an individual enrolled with the organization,

B. described in section 1395l(a)(1)(A) of this title to an individual enrolled with the organization,

C. receiving payments on a prepaid basis, under a demonstration project under section 1395b–1(a) of this title or under section 222(a) of the Social Security Amendments of 1972, to an individual enrolled with the organization,

D. that is a qualified health maintenance organization (within the meaning of section 300e–9(d) of this title) to an individual enrolled with the organization, or

E. that is a Medicare+Choice organization under part C that is offering a coordinated care plan described in section 1395w–21(a)(2)(A) of this title to an individual enrolled with the organization.

4. Other permissible exceptions

In the case of any other financial relationship which the Secretary determines, and specifies in regulations, does not pose a risk of program or patient abuse.

5. Electronic prescribing

An exception established by regulation under section 1395w–104(e)(6) of this title.

e. Exceptions relating to other compensation arrangements

The following shall not be considered to be a compensation arrangement described in subsection (a)(2)(B):

1. Rental of office space; rental of equipment

A. Office space

Payments made by a lessee to a lessor for the use of premises if—

i. the lease is set out in writing, signed by the parties, and specifies the premises covered by the lease,

ii. the space rented or leased does not exceed that which is reasonable and necessary for the legitimate business purposes of the lease or rental and is used exclusively by the lessee when being used by the lessee, except that the lessee may make payments for the use of space consisting of common areas if such payments do not exceed the lessee's pro rata share of expenses for such space based upon the ratio of the space used exclusively by the lessee to the total amount of space (other than common areas) occupied by all persons using such common areas,

iii. the lease provides for a term of rental or lease for at least 1 year,

iv. the rental charges over the term of the lease are set in advance, are consistent with fair market value, and are not determined in a manner that takes into account the volume or value of any referrals or other business generated between the parties,

v. the lease would be commercially reasonable even if no referrals were made between the parties, and

vi. the lease meets such other requirements as the Secretary may impose by regulation as needed to protect against program or patient abuse.

B. Equipment

Payments made by a lessee of equipment to the lessor of the equipment for the use of the equipment if—

i. the lease is set out in writing, signed by the parties, and specifies the equipment covered by the lease,

ii. the equipment rented or leased does not exceed that which is reasonable and necessary for the legitimate business purposes of the lease or rental and is used exclusively by the lessee when being used by the lessee,

iii. the lease provides for a term of rental or lease of at least 1 year,

iv. the rental charges over the term of the lease are set in advance, are consistent with fair market value, and are not determined in a manner that takes into account the volume or value of any referrals or other business generated between the parties,

v. the lease would be commercially reasonable even if no referrals were made between the parties, and

vi. the lease meets such other requirements as the Secretary may impose by regulation as needed to protect against program or patient abuse.

C. Holdover lease arrangements

In the case of a holdover lease arrangement for the lease of office space or equipment, which immediately follows a lease arrangement described in subparagraph (A) for the use of such office space or subparagraph (B) for the use of such equipment and that expired after a term of at least 1 year, payments made by the lessee to the lessor pursuant to such holdover lease arrangement, if—

i. the lease arrangement met the conditions of subparagraph (A) for the lease of office space or subparagraph (B) for the use of equipment when the arrangement expired;

ii. the holdover lease arrangement is on the same terms and conditions as the immediately preceding arrangement; and

iii. the holdover arrangement continues to satisfy the conditions of subparagraph (A) for the lease of office space or subparagraph (B) for the use of equipment.

2. Bona fide employment relationships

   Any amount paid by an employer to a physician (or an immediate family member of such physician) who has a bona fide employment relationship with the employer for the provision of services if—

   A. the employment is for identifiable services,

   B. the amount of the remuneration under the employment—

      i. is consistent with the fair market value of the services, and

      ii. is not determined in a manner that takes into account (directly or indirectly) the volume or value of any referrals by the referring physician,

   C. the remuneration is provided pursuant to an agreement which would be commercially reasonable even if no referrals were made to the employer, and

   D. the employment meets such other requirements as the Secretary may impose by regulation as needed to protect against program or patient abuse.

      Subparagraph (B)(ii) shall not prohibit the payment of remuneration in the form of a productivity bonus based on services performed personally by the physician (or an immediate family member of such physician).

3. Personal service arrangements

   A. In general

      Remuneration from an entity under an arrangement (including remuneration for specific physicians' services furnished to a nonprofit blood center) if—

      i. the arrangement is set out in writing, signed by the parties, and specifies the services covered by the arrangement,

      ii. the arrangement covers all of the services to be provided by the physician (or an immediate family member of such physician) to the entity,

       iii. the aggregate services contracted for do not exceed those that are reasonable and necessary for the legitimate business purposes of the arrangement,

       iv. the term of the arrangement is for at least 1 year,

       v. the compensation to be paid over the term of the arrangement is set in advance, does not exceed fair market value, and except in the case of a physician incentive plan described in subparagraph (B), is not determined in a manner that takes into account the volume or value of any referrals or other business generated between the parties,

       vi. the services to be performed under the arrangement do not involve the counseling or promotion or a business arrangement or other activity that violates any State or Federal law, and

       vii. the arrangement meets such other requirements as the Secretary may impose by regulation as needed to protect against program or patient abuse.

  B. Physician incentive plan exception

       i. In general

       In the case of a physician incentive plan (as defined in clause (ii)) between a physician and an entity, the compensation may be determined in a manner (through a withhold, capitation, bonus, or otherwise) that takes into account directly or indirectly the volume or value of any referrals or other business generated between the parties, if the plan meets the following requirements:

         I. No specific payment is made directly or indirectly under the plan to a physician or a physician group as an inducement to reduce or limit medically necessary services provided with respect to a specific individual enrolled with the entity.

         II. In the case of a plan that places a physician or a physician group at substantial financial risk as determined by the Secretary pursuant to section 1395mm(i)(8)(A)(ii) of this title, the plan complies with any requirements the Secretary may impose pursuant to such section.

         III. Upon request by the Secretary, the entity provides the Secretary with access to descriptive information regarding the plan, in order to permit the Secretary to determine whether the plan is in compliance with the requirements of this clause.

ii. "Physician incentive plan" defined

For purposes of this subparagraph, the term "physician incentive plan" means any compensation arrangement between an entity and a physician or physician group that may directly or indirectly have the effect of reducing or limiting services provided with respect to individuals enrolled with the entity.

C. Holdover personal service arrangement

In the case of a holdover personal service arrangement, which immediately follows an arrangement described in subparagraph (A) that expired after a term of at least 1 year, remuneration from an entity pursuant to such holdover personal service arrangement, if—

i. the personal service arrangement met the conditions of subparagraph (A) when the arrangement expired

ii. the holdover personal service arrangement is on the same terms and conditions as the immediately preceding arrangement; and

iii. the holdover arrangement continues to satisfy the conditions of subparagraph (A).

4. Remuneration unrelated to the provision of designated health services

In the case of remuneration which is provided by a hospital to a physician if such remuneration does not relate to the provision of designated health services.

5. Physician recruitment

In the case of remuneration which is provided by a hospital to a physician to induce the physician to relocate to the geographic area served by the hospital in order to be a member of the medical staff of the hospital, if—

A. the physician is not required to refer patients to the hospital,

B. the amount of the remuneration under the arrangement is not determined in a manner that takes into account (directly or indirectly) the volume or value of any referrals by the referring physician, and

C. the arrangement meets such other requirements as the Secretary may impose by regulation as needed to protect against program or patient abuse.

6. Isolated transactions

In the case of an isolated financial transaction, such as a one-time sale of property or practice, if—

A. the requirements described in subparagraphs (B) and (C) of paragraph (2) are met with respect to the entity in the same manner as they apply to an employer, and

B. the transaction meets such other requirements as the Secretary may impose by regulation as needed to protect against program or patient abuse.

7. Certain group practice arrangements with a hospital

A. In general

An arrangement between a hospital and a group under which designated health services are provided by the group but are billed by the hospital if—

i. with respect to services provided to an inpatient of the hospital, the arrangement is pursuant to the provision of inpatient hospital services under section 1395x(b)(3) of this title,

ii. the arrangement began before December 19, 1989, and has continued in effect without interruption since such date,

iii. with respect to the designated health services covered under the arrangement, substantially all of such services furnished to patients of the hospital are furnished by the group under the arrangement,

iv. the arrangement is pursuant to an agreement that is set out in writing and that specifies the services to be provided by the parties and the compensation for services provided under the agreement,

v. the compensation paid over the term of the agreement is consistent with fair market value and the compensation per unit of services is fixed in advance and is not determined in a manner that takes into account the volume or value of any referrals or other business generated between the parties,

vi. the compensation is provided pursuant to an agreement which would be commercially reasonable even if no referrals were made to the entity, and

vii. the arrangement between the parties meets such other requirements as the Secretary may impose by regulation as needed to protect against program or patient abuse.

8. Payments by a physician for items and services

Payments made by a physician—

A. to a laboratory in exchange for the provision of clinical laboratory services, or

B. to an entity as compensation for other items or services if the items or services are furnished at a price that is consistent with fair market value.[12]

Context: Many of the exceptions to the Stark Law's strict general prohibition against self-referrals concern the business realities of medical practice. Some of the exceptions concern physicians working in a group practice. A "group practice" is defined by the Stark Law as a corporate entity of physicians working in the same space, sharing equipment and staff, providing the same full range of services, collectively billing and maintaining the business, and which the physicians are not compensated based on referrals.[13] Physicians are free to refer physician services (e.g., surgeries and consultations) to other physicians in the same group practice, or ancillary services to physicians or supervised personnel within the group practice, where the treating physician normally furnishes their services or where the treated patient receives their services, and billed using an approved Medicare or Medicare billing number.[14] Other exceptions include the ability for physicians to rent offices and equipment, pay employees, be recruited by hospitals, and provide personal services.[15] Typically, all exceptions concern the unlikelihood that such an arrangement would result in conduct that would take advantage of the federal healthcare system and patients. Importantly, the HHS secretary is authorized to pass regulatory exceptions to the Stark Law, which are found at 42 C.F.R. § 411.357. Section 411.357 includes additional exceptions, such as physician donations to charity, and also expand on the existing statutory exceptions.

Risk Area: General Exceptions to Both Ownership and Investment Prohibitions

42 U.S.C. §§ 1395nn(c),(d)

c. General exception related only to ownership or investment prohibition for ownership in publicly traded securities and mutual funds

Ownership of the following shall not be considered to be an ownership or investment interest described in subsection (a)(2)(A):

1. Ownership of investment securities (including shares or bonds, debentures, notes, or other debt instruments) which may be purchased on terms generally available to the public and which are—

   A.

      i. securities listed on the New York Stock Exchange, the American Stock Exchange, or any regional exchange in which quotations are published on a daily basis, or foreign securities listed on a recognized foreign, national, or regional exchange in which quotations are published on a daily basis, or

      ii. traded under an automated interdealer quotation system operated by the National Association of Securities Dealers, and

   B. in a corporation that had, at the end of the corporation's most recent fiscal year, or on average during the previous 3 fiscal years, stockholder equity exceeding $75,000,000.

2. Ownership of shares in a regulated investment company as defined in section 851(a) of the Internal Revenue Code of 1986, if such company had, at the end of the company's most recent fiscal year, or on average during the previous 3 fiscal years, total assets exceeding $75,000,000.

d. Additional exceptions related only to ownership or investment prohibition

The following, if not otherwise excepted under subsection (b), shall not be considered to be an ownership or investment interest described in subsection (a)(2)(A):

1. Hospitals in Puerto Rico

   In the case of designated health services provided by a hospital located in Puerto Rico.

2. Rural providers

   In the case of designated health services furnished in a rural area (as defined in section 1395ww(d)(2)(D) of this title) by an entity, if—

   A. substantially all of the designated health services furnished by the entity are furnished to individuals residing in such a rural area;

   B. effective for the 18-month period beginning on December 8, 2003, the entity is not a specialty hospital (as defined in subsection (h)(7)); and

C. in the case where the entity is a hospital, the hospital meets the requirements of paragraph (3)(D).

3. Hospital ownership

In the case of designated health services provided by a hospital (other than a hospital described in paragraph (1)) if—

A. the referring physician is authorized to perform services at the hospital;

B. effective for the 18-month period beginning on December 8, 2003, the hospital is not a specialty hospital (as defined in subsection (h)(7));

C. the ownership or investment interest is in the hospital itself (and not merely in a subdivision of the hospital); and

D. the hospital meets the requirements described in subsection (i)(1) not later than 18 months after March 23, 2010.[16]

Context: The Stark Law allows physicians to maintain certain investment and ownership interests that do not constitute a financial relationship under 42 U.S.C. § 1395nn(a)(2). Physicians are permitted to invest in entities through publicly available securities available on the New York Stock Exchange and certain mutual funds. Further, physicians can have an ownership or investment interest in a rural healthcare provider or a hospital in Puerto Rico. Physicians may also have an ownership interest in certain hospitals qualifying under 42 U.S.C. § 1395nn(i)(1).

Consequences for Noncompliance

Subsection (g) of the Stark Law provides for sanctions and civil penalties in the event a violation occurs. Because Stark Law violations often overlap with AKS violations, the latter law may expose healthcare organization officials to criminal liability.

Administrative Proceedings

Penalties

- Payment of a designated health service covered by Medicare or Medicare may be denied.

- Collections of amounts billed in violation of the Stark Law must be refunded to the patient or other party.

- Any person who presents or causes to be presented a bill or claim for a designated health service that the person knew or should have known was an illegal referral or should have been refunded shall be subject to a civil money penalty not exceeding $15,000 for each service.

- Any physician or other entity who enters into an arrangement or scheme that the physician or entity knew or should have known was for securing illegal referrals shall be subject to a civil money penalty not exceeding $100,000 per arrangement or scheme.

- Any person required to report its ownership, investment, or compensation arrangements under 42 U.S.C. § 1395nn(f) and fails to do so is subject to a civil money penalty not exceeding $10,000 for each day for which reporting is required to have been made.

Civil Litigation

Damages

Three times damages for violations involving illegal renumeration under the False Claims Act.

Important Compliance Guidance and Tools

Centers for Medicare & Medicaid Services

Physician Self Referral

CMS covers its regulations interpreting physician self-referral on this site:

https://www.cms.gov/Medicare/Fraud-and-Abuse/PhysicianSelfReferral/index?redirect=/physicianselfreferral/

U.S. Department of Health & Human Services Office of Inspector General

A Roadmap for New Physicians: Fraud & Abuse Laws

This primer for new physicians covers the five main fraud and abuse laws physicians need to understand and comply with in order to avoid criminal penalties, civil fines, federal healthcare program exclusion, or loss of their medical license from state medical boards.

https://oig.hhs.gov/compliance/physician-education/01laws.asp

Relevant Physician Self-Referral Law (Stark Law) Cases and Opinions

United States ex rel. Riedel v. Boston Heart Diagnostics Corp., No. 1:12-cv-1423 (D.D.C.) and United States ex rel. FBH1 v. Boston Heart Diagnostics Corp., No. 2:17-cv-2061 (E.D. Cal.)

Case summary: Between 2015 and 2017, Boston Heart Diagnostics Corporation (Boston Heart), a medical laboratory, entered an agreement with small Texas hospitals to provide lab testing in exchange for per-test payments. In a scheme to generate more patient referrals for itself and its affiliated hospitals, Boston Heart arranged with the hospitals' independent marketers and their management services organizations—entities physicians can join for management services such as billing and collections—in order to identify physicians and offer them payment for patient referrals. The physicians would refer patients either to Boston Heart directly or to one of its affiliated hospitals, which would then refer its patients to Boston Heart. The physicians would be paid through distributions from the management service organizations. Through this complex scheme, Boston Heart performed laboratory tests for referring physicians for compensation, then billed Medicare and Medicare for the covered services.

Opinion issued: November 26, 2019

Link to full text: https://www.justice.gov/opa/pr/ laboratory-pay-2667-million-settle-false-claims-act-allegations-illegal-inducements-referring

Boston Heart would ultimately settle with the Department of Justice for $26.7 million. Commenting on the case, which was brought by qui tam relators under the False Claims Act, Assistant Attorney General Jody Hunt cited the purpose of Federal healthcare laws as to preserve "the integrity of federal healthcare programs."[17] Special Agent C. J. Porter of the Office of Inspector General, commented on violations of federal healthcare laws as "driving up medical costs, wasting taxpayer dollars, and often harming patients."[18] The settlement agreement cited alleged violations of the False Claims Act, Anti-Kickback Statute, and Stark Law. Namely, the financial relationship between the physicians, Boston Heart, and the Texas hospitals failed to meet an exception under Stark Law, and thus violated the law. The whistleblowers who brought the case were compensated under the False Claims Act for $4.36 million.

United States ex rel. Hammett v. Lexington County Health Services District d/b/a Lexington Medical Center, No. 3:14-cv-03653 (D.S.C.)

Case summary: In a case brought by Dr. David Hammett against his former employer, South Carolina hospital Lexington Medical Center (Lexington Medical) allegedly entered into inappropriate financial agreements with 28 physicians. The agreements allegedly violated the Stark Law's limitation that agreements between hospitals and physicians be of fair market value, be commercially reasonable, and, most importantly, are not for the referral of designated health services. Specifically, the government claimed Lexington Medical either acquired or employed certain physicians' practices and factored into its compensation calculation the value and volume of their referrals. Thus, physicians were compensated in excess of their medical talent to the extent they referred covered medical services. The various agreements spanned from as early as January 2011 to as late as September 2015.

Opinion issued: July 28, 2016

Link to full text: https://www.justice.gov/opa/pr/
south-carolina-hospital-pay-17-million-resolve-false-claims-act-and-stark-law-allegations

Lexington Medical agreed to pay $17 million to the government through the Office of Inspector General. The settlement agreement news release explained the Stark Law's intent to "ensure that physician referrals are made based on the medical needs of the patients and are not tainted by certain financial arrangements."[19] Then acting Principal Deputy Assistant Attorney General Benjamin C. Mizner commented on the settlement as ensuring physicians refer patients for tests and procedures for their best interests, and "not because the physician stands to gain financially from the referral."[20] The settlement, memorialized in a Corporate Integrity Agreement, also requires Lexington Medical to "detect future conduct similar to that which gave rise" to the settlement. Hammett received more than $4 million for his role in the action.[21,22]

United States ex rel. Louis Longo v. Wheeling Hospital, Inc., No. 19-cv-192 (N.D.W. Va. 2020).

Case summary: Wheeling Hospital in West Virginia allegedly violated the Stark Law by billing Medicare for designated health services referred by physicians with whom the hospital had a financial relationship. Between 2007 and 2020, Ronald Violi—Wheeling's CEO at the time the alleged violations took place—compensated referring physicians well beyond fair market value for their services. Instead of being compensated solely for their productivity, physicians were instead compensated based on the "downstream revenue" from their patient referrals. Violi's actions were purportedly motivated by a need to turn around Wheeling Hospital's financial situation—the type of profiteering the Stark Law and similar laws were created to prevent.

Opinion issued: September 9, 2020

Link to full text: https://www.leagle.com/decision/infdco20190919c43

Wheeling Hospital would enter into a $50 million settlement agreement with the Department of Justice. The Department of Justice's corporate settlement news release cited the purpose of the Stark Law, which was meant to prohibit hospitals from "billing Medicare for certain services referred by physicians with whom the hospital has a financial relationship, unless that relationship satisfies one of the law's statutory or regulatory exceptions."[23] Assistant Attorney General Jeffrey Bossert Clark said "[i]mproper financial arrangements between hospitals and physicians can influence the type and amount of health care that is provided."[24] Scott Brady, U.S. Attorney for the Western District of Pennsylvania, referred to the trust Medicare and Medicaid patients must have in their healthcare providers, adding that enforcement of the Anti-Kickback Statute helps ensure providers do not breach that trust. The complaint was brought by former Wheeling Hospital executive Louis Longo, who received $10 million under the False Claims Act qui tam provision.

Endnotes

1. **Gabriel Imperato** is managing partner at the Fort Lauderdale office of Nelson Mullins Riley & Scarborough. He is the team leader of the firm's Health Care Criminal and Civil Enforcement, Litigation and Compliance Practice. He has practiced healthcare law in both the public and private sectors for more than 40 years. He is board certified as a specialist in health law by The Florida Bar. Imperato recently served as the general counsel of the North Broward Hospital District, the tenth largest healthcare system in the United States. He has also served as deputy chief counsel for the U.S. Department of Health & Human Services' Office of the General Counsel. Imperato is also a longtime member of the board of directors of Society of Corporate Compliance and Ethics & the Health Care Compliance Association (SCCE & HCCA), where he was also a past president and interim CEO.

2. **Anne Novick Branan** is an of counsel attorney in the Fort Lauderdale office of Nelson Mullins Riley & Scarborough. She has been board certified in health law by The Florida Bar since 1995. Branan counsels healthcare providers about avoiding and responding to allegations of fraud under the Medicare and Medicaid programs. She helps her clients navigate the complex regulatory environment affecting acquisitions and contracting in the healthcare industry. Branan regularly assists healthcare companies in developing and assessing the effectiveness of corporate compliance and ethics programs. She was recognized in *The Best Lawyers in America* for healthcare law, 2015–2020, and selected as Fort Lauderdale Health Care Law "Lawyer of the Year" in 2017.

3. **Richard Sena** is a juris doctor candidate at the Nova Southeastern University Shepard Broad College of Law. He is the editor-in-chief of the *Nova Law Review* and a law clerk at Nelson Mullins Riley & Scarborough in Fort Lauderdale since the summer of 2020. Sena has conducted health law research under the guidance of attorneys Gabriel Imperato and Anne Novick Branan and helped author sections of the "Key Laws in Healthcare Compliance" chapter in the 2021 HCCA *Complete Healthcare Compliance Manual*. He is expected to graduate in May 2021 and plans to continue his career as an associate attorney at Nelson Mullins.

4. **Megan Speltz** is a digital product owner at SCCE & HCCA, where she helps define and deliver new digital products to the COSMOS platform. She graduated from the University of St. Thomas School of Law in May 2020; she obtained her juris doctor with a concentration in organizational ethics and compliance. In addition to working at SCCE & HCCA, Speltz is a licensed attorney practicing in the state of Minnesota and represents small businesses and nonprofit organizations.

5. 42 C.F.R. §§ 411.355, 411.357.

6. 42 U.S.C. § 1320a-7b(b).

7. 31 U.S.C. §§ 3729–3733.

8. 42 U.S.C. § 1395nn(a).

9. 42 C.F.R. § 411.351.

10. 42 U.S.C. § 1395nn(f).

11. 42 U.S.C. § 1395nn(g).

12. 42 U.S.C. §§ 1395nn(b), (e).

13. 42 U.S.C. § 1395nn(h)(4).

14. 42 C.F.R. § 411.355.

15. 42 C.F.R. § 411.357.

16. 42 U.S.C. §§ 1395nn(c), (d).

17. U.S. Department of Justice, "Laboratory to Pay $26.67 Million to Settle False Claims Act Allegations of Illegal Inducements to Referring Physicians," news release, November 26, 2019, http://www.justice.gov/opa/pr/laboratory-pay-2667-million-settle-false-claims-act-allegations-illegal-inducements-referring.

18. U.S. Department of Justice, "Laboratory to Pay $26.67 Million."

19. U.S. Department of Justice, "South Carolina Hospital to Pay $17 Million to Resolve False Claims Act and Stark Law Allegations," news release, July 28, 2016, http://www.justice.gov/opa/pr/south-carolina-hospital-pay-17-million-resolve-false-claims-act-and-stark-law-allegations.

20. U.S. Department of Justice, "South Carolina Hospital to Pay $17 Million."

21. U.S. Department of Justice, "South Carolina Hospital to Pay $17 Million."

22. "Corporate Integrity Agreement Between the Office of Inspector General of the Department of Health and Human Services and Lexington County Health Services District, Inc. D/B/A Lexington Medical Center," U.S. Department of Health & Human Services Office of Inspector General, accessed February 1, 2021, https://www.oig.hhs.gov/fraud/cia/agreements/Lexington_Medical_Center_07202016.pdf.

23. U.S. Department of Justice, "West Virginia Hospital Agrees to Pay $50 Million to Settle Allegations Concerning Improper Compensation to Referring Physicians," news release, September 9, 2020, http://www.justice.gov/opa/pr/west-virginia-hospital-agrees-pay-50-million-settle-allegations-concerning-improper.

24. U.S. Department of Justice, "West Virginia Hospital Agrees to Pay $50 Million."

Chapter 6

Healthcare Compliance Risk Areas

Artificial Intelligence

Artificial Intelligence and Compliance Programs

By Alan Brill,[1] CISSP, CFE, CIPP/US, FAAFS

What is Artificial Intelligence in Relation to Compliance Programs?

Artificial intelligence (AI) is simply the application of computer processing to simulate the actions of a person. One of the earliest AI systems was, in fact, a medical application called "MYCIN." The program was designed to diagnose bacterial infections and recommend appropriate medications, with the dosage adjusted for the patient's body weight. Viewed from current technology, MYCIN was quite primitive, using an inference engine with approximately 600 rules derived from interviews with expert human diagnosticians. MYCIN was originally written as part of a doctoral dissertation at Stanford University and was never used in actual medical practice for legal and ethical reasons (along with limitations related to the technology of the day.) But it formed the basis for continued experimentation and development.

There are aspects of AI that are continuously evolving, but there are some basic terms that are worth understanding.

Machine Learning

This is a subset of AI in which the computer's algorithms (essentially the AI computer program) are able to modify the computer's actions with the objective of improving through experience. In many settings (medicine, aviation, or automobiles for example), learning through actual experience could be counterproductive. For example, imagine stating that a number of airplane crashes happened because the airplane's computer program hadn't learned to deal with unexpected turbulence yet. So, typically machine-learning systems are given what is called "training data" in order to learn how to function. Provided with data and outcomes, the software should be able to modify processing to result in better—or more accurate—performance.

Rule-Based Machine Learning

This involves systems that evolve a set of rules by which a program makes decisions. MYCIN, for example, had hundreds of rules. In a rule-based system, the program uses its experience to identify which rules are more or less useful and to modify the rules or the weights given to them to improve processing outcomes.

Deep-Learning Systems

These systems are generally characterized as having multiple layers of processing, using layers that go from general to specific analysis, that are often being applied to large networks of unstructured data. An example might be a system that is designed to read human handwriting. Clearly, experience tells us that this isn't easy, as there are as many variations in handwriting as there are people. But there are generalizations that can be used to do some preliminary analysis (for example, that a given character is uppercase) that can lead to deeper analysis to try to figure out which character is being represented.

Cognitive Computing

This is generally thought of as an alternative name for AI. There is no widely accepted definition, but you may run into the term as a synonym for AI.

Computer Vision

This is a subset of AI that focuses on how computers use digital images (still or video) in their processing. An assembly line for drug packaging can use computer vision technologies, for example, to inspect sterile vials of injectable medication to ensure that labels have been affixed and that the top is properly sealed. This can be done at the speed of the assembly line, with a mechanical "kicker" used to eject vials not meeting the specifications.

Natural Language Processing (NLP)

This is the part of AI that focuses on enabling interactions with humans by interpreting their language. It includes automated language understanding and interpretation, automated language generation, speech recognition, and responding with spoken responses. In the past few years, this has gone from the lab to millions of homes, with digital assistants like Siri and Alexa ready to listen and respond to requests. In many cases, the vendors of these systems seek user's permission to use recordings of these interactions to improve the system's performance. This has been recognized as a privacy issue. In at least one case, recordings of interactions with a digital assistant have been subpoenaed in connection with a murder trial.

Chatbots

These are very similar to natural language processors, although they were developed to replace human operators in online text-based chat systems. For example, a chat system could be fielded to answer routine questions and to forward difficult or complex ones to human operators, thus reducing the workload on the humans. In some cases, these can use text-to-speech processing to enable spoken responses.

Graphics Processing Units (GPUs)

These are specialized processors operating within computers designed to process image data. A GPU could be used to create the images displayed on a computer's screen. However, these powerful units have been used for many other purposes. A current example is that GPUs are often used to process cryptocurrency transactions (a process known as mining, which can be very profitable). Specialized computers using massive numbers of GPUs have been developed as mining machines for cryptocurrency processing.

Internet of Things

This is a term that refers to the abundance of devices that can connect to a network that are not traditional computers (or smartphones or tablets). Ranging from smart lightbulbs to cameras to refrigerators, they enable remote control and monitoring of connected devices. There has been enormous growth in the number of medical devices that can connect to a network. Unfortunately, there are serious security concerns that have resulted in Food and Drug Administration (FDA) warnings relating to several devices, including network-connected infusion pumps.[2]

Application Programming Interfaces (APIs)

This refers to the connections between devices and the rules by which these connections are made and interpreted. So, for example, if an AI-based analytic engine is to be given access to a particular database, an API defines the way the systems interact, how requests are made, and how they are responded to.

AI and the Compliance Function

When it comes to AI, compliance professionals are presented with what could be characterized as a double-edged sword. On one hand, AI represents an opportunity for compliance professionals to automate certain compliance activities. AI software can perform a compliance function within a given automated function. For example, an AI system could be instructed to issue a report (or email or text message) to a compliance officer if certain values are exceeded or fall below a specified threshold. If regular reports from multiple people are required, the system can monitor whether it has received the reports. It can be programmed to send a notice to those who have not made their report, and eventually to the compliance officer if reports are not received within a specified time period. The system can adjust processing based on an individual reporter's performance. So, for example, more leeway might be given to someone who always files their reports on time versus someone who is frequently late.

For compliance officers, using AI represents what might be called a force multiplier, in that it enables compliance tasks to be assigned to a machine rather than requiring a human to track and identify reports not received on a timely basis. Because typical budgets for compliance are never enough to do everything a compliance officer might like, automating some processes can make those resources go further, which can be a valuable part of the overall compliance process in an organization.

On the other hand, AI software cannot exist in a vacuum. It needs to be properly controlled and carefully examined by a compliance professional. This person should be involved in the development or adoption of the AI software, along with its customization and testing. Compliance professionals should not underestimate the importance of being involved in testing. Problems with data used to train the system can produce results that might seem completely appropriate to the AI technical team, but may be recognized by compliance specialists as reflecting, for example, inherent biases that may be implicit in the training data, which is often historic in nature and may have been obtained from periods where various issues (like racial or gender bias) may not have been recognized. The technical people involved in the AI development process may not be sensitive to these issues. Compliance professionals must be—and can serve as—a vital system of checks and balances to assure that old problems are not carried forward into the new AI-based system.

AI and deep-learning systems can impact the traditional compliance function. Compliance professionals can both protect the organization from AI-related problems and take advantage of AI's potential capability to enhance and serve the compliance function.

Risk Area Governance

In thinking about AI systems, remember that the entire spectrum of AI is still an emerging area of technology. As a result, there are no laws at this time specifically regulating or otherwise uniquely addressing AI systems.

AI systems, however, can violate laws. For example, consider an AI system designed by a bank to make decisions on mortgage loan applications. For example, during the development and training of the system, AI could determine that a significant predictor of whether a mortgage will be successfully paid is the postal code of the borrower. From a technical standpoint, it might be reasonable to let the system make loan decisions—including the interest rate and other terms of a loan with significant weight given to the borrower's postal code. But doing so might be determined to be an unlawful practice called redlining, which is defined as denying a service to someone on the basis that they live in an area believed to be a financial risk to the lender. This discriminatory practice was generally outlawed in the Fair Housing Act of 1968 and the Community Reinvestment Act of 1977.[34] But those developing the AI system may be experts in technology—and not in banking or the application of those laws. This is an example of a system that could perpetuate bias if the problem went unrecognized.

It is necessary to consider AI in terms of the risks associated with:

- Any compliance system (manual or automated)
- Applicable laws and regulations
- The need for controls over that system
- The requirement that a compliance function be able to provide assurance that the necessary controls are working as intended

Common Compliance Risks

AI Development Team May Not Include Sufficient Input from Counsel

AI systems are subject to all relevant laws, regulations, contractual agreements, and company/agency policies covering both the subject matter of the system and any technological issues relating to the system. If a system is created by external specialists as a work made for hire or the system is acquired under some form of a license agreement from the developer/owner of the system, the legal issues regarding the acquisition, ownership, and duties of the parties represent legal issues. For that reason, compliance professionals should consider whether the development of the AI system has received sufficient input from either in-house or outside counsel to assure that the system is in compliance with the applicable laws, regulations, and contractual agreements (such as for remote storage, data breach incidents, and privacy and security requirements).

Compliance professionals are more aware of the potential impact of a system that violates laws, regulations, or contractual agreements than the average person, so it is important that they help assure the AI system has been subject to appropriate review and follow-up by counsel.

AI Development Team May Not Include Sufficient Input from Compliance Professionals

It is not unusual for an AI development team to be largely composed of technology and AI specialists. They are not compliance professionals, and one must not assume that this kind of technology team will adequately design or implement the needed compliance controls. Consider the extent to which non-AI systems require compliance oversight. AI systems often have greater freedom of action based on their rulesets and the experience that they gain during their operation. Compliance professionals have to review in detail the controls being implemented into the AI system to determine whether the properly implemented controls are sufficient. If they aren't, the compliance professional must take whatever steps necessary to get those controls into the system, or to develop compensating controls that can replace missing controls within AI systems.

AI System May Not Be Designed to Retain All Records Required by Law or Regulation

There are many records that a company or governmental body must retain for specified periods of time, as required by law, regulation, or contractual provision. Tax-related information is a good example, but not the only one that is relevant. AI systems being built or licensed may not take all of the relevant laws and regulations into account. Both legal and compliance professionals must work together to understand what the requirements are and the extent to which the existing system design accurately reflects those requirements.

AI System May Not Be Designed to Retain Records That Could Become Important Evidence in the Event of Litigation Relating to the System's Operations

The information that counsel wants preserved in logs or other records of an AI system may go beyond requirements set by laws, regulations, or contractual provisions. For example, there is very little legal guidance on exactly what data an autonomous driving vehicle has to maintain. But counsel may have some very specific ideas on what should be available if—as has happened—the self-driving car kills a pedestrian. What were the sensors seeing? What was the ruleset that led the car to hit the pedestrian? If the data is not stored in a log or other record, it won't be available, and that fact may, in and of itself, be seen as problematic if litigation ensues. History tells us that AI systems are no less likely than other systems to result in litigation, and as a result, thinking in terms of the evidence that counsel would like to have in the event of litigation is very important. The compliance department needs to ensure that those records are being created by the AI system and stored for the time period designated by counsel.

AI System's Learning and Testing Data Sets May Be Ineffective in Preventing Unwanted Behavior or in Identifying Potential Issues with the AI System's Performance

AI systems referred to as having machine-learning or deep-learning attributes are different than traditional AI programs in that these systems modify their functionality over time based on experience. These systems simulate the learning that would happen to a human. The set of rules that is part of the software determines how the system can change as it "learns." What limits are set for these changes? Who has looked at the data used to train and test the system? Unless you actively look at these issues, you can't simply assume that everything will be OK. For example, an AI computer-vision system that inspects vials to ensure that the label was properly attached might need to be adjusted if the label size changes or the dimensions of the vials change to avoid rejecting vials that are acceptable.

Consider the example of AI facial recognition systems. At first, there was a general assumption that these systems worked well. But as facts emerged, that assumption had to be challenged. A federal study demonstrated that facial recognition systems misidentified people of color more than white people.[5] According to a report in *The Washington Post*, "Asian and African American people were up to 100 times more likely to be misidentified than white men, depending on the particular algorithm and type of search."[6] This was not a study of systems that were being considered for use. These systems were in actual use and were misidentifying people of color. It raises a question of how that could have happened and why it was not noticed. Certainly, there was inherent bias in the data, but it's also important to note that the people building these systems either did not understand that (or chose to ignore it). What might seem like an academic issue of how the system works can in reality result in life-or-death situations. For example, an innocent person inaccurately identified as a dangerous criminal who has resisted arrests in the past might lead to a rapidly escalating —and deadly— situation when police attempt to apprehend that innocent person.

Updates and Changes to the AI System May Impact the System's Operations in a Way That Presents Increased Risks That Must Be Evaluated by Counsel and Compliance Professionals

AI and machine-learning systems, as all systems, will be updated at some point or on a regular basis. The changes could be a result of changing the underlying operating systems of the computers on which they run or a change in the desired functionality of the system. Regardless, it's important that compliance personnel be involved to provide assurance that the changes won't result in a degradation of controls or in reporting mechanisms.

Addressing Compliance Risks

During the Developmental Phase of AI System Development

The compliance function plays (or at least should play) an important role during the development (i.e., programming, installation, or customization) of the AI system. Taking an active role to understand what the system does, how it does it, any limitations on the system's freedom of action, designed-in controls, reporting, data logging and preservation, and error reporting is key to being able to accurately report to management on how well the system is controlled and how those controls can be overseen.

During the Testing Phase of AI System Development

The compliance function should be involved in testing. The objective of testing should be to detect problems. All too often, developers want the system to be accepted, and may take shortcuts. For example, the developers may have a large file of data that is relevant to the system. They can take half of the file and use it for training the system, and then use the other half of the file as the test set. The problem with this is that any problems or bias that are consistent throughout the file will most likely not be caught, since the same error that is in the test set was also in the set of data used for testing. Making sure that the test data actively challenge the system is important.

During the Operational Phase of AI System

During the operational life of the system, the compliance function must examine reports coming from the system to understand potential problems. Compliance professionals looking at AI systems must do what they are good at—asking the "What if?" questions that may have been overlooked by the development team. Additionally, those using AI systems may not like the discipline imposed by these systems and develop ways to bypass them or render them less effective. Recognizing this possibility can lead a compliance professional to closely examine how the AI system is operating and be on the lookout for behaviors their experience tells them may be present. At the same time, sufficient testing must be developed that can determine that the right controls are in place and that they are working. AI systems are no different than any other corporate system in this regard.

Updating and Maintaining AI Systems

As AI systems are updated and maintained, compliance specialists should be involved to understand the changes to ensure that the systems do not negatively impact the controls in place and determine whether they require additional controls and whether the overall system of controls will continue to work properly.

Possible Penalties

Legal Penalties

While no current laws focus specifically on AI, there are no exemptions for those systems either. Any violations of law that are attributable to the operation of AI systems are subject to the same penalties as any other violation. Depending on their functionality, AI systems can be subject to multiple laws in multiple countries.

Reputational Costs

Cases in which driverless cars have been involved in accidents—and, in at least one case, killed a pedestrian—are examples of incidents involving AI systems that can produce substantial reputational damage. The same can be said of the revelations of the differing error rates of facial recognition systems based on the role of the individual being matched having had a substantial effect on the developers of those systems. Reputational risk is always a factor to be considered.

Reputational risks cover a broad range of issues. Some examples include:

- Negative publicity from the AI-related incident resulting in a loss of customer confidence.
- Negative publicity from fines or other sanctions imposed by regulators in response to a data breach or other incident. This can also result in loss of confidence or a general degradation of the overall perceived reputation of the organization.
- Loss of market valuation if the incident results in reduction in stock prices. This can be sudden and precipitous. It can then result in higher borrowing costs or access to capital markets.
- The initiation of shareholder and related civil actions based on an incident can also contribute to reputational damage.
- Loss of reputation of executives and board members, which can have a personal effect on them.

Compliance Resources

The use of AI in carrying out the compliance function is fast evolving. Some resources that may be of interest include:

- Balamurugan Balakreshnan et al., "PPE Compliance Detection using Artificial Intelligence in Learning Factories," *Procedia Manufacturing* 45 (2020), 277–282, https://doi.org/10.1016/j.promfg.2020.04.017.

- Tom Butler and Leona O'Brien, "Artificial intelligence for regulatory compliance: Are we there yet?" *Journal of Financial Compliance* 3, no. 1, (Autumn/Fall 2019), 44–59, https://www.henrystewartpublications.com/jfc/v3.
- Alexander L. Fogel and Joseph C. Kvedar, "Artificial intelligence powers digital medicine," *npj Digital Medicine* 1 (2018), https://doi.org/10.1038/s41746-017-0012-2.
- John Kingston, "Using artificial intelligence to support compliance with the general data protection regulation," *Artificial Intelligence and Law* 25 (2017), 429–443, https://doi.org/10.1007/s10506-017-9206-9.

Risk Takeaways

Main points of interest:

Artificial intelligence (AI) is a fast-growing area of technology that has the potential to automate many different compliance functions, saving time and money in a compliance department. Yet it's vital that compliance professionals be involved in the development, testing, and oversight of these systems. Without the involvement of the compliance department, AI systems may cause a company to be noncompliant in numerous areas, resulting in serious penalties and reputational harm.

Areas to watch:

- AI development team may not include sufficient input from counsel.
- AI development team may not include sufficient input from compliance professionals.
- AI system may not be designed to retain all records required by law or regulation.
- AI system may not be designed to retain the records that could become important evidence in the event of litigation relating to the system's operations.
- AI system's learning and testing data sets may be ineffective in preventing unwanted behavior or in identifying potential issues with the AI system's performance.
- Updates and changes to the AI system may impact the system's operations in a way that presents increased risks that must be evaluated by counsel and compliance professionals.
- Also, consider the following during an AI system's development and maintenance:
  - Does the system comply with all relevant laws, regulations, contractual agreements, and company/agency standards?
  - Does the system maintain both the legally required records and the digital evidence that counsel wants available in the event of litigation?

Laws that apply:

There are no current laws focused on AI, but all laws covering the areas of operation of the system are applicable. AI systems don't get a pass if their decisions violate a law or regulation, so avoidance of those circumstances represents best practice.

Addressing compliance risks:

The key to success for compliance professionals is to be involved at the design stage of the system and assure that the appropriate controls are in place, that the system monitors those controls, and to act accordingly when a violation is detected.

Endnotes

1. **Alan Brill** is a senior managing director of the Cyber Risk practice at Kroll, a division of Duff & Phelps, and an adjunct professor at Texas A&M University School of Law. His research at Kroll focuses on the interface of artificial intelligence technology, security, and compliance. He has worked with a wide variety of healthcare-related organizations—from hospital systems to medical device manufacturers—in meeting the evolving challenges of cybersecurity in a rapidly changing environment. Brill is also the founder of Kroll's global high-tech investigations practice and has led engagements that range from large-scale reviews of information security and cyber incidents for multibillion-dollar corporations to criminal investigations of computer intrusions.

2. "Cybersecurity," U.S. Food and Drug Administration, last revised October 22, 2020, https://www.fda.gov/medical-devices/digital-health-center-excellence/cybersecurity.

3. 7 C.F.R. § 1901.203.

4. 12 U.S.C. § 2901 et seq.

5. Patrick Grother, Mei Ngan, and Kayee Hanaoka, "Face Recognition Vendor Test (FRVT) Part 3: Demographic Effects," National Institute of Standards and Technology, U.S. Department of Commerce, December 2019, https://doi.org/10.6028/NIST.IR.8280.

6. Drew Harwell, "Federal study confirms racial bias of many facial-recognition systems, casts doubt on their expanding use," *The Washington Post*, December 19, 2019, https://www.washingtonpost.com/technology/2019/12/19/federal-study-confirms-racial-bias-many-facial-recognition-systems-casts-doubt-their-expanding-use/.

Clinical Research

Financial Conflicts of Interest

By Emmelyn Kim,[1] MA, MPH, MJ, CCRA, CHRC

What Are Financial Conflicts of Interest in Clinical Research?

Financial conflicts of interest (FCOIs) in clinical research are external interests held by the research investigator, and in some cases by the institution, that are financial in nature that could directly and significantly affect and/or appear to affect the design, conduct, and or reporting of research. Individual FCOIs are specifically defined in federal regulations that apply to Public Health Service (PHS)-funded research as external interests of the research investigator that reasonably appear related to their institutional responsibilities and are considered significant financial interests (SFIs).[2] FCOIs can be complex, considering that interactions have become increasingly more common among academia, industry/private sector, and government agencies in pursuit of advancing scientific discoveries using cutting-edge science and technology. The Bayh–Dole Act enacted in 1980 was the key piece of legislation that changed the landscape at academic institutions by allowing institutions and faculty to retain rights to inventions from federally funded research.[3] This provided a pathway toward commercialization through technology licensing and transfer and also opened up a wider door for interactions with industry. Therefore, it is critical to understand where FCOI risks may occur in such interactions and employ strategies to ensure that research remains objective and is ethically conducted.

In clinical research, FCOIs are important to detect and effectively manage in order to prevent bias from negatively or inappropriately affecting the design, conduct, or outcome of the research. These steps are also essential to maintaining the public's trust in the research produced by healthcare or research institutions and individual researchers. Healthcare institutions often participate in clinical research through government, industry, or internal funding mechanisms. The federal government funds clinical research at healthcare institutions through the form of grants that require recipient institutions and research investigators to comply with the terms and conditions of the award, including FCOI disclosure and management. Industry-sponsored clinical research is governed by contracts between the institution and company developing or marketing the drug, device, or biologic under study, and is often bound by disclosure and reporting requirements pursuant to the Food and Drug Administration (FDA) financial disclosure regulations. There may also be other state and local laws or institutional policies that govern conflict of interest (COI) disclosure and management pertaining to business interactions and transactions. Clinical researchers and institutions have a shared responsibility in ensuring compliance with regulatory and other local requirements to promote objectivity in the research conducted at their organizations, which is why this remains an important and complex risk area for compliance professionals.

A number of factors that affect institutional FCOI risk and risk tolerance in clinical research include the overall maturity of compliance and research integrity programs; leadership support and investment; nature and breadth of research programs, including funding sources; degree of interactions with industry and commercialization activity; institutional culture; reporting mechanisms; and reputational impacts. The increasing pressures and complexities of the academic and scientific environments combined with heightened public scrutiny regarding FCOIs require more sophisticated oversight programs to ensure transparency, accountability, and effective management of conflicts.

A comprehensive lens should be applied when evaluating FCOI risks associated with clinical research. This is because other types of individual conflicts (e.g., conflict of commitment, role-based conflicts, conflict of conscience) may arise or be comingled with FCOI in the context of clinical research. Researchers in healthcare environments often have multiple roles, including that of a healthcare provider, faculty member or student, administrator, and institutional official, or serve on institutional review committees. They may have external interests (e.g., start-up companies) and collaborations or relationships (e.g., advisory board roles) that may intersect or conflict with their institutional responsibilities. Growing concerns by the US government over inappropriate influence by foreign governments on federally funded research have led to reinforcement by the National Institutes of Health (NIH) of appropriate disclosure by researchers and review by institutions of foreign support, relationships, and activities that represent an FCOI or conflict of commitment.[4] Institutional FCOIs may also arise from institutionally held investments or equity, royalties, significant donations from or interactions with industry, or from institutional officials who have substantial purchasing or business decision-making authority. There are currently no federal regulations that govern FCOIs on an institutional level, which are often left up to institutional policies. Despite this, there have been mounting concerns over increased institutional FCOIs at academic institutions and the need to ensure effective oversight and management of this particular risk area.[5] Therefore, healthcare institutions should be attuned to the various types of conflicts that may occur and employ ways to comprehensively review and manage these risks in clinical research.

Risk Area Governance

FCOI federal regulations were promulgated in 1995 by the Office of the Secretary of the U.S. Department of Health & Human Services (HHS) to promote objectivity of PHS-funded research. HHS revised the regulations and issued a final rule on August 25, 2011, requiring compliance by institutions applying for or receiving PHS funding by August 24, 2012.[6]

Codified at:

- 42 C.F.R. § 50, subpart F, Responsibility of Applicants for Promoting Objectivity in Research for which Public Health Service Funding is Sought and Responsible Prospective Contractors[7]
- 42 C.F.R. § 94, Responsible Prospective Contractors[8]

The FCOI regulations apply to institutions and research investigators that are recipients of funding from PHS funding agencies such as the NIH. Research investigators are defined by the regulations as the "project director or principal Investigator and any other person, regardless of title or position, who is responsible for the design, conduct, or reporting of research funded by the PHS, or proposed for such funding, which may include, for example, collaborators or consultants."[9] These regulations do not apply to Phase I Small Business Innovation Research (SBIR) and Small Business Technology Transfer Research (STTR) applicants.[10]

Investigators are responsible for complying with their institutional FCOI policy and disclosing any external interests (including those of their spouse and dependent children) that are reasonably related to their professional responsibilities at their institutions and considered SFIs. Review of SFI disclosures must occur no later than at the time of applying for PHS funding, at least annually during the period of the award, and within 30 days of acquiring or discovering a new SFI.[11] Investigators must also complete FCOI training before engaging in PHS-funded research, at least every four years and under certain circumstances. Institutions have additional responsibilities under the regulations, including review of SFIs disclosed by investigators, identifying any COIs that require management or reduction or elimination of the interest as appropriate, and reporting FCOIs to the PHS awarding component prior to expenditure of funds and subsequently as required. Part of this process involves a designated institutional official(s) that determines that the investigator's SFI could directly and significantly affect the design, conduct, or reporting of the PHS-funded research and therefore represents an FCOI. There are other oversight, policy, education and training, and handling of noncompliance requirements that institutions must comply with per the regulation.

SFIs are defined in the PHS regulations, which include the aggregate amount of remuneration received or value of equity interest from publicly traded entities in the past 12 months preceding the disclosure of $5,000 or more. SFIs also include those from non-publicly traded entities where remuneration exceeds $5,000 or any equity interest, intellectual property rights and interests upon receipt of income and reimbursed or sponsored travel from certain entities. Since industry interactions between industry and researchers may be sporadic or ongoing, new information representing an SFI should be disclosed to institutions within 30 days during the period of the research.

Institutions must be aware of any other applicable federal regulations, state or local laws, funding agency requirements, and institutional policies, especially if they differ from PHS rules, impose additional requirements, or govern other types of COIs and transactions. For example, the National Science Foundation, which is a federal agency that provides research funding, requires investigator disclosures of certain external interests in accordance with a higher SFI threshold amount of more than $10,000.[12] The FDA also requires clinical investigators (including their spouse and dependent children) to disclose certain financial interests, payments, or arrangements to the sponsor of a covered clinical study; however, their threshold amounts differ from PHS rules.[13] Investigator interests that require reporting and disclosure to the FDA include equity interests in the sponsor and, for publicly held companies, any interest of more than $50,000 in value, any significant payments of other sorts of more than $25,000 from the sponsor, proprietary interests in the tested product, and other compensation that could be affected by the study outcome.

Requirements for other conflict review and management areas may depend on the institution (e.g., state-funded institutions, nonprofits) and type of individuals covered (e.g., state employees, healthcare providers, institutional officials, key employees). The Physician Payments Sunshine Act, which was passed in 2009 and embedded within the Affordable Care Act, requires applicable drug, device, biological, or medical supply manufacturers and group purchasing organizations (GPOs) to report annually to the Centers for Medicare & Medicaid Services (CMS) any payments or transfers of value to physicians and teaching hospitals worth more than 10 dollars.[14] The legislation was meant to increase transparency of financial relationships between physicians and teaching hospitals and industry. CMS publishes this information on its website.[15]

Certain institutions apply PHS regulations to a subset of research funded by PHS, whereas others apply it to all research activities, regardless of funding source and per institutional policies. Extending regulatory requirements more broadly depends on the risk strategy that an institution takes depending on the type of institution, makeup of researchers, funding, and type of research that is conducted. Many institutions also have policies that cover both individual and institutional FCOIs and include other types of conflicts that may occur within the clinical research environment.

Common Compliance Risks

Lack of Effective Organizational Oversight

Organizations that receive PHS research funding are responsible for complying with FCOI regulations, informing investigators about their FCOI policies, and ensuring effective oversight and management. The authorized organizational representative certifies when submitting a PHS grant application that the applicant's institution is in compliance with the regulations. Other requirements and types of conflicts including intuitional FCOIs require review and management at an organizational level. Due to the complexity of this space, an effective organizational oversight structure for COIs in research must be in place to ensure compliance and mitigate risks.

Not Maintaining Up-to-Date Policies or Education and Training

FCOI policies are required to be written, up to date, and available to the general public via an accessible website or provided within five business days pursuant to a public request. Education and training should be ongoing and also updated to ensure that they contain relevant information and effectively address any conflicts of interests that may arise in the organizational environment. Research investigators must also complete FCOI training requirements for PHS-funded research.

Not Identifying or Managing FCOIs in a Timely Fashion

External financial interests including consulting, employment, remuneration, service on boards, equity interest (such as stock, stock options, or company ownership interest), and any others considered SFIs should be disclosed by investigators in a timely fashion and evaluated for FCOI before submission of a grant application, prior to engaging in any research activity, and annually or regularly thereafter. These steps are important to reduce the risk that the researcher's judgment may be compromised by financial ties they have with industry and negatively affect the objectivity or integrity of the research.

Failure to Fulfill Federal Reporting Requirements

The institution is required to identify, manage, and report FCOIs to the PHS funding agency through initial and annual FCOI reports through eRA Commons.[16] The reports must be submitted prior to expenditure of the funds and when renewals are granted for ongoing projects. Reporting by institutions is also required for any retrospective reviews in cases where FCOIs were not previously disclosed by the investigator and bias was found in the conduct of the research or in instances of noncompliance with the management plan. Clinical investigators who are also considered sponsors of covered clinical trials (sponsor-investigators) must ensure that they fulfill reporting requirements under the FDA financial disclosure rules.

Not Managing Risk of Subrecipient FCOIs

Collaborative PHS-funded research requires the awardee and subrecipients (e.g., subcontractor or consortium members) to either certify that their policy complies with regulations or rely on the awardee's FCOI policy and incorporate which institution's policy will apply in the agreement to identify and manage investigator FCOIs.

Inadequate Compliance Monitoring

Ongoing institutional review of compliance with FCOI management plans is required until the completion of the PHS-funded research.

Not Evaluating Overall COI Risk in Relation to Business and Environmental Changes

When macro-level changes occur that affect the nature of the business at organizations or when the regulatory environment or public perceptions change, this may lead to downstream impacts on an organization's COI compliance risk profile. Certain types of arrangements may increase risk in clinical research:

- Individual or institutional FCOIs related to clinical research, especially the high-profile ones, involve significant financial gains or greater than minimal risk in human subject research.
- Researcher or faculty start-ups, employment or financial interests in companies seeking SBIR and STTR funding that involve subcontracting part of the research work to their departments or institutions, or involving licensing activities and clinical research at the institution.
- Organizational investment arms that seek to invest in investigator or institutional start-ups or innovations that are tied to sponsored research at the organization.
- Foreign collaborations, activities, or support that represent an FCOI or other type of conflict.

Addressing Compliance Risks

Effective Program Oversight and Implementation

FCOIs must be managed by institutions that receive PHS funding, which means investing adequate resources into a COI research compliance program and staff, committees and designated official(s) that can effectively review investigator disclosures to identify any SFIs representing FCOIs that require mitigation or management, and reporting. Conducting regular compliance risk assessments to ensure that the institution has adequate resources and a good level of oversight is key. Reputational harm and risks to research integrity and the rights, safety, and welfare of research participants can occur as a consequence of noncompliance, which is why it is important to implement robust and effective COI compliance programs. Areas to evaluate include the following.

Program and Governance Structure

Ensure programs are structured appropriately and include the following elements:

- Overseen by a centralized department with compliance oversight that is supported by leadership and organization-wide COI policies and procedures.
- Led by an individual with executive-level and board-reporting responsibilities and a close connection to clinical research activities occurring at the organization.
- Adequate resources, systems, and training for COI staff and committees to review both individual and institutional disclosures and mitigate or manage FCOIs.
- Standardized procedures and mechanisms (e.g., hotline, nonretaliation policy) to report, investigate, and handle noncompliance.
- Compliance coordination with other departments and offices across the organization, including, but not limited to: Human Research Protection Programs, Institutional Review Boards (IRBs), Grants and Contracts, Procurement, Foundations, Technology Transfer, Legal, Ventures and Innovations, and Academic and Medical Affairs.

Awareness and Education

Complexities involving both individual and institutional COIs in today's environment require ongoing education and training efforts to reduce risks to objectivity and integrity in clinical research. Education and training on institutional COI policies can raise investigator awareness of regulatory requirements, enhance conflict identification, and foster better FCOI mitigation or management strategies. Education and training can be facilitated through organization-wide learning management systems or programs that track training and notify investigators prior to expiration.

Centralized Disclosure and Review Using Technology

Use of organization-wide technology, such as web-based platforms and electronic systems, to centrally capture and manage investigator disclosures allow for the following:

- Timely disclosure of external interests by investigators, including any updates and real-time review of the information in relation to anticipated or ongoing grants and research activities.
- Documenting FCOI review determinations and any other institutional actions.
- Easy access and maintenance of records for at least three years from the date of submission of the final PHS expenditure report or where otherwise required.
- Cross-referencing other sources of information, such as Open Payments, as part of the review process for any physician researchers.
- Coordinating and sharing up-to-date disclosures and FCOI management plans through automated feeds or reports with IRB offices and committees, grants and contracts offices, and any other organizational departments requiring the information.
- Facilitating posting and updating of information on a publicly available website or fulfilling written requests within five business days of any public requests regarding FCOIs of senior or key personnel that include the required elements.
- Running reports and information to facilitate compliance monitoring and evaluating organizational risks over time.

Effective FCOI Management Strategies

FCOIs in clinical research should be reviewed by the designated official(s) and/or COI committee, and management plans should be developed if they cannot be reduced or eliminated. Management plan strategies should comprehensively cover individual and any institutional conflicts and require certain conditions or restrictions for conducting the research, depending on the nature of the study. These can include, but are not limited to, the following:

- Restricting conflicted individuals from participating in certain aspects of the research study, such as recruiting, enrolling, and obtaining consent from research participants; collecting or analyzing data; or assessing adverse events and safety monitoring.
- Removing conflicted individuals (including institutional officials) from oversight of the research; lines of reporting tied to the research; or certain individuals involved in the design, conduct, or reporting of the research.
- Recusal of conflicted individuals that serve on any institutional research review or other committee when a review is related to the entity or product in which they have a financial interest.
- Modifying the research plan to reduce risk of bias resulting from the FCOI, such as randomization or blinding procedures, independent third-party analysis, or validation of results.
- Ensuring the research team and research participants can approach an unconflicted individual or a compliance representative for any COI concerns.

- For institutional interests, requiring an external IRB review, independent safety monitor/board, or monitoring body.
- Employing an independent monitor or data reviewer or requiring independent audits to ensure the design, conduct, and reporting of the research is protected against bias.
- Disclosing the FCOI:
  - To potential research participants by including language in the informed consent form
  - To collaborators and sponsors
  - To procurement
  - In publications and presentations
  - To any other parties deemed necessary

Compliance Monitoring and Handling of Noncompliance

Institutions are required to establish adequate and appropriate enforcement mechanisms to ensure compliance. This includes ensuring timely disclosure of SFIs and adherence to FCOI management plans by investigators. The following are ways to address these risks:

- Develop institutional policies and procedures for escalation of identified noncompliance and any necessary reporting to IRBs, PHS funding agencies, institutional officials or committees, research integrity officers, and any others as required.
- Perform regular monitoring of compliance with FCOI management plans. This can be done through regular check-in questionnaires with investigators, audits of research documentation at research sites, comparing publicly available information or publications against FCOI management plans, or requesting regular reports from independent monitors.
- Create a tool for retrospective reviews of research that are required within 120 days if an FCOI was not disclosed by the researcher. If the institution determines as a result of the review that there was bias in the design, conduct, or reporting of the research during the noncompliant period, then they need to develop a mitigation report that includes actions taken to eliminate or mitigate the bias. A PHS mitigation report template should be developed that includes all required regulatory elements.

Evaluate and Identify Other Risk Areas

- Regularly review COI processes that may touch other departments to detect any information or process gaps requiring improvements or enhanced coordination.
- Provide additional education and training to sponsor-investigators holding an investigational new drug application or investigational device exemption, who are required by the FDA to collect information regarding financial interests and report appropriately.
- Confirm ongoing review and management of subrecipient investigator FCOIs and any required reporting to PHS by the awardee institution.

- Ensure effective measures are taken to manage other types of conflicts that may arise, such as institutional, commitment, role-based, procurement/purchasing, or others. This may require other disclosure and review mechanisms and additional COI management strategies to be applied in the context of the research.

Possible Penalties

Noncompliance with PHS regulations by investigators may result in the PHS awarding component imposing special award conditions, suspension of funding, or other enforcement action. Institutional-level sanctions could occur and affect an investigator's ability to conduct research at the organization. Sanctions can depend on the seriousness and severity of the noncompliance, taking into account the reasons for noncompliance, whether the noncompliance is continuing, and impact to the objectivity and integrity of the research involved and human subject protections. Remedial measures could include retraining, increased monitoring of the investigator's compliance, or individual disciplinary measures. On a broader level, the impact of noncompliance may result in reputational harm to the institution or researcher and erosion of public trust.

Compliance Resources

CMS Open Payments

Publicly accessible database with search tools to look up information on financial relationships between applicable manufacturers and GPOs and healthcare providers and teaching hospitals.

https://www.cms.gov/OpenPayments

FDA Guidance

"Financial Disclosure by Clinical Investigators: Guidance for Clinical Investigators, Industry, and FDA Staff," interpreting and complying with financial disclosure regulations 21 C.F.R. § 54.

https://www.fda.gov/regulatory-information/search-fda-guidance-documents/financial-disclosure-clinical-investigators

National Institutes of Health

Financial Conflict of Interest

The FCOI policy and compliance website provides comprehensive resources, including:

- Summary of the current regulation 42 C.F.R. § 50, subpart F
- Elements of an FCOI report
- Submitting an FCOI report
- Other resources, frequently asked questions, and checklists

https://grants.nih.gov/grants/policy/coi/index.htm

Protecting U.S. Biomedical Intellectual Innovation

This website regarding requirements for disclosure of other support, foreign relationships, and activities and conflicts of interest. Includes examples of what recipients must disclose to NIH about senior/key personnel on applications and awards and when to review for potential FCOI.

https://grants.nih.gov/policy/protecting-innovation.htm

National Science Foundation

Conflict of Interest Policies

Conflict of interest policies for National Science Foundation grantees can be found on this site.

https://www.nsf.gov/pubs/manuals/gpm05_131/gpm5.jsp#510

Office of Research Integrity

Conflicts of Interest and Commitment

This site contains responsible conduct of research resources, including training on conflict of interest and commitment in research.

https://ori.hhs.gov/conflicts-interest-and-commitment

Risk Takeaways

Main points of interest:

- FCOIs in clinical research are external, significant financial interests of the research investigator that reasonably appear related to their institutional responsibilities or of the institution that could directly and significantly affect and/or appear to affect the design, conduct, and or reporting of research.
- Due to more common interactions between academia and industry, FCOIs are important to detect and effectively manage in order to prevent bias from negatively or inappropriately affecting the design, conduct, or outcome of the research.
- Individual FCOIs should be evaluated in relation to other types of conflicts that may occur in clinical research.

Areas to watch:

- Lack of effective organizational oversight
- Not maintaining up-to-date policies or education and training
- Not identifying or managing FCOIs in a timely fashion
- Failure to fulfill federal reporting requirements
- Not managing risk of subrecipient FCOIs
- Inadequate compliance monitoring
- Not evaluating overall COI risk in relation to business and environmental changes

Laws that apply:

- PHS FCOI Regulations, 42 C.F.R. § 50 subpart F and 42 C.F.R. § 94
- FDA Financial Disclosure by Clinical Investigators, 21 C.F.R. § 54

Addressing compliance risks:

- Effective program oversight and implementation
  - Program and governance structure: Ensure programs are structured appropriately and include key elements.
  - Awareness and education: Complexities involving various COIs in the environment require ongoing education and training efforts.
- Centralized disclosure and review using technology: Use organization-wide technology to centrally capture and manage investigator disclosures.
- Effective FCOI management strategies: FCOIs should be reviewed by the designated official(s) and/or COI committee, and management plans should be developed if they cannot be reduced or eliminated.
- Compliance monitoring and handling of noncompliance: Institutions are required to establish adequate and appropriate enforcement mechanisms to ensure compliance.
- Evaluate and identify other risk areas: Review other COI risk areas that may affect regulatory compliance.

Endnotes

1. **Emmelyn Kim** is AVP of research compliance & privacy officer at Feinstein Institutes for Medical Research, Northwell Health. She has more than 20 years of experience in research and compliance and oversees the research compliance program throughout the organization, including conflicts of interest. This includes reviewing disclosures, managing conflicts of interest in research, and administering the individual and institutional conflict-of-interest committees in partnership with the Office of Corporate Compliance.

2. 42 C.F.R. § 50.603.

3. Bayh–Dole Act, Pub. L. No. 96-517, 94 Stat. 3015 (1980).

4. "Protecting U.S. Biomedical Intellectual Innovation," Policy & Compliance, National Institutes of Health, updated July 31, 2020, https://grants.nih.gov/policy/protecting-innovation.htm.

5. Francisco G. Cigarroa, Bettie Sue Masters, and Dan Sharphorn, "Institutional Conflicts of Interest and Public Trust," *JAMA* 320, no. 22, (2018), at 2305–2306, https://jamanetwork.com/journals/jama/article-abstract/2715796.

6. Responsibility of Applicants for Promoting Objectivity in Research for which Public Health Service Funding is Sought and Responsible Prospective Contractors, 76 Fed. Reg. 53,256 (August 25, 2011).

7. 42 C.F.R. § 50, subpart F.

8. 42 C.F.R. § 94.

9. 42 C.F.R. § 50.603.

10. 42 C.F.R. § 50.603.

11. 42 C.F.R. § 50.604.

12. "Chapter IV - Grantee Standards," National Science Foundation, updated February 2014, https://www.nsf.gov/pubs/policydocs/pappguide/nsf14001/aag_4.jsp#IVA.

13. 21 C.F.R. § 54.4(a)(3).

14. 42 C.F.R. § 403.

15. "Open Payments," Centers for Medicare & Medicaid Services, modified September 21, 2020, https://www.cms.gov/OpenPayments.

16. "Welcome to the Commons," National Institutes of Health, accessed November 25, 2020, https://public.era.nih.gov/commons/.

Human Research Protections

By Emmelyn Kim,[1] MA, MPH, MJ, CCRA, CHRC

What are Human Research Protections in Clinical Research?

Human Research Protections were founded on ethical principles that evolved over time as a result of past atrocities involving humans in research experiments. The Nuremberg Code and the World Medical Association's Declaration of Helsinki were developed after the World War II Nuremberg trials and established ethical codes such as explicit and voluntary consent from patients and guiding principles for physicians.[2,3] The *Belmont Report* was published in 1979 by the National Commission for the Protection of Human Subjects of Biomedical and Behavioral Research and described the basic ethical principles of respect for persons, beneficence, and justice.[4] These principles collectively provided a framework for research ethics that led to today's regulatory framework designed to protect human research participants.

Today, clinical research requires review by an institutional review board (IRB), which is a committee constituted by a group of individuals that ensures that any proposed research involving human subjects is ethical; adheres to established principles and rules; and has procedures in place to adequately protect the rights, safety, and welfare of humans participating in the research. Informed consent from participants is also a requirement under the regulatory framework. Clinical research is critical to contributing to scientific knowledge and advancing medicine. Over time, clinical research has become more fast-paced and complex as a result of advanced technology and expansion to multiple sites due to increased collaborative research efforts with industry and government agencies.

Healthcare institutions often participate in clinical research due to factors such as ties to research institutes and medical schools, provision of options for patients, and prestige. Institutions may participate in research that is funded internally, by the government, or industry. Externally funded research is governed by contracts and agreements that require adherence to various rules and regulations pertaining to human research protections and other areas of research conduct. Clinical researchers at healthcare institutions are required to navigate through a complex regulatory environment because research regulations add another layer on top of the already highly regulated healthcare environment. Therefore, depending on the complexity and extent of research, appropriate levels of monitoring and oversight of the research should be implemented to ensure compliance with regulations and adequate human subject protections during the research period.

Compliance risks for organizations depend on the nature and scale of the research, institutional oversight and culture, researcher qualifications and experience, populations involved, funding mechanisms, and legal and regulatory requirements that apply. Other factors that may affect human research protections, ethical conduct, or objectivity of the research include those related to academic pressures, researcher or institutional financial conflicts of interest, therapeutic misconception from research participants, community and cultural differences, and adequate resources to support and conduct the research. Thus, it is important to understand compliance risks more holistically when evaluating human research protections and consider both internal and external factors.

Risk Area Governance

Federal regulations that govern human research protections were promulgated by the Department of Health & Human Services (HHS) and apply to research conducted or supported by HHS.[5] The subparts of the regulation include:

A. The Common Rule;
B. Additional protections for pregnant women, human fetuses, and neonates;
C. Additional protections for prisoners; and
D. Additional protections for children.[6]

The Common Rule, which is the federal policy for human research protections that defines ethical standards in human subject research, was revised in 2017 with compliance dates of January 19, 2018, and January 20, 2020.[7]

The Office for Human Research Protections (OHRP) within the Office of the Secretary of HHS provides regulatory and compliance oversight and develops policies, guidance, and education for human subject protections. Institutions that are required to comply with federal regulations must promptly report to OHRP "(1) Any unanticipated problems involving risks to human subjects or others; (2) any . . . serious or continuing noncompliance with [the] regulations or the requirements or determinations of the IRB; or (3) any suspension or termination of IRB approval."[8] Institutions that receive HHS support for research involving human subjects must also have a Federalwide Assurance (FWA) or commitment to comply with federal regulations signed by an institutional official and designate an IRB that is registered with OHRP. Institutions may choose to apply Common Rule requirements to all research or just those that are federally funded.

Institutions that operate an IRB must ensure regulatory requirements are met and establish policies and procedures. This includes an appropriate IRB committee constitution and meeting IRB review and approval criteria under the Common Rule. IRB approval criteria include: ensuring that the risks to participants are minimized and reasonable in relation to anticipated benefits, an equitable selection of subjects, ensuring that informed consent is sought from the prospective participant or their legally authorized representative and documented, ensuring that adequate privacy protections are in place to maintain confidentiality of the data, and monitoring the data to ensure subject safety where appropriate. IRBs must also comply with Food and Drug Administration (FDA) regulations.

There are various FDA regulations that apply to clinical research that involves drugs, devices, and biologics. The following are FDA regulatory subparts that are more applicable to human research protections and IRBs:

- 21 C.F.R. § 50 (Informed consent)[9]
- 21 C.F.R. § 54 (Financial disclosure by clinical investigators)[10]
- 21 C.F.R. § 56 (IRBs)[11]
- 21 C.F.R. § 312 (Investigational new drug application)[12]
- 21 C.F.R. § 812 (Investigational device exemptions)[13]

FDA-regulated clinical trials must also adhere to good clinical practice (GCP), which is an "international ethical and scientific quality standard for designing, conducting, recording and reporting trials that involve the participation of human subjects."[14] GCP is a set of international standards that were developed by the International Council for Harmonisation of Technical Requirements for Pharmaceuticals for Human Use (ICH) to ensure that the rights, safety, and well-being of human participants in clinical trials are protected in accordance with ethical principles and the data is credible. There are a variety of ICH GCP guidance documents, and the most relevant one to healthcare institutions conducting clinical research is GCP ICH E6 (R2), which was amended to take into account the modern complexities of clinical research and use of electronic records.

Registration of "applicable clinical trials" on ClinicalTrials.gov, including summary results, is required per the FDA Amendments Act of 2007 and final rule.[15] Registration is required for National Institutes of Health (NIH)-funded clinical trials and posting of a consent form is required for any clinical trial conducted or supported by a Common Rule agency. These requirements are part of efforts to provide the public with greater transparency and access to information about clinical research.

Institutions supported by Public Health Service (PHS) funding must comply with other federal regulations. This includes research misconduct regulations that serve to promote the responsible conduct of research.[16] The Office of Research Integrity oversees PHS research integrity–related activities, and institutions are required to submit reports pertaining to research misconduct when certain criteria are met. Research misconduct is defined as "fabrication, falsification, or plagiarism in proposing, performing, or reviewing research, or in reporting research results," and any such allegations require prompt review by institutions.[17] Other PHS regulations govern financial conflict of interest (FCOI) and aim to promote objectivity in the design, conduct, and reporting of research.[18] See "Clinical Research: Financial Conflicts of Interest" in this chapter for more information about FCOI regulations.

Other federal regulations that pertain to protecting the privacy and security of information may apply to clinical research. The Health Insurance Portability and Accountability Act (HIPAA) Privacy and Security rules govern privacy and security of protected health information (PHI) for institutions that are considered covered entities.[19] Use and disclosure of PHI for research purposes by covered entities can occur through signed HIPAA authorizations (which may be combined with the research consent form) from research participants or waivers or alterations of HIPAA authorization granted by a privacy board or IRB. Covered entities must also implement appropriate administrative, physical, and technical safeguards to ensure the confidentiality, security, and integrity of electronic PHI. Research participant information may also be protected by researchers that have obtained a certificate of confidentiality (CoC) for research funded by HHS agencies (e.g., NIH) that serves to protect the privacy of research participants by prohibiting the disclosure of identifiable, sensitive research information.[20]

Institutions must be aware of any other applicable federal regulations, state and local laws, or funding agency policies that apply to clinical research activities. This will depend on the type of institution that is conducting the research, nature and type of research, funding source, and contract and agreement terms. Special attention should be paid to high-risk or early-phase trials evaluating safety or research involving vulnerable and critically ill populations. Also, international research will require broader evaluation of other human research and data protection rules and regulations specific to the local and cultural context of the locations and populations.

Common Compliance Risks

Lack of Effective Organizational Oversight

Organizations that conduct clinical research are responsible for complying with all applicable federal, state, and local requirements as well as contractual agreements, and therefore, must ensure effective oversight. Lack of knowledge regarding the clinical research portfolio (e.g., federally funded, sponsored by industry, investigator initiated), policies and procedures, or institutional-level infrastructure for oversight and monitoring will leave organizations vulnerable to compliance risks.

Not Maintaining Up-to-Date Policies or Education and Training

Up-to-date and accessible institutional policies and procedures should be available to researchers. Education and training should be ongoing and also updated to ensure that they contain relevant information and effectively address risk areas that may arise in the organizational environment. Research investigators should complete research training in accordance with institutional or funding agency requirements.

Investigator Noncompliance

This can occur due to a variety of reasons including lack of training, qualification, or experience, and not having standard operating procedures (SOPs) or adequate supervision of the research. Noncompliance, protocol deviations or violations can potentially affect the integrity of the research data or safety of the research participants.

Inadequate Protections for Research Participants

Protecting the rights, safety, and welfare of research participants are principal tenets of human research protections. Risks to this can occur if research is initiated without IRB review and approval or informed consent is not obtained appropriately from research participants. Risks pertaining to safety and welfare of research participants can occur if adverse events or unanticipated events that represent a risk to subjects or others are not assessed or reported to the IRB and other parties as required (e.g., sponsor, FDA).

Inadequate Protections of Privacy and Confidentiality

Breaches of research information can cause risks to research participant privacy and confidentiality of sensitive information.

Lack of Institutional IRB Compliance and Reporting

Organizations that operate their own IRB committee(s) and receive federal support for research must register their IRB with OHRP and comply with FWA requirements that include reporting serious and continuing noncompliance to OHRP. IRBs that review research involving FDA-regulated products require adherence to FDA regulations and reporting and are subject to routine FDA inspections.

Failure to Comply with FDA Rules

Clinical research involving FDA-regulated products requires adherence to FDA regulations. FDA rules apply to other uses of investigational products for treatment use under expanded access (including emergency use) or emergency use authorizations pathways. Clinical investigators that conduct clinical research involving FDA-regulated products are routinely inspected by the FDA.

Lack of Procedures to Handle Reports of Research Noncompliance

Organizations that do not have a process to handle and investigate such reports may open themselves up to risk. This is an important element of institutional oversight and institutions should have a process to investigate the allegation; if substantiated, ensure they follow any required reporting to federal agencies and institutional officials. Noncompliance or complaints from whistleblowers, research participants, or the public can be submitted to federal agencies such as OHRP that will then take necessary actions to investigate. Institutions will also need to take measures to investigate any allegations and may need to report back to the agency. PHS-supported institutions must have a program in place for reporting and investigating allegations of research misconduct.

Inadequate Compliance Monitoring

Ongoing institutional review of compliance with regulatory and institutional requirements is necessary to quickly identify issues that may affect human research protections, evaluate organizational risks, and inform education and training of researchers.

Addressing Compliance Risks

Establish Effective Oversight of Clinical Research

Institutions must establish comprehensive oversight for clinical research occurring at the organization, taking into consideration the complexity of the research, involvement of multiple sites or institutions, and use of external or central IRBs. Regulatory, funding, or sponsor requirements must be met, and the rights, safety, and welfare of research participants must be adequately protected. Attention should be paid to the evolution of the research portfolio and researchers over time as new risks may emerge. Considerations for effective institutional oversight include the following:

Institutional Human Research Protection Program Governance
Ensure programs are appropriately structured and include the following elements:

- Oversight by a centralized institutional program and administrator with a compliance oversight function that is supported by leadership and operates under organization-wide policies and procedures.

- If an institution has an internal IRB, the process for review and approval of human subject research is clear and supported by policies and procedures. Institutions that receive federal support for research must register their IRBs with OHRP and obtain an FWA.
- Ensuring that appropriate agreements are in place if using external or central IRBs and external investigators or facilities.
- Oversight programs should coordinate with multiple departments throughout the organization. The program can also evaluate any concerns; unanticipated problems; noncompliance issues; or concerns reported internally, from research participants, sponsors or funding agencies, private or government entities, or the public.

Institutional Review of Clinical Research

Reviews should be comprehensive to ensure any federal, state, and institutional requirements are met prior to and during the research. Considerations include:

- Establishing a review process that ensures, but is separate from, IRB review and approval. Other regulatory requirements and areas that may directly or indirectly affect human research protections should be reviewed prior to implementation. Examples of other areas include ClinicalTrials.gov registration, financial conflicts of interest disclosure and management, device or electronic system information technology security reviews, export controls, biosafety and radiation safety measures or risk assessments, grant or contracted related requirements, research billing or compensation-related reviews, and international research where other regulations and local rules apply or other areas.
- Ensuring that individuals involved in the research have the appropriate qualifications and level of experience and training.
- Allocating appropriate staff and resources to perform the work.
- Obtaining any necessary facility, ancillary department services (e.g., pharmacy or lab), and local community approvals.

Organizational Standards

Policies and procedures pertaining to clinical research should be easily accessible and available to researchers. They should be updated regularly and include regulatory, local, and institutional requirements. Information about clinical research requirements and reporting should also be included in the code of ethical conduct. Regular education regarding these standards can help enhance awareness and promote overall compliance.

Develop and Provide Ongoing Education and Training

Effective education and training are necessary to reduce the risk of research noncompliance. There should be ongoing education and training efforts on regulations, policies, and best practices, as well as new or emerging topics that are relevant to the clinical research community. An online learning management system can be used to disseminate and track training and education throughout the organization.

Provide Support for FDA-regulated Research or Activities

FDA-regulated activities can be complex and researchers and clinicians at healthcare organizations often require additional support to navigate regulatory requirements. Additional education and training may be necessary to ensure the research is conducted in accordance with FDA rules and GCP.

The following are compliance risk areas.

Investigational New Drug (IND) Applications and Investigational Device Exemptions (IDE): Certain clinical research studies for both marketed and experimental products may require an IND application or an IDE, preliminary evaluation and review of requirements, and monitoring to ensure compliance.

Sponsor-Investigators: Investigators that hold an IND application or an IDE are also considered sponsors and take on additional responsibilities. They will often need supplementary education and training to ensure they fulfill sponsor responsibilities such as monitoring, safety reporting, and other requirements.

Expanded Access/Compassionate Use and Emergency Use: Investigational (or non-FDA-approved) drugs, biologics, or devices used for treatment of a patient with a serious disease or condition outside of a clinical trial must meet certain criteria. FDA and IRB review and reporting at certain time points are required.

Safety Monitoring and Reporting: Documenting adverse events, reporting any considered serious, and ensuring adherence to the data and safety monitoring plans are key elements to ensuring safety of research participants.

FDA Inspections: The FDA's Bioresearch Monitoring Program (BIMO) conducts routine and for-cause inspections of clinical investigators and committees that review FDA-regulated research such as IRBs and Radioactive Drug Research Committees (RDRCs). Regular internal reviews should be done to ensure compliance with FDA regulations and prepare for external inspections. Any observations cited by the FDA will require appropriate corrective and preventive actions and an effective response strategy.

Implement a Compliance and Integrity Program

Institutional compliance oversight is necessary not only to ensure that organizational obligations are met and human research participants are adequately protected, but also to guard against more serious issues such as fraud and research misconduct. A comprehensive compliance program for human research protections should encompass the following:

Compliance Oversight: Establish an independent group that performs regular audits and reviews of ongoing clinical research to evaluate compliance of clinical research investigators and IRBs. The group should maintain an independent reporting structure and report to the highest levels of management. Regular risk assessments should be conducted and annual work plans developed that incorporate clinical research reviews.

Routine Compliance Reviews: Establish reviews that are conducted on a routine basis. Reviews can be risk-based to balance resources against research volume and can be comprehensive or focused on a particular area. This allows evaluation of investigator compliance with IRB approvals and reporting, the protocol, any conflict of interest management plans, obtaining informed consent from research participants, drug or device accountability, safety reporting, regulatory documentation, and any other applicable requirements. Higher-risk areas tend to be research:

- Conducted by new or inexperienced researchers
- Involving interventional procedures or products that have a higher risk profile
- In early phase or a complex study
- Of FDA-regulated products
- Involving sponsor-investigator IND/IDE trials
- Involving researchers with prior compliance issues
- Involving vulnerable or critically ill populations

Nonretaliatory Reporting: Allow multiple ways to report noncompliance concerns (even anonymously) through a phone or web-based hotline, supported by institutional nonretaliation policies to ensure an open and safe environment.

Noncompliance Investigations and Reporting: Allegations of noncompliance, research misconduct, or complaints from clinical research participants must be investigated promptly and handled in accordance with institutional policies and applicable federal or state rules. Required reporting should be made within the time period based on any federal assurances and grant or contract requirements.

Organizational Communication: Serious or continuing noncompliance and research misconduct will require communication with other departments, such as legal affairs, human resources, risk management, or other groups. Institutional officials, research integrity officers, management, executive leadership, and the board should be appropriately informed of any issues.

Manage Privacy and Security

Healthcare organizations, which are considered covered entities, must pay attention to HIPAA rules and ensure privacy protections, security requirements, and breach reporting are met. International research requires special attention to local privacy and data protections requirements. This requires coordination with privacy boards, privacy officers, and chief information security officers at an organizational level. Clinical research should be incorporated into larger organizational privacy and security risk assessments, policies and procedures, and breach management and reporting.

The following are areas to pay attention to:

Privacy Boards for Research: Ensure one is appointed (which can be the IRB) that issues waivers or alterations of HIPAA authorization requirements where appropriate.

Agreements: Appropriate agreements for covered entities should be in place when researchers propose use of certain data sets containing PHI, such as data use agreements, and when working with business associates that provide services that involve creating, receiving, maintaining, or transmitting PHI. This ensures that certain safeguards are in place when handling PHI.

Security of Research Information: Ensure that the appropriate controls and systems are in place to secure research data and ensure confidentiality of the information. This includes controlling access to research information, providing HIPAA-compliant tools and platforms for researchers to use, and ensuring appropriate security controls for research charts and devices where research participant information is stored. This can become more complex with increased use of mobile devices, cloud-based storage, and database applications.

Handling and Reporting Privacy and Security Breaches: Incidents must be investigated promptly and reported in accordance with federal and local requirements. Breaches will require notification to the affected research participants, IRB, institutional officials, the Office for Civil Rights, and any other federal or state agencies.

Possible Penalties

Noncompliance with human research protection requirements by investigators may result in suspension or termination of the research by the reviewing IRB, special conditions imposed by the funding agency or sponsor, citations, or debarment by federal agencies. For example, the FDA will issue an observation or warning letter as a result of an inspection, and for more egregious cases will initiate clinical investigator disqualification proceedings. Depending on the severity, this may mean that they are not eligible to conduct FDA-regulated research, engage in product development activities, or may be restricted from receiving investigational products. PHS will take administrative actions against individuals found to have engaged in research misconduct, including debarment from eligibility to receive federal funding, prohibition from service on PHS advisory committees and grant review panels, supervision by the institution, submission of corrections or retraction of published articles, and other actions.

More serious noncompliance that is fraudulent in nature may result in fines and penalties. Violation of the False Claims Act (which qui tam or whistleblower lawsuits are often brought under) can result in civil and sometimes criminal liability for individuals and institutions. This can also lead to reputational harm for the institution or researcher and loss of public trust. Serious or systemic issues at organizations with an FWA could also lead to a halt of all research (or those that are federally funded) occurring at an institution.

Institutional-level sanctions may include limiting an investigator's ability to conduct research at the organization. The type of sanctions will depend on the seriousness and severity of the noncompliance, taking into account the reasons for noncompliance, whether it is continuing noncompliance, and the impact to research integrity and research participants. Remedial measures can include retraining, increased monitoring of the investigator's research, or disciplinary measures on the individual level.

Compliance Resources

FDA Clinical Trials and Human Subject Protection

The following guidance and resources for clinical trials include the following.

Regulations: Good Clinical Practice and Clinical Trials

https://www.fda.gov/science-research/clinical-trials-and-human-subject-protection/
regulations-good-clinical-practice-and-clinical-trials

Good Clinical Practice Education Materials

https://www.fda.gov/science-research/clinical-trials-and-human-subject-protection/
good-clinical-practice-educational-materials

Industry Notices and Guidance Documents

https://www.fda.gov/industry/industry-notices-and-guidance-documents

Clinical Investigations Compliance & Enforcement

https://www.fda.gov/science-research/clinical-trials-and-human-subject-protection/
clinical-investigations-compliance-enforcement

BIMO Inspection Metrics

- ClinicalTrials.gov information
  https://clinicaltrials.gov

- Clinical Trials and Human Subject Protection
  https://www.fda.gov/science-research/science-and-research-special-topics/
  clinical-trials-and-human-subject-protection

- Expanded Access
  https://www.fda.gov/news-events/public-health-focus/expanded-access

- BIMO Compliance Programs and Guidance Manuals used by FDA inspectors https://www.fda.gov/inspections-compliance-enforcement-and-criminal-investigations/compliance-program-guidance-manual-cpgm/bioresearch-monitoring-program-bimo-compliance-programs

- *E6(R2) Good Clinical Practice: Integrated Addendum to ICH E6(R1)* https://www.fda.gov/regulatory-information/search-fda-guidance-documents/e6r2-good-clinical-practice-integrated-addendum-ich-e6r1

Office for Civil Rights

HIPAA Privacy Rule and Research Resources

https://www.hhs.gov/hipaa/for-professionals/special-topics/research/index.html

Office for Human Research Protections

Human research protection resources, including:

- Regulations, policy, and guidance
- Compliance and reporting
- The Secretary's Advisory Committee on Human Research Protections
- International research
- Final rule revising the Common Rule

https://www.hhs.gov/ohrp/

Office of Research Integrity

Human Subject Research
Responsible conduct of research resources are available on this site, including training on human subject research.

https://ori.hhs.gov/human-subject-research

Risk Takeaways

Main points of interest:
- Clinical research requires review by an IRB that ensures that the proposed human subject research is ethical, adheres to established principles and rules, and has procedures in place to adequately protect the rights, safety, and welfare of humans participating in the research. This includes informed consent from participants.
- Healthcare institutions often participate in clinical research. Therefore, appropriate levels of monitoring and oversight of the research should be implemented to ensure compliance with regulations and adequate human subject protections during the period of the research.
- Compliance risks depend on the nature and scale of the research, institutional oversight and culture, researcher qualifications and experience, populations involved, funding mechanisms, and legal and regulatory requirements. Therefore, it is important to understand the risks holistically.

Areas to watch:
- Lack of effective organizational oversight
- Not maintaining up-to-date policies or education and training
- Investigator noncompliance
- Inadequate protections for research participants
- Inadequate protections of privacy and confidentiality
- Lack of institutional IRB compliance and reporting
- Failure to comply with FDA rules
- Lack of procedures to handle reports of noncompliance
- Inadequate compliance monitoring

Laws that apply:
- 45 C.F.R. § 46 (OHRP Common Rule)
- 21 C.F.R. § 50 (Informed consent)
- 21 C.F.R. § 54 (Financial disclosure by clinical investigators)
- 21 C.F.R. § 56 (FDA regulation for IRBs)
- 21 C.F.R. § 312 (FDA regulation for investigational new drugs)
- 21 C.F.R. § 812 (FDA regulation for investigational device exemptions)
- 42 C.F.R. § 11 (Final rule for clinical trials registration and results information submission)
- 42 C.F.R. § 93 (Research misconduct regulations)
- 42 C.F.R § 50, Subpart F, and 42 C.F.R. § 94 (PHS FCOI regulations)
- 45 C.F.R. §§ 160, 164 (HIPAA privacy and security)
- 42 U.S.C. §241(d)

Addressing compliance risks:
- Establish effective oversight of clinical research, including:
  - Institutional Human Research Protection Program governance
  - Institutional review of clinical research
  - Organizational standards
- Develop and provide ongoing education and training to reduce risk of research compliance.
- Provide support for FDA-regulated research or activities, including:
  - Investigational new drug applications (INDs) and investigational device exemptions (IDEs)
  - Sponsor-investigators
  - Expanded access/compassionate use and emergency use
  - Safety monitoring and reporting
  - FDA inspections
- Implement a compliance and integrity program, including:
  - Compliance oversight
  - Routine compliance reviews
  - Nonretaliatory reporting
  - Noncompliance investigations and reporting
  - Organizational communication
- Manage privacy and security, including:
  - Privacy boards for research
  - Agreements
  - Security of research information
  - Handling and reporting privacy and security breaches

Endnotes

1. **Emmelyn Kim** is AVP, Research Compliance & Privacy Officer at Feinstein Institutes for Medical Research, Northwell Health. She has more than 20 years of experience in research and compliance and oversees the research compliance program throughout the organization, including conflict of interest. This includes review of disclosures, management of conflicts of interest in research, and administering the individual and institutional conflict-of-interest committees in partnership with the Office of Corporate Compliance.

2. "WMA Declaration of Helsinki – Principles for Medical Research Involving Human Subjects", World Medical Association, accessed November 9, 2020, https://www.wma.net/policies-post/wma-declaration-of-helsinki-ethical-principles-for-medical-research-involving-human-subjects/.

3. "The Nuremburg Code", National Institutes of Health, Office of NIH History & Stetten Museum, accessed November 9, 2020, https://history.nih.gov/display/history/Nuremburg+Code.

4. "The Belmont Report," Office for Human Research Protections, U.S. Department of Health & Human Services, updated March 15, 2016, https://www.hhs.gov/ohrp/regulations-and-policy/belmont-report/index.html.

5. 45 C.F.R. § 46.

6. 45 C.F.R. § 46.

7. Federal Policy for the Protection of Human Subjects, 82 Fed. Reg. 7,149 (January 19, 2017).

8. 21 C.F.R. § 56.108(b).

9. 21 C.F.R. § 50.

10. 21 C.F.R. § 54.

11. 21 C.F.R. § 56.

12. 21 C.F.R. § 312.

13. 21 C.F.R. § 812.

14. U.S. Department of Health & Human Services, Food and Drug Administration, *E6(R2) Good Clinical Practice: Integrated Addendum to ICH E6(R1), Guidance for Industry*, March 2018, https://www.fda.gov/media/93884/download.

15. 42 C.F.R. § 11.

16. 42 C.F.R. § 93.103.

17. 42 C.F.R. § 93.103.

18. 42 C.F.R. § 50, Subpart F; 42 C.F.R. § 94.

19. 45 C.F.R. §§ 160, 164.102, 164.302, 164.500.

20. 42 U.S.C. §241(d).

Medicare Clinical Trial Policy

By Kelly M. Willenberg,[1] DBA, RN, CHRC, CHC, CCRP

What Is the Medicare Clinical Trial Policy?

Clinical trial billing is one of the highest priorities for research sites that are doing therapeutic trials. This process is defined as a review of all documentation to create a coverage analysis to validate what can be billed out to commercial and government payers on a claim. It includes the coverage analysis with a convergence of documentation within the budget, contract, and consent. After a patient is identified as one who has consented to a particular study, tracking that patient throughout the life cycle of the study to ensure proper billing within the clinical trial policy and rules is best practice.

The clinical trial policy was enacted by President Bill Clinton in October 2000 to enable seniors to have more opportunity to participate in clinical trials.[2] Information gained from important clinical trials is used to inform coverage decisions, so Medicare was instructed to revise rules to expand benefits for qualifying clinical trials.

The types of trials that are of highest importance for compliance are the investigational device exemption (IDE); drug; and coverage with evidence development (CED) studies. The role of the Medicare's National Coverage Determination (NCD) and how it affects a site varies among different institutions. Because of the variety of tasks and responsibilities related to the clinical trial billing process, institutions often need several specialized individuals to maintain all aspects of compliance in billing Medicare and other types of health insurance. Establishing a billing compliance program takes not only expertise in the Centers for

Medicare & Medicaid Services' (CMS) National Coverage Determination for Routine Costs in Clinical Trials (NCD 310.1), but also a significant commitment.[3] Finding expertise in this area can be extremely difficult. The breadth of employees who are involved in the process reach across an institution or site. It will include a principal investigator and research team, the finance staff, and coding department.

Formulations of how this work is performed at each site are based on the electronic medical record, physician–investigator relationship to the site and practice group ownership, a clinical trials management system, the institutional review board's views on identifying costs to patients, and the varying risk profile of the research portfolio. Staff must dedicate significant focus to billing compliance: by not having a solid program, a site can have true risks. By not having an effective program fully implemented, those risk increase. The roles and responsibilities defined by the U.S. Department of Justice Criminal Division's *Evaluation of Corporate Compliance Programs* in June 2020 should be configured by solid policies, procedures, and defined responsibilities of the compliance team.[4]

NCD 310.1 is an established policy that even after 20 years can be difficult to absorb. In order to cover conventional care, and the expanded benefits to monitor and prevent toxicities, one must understand the type of trial that is being done. Sites must designate who will perform the qualifying status and billing nature of the tests and procedures on the schedule of events in a clinical trial protocol. It takes careful review to ensure that all of the items eligible for billing Medicare and commercial insurance are correct and validated. This tedious process is called a coverage analysis. Within the study calendar, the items must be itemized as they will show up on a claim for justification of billing. Reviewing published evidence-based guidelines provides direction on the billing process before the study starts and helps ensure compliant billing once patients are enrolled.

The risk of not providing a coverage analysis and review can lead to liability under the False Claims Act.[5] These risks were brought to national attention when Rush University Medical Center entered into a million-dollar settlement agreement with the Department of Justice in 2005 for clinical trial billing errors in cancer research. This included overpayments related solely to the NCD 310.1. Rush's settlement with the federal government was the first to focus on a clinical trial policy.[6] The potential for noncompliant billing in clinical research became noticeable for sites across the country after the Rush settlement. Many sites began conducting more intense evaluations of qualifying status and determining routine costs. The risks of vague budgets without coverage analysis guidance became more evident as auditing moved forward. The coverage analysis became a powerful, necessary tool. Recognizing the application of NCD 310.1 to research studies as a priority in the study start-up process has become increasingly more important throughout the last 20 years.

Risk Area Governance

False Claims Act (31 U.S.C. §§ 3729–3733)

To mitigate the risk of billing errors, sites need to be aware of the laws that govern clinical trial billing and the False Claims Act. The False Claims Act basically states that if an individual or group knowingly submits a false claim for payment of government funds, they are liable for up to three times the government's damages plus civil penalties. Although the False Claims Act uses the term "knowingly," proof of specific intent to defraud is not required.[7] A coverage analysis is the source of truth for billing to all payers and will help in mitigating billing issues if errors occur.

Centers for Medicare & Medicaid Services

- Centers for Medicare & Medicaid Services, "National Coverage Determination (NCD) for Routine Costs in Clinical Trials (310.1)," transmittal, July 2007
- Centers for Medicare & Medicaid Services, "Clarification of Medicare Payment for Routine Costs in a Clinical Trial," *MLN Matters*, SE0822 Revised, May 16, 2018
- Centers for Medicare & Medicaid Services, "Chapter 15: Covered Medical and Other Health Services," *Medicare Benefit Policy Manual*, Pub. 100-02, revised July 12, 2019
- Centers for Medicare & Medicaid Services, "Chapter 14: Medical Devices," *Medicare Benefit Policy Manual*, Pub. 100-02, revised November 6, 2014
- Centers for Medicare & Medicaid Services, "Chapter 32: Billing Requirements for Special Services," *Medicare Claims Processing Manual*, Pub. 100-04, revised July 21, 2020

The clinical trial policy, or NCD 310.1, is the indication of the terms and conditions for coverage. Effective for items and services furnished on or after July 9, 2007, Medicare covers the routine costs of qualifying clinical trials, which are defined in NCD 310.1, as well as reasonable and necessary items and services (such as a physical exam on day one of a treatment cycle for a patient with cancer, or a glucose lab for a patient with diabetes) used to diagnose and treat complications arising from participation in all clinical trials. It is important to remember that all other Medicare rules apply and that NCD 310.1 does not stand alone among Medicare rules. CMS has many billing guidance documents that guide billing for IDE, drug, and CED trials. The coverage requirements for routine costs of qualifying clinical trial services and how to submit claims lie within the various manuals.

Medical Services Coverage Decisions That Relate to Healthcare Technology

42 C.F.R. §§ 405.201–405.215, 411.15, and 411.406 (for device trials)

Device trial coverage rules lie within the Code of Federal Regulations in 42 C.F.R. §§ 405.201–405.215, 411.15, and 411.406 and are partially dependent upon action by the Food and Drug Administration (FDA).[8] The FDA provides the category status for devices under an IDE of either a Category A (experimental) or Category B (nonexperimental/investigational) study. Understanding the FDA categorization of an IDE device is necessary to know how to bill not only the investigational device, but also the likelihood of CMS approval of the study for billing. CMS must approve billing for an IDE study, which is notated on the approved IDE trial website ClinicalTrials.gov, which is maintained by CMS.[9]

Common Compliance Risks

Billing for an Item or Service that a Sponsor or Grant Has Paid for or Funded

If a sponsor provides a payment in a budget for a service, you cannot submit that item or service on a claim or you may have double billed.

Billing for an Item that is Being Performed for Research Only

Validating all research-related items or services that do not meet the guidelines and identifying them as paid by the sponsor or as a patient liability is important to ensure that you do not bill inappropriately or violate the False Claims Act.

Billing for an Item or Service that is Promised "Free" in the Informed Consent Form

Billing for an item or service that has been identified to a patient in a consent form as "free" or "at no cost" must be provided and not charged to their payer or you may violate the False Claims Act.

Billing Medicare Advantage Plans For an Item or Service that Should Be Billed to and Paid for by the Medicare Administrative Contractor

Medicare has rules surrounding billing drug trials to regular Medicare, while Medicare Advantage plans should cover IDE approved studies. Knowing the particular payer is recommended.

Unknowing Stakeholders Who Can Displace the Process by Not Following Billing Rules in Ordering and Documentation in the Medical Record

The removal of codes, modifiers, national clinical trial number, or an IDE number is sometimes found when coding teams are not provided adequate information on clinical trial billing and coverage analysis.

Allowing Principal Investigators to Assert Standard of Care Services as the Same as Routine Costs in a Qualifying Trial and Not Validating the Billing Status of Protocol Events with a Coverage Analysis

"Standard of care" is not a term that Medicare uses. It covers routine costs in a qualifying trial and items and services that are medically necessary to diagnose or treat illness or injury.

Not Knowing All of the Study Portfolio Occurring and Not Managing All Study-related Activity from a Billing Compliance Perspective

The possibility that research is ongoing in a facility can lead to unknown claims being submitted without the rigorous review against the coverage analysis. This can lead to improper billing to all payers.

Addressing Compliance Risks

Billing for an Item or Service that a Sponsor or Grant has Paid for or Funded

Perform a coverage analysis and ensure that the budget and contract are consistent with it. Then, once a service is performed, ensure that the charges are segregated appropriately against the coverage analysis.

Billing for an Item that is Being Performed for Research Only

Identify services by reviewing the protocol for all items and services being done within the trial that are research driven while removing them from the claim consistent with the coverage analysis.

Billing for an Item or Service that is Promised "Free" in the Informed Consent Form

Understand the "Expected Cost" section of the consent when the patient is consented. Confirm that anything promised at no cost is not submitted on a claim or sent to a patient for payment.

Billing Medicare Advantage Plans for an Item or Service that Should Be Billed to and Paid for by Medicare Fee-For-Service

Recognize a clinical trial patient's payer. If the patient is enrolled in a Medicare Advantage plan, ensure that the routine costs of the clinical trial services are diverted to the site's regular Medicare administrative contractor for payment when they are participating in a drug clinical trial. Bill any remaining amount after Medicare pays to the Medicare Advantage plan to make the patient "whole."[10]

Unknowing Stakeholders Who Can Displace the Process by Not Following Billing Rules in Ordering and Documentation in the Medical Record

Conduct compliance training on the clinical trial billing process. Training is the only method for ensuring that all stakeholders are aware of the clinical trial billing process. From the principal investigator to the coder who releases a claim, all must understand and appreciate the correct billing process, which helps avoid errors in an intended workflow.

Allowing Principal Investigators to Assert Standard of Care Services as the Same as Routine Costs in a Qualifying Trial and Not Validating the Protocol with a Coverage Analysis

Principal investigators should be a part of the billing process. They should provide input and approve the coverage analysis as a commitment to bill all subjects consistently. By permitting them to just provide what they feel is standard of care does not guarantee that what they order is billable within the guidelines or coverage decisions. The only sure method to validate the items in a study is to do a thorough coverage analysis. Inappropriately billing Medicare for items or services in a clinical trial that are ineligible for coverage might constitute a false claim if the claim should not have been submitted in the first place.

Not Knowing All of the Study Portfolio Occurring and Not Managing All Study-related Activity from a Billing Compliance Perspective

Have a complete itemized list of ongoing studies at the site. If a site does not have a complete itemized list of the studies ongoing at a site, then it does not have the capability to safeguard all claims to be placed in a "hold" status or a work queue for the appropriate codes and modifiers to be added. This also warrants that the proper payer is billed for each encounter.

Possible Penalties

The potential penalties for noncompliance with the Medicare clinical trial policy can be significant.

National Coverage Determination (NCD) for Routine Costs in Clinical Trials (310.1)

If a site does not follow the NCD 310.1, errors in billing to Medicare can occur, which may violate the False Claims Act. Those items include:

- Billing for the investigational item or service itself if it is not covered outside the study;
- Items and services provided solely to satisfy data collection;
- Items and services that are not used in the direct clinical management of the patient (e.g., monthly CT scans for a condition usually requiring only a single scan every six months); and,
- Items and services customarily provided by the research sponsors free-of-charge for any enrollee in the trial.[11]

While there is no single correct way to develop process compliance controls to meet federal clinical trials billing regulations around Medicare, standardization of the entire billing process is key. Establishing standards around a comprehensive clinical trial billing compliance program will help mitigate billing non-compliance risks. The risks of not complying with federal clinical trial billing regulations can lead to research suspension, fines, and/or the imposition of corporate integrity agreements.[12]

False Claims Act

The False Claims Act prohibits filing or causing the filing of false claims or creating a false record to get a claim paid.[13] The core of a false claims case is that the government was cheated in one form or another—hence the false claim. This is typically due to double-billing or improper billing in a clinical research study.

The benefits of self-disclosure (e.g., a speedy resolution, lower multiplier, and an exclusion release without integrity agreement obligations) depend on the disclosing party's willingness to work cooperatively with the Office of the Inspector General (OIG) throughout the process.[14] Depending on the facts, OIG "believe[s] that individuals or entities that use the SDP [self-disclosure protocol] and cooperate with OIG during the SDP process deserve to pay a lower multiplier on single damages." OIG will attempt to process the issue faster due to streamlined processes and turnaround times.[15]

The False Claims Act is a punitive statute enforced by the Department of Justice and qui tam relators. For civil violations, its penalties provision authorizes fines of three times the amount the government paid for each false claim, plus an additional penalty of up to $11,000 per false claim.[16]

Compliance Resources

Centers for Medicare & Medicaid Services

Clarification of Medicare Payment for Routine Costs in a Clinical Trial, MLN Matters, SE0822

This CMS bulletin provides clarification on Medicare payment of routine costs associated with clinical trials.

https://www.cms.gov/Outreach-and-Education/Medicare-Learning-Network-MLN/MLNMattersArticles/downloads/se0822.pdf

Medicare Benefit Policy Manual
- **Chapter 15: Covered Medical and Other Health Services, Section 50: Drugs and Biologicals**
  https://www.cms.gov/Regulations-and-Guidance/Guidance/Manuals/downloads/bp102c15.pdf
- **Chapter 14: Medical Devices**
  https://www.cms.gov/regulations-and-guidance/guidance/manuals/downloads/bp102c14.pdf

Medicare Claims Processing Manual
Chapter 32: Billing Requirements for Special Services

https://www.cms.gov/Regulations-and-Guidance/Guidance/Manuals/downloads/clm104c32.pdf

Medicare Clinical Trial Policies
This site provides information about the development of the policy and provides useful links related to the policy.

https://www.cms.gov/Medicare/Coverage/ClinicalTrialPolicies/index

National Coverage Determination (NCD) for Routine Costs in Clinical Trials (310.1)

https://www.cms.gov/medicare-coverage-database/details/ncd-details.aspx?NCDId=1

Health Care Compliance Association

Research Compliance Professional's Handbook, 3rd Edition
This book is a practical guide to building and maintaining a clinical research compliance and ethics program.

https://www.hcca-info.org/store/books/RESEARCHPROF_3

Risk Takeaways

Main points of interest:

- A lack of a billing compliance program can lead to noncompliance.
- Establish policies and procedures that include coverage analysis, document concordance, and a back-end bill hold and review on all clinical trial claims to ensure a solid billing compliance review.

Areas to watch:

- Double billing, misbilling, or underbilling of claims.
- Medicare Advantage errors.
- Document nonconcordance that leads to inconstancy in claims processing.
- Physician/professional fees that do not match up with hospital/facility billing.
- Recognizing all ongoing studies and performing an ongoing audit.
- Know the payer mix and required rules for each.
- Conditional payment clauses that put a site into jeopardy in billing.

Laws that apply:

- The False Claims Act, 31 U.S.C. §§ 3729–3733
- National Coverage Determination (NCD) for Routine Costs in Clinical Trials (310.1) (July 2007)
- "Clarification of Medicare Payment for Routine Costs in a Clinical Trial," *MLN Matters*, SE0822 Revised, May 16, 2018
- *Medicare Benefit Policy Manual*
  - Chapter 15: Covered Medical and Other Health Services, Section 50
  - Chapter 14: Medical Devices
- *Medicare Claims Processing Manual*, Chapter 32: Billing Requirements for Special Services
- 42 C.F.R. §§ 405.201–405.215, 411.15, and 411.406 (for device trials)
- 42 U.S.C. § 1395y(a)(2)
- 42 U.S.C. § 1395y(b)(7),(8) and CMS Alert: Clinical Trials & Liability Insurance

Addressing compliance risks:

- In order to preserve claims processing to all payers, a site must understand that all payers do not have the same specific rules on what is covered or not covered in a clinical research study.
- As Medicare is the largest payer, the framework surrounding the structure outlined in the clinical trial policy is the obvious instruction taught by experts. With the risks associated with noncompliant billing, sites must realize that this part of compliance is of highest priority.
  - There is a high probability of error for double billing when a sponsor covers the cost of an item of service in a budget and contract if there is no adequate collaboration between the research office and the billing office to identify the service.
  - Meeting the challenges with compromise will lead to better compliance in billing within the clinical trial policy.[17] Appreciating the importance of the consent, budget, contract, and coverage analysis being in sync from a language perspective becomes urgent when they differ.
  - One must be prepared to act when something does not coincide in language or a billing error may occur imminently.
  - Training is crucial for staff to know the rules so they are grounded in the context of the billing compliance process.
  - When the claims processing team flawlessly submits claims to Medicare Advantage when a patient is enrolled in a drug clinical trial but they are not aware of the enrollment, it is no small matter. One has to consider future cost when claims must be reversed and repayment to payers is required.
  - Administrators, research staff, and principal investigators must know drug and device rules for billing compliance. Vigilant attention will bring about consistencies that will prevent billing errors and keep the clinical trial policy as a priority for the entire operation.

Endnotes

1. **Kelly Willenberg** is the CEO & Manager of Kelly Willenberg & Associates. She has more than 25 years of clinical trial billing compliance experience. She is an oncology nurse, Certified in Healthcare Research Compliance (CHRC), a faculty member of the HCCA Research Compliance Academies, and a member of the Board of Directors of HCCA. She works with sites across the country to perform coverage analysis and follow the Medicare rules around billing compliance.

2. Angelica P. Herrera et al., "Disparate Inclusion of Older Adults in Clinical Trials: Priorities and Opportunities for Policy and Practice Change," Supplement, *American Journal of Public Health* 100, no 1 (April 2010), S105–S112, https://www.ncbi.nlm.nih.gov/pmc/articles/PMC2837461/#:~:text=In%202000%2C%20an%20executive%20mandate,38%25%20between%201993%20and%202003.

3. Centers for Medicare & Medicaid Services, "National Coverage Determination (NCD) for Routine Costs in Clinical Trials (310.1)," transmittal, July 2007, https://www.cms.gov/medicare-coverage-database/details/ncd-details.aspx?NCDId=1.

4. Elliott C. Kulakowski and Lynne U. Chronister, *Research administration and management* (Sudbury, MA: Jones and Bartlett Publishers, 2006), 466.

5. 31 U.S.C. §§ 3729–3733.

6. Cynthia E. Boyd and Ryan D. Meade, "Clinical trial billing compliance at academic medical centers," *Academic Medicine* 82, no. 7 (July 2007), 646–653, https://pubmed.ncbi.nlm.nih.gov/17595559/.

7. 31 U.S.C. § 3729(b)(1)(B).

8. "Approved IDE Studies," Centers for Medicare & Medicaid Services, last updated August 4, 2015, https://www.cms.gov/Medicare/Coverage/IDE/Approved-IDE-Studies.

9. "Home," ClinicalTrials.gov, United States National Library of Medicine, National Institutes of Health, last accessed December 22, 2020, https://clinicaltrials.gov/.

10. Centers for Medicare & Medicaid Services, "Chapter 32 – Billing Requirements for Special Services," Medicare Claims Processing Manual, Pub. 100-04, revised July 21, 2020, https://www.cms.gov/Regulations-and-Guidance/Guidance/Manuals/downloads/clm104c32.pdf.

11. Centers for Medicare & Medicaid Services, "National Coverage Determination (NCD) for Routine Costs in Clinical Trials (310.1)."

12. Jim Moran, Erika Stevens, and Julie Statzel, "Medicare and the NCD," *Applied Clinical Trials* 22, no. 2 (February 2013), 12, https://www.appliedclinicaltrialsonline.com/view/medicare-and-ncd.

13. "A Roadmap for New Physicians: Fraud & Abuse Laws," Office of Inspector General, U.S. Department of Health & Human Services, last accessed December 22, 2020, https://oig.hhs.gov/compliance/physician-education/01laws.asp.

14. U.S. Department of Health & Human Services, Office of Inspector General, "OIG's Provider Self-Disclosure Protocol," April 17, 2013, https://oig.hhs.gov/compliance/self-disclosure-info/files/Provider-Self-Disclosure-Protocol.pdf.

15. 42 U.S.C. § 1320a–7k(d).

16. "A Roadmap for New Physicians: Fraud & Abuse Laws," Office of Inspector General, U.S. Department of Health & Human Services.

17. R. Meade, K. Willenberg, "The 3 Cs of Research Billing Compliance: Collaboration, Challenges, and Compromise," *Journal of Healthcare Compliance* 12, no. 2 (January–February 2010), 17.

Research Misconduct

By Lynn E. Smith,[1] JD, CHRC

What Is Research Misconduct in Clinical Research?

Research misconduct (sometimes called scientific misconduct) is one of several behaviors related to research activities that are generally considered to be unethical or dishonest. Most people learn early in life that these behaviors are unacceptable. Nevertheless, rules exist to draw a distinct line separating allowable research behavior from research misconduct.

Research misconduct is limited to the following three behaviors: (1) fabrication, (2) falsification, and (3) plagiarism. There are many other unethical or incorrect behaviors that a researcher may engage in, such as noncompliance with research protocols or failing to disclose a significant financial interest with a research sponsor. These and many other fraudulent behaviors, however, are dealt with through other regulatory or administrative mechanisms. The following is a closer look at the three specific behaviors of research misconduct.

Fabrication is making up data or results and, subsequently, recording or reporting them. Fabrication is perhaps the most serious form of research misconduct because it is outright deception—the results are conjured up from the deceiver's imagination. It is science fiction posing as fact because the empirical work from which results have been reported either (1) was never conducted or (2) bore out results that were contrary to and replaced by those reported.

Falsification is manipulating research materials, equipment, or processes, or changing or omitting data or results such that the research is not accurately represented in the research record. Falsification is similar to fabrication inasmuch as it is a form of deliberate deception, but different in its magnitude and often its subtlety. For example, a study that yields merely promising results can be made to look like a major breakthrough by selectively removing data points that are not consistent with the desired outcome—an act of falsification.

Plagiarism is the appropriation of another person's ideas, processes, results, or words without giving appropriate credit. Plagiarism differs from fabrication or falsification in that results or reports may be entirely accurate and true, except for the matter of who actually did the work. Plagiarism is a deception and more; the plagiarist commits a form of theft by taking credit for the work of others.[2]

There are any number of reasons why research misconduct might occur, but some of the most common motivators are pressure to publish or the desire for professional recognition or money. Another reason for misconduct may come from failures at the site level, such as lack of resources, staff turnover, lack of training, or absence of policies and procedures that should be in place to protect both the institution and the researchers.

It is important to remember that research misconduct is narrowly defined. It does not include honest differences of opinion among scientists, inadvertent errors, or disputes about the order of appearance in a list of authors' names. Likewise, the use of sloppy research techniques or suboptimal record keeping, even the republishing of an author's original or collaborative work (so-called "self-plagiarism"), are not considered instances of research misconduct. These activities, however, do represent inappropriate and sometimes unethical behavior, and institutions may choose to develop policies or procedures that address these behaviors, although they are not under the purview of the federal Office of Research Integrity (ORI).[3]

The ORI oversees and directs research integrity activities of the U.S. Public Health Service (PHS) on behalf of the Secretary of the U.S. Department of Health & Human Services (HHS), with the one exception: the regulatory research integrity activities of the U.S. Food and Drug Administration (FDA). Organizationally, the ORI is located within the Office of the Assistant Secretary for Health (OASH), which is in Office of the Secretary of Health and Human Services (OS) in HHS.[4] According to its website,

> ORI carries out its responsibilities by:
>
> - developing policies, procedures and regulations related to the detection, investigation, and prevention of research misconduct and the responsible conduct of research;
> - reviewing and monitoring research misconduct investigations conducted by applicant and awardee institutions, intramural research programs, and the Office of Inspector General in the Department of Health and Human Services (HHS);
> - recommending research misconduct findings and administrative actions to the Assistant Secretary for Health for decision, subject to appeal;
> - assisting the Office of the General Counsel (OGC) to present cases before the HHS Departmental Appeals Board;
> - providing technical assistance to institutions that respond to allegations of research misconduct;

- implementing activities and programs to teach the responsible conduct of research, promote research integrity, prevent research misconduct, and improve the handling of allegations of research misconduct;
- conducting policy analyses, evaluations and research to build the knowledge base in research misconduct, research integrity, and prevention and to improve HHS research integrity policies and procedures;
- administering programs for: maintaining institutional assurances, responding to allegations of retaliation against whistleblowers, approving intramural and extramural policies and procedures, and responding to Freedom of Information Act and Privacy Act requests.[5]

A **finding of research misconduct** requires that:

1. A significant departure from accepted practices of the relevant research community occurred;

2. The misconduct was committed intentionally, knowingly, or recklessly; and

3. The allegation be proven by a preponderance of the evidence.[6]

A robust research compliance program is certainly a key to keeping an institution educated, trained, and on the lookout for any signs of impending research misconduct. Such a program will have policies and procedures ready to identify and manage any allegations of research misconduct, if they arise. Also, the program will have a designated research integrity officer (RIO) to carry out any necessary inquiries and investigations. Each of these aspects of a robust program will be described in greater detail.

Risk Area Governance

This article focuses on standards codified in HHS from 42 C.F.R. § 93, which details PHS Policies on Research Misconduct, and the National Science Foundation (NSF) regulation of 45 C.F.R. § 689, which explains Policies on Scientific Misconduct. Note that the ORI is responsible for oversight of misconduct for PHS agencies, including the National Institutes of Health (NIH). [78] The NSF Office of Inspector General is responsible for NSF-funded research.[9] The Department of Justice (DOJ) and the FDA may also investigate research misconduct related to research supported or funded by those agencies.

Institutions that seek PHS funding are required to have an assurance certifying that the institution has (1) policies and procedures to manage allegations of research misconduct and (2) a designated RIO to implement and manage the process.[10] Prior to 1996, this process required an "initial assurance" form; however, as of 1996, the act of signing the face page of a grant application constitutes a deemed assurance. It is important to note that compliance with these regulations is required when an application for funding is *submitted* and is not contingent upon receiving funding.[11] There also is an annual reporting requirement that describes any allegations and how they were managed in the previous year.

Common Compliance Risks

Treating Allegations Properly

Allegations of research misconduct generally fall into one of three categories: (1) good-faith allegations raised by individuals who have credible evidence for research misconduct; (2) good-faith allegations made by individuals who may be confusing honest disagreement or sloppy research practices with actual misconduct; or (3) allegations not made in good faith.[12] The last is very difficult to prove, therefore, the best practice is to treat all allegations as though they were brought in good faith.

Having Policies and Procedures

Not having policies and procedures in place can put an institution's PHS funding at risk and create an environment ripe for noncompliance. Each institution that seeks PHS funding should have written policies and procedures to handle allegations of research misconduct that are consistent with the federal regulations. The ORI has published a model policy that can be accessed on its website.[13] The sample policy and procedures can be tailored to fit any research institution to outline the process that it will undertake when an allegation of research misconduct arises. The sample policy and procedures also define the individual roles involved in the handling of research misconduct.

Having the Proper Officials Assigned

Institutions must have individuals assigned to investigate allegations of research misconduct to fulfill part of the ORI's requirement to have policies and procedures in place to conduct an inquiry and, if needed, an investigation of the allegation. In an investigation, the **complainant** is the person who brings forward the allegation of research misconduct. The **respondent** is the person accused of the misconduct. The **RIO** is the institutional official assigned the responsibility for carrying out the process described herein for the handling of allegations of research misconduct. The **deciding official** (DO) is the institutional official who makes the final determination on the allegation. The RIO and the DO should be two different individuals, because the RIO is responsible for carrying out the *procedures* involving the inquiry and investigation of the allegation of research misconduct and the DO, who is a higher-level official, is able to review the outcomes of both the inquiry and investigation and *make a decision based on the facts alone.*

Determining the Credibility of an Allegation

Not all allegations are credible, and the RIO needs to perform due diligence to determine which allegations should be pursued. The pursuit of a false one could be quite costly to the institution and the researcher alike. Such inquiries and investigations have the potential to damage careers and reputations, and neither should be taken lightly. Once an institution receives an allegation of research misconduct, it must first determine whether the allegation is sufficiently credible and specific so that evidence of the misconduct can be identified. If so, the RIO should initiate an official *Inquiry* and designate an *Inquiry Committee*. The Inquiry Committee reviews available evidence to determine whether an official *Investigation* is warranted and then prepares a report for the DO. The DO makes the final determination on whether a formal investigation will be conducted.[14]

If the inquiry advances to the investigation stage, a formal examination is conducted and a factual record is created that will result in a determination (1) not to make a finding of research misconduct or (2) to recommend for a finding of research misconduct that may include other administrative actions. The investigation ends when an *Investigation Report* is provided to the DO, who then decides what administrative action(s) to take.[15] There are specific points throughout this process at which the institution is obligated to report its activities and findings to the ORI.

Addressing Compliance Risks

It is important that the research compliance program has in place an adequate program to monitor and address research misconduct—*and* that it trains the research community on this process. This should be part of the ongoing training program, along with an annual review of the process to determine whether any revisions to the established policies and procedures are required. Once a legitimate allegation of research misconduct is found and the institution decides to investigate, the RIO and DO must ensure they take the following actions.

Maintain Complainant Confidentiality and Ensure No Retaliation

An institution is obligated to take reasonable efforts to keep the identity of the complainant confidential; however, this may not always be practical, depending upon the setting and circumstances. It is equally important to protect the complainant from retaliation. Once the respondent is made aware of the inquiry, the RIO should discuss the institution's policy against retaliation with the respondent as well as any others who are involved, particularly those who are more senior in their roles than the complainant. This policy should reflect a zero-tolerance standard regarding retaliation.

Preserve Respondent's Reputation

The institution also has an obligation to preserve the reputation of the respondent throughout the process and ensure that information about the case is shared only with those who have a need to know. Reputations can be damaged for years as a result of an investigation, even when the allegation is ultimately determined not to be research misconduct.[16] Therefore, the inquiry and investigation should be carried out with utmost care in preserving the confidentiality of both the complainant and respondent.

Adhere to ORI Timelines

Specific timelines exist for the inquiry and investigation phases, as well as for reporting to the ORI. This is important, not only from a regulatory perspective, but also from a fairness perspective. Wrapping up the inquiry and investigation in a timely manner will go a long way to protecting the confidentiality of the process, as well as protecting the identity of the complainant and the reputation of the respondent. The inquiry should be completed within 60 calendar days of its initiation, unless extended by the RIO in writing (up to an additional 60 days). The inquiry ends when the *Inquiry Report* is complete and the DO has decided whether or not to move forward with an investigation. If the DO decides to move forward with an investigation, the RIO must notify the ORI within 30 days of the completion of the inquiry. The investigation must also begin within those 30 days. The investigation, Investigation Report, and submission to ORI must be completed within 120 days. Any additional extensions must be requested from and granted by ORI.[17][18]

Form an Impartial Committee

Assembling an impartial committee can be a difficult task. No members of the Inquiry or Investigation Committee should have any personal, financial, or professional biases toward the respondent or the complainant.[19] The members should be acceptable to both sides and may be from within or outside of the institution.

Conduct and Transcribe Interviews

Conducting interviews can also present a challenge. Some interviewees, particularly the respondent, may request to have legal counsel present for the interviews. Since the interviews are not legal proceedings, the institution has no obligation to address counsel or permit that person to participate in the interview. Transcripts of the interviews should be provided to the interviewee(s) so that they may offer any corrections to the record or provide additional information. Transcripts are part of the official record and will also be submitted to the ORI as part of the Investigation Report.[20]

Manage and Sequester Documentation

Sequestering records and materials should start when the decision is made to move forward with an inquiry. The information being sequestered is important for determining whether or not the allegation has a basis in fact and, therefore, should be secured and chain of custody recorded and maintained. At this stage, there is a risk of breaching confidentiality as the physical process of collecting and sequestering documents and materials can be difficult, especially when there is a research team working with the respondent who will have questions and who will need access to some or all of the sequestered documents or materials to continue their work. The RIO will have to determine the best way to protect the documents and materials, while allowing sufficient access to the research team.[21] Record keeping will need to be complete, up to date, and kept in a secure chain of command. Most institutions allow the respondent and complainant a brief period to comment on the draft reports before they are finalized and submitted to the ORI.[22]

Respond Appropriately to ORI Review and Findings

Once the ORI receives a report, it will examine the information to determine whether the institution's findings are defensible, supported by evidence, and an acceptable outcome of the inquiry and investigation. During its review, the ORI may determine it agrees with the institution's report; request additional information; initiate its own review of the allegation; or refer the case to the HHS Office of Inspector General for further investigation. At the end of its review, the ORI will send a copy of the report to the institution and request that the institution directly notify the respondent and whistleblower of the outcome of the investigation. If a finding of research misconduct is made, the ORI may negotiate with the respondent a voluntary exclusion agreement (VEA) in which the respondent accepts the imposition of PHS administrative actions, or, if no agreement is reached, then the ORI makes a finding of research misconduct and recommends to the Assistant Secretary for Health the imposition of administrative actions or submits a charge letter to the HHS Departmental Appeals Board.[23]

Possible Penalties

Possible penalties for research misconduct are divided into three groups and range from minimal restrictions (Group I) to the most severe and restrictive (Group III). The possible penalties listed in the regulations are not exhaustive and do not include possible criminal or other administrative sanctions. Here are some examples of the penalties that may be directed to an individual or an institution within each of the three groups.

Group I penalties include a letter of reprimand to the individual or institution; a condition of an award that for a specified period an individual or institution must obtain special prior approval from NSF for particular activities; or a requirement that, for a specified period, an institutional official other than those guilty of misconduct certify the accuracy of reports generated under an award or provide assurance of compliance with particular policies, regulations, guidelines, or special terms and conditions.[24]

Group II penalties include total or partial suspension of an active award or restriction of designated activities or expenditures under an active award for a specified period. All requests for funding from an affected individual or institution will require special reviews for a specified period to ensure that steps have been taken to prevent repetition of the misconduct—or will require a correction to the research record.[25]

Group III penalties include terminating an active award; prohibiting an individual from participating as an NSF reviewer, advisor, or consultant for a specified period; or debarring or suspending an individual or institution from participation in federal programs for a specified period, after further proceedings under applicable regulations.[26]

Factors that should be considered when determining the appropriate actions to be taken include the seriousness of the misconduct; the degree to which the misconduct was knowing, intentional, or reckless; whether it was an isolated event or part of a pattern; whether it had a significant impact on the research record, research subjects, other researchers, institutions, or the public welfare; and other relevant circumstances.[27]

Interim actions that may be taken include, but are not limited to, totally or partially suspending an existing award; suspending eligibility for federal awards in accordance with debarment-and-suspension regulations; proscribing or restricting particular research activities, as, for example, to protect human or animal subjects; requiring special certifications, assurances, or other, administrative arrangements to ensure compliance with applicable regulations or terms of the award; requiring more prior approvals by the NSF; deferring funding action on continuing grant increments; deferring a pending award; or restricting or suspending participation as an NSF reviewer, advisor, or consultant. For cases governed by the debarment and suspension regulations, the standards of proof in the regulations shall control. Otherwise, NSF will take no final action under this section without a finding of misconduct supported by a preponderance of the relevant evidence. [28]

Compliance Resources

U.S. Department of Health & Human Services, Office of Research Integrity

Assurance Program—Annual Report System
RIOs use this portal within the ORI website to file an annual report and submit any additional information requested by the ORI related to the institution's research misconduct proceedings and the institution's compliance with 42 C.F.R. § 93.[29]

https://ori.hhs.gov/arprm/Login.php

Case Summaries
The ORI website also provides a link to summaries of misconduct cases so an institution can review current and past cases reported to the ORI.[30]

https://ori.hhs.gov/content/case_summary

PHS Administrative Action Bulletin Board
This bulletin board features a list of individuals currently under PHS administrative actions. Which administrative actions and the number and the length of the actions depend on the seriousness of the misconduct, the impact of the misconduct, and whether the misconduct demonstrates a pattern of behavior. Administrative actions usually are imposed for three years but have ranged from one year to a lifetime. Individuals are removed from the bulletin board when the administrative actions expire.[31] This real-time information can be an effective educational tool to highlight the impact that research misconduct can have on an individual's career, as well as on the individual's reputation and the institution's.

https://ori.hhs.gov/ORI_PHS_alert.html?d=update

Sample Policy & Procedures for Responding to Research Misconduct Allegations

The ORI has a sample research misconduct policy, sample procedures for responding to allegations, and a list of RIO responsibilities on its website. The sample documents provide a solid framework that an institution may use to *develop* its own set of policies and procedures for handling allegations of research misconduct. The samples also can be used to *compare* with an institution's established policies and procedures to ensure they meet the requirements of the ORI.

https://ori.hhs.gov/sample-policy-procedures-responding-research-misconduct-allegations

---

Risk Takeaways

Main points of interest:

- The definition of research misconduct is narrow, limited to fabrication, falsification, and plagiarism. It does not include honest differences of opinion among scientists, inadvertent errors, or disputes about the order of appearance in a list of authors' names.
- The requirements for a finding of research misconduct are the following: (1) showing a significant departure from accepted practices of the relevant research community; (2) proving that the misconduct was committed intentionally, knowingly, or recklessly; and (3) proving the allegation of misconduct by a preponderance of the evidence.

Areas to watch:

- Maintaining confidentiality of complainant and reputation of respondent
- Conducting an inquiry and investigation within the established timelines
- Assembling an impartial Inquiry/Investigation Committee
- Keeping accurate and up-to-date records and reports while maintaining chain of command

Laws that apply:

- U.S. Department of Health & Human Services, 42 C.F.R. § 93
- National Science Foundation, 45 C.F.R. § 689

Addressing compliance risks:

- Institutions seeking PHS funding should have written policies and procedures that are consistent with the federal regulations for the handling of research misconduct allegations.
- The organization's RIO will review an allegation of research misconduct to determine whether it is sufficiently credible and specific so that evidence of the misconduct may be identified.

- The RIO should initiate an official Inquiry and designate an Inquiry Committee that will review the available evidence and determine whether an official Investigation is warranted. If so, the Inquiry Committee will prepare an Inquiry Report for the DO, who will determine whether or not to move forward with a formal investigation.
- An Investigation Committee will conduct a formal examination and factual-record review to determine whether there is a finding of research misconduct.
- The DO will make the final determination and decide which administrative actions to take. The full report and record will be submitted to ORI, which may accept the determination made by the institution or conduct its own investigation.
- An institution's best defense against research misconduct is a robust set of policies and procedures to identify and manage misconduct and appropriately skilled officials who will proactively train and educate the research community on the subject of research misconduct, and, when necessary, react promptly to any allegations that are brought forward in good faith.

Endnotes

1. **Lynn E. Smith**, JD, CHRC, is the director, research compliance officer at Tampa General Hospital in Tampa, Florida. Smith is a research professional with 30 years of experience in research administration and regulatory compliance. Her expertise includes management of conflicts of interest, research misconduct, and monitoring of ongoing clinical trials. Additional areas of expertise include transformation of Human Research Protection Programs (HRPP) and institutional review boards (IRBs) focused on regulatory compliance and operational efficiency.
2. 42 C.F.R. § 93.103.
3. 42 C.F.R. § 93.103.
4. "About ORI," The Office of Research Integrity, accessed January 12, 2022, https://ori.hhs.gov/about-ori.
5. "About ORI," The Office of Research Integrity, accessed January 12, 2022, https://ori.hhs.gov/about-ori.
6. 42 C.F.R. § 93.104.
7. 42 C.F.R. § 93.
8. 45 C.F.R. § 689.
9. Marti Arvin et al., *Research Compliance Professional's Handbook, 3rd Edition* (Minneapolis: Health Care Compliance Association, 2019), 41.
10. "Assurance Program," The Office of Research Integrity, accessed January 12, 2022, https://ori.hhs.gov/sample-policy-procedures-responding-research-misconduct-allegations.
11. Marti Arvin et al., *Research Compliance Professional's Handbook, 3rd Edition* (Minneapolis: Health Care Compliance Association, 2019), 45.
12. 42 C.F.R. § 93.210.
13. "Sample Policy & Procedures for Responding to Research Misconduct Allegations," The Office of Research Integrity, accessed January 12, 2022, https://ori.hhs.gov/sample-policy-procedures-responding-research-misconduct-allegations.
14. 42 C.F.R. § 93.307.
15. 42 C.F.R. § 93.310.
16. 42 C.F.R. § 93.304(k)-(l).
17. 42 C.F.R. § 93.307(g).
18. 42 C.F.R. § 93.311.
19. 42 C.F.R. § 93.310 (f).
20. 42 C.F.R. § 93.305.
21. 42 C.F.R. § 93.305.
22. 42 C.F.R. § 93.305.
23. "ORI Oversight Review," The Office of Research Integrity, accessed January 12, 2022, https://ori.hhs.gov/ori-oversight-review.
24. 45 C.F.R. § 689.3.
25. 45 C.F.R. § 689.3.
26. 45 C.F.R. § 689.3.
27. 45 C.F.R. § 689.3.
28. 45 C.F.R. § 689.3.
29. "Assurance Program-Annual Report System," The Office of Research Integrity, accessed January 12, 2022, https://ori.hhs.gov/arprm/Login.php.
30. "Case Summaries," The Office of Research Integrity, accessed January 12, 2022, https://ori.hhs.gov/content/case_summary.
31. "PHS Administrative Action Bulletin Board," The Office of Research Integrity, accessed January 12, 2022, https://ori.hhs.gov/phs-administrative-action-bulletin-board.

Conflicts of Interest

CMS Open Payments

By Betsy Wade,[1] MPH, CHC, CNA

What Are Conflicts of Interest and CMS Open Payments?

The Centers for Medicare & Medicaid Services (CMS) Open Payments database is a public reporting tool that compliance officers should use annually in conjunction with other information and research to monitor potential conflicts of interest between contracted, employed, and other healthcare providers and manufacturers of drugs, medical devices, biological, and medical supplies.[2]

A healthcare provider who benefits personally from payments, gifts, entertainment, or other compensation provided by manufacturers may develop a conflict with their employer or contracted healthcare provider if that remuneration causes them to engage in conduct that benefits them personally and puts their employer and/or patients in harm's way. The CMS Open Payments database does not identify conflicts of interest, but it is the only national resource of its type that allows federal payment program beneficiaries, consumers, physicians, and the public to review and research financial relationships with providers that could cause a conflict.

Compliance officers can use the information reported in the database to validate information disclosed to their organizations in conflicts of interest statements and ultimately as a basis to monitor their providers' prescribing trends and evaluate medical device use. Examples of potential conflicts that can be identified include, but are not limited to:

- A review of a psychiatrist's open payments data shows the provider being paid more than $100,000 a year to talk with other providers at restaurants and conferences about an antidepressant drug that a company manufactures. When the compliance officer reviewed the psychiatrist's prescribing patterns, it showed the provider almost exclusively prescribed the antidepressant drug the provider was being paid to promote. The psychiatrist also did not disclose the financial relationship on the annual conflict of interest statement.
- A review of an orthopaedic surgeon's open payments shows the provider is receiving more than $1 million annually in royalties from a device manufacturer for a knee replacement device the provider developed in conjunction with the manufacturer. When the compliance officer reviewed the orthopaedic surgeon's medical device utilization, it showed the provider chose the knee replacement device the provider was receiving royalties on in 90% of surgical procedures performed by the provider. The orthopaedic surgeon also did not disclose the royalty payments on the annual conflict of interest statement.
- A review of the Open Payments database shows a family practice physician accepted an all-expenses paid trip, including airfare, lodging, food, and entertainment totaling $7,500, from a drug manufacturer to attend a conference to learn about a new medication in violation of the organization's code of conduct and gift policy. Further review by the compliance officer shows the provider began prescribing the medication after the trip.
- A review of the Open Payments database shows a cardiac surgeon received research payments from a device manufacturer. When the compliance officer reviewed the cardiac surgeon's conflicts of interest statement, the compliance officer found that no payments had been disclosed. The cardiac surgeon also did not have any active research studies approved by an institutional review board (IRB) or the organization's research office.

The CMS Open Payments database reported information on physicians and teaching hospitals for the first time on September 30, 2014, after being developed to shine a light on financial relationships and potential conflicts of interest between healthcare providers and manufacturers.[3] The database developed out of the Physician Payments Sunshine Act, which requires manufacturers of biological and medical supplies, drugs, and medical devices that are paid for by federal healthcare programs to collect and track financial relationships with physicians and teaching hospitals and to report the data to CMS.[4] Before the data is published annually, physicians and teaching hospitals have an opportunity to review and dispute the information that has been reported.

Financial relationships reported in the Open Payments database include, but are not limited to:

- Travel and lodging
- Fees, including consulting, speaking, honoraria, teaching, and licenses

- Charitable contributions
- Entertainment (e.g., food, beverages, and gifts)
- Royalties
- Research activities[5]

In addition to reporting data on doctors of medicine/osteopathy, doctors of dental medicine/dental surgery, doctors of podiatric medicine, doctors of optometry, and chiropractors, the Open Payments database will begin reporting data on five additional provider types in 2022:

1. Physician assistants,
2. Nurse practitioners,
3. Clinical nurse specialists,
4. Certified registered nurse anesthetists, and
5. Certified nurse-midwives.[6]

In addition to the added provider types, the types of payment categories will be expanded to include debt forgiveness, long-term medical supply or device loan, and acquisitions.

Risk Area Governance

As noted previously, the CMS Open Payments database grew out of the Physician Payments Sunshine Act—a law focused on provider financial relationships that was introduced in 2007 by U.S. Senators Charles Grassley and Herb Kohl and enacted in 2010 as part of the Patient Protection and Affordable Care Act.[7]

CMS followed by issuing its final rule titled "Transparency reports and reporting of physician ownership or investment interests" on February 8, 2013.[8] The new rule required manufacturers of biologicals, devices, drugs, and medical supplies to report annually to CMS on compensation or remuneration to physicians and teaching hospitals.

Under the rule, manufacturers and group purchasing organizations (GPOs) are also required to disclose any ownership or investment interests held by physicians or their immediate family members, which include:[9]

- Spouse.
- Natural or adoptive parent, child, or sibling.
- Stepparent, stepchild, stepbrother, or stepsister.
- Father-, mother-, daughter-, son-, brother-, or sister-in-law.
- Grandparent or grandchild.
- Spouse of a grandparent or grandchild.

Five years after CMS issued its final rule, President Donald Trump signed the Substance Use-Disorder Prevention that Promotes Opioid Recovery and Treatment for Patients and Communities Act (SUPPORT Act) on October 24, 2018.[10] The SUPPORT Act expanded the

CMS Open Payment database's recipients to include five additional provider types described previously. CMS issued a corresponding final rule under the Medicare physician fee schedule (PFS) on November 1, 2019, that changed the definition of a "covered recipient" to include the five additional provider types, expanded the payment categories as noted previously, and combined two education categories into one.[11] It also added reporting requirements to include the unique device identifier for devices and medical supplies. These changes are applicable for data collection beginning in 2021 and are required to be submitted to CMS on or after January 1, 2022.

Common Compliance Risks

Conflicts of interest between providers and industry are the greatest concern that can be identified through the Open Payments database.

There are many definitions for "conflict of interest." Lexico defines it as "a situation in which a person is in a position to derive personal benefit from actions or decisions made in their official capacity."[12] Section 303A of the New York Stock Exchange corporate governance rules describes it as "when an individual's private interest interferes in any way—or even appears to interfere—with the interests of the corporation as a whole."[13] And, the National Institutes of Health defines a conflict of interest as "a set of circumstances that creates a risk that professional judgment or actions regarding a primary interest will be unduly influenced by a secondary interest."[14]

Regardless of which definition is followed, a conflict of interest can not only harm the involved individual's reputation and employment status but could also have civil and/or criminal legal implications as well as licensure implications. An individual's conflict of interest also could lead to legal implications for the organization, such as civil monetary penalties, criminal charges, and lawsuits.

The financial information in the Open Payments database alone does not determine whether the relationships between the provider and manufacturer are improper or present a conflict of interest. Further review of those financial ties and other information is needed to determine whether a problem exists.

Here are some examples of financial relationships that could become potential conflicts of interest:

- Charitable contributions from manufacturers to tax-exempt organizations
- Compensation to providers for serving as faculty/speaker for an unaccredited/accredited and noncertified/certified continuing education program
- Compensation for services to providers for speaking, training, and education that is not for continuing education
- Consulting payments to providers for offering advice/expertise on a medical product or treatment

- Education support for activities, books, classes, events, and programs that involve skill or knowledge for a particular profession
- Entertainment, such as attendance at cultural (e.g., concerts and theater), recreational, sporting, or other events
- Food and beverage during lunches and dinners
- Gifts, such as promotional items
- Grants to a provider or teaching hospital to support an activity or cause
- Honoraria or one-time payments
- Lodging and travel
- Ownership or investment interest
- Research payments for activities, such as enrolling patients into studies of new drugs or devices
- Royalty or licensure payments based on sales of products using a physician's intellectual property
- Space rental or facility fees

Addressing Compliance Risks

There are many ways that compliance officers can proactively address conflicts of interest to prevent potential conflicts from becoming a risk to the provider or the organization. Steps fall squarely within the seven elements of an effective compliance program and include implementing appropriate policies and procedures, providing education, incorporating conflicts of interest in the annual compliance monitoring plan or internal audit plan, investigating concerns, developing conflict management plans and corrective action plans (CAPs), and recommending disciplinary action. While the following points focus more on relationships between healthcare providers and pharmaceutical companies/device manufacturers, many other types of conflicts of interest can be found in healthcare organization, such as those related to procurement and relationships with competitors. All should be addressed within an organization.

Policies and Procedures

- Include conflicts of interest in the organization's code of conduct to inform employees and providers that financial relationships will be monitored.
- Develop and implement policies and procedures that address conflicts of interest.
- Establish a process to obtain and maintain conflicts of interest questionnaires and data at time of contracting or hire, when changes occur, and, at a minimum, annually.
- Develop and implement policies and procedures that address gifts to providers.
- Ensure informed consent policies and corresponding informed consent forms contain language that a provider may have had involvement with the development of the drug or device being prescribed or ordered.

Education

- Educate providers on the organization's code of conduct.
- Educate providers on the organization's conflicts of interest policy, the organization's conflicts of interest process, and laws and regulations that govern conflicts of interest.
- Educate providers on the CMS Open Payments database, how it reports financial relationships with manufacturers, and how the data from it is used in the organization's compliance monitoring and/or internal audit process.
- Educate providers on the organization's gifts policies.

Monitoring and Auditing

- Review conflict of interest statements annually for disclosure of potential conflicts between providers and manufacturers as part of the compliance monitoring plan.
- Incorporate annual reviews of the CMS Open Payments database in the organization's compliance monitoring plan and/or internal audit plan.
- Include reviews of provider prescribing habits and medical device utilization in the organization's compliance monitoring plan.
- Include reviews of research funding in annual compliance monitoring plan.
- Conduct medical necessity reviews of aberrant prescribing or medical device usage as part of compliance monitoring plan or internal audit plan.

Investigations

- Include conflicts of interest as a category in compliance investigations.
- Investigate allegations of a conflict of interest between providers and manufacturers.
- Investigate potential conflicts of interest that arise from monitoring the annual CMS Open Payments database, provider prescribing habits, and medical device usage.

Corrective Action

- Develop and implement CAPs, including disciplinary action when necessary, to address conflicts of interest related to financial relationships between providers and manufacturers.
- Develop and implement conflict management plans when necessary and monitor compliance with the plans.

Possible Penalties

Ramifications for conflict of interest are varied and can range from disciplinary action for policy violations to exclusion from federal healthcare programs. The CMS Open Payments database is a great tool to begin to examine the financial ties to determine whether the relationship is beneficial to developing new technology, an inappropriate influence on clinical decision-making and research, or one that will ultimately lead to healthcare fraud and abuse.

Consider the orthopaedic surgeon who was being paid more than $1 million annually in royalties from a device manufacturer for a knee replacement device the provider developed in conjunction with the manufacturer. When the compliance officer reviewed the orthopaedic surgeon's medical device usage, it showed that in 90% of the provider's surgical procedures he chose the device that he developed and for which he was receiving royalties. The orthopaedic surgeon also did not disclose the royalty payments on the annual conflicts of interest statement. Here are some additional risks and possible penalties to consider:

- The surgeon may be in violation of policy for failure to notify the healthcare organization of the financial relationship and updating the conflicts of interest statement to reflect the royalties. This can lead to disciplinary action if the surgeon is employed or contracted with the healthcare organization.
- The surgeon may have violated the healthcare organization's policies to notify and obtain consent from patients when using physician-developed or physician-owned devices. This can lead to disciplinary action if the surgeon is employed or contracted with the healthcare organization. It also can put the healthcare organization and surgeon at risk of lawsuits if the patients were not informed and had not consented.
- The surgeon's judgment may have been clouded by the financial gain and medical necessity may not have been met in all of the cases in which the provider used the knee replacement device that the provider helped develop. If medical necessity was not met, the provider and healthcare organization could be at risk for False Claims Act and Civil Monetary Penalties Law violations, medical malpractice litigation, and other action. If the surgeon knowingly implanted devices that were not medically necessary for financial gain, the provider also could face criminal charges. The healthcare organization also could be subject to a corporate integrity agreement (CIA) and/or exclusion from participation in federal healthcare programs.
- Depending on the outcome of the investigation and any actions taken, the provider also could be at risk for licensure restrictions, suspensions, or termination.

Compliance Resources

Educational Programs

Open Payments: Initial Publication of Program Year 2019 Data
This CMS publication is a tutorial on the Open Payments program and how to access its data, tools, and resources.

https://www.cms.gov/OpenPayments/Downloads/OpenPaymentsDataPubTutorial.pdf

Open Payments: Overview and Enhancements
This CMS publication provides important information on the Open Payments program and enhancements.

https://www.cms.gov/files/document/op-overview-and-enhancements-january-2020.pdf

General Information

CMS Open Payments
Information about the Open Payments program and important links.

https://www.cms.gov/OpenPayments

CMS Open Payments Database
Access to the searchable Open Payments database, along with downloadable data sets.

https://openpaymentsdata.cms.gov

CMS Open Payments Frequently Asked Questions
This CMS publication provides answers to common questions on the Open Payments database.

https://www.cms.gov/OpenPayments/Downloads/open-payments-general-faq.pdf

Laws and Regulations

Open Payments Final Rule
Medicare, Medicaid, Children's Health Insurance Programs; Transparency Reports and Reporting of Physician Ownership or Investment Interests, 78 Fed. Reg. 9,458 (February 8, 2013).

https://www.cms.gov/OpenPayments/Downloads/Affordable-Care-Act-Section-6002-Final-Rule.pdf

Updates to the Open Payments Final Rule
Medicare Program; Revisions to Payment Policies Under the Physician Fee Schedule, Clinical Laboratory Fee Schedule, Access to Identifiable Data for the Center for Medicare and Medicaid Innovation Models & Other Revisions to Part B for CY 2015, 79 Fed. Reg. 67,548, 67,758 (November 13, 2014).

https://www.cms.gov/OpenPayments/Downloads/Open-Payments-Revision-Nov-2014.pdf

Open Payments Definitions
Patient Protection and Affordable Care Act, Pub. L. No. 111-148, § 6002, 124 Stat. 689 (2010).

https://www.govinfo.gov/content/pkg/PLAW-111publ148/pdf/PLAW-111publ148.pdf

Open Payments Definitions (Amended: Public Law No. 111-152)
Health Care and Education Reconciliation Act of 2010, Pub. L. No. 111-152, 124
Stat. 1029 (2010).

https://www.ssa.gov/OP_Home/ssact/title11/1128G.htm

Open Payments Definitions (Amended: Public Law No. 115-271)
Substance Use-Disorder Prevention that Promotes Opioid Recovery and Treatment for
Patients and Communities Act, Pub. L. No. 115-271, 132 Stat. 3894 (2018).

https://www.govinfo.gov/content/pkg/PLAW-115publ271/html/PLAW-115publ271.htm

Payment Categories
42 U.S.C. § 1320a-7h(a)(1)(A)(vi).

https://www.ssa.gov/OP_Home/ssact/title11/1128G.htm

Risk Takeaways

Main points of interest:
- The CMS Open Payments database is a tool compliance officers can use to evaluate financial relationships between providers and manufacturers.
- Conflicts of interest are the main compliance risk from financial relationships.

Areas to watch:
- Charitable contributions
- Compensation for serving as faculty/speaker for unaccredited/accredited and non-certified/certified continuing education programs
- Compensation for services to providers for speaking, training, and education that is not for continuing education
- Consulting payments to providers for providing advice and expertise on a medical product or treatment
- Education support
- Entertainment, such as attendance at recreational, cultural, sporting, or other events that would generally have a cost; tickets to sporting events, concerts, or theater shows
- Food and beverage

- Gifts
- Grants
- Honoraria
- Lodging and travel
- Ownership or investment interest by a provider or their immediate family member
- Research payments
- Royalty or licensure
- Space rental or facility fees

Laws that apply:

- Open Payments Final Rule, published February 8, 2013
- Updates to the Open Payments Final Rule, published November 13, 2014
- Open payments definitions: Patient Protection and Affordable Care Act, Pub. L. No. 111-148, § 6002, 124 Stat. 689 (2010)
- Open payments definitions amended:
  - Health Care and Education Reconciliation Act of 2010, Pub. L. No. 111-152, 124 Stat. 1029 (2010)
  - Substance Use-Disorder Prevention that Promotes Opioid Recovery and Treatment for Patients and Communities Act, Pub. L. No. 115-271, 132 Stat. 3894 (2018)
- Payment categories: 42 U.S.C. § 1320a-7h(a)(1)(A)(vi)

Addressing compliance risks:

- Include conflicts of interest in the organization's code of conduct.
- Develop and implement policies and procedures that address conflicts of interest.
- Establish a process to obtain and maintain conflicts of interest questionnaires and data.
- Develop and implement policies and procedures that address gifts.
- Educate providers on conflicts of interest and gifts policies.
- Educate providers on how the CMS Open Payments database is used to monitor financial relationships and potential conflicts of interest.
- Include conflicts of interest as a category in compliance investigations.
- Investigate allegations of conflicts of interest.
- Include monitoring of the CMS Open Payments database and other information to evaluate financial relationships between providers and manufacturers in annual compliance monitoring plan or internal audit plan.
- Develop and implement corrective action plans, including disciplinary action when necessary.
- Develop and implement conflict management plans when necessary and monitor compliance with the plans.

Endnotes

1. **Betsy Wade** is chief compliance & ethics officer at Signature HealthCARE. With more than 20 years of experience in healthcare compliance, Wade has worked in a variety of organizations overseeing compliance in a number of settings—all of which have included oversight of conflicts of interest and identification of potential compliance issues related to conflicts of interest. She also is a faculty member of the Health Care Compliance Association Basic Compliance Academy and Privacy Academy.

2. "Home," OpenPaymentsData.CMS.gov, Centers for Medicare & Medicaid Services, accessed December 29, 2020, https://openpaymentsdata.cms.gov/.

3. Thomas J. Parisi, Isabella M. Ferre, and Harry E. Rubash, "The Basics of the Sunshine Act: How It Pertains to the Practicing Orthopaedic Surgeon," *Journal of the American Academy of Orthopaedic Surgeons* 23, no. 8 (August 2015), 455–467, https://journals.lww.com/jaaos/fulltext/2015/08000/the_basics_of_the_sunshine_act__how_it_pertains_to.1.aspx.

4. Patient Protection and Affordable Care Act, Pub. L. No. 111-148, § 6002, 124 Stat. 689 (2010).

5. "Natures of Payment," Centers for Medicare & Medicaid Services, last modified November 12, 2019, https://www.cms.gov/OpenPayments/About/Natures-of-Payment.

6. "Newly Added Covered Recipients," Centers for Medicare & Medicaid Services, last modified August 21, 2020, https://www.cms.gov/OpenPayments/Program-Participants/Newly-Added-Covered-Recipients.

7. 42 U.S.C. § 18001 et seq.

8. Medicare, Medicaid, Children's Health Insurance Programs; Transparency Reports and Reporting of Physician Ownership or Investment Interests, 78 Fed. Reg. 9,458 (February 8, 2013).

9. Medicare, Medicaid, Children's Health Insurance Programs; Transparency Reports and Reporting of Physician Ownership or Investment Interests, 78 Fed. Reg. 9,458.

10. Substance Use-Disorder Prevention that Promotes Opioid Recovery and Treatment for Patients and Communities Act, Pub. L. No. 115-271, 132 Stat. 3894 (2018).

11. Medicare Program; CY 2020 Revisions to Payment Policies Under the Physician Fee Schedule and Other Changes to Part B Payment Policies; Medicare Shared Savings Program Requirements; Medicaid Promoting Interoperability Program Requirements for Eligible Professionals; Establishment of an Ambulance Data Collection System; Updates to the Quality Payment Program; Medicare Enrollment of Opioid Treatment Programs and Enhancements to Provider Enrollment Regulations Concerning Improper Prescribing and Patient Harm; and Amendments to Physician Self-Referral Law Advisory Opinion Regulations Final Rule; and Coding and Payment for Evaluation and Management, Observation and Provision of Self-Administered Esketamine Interim Final Rule, 84 Fed. Reg. 62,568, 62,915 (November 15, 2019).

12. "conflict of interest," Lexico, accessed December 29, 2020, https://www.lexico.com/en/definition/conflict_of_interest.

13. "303A.10 Code of Business Conduct and Ethics," *NYSE Listed Company Manual*, amended November 25, 2009, https://nyse.wolterskluwer.cloud/listed-company-manual/document?treeNodeId=csh-da-filter!WKUS-TAL-DOCS-PHC-%7B0588BF4A-D3B5-4B91-94EA-BE9F17057DF0%7D--WKUS_TAL_5667%23teid-78.

14. Institute of Medicine, *Conflict of Interest in Medical Research, Education, and Practice* (Washington D.C.: The National Academies Press, 2009), 46, https://www.ncbi.nlm.nih.gov/books/NBK22937/.

Relationships with Industry—Medical Device Manufacturers & Pharmaceutical Companies

By Betsy Wade,[1] MPH, CHC, CNA

What Are the Conflicts of Interest Involving Relationships with Medical Device Manufacturers and Pharmaceutical Companies?

Relationships between healthcare providers and medical device manufacturers and pharmaceutical companies can result in conflicts of interest if the relationship personally benefits the provider and unduly influences the provider's clinical judgment or actions. These conflicts of interest ultimately could lead to patient harm as well as potential compliance issues that could result in civil, criminal, or administrative enforcement actions and financial penalties. The same can be true for relationships between healthcare organizations that are recipients of funding or other compensation from medical device manufacturers and pharmaceutical companies. The financial relationship could cloud the decision-making of healthcare organization leadership because of the incentive.

In fact, the Department of Health & Human Services Office of Inspector General (OIG) issued a special fraud alert November 16, 2020, highlighting the fraud and abuse risks associated with pharmaceutical and medical device companies offering remuneration to healthcare providers for participating in company-sponsored speaker programs about drugs or devices targeted at other healthcare providers.[2] The alert notes that over the past three years, drug and device companies have reported paying nearly $2 billion to healthcare providers for speaking engagements, and the OIG and Department of Justice (DOJ) have investigated and resolved a number of fraud cases involving allegations that remuneration violated the Anti-Kickback Statute.[3] As a result, the government has pursued civil and criminal cases against individuals and companies involved in speaker programs.

Among the cases, the OIG found that drug and device companies:

- Selected high-prescribing healthcare providers to be speakers and paid them well, with some receiving hundreds of thousands of dollars.
- Required speakers to write a minimum number of prescriptions in order to be paid the speaking fee.
- Held programs at entertainment venues (e.g., wineries, adult entertainment facilities, sports stadiums) or during recreational events, such as fishing trips and golf outings, that were not conducive to education.
- Held programs at high-end restaurants that included expensive meals and alcohol. The OIG noted that in one case, the average food and alcohol cost was more than $500 per attendee.
- Invited an audience of healthcare providers who previously had attended the same program or invited the providers' friends, family members, or significant others who did not have a legitimate business reason to participate in the program.

For years, story after story has circulated in the news about inappropriate financial relationships between healthcare providers and industry that led to negative consequences or even patient death. One such example was the story of Jesse Gelsinger, an 18-year-old who had a rare metabolic disorder that caused a high level of ammonia in his blood.[4] His condition was not life-threatening, but he opted to participate in a gene therapy clinical trial at the University of Pennsylvania in 1999. In the study, an adenovirus was injected into Jesse's bloodstream, he developed a severe immune reaction to it, and he died four days later. An investigation revealed ethical, technical, and regulatory issues with the clinical trial and that the principal investigator—who also was the head of the institute where the procedure was performed—had a substantial financial stake in the company providing funds to finance the research—a potential conflict of interest.

Despite industry guidance that emerged in the early 2000s and the passage of Internal Revenue Service (IRS) laws and the Sarbanes-Oxley Act of 2002, which focused on inappropriate financial relationships and conflicts of interest among nonprofits and for-profits, years of allegations of improper relationships between healthcare providers and device and pharmaceutical manufacturers led to a series of probes into conflicts of interest by Senator Chuck Grassley.[56] Grassley compared documentation from manufacturers with data from universities and identified several cases where individuals substantially understated money they had received from pharmaceutical companies, for example.

Among the findings:

- An Emory University physician earned more than $2.8 million from drugmakers between 2000 and 2007, yet failed to report more than $1.2 million to the university and violated federal research rules. [7] The physician signed a letter promising Emory University that he would earn less than $10,000 a year from the pharmaceutical company to comply with federal rules, but on the same day, he was found at the Four Seasons Resort in Jackson Hole, Wyoming, earning $3,000 of what would become $170,000 in income from the company.
- A University of Cincinnati physician disclosed to the university that she made $100,000 from eight drug companies, when she was really paid $238,000 from just one company for the defined period.[8]
- Two Harvard University physicians who practiced at Massachusetts General Hospital reported making several hundred thousand dollars each from drugmakers from 2000 to 2007, when each actually made more than $1.6 million.[9]

Risk Area Governance

One of the reasons why the Anti-Kickback Statute was enacted was to protect patients from prescriptions, referrals, or recommendations from healthcare providers who may have been influenced in their decision-making by inappropriate financial incentives. It is a crime under the Anti-Kickback Statute to knowingly and willfully solicit, receive, offer, or pay any remuneration to induce or reward, among other things, referrals for, or orders of, items or services reimbursable by a federal health care program.[10] Remuneration includes anything of value, directly or indirectly, overtly or covertly, in cash or in kind. Violation of the statute can lead to criminal liability to all parties involved. A violation can result in a felony that is punishable by imprisonment for up to ten years or a maximum fine of $100,000 or both. Conviction can also result in exclusion from participation in federal healthcare programs such as Medicare, Medicaid, and TRICARE.[11] The OIG also may impose civil monetary penalties for violations.[12]

The 2020 OIG special fraud alert on speaker programs was not the first time the government had warned providers that financial relationships with drug and device manufacturers could result in criminal, civil, or administrative penalties. As early as 2003, OIG shared its concerns about such financial relationships—and the possibility they could trigger the Anti-Kickback Statute—in its Compliance Program Guidance for Pharmaceutical Manufacturers.[13] And in 2010, OIG again warned providers that such arrangements with drug or device companies could be an improper inducement to prescribe or use the company's products to be rewarded financially, rather than providing the best treatment for patients.[14]

To help ensure ethical relationships between providers and manufacturers, the Pharmaceutical Research and Manufacturers of America (PhRMA) and the Advanced Medical Technology Association (AdvaMed) both developed voluntary codes of ethics designed to address appropriate relationships between healthcare providers and medical device and pharmaceutical manufacturers.

PhRMA, which represents research-based pharmaceutical and biotechnology companies, adopted its *Code on Interactions with Health Care Professionals* in January 2009.[15] The code has been revised over the years, and the latest revision was released in June 2020. The association also launched the *Principles on Conduct of Clinical Trials and Communication of Clinical Trial Results* for clinical investigators that have relationships with pharmaceutical companies.[16]

AdvaMed is the largest global medical technology industry association, which unveiled its original code of ethics in 2003. The AdvaMed *Code of Ethics on Interactions with U.S. Health Care Professionals* has been revised over the years, with the last revision released in July 2020.[17] AdvaMed also has provided guidance over the years on additional topics such as physician-owned distributorships (PODs).[18] PODs are device companies and distributors that may offer equity to physicians who may be in a position to refer business to the entities. The OIG issued a special fraud alert regarding PODs March 26, 2013.[19]

Following the congressional probes, Grassley and Senator Herb Kohl took the industry guidance a step further and drafted legislation that was introduced in 2007 focusing on provider financial relationships with medical device and pharmaceutical manufacturers. The Physician Payments Sunshine Act was enacted in 2010 as part of the Patient Protection and Affordable Care Act.[20][21]

The Centers for Medicare & Medicaid Services (CMS) issued its Transparency Reports and Reporting of Physician Ownership or Investment Interests final rule on February 8, 2013.[22] Also known as the Physician Payments Sunshine Act, which required manufacturers of biologicals, devices, drugs, and medical supplies to report annually to CMS on compensation or remuneration to physicians and teaching hospitals.

A smattering of guidance, laws, and regulations from government agencies and private industry offer guardrails to protect providers with both for-profit organizations and nonprofit organizations from potential conflicts of interest. All of the guidance and laws, however, share a similar goal: that providers fulfill their duty to act in the best interest of their patients and solely on each patient's medical needs. But there is not one governing authority, so every situation has to be evaluated based on the facts.

Common Compliance Risks

Financial relationships between providers and pharmaceutical and device manufacturers can lead to a variety of compliance risks, including, but not limited to, conflicts of interest, improper inducements, and potential violations of the Anti-Kickback Statute, as well as medically unnecessary care and false claims, all of which can lead to increased costs for the organization.

Remuneration provided by pharmaceutical and device companies to providers can cloud their judgment, leading to providers:

- Prescribing medications in exchange for payments or kickbacks,
- Marketing and prescribing medications or devices off-label,
- Misrepresenting diagnoses to justify services that are not medically necessary, and
- Ordering devices that ultimately could further line their pockets with increased compensation.

Doing so not only can trigger the Anti-Kickback Statute but also could result in care that is not medically necessary and result in violations of the False Claims Act.[23]

Five of the largest pharmaceutical companies in the world—Abbott, Eli Lilly, GlaxoSmithKline, Johnson & Johnson, and Pfizer—for example, all have had to pay settlements totaling $1 billion or more under the False Claims Act for such violations.[24]

Addressing Compliance Risks

Compliance officers who work for healthcare organizations can proactively address compliance risks related to financial relationships between vendors and physicians who serve as medical directors, attendings, consultants, researchers, or are employed by the organization. They should address each of the items under the following categories.

Policies and Procedures

Implement policies and procedures that address financial relationships between pharmaceutical and device manufacturers and physicians.

Education

Provide education on the compliance risks and applicable laws, regulations, guidance, and special fraud alerts that address financial relationships between providers and vendors.

Contract Review

Review contracts between drug and device companies and providers to ensure they are compliant with state and federal laws and regulations as well as company policy.

Conflicts of Interest Statements

- Ensure physicians complete their conflicts of interest statement upon the commencement of their relationship with the healthcare organization and make sure some questions specifically ask about financial relationships with pharmaceutical and device manufacturers.
- Make sure conflict of interest statements are updated when there is a change in the provider's status.
- Ensure providers update their conflicts of interest statements at least annually.
- Have a committee that includes someone from the compliance department review disclosures on conflicts of interest statements to determine whether concerns exist with relationships between providers and pharmaceutical companies and/or device manufacturers.

Corrective Action Plan

- Address any potential conflicts of interest with a corrective action plan or monitoring plan.
- Monitor the provider to ensure the plan is being followed and is effective.

Hotline Reporting

Make sure the organization's hotline includes a reporting category to address conflicts of interest that may be reported.

Monitoring and Auditing

- Monitor payments from drug and device manufacturers to providers through the CMS Open Payments database.[25]
- Conduct data mining to monitor physician prescribing patterns and device usage and look for overutilization or changes in patterns that may be related to financial incentives received from a pharmaceutical or device manufacturing company.
- Conduct medical necessity audits of physician prescribing and device usage and focus on drugs or devices that the physician may have ordered where he or she also has a financial relationship with a pharmaceutical or device manufacturer.

Investigate Concerns and Take Corrective Action

Investigate when there is concern about a financial relationship between a provider and a pharmaceutical or device manufacturing company. Take appropriate corrective action if necessary and follow up to ensure the corrective action addressed the concern and is effective.

Report Findings

Share results of all compliance efforts related to financial relationships between drug and device companies with the organization's compliance committee and the board of directors.

Possible Penalties

Improper financial relationships between pharmaceutical manufacturers and drug companies can lead to a variety of criminal, civil, and administrative penalties.

Violations that trigger the Anti-Kickback Statute can lead to criminal liability to all parties—physician and pharmaceutical or device company—involved. An Anti-Kickback Statute violation can result in a felony punishable by imprisonment for up to ten years, a maximum fine of $100,000, or both. Conviction also can result in mandatory exclusion from participation in federal healthcare programs such as Medicare, Medicaid, and TRICARE.[26] The OIG also may impose civil monetary penalties for violations under the False Claims Act if the matter results in medically unnecessary care, for example.[27]

Healthcare organizations also can impose their own penalties with providers, such as disciplinary action up to and including termination, as well as reporting providers to the state board of medical licensure. Healthcare organizations also may reevaluate their contracts with pharmaceutical and device manufacturers, and terminate the relationship because of an improper relationship.

Compliance Resources

U.S. Department of Health & Human Services, Office of Inspector General

Special Fraud Alert: Physician-Owned Entities

https://oig.hhs.gov/fraud/docs/alertsandbulletins/2013/POD_Special_Fraud_Alert.pdf

Compliance Program Guidance for Pharmaceutical Manufacturers

https://oig.hhs.gov/fraud/docs/complianceguidance/042803pharmacymfgnonfr.pdf

A Roadmap for New Physicians, Avoiding Medicare and Medicaid Fraud and Abuse

https://oig.hhs.gov/compliance/physician-education/roadmap_web_version.pdf

Compliance Program Guidance for Healthcare Providers

https://oig.hhs.gov/compliance/compliance-guidance/index.asp

Measuring Compliance Program Effectiveness: A Resource Guide

https://oig.hhs.gov/compliance/101/files/HCCA-OIG-Resource-Guide.pdf

Pharmaceutical Research and Manufacturers of America

Code on Interactions with Health Care Professionals (June 2020)

https://www.phrma.org/-/media/Project/PhRMA/PhRMA-Org/PhRMA-Org/PDF/A-C/Code-of-Interaction_FINAL21.pdf

Principles on Conduct of Clinical Trials and Communication of Clinical Trial Results

https://www.phrma.org/-/media/Project/PhRMA/PhRMA-Org/PhRMA-Org/PDF/P-R/PhRMAPrinciples-of-Clinical-Trials-7.pdf

Advanced Medical Technology Association

Code of Ethics (July 2020)

https://www.advamed.org/sites/default/files/resource/advamed-code-of-ethics_2020_july20.pdf

Risk Takeaways

Main points of interest:

- Financial relationships between physicians and pharmaceutical manufacturers and device companies are high risk and can lead to conflicts of interest, violations of the Anti-Kickback Statute, and False Claims Act violations.
- OIG has issued special fraud alerts related to financial relationships between providers and pharmaceutical and device companies on more than one occasion.

Areas to watch:

- Conflicts of interest disclosures
- CMS Open Payments database
- Provider prescribing patterns
- Provider use of medical devices
- Provider use of off-label drugs and devices
- Medical necessity of prescriptions and device orders

Laws that apply:

- Anti-Kickback Statute, 42 U.S.C. § 1320a-7b(b)
- False Claims Act, 31 U.S.C. §§ 3729–3733
- Exclusions, 42 U.S.C. § 1320a–7(a)
- IRS regulations for nonprofits, 26 U.S.C. § 501(c)(3)
- Sarbanes-Oxley Act of 2002, Pub. L. 107–204, 116 Stat. 745 (2002)

Addressing compliance risks:

- Develop and implement policies and procedures that address relationships between providers and drug and device manufacturers.
- Include conflicts of interest in the organization's code of conduct.
- Develop and implement policies and procedures that address conflicts of interest.
- Establish a process to obtain and maintain conflicts of interest questionnaires and data.
- Develop and implement policies and procedures that address gifts.
- Educate providers on conflicts of interest and gifts policies.
- Educate providers on how the CMS Open Payments database is used to monitor financial relationships and potential conflicts of interest.
- Include conflicts of interest as a category in compliance investigations.
- Investigate allegations of conflicts of interest.
- Include monitoring of the CMS Open Payments database and other information to evaluate financial relationships between providers and manufacturers in an annual compliance monitoring plan or internal audit plan.
- Develop and implement corrective action plans (CAPs), including disciplinary action when necessary.
- Develop and implement conflict management plans when necessary and monitor compliance with the plans.

Endnotes

1. **Betsy Wade** is chief compliance & ethics officer at Signature HealthCARE. With more than 20 years of experience in healthcare compliance, Wade has worked in a variety of organizations overseeing compliance in a number of settings—all of which have included oversight of conflicts of interest and identification of potential compliance issues related to conflicts of interest. She also is a faculty member of the Health Care Compliance Association Basic Compliance Academy and Privacy Academy.

2. U.S. Department of Health & Human Services, Office of Inspector General, "OIG Special Fraud Alert: Speaker Programs," November 16, 2020, https://oig.hhs.gov/fraud/docs/alertsandbulletins/2020/SpecialFraudAlert-SpeakerPrograms.pdf.

3. 42 U.S.C. § 1320a-7b(b).

4. Sheryl Gay Stolberg, "The Biotech Death of Jesse Gelsinger," *The New York Times Magazine*, November 28, 1999, https://www.nytimes.com/1999/11/28/magazine/the-biotech-death-of-jesse-gelsinger.html.

5. "Exempt Organizations Annual Reporting Requirements - Governance (Form 990, Part VI)," Internal Revenue Service, updated March 19, 2020, https://www.irs.gov/charities-non-profits/exempt-organizations-annual-reporting-requirements-governance-form-990-part-vi.

6. Sarbanes- Oxley Act of 2002, Pub. Law 107–204 (July 30, 2002).

7. Ashutosh Jogalekar, "Emory in a little, Nemeroff in big, trouble," *The Curious Wavefunction* (blog), October 3, 2008, http://wavefunction.fieldofscience.com/2008/10/emory-in-little-nemeroff-in-big-trouble.html.

8. Chuck Grassley, "Grassley floor statement on drug company payments to doctors," United States Senate Committee on Finance, April 2, 2008,https://www.finance.senate.gov/ranking-members-news/grassley-floor-statement-on-drug-company-payments-to-doctors.

9. Chuck Grassley, "Payments to Physicians," Congressional Record 154, no. 91 (June 4, 2008), S5029–S5033, https://www.govinfo.gov/content/pkg/CREC-2008-06-04/html/CREC-2008-06-04-pt1-PgS5029-2.htm.

10. 42 U.S.C. § 1320a-7b(b)(1)-(2).

11. 42 U.S.C. § 1320a-7(a).

12. 42 U.S.C. § 1320a-7(b)(7); 42 U.S.C. § 1320a-7a(a)(7).

13. OIG Compliance Program Guidance for Pharmaceutical Manufacturers, 68 Fed. Reg. 23,731 (May 5, 2003), https://oig.hhs.gov/authorities/docs/03/050503FRCPGPharmac.pdf.

14. U.S. Department of Health & Human Services, Office of Inspector General, *A Roadmap for New Physicians: Avoiding Medicare and Medicaid Fraud and Abuse*, accessed February 19, 2021, https://oig.hhs.gov/compliance/physician-education/roadmap_web_version.pdf.

15. Pharmaceutical Research and Manufacturers of America, *Code on Interactions with Health Care Professionals*, accessed February 19, 2021, https://www.phrma.org/-/media/Project/PhRMA/PhRMA-Org/PhRMA-Org/PDF/A-C/Code-of-Interaction_FINAL21.pdf.

16. Pharmaceutical Research and Manufacturers of America, *Principles on Conduct of Clinical Trials and Communication of Clinical Trial Results*, accessed February 19, 2021, https://www.phrma.org/-/media/Project/PhRMA/PhRMA-Org/PhRMA-Org/PDF/P-R/PhRMAPrinciples-of-Clinical-Trials-7.pdf.

17. Advanced Medical Technology Association, *AdvaMed Code of Ethics on Interactions with U.S. Health Care Professionals*, accessed February 19, 2021, https://www.advamed.org/sites/default/files/resource/advamed-code-of-ethics_2020_july20.pdf.

18. "PODS," Advanced Medical Technology Association, accessed February 19, 2021,https://www.advamed.org/issues/legal-compliance/pods.

19. U.S. Department of Health & Human Services, Office of Inspector General, "Special Fraud Alert: Physician-Owned Entities," March 26, 2013, https://oig.hhs.gov/fraud/docs/alertsandbulletins/2013/POD_Special_Fraud_Alert.pdf.

20. Physician Payments Sunshine Act, Pub. L. No. 111–148 § 6002 (March 23, 2010).

21. 42 U.S.C. § 18001 et seq.

22. Medicare, Medicaid, Children's Health Insurance Programs; Transparency Reports and Reporting of Physician Ownership or Investment Interests, 78 Fed. Reg. 9,458 (February 8, 2013).

23. 31 U.S.C. §§ 3729–3733.

24. "Off-Label Marketing and Promotion of Drugs and Medical Devices," Hagens Berman Sobol Shapiro LLP (blog), accessed February 19, 2021, https://www.hbsslaw.com/whistleblower/pharmaceuticalmedical-device-fraud-including-off-label-promotion.

25. "Open Payments," Centers for Medicare & Medicaid Services, updated February 2, 2021, https://www.cms.gov/OpenPayments.

26. 42 U.S.C. § 1320a-7(a).

27. 42 U.S.C. § 1320a-7(b)(7); 42 U.S.C. § 1320a-7a(a)(7).

Contracts with Referral Sources

Entering into a Proper Physician Arrangement

By Robert A. Wade, Esq.[1]

What Is a Proper Physician Arrangement?

It is vitally important that healthcare organizations have a formal process for entering into financial arrangements with physician referral sources. Merely *offering* a financial arrangement to a referring physician that does not comply with healthcare regulatory requirements, including fair market value and commercial reasonableness, could impose civil and criminal penalties on all persons and entities involved.

By way of example, if an officer for a healthcare entity offers a financial arrangement to a referring physician that is not consistent with fair market value or is not commercially reasonable, the offering entity, officer of the entity, and recipient physician could be subject to criminal prosecution and penalties under the Anti-Kickback Statute.[2] If the offering of the financial terms are not consistent with fair market value or are not commercially reasonable, those responsible within the offering entity for the development of the financial arrangement could exacerbate the potential liability. If a high-ranking officer of a healthcare entity creates a financial arrangement that is not compliant with fair market value or commercial reasonableness principles, individuals subordinate to the officer, believing that the officer's proposal is compliant, could unknowingly document and finalize the inappropriate financial arrangement.

The commencement of financial arrangements involve multiple parties within healthcare organizations. Frequently, operating divisions, finance, legal, and compliance will all be involved in some aspect with respect to the creation of and entering into financial arrangements with physicians. Because multiple departments are involved, the procedures implemented by a healthcare organization should require input and approval by each applicable department. The risk of compliance violations for entering into physician financial arrangements is increased if a single individual determines the terms and conditions of the financial arrangements and asks the other departments (such as finance, legal, and compliance) to simply "paper the deal."

If a financial arrangement involves a sophisticated healthcare entity, physicians contracting with such entity frequently rely on the expertise of the entity, assuming that the entity understands the healthcare regulatory restrictions around fair market value and commercial reasonableness and compliance with other healthcare regulatory requirements. Because the contracting physician may be exposed to potential healthcare regulatory liability, it is important that the contracting physician seeks counsel from independent competent counselors knowledgeable about the healthcare regulatory requirements.

Risk Area Governance

The following laws apply when entering into physician financial arrangements.

Stark Law, 42 U.S.C. § 1395nn

If a physician (or an immediate family member) has a financial arrangement with an entity that performs or bills designated health services, the financial arrangement will need to comply fully with an exception. Otherwise, the physician cannot refer designated health services to the entity, and the entity cannot bill for the designated health services referred by the applicable physician.[3]

Anti-Kickback Statute, 42 U.S.C. § 1320(a)–7b(b)

If a purpose of entering into a physician financial arrangement is to induce the physician to refer services that are reimbursed by Medicare or Medicaid, criminal liability can occur. The Anti-Kickback Statute has a series of safe harbors. Unlike the exceptions to the Stark Law, all financial arrangements are not required to comply with all components of a safe harbor. If all components of a safe harbor are not met, the financial arrangement will be defensible under the Anti-Kickback Statute as long as neither party intended to induce referrals through the offering of or entering into the financial arrangement.[4]

False Claims Act, 31 U.S.C. §§ 3729–3733

If a financial arrangement is entered into that does not comply with the Stark Law or the Anti-Kickback Statute, and if the parties enter into the financial arrangement with actual knowledge, reckless disregard, or intentional indifference to the law, billing for or retention of reimbursement could be trebled and a fine assessed from $11,665 to $23,331.[56]

Civil Monetary Penalties Law, 42 U.S.C. § 1320a–7a

Civil monetary penalties occur when an entity bills Medicare or Medicaid for items or services when the submission of the claim is known to be false or fraudulent.[7]

Common Compliance Risks

The common compliance risks when entering into physician financial arrangements include:

Inappropriate Intent

Entering into a physician financial arrangement motivated in whole or in part by capturing referrals from the physician when there is a connection between the financial arrangement and the physician's referrals.

Fair Market Value

Entering into financial arrangements where, for example, the physician is compensated above market for services rendered or the physician is paying for items or services, like leasing of space or equipment from a referral (i.e., hospital) recipient that is below fair market value.

Commercial Reasonableness

It is inappropriate for an entity to pay a physician, even at fair market value, for items or services that are not commercially reasonable. Financial arrangements should be assessed to determine whether a reasonably prudent healthcare entity would contract with a referring physician for services. By way of example, if only one medical director over a service line is reasonable, it may not be commercially reasonable to enter into a second medical directorship with a referring physician even if the compensation paid to such physician was determined to be fair market value.

Addressing Compliance Risks

Healthcare entities should strictly follow a regimented process when deciding to enter into a financial arrangement with a referring physician.

Determine Business or Medical Justification

A starting point should be to determine the business or medical justification for entering into the physician financial arrangement. The process should require documentation as to the need for the contracted service and whether the service could be provided through another provider. By way of example, the process should determine whether the service requires a physician to perform the duties and responsibilities or whether the service could be performed by a nonphysician practitioner or a nonclinical person.

Determine Extent and Amount of Services

After it has been determined that the financial arrangement is commercially reasonable, the extent and amount of services will need to be determined. By way of example, are the services from the referring physician required on a full-time basis, or can the services be reasonably provided 10 hours per week on a part-time basis?

Determine Fair Market Value Compensation

After the financial arrangement has been determined to be commercially reasonable, the amount of compensation will need to be assessed to ensure that the compensation paid is representative of fair market value. The annual salary, if the services are required on a full-time basis, should be benchmarked to the local market or through the use of national benchmark sources (e.g., SullivanCotter, Medical Group Management Association, American Medical Group Association). If the financial arrangement is part-time, the hourly rate paid should be evaluated to determine whether it is defensible either based upon the type of services performed or the physician's specialty if the services are required to be performed by a physician of a particular specialty. Proof of arm's-length negotiations, including counteroffers from other entities, could be helpful in evaluating fair market value. Objective factors, like hours worked or productivity (e.g., work relative value units (wRVUs), number of patient encounters), can be used to assess fair market value. Subjective factors can also be used, like high demand for a specialty with few providers in the service area. Fair market value can either be assessed and documented internally or through the use of outside third parties.

Submit Financial Arrangement for Committee Review

After the commercial reasonableness justification and fair market value documentation are developed, a way to minimize risk when entering into physician financial arrangements is to have the financial arrangement approved by a committee within the healthcare entity. The committee approving of entering into physician financial arrangements could either be a management committee, board committee, or a mixture of management and board members.

Establish Thresholds for Heightened Security

Another way to address risks when entering into physician financial arrangements is to establish thresholds for heightened scrutiny. By way of example, if the proposed compensation exceeds the 75th percentile from a national benchmarking source, such financial arrangement may require the review and approval from an independent third party. Likewise, if a compensation arrangement exceeds the 75th percentile, instead of having the financial arrangement approved by a management committee, the financial arrangement may require approval from either a board committee or a committee made up of both management and board members.

Possible Penalties

- **Stark Law**: Repayment of reimbursement received as well as possible exclusion from participation in federal healthcare programs.[8]
- **Anti-Kickback Statute**: Up to five years in prison, exclusion from participation in federal healthcare programs, and up to $50,000 per kickback plus three times the amount of the remuneration received.[9]
- **False Claims Act**: Three times the amount of reimbursement received (treble damages) plus up to $23,331 (violations of the Anti-Kickback Statute) or $11,665 (Stark Law violations or actions involving false claims or statements).[10]
- **Civil Monetary Penalties Law**: Generally, not more than $20,000 for each item or service inappropriately billed or reimbursement received.[11]

Compliance Resources

The following resources provide information regarding the primary healthcare regulations that apply to physician compensation arrangements:

Centers for Medicare & Medicaid Services

Stark Law

https://www.cms.gov/Medicare/Fraud-and-Abuse/PhysicianSelfReferral/index

U.S. Department of Health & Human Services, Office of Inspector General

Compliance Guidance

https://oig.hhs.gov/compliance/compliance-guidance/index.asp

Anti-Kickback Safe Harbor Regulations

https://www.oig.hhs.gov/compliance/safe-harbor-regulations/index.asp

Risk Takeaways

Main points of interest:
- Healthcare entities should establish a formal process to develop and enter into physician financial arrangements.
- Penalties for entering into noncompliant arrangements are high, including trebled damages, penalties up to $23,331, and even imprisonment.

Areas to watch:
- The key areas to consider are whether the financial arrangement with the referring physician is commercially reasonable and whether the financial terms can be defended as representative of fair market value.
- Strict compliance with a Stark Law exception is required, including, under most circumstances (with the primary exception being employment), a signed written arrangement.

Laws that apply:
- Stark Law, 42 U.S.C. § 1395nn
- Anti-Kickback Statute, 42 U.S.C. § 1320a–7b(b)
- False Claims Act, 31 U.S.C. §§ 3729–3733
- Civil Monetary Penalties Law, 42 U.S.C. § 1320a–7a

Addressing compliance risks:
- To decrease the risks of entering into inappropriate financial arrangements with referring physicians, healthcare organizations should have:
  - A formal approval process,
  - Commercial reasonableness documentation for each financial arrangement, and
  - Documentation that supports that the financial arrangement is representative of fair market value.
- Use national benchmarking sources and independent third parties to document commercial reasonableness/fair market value.

Endnotes

1. **Bob Wade** is Partner at Barnes & Thornburg LLP, where he provides legal and compliance counsel to multiple types of healthcare providers across the country, including counsel on how to implement a process and monitor the implementation of physician compensation arrangements.
2. 42. U.S.C. § 1320(a)-7b(b).
3. 42 U.S.C. § 1395nn.
4. 42 U.S.C. § 1320(a)-7b(b).
5. 28 C.F.R. § 85.5.
6. 31 U.S.C. 3729.
7. 42 U.S.C. § 1320a-7a.
8. 42 U.S.C. § 1395nn(g).
9. 42 U.S.C. § 1320-7b(b).
10. 31 U.S.C. 3729.
11. 42 U.S.C. § 1320a-7a.

Importance of Monitoring These Arrangements

By Robert A. Wade, Esq.[1]

Why Is it Important to Monitor Contracts with Referral Sources?

Once a financial arrangement is entered into with referral sources, it is vitally important that the financial arrangement be monitored to ensure that it remains compliant with all material laws, rules, and regulations. Healthcare organizations may establish detailed policies and procedures with respect to entry into proper physician financial arrangements. Healthcare organizations may document the fair market value basis for the financial arrangement and why it is commercially reasonable. The entry into financial arrangements with referral sources, including physicians, only begins the journey of compliance. Monitoring each financial arrangement for compliance is a material part of a financial arrangement with referral sources. A healthcare entity, hypothetically, could enter into a financial arrangement with a referring physician that meets fair market value compensation and commercially reasonable standards. By way of example, a healthcare entity may document that entering into a financial arrangement with a referring physician for medical director administrative services at an hourly rate of $150 is fair market value based upon the applicable physician's specialty, and the healthcare entity may adequately document that the financial arrangement is commercially reasonable because the services are reasonable and necessary. Frequently, however, even though the commencement of the financial arrangement with the referring physician may be representative of fair market value and be documented to be commercially reasonable, if the financial arrangement is not carefully monitored during the existence of the arrangement, the arrangement may not meet fair market value and commercial reasonableness standards through the implementation of the financial arrangement. It is also possible that if the arrangement is an independent contractor arrangement, and if the arrangement is not continuously subject to a written arrangement signed by the parties, the arrangement could fall out of compliance for failure to comply with documentation requirements, including the written arrangement signed by the parties requirement under the personal service arrangements exception under the Stark Law.[2]

Using this example, assume that the healthcare entity pays a monthly stipend of $1,500 for 10 hours of administrative services. If the arrangement is not carefully monitored, the healthcare entity could continue to pay $1,500 per month for ten hours of service while the contracted physician only provides five hours of administrative service on average per month, the resulting hourly rate would be $300 per hour as opposed to $150 per hour.

$1,500 [monthly stipend] ÷ 5 hours = $300 per hour

versus

$1,500 [monthly stipend] ÷ 10 hours = $150 per hour

This example shows one way it is possible for a financial arrangement to fall out of compliance and exceed fair market value and commercial reasonableness standards if the administrative medical directorship is not *monitored* by the healthcare entity and the physician. These are requirements under the Stark Law and Anti-Kickback Statute.

Risk Area Governance

The following laws apply when entering into physician financial arrangements.

Stark Law, 42 U.S.C. § 1395nn

If a physician (or an immediate family member) has a financial arrangement with an entity that performs or bills designated health services, the financial arrangement will need to comply fully with an exception. Otherwise, the physician cannot refer designated health services to the entity, and the entity cannot bill for the designated health services referred by the applicable physician.[3]

Anti-Kickback Statute, 42 U.S.C. § 1320(a)-7b(b)

If a purpose of entering into a physician financial arrangement is to induce the physician to refer services that are reimbursed by Medicare or Medicaid, criminal liability can occur. The Anti-Kickback Statute has a series of safe harbors. Unlike the exceptions to the Stark Law, all financial arrangements are not required to comply with all components of a safe harbor. If all components of a safe harbor are not met, the financial arrangement will be defensible under the Anti-Kickback Statute as long as neither party intended to induce referrals through the offering of or entering into the financial arrangement.[4]

False Claims Act, 31 U.S.C. §§ 3729–3733

If a financial arrangement is entered into that does not comply with the Stark Law or the Anti-Kickback Statute, and if the parties enter into the financial arrangement with actual knowledge, reckless disregard, or intentional indifference to the law, billing for or retention of reimbursement could be trebled and a fine assessed from $11,665 to $23,331.[56]

Civil Monetary Penalties Law, 42 U.S.C. § 1320a–7a

Civil monetary penalties occur when an entity bills Medicare or Medicaid for items or services when the submission of the claim is known to be false or fraudulent.[7]

Common Compliance Risks

The common compliance risks when monitoring financial arrangements with referring physicians include:

Compensation above Fair Market Value

If a monthly, quarterly, or annual stipend is paid and if the services provided by the physician do not comply with the anticipated hourly requirements when the financial arrangement was entered into, the compensation arrangement could exceed fair market value parameters. If, alternatively, the healthcare entity compensates the physician based upon hours worked and if the physician either fails to accurately record the hours worked or the healthcare entity pays inconsistently with the hours worked as reported, the compensation paid to the referring physician could exceed fair market value. Monitoring helps assure that the arrangement remains at fair market value.

Commercial Reasonableness

If the physician is compensated based upon projected hours that are higher when compared with the hours actually worked, the stipend compensation arrangement could be determined to be not commercially reasonable. It is commercially unreasonable to compensate a physician above fair market value. It is critical for the healthcare entity to monitor the types of services provided by the physician to ensure that they are consistent with the services anticipated to be provided when the financial arrangement was entered into by the parties. For example, if the physician is a medical director and was expected to attend meetings, draft policies and procedures, and educate staff, but the physician documented hours spent reading medical journals, the documented "reading" services may not be deemed to be commercially reasonable with respect to the types of services the healthcare entity desired when the contractual arrangement commenced. Simply stated, it is important that the services provided by the physician be monitored to ensure the services provided by the physician and compensation by the healthcare entity are consistent with the commercial reasonable determination of the types of services needed when the financial arrangement was entered into by the parties. It is also important for the healthcare entity to ensure that the types of services being performed are reasonably necessary to be performed by the contracted physician. By way of example, if the services can be reasonably provided by the healthcare entity's nonadministrative staff, it may not be commercially reasonable to compensate such physician services performed by a physician.

Inappropriate Tying of Referrals

It is permissible under the Stark Law to require referrals if the referrals are connected with the compensated services performed by the physician.[8] Any mandated referral requirement should be monitored to ensure that the mandated referrals are connected to the compensation arrangement entered into between the healthcare entity and the referring physician. Therefore, if mandated referrals are required by the written arrangement, it is important to monitor the use of the mandated referral requirement to ensure such referrals are connected to the compensation arrangement.[9]

Addressing Compliance Risks

Establish and Follow a Strict Documentation Process

Healthcare entities should establish and strictly follow a process to receive documentation for the compensated services rendered by referring physicians. Documentation can include monitoring of hours worked, studies, and evaluation of patient encounters if the financial arrangement is for physician professional services.

Documentation regarding professional clinical services may be different when documenting administrative services. Clinical services could be established through documenting personally performed work relative value units (wRVUs), patient encounters, or charges/collections for professional services. Administrative services may require different compliance monitoring oversight, including the review of documented hours worked like through a monthly time log. If monthly time logs are used, it is recognized as a best practice for a healthcare entity's administrator to cosign the physician's time log to affirm that the hours worked were actually performed by the physician and were hours related to the contractual arrangement and not, for example, direct patient care services that may be separately reimbursed and paid to the physician. Monitoring is critical to ensure compensated professional hours are distinct from administrative hours.

Monitor Payment Process

It is also important for healthcare entities to monitor the payment process for compensation paid to referral sources. It is possible that a healthcare organization may have separate payment processes depending upon the classification of the physician providing the contracted services. For example, if the physician is a W-2 employee, the physician could be compensated through the healthcare entity's payroll process, but if the physician was a 1099 independent contractor, the physician could be compensated through the healthcare entity's accounts payable process. Frequently, different personnel are responsible for monitoring payroll as opposed to accounts payable. Therefore, monitoring how referring physicians are compensated may involve a different process depending upon whether the physician is classified as a W-2 employee or 1099 independent contractor.

Possible Penalties

- **Stark Law**: Repayment of reimbursement received as well as possible exclusion from participation in federal health care programs.[10]
- **Anti-Kickback Statute**: Up to five years in prison, exclusion from participation in federal health care programs, up to $50,000 per kickback plus three times the amount of the remuneration received, and receipt of a corporate integrity agreement.[11]
- **False Claims Act**: Three times the amount of reimbursement received (treble damages) plus up to $23,331 (violations of the Anti-Kickback Statute) or $11,665 (Stark Law violations or actions involving false claims or statements).[12]
- **Civil Monetary Penalties Law**: Generally, not more than $20,000 for each item or service inappropriately billed or reimbursement received.[13]

Compliance Resources

The following resources provide information regarding the primary healthcare regulations that apply to physician compensation arrangements.

Centers for Medicare & Medicaid Services

Stark Law

https://www.cms.gov/Medicare/Fraud-and-Abuse/PhysicianSelfReferral/index

U.S. Department of Health & Human Services, Office of Inspector General

Compliance Guidance

https://oig.hhs.gov/compliance/compliance-guidance/index.asp

Anti-Kickback Safe Harbor Regulations

https://www.oig.hhs.gov/compliance/safe-harbor-regulations/index.asp

Risk Takeaways

Main points of interest:
- Healthcare entities should establish a formal process to account for the services performed by the referring physicians.
- These processes could differ depending upon whether the referring physician is compensated based upon a monthly/quarterly/annual stipend or hourly rate.
- The monitoring processes can also differ depending upon whether the referring physician is classified as a W-2 employee or 1099 independent contractor.

Areas to watch:
- One key area to watch is whether the amount of services contracted are actually performed by the referring physician during the term of the financial arrangement. If the financial arrangement reasonably estimated that the physician would work 100 hours in the performance of a medical directorship, it is important that the healthcare entity receive documentation to ensure that the physician was working the projected 100 hours.
- Ensure that the types of services being performed and compensated are the same services anticipated when the financial arrangement was entered into between the parties. If, by way of example, the physician was contracted to assist in the implementation of the healthcare entity's electronic health record, the services documented and compensated should be reasonably and materially related to the implementation of the healthcare entity's electronic health record.

Laws that apply:
- Stark Law, 42 U.S.C. § 1395nn
- Anti-Kickback Statute, 42 U.S.C. § 1320a-7b(b)
- False Claims Act, 31 U.S.C. §§ 3729-3733
- Civil Monetary Penalties Law, 42 U.S.C. § 1320a-7a

Addressing compliance risks:
- To decrease monitoring risks, healthcare entities should have a regimented process to receive and evaluate the types and amount of services performed by the physician referral source.
- A best practice is to have the amount and types of services validated by a healthcare entity's executive to ensure that the services being compensated are consistent with the type and amount of services validated as being fair market value and commercially reasonable when the financial arrangement was first entered into.
- It is also a best practice to periodically monitor the payroll and accounts payable processes for compensation paid to referral sources to ensure that the compensation paid is consistent with the terms and conditions when the financial arrangement was determined to be fair market value and commercially reasonable when first entered into by and between the parties.

Endnotes

1. **Bob Wade** is Partner at Barnes & Thornburg LLP, where he provides legal and compliance counsel to multiple types of healthcare providers across the country, including counsel on how to implement a process and monitor the implementation of physician compensation arrangements.
2. 42 U.S.C. § 1395nn.
3. 42 U.S.C. § 1395nn.
4. 42 U.S.C. § 1320(a)-7b(b).
5. 31 U.S.C. § 3729.
6. 28 C.F.R. § 85.5.
7. 42 U.S.C. § 1320a--7a.
8. 42 U.S.C. §1395nn.
9. 42 C.F.R. § 411.354(c)(4).
10. 42 U.S.C. § 1395nn(g).
11. 42 U.S.C. § 1320(a)-7b(b).
12. 31 U.S.C. § 3729.
13. 42 U.S.C. § 1320a-7a.

Real Estate Compliance

By Goran Musinovic,[1] J.D., CHC; Michael E. Honeycutt,[2] CCIM, CRE; and Gregory P. Gheen,[3] CCIM, CRE

What Is Real Estate Compliance?

Healthcare real estate is unique. The Stark Law,[4] the Anti-Kickback Statute,[5] the False Claims Act,[6] and a myriad of other healthcare statutes and regulations create a complex regulatory environment in which healthcare providers must operate daily. A course of action that may be perfectly acceptable in any other type of real estate transaction could, in the context of healthcare real estate, result in serious regulatory violations and expose healthcare providers to significant liability.

Real estate transactions can be subdivided into two broad, general categories: lease transactions and purchase and sale transactions. Although purchase and sale transactions can and do expose healthcare providers to regulatory liability, lease transactions present greater compliance risk for two reasons. First, healthcare providers enter into far more lease transactions with referral sources than purchase and sale transactions. Second, lease transactions are long-term arrangements and, as a result, require constant monitoring and enforcement of their terms to avoid compliance infractions. Consequently, this article will focus on real estate lease arrangements with referral sources and outline the governing laws, common compliance risks with these arrangements, ways to mitigate compliance risks, and compliance resources for healthcare providers.

Risk Area Governance

To avoid violating the Stark Law, lease arrangements between referring physicians and healthcare providers must comply with the rental of office space exception under the Stark Law (Lease Exception), which consists of the following elements:

1. The lease arrangement must be in writing, signed by all parties, and adequately describe the leased premises;
2. The term of the lease arrangement must be at least one year;
3. The leased premises must not exceed that which is reasonable and necessary for the legitimate business purposes of the lease;
4. Leased space must be used exclusively by the lessee;
5. Rent under the lease arrangement must be set in advance and consistent with fair market value (FMV);
6. The rental charges under the lease arrangement cannot be determined in a manner that considers the volume or value of any referrals or other business generated between the parties, uses a formula based on a percentage of the revenue attributable to the services performed or business generated in the office space or is based on per-unit of service rental charges; and
7. The lease arrangement would be commercially reasonable even if no referrals were made between the lessee and the lessor.[7]

One of the key elements of the Lease Exception is the requirement for the lease arrangement to be consistent with FMV, which is defined, in pertinent part, under the Stark Law as follows:

- Fair market value means, "with respect to the rental of office space, the value in an arm's-length transaction of rental property for general commercial purposes (not taking into account its intended use), without adjustment to reflect the additional value the prospective lessee or lessor would attribute to the proximity or convenience to the lessor where the lessor is a potential source of patient referrals to the lessee, and consistent with the general market value of the subject transaction."[8]
- General market value means, "with respect to the rental of equipment or the rental of office space, the price that rental property would bring at the time the parties enter into the rental arrangement as the result of bona fide bargaining between a well-informed lessor and lessee that are not otherwise in a position to generate business for each other."[9]

Additionally, under the Lease Exception, the lease arrangement must be commercially reasonable, which has recently been defined under the Stark Law to mean the following:

Commercially reasonable means that the particular arrangement furthers a legitimate business purpose of the parties to the arrangement and is sensible, considering the characteristics of the parties, including their size, type, scope, and specialty. An arrangement may be commercially reasonable even if it does not result in profit for one or more of the parties.[10]

A lease arrangement between a healthcare provider and a referral source that is not consistent with FMV and/or that is not commercially reasonable can violate the Stark Law, exposing healthcare providers to potential liability to the government.

Regarding lease arrangements, the Anti-Kickback Statute is similar to the Stark Law in that it prohibits space leasing arrangements between healthcare providers and referral sources unless the arrangement meets the space rental safe harbor, which contains similar elements to the Lease Exception.[11] Therefore, the compliance risks outlined in this article not only expose healthcare providers to potential liability under the Stark Law but to potential liability under the Anti-Kickback Statute.

On December 2, 2020, the Department of Health & Human Services Office of Inspector General (OIG) published the Revisions to Safe Harbors Under the Anti-Kickback Statute and Civil Monetary Penalty Rules Regarding Beneficiary Inducements final rule, and the Centers for Medicare & Medicaid Services (CMS) issued the Modernizing and Clarifying the Physician Self-Referral Regulations final rule to reduce regulatory barriers to care coordination and accelerate the transformation of the healthcare system into one that pays for value and promotes the delivery of coordinated care.[12][13] The final rules went into effect on January 19, 2021, and brought several important changes and clarifications affecting real estate lease arrangements with referral sources, including, but not limited to, changes to the definition of FMV for leasing arrangements and the creation of the statutory definition of commercial reasonableness as outlined above, changes to the exclusive use requirements under the Lease Exception clarifying that the exclusive use requirement requires only the lessor to be excluded from the space, and the expansion of certain Stark Law exceptions (i.e., the fair market value exception, the certain arrangements with hospitals exception, and the payments by a physician exception) that could apply to space leases in some circumstances.[14][15][16][17][18][19]

Common Compliance Risks

Real estate lease arrangements between referral sources and healthcare providers present numerous compliance risks, any one of which can trigger a violation under the Stark Law or the Anti-Kickback Statute. Compliance risks associated with lease arrangements can be generally classified as "transactional" or "operational." Transactional compliance risks stem from the lease arrangement itself and the specific structure of the transaction. Operational compliance risks stem from the subsequent administration, or lack thereof, of the terms of the lease arrangement with a referring physician. Both compliance risks are caused by structural deficiencies in healthcare providers' compliance programs, and both can expose healthcare providers to significant liability.

Transactional Compliance Risks

Healthcare providers face a myriad of transactional compliance risks when they enter into lease arrangements with referral sources. Some, such as the lease being signed by all the parties, are easy to identify. Others, particularly compliance risks associated with FMV and commercial reasonableness requirements, are more subtle and have a greater potential to result in violations. Healthcare providers must be especially cognizant of the compliance risks associated with rent rates, commercial reasonableness analyses, square footage measurements of leased premises, and tenant improvement allowances.

Rent Rates

Healthcare providers are legally obligated to charge or pay rent to referral sources that is consistent with FMV. The failure of healthcare providers to procure FMV support from qualified and independent third-party valuation experts or to procure FMV reports that align with the transactions they are supposed to support are common transactional compliance risks relating to rent rates.

Application of the FMV Report

Even if healthcare providers procure and rely on FMV reports from qualified valuation experts, an FMV report that is inaccurate or, as is more often the case, misapplied to the transaction can leave healthcare providers responsible for Stark Law violations. Consequently, healthcare providers should have internal protocols to ensure that they procure high-quality FMV reports that support their real estate lease transactions and apply those reports accurately to those transactions.

Commercial Reasonableness

In addition to charging rent rates consistent with FMV, lease arrangements with referral sources must be commercially reasonable. Many healthcare providers fail to undertake or document commercial reasonableness analyses of real estate lease arrangements with referral sources. Consequently, if a real estate lease arrangement is challenged on commercial reasonableness grounds, the healthcare providers lack documentary evidence to defend the arrangement. Additionally, many healthcare providers are under the mistaken belief that so long as a transaction is consistent with FMV, it is automatically commercially reasonable. That, however, is not always the case. If a healthcare provider enters into a lease arrangement with a referral source that is consistent with FMV, but for space that the healthcare provider does not need, the arrangement may not be commercially reasonable, which is one of the requirements under the Lease Exception.

Square Footage Measurements

While it is critically important for healthcare providers to charge referral sources rent rates per square foot that are consistent with FMV, it is equally important to ensure that the square footage of the leased premises is accurately measured. Remuneration to referral sources can be accomplished by charging rent rates below FMV or by not charging the referral source for the entirety of the space the referral source is occupying. For example, if a referral source leases 10,000 square feet from a healthcare provider but only pays for 9,500 square feet because the space was inaccurately measured or inaccurately accounted for in the lease arrangement, the referral source receives remuneration from the healthcare provider by not having to pay for 500 square feet of space that it occupies.

Tenant Improvement Allowances

Providers should carefully consider the amount of tenant improvement allowances granted to referral source tenants. Failing to account for tenant improvement allowances in FMV reports can result in incorrect FMV rent range determinations. Additionally, overly generous and unnecessary allowances for tenant improvements to referral sources can also lead to transactions not being commercially reasonable (e.g., typically, it would not be commercially reasonable to provide a $100,000 tenant improvement allowance for a lease arrangement that generates $125,000 in total rent revenue). Finally, a healthcare provider's use of internal benchmarks and caps for tenant improvement allowances can create additional compliance risks, especially if those benchmarks are exceeded or if tenant improvement allowances are given for leased spaces that are already in turnkey condition, as this could be perceived as remuneration for inducing or rewarding patient referrals.

Off-Lease Benefits

Healthcare providers should also be aware of providing benefits to referral sources at no cost that are not referenced in a lease arrangement and not accounted for in the rent rate. Examples of off-lease benefits include free hazardous/medical waste removal services, free parking, free meals, free telephone, free cable and internet, and free transportation services. Any benefit that a healthcare provider grants at no cost to the referral source could be interpreted as remuneration to the referral source to induce or reward patient referrals, subjecting the healthcare provider to significant penalties.

Operational Compliance Risks

Structuring lease arrangements properly and in compliance with the Stark Law is only half the battle. The proper administration of the lease arrangements is just as important. A lease arrangement structured in perfect compliance with healthcare regulations can still expose healthcare providers to compliance violations if the arrangement is not properly administered. Common operational compliance risks involve rent collection, operating expense reconciliations, off-lease benefits, space creep, and timeshare arrangements in general.

Rent Collection

To avoid liability under the applicable healthcare regulations, healthcare providers must collect all rent due under their lease arrangements with referring physicians. Despite this requirement, many healthcare providers regularly fail to do so. This failure can manifest in many different forms.

Tenant physicians may fail to pay rent for their spaces for various reasons, yet healthcare providers inadvertently allow them to continue occupying their spaces for extended periods. When this happens, many healthcare providers fail to send notice of default letters and seek available remedies under the law. If and when the delinquent tenants finally decide to pay their outstanding rent, healthcare providers often fail to impose and collect late fees or interest charges on the delinquent amounts despite lease arrangements requiring them to do so. These failures can happen because of administrative oversights or healthcare providers' reluctance to engage in actions that could upset the physicians or result in the healthcare providers garnering a negative reputation with physicians.

Similar issues arise with rent escalators and holdover premiums. Most lease arrangements contain annual lease escalators through which a tenant's base rent increases by a certain percentage (typically between 2% and 4%) each year throughout the term of the lease. However, healthcare providers do not always apply these rent escalations, resulting in tenant physicians paying less in total rent during the term of the lease than required under the lease. Many lease arrangements also require physicians who go into holdover to pay a higher rent, typically set as a percentage of the base rent rate for the year immediately preceding the holdover period (typically between 125% and 200%), during the holdover period. Just like with late fees and rent escalators, these holdover premiums are often not imposed and collected. As a result, physicians pay less rent than required under the lease arrangement.

Tenant Improvement Allowances

Typically, tenant improvement allowances are capped by the landlord, and most lease arrangements require tenants to pay for costs of improvements in excess of the tenant improvement allowance as additional rent. Problems arise when healthcare providers fail to charge these tenant improvement allowance overages as additional rent, resulting in healthcare providers not collecting the full amounts due under the lease arrangements.

Operating Expenses

Healthcare providers face additional compliance risks when they enter into triple net leases and modified gross leases. These types of leases require tenants to pay for a specified share of the enumerated operating expenses based on the amount of space they occupy in the building. Many healthcare providers fail to reconcile operating expenses, resulting in referring physicians not paying the operating expenses for which they are responsible.

Including or excluding certain property expenses in or from operating expenses can also raise compliance concerns. For example, healthcare providers may fail to include estimated insurance premiums in operating expenses when they are self-insured, meaning the tenant physicians will not have to pay for their share of insurance on the property. Another potential issue arises when healthcare providers make repairs inside a physician's leased premises despite the tenant being obligated under the lease to pay for the costs of such repairs. If the healthcare provider inadvertently includes the costs of those repairs in the total operating expenses for the property that are then shared by all the tenants in the building, that certain tenant will not be paying for all expenses according to the terms of the lease arrangement.

Space Creep

Space creep is an issue that arises when healthcare providers allow or fail to recognize that physicians are using or have moved into vacant spaces adjacent to the space covered under their lease arrangement without executing a lease amendment or paying additional rent. Often, space creep involves a physician using storage or administrative spaces. These additional spaces are not covered by the physician's existing lease arrangement with the healthcare provider. As a result, the physician ends up occupying space without a written lease in place, which violates the applicable healthcare regulations. The physician receives remuneration from the healthcare provider by not paying for the additional space.

The best way to prevent space creep is for healthcare providers to conduct regular walkthroughs of their real estate portfolio to ensure that physicians do not occupy more space than provided for under their leases. Additionally, a physician should never be allowed to use any space in a building, regardless of how small or immaterial it may be, without first executing an amendment to their existing lease agreement (or a new lease agreement for such space) that incorporates the additional space into the lease and defines the additional rent the physician must pay.

Lease Expirations

Many healthcare providers fail to track lease expiration dates, and, as a result, referral source tenants may occupy spaces without active lease arrangements in place. This presents several issues. First, even if the lease rates were consistent with FMV and supported by a defensible FMV report when the lease was first entered into, once the lease expires, the rates charged under the expired lease may no longer be consistent with FMV. Second, the healthcare provider may fail to continue collecting rent from tenants occupying the space after lease expiration. Because expired leases are difficult to monitor and may not be reflected on the lists reviewed by healthcare providers' compliance and audit departments, healthcare providers inadvertently allow tenants to occupy spaces for years without a lease in place and without paying rent. Third, where lease arrangements expire through the fault of the healthcare providers or their third-party lease administrators, healthcare providers may be reluctant to impose holdover premiums on the tenants whose leases have expired even though the terms of the lease require them to do so.

Poorly designed leasing policies and procedures are often the root cause when a healthcare provider allows a lease arrangement to expire. Bottlenecks in the leasing process prolong lease renewal discussions and negotiations and can result in the expiration of the lease arrangement before renewal is executed. Additionally, many healthcare providers fail to implement centralized tracking systems that monitor the material terms of leases, such as lease expiration dates, rent escalation dates, payment history, etc., and thus fail to realize that a lease arrangement has expired or is about to expire. Finally, many healthcare providers fail to conduct regular walk-throughs of their real estate portfolios to ensure that the occupied spaces are covered by active lease arrangements and used in the manner prescribed in such lease arrangements.

Timeshare Lease Arrangements

Timeshare lease arrangements, where a physician leases a defined space part-time (e.g., two days a week from 8:00 a.m. to 12:00 p.m.), present significant compliance risks for healthcare providers. Tracking the time spent by a physician in the space covered under a timeshare lease arrangement presents administrative challenges that could result in operational compliance issues. A physician may, for example, advertently or inadvertently use the space for more time than allotted under the timeshare lease arrangement. In such an instance, the healthcare provider could be seen as providing remuneration to the physician through reduced rent.

Space creep issues can be especially prevalent in timeshare lease arrangements. Because physicians do not occupy the spaces full-time, they will often bring patient records and other supplies and materials and ask to store them in closets or spaces not covered by and paid for under their timeshare lease arrangements. Once again, the healthcare providers could be seen as providing remuneration to the physician in the form of free rent on the additional storage space. Similarly, the spaces leased by physicians under timeshare lease arrangements typically include several exam rooms inside a larger suite. The physician should only use the exam rooms covered by the lease arrangement. However, there are situations when the physician uses additional exam rooms inside the suite that are not covered by and paid for under the timeshare lease arrangements.

Addressing Compliance Risks

Retain Qualified and Independent Third-Party Valuation Consultants to Determine FMV of Rent Rates

To help ensure the rent rates charged to referring physicians meet the definition of FMV, healthcare providers should retain qualified and independent third-party valuation consultants to provide supporting FMV reports. The applicable regulations impose no obligations on healthcare providers to hire valuation experts with certain designations or use specific valuation methods to determine rent ranges consistent with FMV. The government will accept any method that is commercially reasonable and provides evidence that the rent rates meet the definition of FMV under the Stark Law.[20] Therefore, when selecting a valuation consultant, the key questions for a healthcare provider should be (1) whether the valuation consultant is qualified to render an opinion and (2) whether the valuation consultant's opinion is supported by defensible analysis.

When selecting a consultant, healthcare providers should closely examine the consultant's experience in the healthcare real estate industry. Prudent healthcare providers will select consultants with multiple years of healthcare real estate experience and hands-on experience performing and providing FMV opinions for healthcare real estate transactions.

In addition to selecting a consultant with significant experience in the healthcare real estate industry, healthcare providers should carefully examine the consultant's analysis to arrive at FMV opinions. The opinion should be based on well-defined and widely accepted standards of practice (e.g., proper use and application of the market, income, and/or cost methods to real estate valuation), supported by reliable sources, and based on the Stark Law's definition of FMV. The opinion should also cover all the material terms of a particular lease arrangement. The strength and the defensibility of the resulting FMV opinion will depend on the consultant's relevant experience and ability to properly customize well-established real estate valuation methodologies to specific healthcare real estate transactions.

Ensure Rent Rate Accuracy of the FMV Report

The rent range in an FMV report should account for factors like the lease structure (i.e., whether the operating expenses are accounted for on a full-service gross, modified gross, or triple net basis), quality of the space, rent escalators, rent abatements, and tenant improvement allowances. Different types of lease structures will command different rent rates. As a result, it is imperative that healthcare providers accurately classify their lease arrangements with referral sources. Leases can be generally subdivided into net leases and gross leases. Under a net lease, the tenant pays base rent for the use of the premises and additional rent, which may, depending on the type of net lease (single, double, or triple net), include operating expenses and common area maintenance fees (CAM), taxes, and property insurance.

Conversely, under a full-service gross lease, the tenant pays a single, "all-in" rent, and the landlord is responsible for paying property CAM, taxes, and property insurance. Modified gross leases can vary and are a hybrid between a net lease and a full-service gross lease. Regardless of which lease structure it chooses to employ, the healthcare provider must ensure that the classification given to the lease arrangement matches its substance so that an appropriate rent rate can be assigned to it. Charging referral sources triple net rent rates for full-service gross leases, for example, will likely result in healthcare providers charging below FMV rates, potentially subjecting them to liability.

Annual rent escalators and rent abatements also impact the FMV of rent rates. In most markets, rent rates increase on an annual basis. A long-term lease arrangement that does not contain annual rent escalators can result in a lease arrangement where the rent rate is consistent with FMV during the first year of the term but falls below FMV in subsequent years because it does not escalate like other rent rates in the market. As a result, the absence of annual rent escalators in lease arrangements can result in compliance violations.

Like annual escalators, rent abatements are market specific. If the market does not typically provide rent abatements, they should not be included in lease arrangements with referral sources. If rent abatements are included in a lease arrangement, accounting for them when determining the FMV of rent rates is critical. Rent abatements result in lower overall revenue for the landlord during the lease term. As a result, a rent rate that may appear to be consistent with FMV on its face may effectively be lower than FMV when accounting for the overall revenues that the landlord will generate during the term of the lease arrangement.

Obtain an Accurate Commercial Reasonableness Opinion

There is some debate in the healthcare industry about what party is best suited to render commercial reasonableness opinions for lease transactions: the valuation consultant, the real estate department, or the legal department. Although the answer to this question depends on different factors, the most defensible position is to have all three parties provide input into the commercial reasonableness of a transaction. A properly qualified valuation consultant experienced in the healthcare real estate industry may opine on the commercial reasonableness of the lease terms and what is customary in a particular market; the real estate department may opine on the commercial reasonableness of the transaction as it relates to tenant selection, the services provided by the tenant, and the overall real estate strategy of the healthcare provider; and the legal department may opine on the commercial reasonableness of the legal rights and obligations of the parties under the lease arrangement. Regardless of what party ultimately opines as to the commercial reasonableness of the transaction, the commercial reasonableness analysis should be well documented and able to withstand challenge.

Accurately Measure Square Footage of Real Estate

Healthcare providers should consider hiring qualified engineering or architecture firms to accurately measure the spaces in their real estate portfolio using a unified standard of measurement approved by reputable organizations like the Building Owners and Managers Association. All measurements should be regularly updated to account for any changes in the spaces caused by tenant improvements, consolidation or separation of spaces, and renovations of medical office buildings.

Similarly, healthcare providers should be consistent internally and within local markets in structuring leases based on "usable square footage" (a measurement that does not include a square footage allocation of common areas of the building to the leased premises) or "rentable square footage" (a measurement that does include a square footage allocation of common areas of the building to the leased premises) and charging appropriate rent rates based on the structure of the lease. For example, rent rates per square foot for leases based on usable square footage will be higher than rent rates based on rentable square footage because the referral source is being charged for less total square footage than it is ultimately using since common areas that the referral source is using are not factored into the total usable square footage.

Address Tenant Improvement Allowances in FMV Reports

As a matter of best practice, tenant improvement allowances should be addressed in FMV reports, and the lease agreements should provide for tenant improvement allowances consistent with the supporting FMV reports. Internal benchmarks for tenant improvement allowances should not be exceeded absent a legitimate and documented business purpose.

Contract with and Task Third-Party Property Managers with Reviewing and Confirming Operating Expense Reconciliations

To mitigate the risks associated with operating expenses, healthcare providers can contract with and task third-party property managers with reviewing and confirming operating expense reconciliations. Similarly, healthcare providers should implement internal protocols through which the property accountants reconcile the operating expenses and work with the healthcare providers' legal counsel to ensure that all costs are accurately passed through to tenants pursuant to the terms of the applicable lease arrangements.

Ensure Timely Rent Collection Practices are Being Followed through Communication, Training, and Third-Party Property Managers

The operational compliance risks associated with rent collection can often be attributed to a lack of communication between different healthcare provider departments. For example, a healthcare provider's billing department may fail to communicate to their legal and real estate departments that a physician is behind in paying rent. Because the legal and real estate departments are unaware that rent is outstanding, they will not send notices of default, assess and collect late fees and interest charges, and, if necessary, commence eviction proceedings because they are unaware of any problem with the lease arrangement. Therefore, it is critically important to avoid silos between different healthcare provider departments and ensure they regularly communicate. Regularly scheduled interdepartmental meetings can help prevent departmental silos.

Additionally, lack of adequate training often results in rent collection problems. Employees tasked with collecting rent may not fully appreciate the compliance considerations for ensuring that all amounts due under a lease arrangement are collected from the physician tenant. Therefore, healthcare providers should regularly conduct educational seminars for their employees on the applicable healthcare regulations.

Another way to mitigate rent collection issues is to hire third-party property managers to collect rent and interact with physician tenants. Experienced property managers will have systems to ensure that all rent due under the leases is collected timely and accurately and that, when necessary, late fees and interest charges are collected and assessed. These independent, third-party property managers can send notice of default letters and interact with nonpaying physician tenants during the rent collection process, thereby eliminating the need for healthcare providers to engage in difficult discussions with nonpaying physicians. Finally, for claims brought under the Anti-Kickback Statute, third-party property managers can help healthcare providers negate the Anti-Kickback Statute's requisite element of intent.

Have Policies and Procedures in Place to Monitor Lease Expirations and Renewals

To mitigate the risks associated with lease expirations, healthcare providers should streamline their leasing policies and procedures to eliminate any existing bottlenecks in the lease renewal process. Additionally, healthcare providers should use property management software that allows them to track important lease information and dates and that can automate many of the functions necessary for proper lease administration. Regular walkthroughs of real estate portfolios should be performed, and a walkthrough checklist should be created to guide the personnel performing the walkthrough. The completed walkthrough checklists should be saved to each individual lease file. Finally, outsourcing property management and lease administration functions to reputable healthcare property management firms may mitigate risks because those firms have the knowledge, experience, resources, and personnel necessary to perform the work effectively and efficiently.

Adopt and Enforce Occupancy Schedules

To mitigate the operational compliance dangers posed by timeshare lease arrangements, healthcare providers should adopt occupancy schedules and have property managers strictly enforce those schedules. These measures help ensure that a physician comes and leaves within the time blocks allotted under the applicable timeshare lease arrangement and that multiple physicians do not use the same space simultaneously. Healthcare providers should also limit physicians' rights to reschedule or cancel the time blocks within which the physician can use and occupy the space to a set number of times per year and require physicians to submit notices several weeks in advance to reschedule a time block. Finally, healthcare providers should not allow the physician to use any space (e.g., storage closets, administrative spaces, or extra exam rooms) that is not covered by and paid for under the timeshare lease arrangement.

Possible Penalties

Healthcare providers face numerous penalties under the law if their real estate lease arrangements with referral sources are noncompliant, as more specifically outlined below:

Stark Law
- Civil sanctions:
  - Denial of payment
  - Refunds of amounts collected
  - $15,000 fine for each bill/claim
  - Treble damages on amount claimed
  - $100,000 fine for each arrangement or "scheme"
  - Program exclusion
- False Claims Act liability[21]

Anti-Kickback Statute
- Civil sanctions:
  - Potential fines of up to $50,000 per violation
  - Minimum $50,000 settlement under OIG Self-Disclosure Protocol
  - Civil assessment of up to three times the kickback
  - Program exclusion
- False Claims Act liability
- Criminal sanctions:
  - Liability for both those offering and those receiving remuneration
  - Fines of up to $25,000 for each violation and prison terms of up to five years[22]

False Claims Act
- Repayment plus interest
- Treble damages
- Civil monetary penalties
- Exclusion from Medicare/Medicaid[23]

It is also worth noting that a study of Voluntary Self-Referral Disclosure Protocol settlement data published by CMS and Provider Self-Disclosure Protocol settlement data published by the OIG revealed that, in the period between 2009 and 2016, the cost of settlement of a potential violation involving a real estate arrangement was 66% higher than the average settlement that did not involve a real estate arrangement.[24] The study also found that, during that period, "the average settlement involving a real estate arrangement was $731,654.17 compared to the average settlement amount of $439,097.43 for matters not involving a real estate arrangement."[25]

Compliance Resources

Centers for Medicare & Medicaid Services

Physician Self-Referral
CMS provides comprehensive information on its website, including, but not limited to, advisory opinions, to help healthcare providers remain compliant with the Stark Law.

https://www.cms.gov/Medicare/Fraud-and-Abuse/PhysicianSelfReferral/index

U.S. Department of Health & Human Services, Office of Inspector General

Advisory Opinions
OIG Advisory Opinions provide feedback and advice on certain applications of the Anti-Kickback Statute to, among other situations, specific healthcare real estate situations.

https://oig.hhs.gov/compliance/advisory-opinions/index.asp

Health Care Fraud Prevention and Enforcement Action Team Provider Compliance Training
The OIG's compliance training consists of videos, podcasts, and PowerPoint presentations concerning the Stark Law and Anti-Kickback Statute and their corresponding exceptions and safe harbors, tips on creating effective healthcare compliance programs, and additional resources for healthcare providers regarding real estate compliance.

https://oig.hhs.gov/compliance/provider-compliance-training/index.asp#materials

Office of Inspector General and Health Care Compliance Association

Measuring Compliance Program Effectiveness: A Resource Guide
This presentation, put together by the OIG and Health Care Compliance Association, provides an extensive overview of elements that may be necessary to craft an effective healthcare real estate compliance program.

https://oig.hhs.gov/compliance/compliance-resource-portal/files/HCCA-OIG-Resource-Guide.pdf

Realty Trust Group

Innovation Center: White Papers
Realty Trust Group regularly posts white papers on various healthcare real estate compliance topics.

https://www.realtytrustgroup.com/innovation-center/#white-paper

Risk Takeaways

Main points of interest:
- Both transactional and operational risks in healthcare real estate compliance
- Rent rates must be consistent with FMV
- FMV reports need to be accurate to support real estate lease transactions
- Lease arrangements need to be commercially reasonable
- Accurate square footage measurements are critically important
- Carefully consider the tenant improvement allowances and account for them on FMV reports
- Be aware of off-lease benefits and their risks
- Ensure rent and holdover premiums are collected and adhere to annual lease escalations
- Avoid space creep and monitor lease expirations
- Timeshare lease arrangements are difficult to monitor and may lead to compliance issues

Areas to watch:
- Updates to the Stark Law
- Updates to co-location of hospital space rules

Laws that apply:

- Stark Law, 42 U.S.C. § 1395nn
- Anti-Kickback Statute, 42 U.S.C. § 1320a–7b
- False Claims Act, 31 U.S.C. §§ 3729–3733

Addressing compliance risks:

- Development of real estate compliance policies and procedures
- Procurement of FMV reports from qualified valuation consultants
- Documenting commercial reasonableness analysis
- Space walkthroughs
- Annual lease audits

Endnotes

1. **Goran Musinovic** is Vice President of Realty Trust Group LLC, where he serves as the leader of Realty Trust Group's Compliance Service Line, providing a broad spectrum of real estate compliance advisory services, which range from helping healthcare providers create, improve, and implement effective real estate compliance programs to minimize their exposure under the Stark Law, the Anti-Kickback Statute, and the False Claims Act to providing real estate due diligence support and fair market value and commercial reasonableness analyses in connection with various real estate arrangements and transactions.

2. **Michael E. Honeycutt** is Senior Vice President, Realty Trust Group LLC, where he co-leads Realty Trust Group's Advisory Service Line, providing real estate strategy and planning services for health systems and physician practices. Leveraging his experience in market analysis, project financing and ownership, and facility development services, Michael helps healthcare providers optimize their real estate portfolios and routinely provides real estate fair market value opinions for health systems and leading healthcare law firms.

3. **Greg P. Gheen** is President of Realty Trust Group LLC. He is one of the founding members of Realty Trust Group and has served as president since its formation in 1998. Greg has more than 31 years of experience in healthcare real estate, including 10 years as the chief real estate professional with a regional healthcare system in Knoxville, Tennessee. His experience includes development of medical office and specialty facilities; strategic real estate planning and physician network development; litigation support on real estate matters relating to legal and regulatory compliance, including fair market value issues and certificate of need preparation; monetization of healthcare portfolios; and syndication of real estate assets involving physician joint ventures.

4. 42 U.S.C. § 1395nn.

5. 42 U.S.C. § 1320a–7b.

6. 31 U.S.C. §§ 3729 – 3733.

7. 42 U.S.C. § 1395nn(e)(1); 42 C.F.R. § 411.357(a).

8. 42 C.F.R. § 411.351.

9. 42 C.F.R. § 411.351.

10. 42 C.F.R. § 411.351.

11. 42 C.F.R. § 1001.952(b).

12. Medicare and State Health Care Programs: Fraud and Abuse; Revisions to Safe Harbors Under the Anti-Kickback Statute, and Civil Monetary Penalty Rules Regarding Beneficiary Inducements, 85 Fed. Reg. 77,684 (December 2, 2020).

13. Medicare Program; Modernizing and Clarifying the Physician Self-Referral Regulations, 85 Fed. Reg. 77,492 (December 2, 2020).

14. 42 C.F.R. § 411.351.

15. 42 C.F.R. § 411.351.

16. 42 C.F.R. § 411.357(a)(3).

17. 42 C.F.R. § 411.357(l).

18. 42 C.F.R. § 411.357(g).

19. 42 C.F.R. § 411.357(i).

20. Medicare and Medicaid Programs; Physicians' Referrals to Health Care Entities With Which They Have Financial Relationships, 66 Fed. Reg. 856, 944–45 (Jan. 4, 2001).

21. 42 U.S.C. § 1395nn.

22. 42 U.S.C. § 1320a–7b.

23. 31 U.S.C. §§ 3729 – 3733.

24. Andrew A. Dick, "OIG Data Confirms That Non-Compliant Real Estate Arrangements Are Costly," Hall, Render, Killian, Heath & Lyman PC, October 20, 2016, https://www.lexology.com/library/detail.aspx?g=fbd-738fb-9868-4ca9-b76c-dec8e67684fe.

25. Andrew A. Dick, "OIG Data Confirms That Non-Compliant Real Estate Arrangements Are Costly," Hall, Render, Killian, Heath & Lyman PC, October 20, 2016, https://www.lexology.com/library/detail.aspx?g=fbd-738fb-9868-4ca9-b76c-dec8e67684fe.

Emergency Medical Treatment and Labor Act

Emergency Medical Treatment and Labor Act (EMTALA)

By Jennifer McAleer,[1] MBA, MS, CHC, CHPC, CCEP, CHRC

What Is the Emergency Medical Treatment and Labor Act (EMTALA)?

The Emergency Medical Treatment and Labor Act (EMTALA), known as the "anti-dumping law," was part of the Consolidated Omnibus Budget Reconciliation Act of 1986, resulting from hospitals "dumping" indigent emergency patients.[2] The statute was amended in 1988, 1989, 2003, and 2011.

The law, signed by President Ronald Reagan, was in response to public outrage over a surge in community hospitals transferring unstable emergency patients to public hospitals for financial purposes. EMTALA was the first law that guaranteed individuals a right to healthcare, though it was and continues to be limited to healthcare treating emergency conditions. EMTALA continues to be an unfunded mandate, and hospitals often absorb the cost of treating these uninsured patients needing emergency care.

EMTALA requires that any Medicare-participating hospital that has a dedicated emergency department (DED) must provide a medical screening examination (MSE) to any individual who presents to the hospital (or anywhere within 250 yards of the hospital's main buildings) requesting treatment. A DED is defined as "any department or facility of the hospital, regardless of whether it is located on or off the main hospital campus, that meets at least one of the following requirements:

1. "It is licensed by the State in which it is located under applicable state law as an emergency room or emergency department;

2. "It is held out to the public (by name, posted signs, advertising, or other means) as a place that provides care for emergency medical conditions on an urgent basis without requiring a previously scheduled appointment; or

3. "During the calendar year immediately preceding the calendar year in which a determination under this section is being made, based on a representative sample of patient visits that occurred during that calendar year . . . at least one-third of all of its outpatient visits [are] for the treatment of emergency medical conditions on an urgent basis without requiring a previously scheduled appointment."[3]

An MSE is defined as an "appropriate medical screening examination within the capability of the hospital's emergency department, including ancillary services routinely available to the emergency department, to determine whether or not an emergency medical condition exists."[4]

Treatment must be provided in a nondiscriminatory way, regardless of the individual's actual or perceived ability to pay for the services, and regardless of diagnosis, race, national origin, or disability. The statute also prohibits "reverse dumping," where a hospital would refuse to receive the transfer of a patient based on the same criteria.

If an individual presents to the emergency department but is unable to, or fails to, request treatment for themselves, the requirement still stands if a prudent layperson would reasonably believe that the individual needs emergency examination or treatment. If an emergency medical condition (EMC) is determined to exist, the patient must then be stabilized prior to being transferred or discharged.[5] An EMC is defined as a "medical condition manifesting itself by acute symptoms of sufficient severity (including severe pain) such that the absence of immediate medical attention could reasonably be expected to result in . . . (i) placing the health of the individual (or, with respect to a pregnant woman, the health of the woman or her unborn child) in serious jeopardy, (ii) serious impairment to bodily [organs] . . . ; or . . . with respect to a pregnant woman who is having contractions, . . . (i) that there is inadequate time to effect a safe transfer to another hospital before delivery, or (ii) that transfer may pose a threat to the health or safety of the woman or the unborn child." Psychiatric disturbances as well as symptoms of substance abuse are also considered under the definition of an EMC.[6]

In some cases, patients can be transferred to another hospital if the EMC that caused the patient to seek care is stabilized (even if an underlying medical condition persists), if the patient requests the transfer, or if the patient requires specialized treatment that cannot be provided at the initial facility, as long as the medical benefits of the transfer outweigh the risks. In all circumstances, a transfer form must be completed prior to the transfer taking place.

Risk Area Governance

The Centers for Medicare & Medicaid Services (CMS) and the U.S. Department of Health & Human Services Office of Inspector General (OIG) have ultimate oversight responsibility for

EMTALA, including conducting investigations and issuing enforcement actions, although violations of EMTALA are also reported to the Department of Justice (for evaluation of possible Hill–Burton Act violations), the Office for Civil Rights (for evaluation of discrimination allegations), the Internal Revenue Service (for evaluation of implications for tax-exempt status), and The Joint Commission (for accreditation review).[7, 8]

CMS has adopted and published interpretive guidelines as part of the *Medicare State Operations Manual*, which provides guidance to state and federal surveyors in their investigation and enforcement of EMTALA. While not considered regulations, the interpretive guidelines are considered the official interpretation of EMTALA and are used to evaluate compliance. CMS published revisions to the interpretive guidelines in 2019.[9] Occasionally, CMS also publishes program memoranda and frequently asked questions regarding EMTALA.[10] The most recent memorandum was published in March 2020 and provides guidance regarding complying with EMTALA during the COVID-19 pandemic.[11] Details of these memoranda are often incorporated into updates of the interpretive guidelines, keeping the these guidelines the most comprehensive source of EMTALA guidance for hospitals and regulators alike.

The enforcement of EMTALA is mainly a complaint-driven process. The interpretive guidelines require a hospital that has received an improper transfer from another hospital to report the violation within 72 hours, or face potential sanctions, including possible misdemeanor charges or termination of its Medicare provider agreement. There is no legal obligation to self-report; however, if a hospital believes that the receiving hospital is likely to report to CMS, there may be some benefit to self-reporting a violation. Hospitals should consider the risks and benefits of self-reporting, which are determined by the specific circumstances and must be evaluated on a case-by-case basis.

If CMS receives a complaint, or otherwise becomes aware of a possible EMTALA violation, CMS most often will direct the state survey agency to conduct a complaint survey of the hospital. CMS may also choose to conduct the survey itself. The surveys are unannounced, and the scope typically expands beyond the violation that was reported. Results of the survey are forwarded to CMS, which then determines whether an EMTALA violation occurred and, if so, determines appropriate penalties. There is sometimes a discrepancy between the state survey agency and CMS due to the depth of EMTALA knowledge of the state survey agency or the interpretation of the regulation. While state survey decisions are important, decision-making authority regarding an EMTALA violation lies solely with CMS. If CMS decides that an EMTALA violation has occurred, it will initiate an investigation that can result in Medicare program exclusion, substantial civil monetary penalties, and corrective actions.

Oftentimes an incident investigated by CMS may lead to the discovery of more than one violation, resulting in significant penalties to a hospital. The physician(s) involved may also face disciplinary actions by state licensing boards' Quality Improvement Organization hearings and disciplinary actions by the hospital's medical staff leadership committee.

Common Compliance Risks

Medical Screening Exams and Emergency Medical Conditions

A hospital with a DED is required to provide an appropriate MSE to determine whether an EMC exists. The MSE is a process that entails a variety of medically appropriate examinations and diagnostic testing based on the symptoms or complaints of the patient, in an effort to rule out an EMC.[12] The MSE must be performed by a qualified medical professional (QMP), as defined in the hospital's bylaws. A QMP is someone formally identified by a hospital to be "qualified to perform the initial medical screening examinations" and who is authorized to request and accept transfers.[13] "While it is permissible for a hospital to designate a non-physician practitioner as [QMPs], the designated non-physician practitioners must be … approved by the governing body of the hospital" to perform MSEs. "Those health practitioners designated to perform [MSEs] are to be identified in the hospital by-laws or in the rules and regulations governing the medical staff following governing body approval."[14]

Before an MSE is considered complete, all necessary testing must be ordered and performed, and any necessary specialty services (including those on call) must be provided. Additionally, the MSE is considered to be in process for patients who require observation or transfer until an MSE is ruled out or stabilized.

While there is no standard MSE form, the documentation of an MSE must include, at a minimum, notes regarding the initial triage of the patient, a brief history and physical examination of the patient, the diagnostic tests and procedures performed, information regarding results as reviewed by a qualified physician, an assessment by a physician detailing the findings and plan of care, and the condition of the patient upon discharge and upon admission to an inpatient setting or transfer to another facility, including recent vital signs.

While it must be individualized based on the patient's presenting symptoms, the MSE must be the same that the hospital would provide to any patient presenting with similar symptoms, regardless of their ability to pay and without consideration of any other factors.

Hospital Property

The EMTALA obligation begins when any person comes to a hospital with a DED and requests treatment for an EMC. The regulation expands the entry point into a hospital to include areas within 250 yards of the main hospital buildings in which inpatient services are provided, which includes the entire main hospital campus, parking lots, sidewalks, driveways, and any building owned by the hospital within these 250 yards of the hospital.[15]

EMTALA obligations also exist if a ground or air ambulance are owned by the hospital, even if they are not located on the hospital grounds. EMTALA does not apply to other spaces within the hospital property, such as physician offices, rural health centers, restaurants, shops, or other clinics that participate separately under Medicare and are not owned by the hospital.[16]

Transferring Under EMTALA

Several factors must be considered, and procedures followed, when deciding whether to transfer a patient to a different hospital. A transfer is "the movement (including the discharge) of an individual outside a hospital's facilities at the direction of any person employed by (or affiliated or associated, directly or indirectly, with) the hospital, but does not include such a movement of an individual who (i) has been declared dead, or (ii) leaves the facility without the permission of any such person."[17]

Generally, transfers are prohibited if a patient's EMC has not been stabilized, unless the patient requests the transfer, or the hospital does not have the capability or capacity to stabilize the EMC and opts to transfer the patient to a higher level of care. With respect to an EMC, "stabilized" or "to stabilize" means that "'no material deterioration of the condition is likely, within reasonable medical probability, to result from or occur during the transfer of the individual from a facility or, with respect to an 'emergency medical condition' as defined in this section under paragraph (2) of that definition, that the woman has delivered the child and the placenta.'"[18]

If the patient's EMC is stabilized, then the EMC ceases to exist, and EMTALA no longer applies. If the patient's EMC is not yet stabilized, then a careful analysis of whether the benefits outweigh the risks of transfer should be conducted by the referring physician, discussed with the patient when possible, and documented.

The general rule is that the referring physician has the authority to decide whether the patient should be transferred. The physician at the receiving hospital cannot require any unnecessary steps (e.g., additional testing) prior to accepting the patient in an attempt to delay or avoid the transfer; however, they are permitted to offer guidance to the referring physician if appropriate. The receiving hospital *must* accept the patient if it has the capacity and capability to treat the patient. During the discussion regarding the patient, the receiving hospital may obtain information to determine whether it has the capacity and capability to meet the needs of the patient. If the receiving hospital believes the referring physician misrepresented the patient's condition, or otherwise transferred the patient inappropriately under EMTALA, it has an obligation to report the transferring hospital or physician to CMS.

Transfer Form/Physician Certification

It is important to comprehensively and accurately document the details of the transfer on the transfer form. Failure to do so puts the transferring physician and transferring hospital at risk. A summary of the benefits and risks should be documented on the transfer form with enough detail to clearly articulate why the transfer took place.

If the patient is in active labor, the physician must certify that the expected benefits of transfer outweigh the risks to both the pregnant patient and unborn child. "'Labor' is defined to mean the process of childbirth beginning with the latent or early phase of labor and continuing through the delivery of the placenta. A woman experiencing contractions is in true labor, unless a physician, certified nurse-midwife, or other qualified medical person acting within his or her scope of practice as defined in hospital medical staff bylaws and State law, certifies that, after a reasonable time of observation, the woman is in false labor."[19]

The patient's vital signs at the time of transfer should be documented as part of the physician's evaluation of the EMC and appropriateness of the transfer. If there is a significant gap between the time when vital signs were last taken and the time of the transfer, it would be difficult for a physician to determine whether the patient's EMC is stable or unstable and whether the benefits and risks remain current and pertinent to the transfer. CMS could find that a violation occurred if the transfer form is incomplete, lacking enough details to outline exactly what the risks and benefits were at the time of transfer, or if the patient's condition upon arrival at the receiving hospital does not match what was documented on the transfer form.

Transfers Between Hospitals with Common Ownership

Common ownership of hospitals is not an exception under EMTALA. Despite EMTALA being silent on the issue, the interpretive guidelines and other industry resources make it clear that even hospitals under the same license (but with separate emergency departments) are expected to individually comply with EMTALA. Transferring patients because a hospital system offers certain specialty services in one hospital versus another is prohibited under EMTALA, unless the patient requests the transfer, or the physician certifies that the benefits of the transfer outweigh the risks for the patient.[20]

Transferring patients for physician's convenience is prohibited. This includes situations in which a physician is providing care to patients in Facility A, but the patient with the EMC has arrived in Facility B. However, a transfer of this nature is permissible if a community call plan exists that allows for these transfers due to limited community resources.[21] A formal community call plan must include a "clear delineation of on-call coverage responsibilities; a description of the geographic area to which the plan applies; a signature by a representative of each hospital participating in the plan; assurance that any emergency medical services (EMS) protocol includes information on community on-call arrangements; a statement specifying that even if an individual arrives at a hospital that is not designated as the on-call hospital, the hospital still has an obligation under EMTALA to provide an MSE and stabilizing treatment within its capacity; and an annual assessment of the community call plan by the participating hospitals.

'Clinically Stable' vs. 'Stable' Under EMTALA

Clinicians point out that there is a discrepancy between standard medical terminology referring to stabilization and the EMTALA definition of stabilization. As noted above, the definition of "stabilized" under EMTALA is that "no material deterioration of the [patient's] condition is likely, within reasonable medical probability, to result from or occur during the transfer" or discharge of the patient from the facility.[22] In the case of a patient in labor, "stabilized" means that the patient has delivered the child, along with the placenta.

To be stabilized does not mean that the underlying medical condition has been resolved, but instead refers to the resolution of the EMC determined to be present at the time of the MSE. Sometimes it will be necessary for those patients classified as unstable under EMTALA to be transferred if the hospital does not have access to the services or equipment needed to evaluate or treat the patient. Patients transferred to higher levels of care are usually not considered stable under EMTALA. In the case of a patient in labor, this means that unless documented benefits outweigh the risks, transferring the patient to another hospital *may* be an EMTALA violation, even if the hospital does not have a designated obstetrics service.

Capacity and Capability

EMTALA defines capacity as "the ability of the hospital to accommodate the individual requesting examination or treatment."[23] It encompasses considerations such as "numbers and availability of qualified staff, beds and equipment and the hospital's past practices of accommodating additional patients in excess of its occupancy limits."[24] CMS's interpretive guidelines further state, "the capacity to render care is not reflected simply by the number of persons occupying a specialized unit, the number of staff on duty, or the amount of equipment on the hospital's premises."[25]

EMTALA defines capability as the "physical space, equipment, supplies, and specialized services that the hospital provides" and "the level of care that the personnel of the hospital can provide within the training and scope of their professional licenses. This includes coverage available through the hospital's on-call roster."[26]

EMTALA requires that a hospital with specialized capabilities must accept patients transferred from a hospital lacking such capabilities if the receiving hospital has the capacity to treat the transferred patient.[27] In order for a hospital to refuse a transfer of a patient due to capability or capacity, a hospital must first be sure there is no way to gain the capability or capacity, and that it does not have a history of increasing capacity that would allow them to accept the transfer. CMS is not sympathetic to the "no capacity" argument, unless the hospital has documentation proving that there was no capacity at the time.

Call Requirements

EMTALA states that hospitals with DEDs are required to maintain a list of physicians who are on medical staff or have privileges at the hospital and who are on call to provide consultation or treatment to stabilize a patient with an EMC as necessary. All specialty services usually offered by the hospital to inpatients are expected to be included in the call schedule and made available to patients being treated in the emergency department. The list must include individual physician names, including specific contact information of how to reach them. Hospitals must have policies that specify who is required to take call, whether physicians can take call at more than one hospital at a time, whether physicians can perform elective surgeries while they are on call, and what the expected time to respond is (usually 30 minutes).[28] Lack of an appropriate call system and disciplinary action against physicians who fail to respond when called puts hospitals at risk for violations. Additionally, physicians who fail to respond to a call (while scheduled to be on call) are also susceptible to citations from CMS.[29]

Pregnant Patients

Understanding the EMTALA requirements regarding pregnant patients is key to ensuring full compliance when treating patients who are pregnant and experiencing labor. While initially EMTALA stood for the "Emergency Medical Treatment and *Active* Labor Act," in an early amendment to the regulation, the word "active" was removed to include all stages of labor, from early contractions through the delivery of the placenta. This eliminated the ability to argue that a patient in early stages of labor were not in "active" labor and therefore that EMTALA didn't apply to the situation. EMTALA now stands for "Emergency Medical Treatment and Labor Act".

A pregnant patient experiencing contractions is considered to be in labor unless the physician observing the patient over a reasonable period of time certifies that the patient is in false labor. In the case of pregnant patients, the labor and delivery unit of a hospital with a DED must also comply with EMTALA. The MSE for pregnant patients presenting to the labor and delivery unit may be modified from the normal MSE that a patient would receive in the DED, unless the physician determines that they should expand the MSE to other areas (e.g., if the patient is experiencing unknown abdominal pain).

Psychiatric Patients

DEDs must treat psychiatric patients according to EMTALA. For patients presenting at an acute hospital with psychiatric symptoms, a full medical assessment must be completed prior to a mental health assessment, as part of the MSE. Patients must be stabilized medically first, their psychiatric conditions determined subsequently. The MSE must rule out any organic traumatic injuries or toxic causes of the psychiatric symptoms. CMS expects, at a minimum, that patients presenting with depression, suicidal ideation, altered mental status, self-mutilation, drug overdose, delusion, or who are violent be provided a mental health assessment as part of the MSE by a QMP. Hospitals must continue to monitor patients with psychiatric symptoms until their departure from the hospital.

Frequent Patients

Even patients who frequently visit the hospital have rights under EMTALA. These patients must receive a full MSE on every unique visit they make to the DED. In cases where the individual has refused care or left against medical advice but then changed their mind, the patient must receive a new MSE for each visit. Depending on the circumstances, prior testing results may be referenced if it is believed that no changes have occurred since the tests were conducted.

Sexual Assault Nurse Examiner (SANE)

If an individual presents to the DED for an examination related to a sexual assault, the hospital must still comply with EMTALA requirements (i.e., MSE, stabilization, or appropriate transfer). Hospitals may decide to incorporate the SANE nurse into the MSE procedure to ensure the MSE meets all of the needs of the patient and law enforcement, if appropriate. If the SANE nurse is at another hospital, the patient must receive an MSE and stabilization prior to transfer to the other hospital for evaluation. Hospitals may decide to set up an arrangement where a SANE nurse would travel to the patient in order to avoid the need to transfer a patient who has experienced trauma.

Scheduled Outpatient Visits

If a patient is presenting to an outpatient setting, even if on hospital property, the hospital is not required to perform an MSE unless the individual requests emergency medical treatment, or a prudent layperson would believe that the individual needs emergency medical treatment. Documentation showing the scheduled appointment should exist and be maintained. Patients being sent to the DED for tests should be considered to need an MSE under EMTALA, even if they have orders for the tests.

Law Enforcement/Blood Draws

If a patient is brought into the DED by law enforcement requesting a blood alcohol test, it is up to the hospital personnel to determine if an MSE is required. If the individual requests treatment, has an obvious injury, is reported to have been unconscious, has impaired memory, has been involved in a major auto accident or significant fall, or has significant impairment from what appears to be intoxication, then the hospital must provide an MSE.

However, if the individual does not present with any of these symptoms or red flags, does not request care, and is brought in by law enforcement for a blood alcohol test only, EMTALA screening is not required.

Hospitals should document their decision regarding these individuals carefully to be able to show CMS that an MSE was either conducted or deemed not appropriate given the presenting factors. Documentation of a law enforcement officer refusing to allow the hospital to perform an MSE should also be entered into the record, if appropriate.

Central Log

EMTALA requires that a hospital maintain a central log of all individuals who have come to the DED seeking treatment to track the care provided to these individuals. The log must indicate whether these individuals were treated, admitted, stabilized, transferred, discharged, refused treatment, or denied treatment. The central log may be kept as multiple logs or within the hospital's electronic medical record, if allowed by state law. The ability to produce the log quickly upon a surveyor request is critical. The interpretive guidelines instruct surveyors to review the central log going back at least six months. Incomplete entries are likely to result in a citation by CMS.

Signage

EMTALA requires hospitals with DEDs to post signs that provide the public with information about their rights under EMTALA. Signs should be posted in conspicuous locations seen by all members of the public entering the hospital, including in the DED and in labor and delivery units. Signs should be written in wording that is clear and understandable by the general public. Signs must be printed in English and in other major languages that are common to the geographic area of the hospital.

A sign must be readable from a distance of 20 feet or from the anticipated angle and distance of members of the public who would be reading it, depending on where the sign is posted. The sign must include a reference to whether the hospital participates in the state Medicaid program.[30] Some states have adopted additional EMTALA signage requirements relating to emergency care. No information that could be interpreted as discouraging individuals from entering the DED for care should be included on the sign.[31]

Sample EMTALA sign language:

It's the Law! If You Have a Medical Emergency or Are in Labor

You have the right to receive, within the capabilities of this hospital's staff and facilities:

- An appropriate medical Screening Examination.

- Necessary Stabilizing Treatment (including treatment for an Unborn child) and if necessary.

- An appropriate Transfer to another facility even if you cannot pay or do not have medical insurance or you are not entitled to Medicare or Medicaid.

This hospital (does/does not) participate in the Medicaid program.[32]

Disasters

During a national emergency, a hospital's EMTALA obligations remain in full effect until all of the following three conditions are met:[33]

- The federal government declares a national emergency.
- The United States Department of Health & Human Services has declared a public health emergency.
- The United States Department of Health & Human Services has issued a waiver that excuses or suspends one or more requirements of EMTALA.

The hospital must be located within the emergency area that is covered by the declaration of the emergency and activate its disaster protocol. Additionally, the state must activate an emergency preparedness plan or pandemic preparedness plan in the emergency area, and the redirection of individuals to other hospitals for medical screening must be consistent with the state plan.[34]

Reporting

A hospital is required to report any hospital it believes to have violated EMTALA to CMS or the state survey agency as soon as reasonably possible. The interpretive guidelines state that reports should be made within 72 hours of the occurrence. Failure to report may subject the receiving hospital to termination of its Medicare provider agreement.

To determine whether the transfer was a violation of EMTALA, the receiving hospital may choose to contact the referring hospital and let its staff know that it is investigating the transfer as a possible violation. It is possible that the transferring hospital will provide information or documentation that reveals that no violation occurred and therefore the receiving hospital has no obligation to report the incident. If the transferring hospital determines that a violation has occurred, it should consider reviewing the incident and implementing corrective actions, if appropriate, prior to the state or CMS survey in an effort to prevent formal findings or termination of the Medicare provider agreement. This notification by the receiving hospital also contributes to the collegial relationship between the two hospitals, which may allow them to problem-solve together the community issues that lead to unintentional violations.

Where No EMTALA Obligations Exist

EMTALA obligations do not exist if an individual presents to an off-campus location of a hospital that is not a DED, if an individual is receiving outpatient services in the hospital (and does not require emergency medical treatment), is or becomes an inpatient within the hospital, or is an individual who presents at a location for a service that is not considered part of the hospital for Medicare purposes (e.g., a skilled nursing facility).[35]

Addressing Compliance Risks

Conduct Relevant Policy Reviews

- Review EMTALA/transfer policies to ensure that they are up to date and comprehensive and that they address EMTALA obligations and transfers.
- Review the call policy to determine if adequate and appropriate coverage is in place to satisfy EMTALA requirements.

Transfer Form Review

- Review the transfer form and confirm compliance with EMTALA requirements.
- Conduct audits of transfers to confirm that the transfer form is properly completed, including documentation of risks and benefits as well as of vital signs taken immediately prior to transfer.

Medical Screening Examinations

Conduct audits to ensure caregivers are conducting an MSE prior to requesting payment information from patients.

Maintain a Central Log

Regularly audit the central log, which ensures that the hospital maintains the required log of all those who come to the emergency department for treatment.

Conduct Compliance Training

Hospital staff should receive training so that they understand the basics of EMTALA. More in-depth training should be provided to emergency department staff and security personnel. Regular refresher trainings should also be conducted.

Conduct Incident Debriefs

Hospitals should conduct an incident debrief if they become aware of an EMTALA violation. The debrief should be focused on determining what lead to the violation, whether the incident should be self-reported, whether disciplinary action is appropriate for those who caused the violation, whether the process needs to be reviewed to ensure it's adequate, and whether additional refresher training is warranted.

Possible Penalties

EMTALA compliance is a condition of the Medicare provider agreement, and as such, violations of EMTALA can result in termination of the Medicare provider agreement by CMS. If CMS has determined that an EMTALA violation has occurred, it may issue a 23-day termination notice, a 90-day termination notice, or no termination at all (most likely option if corrective actions were put in place by the hospital prior to the enforcement survey by CMS or the state).[36] Additional corrective actions (such as staff training or revisions to forms, processes, and/or signs) may be required of the hospital by CMS if no termination notice is issued.

If found to have violated EMTALA, the OIG has the authority to impose civil monetary penalties (CMPs) of up to $111,597 to the violating hospital *or* physician, for each violation.[37] Multiple violations can be found related to the same patient (e.g., failure to screen patient, failure to stabilize patient, and transferring unstable patient). For hospitals with fewer than 100 beds, the maximum fine is $55,800 per violation. The maximum amount of these fines is now subject to annual adjustment for inflation, and was last updated in 2020.[38] The previous maximum amount of $50,000 had not been adjusted for inflation since the passing of EMTALA in 1986; the Federal Civil Penalties Inflation Adjustment Act Improvements Act of 2015 updated the fine for the first time, and it has subsequently been increased each year in accordance with the Consumer Price Index. Additionally, the OIG may exclude a hospital and/or physician from participating in federally funded healthcare programs as a result of serious or repeated EMTALA violations.

Sometimes a situation involving one patient may result in multiple violations of EMTALA, which could mean extensive penalties being issued. Additionally, CMS and the state often review multiple transfer forms, six months of the central log, or other documentation if they are conducting an on-site investigation, and, as a result, they may find additional violations that the hospital or physician(s) could be held accountable for.

Compliance Resources

Stephen A. Frew and Kris Giese, *EMTALA Field Guide, Fourth Edition*

The *EMTALA Field Guide* is an invaluable resource to compliance professionals, in that it provides information about the rule, how the rule is typically applied in hospitals, what the documentation requirements of that rule are, and cautionary advice on what the authors have seen as a consequence of noncompliance.

Brooke Bennett Aziere et al., *AHLA Health Care Compliance Legal Issues Manual, Fifth Edition*, American Health Lawyers Association

This resource provides information and guidance on a variety of healthcare compliance topics, including EMTALA. With a chapter dedicated to EMTALA, it's a great resource focused on the regulation itself, written for healthcare lawyers but useful to healthcare compliance officers as well.

M. Steven Lipton, *EMTALA Manual*, California Hospital Association

M. Steven Lipton is a well-known EMTALA expert, which is why the California Hospital Association asked him to write the EMTALA manual. While the book is intended for California hospitals, it has great information for all hospitals regardless of their state as the California regulations are carved out in separate sections, making it easy to know what information is relevant to hospitals in other states.

Centers for Medicare & Medicaid Services

State Operations Manual
"Appendix A - Survey Protocol, Regulations and Interpretive Guidelines for Hospitals"

https://www.cms.gov/Regulations-and-Guidance/Guidance/Manuals/downloads/som107ap_a_hospitals.pdf

Risk Takeaways

Main points of interest:
- The referring physician has the authority to decide whether the patient should be transferred.
- Lack of an appropriate call system and disciplinary action against physicians who fail to respond puts a hospital at risk for violations.
- As of 2020, physicians and hospitals face penalties of up to $111,597 (or $55,800) for each violation.
- EMTALA requires that a hospital with specialized capabilities accept patients transferred from a hospital lacking such capabilities, as long as the receiving hospital has the capacity.

Areas to watch:
- Medical screening exams and emergency medical conditions
- Hospital property
- Transferring a patient with an EMC
- Transfer forms and physician certification
- Transferring between hospitals with common ownership
- The difference between "clinically stable" vs. "stable" under EMTALA
- EMTALA's definitions of capacity and capability

- Call requirements
- Treatment of pregnant patients, psychiatric patients, and "frequent flyer" patients
- Sexual assault nurse examiners
- Scheduled outpatient visits
- Law enforcement/blood draws
- The hospital's central log
- EMTALA signage
- Emergency care during national disasters
- Reporting noncompliant hospitals

Law that applies:

Emergency Medical Treatment and Labor Act (EMTALA); Examination and treatment for emergency medical conditions and women in labor (42 U.S.C. § 1395dd).

Addressing compliance risks:

- Conduct relevant policy reviews. Review EMTALA/transfer and call policies to ensure they are current and EMTALA compliant.
- Conduct a transfer form review. Review the transfer form and confirm EMTALA compliance.
- Audit the process of Medical Screening Examinations. Audit the process to confirm that caregivers conduct a medical screening examination prior to requesting payment information from patients.
- Audit the central log. Review the central log to ensure the log tracks patients who come to the emergency department for treatment.
- Audit transfers. Conduct audits of transfers to confirm that the transfer form is properly completed.
- Conduct compliance training. Train hospital staff on the basics of EMTALA. Emergency department staff and security personnel should receive more in-depth training.
- Conduct debriefs. Hospitals should conduct an incident debrief if they become aware of an EMTALA violation. The debrief should be focused on determining what lead to the violation, whether the incident should be self-reported, whether disciplinary action is appropriate for those who caused the violation, whether the process needs to be reviewed to ensure it's adequate, and whether additional refresher training is warranted.

Endnotes

1. **Jennifer McAleer** is the Chief Compliance & Privacy Officer at Swedish Health Services. With more than 20 years of experience in healthcare compliance, she has worked in a variety of organizations overseeing compliance with healthcare regulations, including EMTALA. EMTALA is of particular interest to her because it ensures that everyone, regardless of their ability to pay, receives access to basic emergency medical services when they need it, a right that McAleer believes we all should have.

2. 42 U.S.C. § 1395dd.

3. 42 C.F.R. § 489.24(b).

4. 42 C.F.R. § 489.24(a)(i).

5. 42 C.F.R. § 1395dd.

6. 42 C.F.R. §489.24(b).

7. "Hill-Burton Free and Reduced-Cost Health Care," Health Resources & Services Administration, U.S. Department of Health and Human Services, last reviewed April 2019, https://www.hrsa.gov/get-health-care/affordable/hill-burton/index.html.

8. Stephen A. Frew and Kris Giese, *EMTALA Field Guide, Fourth Edition* (Loves Park, IL: Stephen A. Frew, 2019), 27.

9. Centers for Medicare & Medicaid Services, "Appendix V – Interpretive Guidelines – Responsibilities of Medicare Participating Hospitals in Emergency Cases," *State Operations Manual*, Pub. 100-07, revised July 19, 2019, https://www.cms.gov/Regulations-and-Guidance/Guidance/Manuals/downloads/som107ap_v_emerg.pdf.

10. "Policy & Memos to States and Regions," Centers for Medicare & Medicaid Services, last modified January 10, 2018, https://www.cms.gov/Medicare/Provider-Enrollment-and-Certification/SurveyCertificationGenInfo/Policy-and-Memos-to-States-and-Regions.

11. Centers for Medicare & Medicaid Services, Center for Clinical Standards and Quality/Quality, Safety and Oversight Group, "Emergency Medical Treatment and Labor Act (EMTALA) Requirements and Implications Related to Coronavirus Disease 2019 (COVID-19) (Revised)," memorandum, March 30, 2020, https://www.cms.gov/files/document/qso-20-15-hospital-cah-emtala-revised.pdf.

12. 42 C.F.R. § 489.24(a)(i).

13. Centers for Medicare & Medicaid Services, "Appendix V – Interpretive Guidelines – Responsibilities of Medicare Participating Hospitals in Emergency Cases," *State Operations Manual.*

14. Centers for Medicare & Medicaid Services, *State Operations Manual,* "Appendix V – Interpretive Guidelines" (Rev. 191, 07-19-19), https://www.cms.gov/Regulations-and-Guidance/Guidance/Manuals/downloads/som107ap_v_emerg.pdf.

15. 42 C.F.R. § 413.65(a)(2).

16. 42 C.F.R. §489.24(b).

17. Centers for Medicare & Medicaid Services, "Appendix V – Interpretive Guidelines – Responsibilities of Medicare Participating Hospitals in Emergency Cases," *State Operations Manual.*

18. 42 C.F.R. § 489.24(b).

19. Centers for Medicare & Medicaid Services, "Appendix V – Interpretive Guidelines – Responsibilities of Medicare Participating Hospitals in Emergency Cases," *State Operations Manual.*

20. Jennifer McAleer, "EMTALA: What hospitals and physicians need to know," *Compliance Today*, December 2019, https://compliancecosmos.org/emtala-what-hospitals-and-physicians-need-know.

21. 42 C.F.R. § 489.24(j)(2)(iii).

22. 42 C.F.R. § 489.24(b).

23. 42 C.F.R. § 489.24(b).

24. 42 C.F.R. § 489.24(b).

25. Centers for Medicare & Medicaid Services, "Appendix V – Interpretive Guidelines – Responsibilities of Medicare Participating Hospitals in Emergency Cases," *State Operations Manual.*

26. 42 C.F.R. § 489.24(d)(1)(i).

27. 42 C.F.R. § 489.24(f).

28. Centers for Medicare & Medicaid Services, "Appendix V – Interpretive Guidelines – Responsibilities of Medicare Participating Hospitals in Emergency Cases," *State Operations Manual.*

29. 42 C.F.R. § 489.20(r).

30. 42 U.S.C. § 1395cc(a)(1)(N)(iii).

31. 42 C.F.R. § 489.20(q).

32. Medicare Program; Participation in CHAMPUS and CHAMPVA, Hospital Admissions for Veterans, Discharge Rights Notice, and Hospital Responsibility for Emergency Care, 59 Fed. Reg. 32,086, 32,107 (June 22, 1994).

33. Centers for Medicare & Medicaid Services, "Appendix V – Interpretive Guidelines – Responsibilities of Medicare Participating Hospitals in Emergency Cases," *State Operations Manual.*

34. Centers for Medicare & Medicaid Services, "Appendix V – Interpretive Guidelines – Responsibilities of Medicare Participating Hospitals in Emergency Cases," *State Operations Manual.*

35. 42 C.F.R. § 489.24(b).

36. Centers for Medicare & Medicaid Services, "Appendix V – Interpretive Guidelines – Responsibilities of Medicare Participating Hospitals in Emergency Cases," *State Operations Manual.*

37. Annual Civil Monetary Penalties Inflation Adjustment, 85 Fed. Reg. 2,869, 2,876 (January 17, 2020).

38. Annual Civil Monetary Penalties Inflation Adjustment, 85 Fed. Reg. 2,869, 2,876 (January 17, 2020).

Health Information Management

Coding Compliance Audits and Third-Party Reviews

By Ghazal Irfan,[1] MBI, RHIA

What Are Coding Compliance Audits and Third-Party Reviews?

Conducting routine medical coding compliance audits help a healthcare provider identify, assess, and mitigate risks and achieve compliance with federal and state laws, policies, and official coding guidelines. Hospitals, health systems, medical practices, ambulance companies, skilled nursing homes, rehabilitation services providers, laboratories, and others involve medical documentation and coding in their daily operations. The accuracy of this complex information is critically important to their organizations, not only because code assignment should accurately reflect underlying patient treatment and procedures, but because it also affects billing accuracy.

Internal Coding Compliance Audits

Internal coding audits are part of proactive risk management in an effective compliance program to periodically check for assurance that medical codes from an official code set are assigned correctly in the medical record, including insurance billing. Such audits should be performed by qualified personnel, including certified coders with appropriate coding credentials. Operational units, such as a health information management department, may conduct such audits as part of quality assurance efforts. The compliance department also periodically performs coding audits as part of independent oversight, although they are performed more often when systemic issues are expected, in response to allegations, or when operational quality assurance efforts are insufficient or weak.

The frequency and scope of such coding audits will depend, among other things, on identified risks and resources. However, at a minimum, coding audits should occur quarterly and validate coding accuracy of assignment in the medical record and on a bill. These audits test that the medical codes assigned and documented in the medical record are based on the underlying medical documentation of patient treatment; medical management necessary; and services, items, and procedures performed at the date of service, service period, or episode of care.

OIG and Third-Party Coding Audit Reviews

Routine internal coding compliance audits can help a provider succinctly handle or potentially avoid a third-party review such as those from the recovery audit contractors (RACs), Targeted Probe and Educate (TPE), Office of Inspector General (OIG), Medicare administrative contractors (MACs), and unified program integrity contractors, to name a few—although most of these contractors go beyond coding reviews and include billing auditing and potential overpayments to federal healthcare program payers.

For example, RACs review claims on a post-payment basis. They detect and correct past improper payments so that Centers for Medicare & Medicaid Services (CMS) and carriers, fiscal intermediaries, and MACs can implement actions that will prevent future improper payments. TPE audits typically involve the review of 20–40 claims per provider/supplier, per item, or per service.[2] Unlike other Medicare audits, providers and suppliers may be subject to up to three rounds of record reviews. After each round, providers/suppliers are offered individualized education based on the results of their reviews. Providers/suppliers are also offered individualized education during a round to more efficiently fix simple problems. Unified program integrity contractors' (UPICs) primary goal is to investigate instances of suspected fraud, waste, and abuse in Medicare or Medicaid claims. Their focus is investigating fraud and abuse, although they also identify improper payments and conduct overpayment extrapolations.

The OIG Office of Audit Services also conducts audits, either with its own audit resources or by overseeing audit work done by others. These audits are meant to help reduce waste, abuse, and mismanagement and promote economy and efficiency throughout the U.S. Department of Health & Human Services. For example, an ongoing Office of Audit Services auditing focus is a series of hospital compliance audits. Using computer matching, data mining, and other data analysis techniques, the OIG identifies hospital claims it deems at risk for noncompliance with Medicare billing requirements. Data mining of overused codes or unusual coding and billing patterns may trigger such audits, which is why it's important for providers and suppliers to detect unusual or suspicious coding patterns and coding errors internally.[3] This may involve not only chart review, but also data analysis and compliance review of the National Correct Coding Initiative edits. In other words, knowing and auditing one's own coding accuracy is critically important to avoiding government scrutiny.

Inpatient Coding and Audits

Coding compliance audits not only result in clean claims submission and establish best coding and documentation practices, but also improve clinical documentation and code capture, which has a direct impact on a provider's case-mix index (CMI). Hospital or facility coding is divided between inpatient (IP) and outpatient (OP) coding. It is beyond the scope of this article to discuss professional coding, which is used to capture physician care.

IP hospital coding is based on the International Classification of Diseases, Tenth Revision, Clinical Modification (ICD-10-CM) for capturing diagnosis and the International Classification of Diseases, Tenth Revision, Procedure Coding System (ICD-10-PCS) for capturing procedures.[45] Both classification systems were adopted under the Health Insurance Portability and Accountability Act and are updated on October 1 of each year.

Inpatient claims are paid a set reimbursement amount based on the selection of diagnosis-related group (DRG) under the inpatient prospective payment system rule. DRG assignment and reimbursements are dependent upon and affected by the selection of principal diagnosis, secondary diagnosis(es), surgical procedure(s), present on admission (POA) indicators, discharge disposition (DD), and admit type sources.[6] While hospitals use Medicare severity DRG (MS-DRG) codes for IP billing, there are other types of codes used for IP services. Inpatient rehabilitation facilities (IRF) use case-mix group codes for billing and skilled nursing facilities use Health Insurance Prospective Payment System codes for billing, for which "clinical assessment data is the basic input."[7]

RAC, MAC, and third-party payer auditing agencies use Uniform Hospital Discharge Data Set (UHDDS) definitions to review and validate primary diagnosis (PDX) and secondary diagnosis code selection.[8] Presence of secondary diagnosis codes that are either a complication or comorbidity (CC) or a major complication or comorbidity (MCC) indicate patient care that required additional hospital resources such as increased nursing care, monitoring, and extended length of stay (LOS) than an average patient care would routinely require, therefore resulting in additional reimbursement to the healthcare provider.[9]

The enforcement community, including MACs and the OIG, are continuously updating their auditing targets in response to violations and risk areas that they have identified through the Comprehensive Error Rate Testing (CERT) report. The CERT report identifies coding and medical necessity concerns at the national level. For more information on CERT audits, see the "Government Audits" article in the "Revenue Cycle" section of this chapter.

In **Table 1. Inpatient Coding and Medical Necessity Auditing Targets** are some of the most pressing IP areas of concerns that are at a higher risk for overpayment and improper billing in 2022. These targets are identified by government auditing agencies such as CERT, OIG, and CMS-RAC, and more information can be found at their respective websites.

Table 1. Inpatient Coding and Medical Necessity Auditing Targets

Inpatient 2022				
Target	**DRG or ICD-10**	**Indication**	**Coding or Medical Necessity Review**	**Reasoning**
Spinal fusion	DRG: 459, 460 453, 454, 455 471, 472, 473	**CERT medical necessity error:** DRG 459–460: 48.6%; DRG 453–455: 0%; DRG 471–473: 90.5% **CERT coding error:** DRG 459–460: 10.8%; DRG 453–455: 21.7%; DRG 471–473: 0%	Both	<ul><li>Higher-weighted DRG (HWDRG)</li><li>Program for Evaluating Payment Patterns Electronic Report (PEPPER) target area</li></ul>
Heart failure	DRG: 291, 292, 293	**CERT medical necessity error:** 62.4% **CERT coding error:** 37.6%	Both	OIG target—medical necessity: Short stay claims with single MCC
Chest pain	DRG: 313	**CERT medical necessity error:** 100%	Both	Inpatient admission for this low-weighted DRG (LWDRG) is generally not appropriate
Malnutrition	ICD10CM: E40–E43	OIG target and PEPPER target	Both	OIG audit found hospitals over-billed Medicare $1 billion by submitting incorrectly coded claims that lack medical necessity and documentation
COVID-19 and sepsis	DRG: 179, 178, 177	New OIG target New sequencing guideline on sepsis and COVID-19	Both	Official coding guidelines for a COVID-19 infection that progresses to sepsis; see Section I.C.1.d. Sepsis, Severe Sepsis, and Septic Shock. See also ICD-CM/PCS *Coding Clinic*, First Quarter ICD-10 2021, page 33, effective with discharges starting January 1, 2021.

Table 1. Inpatient Coding and Medical Necessity Auditing Targets (cont.)

	Inpatient 2022			
Target	**DRG or ICD-10**	**Indication**	**Coding or Medical Necessity Review**	**Reasoning**
Extensive operating room (OR) procedure unrelated to principal diagnosis	DRG: 981, 982, 983	**CERT medical necessity error**: 34.3% / **CERT coding error**: 52.7%	Both	Complex review of claims where principal diagnosis is unrelated to an extensive OR procedure
Simple pneumonia & pleurisy	DRG: 193, 194, 195	**CERT medical necessity error**: 55.8% / **CERT coding error**: 19.1%	Both	RAC and PEPPER target due to sequencing error
Impella Ventricular Assist Device	DRG: 003 ICD10PCS: 02HA0QZ–02HA4RZ, 02PA0QZ–02PA4RZ, 02WA0QZ–02WAXRZ, 5A02116, 5A0211D, 5A02216, 5A0221D	High-weighted DRG New coding guideline	Both	A ventricular assist device (VAD) is surgically attached to one or both intact ventricles and is used to assist or augment the ability of a damaged or weakened native heart to pump blood. Improvement in the performance of the native heart may allow the device to be removed. The documentation will be reviewed to determine if a left ventricular assist device (LVAD) was placed for a Medicare-covered indication.
Kidney & urinary tract infections	DRG: 689, 690	**CERT medical necessity error**: 81.4% **CERT coding error**: 18.6%	Both	Claims lacking medical necessity

In the following sections, detailed explanations are provided on how to properly address coding audits (e.g., malnutrition) and medical necessity audits (e.g., total knee replacement). These processes and guidance can be used to identify and improve any coding or medical necessity audits.

Malnutrition Coding Audits

In recent years, the OIG has visited the diagnosis of malnutrition twice, in 2017 and in 2020. In 2017, an OIG review identified that healthcare providers were increasingly coding a specific type of MCC malnutrition known as Kwashiorkor that is rarely found in the United States but generally affects populations in famine-stricken regions.[10] That review resulted in healthcare providers returning millions of dollars to the Medicare trust funds.[11]

More recently, OIG review has shifted attention toward nutritional marasmus (an MCC that codes to E41) and unspecified severe protein-calorie malnutrition (an MCC that codes to E43), alleging that CMS was billed more than a billion dollars for incorrect malnutrition code assignment. Like Kwashiorkor, nutritional marasmus is rarely seen in the United States but is commonly seen in developing, famine-stricken nations. As far as the severe protein-calorie malnutrition code assignment is concerned, if a healthcare provider coded E43 but didn't provide documentation to support its code assignment based on UHDDS's definition of secondary code assignment, then the provider should get ready to start returning hundreds or thousands of dollars back to the Medicare trust funds.

To ensure compliance with Medicare payment rule and to meet medical necessity, providers must ensure that registered dietician's nutrition assessment (such as body mass index, past surgical history, muscle wasting), nutrition intervention (such as enteral or parenteral nutrition, shakes, meal plan), and nutrition goals (such as weight gain interventions, food intake plan) are documented in the medical record.[12] These plans need to be validated by the attending provider who needs to document the diagnosis throughout the medical record, especially in the discharge summary.

The UHDDS's core elements for reporting malnutrition as a secondary diagnosis are met through documenting clinical evaluation (nutrition assessment), therapeutic treatment (nutrition intervention), and increased nursing care and/or monitoring (nutrition goals and plans). Medicare has no issues reimbursing additional payment to healthcare providers who provide and document extensive patient care in the medical record. However, if providers are lax about capturing all aspects of patient care, then Medicare has no issues rejecting or recouping payment. For now, it looks like the malnutrition review is more of a coding-related review with some medical necessity review aspects involved. Providers need to ensure malnutrition is evaluated and monitored throughout the patient care and consistently documented, from history and physical (H&P) to discharge summary (DS).

Medical Necessity Audits

Medicare, Medicaid, and commercial insurers use medical necessity as a key factor for paying claims for medical services. Section 1862(a)(1)(A) of the Social Security Act directs that Medicare will not cover services that "are not reasonable and necessary for the diagnosis or treatment of illness or injury or to improve the functioning of a malformed body member."[13]

That means the provider's or supplier's documentation must "support the medical need for the service rendered. . . . The documentation may include clinical evaluations, physician evaluations, consultations, progress notes, physician's office records, hospital records, nursing home records, home health agency records, records from other healthcare professionals and test reports. It is maintained by the physician and/or provider."[14]

Medical necessity audits often fail when medical documentation is simply insufficient or incomplete, or not present at all in the record to substantiate the claim. Payers may define this further; in the words of one MAC, medical necessity means treatments must be:

- Safe and effective;
- Not experimental or investigational; and
- Appropriate, including the duration and frequency in terms of whether the service or item is:
  - Furnished in accordance with accepted standards of medical practice for the diagnosis or treatment of the beneficiary's condition or to improve the function of a malformed body member;
  - Furnished in a setting appropriate to the beneficiary's medical needs and condition;
  - Ordered and furnished by qualified personnel; and
  - One that meets, but does not exceed, the beneficiary's medical need.[15]

For any service reported to Medicare, it is expected that the medical documentation clearly demonstrates that the service meets all of the above criteria. All documentation must be maintained in the patient's medical record and be available to the contractor upon request.

Total knee replacement (TKR) audits are heavily based on medical necessity and documentation review. Effective January 2018, TKRs were removed from Medicare's IP–only procedures list, allowing healthcare entities to perform TKRs on the IP as well as on the OP side.[16]

Recently, healthcare entities have noticed increased scrutiny and claims denial for TKRs, especially if performed on the IP side. A majority of IP claim denials are not related to coding and instead are due to a lack of medical necessity surrounding the two-midnight rule. Per CMS, a provider's decision to admit a patient to perform TKR on IP basis is complex but must involve review and documentation of multiple medical risk factors, such as a patient's history, comorbidities, and/or risk of complications. IP TKR claims must support the two-midnight rule by physician clearly documenting patient needing two or more midnights of hospital care because of patient's risk of developing intra-operative or postsurgical complications due to medical history. IP TKR claims without significant complication or risk documentation, or claims lacking medical necessity as per local coverage determination (LCD) L36575, providers will have a difficult time challenging or overturning any claims denial or appeal. Per LCD L36575, a TKR surgery is considered medically necessary if it meets the following criteria:

- Performed due to advanced joint disease demonstrated through radiological imaging such as a magnetic resonance imaging (MRI) and/or computed tomography (CT);
- Documentation of pain impacting activities of daily living (ADL); and

- Failure to respond to conservative therapy such as anti-inflammatory medications or supervised physical therapy.[17]

This is not an all-inclusive list, and L36575 should be reviewed for a complete list of criteria LCDs.

Outpatient Coding and Audits

Outpatient coding is based on ICD-10-CM for capturing diagnosis; Current Procedural Terminology (CPT) and Healthcare Common Procedure Coding System (HCPCS) for capturing diagnostic, medical, and surgical services; and modifiers to capture supplemental information.[18] Like IP coding, coders coding OP records must adhere to the ICD-10-CM classification instructions and conventions, official coding guidelines, and for additional guidance and clarification, follow *Coding Clinic for ICD-10-CM*, *Coding Clinic for HCPCS*, and *CPT Assistant* for CPT advice. Under the Outpatient Prospective Payment System (OPPS), healthcare providers are paid for OP services through ambulatory payment classification (APC) system. Unlike the IP DRG payment system where a single DRG determines the payment for an entire IP service, an OP claim may have multiple APCs assigned based on CPT selection and could get paid separately for each APC. APCs group together services with similar clinical intensity, resource utilization, and cost. To ensure correct APC assignment, coders need to be educated and trained on new and updated code changes. OP coders cannot pick up "suspected," "probable," or "questionable" diagnoses, but they can and should code a diagnosis to the highest level of certainty.[19]

Medical Necessity Coding Audit Review

Coders should not code "signs and symptoms" if a more definitive diagnosis has been provided by the provider to ensure medical necessity is captured. Time and time again, healthcare providers see their OP claims denied because of lack of medical necessity. Let's take cataract surgery as an example. RAC has been denying cataract surgical claims by stating medical necessity not met per LCD L37027.[20]

The LCD contains a list of all CPT/HCPCS codes and ICD-10-CM codes that support medical necessity for cataract surgery claims to Medicare. Once you click on L37027, scroll to the "Associated Documents" section to get to "A57196 - Billing and Coding: Cataract Surgery in Adults." If a claim is submitted without any of the listed ICD-10-CM codes, then the chances of a provider being reimbursed become very slim. So, is it difficult to show medical necessity on a claim? The answer is simply, "no."

By educating coders and physicians on LCD L37027 and documentation requirements, it is very possible to support medical necessity and compliance with Medicare. A provider may document "patient with type II diabetes" in a cataract-suffering patient, but a coder who lacks understanding of coding guideline "13. Etiology/manifestation convention ('code first,' 'use additional code,' and 'in diseases classified elsewhere' notes)" may not pick the casual relationship between diabetes and cataract and not code E11.36 - Type 2 diabetes mellitus with diabetic cataract.[21] Instead, the coder may code diabetes as E11.9 - Type 2 diabetes mellitus without complication and H26.9 - Unspecified cataract. Neither E11.9 nor H26.9 are part of ICD-10 codes housed under the L37027 LCD. This basic lack of coding guideline knowledge and understanding causes a cataract claim to be submitted with codes that don't support medical necessity and in return, heighten a provider's chance of claim denial.

On a more basic level, medical necessity could simply fail if there is no valid physician (signed and dated) order that is required for a procedure or service. Good record-keeping and explaining reasons for the care go a long way toward correct coding and eventually appropriate billing.

In **Table 2. Outpatient Coding and Medical Necessity Targets**, some of the most commonly denied OP targets by government auditing agencies are captured. RAC has been aggressively pursuing the review of cataract, pacemaker/AICD, and TKR claims and denying payment.

Table 2. Outpatient Coding and Medical Necessity Targets

Outpatient 2022				
Target	**Indication**	**CPT/HCPCS**	**Coding or Medical Necessity Review**	**Reasoning**
Ventricular assist device	CMS-approved topic for 2022 RAC review	CPT: 33975–33983, 33990– 33993	Both	A ventricular assist device (VAD) is surgically attached to one or both intact ventricles and is used to assist or augment the ability of a damaged or weakened native heart to pump blood. Improvement in the performance of the native heart may allow the device to be removed. The documentation will be reviewed to determine whether a left ventricular assist device (LVAD) was placed for a Medicare-covered indication.
PT/OT	**Noridian TPE error rate 97530:** 38% **Post-pay review 97110:** 45.48%	CPT: 97110, 97530	Both	Top denial reasons: ▪ Failure to return records ▪ Documentation did not support a plan of care (POC) that was certified/signed by the physician or nonphysician practitioner ▪ Documentation did not clearly reflect total direct and indirect time[22]

Table 2. Outpatient Coding and Medical Necessity Targets (cont.)

Outpatient 2022				
Target	**Indication**	**CPT/HCPCS**	**Coding or Medical Necessity Review**	**Reasoning**
Therapeutic, prophylactic, and diagnostic injections and infusions	RAC target	CPT: 96360, 96361	Both	Necessity for administration of hydration should be supported within medical documentation. Routine administration of IV fluids, pre/postoperatively while the patient is NPO, for example, without documentation, supporting signs, and/or symptoms including those of dehydration or fluid loss is not supported as medically necessary.[23]
Cataract removal	RAC target	CPT: 66830, 66840, 66850, 66852, 66920, 66930, 66940, 66982, 66983, 66984 (CERT target)	Both	Documentation will be reviewed to determine whether cataract surgery meets Medicare coverage criteria, meets applicable coding guidelines, and/or is medically reasonable and necessary.
Spinal cord stimulation	CMS-approved topic for RAC review	CPT: 63685, 63650, 63655	Both	Spinal cord neurostimulators (SCS) may be covered as therapies for the relief of chronic intractable pain, and medical records will be reviewed to determine whether the implantation of SCS meets Medicare coverage criteria and documentation requirements.
AICD/Pacemaker	RAC target	CPT: 33240, 33241, 33243, 33244, 33249, 33216, 33217	Both	Documentation will be reviewed to determine whether implantable automatic defibrillators meet Medicare coverage criteria, meet applicable coding guidelines, and/or are medically reasonable and necessary.
Deep brain stimulation	CMS-approved topic for RAC review	CPT: 61885, 61886, 95970, 95971, 95972, 95973	Both	Medicare will consider whether the initial placement of deep brain stimulation is reasonable and necessary for the treatment of Parkinson's disease and essential tremor, under certain conditions.

Table 2. Outpatient Coding and Medical Necessity Targets (cont.)

Outpatient 2022				
Target	**Indication**	**CPT/HCPCS**	**Coding or Medical Necessity Review**	**Reasoning**
Polysomnography	CMS-approved topic for RAC review	CPT: 95810, 95811	Both	This review will determine whether polysomnography is reasonable and necessary for the patient's condition based on the documentation in the medical record. When the documentation does not meet the criteria for the service rendered, or the documentation does not establish the medical necessity for the services, such services will be denied.
Leadless pacemakers	RAC target	CPT: 0387T–0391T, 33274, 33275, 33207, 33208, 33213, 33214, 33999	Both	The documentation will be reviewed to determine whether the use of a leadless pacemaker meets Medicare coverage guidelines and applicable coding guidelines.
Intensity-modulated radiation therapy (IMRT)	Expensive procedure	CPT: 77301	Both	Payment amounts for the services identified by CPT codes 77014, 77280, 77285, 77290, 77295, 77305 through 77321, 77331, and 77370 are included in the ambulatory payment classification (APC) payment for CPT 77301 (intensity modulated radiotherapy plan, including dose volume histograms for target and critical structure partial tolerance specifications). These codes should not be reported in addition to CPT 77301 when provided prior to, or as part of, the development of the IMRT plan.

Table 2. Outpatient Coding and Medical Necessity Targets (cont.)

Outpatient 2022				
Target	**Indication**	**CPT/HCPCS**	**Coding or Medical Necessity Review**	**Reasoning**
Pulmonary rehab	RAC target	HCPCS: G0424	Both	Pulmonary rehabilitation is a physician-supervised program for chronic obstructive pulmonary disease (COPD) and certain other chronic respiratory diseases designed to optimize physical and social performance and autonomy. Medical documentation will be reviewed to determine whether pulmonary rehabilitation is medically reasonable and necessary and meets federal guidelines and Medicare coverage criteria.
Magnetic Resonance Imaging (MRI)	CMS-approved topic for RAC review **CERT improper payment rate**: 11.1%	CPT: 70540, 70544, 70547, 70551, 70557, 71550, 72141, 72146, 72148, 72195, 73218, 73221, 73718, 73721, 74181	Both	When a more extensive MRI is performed on the same site as a less extensive MRI, the less extensive MRI is bundled into the more extensive MRI.
Arthroscopy limited shoulder debridement	CMS-approved topic for RAC review	CPT: 29822, 29805, 29806, 29807, 29819, 29820, 29821, 29823, 29824, 29825, 29827, 29828	Coding	Shoulder arthroscopy procedures include a limited debridement that is not separately payable when another shoulder arthroscopy procedure is billed and paid on the same shoulder for the same day for the same beneficiary at the same encounter.
Total knee arthroplasty	CMS-approved topic for RAC review	CPT: 27445, 27447, 27486, 27487	Coding, medical necessity, and documentation review	The documentation will be reviewed to determine whether a TKA is medically necessary according to the guidelines outlined in the LCDs and local coverage articles (LCAs).

Risk Area Governance

To prevent fraud, waste, and abuse, the government can bring suit against a healthcare provider under the False Claims Act.[24] Qui tam or whistleblower suits are filed by private citizens on behalf of the government to combat unlawful claims submission where a provider knowingly submits false claims to the government. OIG is on a mission to address fraud, waste, and abuse in the healthcare sector by routinely conducting complex audits on healthcare claims. An audit report is sent to CMS and released to the public after completion of such audit. This report details coding, billing, and compliance trends (such as upcoding or lack of documentation to support medical necessity) that the OIG observed. In addition, the report details the monetary amounts the hospital owes (overpayment) to CMS for submitting incorrect claims. According to Medicare's 60-day Overpayment Rule, once an overpayment is identified by a healthcare provider, it needs to be returned to CMS within 60 days since identification of the overpayment.[25]

Coding irregularities may also affect a healthcare organization's compliance with the following laws and could result in civil, criminal, and administrative penalties and corrective actions:

- Anti-Kickback Statute, 42 U.S.C. § 1320a-7b(b)
- Physician Self-Referral Law (Stark Law), 42 U.S.C. § 1395nn
- Criminal Health Care Fraud Statute, 18 U.S.C. § 1347
- Exclusion Statute, 42 U.S.C. § 1320a-7
- Civil Monetary Penalties Law (CMPL), 42 U.S.C. § 1320a-7a

Common Compliance Risks

Lack of Timely Training and Education on Coding Updates and Regulations

Coding guidelines change, and new codes are often added. Coders must have ongoing education and training and maintain their coding certification. For example, in January 2021, major changes by the American Medical Association in the evaluation and management (E/M) office visit codes went into effect.[26] Incorporating these groundbreaking revisions into physician and coder workflows involved software, which was vital for the success. This included familiarizing and educating coders. Telehealth coding (e.g., 99441–99443) and COVID-19–related CPT coding guidelines that were added during the pandemic are another example. Staying up to date on regulatory updates and coding guidelines is a must to avoid denials and government audits.

Inadequate Physician Documentation

Physician documentation is critical to support medical necessity. Examples of inadequate documentation include, but are not limited to insufficient medical history, illegible signature or handwriting, insufficient or shortage of physician notes that would outline what care was provided and why, testing, assessment, interpretation, patient education, no physician order, and inadequate description of prescriptions to be filled.

Inadequate Documentation for MCC and CC codes

DRGs for inpatient claims with high severity are often targeted by the OIG in hospital compliance audits. If CC or MCC, when used in secondary diagnoses, are not supported in the record, they may not justify a billed DRG and lead to denials or overbilling.

Improper Type-of-Admission Codes on Claims

Admission type codes have a deep impact on a healthcare provider's mortality measures and scores, which is why it is crucial to have these codes listed correctly.

Improper DD Reported on Claims

These codes allow Medicare to split reimbursement between the hospital and the post-acute care setting. If an incorrect DD is assigned, a provider may end up receiving an overpayment. For example, one of the most common DD errors is when a patient is discharged on home health (HH) (06) but home (01) is submitted on the claim. This happens because at the time of writing the discharge, the patient refused HH and hence provider documented the home as the place of discharge. However, after a while the patient changes their mind and decides to go to HH. This gets documented in the medical record by the care management (CM) or nursing team, but it contradicts the provider's discharge summary documentation. A coder may not look through the CM or nursing notes to verify the patient's DD and code the status as 01 when it should be 06.

Improper Diagnosis Coding and RADV Audits

With a trend to more managed Medicaid and managed Medicare (MA) payment model, the hierarchical condition categories (HCC) coding accuracy and risk adjustment data validation (RADV) audits by third parties should be considered in risk management along with traditional fee-for-service (FFS) claims coding.[27] As opposed to FFS model where payment is paid for each encounter by unbundling and charging for services separately, under an MA payment model, CMS uses HCC risk adjustment scores from prior year to reimburse MA organizations for each enrollee. HCC scores are captured through ICD-10-CM coding and calculated based on absence or presence of chronic conditions such as diabetes, chronic obstructive pulmonary disease, and congestive heart failure (CHF). CMS performs RADV audits to ensure data submitted for risk adjustment scores is accurate and valid. OIG also conducts audits on MA organizations to ensure diagnosis codes are correctly coded and risk scores are reported accurately, in compliance with federal and state guidelines. In May 2021, the OIG conducted an audit on seven high-risk groups that have been identified as high risk for miscoding that results in inflated risk adjustment scores.[28] These high-risk groups of diagnoses are:

- Acute stroke,
- Acute heart attack,
- Acute stroke and acute heart attack combination,
- Embolism,
- Vascular claudication,
- Major depressive disorder, and
- Potentially mis-keyed diagnosis codes.[29]

To avoid miscoding and risk calculation, providers need to ensure diagnoses are coded based on provider documentation. Chronic conditions, cause and effect relationships, complications, or manifestations of a disease process are monitored, evaluated, assessed, and treated by the provider throughout the calendar year and documented as such in the medical record.

Addressing Compliance Risks

Provide Coding Education and Training

Coding professionals need to receive education and training by October 1 each year on coding updates and regulations. Providers must ensure that coding professionals are educated and trained on ICD-10-CM and ICD-10-PCS coding updates well ahead of the October 1 due date to ensure compliance with coding requirements and federal regulations. It is vital to note that coding guidelines complement the coding instructions and conventions; the coding instructions and conventions take precedence over guidelines.

Have the Right Documentation for MCC and CC Codes

Ensure that MCC or CC codes are backed by solid, complete, and consistent documentation, clinical indicators, and complaint queries, if needed. When conducting an audit of IP claims, compliance professionals need to ask whether the review is coding related or medical necessity and documentation review related. Having certified inpatient coders on the review team will also be a tremendous help.

Collect Consistent and Adequate Physician Documentation

The only way a healthcare provider can pass a CC or MCC audit review is by having concrete, complete, and consistent physician documentation in the medical record to support additional and extensive patient care per UHDDS definitions; otherwise, providers risk losing hundreds of thousands of dollars per claim. And if physician documentation is sloppy on a more systemic level, more is at risk than a few particular claims. It could potentially become a due diligence issue that can even give rise to False Claims Act allegations if not remedied quickly. Solid physician documentation is the secret sauce to good medical record-keeping.

Ensure DD and Type-of-Admission Codes Are Reported Correctly on Claims

These codes have an impact on provider's reimbursement. Patients that are discharged from an acute care setting (hospital) to a post-acute care setting (such as a skilled nursing facility (SNF) or an HH agency) are reported out to Medicare with different DD codes: 03 for SNF and 06 for HH discharges. Recently, RACs have started to deny claims where the DD was incorrectly reported and recouping reimbursement. To avoid such mishaps, CM or nursing needs to communicate with the provider to ensure the correct DD is documented and updated in the patient's medical record.

Select Proper Codes for POA Indicators, DD, and Type of Admission

These elements affect reimbursement and a healthcare organization's quality scores and reporting. POA indicators are assigned to ICD-10-CM codes to indicate whether a diagnosis was present on admission (Y), developed after admission (N), unable to determine (U), clinically undetermined (W), or exempt from POA reporting (1).[30] Healthcare providers wanting to review their quality data through hospital-acquired conditions (HACs) and patient safety indicators (PSIs) may want to start off by ensuring that the POA indicators are correctly assigned. Certain conditions that develop after an IP admission are assigned POA N. Though they may be an MCC code, they are not paid by Medicare—in fact, the provider is penalized for not taking steps to prevent such condition from developing in admitted patients. Catheter-associated urinary tract infection (CAUTI) is one such example of a condition that, if developed after an IP admission, will cost healthcare providers money and possible fines.

Since these codes carry significant implications on a healthcare provider's quality reporting, it is crucial to have an established set of protocols in place to ensure clear and consistent documentation throughout the medical record. For conditions developing during a procedure, providers need to clearly and consistently document whether the condition was inherent, expected, necessary, unavoidable, integral to the procedure, or whether it is a complication due to an unexpected outcome of a procedure. An integral, expected, necessary, unavoidable, or inherent condition is not coded as a complication; a complication is identified as a HAC or PSI, attracting scrutiny and negative quality reporting. If a condition is not clearly documented, coders need to query the provider for clarification before coding a condition as a complication or a postsurgical complication. For example, coders may query the provider to clarify CAUTI's POA status. A provider can review patient's labs taken on admission to confirm whether the CAUTI was POA Y or N. Receiving clarification can result in a condition being reported as an HAC, PSI, or any other condition. Provider communication and cooperation is key here.

Check That Admit Type Codes Are Listed Correctly

The six main admit type codes for admission/visit include: emergency (1), urgent (2), elective (3), newborn (4), trauma center (5), or information not available (9).[31] [*Note: Codes 6–8 are reserved for national assignment.*] The first three admit type codes have the most impact on mortality and quality outcomes reporting. Let's say an 86-year-old patient with multiple comorbidities is brought to the emergency department in grave condition and the provider rushes that person to the ICU. Unfortunately, the patient dies within 24 hours of hospital admission in the ICU. The admit type code is erroneously selected as elective, causing this death to be counted as an in-hospital death. This negatively influences the mortality score. When the admit type code is correctly selected as either emergent or urgent, the death becomes an expected death that does not influence the hospital's mortality score and measures. A probe audit on admit type codes can identify whether coders (or whoever is responsible for admit type data abstraction) are reporting these codes correctly. If appropriate, education needs to be provided on correct assignment of admit type codes and their definition to ensure correct data capture and compliance.

Perform a Root Cause Analysis on Coding Concerns

Compliance associates need to perform a root cause analysis on internal coding audits, RAC claims, or any other coding concern to identify the cause of and cure for the problem and determine solutions so that the pattern does not repeat. A good way to conduct root cause analysis is by asking why a pattern or coding error occurred several times to understand all angles of the issue and receive different answers for the causes of the problem. This will likely lead to where the documentation process internal control failures occurred. Based on the root cause analysis feedback, create an action plan to address coding, billing, or documentation concerns. It is best to prioritize risk based on significance to allow appropriate allocation of resources from the most to least critical issues.

Review Policies and Procedures

Ensure all coding policies and procedures are updated and compliant with federal and state regulations and that coders adhere to the coding policies. It is very common for a healthcare provider to have coding policies that sit in a folder, collecting "e-dust," but which are never shared with the coding staff. Ensure you have a domain owner and set review schedules for these procedures and policies. The compliance office may conduct simple test audits of health information management policies or coding policies that were recently updated or consistent with policy expectation. This is part of coding process auditing rather than coding claims auditing, but it is necessary. Also check the coding training policy.

Encourage and Educate Coders on Reporting Noncompliance

Coders should be educated on ways to report noncompliant activities and observations. In certain instances, coders have been instructed to append a modifier to a Medicare claim to avoid edits or having a claim returned for resubmission. Coders find themselves in conflict when given such instructions, especially if those instructions come from leadership. In these circumstances, coders need to be armed with resources to anonymously report such behaviors without fear of being punished or retaliated against. A hotline is important to report such concerns to the compliance department, but coders must be educated on its usage and reliability.

Mind COVID-19 Blanket Waiver Policies

While the CMS COVID-19 blanket waiver policies are in effect, providers of all types must ensure they comply with the conditions of the waivers, in particular the documentation requirements.[32] The COVID-19 waiver reduces burden on a provider for claim submission, but the OIG is already conducting audits on services rendered during the public health emergency. In 2022, OIG is expected to conduct nationwide audits on the following list of targets:

- Audits of Medicare Part B Telehealth Services During the Covid-19 Public Health Emergency
- Audit of Home Health Services Provided as Telehealth During the Covid-19 Public Health Emergency
- Audit of Medicare Payments for Inpatient Discharges Billed by Hospitals for Beneficiaries Diagnosed With COVID-19
- Trend Analysis of Medicare Laboratory Billing for Potential Fraud and Abuse With COVID-19 Add-on Testing[33]

This is not an all-inclusive list. A complete listing of OIG's workplan and targets can be found on the OIG website.

Possible Penalties

In 2020, the U.S. Department of Justice updated the civil violations which now range between $11,665 and $23,331 per violation.[34] Violators are not only subject to jail time and monetary fines, but also risk exclusion from participating in all federal healthcare programs, including Medicare and Medicaid. In summary, the OIG has the authority to enforce the following penalties on a healthcare provider or an entity that it deems a violator(s) of the federal healthcare program:

- Impose civil monetary violations ranging between $11,665 and $23,331 per violation; and/or
- Impose jail time; and/or
- Enter into a corporate integrity agreement contract with the OIG requiring the violator to implement an effective compliance program that's based on OIG's compliance program guidance; and/or
- Exclude the provider or entity from participating in any federal healthcare program by adding the violator to the List of Excluded Individuals/Entities.

Compliance Resources

Centers for Medicare & Medicaid Services

CERT Comprehensive Error Rate Testing
https://www.cms.gov/Research-Statistics-Data-and-Systems/Monitoring-Programs/
Improper-Payment-Measurement-Programs/CERT

CMS Transmittals
https://www.cms.gov/Regulations-and-Guidance/Guidance/Transmittals/2021-Transmittals

Medicare Administrative Contractor
https://www.cms.gov/Medicare/Medicare-Contracting/
Medicare-Administrative-Contractors/What-is-a-MAC

Medicare Fee-for-Service Recovery Audit Program
https://www.cms.gov/Research-Statistics-Data-and-Systems/Monitoring-Programs/
Medicare-FFS-Compliance-Programs/Recovery-Audit-Program

Medicare Risk Adjustment Data Validation Program
https://www.cms.gov/Research-Statistics-Data-and-Systems/Monitoring-Programs/
Medicare-Risk-Adjustment-Data-Validation-Program/Overview

RAC Recovery Audit Program
https://www.cms.gov/Research-Statistics-Data-and-Systems/Monitoring-Programs/
Medicare-FFS-Compliance-Programs/Recovery-Audit-Program

Targeted Probe and Educate
https://www.cms.gov/Research-Statistics-Data-and-Systems/Monitoring-Programs/
Medicare-FFS-Compliance-Programs/Medical-Review/Targeted-Probe-and-EducateTPE

Coding Resources

Coding Conventions
https://icd.who.int/browse10/2019/en

Coding Clinics
https://www.codingclinicadvisor.com/

CPT Assistant
https://commerce.ama-assn.org/store/ui/catalog/
productDetail?product_id=prod270004&sku_id=sku270043

Official Guidelines for Coding and Reporting
https://www.cms.gov/medicare/icd-10/2022-icd-10-cm

Program for Evaluating Payment Patterns Electronic Report (PEPPER)

https://pepper.cbrpepper.org

U.S. Department of Health & Human Services, Office of Inspector General

Work Plan
https://oig.hhs.gov/reports-and-publications/workplan/index.asp

Risk Takeaways

Main points of interest:
- Complete and consistent provider documentation is key to passing any type of audits and reviews.
- Collaboration between provider, coding, billing, care management, and compliance is essential to meeting state and federal compliance.
- A claim cannot withstand external audit scrutiny if it's not supported by medical necessity.

Areas to watch:
- Unbundling procedures
- Upcoding ICD-10-CM, ICD-10-PCS, or CPT/HCPCS
- Lack of or inconsistent provider documentation
- Improper risk score based on incorrect diagnoses code assignment
- Lack of coding training and education

Laws that apply:
- False Claims Act: 31 U.S.C §§ 3729–3733

- Anti-Kickback Statue: 42 U.S.C. § 1320a-7b(b)
- Physician Self-Referral Law (Stark Law): 42 U.S.C. § 1395nn
- Criminal Health Care Fraud Statute: 18 U.S.C. § 1347
- Exclusion Statute: 42 U.S.C. § 1320a-7
- Civil Monetary Penalties Law: 42 U.S.C. § 1320a-7a

Addressing compliance risks:
- Provide coding education and training.
- Ensure the proper documentation backs MCC and CC codes.
- Collect consistent and adequate physician documentation.
- Ensure DD and type-of-admission codes are reported correctly on claims.
- Select proper codes for POA indicators, DD, and type of admission.
- Check that admit type codes are listed correctly.
- Perform a root cause analysis on coding concerns.
- Review policies and procedures.
- Encourage and educate coders on reporting noncompliance.
- Mind COVID-19 blanket waiver policies.

Endnotes

1. **Ghazal Irfan** is the hospital-revenue cycle compliance manager at Adventist Health-West. Irfan's key areas of expertise include coding data quality and compliance, clinical documentation improvement, medical staff documentation review, prospective payment reviews, and revenue capture. Irfan has extensive experience in the qualitative and quantitative analysis of medical record clinical data, coding guidelines, diagnosis-related group reimbursement, Medicare policies and regulations, and data collection.

2. Centers for Medicare & Medicaid Services, "Targeted Probe and Educate (TPE) Q & A's," accessed December 15, 2021, https://www.cms.gov/Research-Statistics-Data-and-Systems/Monitoring-Programs/Medicare-FFS-Compliance-Programs/Medical-Review/Downloads/TPE QAs.pdf.

3. "Hospital Compliance Reviews," Office of Inspector General, U.S. Department of Health & Human Services, accessed December 15, 2021, https://oig.hhs.gov/newsroom/podcasts/hospital-compliance/.

4. Centers for Disease Control and Prevention, "ICD-10-CM Official Guidelines for Coding and Reporting FY 2020 (October 12019 – September 30, 2020)," accessed December 15, 2021,https://www.cdc.gov/nchs/data/icd/10cmguidelines-FY2020_final.pdf.

5. Centers for Medicare & Medicaid Services, "ICD-10-PCS Official Guidelines for Coding and Reporting *2020*," accessed December 15, 2021, https://www.cms.gov/Medicare/Coding/ICD10/Downloads/2020-ICD-10-PCS-Guidelines.pdf.

6. "MS-DRG Classifications and Software," Centers for Medicare & Medicaid Services, accessed December 15, 2021,https://www.cms.gov/Medicare/Medicare-Fee-for-Service-Payment/AcuteInpatientPPS/MS-DRG-Classifications-and-Software.

7. Centers for Medicare & Medicaid Services, Division of Institutional Claims Processing, "Definition and Uses of Health Insurance Prospective Payment System Codes (HIPPS Codes)," May 28, 2021, https://www.cms.gov/Medicare/Medicare-Fee-for-Service-Payment/Prosp-MedicareFeeSvcPmtGen/Downloads/hippsuses.pdf.

8. ICD Centers for Disease Control and Prevention, "ICD-10-CM Official Guidelines for Coding and Reporting FY 2020."

9. Centers for Disease Control and Prevention, "ICD-10-CM Official Guidelines for Coding and Reporting FY 2020."

10. "Payments for Patients Diagnosed with Malnutrition," Office of Inspector General, U.S. Department of Health & Human Services, accessed December 15, 2021, https://oig.hhs.gov/reports-and-publications/workplan/summary/wp-summary-0000092.asp.

11. "CMS Did Not Adequately Address Discrepancies in the Coding Classification for Kwashiorkor," Office of Inspector General, U.S. Department of Health & Human Services, November 28, 2017,https://oig.hhs.gov/oas/reports/region3/31400010.asp.

12. Wendy Phillips and Maria Browning, "A Clinician's Guide to Defining, Identifying and Documenting Malnutrition in Hospitalized Patients," *Nutrition Issues in Gastroenterology* 169 (November 2017), https://med.virginia.edu/ginutrition/wp-content/uploads/sites/199/2014/06/Documenting-Malnutrition-November-17.pdf.

13. 42 U.S.C. § 1395y(a)(1)(A).

14. "Medical Necessity Documentation," Centers for Medicare & Medicaid Services, January 31, 2012.

15. "Reasonable & Necessary Guidelines," Novitas Solutions, last modified November 1, 2019,https://www.novitas-solutions.com/webcenter/portal/MedicareJH/pagebyid?contentId=00099545.

16. "Total Knee Arthroplasty (TKA) Removal from the Medicare Inpatient-Only (IPO) List and Application of the 2-Midnight Rule," Centers for Medicare & Medicaid Services, January 24, 2019, https://www.cms.gov/Outreach-and-Education/Medicare-Learning-Network-MLN/MLNMattersArticles/downloads/SE19002.pdf.

17. "Total Knee Arthroplasty," Local Coverage Determination (LCD), Medicare Coverage Database, Centers for Medicare & Medicaid Services, accessed December 15, 2021, https://www.cms.gov/medicare-coverage-database/view/lcd.aspx?LCDId=36575&ver=17&NCDId=177&ncdver=1&SearchType=Advanced&CoverageSelection=Both&NCSelection=NCD&ArticleType=Ed%7CKey%7CSAD%7CFAQ&PolicyType=Final&s=-%7C5%7C6%7C66%7C67%7C44&KeyWord=Computed+Tomography&KeyWordLookUp=Doc&KeyWordSearchType=Exact&kq=true&bc=IAAAACgAAAAA&.

18. Centers for Medicare & Medicaid Services, "Chapter 23 – Fee Schedule Administration and Coding Requirements," *Medicare Claims Processing Manual*, Pub. 100-04, revised July 15, 2021,https://www.cms.gov/Regulations-and-Guidance/Guidance/Manuals/downloads/clm104c23.pdf.

19. ICD Centers for Disease Control and Prevention, "ICD-10-CM Official Guidelines for Coding and Reporting FY 2020."

20. "Cataract Surgery in Adults," Local Coverage Determination (LCD), Medicare Coverage Database, Centers for Medicare & Medicaid Services, accessed December 15, 2021, https://www.cms.gov/medicare-coverage-database/details/lcd-details.aspx?LCDId=37027&ContrId=345&ver=11&ContrVer=1&CntrctrSelected=345*1&Cntrctr=345&s=5&DocType=1&bc=AAAAAACAAAAA&.

21. "Cataract Surgery in Adults," Local Coverage Determination (LCD), Medicare Coverage Database, Centers for Medicare & Medicaid Services, accessed December 15, 2021, https://www.cms.gov/medicare-coverage-database/details/lcd-details.aspx?LCDId=37027&ContrId=345&ver=11&ContrVer=1&CntrctrSelected=345*1&Cntrctr=345&s=5&DocType=1&bc=AAAAAACAAAAA&.

22. "Therapeutic Activities Targeted Probe and Educate Review Results," Noridian Healthcare Solutions, last updated February 25, 2020, https://med.noridianmedicare.com/web/jfb/cert-review/mr/review-results/therapeutic-activities-quarterly-results-of-tpe-review.

23. "Hydration," Noridian Healthcare Solutions, last updated March 6, 2020, https://med.noridianmedicare.com/web/jfa/topics/drugs-biologicals-injections/hydration.

24. 31 U.S.C. §§ 3729–3733.

25. Centers for Medicare & Medicaid Services, "Medicare Reporting and Returning of Self-Identified Overpayments," fact sheet, February 11, 2016, https://www.cms.gov/newsroom/fact-sheets/medicare-reporting-and-returning-self-identified-overpayments.

26. "CPT Evaluation and Management (E/M) Office or Other Outpatient (99202-99215) and Prolonged Services (99354, 99355, 99356, 99417) Code and Guideline Changes," American Medical Association, accessed January 21, 2022, https://www.ama-assn.org/system/files/2019-06/cpt-office-prolonged-svs-code-changes.pdf.

27. "Medicare Risk Adjustment Data Validation Program," Centers for Medicare & Medicaid Services, last modified December 1, 2021, https://www.cms.gov/Research-Statistics-Data-and-Systems/Monitoring-Programs/Medicare-Risk-Adjustment-Data-Validation-Program/Overview.

28. Amy J. Frontz, "Medicare Advantage Compliance Audit of Specific Diagnosis Codes That Anthem Community Insurance Company, Inc. (Contract H3655) Submitted to CMS," A-07-19-01187, Office of Inspector General, U.S. Department of Health & Human Services, May 2021, 4–5, https://oig.hhs.gov/oas/reports/region7/71901187.pdf.

29. "Medicare Advantage Compliance Audit of Specific Diagnosis Codes That Anthem Community Insurance Company, Inc. (Contract H3655) Submitted to CMS," A-07-19-01187, Office of Inspector General, U.S. Department of Health & Human Services, May 2021, https://oig.hhs.gov/oas/reports/region7/71901187.pdf.

30. "Present on Admission Indicators," Noridian Healthcare Solutions, last updated February 24, 2020,https://med.noridianmedicare.com/web/jea/provider-types/acute-ipps-hospital/present-on-admission-indicators.

31. Centers for Medicare & Medicaid Services, "Point of Origin Codes Update to the UB-04 (CMS-1450) Manual Code List," Trans. 1775, Medicare Claims Processing, Pub. 100-04, July 24, 2009, https://www.cms.gov/Regulations-and-Guidance/Guidance/Transmittals/Downloads/R1775CP.pdf.

32. "Coronavirus waivers & flexibilities," Centers for Medicare & Medicaid Services, last modified June 3, 2021, https://www.cms.gov/about-cms/emergency-preparedness-response-operations/current-emergencies/coronavirus-waivers.

33. "Active Work Plan Items," Office of Inspector General, U.S. Department of Health & Human Services, accessed December 15, 2021, https://oig.hhs.gov/reports-and-publications/workplan/active-item-table.asp#example=f-during%20the%20covid-19%20public%20health%20emergency%20.

34. Civil Monetary Penalties Inflation Adjustment, 85 Fed. Reg. 37,004 (June 19, 2020).

Coding with ICD-10 Clinical Modification (ICD-10-CM)

By Sonal Patel,[1] CPMA, CPC, CMC

What Is the ICD-10-CM?

Currently in the United States, certified medical coders abide by the International Classification of Diseases, 10th Revision, Clinical Modification (ICD-10-CM). ICD-10-CM was modified by the National Center for Health Statistics (NCHS) from the World Health Organization's (WHO) ICD-10 to report diagnoses for reimbursement purposes. Although WHO authorized the publication of ICD-10 for mortality coding and classification based on death certificates in the United States in 1999, it was not until October 1, 2015, that ICD-10-CM was implemented. In fact, it was the U.S. Department of Health and Human Services (HHS) that mandated all entities covered by the Health Insurance Portability and Accountability Act (HIPAA) must transition to this new code set from ICD-9-CM for all electronic healthcare claims.[2]

To reflect ongoing changes in the medical field, ICD has, in fact, been revised over the years.[3] There have been numerous advancements and developments in U.S. healthcare since 1979 that have warranted increasing clinical accuracy, adding more codes, and revising code structure by expansion. Integral to our current clinical modification of ICD-10-CM is the notable differences in the quality of data reporting. For instance, there are expanded injury codes for tracking public health conditions; additions of sixth and seventh characters for greater specificity; laterality capability; and the creation of combination codes for better epidemiological research. Moreover, since the transition, the U.S. can finally compare morbidity diagnosis data at the international level, because many developed countries adopted ICD-10 code sets much earlier than the U.S. did. As an additional bonus, ICD-10-CM allows for further expansion.

Certified medical coders are prepared for new ICD-10-CM additions, deletions, and revisions on October 1 each year, as well as any periodic updates made throughout the year.

Characteristics of ICD-10-CM

ICD-10-CM is an exceptional representation of the best minds in medicine, epidemiology, and nosology. It captures current healthcare concepts and codes that reflect the breadth of modern medicine. Continuous involvement and maintenance are required by the Centers for Disease Control and Prevention (CDC). It is the CDC that approves of all code extensions, interpretations, modifications, addenda, or errata.[4]

The 2021 code book totals 1,360 pages and contains more than 70,000 codes. It includes the Tabular List, Alphabetic Index to Diseases and Injuries, Table of Neoplasms, Table of Drugs and Chemicals, and Index to External Causes of Injuries.

There are also ICD-10-CM official guidelines for coding and reporting that are issued by the CDC as an official accompaniment to the official version of the ICD-10-CM as published on the NCHS website.[5] Adherence to guidelines is a requirement under HIPAA; specifically, the diagnosis codes found in the Tabular List and Alphabetic Index of the ICD-10-CM manual, have been adopted under HIPAA for all healthcare settings. The "ICD-10-CM Official Coding Guidelines for Coding and Reporting" always takes precedence over any and all other coding advice, including the American Health Association's, *Coding Clinic Advisor*.

The information is structured to assist the certified medical coder. There are 22 chapters, as well as three appendices that detail the diagnosis codes.

ICD-10-CM Guidelines

The guidelines are organized into four sections. Section I covers the structure and conventions of the classification; general guidelines that apply to the entire classification; and chapter-specific guidelines that correspond to the chapters as they are arranged in the classification. Section II has guidelines for selection of principal diagnoses for non-outpatient settings. Section III contains guidelines for reporting additional diagnoses in non-outpatient settings. Section IV is highly detailed for outpatient coding and reporting. Certified coders must review all sections of the guidelines to fully understand all of the rules and instructions needed to code correctly and compliantly.

Certified medical coders must know these guidelines in order to understand and follow sequencing and specificity within the codes that change annually.

ICD-10-CM Structure

ICD-10-CM codes are composed of alphanumeric characters that describe the diagnosis, or signs and symptoms, and other conditions documented by the physician or other qualified healthcare professional in code format. There are seven characters in the code sequence. Character 1 is identified with capital letters A–Z. Characters 2 and 3 are captured with a numerals. Characters 4–6 are identified with either numerals or letters (capital or lowercase). And Character 7 is used only in specific chapters (which include Pregnancy, Musculoskeletal, Injuries, and External Causes of Morbidity) and is captured with either numerals or letters (capital or lowercase).

Documentation and ICD-10-CM Coding

Proper clinical documentation is critical for certified medical coders to correctly assign ICD-10-CM codes. After all, accurate, concise, and complete clinical documentation is central to reflecting patient care, as well as for coding and billing medical encounters. Unfortunately, many diseases, signs and symptoms, even conditions and injuries require specific and detailed documentation. This specific and detailed documentation is needed for compliance not only with the ICD-10-CM code structure, but also for compliance with capturing the highest level of specificity available within ICD-10-CM for accurate reporting and correct reimbursement.

Therefore, insufficient clinical documentation is one of the highest areas of risk due to the many inadvertent holes in documentation capture. Certified medical coders must abstract codes with less-than-acceptable accuracy, despite multiple queries from clinical documentation specialists. When this happens, the claim is billed despite an incomplete medical picture, and the inevitable denial or post-payment audit ensues.

There are areas of improvement that can be made to reduce compliance risks. First, continued education for certified medical coders and physicians alike is required. It is critical that both parties understand the myriad of documentation requirements, changes, and updates; support them all; and find mutual benefits. Second, certified medical coders, clinical documentation integrity specialists, and other health information management professionals should be allowed to communicate freely amongst one another and break down the silos that currently exist in healthcare. Once all of the instrumental players in the revenue cycle provide their insights, it will become evident that all have one identical goal: protecting the provider. Third, documentation improvements can be made after developing an internal self-auditing and self-monitoring plan that isolates targeted areas of deficiencies. And finally, all three of these actions must be supported at the highest level within the organization. It is the compliance team that should spearhead the movement to see greater accuracy in medical documentation that is driven by medical necessity for each and every encounter. Inevitably, once documentation accuracy increases, the correct coding levels will increase accordingly.

Risk Area Governance

HIPAA, 45 C.F.R. § 162

The Final Rule issued on January 16, 2009, by HHS mandated that all entities covered by HIPAA implement ICD-10.[6] All electronic healthcare claims had to be upgraded to Version 5010 by January 1, 2012, and as of that date, all HIPAA-covered entities needed to be in compliance with Version 5010.[7]

The Stark Law, 42 U.S.C. § 1395nn

The Physician Self-Referral Law, commonly referred to as the Stark Law, prohibits physicians from referring patients to receive "designated health services" payable by Medicare or Medicaid from entities with which the physician or an immediate family member has a financial relationship—unless an exception applies. Financial relationships include both ownership/investment interests and compensation arrangements. For example, if someone invests in an imaging center, the Stark Law requires the resulting financial relationship to fit within an exception or that person may not refer patients to the facility and the entity may not bill for the referred imaging services.

Designated health services include:

- Clinical laboratory services
- Physical therapy, occupational therapy, and outpatient speech-language pathology services
- Radiology and certain other imaging services
- Radiation therapy services and supplies
- Durable medical equipment (DME) and supplies
- Parenteral and enteral nutrients, equipment, and supplies
- Prosthetics, orthotics, and prosthetic devices and supplies
- Home health services
- Outpatient prescription drugs
- Inpatient and outpatient hospital services

The Stark Law is a strict liability statute, which means proof of specific intent to violate the law is not required. The Stark Law prohibits the submission or causing the submission of claims in violation of the law's restrictions on referrals. Penalties for physicians who violate the Stark Law include fines as well as exclusion from participation in the federal healthcare programs.[8]

Civil False Claims Act (FCA), 31 U.S.C. §§ 3729–3733

The civil FCA makes it illegal to submit claims for payment to Medicare or Medicaid that a person knows or should know are false or fraudulent. Providers that file false claims may be fined of up to three times the programs' loss plus $11,000 per claim filed. According to the HHS Office of Inspector General (OIG):

> Under the civil FCA, each instance of an item or a service billed to Medicare or Medicaid counts as a claim, so fines can add up quickly. The fact that a claim results from a kickback or is made in violation of the Stark Law also may render it false or fraudulent, creating liability under the civil FCA as well as the AKS or Stark Law.

> Under the civil FCA, no specific intent to defraud is required. The civil FCA defines "knowing" to include not only actual knowledge, but also instances in which the person acted in deliberate ignorance or reckless disregard of the truth or falsity of the information. Further, the civil FCA contains a whistleblower provision that allows a private individual to file a lawsuit on behalf of the United States and entitles that whistleblower to a percentage of any recoveries. Whistleblowers could be current or ex-business partners, hospital or office staff, patients, or competitors.[9]

Criminal False Claims Act, 18 U.S.C. §§ 287, 286

Section 287 of the False Claims Act is for false, fictions, or fraudulent claims and it states:

> "Whoever makes or presents to any person or officer in the civil, military, or naval service of the United States, or to any department or agency thereof, any claim upon or against the United States, or any department or agency thereof, knowing such claim to be false, fictitious, or fraudulent, shall be imprisoned not more than five years and shall be subject to a fine in the amount provided in this title."[10]

Section 286 of the False Claims Act is for conspiracy to defraud the government with respect to claims and it states:

> Whoever enters into any agreement, combination, or conspiracy to defraud the United States, or any department or agency thereof, by obtaining or aiding to obtain the payment or allowance of any false, fictitious or fraudulent claim, shall be fined under this title or imprisoned not more than ten years, or both.

> In order for the government to prove a case under § 287, three elements must exist:

1. An individual made or presented a claim to a department or agency of the United States for money or property,

2. The claim was false, fictitious, or fraudulent, and

3. An individual knew at the time that the claim was false, fictitious, or fraudulent.[11]

Healthcare Fraud Statute, 18 U.S.C. § 1347

Section 1347 for the healthcare fraud statute states:

(a) Whoever knowingly and willfully executes, or attempts to execute, a scheme or artifice—

(1) to defraud any health care benefit program; or

(2) to obtain, by means of false or fraudulent pretenses, representations, or promises, any of the money or property owned by, or under the custody or control of, any health care benefit program, in connection with the delivery of or payment for health care benefits, items, or services, shall be fined under this title or imprisoned not more than 10 years, or both. If the violation results in serious bodily injury (as defined in section 1365 of this title), such person shall be fined under this title or imprisoned not more than 20 years, or both; and if the violation results in death, such person shall be fined under this title, or imprisoned for any term of years or for life, or both.

(b) With respect to violations of this section, a person need not have actual knowledge of this section or specific intent to commit a violation of this section.[12]

Exclusion Statute, 42 U.S.C. § 1320a-7

The OIG is required to exclude individuals and entities from participating in federal healthcare programs if they are convicted of these kinds of criminal offenses:

1. Medicare or Medicaid fraud, as well as any other offenses related to the delivery of items or services under Medicare or Medicaid
2. Patient abuse or neglect
3. Felony convictions for other healthcare-related fraud, theft, or other financial misconduct

4. Felony convictions for unlawful manufacture, distribution, prescription, or dispensing of controlled substances[13]

The OIG can also exclude individuals and entities for several other reasons, including:

- Misdemeanor convictions related to healthcare fraud other than Medicare or Medicaid fraud or misdemeanor convictions in connection with the unlawful manufacture, distribution, prescription, or dispensing of controlled substances
- Suspension, revocation, or surrender of a license to provide healthcare for reasons bearing on professional competence, professional performance, or financial integrity and provision of unnecessary or substandard services
- Submission of false or fraudulent claims to a federal healthcare program and engaging in unlawful kickback arrangements
- Defaulting on health education loan or scholarship obligations[14]

Exclusion means that Medicare, Medicaid, and other federal healthcare programs will not reimburse for items or services that individuals and entities furnish, order, or prescribe. According to the OIG, "excluded physicians may not bill directly for treating Medicare and Medicaid patients, nor may their services be billed indirectly through an employer or a group practice. In addition, if you furnish services to a patient on a private-pay basis, no order or prescription that you give to that patient will be reimbursable by any Federal health care program."[15]

Individuals and entities are also responsible for "ensuring that [they] do not employ or contract with excluded individuals or entities, whether in a physician practice, a clinic, or in any capacity or setting in which Federal health care programs may reimburse for the items or services furnished by those employees or contractors. This responsibility requires screening all current and prospective employees and contractors against OIG's List of Excluded Individuals and Entities."[16]

Social Security Act, Medicare and Medicaid Program Integrity Provisions, 42 U.S.C. § 1320a-7k

The Social Security Act regulations require that services be medically necessary and ordered by physicians, as well as have medical documentation to support all billed claims. Medicare and Medicaid Program Integrity Provisions are often cited throughout OIG reports, such as those included in this article.[17]

Requirements for Reporting and Returning of Overpayments, 42 C.F.R. § 401.305

This law details the requirements for reporting and returning overpayments, and it has been cited throughout OIG reports as well.

Medicare Claims Processing Manual

This manual must be adhered to when filing claims to Medicare.

Medicare Program Integrity Manual

This manual must be adhered to when filing claims to Medicare.

Medicare Administrative Contractors (MACs)

Providers need to follow their local coverage determinations (LCDs) through their MACs when it comes to medical necessity and ICD-10-CM coding. National coverage determinations (NCDs), as applicable, must be followed.

ICD-10-CM Official Guidelines for Coding and Reporting

The ICD-10 guidelines should be strictly adhered to, as they are required under HIPAA.[18] The instructions and conventions of the classification take precedence over the guidelines.

Common Compliance Risks

Based on the complexities involved in our healthcare system, which include the myriad of regulations and rules at the federal, state, and local levels, the compliance risks faced in the business of medicine are manifold. However, for ICD-10-CM specifically, current 2020 OIG reports issued for both hospital inpatient and outpatient audits for compliance reveal areas of significant deficiency.[19][20] Here is a list of common compliance risks:

1. **Upcoding**: Erroneous diagnoses for severity of illness to garner increased reimbursement
2. **Diagnosis-Related Groups (DRG) optimization**: Upcoding leads to DRG optimization by adding complication/comorbidity (CC) and major complication/comorbidity (MCC) for increased reimbursement
3. **Incorrect coding**: Nave diagnosis coding errors leads to significant levels of DRG impact
4. **Poor query techniques:** Leading physicians to document a certain way, often for DRG optimization
5. **Oversight deficiency**: Poor leadership and management of coding, clinical documentation improvement (CDI), and health information management (HIM) professionals involved in compliant documentation and correct coding practices
6. **Insufficient continued education**: For CDI, coders, and providers alike

7. **CDI professional deficiencies**: A compliance risk due to deficiencies in provider education regarding compliant documentation practices
8. **Clinical coder errors**: A compliance risk due to coding-error rates
9. **Outpatient coder errors**: A compliance risk due to coding-error rates
10. **Problematic documentation/medical record**: Missing or insufficient documentation in medical records to support secondary diagnoses that are monitored, evaluated, assessed, and treated
11. **Claims denial:** Claims not properly scrubbed, poor demographic intake, lack of prior authorization, and numerous other compliance risk factors
12. **Erroneous reimbursements**: A compliance risk due to financial impacts
13. **Overpayments**: A compliance risk from not abiding by the 60-day rule to return monies
14. **Data mining**: A compliance risk as payors take the upper hand by mining provider data and leveraging data to their advantage

Addressing Compliance Risks

Develop a Coding Compliance Plan

An organization's overarching compliance program should include the seven fundamental elements developed by the OIG. A strong coding compliance plan also should be developed and maintained to reflect dedicated commitment to adherence to all federal, state, and local rules and regulations.[21] Maintaining a robust compliance program reflects a strong culture of compliance and ethics within a private practice or hospital system of any size.

Certified coders should be trained with this coding compliance plan. They should be provided access to this plan and be required to read it quarterly or annually, and as often as it is updated in the organization. Items in the coding compliance plan can include:

- Visionary statement (from leadership in coding team)
- Leadership and oversight (identifying organizational structure and reporting details of medical coding team)
- Communication policies and procedures (emphasizing transparency)
- Auditing and monitoring (stressing these integral functions and perhaps appointing specific team members to perform either/or both)
- Education and training (critical to addressing continued education throughout the year for the team and individuals for certification maintenance)
- Investigation and corrective actions (identifying necessity of quality assurance audits for coder performance and levels of corrective actions for individual coders who are deficient)
- Prevention and disciplinary actions (ensuring steps are clearly outlined by coding leadership, reflecting greater organization's policy on disciplinary action)

Additionally, the American Health Information Management Association (AHIMA) abides by a code of ethics, which should be utilized when crafting a strong coding compliance plan. The AHIMA code:

1. Promotes high standards of HIM practice
2. Summarizes broad, ethical principles that reflect the profession's core values
3. Establishes a set of ethical principles to be used to guide decision-making and actions
4. Establishes a framework for professional behavior and responsibilities when professional obligations conflict or ethical uncertainties arise
5. Provides ethical principles by which the general public can hold the HIM professional accountable
6. Helps mentor practitioners new to the field to HIM's mission, values, and ethical principles[22]

Further still, organizations should reflect on AHIMA's Standards of Ethical Coding.[23] They are the industry ideal with 11 principles that make up the basis of ethical coding and say AHIMA will:

1. Apply accurate, complete, and consistent coding practices that yield quality data.
2. Gather and report all data required for internal and external reporting, in accordance with applicable requirements and data set definitions.
3. Assign and report, in any format, only the codes and data that are clearly and consistently supported by health record documentation in accordance with applicable code set and abstraction conventions, and requirements.
4. Query and/or consult as needed with the provider for clarification and additional documentation prior to final code assignment in accordance with acceptable healthcare industry practices.
5. Refuse to participate in, support, or change reported data and/or narrative titles, billing data, clinical documentation practices, or any coding related activities intended to skew or misrepresent data and their meaning that do not comply with requirements.
6. Facilitate, advocate, and collaborate with healthcare professionals in the pursuit of accurate, complete and reliable coded data and in situations that support ethical coding practices.
7. Advance coding knowledge and practice through continuing education, including but not limited to meeting continuing education requirements.
8. Maintain the confidentiality of protected health information in accordance with the Code of Ethics.
9. Refuse to participate in the development of coding and coding related technology that is not designed in accordance with requirements.
10. Demonstrate behavior that reflects integrity, shows a commitment to ethical and legal coding practices, and fosters trust in professional activities.
11. Refuse to participate in and/or conceal unethical coding, data abstraction, query practices, or any inappropriate activities related to coding and address any perceived unethical coding related practices.[24]

Develop Coding Documentation and Standards Policies and Procedures

Each organization should develop and implement standards for documentation and coding through written policies and procedures that reflect the practice's commitment to integrity, ethics, and compliance.

Emphasis should be placed on an accuracy rate of 95% for coded claims, because that rate is the standard set forth by the OIG. To achieve this high level of accuracy, clinical documentation standards must rise up to meet all coding conventions and guidelines.

Conduct Focused and Random Internal Audits

Data mining has taken over the analysis of healthcare claims. With this surge, it is critical for providers to take back their data and understand it for their own benefit. Review current OIG audit and compliance reports to identify what diagnoses are in the spotlight. If your organization shares the spotlight, best practice recommendations include:

- Identify deficiencies by tracking and trending the organization's data
- Conduct DRG-focused audits (e.g., malnutrition, pressure ulcers, acute respiratory failure, chronic kidney disease, acute blood loss anemia)
- Generate reports to monitor error rates
- Quantify by percentage
- Provide quality feedback
- Aim for 95% correct coding rate
- Develop findings report
- Disseminate corrective action plan

Require Coders to Read Coding Resources

It's imperative that your team of certified medical coders stays up to date and has access to the required resources below. These are the main coding books and resources for both the inpatient and outpatient settings.

- Official Guidelines for Coding and Reporting ICD-10-CM, current year(s)
- ICD-10-CM: The Complete Official Code Book, current year(s)
- AHA Coding Clinic Advisor
- AMA CPT® Manual, current year(s)
- AMA CPT® Assistant
- HCPCS Level II Manual, current year(s)
- ICD-10-PCS: The Complete Official Code Book, current year(s)

Require Coders to Receive Compliance Education and Training

Continued education and training is fundamental to an organization's commitment to compliance. Certified coding professionals need to stay current on trends and trainings to ensure accuracy of reimbursement levels the first time. Provide education and training for:

- Each specialty coder, in-house
- Each specialty coder, external and vendor coding personnel
- Physician querying
- Auditing and monitoring
- Corrected claims, rebilling, and appeals
- Ongoing continued education unit (CEU) requirements, maintenance, and support

Dedicate Funds for Promoting a Culture of Compliance

Current books and resources, continued education, and trainings all require organizational funds that help to promote and foster a culture of compliance. Set aside budgetary monies each year to maintain your commitment to compliance. Allow your certified coders to write letters of resource requests to leadership and reimburse them promptly after leadership approval. Or, allot a lump sum that covers all of the educational resources your certified coders require. There are many ways to dedicate compliance funds so ensure your coding compliance plan provides the specific details for your organization.

Possible Penalties

In today's landscape, clinical documentation and coded and billed healthcare claims miss the mark when millions, if not billions, of dollars are at risk in the eyes of the OIG. The errors found in both insufficient clinical documentation, the lack of medical necessity, as well as the inaccuracies in coding capture have led to the many financial repercussions to physicians, qualified healthcare providers, and hospital systems. Examples include:

- Fraud, waste, and abuse violations (with each FCA penalty ranging from $11,665 - $23,331 per violation)[25]
- Overpayment requests (letters from CMS stating an overpayment has been made)
- Unified Program Integrity Contractor (UPIC) audits (letters from UPICS whose primary goal is to investigate possible fraud, waste, and abuse in Medicare or Medicaid claims)
- Special Investigation Units (SIU) investigations, usually from private payors, looking into possible fraud, waste, and abuse)
- Referrals to Exclusion (the OIG has authority to exclude providers and entities from federally funded healthcare programs for a variety of reasons, including a conviction of Medicare or Medicaid fraud)

Compliance Resources

U.S. Department of Health & Human Services Office of the Inspector General

Audit Reports

https://oig.hhs.gov/reports-and-publications/oas/cms.asp

Compliance Resources

https://oig.hhs.gov/compliance/compliance-resource-portal/index.asp

Centers for Disease Control and Prevention

ICD-10-CM Official Guidelines for Coding and Reporting FY2021

https://www.cdc.gov/nchs/data/icd/10cmguidelines-FY2021.pdf

American Hospital Association

Coding Clinic Advisor

https://www.codingclinicadvisor.com/

Books

- American Medical Association, *ICD-10-CM 2021: The Complete Official Codebook* (Chicago: American Medical Association, 2021).
- American Academy of Professional Coders, *ICD-10-CM Expert Manual 2021* (Salt Lake City: American Academy of Professional Coders, 2021).
- American Academy of Professional Coders, *ICD-10-PCS Expert Manual 2021* (Salt Lake City: American Academy of Professional Coders, 2021).
- American Academy of Professional Coders, *HCPCS Level II 2021 Expert* (Salt Lake City: American Academy of Professional Coders, 2021).
- American Medical Association, *Principles of ICD-10-CM Coding* (Chicago: American Medical Association, 2016).
- American Medical Association, *ICD-10-CM Documentation 2021: Essential Charting Guidance to Support Medical Necessity* (Chicago: American Medical Association, 2021).
- American Medical Association, *CPT Assistant* (Chicago: American Medical Association, 2021).

Risk Area Takeaways

Main points of interest:
- All entities covered by the HIPAA must abide by the International Classification of Diseases, 10th Revision, Clinical Modification (ICD-10-CM).
- The 2021 code book totals 1,360 pages and contains more than 7,000 codes.
- The ICD-10-CM official guidelines for coding and reporting are issued by the CDC as an official accompaniment to the official version of the ICD-10-CM.
- Proper clinical documentation is critical for certified medical coders to correctly assign ICD-10-CM codes.

Areas to watch:
- Overcoding
- DRG optimization
- Incorrect coding
- Poor query techniques
- Oversight deficiency
- Lack of education
- Insufficient documentation
- Overpayments
- Erroneous reimbursements
- Denied claims

Laws that apply:
- HIPAA, 45 C.F.R. § 162
- Stark Law, 42 U.S.C. § 1395nn
- Civil False Claims Act (FCA), 31 U.S.C. §§ 3729–3733
- Criminal False Claims Act, 18 U.S.C. §§ 287, 286
- Healthcare Fraud Statute, 18 U.S.C. § 1347
- Exclusion Statute, 42 U.S.C. § 1320a-7
- Social Security Act Medicare and Medicaid Program Integrity Provisions, 42 U.S.C. § 1320a-7k
- Requirements for Reporting and Returning of Overpayments, 42 C.F.R. § 401.305

Addressing compliance risks:
- Improve diagnosis coding oversight from management
- Provide diagnosis updates and physician-query trainings regularly
- Develop and implement a coding-compliance plan
- Promote a culture of compliance through continued coding education and training
- Develop internal auditing team to conduct audits and swiftly identify coding deficiencies before claims submission
- Require coders to read coding resources
- Dedicate funds for promoting a culture of compliance

Endnotes

1. **Sonal Patel** is a healthcare coder and compliance consultant at Nexsen Pruet LLC, where she serves as the firm's remote expert coding and compliance consultant. She is committed to providing her clients coding and documentation guidance based on government and private payer regulations. Patel provides detailed, high-level findings reports for practices under zone program integrity contractor, unified program integrity contractor, and recovery audit contractor audit reviews, as well as risk-adjustment audits. She creates custom corrective action plans for both Part A and Part B providers. At the request of many physicians, Patel conducts baseline audits to assure compliance. She is an avid educator and provides individualized PowerPoint presentations for physician billing and coding education.

2. "International Classification of Diseases, (ICD-10-CM/PCS) Transition–Background," Centers for Disease Control and Prevention National Center for Health Statistics, updated November 6, 2015, https://www.cdc.gov/nchs/icd/icd10cm_pcs_background.htm#:~:text=World%20Health%20Organization%20(WHO)%20authorized,in%20the%20U.S.%20in%201999.

3. " International Classification of Diseases, Ninth Revision (ICD-9)," Centers for Disease Control and Prevention National Center for Health Statistics, updated November 6, 2015, https://www.cdc.gov/nchs/icd/icd9.htm.

4. American Academy of Professional Coders, *ICD-10-CM Expert Manual* (Salt Lake City: American Academy of Professional Coders, 2021), 1.

5. "ICD-10-CM Official Guidelines for Coding and Reporting FY 2021," Centers for Disease Control and Prevention National Center for Health Statistics, accessed February 18, 2021, https://www.cdc.gov/nchs/data/icd/10cmguidelines-FY2021.pdf.

6. 45 C.F.R. § 162.

7. "Statute and Regulations, ICD-10 Final Rule," Centers for Medicare & Medicaid Services, updated August 4, 2020, https://www.cms.gov/Medicare/Coding/ICD10/Statute_Regulations.

8. "A Roadmap for New Physicians, Fraud & Abuse Laws," U.S. Department of Health & Human Services Office of Inspector General, https://oig.hhs.gov/compliance/physician-education/01laws.asp.

9. "A Roadmap for New Physicians, Fraud & Abuse Laws," U.S. Dep't of Health & Human Services.

10. 18 U.S.C. § 287.

11. 18 U.S.C. § 286.

12. 18 U.S.C. § 1347.

13. "A Roadmap for New Physicians: Fraud & Abuse Laws," U.S. Dep't of Health & Human Services.

14. "A Roadmap for New Physicians, Fraud & Abuse Laws," U.S. Dep't of Health & Human Services.

15. "A Roadmap for New Physicians, Fraud & Abuse Laws," U.S. Dep't of Health & Human Services.

16. "A Roadmap for New Physicians, Fraud & Abuse Laws," U.S. Dep't of Health & Human Services.

17. "Medicare and Medicaid Program Integrity Provisions," Social Security Administration, accessed February 18, 2021, https://www.ssa.gov/OP_Home/ssact/title11/1128J.htm.

18. American Academy of Professional Coders, *ICD-10-CM Expert Manual* (Salt Lake City: American Academy of Professional Coders, 2021), G1.

19. "Hospitals Overbilled Medicare $1 Billion by Incorrectly Assigning Severe Malnutrition Diagnosis Codes to Inpatient Hospital Claims," U.S. Dep't of Health & Human Services Office of Inspector General, July 13, 2020, https://oig.hhs.gov/oas/reports/region3/31700010.asp.

20. "Medicare Hospital Provider Compliance Audit: The Ohio State University Hospital," U.S. Dep't of Health & Human Services Office of Inspector General, May 22, 2020, https://oig.hhs.gov/oas/reports/region5/51800042.asp.

21. "Health Care Compliance Program Tips," U.S. Dep't of Health & Human Services Office of Inspector General, accessed February 18, 2021, https://oig.hhs.gov/compliance/provider-compliance-training/files/compliance101tips508.pdf.

22. "AHIMA Code of Ethics," American Health Information Management Association, accessed February 18, 2021, https://bok.ahima.org/doc?oid=105098#.X471XIeWyUk.

23. "American Health Information Management Association Standards of Ethical Coding [2016 version]," American Health Information Management Association, accessed February 18, 2021, https://bok.ahima.org/CodingStandards#.X472loeWyUk.

24. "American Health Information Management Association Standards of Ethical Coding [2016 version]," American Health Information Management Association.

25. Civil Monetary Penalties Inflation Adjustment, 85 Fed. Reg. 37,004 (June 19, 2020).

Coding with ICD-10 Current Procedural Terminology/ Healthcare Common Procedure Coding System (ICD-10-CPT/HCPCS)

By Nancy L. Freeman,[1] RHIA, CHC, CRC

What Is the Current Procedural Terminology/ Healthcare Common Procedure Coding System?

The Healthcare Common Procedure Coding System (HCPCS) is a standardized coding system for describing and identifying healthcare services and supplies. It is designed to allow for the efficient processing of claims from Medicare as well as other payers. There are three recognized levels of this coding system:

- **Level I**: *Current Procedural Terminology* (CPT) is maintained and published by the American Medical Association (AMA). The Health Insurance Portability and Accountability Act (HIPAA) mandates the use of CPT reporting of outpatient services and procedures.
- **Level II**: HCPCS is published and maintained by the Centers for Medicare & Medicaid Services (CMS). HCPCS Level II codes were developed to provide a mechanism for

suppliers other than physicians to bill for products and services that are not identified in CPT. Use is mandated by HIPAA for standardized billing of healthcare equipment and supplies as well as services not covered by CPT.

- **Level III**: HCPCS codes are utilized by local carriers and payers.

Level 1: HCPCS/CPT

Level I HCPCS/CPT is a set of codes, descriptions, and guidelines that describe procedures and services performed by physicians, other medical professionals, and facilities. The code set is updated annually and published in the fall. Updates generally are based upon input from practicing physicians, other healthcare providers, specialty associations, state medical associations, and others who use the CPT code set. The new code application process can be found at https://www.ama-assn.org/practice-management/cpt. The new codes are effective with encounters on or after January 1 of the following year.

General instructions for using CPT that apply across the entire code set are provided in the introduction to the code set. More specific guidance is presented within the body of the code set and may apply to one or more chapters. For example, the Anesthesia Guidelines only apply to the Anesthesia section of the CPT; however, the Surgery Guidelines apply to all surgical services. Section guidance applies to an even more limited part of the code set.

There are three categories of CPT codes. Category I codes are 5-digit numeric codes representing procedures and services that are consistent with contemporary medical practice and are performed by many practitioners in clinical practice in many locations. This category is the standard used to bill most professional and outpatient-facility services. Category II codes are supplemental codes used for tracking and performance measurement. Category II codes are alphanumeric, and their use is optional. Category III codes are temporary codes used for emerging technology, services, procedures, and service paradigms. They are alphanumeric and should be used in lieu of an unlisted Category I code.

The Category I codes are subdivided into six distinct sections:

1. Evaluation and Management (E&M) Services
2. Anesthesia Services
3. Surgery
4. Radiology Services
5. Pathology and Laboratory Services
6. Medical Services and Procedures

The E&M codes depict a variety of provider visits: office visits, hospital visits, emergency department visit, critical care, etc. This area of CPT has recently changed significantly beginning in 2021.

Prior to January 1, 2021 most E&M codes were based upon documentation of history, physical examination, and Medical Decision Making (MDM). For most E&M services time was a factor for selecting the correct code only when greater than 50% of the visit is spent counseling and coordinating care. The two exceptions are instances in which:

1. The code is a time-based code, such as critical care management or discharge day management.
2. The service was a telehealth service performed during the COVID-19 Public Health Emergency.

CPT provides the definition for the codes; however, CMS provided guidelines in 1995 and 1997 that further refined the requirements for code assignment (such as what documentation is required for a comprehensive history or physical examination).[23] These guidelines are required for government payors but are adopted by most commercial payers as well. Of note, each Medicare Administrative Contractor (MAC) as well as Medicaid programs and private payers have interpreted the guidelines differently—some are more restrictive than others— and this has led to inconsistent application.

In January 2021, the basis for code selection in the office and outpatient settings (CPT codes 99202–99215) changed to total time of the visit or MDM. When determining total time for code selection, the amount should include both face-to-face and non-face-to-face time. If an advanced practice professional (e.g., nurse practitioner or physician assistant) participates in the visit, the time spent by both the physician and the advanced practice professional can be included, *except for time jointly spent* with the patient (this would represent double billing). Additionally, a prolonged service code was created. The CPT states that the prolonged service code 99417 is used when the *minimum* time associated with 99205 or 99215 is reached. This code may be used for commercial payers. CMS created a new code, G2212, to be used for prolonged visits for time-based services for federal beneficiaries (e.g. Medicare patients). The CMS guidance, however, is that the *maximum* time associated with 99205 or 99215 is reached before the prolonged service code G2212 can be used. If using MDM rather than time for code selection, a new MDM grid was developed that is similar in appearance to the Risk Table used in determining MDM prior to January 1, 2021. However, it is designed to be less complicated and the AMA published definitions for terms used in the new MDM to promote consistency in application.

The CPT 2023 incorporates massive changes to the E&M section intended to reduce the administrative burden for providers. The following families of E&M are affected:

- Hospital Inpatient – revised
- Hospital Observation – deleted (incorporated into inpatient)
- Consultation – deleted and reviewed
- Emergency Department - revised
- Nursing Facility – deleted and revised
- Domiciliary, Rest Home, Custodial Care– deleted
- Home or Residential Services – deleted and revised
- Deletion of Prolonged Services – added, deleted and revised

While the changes to CPT have been adopted by the CPT Editorial Board, the changes have not yet completed the process for acceptance for Medicare. As of 10/31/2022 the Medicare Physician Fee Schedule (MPFS) CY 2023 Final Rule has not yet been published. However, the MPFS Proposed Rule published 07/07/22 stated the following:

> "As part of the ongoing updates to E/M visits and related coding guidelines that are intended to reduce administrative burden, the AMA CPT Editorial Panel approved revised coding and updated guidelines for Other E/M visits, effective January 1, 2023. Similar to the approach we finalized in the CY 2021 PFS final rule for office/outpatient E/M visit coding and documentation, we are proposing to adopt most of these changes in coding and documentation for Other E/M visits (which include hospital inpatient, hospital observation, emergency department, nursing facility, home or residence services, and cognitive impairment assessment) effective January 1, 2023. This revised coding and documentation framework would include CPT code definition changes (revisions to the Other E/M code descriptors), including:
>
> New descriptor times (where relevant).
>
> Revised interpretive guidelines for levels of medical decision making.
>
> Choice of medical decision making or time to select code level (except for a few families like emergency department visits and cognitive impairment assessment, which are not timed services).
>
> Eliminated use of history and exam to determine code level (instead there would be a requirement for a medically appropriate history and exam).
>
> We are proposing to maintain the current billing policies that apply to the E/Ms while we consider potential revisions that might be necessary in future rulemaking. We are also proposing to create Medicare-specific coding for payment of Other E/M prolonged services, similar to what CMS adopted in CY 2021 for payment of Office/Outpatient prolonged services."

While Medicare may not adopt all of the proposed changes – or may create Medicare specific codes for certain services such as the prolonged services – it is expected that most of the suggested changes will be accepted by the Medicare Program as well as commercial payers.

The Anesthesia codes are used for reporting the administration of anesthesia and include all routine services, such as pre- and post-operative visits, intra-operative care, and fluid administration. Nonroutine services are billed separately. Additionally, physical status modifiers are reported with the anesthesia codes and reflect the severity/complexity of the anesthesia service. The anesthesia codes start with the numeral 0.

The largest section of CPT, Surgery, is organized into sections by body system. The range of codes per sections are as follows.

Codes	Section
10004–19499	Integumentary System
20100–29999	Musculoskeletal System
30000–32999	Respiratory System
33016–39599	Cardiovascular System
40490–49999	Digestive System
50010–53899	Urinary System
54000–55899	Male Genital System
55920	Reproductive System Procedures
55970–55980	Intersex Surgery
56405–58999	Female Genital System
59000–59899	Maternity Care and Delivery
60000–60699	Endocrine System
61000–64999	Nervous System
65091–68899	Eye and Ocular Adnexa
69000–69979	Auditory System
69990	Microsurgical Techniques

The Surgery guidelines are found at the beginning of the Surgery section. They provide guidance and definitions unique to surgery (i.e., separate procedures or the global surgical package). Additionally, chapter-specific and subchapter-specific guidance is covered throughout. The Surgery section provides codes for commonly performed surgical procedures. In the event that no code accurately defines the surgical procedure performed, Unlisted Procedure codes within most chapters and subchapters should be used.

The codes for Radiology Services are found in the 70000 series. In addition to the introductory CPT guidelines, this section has radiology-specific guidance applicable to the entire chapter as well as subsection guidance that provides special instruction for complex and unique areas, such as vascular procedures.

The main sections are Diagnostic Radiology, Diagnostic Ultrasound, Radiologic Guidance, Breast Mammography, Bone and Joint Studies, Radiation Oncology, Nuclear Medicine, and Therapeutic Procedures.

The codes for Laboratory and Pathology Services are found in the 80000 series. This chapter begins with an extensive table of molecular-pathology gene tables with information about genes, related diseases, and CPT codes. Most of the remaining specific guidance relating to laboratory and pathology lies at the section and subsection level, due to the varying modalities. Also included in this chapter are the Proprietary Laboratory Analysis codes (PLA). These codes are alphanumeric and are specific to manufacturers and laboratories to identify their tests, including codes for multianalyte assays with algorithmic analysis and genomic sequencing procedures. An area of recent focus is the appropriate billing of drug assays and molecular/genomic testing.

The codes for Medicine Services are found in the 90000 series. This chapter includes a variety of nonsurgical services that may be performed by and under the supervision of a physician. It includes the following sections.

Medicine Services (Nonsurgical):

- Immune globulins, serum or recombinant products
- Immunization Administration for Vaccine/Toxoids
- Vaccines, Toxoids
- Psychiatry
- Biofeedback
- Dialysis
- Gastroenterology Services
- Ophthalmology Services
- Special Otorhinolaryngologic Services
- Cardiovascular Services
- Noninvasive Vascular Diagnostic Services
- Pulmonary Services
- Allergy and Clinical Immunology Services
- Endocrinology Services
- Neurology and Neuromuscular Procedures
- Medical Genetics and Genetic Counseling Services
- Adaptive Behavior Services
- Central Nervous Systems Assessment/Testing
- Health Behavior Assessment and Intervention
- Hydration/Therapeutic Prophylactic, Diagnostic Injections and Infusions and Chemotherapy and Other Highly Complex Drug or Highly Complex Biologic Agent Administration
- Photodynamic Therapy
- Special Dermatological Procedures
- Physical Medicine and Rehabilitation
- Medical Nutrition Therapy
- Acupuncture
- Osteopathic Manipulative Treatment
- Chiropractic Manipulative Treatment
- Education and Training for Patient Self-Management
- Non-Face-to-Face Nonphysician Services
- Special Services, Procedures and Reports

- Qualifying Circumstances for Anesthesia
- Moderate (Conscious) Sedation
- Other Services and Procedures
- Home Health Procedures/Services
- Medication Therapy Management Services

Because of the lack of commonality between the various subchapters, the chapter guidance is limited. However, most subchapters do have code-specific guidance.

Level II: HCPCS

Level II of the HCPCS is a standardized coding system that is used to identify products, supplies, and services not included in the CPT® code set, such as ambulance services and durable medical equipment (DME), drugs, prosthetics, orthotics, and supplies when used outside a physician's office. They are also often used as temporary codes prior to a code being assigned by the CPT. HCPCS Level II provides a mechanism for providers and suppliers to bill for items covered by Medicare and by other payers, but for which there is no CPT code. For example, when the COVID-19 public health emergency began, CMS was able to quickly create HCPCS codes for laboratory testing specific to the virus that causes COVID-19. It was selected as a part of HIPAA as the standardized coding system for reporting items and services not identified by CPT.[4]

Level II HCPCS has several types of codes:

- **Permanent National Codes**: Maintained by the CMS HCPCS Workgroup, which includes representatives from private and public insurers, and updated annually.
- **Dental Codes**: Maintained and published by the American Dental Association (ADA) and used for billing dental procedures and supplies.
- **Miscellaneous Codes**: A category of codes used for billing for items or services with no existing national code. These codes allow suppliers to begin billing as soon as U.S. Food and Drug Administration (FDA) approval is received. Claims are manually reviewed, and documentation describing the item and pricing must be provided.
- **Temporary National Codes**: Temporary codes maintained by the CMS HCPCS Workgroup and used to address national program operational needs. Temporary codes are provided quarterly, while permanent codes are updated only once per year, effective January 1. There is no expiration date for a temporary code, and the codes may be replaced with a permanent code if they receive Workgroup approval. There are several types of temporary codes:
  - **C codes**: Established to report drugs, biologicals, magnetic resonance angiography (MRA), and devices used by OPPS hospitals. C codes are reported for device categories, new technology procedures, and drugs, biologicals, and radiopharmaceuticals that do not have existing HCPCS codes.
  - **G codes**: Used to report professional healthcare procedures and services that would otherwise be coded in CPT but have no existing code.
  - **H codes**: Used by state Medicaid agencies for identifying mental health services.

- **K codes**: Used by the DME MACs when there is not a permanent code and the DME MAC needs a code for purposes of medical review policy.
- **Q codes**: Used for items that will not have a CPT code and do not currently have a permanent Level II code.
- **S codes**: Used by private insurers to report products or services for which there is no national code.

Level III: HCPCS

Level III HCPCS are codes developed and utilized at the state or local level. Published guidance is available only at the state level.

Modifiers

Both CPT (numeric) and HCPCS (alphanumeric or two letters) have two-character modifiers that are required to supplement the code definition or identify special circumstances. Some modifiers affect payment while others do not. Failure to apply a modifier when needed or applying a modifier when not appropriate can result in overpayments or underpayments.

Risk Area Governance

The False Claims Act (FCA) is a federal statute originally enacted in 1863 in response to defense contractor fraud during the American Civil War.[5] The FCA provided that any person who knowingly submitted false claims to the government was liable for double the government's damages plus a penalty of $2,000 for each false claim. The FCA has been amended several times and now provides that violators are liable for treble damages plus a penalty linked to inflation. The FCA allows private citizens to file suits (called *qui tam* or whistleblower suits) on behalf of the government against those who have defrauded the government. Private citizens who successfully bring *qui tam* actions may receive a portion of the government's recovery. Many Department of Justice (DOJ) Fraud Section investigations and lawsuits arise from such *qui tam* actions. The DOJ obtained more than $5.6 billion in settlements and judgments from civil cases involving fraud and false claims against the government in the fiscal year ending September 30, 2021.[6]

In addition, many states have enacted their own false claims acts. These laws are generally fashioned after the federal FCA and may, if approved by the U.S. Department of Health & Human Services (HHS) Office of the Inspector General (OIG) and U.S. Attorney General, entitle the state to an incentive of their share of any compensation received.[7] Most were implemented for the purpose of giving whistleblower protections for claims on behalf of the state.

Even though other healthcare laws that have some coding component, such as the Stark Law or Anti-Kickback Statute (AKS), recoupments are most often through the FCA.

Common Compliance Risks

Incorrect CPT/HCPCS Code Selection

Incorrect reporting of CPT/HCPCS codes may result in inaccurate payments to the provider(s). Incorrect code assignment may be made by the provider, a coder, or through a charge description master and may result in inaccurate payments to the physician, physician extender, and/or hospital.

Upcoding CPT/HCPCS

Upcoding involves the selection of a CPT/HCPCS code that describes a more complex service or supply than was provided (e.g., assigning a higher-level E&M code than the documentation supports or billing for more drug units than were given).

Incorrect Application of a Modifier

In addition to selecting the correct code, coders must apply CPT *modifiers* in certain circumstances. Modifiers may or may not affect payment and, when incorrectly applied, may result in an overpayment or an underpayment. For example, modifiers such as RT (right) or LT (left) do not generally affect payment. However, modifiers such as 52 (reduced service) should result in a reduction in payment while 59 (distinct procedural service) may result in an increased payment.

Unbundling (Fragmenting) the Procedure

Another risk area is unbundling of procedures. Unbundling is coding each of the component parts of a procedure separately when a single inclusive code should be used instead. Even if the unbundling occurs unintentionally, it creates a risk area.

Lack of Adequate Documentation

While the quality of coding often reflects the coder's knowledge base and experience, the completeness and accuracy of the *provider's* documentation is also a key factor in coding quality. Poor quality documentation of a procedure may lead to:

- No code assignment, risking a loss of reimbursement
- Inaccurate code assignment, risking payment
- Delayed billing, risking delayed payment while the coder waits for more specific documentation
- Code assignment based upon a best guess, risking a claim without supporting documentation

Addressing Compliance Risks

The best defense against the risk of false claim submission is a robust compliance program composed of education and communication, policies and procedures, monitoring, internal and external auditing, and enforcement of documentation standards.

Policies and Procedures

All providers, regardless of size, should have policies and procedures for documentation and coding standards. These should be comprehensive and enforceable and provide a roadmap for coders, especially where the guidance is ambiguous. The American Health Information Management Association (AHIMA) and American Academy of Professional Coders (AAPC) websites publish standards of ethical coding and have many educational programs for both coders and providers.[89] Policies and procedures should have buy-in from the medical staff, health information management team, and compliance team. These policies and procedures should be reviewed annually and updated when industry guidelines change.

Education and Training

Continuing education for providers, coders, and auditors can be an effective way to stay current and can create a path for communication between those who create documentation and those who assign codes based upon it. In addition to receiving educational opportunities, coders should be provided access to resources such as the AMA *CPT Assistant*, AHA Coding Clinic for HCPCS, and *MLN Matters* (published by CMS) for current interpretation of the coding requirements. Coders also should have access to medical, surgical, and pharmaceutical reference materials.

Internal and External Monitoring of Coding

Periodic internal monitoring by coding management can identify gaps in provider documentation, coding education and training, and claim submission. As internal staff are accustomed to monitoring activities, there is flexibility regarding auditing topics and frequency. The compliance department may also have coders who can perform periodic audits of coding. The compliance work plan should include periodic audits of coding activities based upon high-risk/high-volume areas; well as OIG Work Plan audits; Program for Evaluating Payment Patterns Electronic Report (PEPPER); previously identified problem areas; and other topics of interest. External auditors are considered more objective (and are more expensive), but annual external coding audits are part of many hospital systems' compliance programs.

Enforce Corrective Action Plan Requirements

Regardless of the audit program a facility undertakes, one of the most important elements is a corrective action plan that is clear and enforceable. Recurring offenders should be held accountable regardless of position or standing. Enforcing policies shows respect for the work that goes into a compliance program and the staff tasked with maintaining it.

Possible Penalties

In today's landscape, coded and billed healthcare claims miss the mark when millions, if not billions, of dollars are at risk in the eyes of the OIG. The errors due to a lack of medical necessity, as well as the inaccuracies in coding, have led to many financial repercussions for physicians, qualified healthcare providers, and hospital systems. Financial repercussions include:

- Fraud, waste, and abuse violations (with each FCA penalty ranging from $12,537–$25,076 per violation)
- Overpayment requests (letters from CMS stating an overpayment has been made)
- Unified Program Integrity Contractor (UPIC) audits (letters from UPICs, whose primary goal is to investigate possible fraud, waste, and abuse in Medicare or Medicaid claims)
- Special Investigation Unit (SIU) investigations (usually from private payers investigating possible fraud, waste, and abuse)
- Referrals to Exclusion (related to the OIG's authority to exclude providers and entities from federally funded healthcare programs for a variety of reasons, including a conviction of Medicare or Medicaid fraud)

Compliance Resources

American Medical Association

2021 CPT
This site contains links to a variety of practice management tools, including information on CPT.

https://www.ama-assn.org/practice-management

CPT Assistant
Official AMA publication for providing CPT education.

https://commerce.ama-assn.org/store/ui

American Hospital Association

AHA Coding Clinic

The *AHA Coding Clinic* for HCPCS is a quarterly newsletter and is the official publication for coding guidelines and advice.

https://www.codingclinicadvisor.com/

Department of Health & Human Services, Office of the Inspector General

OIG Work Plan

The OIG Work Plan includes the agency's current and upcoming audits and evaluations.

https://oig.hhs.gov/reports-and-publications/workplan/index.asp

Program for Evaluating Payment Patterns Electronic Report (PEPPER)

PEPPER reports supply Medicare data statistics that can help providers identify potential overpayments and underpayments.

https://pepper.cbrpepper.org

Risk Takeaways

Main points of interest:
- CPT/HCPCS codes are used for coding of professional and technical services.
- CPT is published and maintained by the AMA.
- HCPCS is published by CMS.

Areas to watch:
- Incorrect CPT/HCPCS code selection
- Upcoding CPT/HCPCS
- Fragmenting or unbundling procedures
- Lack of adequate documentation
- Improper use of modifiers

Laws that apply:
- False Claims Act (FCA), 31 U.S.C. §§ 3729–3733
- State false claims acts (varies per state)
- Stark Law, 42 U.S.C. § 1395nn
- Anti-Kickback Statute, 42 U.S.C. § 1320a-7b(b)

> **Addressing compliance risks:**
> - Have policies and procedures for documentation and coding standards.
> - Provide continuing education for providers, coders, billers, and auditors.
> - Conduct internal and external monitoring of coding.
> - Enforce corrective action plan requirements.

Endnotes

1. **Nancy Freeman** is a managing director in the Health Solutions practice at FTI Consulting. She is based in Atlanta. Nancy has more than 30 years of healthcare consulting experience primarily relating to coding and billing compliance. She is an approved ICD-10-CM/PCS trainer from American Health Information Management Association.

2. "1995 Documentation Guidelines for Evaluation and Management Services," Centers for Medicare & Medicaid Services, accessed February 23, 2021, https://www.cms.gov/Outreach-and-Education/Medicare-Learning-Network-MLN/MLNEdWebGuide/Downloads/95Docguidelines.pdf.

3. "1997 Documentation Guidelines for Evaluation and Management Services," Centers for Medicare & Medicaid Services, accessed February 23, 2021, https://www.cms.gov/Outreach-and-Education/Medicare-Learning-Network-MLN/MLNEdWebGuide/Downloads/97Docguidelines.pdf.

4. American Academy of Professional Coders, *HCPCS Level II Expert* (Salt Lake City: American Academy of Professional Coders, 2021).

5. 31 U.S.C. §§ 3729–3733.

6. "The False Claims Act," U.S. Department of Justice, updated January 10, 2020, https://www.justice.gov/civil/false-claims-act.

7. "State False Claims Acts Reviews" Office of the Inspector General, U.S. Department of Health and Human Services, accessed December 15, 2020, https://oig.hhs.gov/fraud/state-false-claims-act-reviews/.

8. "American Health Information Management Association Standards of Ethical Coding [2016 version]," American Health Information Management Association, updated December 12, 2016, http://bok.ahima.org/doc?oid=302237#.YAXwti2ZOjR.

9. "AAPC Code of Ethics," American Academy of Professional Coders, accessed January 18, 2021, https://www.aapc.com/aboutus/code-of-ethics.aspx.

Coding with ICD-10 Procedure Coding System (ICD-10-PCS)

By Nancy L. Freeman,[1] RHIA, CHC, CRC; and Kim Stafford,[2] CCS, CRC

What Is the ICD-10 Procedure Coding System?

Since 1984, the Medicare program has reimbursed hospitals for inpatient acute-care services using the inpatient prospective payment system (IPPS). Under IPPS, diagnosis-related groups (DRGs) were initially the mechanism for payment. In 2008, the IPPS was updated to Medicare Severity–Diagnosis Related Groups (MS-DRGs) to better account for severity of illness. Both the DRG and the MS-DRG systems rely on the International Classification of Diseases, 10th Revision (ICD-10) codes (which were ICD-9 prior to October 1, 2015) to determine which MS-DRG is assigned and, ultimately, the reimbursement amount for the hospital stay. If the discharge is medical (nonsurgical), the ICD-10 Clinical Modification (ICD-10-CM) diagnosis codes drive reimbursement. Surgical discharges are assigned ICD-10 Procedure Coding System (ICD-10-PCS) procedure codes, which then drive the MS-DRG assignment and reimbursement amounts.

The ICD-10-PCS coding system was developed for the Centers for Medicare & Medicaid Services (CMS) by 3M Health Information Systems. The guidelines governing ICD-10-PCS code assignment are provided by CMS after approval by the four groups that make up the ICD-10 Cooperating Parties: CMS, the National Center for Health Statistics (NCHS), the American Health Information Management Association (AHIMA), and the American Hospital Association (AHA). Generally, guidelines are updated annually, as is the ICD-10-PCS system.[3] ICD-10-PCS is used only for coding surgical procedures for hospital inpatients.

The material difference between ICD-9-CM and ICD-10-PCS for reporting surgical procedures is the structure of the systems. Unlike its predecessor—ICD-9-CM Volume 3—ICD-10-PCS is not a closed classification. A closed classification has a code for virtually every procedure description, regardless of ambiguity. ICD-9-CM provided codes for terminology that was not otherwise specified. For example, if the patient's body system was known (e.g., respiratory), a procedure could be coded even if the specific root operation (e.g., excision) or site (e.g., bronchus) was not documented. In contrast, ICD-10-PCS is a table-driven, multiaxial code system with specific valid options in each character position. In this example, unless the specific root operation and body site of the skin is documented, a coder cannot assign an ICD-10-PCS code. Prior to October 1, 2015, if a coder read in the progress notes that an incision and drainage of a skin abscess was performed, even though there was no documentation of the site, the coder could assign ICD-9-CM's 86.04: "Other incision with drainage of skin and subcutaneous tissue." The procedure was captured, even with little documentation. However, a procedure code for this case could not be assigned in ICD-10-PCS, because the body site of the skin abscess is required.

Each ICD-10-PCS code is composed of a sequence of seven alphanumeric characters. The position of each character has a specific meaning, as does the value assigned to it. Characters can be assigned one of 34 values: numerals 0–9 and letters (excluding I and O). ICD-10-PCS is organized in 16 separate sections (e.g., Medical and Surgical, Obstetrics, Imaging). Within each section the value definitions may change. The Medical and Surgical section is the most commonly used (see **Table 1** for these characters).

Table 1. ICD-10-PCS Medical and Surgical Section						
Character 1	Character 2	Character 3	Character 4	Character 5	Character 6	Character 7
Section	Body System	Root Operation	Body Part	Approach	Device	Qualifier

The remaining sections are: Obstetrics, Placement, Administration, Measuring and Monitoring, Extracorporeal Assistance and Performance, Extracorporeal Therapies, Osteopathic, Other Procedures, Chiropractic, Imaging, Nuclear Medicine, Radiation Oncology, Physical Rehabilitation and Diagnostic Audiology, Mental Health, and Substance Abuse Treatment. While the character definitions in certain sections may resemble those in the Medical-Surgical section, the definitions for those characters in the ancillary areas often differ.

The ICD-10-PCS is a table-based classification. The tables are organized by the first three characters, shown at the top of the table. The remaining characters are in a four-column format. There may be multiple rows to specify the valid choices for the remaining characters. The coder must build the code based upon the choices provided for each character. There is an index provided to assist the coder in selecting the right table; however, use of the index is not required. Selection of the correct table is essential to identifying the correct ICD-10-PCS code. And the correct code is essential for determining the right MS-DRG, which leads to the correct reimbursement. An example of two similar tables is shown in **Table 2** and **Table 3**. Selection of the correct table is essential to identifying the correct ICD-10-PCS code.

Table 2. ICD-10-PCS Table Example			
0 Medical and Surgical (Character 1) L Tendons (Character 2) H Insertion: Putting in a nonbiological appliance that monitors, assists, performs, or prevents a physiological function but does not physically take the place of the body part (Character 3)			
Body Part	Approach	Device	Qualifier
Character 4	Character 5	Character 6	Character 7
X Upper Tendon Y Lower Tendon	0 Open 3 Percutaneous 4 Percutaneous Endoscopic	Y Other Device	Z No Qualifier

Table 3. ICD-10-PCS Table Example			
0 Medical and Surgical (Character 1) L Tendons (Character 2) J Inspection: Visually and/or manually exploring a body part (Character 3)			
Body Part	Approach	Device	Qualifier
Character 4	Character 5	Character 6	Character 7
X Upper Tendon Y Lower Tendon	0 Open 3 Percutaneous 4 Percutaneous Endoscopic X External	Z No Device	Z No Qualifier

Risk Area Governance

The False Claims Act (FCA) is a federal statute originally enacted in 1863 in response to defense contractor fraud during the American Civil War.[4] The FCA provided that any person who knowingly submitted false claims to the government was liable for double the government's damages plus a penalty of $2,000 for each false claim. The FCA has been amended several times and now provides that violators are liable for treble damages plus a penalty linked to inflation. The FCA allows private citizens to file suits on behalf of the government (called *qui tam* or whistleblower suits) against those who have defrauded the government. Private citizens who successfully bring qui tam actions may receive a portion of the government's recovery. Many Fraud Section investigations and lawsuits arise from such qui tam actions. The U.S. Department of Justice (DOJ) obtained more than $5.6 billion in settlements and judgments from civil cases involving fraud and false claims against the government in the fiscal year ending September 30, 2021.[5]

In addition to federal laws, many states have enacted their own false claims acts. These laws are generally fashioned after the federal FCA, and may, if approved by the Office of the U.S. Department of Health & Human Services (HHS) Inspector General (OIG) and U.S. Attorney General entitle the state to an incentive of their share of any compensation received.[6] Most were implemented for the purpose of giving whistleblower protections for claims on behalf of the state.

Other healthcare laws, such as the Stark Law or Anti-Kickback Statute (AKS), may have some coding component, but recoupments are most often through the FCA.

Common Compliance Risks

Incorrect MS-DRG Selection

Incorrect coding of ICD-10-PCS may result in an inaccurate MS-DRG selection. Selection of an incorrect value for a character may result in the identification of the wrong procedure, wrong site, wrong approach—any of which could lead to an incorrect ICD-10-PCS code and may affect the MS-DRG assignment, which determines reimbursement. Even when the coder is provided a complete descriptive operative report, there is still risk. ICD-10-PCS has a unique set of definitions for root operations (as well as for other positions that make up the complete seven-character code. Without understanding the differences between the many similar-seeming root operations, there is a risk of inaccurate code assignment and possible false claim.

For example, a surgeon may document the term "excision" of a blood clot to indicate the removal of the clot. In ICD-10-PCS, excision is defined as "cutting out or off, without replacement, a portion of a body part."[7] Since a blood clot is not a body part, excision should not be reported. So should "removal" of a blood clot be reported? No, because the ICD-10-PCS definition of removal is "taking out or off a device from a body part."[8] The clot is not a device. The correct root operation for this procedure is "extirpation," defined as "taking or cutting out solid matter from a body part." The coding guidelines place on the coder the responsibility for translating the operative note into the correct ICD-10-PCS terminology. If the MS-DRG is incorrect, then the hospital may receive an overpayment or an underpayment, depending on the weight assigned to the MS-DRG.

Incorrect Selection of the Principal Procedure

In addition to assigning the correct code, selection of the correct principal procedure is another risk factor for MS-DRG assignment. The "ICD-10-PCS Official Guidelines for Coding and Reporting 2021" state the following:

The following instructions should be applied in the selection of principal procedure and clarification on the importance of the relation to the principal diagnosis when more than one procedure is performed:

1. Procedure performed for definitive treatment of both principal diagnosis and secondary diagnosis
    a. Sequence procedure performed for definitive treatment most related to principal diagnosis as principal procedure.
2. Procedure performed for definitive treatment and diagnostic procedures performed for both principal diagnosis and secondary diagnosis.
    a. Sequence procedure performed for definitive treatment most related to principal diagnosis as principal procedure
3. A diagnostic procedure was performed for the principal diagnosis and a procedure is performed for definitive treatment of a secondary diagnosis.
    a. Sequence diagnostic procedure as principal procedure, since the procedure most related to the principal diagnosis takes precedence.
4. No procedures performed that are related to principal diagnosis; procedures performed for definitive treatment and diagnostic procedures were performed for secondary diagnosis
    a. Sequence procedure performed for definitive treatment of secondary diagnosis as principal procedure, since there are no procedures (definitive or nondefinitive treatment) related to principal diagnosis.[9]

The assignment of a principal procedure (or first listed procedure) may drive MS-DRG assignment in certain instances. With a few exceptions, the grouper software uses a complex algorithm to assign the MS-DRG. If multiple procedures are reported, the software's surgical hierarchy will select the procedure that assigns the more highly weighted MS-DRG, regardless of position. But even when the sequencing of procedures does not affect payment, the principal procedure is important for core-measure (healthcare quality metrics) reporting. It is the responsibility of the coder to validate that the code in the principal position meets the definition of principal procedure as outlined.

Fragmenting or Unbundling the Procedure

Another risk area is fragmenting the procedure, or "unbundling" as it is called in Current Procedural Terminology (CPT), a code set developed by the American Medical Association (AMA) to bill outpatient and office procedures. The "ICD-10-PCS Official Guidelines for Coding and Reporting" define which components of a procedure should be separately coded vs. what is integral to the procedure. However, the guidance is difficult to apply, resulting in multiple reporting of procedures, as well as potentially missed procedures.

The "ICD-10-PCS Official Guidelines for Coding and Reporting 2021" state the following:

B3.1b Components of a procedure specified in the root operation definition or explanation as integral to that root operation are not coded separately. Procedural steps necessary to reach the operative site and close the operative site, including anastomosis of a tubular body part, are also not coded separately. Examples: Resection of a joint as part of a joint replacement procedure is included in the root operation definition of Replacement and is not coded separately. Laparotomy performed to reach the site of an open liver biopsy is not coded separately. In a resection of sigmoid colon with anastomosis of descending colon to rectum, the anastomosis is not coded separately.[10] [*Note this exception: Mastectomy followed by breast reconstruction, both resection and replacement of the breast are coded separately.B3-18*]

Lack of Adequate Documentation

While the quality of coding often reflects the coder's knowledge base and experience, the completeness and accuracy of the documentation is a key factor in coding quality. Poor quality documentation of a procedure may lead to:

- No code assignment, risking a loss of reimbursement

- Inaccurate code assignment, risking wrong MS-DRG assignment and payment

- Delayed billing as the coder waits until more specific documentation

- Code assignment based upon a best guess, risking a claim without supporting documentation

Addressing Compliance Risks

The best defense against the risk of false claim submission is a robust compliance program composed of education and communication, policies and procedures, monitoring, internal and external auditing, and enforcement of documentation standards.

Policies and Procedures

All facilities should have policies and procedures for documentation and coding standards. They should be comprehensive and enforceable and should provide a roadmap for coders, especially where the guidance is ambiguous. The AHIMA website publishes standards of ethical coding and has many educational programs for both coders and providers. Policies and procedures should have buy-in from the medical staff, health information management team, and the compliance team. These policies and procedures should be reviewed annually and updated when there are changes to industry guidelines.

Education and Training

Continuing education for providers, coders, auditors, and members of the clinical documentation team can be an effective way to stay current and can create a path for communication between those who create documentation and those who assign codes based upon it. In addition to providing educational opportunities, coders should be provided access to resources such as the AHA Coding Clinic Advisor for current interpretation of the coding requirements as well as medical, surgical, and pharmaceutical reference materials.

Internal and External Monitoring of Coding

Periodic internal monitoring by coding management can identify gaps in provider documentation, coding education and training, and claims submissions. As internal staff are used to monitor, there is flexibility regarding audit topics and frequency. The compliance department may also have coders who can perform periodic audits of coding. The compliance work plan should include periodic audits of coding activities based upon high-risk and high-volume areas as well as the U.S. Department of Health and Human Services (HHS) Office of Inspector General (OIG) Work Plan audits, Program for Evaluating Payment Patterns Electronic Report (PEPPER), and previously identified problem areas. External auditors are considered more objective (and more expensive), but annual external coding audits are part of many hospital systems' compliance programs.

Enforce Corrective Action Plan Requirements

Regardless of the audit program a facility undertakes, one of the most important elements is a corrective action plan that is clear and enforceable. Recurring offenders should be held accountable regardless of position or standing. When policies are enforced, it shows respect for the work that goes into a compliance program and the staff who are tasked with maintaining it.

Possible Penalties

In today's landscape, clinical documentation and coded-and-billed healthcare claims often miss the mark, leaving millions, if not billions, of dollars at risk in the eyes of the OIG. The errors found in insufficient clinical documentation, lack of medical necessity, as well as inaccurate code assignment have led to significant financial repercussions for hospitals. The complexities associated with ICD-10-PCS coding create a prime environment for inaccurate code assignment which may lead to an incorrect MS-DRG assignment and resulting payment. The types of penalties hospitals may face include:

- **Fraud, waste, and abuse violations**: With each FCA penalty ranging from $12,537–$25,076 per violation[11]

- **Overpayment requests:** Letters from CMS or Medicare Administrative Contractors (MACs) stating an overpayment has been made
- **Recovery Audit Contractor recoupments**
- **UPIC audits:** Letters from Unified Program Integrity Contractor (UPIC) whose primary goal is investigate possible fraud, waste, and abuse in Medicare or Medicaid claims
- **SIU investigations:** Special Investigation Units (SIUs), usually from the private payors, investigating possible fraud, waste, and abuse
- **Referrals to exclusion:** OIG has authority to exclude providers and entities from federally funded healthcare programs for a variety of reasons, including a conviction of Medicare or Medicaid fraud.

Compliance Resources

American Health Information Management Association (AHIMA)

Inpatient Coding
AHIMA offers education on training for inpatient coding, including ICD-10-PCS.

https://www.ahima.org/education-events/education-by-topic/coding/

American Hospital Association (AHA)

Coding Clinic Advisor
The AHA's Coding Clinic publications offer coding guidance for signs and symptoms, diseases, disorders, and more including basic coding guidelines for ICD-10 and supplementary classifications.

https://www.codingclinicadvisor.com/

Centers for Medicare & Medicaid Services

2021 ICD-10-PCS
This site contains links to CMS updates for ICD-10-PCS, including the "ICD-10-PCS Official Guidelines for Coding and Reporting."

https://www.cms.gov/medicare/icd-10/2021-icd-10-pcs

Program for Evaluating Payment Patterns Electronic Report

PEPPER Reports supply Medicare data statistics that can help providers identify potential overpayments and underpayments.

https://pepper.cbrpepper.org

U.S. Department of Health & Human Services

OIG Work Plan
The OIG's Work Plan includes their current and upcoming audits and evaluations.

https://oig.hhs.gov/reports-and-publications/workplan/index.asp

Risk Takeaways

Main points of interest:
- Surgical discharges are assigned ICD-10 Procedure Coding System (ICD-10-PCS) procedure codes that drive the Medicare Severity–Diagnosis Related Groups (MS-DRG) assignment and reimbursement amounts.
- ICD-10-PCS code has seven alphanumeric characters, each of which has a specific meaning. Characters can be assigned one of 34 values: numerals 0–9 and letters (excluding I and O). There are 16 separate sections in the classification. The Medical and Surgical section is the most commonly used.
- The ICD-10-PCS is a table-based classification. Selection of the correct table is essential to identifying the correct ICD-10-PCS code.

Areas to watch:
- Incorrect MS-DRG selection
- Incorrect selection of the principal procedure
- Fragmenting or unbundling the procedure
- Lack of adequate documentation

Laws that apply:
- False Claims Act, 31 U.S.C. §§ 3729–3733
- State false claims acts (varies per state)
- Stark Law, 42 U.S.C. § 1395nn
- Anti-Kickback Statute, 42 U.S.C. § 1320a-7b(b)

Addressing compliance risks:
- Have policies and procedures for documentation and coding standards.
- Provide continuing education for providers, coders, clinical documentation improvement team members, and auditors.
- Conduct internal and external monitoring of coding.
- Enforce corrective action plan requirements.

Endnotes

1. **Nancy Freeman** is a managing director in the Health Solutions practice at FTI Consulting. She is based in Atlanta. Nancy has more than 40 years of healthcare consulting experience primarily relating to coding and billing compliance. She is an approved ICD-10-CM/PCS trainer from American Health Information Management Association.

2. **Kim Stafford** is a director at FTI Consulting and is based in Florida. She is part of the Health Solutions segment. She has more than 35 years of healthcare experience, with expertise in medical classification systems; coding and diagnosis-related group compliance audits; risk-adjusted coding models; charge capture and billing compliance audits; clinical documentation improvement in the inpatient setting; and ICD-10 education and training for physicians, nurses, coders, and ancillary staff.

3. "2021 ICD-10-PCS," Centers for Medicare & Medicaid Services, updated December 2, 2021, https://www.cms.gov/medicare/icd-10/2021-icd-10-pcs.

4. 31 U.S.C. §§ 3729–3733.

5. "The False Claims Act," U.S. Dep't of Justice, last updated January 10, 2020, https://www.justice.gov/civil/false-claims-act.

6. "State False Claims Acts Reviews" Office of the Inspector General, U.S. Dep't of Health and Human Services, accessed December 15, 2020, https://oig.hhs.gov/fraud/state-false-claims-act-reviews/.

7. American Medical Association, "Appendix A: Root Operations Definitions," *ICD-10-PCS 2021* (Chicago: American Medical Association, 2021).

8. American Medical Association, "Appendix A: Root Operations Definitions," *ICD-10-PCS 2021*.

9. "ICD-10-PCS Official Guidelines for Coding and Reporting 2021," Centers for Medicare & Medicaid Services, accessed December 15, 2020, https://www.cms.gov/files/document/2021-official-icd-10-pcs-coding-guidelines-updated-december-1-2020.pdf.

10. "ICD-10-PCS Official Guidelines for Coding and Reporting 2021."

11. 15 C.F.R. § 6.3(a)(3).

Effects of Complex Coding Guidelines and Increased Workloads

By Sonal Patel,[1] CPMA, CPC, CMC

What Are the Complexities of Coding Guidelines and Effects on Increased Workloads?

A certified medical coder abides by the coding guidelines set forth in the American Medical Association (AMA) *Current Procedural Terminology (CPT) Professional Edition* code set, effective January 1 every year. The AMA first developed and published the CPT code set in 1966.[2] The intended goal of the coding system was to standardize descriptions of services and procedures through alphanumeric codes to convey accurate health information that various agencies could use for statistical and actuarial purposes.

AMA still defines *CPT, Fourth Edition*, as a listing of descriptive terms and identifying codes for reporting medical services and procedures performed by physicians and other qualified health care professionals.[3] The overall purpose of these codes is to provide a uniform language to effectively communicate to physicians, other qualified healthcare professionals, patients, and third parties alike. The CPT code set also is useful for administrative purposes, such as claims processing and the development of medical-service guidelines. And further still, it is useful for the purposes of capturing public health data at local, regional, and national levels.

Certified coders are educated and trained to abstract various codes from patient medical records. It is this clinical documentation that contains the medical services and procedures that directly correlate to the five-digit CPT codes.

The CPT code set is released annually in October but is not effective until January 1 of each new year. Certified coders are trained with instructions about how to use the book effectively and efficiently. Certified coders are also apprised of the many guidelines that accompany each of CPT's six main sections: Evaluation and Management, Anesthesia, Surgery, Radiology, Pathology and Laboratory, and Medicine. There are also additional sections for Category II and III Codes, as well as 16 Appendices for a certified coder to be use.

There is another set of codes contained in the Healthcare Common Procedure Coding System (HCPCS) Level II code book. Developed by the Centers for Medicare & Medicaid Services (CMS), it contains codes for services, supplies, durable medical equipment, and drugs. New HCPCS books are released in January of each new year, but quarterly updates are made available on the CMS website.

Certified coders are educated and trained to understand both the code structure and code selection process. HCPCS codes are made up of five alphanumeric characters, starting with a letter that represents a category of similar codes, followed by four numerals.[4]

Certified coders need to understand all applicable CPT guidelines before assigning codes to services and procedures that are documented in the medical record. The complexity of each section guideline and the effort to master new and revised codes have an impact on coders in the everyday work they perform.

A medical practice must maintain a well-regulated cash flow by submitting claims in a timely fashion. Certified medical coders are instructed to code by *volume*, in other words, to code all of the successful number of patient encounters on the same day they occurred. This approach is critical to the health and vitality of the revenue cycle.

However, without an emphasis on addressing attention to detail and thorough research on various coding guidelines, the implicit message of production increases coding errors. Therefore, placing importance of volume production over valuable performance accuracy poses the greatest area of risk to coding compliance. Coding errors can be categorized into areas of risk that involve upcoding, downcoding, and miscoding—resulting in Medicare and Medicaid claims denials, as well as significant overpayments and potential recoupments in subsequent years. These kinds of coding errors can cost healthcare organizations significant financial loss.

Risk Area Governance

Health Insurance Portability and Accountability Act (HIPAA), Health Insurance Reform: Standards for Electronic Transactions, 45 C.F.R. §§ 160, 162

The Final Rule for transactions and code sets was issued on August 17, 2000.[5] This rule requires the Department of Health & Human Services (HHS) to provide national standards for the electronic transactions of healthcare information. Further, CPT codes and modifiers, along with HCPCS codes, are defined as the procedure code sets for:

- Physician services
- Physical and occupational therapy services
- Radiological procedures
- Clinical laboratory tests
- Other medical diagnostic procedures
- Hearing and vision services
- Transportation services including ambulance

False Claims Act, 18 U.S.C. §§ 287, 286

Section 287 of the False Claims Act (FCA) is for false, fictions, or fraudulent claims and it states the following:

> Whoever makes or presents to any person or officer in the civil, military, or naval service of the United States, or to any department or agency thereof, any claim upon or against the United States, or any department or agency thereof, knowing such claim to be false, fictitious, or fraudulent, shall be imprisoned not more than five years and shall be subject to a fine in the amount provided in this title.[6]

Section 286 of the False Claims Act is for conspiracy to defraud the government with respect to claims and it states:

> Whoever enters into any agreement, combination, or conspiracy to defraud the United States, or any department or agency thereof, by obtaining or aiding to obtain the payment or allowance of any false, fictitious or fraudulent claim, shall be fined under this title or imprisoned not more than ten years, or both.
>
> In order for the government to prove a case under § 287, three elements must exist:

1. An individual made or presented a claim to a department or agency of the United States for money or property,
2. The claim was false, fictitious, or fraudulent, and

An individual knew at the time that the claim was false, fictitious, or fraudulent.[7]

Common Compliance Risks

Based on the complexities involved in our healthcare system, which include the myriad of regulations and rules at the federal, state, and local levels, the compliance risks faced in the business of medicine are manifold. However, for CPT and HCPCS code sets specifically, recent OIG reports issued for both hospital inpatient and outpatient audits for compliance reveal areas of significant deficiency. Some of the biggest risks include placing certified coders in stressful situations of unrealistic coding demands, as well as not providing certified coders with continuing education to meet rapid changes in guidelines and new codes. Here is a significant list of risks:

1. **Unrealistic coding demands on coders.**
2. **Coders' lack of familiarity with guidelines for coding patient encounters.**
3. **Instances of upcoding levels for evaluation and management (E&M) services**: For example, if all codes are a level 4 or 5, that is significant for lack of individuality from patient encounter to patient encounter.
4. **Instances of downcoding levels for E&M services**: For example, if playing it safe and all codes are a level 2, that is a significant indication for lack of individuality from patient to patient.
5. **Instances of unbundling services (with modifier 59)**: An example is trying to carve out a smaller procedure that is already included as part of greater procedure.
6. **Use of modifier 25 and all other modifiers**: This points to continued misunderstanding and continued confusion.
7. **Incorrect coding**: This places a practice at risk for claims rejects and claims denials, at the minimum.
8. **Technology issues (with electronic medical records [EMRs], computer-assisted coding)**: For example, continued copy/paste and carry/forward abuses result in lack of individuality from patient record to patient record.
9. **Oversight deficiency**: This leads to voluminous errors based on poor practice management and lack of leadership.
10. **Lack of continued education**: This applies to coders, clinical documentation improvement personnel, and providers.
11. **Outpatient coders**: They can create a risk due to coding error rates.
12. **Missing or insufficient documentation in medical records**: For example, lack of documentation to support services and procedures.
13. **Claims denials**: This includes improperly scrubbed, poor demographic intake, lack of prior authorization, numerous other compliance risk factors.
14. **Erroneous reimbursements**: The financial impacts are always a compliance risk.
15. **Overpayments**: For example, the 60-day rule to return monies and financial impact are always a compliance risk.
16. **Data mining**: This applies to payers taking the upper hand by data mining providers' data and leveraging the data to their advantage.

Addressing Compliance Risks

Develop a Coding Compliance Plan

As a part of an organization's overarching compliance program, a coding compliance plan should be developed and maintained to reflect dedicated commitment to adhering to all federal, state, and local rules and regulations. Maintaining a robust compliance program reflects a strong culture of compliance and ethics within private practices or hospital systems of any size. Items on the plan can include:

- **Visionary statement**: from leadership in coding team
- **Leadership and oversight**: identifies organizational structure and reporting details of medical coding team
- **Communication policies and procedures**: emphasizes transparency
- **Auditing and monitoring**: stresses these integral functions and may include appointing specific team members to perform either and/or both
- **Education and training**: emphasizes critical need to address continued education throughout the year for the team, as well as the individual for certification maintenance
- **Investigation and corrective actions**: identifies necessity of quality assurance audits for coder performance and levels of corrective actions for individual coders who are deficient
- **Prevention and disciplinary actions**: emphasizes that steps must be clearly outlined by coding leadership and may reflect greater organization's policy on disciplinary action

Additionally, the American Academy of Professional Coders (AAPC) abides by a Code of Ethics, which should be utilized when creating a strong coding compliance plan. The code states:

> It shall be the responsibility of every AAPC member, as a condition of continued membership, to conduct themselves in all professional activities in a manner consistent with ALL of the following ethical principles of professional conduct:
>
> - Integrity
> - Respect
> - Commitment
> - Competence
> - Fairness
> - Responsibility
>
> Adherence to these ethical standards assists in assuring public confidence in the integrity and professionalism of AAPC members. Failure to conform professional conduct to these ethical standards,

as determined by AAPC's Ethics Committee, may result in the loss of membership with AAPC.[8]

Emphasize Coding Accuracy over Speed

Coding leadership and management must strive to improve the quality of their coders' coding functionality for greater success in achieving compliance. This can be done by developing and implementing policies that stress a new paradigm shift—one that places value on coding accuracy vs. simply high coding production. The culture of practices must embrace this new focus on compliant coding capture the first time.

Conduct Focused Internal Audits

Analyzing and looking critically at a practice's claims and coordinating documentation can help improve a practice from within. By conducting focused internal assessments, monitoring, and audits, a practice can identify any deficiencies and make swift corrections before claims are submitted. These audits should focus on each unique practice by:

- Identifying deficiencies by tracking and trending the organization's data
- Isolating E&M services
- Isolating procedures
- Isolating new providers
- Isolating modifiers (25, 59, or any other overly used modifier at the practice)
- Generating reports to monitor error rates
- Quantifying by percentage
- Providing quality feedback
- Aiming for 95% correct coding rate
- Developing a findings report
- Disseminating a corrective-action plan

Conduct Random Internal Audits

It is always important to track and trend your own data – before a data miner does. Best practice recommendations always involve audits that focus on:

- All payers
- All settings and places of service
- New CPT or HCPCS codes issued

Develop an Internal Auditing Team

Assign Medicare/Medicaid/Tricare Leader(s)

Appointing a government payer-policy lead on the coding team will ensure significant compliance improvements when coding for services and procedures for those who have Medicare,

Medicaid, or Tricare insurance. A Medicare/Medicaid/Tricare leader is knowledgeable about and understands all things regarding government payer policies (e.g., reimbursement, clinical, administrative areas).

Assign Commercial Leader(s)

Appointing a commercial payer policy lead or two on the coding team will provide significant compliance improvements when coding for patient services and procedures among Blue Cross Blue Shield, Cigna, Aetna, Humana, UnitedHealthcare, and thousands of other commercial carriers in the United States. A commercial leader is knowledgeable about and understands all things regarding commercial-payer policies (e.g., reimbursement, clinical, administrative areas).

Provide Coding Resources to Coders

To ensure medical coders stay informed on the latest coding guidelines, it is highly recommended that certified medical coders have easy access to these vital resources:

- Official Guidelines for Coding and Reporting ICD-10-CM, current year(s)
- *ICD-10-CM: The Complete Official Code Book*, current year(s)
- AHA Coding Clinic Advisor
- *AMA CPT® Manual*, current year(s)
- *AMA CPT® Assistant*

Provide Required Compliance Education and Training

Continued education and training is fundamental to an organization's commitment to compliance. Certified coding professionals need to stay current on trends and attend trainings to ensure accuracy of reimbursement levels the first time.

Your compliance training and educations should include separate sessions and materials for the following:

- Each specialty coder, in-house
- Each specialty coder, external, and vendor coding personnel
- Auditing and monitoring
- Corrected claims, rebilling, and appeals
- Ongoing continued education unit (CEU) requirements, maintenance, and support

Dedicate Funds for Culture of Compliance

Current books and resources, continued education, and training all require organizational funds that help to promote and foster a culture of compliance. Set aside budgetary monies each year to maintain your commitment to compliance. Allow your certified coders to write letters of resource requests to leadership and reimburse them promptly after leadership approval. Or, allot a lump sum that covers all of the educational resources your certified coders require. There are many ways to dedicate compliance funds, so ensure your coding-compliance plan provides the specific details for your organization.

Possible Penalties

In today's landscape, coded and billed healthcare claims miss the mark when millions, if not billions, of dollars are at risk in the eyes of the Office of Inspector General (OIG). The errors found in both insufficient clinical documentation, lack of medical necessity, as well as the inaccuracies in coding capture, have led to many financial repercussions to physicians, qualified healthcare providers, and hospital systems. These penalties include:

- **Fraud, waste, and abuse**: with each FCA penalty ranging from $11,665–$23,331 per violation[9]
- **Overpayment requests**: letters from CMS stating an overpayment has been made
- **Unified Program Integrity Contractor (UPIC) audits:** letters from UPICs whose primary goal is investigating possible fraud, waste, and abuse in Medicare or Medicaid claims
- **Special Investigation Units (SIU) investigations:** usually from private payers investigating possible fraud, waste, and abuse
- **Referrals to Exclusion:** related to the OIG authority to exclude providers and entities from federally funded healthcare programs for a variety of reasons, including a conviction of Medicare or Medicaid fraud

Compliance Resources

Centers for Disease Control and Prevention

ICD-10-CM Official Guidelines for Coding and Reporting FY2021

https://www.cdc.gov/nchs/data/icd/10cmguidelines-FY2021.pdf

American Hospital Association

Coding Clinic Advisor

https://www.codingclinicadvisor.com/

Office of Inspector General

Office of Audit Services: Centers for Medicare & Medicaid Services

https://oig.hhs.gov/reports-and-publications/oas/cms.asp

Books

- Deborah J. Grider, *Principles of ICD-10-CM Coding* (Chicago: American Medical Association, 2016).
- American Medical Association, *ICD-10-CM Documentation 2021: Essential Charting Guidance to Support Medical Necessity* (Chicago: American Medical Association, 2021).
- American Academy of Professional Coders, *ICD-10-CM Expert Manual2021* (Salt Lake City: American Academy of Professional Coders, 2021).
- American Medical Association, *CPT Assistant* (Chicago: American Medical Association, 2021).
- American Medical Association, *ICD-10-CM 2021: The Complete Official Codebook* (Chicago: American Medical Association, 2021).

Risk Area Takeaways

Main points of interest:
- A certified medical coder abides by the coding guidelines set forth in the American Medical Association (AMA) *Current Procedural Terminology (CPT) Professional Edition* code set effective January 1 every year.
- Certified coders need to understand all applicable CPT guidelines before assigning codes to services and procedures documented in the medical record.
- The complexity of each section's guidelines and the effort to master new and revised codes, affect coders in the everyday work they perform.
- Certified medical coders are instructed to code by volume, meaning to code all of the successful number of patient encounters occurring on that day.
- Implicit message of production without also stressing attention to detail and thorough research on various coding guidelines increases coding errors.

Areas to watch:
- Setting unrealistic demands for coders
- Providing insufficient coding education for coders
- Upcoding
- Downcoding
- Unbundling
- Using modifiers improperly
- Having insufficient documentation
- Using computer-assisted coding

Laws that apply:
- Health Insurance Portability and Accountability Act (HIPAA), Health Insurance Reform: Standards for Electronic Transactions, 45 C.F.R. §§ 160, 162
- False Claims Act, 18 U.S.C. §§ 287, 286
- Health Care Fraud, 18 U.S.C. § 1347

Addressing compliance risks:
- Focus on coding accuracy over speed
- Allow for continued education and improved oversight to maintain compliance
- Reduce compliance risks by implementing an internal audit team
- Conduct focused and random internal audits
- Develop a coding compliance plan
- Improve CPT and HCPCS oversight from management
- Provide CPT and HCPCS code updates and continued education and trainings to certified coders
- Dedicate funds for a culture of compliance

Endnotes

1. **Sonal Patel** is a healthcare coder and compliance consultant at Nexsen Pruet LLC, where she serves as the firm's remote expert coding and compliance consultant. She is committed to providing her clients coding and documentation guidance based on government and private payer regulations. Patel provides detailed, high-level findings reports for practices under zone program integrity contractor, unified program integrity contractor, and recovery audit contractor audit reviews, as well as risk-adjustment audits. She creates custom corrective action plans for both Part A and Part B providers. At the request of many physicians, Patel conducts baseline audits to assure compliance. She is an avid educator and provides individualized PowerPoint presentations for physician billing and coding education.

2. "CPT purpose & mission," American Medical Association, accessed December 30, 2020, https://www.ama-assn.org/about/cpt-editorial-panel/cpt-purpose-mission.

3. American Medical Association, *CPT 2021 Professional Edition* (Chicago: American Medical Association, 2021), vi.

4. American Academy of Professional Coders, *HCPCS Level II Expert 2021* (Salt Lake City: American Academy of Professional Coders, 2021), 5.

5. "CPT purpose & mission," American Medical Association.

6. 18 U.S.C. § 287.

7. 18 U.S.C. § 286.

8. "AAPC Code of Ethics," American Academy of Professional Coders, accessed March 10, 2021, https://www.aapc.com/aboutus/code-of-ethics.aspx.

9. Civil Monetary Penalties Inflation Adjustment, 85 Fed Reg. 37,004 (June 19, 2020).

Electronic Health Record Systems

By K. Mark Jenkins,[1] CPA (TN), CHC, CHPC, CHRC, CIA, CFE, CGMA, CHCO

What Are Electronic Health Record Systems?

Prior to electronic health records (EHR), all medical records were kept as paper copies in manual filing systems with each clinician's (doctor, nurse practitioner, etc.) office and hospital, clinic, or surgery center that a patient utilized over the course of the patient's healthcare. From the healthiest individuals who only sought episodic care to treat things such as ear infections and the flu to the sickest individuals with multiple illnesses and comorbid conditions, their medical histories (care notes, lab results, medications, etc.) were all written and maintained on paper in various locations.

In the mid-1960s, various technology and engineering companies began developing EHR systems. This was not an overnight one-stop shop for medical records. Many independent systems were developed for medical specialty areas that performed to improve care, but they each were independent systems. These standalone systems (called "subsystems") were in many cases connected to a core medical record system. In many large healthcare systems, this has meant that up to 400 independent subsystems were linked to form a consolidated view of a patient's medical record. In many cases, the billing component of healthcare services was not integrated into the EHR system until long after the systems were created, resulting in unique compliance challenges for compliant records and billing.

As EHRs advanced and funding increased to implement these systems, the field of EHR system developers reduced and consolidated, and today a few more fully integrated systems are primarily utilized by healthcare organizations. Although these systems all have primary functionality (which house patient encounters and episodes of care, orders, lab tests, radiological images, billing and collection records, etc.), all have also been implemented uniquely by different healthcare organizations. The core systems, as well as the implemented customizations at each entity, increase compliance and other risks, which must be mitigated.

Often EHR system implementation involves building the new system to do things as the organization did them in the past (either through paper documentation or older EHR systems), which can create or even further compliance issues and concerns. There are also features built within each EHR core system, which were developed by well-meaning engineers with clinician input, that can be manipulated by in-house system designers. These features are intended to increase productivity and reduce documentation and other burdens, but they cause increased documentation risks.

EHR systems have revolutionized healthcare in many ways: theoretically providing real-time access to complete medical records and history to healthcare providers and patients; increasing the capability to diagnose diseases, reduce medical errors, and improve outcomes; allowing multiple clinicians access to medical record information at the same time; and many other ways.

Most EHR systems allow for a wide variety of implementation, from out-of-the-box (standard) implementation to customized implementation. Compliance needs to be involved in decisions about a healthcare organization's EHR system from the start. Even out-of-the-box implementations can have features that do not align with good internal controls and processes. The higher the customization, the higher the compliance risk. With a fully integrated EHR system (where one system has clinician documentation (for clinic and inpatient services), billing module(s), subsystems such as radiology, etc.), there are increased opportunities for a single change in the system to help or fix one situation that may impact downstream processes or outputs. Therefore, it is critical that compliance professionals be included in development, deployment, and ongoing changes with EHR systems.

EHR systems promise capabilities to streamline documentation; however, most clinicians find documentation in these systems to be extremely labor and time extensive. This has caused many tools and templates to be developed, which tend to increase compliance risks and the need for compliance to be involved at the beginning of an EHR implementation as well as when templates and other tools are updated.

Risk Area Governance

Health Information Technology for Economic and Clinical Health (HITECH) Act, 42 U.S.C. § 139w-4(o)(2)

This act provides the U.S. Department of Health & Human Services with the authority to establish programs to improve healthcare quality, safety, and efficiency through the promotion of health IT, including EHRs and private and secure electronic health information exchange. EHRs must comply with various provisions of the HITECH Act. The act also increased penalties for violations of the Health Insurance Portability and Accountability Act (HIPAA) Privacy and Security Rules.[2]

Many rules govern documentation standards for medical records to support billing for medical services. These include the following: False Claims Act (FCA), Health Insurance Portability and Accountability Act of 1996 (HIPAA), Joint Commission and the Centers for Medicare & Medicaid Services (CMS), and 42 C.F.R. § 482.24, Condition of participation: Medical record services.

False Claims Act, 31 U.S.C. §§ 3729-3733

The FCA makes it a crime for any person or organization to knowingly make a false record or file a false claim regarding any healthcare program that is funded directly by the United States government or any state healthcare system. There has been a significant increase in FCA cases regarding allegations of false claims to Medicare and Medicaid, pursuant to the Electronic Health Records Incentive Program. In addition, the FCA has also been triggered related to fraudulent arrangements tied to implementation and use of EHRs. Inappropriately configured EHRs can cause false claims to be submitted due to documentation inconsistencies or inaccuracies.[3]

Health Insurance Portability and Accountability Act of 1996, Pub. L. No. 104-191, 110 Stat. 1936

HIPAA rules relate to privacy, security, and EHRs. EHRs must have appropriate controls to protect the data internally and externally. It is imperative that health systems have access controls, encryption, and the ability to track all access to records.[4]

Joint Commission and the Centers for Medicare & Medicaid Services

Both have medical record signature requirements that extend to paper and electronic signatures. EHRs must have the ability to track various forms of authentication (of orders, reviews, documentation, etc.). The signature must include the date and time.

CMS Condition of Participation: Medical Record Services

42 C.F.R. § 482.24
This rule requires hospitals to have administrative responsibilities for medical records and that a medical record has to be maintained for every individual evaluated or treated.[5]

Common Compliance Risks

All documentation systems have inherent risks. EHRs have tools and functionality that can increase the risk that the tools are utilized in a noncompliant manner. Compliance programs should ensure the organization has clearly defined policies and procedures that define the appropriate utilization of these tools. Here are a few of the common risks (not an all-inclusive listing).

Copy, Paste, and Carryforward

These tools are intended to help clinicians easily bring relevant data forward without reentering. The risk is that these tools will create note bloat with information that is not relevant to the encounter or, worse, create inconsistencies in documentation that was written today versus information brought forward and unedited.

Templates

A template is an electronic documentation form that is built with the intent to facilitate accurate and complete documentation. Templates can be controlled at the entity level (only templates approved by the organization can be utilized), but more often, anyone can create their own template. Templates can quickly replicate the same issue over and over when not vetted for compliant documentation. Some template functionality can cause self-populating entries. These are not necessarily bad when the data is automatically populated from updated data in the patient's medical record; however, our recommendation is that these not be implemented unless they are required to be activated by the clinician while documenting.

Authentication of Medical Record Documentation

Signatures are required, as indicated previously. It is important that controls be built into the EHR to require authentication before a medical record is considered complete for billing. In academic medical centers, appropriate authentication rules have to be built to include trainee authentication of documentation, as well as attestations and authentication by the attending clinician.

Billing and Coding Issues

These issues can occur when appropriate controls are not built in to require documentation, signatures, etc., before a bill can be generated; however, most systems are not sophisticated enough to determine if complete and accurate documentation has been entered. When independent coders are utilized to code and bill claims, they can act as an additional layer of review; however, when clinicians code their own claims, compliance needs to have testing to reduce the risk of billing and coding concerns.

Documentation Timeliness

This can be helped with EHR tracking and denoting when documentation has not been completed and authenticated timely, allowing leadership to work with clinicians to complete their documentation for billing.

EHR systems are primary in the exchange of personal health information (release of medical records, for treatment and administrative purposes, etc.). Addressing compliance risks with EHRs is complicated and requires compliance involvement in multiple areas. As our EHR implementation has expanded to new modules/components and "bolt-on" subsystems being added, the risk of a tweak in one area impacting other areas increases. Being involved in the decision-making, providing risk assessment and evaluation, and implementing auditing and monitoring programs are all essential to help reduce the risks with EHRs.

Addressing Compliance Risks

EHR systems have helped revolutionize healthcare delivery, making medical record documentation available to patients and other healthcare providers. These systems allow for better medical decisions and outcomes and enhance the amount of data that can be used for research and other healthcare purposes. EHRs come with many tools that are intended to improve documentation by clinicians but can be utilized in ways that increase risks of validity and appropriateness in all areas of the seven elements of an effective compliance program. Here are some ways an organization may address those risks within each element:

1. **Implement Written Policies, Procedures, and Code.** EHR systems require policies and procedures and standards of conduct to be reviewed, rewritten, or added to accommodate how the system handles clinician orders, electronic signature requirements, etc.
2. **Designate Compliance Officer and Committee.** The compliance officer and compliance committee may need to add knowledgeable IT or EHR personnel to help ensure informed decisions are made regarding the compliance program related to how the EHR system functions.
3. **Conduct Effective Training and Education.** Effective training and education are critical to the success of an EHR system. Many controls can be built into an EHR, but there is likely a way around the control that someone will find and manipulate.

4. **Develop Effective Lines of Communication.** Effective communication is key in the early deployment of the EHR system, but it is as critical that the communication lines remain open as the EHR is refined and updated and as issues/concerns are noted.

5. **Conduct Internal Monitoring and Auditing.** Internal monitoring and auditing processes are impacted significantly by the EHR system. Audit teams must be educated in how the system is designed to perform so they can plan and conduct their reviews in a manner to detect issues and concerns. Further, trends need to be analyzed before implementation of the EHR system and after to help ensure the new system is not leading to over- or undercoding or other documentation concerns.

6. **Enforce Standards through Well-publicized Disciplinary Guidelines.** Enforcing standards is critical. Given the review and need for new policies and standard operating procedures in the world of EHRs, having methods to correct and, when necessary, enforce standards is a key control.

7. **Respond Promptly to Detected Offenses and Take Corrective Action.** Responding promptly to detected concerns involves not only concerns that are reported, but also issues noted in reviews, trend analysis, etc. It is critical that compliance programs be prepared for new concerns with an EHR system regardless of if it is the first deployment of an EHR system or a replacement system.

Some specific areas to address include the following.

Understanding the Risks of Templates, Shortcuts, and Documentation Tools

These tools come in a wide variety and are often proprietary to specific EHR system software. These tools are often out of the box, customizable, and developed by the health system. Some compliance risks that have been noted with these are the following.

Electronic Signatures

In the paper record days, a clinician's signature had to be written along with the date and time. EHR systems have signature mechanisms that when initiated by the clinician writing the documentation, include a signature, date, and time. Often, the functions and processes within documentation templates and tools may not require authentication (signature, date, and time). This allows the documentation to appear complete and ready, but upon further evaluation, the documentation will not have been appropriately authenticated.

Self-Populating Entries

In many cases, EHR systems have tools that allow medical record documentation to populate with commands or phrases. Generally, these entries are initiated by either a command or phrase, but they can be embedded in templates to happen automatically when that template is initiated. These entries often create unnecessary or conflicting documentation. In some cases, the author does not directly see these items populating in their "live" note documentation, but they do appear in the completed and authenticated documentation. This can lead to inaccurate or inconsistent documentation, note bloat, and other concerns with the accuracy of the data recorded for the encounter.

Cloning, Copy, Paste, and Carryforward

These are all unique terms that have individual meanings and, in many cases, refer to similar documentation elements. When a clinician through affirmative action brings forward documentation in the patient's medical record, which may have been authored by that clinician in the past or could have another author, this documentation is tracked. These tools can provide a relatively completer and more accurate picture of the patient's condition/treatments, but often they cause bloat of the note and provide conflicting information related to the specific encounter. Upon review, many of these tools cause irregularities, which appear as multiple authors in the note, etc.

These are merely a few examples of documentation tools EHR systems have that may cause clinician documentation to be noncompliant to support the services performed and billed.

Be Aware of New Evaluation and Management (E/M) Codes for Clinic Visits

New codes became active in January 2021. These are the first changes to these codes since the 1995 and 1997 E/M documentation guidelines. The E/M codes are determined by the American Medical Association (AMA). The 2021 changes impact a specific set of codes and change the requirements for leveling of these codes. They will no longer require a number of specific elements of documentation (Review of Systems, History, Exam, Medical Decision Making, etc.) where elements must meet various standards in order to meet a level. Under the new guidelines, "documentation of time" (new definition of elements of time spent on the same day as the clinic encounter, no longer face-to-face, and focused on counseling) or "medical decision-making" will be the key factors in leveling E/M codes. The new coding rules are intended to streamline note writing to the most relevant elements to patient care and reduce note bloat. Many EHR system templates are set to bring forward elements to aid the clinician in meeting the 1995 or 1997 documentation elements (history, exam, review of systems, etc.), which may need to be altered to document under the new requirements and receive the advantages intended by these changes. The intent under the new guidelines for these clinic visit codes is that a relevant, clinically appropriate note will be completed.

Have a Physician Champion Working with Compliance

Physicians often see their documentation as being complete ("I always do X when a patient has Y."), when a reviewer may not see X and Y documented. Having a physician champion who understands compliance and can communicate with other clinicians the important differences is imperative. With EHR implementations and ongoing improvement, a physician champion can be vital to provide insights to compliance and other clinicians on a variety of topics. When reviews occur, having a physician who can help interpret and find ways to solve issues can facilitate faster progress.

Ensure Automated Coding Software Is Compliant

This software is either integrated within the EHR system or is a subsystem that has been "bolted" onto to the existing EHR system. Compliance professionals need to ensure these coding software systems are revised to compliantly code under the new rules and gain some comfort that the tools render accurate codes. In many cases, compliance professionals recommend the clinician must actively code their own account and may only utilize software to help; however, it has become vital that compliance review these programs and work to ensure compliant coding is being generated. With the new coding rules for some codes, it is imperative to have confidence the documentation and coding are yielding consistent and accurate billing.

Training and Education

Training clinicians to understand what the EHR system tools are, how they are compliantly utilized, and, in many cases, how tools can be misused are keys to an effective compliance program and in utilizing the EHR system's capabilities. In addition, compliance should partner with the professional coding team(s) and revenue cycle team not only to help ensure clinicians are trained, but also to address new issues with these partners to assess the situation, determine the risk, and implement corrective action when needed.

Possible Penalties

The possible penalties vary depending on the applicable rule(s) that have been violated. For instance, the FCA can impose a minimum penalty for a single false claim of $11,665 to the maximum penalty of $23,331. The key is understanding the documentation and coding (billing) guidelines and endeavoring to ensure clinicians and coding professionals are up-to-date with the rules and review the documentation generated by the EHR before submitting the claim for billing.

Compliance Resources

The Centers for Medicare & Medicaid Services

EHR Incentive Programs
An Introduction to the Medicaid EHR Incentive Program for Eligible Professionals
This guide covers the Medicaid EHR Incentive Program, how to participate, meaningful use, attestation, resources, and more.

https://www.cms.gov/regulations-and-guidance/legislation/ehrincentiveprograms/downloads/medicaid-ehr-guide.pdf

Medicare Learning Network
Complying with Medical Record Documentation Requirements
This Medicare Learning Network (MLN) fact sheet details common Comprehensive Error Rate Testing (CERT) Program errors related to medical record documentation, including third-party additional documentation requests and insufficient documentation errors.

https://www.cms.gov/Outreach-and-Education/Medicare-Learning-Network-MLN/MLNProducts/Downloads/CERTMedRecDoc-FactSheet-ICN909160.pdf

Complying with Medicare Signature Requirements
This MLN fact sheet details common CERT Program errors related to signature requirements.

https://www.cms.gov/Outreach-and-Education/Medicare-Learning-Network-MLN/MLNProducts/downloads/signature_requirements_fact_sheet_icn905364.pdf

The Office for Health Information Technology

Certification of Health IT
Learn about the Office of the National Coordinator for Health Information Technology (ONC) Health IT Certification Program on this site.

https://www.healthit.gov/topic/certification-ehrs/certification-health-it

Risk Takeaways

Main points of interest:
- EHR systems have enhanced clinician documentation, but they have also increased the risks facing organizations in staying compliant with medical record documentation in many ways.
- EHR systems can be customized (although this may present new compliance issues) or used out of the box. The higher the customization, the higher the compliance risk.
- Tools, templates, and other features often cause increased documentation risks.
- Compliance professionals should be included in development, deployment, and ongoing changes with EHR systems.

Areas to watch:
- EHR system implementation and updates
- Copy and paste, cloning, and signatures

- Billing and coding issues (services not performed, upcoding, cloning/fraud in EHRs outpatient coding and professional fee coding, etc.)
- Lack of timely documentation
- Incentive monies
- Retrospective auto-reporting entries

Laws that apply:
- HITECH, 42 U.S.C. § 139w-4(o)(2)
- HIPAA, Pub. L. No. 104-191, 110 Stat. 1936
- False Claims Act, 31 U.S.C. §§ 3729-3733
- Joint Commission and Centers for Medicare & Medicaid Services (CMS) medical record signature requirements
- Condition of participation: Medical record services, 42 C.F.R. § 482.24

Addressing compliance risks:
- Compliance should be involved during implementation and major system changes and enhancements.
- Train and educate staff on EHR systems, their risks, and how to compliantly utilize them.
- Analyze templates, shortcuts, and documentation tools for any noncompliant issues.
- Be aware of new E/M codes for clinic visits published in January 2021.
- Find a physician champion to help compliance combat note bloat.
- Ensure automated coding software is compliant.
- EHR certification

Endnotes

1. **K. Mark Jenkins** is the compliance officer, adult enterprise, at Vanderbilt University Medical Center. Implementing a new electronic health record (EHR) system involves many areas to be successful. Jenkins's background in internal audit and compliance has allowed him to be involved in several over the years, focusing on internal controls as well as compliance risks. Along with compliance leaders in other organizations, Jenkins has spoken on a number of EHR topics at Health Care Compliance Association (HCCA) Compliance Institute events, as well as at a user conference for a major EHR along with clinicians and information technology professionals.

2. 42 U.S.C. § 139w-4(o)(2).
3. 31 U.S.C. §§ 3729-3733.
4. Health Insurance Portability and Accountability Act of 1996, Pub. L. No. 104-191, 110 Stat. 1936 (1996).
5. 42 C.F.R. § 482.24.

Patient Access, Information Blocking, and the 21st Century Cures Act

By Patricia A. Markus,[1] JD, CIPP/US

What Are the Patient Access and Information Blocking Requirements of the 21st Century Cures Act?

Since 2003, under the Health Insurance Portability and Accountability Act (HIPAA) Privacy Rule, individuals have had the right to access and obtain a copy of their own protected health information (PHI) from a healthcare provider or a provider's business associate, subject to a few narrow exceptions.[2] However, due to a misunderstanding of HIPAA requirements and, in some cases, a desire to protect against competition, providers over the last few years have repeatedly been fined by federal regulators for Privacy Rule infractions. These include failing to provide access to PHI in a timely manner; denying access when access is permitted; failing to provide access in the format requested; failing to provide access to individuals' personal representatives as required by HIPAA; and charging excessive fees for copies of medical records.[3]

More recently, regulations under the 21st Century Cures Act (Cures Act), which prohibit healthcare providers from engaging in "information blocking," have complicated whether and how providers give access to individuals' electronic health information (EHI).[4] The final rule addresses interoperability, information blocking, and the Office of the National Coordinator for Health Information Technology (ONC) Health IT Certification Program under the Cures Act. The final rule was published in the *Federal Register* on May 1, 2020, and, following a six-month implementation delay due to COVID-19, became effective on April 5, 2021.[5] The information blocking provisions of the Cures Act responded to concerns about healthcare industry practices that were unreasonably limiting the availability and use of EHI for permitted purposes, including use by individuals and other appropriate persons within the healthcare ecosystem.[6] These industry practices include contract terms, policies, or processes that interfered with individuals' rights to access their own PHI for permitted purposes under HIPAA; fees that made the access, exchange, or use of PHI cost prohibitive; and nonstandard implementation of health information technology that substantially increased the cost, complexity, and burden of sharing health data.

A significant emphasis in the Cures Act's Information Blocking Rule is ensuring the rights of individuals and their personal representatives to access their PHI without unnecessary delay, without special effort on the individuals' part, and at a minimal cost or, in certain circumstances, no cost. This protection of individuals' right of access expands upon the right originally set forth in the HIPAA Privacy Rule and furthered by the Health Information Technology for Economic and Clinical Health Act (HITECH). The Information Blocking (IB) Rule builds upon this right of access; it prohibits charging individuals, their personal representatives, or another person or designated entity for providing "electronic access" to the individual's EHI.

Compliance with the IB Rule requires a paradigm shift in the way healthcare industry stakeholders and compliance officials think about when and how to make EHI available to third parties. For 19 years, the healthcare industry worked with the HIPAA Privacy Rule, which specifies when PHI **may** be used and disclosed. The IB Rule, on the other hand, **requires** healthcare providers and others governed by the rule to make EHI available for access, use, or disclosure when appropriate to do so and when not otherwise prohibited by law. Thus, the analysis regarding whether to use and disclose PHI in certain situations transitions from the HIPAA-based presumption that PHI **should not** be used or disclosed unless doing so is specifically permitted or required, to a presumption that EHI **must** be made available unless the access, use, or disclosure is specifically *prohibited* by law or if the circumstances surrounding the decision not to make EHI available fit within an exception to the definition of information blocking.

The IB Rule includes a significant number of defined terms that need to be understood to determine what conduct may be problematic and what conduct may fall within one of its eight exceptions. Before the enforcement mechanisms for the IB Rule are finalized, compliance officers need to understand the requirements of the IB Rule and the limitations of its exceptions. Simultaneously, compliance officers must watch for guidance to be issued by the ONC and other agencies within the U.S. Department of Health and Human Services (HHS) that address how to comply with different aspects of the rule and its exceptions.

Risk Area Governance

The IB Rule generally prohibits "actors" from engaging in "information blocking." Its definition of "actor" includes a healthcare provider, a developer of certified health IT, and a health information network or a health information exchange (HIE). (Health information *networks* and health information *exchanges* are collectively referred to as HIEs).[7]**The term "information blocking" is defined, in part, as a practice that, except as required by law or covered by an exception set forth in the IB Rule, "is likely to interfere with access, exchange, or use of electronic health information."**[8] "Interfere with" means to prevent, materially discourage, or otherwise inhibit.[9] A "practice" is defined as "an act or omission by an actor."[10]

The IB Rule is an intent-based statute. This means that an actor engages in information blocking only if the actor (while engaging in a practice that is likely to interfere with access, exchange, or use of EHI) has the level of intent specified in the IB Rule. *Healthcare providers* engage in information blocking only if they know that the practice is unreasonable and is likely to interfere with the access, exchange, or use of EHI.[11]*Health IT developers and HIEs* engage in information blocking only if they know or should know that a practice is likely to interfere with the access, exchange, or use of EHI.[12]

EHI was not defined in the Cures Act or the other statutes to which it refers,[13] so a definition of EHI was included in the IB Rule.[14] The definition of EHI is a subset of electronic protected health information (ePHI) as defined in the HIPAA Privacy Rule,[15] in that EHI is limited to ePHI that would be included in a designated record set (DRS), whether or not the actor is a HIPAA-covered entity.[16] The Privacy Rule defines a designated record set as follows:

1. A group of records maintained by or for a **covered entity** that involve:
   i. Medical and billing records about individuals and maintained by or for a covered healthcare provider;
   ii. Enrollment, payment, claims adjudication, and case or medical management record systems that are maintained by or for a health plan or are used, in whole or in part, by or for the covered entity to make decisions about individuals.
2. The term "record" here means any item, collection, or grouping of information that includes protected health information and is maintained, collected, used, or disseminated by or for a **covered entity**.[17]

The definition of EHI specifically *excludes* psychotherapy notes and information compiled in anticipation of or for use in a civil, criminal, or administrative action or proceeding.[18]

The ONC did not limit the scope of EHI to records that are used or maintained by or for covered entities: "actors" who are regulated by the IB Rule include noncovered entities such as HIEs, certified health IT developers, and healthcare providers who do not take insurance. This, in turn, means that what constitutes EHI is much broader than the definition of ePHI under HIPAA: EHI may encompass medical and billing records, health plan records, and other records used to make decisions about individuals when such records are maintained by developers of certified health IT, HIEs, and healthcare providers that are not covered entities.

Related Laws

Health Insurance Portability and Accountability Act of 1996, Pub. L. No. 104–191 (HIPAA), as amended by the Health Information Technology for Economic and Clinical Health Act of 2009, Pub. L. No. 111–5 (HITECH)

Although HIPAA restricts the unauthorized use and disclosure of patients' PHI, it expressly requires covered entities and business associates to provide individuals and their personal representatives access to such individuals' PHI in a DRS, with the exception of psychotherapy notes[19] and information compiled in reasonable anticipation of, or for use in, a civil, criminal, or administrative action or proceeding.[20] After an individual requests access, under the HITECH Act's implementing regulations, a covered entity or business associate must act on the request within 30 days, unless the entity is unable to make the information available within that period (e.g., if the information is stored offsite or must be compiled from a variety of paper and electronic files). In that instance, the entity has an additional 30 days to provide access to the PHI if it notifies the individual and states the reason for the delay and the expected date on which the PHI will be provided.[21] The HITECH regulations also specify that any fee to produce an electronic copy of PHI may not be greater than the labor costs involved in responding to the request for the copy plus any costs for supplies for creating an electronic copy on portable media.[22] HITECH additionally requires providers, upon an individual's request, to send a copy of PHI directly to a person or entity designated individual so long as the individual's request to do so is "clear, conspicuous, and specific."[23] Finally, HITECH requires covered entities and business associates to provide access to PHI in the *form and format* (e.g., electronically on a flash drive) requested by the individual, if feasible. If doing so is not feasible, the entity must provide the PHI in a readable form and format agreed upon by the entity and the requestor.[24]

Common Compliance Risks

Information Blocking Examples

The Final Rule specifies that an action or practice by an actor "implicates" information blocking if the practice limits—by contract, license, or policy—availability of EHI that is not prohibited from being made available, or if the practice involves either ignoring a request to share information or charging an exorbitant sum to make EHI available. **Implicates** does not necessarily mean **violates**. As with HIPAA, where a violation is not necessarily a reportable breach, a practice that implicates the IB Rule may not violate the rule, but a fact-specific evaluation must be undertaken to determine whether such an action or practice is required by law or complies with an exception to the IB Rule.

A few examples of practices that "implicate" the IB Rule include:

- A hospital's internal policy requiring staff to obtain the patient's written consent before sharing the patient's EHI with unaffiliated providers for treatment, where such consent is not required by law.
- A practice's failure, upon receiving a patient's request, to forward the patient's EHI to a former shareholder of the practice who recently joined a competitor practice.
- A hospital's choosing not to enable a function of its patient portal that allows patients to transmit their EHI directly to third parties. A practice's ignoring or unreasonably delaying response to a request for EHI.

Exceptions to Information Blocking

The ONC has identified eight exceptions to the IB Rule describing "reasonable and necessary" practices that do not constitute information blocking. The exceptions apply to certain activities that are likely to interfere with, prevent, or materially discourage the access, exchange, or use of EHI, but that would be reasonable and necessary if certain conditions are met. The first five exceptions involve *not fulfilling requests* to access, exchange, or use EHI, while the final three exceptions specify procedures for *fulfilling requests* to access, exchange, or use EHI.[25] An actor's practice that does not meet the conditions of an exception will not automatically constitute information blocking; the practice will be evaluated on a case-by-case basis to determine whether the practice rises to the level of an interference and whether the actor acted with the requisite intent.[26]

a. Preventing Harm Exception

b. Objective: This exception recognizes that the public interest in protecting patients and other persons against unreasonable risks of harm can justify practices that are likely to interfere with access, exchange, or use of EHI.[27]

c. Exception and Key Conditions: Under this exception, a provider may refuse to make EHI available if it has a reasonable belief denying access will substantially reduce risk of harm to a patient or another person that otherwise would arise from making the EHI available. The risk must be that corrupt or inaccurate data will be included in a patient's record or that, based on a licensed professional's determination, disclosing EHI is likely to endanger the life or physical safety of the patient or others. A provider's practice involved in refusing to make EHI available must be no broader than necessary to substantially reduce the risk of harm that the practice is implemented to reduce, and the provider's practice must either be based on an organizational policy or on an individual determination that concerns the circumstances of an incident. Specific additional criteria apply.[28]

d. The Privacy Exception

e. <u>Objective</u>: This exception recognizes that if an actor is permitted to provide access, exchange, or use of EHI under a privacy law, then the actor should do so. However, an actor should not be required to use or disclose EHI in a manner that is prohibited under state or federal privacy laws.[29]

f. <u>Exception and Key Conditions</u>: Under this exception, a provider may refuse to make EHI available if (i) federal or state privacy laws impose preconditions to access (such as consents or authorizations) that have not been satisfied; (ii) HIPAA allows the provider to deny access to an individual; or (iii) the patient has requested that their information not be shared. In each circumstance, specific additional conditions apply.[30]

g. The Security Exception

h. <u>Objective</u>: This exception is intended to cover all legitimate security practices by actors; however, it does not prescribe a maximum level of security or dictate a one-size-fits-all approach.[31]

i. <u>Exception and Key Conditions</u>: Under this exception, a provider may refuse to make EHI available if doing so is necessary to safeguard the confidentiality, integrity, and availability of the EHI consistent either with (i) the provider's organizational policies or (ii) a specific determination that no reasonable, less-obstructive alternatives exist for securing the EHI. The practice must directly relate to safeguarding the confidentiality, integrity, and availability of EHI and be tailored to specific security risks.[32]

j. Infeasibility Exception

k. <u>Objective</u>: This exception recognizes that legitimate and practical challenges may limit an actor's ability to comply with requests for access, exchange, or use of EHI.[33]

l. <u>Exception and Key Conditions</u>: Under this exception, a provider may refuse to make EHI available if (i) an extraordinary event beyond its control (i.e., a natural disaster) prevents it from fulfilling the request for access; (ii) it cannot segregate the requested EHI from other information that is not subject to access (e.g., the other information that may not be disclosed pursuant to law); or (iii) it shows that responding to the request is not feasible (e.g., due to the type of information sought, the cost involved in providing it, available resources, and many other factors).[34]

m. <u>Note</u>: To meet this exception, within 10 days of receiving a request for access, a provider must notify the requestor in writing of the reason why it is infeasible to provide the access sought.

n. Health IT Performance Exception

o. <u>Objective</u>: This exception recognizes that for health IT to perform properly and efficiently, it must be maintained, and in some instances improved. This may require that health IT be taken offline temporarily. Actors should not be deterred from taking reasonable and necessary measures to make health IT temporarily unavailable or to degrade the health IT's performance for the benefit of the overall performance of health IT.[35]

p. Exception and Key Conditions: Under this exception, a provider is not engaging in information blocking if it takes reasonable and necessary measures to make health IT temporarily unavailable, so long as such unavailability lasts no longer than necessary and is in accordance with additional conditions.[36]

q. Note: If a provider is acting as a health IT developer or an HIE, it may temporarily block access to EHI if necessary for maintenance of the platform/system and to improve health IT performance. The unavailability may be for no longer than necessary.[37]

r. The Content and Manner Exception

s. Objective: This exception provides clarity and flexibility regarding the required *content* (i.e., scope of EHI) of an actor's response to a request to access, exchange, or use EHI and the *manner* in which the actor may fulfill the request.[38]

t. Exception and Key Conditions: Under this exception, a provider generally must provide access to EHI in the manner requested, unless the provider is technically unable to fulfill the request or cannot reach agreeable terms with the requestor. If unable to provide access as requested or as agreed, the provider must take reasonable steps to fulfill the request in an alternative manner, consistent with additional specified technical standards. The requirements of the "Fees and Licensing" exceptions will apply to such alternative access.[39]

u. Fees Exception

v. Objective: This exception enables actors to charge fees related to the development of technologies and the provision of services that enhance interoperability, while not protecting rent-seeking, opportunistic fees, or exclusionary practices that interfere with access, exchange, or use of EHI.[40]

w. Exception and Key Conditions: Under this exception, a provider may charge a reasonable fee for making EHI available, as long as the fee is based on its costs and applied to similarly situated requestors in a nondiscriminatory manner. Other standards apply.[41]

x. Note: Providers may not charge a fee "based in any part on the electronic access of an individual's EHI" by individuals, their personal representatives, or another person or entity designated by such individuals.[42] "Electronic access" means an "internet-based method" that makes EHI available at the time EHI is requested "and where no manual effort is required to fulfill the request."[43] An example of electronic access is a healthcare provider's patient portal.

y. Licensing Exception

z.   Objective: This exception allows actors to protect the value of their innovations and charge reasonable royalties in order to earn returns on the investments they have made to develop, maintain, and update those innovations.[44]

aa. Exception and Key Conditions: Under this exception, a provider must agree to license certain technologies (***"interoperability elements,"***), which include certified EHR technology and most application programming interfaces (APIs), as well as hardware, software, intellectual property, upgrades, or services controlled by the provider that may be necessary to access, exchange, or use EHI that enable access to EHI upon a third party's request for a license, **except** where the third party intends to develop a competing product through the license. Any license fees must be reasonable, and the license terms must be nondiscriminatory. Certain other limitations apply.[45]

ab. Note: To meet this exception, within 10 business days of receipt of a request for a license of interoperability elements, a provider must begin negotiations for such a license and work in good faith to conclude such negotiations within 30 business days.

Addressing Compliance Risks

Areas to Prioritize

The IB Rule states that information blocking will "almost always" be implicated if an actor's practice interferes with access, exchange, or use of EHI for any of these purposes that follow.[46] It may be efficient, therefore, for compliance officers to prioritize compliance activities with respect to the following areas:

1. Ensure that policies and practices generally do not inappropriately delay or unreasonably restrict sharing of EHI. In this regard, be sure that:
    a. Patients may access their own EHI and exchange and use it without special effort.
    b. Healthcare professionals and other authorized persons have the EHI they need, when and where they need it, to make treatment decisions, coordinate/manage care, and use the EHI they receive from other sources.
    c. Payers and other purchasers of healthcare services can obtain EHI needed to effectively assess clinical value and promote transparency regarding quality and costs.
    d. Healthcare providers can access, exchange, and use EHI for quality improvement and population health management.
    e. EHI is made available for patient safety and public health.
2. Evaluate for possible information blocking the provider's policies and practices involving the availability of EHI. Determine whether an exception applies in each instance.

3. Compare operational policy provisions (including HIPAA policies) to IB Rule requirements; update policies where needed. Examples include the following:
    a. Preventing Harm Exception

    i.   Review policy on individual's right to access information. Ensure that it includes provisions that conform to the exception regarding preventing harm. Examples could include situations involving abuse (when access is requested by a parent or personal representative) or when a clinician has determined a risk of harm to the individual or another person.

    ii. Remember that the exception will be met with either a policy outlining limitations that are no broader than needed to prevent harm **or** with an individualized determination of harm in a given circumstance.

    iii. Evaluate how quickly test results are made available to individuals and consider creating a policy noting that test results will be made available without delay unless a clinician makes a good faith, individualized determination of a substantial likelihood of harm arising in a given instance.

        1. Individualized determinations should be *documented in writing* (to defend against potential information-blocking complaints) and *maintained* in the patient's record. Some providers are working with their electronic health record system vendors to add drop-down menus that enable clinicians to describe individualized determinations of harm in different circumstances.

        2. Be cautious about implementing a policy stating that certain categories of test results will be delayed—unless such delays are required by other laws (i.e., state law).

b. Privacy Exception

    i.   Revise (or create) policies for notifying patients or others requesting EHI that is subject to a precondition when the consent or authorization that was submitted to satisfy the precondition requires modifications. Consider providing requestors a form that satisfies the elements of the required consent/authorization or other precondition when appropriate to do so.

    ii. Determine whether and how information about minors may be appropriate to make available but needs to be withheld when required by law (use the Infeasibility or Content and Manner Exceptions as needed).

c. Security Exception

    i.   Consider whether terms in Business Associate Agreements (BAAs) and other documents that address information security improperly interfere with the access, exchange, or use of EHI (i.e., are unreasonable or improperly obstructive). Update where necessary.

d. Infeasibility Exception

    i.   Identify situations where data segmentation may be needed to comply with requests for access to EHI while also staying compliant with applicable laws that restrict such access, but where such segmentation isn't feasible. This might include documents scanned into a provider's system that contain some information that, by law, may not be disclosed.

    ii. When a request is determined to be infeasible, ensure that the provider has a process for responding in writing within 10 business days of receiving the request.

    iii. Remember that EHI may be made available in an alternative fashion if possible (and if the recipient agrees) under the Content and Manner Exception; in such a case, the provider will be subject to the requirements of the Fees and Licensing Exceptions if EHI is made available in an alternative fashion.

 e. Health IT Performance Exception

  i. Determine whether service-level agreements and other uptime standards in technology contracts—both in instances where the provider is the recipient of the software/services and where it is responsible for providing them (if any)—comply with the requirements of the exception.

 f. Fees Exception

  i. Establish processes to evaluate and respond to requests for access to EHI, and determine appropriate costs for or limitations of such access.

  ii. Where no manual effort is needed to provide electronic access to EHI, **individuals and their personal or legal representatives may not be charged a fee**. Review policies and processes regarding fees for making EHI available; update them as needed, ensuring that fees are reasonable. (Note that manual effort includes collating or assembling EHI from various systems in response to a request.)

  iii. In licensing contracts, the parties should agree in advance (i.e., at the time the contract is signed) on the fee, if any, for export or conversion of the requestor's data.

 g. Licensing Exception

  i. Determine what hardware, software, or services a provider may license to third parties that are "interoperability elements."

  ii. Identify and revise contract terms and conditions that discourage the use of interoperability elements.

  iii. If applicable, establish policies for responding to requests from third parties for licenses of interoperability elements. Remember that actors have 10 business days to start license negotiations after a request and they have 30 business days to complete those negotiations in good faith.

  iv. Review the functionality of platforms and systems containing EHI. Ensure that such functionality has not been configured or disabled in a manner that would constitute information blocking. For example, check whether some physicians or physician offices provide patients their clinical notes while others do not or have not configured their systems to permit sharing of such information.

 h. Licensing and Fee Exceptions

  i. Assess whether pricing and fees in contracts that address access to EHI or licensing interoperability elements are appropriate or need modification.

  ii. Remember that pricing may not be discriminatory and that the licensor may not, as a condition of offering the license, require the licensee to obtain other licenses or products that are unrelated to the requested interoperability elements or to give away the licensee's intellectual property.

4. Identify capabilities and limitations of platforms and systems containing EHI that could justify a denial of certain requests for access. For example, if the version of software used doesn't permit the export of EHI in a certain file format or can't otherwise accommodate a request for EHI and it is cost-prohibitive to upgrade to a different version of the software (and where the upgrade isn't required to comply with other laws).

5. Respond appropriately to requests for sharing of EHI. Develop a process for routing different requests to an individual or group of individuals who understand the requirements of the IB rule and who can set in motion an appropriate response to such requests

6. Plan to identify and educate personnel within multiple departments who are likely to be affected, including clinicians and individuals in the C-suite, as well as staff in finance, legal, IT, contracts, risk management, and records management. Those involved in contracting, compliance, IT, patient care, and health information management likely will require more robust education, but other leaders certainly should be aware of the new rule and its implications and should participate in decisions regarding compliance, where appropriate. All employees should be trained on which personnel (e.g., supervisor, department head) to contact about possible information-blocking concerns.

Possible Penalties

Penalties or other consequences for information blocking will apply depending on the type of actor involved in the activity that is determined to constitute information blocking. HIEs and developers of certified health IT are subject to substantial monetary penalties of up to a million dollars per violation, with the Office of Inspector General (OIG) serving as the enforcement agency. The OIG has yet to issue a final rule to establish parameters and enforcement dates pertaining to the civil monetary penalties to which health IT developers and HIEs will be subjected. The penalty determination will take into account factors such as the nature and extent of the information blocking and the resultant harm, including the number of patients and providers affected and the number of days the information blocking persisted.[47] Healthcare providers will be subject to different penalties and "appropriate disincentives" for information blocking, but these penalties and disincentives have not yet been definitively identified.

Significantly, an entity might fall into more than one category of actor depending on its activities. For example, a healthcare provider may also operate an HIE or fall within the definition of a developer of certified health IT; if the provider violates the IB Rule when it is acting as an HIE or developer of certified health IT, it will be subject to the substantial civil monetary penalty described above.

Compliance Resources

Information about the 21st Century Cures Act's Information Blocking final rule for patients, providers, and IT developers, along with links to other resources can be found here:

https://www.healthit.gov/curesrule/.

Fact Sheets are located at https://www.healthit.gov/curesrule/resources/fact-sheets are particularly useful.

Look for additional guidance from ONC and CMS on the rules at these web sites: https://www.healthit.gov/topic/information-blocking and https://www.healthit.gov/curesrule/resources/information-blocking-faqs.

Such guidance has been promised and will be needed to understand the nuances of the IB Rule and its interplay with HIPAA.

Risk Takeaways

Main points of interest:
- Individuals have had the right under HIPAA since 2003 to access and obtain copies of their health information, with limited exceptions.
- The IB Rule enhances individuals' rights of access to their health information but makes determining when to share information with individuals, and others permitted to receive it, more challenging.
- The exceptions to the IB Rule provide "safe harbors" against allegations of information blocking if complied with in their entirety.

Areas to watch:
- Avoid improperly withholding or delaying the provision of copies of EHI from individuals and their personal representatives, as OCR is receiving and investigating a wide variety of complaints in this area.

- Be on the lookout for updated FAQs from ONC addressing the IB Rule.

- Be on the lookout for more information from OIG and CMS regarding penalties that may be imposed under the IB Rule and the date on which such penalties may start.

Laws that apply:
- 21st Century Cures Act
- *HIPAA, as amended by the HITECH Act*

Addressing compliance risks:
- Review HIPAA policies for compliance with the IB Rule and its exceptions, and update or create new policies as needed.
- Review IT systems to determine how information may be shared from them, and review contracts to ensure that they do not implicate the IB Rule.
- Educate all members of the organization regarding who to contact if there is a question about releasing PHI.

Endnotes

1. **Patricia A. Markus** is a partner in the Raleigh office of Nelson Mullins Riley & Scarborough LLP. She represents healthcare providers and health technology companies on wide-ranging regulatory compliance, reimbursement, licensure, and operational matters. She regularly advises clients on ways to use technology to improve healthcare access and outcomes while assuring compliance with applicable data privacy and security laws and other healthcare regulatory requirements. Trish serves as the President-Elect of the American Health Law Association for 2022–2023.

2. 45 C.F.R. § 164.524.

3. U.S. Department of Health & Human Services, Office of Civil Rights, "OCR Settles Three Cases with Dental Practices for Patient Right of Access under HIPAA," September 20, 2022, https://www.hhs.gov/about/news/2022/09/20/ocr-settles-three-cases-dental-practices-patient-right-access-under-hipaa.html.U.S. Department of Health & Human Services, Office of Civil Rights, "Eleven Enforcement Actions Uphold Patients' Rights Under HIPAA," July 15, 2022, https://www.hhs.gov/about/news/2022/07/15/eleven-enforcement-actions-uphold-patients-rights-under-hipaa.html.

4. 21st Century Cures Act, Pub. L. No. 114–255, § 4004, 130 Stat. 1033 (2016).

5. 21st Century Cures Act: Interoperability, Information Blocking, and the ONC Health IT Certification Program, 85 Fed. Reg. 25642 (May 1, 2020) (codified at 45 C.F.R. §§ 170, 171), https://www.federalregister.gov/documents/2020/05/01/2020-07419/21st-century-cures-act-interoperability-information-blocking-and-the-onc-health-it-certification.

6. 21st Century Cures Act, 85 Fed. Reg. at 25790.

7. 45 C.F.R. § 171.102.

8. 45 C.F.R. § 171.103.

9. 45 C.F.R. § 171.102.

10. 45 C.F.R. § 171.102.

11. 45 C.F.R. § 171.103.

12. 45 C.F.R. § 171.103.

13. 21st Century Cures Act, 85 Fed. Reg. at 25803.

14. 45 C.F.R. § 171.102.

15. 45 C.F.R. § 160.103.

16. 45 C.F.R. § 171.102.

17. 45 C.F.R. § 164.501 (*emphasis added*).

18. 45 C.F.R. § 171.102.

19. 45 C.F.R. § 164.501. Psychotherapy notes are defined as notes recorded by a mental health professional documenting or analyzing a conversation during a counseling session, and which are separated from the remainder of the individual's medical record.

20. 45 C.F.R. § 164.524(a)(1).

21. 45 C.F.R. § 164.524(b)(2).

22. 45 C.F.R. § 164.524(c)(4).

23. 42 U.S.C. § 17935(e).

24. 45 C.F.R. § 164.524(c)(2).

25. 21st Century Cures Act, 85 Fed. Reg. at 25821.

26. 21st Century Cures Act, 85 Fed. Reg. at 25820.

27. "Cures Act Final Rule Information Blocking Exceptions," Office of the National Coordinator for Health Information Technology, (last reviewed October 31, 2022), https://www.healthit.gov/sites/default/files/2022-07/InformationBlockingExceptions.pdf.

28. 45 C.F.R. § 171.201.

29. 45 C.F.R. § 171.202.

30. 45 C.F.R. § 171.202.
31. 45 C.F.R. § 171.203.
32. 45 C.F.R. § 171.203.
33. 45 C.F.R. § 171.204.
34. 45 C.F.R. § 171.204.
35. 45 C.F.R. § 171.205.
36. 45 C.F.R. § 171.205.
37. 45 C.F.R. § 171.205.
38. 45 C.F.R. § 171.301.

39. 45 C.F.R § 171.301.
40. 45 C.F.R. § 171.302.
41. 45 C.F.R. § 171.301.
42. 45 C.F.R. § 171.302(b)(2).
43. 45 C.F.R. § 171.302(d).
44. 45 C.F.R. § 171.303.
45. 45 C.F.R. § 171.303.
46. 21st Century Cures Act, 85 Fed. Reg. at 25810.
47. 42 U.S.C. § 300jj-52(b)(2)(A).

Patient Care

Medical Necessity and Patient Status

By Donna Abbondandolo,[1] CHC, CHPC, CPHQ, RHIA, CCS, CPC

What Are Medical Necessity and Patient Status?

The Social Security Act (SSA) outlines that all services provided under Medicare must be reasonable and necessary as a basis for payment.[2] Section 1862(a)(1)(A) of the SSA further defines that payment may not be made for any expenses incurred for items or services which are not reasonable and necessary for the evaluation and management of a disease, condition, illness, or injury.[3] It is important to note this clarification, as the focus is on payment and not the quality of care received. For compliance professionals, this key point is center stage when discussing medical necessity with providers, ensuring proper documentation that supports medical necessity is within the medical record, and ensuring understanding that medical necessity is not a reflection of the care provided.

Medical necessity for healthcare services is evidenced through documentation. Documentation within the medical record serves several key functions—it is the communication vehicle between members of the team providing care to a patient across multiple settings to ensure continuity of patient care, serves as the legal document to support services provided, and demonstrates the justification to support payment for the medical care and services provided to the patient. Care must be considered reasonable when compared against current medical standards of care.

The Centers for Medicare & Medicaid Services (CMS) Conditions of Participation for Medicare and Medicaid and the SSA require that hospitals and health systems have an effective utilization review (UR) plan/UR function in place, with specific processes to review medical necessity, resource use, length of stay (LOS), denials, and outcomes, which directly affect reimbursement.[4] In addition, payers and health plans have contractual requirements that affect reimbursement. Given the role of the UR function and the regulatory complexities within healthcare, UR can be the bridge between quality, medical necessity, resources, coverage, and reimbursement and facilitate compliance with regulatory, risk, and quality requirements.

Coordination among UR, care management, revenue cycle, and the physician is imperative. Medicare reimbursement for inpatient and outpatient hospital services differ, with CMS providing payment for inpatient stays under the hospital inpatient prospective payment system (IPPS) in the Medicare Part A program or under payment structures for critical access hospitals, inpatient rehab, long term acute care, cancer, religious, or inpatient psych.[5] Whereas hospital outpatient visits are paid under the hospital outpatient prospective payment system (OPPS) under the Medicare Part B program.[6] When a patient presents to a hospital in need of medical care, the physician must determine whether the patient needs inpatient care or can be treated in an outpatient setting. This decision has implications for hospital payment and beneficiary cost sharing, and the physician documentation must support the level of care provided and that services are medically necessary regardless of the setting where the patient receives those services.

Two main clinical criteria are used as guidance for determining level of care: McKesson's InterQual Criteria and MCG. Both are evidence-based clinical guidelines used to assess whether a patient's level of care was appropriate. As these are guidelines, each physician must use their expertise to determine appropriate level of care, which may not align with clinical criteria. This is where it becomes critical for physicians to document their thought processes when making determinations of level of care and include in their documentation their evaluation of the patient, prior patient history, current symptoms or course of illness, and the details behind their clinical decisions. Patient evaluation does not always need to meet InterQual or MCG to admit the person as an inpatient.

CMS has two requirements to document and validate medical necessity of inpatient admission:

1. Reasonable expectation based on clinical standards of medical practice that the patient is likely to require two midnights or more of inpatient care, and

2. Specific explanation of the clinical conditions, circumstances, complications, comorbidities, and risks to the patient upon which that expectation is based.

Payment under Medicare Part A is generally not appropriate for hospital stays expected to span less than two-midnights, unless the admission falls into an exception as outlined by CMS, as either a procedure on the "inpatient only" list or qualifies for a case-by-case exception. To meet the qualification for the case-by-case exception, the medical record documentation must clearly support the physician's determination that the patient required hospital services in the inpatient setting regardless of the expectation of staying at least two-midnights. CMS' expectation is that an inpatient admission less than 24 hours would seldom qualify for the case-by-case exception to the two-midnight benchmark.

Effective October 1, 2018, CMS updated regulations that govern hospital admissions under Medicare Part A.[7] The changes removed the requirement that an inpatient admission order "must be present in the medical record and be supported by the physician admission and progress notes, in order for the hospital to be paid for hospital inpatient services under Medicare Part A."[8] More importantly, CMS did not change the standard in that same regulation that an individual becomes an inpatient when formally admitted under an order for inpatient admission by a physician. According to CMS, this regulatory standard remains significant because it reflects a determination by the treating physician that inpatient services are medically necessary.

A physician order to admit a patient for inpatient services is binding and inpatient status begins at formal admission pursuant to the order. If after admission it is determined that the inpatient admission decision was incorrect or cannot be supported, the hospital can use the Condition Code 44 process to change the status to outpatient if the patient is still a patient in the hospital. To use the Condition Code 44 process, the attending physician and a UR Committee physician must both concur.[9] If the patient has already been discharged or the attending physician does not concur with the change to outpatient, the hospital may self-deny and rebill to Medicare part B.[10] In order to rebill, the attending physician must be afforded the opportunity to express his or her views but two physician members of the UR committee may approve self-denial without concurrence of the physician.[11] In both scenarios, the patient must be notified.

Prolonged Observation Services Guidance

Several CMS policies provide guidance relating to prolonged observation services: the definition provided for "observation services," Medicare Outpatient Observation Notice (MOON), comprehensive Ambulatory Payment Classification (APC) C-APC-8011, two-midnight rule, and Notice of Observation Treatment and Implication for Care Eligibility Act (NOTICE Act).

Observation Services and Medicare Outpatient Observation Notice (MOON)

To be covered by Medicare, observation services must be reasonable and necessary. Observation is a short-term treatment that allows for assessment to determine whether a patient needs additional treatment as a hospital inpatient. An order by a qualified provider is required to place the patient in observation and start the clock to calculate the hours the patient is in observation for billing purposes. General supervision by the physician is required by CMS for observation services, and the presence of the physician is not required.[12] Notification to the patient if observation extends beyond 24 hours must occur through the MOON. Decisions to admit the patient to inpatient level of care or discharge the patient rarely extend beyond 48 hours.

Ambulatory Payment Classification (APC) C-APC-8011

Observation services are reported using HCPCS code G0378 for hourly observation services and is assigned a status indicator of N, identifying that payment is always packaged. As part of the CMS Comprehensive Ambulatory Payment Classification (C-APC) payment policy methodology, C-APC 8011 was established to capture claims that contain a specific combination of services provided to a patient during the same encounter; one of which must be eight or more units of service for G0378. In addition, the other criteria that qualify claims for payment under C-APC 8011 are: 1) HCPCS codes with a status indicator of T are not listed on the claim; 2) the claim contains one of the following codes: G0379 on the same date of service; 99281 – 99285 (emergency department visit); G0380--G0384 (type B emergency department visit); 99291 (critical care); or G0463 (hospital outpatient clinic visit) provided on the same date of service or 1 day before the date of service for G0378; and 3) HCPCS codes with status indicator J1 are not listed on the claim.

Two-Midnight Rule

Length of stay plays a key role in inpatient care decision-making, as outlined in the two-midnight rule adopted by CMS in 2014.[13] CMS recognizes that a patient with a hospital stay that does not cross two midnights may be appropriately considered an inpatient, if the medical record documentation supports the inpatient stay and it meets certain circumstances (such as death, transfer, leaving against medical advice, undergoing an inpatient-only procedure, or receiving ventilation). There are three concepts to consider:

1. Stays that are expected to last less than 24 hours should rarely be provided as an inpatient, except for patients undergoing a procedure on the Medicare inpatient-only list or medically necessary with extenuating circumstances where the physician determines inpatient admission is warranted. The patient should be admitted regardless of the expected length of stay.

2. Stays greater than 48 hours should rarely be considered an outpatient unless there are concerns regarding medical necessity.

3. Any stay between 24 and 48 hours should be under close observation of the physician.

Notice of Observation Treatment and Implication for Care Eligibility Act (NOTICE Act)

In 2016, Bill H.R. 876, the NOTICE Act, amended Title XVIII of the SSA to require hospitals to notify patients verbally and in writing if they have been in observation more than 24 hours and also outlined several other requirements to provide patients with information on their status, financial obligations, and documentation and signature specifications for compliance under the act.[14]

Utilization Review (UR) Function

Each hospital must also comply with the hospital conditions of participation (CoPs) in order to participate in the Medicare and Medicaid programs. 42 C.F.R. § 482.30 (Condition of Participation: Utilization Review) outlines the requirements of the hospital to establish a UR function: "The hospital must have in effect a utilization review (UR) plan that provides for review of services furnished by the institution and by members of the medical staff to patients entitled to benefits under the Medicare and Medicaid programs." This includes establishment of a UR committee for medical necessity reviews, denials, and internal processes for UR and physician advisor (PA) reviews.[15]

Risk Area Governance

Medical necessity and associated payment mechanisms related to both inpatient and outpatient services are defined by CMS in several federal regulations governing the Medicare and Medicaid programs in healthcare, including the SSA, the two-midnight rule, the *Medicare Benefit Policy Manual*, and the *Medicare Claims Processing Manual*. In addition, the Medicare Conditions of Participation also outline the expectations of hospitals and health systems to design and implement a UR program with direct responsibility for review of medical necessity of inpatient admissions.

Title XVIII of Social Security Act, Section 1862(a)(1)(A)

The SSA defines medical necessity as follows: "Notwithstanding any other provision of this subchapter, no payment may be made under part A or part B for any expenses incurred for items or services which...are not reasonable and necessary for the diagnosis or treatment of illness or injury or to improve the functioning of a malformed body member."[16]

NOTICE Act, H.R. 876

Amendment to Title XVIII of the SSA that required hospitals to notify patients verbally and in writing of their observation status exceeding 24 hours, the reasons why they are in outpatient status, any financial obligations under Medicare Part B, as well as implications for impact on Medicare noncovered services and that outpatient observation hours do not count toward the three-day acute care qualifying stay requirement for skilled nursing facility coverage.[17]

Condition of Participation: Utilization Review, 42 C.F.R. § 482.30

1. The UR plan must provide for review for Medicare and Medicaid patients with respect to the medical necessity of—

   i.   Admissions to the institution;

      i.   The duration of stays; and

      ii. Professional services furnished, including drugs and biologicals.

2. Review of admissions may be performed before, at, or after hospital admission.[18]

Two-Midnight Rule, Final Rule CMS-1599-F

Effective for admission beginning on or after October 1, 2013, the rule established payment policy regarding the benchmark criteria to use when determining whether inpatient admission is reasonable and necessary for purposes of payment under Medicare Part A. An inpatient stay is presumed appropriate if the patient requires hospital care that will cross two midnights.[19]

Common Compliance Risks

- **Medical necessity denials** (from complex medical reviews).

- **Technical denials** (from lack of response to government or quality improvement organization requests).

- **Inadequate UR and PA internal controls** (i.e., those that assess the effectiveness and timeliness of reviews).

- **Breakdown in UR function** (UR process not comprehensive or does not provide adequate coverage).

- **Consistent billing irregularities** (the federal government's ability to investigate hospital-specific data for referral to the Office of Inspector General to pursue under the False Claims Act).

- **Lack of adherence to regulatory requirements** (for level of care assignment, patient notification, and billing).

- **Lack of robust monitoring efforts** (to ensure compliant processes).

- **Cloning or overdocumentation** (implementation of electronic medical records (EMR) has facilitated ease of incorporating ancillary and provider documentation within the EMR).

- **Systemic abuse or delays in the provision of care (in an attempt to qualify for the two-midnight presumption)** (CMS may identify such trends through probe reviews and data provided by the Comprehensive Error Rate Testing (CERT) contractor, First-look Analysis Tool for Hospital Outlier Monitoring (FATHOM), and Program for Evaluating Payment Patterns Electronic Report (PEPPER).)

- **Referral from beneficiary and family centered care quality improvement organization (BFCC-QIO) to the Medicare administrative contractor (MAC)/recovery audit contractor (RAC)** (Enforcement of the two-midnight rule is delegated to one national BFCC-QIOs—Livanta.[20] These organizations are charged with evaluating the appropriateness of inpatient claims for hospital stays that do not cross two midnights. The BFCC-QIOs choose samples of one-day inpatient claims, often from hospitals whose percentage of short stay admissions is higher than the national average. If the sampled claims indicate that a hospital's short-stay admissions are not appropriate, the BFCC-QIO meets with the hospital to share its concerns when they identify that a short-stay admission is not appropriate. Referral to the MACs for further review occurs when there is no improvement after a six-month period, the issue persists, and then is eventually referred to the RACs.)

Addressing Compliance Risks

Hospitals can address potential compliance risks through a variety of data analysis as well as process assessment and education.

Assess the UR Function

The UR function should undergo an assessment and evaluation of policies and procedures, as well as compliance with the CoPs. These are best practice to identify opportunities to improve organizational oversight, standardize processes, improve training, and create a feedback mechanism to the UR and PA leaders. Frequently, quick wins are to address appropriate patient status and adhering to the two-midnight rule. Monitoring of denials and observation rates can identify concerns in the UR process.

Educate Physicians

An effective UR process uses internal and external data to ensure physicians are aware of their responsibilities with respect to appropriate documentation and to prioritizing updates and guidance of the two-midnight rule to routinely educate physicians on applicability to patient services.

Robust Monitoring Activities to Ensure Compliance Processes

Several areas of focus for monitoring activities can include some of the following:

- Observation to inpatient ratio can give insight to how well an organization is performing.
- Benchmarking the number of patient admissions that did not undergo a first-level review by UR and PA.
- Length-of-stay reviews with an additional component for outliers.
- Condition Code 44 rates can sometimes indicate physicians placing orders for incorrect status.

Use Tools to Evaluate Medical Necessity

Use national coverage determinations, local coverage determinations, CMS Internet-only manuals, clinical screening tools (MCG and InterQual), industry best practices, and clinical practice standards as tools to evaluate medical necessity.

Denial Analysis

Most CMS denials are based on the lack of documentation for reasonable and medically necessary inpatient admissions. Ongoing review of the various categories of denials include:

- Short inpatient stays (fewer than two midnights).
- Inpatient stays that are not medically necessary due to unreasonable care delays.
- Three-midnights-long inpatient admission that are transferred to a skilled nursing facility. (Is there significant volume, and were these admissions reviewed by UR?)
- Observation services longer than 48 hours (can assist the hospital in identifying areas to focus UR efforts).

Provide Proper Documentation to Avoid QIO/MAC/RAC Audits

Physicians and hospitals are at risk of being audited, or even sanctioned, by Medicare if they file claims for inpatient care when Medicare's criteria are not met. Documenting a reasonable and legitimate expected length of stay of at least two days and identifying the clinical basis for it will substantiate the medical necessity of the inpatient care provided.

Monitor for Cloning/Overdocumentation

The implementation of electronic medical records (EMRs) and the use of templates, check-off boxes for provider documentation, and the ease with which to incorporate documentation from other areas of the record have introduced problems associated with cloning and over-documentation of provider notes. The volume of documentation should never be the primary reason upon which a specific level of care is assigned and/or billed.

Possible Penalties

Sanctions can be imposed by the government related to noncompliance, which can range from education requirements to corrective action plans to expulsion from governmental programs. These penalties include:

- Referral to the recovery audit program to conduct patient status reviews for those providers referred by the QIO for persistent noncompliance with Medicare payment policies, including, but not limited to, consistently failing to adhere to the two-midnight rule or failing to improve their performance after a QIO educational intervention.
- Exclusion from governmental healthcare programs for not meeting the Conditions of Participation.

Compliance Resources

Centers for Medicare & Medicaid Services

The CMS manuals are available on the CMS website and can be located under the Internet-only manuals, which are a replica of the official agency copies. The manuals are available to the general public and contain a wealth of information on Medicare and Medicaid. In addition, the manuals contain CMS's program memoranda, policies and procedures, and day-to-day operating instructions derived from regulations, statutes, guidelines, and directives. They provide direction for administration of CMS programs to providers, state surveyors, contractors, various program components, and Medicare Advantage programs.

https://www.cms.gov/Regulations-and-Guidance/Guidance/Manuals/
Internet-Only-Manuals-IOMs

Medicare Benefit Policy Manual
The *Medicare Benefit Policy Manual* provides details relating to the types of services covered by Medicare within various care settings and outlines requirements needed for coverage.

https://www.cms.gov/Regulations-and-Guidance/Guidance/Manuals/
Internet-Only-Manuals-IOMs-Items/CMS012673

Medicare Claims Processing Manual
The *Medicare Claims Processing Manual* outlines specific billing requirements and payment methodologies for various care settings. In addition, the manual details claims processing requirements.

https://www.cms.gov/Regulations-and-Guidance/Guidance/Manuals/
Internet-Only-Manuals-IOMs-Items/CMS018912

Conditions of Participation

The CMS conditions that healthcare organizations must meet in order to begin and continue participating in the Medicare and Medicaid programs.

https://www.cms.gov/Regulations-and-Guidance/Legislation/CFCsAndCoPs

MCG Care Guidelines

The MCG Care Guidelines provide access to evidenced-based knowledge and best practices across care settings to assist facilities in care coordination and decision-making on patient settings.

https://www.mcg.com/care-guidelines/care-guidelines/

InterQual

InterQual are level of care criteria that assist healthcare providers with decision-making of the most clinically appropriate patient care level based on the clinical condition.

https://www.changehealthcare.com/solutions/clinical-decision-support/interqual

---

Risk Takeaways

Main points of interest:
- The Medicare Conditions of Participation require hospitals to have a utilization review program responsible for ensuring the hospital is providing medical necessary healthcare services.
- Medical necessity for healthcare services is evidenced through documentation and is determined by the physician's clinical assessment and determination of the clinical course of treatment.

Areas to watch:
- Increase in medical necessity denials and the type of denial
- Percent of patients receiving observation services longer than 48 hours
- Condition Code 44 rates
- Observation/inpatient admission ratio
- Number of observation and inpatient admissions without first-level screening by UR/PA
- CMS Targeted Probe and Educate (TPE) program results

Laws that apply:

All healthcare services must be reasonable and medical necessary to be reimbursed under the Medicare and Medicaid programs. Specific determination of the appropriate level of care provided to a patient, hospitals must comply with the following:

- Title XVIII of Social Security Act § 1862(a)(1)(A)
- NOTICE Act, H.R. 876
- Condition of participation: Utilization review, 42 C.F.R. § 482.30
- Two-Midnight Rule Coordination and Improvement Act of 2014, S. 2082, 113th Cong., Final Rule CMS-1599-F

Addressing compliance risks:

- Continuously assess the UR function to improve processes.
- Educate physicians.
- Implement a robust monitoring program that includes denial analysis, key metrics, and education.
- Provide proper documentation to avoid QIO/MAC/RAC audits.
- Utilize tools to evaluate medical necessity.
- Monitor for cloning/overdocumentation.

Endnotes

1. **Donna Abbondandolo** is the Chief Compliance Officer at Bon Secours Mercy Health. As a healthcare compliance professional, she brings more than 30 years of experience in the healthcare industry, serving in various compliance and leadership roles. Prior to joining Bon Secours Mercy Health, Abbondandolo served in compliance leadership positions for several large healthcare networks in New York. She also served as Program Director for the health information management bachelor's degree program and adjunct faculty for Long Island University, C.W. Post, holding this role for nine years. She has a master of business administration in finance degree from Hofstra University and a bachelor of science in health information management from Long Island University, C.W. Post. She has participated in national and state initiatives relative to healthcare compliance, privacy, reimbursement, and certification standard setting processes. Abbondandolo also serves on the editorial board for *Compliance Today* magazine.

2. 42 U.S.C. §§ 301–1305.

3. 42 U.S.C. § 1395y.

4. 42 C.F.R. § 482.30

5. "Acute Inpatient PPS," Centers for Medicare & Medicaid Services, updated February 20, 2020, https://www.cms.gov/Medicare/Medicare-Fee-for-Service-Payment/AcuteInpatientPPS.

6. "Hospital Outpatient PPS," Centers for Medicare & Medicaid Services, updated February 24, 2021, https://www.cms.gov/Medicare/Medicare-Fee-for-Service-Payment/HospitalOutpatientPPS.

7. Medicare Program; Hospital Inpatient Prospective Payment Systems for Acute Care Hospitals and the LongTerm Care Hospital Prospective Payment System and Policy Changes and Fiscal Year 2019 Rates; Quality Reporting Requirements for Specific Providers; Medicare and Medicaid Electronic Health Record (EHR) Incentive Programs (Promoting Interoperability Programs) Requirements for Eligible Hospitals, Critical Access Hospitals, and Eligible Professionals; Medicare Cost Reporting Requirements; and Physician Certification and Recertification of Claims, 83 Fed. Reg. 41,144 (August 17, 2018), https://www.govinfo.gov/content/pkg/FR-2018-08-17/pdf/2018-16766.pdf.

8. Medicare Program; Hospital Inpatient Prospective Payment Systems for Acute Care Hospitals and the LongTerm Care Hospital Prospective Payment System and Policy Changes and Fiscal Year 2019 Rates; Quality Reporting Requirements for Specific Providers; Medicare and Medicaid Electronic Health Record (EHR) Incentive Programs (Promoting Interoperability Programs) Requirements for Eligible Hospitals, Critical Access Hospitals, and Eligible Professionals; Medicare Cost Reporting Requirements; and Physician Certification and Recertification of Claims, 83 Fed. Reg. 41,507.

9. 42 C.F.R. § 482.30(b).

10. Centers for Medicare & Medicaid Services, "Chapter 1: General Billing Requirements," § 50.3, *Medicare Claims Processing Manual*, Pub. 100-04, revised July 31, 2020, https://www.cms.gov/Regulations-and-Guidance/Guidance/Manuals/Downloads/clm104c01.pdf

11. 42 C.F.R. § 482.30(d)(2).

12. Centers for Medicare & Medicaid Services, "Chapter 6: Hospital Services Covered Under Part B," § 20.5.3, *Medicare Benefit Policy Manual*, Pub. 100-02, revised December 31, 2020, https://www.cms.gov/Regulations-and-Guidance/Guidance/Manuals/Downloads/bp102c06.pdf.

13. Two-Midnight Rule Coordination and Improvement Act of 2014, S. 2082, 113th Cong. (2014).

14. Notice of Observation Treatment and Implication for Care Eligibility Act, Pub. L. No. 114-42, 129 Stat. 468 (August 6, 2015).

15. 42 C.F.R. § 482.30.

16. 42 U.S.C. § 1395y.

17. Notice of Observation Treatment and Implication for Care Eligibility Act, Pub. L. 114-42 129 Stat. 468 (August 6, 2015).

18. 42 C.F.R. § 482.30(c).

19. Medicare Program; Hospital Inpatient Prospective Payment Systems for Acute Care Hospitals and the Long-Term Care Hospital Prospective Payment System and Fiscal Year 2014 Rates; Quality Reporting Requirements for Specific Providers; Hospital Conditions of Participation; Payment Policies Related to Patient Status, 78 Fed. Reg. 50,596 (August 19, 2013), https://www.federalregister.gov/documents/2013/08/19/2013-18956/medicare-program-hospital-inpatient-prospective-payment-systems-for-acute-care-hospitals-and-the.

20. Centers for Medicare & Medicaid Services, "Chapter 3: Verifying Potential Errors and Taking Corrective Actions," § 3.2.3, *Medicare Program Integrity Manual*, Pub. 100-08, revised October 2, 2020, https://www.cms.gov/Regulations-and-Guidance/Guidance/Manuals/Downloads/pim83c03.pdf.

Rehab

By Nancy J. Beckley,[1] MS, MBA, CHC

What Is Rehab?

Rehab is an enigma—it's both a program and a service offering. It is more popularly described as therapy, or more specifically as physical therapy (PT), occupational therapy (OT), or speech-language pathology (SLP). How this therapy is delivered, billed for, and paid for is described in U.S. Statute; U.S. Code of Federal Regulations (C.F.R.); Centers for Medicare & Medicaid Services (CMS) policy manuals, including the *Benefit Policy Manual* and *Claims Processing Manual*; as well as in Medicare national coverage determinations (NCDs) and local coverage determinations (LCDs).[2] Risk identification, risk assessment, and risk mitigation spin on the specific single disciplinary or multidisciplinary rehab service or program.

What are the major areas of therapy, and how are they delivered? Table 1 shows Medicare venues and payment, including the type of rehab service delivery venue, the Medicare category, and the applicable Medicare payment methodology. The final column contains information from the October 2020 Medicare Payment Advisory Commission (MedPAC) *Payment Basics* fact sheets (per program) that give context to the complexity of Medicare rules, regulations, and payment criteria, and therefore the complexity of compliance risk across the therapy and rehabilitation spectrum.

Chart 1: Medicare Venues and Payment

Rehab Service Delivery Venue	Medicare Category	Medicare Payment Methodology	MedPAC *Payment Basics* Fact Sheet
Acute care hospital	Inpatient, outpatient	**Inpatient:** Prospective payment system (PPS) **Observation:** Physician fee schedule[3] **Outpatient:** Physician fee schedule	Hospital acute inpatient services payment system[4]
Critical access hospital (CAH)	Inpatient, outpatient	CAH cost-based	Critical access hospitals payment system[5]
Inpatient rehabilitation facility (IRF)	Inpatient, outpatient	**Inpatient:** PPS **Outpatient:** Physician fee schedule	Inpatient rehabilitation facilities payment system[6]
Long-term care hospital	Inpatient, outpatient	**Inpatient:** PPS **Outpatient:** Physician fee schedule	
Home health agency (HHA)	Patient-driven grouping models (PDGM), outpatient	**Home health episode:** PDGM **Outpatient:** Physician fee schedule	Home health care services payment system[7]
Skilled nursing facility (SNF)	Patient-driven payment model (PDPM), outpatient	**Skilled nursing Part A episode:** PDPM **Outpatient:** Physician fee schedule	Skilled nursing facility payment system[8]

Chart 1: Medicare Venues and Payment (cont.)

Rehab Service Delivery Venue	Medicare Category	Medicare Payment Methodology	MedPAC *Payment Basics* Fact Sheet
Comprehensive outpatient rehabilitation facility (CORF)	Outpatient, Part A provider	**Outpatient:** Physician fee schedule	Outpatient therapy services payment system[9]
Rehabilitation agency, also known as rehab agency (RA), outpatient physical therapy (OPT), or outpatient rehab facility (ORF)	Outpatient, Part A provider	**Outpatient:** Physician fee schedule	Outpatient therapy services payment system
Private practice, including group, PT-OT group, also known as physical therapist in private practice (PTPP), occupational therapist in private practice (OTPP), or speech-language pathologist in private practice (SLPPP)	Outpatient, Part B Supplier	**Outpatient:** Physician fee schedule	Outpatient therapy services payment system
Physician practice	Outpatient, Part B supplier	**Outpatient:** Physician fee schedule	Physician and other health professional payment system[10]

All therapy venues, in general, provide outpatient therapy, or at least have the ability to provide outpatient therapy. Outpatient therapy is paid under the physician fee schedule, with the exception of critical access hospitals, which are paid on the basis of cost.[11] Documentation, coding, and billing guidance for outpatient therapy is provided by CMS in the *Medicare Benefit Policy Manual* (MBPM) and the *Medicare Claims Processing Manual* (MCPM).[12][13] Guidance in the MBPM and the MCPM discuss the presence of varying regulations, such as supervision requirements, provision of maintenance therapy, or statutory requirements or limitations.

Many identified compliance risks associated with therapy programs and/or therapy services are universal to all providers of therapy programs and services, such as:

- Therapy is not medically necessary
- Billing for therapy not provided
- Lacking required certifications
- Not meeting supervision requirements

- Misrepresenting time (therapy minutes) to obtain higher reimbursement

Likewise, compliance risks that would be identified for outpatient therapy programs and services are often universal risks, such as:

- Compliance with the Health Insurance Portability and Accountability Act Privacy, Security, and/or Breach Notification rules
- Updating Medicare enrollment records as required
- Medical director contracts and agreements
- Excluded providers and entities
- Offering free or discounted services to induce referrals

This article will focus on compliance risks from the viewpoint of outpatient therapy programs and services, including physical therapy, occupational therapy, and speech language pathology.

Risk Area Governance

Outpatient therapy providers and services are not governed under a single law or regulation—as noted before, therapy is both a program and a service. Providers are often confused in the process of determining applicable governance. The relevant areas of governance are found in applicable Conditions for Participation for hospitals, skilled nursing facilities, home health agencies, rehabilitation agencies, and CORFs, as well as in applicable conditions for coverage and conditions for payment.

Other laws and regulations that govern risk include the following.

False Claims Act, 31 U.S.C. §§ 3729–3733

Submitting claims for therapy not provided, upcoding to receive higher reimbursement, duplicate billing, and therapy that is not medically necessary may constitute the submission of a false claim. In therapy practices, there are many examples of whistleblowers who are often ex-business partners, competitors, or staff members. Whistleblowers may receive up to 30% of any False Claims Act settlement.[14]

Anti-Kickback Statute, 42 U.S.C. § 1320a–7b(b)

The Anti-Kickback Statute (AKS) prohibits asking for or receiving anything of value in exchange for the referral of federal healthcare program (Medicare, Medicaid) business. The AKS applies to both payers and recipients. Asking for or offering a kickback could violate the AKS. A routine waiver of patient copayments could be considered a violation of the AKS.

Offering a physician a medical director position in exchange for referrals may be considered a violation of the AKS.[15]

Civil Monetary Penalties Law, 42 U.S.C. § 1320a–7a

The Office of Inspector General (OIG) may seek civil monetary penalties for a wide variety of abusive conduct, such as failing to report and turn an overpayment.[16]

Exclusion Statute, 42 U.S.C. § 1320a–7

Under its exclusion authorities, the OIG may exclude providers and others from participation in federal healthcare programs. Mandatory exclusions are imposed on the basis of certain criminal convictions, and permissive exclusions are based on sanctions by other agencies, such as the applicable state licensing board.[17]

Physician Self-Referral Law (Stark Law), 42 U.S.C. § 1395nn

The Stark Law is a "strict liability" statute. The Stark Law limits physician referrals in instances where the physician has a financial relationship with an entity. PTs, OTs, and SLPs are included in the in-office ancillary exception to Stark.[18]

Mandatory Claims Submission, 42 U.S.C. § 1395w-4; *Medicare Claims Processing Manual*, Chapter 1, Section 70.8.8

As suppliers that are not eligible to opt out, physical therapists, occupational therapists, and speech-language pathologists must comply with mandatory claims submission.[19] [20]

Professional State Practice Acts

State practice acts provide additional laws and regulations regarding the practice of physical therapy, occupational therapy, and speech-language therapy. In instances where rules are stricter than Medicare, the stricter rules apply. Relevant state practice acts should be reviewed and assessed for compliance risk. Relevant state practice acts for:

- Physical therapy's are at the **Federation of State Boards of Physical Therapy**: https://www.fsbpt.org/Free-Resources/Licensing-Authorities-Contact-Information
- Occupational therapy's are at **American Occupational Therapy Association**: https://www.aota.org/Advocacy-Policy/State-Policy/Licensure/StateRegs.aspx
- Speech-language pathology's are at **American Speech-Language-Hearing Association**: https://www.asha.org/advocacy/state/

Telehealth and Telehealth Waivers

During the COVID-19 public health emergency, CMS has issued a number of waivers related to the provision of telehealth, including expansion of telehealth capability to PT, OT, and SLP who are not recognized as telehealth providers. Provider risks include compliance with telehealth waivers and applicability to private practice settings and institutional settings, including documentation, coding, and billing. Providers are cautioned to keep up to date on state practice acts regarding telehealth, as well as CMS waiver updates.[21]

Common Compliance Risks

Risks in therapy are around every corner. However, CMS guidance in the MBPM and MCPM provides insight into risk areas within their respective sections on "Conditions of Coverage" and "Conditions for Payment."[22][23] Various sections include relevant citations to the C.F.R. and to the statute. These manuals offer a process for understanding the basis of the risk, and the C.F.R. and/or statute provide the underlying regulator and/or law. For Part A providers, the respective Conditions of Participation and Interpretive Guidelines for Rehabilitation Agencies and Comprehensive Outpatient Rehabilitation Facilities (CORF) are ready reference points for assessing compliance risk.[24][25] Some common compliance risks for outpatient therapy follow.

Plan of Care Certification

Providers must certify the plan of care on a timely basis or meet the qualifications for delayed certification. They must meet CMS signature requirements, including date of certification.

Therapy Minutes Calculations

The daily note must contain information to support the billing of therapy codes by the use of two tallies:

1. Total of timed code treatment minutes
2. Total treatment time, including time code treatment minutes and untimed code treatment minutes

Unqualified Personnel

Therapy must be provided by qualified personnel. Per CMS, a qualified professional is a "physical therapist, occupational therapist, speech-language pathologist, physician, nurse practitioner, clinical nurse specialist, or physician's assistant, who is licensed or certified by the state to furnish therapy services, and who also may appropriately furnish therapy services under Medicare policies. Qualified professional may also include a physical therapist assistant (PTA) or an occupational therapy assistant (OTA) when furnishing services under the supervision of a qualified therapist, who is working within the state scope of practice in the state in which the services are furnished. Assistants are limited in the services they may furnish . . . and may not supervise other therapy caregivers."[26]

Group Therapy vs. Individual Therapy

Corporate integrity agreements/integrity agreements (and their underlying whistleblower complaints) are often the result of billing for therapy as if it was provided on a one-on-one basis as described in the applicable Current Procedural Terminology (CPT) code, when in fact the therapy was provided in a group setting.[27] CMS has provided guidance on group therapy vs. individual therapy since 2002 in "11 Part B Billing Scenarios for PTs and OTs."[28]

Coding for Dry Needling

Beginning in 2020, there are new "dry needling codes" (CPT 20560 and CPT 20561) describing needle insertions without injections. Medicare has listed these codes as nonpayable. A voluntary advance beneficiary notice (ABN) may be issued to the beneficiary to indicate noncoverage.[29]

Therapy Evaluation Coding and Documentation Requirement

CMS documentation specifies what is required for the therapy evaluation and plan of care. New physical therapy and occupational therapy CPT codes for evaluation were put in place in 2018. For both physical and occupational therapy, the single evaluation code was replaced with three evaluation codes based on level of evaluation complexity: low, moderate, or high. CMS has not differentiated payment for the respective complexity codes for physical therapy or occupational therapy evaluation. Therapists should accurately reflect the level of evaluation complexity regardless of payment.[30]

Aquatic Therapy and Use of Community Pools

CMS policy allows for aquatic therapy to be provided at community pools.[31] The therapy practice must enter into an agreement with the community pool. However, CMS differentiates between the requirements for private practice (enrolled as a supplier under Medicare) and a rehab agency (enrolled as a provider under Medicare). If a physical therapist assistant or occupational therapy assistant is providing the aquatic therapy, service supervision rules apply. In private practice, direct supervision is required. In a rehab agency, general supervision is required.

Therapy Assistant Supervision

Physical therapist assistants and occupational therapy assistants provide services under the direction and supervision of the physical therapist and occupational therapist. Services provided in private practice by the assistant are billed under the national provider identifier (NPI) of the supervising therapist, who is present in the clinic and providing direct supervision. In all other settings, general supervision requirements are applicable, unless the relevant state practice act requires more stringent supervision.

Therapy Assistants Coding and Billing

Beginning in 2020, CMS required the use of a modifier to be appended to the claim line for professional and institutional claims for services that were provided in whole or in part by a physical therapist assistant or occupational therapist assistant.

Opt-Out Affidavits and Private Contracts

Physical therapists, occupational therapists, and speech-language pathologists are not among the allowed opt-out providers, and therefore cannot file an opt-out affidavit, nor enter into a private contract with Medicare beneficiaries.

Incident-to Therapy in Physician Offices

Therapy provided in a physician's office is subject to compliance with the Stark Law in-office ancillary exception and must be provided by a PT, OT, or SLP. A PTA or an OTA may not provide incident-to therapy as physician services. If a PT or OT is enrolled in a physician group practice and has reassigned benefits to the practice, a PTA or an OTA may provide services under the direct supervision of the PT or OT.[32]

Free Services, Discounted Services, and Hardship Waivers

The federal AKS does not prohibit the provision of free or discounted services. Discounted and free services should be based on a consistent application of a financial hardship policy.

Renting from a Referring Physician

OIG issued a special fraud alert specifically to address the "Rental of Space in Physician Offices by Persons or Entities to Which Physicians Refer."[33]

Relationships with Referring Physicians

The CMS CORF conditions of participation require the services of a physician related to the CORF program oversight and quality. The rehab agency conditions of participation require a physician (who refers to the rehab agency) to participate as a member of the committee that annually reviews policies and procedures. There are no CMS-imposed requirements for physician participation in a physical or occupational therapy practice.

Therapy Practice Enrolled as Medicare DME Supplier

PTs and OTs in private practice may choose to enroll in Medicare as a durable medical equipment (DME) supplier via the National Supplier Clearinghouse.[34] Several exemptions related to surety bonds and accreditation apply for therapists. These exceptions should be reviewed prior to application, as well as any state regulations limiting the ability of a physical therapist and/or occupational therapists from fabricating orthoses.[35]

When assessing compliance risk and governing laws and regulations, providers are encouraged to seek the guidance of competent legal counsel to ensure proper review and application.

Addressing Compliance Risks

Compliance Risk Assessment

The first step in assessing compliance risk is conducting a risk assessment on an annual, or as-needed, basis. Therapy providers should look to assess risks in therapy at the national level (Medicare regulations and policy pertaining to therapy, OIG audit reports, OIG corporate integrity/integrity agreements, OIG exclusions, OIG self-disclosures); the regional level (the relevant Medicare administrative contractors (MAC) and TRICARE contractor resources, MAC and recovery audit contractors (RAC) posted review topics for therapy); and the state level (Medicaid program, practice acts).

Establish Compliance Program

- Establish policies and procedures specific to compliance.
- Identify and apply existing policies and procedures in compliance.
- Identify and implement additional compliance policies.

Compliance Program Oversight

- Establish a compliance charter.
- Establish oversight function (committee or officer).

Screening & Evaluation

- Establish a process to query exclusions lists, including the OIG's List of Excluded Individuals and Entities (LEIE).
- Review relevant Medicaid exclusion lists that are not reported to the OIG LEIE, such as the California's Medi-Cal Suspended and Ineligible Provider List.[36]
- Verify professional licenses of staff or job applicants per the state licensing authority.

Communication, Education, and Training

- Implement new employee and annual compliance training specific to rehab to prevent fraud, waste, and abuse. Use "A Roadmap for New Physicians: Avoiding Medicare and Medicaid Fraud and Abuse" as a training model.[37]
- Conduct annual compliance training specific to rehab to address high-risk areas, including documentation, coding, and billing. Use CMS therapy policies and MAC local coverage determination in the training materials.[38][39]
- Customize compliance training related to rehab for the marketing and sales force.

Monitoring, Auditing, and Reporting

- Routinely review OIG cases, audit reports, corporate integrity agreements, settlement agreements, and self-disclosures to determine areas of identified therapy risk.
- Review MAC published results of Targeted Probe and Educate related to identified therapy denials (e.g., plan of care was not certified) and replicate internal audit of topics.

Discipline for Noncompliance

- Establish and communicate discipline for noncompliance.
- Implement disciplinary process for noncompliance.

Investigations and Remedial Measures

- Create a cycle of "prevent, detect, correct." Actively refund overpayments as result of chart reviews or from other overpayment identification methods.

Possible Penalties

Sanctions imposed related to noncompliance can range from corrective action plans to financial penalties to expulsion from the Medicare program. These include, but may not be limited to, the following.

Pre-payment or Post-payment Review

As a result of an audit finding, the Medicare administrative contactor may require that all claims be reviewed prior to payments. Alternatively, the Medicare administrative contractor may require additional rounds of post-payment review until the provider error rates drops to an acceptable level as identified by the Medicare administrative contractor.

Repayment

As a result of an audit finding as appropriate, the provider should identify and refund overpayments to which they are not entitled.

Self-Disclosure

As a result of an audit finding a provider may opt to self-disclose to either CMS or the OIG using their respective self-disclosure protocols.

Involuntary Termination of Medicare Enrollment

In certain circumstances, CMS will elect to terminate providers from participation as a Medicare supplier or provider. Termination legal notices are published to the CMS website's "Termination Notices" page.[40]

Settlement Agreement

A settlement agreement resolves False Claims Act cases in which the "government alleges fraudulent conduct and the settling parties do not admit liability."[41]

Integrity Agreement or Corporate Integrity Agreement

OIG negotiates integrity agreements and corporate integrity agreements with healthcare providers (and other entities) as part of the "settlement of Federal health care program investigations arising under a variety of civil false claims statutes."[42]

Exclusion under the OIG Exclusion Authorities for Mandatory or Permissive Exclusions

Mandatory exclusions include those convicted of program-related crimes, patient abuse, or neglect. Permissive exclusions include license revocation, suspension, or surrender or conviction relating to obstruction of an investigation or audit. The OIG exclusion authorities are described in further detail on the OIG website.[43]

Compliance Resources

Centers for Medicare & Medicaid Services

Medicare Benefits Policy Manual
Chapter 12: Comprehensive Outpatient Rehabilitation Facility (CORF) Coverage

This chapter is specific to CORFs and provides additional CMS guidance on coverage of services to include CORF required and optional services, rules for provision and payment of CORF services, and services that are covered as a CORF benefit.

https://www.cms.gov/Regulations-and-Guidance/Guidance/Manuals/Downloads/bp102c12.pdf

Chapter 15: Covered Medical and Other Health Services

This chapter identifies and specifies requirements for outpatient therapy, including requirements for each therapy documentation note (evaluation, plan of care, daily encounter note, progress report, and discharge report). Also specified are plan-of-care certification and delayed certification requirements.

https://www.cms.gov/Regulations-and-Guidance/Guidance/Manuals/Downloads/bp102c15.pdf

Medicare Claims Processing Manual
Chapter 5: Part B Outpatient Rehabilitation and CORF/OPT Services

This chapter provides information on therapy financial limitations, special claims processing rules, specific Healthcare Common Procedure Coding System (HCPCS) coding requirements, and special rules for services in CORFs.

https://www.cms.gov/Regulations-and-Guidance/Guidance/Manuals/Downloads/clm104c05.pdf

11 Part B Billing Scenarios for PTs and OTs (Individual vs. Group Treatment)

This is an essential document to understand CMS requirements for coding and billing for therapy services using the Medicare eight-minute rule. The document provides various scenarios for the tally of minutes and their apportionment to codes that are submitted on claims. This document also provides guidance on the difference between individual therapy and group therapy.

https://www.cms.gov/Medicare/Billing/TherapyServices/billing_scenarios

Annual Therapy Update
This CMS reference page provides a historical listing (on an annual basis) of codes indicating whether they are "sometimes or always therapy services."

https://www.cms.gov/Medicare/Billing/TherapyServices/AnnualTherapyUpdate

Medicare Learning Network
Outpatient Rehabilitation Therapy Services: Complying with Documentation Requirements
This *MLN Booklet* spells out common therapy errors identified in the Comprehensive Error Rate Testing (CERT)program. For error identified, there is a corresponding "prevention" tip. This MLN article also provides a summary listing of therapy documentation, coding and billing requirements, and links to CMS therapy references and resources.

https://www.cms.gov/Outreach-and-Education/Medicare-Learning-Network-MLN/MLNProducts/Downloads/OutptRehabTherapy-Booklet-MLN905365.pdf

Complying with Medicare Signature Requirements
This resource provides guidance on CMS acceptable signatures. For therapy documentation, this includes all therapy notes, as well as the physician certification on the plan of care.

https://www.cms.gov/Outreach-and-Education/Medicare-Learning-Network-MLN/MLNProducts/downloads/signature_requirements_fact_sheet_icn905364.pdf

Jimmo Settlement (Maintenance Therapy)
As a result of the Jimmo v. Sebelius settlement agreement, CMS was required to notify contractors of the coverage requirements for maintenance therapy. This CMS page provides additional resources for the therapy provider to understand maintenance therapy and how to document the medical necessity of maintenance therapy vs. rehabilitative therapy.

https://www.cms.gov/Center/Special-Topic/Jimmo-Center

U.S. Department of Health & Human Services, Office of Inspector General

OIG Exclusions Database, List of Excluded Individuals and Entities (LEIE)
The OIG exclusions database can be queried for up to five individuals or five groups at a time. This database is updated on a monthly basis, so the OIG recommends that providers access it on a monthly basis. The database may also be downloaded for matching against a provider list. Larger providers may choose to contact with a vendor providing exclusion searches.

https://oig.hhs.gov/exclusions/

A Roadmap for New Physicians

OIG created a physician education training set to include a booklet for physician self-study, a companion PowerPoint presentation, and speaker notes to the presentation. While specific to physicians, outpatient therapy providers are encouraged to adapt the presentation using therapy language and case study examples.

https://oig.hhs.gov/compliance/physician-education/index.asp

Health Care Compliance Association

Compliance Today

Articles that address various topics of outpatient therapy compliance and risk:

- "Outpatient therapy: Myths and risks"[44]

- "Rehab under review: The devil is in the details"[45]

Private Practice Section of the American Physical Therapy Association

Impact Magazine
- "Dry Needling Codes: Compliance Implications"[46]

- "COVID-19 and Compliance: Resources Hiding in Plain Sight"[47]

MAC	Jurisdictions	LCD #	Title
CGS	J15	L34049	Outpatient physical and occupational therapy services
FCSO	JN	L33413	Therapy and rehabilitation services
NGS	JK, J6	L33631	Outpatient physical and occupational therapy services
Noridian	JE, JF	N/A	Retired
Novitas	JH, JL	L35036	Therapy and rehabilitation services (PT, OT)
Palmetto	JJ, JM	L34428	Outpatient physical therapy
		L34427	Outpatient occupational therapy
WPS	J5, J8	N/A	Retired

Risk Takeaways

Main points of interest:

- Therapy is both a service and a program.
- Outpatient therapy by providers and suppliers is generally subject to the same requirements, with some variance in regulation per provider/program type.
- Outpatient therapy is high risk for documentation, coding, and billing errors.
- Understanding compliance risks is specific to therapy program, provider type, and venue.

Areas to watch:

- Therapy as opt-out providers
- Therapists to be included as telehealth providers
- Delegation, supervision, and coding for assistants

Laws that apply:

- Anti-Kickback Statute, 42 U.S.C. § 1320a-7b(b)
- False Claims Act, 31 U.S.C. §§ 3729–3733
- Exclusion Statute, 42 U.S.C. § 1320a-7
- Civil Monetary Penalties Law, 42 U.S.C. § 1320a-7a
- Physician Self-Referral Law (Stark Law), 42 U.S.C. § 1395nn
- CMS Mandatory Claims Submission, 42 U.S.C. § 1395w-4
- CMS telehealth waivers
- Therapy state practice acts

Addressing compliance risks:

- Conduct a risk assessment assessing outpatient therapy, including specific risks that pivot on provider/supplier type.
- Update risk assessments and audit plans to reflect enforcement trends and audit reports.

Endnotes

1. **Nancy Beckley** is President of Nancy Beckley & Associates LLC. She is certified in healthcare compliance by the HCCA Compliance Certification Board and was among the first in therapy industry to do so. She's worked with more than 125 provider groups in their quest for survey, certification, accreditation, policies and procedures, plan of correction, and certification appeals. Clients include providers under Medicare probe review, progressive corrective action plans, corporate integrity agreements, ZPIC investigations, and RAC audits. Beckley served on the CMS Technical Expert Panel for Comprehensive Outpatient Rehabilitation Facilities (CORF), advising CMS on the opportunities and potential for CORFs from a policy and regulatory perspective.

2. "Welcome to the MCD Search," Medicare Coverage Database, Centers for Medicare & Medicaid Services, accessed February 2, 2021, https://www.cms.gov/medicare-coverage-database/new-search/search.aspx.

3. "Physician Fee Schedule," Centers for Medicare & Medicaid Services, updated January 7, 2021, https://www.cms.gov/Medicare/Medicare-Fee-for-Service-Payment/PhysicianFeeSched.

4. "Hospital Acute Inpatient Services Payment System," *Payment Basics*, MedPAC, October 2020, http://www.medpac.gov/docs/default-source/payment-basics/medpac_payment_basics_20_hospital_final_sec.pdf.

5. "Critical Access Hospitals Payment System," *Payment Basics*, MedPAC, October 2020, http://www.medpac.gov/docs/default-source/payment-basics/medpac_payment_basics_20_cah_final_sec.pdf.

6. "Inpatient Rehabilitation Facilities Payment System," *Payment Basics*, MedPAC, October 2020, http://www.medpac.gov/docs/default-source/payment-basics/medpac_payment_basics_20_irf_final_sec.pdf.

7. "Home Health Care Services Payment System," *Payment Basics*, MedPAC, October 2020, http://www.medpac.gov/docs/default-source/payment-basics/medpac_payment_basics_20_hha_final_sec.pdf.

8. "Skilled Nursing Facility Services Payment System," *Payment Basics*, MedPAC, October 2020, http://www.medpac.gov/docs/default-source/payment-basics/medpac_payment_basics_20_snf_final_sec.pdf.

9. "Outpatient Therapy Services Payment System," *Payment Basics*, MedPAC, October 2020, http://www.medpac.gov/docs/default-source/payment-basics/medpac_payment_basics_20_opt_final_sec.pdf.

10. "Physician and Other Health Professional Payment System," *Payment Basics*, MedPAC, October 2020, http://www.medpac.gov/docs/default-source/payment-basics/medpac_payment_basics_20_physician_final_sec.pdf.

11. "Physician Fee Schedule," Centers for Medicare & Medicaid Services.

12. Centers for Medicare & Medicaid Services, *Medicare Benefits Processing Policy Manual*, Pub. 100-02, https://www.cms.gov/Regulations-and-Guidance/Guidance/Manuals/Internet-Only-Manuals-IOMs-Items/CMS012673. .

13. Centers for Medicare & Medicaid Services, *Medicare Claims Processing Manual*, Pub. 100-04, https://www.cms.gov/Regulations-and-Guidance/Guidance/Manuals/Internet-Only-Manuals-IOMs-Items/CMS018912.

14. 31 U.S.C. §§ 3729–3733.

15. 42 U.S.C. § 1320a-7b(b).

16. 42 U.S.C. § 1320a-7a.

17. 42 U.S.C. § 1320a-7.

18. 42 U.S.C. § 1395nn.

19. Centers for Medicare & Medicaid Services, "Chapter 1 – Ge: General Billing Requirements," § 70.8.8, *Medicare Claims Processing Manual*, Pub. 100-04, revised July 31, 2020, https://www.cms.gov/Regulations-and-Guidance/Guidance/Manuals/Downloads/clm104c01.pdf. .

20. 42 U.S.C §§ 1395w-4, 1848(g)(4)(A).

21. "Physicians and Other Clinicians: CMS Flexibilities to Fight COVID-19," Centers for Medicare & Medicaid Services, January 28, 2021, https://www.cms.gov/files/document/covid-19-physicians-and-practitioners.pdf.

22. Centers for Medicare & Medicaid Services, *Medicare Claims Processing Manual.*, Pub. 100-04, https://www.cms.gov/Regulations-and-Guidance/Guidance/Manuals/Internet-Only-Manuals-IOMs-Items/CMS018912.

23. Centers for Medicare & Medicaid Services, *Medicare Benefits Processing Policy Manual*, Pub. 100-02, https://www.cms.gov/Regulations-and-Guidance/Guidance/Manuals/Internet-Only-Manuals-IOMs-Items/CMS012673.

24. Centers for Medicare & Medicaid Services, "Appendix E - Guidance to Surveyors: Outpatient Physical Therapy or Speech Pathology Services," *State Operations Manual*, Pub. 100-07, revised July 25, 2014, https://www.cms.gov/Regulations-and-Guidance/Guidance/Manuals/downloads/som107ap_e_opt.pdf.

25. Centers for Medicare & Medicaid Services, "Appendix K - Guidance to Surveyors: Comprehensive Outpatient Rehabilitation Facilities," *State Operations Manual*, Pub. 100-07, revised February 21, 2020, https://www.cms.gov/Regulations-and-Guidance/Guidance/Manuals/downloads/som107ap_k_corf.pdf.

26. Centers for Medicare & Medicaid Services, "Chapter 15 - Covered Medical and Other Health Services," § 220, *Medicare Benefit Policy Manual*, Pub. 100-02, revised August 7, 2020, https://www.cms.gov/Regulations-and-Guidance/Guidance/Manuals/Downloads/bp102c15.pdf.

27. Department of Justice, U.S. Attorney's Office for the District of South Carolina, "Drayer Physical Therapy Institute, LLC Settle False Claims Act Case for $7,000,000," news release, July 5, 2016, https://www.justice.gov/usao-sc/pr/drayer-physical-therapy-institute-llc-settle-false-claims-act-case-7000000.

28. Centers for Medicare & Medicaid Services, "11 Part B Billing Scenarios for PTs and OTs," last reviewed September 2009, https://www.cms.gov/medicare/billing/therapyservices/downloads/11_part_b_billing_scenarios_for_pts_and_ots.pdf.

29. Nancy J. Beckley, "Dry Needling Codes: Compliance Implications," *Impact Magazine*, February 2020, http://www.ppsimpact.org/dry-needling-codes-compliance-implications/.

30. Centers for Medicare & Medicaid Services, "2017 Annual Update to the Therapy Code List," *MLN Matters*, MM9782, November 10, 2016, https://www.cms.gov/Outreach-and-Education/Medicare-Learning-Network-MLN/MLNMattersArticles/downloads/MM9782.pdf.

31. Centers for Medicare & Medicaid Services, "Chapter 15 - Covered Medical and Other Health Services," § 220, *Medicare Benefit Policy Manual*.

32. 42 C.F.R. § 411.355.

33. U.S. Department of Health & Human Services, Office of Inspector General, "Special Fraud Alert: Rental of Space in Physician Offices by Persons or Entities to Which Physicians Refer," February 2000, https://oig.hhs.gov/fraud/docs/alertsandbulletins/office%20space.htm.

34. "National Supplier Clearinghouse MAC," Palmetto GBA, accessed January 29, 2021, https://www.palmettogba.com/nsc.

35. Centers for Medicare & Medicaid Services, "DMEPOS Accreditation," Medicare Learning Network, September 2020, https://www.cms.gov/Outreach-and-Education/Medicare-Learning-Network-MLN/MLNProducts/downloads/DMEPOS_Basics_FactSheet_ICN905710.pdf.

36. "Suspended and Ineligible Provider List," Medi-Cal Providers, California Department of Health Care Services, accessed January 29, 2021, http://bit.ly/3cBmODg.

37. "A Roadmap for New Physicians: Avoiding Medicare and Medicaid Fraud and Abuse," Office of Inspector General, U.S. Department of Health & Human Services, accessed January 29, 2021, https://oig.hhs.gov/compliance/physician-education/index.asp.

38. "Therapy Services," Centers for Medicare & Medicaid Services, updated December 21, 2018, https://www.cms.gov/Medicare/Billing/TherapyServices. .

39. "Local Coverage Determinations (LCDs) by State Index," Medicare Coverage Database, Centers for Medicare & Medicaid Services, accessed January 29, 2021, https://www.cms.gov/medicare-coverage-database/indexes/lcd-state-index.aspx.

40. "Termination Notices," Centers for Medicare & Medicaid Services, last modified January 20, 2021, https://www.cms.gov/Medicare/Provider-Enrollment-and-Certification/SurveyCertificationGenInfo/Termination-Notices.

41. "Fraud Risk Indicator," Office of Inspector General, U.S. Department of Health & Human Services, accessed January 29, 2021, https://oig.hhs.gov/compliance/corporate-integrity-agreements/risk.asp.

42. "Corporate Integrity Agreements," Office of Inspector General, U.S. Department of Health & Human Services, accessed January 29, 2021, https://oig.hhs.gov/compliance/corporate-integrity-agreements/index.asp.

43. "Exclusion Authorities," Office of Inspector General, U.S. Department of Health & Human Services, accessed January 29, 2021, https://oig.hhs.gov/exclusions/authorities.asp.

44. Nancy J. Beckley, "Outpatient therapy: Myths and risks," *Compliance Today*, August 2019, https://compliancecosmos.org/outpatient-therapy-myths-and-risks.

45. Nancy J. Beckley, "Rehab under review: The devil is in the details," *Compliance Today*, August 2017, 68–72, https://compliancecosmos.org/compliance-today-august-2017.

46. Nancy J. Beckley, "Dry Needling Codes: Compliance Implications," *Impact Magazine*, February 2020.

47. Nancy J. Beckley, "COVID-19 and Compliance: Resources Hiding in Plain Sight," *Impact Magazine*, August 2020, http://www.ppsimpact.org/covid-19-and-compliance-resources-hiding-in-plain-sight/.

Telehealth and Telemedicine

By Raul G. Ordonez, CHC; Vice President
& Chief Compliance Officer; Jackson Health System[1]

What are Telehealth and Telemedicine?

The terms "telehealth" and "telemedicine" are commonly used interchangeably, and their definitions may vary depending on the location or jurisdiction where defined. Generally, "telemedicine" refers to the delivery of healthcare whereby the healthcare provider can care for the patient from a remote location through the use of electronic telecommunication. The term "telehealth" commonly has a broader connotation that includes both provider-patient encounters as well as the use of electronic telecommunication for other health-related interactions including provider education, public health, and health administration."[2] For purposes of this article, the terms will be used interchangeably, but with a narrower focus in the context of provider-patient care.

For years, advocates of telehealth have emphasized its ability to expand access to healthcare services not readily available, improve patient convenience and experience, and lower provider costs. Moreover, they have continually predicted that telehealth will feature prominently in the future delivery of healthcare. Meanwhile, consistent with those predictions, the use of telehealth has grown considerably in just a few years with more insurance plans covering telehealth services, more providers offering them, and more states regulating the services in their respective jurisdictions.[3] The predicted growth in telehealth was further intensified by the COVID-19 pandemic. Despite its increasing availability and practice prior to COVID-19, Medicare reimbursement was primarily limited to services for patients located in qualifying rural areas. However, in response to the COVID-19 pandemic, the Centers for Medicare & Medicaid Services (CMS) relaxed a number of the requirements that had been necessary for reimbursement and temporarily expanded the types of telehealth services for which Medicare reimbursement is available.[4] Almost three years after the onset of the public health emergency (PHE), though the permanence of Medicare reimbursement for specific services may still be unclear, there is a general consensus that the pandemic has accelerated the practice of telehealth in a manner that is to some degree irreversible. As stated by then CMS Administrator Seema Verma in 2020, the COVID-19 pandemic has taken telehealth to a new frontier, and, "there's absolutely no going back."[5] The same general sentiment is still present as of the time of this writing.

Correspondingly, the growth in telehealth over the years has resulted in increasing government scrutiny. Even prior to the pandemic in April 2018, when Medicare reimbursement was far more limited, the HHS Office of Inspector General (OIG) already had an interest in telehealth due to its relatively rapid expansion up to that point. At the time, the OIG published its audit findings identifying the failure by providers to meet various Medicare requirements.[6] Subsequently, as a result of the substantial expansion of services during the PHE, the OIG has signaled an even greater interest in telehealth by adding thirteen telehealth-related reviews to its annual work plan since the onset of the pandemic.[7] In addition, there have been a number of large-scale prosecutions by the Department of Justice (DOJ) alleging over $1 billion in fraudulent activity involving telemedicine companies and fraudulent relationships with physicians.[8] Correspondingly, the OIG published a Special Fraud Alert regarding fraudulent contractual arrangements between physicians and telemedicine companies.[9] All in all, there is considerable evidence that telehealth-related noncompliance is a growing government enforcement priority. Given the continued growth of telehealth happening even before and especially during the COVID-19 public health emergency, it is reasonable to expect government enforcement efforts to further intensify.

Risk Area Governance

Medicare and Medicaid Program Integrity Provisions

Social Security Act § 1128J(d)[10]

This law requires that any self-identified Medicare overpayments resulting from incorrect coding, insufficient documentation, and medical necessity errors be returned within 60 days of identification.

Anti-Kickback Statute

42 U.S.C. § 1320a-7(b)[11]

The Statute prohibits offering, paying, soliciting, or receiving anything of value to induce or reward referrals to generate federal healthcare program business.

See article "Anti-Kickback Statute" in Chapter 5 for more information about the law.

The Stark Law

42 U.S.C. § 1395nn[12]

The Stark Law prohibits a physician from referring Medicare patients for designated health services to an entity with which the physician (or physician's immediate family member) has a financial relationship, unless an exception applies.

See article "Physician Self-Referral Law (Stark Law)" in Chapter 5 for more information about the law.

False Claims Act

31 U.S.C. §§ 3729–3733[13]

The False Claims Act prohibits, among other things, (1) the submission of false or fraudulent claims and (2) knowingly making, using, or causing to be made false statements or information to obtain fraudulent claims payment. False Claims Act violations occur when providers knowingly bill for services improperly. In addition, violations of both the Anti-Kickback Statute and the Stark Law as well as the failure to refund overpayments can each result in False Claims Act liability.

See article "False Claims Act" in Chapter 5 for more information about the law.

Health Insurance Portability and Accountability Act (HIPAA)

Pub.L. No. 104-191, 110 Stat. 1938[14]

HIPAA imposes requirements upon "covered entities" including healthcare providers, healthcare plans, and clearinghouses regarding their transmission of protected health information (PHI). PHI is information created or received by the covered entity that identifies an individual and relates to the individual's health or healthcare provision, or payment thereof. Under HIPAA, covered entities must handle PHI as required by the Privacy Rule[15], Security Rule[16], and Breach Notification Rule[17]. Under the Privacy Rule, covered entities can only use and share PHI after obtaining patient authorization unless a specific HIPAA exception applies. The Security Rule requires covered entities to maintain administrative, physical, and technical safeguards to assure the confidentiality, integrity, and availability of the PHI. The Breach Notification Rule requires covered entities to notify the Secretary for Health and Human Services in the event of a breach of unsecured PHI.

See article "Health Insurance Portability and Accountability Act of 1996" in Chapter 5 for more information about the law.

Ryan Haight Act

21 U.S.C. § 829(e)[18]

This act amended the Controlled Substances Act to prohibit the delivering, distribution, or dispensing of a controlled substance by means of the Internet without a valid prescription.[19] This requires that the prescription be issued for a legitimate medical purpose either by a practitioner having conducted at least one in-person medical evaluation or by a covering practitioner. The regulations provide seven telemedicine exceptions to the in-person examination requirement.[20] They include:

- The practice of telemedicine while the patient is being treated by and physically located in a qualifying hospital or clinic.
- The practice of telemedicine while the patient is in the physical presence of a practitioner.
- The practice of telemedicine by a practitioner who is an employee or contractor of the Indian Health Service.
- The practice of telemedicine during a public health emergency as declared by the Secretary of HHS.
- The practice of telemedicine when conducted by a practitioner who has received a special registration from the DEA Administrator.
- The practice of telemedicine that occurs in a Department of Veterans Affairs medical emergency.
- The practice of telemedicine in circumstances specified by DEA regulation.[21]

State Law Equivalents of Anti-Kickback Statute, Stark Law, and False Claims Act

Some states have enacted versions of the federal Anti-Kickback Statute, Stark Law, and False Claims Act. State laws may be broader in scope and apply both to state programs such as Medicaid as well as to claims submitted to commercial payers.[22]

State Licensing, Modality, and Prescribing Laws

States have varying licensing requirements for out-of-state physicians to practice telemedicine.[23] Some states require out-of-state physicians to be licensed where the patient will receive the services, while other states issue special telemedicine licenses.[24] Other states allow out-of-state physicians to perform telehealth follow-up without a state license if the onset of medical services first occurred in a state where the physician is licensed, while yet others do not require licensure when the telehealth physician is in consult with a physician who is licensed in-state.[25] States also differ as to the type of technology that must be utilized to establish a valid doctor-patient relationship (real-time audio-video, interactive audio, or store-and-forward technologies), as well as the treatment standards necessary to prescribe medications.[26]

Common Compliance Risks

Medicare/False Claims Act

The following list consists of common compliance errors that result in a failure to meet Medicare requirements. Medicare reimbursement received in these circumstances constitutes a Medicare overpayment. Failure to return a Medicare overpayment can result in False Claims Act liability.

Beneficiaries receiving services at nonrural originating sites.

Medicare defines the "originating site" as the location where a Medicare beneficiary receives physician or practitioner medical services through a telecommunications system. With few exceptions, in order to receive Medicare reimbursement for telehealth services, the services must occur with an originating site that is either (1) a Health Professional Shortage area that is outside a Metropolitan Statistical Area (MSA) or within a rural census tract of an MSA or (2) a county that is not included in an MSA as of December 31 of the preceding year.[27] The geographic requirement does not apply to patients receiving home dialysis monthly clinical assessment services for end stage renal disease, diagnosis, evaluation, or treatment of symptoms of an acute stroke, and treatment of substance abuse disorder or co-occurring mental health disorder.[28] (Note that as a result of the COVID-19 public health emergency, CMS has temporarily expanded the eligible geographic locations for an originating site to include all geographic areas; the extension of the waiver of the geographic restrictions is set to lapse after December 31, 2024)[29]

Institutional providers ineligible to bill.

Generally, Medicare reimburses the telehealth provider for services, but not institutional facilities. Institutional facilities may only bill Medicare for telehealth services upon two conditions: (1) the facility is a critical access hospital (CAH) that elected the Method II payment option and the practitioner reassigned his or her benefits to the CAH, or (2) the facility provided medical nutrition therapy (MNT) services.[30] When neither of the above conditions are present, the institutional facility is not eligible to bill for telehealth services.

Ineligible distant site practitioners.

To receive Medicare reimbursement, the distant site practitioner who performs the telehealth service must be one of the following: a physician, nurse practitioner (NP), physician assistant (PA), nurse-midwife, clinical nurse specialist (CNS), certified registered nurse anesthetist (CRNA), clinical psychologist (CP), clinical social worker (CSW), or a registered dietitian or nutrition specialist.[31] Telehealth services performed by someone not within one of those categories are not reimbursable. (Note that as a result of the COVID-19 public health emergency, CMS has temporarily expanded the eligible distant site practitioners to include federally qualified health centers, rural health centers, physical therapists, occupational therapists, speech language pathologists and audiologists; the extension of the waiver of eligible distant site practitioners is set to expire after December 31, 2024.)[32]

Beneficiaries receiving services at unauthorized originating sites.

For a provider to receive Medicare reimbursement for telehealth services, the originating site must be one of the following: the office of a practitioner; a hospital; a CAH; a rural health clinic; a federally qualified health center; a hospital-based or CAH-based renal dialysis center; a skilled nursing facility; a community mental health center, a renal dialysis facility; a home beneficiary with end-stage renal disease; a mobile stroke unit; or the home of an individual only for purposes of treatment of a substance use disorder or a co-occurring mental health disorder, furnished on or after July 1, 2019, to an individual with a substance use disorder diagnosis.[33] (Note that as a result of the COVID-19 public health emergency, CMS temporarily expanded eligible originating sites to include any healthcare facility, as well as the patient's home; the extension of the waiver of eligible originating sites is set to expire after December 31, 2024).[34]

Providers using unallowable means of communication.

In general, to bill Medicare, practitioners must provide telehealth services using at a minimum, audio and video equipment permitting two-way, real-time interactive communication between the patient and distant site physician or practitioner.[35] However, providers may use two-way, real time audio-only technology for diagnosis and treatment of a mental health disorder when the distant site physician has the capability to use an audio and visual system but the patient is not capable of, or does not consent to, the use of video technology.[36] There is also an exception for federal telemedicine demonstration programs in Alaska or Hawaii which do allow for asynchronous store-and-forward technology. Nonetheless, a practitioner who utilizes noncompliant technology to perform telehealth services cannot bill Medicare for those services. (Note that in response to the PHE, CMS has provided additional flexibility in reimbursing providers for services not meeting the regulatory standards of real-time audio and video interaction such as audio-only telehealth using telephone, for example. Reimbursement for audio-only telehealth is set to expire on December 31, 2024.)[37]

Practitioner providing a noncovered service.

The list of Medicare reimbursable telehealth services is made available through the annual physician fee schedule rulemaking process. Services provided to a patient that are not included in the annual physician fee schedule are not reimbursable. (Note that CMS has temporarily expanded the list of telehealth covered services in response to the COVID-19 public health emergency.[38] CMS has traditionally reimbursed for two categories of telehealth services. They are Category 1, consisting of services similar to office visits, professional consultations, and office psychiatry services currently on the list of telehealth services and Category 2, consisting of services not similar to the current list of telehealth services but which are demonstrated to provide a clinical benefit to the patient. In response to the unique circumstances of the PHE and the lack of data regarding the benefits of the temporarily expanded services, CMS created a third category, Category 3, for purposes of evaluating the expanded services and potentially adding them permanently to either Category 1 or Category 2. Category 3 services that are not added to Category 1 or Category 2 will remain reimbursable through the end of calendar year 2023.[39] In response to the COVID-19 pandemic, CMS also added certain services to the telehealth list without designating them in any category. Those services will stay on the telehealth list until 151 days after the termination of the Public Health Emergency.[40])

Coding errors.

Telehealth claims must be submitted with the appropriate CPT/HCPCS code published by CMS every year. Providers must add the -GQ modifier with the professional service CPT or HCPCS code when performing a telehealth service through an asynchronous telecommunications system.[41] In addition, providers must add Place of Service (POS)-02 to indicate that the service was performed via telehealth from a distant site. Miscoded telehealth claims can result in overpayment.

Telefraud.

As discussed above, both the Department of Justice and the HHS OIG have prosecuted providers under the False Claims Act for their role in fraudulent arrangements with telehealth companies commonly known as 'telefraud.' Cases typically involve physicians employed by telemedicine companies ordering medically unnecessary items or services despite little or no patient interaction.[42] The types of services ordered have varied from genetic testing to durable medical equipment, wound care medication, and prescription medications. Generally, these schemes have not involved billing for telehealth services; instead, telemedicine has served as a conduit for the physicians to efficiently connect with a large volume of patients and order non-telehealth items and services.

Anti-Kickback Statute

Providing telehealth technology to other providers in exchange for referrals of federal program business.

Healthcare providers may seek to collaborate by entering into telehealth arrangements. Typically, one provider will make telehealth technology available to another provider in order to make their services available via telehealth to the receiving provider's patients. Through its

Advisory Opinion process, the HHS-OIG has analyzed a number of proposals between providers involving the provision or subsidizing of telemedicine equipment by one provider to another, or the provision of a telehealth screening service.[43] Although electing not to prohibit the individual arrangements in question, the OIG has stated that such arrangements could potentially generate prohibited remuneration under the Anti-Kickback Statute if the requisite intent to induce referrals of federal healthcare program business were present.

Telefraud.

In addition to False Claims Act liability, physicians implicated in telefraud schemes have faced liability under the Anti-Kickback Statute. As discussed above, various schemes have involved telemedicine companies paying individual providers a per-patient fee while encouraging the provider to order a specific service or product.[44] The Department of Justice and OIG have alleged that the payments from the telemedicine company to the providers constituted kickbacks for the physician's ordering of items and services.

Stark Law

Providing telehealth technology to physicians and failing to meet a Stark Law exception.

Any telehealth arrangement between a healthcare entity and a physician may implicate the Stark Law to the extent that the provision of telehealth equipment creates a financial relationship between the provider and entity, and the physician is a referral source to the entity. In such instances, the relationship must satisfy a Stark Law exception, or the law will be violated regardless of intent. (Note that CMS has published temporary blanket waivers to the Stark Law in response to the COVID-19 public health emergency.[45] To take advantage of the blanket waiver, the arrangements must be implemented as a response to the effects of COVID-19. As an example of an arrangement that would be protected under the blanket waiver, CMS described an entity that provides free telehealth equipment to a physician practice to facilitate telehealth visits for patients who are observing social distancing, in isolation, or in quarantine.)

HIPAA

Use of non-HIPAA-compliant telehealth platforms.

Providers must ensure that the telehealth technology utilized to store and communicate PHI is HIPAA-compliant. Thus, providers must typically enter into a business associate agreement with the technology company that provides satisfactory assurances that the company maintains the necessary safeguards to protect the information. Both utilization of a technology that does not maintain the security requirements and the failure to obtain satisfactory assurances in a business associate agreement result in HIPAA noncompliance. (Note that in response to the COVID-19 public health emergency, the Office for Civil Rights has stated that it will not impose penalties on those utilizing telehealth for the good faith provision of services during the public health emergency, and providers are allowed to use non-public facing audio and video telecommunication products despite possible security risks).[46]

Ryan Haight Act

Failure to provide an in-person examination prior to issuing a prescription for a controlled substance without meeting the "practice of telemedicine" exception.
The Ryan Haight Act requires that a provider can only prescribe controlled substances after having performed one in-person examination unless an exception applies. Prescribing controlled substances without performing the in-person examination while failing to meet one of the exceptions causes noncompliance. (Note: In response to the COVID-19 public health emergency, the Drug Enforcement Agency (DEA) is temporarily allowing providers the choice to evaluate patients either in-person or via telemedicine prior to issuing a prescription for a controlled substance.)[47]

State Laws

Noncompliance with state licensing law.
States maintain laws that govern the licensing necessary to perform a telehealth consult for an originating site located in that state. Noncompliance occurs when a physician performs telehealth services without having the state-required licensure.

Noncompliance with state-required telehealth modalities.
States maintain laws governing the necessary technology needed to perform a valid telehealth consult in that state. Providers engage in noncompliance when the provider performs telehealth services in a manner inconsistent with the modality required by state laws, rules, and regulations.

Noncompliance with state prescribing law.
States maintain their own prescribing standards for controlled substances which may be even more restrictive than the federal Ryan Haight Act. Providers must ensure they meet state-specific standards as well.

Addressing Compliance Risks

Policies and Procedures

Healthcare entities providing telehealth services should maintain policies and procedures to ensure compliance. As an example, the policies and procedures can be structured to reinforce the Medicare requirements regarding originating sites of service, eligible telehealth practitioners, appropriate communication technology, coding requirements, and covered services. The policies should also reinforce the state and federal prescribing requirements, as well as the procedure to confirm that providers maintain the appropriate licensing requirements prior to performing telehealth services in a certain area. Policies should also detail the process to return any identified Medicare overpayments. In addition, a policy should delineate the appropriate internal review process for arrangements with referral sources to ensure compliance with the Stark Law and Anti-Kickback Statute. Any proposed telehealth arrangement or collaboration that involves the provision or receipt of telehealth equipment from or to another provider should be governed by such policy.

Auditing and Monitoring

Healthcare providers performing telehealth services should consider auditing claims to ensure compliance with the various telehealth billing requirements. They should also monitor provider licensing to ensure practitioners are eligible to provide telehealth services throughout targeted originating sites. In addition, the organization's compliance with the HIPAA Security Rule should be revisited on a yearly basis to ensure that the telehealth technologies utilized by the healthcare entity are appropriate.

Education and Training

In order for policies and procedures to be effective, the appropriate stakeholders must be trained and educated on them. Providers must be trained on the necessary billing requirements and telehealth practice standards. Organizational employees must know how to recognize a potential referral source arrangement and who should review the arrangement. Organizations that employ physicians and advanced practice providers should educate them on the 2022 OIG Special Fraud Alert regarding the risks of entering into telefraud arrangements.[48]

Stark Exceptions and Anti-Kickback Safe Harbors

Any telehealth arrangement that includes the sharing or providing of telehealth equipment to a referral source should be tailored to fit a Stark Law exception or Anti-Kickback safe harbor. Commenters have noted that the most recent Final Rules updating the Stark and Anti-Kickback laws included new exceptions and safe harbors which may potentially facilitate compliant telehealth arrangements, specifically those focusing on value-based arrangements.[49] Examples of the new potentially promising safe harbors for the Anti-Kickback Statute include the Care Coordination safe harbor and the Patient Engagement Tools and Support safe harbor. Similarly, CMS stated that it expected the value-based exceptions to the Stark Law to result in arrangements for hospitals to provide free telehealth equipment to physicians to prevent unnecessary ambulance transports, ER visits, and patient complications that occur in the physician office.[50] CMS also identified the potential for sharing telehealth equipment among physicians in order to obtain specialist consults in the primary care setting as another arrangement likely resulting from the new exceptions.[51]

Possible Penalties

Payback of claims resulting from Medicare Review Contractors Audits (i.e. Medicare Administrative Contractors, Comprehensive Error Rate Testing Contractors, Recovery Auditor Contractors, Zone Program Integrity Contractors, etc.)

False Claims Act:

- $12,537-$25,076 per claim plus treble damages.[52]

Anti-Kickback Statute:

- Penalties may include fines, imprisonment, and exclusion from participation in the Federal health care program.
- Under the Civil Monetary Penalties Law, penalties for violating the Anti-Kickback Statute may include three times the amount of the kickback plus up to $25,076 per kickback.[53]

Stark Law:

- Penalties up to $27,750 for each service[54]
- Repayment of claims
- Potential exclusion from participation in federal healthcare programs

HIPAA:

- Minimum penalty: $127
- Maximum penalty: $ 1,919,173[55]

Controlled Substances Act (Ryan Haight Act):

- Penalties up to $72,683 per violation.[56]
- Imprisonment
- Fine
- Temporary or permanent loss of DEA Registration

Compliance Resources

Centers for Medicare & Medicaid Services

Medicare Telehealth
This web page contains a list of covered Telehealth Services and information on submitting services to the Physician Fee Schedule.

https://www.cms.gov/Medicare/Medicare-General-Information/Telehealth

Medicare Telemedicine Health Care Provider Fact Sheet
This fact sheet covers the three main types of virtual services physicians and other professionals can provide to Medicare beneficiaries: Medicare telehealth visits, virtual check-ins and e-visits.

https://www.cms.gov/newsroom/fact-sheets/
medicare-telemedicine-health-care-provider-fact-sheet

U.S. Department of Health and Human Services

Health Resources and Services Administration

Telehealth: For Providers

Find resources for healthcare providers offering telehealth services, including updates on policy changes, billing and reimbursement, and legal considerations on this site.

https://telehealth.hhs.gov/providers/

Risk Takeaways

Main Points of Interest
- Telehealth continues to grow both in practice and CMS reimbursement.
- The COVID-19 public health emergency has intensified the use of telehealth services.
- Government scrutiny of telehealth has and will continue to increase.

Areas to Watch:
- Equipment usage
- Patient privacy and PHI

- Licensing, modality, and prescribing requirements
- Coding errors
- Collaborative telehealth arrangements
- Providing Medicare noncovered services
- Medicare rules regarding telehealth
- Many laws governing telehealth practice have been altered or relaxed for the COVID-19 public health emergency. Telehealth providers should monitor how these laws evolve once the public health emergency ends.

Laws that Apply:
- False Claims Act[57]
- Stark Law[58]
- Anti-Kickback Statute[59]
- HIPAA[60]
- Ryan Haight Act[61]
- State licensing, modality, and prescribing laws

Addressing Compliance Risks of Telehealth and Telemedicine:
- Providers should develop policies and procedures to reinforce telehealth reimbursement requirements. They should audit and monitor for compliant billing and licensing, and educate necessary stakeholders regarding billing and prescribing requirements as well as the elevated risk of fraudulent arrangements.

Endnotes

1. Ordonez is a licensed attorney in Florida. He began his career at the Jackson Health System negotiating clinical trial agreements for the hospital system and subsequently transitioned into compliance, where he now oversees the program for the health system.

2. "Telehealth Programs," Federal Office of Rural Health Policy, Health Resources & Services Administration, updated October 2020, https://www.hrsa.gov/rural-health/telehealth.

3. Looney, Kim Harvey, and Molly August Huffman, "That Was Then and This Is Now-How the COVID-19 Crisis Changed Telehealth Services: Are the Changes Here To Stay?" *Health Law Connections* (September 2020) 10, https://www.americanhealthlaw.org/content-library/connections-magazine/article/55a5ad47-302e-41f4-8e83-c1c1813c48a4/that-was-then-and-this-is-now-how-the-covid-19-cri.

4. "Medicare Telemedicine Health Care Provider Fact Sheet," Newsroom, Centers for Medicare & Medicaid Services, March 17, 2020, https://www.cms.gov/newsroom/fact-sheets/medicare-telemedicine-health-care-provider-fact-sheet.

5. Looney, Kim Harvey, and Molly August Huffman, "That Was Then and This Is Now-How the COVID-19 Crisis Changed Telehealth Services: Are the Changes Here To Stay?" Health Law Connections (September 2020) 10, https://www.americanhealthlaw.org/content-library/connections-magazine/article/55a5ad47-302e-41f4-8e83-c1c1813c48a4/that-was-then-and-this-is-now-how-the-covid-19-cri.

6. Department of Health and Human Services Office of Inspector General, "CMS Paid Practitioners for Telehealth Services That Did Not Meet Medicare Requirements" (A-05-16-0058), April 2018, https://oig.hhs.gov/oas/reports/region5/51600058.pdf.

7. Alliance for Connected Care, "HHS OIG Telehealth Work Plan Items," December 19 2021 https://connectwithcare.org/hhs-oig-telehealth-work-plan-items/.

8. "Federal Law Enforcement Action Involving Fraudulent Genetic Testing Results in Charges Against 35 Individuals Responsible for Over $2.1 Billion in Losses in One of the Largest Health Care Fraud Schemes Ever Charged," Office of Public Affairs, Department of Justice, September 27, 2019, https://www.justice.gov/opa/pr/federal-law-enforcement-action-involving-fraudulent-genetic-testing-results-charges-against#:~:text=A%20federal%20law%20enforcement%20action,the%20largest%20health%20care%20fraud; "Federal Indictments & Law Enforcement Actions in One of the Largest Health Care Fraud Schemes Involving Telemedicine and Durable Marketing Executives Results in Charges Against 24 Individuals Responsible for Over $1.2 Billion in Losses," Office of Public Affairs, Department of Justice, April 9, 2019, https://www.justice.gov/opa/pr/federal-indictments-and-law-enforcement-actions-one-largest-health-care-fraud-schemes. "National Health Care Fraud and Opioid Takedown Results in Charges Against 345 Defendants Responsible for More than $6 Billion in Alleged Fraud Losses" Office of Public Affairs, Department of Justice September 30, 2020 https://www.justice.gov/opa/pr/national-health-care-fraud-and-opioid-takedown-results-charges-against-345-defendants"Justice Department Charges Dozens for $1.2 Billion in Health Care Fraud: Nationwide Coordinated Law Enforcement Action to Combat Telemedicine, Clinical Laboratory, and Durable Medical Equipment Fraud,"Office of Public Affairs, Department of Justice, July 20, 2022 https://www.justice.gov/opa/pr/justice-department-charges-dozens-12-billion-health-care-fraud

9. Department of Health and Human Services Office of Inspector General, *Special Fraud Alert: OIG Alerts Practitioners To Exercise Caution When Entering Into Arrangements With Purported Telemedicine Companies*, July 20, 2022, https://oig.hhs.gov/documents/root/1045/sfa-telefraud.pdf

10. 42 U.S.C. § 1320a-7k.

11. 42 U.S.C. § 1320a-7(b).

12. 42 U.S.C. § 1395nn.

13. 31 U.S.C. §§ 3729–3733.

14. Pub.L. No. 104-191, 110 Stat. 1938.

15. 45 C.F.R. §§ 160, 164.102-164.106, 164.500-164.534.

16. 45 C.F.R. §§ 160, 164.102-164.106, 164.302-164.318.

17. 45 C.F.R. §§ 164.400-164.414

18. 21 U.S.C. § 829(e).

19. 21 U.S.C. § 812.

20. Faget, Kyle Y., "Telemedicine Compliance: The Practice Requirements," *Journal of Health Compliance*, vol. 22, n. 2, (March-April 2020) 2.

21. 21 U.S.C. § 829(e).

22. Grimm, Douglas, and Hillary Stemple, "Telemedicine: A Review of the Fraud and Abuse Landscape," *Compliance Today*, March 2019, https://compliancecosmos.org/telemedicine-review-fraud-and-abuse-landscape.

23. Faget, Kyle Y., "Telemedicine Compliance: The Practice Requirements," *Journal of Health Compliance*, vol. 22, n. 2, (March-April 2020) 2.

24. Faget, Kyle Y., "Telemedicine Compliance: The Practice Requirements," *Journal of Health Compliance*, vol. 22, n. 2, (March-April 2020) 2.

25. Faget, Kyle Y., "Telemedicine Compliance: The Practice Requirements," *Journal of Health Compliance*, vol. 22, n. 2, (March-April 2020) 2.

26. Faget, Kyle Y., "Telemedicine Compliance: The Practice Requirements," *Journal of Health Compliance*, vol. 22, n. 2, (March-April 2020) 3.

27. 42 C.F.R. § 410.78(b)(4)

28. 42 C.F.R. § 410.78(b)(4)

29. Centers for Medicare & Medicaid Services, "Medicare Telemedicine Health Care Provider Fact Sheet," https://www.cms.gov/newsroom/fact-sheets/medicare-telemedicine-health-care-provider-fact-sheet

30. Centers for Medicare & Medicaid Services, Medicare Claims Processing Manual, Chapter 12-Physicians/Nonphysician Practitioners § 190.6.1, Revised 11-01-19, https://www.cms.gov/Regulations-and-Guidance/Guidance/Manuals/Downloads/clm104c12.pdf.

31. Faget, Kyle Y., "Telemedicine Compliance: The Practice Requirements," *Journal of Health Compliance*, vol. 22, n. 2, (March-April 2020) 7.

32. Enyeart, Amanda, Marshall E. Jackson Jr., Lisa Mazur, Rachel Stauffer, Grayson I. Dimick, Jayda Greco, Abby Higgins, Ashley Ogedegbe, Sarah G. Raaii, Angela Irene Theodoropoulos, "Omnibus Bill Extends Medicare Telehealth Flexibilities And HDHP Telehealth Safe Harbor." December 23, 2022, https://www.mwe.com/insights/omnibus-bill-extends-medicare-telehealth-flexibilities-and-hdhp-telehealth-safe-harbor/

33. 42 C.F.R. § 410.78(b)(3)

34. Centers for Medicare & Medicaid Services, "Medicare Telemedicine Health Care Provider Fact Sheet," https://www.cms.gov/newsroom/fact-sheets/medicare-telemedicine-health-care-provider-fact-sheet.

35. 42 C.F.R. § 410.78(b).

36. 42 C.F.R. § 410.78(b).

37. Enyeart, Amanda, Marshall E. Jackson Jr., Lisa Mazur, Rachel Stauffer, Grayson I. Dimick, Jayda Greco, Abby Higgins, Ashley Ogedegbe, Sarah G. Raaii, Angela Irene Theodoropoulos, "Omnibus Bill Extends Medicare Telehealth Flexibilities And HDHP Telehealth Safe Harbor." December 23, 2022, https://www.mwe.com/insights/omnibus-bill-extends-medicare-telehealth-flexibilities-and-hdhp-telehealth-safe-harbor/

38. "List of Telehealth Services," Centers for Medicare & Medicaid Services, updated November 2, 2022, https://www.cms.gov/medicare/medicare-general-information/telehealth/telehealth-codes

39. Medicare and Medicaid Programs; CY 2023 Payment Policies under the Physician Fee Schedule and Other Changes to Part B Payment and Coverage Policies; Medicare Shared Savings Program Requirements; Implementing Requirements for Manufacturers of Certain Single-dose Container or Single-use Package Drugs to Provide Refunds with Respect to Discarded Amounts; and COVID-19 Interim Final Rules, 87 FR 69404, 69446 November 18, 2022

40. Id. At 69450

41. Faget, Kyle Y., "Telemedicine Compliance: The Practice Requirements," *Journal of Health Compliance*, vol. 22, n. 2, (March-April 2020) 7.

42. Department of Health and Human Services Office of Inspector General, Special Fraud Alert: OIG Alerts Practitioners To Exercise Caution When Entering Into Arrangements With Purported Telemedicine Companies, July 20, 2022, https://oig.hhs.gov/documents/root/1045/sfa-telefraud.pdf

43. OIG Advisory Op. No. 18-03 (May 31, 2018), https://oig.hhs.gov/fraud/docs/advisoryopinions/2018/AdvOpn18-03.pdf; OIG Advisory Op. No. 04-07 (June, 24, 2004), https://oig.hhs.gov/fraud/docs/advisoryopinions/2007/AdvOpn07-04.pdf; OIG Advisory Op. No.11-12 (September 6, 2011), https://oig.hhs.gov/fraud/docs/advisoryopinions/2011/AdvOpn11-12.pdf.

44. Department of Health and Human Services Office of Inspector General, Special Fraud Alert: OIG Alerts Practitioners To Exercise Caution When Entering Into Arrangements With Purported Telemedicine Companies, July 20, 2022, https://oig.hhs.gov/documents/root/1045/sfa-telefraud.pdf

45. "Blanket Waivers of Section 1877(g) of the Social Security Act Due to Declaration of COVID-19 Outbreak in the United States as a National Emergency," Center for Medicare and Medicaid Services, March 30, 2020, https://www.cms.gov/files/document/covid-19-blanket-waivers-section-1877g.pdf.

46. "Notification of enforcement Discretion for Telehealth Remote Communications During the COVID-19 Nationwide Public Health Emergency," U.S. Department of Health & Human Services, Last Reviewed: March 30, 2020, https://www.hhs.gov/hipaa/for-professionals/special-topics/emergency-preparedness/notification-enforcement-discretion-telehealth/index.html

47. "How to Prescribe Controlled Substances to Patients During the COVID-19 Public Health Emergency," U.S. Department of Justice, Drug Enforcement Administration, March 31, 2020, https://www.deadiversion.usdoj.gov/GDP/(DEA-DC-023)(DEA075)Decision_Tree_(Final)_33120_2007.pdf.

48. Department of Health and Human Services Office of Inspector General, Special Fraud Alert: OIG Alerts Practitioners To Exercise Caution When Entering Into Arrangements With Purported Telemedicine Companies, July 20, 2022, https://oig.hhs.gov/documents/root/1045/sfa-telefraud.pdf

49. Eric Wicklund, "Stark Law Changes Should Benefit Telehealth, Remote Patient Monitoring" mhealthintelligence Nov. 24, 2020 https://mhealthintelligence.com/news/stark-law-changes-should-benefit-telehealth-remote-patient-monitoring

50. Modernizing and Clarifying the Physician Self-Referral Regulations, 85 Fed. Reg. 77492, 77647, December 2, 2020 https://www.federalregister.gov/documents/2020/12/02/2020-26140/medicare-program-modernizing-and-clarifying-the-physician-self-referral-regulations

51. Modernizing and Clarifying the Physician Self-Referral Regulations, 85 Fed. Reg. 77492, 77647, December 2, 2020 https://www.federalregister.gov/documents/2020/12/02/2020-26140/medicare-program-modernizing-and-clarifying-the-physician-self-referral-regulations

52. Department of Justice; Civil Monetary Penalties Inflation Adjustment 2022 (May 9, 2022) https://www.govinfo.gov/content/pkg/FR-2022-05-09/pdf/2022-09928.pdf.

53. Department of Justice; Civil Monetary Penalties Inflation Adjustments for 2022; 87 Fed. Reg. 27513, 27516 (May 9, 2022) https://www.govinfo.gov/content/pkg/FR-2022-05-09/pdf/2022-09928.pdf.

54. Department of Health and Human Services; Annual Civil Monetary Penalties Inflation Adjustment 2022, 87 Fed. Reg. 15100, 15107 (March 17, 2022) https://www.govinfo.gov/content/pkg/FR-2022-05-09/pdf/2022-09928.pdf

55. Department of Health and Human Services; Annual Civil Monetary Penalties Inflation Adjustment 2022, 87 Fed. Reg. 15100, 15109 (March 17, 2022) https://www.govinfo.gov/content/pkg/FR-2022-05-09/pdf/2022-09928.pdf

56. Department of Justice; Civil Monetary Penalties Inflation Adjustments for 2022; 87 Fed. Reg. 27513, 27517 (May 9, 2022) https://www.govinfo.gov/content/pkg/FR-2022-05-09/pdf/2022-09928.pdf.

57. 31 U.S.C. §§ 3729–3733

58. 42 U.S.C. § 1395nn.

59. 42 U.S.C. § 1320a-7(b).

60. Pub.L. No. 104-191, 110 Stat. 1938.

61. 21 U.S.C. § 829(e)

Patient Privacy and Security

Business Associates

By Isabella A. Porter,[1] JD, CHC, CHPC

What Are Business Associates in Relation to Patient Privacy and Security?

When the Health Insurance Portability and Accountability Act (HIPAA) was enacted in 1996, the world of healthcare operations vis-à-vis technology differed vastly from today. How healthcare entities functioned shifted between then and 2009, when the Health Information Technology for Economic and Clinical Health Act (HITECH) was passed by Congress within the omnibus American Recovery and Reinvestment Act (ARRA). The healthcare industry was eager to acquire technology and to contract for services that would facilitate patient care, support efficient healthcare operations, enhance organizations' ability to collect revenue, and minimize their risks.

Advances in technologies during the last 10 years have changed the healthcare industry with such developments as moving from web applications to mobile apps, handling data analytics and data increasingly through cloud-based services, and the rise of telework opportunities (especially in the context of COVID-19). The advances also have posed challenges—managing cyber risk, vendor risk, and various other threats. Healthcare providers often contract with entities to perform or outsource certain functions related to treatment, payment, and operations if the covered entities lack the necessary internal capabilities or skill sets, or need assistance with activities that are out of scope of the healthcare entity's normal business. If these functions involve individual health information of patients, which is often the case, contractors or vendors engaged to perform such functions on behalf of the healthcare organization are known as **business associates**.

Business Associates and Their Roles

Business associates are individuals or entities that perform services on behalf of covered entities involving the use or disclosure of the covered entity's protected health information (PHI) and electronic PHI (ePHI). Business associates are vendors or contractors that are not directly involved in the treatment of a covered entity's patients or members. For instance, their services include such functions as claims processing or administration, quality assurance, billing, practice management, legal, and accounting.[2] A legal definition of "business associate" can be found in 45 C.F.R. § 160.103.[3]

Common examples of business associates include:

- Certified public accountants (CPAs)
- Attorneys
- Consultants
- Auditors
- Coding companies
- Third-party administrators (TRAs) performing billing
- Security consultants
- IT support contractors
- Data aggregation services (such as population health and de-identification)
- Transcription services
- Contracted ambulance companies
- Electronic health record (EHR) vendors that support their applications/tools and can view PHI

Owing to the sensitive nature of information that business associates need to perform their contracted services, covered entities are required to obtain satisfactory assurances that business associates will protect the privacy and security of the PHI they access, use, and disclose. These assurances are codified in a business associate agreement that essentially supports the PHI chain of trust for PHI that a business associate receives from a covered entity. Lastly, depending on the services provided, one covered entity can be considered a business associate of another covered entity, and subcontractors that are creating, receiving, maintaining, or transmitting PHI on behalf of a business associate may also be considered a business associate.[4][5][6]

Business Associates After HITECH

Before HITECH was enacted, healthcare providers were required to obtain satisfactory assurances that business associates would protect PHI before contracting and sharing PHI with them. Providers, however, soon learned that contracting for services and technology from business associates carried its own set of risks. Namely, the HIPAA security standards and penalties applicable to healthcare providers did not apply to contracted business associates accessing PHI to perform services on their behalf.[7] In fact, prior to HITECH, a business associate could be held liable for a HIPAA breach by a covered entity only under a breach of contract claim.[8] HITECH made business associates directly responsible for HIPAA compliance within their individual businesses that would not otherwise be subject to HIPAA regulations and penalties.[9]

Even if no written contract exists between the covered entity and a contracted company performing services related to handling PHI in some form, the company is deemed a business associate by law. This deemed status essentially classifies contracted vendors or individuals as business associates solely by the nature of the services they provide to a covered entity, regardless of whether they intended to be classified as business associates or were aware of their status as such. HIPAA and HITECH may hold these vendors to business associate obligations as long as they *act* as business associates.

To protect healthcare entities and their patients, a robust compliance program is essential for monitoring business-associate relationships and contracts.

Risk Area Governance

In the context of business associates, HIPAA, HITECH, and the Omnibus Final Rule all work in concert to expand statutory requirements surrounding privacy and security protections of PHI to include vendors indirectly involved in the treatment of patients. While HITECH enhanced HIPAA by extending its Privacy and Security Rules' penalties to contracted business associates and their subcontractors accessing a covered entities' PHI, the Omnibus Final Rule added direct liability to noncompliant business associates, which includes imposing fines by the U.S. Department of Health & Human Services (HHS) Office for Civil Rights (OCR). Additionally, 45 C.F.R. § 160 and Subparts A and C of 45 C.F.R. § 164 detail the HIPAA Security Rule. These sections explain the basic standards required by statute to protect ePHI by covered entities and their business associates. Further, they require both to incorporate appropriate physical, administrative, and technical safeguards to protect the confidentiality, integrity, and security of ePHI.[10][11]

The HIPAA Privacy Rule only applies to covered entities that are defined as health plans, healthcare clearinghouses, and healthcare providers "who transmit any health information in electronic form in connection with a transaction for which the HHS has adopted a standard."[12][13] Business associates are defined as "person[s] or entit[ies] that [perform] certain functions or activities . . . involv[ing] the use or disclosure of [PHI] on behalf of, or [provide] services to, a covered entity."[14]

The HIPAA Privacy Rule permits covered entities to disclose PHI to business associates if they "obtain satisfactory assurances that the business associate will use the information only for the purposes for which it was engaged by the covered entity, will safeguard the information from misuse, and will help the covered entity comply with some of the covered entity's duties under the Privacy Rule."[15] These satisfactory assurances are met through the explicit prerequisite that a covered entity obtain a business associate agreement "or other arrangement with the business associate that establishes specifically what the business associate has been engaged to do and requires the business associate to comply with the [HIPAA] Rules' requirements to protect the privacy and security of [PHI]," and "[i]n addition to these contractual obligations, business associates are directly liable for compliance with certain provisions of the HIPAA Rules."[16][17] On the condition that a covered entity has obtained a valid and appropriate business associate agreement, "[c]overed entities may disclose [PHI] to an entity in its role as a business associate only to help the covered entity carry out its health care functions—not for the business associate's independent use or purposes, except as needed for the proper management and administration of the business associate."[18] Conversely, if a covered entity only plans to disclose a limited data set to the business associate, as specified in 45 C.F.R. § 164.514(e)(2) and 45 C.F.R. § 164.514 (e)(3), then a business associate agreement is not required and a data use agreement may be obtained in its place.[19]

Under HIPAA and HITECH, individuals or entities who have been identified as business associates are obligated to enter into a business associate agreement with their contracted covered entities. At a minimum, the business associate agreement must do the following:

1. Address permitted and required uses and disclosures of PHI by the business associate.

2. Restrict business associate from disclosing PHI in a manner not permitted or required under the agreement or as required by law.

3. Require appropriate safeguards be implemented by the business associate to prevent unauthorized use or disclosure of PHI, which would include HIPAA Security Rule provisions concerning ePHI.

4. Require business associates to report any use or disclosure of PHI to the covered entity that is inconsistent with the permitted uses and disclosures allowed for by the agreement (e.g., breaches of unsecured PHI). At this time, there is no statutory timeframe specifying what is a reasonable turnaround for a business associate to notify a covered entity, so it is crucial for covered entities to consider a timeframe that would allow it to comply with the totality of its breach notification obligations under the law. This task can be extremely constricted if it concerns a breach of PHI of more than 500 patients and patients from different states with separate breach reporting mandates.

5. Require business associates to disclose PHI in order to fulfill a covered entity's patient request for copies of their information, amendments to their information, and/or accounting of disclosures.

6. Require the business associate to comply with the applicable obligation(s) in the event that the business associate is to fulfill a covered entity's obligation as specified under the Privacy Rule.

7. Require the business associate to make available to HHS its internal practices, books, and records related to the use and disclosure of the covered entity's PHI for HHS to determine the covered entity's compliance with the HIPAA Privacy Rule.

8. Require business associates to return or destroy all PHI received from the covered entity at the termination of the agreement, if feasible. If a covered entity does opt for the destruction option, they should consider requesting a certificate of destruction upon completion. If not feasible, then covered entities should ensure that the agreement contains language extending the protections of the agreement to the PHI *beyond* its termination.

9. Require business associates to impose on their subcontractors the same restrictions from their agreement on accessing PHI, so as to ensure that the information will be consistently protected at the same level of care from covered entity to business associate to its subcontractor. It should be noted that per the OCR, "contracts between business associates and business associates that are subcontractors are subject to these same [overall business associate agreement] requirements."[20]

10. Authorize termination of the agreement by the covered entity should the business associate commit a material breach of contract or violate an essential term of the agreement. Some business associate agreements will indicate a cure period prior to termination for a material breach of this agreement (such as 30 days to cure an identified material breach); covered entities should consider whether there would be instances when a cure would be inconceivable, thus immediate or expedited termination of an agreement would be preferred.[21]

In addition, while it is important to recognize when a relationship with an individual or entity triggers the business associate agreement mandate under the HIPAA Privacy Rule, it is equally important to be cognizant of its exceptions. For instance, according to HHS, "a covered entity is not required to have a business associate [agreement] or other written agreement in place before [PHI] may be disclosed to the person or entity" for the following situations:

- Disclosures of an individual's PHI by a covered entity to another healthcare provider for the purposes of treating that individual.
- When appropriate, disclosures by a group health plan (or similarly situated insurers) to a health plan sponsor.
- When appropriate, the gathering and transmission of PHI by a public benefits program health plan and the agencies that assist with determining eligibility and enrollment.
- Disclosures made for payment purposes by a healthcare provider to a health plan.
- Relationships with individuals or entities providing services to the covered entity that do not involve the use or disclosure of PHI, but the services are being performed in or around the covered entity's physical location (e.g., building maintenance). [*Note: In these situations, while a business associate agreement would not be necessary, it is still advisable for covered entities to execute confidentiality agreements with these individuals/entities and perform routine vendor screening and due diligence on them.*]
- When individuals or entities act solely as conduits of PHI (e.g., the U.S. Postal Service delivering letters containing PHI).
- When appropriate, disclosures by covered entities participating in an organized healthcare arrangement (OHCA).
- Disclosures made to a health insurer by a group plan purchasing insurance.

- Disclosures made to an insurer through the purchase of a health plan product or other insurance by a covered entity.
- When appropriate and as provided for under HIPAA, disclosures made to a researcher solely for research purposes.[22][23]
- Disclosures made by a financial institution pursuant to any activity directly affecting or assisting with the application of funds for payment for healthcare or health plan premiums.[24]

In sum, it behooves covered entities to be familiar with the circumstances that either require or exempt an individual or entity from executing a business associate agreement.

Common Compliance Risks

Common compliance risks associated with business associates can be grouped into the following categories.

Failure to Identify Business Associates

While it may seem elementary to some, especially since HITECH was finalized in 2013, many people still do not entirely understand when certain vendor relationships trigger the requirement for a business associate agreement. Consequently, often vendors will seek a contract with a covered entity which does not recognize the vendor as a business associate and thus never executes a business associate agreement with the covered entity. Furthermore, this risk extends even beyond new vendor contracting, especially for covered entities organized in years prior to 2013. Vendors who have performed services on behalf of a covered entity for many years might have contracts in place that have never been evaluated for business-associate classification and validation of an active current business-associate agreement. For covered entities with contracts that have not been regularly reviewed, the likelihood is high that it has vendors that are unidentified business associates. This category also poses a particularly special risk because even if these vendors are not business associates, they still may require updated contracts addressing confidentiality regarding the contracted services they perform for the covered entity.

Moreover, even if a covered entity performed its due diligence in identifying all vendors that operate as business associates on behalf of the organization, it is equally important that the covered entity review the executed business associate agreements as well. Covered entities that maintain a business associate agreement template should review it concurrently with their business associate policy. They may find that they have updated their business associate agreement template since 2013, which could result in different versions of business associate agreements being maintained by the organization. This can happen as the result of a lack of coordination of the updated business associate agreement template to the individuals responsible for securing these agreements or because of the inability to update outdated agreements. As with any template or form used internally, organizations must ensure they effectively (1) communicate changes and updates to all individuals involved with the contracting process, (2) share updated business associate agreement templates with these individuals, and then (3) validate through internal auditing and monitoring efforts that the newer template is being utilized. Upon review, covered entities may also find that some vendors need to execute updated business associate agreements with more updated terms, such as shortening the breach notification period that was deemed to be reasonable back in 2013 but is by no means reasonable in the context of 2022.

In addition, some contracted vendors offer an array of services, some of which require access to PHI and others that can be performed without it. The risk emerges when a covered entity initially contracted for services that do not require access to PHI, but then the covered entity later augments with the vendor activities that now do require access to the covered entity's PHI. In this situation, covered entities may fail to reevaluate the existing contract with the vendor to confirm that a business associate agreement has been obtained. This oversight results in a newly classified business associate performing services on behalf of the covered entity without the required business associate agreement.

On the other hand, some covered entities are so aware of the requirement to execute business associate agreements, they often request them from *all* vendors with whom they contract—as a safeguard. Such an approach may be well-meaning and strategic, but it poses risks primarily for true nonbusiness associates entering into these agreements.

If vendors that are not considered business associates under the statute do agree to execute a business associate agreement, they take on not only the expenses of complying with the agreement's standards, they also incur the contractual liabilities, including damages for the inability to comply with any of the contract's terms.[25] Further, these entities place unnecessary limits on how they disclose information subject to their relationship with the covered entity, while also labeling themselves as a business associate under the law, which exposes them to possible HIPAA penalties for noncompliance.[26]

Lastly, even while covered entities often zealously evaluate vendors for potential business associate activities, they tend to overlook other covered entities that act as business associates. A classic example of this situation is a physician working for a covered entity solely in an administrative position, such as a medical director. Even if the physician continues to practice medicine elsewhere (in a self-owned practice, for example), the covered entity contracting with the physician to be medical director still must obtain a business associate agreement with the physician (who is also a covered entity). Another example may be an ambulance company under contract with a hospital. For this reason, it is crucial that all aspects of contracting, even for services provided by other covered entities, be reviewed for potential business associate activity.

Lack of Appropriate Review in the Contracting Process

With the hasty deadlines that regularly come when contracting for new services, many covered entities do not perform detailed reviews of contracts and submitted attachments, which creates a risk concerning business associate agreements. For example, many business associates may automatically include their own business associate agreement template as an attachment to their contracting documentation, and some covered entities assume that the terms are consistent with standard business associate agreement terms. Without proper review and scrutiny of these terms, covered entities could be entering into business associate agreements potentially lacking required elements and consistency with their other executed contracts. In addition, many large vendors have business associate agreements they'd prefer to use and often are unwilling to amend terms or customize their business associate agreements for specific covered entities. In these instances, it is important that covered entities perform an appropriate assessment of the risks posed to the organization if they forego certain terms and then determine whether or not to continue pursuing a contract with a particular vendor (e.g., a vendor that is unwilling to shorten the breach notice period requirement or that limits potential damages the covered entity can collect to what the vendor was paid in a 12-month period).

Lack of Continuous Oversight over Business Associate Activities

Serious risks to covered entities could go undetected without appropriate oversight of business associates. Problems could include a covered entity's inability to (a) maintain a centralized and readily available repository for business associate agreements; (b) perform continuous auditing and monitoring of business associates' activities and compliance with business associate agreement requirements, (c) perform effective vendor risk management, and (d) monitor compliance with termination provisions of business associate agreements, such as determining whether certificates of destruction were provided upon termination.

Continuous-oversight activities allow covered entities the opportunity to better detect, assess, and correct risks posed to them by business associates. For covered entities in the initial stages of performing oversight of its business associates, it would be advisable to start small before delving into in-depth oversight activities. For instance, a covered entity could send a business associate a preliminary questionnaire asking it to confirm whether its organization has policies and procedures addressing physical, administrative, and technical safeguards, Later, the covered entity can follow up with a request for the business associate to provide specific policies, such as one concerning its use of the minimum necessary standard and its policy regarding subcontractors' onboarding/offboarding and access to PHI. Other sensible areas of inquiry could be whether a business associate has offshoring activities or subcontracts with vendors located offshore, or whether it has obtained cybersecurity insurance that would apply to its activities with a covered entity and would be sufficient coverage to address a cybersecurity incident concerning the covered entity's patients. Without continuous oversight, it would be difficult for covered entities to demonstrate that they exercised an appropriate amount of due diligence over a business associate should the entities experience a security incident resulting in a massive PHI breach. Failing to identify these risks and perform continuous assessments surrounding covered entities' contracting activities is guaranteed to lead to noncompliance with regulatory requirements and, ultimately, expose patients to risks concerning PHI privacy and security.

Moreover, a trend toward more oversight is suggested by the fact that it has become more customary in recent years for covered entities to request that their business associates annually complete a survey or questionnaire to assess their compliance with the privacy and security provisions of the applicable business associate agreement. Questions on this assessment can probe whether a business associate performs an annual security risk assessment; maintains business continuity or disaster recovery plans; has policies regarding appropriate PHI uses and disclosures among its workforce; and monitors subcontractors that have access to the covered entity's PHI. The purpose of these questions is to proactively allow covered entities to exercise due diligence and more effectively perform risk management oversight of their contracted vendors.

Addressing Compliance Risks

Covered entities can develop routine and consistent methods for supporting privacy programs that ultimately reduce risks posed by contracting with business associates. Among these methods, continuous communication is key to reducing the risks posed by contracting with business associates. For example, providing routine education or annual refreshers with management and individuals responsible for contract execution in the organization can help reinforce the importance of business associate identification. It can assist with collecting required business associate agreements from contracted individuals and entities. Additionally, routine communication reinforces the knowledge base of the individuals involved with contracting, as consideration of business associate issues could be forgotten due to employee attrition and prolonged periods without new contracting.

Furthermore, implementing systematic controls within the contracting process, such as requiring all contracts to undergo a vendor risk assessment in the initial contracting and renewal phases, could assist covered entities with continuous assessment of risks posed to their organizations though their business associates. To illustrate, one component of these controls could involve the requisite that only the covered entity's privacy officer (or suitable designee) be granted signatory authority for business associate agreements. This action would help to ensure that all business associate agreements executed are appropriate to the organization's privacy program. Two other examples of these controls are (1) automatically requiring that the covered entity's business associate agreement template be used rather than the business associate's and (2) ensuring all vendors (regardless of whether they have been classified as business associates) undergo routine basic vendor assessments by the group or individual responsible for the covered entity's contracting activities. If a vendor is determined to be a business associate, it can be prioritized for more in-depth vendor risk-management reviews. For larger organizations with in-house Risk Management, Legal, and Security Departments, it is highly recommended that they be included in vendor risk management and vendor risk assessments.

Possible Penalties

Given that business associates can still "be sued by their [contracted] [c]overed [e]ntities for breaching the terms of their [business associate agreements]," HITECH has made business associates subject to civil and (when applicable) criminal penalties for violating business associate agreements and/or for HIPAA requirements through inappropriate uses and disclosures of PHI. Monetary penalties can be as high as $1.5 million.[27][28][29] Some recent settlements include the following:

- April 2016: Raleigh Orthopedic Clinic agreed to a $750,000 settlement and a corrective action plan with the OCR over HIPAA violation allegations regarding the transfer of thousands of X-rays and related PHI to a vendor that had not entered into a business associate agreement with the provider.[30]
- March 2016: North Memorial Health Care of Minnesota agreed to pay a $1.55 million settlement and enter into a corrective action plan with the OCR over HIPAA violation allegations regarding disclosure of PHI to its business associate, Accretive Health, without having a business associate agreement in place before the transfer.[31]
- March 2020: A solo physician practitioner's $100,000 settlement with the OCR included an agreement to adopt a corrective action plan for a potential HIPAA violation regarding a business associate and its use of the physician's patients' ePHI.[32]

Under HITECH, business associates failing to safeguard ePHI as required under the HIPAA Security Rule can be directly liable and subject to civil penalties. Also, the law permits state attorneys general to pursue remedies for a HIPAA violation in the event HHS or another federal agency declines to pursue such remedies available to them.[33][34][35] Further, while there is no private right of action under HIPAA for individuals whose PHI had been compromised while under the control of a covered entity and/or business associate, these individuals can sue covered entities and business associates "for violations under the common law principles of invasion of privacy, defamation, negligence and breach of fiduciary duty, among others."[36] It should also be noted that lack of execution of a business associate agreement does not necessarily relieve a business associate from liability under HITECH.[37]

Further, under HITECH and the HHS Office for Civil Rights' (OCR) final rule, business associates are directly liable and the "OCR has authority to take enforcement action against business associates" for the following violations:[38]

- Failure to provide the HHS Secretary with records and compliance reports; cooperate with complaint investigations and compliance reviews; and permit access by the Secretary to information, including . . . [PHI], pertinent to determining compliance.
- Taking any retaliatory action against any individual or other person for filing a HIPAA complaint, participating in an investigation or other enforcement process, or opposing an act or practice that is unlawful under the HIPAA Rules.
- Failure to comply with the requirements of the Security Rule.
- Failure to provide breach notification to a covered entity or another business associate.
- Impermissible uses and disclosures of PHI.

- Failure to disclose a copy of electronic PHI (ePHI) to either (a) the covered entity or (b) the individual or the individual's designee (whichever is specified in the business associate agreement) to satisfy a covered entity's obligations under 45 C.F.R. § 164.524(c)(2)(ii) and 3(ii), respectively, with respect to an individual's request for an electronic copy of PHI.
- Failure to make reasonable efforts to limit PHI to the minimum necessary to accomplish the intended purpose of the use, disclosure, or request.
- Failure, in certain circumstances, to provide an accounting of disclosures.
- Failure to enter into business associate agreements with subcontractors that create or receive PHI on their behalf, and failure to comply with the implementation specifications for such agreements.
- Failure to take reasonable steps to address a material breach or violation of the subcontractor's business associate agreement.[39]

On the other hand, covered entities must be aware that the "OCR lacks the authority to enforce the 'reasonable, cost-based fee' limitation in 45 CFR §164.524(c)(4) against business associates because the HITECH Act does not apply the fee limitation provisions to business associates."[40] Consequently, in situations where a business associate is tasked by a covered entity with fulfilling an individual's request for access to their PHI, but the business associate charges an individual in excess of the fee limitation, the OCR can only take enforcement action against the covered entity.[41] Additionally, covered entities can face penalties for not obtaining a business associate agreement, as well as not exercising the appropriate oversight over the business associate should a breach of the covered entity's PHI occur.[42][43]

Compliance Resources

U.S. Department of Health & Human Services

Business Associates
The FAQ page on the OCR website specifically concerns questions about business associates. The OCR's responses to these questions offer guidance and insight regarding its expectations and interpretations of HIPAA and HITECH.

https://www.hhs.gov/hipaa/for-professionals/faq/business-associates/index.html

Business Associate Contracts
This resource offers a link to a sample Business Associate Agreement template provided on the OCR website. It can be used by covered entities that do not have an official in-house Business Associate Agreement template, or it can be used to reevaluate the current template utilized by the covered entity. Additionally, this sample agreement can be used as a basis to create an internal tool that covered entities may reference when evaluating whether a template provided by a business associate meets the OCR's requirements concerning the necessary elements of a business associate agreement.

https://www.hhs.gov/hipaa/for-professionals/covered-entities/sample-business-associate-agreement-provisions/index.html

Risk Takeaways

Main points of interest:
- Covered entities must maintain oversight over business associates
- Covered entities can be liable for breaches caused by business associates
- HIPAA Privacy and Security Rules
- HIPAA/ HITECH penalties
- HIPAA Privacy Rule application

Areas to watch:
- Business associate agreements
- Covered entity oversight
- Covered entity and business associate liabilities

Laws that apply:
- Health Insurance Portability and Accountability Act of 1996 (HIPAA), Pub. L. No. 104–191
- Health Information Technology for Economic and Clinical Health (HITECH), Pub. L. No. 111–5, 123 Stat. 226 (codified as amended in scattered sections of U.S.C.)
- Omnibus Final Rule: Modifications to the HIPAA Privacy, Security, Enforcement, and Breach Notification Rules Under the Health Information Technology for Economic and Clinical Health Act and the Genetic Information Nondiscrimination Act; Other Modifications to the HIPAA Rules; Final Rule, 45 C.F.R. §§ 160, 164

Addressing compliance risks:
- Covered entities must exercise adequate oversight over contracting activities involving the access of PHI.
- Covered entities need to implement processes that adequately identify business associates so that business associate agreements can be obtained and updated, and risks posed to the organization can be adequately assessed.

Endnotes

1. **Isabella A. Porter**, JD, CHC, CHPC, is the director of compliance and privacy officer of District Medical Group in Phoenix, Arizona. Porter is an Arizona licensed attorney who has been working in healthcare compliance since 2012. Her expertise includes vendor risk management, contract compliance, and privacy program compliance. Additional areas of expertise consist of compliance program administration in pediatric and behavioral health settings, policy and procedure development, cultural competency compliance, and program development in the following areas: internal audit, e-learning, and compliance and ethics for outpatient clinics and physician practice groups.

2. "Business Associates," U.S. Department of Health & Human Services Office for Civil Rights, last reviewed May 24, 2019, https://www.hhs.gov/hipaa/for-professionals/privacy/guidance/business-associates/index.html.

3. 45 C.F.R. § 160.103.

4. 45 C.F.R. § 160.103.

5. Modifications to the HIPAA Privacy, Security, Enforcement, and Breach Notification Rules Under the Health Information Technology for Economic and Clinical Health Act and the Genetic Information Nondiscrimination Act; Other Modifications to the HIPAA Rules, 78 Fed. Reg. 5572 (January 25, 2013).

6. Kim Stanger, "Avoiding Business Associate Agreements," *News and Insights*, Holland & Hart LLP, November 26, 2013, https://www.hollandhart.com/avoiding-business-associate-agreements.

7. Megan Bradshaw and Benjamin K. Hoover, "Not So Hip?: The Expanded Burdens on and Consequences to Law Firms as Business Associates Under HITECH Modifications to HIPAA," *Richmond Journal of Law and the Public Interest* vol. 13 (Spring 2010): 328.

8. Megan Bradshaw and Benjamin K. Hoover, "Not So Hip?: The Expanded Burdens on and Consequences to Law Firms as Business Associates Under HITECH Modifications to HIPAA," *Richmond Journal of Law and the Public Interest* vol. 13 (Spring 2010): 328.

9. Megan Bradshaw and Benjamin K. Hoover, "Not So Hip?: The Expanded Burdens on and Consequences to Law Firms as Business Associates Under HITECH Modifications to HIPAA," *Richmond Journal of Law and the Public Interest* vol. 13 (Spring 2010): 329.

10. "The Security Rule," U.S. Department of Health & Human Services Office for Civil Rights, last reviewed September 23, 2020, https://www.hhs.gov/hipaa/for-professionals/security/index.html.

11. "Summary of the HIPAA Security Rule," U.S. Department of Health & Human Services Office for Civil Rights, last reviewed July 26, 2013, https://www.hhs.gov/hipaa/for-professionals/security/laws-regulations/index.html.

12. "Business Associates," U.S. Department of Health & Human Services Office for Civil Rights, last reviewed May 24, 2019, https://www.hhs.gov/hipaa/for-professionals/privacy/guidance/business-associates/index.html.

13. "Covered Entities and Business Associates," U.S. Department of Health & Human Services Office for Civil Rights, last reviewed June 16, 2017, https://www.hhs.gov/hipaa/for-professionals/covered-entities/index.html.

14. "Business Associates," U.S. Department of Health & Human Services Office for Civil Rights, last reviewed May 24, 2019, https://www.hhs.gov/hipaa/for-professionals/privacy/guidance/business-associates/index.html.

15. "Business Associates," U.S. Department of Health & Human Services Office for Civil Rights, last reviewed May 24, 2019, https://www.hhs.gov/hipaa/for-professionals/privacy/guidance/business-associates/index.html.

16. "Business Associates," U.S. Department of Health & Human Services Office for Civil Rights, last reviewed May 24, 2019, https://www.hhs.gov/hipaa/for-professionals/privacy/guidance/business-associates/index.html.

17. "Covered Entities and Business Associates," U.S. Department of Health & Human Services Office for Civil Rights, last reviewed June 16, 2017, https://www.hhs.gov/hipaa/for-professionals/covered-entities/index.html.

18. "Business Associates," U.S. Department of Health & Human Services Office for Civil Rights, last reviewed May 24, 2019, https://www.hhs.gov/hipaa/for-professionals/privacy/guidance/business-associates/index.html.

19. 45 C.F.R. § 164.514(e).

20. "Business Associate Contracts," U.S. Department of Health & Human Services Office for Civil Rights, last reviewed June 16, 2017, https://www.hhs.gov/hipaa/for-professionals/covered-entities/sample-business-associate-agreement-provisions/index.html.

21. "Business Associate Contracts," U.S. Department of Health & Human Services Office for Civil Rights, last reviewed June 16, 2017, https://www.hhs.gov/hipaa/for-professionals/covered-entities/sample-business-associate-agreement-provisions/index.html.

22. 45 C.F.R. § 164.512(i).

23. 45 C.F.R. § 164.514(e).

24. "Business Associate Contracts," U.S. Department of Health & Human Services Office for Civil Rights, last reviewed June 16, 2017, https://www.hhs.gov/hipaa/for-professionals/covered-entities/sample-business-associate-agreement-provisions/index.html.

25. Kim Stanger, "Avoiding Business Associate Agreements," *News and Insights*, Holland & Hart LLP, November 26, 2013, https://www.hollandhart.com/avoiding-business-associate-agreements.

26. Kim Stanger, "Avoiding Business Associate Agreements," *News and Insights*, Holland & Hart LLP, November 26, 2013, https://www.hollandhart.com/avoiding-business-associate-agreements.

27. Notification of Enforcement Discretion Regarding HIPAA Civil Money Penalties, 84 Fed Reg 18151 (April 30, 2019).

28. Health Information Technology for Economic and Clinical Health (HITECH), Pub. L. No. 111–5, 123 Stat. 226 § 13404.

29. Deven McGraw, Susan Ingargiola, and Kier Wallis, *Business Associate Compliance With HIPAA: Findings from a Survey of Covered Entities and Business Associates,*

(Los Angeles: Manatt, 2022), 2, https://www.manatt.com/getattachment/0b19cc2d-ed14-458b-a4bc-7b4436437c4f/attachment.aspx.

30. "Raleigh Orthopaedic Resolution Agreement," U.S. Department of Health & Human Services, accessed January 13, 2022, https://www.hhs.gov/sites/default/files/raleigh-orthopaedic-racap.pdf.

31. "North Memorial Resolution Agreement," U.S. Department of Health & Human Services, accessed January 13, 2022, https://www.hhs.gov/sites/default/files/north-memorial-ra-and-cap-march-2016.pdf.

32. "Porter Resolution Agreement," U.S. Department of Health & Human Services, accessed January 13, 2022, https://www.hhs.gov/sites/default/files/porter-ra-cap-508.pdf.

33. Health Information Technology for Economic and Clinical Health (HITECH), Pub. L. No. 111–5, 123 Stat. 226 § 13401.

34. Deven McGraw, Susan Ingargiola, & Kier Wallis, "Business Associate Compliance With HIPAA: Findings From a Survey of Covered Entities and Business Associates," Manatt and The California HealthCare Foundation, accessed January 13, 2022, 2, https://www.manatt.com/getattachment/0b19c-c2d-ed14-458b-a4bc-7b4436437c4f/attachment.aspx.

35. Health Information Technology for Economic and Clinical Health (HITECH), Pub. L. No. 111–5, 123 Stat. 226 §§ 13410, 13411.

36. Deven McGraw, Susan Ingargiola, and Kier Wallis, *Business Associate Compliance With HIPAA: Findings from a Survey of Covered Entities and Business Associates*, (Los Angeles: Manatt, 2022), 2, https://www.manatt.com/getattachment/0b19cc2d-ed14-458b-a4bc-7b4436437c4f/attachment.aspx.

37. Modifications to the HIPAA Privacy, Security, Enforcement, and Breach Notification Rules Under the Health Information Technology for Economic and Clinical Health Act and the Genetic Information Nondiscrimination Act; Other Modifications to the HIPAA Rules, 78 Fed. Reg. 5574 (January 25, 2013).

38. "Direct Liability of Business Associates," U.S. Department of Health & Human Services Office for Civil Rights, last reviewed July 16, 2021, https://www.hhs.gov/hipaa/for-professionals/privacy/guidance/business-associates/factsheet/index.html.

39. "Direct Liability of Business Associates," U.S. Department of Health & Human Services Office for Civil Rights, last reviewed July 16, 2021, https://www.hhs.gov/hipaa/for-professionals/privacy/guidance/business-associates/factsheet/index.html.

40. "Direct Liability of Business Associates," U.S. Department of Health & Human Services Office for Civil Rights, last reviewed July 16, 2021, https://www.hhs.gov/hipaa/for-professionals/privacy/guidance/business-associates/factsheet/index.html.

41. "Direct Liability of Business Associates," U.S. Department of Health & Human Services Office for Civil Rights, last reviewed July 16, 2021, https://www.hhs.gov/hipaa/for-professionals/privacy/guidance/business-associates/factsheet/index.html.

42. Kim Stanger, "Ensure You Have Business Associate Agreements or Face HIPAA Penalties," *News and Insights*, Holland & Hart LLP, May 12, 2016, https://www.hollandhart.com/ensure-you-have-business-associate-agreements-or-face-hipaa-penalties.

43. Madison M. Pool, "No Good Deed Goes Unpunished: Reporting Business Associate's HIPAA Breach Results in Liability for Covered Entity," Arnall Golden Gregory LLP, March 9, 2020, https://www.agg.com/news-insights/publications/no-good-deed-goes-unpunished-reporting-business-associates-hipaa-breach-results-in-liability-for-covered-entity/.

Cyberattacks

By Michelle O'Neill[1]

What Are the Effects of Cyberattacks on Patient Privacy and Security?

Cyberattacks are attacks, via the internet, targeting an enterprise's use of cyberspace for the purpose of disrupting, disabling, destroying, or maliciously controlling a computing environment or infrastructure—or destroying the integrity of the data or stealing controlled information. The individuals or organizations that carry out cyberattacks are typically called cybercriminals, and they use cyberattacks to cause damage, to create disruption, to enact revenge, for financial gain, and for purposes of cyberwarfare. Unfortunately, the healthcare sector remains the number one target for cyberattacks. This is primarily due to the value of the data that can be obtained from a successful attack and the fact that cybercriminals are aware that if they lock up systems and patient data, it significantly affects operations and ultimately patient care.

Cyberattacks are continuing to increase and cause massive chaos to the healthcare industry. In 2017, the Healthcare Industry Cybersecurity Task Force concluded that the industry was in "critical condition," and the 2017 WannaCry cyberattack is a prime example of an attack that crippled the healthcare industry.[2] The WannaCry attack infected thousands of computers throughout the world and threw the United Kingdom's National Health Service into some chaos. Although there was no evidence that patients died as a result of WannaCry, the attack still hijacked thousands of hospital computers and diagnostic equipment.[3] NotPetya was another cyberattack in 2017 and was one of the largest cybercrimes of all time. It caused $10 billion in damage to companies and affected computers around the world.[4] The company's systems were shut down for weeks and left healthcare systems unable to use their programs, including Sutter Health. Sutter Health was prepared to respond to the attack, but even with preparation, they dealt with a backlog of more than one million files that needed to be transcribed. There are times when these notes were needed urgently, and this could have been a huge patient safety issue, and from an operational perspective, how do you recover from a backlog of one million files?

Ransomware attacks and vendor-related breaches also rose in 2019. In addition, phishing campaigns tied to the Covid-19 pandemic peaked in mid-April 2020. In 2020, US federal agencies sent an alert that there was "credible information of an increased and imminent cybercrime threat" to hospitals and healthcare providers.[5] Federal agencies urged institutions to take necessary precautions to protect their networks. The agencies stated that the hackers were using a malicious software used to encrypt and lock up data. Throughout 2020, US hospitals have been targeted in a rising wave of ransomware attacks. Hospitals have been consistently hit by ransomware attacks designed designed to infect systems. As a result of these hits, healthcare providers and hospitals were strongly urged to take necessary precautions to protect their networks.

In addition to healthcare moving to the top of the list of the most expensive data breaches, cyberattacks against the healthcare industry also have the greatest impact and risk of harm to individuals. These attacks cause damage to an organization's reputation within the community that it services and threaten patient privacy, clinical outcomes, and healthcare organizations' financial resources. Losing access to patient information or having patient information held hostage greatly affects the ability of healthcare organizations to effectively care for patients. Inappropriate access to private patient information not only violates the patient's privacy but can also open the door for cybercriminals to alter patient data, which can lead to severe effects on clinical outcomes for patients.

There are many compliance risks associated with a cyberattack of patient information. The first and most important is the fact that patient safety could be affected by an attack. If a provider and/or healthcare organization is unable to effectively treat a patient because information is altered or unavailable, this can be a serious issue for the patient and ultimately affects patient safety. In addition, a cyberattack could result in a privacy breach, which affects the patient's privacy and puts the patient at risk for identity theft and other fraudulent activity.

Also take into consideration the fact that a cyberattack could result in negative press against the organization and loss of trust among patients. A cyberattack shakes patient confidence in the organization. If patients do not feel that their information is private and secure, they will not continue to seek care at the organization. This impacts patient care and ultimately can hurt the organization financially.

Risk Area Governance

The National Institute of Standards and Technology (NIST) Cybersecurity Framework provides cybersecurity best practices along with a framework for managing risk.[6] The NIST Cybersecurity Framework was developed as a guide to provide a voluntary risk-based approach based on existing standards and guidelines. It also gives organizations the ability to tailor this framework based on the specific organization and the specific security needs. The framework includes updated recommendations on authentication, cyber-risk assessments, and vulnerability disclosures. While NIST is applicable to many different sectors, there are also many sector-specific rules that apply to the privacy and security of information and cyberattacks. Although NIST Cybersecurity Framework standards are best practice and what organizations should follow to prevent healthcare breaches, this is only voluntary guidance, and organizations will not be penalized for not adhering to this framework. Interestingly, a study done by CynergisTek in 2020 found that only 44% of hospitals and healthcare entities were following the NIST Cybersecurity Framework.[7] This number is concerning, and CynergisTek commented on the results of the study, stating that "in cybersecurity, if you are not improving, you are falling behind in managing your risks."[8]

In healthcare, the main federal laws that protect health information are the Health Insurance Portability and Accountability Act of 1996 (HIPAA) Privacy, Security, and Breach Notification rules. [9][10][11] The Privacy Rule sets limits on how patient health information can be used and shared with others and gives patients rights in respect to their health information. The Security Rule sets how patients' health information must be kept secure with administrative, technical, and physical safeguards. The Breach Notification Rule requires HIPAA-covered entities and their business associates to provide notification following a breach of unsecured protected health information. Breaches are generally defined as any impermissible use and disclosure that compromises the privacy or security of protected health information. Privacy and security violations are determined to be breaches following a risk assessment. If there is a high probability that the protected health information has been compromised, notification must occur as per the Breach Notification Rule. This notification includes the affected individual, and in cases where the breach affects over 500 individuals, notification must also be made to the secretary of the Department of Health & Human Services and the media.[12] If a breach of unsecured protected health information occurs by a business associate, the business associate must notify the covered entity following the discovery of the breach.

The Office for Civil Rights (OCR) is the entity that oversees HIPAA, and the OCR's major goal is to ensure that patients' health information is properly protected while allowing for the flow of health information needed to provide and promote high-quality healthcare and to protect the public's health and well-being. In addition to providing guidance on how to protect patient information, the OCR also provides excellent guidance on steps to take if an entity experiences a cyberattack. This includes executing a response, mitigation efforts, and contingency plans, as well as reporting obligations, and these mitigation efforts are taken into consideration in an event where OCR investigates a cybersecurity event or breach investigation.

Common Compliance Risks

Human error is one of the biggest risk factors in cybersecurity attacks. A recent study by the Ponemon Institute and IBM Security found that human error accounted for 95% of cybersecurity breaches.[13] Many of the successful security attacks occur as a result of an employee falling victim to an external hacker. These cybercriminals count on human error and weakness to carry out their attacks. This can be an employee clicking on a phishing email or having their system infected with malware by opening up a suspicious attachment. A HIPAA breach can also occur if an employee emails protected health information to the incorrect recipient or faxes to the wrong entity. These errors are unfortunately very common. It is important for organizations to place focus on human behavior and the "people" part of the organization, as they are not only the biggest risk factor but also often your first line of defense. If employees are aware of the threats they face and equipped with the tools to detect them, they can prevent cybersecurity attacks from occurring.

Other compliance risks include not being prepared for a cyberattack. This would be neglecting to have a privacy and security program in place—including a business continuity plan and proactive breach response plan. Risk assessments must also be done to assess risk and determine the best approach to mitigate that risk. The plan should be documented and continuously monitored and audited. Employees also need to be aware of how and when to report privacy and security issues or concerns, as these can lead to more serious consequences if they are not mitigated or prevented going forward.

Addressing Compliance Risks

There are several ways to effectively address the compliance risks associated with human error. The most important strategy is to be proactive in handling privacy and security concerns and preventing cybercrimes.

Have HIPAA Policies and Procedures

It is also imperative to have a strong privacy and security program in place, which includes policies and procedures supporting the program. Healthcare organizations are required to have HIPAA policies and procedures in place to ensure that all workforce members understand and follow the privacy laws and regulations. This is done by providing all workforce members with training upon hire, annually, and with periodic reviews throughout the year. Organizations should also make these policies available to all employees, either by intranet, email, or hard copy. These policies do need to be reviewed as needed for updates and changes to regulations and policies.

Educate Leadership About Compliance, Privacy, and Security Issues

Compliance, privacy, and security need to be important cultural values at the organization. This piece is often the most challenging but also the most valuable. Privacy and security should start with executive leadership. Organizations should have leadership at the organization engaged and should regularly meet to discuss privacy and security issues, news, updates, and trends. This can occur by discussing privacy and security at executive meetings and having the leaders weigh in on communicating to the organization. It's also important for privacy and security officers to update leadership as there are constant changes, updates, and threats that they need to be aware of. The staff in an organization look up to leadership, and having that executive-level buy-in creates a "lead by example" approach that helps maintain the privacy and security culture that an organization strives to have.

Educate Employees About Cyberattacks and the Privacy and Security Program

Employees should be aware of the privacy and security program and should look at protecting the privacy and security of patients as one of the most important aspects of their job. Part of the program should also make employees aware of their duty to report any privacy or security concerns as soon as they become aware. The program should give employees the tools to recognize a cyberattack, which could be a phishing attack, malware, a hacking incident—anything that could jeopardize the privacy and security of the systems and patient information. Employees should know that they can reach out when they have concerns or questions and be willing to change behaviors that may put the organization at risk. An open-door policy is key. If employees feel that they can reach out with questions and concerns in a nonpunitive manner, privacy and security officers are better able to proactively correct and/or assist with issues before they become privacy or security violations or breaches. It's so important that employees feel comfortable reaching out because they are often the first line of defense in preventing a data breach. Having this strong culture of compliance and privacy also empowers employees to do their best to be aware of privacy and security in their day-to-day work, detect potential issues, and prevent issues from occurring.

Provide Training on Privacy and Security

Training and education are very important. New hire, annual, and periodic trainings on privacy and security help, but this is the bare minimum that should be provided. It is important that these trainings are not just check-the-box trainings but are effective and engaging. This can be done by continuously updating and reviewing the training that is in place. Videos have been well received in many organizations, and the real-life scenarios often help employees understand and relate to the material better. Phishing campaigns are also very helpful in not only educating employees about not clicking on links and providing credentials but also help organizations track how likely a phishing attack would be successful and where training needs to occur.

Another important proactive step would be to ensure that there is a business continuity plan and breach response plan in place prior to a cyberattack. A common statement in the security world is, "it's not if, but when," and being prepared is vital to responding to and mitigating the damage caused by cyberattacks. A plan will help handle the crisis caused by a cyberattack and help get backup patient data available quickly, if necessary, and assist in understanding what data was affected so that the appropriate processes can be followed.

Possible Penalties

Cyberattacks are extremely expensive to healthcare organizations, often costing millions. The impact of a breach can be divided into three categories: financial, reputational, and legal. The economic cost is related to theft of financial information and/or money. Also, if there is a disruption in business, this can also affect a healthcare organization financially. Reputational damage can include loss of patients and business, and legal costs related to a cybersecurity breach can be high: fees from outside counsel, notification costs to patients, and any fines that need to be paid as a result of the breach. The global average cost of a data breach is around $3.5–$4 million per the Ponemon Institute's *Cost of a Data Breach Report 2020*.[14] This can greatly affect organizations financially. The other interesting piece that the Ponemon/IBM Security report touched on was the fact that the healthcare industry was also identified as having the longest time to identify a violation. This is quite concerning, as this is patient information, and this can really affect patient safety and create all sorts of risks for the patient, including medical identity theft. The delay in identifying a violation would also affect the settlement and/or cost of recovery for a significant breach.

HIPAA Penalties

Penalties for HIPAA violations or breaches can be issued by the OCR and state attorneys. In addition to financial penalties, healthcare entities can be required to adopt a corrective action plan to ensure that their policies and procedures reflect the requirements of the HIPAA rule. The purpose of these penalties is to act as a deterrent to prevent violations and also hold covered entities accountable. The penalties are based upon many different factors, including whether the covered entity had knowledge of the violation, and is ultimately impacted by the seriousness of the violation. In addition to the financial penalties, criminal penalties can also be issued. Criminal penalties come into play when an individual knowingly violated HIPAA. An example of a criminal HIPAA violation would be theft of patient information for financial gain and/or to cause harm.

Compliance Resources

U.S. Department of Health & Human Services

Health Information Privacy

www://www.hhs.gov/hipaa/index.html

U.S. Department of Commerce

National Institute of Standards & Technology (NIST) Cybersecurity Framework

https://www.nist.gov/cyberframework

Risk Takeaways

Main points of interest:
- Cyberattacks are increasing and cause massive chaos to the healthcare industry.
- Due to phishing campaigns tied to the pandemic, hospitals and healthcare providers are at an elevated risk for cyberattacks.
- Cyberattacks threaten patient privacy, clinical outcomes, financial resources, and the organization's reputation within the community that it serves.
- If a provider and/or healthcare organization is unable to effectively treat a patient because information is altered or unavailable, this can be a serious issue for the patient that ultimately affects patient safety. A cyberattack could also result in a privacy breach, which puts patients at risk for identity theft and other fraudulent activity.
- A cyberattack could result in negative press against the organization and lack of trust from patients.

Areas to watch:
- Human error

Laws that apply:
- NIST Cybersecurity Framework
- HIPAA Privacy Rule: 45 C.F.R. §§ 160, 164.102, 164.500
- HIPAA Security Rule: 45 C.F.R. §§ 160, 164.102, 164.302
- HIPAA Breach Notification Rule: 45 C.F.R. §§ 164.400-414

Addressing compliance risks:
- Organizations should have a strong privacy and security program in place that includes policies and procedures supporting the program.
- Leadership at the organization should be engaged and should regularly meet to discuss privacy and security issues, news, updates, and trends.
- Employees should be aware of the privacy and security program and should look at protecting the privacy and security of patients as one of the most important aspects of their job. The program should also give employees the tools to recognize a cyberattack, which could be a phishing attack, malware, a hacking incident—anything that could jeopardize the privacy and security of the systems and patient information. Employees should know they can reach out when they have concerns or questions and be willing to change behaviors that may put the organization at risk.
- Training and education on privacy and security should be provided to new hires, as well as annually and periodically to staff.
- Ensure that there is a business continuity plan and breach response plan in place prior to a cyberattack.

Endnotes

1. **Michelle O'Neill** is the vice president of corporate compliance & privacy at Summit Medical Group and CityMD. She is an experienced compliance and privacy officer who lays the foundation for the culture of compliance at the nation's premier independent-owned multispecialty medical group and the largest urgent care company in the New York City metro area. She is focused on education and training; fraud, waste, and abuse; patient and employee privacy and security; and nondiscrimination in healthcare.

2. Healthcare Industry Cybersecurity Task Force, *Report on Improving Cybersecurity in the Health Care Industry*, June 2017, https://www.phe.gov/preparedness/planning/cybertf/documents/report2017.pdf.

3. Selena Larson, "Why hospitals are so vulnerable to ransomware attacks," CNN, May 16, 2017, https://money.cnn.com/2017/05/16/technology/hospitals-vulnerable-wannacry-ransomware/index.html.

4. Andy Greenberg, "The Untold Story of NotPetya, the Most Devastating Cyberattack in History," *Wired*, August 22, 2018, https://www.wired.com/story/notpetya-cyberattack-ukraine-russia-code-crashed-the-world/.

5. Cybersecurity and Infrastructure Security Agency, "Alert (AA20-302A): Ransomware Activity Targeting the Healthcare and Public Health Sector," news alert, last revised November 2, 2020, https://us-cert.cisa.gov/ncas/alerts/aa20-302a.

6. "Cybersecurity Framework," National Institute of Standards and Technology, accessed January 13, 2021, https://www.nist.gov/cyberframework.

7. CynergisTek, *Moving Forward: Setting the Direction, 2020 Annual Report*, September 7, 2020, https://insights.cynergistek.com/i/1288397-2020-annual-report/1?.

8. CynergisTek, *Moving Forward: Setting the Direction*, 1.

9. 45 C.F.R. §§ 160, 164.102, 164.500.

10. 45 C.F.R. §§ 160, 164.102, 164.302.

11. 45 C.F.R. §§ 164.400-414.

12. 45 C.F.R. § 164.40.

13. IBM Security and Ponemon Institute, *Cost of a Data Breach Report 2020*, July 29, 2020, https://www.ibm.com/security/digital-assets/cost-data-breach-report/#/.

14. IBM Security and Ponemon Institute, *Cost of Data Breach Report 2020*.

Hybrid Work Environment

By Sheila Price Limmroth,[1] CHC, CIA

What Is a Hybrid Work Environment and Its Effect on Patient Privacy and Security?

Traditionally, employers have set expectations that employees physically show up at an office to perform their work assignments. Even jobs that could lend themselves to remote work have required an in-person presence. In 2020, however, such workforce expectations changed with the onset of the COVID-19 pandemic. That summer, Owl Labs and Global Workplace Analytics (GWA) surveyed 2,025 full-time workers in the United States between the ages 21 and 65 at companies with 10 or more employees. The survey found that 92% of respondents expected to work from home at least one day per week after COVID-19 restrictions lifted and workplaces reopened; 80% expected to work from home at least three days per week.[2] Hence, expectations are that the hybrid work environment will become the norm at most companies, allowing employees to work not just from their homes but also from anywhere in addition to their workplace office.

Working in a hybrid environment requires collaboration and communication technology. Employees must have the tools to be productive from wherever they are working when not in the traditional office setting. An organization may provide equipment that meets the requirements of the Health Insurance Portability and Accountability Act of 1996 (HIPAA) Security Rule (such as a company-owned cell phone, computer, or tablet). Most likely, the organization will permit employees to use their own equipment but require safeguards to protect the data accessed by the home computer and personal mobile devices. The organization should provide processes employees can follow to safeguard electronic information accessed from outside the organization. In 2021, a report on a Webex by Cisco survey of 2,366 knowledge workers noted that 57% (of workers) expect to be in the office 10 days or fewer each month and 98% believe future meetings will include remote participants.[3] Thus, setting expectations for hybrid workers is imperative in protecting the organization's data.

A hybrid work environment can create positive goodwill and loyalty for employees looking for work-life balance. In the healthcare arena, a hybrid work environment can also pose significant risk for employers that must comply with HIPAA. Employers must emphasize patient privacy and security risks inherent in the hybrid working environment and provide guidance to employees on how to avoid the risks. In the healthcare arena, it is imperative that patient privacy is protected by maintaining the confidentiality of protected health information (PHI). PHI refers to individually identifiable health information, including demographic data, related to the past, present, or future physical or mental health or condition; the provision of healthcare to an individual; or the past, present, or future payment for such healthcare, which is created or received by the covered entity.[4] This article focuses on risks to PHI in the healthcare setting and how the risks can be mitigated through privacy protections and administrative, technical, and physical safeguards listed in the HIPAA Security Rule.

Healthcare Workers and the Hybrid Work Environment

Remote workers with access to PHI may create significant risks for the covered entity. The risks are not limited to electronic PHI (ePHI); paper documents carried back and forth can pose risks, as can verbal conversations in the home office. In the past, the typical remote worker in the healthcare setting was the medical records coder. With the COVID-19 pandemic, the dynamic changed and additional types of healthcare workers now find themselves enjoying the benefits of remote or hybrid work. Because of the pandemic, the typical hybrid worker in the healthcare setting may be accessing billing information, working with customer/patient complaints and grievances, performing quality improvement audits, or coordinating patient care upon discharge. These tasks involve significant use of PHI combined with verbal conversations, and, in some instances, print capability. PHI risks are increased with the new tasks that are completed outside the entity's physical building.

Because a hybrid work environment can result in additional physical movement of PHI beyond the work environment and access to a covered entity's network from external sources, the risks that medical information is unsecured increases. Unsecured PHI is subject to breach, and the reporting that is necessary to individuals and the U.S. Department of Health & Human Services (HHS) Office for Civil Rights (OCR) has several potential negative ramifications, including reputational harm. Risks should be assessed for the hybrid work environment so that they may be addressed prior to a breach.

Risk Area Governance

The HIPAA Security Rule and Privacy Rule apply if employees who work remotely have access to PHI as defined in the Privacy Rule. HIPAA describes what should be protected through the Privacy Rule and specifically addresses safeguards necessary for ePHI in the Security Rule.

HIPAA Privacy Rule, 45 C.F.R. §§ 160, 164 (Subparts A and E)

The HIPAA Privacy Rule applies to individually identifiable health information held or transmitted by a covered entity (provider, health plan, healthcare clearinghouse, or business associate) in *any form or media*, whether electronic, paper, or verbal. This information is called protected health information (PHI). According to the OCR,

> "Individually identifiable health information" is information, including demographic data, that relates to:
>
> - the individual's past, present or future physical or mental health or condition
> - the provision of health care to the individual, or
> - the past, present, or future payment for the provision of health care to the individual,
>
> and that identifies the individual or for which there is a reasonable basis to believe can be used to identify the individual. Individually identifiable health information includes many common identifiers (e.g., name, address, birth date, Social Security Number).[5]

HIPAA Security Rule, 45 C.F.R. §§ 160, 164 (Subparts A and C)

The HIPAA Security Rule protects a subset of information covered by the Privacy Rule, which is all individually identifiable health information a covered entity creates, receives, maintains, or transmits in *electronic* form. The Security Rule calls this information "electronic protected health information" (ePHI). The Security Rule does not apply to PHI transmitted verbally or in writing.

The Security Rule requires covered entities to maintain reasonable and appropriate administrative, technical, and physical safeguards for protecting ePHI. Specifically, covered entities must comply with all of the following:

1. Ensure the confidentiality, integrity, and availability of all ePHI they create, receive, maintain, or transmit.

2. Identify and protect against reasonably anticipated threats to the security or integrity of the information.

3. Protect against reasonably anticipated, impermissible uses or disclosures.

4. Ensure compliance by their workforce.[6]

Covered entities must determine how they will address the administrative, technical, and physical safeguards described in the HIPAA Security Rule when permitting a hybrid work environment in which the remote worker has access to ePHI.

Office for Civil Rights Guidance on Remote Use

In 2006, the OCR recognized the need for guidance for remote workers with access to ePHI. In the guidance, the OCR states that a covered entity, when deciding on security strategies, should consider the size and complexity of the organization, its technical infrastructure, costs of security measures, and probability and criticality of potential risks to ePHI.

The OCR suggests significant emphasis should be placed on three areas of compliance:

1. Risk analysis and risk management

2. Policies and procedures for safeguarding ePHI

3. Security awareness and training on the policies and procedures[7]

Common Compliance Risks

Use of Personal Devices Without Encryption

Employees may download ePHI to their personal devices and take screenshot photos with mobile devices. The unencrypted ePHI is left vulnerable to viewing by those who have no reason to view the information.

Use of Personal Devices Without Appropriate Protections

Employees may not have protections from malware on their personal devices. They may not pay for anti-virus protection or update their personal devices as necessary. Software updates are critical as they often patch known vulnerabilities in the software.

Print Capability

Employees may be granted print access for their remote location. Whether the printed PHI represents billing details or coding information, for example, the risks are significant that family members or visitors may view the paper documents. When on-site, employees may have access to shredders or locked shred bins. This may not be the case in the remote environment. Such risks could result in breach of confidentiality and a HIPAA violation.

Ransomware and Phishing Attacks

Whether working remotely or in the workplace office, employees who have not been educated about the risks may inadvertently allow the infiltration of bad actors by simply clicking on a fake email. With COVID-19 came an influx of phishing scams.[8] Phishing is a cybercrime in which a target or targets are contacted by email, telephone, or text message by someone posing as a legitimate institution to lure individuals into providing sensitive data, such as personally identifiable information, banking and credit card details, and passwords. The information is then used to access important accounts and can result in identity theft and financial loss. Some of the more notable email phishing schemes during the pandemic have included emails claiming to be sent from the Centers for Disease Control and Prevention (CDC) and the World Health Organization (WHO); scams offering reduced pricing on personal protective equipment (PPE); and fake invoices attached to scam vendor emails.

IT Department Failure to Track Users and Secure Networks

An increase in the remote workforce increases the need for security utilizing technical safeguards described in the HIPAA Security Rule. An organization's IT personnel must ensure that remote access is compliant with the HIPAA Security Rule. This includes verification that access to company software is through a secured network. Typically, employees gain access to the company's software and their computer through virtual private network (VPN) technologies. Users must have VPN software on their device and be authenticated prior to being granted access.

Physical Movement

Working remotely followed by a day in the office sounds like a win-win for employee and employer. The physical movement, however, can create risks. If permitted, the employee may have the ability to move data back and forth between home and work offices using technology such as USB storage devices and cloud-based sites or physical paper. Such movement of ePHI becomes difficult to manage and for the employer to track.

Verbal PHI Discussions

During the COVID-19 pandemic, Zoom, Microsoft Teams, and other virtual meetings became the everyday norm. No topic was off limits, including discussions involving PHI. Such meetings pose a compliance risk for the remote worker because the information can be overheard. This is especially concerning if the employee is working not just from home, but also at a coffee shop, bookstore, or other businesses. These locations can increase the risk that PHI will not be adequately protected.

Documenting and Discussing Credit Card Information

HIPAA is not the only law that should be considered when protecting the confidentiality of data. The Payment Card Industry Data Security Standards (PCI DSS) should also be considered. According to Investopedia, "PCI compliance standards require merchants and other businesses to handle credit card information in a secure manner that helps reduce the likelihood that cardholders would have sensitive financial account information stolen. If merchants do not handle credit card information according to PCI Standards, the card information could be hacked and used for a multitude of fraudulent actions."[9] Healthcare organizations should assess whether they must meet the requirements of the PCI Standards. An excellent resource for additional information on PCI compliance is the PCI Security Standards Council.[10]

Regardless of whether the organization is required to meet the PCI Standards, a best practice is to ensure the employee is working in a secure location where credit card information obtained and repeated in phone conversations cannot be compromised. Additionally, employees should be reminded that they should not write down credit card numbers and that credit card information should not be stored outside of approved systems.

Addressing Compliance Risks

IT Controls

Compliance departments can verify that the privacy and security risks associated with the hybrid work environment are being managed through discussions with appropriate management. Discussions should occur with HIPAA privacy and security personnel as well as members of the IT Department, including the chief information officer, Human Resources Department, and members of a compliance oversight committee.

One of the first steps in addressing risks related to the hybrid work environment is determining how remote workforce issues have been incorporated into the IT risk assessment. The Security Rule requires entities to evaluate risks and vulnerabilities in their environments and to implement reasonable and appropriate security measures to protect against reasonably anticipated threats or hazards to the security or integrity of ePHI.[11] External consultants or internal staff may perform the IT risk assessment. It represents the covered entity's unique risk profile based on the size and complexity of the organization.

The risk assessment process includes data mapping to ensure all ePHI in motion (transmitted) and at rest (stored) is captured. Once all ePHI has been catalogued for the entire organization and includes transmission and storage by the remote workforce, the focus should be on documenting potential threats to the organization's ePHI, the likelihood that the threats could occur, the resulting harm from them, and the mitigating controls that can be placed in operation to neutralize threats. Specific to the hybrid work environment, the compliance professional should discuss controls to minimize threats as the result of telework, which include requiring the following:

- Firewalls and anti-virus software on the remote worker's personal devices

- Encryption and password protection on home routers

- Encryption and strong passwords/facial recognition/retina scans to protect personal devices used to access ePHI (e.g., cell phones, tablets)

- Timed screen locks on personal computers in the home office (similar to what is required in the on-site work office)

- Privacy screens for hybrid remote workers who have limited space within their home

- VPN log-off when employee is not working

- Encryption for emails that contain ePHI

- IT maintenance of remote activity logs and routine disabling of inactive accounts after a predefined time

- Multifactor authentication on all platforms that are accessed remotely

In addition to having these remote work requirements to minimize privacy and security risks to ePHI, compliance professionals will also want to address the remote-worker approval process. One of the administrative safeguards under the HIPAA Security Rule addresses workforce security.[12] Role-based access ensures that only those workers, including workers in a hybrid environment, have access to ePHI if it is necessary for them to perform assigned duties. The minimum necessary standard should also be addressed for remote workers, just as it is for workers on-site at the covered entity. The minimum necessary requirement dictates, "protected health information should not be used or disclosed when it is not necessary to satisfy a particular purpose or carry out a function. The minimum necessary standard requires covered entities to evaluate their practices and enhance safeguards as needed to limit unnecessary or inappropriate access to and disclosure of protected health information."[13][14] The compliance professional can review the approval process for remote access requests to ensure compliance with role-based access to ePHI and the minimum necessary standard.

The IT personnel should be able to discuss their processes for monitoring access to the network and software systems that house ePHI. In the hybrid environment, remote-access logs should also be reviewed and inactive accounts disabled as part of the review process.

Videoconferencing Controls

The COVID-19 pandemic resulted in significant usage of videoconferencing as a means for remote workers to stay in touch with their employers and continue to be productive members of the workforce. As employees return to work on-site full-time or a combination of on-site and remote sites (hybrid), videoconferencing remains a preferred method of communication for many covered entities. The following steps protect ePHI discussed in video conferences in the hybrid work environment:

- Require use of only approved video-conferencing solutions and telehealth solutions (the IT security official should publish the approved solutions that meet the HIPAA Security Rule requirements).

- Require a personal identification number (PIN) for access to the conference.

- Disable screenshots.

- Keep the software used for videoconferencing updated (latest version).

- Review the list of attendees prior to sharing the host's screen.

- Lock the conference once everyone has arrived.

- Remind the remote worker to be aware of the confidentiality of the discussion (ensuring the remote worker is in a secure area so that verbal PHI cannot be overheard by family members or other people).

Videoconferencing is an easy way to conduct meetings, as the workforce has discovered, and these simple steps can protect the privacy and security of videoconference discussions.

Policies and Procedures

Policies and procedures should be reviewed to ensure that appropriate ones exist for the hybrid work environment and that any necessary updates have been made. Organizations should utilize the results of the risk assessment and determine, based on the organization's unique size and complexity, what policies and procedures best address threats to the organization. Compliance professionals should discuss with appropriate security, privacy, IT, and HR personnel the need for the following policies and procedures.

Bring Your Own Device (BYOD) Policy

Consideration should be given to the types of personal devices the organization permits employees to use to access networks and systems that house ePHI. Once parameters have been set based upon risk tolerance, the BYOD policy can be developed.

Remote Wipe Policy

If personal devices can be used to log in to networks, the IT Department should consider a remote wipe policy that permits IT personnel to delete data from an employee's personal device that has been lost or stolen.

Work from Home or Telecommuting Policy

This policy should outline expectations for all employees who will work at home all or part of the time for an employer. The policy should outline eligibility for telecommuting and set expectations and responsibilities for the employee. The policy and procedures should also outline security and privacy expectations such as the requirement that public Wi-Fi should not be used for remote work. Physical environment expectations should be listed. Finally, telecommuters should be given contact information for technical support so they have a method to report suspicious activity such as phishing. The policy should be tailored to the organization's needs and may incorporate a signed attestation by the employee. Attestations that employees understand their responsibilities are especially important for covered entities that must adhere to HIPAA. See the **Resource: Sample Temporary Remote Work Agreement** after this article for an example.

PHI Policy

Some organizations do not permit hybrid workers to work beyond a certain mileage radius of the home office. Other organizations only permit work from the employee's home. Once permitted access to and use of PHI, employees may be tracked through geofencing to ensure compliance with the organization's policy. Geofencing sets up a virtual perimeter and tracks the employee's location using GPS, Wi-Fi, cellular data, and radio frequency identification (RFID). Whether a covered entity permits work from home only or work from anywhere, a PHI policy may be implemented.

The policy protects verbal conversations by reminding employees that verbal conversations involving PHI should be protected from unauthorized disclosure. The policy should address PHI in relation to household members and guests when employees are working from home, as well as conversations in public areas. The most common type of unauthorized access to PHI is verbal conversations in dressing rooms, restaurants, and cafes where an exempt employee accepts a phone call and begins a discussion that eventually involves PHI. This scenario is not limited to hybrid work environments. The policy is applicable to all employees (including vacationing exempt employees) who accept phone calls in public areas when not working on-site. The policy can also incorporate work expectations when on-site; risky conversations involving confidential information often occur in hallways, work cafeterias, and elevators. A PHI policy serves to set expectations for all workforce members.

Print at Home Policy

For employees who must access ePHI as part of their remote work, the covered entity should address whether print capability will be enabled for the home office. Additionally, the organization should determine if job roles require that an employee be allowed to print PHI or sensitive information. PHI and other sensitive information should only be printed from outside the organization when deemed absolutely necessary as established by policy. If print access is permitted, the organization may choose to exclude use of wireless printers due to the risk that the information could be intercepted during transmission. The organization can help employees protect their wireless printers against wireless printer hacking by educating them on how to guard against malicious malware. To do this, the home or area should have a secure Wi-Fi connection. The organization's designated security official should provide an educational checklist for securing home networks and related networked devices. Other risks when home printers are used include the possibility that the printer has an internal hard drive that stores what it prints. This becomes problematic when saved print job(s) involve PHI and the printer is discarded without proper hard drive destruction.

If printing at home is permitted, the policy should set expectations for information that no longer needs to be printed or retained in a paper copy. The policy can also emphasize a "clean desk" expectation at home. The importance of not leaving paper documents in areas used by family, friends, and guests is an important part of the policy.

The covered entity should determine if a locked file cabinet will be necessary, as well as how and when paper should be destroyed. In some cases, the covered entity may require the home office to be equipped with a crosscut shredder. Other organizations may set expectations that the paper be transported and shredded at the on-site office. The OCR provides on its website specific destruction guidance entitled, "Guidance to Render Unsecured Protected Health Information Unusable, Unreadable, or Indecipherable to Unauthorized Individuals."[15] Following the OCR's guidance can assist in preventing HIPAA breaches that must be reported to individuals as well as to the OCR.

Sanctions Policy

The HIPAA Security Rule requires that covered entities have a documented sanctions policy addressing noncompliance with established privacy and security policies by the covered entity's workforce. The HHS issued remote access guidance in 2006 that states:

> A sanction policy must be in place and effectively communicated so that workforce members understand the consequences of failing to comply with the security policies and procedures of the covered entity related to offsite use of, or access to ePHI. When addressing the development and implementation of sanction policies, a covered entity should consider at least requiring employees to sign a statement of adherence to security policies and procedures as a prerequisite to employment.[16]

The compliance professional can reduce risks by reviewing the Work from Home Policy to verify that remote work expectations are aligned with the Sanctions Policy for noncompliance.

Retention Policies

Covered entities must understand state laws about the retention of documents, as well as HIPAA document retention requirements. The compliance professional should review state and federal retention laws that pertain to documents generated by remote workers to ensure compliance with all retention laws and regulations.

Use of External Media Policy

The organization's policy related to use of external media, such as flash drives, should be documented and updated for the hybrid work environment. Some organizations may require all PHI to remain on the organization's network and not permit PHI to be copied to external media. If the PHI is required and needs to be placed on external media, the organization may require approval from the company's security official. Owing to employee turnover occurring in healthcare, it is important that the organization convey specific policies such as a Use of External Media Policy to all employees to avoid confusion. For example, may workers download ePHI to a cloud service to work on from home or transport flash drives back and forth from the home office to the work office? A well-documented policy is necessary to enforce sanctions for noncompliance.

Media Sanitization Policy

This policy should be aligned with the Use of External Media Policy. A covered entity should determine parameters for destroying or erasing sensitive data, including individually identifiable information, from storage media such as CDs, DVDs, ZIP drives, and other media prior to the media being recycled, reused, or disposed of through regular trash. To reduce risks for media storage used by the remote worker, the compliance professional should determine the sanitization process and how it is enforced by the covered entity. The compliance professional may review the National Institute of Standards and Technology (NIST) Special Publication 800-88 Revision 1, "Guidelines for Media Sanitization," which provides best practices for media sanitization.[17]

Policies and procedures should already exist within the covered entity to address the HIPAA Privacy Rule and the HIPAA Security Rule. Compliance professionals can review the policies to verify if any gaps exist related to the hybrid work environment that need to be addressed.

Education and Training

The HIPAA Security Rule includes a Security Awareness and Training standard that states covered entities must, "implement a security awareness and training program for all members of its workforce (including management)."[18] Privacy and security training for employees should encompass hybrid/remote work employee expectations established by the covered entity through its policies and procedures. Employees must receive education on policies and procedures in order to be accountable for compliance with those policies. The compliance professional should review the training and education program for hybrid/remote employees. Additional targeted training should be considered for those members of the workforce who have high-risk roles, meaning the employee performs significant duties that involve significant access to ePHI in the hybrid environment.

Routine security awareness training for all employees, including remote and hybrid employees, is necessary. The training can be computer-based or in-person and supplemented throughout the year through mass emails and newsletters. The training should cover how to reduce security risks from ransomware attacks as well as phishing attacks. Even with spam filters used by the IT team to reduce this risk, phishing awareness training is necessary for the workforce. This training should help employees understand how to identify a phishing email. While misspelled words have helped employees identify such emails, recent phishing scams have improved their email techniques. Employee awareness training should include not clicking on attachments or embedded links if employees are not expecting such emails, even if the email appears to be from a known source. The employee should be taught to hover on the sender's email address to determine if it matches the sender's known email address.

Emails involving prizes (e.g., a day off without pay) when the recipient has not signed up for a prize or emails stating the recipient has won a prize that appears too good to be true are often phishing scams. Awareness training for all new techniques used by malicious actors is necessary for the workforce, regardless of an employee's status as remote, on-site, or hybrid worker.

Possible Penalties

The hybrid work environment is here to stay for many covered entities. PHI must be protected in accordance with HIPAA's Privacy and Security Rules, regardless of the worker's location when performing work assignments. Protection includes implementation of the administrative, technical, and physical safeguards as documented in the HIPAA Security Rule. Compliance professionals with HIPAA knowledge understand there are a number of risks related to PHI maintained by covered entities. The risks increase with a hybrid work environment. The compliance professional and management must address the risks through appropriate analyses.

Recent OCR settlements have proven the need for risk assessment, documented policies and procedures, and education and training for the remote workforce. These settlements indicate that risks can have significant repercussions for a covered entity, whether in the form of a costly corrective action plan (CAP) and/or financial penalty—both of which are levied by the OCR. An OCR press release on November 15, 2019, began with the headline, "Failure to Encrypt Mobile Devices Leads to a $3 Million HIPAA Settlement." This case is an example of HIPAA noncompliance penalties. These resulted from the University of Rochester Medical Center's (URMC's) report that an unencrypted flash drive containing ePHI was lost in 2013. In 2017, URMC reported an unencrypted personally owned laptop containing URMC ePHI was stolen from a treatment center. An OCR investigation into the URMC led to a CAP effective for two years along with a fine.[19] More examples can be found on the OCR website under "OCR News Releases & Bulletins." These settlements demonstrate the risks of ePHI in motion beyond the four walls of an individual locked office.

Compliance Resources

U.S. Department of Health & Human Services, Office for Civil Rights

Security Rule Guidance Material
The guidance includes documents on the following topics:

- Security 101 for covered entities
- Administrative safeguards
- Technical safeguards
- Physical safeguards
- Organizational policies, procedures, and documentation requirements

- Basics of risk analysis and risk management
- Security standards: implementation for the small provider
- Remote use
- Mobile devices
- Ransomware
- HHS security risk assessment tool

www.hhs.gov/hipaa/for-professionals/security/guidance/index.html

National Institute of Standards and Technology Special Publications
On the same page are links to relevant National Institute of Standards and Technology (NIST) publications for additional security guidance. They include:

- NIST Special Publication 800-30, "Risk Management Guide for Information Technology Systems"
  https://www.hhs.gov/sites/default/files/ocr/privacy/hipaa/administrative/securityrule/nist800-30.pdf?language=es
- NIST Special Publication 800-66, "An Introductory Resource Guide for Implementing the Health Insurance Portability and Accountability Act (HIPAA) Security Rule"
  https://www.hhs.gov/sites/default/files/ocr/privacy/hipaa/administrative/securityrule/nist80066.pdf?language=es
- NIST Special Publication 800-77, "Guide to IPsec VPNs"
  https://www.hhs.gov/sites/default/files/ocr/privacy/hipaa/administrative/securityrule/nist80077.pdf?language=es
- NIST Special Publication 800-88, "Computer Security: Guidelines for Media Sanitization"
  https://www.hhs.gov/sites/default/files/ocr/privacy/hipaa/administrative/securityrule/nist80088.pdf?language=es
- NIST Special Publication 800-111, "Guide to Storage Encryption Technologies for End User Devices"
  https://www.hhs.gov/sites/default/files/ocr/privacy/hipaa/administrative/securityrule/nist800111.pdf?language=es
- NIST HIPAA Security Rule Toolkit Application
  https://csrc.nist.gov/projects/security-content-automation-protocol/hipaa

OCR Cyber Awareness Newsletters
The OCR also publishes a quarterly cybersecurity newsletter. You can sign up for the newsletters to be delivered to your inbox. Each newsletter has links to related resources. Relevant issues of the OCR *Cybersecurity Newsletter* include the following:

- Summer 2021, Controlling Access to ePHI: For Whose Eyes Only?
  https://www.hhs.gov/hipaa/for-professionals/security/guidance/cybersecurity-newsletter-summer-2021/index.html
- Summer 2019, Managing Malicious Insider Threats
  https://www.hhs.gov/hipaa/for-professionals/security/guidance/cybersecurity-newsletter-summer-2019/index.html

- Fall 2019, What Happened to My Data?: Update on Preventing, Mitigating and Responding to Ransomware
  https://www.hhs.gov/hipaa/for-professionals/security/guidance/cybersecurity-newsletter-fall-2019/index.html
- Summer 2020, Making a List and Checking it Twice: HIPAA and IT Asset Inventories
  https://www.hhs.gov/hipaa/for-professionals/security/guidance/cybersecurity-newsletter-summer-2020/index.html

For all issues of this newsletter, visit: www.hhs.gov/hipaa/for-professionals/security/guidance/index.html

National Institute of Standards and Technology

Guide to Enterprise Telework, Remote Access, and Bring Your Own Device (BYOD) Security

This 2016 publication provides information on security considerations for several remote access solutions. It also provides recommendations for securing a variety of telework, remote access, and bring your own device (BYOD) technologies. The document can assist chief information officers when considering risks to ePHI within the hybrid work environment.

https://csrc.nist.gov/publications/detail/sp/800-46/rev-2/final

---

Risk Takeaways

Main points of interest:
- Obligations to safeguard PHI—whether verbally, on paper, or in electronic form—exist for covered entities that permit telework.
- The OCR issued remote use guidance on December 28, 2006, that can help covered entities develop strategies to mitigate PHI risks for the remote workforce.
- OCR settlements have shown the need to protect PHI during transmission. This is a high-risk area for organizations that have adopted a hybrid work environment.

Areas to watch:
- Compliance professionals should review the HIPAA Privacy and Security rules in relation to the hybrid work environment and verify policies and procedures that protect PHI have been updated and revised as needed.
- Covered entities should have an education and training program for teleworkers to set expectations and discuss required processes to protect PHI.
- Organizations should consider requiring remote workers to sign an attestation statement outlining the remote worker's responsibilities. The attestation should be aligned with policies and procedures, including the organization's Sanctions Policy.

> **Laws that apply:**
> - HIPAA Privacy Rule, 45 C.F.R. §§ 160, 164 (Subparts A and E)
> - HIPAA Security Rule, 45 C.F.R. §§ 160, 164 (Subparts A and C)
> - Office for Civil Rights (OCR) Guidance on Remote Use
> - Payment Card Industry Data Security Standards
>
> **Addressing compliance risks:**
> - Review the IT risk assessment and risk management program to ensure incorporation of the risks associated with the hybrid work environment.
> - Verify that policies and procedures exist and have been revised as necessary to address the hybrid workforce.
> - Verify that hybrid workforce members receive education and training on how to safeguard PHI, whether verbally, on paper, or in electronic form.

Endnotes

1. **Sheila Price Limmroth** is a part-time Privacy Specialist for DCH Health System in Tuscaloosa, Alabama. She oversees privacy investigations, continually develops privacy training and education programs, and audits employee access to electronic systems that house protected health information. She has worked at DCH 29.8 years, serving as the Corporate Director of Internal Audit, Corporate Director of Internal Audit/Compliance Officer, and also in the role of Privacy Officer prior to semi-retirement. Prior to DCH, Limmroth worked for Ernst & Young in the audit division.

2. Owl Labs and Global Workplace Analytics, *State of Remote Work: 2020 COVID Edition*, accessed January 7, 2022, https://owllabs.com/state-of-remote-work/2020.

3. Webex by Cisco and Dimensional Research, *Entering the Era of Hybrid Work: Understanding How the Workplace Must Evolve*, September 2021, accessed January 7, 2022, https://www.webex.com/content/dam/wbx/us/gated/analyst-report/dimensional-research-entering-the-era-of-hybrid-work-cm-2220.pdf.

4. 45 C.F.R. § 160.103.

5. U.S. Department of Health & Human Services, Office of Civil Rights, *OCR Privacy Brief: Summary of the HIPAA Privacy Rule*, last revised May 2003, https://www.hhs.gov/sites/default/files/privacysummary.pdf.

6. "Summary of the HIPAA Security Rule," U.S. Department of Health & Human Services, Office of Civil Rights, updated July 26, 2013, https://www.hhs.gov/hipaa/for-professionals/security/laws-regulations/index.html.

7. U.S. Department of Health & Human Services, Office of Civil Rights, *HIPAA Security Guidance*, December 28, 2006, https://www.hhs.gov/sites/default/files/ocr/privacy/hipaa/administrative/securityrule/remoteuse.pdf?language=es.

8. "What Is Phishing?," Phishing.org, accessed January 7, 2022, https://www.phishing.org/what-is-phishing.

9. Julia Kagan, "PCI Compliance," Investopedia, March 4, 2021, https://www.investopedia.com/terms/p/pci-compliance.asp .

10. "Document Library," PCI Security Standards Council, accessed December 21, 2021, https://www.pcisecurity-standards.org/document_library.

11. 45 C.F.R. § 164.308(a)(1)(ii)(A).

12. 45 C.F.R. § 164.308(a)(3)(i).

13. 45 C.F.R. § 164.502(b).

14. 45 C.F.R. § 164.514(d).

15. "Guidance to Render Unsecured Protected Health Information Unusable, Unreadable, or Indecipherable to Unauthorized Individuals," U.S. Department of Health & Human Services, Office for Civil Rights, July 26, 2013, https://www.hhs.gov/hipaa/for-professionals/breach-notification/guidance/index.html.

16. U.S. Department of Health & Human Services, Office of Civil Rights, *HIPAA Security Guidance*, December 28, 2006, https://www.hhs.gov/sites/default/files/ocr/privacy/hipaa/administrative/securityrule/remoteuse.pdf?language=es.

17. NIST Computer Resource Center, NIST Special Publication 800-88 Revision 1, Guidelines for Media Sanitization, February 2015, https://csrc.nist.gov/CSRC/media/Publications/Shared/documents/itl-bulletin/itlbul2015-02.pdf.

18. 45 C.F.R. § 164.308(a)(5).

19. U.S. Department of Health & Human Services, "Failure to Encrypt Mobile Devices Leads to $3 Million Fine," news release, November 5, 2019, https://www.hhs.gov/hipaa/for-professionals/compliance-enforcement/agreements/urmc/index.html.

Resource: Sample Temporary Work from Home Agreement

Employee Name:_____ Job Title: _____

Employee ID #: _____

Department: _____ Supervisor: _____

Effective Date:_____ Expire Date: _____

During unforeseen or uncontrollable circumstances such as natural disaster, unforeseen work site unavailability, or pandemic, [ORGANIZATION NAME] recognizes that for business continuity and the safety of its employees, employees with non-direct patient care duties may be required to work from home. This allowance of remote work is for a limited time as indicated above (not to exceed 30 days).

This Work from Home Agreement is voluntarily entered into between you and [ORGANIZATION NAME] for the purpose of allowing you to work from your home to the best of your abilities while setting out [ORGANIZATION NAME's] expectations of you to maintain maximum productivity and professionalism in your work.

You must understand that working from home is a privilege, and [ORGANIZATION NAME] reserves the right to end this relationship at any time based on its operational needs or in its discretion.

YOUR STATUS: You remain employed at the will of [ORGANIZATION NAME]. Nothing in this Agreement alters or in any way changes your status as an at-will employee. The only change in your status is that you will work primarily from your home, not from [ORGANIZATION NAME], while this Agreement is in effect. At all times you remain subject to the same policies, procedures, and Standards of Conduct as all other [ORGANIZATION NAME] employees.

YOUR DUTIES: You agree to perform to the best of your abilities and to devote all such time as necessary to perform all duties set out in your position's job description just as you would if you were working at [ORGANIZATION NAME]. You will also perform to the best of your abilities any other duties asked of you by your supervisor.

COMMUNICATIONS: As set out above, for this Agreement to work, it is imperative that communications between you and your supervisors remain strong and effective. For this reason, you agree to the following:

Resource: Sample Temporary Work from Home Agreement

- You understand that effective communication and satisfactory completion of stated objectives are keys to successful telecommuting or working from home.
- You will contact your Supervisor at least once per workday, either via email or telephone, as directed by your supervisor. It will be grounds for canceling this Agreement if you fail to communicate effectively and timely with your department in your supervisor's determination.
- You can live/office no further than one hour from your normal home facility. If there is an electronic failure or if we need you here at the regional office, you must be no more than one hour from the facility.

HOURS OF WORK/COMPENSATION: You agree that, among other things, you are responsible for establishing clear and certain working hours with your department. Currently the hours you are assigned to work are from_____ a.m. or p.m. to _____ a.m. or p.m. on scheduled days. Effective date:_____ [*please circle a.m. or p.m. when noting time*]

It is important that you work during [ORGANIZATION NAME's] core business hours. Thus, it is not acceptable under this Agreement to complete your hours randomly or at odd times of the night. You will not be compensated under any Shift Differential unless your primary hours set out above are evening or night shift hours according to [ORGANIZATION NAME] policy. If you alter your hours to complete your work at night, you will not be paid a differential.

You agree to observe Federal Wage and Hour provisions as they apply:

- No overtime will be worked unless approved in advance by your supervisor or Department Head.
- Based on an agreement with your supervisor, you may submit time by manually entering clockings into Time and Attendance OR use the approved Time Sheet to keep up with your time. You must still comply with all [ORGANIZATION NAME] Standards and Policies, knowing that you are provided with one 30-minute lunch period (unpaid) during which work is not to be performed, and two 15-minute breaks which are paid.
- You will certify each week that you have worked all time reported, that you are not claiming time not worked, and that no one from [ORGANIZATION NAME] asked you to work off the clock.
- You will be working on the honor system under this Agreement. Therefore, for any time that you are not working and pursuing personal endeavors, you promise not to claim as time worked and to so note this on your time sheets each week.
- You agree that travel between the home or remote work location and the primary worksite shall not be reimbursed. If called to any meetings or to work at [ORGANIZATION NAME], you agree to comply with any such directive and understand that travel time or mileage will not be paid.

SAFE WORKSITE/ERGONOMICS: You agree that your work area will be safe and ergonomically acceptable. You agree to perform a safety analysis of your work site and office

Resource: Sample Temporary Work from Home Agreement

ergonomics and certify that your working conditions are safe and pose no ascertainable harm to you or to [ORGANIZATION NAME] equipment. If injured at home doing [ORGANIZATION NAME] business under this Agreement, you agree to report any such injury to the [ORGANIZATION NAME] Director of Employee Health immediately. You also agree to provide access to your work site by any agent of [ORGANIZATION NAME] to conduct post-accident or other investigations.

USE OF [ORGANIZATION NAME] EQUIPMENT: If required, you will be provided with certain equipment and supplies from [ORGANIZATION NAME] to enable you to work from home. A list of that equipment and serial numbers should be listed on the Temporary Remote Work approval form. You agree to treat this as you would any [ORGANIZATION NAME] property and are responsible for any damage that results to it from your negligence or improper operation. You agree not to use any [ORGANIZATION NAME] equipment for personal or private purposes, nor to allow family members or friends access to that equipment. The [ORGANIZATION NAME] Policy on Confidentiality applies strictly to any equipment or reports or documents in your home. You understand [ORGANIZATION NAME] may pursue recovery for any [ORGANIZATION NAME] property that is deliberately or negligently damaged or destroyed while in your care, custody and control. You shall promptly return all [ORGANIZATION NAME] equipment and data documents when requested by your supervisor. You also agree to follow all software licensing provisions agreed to by [ORGANIZATION NAME]. You agree to notify your supervisor promptly when you are unable to perform work assignments due to equipment failure, loss of power, or other circumstances.

If [ORGANIZATION NAME] property is not returned or not returned in proper working condition, the employee will owe [ORGANIZATION NAME] the replacement cost for the item(s).

INSURANCE: You agree to carry insurance in an amount sufficient to cover any loss of [ORGANIZATION NAME] property or equipment or for injuries to any invitees to your home. You agree not to conduct any meetings for business reasons at your home for reasons of insurance. If you do conduct any such meetings and if any such person is injured, you understand that you will be liable for any such injuries and will defend and hold [ORGANIZATION NAME] harmless for any such injuries or damages.

CONFIDENTIALITY: Patient and hospital confidentiality is paramount. You remain bound by all [ORGANIZATION NAME] Policies and Guidelines regarding Confidentiality and must remain vigilant to protect Confidentiality in your home. No guests or family members can see or read contents of any record or document relating to your work. Computer screens must be hidden from others' view should you be working on [ORGANIZATION NAME] matters. You may not make or keep unauthorized copies of any [ORGANIZATION NAME] or patient records or documents in any form without express approval.

Resource: Sample Temporary Work from Home Agreement

Violation of [ORGANIZATION NAME] Confidentiality Policies or this Confidentiality Agreement is grounds for canceling this Agreement and for termination of employment.

PROFESSIONALISM/CARING FOR DEPENDENTS: You fully understand and agree that telecommuting is not a substitute for child or dependent care and that other arrangements are necessary for regular dependent care. It will not be acceptable and will constitute grounds for immediate termination of this Agreement if it is discovered that you are using your compensable time at home to care for children or dependents or if other purely personal or domestic duties interfere with the primary purpose of your work for [ORGANIZATION NAME].

I have read and understand the terms of this Work at Home Agreement and agree to the duties, obligations, responsibilities, and conditions described in the policy.

Employee Signature: _____ Date: _____

Supervisor Signature: _____ Date: _____

[Department of record retains original document and submits photocopy to Human Resources.]

For Human Resources Use Only

Date received in HR: _____ FLSA Status: Exempt or Non-exempt [*circle one*]

FTE: _____

Identity Theft

By Connie Barrera,[1] MBA, CISSP, CISA

What Is Identity Theft in Relation to Patient Privacy and Security?

Despite continued efforts to stop them, we break data breach and identity theft records year after year. The Federal Trade Commission 2019 "Consumer Sentinel Network" report identified a surge of identity theft reports for 2019, totaling 20.3% of all reports.[2] This figure accounts for the largest percentage of any other filing category.[3] Sorting through the data and focusing in on data breaches in healthcare, based on a Protenus 2020 breach barometer report, more than 41 million patient records were affected by data breaches in 2019.[4] The causes of breach of privacy and security incidents are 58% hacking, 19% insiders, 10% loss/theft, and 13% unknown.[5]

Whenever a data theft incident occurs within healthcare, it is a goldmine for thieves because of the extensive nature of the data. Healthcare not only houses basic personally identifiable information (e.g., full names, addresses, and dates of birth), but also Social Security numbers and many aspects of financial data. This full and extensive data set is what attracts adversaries around the globe to target healthcare organizations everywhere. While we focus on the HIPAA regulation within healthcare, because of the extensive nature of the data, many other regulations apply, such as the Gramm-Leach-Bliley Act (aimed to safeguard financial data), Federal Trade Commission Red Flag Rules (meant to help prevent identity theft), and even the Payment Card Industry Data Security (PCI/DSS) Standard (developed to safeguard credit card information).

While there are clear distinctions between the scope of a HIPAA privacy officer and HIPAA security officer, the anatomy of identity theft incidents tightly weaves both functions and requires extensive and continued collaboration. A vast number of risks emerging from medical identity theft affect both HIPAA privacy and security. These risks result in substantial hardships for patients, providers, and health plans. More often, breaches of medical health data result in direct healthcare fraud, even if the data are still being used in tandem for traditional financial gain. Healthcare fraud is also dangerous because it may result in erroneous health data becoming part of a victim's medical record and lead to treatment errors or diminished benefits they are actually entitled to. Not only do patients experience negative credit issues, which are very difficult to correct, but they can also experience legal issues whenever prescription drugs are obtained via medial ID theft (many times later sold on the black market).

Compliance professionals not only need to ensure current controls are functioning as expected, but also need to constantly brainstorm ways to identify how new risks affect the current environment. Although it's not possible to monitor every system, folder, and file throughout the digital environment, ensuring auditing and monitoring capabilities provide sufficient visibility to user actions and behavior is more important than ever. Without knowing the normal thresholds, it is almost impossible to quickly identify security and privacy issues when they occur.

Risk Area Governance

Healthcare providers and payers have a legal and moral obligation to protect patient records at all times. Federal, state, and localized policies have evolved over the years to compel organizations to continually monitor and ensure the privacy and security of patient health data. Key legislation include the following.

HIPAA Regulation (Security and Privacy), 45 C.F.R. §§ 164.102–164.534

The relevant sections from a privacy and security perspective include 45 C.F.R. §§ 164.500, 164.501, 164.514.[6]

Health Information Technology for Economic and Clinical Health (HITECH) Act of 2009, Pub. L. No. 111-5, § 13,001, 123 Stat. 227, at 13,301, Subtitle B – Incentives for the Use of Health Information Technology

HITECH encourages healthcare organizations to implement electronic healthcare record solutions with an intention to improve privacy and security.[7]

Congressional Statute, 42 U.S.C. § 1320d-5 (Covers Civil Violations)

This is the enforcement provision that allows for the application of civil penalties for relevant violations of the HIPAA regulation.[8]

Congressional Statute, 42 U.S.C. § 1320d-6 (Covers Criminal Violations)

This establishes the enforcement provision, which allows for the application of penalties for criminal violations of the HIPAA regulation.[9]

Wire and Mail Fraud Statutes, 18 U.S.C. §§ 1341, 1343

This regulation would apply to situations of mailing fraudulent bills or claims, or, alternatively, the act of a breach via the internet would be an act of wire fraud.[10]

False Claims Act, 31 U.S.C. §§ 3729–3733

This would apply if an external adversary started to submit false claims with stolen information.[11]

Identity Theft Rules, 16 C.F.R. § 681

These rules require organizations to establish and maintain adequate controls and training to prevent identity theft.[12]

State-Based Identity Theft Protection Laws

Every state has legislation regarding identity theft crimes. Certain states have specific provisions for restitution. A few states have even created programs to help victims from continuing identity theft issues, such as Iowa and Ohio.

Common Compliance Risks

Numerous compliance risks affect healthcare data. One of the biggest reasons why is that the average price for a healthcare record on the black market is $250, according to the 2017 Trustwave *The Value of Data* report.[13] While the enumeration of compliance risks is arguably an endless list, the following are key areas of high risks.

Business Associates

Business associates pose considerable risk due to inappropriate handling, errors, and/or breaches of their respective environment. In 2019, the largest breach occurred due to the hacking of one of the country's largest patient collections agencies—American Medical Collection Agency (AMCA). The AMCA breach resulted in the unauthorized disclosure of more than 20 million medical records.[14] This breach was a result of an internet attack. It was first discovered when the company was notified of a disproportionate number of fraudulent credit card transactions, for cards that had used the AMCA web portal. This company ultimately filed for bankruptcy.

Insider Errors and Malicious Acts

This risk continues to cause substantial issues for all organizations. According to a Protenus report, close to 4 million records were disclosed by insiders.[15] Perhaps surprisingly, the majority of the disclosures where a result of human error and not malicious insiders. Error-based disclosures resulted in 3,659,962 medical records exposed.[16] Despite commitment and rigorous effort, too many individuals in a given organization require extensive access to data elements such as a Social Security numbers. If appropriate IT controls are not in place (such as preventing data from being saved locally), individuals with mobile devices could save patient data directly on individual computers. This is not a theory—there are countless stories involving lost or stolen devices with hundreds or thousands of patient records out in the wild. Many times, individuals saved the data in order to work at home or while traveling, always with good intentions to do more. Unfortunately, it is still a data breach. Likewise, performing basic tasks such as sending emails to patients can be tricky if the system does not always send secured messages. This could yield high numbers of data breaches simply by emailing the wrong person with the wrong information.

Hacking Incidents

These incidents result in exposing medical records, and these attacks continue to grow. From 126 hacking incidents in 2016, they've risen to 330 in 2019.[17] One of the biggest threats leading to system compromise continues to result from phishing emails and ransomware.

Addressing Compliance Risks

Every organization can take proactive action and improve its security, privacy, and compliance posture. A critical factor in the fight against identity theft is having a governance structure that supports the Privacy and IT Division in enacting and enforcing a robust compliance program that can minimize risk and effectively deal with current and evolving threats. The following are specific tangible ways to reduce risks associated with the aforementioned common compliance risks.

Business Associate Agreements

Ensure business associate agreements protect your organization and adhere to all HIPAA requirements, as well as other relevant legislation discussed previously and applicable to your health system. It's also prudent to require business associates to maintain a certain level of cyber liability insurance as a requirement for doing business with your organization.

Cyber Liability Insurance

Every organization should work to obtain cyber liability insurance. If an organization is a service provider, it is critical it has cyber liability insurance in the event it experiences a breach involving your data and needs to be able to provide restoration and/or cover penalties it may owe corporate customers. If a business does not have cyber Insurance, you should be very cautious about sharing any data with it. For individual health organizations, having this insurance will be instrumental in helping with the burden and cash outlay involved in handling of a particular breach. In the case of AMCA, previously discussed, it's reported it was required to pay $3.8 million to inform 7 million individuals of potential identity theft.[18]

Minimize Insider Threats

They can be minimized through the following actions:

- Ensure appropriate logging and alerting is in place for all relevant systems, typically leveraging a SIEM (Security Information Event Management) solution.
- On the IT side, log correlation to identify multiple simultaneous log-ons for the same user ID performed in real time.
- Use multi-factor authentication and tap-in technologies. They will eliminate finger-pointing and statements that someone else accessed the medical record with using someone else's credentials.
- User activity benchmarking will identify excessive access to patient medical records, which could indicate malicious insiders harvesting patient information.
- Activate logging and alerting on printing associated with patient data.
- Data loss prevention technologies ensure that patient data are not inappropriately transmitted outside of established and approved business processes.
- Enterprise computers should be locked down to prevent the ability to connect external storage media.
- All mobile endpoints should be encrypted with whole-disk encryption to safeguard data in the event the device is lost or stolen.
- All users should receive robust security awareness and privacy training yearly. In addition to yearly training, monthly and quarterly content updates are extremely important to keep the topics fresh and evolving to meet the changing threat climate.
- All users should receive ample education and practice on how to detect and report malicious emails since this is the primary vector for current attacks and the number of phishing emails and their sophistication continues to grow.
- Conduct a periodic access review of all user access on a quarterly basis.
- Monthly control audits of user access should be performed for everyone who has access to the digital environment. This is especially true for contractors and business associates.

Protect your organization from hacking

To safeguard organizations from being hacked, the following measures should be strongly considered:

- Minimize the number of firewall ports that are open (ingresses) into the environment.
- Ensure all assets are appropriately patched and kept up to date with supported operating systems and application software.
- Ensure centralized logging, correlation, and alerting are available with a SIEM solution.
- Leveraging behavioral analytics will allow your organization a huge advantage whenever anomalous action occurs.
- Because the end user continues to be the weakest link, a robust endpoint detection and response solution are absolutely needed to isolate and contain an incident to the device in question.
- Minimize remote connectivity capabilities to what is supported and approved. This is especially important because most vendors will want to use a remote support application of their choosing, which may not be in the best interest of your organization. Third parties must conform to your security architecture (and not the other way around).

Possible Penalties

Depending on the type of breach and the motivations behind it, whether it is malicious and intentional or the result of human error, substantial monetary penalties and even jail time are possible.

Depending on the type of breach and the motivations behind it, whether it is malicious and intentional, or if it is the result of human error, substantial monetary penalties and even jail-time are possible. The following table includes HIPAA violation fines per violation category, as provided by the *Federal Register*:[19]

Violation Category: Section 1176(a)(1)	Fine for Each Violation	Fine for All Such Violations of an Identical Provision in a Calendar Year
(A) Did Not Know	$100–$50,000	$1,500,000
(B) Reasonable Cause	$1,000–$50,000	$1,500,000
(C)(i) Willful Neglect–Corrected	$10,000–$50,000	$1,500,000
(C)(ii) Willful Neglect–Not Corrected	$50,000	$1,500,000

Compliance Resources

Federal Trade Commission

Medical Identity Theft: FAQS for Health Care Providers and Health Plans

Provides concise information on specific events that indicate patient information has been breached. Also includes valuable websites that organizations should be sharing with relevant patients.

https://www.ftc.gov/tips-advice/business-center/guidance/
medical-identity-theft-faqs-health-care-providers-health-plans

Medical Identity Theft

Helpful website that provides different considerations for both consumers and organizations dealing with identity theft. The site includes helpful information on correcting mistakes in medical records, which is often an issue caused by ID theft.

https://www.consumer.ftc.gov/articles/0171-medical-identity-theft

Consumer Sentinel Network Data Book 2019

This is a valuable resource for any organization because it enumerates types of identity theft crimes, trends over time and even breaks up the data by states (within the United States). Magnitude and severity of risks are very important when planning and implementing a privacy and security program.

https://www.ftc.gov/system/files/documents/reports/consumer-sentinel-network-data-book-2019/consumer_sentinel_network_data_book_2019.pdf

National Conference of State Legislatures

Identity Theft

Use this site to look up state regulations regarding identity theft.

https://www.ncsl.org/research/financial-services-and-commerce/identity-theft-state-statutes.aspx

Protenus

2020 Breach Barometer

This report is ideal for both justifying privacy and security expenditures in support of preventing breaches and associated fraud as well as gauging that when planning and deploying your program, you are accounting for all the different vectors and risks that evolve over time.

https://www.protenus.com/resources/2020-breach-barometer/

Trustwave

The Value of Data: A Cheap Commodity or a Priceless Asset?

This report is also a valuable tool for justifying expenditures in support of compliance and security programs and especially for providing a realistic view of the impressive value of medical data.

https://www.infopoint-security.de/media/TrustwaveValue_of_Data_Report_Final_PDF.pdf

Risk Takeaways

Main points of interest:
- The number of data breaches and instances of identity theft steadily rise year after year.
- More than 41 million patient records were affected by data breaches in 2019.
- Data breaches and identity theft can have significant negative impacts on patents' lives, providers, and health plans for many years.

Areas to watch:
- Business associates handling of patient data
- Insider errors and malicious attacks
- Hacking incidents

Laws that apply:
- HIPAA regulation (security and privacy), 45 C.F.R. §§ 164.102–164.534
- Congressional statute,42 U.S.C. § 1320d-5 (covers civil violations)
- Congressional statute, 42 U.S.C. § 1320d-6 (covers criminal violations)
- Wire and mail fraud statutes, 18 U.S.C. §§ 1341, 1343
- False Claims Act, 31 U.S.C. §§ 3729–3733
- Identity Theft Rules, 16 C.F.R. § 681
- State-based identity theft protection laws

Addressing compliance risks:
- Ensuring that business associate agreements adhere to HIPAA requirements and other relevant legislation.
- Obtain cyber liability insurance.
- Minimize insider threats through a number of IT actions, such as periodic access reviews and whole-disk encryption.
- Provide yearly training and education on security awareness and privacy.
- Protect your organization from hacking through a number of IT actions, SIEM solution, and minimizing remote connectivity capabilities.

Endnotes

1. **Connie Barrera** is Chief Information Security Officer at Jackson Health System. She has over more than 25 years of experience in the IT industry. As the CISO at Jackson Health System, she is responsible for security architecture and operations, as well as developing policy and standards related to privacy, confidentiality, integrity, and availability of the IT services throughout the enterprise. To this end, Connie develops and maintains risk management, security awareness, and compliance programs to effectively deal with the implications of legislated requirements that affect security for the institution. This includes, but is not limited to, HIPAA, PCI, FDA Part 11 and the Red Flag Rules.

2. Federal Trade Commission, "Consumer Sentinel Network Data Book 2019," January 2020, https://www.ftc.gov/system/files/documents/reports/consumer-sentinel-network-data-book-2019/consumer_sentinel_network_data_book_2019.pdf.

3. Federal Trade Commission, "Consumer Sentinel Network Data Book 2019," January 2020, https://www.ftc.gov/system/files/documents/reports/consumer-sentinel-network-data-book-2019/consumer_sentinel_network_data_book_2019.pdf.

4. Protenus, "2020 Breach Barometer," accessed January 11, 2021, https://www.protenus.com/resources/2020-breach-barometer/.

5. Protenus, "2020 Breach Barometer," accessed January 11, 2021, 13.

6. 45 C.F.R. §§ 164.500, 164.501, 164.514.

7. Pub. L. No. 111-5, § 13,001, 123 Stat. 226, Sec. 13301, Subtitle B.

8. 42 U.S.C. § 1320d-5.

9. 42 U.S.C. § 1320d-6.

10. 18 U.S.C. §§ 1341 & 1343.

11. 31 U.S.C. § 3729.

12. 16 C.F.R. § 681.

13. Trustwave, *The Value of Data: A Cheap Commodity Or A Priceless Asset?*, 2017, https://www.infopoint-security.de/media/TrustwaveValue_of_Data_Report_Final_PDF.pdf. .

14. Jessica Davis, "AMCA Files Chapter 11 After Data Breach Impacting Quest, LabCorp," Health IT Security, June 18, 2019, https://healthitsecurity.com/news/amca-files-chapter-11-after-data-breach-impacting-quest-labcorp#:~:text=After%20an%20eight-month%20data,11%20protection%20-%20aiming%20to%20liquidate.

15. Protenus, "2020 Breach Barometer," 9.

16. Protenus, "2020 Breach Barometer."

17. Protenus, "2020 Breach Barometer."

18. Jessica Davis, "AMCA Files Chapter 11 After Data Breach Impacting Quest, LabCorp."

19. Modifications to the HIPAA Privacy, Security, Enforcement, and Breach Notification Rules Under the Health Information Technology for Economic and Clinical Health Act and the Genetic Information Nondiscrimination Act; Other Modifications to the HIPAA Rules, 78 Fed. Reg. 5,566, 5,583 (January 25, 2013), https://www.federalregister.gov/documents/2013/01/25/2013-01073/modifications-to-the-hipaa-privacy-security-enforcement-and-breach-notification-rules-under-the#h-95.

Protected Health Information

By Connie Barrera,[1] MBA, CISSP, CISA

What Is Protected Health Information?

The risk area involving patient privacy, security, and protected health information (PHI) is greater than ever. This is, in no small part, due to the adoption of electronic health record (EHR) solutions, which brought exceptional opportunities for adversaries to compromise large quantities of patient data from anywhere in the world. In addition, the traditional internal threat actor risk also grew. Now, instead of having to take huge stacks of paper patient records, anyone with the right access but the wrong motivation can steal large quantities of patient data. Even the unfortunate, user error–based/nonmalicious breach became much more serious once patient records went electronic.

PHI under U.S. laws includes any health-related information that can be linked back to a specific individual. If the information is maintained electronically, it would be referred to as electronic protected health information (ePHI). The Health Insurance Portability and Accountability Act (HIPAA) identifies the following 18 data elements that must be safeguarded in order to ensure patient privacy:

1. Names
2. Dates (except year)
3. Telephone numbers
4. Geographic data
5. Fax numbers
6. Social Security numbers
7. Email addresses
8. Medical record numbers

9. Account numbers
10. Health plan beneficiary numbers
11. Certificate/license numbers
12. Vehicle identifiers and serial numbers, including license plates
13. Web addresses
14. Device identifiers and serial numbers
15. Internet protocol (IP) addresses
16. Full face photos and comparable images
17. Biometric identifiers (e.g., retinal scan, fingerprints)
18. Any unique identifying number or code[2]

A process of continual vigilance must be put in place to prevent disclosure of PHI (whether on paper or stored electronically). With the extensive spectrum of data elements on every patient, it's no wonder that healthcare organizations are constantly being attacked by external hackers or exploited by malicious insiders. Malicious insiders will sell the data to make some money, causing damage to each individual whose data will be used for identity theft or other related fraud. Hackers will extract data from health organizations and typically sell the data on the dark web. The breach itself is certainly serious, but industry metrics show that an organization may not realize it has been breached for nine to 18 months. Following the breach, forensically identifying the scope and magnitude of the breach will be difficult and certainly very costly.

In addition to the adversaries mentioned, avoidable breaches continue to occur despite everyone knowing the key issues. Despite a plethora of technical controls available for many years, the announcements of lost or stolen devices with unsecured data continues to be common and often. Other threat vectors to patient privacy include, but are not limited to, weak passwords, unsecured email, unauthorized cloud storage, and USB devices. It's important to point out that all of the traditional paper-based risks still exists, and so more than ever it is vital that every organization ensure it identifies and measures risk on a yearly basis.

Having a compliance program that continually addresses and mitigates threats will greatly help to reduce the risk of data compromise. While some risks may be common to all or most organizations, providers cannot leverage a cookie-cutter approach. Even when two providers or health systems have similar software, depending on the specifics of the technical configuration, business process, and access roles that users are granted, it could yield drastically different risk profiles for each organization. Therefore, deliberate and thorough analysis of threats versus administrative, technical, and physical controls is the essential first step in safeguarding patient privacy and mitigating potential breaches.

Risk Area Governance

HIPAA Privacy Rule, 45 C.F.R. §§ 160, 164.500–164.534

This rule was promulgated to establish global standards and protect the privacy of personal health information.[3]

HIPAA Security Rule, 45 C.F.R. §§ 160, 164.302–§164.318

This rule was promulgated to establish standards aimed to protect electronic health data. The security rules establish administrative, physician, and technical safeguards that are required for compliance.[4]

Health Information Technology for Economic and Clinical Health (HITECH) Act

HITECH was part of the American Recovery and Reinvestment Act, which provided financial incentives amounting to billions of dollars for health systems to implement and meaningfully use health information technology (IT) solutions.[5]

Meaningful Use, 42 C.F.R. §§ 412, 413, 422, 495

These sections of the HITECH Act established requirements for incentive-based payments for the adoption of health IT solutions meant to digitize patient records.[6]

State-Based Identity Theft Protection Laws

Every state has legislation regarding identity theft crimes. Certain states have specific provisions for restitution. A few states have even created programs to help victims from continuing identity theft issues, such as Iowa and Ohio.

Identity Theft Rules, 16 C.F.R. § 681

These rules require organizations to establish and maintain adequate controls and training to prevent identity theft.[7]

Common Compliance Risks

Access, Identity, and Operation

Operationally, a significant and yet common compliance risk relates to access and authorization. Many individuals understand this in the larger context of identity governance. The principles of "least privilege" and "need to know" are paramount in complying with the HIPAA regulations. Providing workforce members and providers with the right access is at times easier said than done. A nurse is not just a nurse from one unit to the other. For example, Nurse Betty may perform a specific set of duties, while Nurse Jeffrey may have a number of other "duties as assigned" that could result in the need to grant him a broader level of access. Access for employees in one unit may require different privileges in other units.

Administratively, this may be difficult to manage but attainable to a point. Yet there is an entire other layer of complexity in organizations where employees have a high transfer rate between units. This does not even consider clinical staff floating to different areas of a hospital on an almost daily basis. In addition to workforce member identity management, it may be more challenging to manage identities for loosely affiliated individuals, such as third-party contractors and payers with access to the health system's EHR.

How do you have any assurance that individuals continue to be employed by the third party on any given day and should continue to have the same level of access? Whether a result of malicious intent or not, unauthorized access and disclosure by authorized parties presents serious challenges that are difficult to address. The inability of some healthcare systems to control identity and access for their users has caused significant fines being imposed by the Office for Civil Rights. Although identity governance is the start of the problem, many more downstream issues may go unaddressed. The number of risks is far too great to enumerate and discuss, but a sample of common serious issues includes weak or default passwords, unpatched systems, weak ciphers, unencrypted endpoints, unsupported operating systems, personal devices, and data being saved everywhere and anywhere.

Lack of Visibility into User Activity

Another series of compliance risks surface from the lack of visibility into user activity. Organizations that are not monitoring user access to the digital environment and their EHR are, in essence, sitting and waiting for a problem to erupt. It may or may not be a lack of audit log capability, but some organizations do not have the personnel or expertise to monitor the endless stream of logs produced by disparate solutions. System security and audit monitoring is also critical in identifying and mitigating cybersecurity threats.

For many years now, the FBI has reported that the healthcare sector is a target of cyberattacks. And in October 2020, "the FBI and other federal agencies warned that cybercriminals are unleashing a wave of data-scrambling extortion attempts against the U.S. healthcare system."[8] Despite the plethora of costly niche tools, breach analysis conducted by IBM reveals that most companies are unaware of any breaches for 197 days and require an average of 69 days to contain the intrusion.[9]

All of the organization's data can be compromised in that period of time. Even more striking, IBM contends that organizations are far more likely to experience a data breach of at least 10,000 records than the average person is likely to catch the flu during winter.[10] The latest report from IBM estimates an average total cost of $3.86 million to deal with a data breach and points out that healthcare leads all other industries, with the highest associated costs to deal with all the fallout.[11]

Addressing Compliance Risks

Recognizing the scope and sheer number of threats constantly at play to compromise any healthcare environment can be overwhelming. The good news is that a deliberate set of practices, planned and executed effectively, will make the difference between timely identification of possible intrusion (almost in real time) and the realization of a breach only when a patient submits a complaint or the secret service or FBI calls. Here are some ways to proactively address those risks.

Strong and Vocal Executive Leadership Support

Without visible board members and executive leader support for all privacy and security issues, buy-in from the rest of the organization will usually be marginal.

Policies and Procedures

It's critical to have the right set of policies and procedures, as every member of the workforce will cite the lack of awareness and/or policies as a reason they acted in any unauthorized way.

Use a Tool to Manage All User Accounts and Passwords

To mitigate the risk of weak identity governance, the organization should deploy a tool or develop one in house that will manage all user accounts and passwords throughout the digital environment. In additional, appropriate password complexity and enhanced authentication will greatly improve the organization's security posture. It's critical, at any given moment, to be able to see who has access to what and confirm that the access is appropriate.

Perform Key Auditing Activities

A monthly control audit should compare your user identity and governance source of truth (who is an active workforce, third party, physician, etc.) with each of the accounts that are live throughout the digital environment. If any accounts are enabled for users that are no longer active (i.e., employed, credentialed, etc.), then those accounts should be immediately terminated. Also perform a quarterly access validation. Historically, it's been a toss-up in many organizations when granting access. Most of the times those requesting access will say, "Make Susie (the new employee) like Sally (an established employee)." All they know is that Sally is functional, and so the new employee—Susie—will probably be okay if granted the same access, whether or not that access meets the standard of "least privilege" and "need to know." Developing an automated quarterly access validation can be taxing, as it requires educating anyone with individuals reporting to them to understand the different roles within any number of applications, as well as keeping them motivated to comply with the exercise. Over time though, putting the responsibility regarding who has access to what on leaders across the organization, and also making them aware of the risks and sensitivity of the data, will enable a culture that champions privacy and security consistently. This validation exercise is critical in ensuring that user roles continue to be appropriate and necessary over time for each user on a network.

Have a Security Architecture in Place

To mitigate the risks associated with lack of visibility and cybersecurity threats, a layered security architecture is required. Some of the key components essential in this architecture include a well-deployed and managed security, information, and event management solution (SIEM). Many details go into this environment, but all systems should be reporting appropriate audit log information into a centralized repository. This repository may be as simple as regular hard disk storage, or it may be a mature data warehouse.

Events from across the spectrum should be parsed and then correlated to yield actionable intelligence. For example, John Smith just logged into a computer in the operating room (OR), immediately accessed the EHR, and started to insert data into a patient's record. Moments later, log entries are captured showing his account is attempting to initiate a connection via the organization's remote connection services (VPN), having provided a correct password but failing to produce a valid enhanced authentication token. Since John is still in the OR, how can this be possible? If the organization had a mature logging, correlation, and analysis environment, it would be able to see that John's RFID identification badge is tagging him physically in the OR and that it's impossible to establish a VPN session from within the network. Therefore, either an external user may be mistyping a user ID (since users with common names will have user IDs that are extremely similar) or it's a purposeful and malicious actor trying to break in. This situation is very common, and having alerts in real time and delivered to technical resources for action will mean the difference between a breach and foiling the intrusion attempt.

Even more challenging is identifying malicious external actors once they have made their way onto the network. For this, a robust behavioral analytics solution is imperative. Knowing what is "normal behavior" is the only way to identify anomalous behavior. Gauging the behavior of all assets and users on the network over time and establishing a benchmark are essential in being able to identify the possibility of an active attack. It's also imperative to train technical resources on the different phases of an attack and provide those individuals with opportunities to continually practice and tune the environment after each penetration test exercise. With the reality of ever-evolving threats and maturity of attacks, continually building skills and tuning systems is invaluable.

Limit Employee Internet Access as Needed

Ultimately, common sense decisions will go a long way. Every organization takes a different stance on what Internet resources will be allowed to its users. Some organizations allow employees to access most Internet sites, including social media, while others do not. At a time when everyone has a minicomputer in their pocket, and sometimes more than one (with their smartphones or other devices), there is really no need to be so indiscriminate on the organization's network. One huge area of risk is allowing employees to access unauthorized email services. No good will come from allowing employees to access personal email accounts on the organization's network. This just opens the door to phishing emails and malware, which have become the easiest way to compromise even the most secure environments. The only applications, data, and services that should be allowed on the network are those that are part of an authorized business process, including patient care. Everything else should be blocked. Taking these purposeful and fundamental steps will help lay the foundation to preserving patient privacy and the confidentiality, integrity, and availability of the computing environment.

Conduct a Yearly HIPAA Risk Assessment

Every organization needs to conduct a yearly HIPAA risk assessment in order to gauge the effectiveness of controls and actual risks that should be remediated for both HIPAA privacy and security. Depending on budget constraints and the organization's size, strong consideration for outsourcing this initiative to an independent third party is highly recommended.

Possible Penalties

Depending on the type of breach and the motivations behind it, whether it is malicious and intentional or the result of human error, substantial monetary penalties and even jail time are possible. The following table includes HIPAA violation fines per violation category, as provided by the *Federal Register*:[12]

Violation Category: Section 1176(a)(1)	Fine for Each Violation	Fine for All Such Violations of an Identical Provision in a Calendar Year
(A) Did Not Know	$100–$50,000	$1,500,000
(B) Reasonable Cause	$1,000–$50,000	$1,500,000
(C)(i) Willful Neglect–Corrected	$10,000–$50,000	$1,500,000
(C)(ii) Willful Neglect–Not Corrected	$50,000	$1,500,000

Compliance Resources

Centers for Medicare & Medicaid Services

Security Risk Analysis Tipsheet: Protecting Patients' Health Information
This security risk analysis tip sheet provides sound information to consider related to risk analysis and also dispels myths that may lead organizations toward noncompliance.

https://www.cms.gov/files/document/security-risk-assessment-fact-sheetupdated-2014-04-18pdf

StatPearls Publishing

Patient Confidentiality
This peer-reviewed article covers significant points of risk and considerations related to patient privacy and security risk.

https://www.ncbi.nlm.nih.gov/books/NBK519540/

IBM Security

Cost of a Data Breach Report 2020
Helpful data in quantifying the scope of the impact that can result from a data breach for leaders and privacy/security professionals.

https://www.ibm.com/downloads/cas/RZAX14GX

Federal Register

C. Section 160.404—Amount of a Civil Monetary Penalty Interim Final Rule
Provides helpful information regarding HIPAA in general and especially the associated penalties for noncompliance.

https://www.federalregister.gov/documents/2013/01/25/2013-01073/modifications-to-the-hipaa-privacy-security-enforcement-and-breach-notification-rules-under-the#h-95

National Conference of State Legislatures

Identity Theft
This web page maintains information regarding state laws and is helpful in researching state identity protection laws.

https://www.ncsl.org/research/financial-services-and-commerce/identity-theft-state-statutes.aspx

U.S. Department of Health & Human Services

Health Information Privacy
This web page links to HIPAA information for providers, patients, and more.

https://www.hhs.gov/hipaa/index.html

FindLaw

State Identity Theft Laws
Search for state identity theft laws on this site.

https://statelaws.findlaw.com/criminal-laws/identity-theft.html

Risk Takeaways

Main points of interest:

- Protected health information (PHI) and electronic protected health information (ePHI) include any health-related data that, when combined, can identify a specific individual.
- There are 18 identifiers that must be protected as part of the HIPAA security and privacy compliance efforts.
- The principles of "need to know" and "least privilege" are paramount in preventing and mitigating unauthorized disclosures of PHI/ePHI. Therefore, identity and access management is critical.
- A defense-in-depth strategy will provide a competitive edge to organization's efforts to protect patient data.

Areas to watch:

- User behavioral analytics and patterns of data access to identify anomalous excessive use or other undesired behaviors that could lead to compromise.
- Ensure vulnerabilities and risks identified as part of gap assessments or audits are promptly remediated.
- Incident response processes are vital in identifying and mitigating external attacks.

Laws that apply:

- HIPAA Privacy Rule, 45 C.F.R. §§ 160, 164.500–§164.534
- HIPAA Security Rule, 45 C.F.R. §§ 160, 164.302–§164.318
- HITECH Act, Meaningful Use, 42 C.F.R. §§ 412, 413, 422, 495
- Congressional statute: 42 U.S.C. § 1320d-5 (covers civil violations)
- Congressional statute: 42 U.S.C. § 1320d-6 (covers criminal violations)
- Wire and mail fraud statutes: 18 U.S.C. §§ 1341, 1343
- False Claims Act: 31 U.S.C. §§ 3729–3733
- Identity Theft Rules, 16 C.F.R. § 681
- State-based identity theft protection laws

Addressing compliance risks:

- Conduct a yearly HIPAA risk assessment
- Compliance requires strong executive leadership champions
- Have policies and procedures in place
- Deploy a defense-in-depth strategy
- Have a layered security architecture in place
- Limit unnecessary internet access
- Automate a robust identity and access management solution to manage user identities based on the principles of "least privilege" and "need to know"
- Identify and run key audit validation exercises that will ensure controls and processes are optimal and any risks are minimized or eliminated

Endnotes

1. **Connie Barrera** is the Chief Information Security Officer (CISO) at Jackson Health System. She has more than 25 years of experience in the IT industry. As the CISO at Jackson Health System, she is responsible for security architecture and operations, as well as developing policy and standards related to privacy, confidentiality, integrity, and availability of the IT services throughout the enterprise. To this end, Barrera develops and maintains risk management, security awareness, and compliance programs to effectively deal with the implications of legislated requirements that affect security for the institution. This includes but is not limited to HIPAA, PCI, FDA Part 11, and the Red Flag Rules.

2. 45 C.F.R. § 164.514.

3. "Summary of the HIPAA Privacy Rule," U.S. Department of Health & Human Services, reviewed July 26, 2013, https://www.hhs.gov/hipaa/for-professionals/privacy/laws-regulations/index.html.

4. "Summary of the HIPAA Security Rule," U.S. Department of Health & Human Services, reviewed July 26, 2013, https://www.hhs.gov/hipaa/for-professionals/security/laws-regulations/index.html?language=es.

5. American Recovery and Reinvestment Act of 2009, Pub. L. No. 111-5, §§ 13001, 4001, 123 Stat. 115, 226, 467 (2009).

6. 42 C.F.R. §§ 412, 413, 422, 495.

7. 16 C.F.R. § 681.

8. Associated Press, "FBI Warns Ransomware Assault Threatens US Health Care System," U.S. News and World Report, Ocotber 29, 2020, https://www.usnews.com/news/business/articles/2020-10-29/fbi-warns-ransomware-assault-threatens-us-healthcare-system#:~:text=In%20a%20joint%20alert%20Wednesday,hospitals%20and%20health%20care%20providers.&text=Previous%20such%20attacks%20on%20health,the%2.

9. Larry Ponemon, "IBM Study: Hidden Costs of Data Breaches Increase Expenses for Businesses," news release, IBM, July 11, 2018, https://newsroom.ibm.com/IBM-security?item=30567.

10. Larry Ponemon, "IBM Study: Hidden Costs of Data Breaches Increase Expenses for Businesses," news release, IBM, July 11, 2018, https://newsroom.ibm.com/IBM-security?item=30567.

11. IBM, *Cost of a Data Breach Report 2020*, July 29, 2020, https://www.ibm.com/security/digital-assets/cost-data-breach-report/#/.

12. Modifications to the HIPAA Privacy, Security, Enforcement, and Breach Notification Rules Under the Health Information Technology for Economic and Clinical Health Act and the Genetic Information Nondiscrimination Act; Other Modifications to the HIPAA Rules, 78 Fed. Reg. 5,566, 5,583 (January 25, 2013), https://www.federalregister.gov/documents/2013/01/25/2013-01073/modifications-to-the-hipaa-privacy-security-enforcement-and-breach-notification-rules-under-the#h-95.

Right to Access

By Kimberly White,[1] CHC

What Is a Patient's Right to Access?

A patient's right to access their medical records is critical to their ability to control their own healthcare. The efficient access to one's medical record assists in monitoring serious health conditions, tracking disease progression, enhancing doctor-patient communications, and adhering to treatment plans.

Yet, according to the U.S. Department of Health & Human Services (HHS) Office for Civil Rights (OCR), one of the most common patient complaints they receive relates to patients' inability to obtain access to their medical records. Historically, the OCR has focused its enforcement actions on privacy and security breaches, rather than patients' right to access, but this changed in 2019 with the Right of Access Initiative and significant penalties levied against healthcare institutions for noncompliance.[2]

With the OCR's announcement of the Right of Access Initiative, the OCR promised to vigorously enforce patients' right to receive their medical records quickly, without being overcharged, and in a readily producible format of their choosing. According to OCR Director Roger Severino, "For too long, healthcare providers have slow-walked their duty to provide patients their medical records out of a sleepy bureaucratic inertia. We hope our shift to the imposition of corrective actions and settlements under our Right of Access Initiative will finally wake up healthcare providers to their obligations under the law."[3] The OCR has thus far made good on this promise, announcing 16 right of access settlements as of February 12, 2021.[4] This area of the law is proving to be a critical tool in the government's enforcement arsenal. In order to avoid hefty fines and provide more positive patient outcomes, entities should be aware of the legal requirements associated with their patients' right to prompt, affordable access to their medical records and establish policies and procedures to empower patients to exercise that right effectively and efficiently.

Risk Area Governance

HIPAA Privacy Rule

Pursuant to the Health Insurance Portability and Accountability Act of 1996 (HIPAA), covered entities must provide individuals, upon request, access to the protected health information (PHI) about them in one or more designated record sets maintained by or for the covered entity.[5] This includes the right to inspect or obtain a copy (or both) of the PHI, as well as direct the covered entity to transmit a copy to a designated person or entity of the individual's choice. A designated record set may include medical and billing records, enrollment, payment, claims, or medical management record systems and other records used by a covered entity to make decisions about an individual's health.

Individuals do not have a right to access PHI contained in quality assessment or improvement records; patient safety activity records; or business planning, development, and management records because they are not used to make decisions about individuals. Expressly excluded from the patient's right of access are psychotherapy notes and information compiled in reasonable anticipation of litigation.[6]

While covered entities should respond to a patient's request for access as soon as possible, access should be provided no later than 30 days after the patient makes the request.[7] If, however, an entity is unable to provide access during the 30-day timeline, they may extend the time by an additional 30 days if they notify the patient in writing during the initial 30-day period. They must advise the requestor of the reason for the delay and the date upon which they will provide the patient the requested access.

In securing a patient's right of access, a covered entity may not impose unreasonable measures on an individual requesting access that serve as barriers to or which unreasonably delay the individual from obtaining access. For example, a doctor may not require individuals who want a copy of their medical records mailed to their home to physically come to the doctor's office and provide proof of identity in person; to use a web portal for requesting access, as not all individuals will have ready access to the portal; or to mail an access request, as this would unreasonably delay the access. However, a covered entity may require individuals to request access in writing, provided the covered entity informs individuals of this requirement before transmitting.[8] Again, this requirement should not create an artificial barrier to the patient's right of access. To better facilitate a patient's ability to request a medical record, a covered entity also may offer individuals the option of using electronic means, such as a secure web portal, to make requests for access.

Form and Format

HIPAA's Privacy Rule requires a covered entity to provide an individual with access to PHI in the form and format requested, if readily producible in that form and format.[9] Notably, whether or not it is "readily producible" is based on the entity's capability to provide in the format requested, not its willingness. A covered entity is not required to purchase new software or equipment to cover all potential requests. As a baseline requirement, however, if the information is maintained electronically, the covered entity must have the capability to provide *some* form of electronic copy of PHI.

To the extent that the PHI is not readily producible by the covered entity, it may produce the information in a readable format as agreed to by the covered entity and the requesting individual. Where an individual requests access to PHI that is maintained electronically by a covered entity, the covered entity may provide the individual with a paper copy of the PHI to satisfy the request only in cases where the individual declines to accept any of the electronic formats readily producible by the covered entity.[10]

Manner of Access

Under the Privacy Rule, a covered entity must provide patients access to their medical records in the manner requested.[11] This would include, for example, arranging a convenient time and place for the patient to pick up a copy of the PHI, or having a copy of the PHI mailed or emailed. It should be noted that mail and email are generally considered readily producible by all covered entities.

In addition, when requesting PHI by email, an individual has the right to request that it be sent unencrypted. In such cases, the covered entity must provide the requestor a brief warning that there is a level of risk that the individual's PHI could be read or otherwise accessed by a third party while in transit, and confirm that the individual still wants to receive his or her PHI by unencrypted email. If the individual consents, the covered entity must comply with the request. If the individual was warned of and accepted the security risks associated with the unsecure transmission, the entity is not responsible for breach notification or liable for disclosures that occur while the PHI is in transit.

A Reasonable Cost-Based Fee

The Privacy Rule permits a covered entity to impose a reasonable, cost-based fee when providing a patient a copy of his or her medical record. Generally, this fee will be based on the cost of actual labor costs, supplies, postage, and (if requested by an individual) the preparation of an explanation or summary of the PHI.[12] A covered entity may also use average labor costs, supplies, and postage—or a flat fee—for electronic copies of PHI maintained electronically. The flat fee is capped at $6.50.[13] The OCR has tended to be strict in its interpretation of labor, stating that it only includes labor for creating and delivering the electronic or paper copy, once the PHI that is responsive to the request has been identified, retrieved or collected, compiled and/or collated, and is ready to be copied. A covered entity may not account for such things as overhead, quality reviews, or costs associated with searching for and retrieving the PHI, even when such costs are permitted under state law.

Rather than calculating labor costs for each request, the OCR has said that a covered entity may develop a schedule of costs for labor based on average labor costs to fulfill standard types of access requests, as long as the types of labor costs included are the ones that the Privacy Rule permits to be included in a fee and are reasonable. Covered entities may then add to that amount any applicable postage or supply costs, such as thumb drives. According to the OCR, covered entities should not use a per-page fee except when the PHI is maintained in paper form and the individual requests a paper copy of the PHI or asks that the paper PHI be scanned into an electronic format. Therefore, OCR does not consider per-page fees for copies of PHI maintained electronically to be reasonable.[14]

The OCR has advised entities that ideally they should forego fees for all individuals for access to their medical records. This is especially vital in situations where the financial standing of the individual requesting the record would make it difficult or impossible for the individual to afford the fee. Further, an individual should never be denied access to his or her medical record due to having not paid a bill for services provided by the covered entity. The OCR has said it will continue to assess whether covered entities are charging fees to individuals that are creating barriers to the right of access, and will take enforcement action where deemed necessary.

Individual's Right to Direct the PHI to Another Person

An individual, or the individual's personal representative, may direct a covered entity to transmit the individual's PHI directly to another person or entity. Such a request must be in writing, be signed by the individual, clearly identify the person or entity being designated to receive the PHI, and state where the PHI should be sent. A covered entity may accept an electronic copy of a signed request, as well as an electronically executed request that includes an electronic signature.

The OCR previously held the position that the same requirements for providing the PHI to the individual, such as fee limitations, apply when an individual directs that the PHI be sent to another person or entity, such as a law firm representing the individual.[15] On January 23, 2020, however, a federal court vacated the "third-party directive" within the individual right of access to the extent it expanded the Health Information Technology for Economic and Clinical Health Act (HITECH) beyond requests for a copy of an electronic health record with respect to PHI of an individual in an electronic format.[16] Further, the court stated that the fee limitations set forth at 45 C.F.R. § 164.524(c)(4) only apply to an individual's request for access to their own records, and does not apply to an individual's request to transmit records to a third party. While the OCR did not appeal this decision during the applicable time frame, it is not yet known whether it will accept the court's decision or promulgate new regulations. In the meantime, however, the fee restrictions still apply to patients who request their own medical records.

Entities should also be mindful of relevant state laws to the extent they are more stringent than, and not preempted by, HIPAA.

Common Compliance Risks

For the past several years, complaints regarding the right to access have been among the top five complaints received and investigated by the OCR. Indeed, in 2016, patient complaints about their inability to access records were the top category of OCR complaints, surpassing inappropriate uses and disclosures for the first time.[17] Some of the most common patient complaints regarding barriers to a right of access include burdensome request procedures, improper format of records provided, untimely responses, and exorbitant fees. The compliance risks involved with these top complaints include manner of requests, form and format, and fees.

Manner of Requests

The OCR has stated that an individual should not be required to request a medical record in person or through the mail. Thus, entities should provide patients options for requesting medical records in various formats, such as via fax, phone, or through an online patient portal. This ensures that more individuals will be able to request their records in the manner in which they are most comfortable.

Form and Format

One of the most challenging issues for covered entities is the ability to provide medical records in the form and format requested by the individual, to the extent readily producible. As evidence of this fact, in a recent study conducted by Ciitizen Corporation, nearly one-half of entities surveyed were unable to provide records in the form and format requested by the patients.[18] Reasons cited by the survey included failure to provide records via unsecure email or secure portal as requested by the patient. When entities have the ability to send in the form and format requested by the patient, they should do so. The OCR has made it clear that concerns related to sending patient information via unsecure email are superseded by the patient's desire for prompt access to their record when the patient has consented to the associated risks. Thus, entities should make every effort to comply with such requests and document the patient's consent of the risks. Entities also should make every effort to have available technologies to provide patients access to medical records electronically. Many institutions cannot keep up with these demands due to using outdated technologies or siloed applications that do not readily share information. Over the last few years, however, federal agencies have encouraged the adoption of seamless mechanisms for digital access to medical records—from incentive payments for data provided via patient portals to ensuring patients have an increasing amount of their health information available to them via their chosen application and penalizing providers that participate in information blocking, essentially acting as a barrier to a patient's right of access.

Fees

Institutions should be careful to only charge individuals a reasonable, cost-based fee for access to their medical records. Such costs should only cover costs for labor and any associated supplies. The easiest way to comply with this demand is providing records free of charge, thus doing away with the requirement altogether. When that is not possible, a $6.50 flat fee for electronic records is a simple way to ensure compliance. Finally, charging a specified rate per hour for copying would be an efficient way to accurately reflect labor costs. Remember, an entity should never apply a per-page fee when providing digital copies of records maintained electronically.

Addressing Compliance Risks

There are a number of steps that compliance departments can take to support an individual's prompt and cost-efficient right to access their medical records. Such steps include, at a minimum:

- An assessment of available technologies and data systems
- An establishment of extensive and sound policies
- Training of applicable workforce members or provision of guidance to business associates

Assess Technologies and Data Systems

Covered entities should assess their available technology and adopt mechanisms to make data sharing more efficient. This will reduce the cost and timing of complying with medical record requests and enhance patient satisfaction and care.

Another step entities can take to facilitate compliance would be to ensure all data systems are appropriately backed up in case of natural disasters or security incidents, such as ransomware attacks. Such challenges could take medical records systems offline, thus compromising the ability to provide a patient prompt access to medical records.

Establish Policies

Entities should draft policies that establish requirements for empowering patients, or their legal representatives, to obtain a copy of their health information or to direct it to a third party. A general policy should be adopted that outlines the rights of the patient, explains the process for requesting one's medical record or directing it to a third party, and reflects the Privacy Rule requirements related to the form and manner of production and the permissible fees. The policy should provide special considerations related to the transmission of the record and steps the workforce can take to protect the confidentiality of the information, such as double-checking addresses and reviewing each page of the record to ensure all information pertains to the intended recipient. Finally, the policy should establish verification procedures and describe when a request for a medical record may be denied.

Entities should also consider developing separate policies that may have special considerations due to, for example, more stringent state laws. Potential categories include policies related to minors, deceased individuals, student immunizations, behavioral health, HIV/AIDS, and drug and alcohol treatment. Finally, if entities use a written form for record requests, they should consider making a patient FAQ available so that patients can more easily navigate the request process.

Train Health Information Management Department and Medical Record Vendors

Education is always one of compliance's greatest tools to prevent regulatory and policy failures. Compliance departments should be sure to provide training materials to their health information management departments and, to the extent such services are outsourced, to their medical record vendor business associates, outlining the OCR guidance and the expectations when responding to requests for medical record access. For example, it may be counterintuitive to an employee that patients are entitled to have their medical records sent by unsecure email. However, the guidance on this issue is clear that this is compliant. Providing employees relevant guidance before running into such demands ensures a more seamless and timely patient experience.

Possible Penalties

Since announcing the HIPAA Right of Access Initiative in 2019, the OCR has settled 16 enforcement actions with covered entities, with penalties ranging from $3,500 to $200,000. In September 2019, the OCR announced a settlement with Bayfront Health St. Petersburg. Bayfront agreed to pay $85,000 to the OCR and adopt a corrective action after failing to provide a mother timely access to the records about her unborn child. The OCR initiated its investigation based on a complaint from the mother. After first asserting that Bayfront lost the fetal heart monitor records, Bayfront later produced the requested health information more than nine months after the initial request, well beyond the 30-day deadline.[19]

On December 12, 2019, the OCR announced a second settlement related to the Right of Access Initiative. Korunda Medical LLC agreed to adopt corrective actions and to pay $85,000 for failing to provide a patient's medical records in electronic format to a third party. Not only did Korunda fail to timely provide the records to the third party despite numerous requests, but it also failed to provide them in the requested electronic format and charged more than the reasonable cost-based fees permitted under HIPAA. Initially, the OCR provided Korunda with technical assistance on how to correct these matters and closed the complaint. Despite OCR's assistance, however, Korunda continued to fail to provide the requested records, resulting in another complaint to the OCR. As a result of OCR's second intervention, the requested records were provided for free in May 2019 in the format requested.[20]

On September 15, 2020, the OCR announced an additional five settlements with entities pursuant to the Right of Access Initiative. "Patients can't take charge of their health care decisions, without timely access to their own medical information," said Severino. "Today's announcement is about empowering patients and holding health care providers accountable for failing to take their HIPAA obligations seriously enough."[21]

The OCR settled with Housing Works Inc., a nonprofit organization that provides services and legal aid support for people living with and affected by HIV/AIDS, for $38,000. Housing Works neglected to provide an individual his medical record even after the OCR sent a letter to the entity providing technical assistance. Eventually, Housing Works provided the record to the individual only after two OCR complaints and four months had passed.[22]

Additionally, All Inclusive Medical Services Inc. paid $15,000 for providing a patient's medical record more than two years after the initial request. Beth Israel Lahey Health Behavioral Services paid $70,000, King MD paid $3,500, and Wise Psychiatry PC paid $10,000 to the OCR—all for violating a patient's right to access his or her medical record. All entities were also subject to a corrective action plan.[23]

In January 2021, Banner Health agreed to "take corrective actions and pay $200,000 to settle potential violations of the HIPAA Privacy Rule's right of access standard."[24]

These enforcement actions demonstrate that the OCR will continue to make the right of access a top priority for the foreseeable future. As a result, healthcare entities must assess their compliance programs and health information management departments to ensure that adequate measures have been taken to secure this vital healthcare right and empower patients to take advantage of the right of access for the best possible patient outcomes.

Compliance Resources

Administrative Office of the United States Courts

Ciox Health, LLC v. Azar, No. 18-cv-0040
This is the electronic case file for the *Ciox Health* case.

https://ecf.dcd.uscourts.gov/cgi-bin/show_public_doc?2018cv0040-51

medRxiv

Health Care Provider Compliance with the HIPAA Right of Individual Access: A Scorecard and Survey (Revised)
This article provides the results of the Ciitizen Corporation's 2019 study.

https://www.medrxiv.org/content/10.1101/19004291v2.full.pdf

U.S. Department of Health & Human Services

HIPAA FAQs for Professionals
The following questions are answered on the HHS site and are central to the right of access issue:

- "Do individuals have the right under HIPAA to have copies of their PHI transferred or transmitted to them in the manner they request, even if the requested mode of transfer or transmission is unsecure?"

  https://www.hhs.gov/hipaa/for-professionals/faq/2060/do-individuals-have-the-right-under-hipaa-to-have/index.html

- "How can covered entities calculate the limited fee that can be charged to individuals to provide them with a copy of their PHI?"

  https://www.hhs.gov/hipaa/for-professionals/faq/2029/how-can-covered-entities-calculate-the-limited-fee/index.html

Health Information Privacy
Important Notice Regarding Individuals' Right of Access to Health Records
This page includes the OCR notice regarding the *Ciox Health* decision.

https://www.hhs.gov/hipaa/court-order-right-of-access/index.html

HIPAA Guidance Materials
Individuals' Right under HIPAA to Access their Health Information 45 CFR § 164.524
This page includes the latest guidance for compliance with HIPAA's right of access regulations.

https://www.hhs.gov/hipaa/for-professionals/privacy/guidance/access/index.html

Risk Takeaways

Main points of interest:
- Patients have a right to receive their medical records quickly, without being over-charged, and in a readily producible format of their choosing.
- In 2019, the OCR's Right of Access Initiative launched, and significant penalties were levied against healthcare institutions for noncompliance.
- Sixteen right of access settlements have been reached seen the initiative launched, with penalties ranging from $3,500 to $200,000.

Areas to watch:
- Manner of requests: Entities should provide patients options for requesting medical records in various formats, such as via fax, phone, or through an online patient portal.
- Form and format: When entities have the ability to send medical records in the form and format requested by the patient, they should do so. Entities also should make every effort to have available technologies to provide patients access to medical records electronically.
- Fees: Institutions should be careful to only charge individuals a reasonable, cost-based fee for access to their medical records. A covered entity may charge for average labor costs, supplies, and postage, or a flat fee for electronic copies of PHI maintained electronically, which is capped at $6.50.

Laws that apply:
- HIPAA Privacy Rule,45 C.F.R. §§ 160, 164.102, 164.500
- 45 C.F.R. § 164.524(c)(4)
- 21st Century Cures Act, 42 U.S.C. § 300jj-52(a)

Addressing compliance risks:
- Assess available technologies and data systems to make data sharing more efficient.
- Establish extensive and sound policies.
- Train applicable workforce members or provide guidance to business associates outlining the OCR guidance and the expectations when responding to requests for medical records access.

Endnotes

1. **Kimberly White** is Corporate Privacy Officer at Northwell Health. She oversees privacy investigations and implementing initiatives aimed at empowering patients to gain access to their medical information, protecting patient privacy, and ensuring compliance with HIPAA and other privacy-related regulations. Prior to joining Northwell Health, White worked as an attorney representing clients in litigation, employment disputes, and governmental investigations. She received her Juris Doctor from Northwestern University. The views expressed herein are her own and do not necessarily reflect the views of Northwell Health.

2. U.S. Department of Health & Human Services, "OCR Settles Ninth Investigation in HIPAA Right of Access Initiative," news release, October 9, 2020, https://www.hhs.gov/about/news/2020/10/09/ocr-settles-ninth-investigation-hipaa-right-access-initiative.html#:~:text=OCR%20announced%20this%20initiative%20as,under%20the%20HIPAA%20Privacy%20Rule.&text=%E2%80%9CNo%20one%20should%20have%20to,copies%20of%20their%20medical%20records.

3. Office for Civil Rights, "OCR Settles Second Case in HIPAA Right of Access Initiative," news release, U.S. Department of Health & Human Services, June 8, 2020, https://www.hhs.gov/guidance/document/ocr-settles-second-case-hipaa-right-access-initiative.

4. Office for Civil Rights, "OCR Settles Sixteenth Investigation in HIPAA Right of Access Initiative," news release, U.S. Department of Health & Human Services, February 12, 2021, https://www.hhs.gov/about/news/2021/02/12/ocr-settles-sixteenth-investigation-in-hipaa-right-of-access-initiative.html.

5. 45 C.F.R. §§ 164.524, 164.501.

6. 45 C.F.R. § 164.524(a)(1).

7. 45 C.F.R. § 164.524(b)(2).

8. 45 C.F.R. § 164.524(b)(1).

9. 45 C.F.R. § 164.524(c)(2).

10. "Under the HIPAA Privacy Rule, do individuals have the right to an electronic copy of their PHI?" U.S. Department of Health & Human Services, last reviewed January 31, 2020, https://www.hhs.gov/hipaa/for-professionals/faq/2054/under-the-hipaa-privacy-rule-do-individuals/index.html.

11. "Individuals' Right under HIPAA to Access their Health Information 45 CFR § 164.524," U.S. Department of Health & Human Services, last reviewed January 31, 2020, https://www.hhs.gov/hipaa/for-professionals/privacy/guidance/access/index.html.

12. 45 C.F.R. § 164.524(c)(4).

13. "Individuals' Right under HIPAA," U.S. Department of Health & Human Services.

14. 45 C.F.R. § 164.524(c)(4).

15. 45 C.F.R. 164.524(c)(3).

16. "Important Notice Regarding Individuals' Right of Access to Health Records," U.S. Department of Health & Human Services, last reviewed January 28, 2020, https://www.hhs.gov/hipaa/court-order-right-of-access/index.html#:~:text=On%20January%2023%2C%202020%2C%20a,individual%20.%20.%20.%20in%20an%20electronic.

17. "Top Five Issues in Investigated Cases Closed with Corrective Action, by Calendar Year," U.S. Department of Health & Human Services, last reviewed March 30, 2020, https://www.hhs.gov/hipaa/for-professionals/compliance-enforcement/data/top-five-issues-investigated-cases-closed-corrective-action-calendar-year/index.html.

18. Deven McGraw, Nasha Fitter, and Lisa Belliveau Taylor, "Health Care Provider Compliance with the HIPAA Right of Individual Access: a Scorecard and Survey (Revised)," November 11, 2019, MedRxiv, https://www.medrxiv.org/content/10.1101/19004291v2.full.pdf.

19. U.S. Department of Health & Human Services, "OCR Settles First Case in HIPAA Right of Access Initiative," news release, September 9, 2019, https://www.hhs.gov/about/news/2019/09/09/ocr-settles-first-case-hipaa-right-access-initiative.html.

20. U.S. Department of Health & Human Services, "OCR Settles Second Case in HIPAA Right of Access Initiative," news release, last reviewed December 12, 2019, https://www.hhs.gov/about/news/2019/12/12/ocr-settles-second-case-in-hipaa-right-of-access-initiative.html.

21. U.S. Department of Health & Human Services, "OCR Settles Five More Investigations in HIPAA Right of Access Initiative," news release, September 15, 2020, https://www.hhs.gov/about/news/2020/09/15/ocr-settles-five-more-investigations-in-hipaa-right-of-access-initiative.html.

22. U.S. Department of Health and Human Services, "OCR Settles Five More Investigations."

23. U.S. Department of Health and Human Services, "OCR Settles Five More Investigations."

24. U.S. Department of Health & Human Services, "OCR Settles Fourteenth Investigation in HIPAA Right of Access Initiative," news release, January 12, 2021, https://www.hhs.gov/about/news/2021/01/12/ocr-settles-fourteenth-investigation-in-hipaa-right-of-access-initiative.html.

Social Media

By Sheila Price Limmroth,[1] CHC, CIA

What Issues Are Associated with Social Media and Patient Privacy and Security?

When the Health Insurance Portability and Accountability Act (HIPAA) originally passed in 1996, discussions surrounding patient privacy in the context of social media were nonexistent.[2] It wasn't until MySpace launched in 2003, followed by Facebook in 2004, that "social media" became a common buzzword and way to communicate virtually. *Merriam-Webster Dictionary* defines social media as forms of electronic communication (such as websites for social networking and microblogging) through which users create online communities to share information, ideas, personal messages, and other content (such as videos).[3]

In February 2009, Congress passed the American Recovery and Reinvestment Act of 2009 (ARRA).[4] ARRA contains the Health Information Technology for Economic and Clinical Health (HITECH) Act. The HITECH Act provided some needed clarification to HIPAA. While HITECH does not specifically address social media concerns in the healthcare environment, both the HIPAA Privacy and Security Rules can be analyzed and applied to the current social media environment.

When discussing social media in terms of HIPAA, covered entities are typically concerned with two distinct components: (1) employee, physician, or vendor social media posts and (2) the entity's own approved website and organizational presence on social media platforms and the internet. This article will discuss the risks associated with both unauthorized and authorized use of social media platforms and the internet by covered entities.

Risk Area Governance

Although social media usage in relation to patient privacy and confidentiality is not specifically addressed by HIPAA, we can determine the need for compliance through a thoughtful review of both the HIPAA Privacy and Security Rules.

Defining Protected Health Information

HIPAA defines protected health information (PHI) as individually identifiable information, including demographic information related to the:

- Past, present, or future physical, mental health, or medical condition of a patient
- Provision of healthcare to a patient
- Past, present, or future payment for such healthcare created or received by a covered entity

PHI may exist verbally, electronically, or physically. The U.S. Department of Health and Human Services (HHS) lists individually identifiable information as including the following 18 patient identifiers:

1. Patient names
2. Geographical elements (such as a street address, city, county, or zip code)
3. Dates related to the health or identity of individuals (including birthdates, date of admission, date of discharge, date of death, or exact age of a patient older than 89)
4. Telephone numbers
5. Fax numbers
6. Email addresses
7. Social Security numbers
8. Medical record numbers
9. Health insurance beneficiary numbers
10. Account numbers
11. Certificate/license numbers
12. Vehicle identifiers
13. Device attributes or serial numbers
14. Digital identifiers, such as website URLs
15. IP addresses
16. Biometric elements, including finger, retinal, and voiceprints
17. Full-face photographic images
18. Other identifying numbers or codes[5]

Covered entities (health plans, providers, healthcare clearinghouses, and business associates) have an obligation to protect PHI. This duty to protect PHI extends to electronic PHI posted to social media.

Covered entities must consider also how PHI is used without a patient's consent. Covered entities may use and disclose PHI for treatment, payment, and certain healthcare operations without written consent.[6] The use of PHI on social media does not fall within the HIPAA defined uses and disclosures exempt from written consent. Based on a review of the uses and disclosures language within HIPAA, one can infer social media posts related to PHI require the patient's consent via a valid written authorization.

The HIPAA Security Rule specifically protects electronic PHI (ePHI), and PHI shared on social media is ePHI. The security regulations specifically require that covered entities and business associates must:

1. Ensure the confidentiality, integrity, and availability of all electronic protected health information the covered entity or business associate creates, receives, maintains, or transmits.
2. Protect against any reasonably anticipated threats or hazards to the security or integrity of such information.
3. Protect against any reasonably anticipated uses or disclosures of such information that are not permitted or required under the Privacy regulations; and
4. Ensure workforce complies with the Security Rule.[7]

Beyond HIPAA, the Centers for Medicare & Medicaid Services (CMS) provides for patient rights as part of conditions of participation in federally funded programs. Hospitals, which bill federally funded programs, must promote and protect each patient's rights. These include, but are not limited to, the right to personal privacy, to be free from all forms of abuse or harassment, and the right to confidentiality of their clinical records.[8]

Common Compliance Risks

Unauthorized Use of Social Media

Generation Z (born between 1997 and 2012) grew up with the internet. This generation used and continues to use social media to connect with friends, express themselves, and find jobs. However, this is not the only generation using social media to connect with friends and blog about their day, often posting experiences (humorous and otherwise) from their work environment. People of all generations may have difficulty distinguishing between their personal and professional lives when using social media platforms. After all, it is easy to make a social media post without much thought.

The consequences of work-related social media posts in healthcare can range from job loss to civil and criminal liability. While HIPAA does not specifically address the use of social media, compliance must apply the Privacy and Security Rules to social media content. News reports from across the nation provide insight into what is considered inappropriate as it relates to sharing a patient's PHI on social media.

Headlines Related to Social Media

News headlines indicate the dire results for employees who post PHI on social media. In 2018, for example, a Texas nurse was terminated for remarks she posted on Facebook about a toddler who contracted measles after overseas travel.[9] Her comments, posted to the group, "Proud Parents of Unvaccinated Children—Texas," divulged detailed information from her treatment of the patient. "The kid was super sick. Sick enough to be admitted to the ICU and he looked miserable," the nurse posted to an antivaccine Facebook page. The nurse's employing hospital stated they were "made aware that one of our nurses posted protected health information regarding a patient on social media."[10]

A nurse in Massachusetts routinely posted TikTok videos she labeled "humorous skits," which others described as "videos that appeared to show [her] joking about mistreating her patients."[11] Her employer released a statement stating, "Be assured we have handled the situation and reported her actions to all appropriate state and federal agencies."[12] This case indicates that using a patient's name is not necessary for an employer to consider a social media post as compromising both a patient's right to privacy and right to dignity.

In 2021, a group of resident physicians posted on Instagram photos of body parts removed from patients in the operating room. The covered entity released a statement, saying it was "shocked and dismayed" by the incident, had already taken "corrective action," and was "actively and comprehensively investigating this unfortunate incident."[13]

In 2019, a Chicago nursing home terminated two employees after a Snapchat video surfaced showing them taunting a 91-year-old resident with dementia .[14] The video resulted in a lawsuit against the nursing home for abuse.

Authorized Use of Social Media

Most covered entities have a social media presence, whether it's an organizational website, company-sponsored social media pages, or online reviews pages (e.g., Yelp, Google). It is important that organizations follow the HIPAA Privacy Rule when developing and responding to content on these platforms, as demonstrated in recent Office for Civil Rights (OCR) settlements.

In March 2022, the OCR issued a press release stating, "a dental practice with offices in Charlotte and Monroe, North Carolina, impermissibly disclosed a patient's PHI on a webpage in response to a negative online review."[15] The practice was assessed a civil monetary penalty.

In 2019, a dental practice in Dallas, Texas, released PHI without authorization when it responded to online reviews. The practice received a monetary penalty and was placed under a corrective action plan (CAP) that included two years of monitoring by the OCR. The OCR investigation found that dental practice impermissibly disclosed the PHI of multiple patients in response to patient reviews on the practice's Yelp review page. Additionally, the practice did not have a policy and procedure regarding disclosures of PHI to ensure that its social media interactions protect the PHI of its patients.[16]

Addressing Compliance Risks

Privacy Violations on Social Media

There are many more examples of social media HIPAA violations indicating unauthorized disclosure of PHI by workforce members at covered entities. Steps can be taken to minimize the risk social media presents in the healthcare environment. The steps follow The U.S. Department of Health & Human Services Office of Inspector General's (HHS OIG) seven elements of an effective compliance program. As a reminder, the elements are as follows:

1. Create and implement written policies and procedures.
2. Designate a compliance officer and compliance committee.
3. Develop reporting systems that can be used without fear of retaliation.
4. Provide employee education and effective lines of communication.
5. Conduct internal monitoring and auditing.
6. Enforce policies using disciplinary guidelines.
7. Respond promptly to offenses and undertake corrective action

Utilizing the seven elements, a covered entity should address social media expectations in relation to the HIPAA Privacy Rule through detailed policies and procedures. A best practice is to acknowledge expectations regarding social media in the covered entity's code of conduct. It is important to review for congruency the code of conduct and any other related policies and procedures within the organization. For example, a social media policy should align with the covered entity's policies related to disciplinary action, email, confidentiality, portable devices (e.g., cell phones, tablets, laptops), internet usage, harassment, minimum necessary standard, and patient authorization. At a minimum, organizations should consider addressing the following within a social media policy:

- Expectations regarding photography and audio recordings of patients and visitors
- Expectations that PHI will not be shared on social media
- Use of devices to participate in social media during work hours
- Obligation to follow federal and state laws
- Permanence of published social media posts, even if made to private groups (search engines can reveal posts years after they were created)
- Expectations about whether or not workforce members are authorized to "speak" on behalf of the organization
- Disciplinary consequences for violations of the social media policy

In addition to a written policy and procedure, a healthcare provider may also reference national guidance such as *A Nurse's Guide to the Use of SocialMedia.*[17] This guide, published by the National Council of State Boards of Nursing (NCSBN), provides detailed examples of social media posts that violate a patient's right to privacy; lists the potential consequences related to inappropriate use of social media; discusses common myths and misunderstandings of social media; and concludes with tips on how to avoid disclosing confidential patient information. Although the guide's target audience is licensed nurses, it can be referenced by covered entities to help develop a social media policy and subsequent training tools.

A section of the guide addresses common myths and misunderstandings, including several erroneous types of social-media decisions made by workforce members of covered entities. For example, one is the mistaken belief that a post is private or accessible only by the intended recipient and audience. Social media posts can be captured via photography, images, text, or email. Deleting a post does not mean a HIPAA violation did *not* occur. The content, although deleted by the author, can be distributed by an individual who captured the information. Additionally, PHI may continue to live on a server even after the post is deleted.

The guide also notes that there is a "mistaken belief that it is acceptable to discuss or refer to patients if they are not identified by name, but referred to by a nickname, room number, diagnosis, or condition."[18] It is imperative that HIPAA training address the definition of PHI and the 18 identifiers. In one of the guide's examples, a hospital employee is celebrating a work anniversary, a photograph is taken in the department to mark the anniversary, and in the background is a full-face photographic image of a patient. The photograph is posted on a social media platform with no intention to violate the HIPAA Privacy Rule. Social media training should address this type of example to reduce risk and provide workforce members the opportunity to ask questions about the discipline for *unintentional* social media violations.

Compliance education and policies should also include repercussions for licensed personnel, beyond those of internal policies and procedures. The previously mentioned guidance issued by the NCSBN explains that licensed nurses may face disciplinary action by a board of nursing that could include "a reprimand or sanction, assessment of a monetary fine, or temporary or permanent loss of licensure."[19]

Additionally, HIPAA violations subject workforce members to civil and criminal penalties, including fines and jail time, depending upon the nature of the violation. Some social media posts could implicate state and federal regulations related to patient abuse or exploitation, as noted in the 2019 incident at a nursing home described earlier.

Social media posts typically involve an audience and can be quickly publicized throughout the community, either through word of mouth or via media outlets. Training and education should incorporate the damage that individual actions can create for healthcare organizations in the community (i.e., reputational harm) as well as harm to the individual subject of the social media content. To protect the covered entity, training and education should include various channels (e.g., compliance hotline) that workforce members can use to report potential social media HIPAA violations.

Effectiveness of a social media policy depends on the disciplinary action associated with violations. Some covered entities address social media violations utilizing a "Just Culture" approach in which mistakes are viewed as opportunities to learn and identify "contributing system factors," rather than to punish.[20] In healthcare, this approach is often used to reduce errors that have an impact on patient safety. When applied to HIPAA, the approach can encourage additional compliance violation reporting, and if the incident is an innocent mistake, such an approach may not result in automatic termination. Social media issues can be opportunities to improve the existing HIPAA training and education program. Consider the example of a workforce member who makes a social media post that involves PHI, with a patient who gave verbal permission. This type of post typically does not follow covered-entity policies and procedures, especially as relates to written patient authorization requirements. Instead of focusing upon disciplinary action, the Just Culture approach uses the post as a learning opportunity for the individual who made the social media post—and for all employees. Compliance should revisit its training to assess and address gaps needing clarifications.

Many covered entities utilize a HIPAA disciplinary committee that includes representatives from human resources, privacy, and legal departments and the director and/or manager who supervises the individual who violated the social media policy. The committee determines application of the disciplinary policy to ensure fairness. Other organizations leave the discipline to the human resources department after investigation by a privacy official. Regardless of the structure, the covered entity should ensure workforce members are educated on the disciplinary process. Compliance should review discipline for social media violations to ensure the application of discipline is fair and consistent.

To address auditing and monitoring within the seven effective elements of a compliance program, many covered entities utilize content management tools to monitor online content (comments or discussions about the organization) across various social media platforms. These tools can reveal potential privacy violations made by employees. Because such tools are readily available from vendors, covered entities should educate employees not to expect any social media posts to be private. Covered entities should also perform due diligence prior to selecting a content management vendor. The vendor should have knowledge of HIPAA in the healthcare space. An area of concern is how a covered entity responds to commentary about the organization made by commenters.

Covered entities should be aware of and address expectations regarding employees "friending" patients on social media. This behavior can quickly lead to conversations that violate HIPAA Privacy and Security Rules. Setting expectations can reduce the risks of blurring the lines between personal and professional lives. For example, a patient may ask the workforce member's opinion regarding past treatment, current medications related to a recent visit, or a question regarding recent treatment. Even if the workforce member can professionally answer the questions, doing so via social media or electronically (i.e., through Facebook messenger feature or by texting) can run afoul of the HIPAA Security Rule. The communication of ePHI in the circumstances described is typically not made through a secured method. HHS expects transmissions of ePHI to be encrypted to reduce the risk of unauthorized access.[21] Education and documented policy should address this issue.

Documentation should clearly state that even if the patient initiates contact, communication should be made through covered entity-approved communication channels that meet HIPAA Security Rule requirements. This includes encryption in accordance with the Security Rule. While encryption is not required, breaches are not generally reportable if they involve encrypted ePHI.[22] This is a strong incentive to use encryption for data at rest and data in motion.

Authorized Use of Social Media

Covered entities have a duty to formulate marketing policies addressing not only organizational goals to promote services offered, but to do so in a HIPPA-compliant manner. Compliance professionals should review marketing policies to ensure processes do not involve the inappropriate disclosure of PHI. Marketing policies and communication plans should be aligned with privacy policies, including a thorough understanding of impermissible disclosures. As part of this understanding, marketing staff should be educated on the need for patient authorizations for using PHI in marketing materials, including social media.

A privacy risk assessment should include whether the covered entity responds to social media posts made by patients and others. For instance, say, a patient posts to social media that they had a terrible (or a great) experience when obtaining an MRI. Does the covered entity utilize a content management vendor that posts automatic comments? Do those comments violate HIPAA by acknowledging the individual as a patient? Marketing employees typically provide "stock" responses for various scenarios. These responses should be reviewed to ensure HIPAA compliance. As an example, an individual's poster may state, "My inpatient stay at [name] Medical Center was less than perfect because of..." Covered entities must be careful that their response does not violate HIPAA. An automated response such as "Please reach out to our Patient Liaison at [phone number]" is more appropriate than responding, "We are sorry about your experience during your recent visit to [name] Medical Center," a statement which, it could be argued, confirms the individual was a patient at [name] Medical Center.

If the covered entity uses a content management vendor to boost brand recognition and provide responses on their social media accounts, compliance should determine if the vendor's product is HIPAA-compliant. The vendor may also provide an instant messaging platform. If so, compliance should determine if the platform is encrypted and HIPAA-compliant. If an employee is responsible for overseeing social media traffic, the privacy official should provide targeted education to the individual(s). Monitoring a covered entity's websites should include a review of any "Contact Us" buttons to determine what information is requested by the covered entity. If the covered entity requests an individual provide ePHI via an online fillable form, the compliance official should determine if the ePHI is protected in accordance with the HIPAA Security Rule. The covered entity should not request that a patient or potential patient provide information through unencrypted means, such as regular email correspondence.

Social media platforms should also be monitored for comments that can suggest privacy violations. Patients sometimes post their grievances to social media instead of contacting the facility and formally reporting the issue through proper channels. As part of the risk assessment process, compliance should determine how complaints are culled from social media platforms and whether posted privacy concerns are immediately forwarded to the privacy officer for investigation.

Education for authorized use of social media extends beyond the marketing department. As the previous examples demonstrate, it is important for providers to understand HIPAA obligations related to online reviews. All workforce members should be educated on the appropriate channels for posting content to the company website and social media.

In addition to privacy issues that can occur when PHI is impermissibly disclosed on social media, some HIPAA Security Rule concerns should also be addressed. Recent headlines demonstrate the importance of security when a covered entity maintains an online presence.

On June 16, 2022, *The Markup* reported finding a tracking tool called Meta Pixel on one-third of the hospital websites on *Newsweek's* list of top 100 hospitals in American. "A tracking tool installed on many hospitals' websites has been collecting patients' sensitive health information—including details about their medical conditions, prescriptions, and doctor's appointments—and sending it to Facebook."[23] Because covered entities were not aware of the tracking tool, there was no business associate agreement in place or patient authorization to permit the sharing of PHI in accordance with the HIPAA Privacy Rule. Meta, which owns Facebook, Instagram, and WhatsApp, is facing class action lawsuits over the data collection. Covered entities also are being sued by patients. Additionally, covered entities have filed breach reports with the OCR and notified affected patients as a result of *The Markup's* article. On August 19, 2022, *HIPAA Journal* reported that, "Novant Health notified 1,362,296 patients about a breach of their PHI due to the incorrect configuration of Meta Pixel code on its patient portal."[24]

The Meta Pixel incident in healthcare indicates the need for covered entities to understand the privacy policies of any online platforms used and the privacy settings within those systems. Covered entities may also, as a best practice, remind patients they can turn off location tracking on their cell phone during appointments. This practice would be particularly useful for patients seeking treatment from a specialized provider, such as an oncologist or a mental health professional. Recently, HHS issued guidance to individuals entitled, "Protecting the Privacy and Security of Your Health Information When Using Your Personal Cell Phone or Tablet."[25] The guidance reminds individuals that, "the HIPAA Rules generally *do not* protect the privacy or security of your health information when it is accessed through or stored on *your* personal cell phones or tablets." The guidance provides steps individuals can take to increase privacy when using mobile devices.

Possible Penalties

Social media use is extensive across all industries, and in the healthcare arena it is imperative that the use of social media does not result in costly HIPAA violations. Past settlements with the HHS OCR demonstrate HIPAA penalties involving social media can result in both civil monetary penalties *and* corrective action plans for covered entities. For example, the small dental practice that responded to a social media review agreed to pay the OCR $10,000 and to adopt a corrective action plan (CAP) to settle potential violations of the HIPAA Privacy Rule. The CAP, which required periodic reporting to the OCR, included development of policies and procedures, development of a training program, and other requirements. A press release from the OCR states the dental practice, "did not have a policy and procedure regarding disclosures of PHI to ensure that its social media interactions protect the PHI of its patients."[26] This press release reminds covered entities that although social media may not be specifically mentioned within HIPAA, the OCR expects covered entities to address the privacy and security issues that social media presents. It also included two years of monitoring by the OCR for compliance with HIPAA.

As another example, a physical therapy practice agreed to a payment of $25,000 as well as implementation of a corrective action plan, and annual reporting of compliance efforts to the OCR for a one-year period.[27] The practice, "impermissibly disclosed numerous individuals' protected health information (PHI), when it posted patient testimonials, including full names and full-face photographic images, to its website without obtaining valid, HIPAA-compliant authorizations.

Regardless of covered entity size, one should expect to be monitored under a CAP if social media violations occur and where a covered entity has no process to address and attempt to prevent such behavior. The size of monetary penalties will depend upon the size of the covered entity.

Compliance Resources

Resources related to this topic include the following:

- Review of compliance enforcement actions can be viewed on the HHS.gov website at: https://www.hhs.gov/hipaa/for-professionals/compliance-enforcement/agreements/index.html

- Review of HIPAA News Releases & Bulletins at: https://www.hhs.gov/hipaa/newsroom/index.html

- Summaries of 15 examples of HIPAA violations involving social media at:

  https://etactics.com/blog/social-media-hipaa-violations

- "Protecting the Privacy and Security of Your Health Information When Using Your Personal Cell Phone or Tablet" at:

  https://www.hhs.gov/hipaa/for-professionals/privacy/guidance/cell-phone-hipaa/index.html

- "Social Media in Health Care: Time for Transparent Privacy Policies and Consent for Data Use and Disclosure," in *Applied Clinical Informatics (2018)* https://www.ncbi.nlm.nih.gov/pmc/articles/PMC6261737/

- "Social Media and Health Care Professionals: Benefits, Risks, and Best Practices," in *Pharmacy and Therapeutics (2014)*

  https://www.ncbi.nlm.nih.gov/pmc/articles/PMC4103576/

Risk Takeaways

Main points of interest:
- Compliance departments should review social media in the context of both authorized and unauthorized use.
- HIPAA Privacy and Security Rules govern how protected health information can be used and transmitted by healthcare organizations.
- Recent news reports demonstrate the repercussions for healthcare organizations in response to inappropriate social media posts made by employees.

Areas to watch:
- Authorized social media includes covered entity website(s) and other entity-sponsored instances of online presence.
- Unauthorized social media include posts made by workforce members that violate HIPAA.

Laws that apply:
- HIPAA Privacy Rule, 45 C.F.R. §§ 160, 164 (Subparts A and E)
- HIPAA Security Rule, 45 C.F.R. §§ 160, 164 (Subparts A and C)

Addressing compliance risks:

- To decrease the risk of both authorized and unauthorized social media participation requires policies and procedures, risk assessment, and training and education to ensure HIPAA compliance.
- Use of social media requires an assessment from a HIPAA Security perspective to verify whether data is encrypted and safeguarded to prevent unauthorized access.
- Workforce members should understand impermissible disclosures and the need for written patient authorization to use any type of ePHI on social media, even if the individual is not named. Education is an ongoing process because of the changing work environment.

Endnotes

1. **Sheila Price Limmroth** is the Compliance Officer for Pinnacle Healthcare Consulting, Inc. She has over 30 years of experience in internal audit, privacy, and compliance. Prior to joining Pinnacle, she served as the Corporate Director of Internal Audit and Compliance for DCH Health System in Tuscaloosa, Al. Prior to DCH she worked for Ernst & Young in the audit services division.

2. Health Insurance Portability and Accountability Act of 1996, Pub. L. No. 104-191.

3. Merriam-Webster.com Dictionary, s.v. "social media," accessed December 15, 2022, https://www.merriam-webster.com/dictionary/social%20media.

4. American Recovery and Reinvestment Act of 2009, Pub. L. No. 111-005.

5. U.S. Department of Health & Human Services, *Guidance Regarding Methods for De-identification of Protected Health Information in Accordance with the Health Insurance Portability and Accountability Act (HIPAA) Privacy Rule*, accessed December 15, 2022, https://www.hhs.gov/hipaa/for-professionals/privacy/special-topics/de-identification/index.html.

6. 45 C.F.R. § 164.502.

7. 45 C.F.R. § 164.306(a).

8. 42 C.F.R. § 482.13

9. Stephan Morgan, "Texas Children's Hospital nurse fired after social media post," Fox26 Houston, August 29, 2018,https://www.fox26houston.com/news/texas-childrens-hospital-nurse-fired-after-social-media-post

10. Maggie Fox, "Texas Children's Hospital Nurse Fired After Post About Measles Patient," ABC News, August 30, 2018, https://www.nbcnews.com/storyline/measles-outbreak/texas-children-s-hospital-nurse-fired-after-post-about-measles-n905146.

11. Ford Hatchett, "Triad Nurse Says She Was Suspended Over Tiktok Videos," WXII 12 News, June 28, 2021, https://www.wxii12.com/article/triad-nurse-says-she-was-suspended-over-joke-tiktok-videos/36867564#.

12. Ford Hatchett, "Triad Nurse Says She Was Suspended Over Tiktok Videos," WXII 12 News, June 28, 2021, https://www.wxii12.com/article/triad-nurse-says-she-was-suspended-over-joke-tiktok-videos/36867564#.

13. Susan Samples, "Graphic Surgery Photos Spectrum Doctors Posted Online May Violate Privacy Laws," Target 8, WoodTV8, March 15, 2021, https://www.woodtv.com/news/target-8/graphic-surgery-photos-spectrum-doctors-posted-online-may-violate-privacy-laws/.

14. "Outrage After Video Shows Staffers Taunting, Terrorizing Woman, 91, at Glenview Nursing Home," CBS News Chicago, August 8, 2019, https://www.cbsnews.com/chicago/news/glenview-nursing-home-abuse/

15. U.S. Department of Health & Human Services, Office of Civil Rights, "Four HIPAA Enforcement Actions Hold Healthcare Providers Accountable with Compliance," news release, March 28, 2022, https://www.hhs.gov/about/news/2022/03/28/four-hipaa-enforcement-actions-hold-healthcare-providers-accountable-with-compliance.html.

16. U.S. Department of Health & Human Services, Office of Civil Rights, "Dental Practice Pays $10,000 to Settle Social Media Disclosures of Patients' Protected Health Information," new release, June 8, 2020, https://www.hhs.gov/guidance/document/dental-practice-pays-10000-settle-social-media-disclosures-patients-protected-health.

17. National Council of State Boards of Nursing, Inc., *A Nurse's Guide to the Use of Social Media*, June 2018,https://www.ncsbn.org/public-files/NCSBN_SocialMedia.pdf.

18. National Council of State Boards of Nursing, Inc., *A Nurse's Guide to the Use of Social Media*, June 2018, https://www.ncsbn.org/public-files/NCSBN_SocialMedia.pdf.

19. National Council of State Boards of Nursing, Inc., *A Nurse's Guide to the Use of Social Media*, June 2018,https://www.ncsbn.org/public-files/NCSBN_SocialMedia.pdf.https://www.ncsbn.org/public-files/NCSBN_SocialMedia.pdf

20. "Just Culture in Healthcare: Balancing Safety and Accountability," Just Culture, accessed December 18, 2022, https://www.justculture.healthcare

21. Health Insurance Reform: Security Standards, 68 Fed. Reg. 8357 (Feb. 20, 2003).

22. 45 C.F.R. § 164.304.

23. Todd Feathers, Simon Fondrie-Teitler, Angie Waller, et al., "Facebook Is Receiving Sensitive Medical Information from Hospital Websites," *The Markup*, June 16, 2022, https://themarkup.org/pixel-hunt/2022/06/16/facebook-is-receiving-sensitive-medical-information-from-hospital-websites.

24. "Novant Health Notifies 1.36 Million Patients About Unauthorized Disclosure of PHI via Meta Pixel Code on Patient Portal," *HIPAA Journal*, August 16, 2022, https://www.hipaajournal.com/novant-health-notifies-patients-about-unauthorized-disclosure-of-phi-via-meta-pixel-code-on-patient-portal/.

25. U.S. Department of Health & Human Services, Office of Civil Rights, *Protecting the Privacy and Security of Your Health Information When Using Your Personal Cell Phone or Tablets*, last reviewed June 29, 2022, https://www.hhs.gov/hipaa/for-professionals/privacy/guidance/cell-phone-hipaa/index.html.

26. "Dental Practice Pays $10,000 to Settle Social Media Disclosures of Patients' Protected Health Information," new release, June 8, 2020, https://www.hhs.gov/guidance/document/dental-practice-pays-10000-settle-social-media-disclosures-patients-protected-health.

27. U.S. Department of Health & Human Services, Office of Civil Rights, "Physical Therapy Provider Settles Violations That It Impermissibly Disclosed Patient Information," HHS-0945-1905-F-6184, news release, https://www.hhs.gov/guidance/document/physical-therapy-provider-settles-violations-it-impermissibly-disclosed-patient.

Pharmacy

340B Drug Pricing Program

By Megan La Suer,[1] Mark Ogunsusi,[2]
William von Oehsen,[3] and Barbara Straub Williams[4]

What Is the 340B Drug Pricing Program?

Section 340B of the Public Health Services Act, enacted in 1992, entitles certain safety-net hospitals and clinics, referred to as "covered entities," to purchase outpatient drugs at discounted prices from drug manufacturers.[5] Companion legislation that amended Section 1927 of the Social Security Act requires drug manufacturers to enter into a Pharmaceutical Pricing Agreement (PPA) with the U.S. Department of Health & Human Services (HHS) to provide such drugs at or below a statutorily defined ceiling price as a condition of the manufacturers' drugs being reimbursable under the Medicaid program and Medicare Part B.[6] These two pieces of legislation launched a new federal program that is known today as the "340B program." The intent of the 340B program is to allow covered entities serving vulnerable populations to "stretch scarce federal resources as far as possible, reaching more eligible patients and providing more comprehensive care."[7]

The 340B program is administered by the Office of Pharmacy Affairs (OPA), which is a division of the Health Resources and Services Administration (HRSA) of HHS.[8] HRSA also relies on a government contractor to help administer the 340B program. The government contractor, which is currently Apexus, Inc. (Apexus), is the 340B prime vendor and responsible for operating a program that provides a range of services to covered entities, including distribution of 340B drugs and negotiation of purchasing terms for both 340B and non-340B products.[9] The 340B prime vendor is also responsible for staffing a call center and providing education, training, and technical assistance to the broader 340B stakeholder community.[10]

This article provides a high-level overview of the requirements and compliance issues applicable to covered entities as well as resources available to covered entities for meeting their 340B program obligations. It also briefly discusses 340B program requirements applicable to manufacturers.

Risk Area Governance

Most of the 340B program's compliance requirements applicable to covered entities and manufacturers are set forth in the 340B statute.[11] Congress gave HRSA rulemaking authority to implement program requirements but only in three narrow areas: (1) the establishment of an administrative dispute resolution process; (2) the development of a methodology for calculating ceiling prices; and (3) the imposition of manufacturer civil monetary penalties.[12] HRSA has adopted regulations in each of these areas.[13][14][15] Because HRSA has limited regulatory authority, many of HRSA's policies governing covered-entity compliance with the 340B program are published in guidance documents and frequently asked questions (FAQs) issued by HRSA and Apexus.

The 340B statute imposes not only general compliance responsibilities on all covered entities, but also more specific requirements that are unique to certain categories of covered entities. The general compliance obligations include the following:

- Prohibition against reselling 340B drugs to anyone other than the covered entity's patients, a practice commonly known as "diversion."[16]
- Obligation of the covered entity to protect a manufacturer from "duplicate discounts" which occurs when a company gives both a 340B discount and Medicaid rebate on the same drug.[17]
- Requirement that the covered entity maintains auditable records of its 340B program activities.[18]

Covered entities are also responsible for complying with OPA's Information System (OPAIS) registration requirements, ensuring the accuracy and completeness of information submitted to and contained in OPAIS, and certifying to the accuracy of the information on OPAIS annually.[19] Compliance obligations that are specific to certain types of covered entities include (1) the prohibition against purchasing drugs through a group purchasing organization (GPO), which only applies to disproportionate share hospitals (DSHs) and children's and cancer hospitals, and (2) the prohibition against purchasing orphan drugs, which only applies to sole community hospitals (SCHs), critical access hospital (CAHs), rural referral center (RRCs), and cancer hospitals. [20][21]

340B Program Eligibility

Only certain categories of safety-net providers are eligible to participate in the 340B program under the 340B statute. A drug company's eligibility to participate in the program, by contrast, extends to any manufacturer willing to enter into and comply with a PPA with HHS. This section outlines the eligibility requirements applicable to both covered entities and manufacturers.

Eligibility and Registration of Covered Entities and Their Contract Pharmacies
Discounted pricing on drugs purchased through the 340B program is only available to safety-net providers that *qualify for* and *register in* the program. Although only covered entities are eligible to purchase 340B drugs, they are entitled to dispense their discounted drugs through any pharmacy willing to contract with the covered entity and to abide by 340B program requirements and terms of the contract. The requirements applicable to a covered entity's eligibility, registration, and contract pharmacy arrangements include the following.

Eligibility

Prior to 2010, participation in the 340B program was statutorily limited to the following categories of healthcare entities:

- Federally qualified health centers (FQHCs) and FQHC look-alikes (FQHC-LAs)[22]
- Native Hawaiian health centers
- Tribal/urban Indian health centers
- Ryan White HIV/AIDS program grantees
- Disproportionate share hospitals (DSH)
- Black lung clinics
- Comprehensive hemophilia diagnostic treatment centers
- Title X family planning clinics
- AIDS drug-assistance programs
- Sexually transmitted disease (STD) clinics
- Tuberculosis clinics[23]

In 2010, Congress expanded the list of eligible covered entities when it included in the Affordable Care Act (ACA) five additional categories of hospitals:

- Children's hospitals
- Cancer hospitals
- Sole community hospitals (SCHs)
- Rural referral centers (RRCs)
- Critical access hospitals (CAHs)[24]

Hospitals are the largest purchasers of 340B drugs and comprise the largest share of covered entity sites participating in the 340B program. To be eligible, hospitals must satisfy an array of requirements that vary depending on the category in which they fall. For example, with the exception of CAHs, every hospital must have a payer mix that, when used to calculate its reimbursement adjustment through the Medicare DSH program, generates an *adjustment percentage* that meets or exceeds a threshold set forth in the 340B statute. DSH, children's hospitals, and cancer hospitals must have a DSH adjustment percentage that exceeds 11.75%. SCHs and RRCs must have a DSH adjustment percentage of at least 8%. [25] [26]

(Please note: The DSH payment percentage is not the same as the DSH patient percentage. A hospital must have a DSH patient percentage of (1) .2733 to have a DSH adjustment percentage of at least 11.75% and (2) .2277 to have a DSH adjustment percentage of at least 8%. If a hospital's DSH adjustment percentage falls below the requisite level based on its most recently filed Medicare cost report, it must notify HRSA and stop purchasing 340B drugs immediately.)

Hospitals are also subject to organizational standards. A 340B hospital must be (1) owned or operated by a state or local government; (2) a private nonprofit organization under contract with a unit of state or local government to provide healthcare services to low-income individuals who are not Medicare or Medicaid beneficiaries; or (3) a public or private nonprofit corporation that is formally granted governmental powers by a unit of state or local government. [27] [28] [29] Another condition of eligibility for DSH, children's hospitals, and cancer hospitals is that they are prohibited from obtaining covered outpatient drugs through a GPO or other group purchasing arrangement.[30]

Nonhospital covered entities are subject to far fewer eligibility requirements under the 340B statute. With the exception of FQHC-LAs, they are eligible to participate in the program simply as a result of receiving federal funding under one of the federal grant programs enumerated in the statute.[31] FQHC-LAs meet all the federal requirements applicable to FQHCs but, unlike FQHCs, are not federally funded. STD clinics may also be eligible to participate by virtue of receiving an "in-kind," or nonmonetary, contribution that is funded under Section 318 of the Public Health Service Act.[32] If a grantee loses its grant or if an FQHC-LA no longer qualifies as an FQHC-LA, the grantee must immediately notify HRSA and stop purchasing 340B drugs. Importantly, 340B grantees and subgrantees may only purchase and use 340B drugs within the scope of their qualifying federal grant.[33] [34]

Registration

Entities eligible to participate in the 340B program must first register through HRSA's 340B Office of Pharmacy Affairs Information System (OPAIS). OPAIS provides a listing of and information about covered entities that are eligible to purchase 340B drugs.[35] During registration, covered entities must attest that their entries in OPAIS are complete and accurate. [36]

HRSA requires covered entities to register for the 340B program during one of four registration periods available each year. The registration periods are:

- January 1–15 for an effective start date of April 1
- April 1–15 for an effective start date of July 1
- July 1– 15 for an effective start date of October 1
- October 1–15 for an effective start date of January 1[37]

A hospital must register its main facility as well as all outpatient departments located outside of the "four walls" of the main facility that will be dispensing, administering, or prescribing 340B drugs. [38] [39] OPA refers to these clinics as "child sites." HRSA will not register these child sites on OPAIS until the costs and charges for the sites appear on a filed Medicare cost report. However, hospitals may begin using 340B drugs at new outpatient department sites that are eligible to participate in the 340B program but are not yet reflected on a filed Medicare cost report.[40] [41] The 340B registration requirements applicable to federal grantees and subgrantees are similar to the hospital requirements. If a grantee or FQHC-LA operates more than one service location that uses 340B drugs, it must *register each location* on OPAIS.[42]

Contract Pharmacy Program

When Congress created the 340B program, it did not consider that some covered entities—especially FQHCs, Ryan White and STD clinics, and other smaller facilities—would be unable to participate because they lacked pharmacies capable of purchasing and dispensing 340B drugs. Soon after the 340B program began, these facilities expressed concerns to OPA over the cost and expertise required to build and operate an in-house pharmacy. They feared that these costs would offset the benefits of participating in the program. They began pressuring OPA to find a way for them to participate without having to incur the start-up and overhead costs of running their own pharmacies.

In 1996, HRSA responded to these complaints by publishing guidelines that allowed covered entities to use third-party contract pharmacies to dispense their 340B drugs.[43] Under the 1996 guidelines, a covered entity could enter into a "ship to, bill to" arrangement with a pharmacy contractor in which manufacturers would bill the covered entity for the 340B drugs that the entity purchases, but ship the drugs to the pharmacy with which the entity contracts.[44] Patients of the covered entity could then receive the 340B drugs from the entity's contract pharmacy, although the pharmacy would not be entitled to dispense the discounted drugs to its other customers.[45] Though the contract-pharmacy program was primarily intended for covered entities that did not own and operate their own outpatient pharmacies, all covered entities were permitted to enter into a contract-pharmacy arrangement.[46]

HRSA initially only permitted covered entities to work with a single contract pharmacy.[47] However, on March 5, 2010, HRSA expanded the contract-pharmacy program by allowing covered entities to contract with an unlimited number of pharmacies.[48] HRSA's 2010 guidelines also increased covered entities' responsibility to monitor compliance of their contract pharmacy arrangements.[49]

Because contract pharmacies are retail pharmacies that are not part of the same legal entity as the covered entity and are not covered entities themselves, they must be registered in the OPAIS under the covered entity's registration. Contract pharmacies act as agents of the covered entity by dispensing drugs to the covered entity's patients. The contract pharmacy typically orders, receives, and dispenses 340B drugs, but only in its capacity as the covered entity's agent. The contract pharmacy also bills insurers, collects reimbursement, and maintains 340B drug inventories on behalf of the covered entity.

Manufacturer Participation

As previously mentioned, manufacturer participation in the 340B program is subject to fewer eligibility requirements. Section 1927 of the Social Security Act states that a manufacturer's drugs will not be covered by Medicaid or Medicare Part B unless the manufacturer signs a PPA with HHS.[50] The PPA requires the drug manufacturer to provide 340B covered entities with "covered outpatient drugs for purchase at or below the applicable ceiling price if such drug is made available to any other purchaser at any price."[51] Manufacturers must offer these discounted prices without any restrictions with respect to where the covered entity requests that they be delivered, including to contract pharmacies.[52] Manufacturers, like covered entities, must register in OPAIS and keep their OPAIS entries up-to-date and accurate.[53]

Diversion

The 340B statute prohibits a covered entity from reselling or otherwise transferring 340B drugs to any person or entity other than its "patient." There is no definition of "patient" in the statute. Because covered entities are only entitled to 340B discounts on "covered outpatient drugs," administration of 340B drugs to a hospital inpatient is also considered diversion even though an inpatient is as much a hospital "patient" as an outpatient.

In 1996, HRSA issued patient definition guidance that describes which individuals are eligible to receive 340B drugs. Under the guidance, an individual must satisfy three criteria in order to be eligible to receive discounted drugs, although the third criterion only applies to the grantees and subgrantees.[54] First, the covered entity must maintain records of the individual's healthcare. Second, the individual must be under the care of a physician or other healthcare professional who is employed by, under contract with, or in a referral relationship with the covered entity such that responsibility for the individual's care remains with the covered entity. Third, the individual must receive a healthcare service or range of services that are consistent with the service or range services for which grant funding or FQHC-LA status has been provided to the covered entity.[55] An individual is not eligible to receive discounted drugs if the only healthcare service received by the individual from the covered entity is the dispensing of a drug for self-administration or administration in the home setting.[56]

Historically, in applying the patient definition guidance to prescriptions for self-administered drugs, HRSA has required that the prescription be written as the result of services provided within an OPAIS-registered location. However, based on a decline in the number of diversion findings in recent HRSA audits and HRSA's decision in 2019 to withdraw its diversion finding against an FQHC that challenged the finding in court, it appears that HRSA is taking a more lenient approach to identifying 340B eligible prescriptions.[57][58] With respect to infusion and injectable products, often referred to as "physician-administered drugs," HRSA has consistently permitted covered entities to use the 340B program for such drugs if the covered entity administers the drug within the covered entity's registered facility, even if the drug is ordered by an outside prescriber.

Duplicate Discounts

Under section 1927 of the Social Security Act, drug manufacturers are required to give rebates to state Medicaid programs on covered outpatient drugs reimbursed either through a state's fee-for-service (FFS) program or by a managed care organization (MCO) under contract with the state. The obligation to pay a rebate, however, is lifted if the rebatable drug was sold at a 340B discount.[59] Manufacturer protection against duplicate discounts differs depending on whether the drug is reimbursed on an FFS basis or by an MCO. With respect to FFS drugs, the obligation to protect against duplicate discounts is set forth in the 340B statute and placed squarely on the shoulders of the covered entity.[60] Protection against MCO duplicate discounts, on the other hand, is addressed in the Medicaid drug rebate statute and is the responsibility of states.

The Medicaid MCO duplicate discount problem did not arise until Congress decided to expand the Medicaid drug rebate program to include MCO drugs in 2010 under the ACA.[61] The language used to expand the program—which was added to section 1927 of the Social Security Act, not the 340B statute—includes a provision stating that such drugs are not subject to a Medicaid rebate if they are purchased under Section 340B.[62] Thus, the duplicate discount provision in the 340B statute does not apply to MCO drugs because, under the Medicaid drug rebate statute, the drugs are not "subject to the payment of a rebate to the State."[63] Manufacturers are protected from duplicate discounts on MCO drugs because the drugs purchased through the 340B program are categorically ineligible for Medicaid drug rebates.

Carve In/Carve Out Election and Use of the Medicaid Exclusion File

HRSA allows covered entities to decide whether they will use 340B drugs for Medicaid FFS beneficiaries. A covered entity's decision to use 340B drugs for its Medicaid population is generally referred to as "carving in," whereas excluding drugs for Medicaid beneficiaries from the covered entity's 340B program is called "carving out."[64] Covered entities are required to keep HRSA informed of their election. They must answer "yes" or "no" to the question on OPAIS regarding whether they will use 340B drugs for Medicaid beneficiaries.[65] Shortly after the 340B program was launched, HRSA created the Medicaid Exclusion File (MEF) as a tool for documenting a covered entity's decision to carve in or carve out.[66] Covered entities that carve in are listed on the MEF, along with their Medicaid billing numbers and national provider identifiers (NPIs). In addition to affording state Medicaid programs and drug manufacturers visibility into a covered entity's decision to use 340B drugs for its FFS Medicaid patients, the MEF actually protects against duplicate discounts because state Medicaid programs are prohibited from seeking rebates for claims submitted under the NPIs and billing numbers reflected in the MEF. In 2014, HRSA clarified that the MEF is not intended to provide information about whether a covered entity dispenses or administers 340B drugs to beneficiaries enrolled with a Medicaid MCO.[67]

A covered entity has less discretion to carve in its Medicaid FFS drugs when those drugs are dispensed by a contract pharmacy. Under HRSA's contract-pharmacy guidelines, covered entities may not use 340B drugs to fill FFS Medicaid prescriptions at contract pharmacies, unless (1) the covered entity, state Medicaid agency, and contract pharmacy have an arrangement in place to prevent duplicate discounts and (2) the covered entity has reported the arrangement to HRSA.[68] Nothing in the guidelines, however, precludes them from carving in FFS claims at their in-house retail pharmacies.

Claims Identification

Many state Medicaid agencies have regulations or policies governing identification of 340B claims for both FFS and MCO beneficiaries. For example, some states require that a covered entity's "carve in" or "carve out" election be the same for Medicaid FFS and Medicaid MCO beneficiaries, and they use the MEF to determine whether a covered entity has elected to carve in or carve out for both categories of beneficiaries.[69] Other states require the covered entity to identify 340B drug claims by use of a claims-level modifier, typically either the UD modifier for 340B physician-administered drug claims or a value of 20 in the submission clarification code field for self-administered drug claims.[70][71] These requirements generally are found in a Medicaid state plan, regulations, or guidance issued by the state Medicaid agency or in Medicaid MCO contracts.

GPO Prohibition

DSH, children's hospitals, and cancer hospitals are prohibited from obtaining covered outpatient drugs through a GPO or other group purchasing arrangement.[72] Because the GPO prohibition is an eligibility requirement, noncompliance can expose the hospital to a risk of being terminated from the program. The GPO prohibition only applies to purchases of "covered outpatient drugs," which means a hospital subject to the GPO prohibition may use a GPO to purchase inpatient drugs or drugs that otherwise fall outside the definition of a "covered outpatient drug."[73][74]

HRSA has recognized several exceptions to the GPO prohibition. For example, hospitals subject to the GPO prohibition may take advantage of the discounts that Apexus has negotiated through the prime vendor program even though the prime vendor program clearly operates as a "group purchasing arrangement" if not a GPO. HRSA also gives hospitals a fair amount of discretion in excluding certain drugs—primarily those that are billed with services and not as separate claims—from the definition of a "covered outpatient drug" so that they can be purchased at GPO prices.[75] Another exception is available if the hospital is initially unable to obtain a covered outpatient drug at a 340B price. In those instances, the hospital must work with the manufacturer to try to obtain 340B pricing and, if unsuccessful, purchase the drug at a non-340B, non-GPO price which, according to HRSA, is the drug's wholesale acquisition cost (WAC).[76] If the hospital cannot obtain the drug on its WAC account, it may then purchase the drug through a GPO. In these instances, the hospital must immediately notify OPA of the details of its prior attempts, communications, and the transaction—all of which must be properly documented and auditable.[77]

Lastly, HRSA established a widely publicized policy release in 2013 that allowed the offsite locations of 340B hospitals to opt out of the 340B program, including the program's prohibition against group purchasing. According to the policy release, hospitals subject to the GPO prohibition may elect not to use 340B and instead use GPO drugs at outpatient facilities that meet the following four requirements:

1. The facility is located at a different physical address than the parent facility.
2. The facility is not registered on the OPAIS as participating in the 340B program.
3. The facility purchases drugs through a separate pharmacy wholesaler account than the 340B participating parent.
4. The hospital maintains records demonstrating that any covered outpatient drugs purchased through the GPO at the facility sites are not used or otherwise transferred to the parent hospital or any outpatient facilities registered in the OPAIS.[78]

It is important to note that contract pharmacies may purchase their own drug inventory through a GPO; however, those drugs should not be dispensed to patients of a hospital subject to the GPO prohibition if they are purchased on behalf of the hospital. Stated differently, a hospital may not try to circumvent the GPO prohibition by purchasing GPO drugs through a contract pharmacy for its patients.[79]

OPAIS Data Errors

HRSA requires that the information included in a covered entity's OPAIS listing be accurate and complete. Inaccurate or incomplete database entries can result in an adverse audit finding. As discussed previously, covered entities can register additional locations during four registration periods available each year. In between those periods, covered entities can request changes to the information in the OPAIS. Covered entity medical practices that share a common building or street address must include suite numbers to help distinguish between them. Failure to separately list clinics, departments, and service lines can also lead to an OPAIS database finding.

Another risk area relates to contract pharmacy registration data. When a covered entity registers a contract pharmacy, OPAIS pulls information from the pharmacy's Drug Enforcement Agency (DEA) records to ensure that it matches the information submitted on OPAIS. That information is then crosschecked against the pharmacy services agreement between the covered entity and contract pharmacy during a HRSA audit. Discrepancies can result in an audit finding or area for improvement.

The individuals that HRSA views as responsible for OPAIS accuracy are the covered entity's Authorizing Official (AO) and Primary Contact (PC). HRSA requires covered entities to designate an AO and PC and these individuals are listed in OPAIS. The AO must be an individual who has authority to legally bind the organization, for example, a chief executive officer, chief operating officer, chief financial officer, president, vice president, senior vice president, clinic administrator, or program manager.[80] The PC must be an employee of the organization and may not be the same person as the AO. Either the AO or the PC can register a covered entity or make changes to the information in OPAIS, but the AO must attest to these actions if the PC makes them. The covered entity assumes a compliance risk if its AO or PC are unfamiliar with applicable 340B program responsibilities, including maintaining its entries in the OPAIS.

Recertification

HRSA has implemented an annual recertification process that requires the AOs at covered entities to certify to the accuracy of several statements relating to the entity's compliance status. Among other statements, AOs must attest that the information reflected on the covered entity's OPAIS entries is correct, that the covered entity is in compliance with all 340B program requirements, and that it will notify OPA if it is in material breach of any 340B program requirements. HRSA implemented the recertification requirement to comply with two program-integrity requirements added to the 340B statute under the ACA—HRSA must "enable and require" covered entities to regularly update their 340B database entry, and HRSA must develop a system to verify the accuracy of the information listed in the database.[81] OPA sends email notifications with information about the recertification process to the AO and PC prior to the recertification period.[82] A covered entity that does not recertify is terminated from the 340B program.[83]

AOs must be careful when certifying to the compliance status of their facilities during the recertification process. Although unlikely, AOs may incur criminal liability if they falsely attest to one or more of the representations required to recertify.[84] If convicted, the AO could be fined or subject to imprisonment.[85]

Orphan Drug Exclusion

Federal law provides incentives to manufacturers for developing a class of drugs, commonly known as "orphan drugs." These are drugs the FDA has determined can treat a rare disease or condition affecting fewer than 200,000 people in the U.S., or more than 200,000 people if there is no reasonable expectation that the costs of developing a drug for such disease or condition would be recouped from sales of the drug in the United States.[86] Physicians often prescribe orphan drugs to treat diseases or conditions other than the one for which the FDA granted the orphan drug designation. The 340B statute prohibits CAHs, RRCs, SCHs, and cancer hospitals from purchasing orphan drugs with 340B discounts.[87] HRSA provides quarterly updates regarding its list of drugs designated as orphan drugs.[88]

In 2014, pharmaceutical manufacturers challenged a HRSA policy allowing hospitals subject to the orphan-drug prohibition to purchase an orphan drug on the hospital's 340B account if the drug was not being used for the purpose for which the drug received orphan designation.[89] The court ruled in favor of the manufacturers and held that the statutory language clearly applies the prohibition regardless of the purpose for which the drug is being prescribed. Although manufacturers are not required to provide 340B discounts on orphan drugs to CAHs, RRCs, SCHs, and cancer hospitals, manufacturers often voluntarily provide "340B-like" discounts to hospitals subject to the orphan-drug prohibition.

A CAH, RRC, SCH, or cancer hospital that purchases an orphan drug with 340B discounts runs the risk of receiving an audit finding from HRSA, even if the drug is not being used for its orphan purpose. HRSA characterizes these instances as diversion although, from a legal perspective, the hospital is technically not violating the prohibition against diversion. If a hospital subject to the orphan-drug restriction receives a 340B-like discount on an orphan drug, it should maintain documentation demonstrating that the discount was voluntary.

Auditable Records

Covered entities must retain auditable records of their 340B operations to maintain eligibility in the 340B program.[90] Covered entities that are audited by HRSA receive a "Data Request" that lists the information and documents that the covered entity must produce prior to the audit. Among the documentation that must be given to the auditor is a spreadsheet of all the covered entity's 340B drug purchases. The auditors then review a sample of 340B drug purchases in more detail to determine compliance with the diversion and duplicate-discount prohibitions. The covered entity must be able to show that its 340B purchases were proper by tracking the drug from when it was ordered to the point of administration or dispensation. HRSA requires a staff member who is knowledgeable about navigating electronic health records (EHRs) (including billing information) and the split-billing software/third-party software to be available during an audit. This requirement is included in HRSA's Fiscal Year 2021 Data Request List, which is provided before the on-site audits.

Operational Issues to Consider

Operationalizing a 340B pharmacy program can be challenging, especially for complex organizations such as hospitals or underfunded clinics such as FQHCs, FQHC-LAs, or Ryan White clinics. Improper planning and/or implementation of a 304B program can lead to compliance problems. The risk of noncompliance is particularly high in the areas of inventory management and contract-pharmacy oversight.

Inventory Management

As is evident from the previous discussion, a covered entity must maintain documentation in order to demonstrate that it is in compliance with the diversion, duplicate-discount, GPO, and orphan-drug restrictions. Compliance with this documentation standard requires the covered entity to maintain controls over its 340B drug inventory. Covered entities track their 340B inventory by using either a physical inventory-management system or a virtual system that manages drug inventories using split-billing software. Under the physical inventory management system, 340B drug inventory is physically stored in a separate location from non-340B drug inventory, or 340B and non-340B inventory is kept in the same space but labeled so that it can be identified and used separately.

A virtual inventory system, by contrast, tracks use of covered outpatient drugs by patients through a computerized software-operated "accumulator." Use of drugs for individuals who are eligible patients under HRSA guidelines is counted under the 340B accumulator and use of all other drugs is counted under non-340B accumulators. Once a sufficient number of 340B dispenses are recorded in the accumulator to allow the covered entity to repurchase a full package size of the drug, the package is purchased "or replenished" with 340B discounts. HRSA requires that covered entities that use a virtual inventory system track drugs at an 11-digit National Drug Code (NDC) level. Therefore, the covered entity purchases and retains title to the drug only after a sufficient number of 340B-eligible prescriptions have been dispensed. Records of a virtual inventory system must demonstrate that the appropriate quantity of a drug was replenished from the correct manufacturer.[91]

A virtual inventory system provides flexibility to covered entities because it allows the covered entity to physically mix its 340B and non-340B inventory and to determine whether a patient is eligible to receive 340B drugs after the drug has been dispensed or administered. A virtual inventory system creates some additional compliance risks, however. For example, if a hospital that is subject to the GPO prohibition uses a virtual inventory system, it must ensure that each initial purchase of a drug that carries a new NDC is at WAC.[92] Similarly, if the hospital under-replenishes 340B drugs by mistakenly under-accumulating its 340B eligible dispenses or administrations, the hospital could violate the GPO prohibition by over-purchasing covered outpatient drugs on its GPO account. Over-replenishment on the 340B account, which is considered to be diversion, is another risk.

Efficient inventory management is essential for a covered entity to maintain compliance with the diversion, duplicate-discount, orphan-drug, and GPO prohibitions. Covered entities typically use a 340B administrator to track and manage records of inventories through processing software and platform integration. Moreover, selection of the appropriate inventory management system can reduce compliance risk.

Contract Pharmacy Oversight

Risks of noncompliance with 340B program requirements may increase if the covered entity uses a contract pharmacy to dispense 340B drugs to its patients, because the covered entity is responsible for 340B compliance at the pharmacy and will be responsible for any 340B compliance violations related to prescriptions filled by the contract pharmacy.[93] A covered entity must maintain auditable records to demonstrate 340B compliance and verify that the contract pharmacy has a tracking system to ensure that the covered entity's 340B drugs are not diverted to non-patients or that a manufacturer is not subject to duplicate discounts.[94] HRSA expects covered entities to have policies and procedures describing their oversight of any contract pharmacies with which they contract, and to conduct annual independent audits of their contract pharmacies to ensure compliance with 340B program requirements.[95]

Audits and Enforcement

The 340B statute requires covered entities to repay their 340B discounts to drug manufacturers if the entities fail to comply with the program's anti-diversion and duplicate-discount requirements.[96] Covered entities may also be required to pay interest on the 340B discounts they improperly receive if the violation is "knowing and intentional."[97] HRSA may terminate a covered entity from the 340B program if there is evidence that the violations are not only knowing and intentional, but also systemic and egregious.[98] A covered entity may also be terminated if it fails to maintain auditable records or to satisfy eligibility requirements, including the GPO prohibition.[99] HRSA may only impose these sanctions after an audit, notice of findings, and a hearing.[100]

HRSA Audits of Covered Entities

The 340B statute gives HRSA the authority to audit covered entities for compliance with 340B program requirements. HRSA's 340B program audits review covered-entity compliance with respect to, among other things, eligibility status; compliance with the duplicate-discount and diversion prohibitions; and contract pharmacy oversight. As stated previously, HRSA holds the covered entity responsible for any compliance issues at the covered entity's contract pharmacies.

HRSA also has authority to audit drug manufacturers for compliance; however, these types of audits are far less common. HRSA has audited more than 1,000 covered entities but only a few manufacturers.

Audit Process

Covered entities are selected for a HRSA audit either through a random selection process or based on information that indicates that the covered entity may have compliance issues. Covered entities that are selected for a HRSA audit receive a letter notifying the covered entity of the audit. HRSA auditors have a preliminary call with the covered entity to discuss logistics, then send a data-request list containing any documents or information that the auditor requires initially. Auditors may request other records during the audit. HRSA typically audits a recent six-month period. Onsite HRSA visits typically last one to three days.

Post-Audit Process

Following an audit, HRSA issues an initial report that may include audit "finding(s)" or "area(s) for improvement." An audit finding, if not reversed, requires the covered entity to take corrective action. Findings reflect a determination by HRSA that the covered entity violated the 340B statute. As its name implies, an area for improvement is a suggestion from HRSA for improvement with respect to 340B compliance. An area for improvement does not require the covered entity to make any repayments. For example, HRSA may issue in its report an area for improvement if auditors believe that the covered entity's 340B policies and procedures are not sufficiently comprehensive.[101]

If HRSA's audit report contains findings of noncompliance, the covered entity may dispute the findings by submitting a notice of disagreement within 30 days. HRSA will review the arguments presented by the covered entity and issue an updated final report that incorporates any changes HRSA may make in response to the covered entity's appeal. After the audit report is finalized, or if the covered entity does not dispute HRSA's findings, the covered entity has 60 days to submit a corrective-action plan explaining how it will address and remedy the noncompliance issues identified in the report. Covered entities are not required to submit a corrective action plan to address areas for improvement.[102]

Covered entities that submit a corrective action plan are expected to complete the plan within six months of the date HRSA approves the corrective action plan. It is the covered entity's responsibility to identify and contact all manufacturers regarding a possible violation of 340B program requirements and negotiate potential remedies. HRSA closes out the audit once it has determined that the covered entity has fully implemented the corrective action plan and the covered entity has reached an agreement with any manufacturers regarding repayment. HRSA posts a listing of the audits conducted each year and the results of the audits.[103]

HRSA may re-audit a covered entity to determine whether it has corrected the compliance issues found in the first audit. If HRSA finds that the covered entity has not corrected a diversion and/or duplicate-discount violation in the second audit, the violation may be considered "systematic and egregious as well as knowing and intentional," justifying removal from the program.[104]

Self-Disclosures

Covered entities are required to disclose a breach to HRSA if noncompliance meets the definition of "material breach."[105] Neither the 340B statute nor HRSA provides a definition for material breach. So HRSA permits each covered entity to adopt its own definition of material breach. Apexus provides a tool to help covered entities establish a "framework to guide the definition of a material breach of compliance and the process for self-disclosure to HRSA."[106] Covered entities are strongly encouraged to define "material breach" in their 340B policies and procedures.

If a covered entity discovers a material breach of 340B program requirements, it must submit a comprehensive self-disclosure to HRSA that contains the following:

- Letter to HRSA noting the covered entity's 340B ID
- Description of the potential violation of 340B program requirements
- Corrective action plan addressing how the problem will be fixed
- Description of strategy to work with manufacturers that includes plans for financial remedy if repayment is necessary[107]

In contrast to a HRSA audit finding, violations addressed in a covered entity's self-disclosure are not posted on HRSA's website.

Importantly, covered entities must remedy any violation they uncover, including violations that fall short of a material breach. They are obligated to repay manufacturers, for example, for engaging in diversion or causing duplicate discounts even if the repayment amount is small.

Manufacturer Audits of Covered Entities

As stated previously, the 340B statute allows manufacturers to audit covered entities, but only with respect to compliance with the diversion and duplicate-discount prohibitions.[108] Before auditing a covered entity, the manufacturer must submit to HRSA an audit work plan and show that the manufacturer has "reasonable cause" to believe that the covered entity has violated the diversion and duplicate-discount prohibitions.[109] If HRSA grants the manufacturer's audit request, the manufacturer must hire an independent auditor to conduct the audit and prepare a final report. The covered entity has the opportunity to dispute any of the independent auditor's findings. Notably, manufacturers do not have the authority to take action against a covered entity based on the outcome of its audit.[110]

Manufacturer Compliance Obligations

Manufacturers are subject to far fewer requirements under the 340B program than covered entities. Essentially, they only have one requirement to meet—to sell their products at or below the 340B statutory ceiling price. Section 1927 of the Social Security Act, which is where the Medicaid drug rebate statute resides, states that a manufacturer's drugs will not be covered by Medicaid or Medicare Part B unless the manufacturer signs a PPA with HHS.[111] The PPA requires a drug manufacturer to provide covered entities with "covered outpatient drugs for purchase at or below the applicable ceiling price if such drug is made available to any other purchaser at any price."[112] HRSA has interpreted this so-called "must offer" provision to mean that manufacturers may not discriminate against 340B covered entities when allocating drugs in short supply or otherwise balancing the demand for products between 340B and non-340B purchasers. HRSA requests, but does not require, that manufacturers submit a written notice of any plan to limit distribution of covered outpatient drugs to HRSA at least four weeks in advance of implementation. These limited distribution plans should provide "[d]etails for a nondiscriminatory practice for restricted distribution to all purchasers, including 340B covered entities."[113]

Until recently, manufacturers have been under no obligation to share their 340B ceiling prices with covered entities, making it difficult for covered entities to validate whether they are receiving the discounts to which they are entitled. That changed in 2019 when HRSA created a secure website for covered entities to verify the quarterly 340B ceiling price for each covered outpatient drug available for purchase.[114] Only the covered entity's AO and PC have access to the website. Participating manufacturers are required to submit quarterly pricing reports that HRSA uses to populate the data on the website.[115][116][117]

Manufacturers sometimes miscalculate the 340B ceiling price, which may result in an overcharge to covered entities.[118][119] The 340B statute requires HRSA to create a system that manufacturers can use for refunding the overcharged amount to covered entities and for recalculating ceiling prices in the event post-sale rebates and discounts have the effect of lowering the 340B ceiling price.[120] Notices informing covered entities of manufacturer overcharges are often posted on the HRSA website.[121] Manufacturers that have overcharged a covered entity must make repayments to the covered entity.[122][123] HRSA may recommend to the OIG that the OIG impose civil monetary penalties on a manufacturer of up to $5,000 for each instance of knowingly and intentionally overcharging a covered entity.[124]

Manufacturers are also expected to maintain accurate information on OPAIS, although HRSA does not have the authority to require them to do so. Nevertheless, HRSA strongly urges manufacturers to verify their database information because it is the source of data that covered entities use to contact them regarding compliance issues, pricing and distribution inquiries, and repayment.[125]

Common Compliance Risks

Common Diversion Risk Areas

The following describes some common risk areas that covered entities should be aware of when addressing compliance with the 340B program's anti-diversion requirement. Diversion is currently the third most common audit finding, although HRSA audit results have shown a dramatic decrease in the number of diversion findings recently.[126][127] Approximately 16% of hospital audits in 2019 resulted in diversion findings, representing more than a 60% decrease in such findings from the previous year.[128] In particular, HRSA issued fewer diversion findings in circumstances in which a prescription for a self-administered drug was written as the result of services provided outside the covered entity.

Hospital Departments Providing Both Inpatient and Outpatient Services

Covered entities are responsible for ensuring that drugs purchased at 340B prices are limited to outpatient use only. So, avoiding diversion can be complicated for covered entities that provide both inpatient and outpatient services. This is especially true for hospitals where a patient's status may switch from outpatient to inpatient or vice versa. Examples of these "mixed-use" hospital settings include surgery and radiology departments, emergency rooms, and areas that are used for both observation services and inpatient care.

HRSA does not dictate how a hospital determines whether an individual qualifies as an outpatient and is therefore eligible to receive 340B drugs in a mixed-use setting.[129] Hospitals use a variety of approaches for determining a drug's outpatient status, including the time of dispensation of the drug, the time of the drug's administration, or whether the drug is billed on an outpatient claim.[130] In its FAQs, Apexus recommends inclusion of certain elements in a tracking system to help reduce compliance risks in mixed-use settings.[131] Hospitals have the flexibility to develop a tracking method that is most appropriate for their facilities, but must always maintain auditable records showing that the method is consistently and accurately applied.[132][133]

Prescriptions for Self-Administered Drugs Written Outside the Covered Entity

Historically, 340B prescriptions for self-administered drugs—drugs that are dispensed by a pharmacy for administration by the patient—must be written as the result of services provided by the covered entity. For 340B hospitals, such services may be rendered in the hospital's main facility or any facility considered by the Medicare program as a hospital outpatient department.[134] Some hospitals have closely affiliated physician clinics that are not hospital outpatient departments for purposes of the Medicare and 340B programs, making it difficult to distinguish between prescriptions written as the result of services by a hospital outpatient department from those written at a physician clinic. Federal grantees and subgrantees that are part of larger health systems face similar challenges. For freestanding grantees, the issue of whether a healthcare service is provided by the covered entity is usually simpler to address because its operations and affiliations are less complex.

HRSA's insistence that 340B prescriptions originate from OPAIS-registered sites was subject to only one narrow exception. HRSA permitted covered entities to use 340B drugs to fill prescriptions written outside the covered entity's registered facilities if (1) there is a written referral in the covered entity's medical records to the prescriber or prescriber's medical practice and (2) the prescriber shares with the covered entity a copy of the medical records, or a summary of that record, for the healthcare visit that resulted in the prescription.[135]

Evidence that HRSA was beginning to relax its strict construction of the 340B prohibition against diversion emerged in 2018 when the agency faced a lawsuit by an FQHC, Genesis Health Care (Genesis), challenging the agency's audit findings. One of the contested findings involved an allegation that Genesis had engaged in diversion by filling prescriptions with 340B drugs that were written by prescribers who were not practicing at the FQHC.[136] Based on court filings, it appears that the individuals for whom the prescriptions were written were patients of Genesis but received both healthcare services and prescriptions outside the FQHC.[137] The FQHC's contract pharmacies used 340B drugs to fill the prescriptions even though they failed to meet HRSA's location test.[138] Genesis argued that its long history of providing primary care services to these individuals demonstrated that they were the FQHC's patients for purposes of the 340B program. Rather than defend its diversion claim, HRSA withdrew its audit findings and the case was dismissed as moot.[139]

Based on a review of the HRSA webpage summarizing the results of recent audits of covered entities, HRSA appears to have issued fewer diversion findings related to prescriptions written outside covered-entity facilities since the *Genesis* case was decided.[140] The number of diversion findings decreased significantly in 2019, which coincides with HRSA's withdrawal of the Genesis audit report on June 6, 2019.[141] [142] The decrease may also be attributable to an Executive Order issued in October 2019 advising federal agencies not to bring enforcement actions unless based on a statutory or regulatory requirement.[143] Regardless of the reasons, it is clear that HRSA is more likely to recognize the eligibility of prescriptions written outside a covered entity's facility today than just two years ago.

Common Duplicate Discount Risk Areas

Covered entities have experienced a recent increase in HRSA audit findings for duplicate discounts. In 2019, 26% of hospital audits resulted in findings of violations of the duplicate-discount prohibition.[144] State Medicaid agencies and Medicaid MCOs typically have policies related to identifying claims for 340B drugs, but those policies are often difficult to locate and, in some cases, vulnerable to legal challenge. Covered entities should contact their state Medicaid agency and Medicaid MCO and also consult legal counsel to ensure they are in compliance with the requirements related to identifying 340B drugs to avoid duplicate discounts.

Medicaid FFS Billing

Covered entities that elect to carve in (i.e., use 340B) for Medicaid FFS beneficiaries are at risk of violating the duplicate-discount prohibition if their election is not properly reflected in OPAIS or they provide inaccurate information for the MEF. Covered entities must provide the Medicaid billing numbers and NPIs for each registered site that participates in the 340B program and for each state Medicaid agency that the covered entity bills.[145] [146] Covered entities that carve out (i.e., do not use 340B) for Medicaid FFS beneficiaries have to ensure that they do not inadvertently provide 340B drugs to Medicaid FFS beneficiaries. Their obligation to carve out often extends to claims for which Medicaid is a secondary payer because most states seek rebates on such claims. Covered entities also need to be aware that some states rely on their own claims identification requirements rather than the MEF to avoid FFS duplicate discounts. HRSA still expects covered entities in those states to keep their MEF entries complete and up-to-date and will issue a duplicate-discount finding if they are not, even if the inaccuracies do not actually result in a duplicate discount.

In 2019, approximately 3% of audited hospitals were found to have violated the GPO prohibition.[147] [148] Although the risk of being cited for a GPO-prohibition violation is limited to hospitals and is otherwise low, the consequences of noncompliance are potentially severe. HRSA takes the position that a hospital violates the GPO prohibition even if it purchases a single covered outpatient drug through a GPO. As previously mentioned, compliance with the GPO prohibition is a condition of eligibility. Therefore, if one of those types of hospitals is out of compliance with the GPO prohibition, it places itself at risk of being terminated from the 340B program. According to the OPA, the GPO prohibition applies even when a covered outpatient drug is not available at the 340B price or is dispensed by the hospital to someone who does not meet the 340B definition of "patient."[149] HRSA will not terminate the hospital, however, if the noncompliance relates solely to past practices and the hospital is currently in compliance.

Medicaid MCO Billing

As previously mentioned, state Medicaid agencies (not covered entities) are responsible for protecting against duplicate discounts for Medicaid MCO claims.[150] Therefore, if a duplicate discount arises on a state Medicaid MCO claim, the state Medicaid agency is responsible for making repayment to the manufacturer of the drug. For this reason, HRSA has generally refrained from auditing for duplicate-discount issues associated with Medicaid MCO claims. Manufacturers, however, sometimes investigate potential Medicaid-MCO duplicate discounts independently by making inquiries to covered entities about whether MCO drugs are being carved in or out. They may even demand repayment from the covered entity when they uncover evidence of a duplicate discount. In addition, under Medicaid MCO contracts, covered entities may be subject to recoupment on improperly billed 340B claims found by the MCO.

As with Medicaid FFS claims, covered entities have to ensure that they follow state billing requirements for identifying 340B claims submitted to Medicaid MCOs. Doing so may be challenging because such policies may be difficult to find, hard to understand, and/or unenforceable. The covered entity's contract with the Medicaid MCO may also include requirements related to identifying 340B drugs on claims submitted to the MCO. Complying with these contractual requirements may be challenging as well because private insurers that offer both Medicaid MCO and private-insurance product lines often use the same bank identification numbers (BINs) and processor control numbers (PCNs) for both plans, making it difficult for covered entities and their contract pharmacies to distinguish between Medicaid and non-Medicaid MCO beneficiaries.[151]

Addressing Compliance Risks

Covered entities need to be prepared to meet the compliance demands of participating in the 340B program before they register. Being prepared is not an easy undertaking, given both the legal and operational complexities of the program. This section provides an overview of necessary steps and best practices that covered entities should implement to meet the challenges of operating a compliant 340B pharmacy program.

340B Policies and Procedures

Covered entities participating in the 340B program should implement a comprehensive set of policies and procedures that address the organization's 340B operations. Without exception, HRSA auditors request a copy of the covered entity's 340B policies and procedures as part of the HRSA audit. Policies and procedures should address every aspect of 340B program compliance, including, but not limited to, a statement that the covered entity will comply with the 340B statute and relevant guidance; the procedure for enrollment in the 340B program (including enrollment of off-site locations and child sites); the process for updating OPAIS records; the process for annual recertification; the procedures for identifying patients eligible to receive 340B drugs and avoiding duplicate discounts; identification of staff members who are responsible for 340B program oversight; management of 340B inventory management; and oversight of contract pharmacy arrangements. Covered entities should review and update their policies and procedures on a regular basis and as needed in response to either an internal or external independent audit or changing HRSA policies.

Internal Compliance Monitoring and Self-Audits

Frequent monitoring of 340B operations—including internal audits of the covered entity's main facility, its off-site locations, as well as its contract pharmacies—is essential for maintaining compliance with applicable 340B standards. Monitoring activities should be tailored to the unique structure of the covered entity's 340B program operations, but should include, at a minimum, the following:

- A sample audit of 340B prescriptions filled at retail pharmacies or administered at the covered entity for compliance with the diversion prohibition, including review of medical records to demonstrate that individuals who received the 340B drug are patients of the covered entity
- A sample audit of claims submitted to the Medicaid state agency for compliance with the duplicate-discount prohibition, including use of required 340B claim identifiers for covered entities that use 340B drugs for Medicaid FFS beneficiaries
- Regular review of OPAIS and the MEF for accuracy and completeness
- Regular review of OPA and Apexus websites for updates and changes in guidance
- Quality assurance analysis of the procedures established to comply with the GPO prohibition for DSH, children's hospitals, and cancer hospitals

- Quality assurance analysis of the procedures established to comply with the orphan drug prohibition for CAHs, RRCs, SCHs, and cancer hospitals

Covered entities should set a regular schedule for these monitoring activities, one that is reasonable given the complexity of its 340B program, but no less often than annually. Many covered entities contract with independent auditors to supplement their internal monitoring activities. With respect to contract pharmacies, HRSA's contract-pharmacy guidelines permit a covered entity to determine "the exact method of ensuring [contract pharmacy] compliance."[152] However, HRSA encourages all covered entities to hire an "independent, outside auditor with experience auditing pharmacies" to conduct annual audits of the covered entity's contract pharmacies.[153]

Oversight Committee

Covered entities should organize a 340B oversight committee made up of staff members who are responsible for overseeing 340B operations and compliance. The oversight committee should have as members individuals who are involved in the day-to-day implementation of the 340B program as well as more senior executives. Typical committee members include the director of pharmacy, 340B manager, procurement officer, representatives from finance and materials management, chief operating officer, and legal counsel. If the covered entity has a compliance officer, that individual should serve on the committee as well.

Education

Along with a compliance committee that oversees 340B operations and compliance in general, covered entities should ensure that all staff involved in the entities' 340B operations receive comprehensive training on 340B program requirements. Such training should be furnished initially upon hire and on a regular schedule thereafter. Covered entities should also support continuing 340B compliance education for staff by attending conferences and educational webinars hosted by HRSA, Apexus, the 340B Coalition, and/or other national organizations.

Possible Penalties

The primary stakeholders in the 340B program are covered entities and manufacturers—the purchasers and sellers of 340B drugs, respectively. In drafting the 340B statute, Congress established very different types of penalties for these two stakeholder groups.

Covered Entity Penalties

Covered entities are subject to a range of penalties under the 340B statute and HRSA guidance. The type of penalty applicable to a covered entity depends on the nature of the violation.

Manufacturer Repayment

If covered entities engage in diversion or cause a duplicate discount involving a Medicaid FFS drug, they are required to return to the manufacturer the discount that they received on the drug. This is the most common penalty that covered entities face within the program.

Interest or Termination

In addition to repaying the 340B discounts covered entities receive from manufacturers, they must pay interest on those repayments if the violation is knowing and intentional. If the non-compliance is also systematic and egregious, the covered entity can be terminated from the program. Termination may also result from a violation of the GPO prohibition, although, according to HRSA, this penalty is only applied if the violation is ongoing, not just in the past. Failure to maintain auditable records or to recertify can also lead to termination. However, since HRSA began auditing covered entities in 2012, we are not aware of any circumstances in which HRSA required a covered entity to pay interest on repayments or terminated a covered entity based on a finding of diversion, duplicate discounts, a GPO-prohibition violation, inauditable records, or failure to recertify.

Update OPAIS

Inaccurate or out-of-date database entries can lead to an adverse audit finding by HRSA. The proper remedy for such a finding is simply to update OPAIS with the proper information. Repayment and other more serious penalties do not apply to database errors.

Improve Policies and Procedures

Covered entities are expected to take corrective action for any noncompliance that they uncover or that is found by HRSA or a manufacturer. Central to a covered entity's corrective action plan is revising and expanding its 340B policies and procedures so that the violation does not reoccur. HRSA audits always entail a review of the covered entity's policies and procedures to ensure they are complete and adequately address past problems.

Authorizing Official Criminal Sanctions

HRSA has implemented an annual recertification process that requires AOs to certify to the accuracy of several statements relating to the covered entity's compliance status. AOs must be careful when making these certifications to avoid making a false statement to the government. Although unlikely, AOs may incur criminal liability if they falsely attest to one or more of the representations required to recertify. Criminal risks include financial penalties and potential imprisonment.

Manufacturer Penalties

Manufacturers are subject to two different types of sanctions—civil monetary penalties and exclusion from the Medicaid and Medicare Part B programs.

Civil Monetary Penalties

When Congress expanded the 340B program under the ACA, it added language to the statute explicitly authorizing HHS to impose civil monetary penalties against manufacturers that overcharge covered entities. The relevant provision allows HHS to levy fines not to exceed

$5,000 for each instance of overcharging. However, such civil monetary penalties only apply when a manufacturer "knowingly and intentionally" charges a covered entity a price in excess of the drug's ceiling price. The rule allowing HHS to levy civil monetary penalties went into effect on January 1, 2019. To date, no manufacturer has been subject to such penalties.

Exclusion from Medicaid and Medicare Part B

Prior to enactment of the ACA, HHS only had one remedy for punishing manufacturers that overcharged. HHS could terminate the manufacturer's PPA which, in turn, would result in the manufacturer's drugs not being covered and reimbursed by the Medicaid and Medicare Part B programs. This remedy is largely viewed as unrealistic because Medicaid recipients who need a company's drugs are generally unable to afford to such drugs if not covered and reimbursed by Medicaid. Consequently, this remedy has never been imposed on a manufacturer for overcharging covered entities.

Compliance Resources

The following is a non-exhaustive list of resources available to covered entities for helping to establish and maintain a compliant 340B program.

Health Resources & Services Administration

Office of Pharmacy Affairs (OPA)

OPA's website provides essential compliance information, including links to the 340B statute, regulations, HRSA policy notices, FAQs, OPAIS, MEF, and updates related to the program. On the OPAIS website under "Help," HRSA offers various resources, including a 340B Public User Guide to assist the public with using and understanding OPAIS, a 340B glossary of terms, and covered entity acronyms. HRSA also provides a 340B OPAIS User Guide for External Users, which explains details about registration and recertification processes. The following are links to some of these resources:

- **OPA Site**: https://www.hrsa.gov/opa/index.html
- **OPAIS Site**: https://340bopais.hrsa.gov/
- **340B Public User Guide**: https://340bopais.hrsa.gov/help/Resources/PDFUserGuides/340BPublicUserGuide.pdf
- **340B OPAIS User Guide for External Users**: https://340bregistration.hrsa.gov/help/external/Resources/PDFUserGuides/ExternalUserGuide.pdf
- **Federal Register Notices**: https://www.hrsa.gov/opa/program-requirements/federal-register-notices/index
- **Policy Releases**: https://www.hrsa.gov/opa/program-requirements/policy-releases/

Apexus Prime Vendor Program

The Apexus 340B prime vendor program, through a contract awarded by HRSA, is responsible for providing program support and resources under the 340B program. The Apexus website includes FAQs, educational and training resources, compliance tools and documents, and many other resources. Covered entities may submit compliance questions to Apexus through a chat line, email, or by calling a help line.

https://www.apexus.com/

Trade Associations

340B Health
340B Health represents public and private nonprofit hospitals that participate in the 340B program. 340B Health members have access to a variety of compliance related tools, ranging from compliance outlines and educational webinars and studies on 340B program best practices.

https://www.340bhealth.org/

Ryan White Clinics for 340B Access (RWC-340B)
RWC-340B is a national organization of HIV/AIDS healthcare clinics and service providers receiving support under the Ryan White Comprehensive AIDS Resources Emergency Act (CARE). RWC-340B's website provides educational materials and analyses of various 340B program issues, as well as alerts on recent developments.

http://www.rwc340b.org/

National Association of Community Health Centers (NACHC)
NACHC serves as the leading national advocacy organization in support of community-based health centers. NACHC's website provides a range of compliance tools and resources, including FAQs and the NACHC *340B Manual* for health centers.

https://www.nachc.org/

National Alliance of State & Territorial AIDS Directors (NASTAD)
NASTAD is a leading nonpartisan nonprofit association that represents public health officials who administer state AIDS drug assistance programs in the U.S. NASTAD's website provides compliance documents and training materials.

https://www.nastad.org/

National Coalition of STD Directors (NCSD)
NCSD is a national public health membership organization representing health department STD directors, their support staff, and community-based partners across 50 states and five U.S. territories. NCSD offers a multitude of resources that may assist covered entities that provide STD-related services.

https://www.ncsddc.org/

National Family Planning and Reproductive Health Association (NFPRHA)

NFPRHA is a membership organization representing providers and administrators committed to helping people obtain family planning education and care. NFPRHA offers 340B program resources and guides.

https://www.nationalfamilyplanning.org/

Planned Parenthood

Planned Parenthood consists of 49 locally governed affiliates that operate more than 600 health centers, which provide a wide range of family planning and STD-related healthcare services. Planned Parenthood provides educational resources and guides for covered entities, including Title X family planning clinics and STD clinics.

https://www.plannedparenthood.org/get-involved

Other Compliance Resources

Experienced Legal Counsel

Competent legal advice before, during, and after registration in the 340B program is essential for covered entities that are serious about meeting their 340B compliance responsibilities. Many aspects of the 340B program are complex, regularly changing, and subject to different interpretations. Therefore, each covered entity should consult experienced legal counsel with a background in and understanding of the 340B program. Experienced legal practitioners can provide practical guidance on issues that directly and materially impact compliance under the 340B program.

State Medicaid Websites

Covered entities should review the state Medicaid website and Medicaid state plan amendments for the states to which they plan to bill Medicaid. These sites often provide notices and Medicaid policies regarding the 340B program. Generally, states will clarify 340B billing requirements that are relevant to the duplicate-discount prohibition.

Medicaid Managed Care Contracts

Medicaid managed care contracts often list 340B billing and claim identification requirements, among other things. Compliance with these requirements is essential to prevent duplicate discounts and to avoid remedial action from the Medicaid MCO, such as recoupments or claw backs. Therefore, covered entities should review and incorporate the terms of the Medicaid MCO contract into their compliance plans. Experienced legal counsel is usually required to interpret the language of these contracts, which is often complex and rife with legalese.

National Council for Prescription Drug Programs (NCPDP)

NCPDP is a not-for-profit, multi-stakeholder forum for developing and promoting industry standards and consensus related to health information technology, among other things. NCPDP's website offers 340B billing tools and reference guides that may be helpful for retail pharmacies during prescription-data entry and claim-adjudication processes.

https://www.ncpdp.org/

Risk Takeaways

Main points of interest:

- Section 340B of the Public Health Services Act entitles certain safety-net hospitals and clinics, referred to as "covered entities," to purchase outpatient drugs at discounted prices from drug manufacturers. Drug manufacturers enter into a Pharmaceutical Pricing Agreement (PPA) with the U.S. Department of Health & Human Services (HHS) to provide such drugs at or below a statutorily defined ceiling price as a condition of the manufacturers' drugs being reimbursable under the Medicaid program and Medicare Part B.
- The 340B program is administered by the Office of Pharmacy Affairs (OPA), which is a division of the Health Resources and Services Administration (HRSA) of HHS.

Areas to watch:

- Diversion
- Duplicate discount
- GPO prohibition (applicable to some categories of hospitals)
- OPA database accuracy
- Recertification
- Orphan drugs (applicable to some categories of hospitals)
- Auditable records

Laws that apply:

- 340B Drug Pricing Program, 42 C.F.R. § 10
- Limitation on prices of drugs purchased by covered entities, 42 U.S.C. § 256b
- Definition of Covered Outpatient Drugs, 42 U.S.C. § 1396r-8
- State Medicaid agency regulations or policies that govern payment for and identification of 340B claims for FFS and MCO beneficiaries

Addressing compliance risks:

- Implement a comprehensive set of policies and procedures that address the organization's 340B operations.
- Conduct internal compliance monitoring and self-audits of the covered entity's main facility, its offsite locations, as well as its contract pharmacies.
- Organize a 340B oversight committee comprised of staff members who are responsible for overseeing 340B operations and compliance.
- Ensure that all staff involved in the entity's 340B operations receive comprehensive training on 340B program requirements.

Endnotes

1. **Megan La Suer** is an associate at Powers Pyles Sutter & Verville PC. She focuses her practice primarily on transactional and regulatory healthcare matters. La Suer's range of legal and legislative advocacy experience includes providing counsel on compliance issues related to the 340B Drug Pricing Program and Ryan White program, state Medicaid policy and licensure requirements, HIPAA Privacy and Security rules and the General Data Protection Regulation, and Medicare enrollment and reimbursement matters.

2. **Mark Ogunsusi** is an associate at Powers Pyles Sutter & Verville PC. He focuses his practice primarily on regulatory matters involving pharmaceutical pricing and, specifically, the 340B federal drug discount program. Ogunsusi regularly advises an array of healthcare entities on the nuances of the 340B program, the Medicaid drug rebate program, federal pharmacy law, food and drug law, and state pharmacy law. In addition to his legal degree, Ogunsusi is a doctor of pharmacy.

3. **William von Oehsen** is principal at Powers Pyles Sutter & Verville PC. He has extensive experience in general health law, legislation, and policy, especially in the areas of pharmaceutical pricing, food and drug law, materials management, managed care, and third-party reimbursement. Von Oehsen has more than 30 years of experience on pharmaceutical pricing and reimbursement matters, including the 340B drug discount program, the Medicaid drug rebate program, Medicare Part D, Robinson-Patman, and state Medicaid and pharmacy laws. He played a key role in helping to enact the 340B program in 1992, as well as to expand the law in 2010 under the Affordable Care Act.

4. **Barbara Straub Williams** is principal at Powers Pyles Sutter & Verville PC. She regularly advises 340B covered entities on compliance issues related to the 340B drug discount program. More recently, she has been involved in litigation challenging manufacturer actions to limit the 340B program, including submitting petitions before the 340 Administrative Dispute Resolution Panel. She assists clients in conducting internal audits on a variety of compliance issues and in making disclosures to the Department of Health & Human Services Office of Inspector General, the Office of Pharmacy Affairs, and other federal and state government entities.

5. Veterans Health Care Act of 1992, Pub. L. 102-585, § 602, 106 Stat. 4,943, 4,967. It is called the "340B program" because it is governed under Section 340B of the Public Health Service Act. 42 U.S.C. § 256b.

6. 42 U.S.C. § 1396r-8(a).

7. H.R. Rep. No. 102-384, 102d Cong., 2d Sess., pt. 2, at 16 (1992).

8. "340B Drug Pricing Program," Health Resources & Services Administration, last reviewed March 2021, https://www.hrsa.gov/opa/.

9. "Apexus 340B Prime Vendor Program," accessed January 26, 2021, https://www.340bpvp.com.

10. "Apexus Answers," Apexus 340B Prime Vendor Program, accessed January 26, 2021, https://www.340bpvp.com/apexus-answers.

11. 42 U.S.C. § 256b.

12. Pharm. Research v. Dep't. of Health & Human Serv., 43 F. Supp. 3d 28, 41 (D.D.C. 2014).

13. 42 C.F.R. § 10.11. (Regulations on imposition of manufacturer civil monetary penalties)

14. 42 C.F.R. § 10.10. (340B ceiling price for a covered outpatient drug definition)

15. 42 C.F.R. §§ 10.20–24. (Administrative dispute resolution process regulations)

16. 42 U.S.C. § 256b(a)(5)(B).

17. 42 U.S.C. § 256b(a)(5)(A).

18. 42 U.S.C. § 256b(a)(5)(C).

19. 42 U.S.C. § 256b(a)(7).

20. 42 U.S.C. § 256b(a)(4)(L)(iii).

21. 42 U.S.C. § 256b(e).

22. 42 U.S.C. § 1396d(l)(2)(B)(iii). (An FQHC-LA is category of FQHC that meets the requirements to be designated as an FQHC but does not receive federal grant funding.)

23. 42 U.S.C. § 256b(a)(4).

24. Patient Protection and Affordable Care Act, Pub. L. 111-148, 124 Stat. 119 (Mar. 23, 2010), as amended by the Health Care and Education and Education Reconciliation Act of 2010, 124 Stat. 1029 (Mar. 25, 2010). (Congress intended to add children's hospitals to the program under the Deficit Reduction Act of 2005 (DRA), but HRSA delayed implementing this directive due to legal complications surrounding how the relevant DRA provision was drafted. Under the DRA, they were added indirectly to the 340B program by including them in manufacturer pharmaceutical pricing agreements, but they were not included in section 340B directly.); Deficit Reduction Act of 2005, Pub. L. No. 109-171, § 6004, 120 Stat. 61.

25. 42 U.S.C. §§ 256b(a)(4)(L), (N), (M). (A cancer or children's hospital that does not file a Medicare cost report must demonstrate through independent verification that if the DSH percentage was calculated, it would be greater than 11.75%. Notice Regarding 340B Drug Pricing Program – Children's Hospitals, 74 Fed. Reg. 45,206, 45,207.)

26. 42 U.S.C. §§ 256b(a)(4)(L), (N), (M).

27. 42 U.S.C. § 256b(a)(4)(L)(i). (The contract must include: 1) Names of the hospital and the government agency; 2) Signatures of hospital and government agency representatives; and 3) Effective dates of the contract.)

28. HRSA, "340B Program Hospital Registration Instructions," Health Resources & Services Administration, updated February 11, 2019, https://www.hrsa.gov/sites/default/files/hrsa/opa/hospital-registration-instruction-details.pdf.

29. HRSA, "340B Program Hospital Registration Instructions," Health Resources & Services Administration, updated February 11, 2019, https://www.hrsa.gov/sites/default/files/hrsa/opa/hospital-registration-instruction-details.pdf.

30. 42 U.S.C. § 256b(a)(4)(L)(iii); 42 U.S.C. § 256b(a)(4)(M).

31. 42 U.S.C. § 256b(a)(4)(A)–(K).

32. "340B Drug Pricing Program FAQs, Program Eligibility, FAQ 3," Health Resources & Services Administration, last reviewed July 2020, https://www.hrsa.gov/opa/faqs/index.html.

33. Final Notice Regarding Section 602 of the Veterans Health Care Act of 1992 Patient and Entity Eligibility, 61 Fed. Reg. 55,156, 55,157 – 55,158 (Oct. 24, 1996).

34. "Apexus FAQ 2656," Apexus, last modified November 1, 2019, https://www.340bpvp.com/hrsa-faqs/faq-search?Ntt=2656.

35. "340B OPAIS," Health Resources & Services Administration, accessed March 9, 2021, https://340bopais.hrsa.gov/.

36. "340B OPAIS User Guide for External Users, Authorizing Official Signature," Health Resources & Services Administration, 149.

37. "Registration," Health Resources & Services Administration, last reviewed August 2019, https://www.hrsa.gov/opa/registration/index.html. (HHS sometimes makes an exception during a Public Health Emergency to allow covered entities to register outside of these periods.)

38. "FAQs: Do clinics/departments located within the four walls of a registered 340B hospital have to be registered in the 340B database?" Health Resources & Services Administration, accessed March 9, 2021, https://www.hrsa.gov/opa/faqs/index.html. (HRSA considers outpatients departments to be inside the "four walls" of the main facility if it has the same physical address of the registered parent 340B hospital.)

39. "FAQs: May an outpatient facility that is reimbursed by CMS as a provider based facility, but not included on the most recently filed cost report, access 340B Drugs under the final guidance published in 1994?" Health Resources & Services Administration, accessed March 9, 2021, https://www.hrsa.gov/opa/faqs/index.html.

40. "COVID-19 Resources," Health Resources & Services Administration, last reviewed June 2020, https://www.hrsa.gov/opa/COVID-19-resources.

41. "FAQ 4301," Apexus, updated June 4, 2020, https://www.340bpvp.com/resourceCenter/faqSearch.html?category=content&Ntt=4301. (These FAQs intimate that a hospital's facilities and departments that have "not yet" appeared on the most recently filed Medicare Cost Report should appear on the next cost report. These locations must be provider-based under 42 C.F.R. § 413.65 to be eligible for their costs and charges to appear on the MCR. Hospitals are encouraged to review provider-based requirements (e.g., the hospital owns and controls the provider-based facility and the facility is located no more than 35 miles from the main hospital.))

42. "FAQs: May an outpatient facility that is reimbursed by CMS as a provider based facility, but not included on the most recently filed cost report, access 340B Drugs under the final guidance published in 1994?" Health Resources & Services Administration, accessed March 9, 2021, https://www.hrsa.gov/opa/faqs/index.html.

43. Notice Regarding Section 602 of the Veterans Health Care Act of 1992; Cont. Pharmacy Serv., 61 Fed. Reg. 43,549 (August 23, 1996). (HRSA included in its initial guidelines a model agreement for covered entities to use when entering into contract pharmacy arrangements.)

44. Notice Regarding Section 602 of the Veterans Health Care Act of 1992; Cont. Pharmacy Serv., 61 Fed. Reg. 43,555 (August 23, 1996).

45. Notice Regarding Section 602 of the Veterans Health Care Act of 1992; Contract Pharmacy Services, 61 Fed. Reg. 43,549, 43,555 (August 23, 1996).

46. Notice Regarding Section 602 of the Veterans Health Care Act of 1992; Contract Pharmacy Services, 61 Fed. Reg. 43,549, 43,551 (August 23, 1996).

47. Notice Regarding Section 602 of the Veterans Health Care Act of 1992; Contract Pharmacy Services, 61 Fed. Reg. 43,549, 43,555 (August 23, 1996).

48. Notice Regarding 340B Drug Pricing Program-Contract Pharmacy Services, 75 Fed. Reg. 10,272 (March 5, 2010).

49. Notice Regarding 340B Drug Pricing Program-Contract Pharmacy Services, 75 Fed. Reg. 10,272 (March 5, 2010).

50. 42 U.S.C. § 1396r-8(a)(1).

51. 42 U.S.C. § 256b(a).

52. Notice Regarding Section 602 of the Veterans Health Care Act of 1992; Contract Pharmacy Services, 61 Fed. Reg. 43,549 (August 23, 1996).

53. "Manufacturer Resources," Health Resources & Services Administration, updated January 2019, https://www.hrsa.gov/opa/manufacturers/index.html.

54. Notice Regarding Section 602 of the Veterans Health Care Act of 1992 Patient and Entity Eligibility, 61 Fed. Reg. 55,156 (October 24, 1996).

55. Notice Regarding Section 602 of the Veterans Health Care Act of 1992 Patient and Entity Eligibility, 61 Fed. Reg. 55,156 (October 24, 1996).

56. Notice Regarding Section 602 of the Veterans Health Care Act of 1992 Patient and Entity Eligibility, 61 Fed. Reg. 55,156 (October 24, 1996).

57. "Program Integrity: Audits of Covered Entities Results," Health Resources & Services Administration, updated April 2020, https://www.hrsa.gov/opa/program-integrity/index.html.

58. Amended Verified Petition for Judicial Review, *Genesis Health Care v. Azar*, No. 4:19-cv-1531, 1-2 (D.S.C. May 24, 2019).

59. 42 U.S.C. § 1396r-8(a)(1).

60. 42 U.S.C. § 256b(a)(5)(A).

61. 42 U.S.C. § 1396r-8(b)(1)(A).

62. 42 U.S.C. § 1396r-8(j)(1).

63. 42 U.S.C. §§ 256b(a)(5)(A)(i), 1396r-8(j)(1).

64. "340B OPAIS User Guide for External Users, Authorizing Official Signature," Health Resources & Services Administration, 143-146.

65. "340B OPAIS User Guide for External Users, Authorizing Official Signature," Health Resources & Services Administration, 143-146.

66. Final Notice Regarding Section 602 of the Veterans Health Care Act of 1992 Duplicate Discounts and Rebates on Drug Purchases, 58 Fed. Reg. 34,058 (June 23, 1993).

67. "340B Drug Pricing Program Notice, Release 2014-1, Clarification on Use of the Medicaid Exclusion File," 12, Health Resources & Services Administration, December 12, 2014, https://www.hrsa.gov/sites/default/files/opa/programrequirements/policyreleases/clarification-medicaid-exclusion.pdf.

68. Notice Regarding 340B Drug Pricing Program-Contract Pharmacy Services, 75 Fed. Reg. 10,278 (March 5, 2010).

69. "Informational Letter No. 1638-MC, RE: Update - 340B Drug Pricing Program," Iowa Department of Human Services, March 21, 2016, http://www.iowamedicaidpdl.com/sites/default/files/ghs-files/2020-02-10/1638-MC_Update-340B_DrugPricing%20Program.pdf.

70. U.S. Gov't Accountability Off., *GAO-20-212, 340B Drug Discount Program: Oversight of the Intersection with the Medicaid Drug Rebate Program Needs Improvement* (January 21, 2020) 34–43, https://www.gao.gov/products/gao-20-212.

71. "340B Information Exchange," National Council for Prescription Drug Programs, Inc., 13, June 2019, https://www.ncpdp.org/NCPDP/media/pdf/340B_Information_Exchange_Reference_Guide.pdf.

72. 42 U.S.C. §§ 256b(a)(4)(L)(iii), 256b(a)(4)(M).

73. 42 U.S.C. §256b(b)(1). (Although the 340B statute incorporates the definition of covered outpatient drugs from provisions of the MDRP, HRSA has a different interpretation under the 340B program. While the MDRP's definition excludes certain drugs billed and paid as part of a bundled service, under the 340B program, HRSA gives a covered entity some discretion in determining whether a drug is billed in a bundled manner or not. This is because Medicaid is not the only payer of 340B drugs, and certain payers may require drugs to be separately billed and paid, while others may require the same drugs to be billed as part of a bundled service.)

74. "FAQ 1355," Apexus, November 1, 2019, https://www.340bpvp.com/hrsa-faqs/faq-search?Ntt=1355. (HRSA permits covered entities to develop their own policies, provided that the policies are "defensible, consistently applied, documented in policy/procedures, and auditable.")

75. 42 U.S.C. §§ 256b(a), 256b(b). (Such drugs would not be eligible for 340B pricing, however, because a manufacturer's obligation to sell at 340B discounts only applies to "covered outpatient drugs.")

76. 42 U.S.C. §§ 256b(a), 256b(b).

77. 42 U.S.C. §§ 256b(a), 256b(b).

78. "340B Drug Pricing Program Notice Release No. 2013-1, Statutory Prohibition on Group Purchasing Organization Participation," Health Resources & Services Administration, February 7, 2013, http://www.hrsa.gov/opa/programrequirements/policyreleases/prohibition-ongpoparticipation020713.pdf.

79. "FAQ 1298," Apexus, updated November 11, 2014, https://www.340bpvp.com/hrsa-faqs/faq-search?Ntt=1298.

80. "FAQ 1515," Apexus, updated October 24, 2014, https://www.340bpvp.com/hrsa-faqs/faq-search?Ntt=1515.

81. 42 U.S.C. § 256b(d)(2)(B)(i), (ii).

82. "340B OPAIS User Guide for External Users," Health Resources & Services Administration.

83. "FAQ 1434," Apexus, updated August 14, 2014, https://www.340bpvp.com/resourceCenter/faqSearch.html?category=content&Ntt=1434.

84. 18 U.S.C. § 1001.

85. 18 U.S.C. § 1001(a).

86. 21 U.S.C. § 360bb(a)(2).

87. 42 U.S.C. § 256b(e).

88. "Orphan Drugs," Health Resources & Services Administration, updated December 2020, https://www.hrsa.gov/opa/program-requirements/orphan-drug-exclusion/index.html.

89. *Pharmaceutical Research and Manuf. of Am. v. HHS*, 138 F. Supp. 3d 31 (D.D.C. 2015). (PhRMA II)

90. 42 U.S.C. § 256b(a)(4). incorporating the audit authority in section (5) (The 340B statute states that covered entities must allow HRSA and drug manufacturers to audit the covered entity as a condition of eligibility. HRSA interprets this provision as requiring covered entities to maintain auditable records.)

91. "FAQ 1222," Apexus, updated November 10, 2014, https://www.340bpvp.com/resourceCenter/faqSearch.html?category=content&Ntt=1222.

92. "340B Drug Pricing Program Notice Release No. 2013-1, Statutory Prohibition on Group Purchasing Organization Participation," Health Resources & Services Administration, February 7, 2013, http://www.hrsa.gov/opa/programrequirements/policyreleases/prohibition-ongpoparticipation020713.pdf.

93. Notice Regarding 340B Drug Pricing Program—Contract Pharmacy Services, 75 Fed. Reg. 10,272, 10,273–10,274 (March 5, 2010).

94. Notice Regarding 340B Drug Pricing Program—Contract Pharmacy Services, 75 Fed. Reg. 10,272, 10,275 (March 5, 2010).

95. "Contract Pharmacy Oversight," Health Resources & Services Administration, Office of Pharmacy Affairs, February 6, 2014, http://www.hrsa.gov/opa/updates/contractpharmacy02052014.html.

96. 42 U.S.C. § 256b(a)(5)(D).

97. 42 U.S.C. § 256b(d)(2)(B)(v)(I).

98. 42 U.S.C. § 256b(d)(2)(B)(v)(II).

99. 42 U.S.C. § 256b(a)(4).

100. 42 U.S.C. § 256b(a)(5)(C), (D).

101. "Program Integrity: Audits of Covered Entities," Health Resources & Services Administration, April 2020, https://www.hrsa.gov/opa/program-integrity/index.html.

102. "Program Integrity: Audits of Covered Entities," Health Resources & Services Administration, April 2020, https://www.hrsa.gov/opa/program-integrity/index.html.

103. "Program Integrity: Audits of Covered Entities," Health Resources & Services Administration, April 2020, https://www.hrsa.gov/opa/program-integrity/index.html.

104. 42 U.S.C. § 256b(d)(2)(B)(v).

105. In public remarks at the 340B Coalition Conference in July 2016, however, the Director of HRSA's Office of Pharmacy Affairs clarified that self-disclosure of 340B program violations is required only when a material breach of compliance has occurred.

106. "Establishing Material Breach Threshold," Apexus, 2018, https://www.340bpvp.com/Documents/Public/340B%20Tools/establishing-material-breach-threshold.docx.

107. "Entity Self-Disclosures," Health Resources & Services Administration, updated August 2018, https://www.hrsa.gov/opa/self-disclosures/self-disclosure.html.

108. 42 U.S.C. § 256b(a)(5)(C).

109. Manufacturer Audit Guidelines and Dispute Resolution Process, 61 Fed. Reg. 65,406, 65,409 (December 12, 1996).

110. Manufacturer Audit Guidelines and Dispute Resolution Process, 61 Fed. Reg. 65,406, 65,410 (December 12, 1996).

111. 42 U.S.C. § 1396r-8(a)(1).

112. 42 U.S.C. § 256b(a).

113. "340B Drug Pricing Program Notice, Release No. 2011-1.1: Clarification of Non-Discrimination Policy," Health Resources & Services Administration, May 23, 2012, https://www.hrsa.gov/sites/default/files/opa/programrequirements/policyreleases/nondiscrimination05232012.pdf.

114. 42 U.S.C. § 256b(d)(1)(B)(i).

115. "December 2016—Office of Pharmacy Affairs Update," Health Resources & Services Administration, December 2016, https://www.hrsa.gov/opa/updates/2016/december.html.

116. "General Instructions for Completing the 340B Drug Pricing Program Pharmaceutical Pricing Agreement – Addendum," Health Resources & Services Administration, accessed March 9, 2021, https://www.hrsa.gov/sites/default/files/hrsa/opa/pdf/ppa-addendum-example.pdf.

117. "Manufacturer Resources," Health Resources & Services Administration, updated January 2019, https://www.hrsa.gov/opa/manufacturers/index.html.

118. 42 C.F.R. § 10.11. ("Any manufacturer with a pharmaceutical pricing agreement that knowingly and intentionally charges a covered entity more than the ceiling price, as defined in § 10.10, for a covered outpatient drug, may be subject to a civil monetary penalty not to exceed $5,000 for each instance of overcharging.")

119. 42 C.F.R. § 10.10.

120. 42 C.F.R. § 256b(d)(1)(B)(ii), (iv).

121. "Manufacturer Notices to Covered Entities," Health Resources & Services Administration, updated October 2020, https://www.hrsa.gov/opa/manufacturer-notices/index.html.

122. 42 U.S.C. § 256b(d)(1)(B)(ii).

123. "Program Integrity, Audits of Manufacturers," Health Resources & Services Administration, updated April 2020, https://www.hrsa.gov/opa/program-integrity/index.html.

124. 42 C.F.R. § 10.11(a).

125. "April 2016—340B Pricing System: Manufacturers 340B Database Verification and Other Updates," Health Resources & Services Administration, updated April 2017, https://www.hrsa.gov/opa/updates/2016/april.html.

126. "April 2016—340B Pricing System: Manufacturers 340B Database Verification and Other Updates," Health Resources & Services Administration, updated April 2017, https://www.hrsa.gov/opa/updates/2016/april.html. (This decline in diversion findings may be due to HRSA's recognition of its lack of broad enforcement authority under the 340B statute.)

127. Examining HRSA's Oversight of the 340B Drug Pricing Program: Hearing Before the Subcomm. on Oversight and Investigations, 115 Cong. 12 (2017). (Statements of Director Krista Pedley, Director Debra Draper, and Assistant Inspector General Erin Bliss)

128. HRSA, OPA, *Program Integrity: FY19 Audit* Results, https://www.hrsa.gov/opa/program-integrity/audit-results/fy-19-results. Fewer than 20 diversion findings were the result of prescriptions having been written at ineligible sites in 2019, as compared to nearly 40 findings in 2018 and 70 findings in 2017.

129. "FAQ 1538," Apexus, updated September 30, 2020, https://www.340bpvp.com/hrsa-faqs/faq-search?Ntt=1538. (Which states that the covered entity defines "

130. in policies and procedures as time of patient status determination for 340B purposes.")

131. "FAQ 1538," Apexus, updated September 30, 2020, https://www.340bpvp.com/hrsa-faqs/faq-search?Ntt=1538.

132. "FAQ 1538," Apexus, updated September 30, 2020, https://www.340bpvp.com/hrsa-faqs/faq-search?Ntt=1538.

133. "FAQ 1538," Apexus, updated September 30, 2020, https://www.340bpvp.com/hrsa-faqs/faq-search?Ntt=1538.

134. "FAQ 1559," Apexus, updated September 30, 2020, https://www.340bpvp.com/hrsa-faqs/faq-search?Ntt=1559.

135. Final Notice Regarding Section 602 of the Veterans Health Care Act of 1992 Entity Guidelines, 59 Fed. Reg. 25,110 (May 13, 1994).

136. " FAQ 1493," Apexus, updated September 30, 2020, https://www.340bpvp.com/hrsa-faqs/faq-search?Ntt=1493.

137. Exhibit 1 of Petitioner's Verified Petition for Judicial Review and Emergency Motion to Stay, *Genesis Health Care v. Azar*, No. 4:18-mc-235-RBH, 3-4 (D.S.C. Jun 28, 2018). (HRSA's findings contained in its Final Report was included in court filings as Exhibit 1.)

138. Petitioner's Verified Petition for Judicial Review, Emergency Motion to Stay, and Petition for Declaratory Relief, *Genesis Health Care v. Azar*, No. 4:18-mc-235-RBH (D.S.C. Jun 28, 2018).

139. Petitioner's Verified Petition for Judicial Review, Emergency Motion to Stay, and Petition for Declaratory Relief, *Genesis Health Care v. Azar*, No. 4:18-mc-235-RBH (D.S.C. Jun 28, 2018), 5.

140. *Genesis Health Care v. Azar*, No. 4:19-cv-1531 2019 WL 6909572 (D.S.C. Dec. 19, 2019).

141. Defendants' Motion to Dismiss, *Genesis Health Care v. Azar*, No. 4:19-cv-1531-RBH (D.S.C. June 17. 2019) (HRSA's letter revoking Genesis' audit findings was included as Exhibit A of the motion to dismiss.)

142. "Program Integrity: FY19 Audit Results," Health Resources & Services Administration, updated January 2021, https://www.hrsa.gov/opa/program-integrity/audit-results/fy-19-results.

143. "Program Integrity: FY20 Audit Results," Health Resources & Services Administration, updated January 2021, https://www.hrsa.gov/opa/program-integrity/audit-results/fy-20-results.

144. Promoting the Rule of Law Through Improved Agency Guidance Documents, 84 Fed. Reg. 55,235 (October 15, 2019).

145. "Program Integrity: FY19 Audit Results," Health Resources & Services Administration, updated January 2021, https://www.hrsa.gov/opa/program-integrity/audit-results/fy-19-results.

146. "Program Integrity: FY19 Audit Results," Health Resources & Services Administration, updated January 2021, https://www.hrsa.gov/opa/program-integrity/audit-results/fy-19-results.

147. "340B Medicaid Exclusion File," Health Resources & Services Administration, updated April 2017, https://www.hrsa.gov/opa/updates/2015/october.html. ("It is a covered entity's responsibility to ensure the information is accurate in order to avoid duplicate discounts and possible repayment to manufacturers.")

148. "Program Integrity: FY19 Audit Results," Health Resources & Services Administration, updated January 2021, https://www.hrsa.gov/opa/program-integrity/audit-results/fy-19-results. (It is important to note that contract pharmacies are permitted to purchase drugs through a GPO on their own behalf, rather than through an account for or on behalf of the covered entity.)

149. "340B Drug Pricing Program Notice Release No. 2013-1, Statutory Prohibition on Group Purchasing Organization Participation," Health Resources & Services Administration, February 7, 2013, http://www.hrsa.gov/opa/programrequirements/policyreleases/prohibition-ongpoparticipation020713.pdf.

150. " 340B Drug Pricing Program FAQs, GPO Prohibition," Health Resources & Services Administration, updated July 2020, https://www.hrsa.gov/opa/faqs/index.html.

151. Medicaid Program; Covered Outpatient Drugs, 81 Fed. Reg. 5,170, 5,273 (February 1, 2016).

152. "NCPDP Processor ID (BIN)," NCPDP, updated May 15, 2020, https://www.ncpdp.org/NCPDP/media/pdf/Resources/NCPDP-Processor-ID-(BIN).pdf?ext=.pdf. (The BIN and PCN numbers are used by the pharmacy to identify and submit claims to payers. These numbers may be found on the front or back of the patient's pharmacy insurance card.)

153. Notice Regarding 340B Drug Pricing Program-Contract Pharmacy Services, 75 Fed. Reg. 10,272, 10,278 (March 5, 2010).

154. Notice Regarding 340B Drug Pricing Program-Contract Pharmacy Services, 75 Fed. Reg. 10,272, 10,278 (March 5, 2010).

Drug Diversion

By Kimberly New,[1] JD, BSN, RN

What Is Drug Diversion?

Drug diversion by healthcare personnel involves stealing or taking medication from patients or healthcare settings for personal or unauthorized use. There are no valid statistics for how often healthcare personnel divert controlled substances, largely because diversion often goes undetected, and when it is identified, it is often underreported. When considering measures to combat drug diversion, it is important to understand that this is a very real risk in any healthcare facility that uses controlled substances. All facilities should expect to have diversion; if a facility isn't identifying diversion, it should review its processes and improve its controlled substance handling and auditing efforts.

Diversion is a substantial patient, staff, and community safety risk. There have been several outbreaks of hepatitis C and gram-negative bacteremia attributable to diversion in hospitals across the country.[2,3,4] Many facilities have faced tragedies in which staff have overdosed and died.[5,6] Risk to the community arises when healthcare personnel drive under the influence of diverted drugs.[7] Many diverting staff have admitted to me that they regularly drove to and from work in an impaired state.

Given the threats posed by diversion to patients, staff, facilities, and communities, instituting and maintaining a robust drug diversion prevention, detection, and response program is vital. Patient and staff safety considerations require that diversion be detected quickly and handled with effective, uniform procedures.

Risk Area Governance

The Controlled Substances Act is the foundation of regulatory guidance for pharmacies and health care facilities that use controlled substances.[8] The Drug Enforcement Administration (DEA) is the federal agency responsible for administering and enforcing the provisions of the Controlled Substances Act.[9] In several areas DEA recommendations are explicit and should be followed to the extent possible, even if they don't rise to the level of being officially required. In addition, the Medicare Conditions of Participation for Hospitals contain numerous regulations that are relevant to diversion prevention, detection, and response.[10]

Pharmacies should pay close attention to the specific requirements set forth regarding the authorization to manage controlled substances, how to manage them, and how to complete and maintain associated paperwork and documentation.[11] They must follow regulations for registration, inventory management, and record keeping. [12] [13] [14]

Paperwork

Each application, attachment, or other document filed as part of an application, shall be signed by the applicant, if an individual; by a partner of the applicant, if a partnership; or by an officer of the applicant, if a corporation, corporate division, association, trust or other entity. An applicant may authorize one or more individuals, who would not otherwise be authorized to do so, to sign applications for the applicant by filing with the Registration Unit of the Administration a power of attorney for each such individual. The power of attorney shall be signed by a person who is authorized to sign applications under this paragraph and shall contain the signature of the individual being authorized to sign applications. The power of attorney shall be valid until revoked by the applicant.[15]

Power of Attorney

A registrant may authorize one or more individuals, whether or not located at his or her registered location, to issue orders for Schedule I and II controlled substances on the registrant's behalf by executing a power of attorney for each such individual, if the power of attorney is retained in the files, with executed Forms 222 where applicable, for the same period as any order bearing the signature of the attorney. The power of attorney must be available for inspection together with other order records.[16]

Inventory Management

Biennial inventory date. After the initial inventory is taken, the registrant shall take a new inventory of all stocks of controlled substances on hand at least every two years. The biennial inventory may be taken on any date which is within two years of the previous biennial inventory date.[17]

Record Keeping

> Every registrant required to keep records pursuant to §1304.03 shall maintain, on a current basis, a complete and accurate record of each substance manufactured, imported, received, sold, delivered, exported, or otherwise disposed of by him/her, and each inner liner, sealed inner liner, and unused and returned mail-back package, except that no registrant shall be required to maintain a perpetual inventory.[18]

Facilities are expected to adequately screen prospective employees who will have access to controlled substances. Specifically, they should assess each potential employee for the likelihood of a drug security breach.[19]

Facilities must keep controlled substances secure from procurement to administration and disposal.[20] Facilities should limit the quantities of controlled substances available to what is necessary to meet the needs of the patients being served. They must track and review procurement and usage so that diversion can be readily identified.

Staff with knowledge of diversion are expected to report that information to a security officer or supervisor.[21] Facilities, in turn, must immediately report theft or significant loss externally to the DEA.[22] They should also report diversion internally to the director of the pharmacy and to the CEO as appropriate.[23]

Common Compliance Risks

Pharmacy Awareness of the Regulations

In the pharmacy, compliance with the fine details of the regulations is often the greatest challenge. For instance, many pharmacy managers are aware of the requirement to keep controlled substance records on the premises for two years, but many don't realize that records relating to controlled substances listed in Schedule II must be kept physically separate from all other records of the business.[24] Unless the regulatory requirements are built into pharmacy policies and procedures, the pharmacy is likely to fall short of these requirements.

Security and Accountability in Clinical Anesthesia Areas

Risks outside the pharmacy are generally related to security and accountability in clinical anesthesia areas. The greatest risks concern keeping controlled substance secure until the moment they are used and being able to track every milligram or microgram of each controlled substance used. Effective diversion detection is often a challenge since auditing is generally a very labor-intensive endeavor.

Missing Reporting Requirements

Finally, appropriate and timely reporting of known or suspected diversion is frequently a challenge for facilities. Each state has unique requirements and reporting avenues in addition to standard federal requirements, and depending on the diversion scheme, there may be requirements to report to professional licensing boards as well.

Addressing Compliance Risks

Follow Industry Best Practices

There are a number of best practices and guidelines available to provide direction and support for diversion program development. Some sources include the American Society of Health-System Pharmacists, Centers for Disease Control and Prevention (CDC), and the Institute for Safe Medication Practices (ISMP). In general, facilities should adhere to best practices for patient safety and drug security, whether or not those practices are specifically spelled out in published regulations.

Develop a Comprehensive Diversion Program

All facilities, including pharmacies, should develop a formal diversion prevention, detection, and response program. A comprehensive diversion program must be multidisciplinary and collaborative. The diversion oversight committee, diversion response team, and diversion specialist form the foundation of the program.

Have a Diversion Oversight Committee

The diversion oversight committee guides and develops the diversion program. It should be composed of high-level leadership, those with the authority to execute measures necessary to establish and maintain a robust program. This committee may include representation from the following departments (as a member or ad hoc member) and, depending on the facility, may include others not listed here:

- Anesthesia
- Nursing
- Pharmacy
- Public safety/security
- Risk management/legal
- Accreditation/quality
- Chief medical officer
- Compliance/internal audit

- Human resources
- Employee health/infection prevention
- Research

Set Annual Goals and Monitor Risks and the Program

The diversion oversight committee typically sets annual goals for the program and, on an ongoing basis, monitors policy development, directs process improvement, and maintains a dashboard that includes metrics for pharmacy, nursing, and anesthesia. The diversion oversight committee monitors progress as risk is addressed and diversion program goals are achieved.

Have a Diversion Response Team

Many facilities struggle with diversion response and have a tendency to follow a standard human resources disciplinary workflow. Unfortunately, this does not necessarily include all stakeholders who should be involved given the unique circumstances of diversion cases. Without a defined response process tailored to diversion, there is a risk that facilities might have disparate outcomes for similar cases, and internal and external reporting may not be sufficiently broad. For these reasons, all facilities should have a diversion response team with a defined diversion response workflow.

The diversion response team should be a small, multidisciplinary group that examines data suggestive of diversion (reasonable suspicion) and determines what action to take. Data-based suspicion differs from suspicion that is based strictly on behavior. Behavior suggestive of impairment should be handled immediately per institutional policy. The possibility that diversion occurred should then be considered after the behavior has been addressed, if appropriate. Having a response team in place to analyze all potential diversion cases ensures consistency and allows the facility to benefit from a knowledge base that is acquired over time.

Patient and staff safety considerations require that the diversion response team be able to convene on very short notice and after routine business hours. If there is reasonable suspicion of diversion, the suspected staff member should be removed from patient contact and have their access to medications, medication storage areas, and the electronic health record suspended until the concern can be investigated.

At the outset of each case, the diversion response team should assess the possibility that patient harm may have occurred, and also consider whether the suspected staff member has adequate support systems in place (i.e., whether they may be vulnerable to self-harm or harm from others).

Investigate All Potential Diversion Cases

The diversion response team should ensure that all potential diversion is fully investigated. The leader of the response team (typically the diversion specialist) should assign tasks and deadlines to other team members.

Have a Diversion Specialist on Staff

For all facilities it is vital to have an individual with accountability for all of the operations of the diversion program. For very small facilities, this role may be assigned to a staff member who has other duties. In most facilities that are 100 beds or larger, the diversion specialist should be a full-time position.

The diversion specialist oversees surveillance and auditing activities and provides an objective perspective. Immediate supervisors looking at the same data may be susceptible to inherent investigator bias. The diversion specialist collects suspicious or diversion-related data from across the system for tracking and trending purposes, provides or directs ongoing staff education, is actively involved in policy development, and serves as an institutional diversion resource. The diversion specialist also convenes the diversion response team when diversion is suspected. To avoid a conflict of interest, the diversion specialist usually reports through compliance, risk, internal audit, or safety/quality.

Conduct Diversion Risk Rounds

An important preemptive approach to diversion is to conduct diversion risk rounds. Risk rounds help uncover noncompliance, workarounds, complacency, and knowledge deficits. Risk rounds help ensure fulfillment of regulatory requirements.

Diversion risk rounds involve observation of areas where controlled medications are received, stored, prescribed, used, or destroyed. They also involve interaction with staff in these locations. The main objectives are to evaluate security, staff awareness, regulatory compliance, and compliance with institutional policy, and to also initiate process improvement where warranted.

Rounds are best conducted by the diversion specialist and a pharmacy staff member (often a pharmacy technician) who can sign into the automated dispensing cabinets and gain access to controlled substances for the purpose of assessing their integrity and conducting impromptu inventories. Since the rounding team is small, rounds can be accomplished with minimal disruption.

The rounds should occur wherever controlled substances are located. High-risk areas should be visited often, which include procedural areas (e.g., operating room (OR), post-anesthesia care unit (PACU),interventional radiology), critical care units, and the pharmacy. Rounds should also include outpatient care settings, retail pharmacies, and specialty care settings (such as transport services). To be effective, diversion risk rounds must be done unan-nounced. Immediately before an area is reviewed, the manager should be notified that rounds are occurring. To promote frank discussion with staff, the manager should not accompany the risk rounds team. After the rounds, the manager should be briefed on the findings. Handling findings in a nonpunitive manner helps ensure that staff are invested in the process and are receptive to change.

Use a Secured Shared Drive for Diversion Program Materials

Facilities should establish a secure shared drive for storing diversion program–related pol-icies, diversion investigation files, meeting minutes, analytics reports, reports to external authorities, and other diversion-related data. Having all documents in a central location that is accessible to select stakeholders is essential in the event of a regulatory inspection.

Have an Ongoing Auditing and Surveillance Program for Diversion

Each facility that handles controlled substances must have an ongoing auditing and surveil-lance program. Auditing should be multidisciplinary and is usually undertaken by pharmacy staff, clinical managers, and the diversion specialist. Clinical and pharmacy managers are in a unique position to know about staffing, workflows, and other factors that affect controlled substance handling, so their input is valuable. These individuals may also be prone to bias; consequently, the diversion specialist should take the lead in diversion auditing and surveil-lance, serving as an independent auditor not closely involved with the staff being audited. The diversion specialist should have responsibility for tracking and trending suspicious transactions that might otherwise be treated as one-off events. Patterns of poor practice should be identified and followed up on. Pervasive poor practice that goes unchecked is often a reason facilities do not detect diversion.

Possible Penalties

Diversion poses an ever-present risk to facilities and healthcare systems in the form of nega-tive publicity, prolonged regulatory investigations, and regulatory liability. Investigations are often extremely disruptive and can go on for years. Settlement amounts with the Department of Justice can be staggering and have often involved requirements for major changes in the way diversion is addressed.[25][26][27]

In 2015, Massachusetts General Hospital (MGH) entered a settlement with the DEA for $2.3 million over allegations of noncompliance with DEA regulations.[28] A three-year corrective action plan was part of the settlement. Under the terms of the corrective action plan, MGH was required to take several specific steps aimed at enhancing its diversion prevention, detection, and response processes. Some of the requirements were to hire a full-time diver-sion specialist, develop a diversion committee or team, conduct mandatory annual education, purchase surveillance software, undertake daily reviews of drug cabinet dispensing reports by pharmacy leadership and weekly reviews of anomalous usage reports by nursing leadership, and replace existing anesthesia carts.

In 2018, the DEA announced a $4.1 million settlement with Effingham Health System.[29] The corrective action plan associated with the settlement required extensive record-keeping and auditing measures aimed at enforcing controlled substance accountability across the organization.

Shortly after the announcement of the settlement with Effingham Health System, the DEA announced a $4.3 million settlement with the University of Michigan Health System (UMHS).[30] The investigation started in 2013 after DEA gained knowledge that two UMHS employees had overdosed on controlled substances. The settlement agreement contained numerous requirements, including a requirement that UMHS hire an external auditor at its own expense to conduct five unannounced audits each quarter. Many very specific anesthesia medication handling procedures were mandated. UMHS was also required to allow DEA representatives to perform inspections with only a 24-hour notice at any time during the period of the agreement without an administrative inspection warrant.

Compliance Resources

American Society of Health-System Pharmacists

Guidelines on Preventing Diversion of Controlled Substances
These guidelines address best practices in all settings in which health system pharmacies typically have responsibility for purchasing, procuring, and distributing controlled substances, including inpatient settings, outpatient and community pharmacies, organization-owned clinics, and physician practices.

https://www.ashp.org/-/media/assets/policy-guidelines/docs/guidelines/preventing-diversion-of-controlled-substances.ashx

Centers for Disease Control and Prevention

Drug Diversion
This CDC page lists data, resources, reports, and more information about drug diversion.

https://www.cdc.gov/injectionsafety/drugdiversion/

Prescription Drugs
This CDC list of resources provides information on state laws on prescription drug misuse and abuse.

https://www.cdc.gov/phlp/publications/topic/prescription.html

Drug Enforcement Administration

Diversion Control Division
This is an excellent source for regulatory requirements, manuals, and up-to-date guidance on diversion prevention, detection, and response in all settings.

https://www.deadiversion.usdoj.gov

Institute for Safe Medication Practices

Guidelines for the Safe Use of Automated Dispensing Cabinets
These ISMP guidelines direct providers on best practices for drug diversion prevention, injection safety, and the use of automated dispensing cabinets.

https://www.ismp.org

Risk Takeaways

Main points of interest:
- Diversion occurs in every institution where controlled substances are handled.
- Diversion poses a risk to patients, staff, the facility, and the community.
- Every facility needs a dedicated diversion program.

Areas to watch:
- DEA regulatory compliance in the pharmacy
- Security and accountability in clinical areas

Laws that apply:
- Controlled Substances Act,
- 21 U.S.C. § 801 et seq.
- Medicare Conditions of Participation for Hospitals,
- 42 C.F.R. § 485.601

> **Addressing compliance risks:**
> - Establish a robust program for the prevention, detection, and response to diversion.
> - Have a diversion oversight committee and diversion specialist.
> - Conduct diversion risk rounds.
> - Use a secured shared drive for diversion program materials.
> - Have an ongoing auditing and surveillance program for diversion.
> - Report diversion promptly, both internally and to regulatory agencies.
> - If you are not finding diversion, you are probably not looking hard enough.

Endnotes

1. **Kimberly New** is a founding partner at Diversion Specialists LLC. She is a specialist in controlled substance security and Drug Enforcement Administration regulatory compliance. New assists facilities across the country with diversion investigations, diversion program development, staff education, crisis management, and remote auditing. She is a nurse and an attorney. She is the cofounder and executive director of the International Health Facility Diversion Association.

2. Sean Robinson, "Puyallup hospital links nurse to 2 patients infected with hepatitis C; 2,600 patients urged to seek testing," *The News Tribune*, April 30, 2018, http://www.thenewstribune.com/news/local/article210158984.html.

3. "Drug Diversion," Centers for Disease Control and Prevention, updated November 26, 2019, https://www.cdc.gov/injectionsafety/drugdiversion/index.html.

4. Allyson Chiu, "Cancer patients contracted a rare blood infection. Officials say a nurse diluting opioids with tap water is to blame," *The Washington Post*, August 8, 2019, https://www.washingtonpost.com/nation/2019/08/08/cancer-blood-infection-opioids-buffalo-new-york/.

5. Sue Ambrose and Holly K. Hacker, "Two nurses died of overdoses inside a Dallas hospital. What went wrong?," *The Dallas Morning News*, December 2, 2018, https://www.dallasnews.com/news/investigations/2018/12/02/two-nurses-died-of-overdoses-inside-a-dallas-hospital-what-went-wrong/.

6. John Counts, "Drug thefts at U-M hospital: Nurse who died from overdose hoped to get off night shift," *Michigan Live*, April 3, 2019, https://www.mlive.com/news/ann-arbor/2014/10/u-m_hospital_nurse_who_died_fr.html.

7. "Former nurse apologizes after causing crash while high on propofol," WSB-TV Atlanta, August 6, 2014, https://www.wsbtv.com/news/local/nurse-apologizes-after-causing-crash-while-high-pr/137588004/.

8. 21 U.S.C. § 801 et seq.

9. "Diversion Control Division," Drug Enforcement Administration, U.S. Department of Justice, accessed March 4, 2021, https://www.deadiversion.usdoj.gov/index.html.

10. 2 C.F.R. § 482 et seq.

11. 21 C.F.R. § 1301.13(j).

12. 21 C.F.R. § 1304.11(c).

13. 21 C.F.R. § 1305.05.

14. 21 C.F.R. § 1304.21(a).

15. 21 C.F.R. § 1301.13(j).

16. 21 C.F.R. § 1305.05(a).

17. 21 C.F.R. § 1304.11(c).

18. 21 C.F.R. § 1304.21(a).

19. 13 C.F.R. § 1301.90 et seq.

20. 42 C.F.R. § 482.25(a) et seq.

21. 21 C.F.R. § 1301.91.

22. 21 C.F.R. § 1301.76.

23. 42 C.F.R. § 482.25(b)(7).

24. 21 C.F.R. § 1304.04(h)(1)-(2).

25. U.S. Department of Justice, "MGH to Pay $2.3 Million to Resolve Drug Diversion Allegations," news release, September 28, 2015, https://www.justice.gov/usao-ma/pr/mgh-pay-23-million-resolve-drug-diversion-allegations.

26. U.S. Department of Justice, "Southern District Of Georgia Announces Largest Hospital Drug Diversion Civil Penalty Settlement in U.S. History," news release, May 16, 2018, https://www.justice.gov/usao-sdga/pr/southern-district-georgia-announces-largest-hospital-drug-diversion-civil-penalty.

27. U.S. Drug Enforcement Administration, "Record settlement reached in University of Michigan hospital drug diversion civil penalty case," news release, August 30, 2018, https://www.dea.gov/press-releases/2018/08/30/record-settlement-reached-university-michigan-hospital-drug-diversion.

28. U.S. Department of Justice, "MGH to Pay $2.3 Million to Resolve Drug Diversion Allegations," news release, September 28, 2015, https://www.justice.gov/usao-ma/pr/mgh-pay-23-million-resolve-drug-diversion-allegations.

29. U.S. Department of Justice, "Southern District of Georgia Announces Largest Hospital Drug Diversion Civil Penalty Settlement in U.S. History," news release, May 16, 2018, https://www.justice.gov/usao-sdga/pr/southern-district-georgia-announces-largest-hospital-drug-diversion-civil-penalty.

30. U.S. Drug Enforcement Administration, "Record settlement reached in University of Michigan hospital drug diversion civil penalty case," news release, August 30, 2018, https://www.dea.gov/press-releases/2018/08/30/record-settlement-reached-university-michigan-hospital-drug-diversion.

The Opioid Crisis and the Risk of Diversion

By Seth Whitelaw,[1] JD, LLM, SJD

What Is the Opioid Crisis and the Risk of Diversion?

In 2018, Congress declared that prescription opioids have created the "worst drug crisis in America's history."[2] It is a complex crisis of staggering proportions. According to recent statistics from the Centers for Disease Control and Prevention (CDC), the opioid crisis has claimed nearly 841,000 lives during the 10-year period from 1999 to 2019, with no end in sight.[3]

At the heart of the crisis is the use and misuse of legal (i.e., prescription) opioid products. It includes both naturally derived compounds (e.g., morphine) and synthetic compounds (e.g., fentanyl). The uses of these products include legitimate medical use by patients as a treatment regimen for chronic pain as well as nonmedical (i.e., illegitimate) use by individuals with substance-abuse disorders (i.e., addiction). The misuse of prescription opioids often culminates in overdose injuries or death. It affects rural and urban communities in every state, ultimately costing taxpayers billions of dollars.[4] Therefore, Dan Aaron Polster, senior US district judge of the Northern District of Ohio, who presides over the Opioid Multidistrict Litigation (MDL), stated it is "accurate to describe the opioid epidemic as a man-made plague."[5][6]

Opioid abuse in the US, however, is not a new public health issue. In the late 1860s and 1870s, the country experienced an opioid epidemic fueled largely by the ravages of the American Civil War, and by "1870, opium was more available in the United States than tobacco was in 1970."[7] Therefore, according to contemporary accounts, that epidemic "was probably more widespread, if far less intense, than today's."[8] However, from 1840 to 1915, the use of opium and opiates was legal in the United States, and opiates were included in mainstream medicinal products such as cough suppressants until restricted under the Harrison Narcotics Act of 1914.[9] Consequently, American opioid abuse is not a new phenomenon.

The Modern-Day Opioid Abuse Crisis

The United States is unique for the volume of opioid medicinal products used. A report by the International Narcotics Control Board (the independent, quasi-judicial body charged with supporting and monitoring government compliance with international drug control treaties) noted that in "2016, the country with the highest consumption of hydrocodone continued to be the United States, with 33.4 tons, equivalent to 99.1 percent of total global consumption."[10] During that same period, the United States accounted for 72.9% of the world's total consumption of oxycodone.[11]

"The poppy's power, in fact, is greater than ever. The molecules derived from it have effectively conquered contemporary America. Opium, heroin, morphine, and a universe of synthetic opioids, including the superpowerful painkiller fentanyl, are its proliferating offspring. More than 2 million Americans are now hooked on some kind of opioid . . . "[12]

—Author Andrew Sullivan

The rapid onset and pervasiveness of the current crisis are illustrated by National Institute on Drug Abuse (NIDA) statistics that show a precipitous rise in prescription opioid abuse beginning in 1999 (see **Figure 1. National Drug-Involved Overdose Deaths, Number Among All Ages, 1999-2019**).[13] NIDA is a federal scientific research institute under the National Institutes of Health (NIH).

This rapid onset of the current opioid crisis corresponds with Purdue Pharma's introduction of OxyContin (a controlled-release formulation of oxycodone), although the company disputes the connection. OxyContin was originally approved by the U.S. Food and Drug Administration (FDA) in 1995 to treat "moderate-to-severe pain lasting more than a few days."[15] Following OxyContin's launch in 1996, product sales grew rapidly, and by 2001, "sales had exceeded one billion [dollars] annually, and OxyContin had become the most frequently prescribed brand-name narcotic medication for treating moderate-to-severe pain in the United States."[16] This growth was fueled by Purdue Pharma's aggressive marketing campaign that used "an expanded sales force and multiple promotional approaches to encourage physicians, including primary care specialists, to prescribe OxyContin as an initial opioid treatment for noncancer pain."[17]

Figure 1. National Drug-Involved Overdose Deaths, Number Among All Ages, 1999-2019 [14]

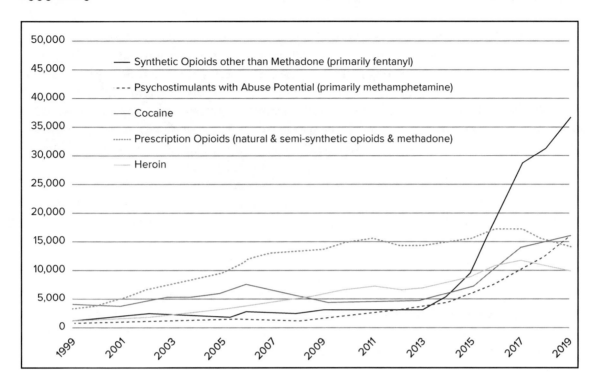

However, since 2010, the nature of the epidemic has shifted dramatically. From 2010 to 2019, prescription opioid deaths declined by 4.5%, but deaths from synthetics opioids, such as fentanyl and heroin, increased by 1040% and 461% respectively.[18] More detailed research indicates that prescription opioid deaths increasingly involve opioid use in combination with other dangerous substances such as heroin, fentanyl, cocaine, barbiturates, benzodiazepines, and even alcohol.[19]

The current epidemic is also unique in its pervasiveness. It is a seemingly boundless public health crisis exacerbated by the rise of modern technology (e.g., automobiles and the internet). Thus, the purchase of opioid products may be tied to one location, while consumption may be tied to another city, county, or state, otherwise known as "opioid diversion." Consequently, opioid diversion in one location can have an impact on jurisdictions many miles or even states away and resembling Prohibition-era bootlegging.

Like alcohol bootlegging before it, opioid diversion follows a risk-mitigation approach of moving from areas with strong enforcement to areas with weaker controls. Consequently, while Florida started out as "ground zero" for diversionary pharmacies, the problem ultimately spread to pharmacies in other states such as Kentucky, West Virginia, and Ohio.[20] This phenomenon, known as the "oxy express," describes the frequent trips made by thousands of individuals to states like Florida to purchase opioids easily and take them back to the states where they reside.[21][22] As a result during a five-year period (2007–2012), 780 million dosage units of hydrocodone and oxycodone were distributed to West Virginia, a state of 1.8 million residents.[23]

Risk Area Governance

Before diving into specific requirements and risk areas, there is the need to address an ongoing misconception that somehow the risks associated with controlled substances do not fall within the holistic risk universe of an effective compliance program, and thus, the well-established compliance elements outlined by the United States Sentencing Commission do not apply.[24] While it is difficult to pinpoint the basis for this misconception, it appears in part due to the fact that the Drug Enforcement Administration (DEA), unlike the FDA, does not think in terms of the Federal Sentencing Guidelines' ubiquitous compliance framework. However, the pervasiveness of the epidemic, its impact on public health, and magnitude of the risks for noncompliance all suggest that organizations involved with controlled substances need to incorporate this risk area into their corporate compliance program and closely monitor it.

The Controlled Substances Act, 21 U.S.C. § 801, et seq.

Enacted in 1970 near the end of the Vietnam War, the Controlled Substances Act (CSA) is the primary federal statute governing controlled substances, which include opioids.[25] The primary goal of the CSA is preventing the diversion of controlled substances "while also ensuring access to controlled substances for legitimate purposes."[26]

The Chemical Diversion and Trafficking Act of 1988 (CDTA) amended the CSA to encompass the regulation of controlled substance analogs and listed chemicals (i.e., controlled substances precursors).[27] In 2018, the SUPPORT for Patients and Communities Act (SUPPORT Act) was enacted.[28] While the act addressed a wide variety of issues across multiple statutes, for CSA purposes, it clarified the all-important definition of suspicious orders and prescribed new civil and criminal penalties for ignoring the most recent DEA data when evaluating opioid orders.[29]

Under the CSA, enforcement authority was vested in the U.S. attorney general who, in turn, delegated it to the Bureau of Narcotics and Dangerous Drugs (BNDD), the predecessor of the DEA.[30] Less than a year after passage of the CSA, the BNDD finalized regulations to implement the statutory requirements.[31] Two years later, in 1973, following several high-profile heroin seizures in France (the so-called French Connection), President Richard M. Nixon declared "an all-out global war on the drug menace," that resulted in the formation of today's DEA.[32]

Scheduling

The classification system is the foundation of the CSA's regulatory framework and, therefore, "nearly all the obligations and penalties that the act establishes flow from" it.[33] Under that foundation, controlled substances are classified into one of five schedules based on three criteria: (a) medical use, (b) psychological or physical dependence, and (c) the potential for abuse.[34] Regardless of which schedule applies, scheduling of a medicinal product means that the DEA has concluded that additional controls regarding the manufacture, distribution, dispensing, and prescribing of the drug are necessary to safeguard public health.[35] These DEA controls are in addition to the usual drug approval process and general controls (e.g., Current Good Manufacturing Practices) under the Federal Food, Drug, and Cosmetic Act (FFDC). [36]

Schedule I drugs are those drugs having no currently accepted medical use and a high potential for abuse.[37] Possession or use of these so-called "illicit or street drugs" is illegal under all circumstances, and healthcare practitioners may not prescribe them.

Schedule II drugs are those drugs with an accepted medical use that have a high potential for abuse that can lead to severe psychological or physical dependence.[38] The primary difference between a Schedule I and II drug is whether a medically acceptable use exists for the drug.

Schedule III drugs have a medium potential for abuse and a moderate potential for physical or psychological dependence.[39] Schedule IV and V drugs have a low risk of abuse relative to the immediately preceding schedule, and, if abused, may cause limited physical or psychological dependence.[40]

Applying the classification system to opioids, the CSA defines an opiate as "any drug or other substance having an addiction-forming or addiction-sustaining liability similar to morphine or being capable of conversion into a drug having such addiction-forming or addiction-sustaining liability."[41] Apart from Tramadol, the main opioids making headlines in the current crisis are either Schedule II or III drugs (see **Table 1. Opioids Involved in the Current Crisis**).

Table 1. Opioids Involved in the Current Crisis

Family	Schedule	Products
Heroin	I	N/A
Morphine	II	Morphine Sulfate Dilaudid (hydromorphone) MS Contin (controlled-release morphine)
Oxycodone	II	OxyContin (controlled-release oxycodone) Percocet (oxycodone + acetaminophen) Percodan (oxycodone + aspirin)
Hydrocodone	II	Vicodin (hydrocodone + acetaminophen)
Fentanyl	II	Duragesic Sublimaze
Methadone	II	Dolophine
Buprenorphine	III	Suboxone
Codeine	III	Tylenol #3 and #4 (codeine + acetaminophen)
Tramadol	IV	Ultram, Ultram ER, Ryzolt, ConZip

[Note: This is not an exhaustive list.]

The five schedules also are updated and published on an annual basis.[42] When updating the schedules, the DEA can shift a drug from one schedule to another depending on new information.[43][44] In the opioid crisis context, in October 2014, the DEA rescheduled hydrocodone combination products moving them from Schedule III to Schedule II based on data showing significant product abuse.[45]

Registration

The statute also requires all major participants in the controlled-substance supply chain (manufacturers, distributors, dispensers (i.e., pharmacies), and prescribers to register with and receive a license from the DEA to handle controlled substances.[46] This series of interlocking registrations creates what is known as the "closed loop" system, which has as its goal ensuring that only authorized users handle controlled substances (see **Figure 2. The DEA "Closed Loop" System**).[47]

Multiple registrations are required in certain situations. For example, each principal place of business that manufactures, distributes (including import or export facilities), or dispenses controlled substances must have a separate registration.[48] Also, certain activities, such as operating a methadone clinic, require a special registration.[49]

Types of Registrants

The DEA separates registrants into two broad segments—the Retail Level and Wholesale Level. The Retail Level includes retail pharmacies, hospitals, clinics, practitioners, teaching institutions, and mid-level practitioners.[50] Manufacturers, distributors, researchers, analytical laboratories, importers/exporters, reverse distributors, and narcotic treatment programs comprise the Wholesale Level. Based on DEA statistics, the Retail Level contains, by far, the most registrants (see **Table 2. DEA Summary of Registrants as of September 2021**).

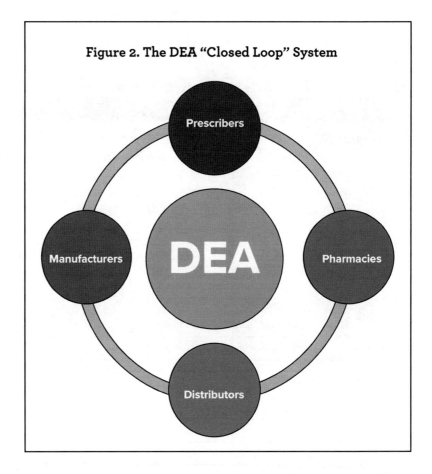

Figure 2. The DEA "Closed Loop" System

Table 2. DEA Summary of Registrants as of September 2021

Retail Level		Wholesale Level	
Retail Pharmacy	70,177	Manufacturer	581
Hospital/Clinic	18,667	Distributor	785
Practitioner	1,364,699	Researcher	11,755
Teaching Institute	254	Analytical Labs	1,526
Mid-Level Practitioner	474,639	Importer	261
		Exporter	266
		Reverse Distributor	72
		Narcotic Treatment Program	1,900
Total	1,928,436	Total	17,146

Within the Retail Level, the retail pharmacy segment not only includes large, national pharmacy chains (e.g., CVS, Walgreens, Rite-Aid, and Walmart), but also smaller, regional chains (e.g., Giant Eagle), as well as local, independently owned pharmacies. Putting it into perspective, in 2020, CVS, Walgreens, Walmart, and Rite-Aid controlled 51.1% all prescription drugs dispensed in the US through a network of more than 26,000 individual pharmacy locations.[52][53]

The large national and some regional pharmacy chains operated their own internal distribution centers for opioids prior to the rescheduling of hydrocodone in 2014. During that time, they simultaneously fell under both the Retail Level (retail pharmacy) and Wholesale Level (distributor). After 2014, the large pharmacy chains shifted from self-distributing opioids to using independent distributors (e.g., McKesson, Cardinal Health, AmerisourceBergen, etc.).

Registrant Obligations

The closed loop system imposes certain basic obligations on controlled-substances registrants. The basics include recordkeeping, reporting, and physical security requirements.[54]

However, there also are more specific requirements depending on the type of registrant. For example, pharmacies are allowed to dispense controlled substances only upon receiving a valid prescription from a practitioner.[55] Schedule II substances (e.g., morphine, oxycodone, and hydrocodone) require a written prescription except in emergency situations.[56] However, Schedule III or IV substances (e.g., codeine and tramadol) may be dispensed via a written or an oral prescription.[57]

Common Compliance Risks

The central compliance risk posed by the opioid epidemic is diversion. This risk affects all registrants involved with opioids. To quote U.S. Senior District Judge Dan Polster, "Everyone shares some of the responsibility, and no one has done enough to abate it."[58]

The lawful dispensing of opioids requires a valid prescription.[59] To be valid, a controlled substance prescription must be issued for a legitimate medical purpose by a practitioner in the usual course of their professional practice.[60][61] Although the primary responsibility for determining a legitimate medical purpose rests with the prescribing practitioner, the DEA's regulations clearly state that "a corresponding responsibility rests with the pharmacist who fills the prescription."[62] Thus, pharmacists face potential prosecution if they deliberately ignore the high probability that a prescription is invalid.[63]

Having the crucial goal of preventing the diversion of controlled substances, the CSA also expressly mandates manufacturers and distributors of legal controlled substances (Schedules II-V) maintain "effective controls against diversion of particular controlled substances into other than legitimate medical, scientific, and industrial channels."[64] While the CSA contains no similarly worded requirement for pharmacies and pharmacists, the DEA by regulation has expanded the statutory mandate to require "**all** applicants and registrants . . . 'provide effective controls and procedures to guard against theft and diversion of controlled substances.'"[65][66]

Diversion

At the outset, it is essential to define what constitutes "diversion." The CSA does not specifically define the term. However, for compliance purposes, the definition of diversion can be inferred from the statutory language. Thus, diversion occurs when a controlled substance is distributed or dispensed into an illegitimate channel.

In the search for clarity, the Uniform Controlled Substances Act of 1994 provides a somewhat more helpful definition, stating that "diversion means the transfer of a controlled substance from a lawful to an unlawful channel of distribution or use."[67] But in the end diversion resembles obscenity, as U.S. Supreme Court Justice Potter Stewart described it, in that we know it when we see it.[68]

Recognizing Diversionary Behavior

In the absence of a precise definition of diversion, the DEA has provided guidance to manufacturers and distributors on what it believes are characteristics indicative of diversionary behavior. These characteristics include:

- Ordering "excessive quantities of a limited variety of controlled substances . . . while ordering few, if any other drugs."
- Ordering controlled substances in quantities disproportionate to the quantities of non-controlled medications.
- Ordering excessive quantities of some controlled substances together with an excessive quantity of lifestyle drugs.
- Ordering the same controlled substance from multiple distributors.[69]

The DEA also has urged distributors to ask a series of probing questions about their pharmacy customers including:

- What percentage of the pharmacy's business does the dispensing controlled substance constitute?
- Is the pharmacy complying with all applicable state laws in the jurisdictions where it does business?
- Is the pharmacy soliciting buyers of controlled substances via the internet—either directly or in association with another internet site?
- Does the pharmacy offer to facilitate the prescription from a practitioner that has no connection to the patient?
- Does the pharmacy fill prescriptions from practitioners based solely on a questionnaire without a medical examination?
- If the controlled substances are being shipped, do the practitioners have a state license in good standing, if required?
- Are one or more practitioners writing a disproportionately large share of the controlled substances prescriptions filled by the pharmacy?
- Does the pharmacy offer to sell controlled substances without a prescription?
- Does the pharmacy charge reasonable prices for controlled substances?
- Does the pharmacy accept insurance payments for purchases made via the internet?[70]

Highlighting the difficulty of identifying diversion, the DEA stressed that the list of suggested questions is not all inclusive, nor are the answers necessarily determinate of whether the prescription is valid.[71] Consequently, the DEA "encourages all registrants to take an integrated approach" to combatting diversion.[72]

DEA Controls for Diversion Prevention

The DEA has established controls specific to the various types of registrants. However, taking an integrated approach to prevent diversion requires examining the full spectrum of controls and DEA guidance across registrant types.

Fraudulent or "Out of Scope" Prescriptions

The DEA has developed a manual for pharmacists as a guide to understand the CSA and its implementing regulations.[73] The *Pharmacist's Manual* provides guidance to identify fraudulent prescriptions and prescriptions not issued for legitimate medical purposes (so-called "out of scope" prescriptions.")[74]

The *Pharmacist's Manual* identifies the following criteria as potential fraud indicators:

1. The prescription looks "too good." For example, the prescriber's handwriting is too legible.

2. The quantities, directions, or dosages differ from usual medical usage.

3. The prescription does not comply with the acceptable standard abbreviations or appears to be textbook presentations.

4. The prescription appears to be photocopied.

5. The directions are written in full and contains no abbreviations.

6. The prescription is written in different color inks or contains different handwriting.[75]

For "out of scope" prescriptions, the *Pharmacist's Manual* highlights the following criteria:

1. The prescriber writes significantly more prescriptions (or in larger quantities) compared to other practitioners in the same specialty in the area.

2. The patient appears to be returning too frequently.

3. The prescriber writes prescriptions for antagonistic drugs, such as depressants and stimulants, at the same time.

4. The patient presents prescriptions written in the names of other people.

5. Multiple people appear simultaneously, or within a short time, all bearing similar prescriptions from the same physician.

6. People who are not regular patrons or residents of the community show up with prescriptions from the same physician (the "oxy-express" situation).[76]

Due Diligence

Like pharmacies, manufacturers and distributors have a duty to make a good faith inquiry to ensure all customers are registered and entitled to possess controlled substances before distributing them.[77] However, the DEA also emphasizes that "a distributor may not simply rely on the fact that the person placing a suspicious order is a DEA registrant and turn a blind eye to the suspicious circumstances."[78]

Instead, there is an obligation to "exercise due diligence" to prevent filling orders that might be diverted, because "distributors are uniquely situated to perform due diligence in order to help support the security of the controlled substances . . . and reduce the possibility that controlled substances within the supply chain will reach locations they are not intended to reach."[79] This due diligence obligation is often referred to as "Know Your Customer" or "KYC."

Suspicious Orders

Another manufacturer/distributor control mechanism involves identifying and mitigating suspicious controlled substances orders. The DEA requires nonpractitioner registrants to "design and operate a system to disclose to the registrant suspicious orders of controlled substances," and to report suspicious orders to the DEA when "discovered."[80] This requirement is commonly referred to as suspicious order monitoring (SOM).

However, the SOM regulation only applies to "nonpractitioners." The term "practitioner" under the CSA includes physicians, dentists, veterinarians, scientific investigators, pharmacies, and hospitals.[81] Therefore, under the closed-loop system, the SOM requirement applies only to manufacturers and distributors.

In addition, while the SOM principles are relatively straightforward, implementation can be challenging.

What Constitutes a Suspicious Order?

One challenge involves the definition of a suspicious order. The SOM regulation provides only general criteria, stating that suspicious orders "include orders of unusual size, orders deviating substantially from a normal pattern, and orders of unusual frequency."[82] However, the regulation fails to provide further granularity on what those criteria mean.

In 2018, Congress expanded the definition of a "suspicious order" under the CSA to include, but not be limited to, an order of unusual size, pattern, or frequency.[83] While the expansion made it clear that more than factors of size, pattern, and frequency applied, the amendment added no additional clarifications.

Drilling deeper requires examining the DEA's guidance documents. However, overall, these documents are of limited help and, in some cases, are difficult to locate.

When providing SOM guidance, the DEA has steadfastly refused "to approve or otherwise endorse any specific [SOM] system," because: [84]

> Registrants who rely on rigid formulas to identify suspicious orders may fail to detect suspicious orders. For example, this system might not identify suspicious orders placed by a pharmacy, if that pharmacy placed unusually large orders from the beginning of its relationship with the supplier. This system might not identify orders as suspicious if the orders were solely for one highly abused controlled substance. [85]

Therefore, "[t]he determination of whether an order is suspicious depends not only on the ordering patterns of the particular customer, but also on the patterns of the registrant's customer base and the patterns throughout the relevant segment of the regulated industry."[86]

The closest that DEA has come to providing truly granular guidance can be found in the *Chemical Handler's Manual* created after the enactment of the CDTA.[87] But the voluntary formula articled in the manual is of limited utility.

The DEA and Thresholds

In an appendix to the *Chemical Handler's Manual*, the DEA sets out a voluntary formula for creating thresholds for controlled substances purchase levels.[88] The formula outlines setting threshold purchase levels based on the last 12 months purchases by the same customer type from the same distribution center (e.g., the customer group). That amount is divided by the total number of customer months (months in which purchases are above zero) and multiplied by a factor to determine the maximum amount a customer may purchase.[89] According to the manual, the "[f]actor equals 3 for C-II and C-III Controlled Substances **containing List I Chemicals**."[90] However, the manual gives no indication of how a level 300% above the base threshold is appropriate.

Perhaps more importantly, since most prescription opioid products do not contain List I chemicals, a plain reading of the appendix reveals that using so-called "Factor of 3" formula to set opioid purchase levels is not appropriate. Despite these limitations and in the absence of other express guidance surrounding purchase levels, the Factor of 3 formula was widely adopted by opioid distributors and is a matter of contention in the current opioid litigation.

Discovery & Reporting

Yet another challenge is that the SOM regulation is unclear on when a suspicious order is considered "discovered" for reporting purposes.[91] The *Chemical Handler's Manual* provides some guidance stating:

> When a regulated person suspects that an order may be intended for illicit purposes, good practice requires that every reasonable effort be made to resolve those suspicions. In addition to making the required reports, the transaction should not be completed until the customer is able to eliminate the suspicions.[92]

The *Masters Pharmaceuticals* case provides additional clarity with DEA's Acting Administrator Chuck Rosenberg concluding that "an order has been discovered to be suspicious and the regulation has been violated where the registrant has obtained information that an order is suspicious but then chooses to ignore that information and fails to report the order."[93] Thus, the purpose of the language in the regulation is "to impose a time period for 'informing' the Agency about a specific suspicious order."[94]

The DEA further clarified that the suspicion "as to the existence of a circumstance (i.e., that a customer is engaged in diversion) is simply a far lower standard of proof than whether it is 'likely' that the circumstance exists . . . [and] does not even rise to the level of probable cause."[95] Based upon this guidance, it is reasonable to assume that registrants are permitted a brief investigatory period to avoid the submission of reports that have been flagged by an SOM system, but clearly are not suspicious when determined through verifiable and documented means. However, neither the regulation, guidance, or case law provide a firm time frame for that investigatory period.

Euclid Family Pharmacy

The story of Euclid Family Pharmacy illustrates the interplay between the requirements of due diligence, SOM, and the characteristic diversionary behavior. The pharmacy, located in Cuyahoga County, Ohio, sits in the lobby of a medical building that serves a Cleveland suburb of approximately 50,000 people. The medical building where the pharmacy is located also houses various pain clinics. Since 1995, Timothy Williams, a licensed Ohio pharmacist, has owned and operated Euclid.

As a result of Euclid's advantageous location, various opioid manufacturers have long targeted the pharmacy as having a "high opioid potential." From 2005 to 2012, Euclid's primary distributor was AmerisourceBergen (ABC), but in 2013, Euclid switched to McKesson. During the 13-year period (2005–2018), Euclid substantially increased its purchases of oxycodone (including OxyContin), reaching a high of 18,000 dose units per month in late 2013. See **Figure 3. ARCOS Data Showing Oxycodone Distribution to Euclid by Distributor**.

Both ABC and McKesson allowed Euclid to steadily increase its purchases even though:

- Williams told a reporter in 2006 that he believed OxyContin was more addictive than other prescription opioids.
- Many were on Medicare/Medicaid or worker's compensation.
- Euclid's overall controlled substances purchases were more than double the average for that geographic area.
- Eighty percent of Euclid's oxycodone prescriptions came from a single physician's office in the building catering to worker's compensation cases and pain management.

By switching distributors, Euclid was able to take advantage of the change to obtain suspiciously high amounts of opioids that were not confirmed to be legitimate by either distributor. [104]

Figure 3. ARCOS Data Showing Oxycodone Distribution to Euclid by Distributor [105] [106]

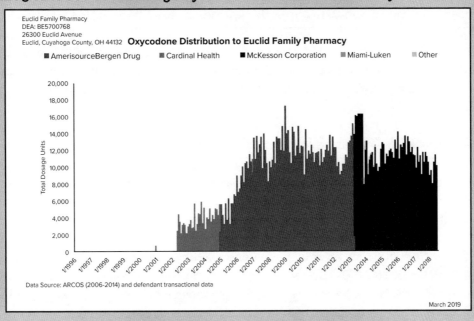

Euclid Family Pharmacy
DEA: BE5700768
26300 Euclid Avenue
Euclid, Cuyahoga County, OH 44132 **Oxycodone Distribution to Euclid Family Pharmacy**

■ AmerisourceBergen Drug　■ Cardinal Health　■ McKesson Corporation　■ Miami-Luken　□ Other

Data Source: ARCOS (2006-2014) and defendant transactional data

March 2019

Responding to Suspicious Orders

A final challenge presented by the SOM regulation is the action a manufacturer or distributor must take after determining a particular order is suspicious. Other than reporting the order to the local DEA Field Division Office, the regulation is silent on additional actions the registrant must undertake such as not shipping the order. [96] In the SUPPORT Act of 2018, Congress stated that registrants have a responsibility to "identify, **stop**, and report suspicious orders," but Congress stopped short of amending the CSA to say that.[97]

The DEA, however, through guidance has interpreted the statutory requirement to maintain "effective controls against diversion" means that suspicious orders must be held and not shipped.[98] The DEA reiterated this position in letters to manufacturers and distributors in the *Masters Pharmaceuticals* case, and the *Chemical Handler's Manual*.[99][100][101][102] As articulated in the *Chemical Handler's Manual*, "[i]n addition to making the required reports, the transaction should not be completed until the customer is able to eliminate the suspicions. [Thus the] distributor may have to forego some transactions."[103]

Addressing Compliance Risks

The essential mechanism for pharmacies to avoid controlled substances violations is to maintain a robust and effective anti-diversion compliance program. Consequently, pharmacies need to take the eight elements of an effective compliance outlined in the Federal Sentencing Guidelines for Organizations and DOJ's guidance on evaluating corporate compliance programs and put them together in the context of controlled substances.[107] Therefore, some controlled substance-specific actions are outlined below. As the DEA correctly notes, "[p]roper controls can be accomplished by following common sense, sound professional practice, and proper dispensing procedures."[108] Specifically, pharmacies should take the following actions.

Employee Training: Apply DEA Specific Guidance for Pharmacies

A pharmacy anti-diversion program needs to incorporate the specific guidance contained in the DEA's *Pharmacist's Manual*. In addition, pharmacies need to train employees on and monitor for the characteristics of fraudulent or "out of scope" prescriptions.[109]

Adapt and Use DEA Guidance for Manufacturers and Distributors

While the due diligence and SOM control mechanisms together with the characteristics of diversionary behavior outlined in the Rannazzisi letters were focused on manufacturers and distributors, they contain elements useful to pharmacies seeking to prevent diversion.

In 2019, Don Bell, senior vice president and general counsel of the National Association of Chain Drug Stores (NACSD) presented on the topic of opioids and compliance.[110] In his presentation, Bell described a series of patient, prescriber, and pharmacy "red flags" that could indicate diversion was occurring.[111] The "red flags" Bell highlighted mirrored the prior guidance provided by the DEA to manufacturers and distributors, which indicates that those principles also are relevant for pharmacy operations.

Use Common Sense to Avoid Diversion

There also are common sense approaches pharmacies and pharmacists can take to avoid possible diversion. Ensure employees are aware of these approaches. They include:

1. It is essential to maintain the primary focus on patients and not on profits.

2. The CSA and its implementing regulations are a floor and not the ceiling for compliance. Compliance with the statute and the regulations are "table stakes," and it is always possible to do more.

3. Shortcomings in regulatory framework do not relieve a company from the responsibility of complying.

4. When confronted with anomalies, it is critical to ask "why" and continue to push for answers that make sense.

5. Pharmacies and pharmacists need to use available internal and external data honestly. Even if doing so results in rejecting prescriptions or refusing to fill prescriptions from questionable prescribers and reporting those situations to the DEA.

6. Pharmacies need to hold employees accountable for noncompliance regardless of employees' past performance, because at its heart, the opioid crisis was a crisis of poor human behavior.

Possible Penalties

Potential violations of the CSA by pharmacies, manufacturers, and distributors can encompass a wide range of activities. Therefore, Congress has provided the DOJ and DEA with a broad set of potential remedies, including administrative, civil, and criminal sanctions, to draw upon.

The government can also employ multiple remedies simultaneously, depending on the type, seriousness, and potential impact of the alleged violations.[112] Therefore, even if the DOJ and DEA seek a civil penalty or administrative sanction, they may still pursue criminal charges. The bottom line is that controlled substances violations can result in substantial negative consequences including fines, forfeitures, and prison time for violators.

Administrative Sanctions

The primary administrative sanction is the suspension or revocation of a registrants' authorization by the DEA to manufacture, distribute, or dispense a controlled substance.[113] Grounds for suspension or revocation include, but are not limited to (a) a material falsification on a registration application, (b) conviction of a felony involving a controlled substances or list I chemical, or (c) revocation or suspension of a required state license.[114] The statute also provides a "catch-all," allowing for suspension or revocation if the registrant "has committed such acts as would render his registration . . . inconsistent with the public interest."[115]

To impose a suspension or revocation, the DEA utilizes two approaches—an Order to Show Cause (OSC) or an Immediate Suspension Order (ISO). An OSC, as the name suggests, is an order from the DEA to a registrant to demonstrate why the DEA should not revoke the registrant's license.[116][117] Upon receipt of the OSC, the registrant must either file a written response within 30 days or request a full hearing before an Administrative Law Judge.[118] Typically, OSCs are resolved by settlement and submission of a corrective action plan.[119][120]

An ISO, on the other hand, is an immediate revocation or suspension of the registrant's license before the registrant has the opportunity to respond or a hearing is held.[121][122] Therefore, the registrant immediately must suspend all handling of controlled substances until the underlying OSC is resolved.[123]

To issue an ISO, the DEA must determine that there is "an imminent danger to public health and safety" if the registrant is allowed to continue controlled substances operations.[124] As clarified in 2016, an "imminent danger" means that:

> [D]ue to the failure of the registrant to maintain effective controls against diversion or otherwise comply with the obligations of a registrant . . . there is a substantial likelihood of an immediate threat that death, serious bodily harm, or abuse of a controlled substance will occur in the absence of an immediate suspension of the registration.[125]

Application in the Context of the Opioid Crisis

Of the two approaches, the DEA employs OSCs more frequently than ISOs (see **Figure 4. ISOs and OSCs Issued by the DEA (FY 2008 to FY 2017)**). In 2019, the DOJ OIG determined that the use of ISOs declined 80% between fiscal years 2010 and 2017.[126] Thus, the DOJ OIG concluded that "beginning in 2013, DEA rarely used its strongest enforcement tool . . . to stop registrants from diverting prescription drugs."[127]

Figure 4. ISOs and OSCs Issued by the DEA (FY 2008 to FY 2017)[128]

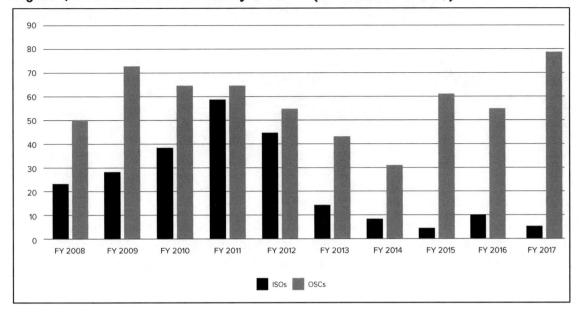

Civil Sanctions

The CSA also allows the DEA to impose civil monetary penalties (CMPs) for violations.[129] As of 2020, the DEA can impose a fine of $64,820 per violation for non-recordkeeping violations, such as filling invalid prescriptions.[130][131] For recordkeeping violations, the DEA can impose a fine of $15,040 per violation.[132] Since each prescription can constitute a separate violation, the fines can quickly accumulate.

For example, in 2013, Walgreens agreed to pay $80 million in civil penalties for violations involving its in-house distribution center and six retail pharmacies.[133] Setting aside the distribution center issues, the DEA alleged that the six pharmacies "received the suspicious drug shipments . . . [and], in turn, filled customer prescriptions that they knew or should have known were not for legitimate medical use."[134] At the time, it was billed as the largest fine paid by a registrant.

Although fines levied against Walgreens were extraordinary, DEA routinely levies fines against smaller pharmacy chains. For example, in September 2019, two pharmacy chains (Osco Pharmacy and a Rite-Aid franchise) were fined $30,000 and $22,500 respectively for filling fraudulent prescriptions.[135] Osco had filled 13 prescriptions, while the Rite-Aid filled 15.[136] In another example, Mountaineer Drug, Inc., in May 2021, agreed to pay $250,000 to resolve claims it had filled invalid prescriptions for Schedule II and III substances.[137]

Criminal Sanctions & Forfeitures

At its heart, the CSA is a criminal statute that divides offenses into various categories of prohibited acts. In addition, the CSA also provides that anyone attempting or conspiring to commit a controlled substances offense is subject to the same penalties as if they committed the offense.[138]

Prohibited Acts A
Under Section 841 of the CSA, any person who knowingly or intentionally manufacturers, distributes, or dispenses a controlled substance except as authorized by the CSA is subject to fines and imprisonment.[139] Fines and prison sentences are based upon the type of controlled substances involved.

For Schedule II substances, a violator faces up to 20 years in prison, or if death or serious injury occurs, up to a life sentence, while the maximum fines can range from a minimum of $1 million for individuals and $5 million for corporations.[140] For Schedule III substances, violators face up to 10 years in prison, or if death or serious injury occurs, up to 15 years, while the maximum fines can range from a maximum of $500,000 for individuals and $2.5 million for corporations.[141] Repeat offenders can face even harsher prison terms and fines.[142]

Prohibited Acts B
Section 842 (Prohibited Acts B) of the CSA encompasses a wide range of activities including:

1. Dispensing controlled substances via invalid prescriptions.[143]

2. Distributing or dispensing a controlled substance outside of their registration or violating the packaging and labeling requirements.[144]

3. Failing to maintain required records or make required reports.[145]

4. In the case of opioids, failing to maintain effective controls against diversion and an SOM program.[146]

Under Section 842, if the DEA can establish a violation was committed knowingly, the individual may face up to one year in prison (or two if it was committed after a prior conviction).[147]

Asset Forfeitures
In addition to fines and imprisonment, the CSA also allows the government upon conviction to reclaim any property "constituting or derived from . . . any proceeds the person obtained . . . as a result of such violation."[148] The property connection can be direct or indirect.[149]

The DEA uses asset forfeiture "to seize . . . property from those involved in crime which benefits law enforcement and the public."[150] Thus, according to the DEA, asset forfeitures deter crime, can dismantle or weaken criminal enterprises, and punishes the criminals.[151]

Application in the Context of the Opioid Crisis
Consistent with the DOJ drive to hold individuals accountable as articulated in the Yates memorandum and its progeny, the DOJ and DEA increasingly have responded to the epidemic by criminally charging individuals.[152][153] For example, in April 2019, the Appalachian

Regional Prescription Opioid Strike Force announced charges against 60 individuals, including doctors, nurse practitioners, and pharmacists, across 11 federal districts.[154]

Manufacturer and distributor companies and their executives also have faced criminal charges. Two notable executive examples are John Kapoor, the founder of Insys Therapeutics, and Laurence Doud, III, the former CEO of Rochester Drug Co-Operative.[155][156] Because of the well-established dangers posed to public health from opioid diversion, the DOJ has shown an increased willingness to pursue individual criminal prosecutions.

Furthermore, when bringing criminal cases, the DOJ often charges violators with a host of other criminal and civil offenses outside of the strict confines of controlled substances (see **Table 3. Non-CSA Offenses Charged in Recent Opioid Cases**).

Table 3. Non-CSA Offenses Charged in Recent Opioid Cases

Individual	Company	Registrant Type	Non-CSA Offenses Charged
John Kapoor	Insys Therapeutics	Manufacturer	Racketeering conspiracy[157] Mail fraud and wire fraud[158] Honest Services mail and wire fraud[159]
N/A	Insys Therapeutics	Manufacturer	Mail fraud False Claims (civil)[160]
Laurence Doud, III	Rochester Drug Co-Operative	Distributor	Conspiracy to defraud the U.S.[161]
N/A	Rochester Drug Co-Operative	Distributor	Conspiracy to defraud the U.S.
N/A	Purdue Pharma	Manufacturer	Conspiracy to violate the FFDCA[162] Conspiracy to violate the Anti-Kickback Statute (AKS)[163]
Shaun Thaxter[164]	Indivior	Manufacturer	Introduction of misbranded drug into interstate commerce[165]
N/A	Indivior	Manufacturer	Healthcare fraud[166] Mail fraud Wire fraud

Table 3. Non-CSA Offenses Charged in Recent Opioid Cases (cont.)

Individual	Company	Registrant Type	Non-CSA Offenses Charged
Xiulu Ruan John Patrick Couch[167]	Physicians Pain Specialists of Alabama	Practitioner	Racketeering conspiracy Conspiracy to violate the AKS
	C&R Pharmacy	Pharmacy	Healthcare fraud Mail fraud Wire fraud Conspiracy to commit money laundering and substantive money laundering (Ruan only)[168]

[Note: This is not an exhaustive list.]

While it is not surprising that mail and wire fraud are common ancillary charges, it is striking that the DOJ is now employing the Racketeer Influenced and Corrupt Organizations (RICO) statute, typically reserved for organized crime, gangs, and drug cartels, against healthcare organizations engaging in opioid diversion.[169]

The DEA also has employed asset forfeitures with increasing effect (see **Table 4. DEA Asset Forfeiture Statistics as of September 2021**). From FY 2019 to FY 2021, the number of forfeitures has increased by more than 16% and recoveries by more than 26%.

Table 4: DEA Asset Forfeiture Statistics as of September 2021[170]

Fiscal Year	Number of Seizures	Value
FY 2021	11,760	~ $744 million
FY 2020	11,699	~ $608 million
FY 2019	10,091	~ $594 million

Thus, the risks and potential penalties for pharmacies and pharmacists have dramatically increased.

Compliance Resources

Drug Enforcement Agency

Pharmacist's Manual

The manual provides important guidance for pharmacists to comply with controlled substances regulation.

https://www.deadiversion.usdoj.gov/pubs/manuals/(DEA-DC-046)(EO-DEA154)_Pharmacist_Manual.pdf

Chemical Handler's Manual (2004)

This manual provides guidance on compliance involving controlled substances and listed chemicals. Currently, DEA is updating its manuals normally available at https://deadiversion.usdoj.gov/pubs/manuals/index.html.

However, the 2004 version is still available and is useful until the new manual is issued.

https://www.justice.gov/sites/default/files/open/legacy/2014/05/09/2004-chemical-handlers-manual.pdf

Congressional Research Service

Legal Overview of the Controlled Substances Act

This report from the Congressional Research Service provides a good introduction to the legal framework of controlled substances regulation and the opioid crisis.

https://sgp.fas.org/crs/misc/R45948.pdf

Risk Takeaways

Main points of interest:

- Opioid abuse in the United States is not a new phenomenon; it dates back more than 150 years.
- The modern framework for regulating controlled substances dates to the 1970s and President Richard M. Nixon's War on Drugs.
- The current epidemic is unique both for its rapid onset and pervasiveness.
- Diversion is the main risk area related to the opioid crisis in pharmacies.

Areas to watch:
- Individual accountability including criminal sanctions on the rise.
- The increasing use of RICO, healthcare fraud, and other laws specific to noncontrolled substances that hold healthcare organizations and their executives accountable for diversion.
- Future clarifications of the ambiguities found in the CSA and its implementing regulations.
- Continuing opioid litigation at both the federal and state level.

Laws that apply:
- Controlled Substances Act, 21 U.S.C. § 801 et seq.
- DEA Controlled Substances Regulations, 21 C.F.R. §1300 et seq.
- Substance Use–Disorder Prevention that Promotes Opioid Recovery and Treatment for Patients and Communities Act, Pub. L. 115-271, 132 Stat. 3894 (Oct. 24, 2018).

Addressing compliance risks:
- Establish a robust pharmacy compliance program to combat the potential for diversion.
- When implementing the compliance program:
  - Apply DEA specific guidance for pharmacies.
  - Adapt and use the DEA guidance for manufacturers and distributors.
  - Use common sense.

Endnotes

1. **Seth Whitelaw** is president and CEO of Whitelaw Compliance Group LLC.; a Senior Fellow & Adjunct Professor, Life Science Compliance, at Mitchell Hamline School of Law; and the editor of *Policy & Medicine Compliance Update*. With more than 30 years working in the life sciences industry, Whitelaw started his career in life science compliance in 1993, when he became the compliance coordinator for C.R. Bard, Inc. His career has encompassed a wide variety of roles from in-house compliance officer with C.R. Bard, Inc., SmithKline Beecham NA; GlaxoSmithKline; and Misonix, Inc.; to industry consultant with Deloitte and his own firm; to editor of a widely read industry compliance publication; and finally, as a law professor where he currently teaches students about healthcare compliance. He also served as an expert compliance witness in the ongoing National Prescription Opiate MDL.

2. U.S. House Energy and Commerce Committee, 115th Congress, *Red Flags and Warning Signs Ignored: Opioid Distribution and Enforcement Concerns in West Virginia*, December 19, 2018, 4, https://www.ruralhealthinfo.org/assets/2616-9819/Opioid-Distribution-Report-Final-REV.pdf

3. "America's Drug Overdose Epidemic: Putting Data to Action," Centers for Disease Control & Prevention, last updated March 8, 2021, https://www.cdc.gov/injury/features/prescription-drug-overdose/index.html.

4. Alex Brill and Scott Ganz, "The Geographic Variation in the Cost of the Opioid Crisis," *American Enterprise Institute*, March 2018, https://www.aei.org/wp-content/uploads/2018/03/Geographic_Variation_in_Cost_of_Opioid_Crisis.pdf?x91208.

5. In re: National Prescription Opiate Litigation, MDL No. 2804 (N.D. Ohio, E.D.).

6. Amanda Bronstad, "Opioid Judge Refuses to Dismiss Claims That Drug Companies Caused 'Man-Made Plague,'" *Law.com*, December 20, 2018, https://www.law.com/2018/12/20/opioid-judge-refuses-to-dismiss-claims-that-drug-companies-caused-man-made-plague/.

7. Andrew Sullivan, "The Poison We Pick," *New York Magazine Intelligencer*, February 19, 2018, https://nymag.com/intelligencer/2018/02/americas-opioid-epidemic.html.

8. Andrew Sullivan, "The Poison We Pick," *New York Magazine Intelligencer*, February 19, 2018, https://nymag.com/intelligencer/2018/02/americas-opioid-epidemic.html.

9. David F. Musto, "The American Experience with Stimulants and Opiates," *Perspectives on Crime & Justice*, Vol. 2 (Washington, D.C.: U.S. Department of Justice, National Institute of Justice: 1998), 51, 56. [In 1898, the Bayer Company introduced heroin as a powerful cough suppressant.]

10. International Narcotics Control Board, *Narcotic Drugs:*

Estimated World Requirements for 2018; Statistics for 2016, (New York, NY: United Nations, 2017), 36.

11. International Narcotics Control Board, *Narcotic Drugs: Estimated World Requirements for 2018; Statistics for 2016,* ((New York, NY: United Nations, 2017), 37.

12. Andrew Sullivan, "The Poison We Pick," *Intelligencer— New York Magazine,* February 2018, http://nymag.com/intelligencer/2018/02/americas-opioid-epidemic.html.

13. "Overdose Death Rates," National Institute on Drug Abuse, January 29, 2021, https://www.drugabuse.gov/drug-topics/trends-statistics/overdose-death-rates#:~:text=Drug%20overdose%20deaths%20involving%20prescription%20opioids%20rose%20from,gender%20from%201999%20to%202019%20%28Source%3A%20CDC%20WONDER%29.

14. "Overdose Death Rates," National Institute on Drug Abuse, January 29, 2021, https://www.drugabuse.gov/drug-topics/trends-statistics/overdose-death-rates#:~:text=Drug%20overdose%20deaths%20involving%20prescription%20opioids%20rose%20from,gender%20from%201999%20to%202019%20%28Source%3A%20CDC%20WONDER%29.

15. U.S. General Accounting Office, *Prescription Drugs: OxyContin Abuse and Diversion and Efforts to Address the Problem,* GAO-04-110, December 2003, 8, https://www.gao.gov/new.items/d04110.pdf.

16. U.S. General Accounting Office, *Prescription Drugs: OxyContin Abuse and Diversion and Efforts to Address the Problem,* GAO-04-110, December 2003, 2, https://www.gao.gov/new.items/d04110.pdf.

17. U.S. General Accounting Office, *Prescription Drugs: OxyContin Abuse and Diversion and Efforts to Address the Problem,* GAO-04-110, December 2003, 44, https://www.gao.gov/new.items/d04110.pdf.

18. U.S. Centers for Disease Control and Prevention, National Center for Health Statistics, "Multiple Cause of Death 1999-2019" on CDC WONDER Online Database, released December 2020, https://wonder.cdc.gov/controller/datarequest/D77.

19. Jeffrey A. Singer, Jacob Z. Sullum, and Michael E. Schatman, "Today's Nonmedical Opioid Users Are Not Yesterday's Patients: Implications of Data Indicating Stable Rates of Nonmedical and Pain Reliever Use Disorder," *Journal of Pain Research* 12 (February 7, 2019): 617–620, https://www.ncbi.nlm.nih.gov/pmc/articles/PMC6369835/.

20. U.S. House Energy and Commerce Committee, 115th Congress, *Red Flags and Warning Signs Ignored: Opioid Distribution and Enforcement Concerns in West Virginia,* December 19, 2018, 4.

21. "The 'Oxy Express': Florida's Drug Abuse Epidemic," *National Public Radio,* March 2, 2011, https://www.npr.org/2011/03/02/134143813/the-oxy-express-floridas-drug-abuse-epidemic.

22. Pat Beall," Florida cuts of oxy: Death, Devastation follow," *The Palm Beach Post,* https://heroin.palmbeachpost.com/florida-cuts-off-oxycodone-death-devastation-follow/?ref=lowerTeases.

23. Andrew Sullivan, "The Poison We Pick," *New York Magazine Intelligencer,* February 20, 2018, https://nymag.com/intelligencer/2018/02/americas-opioid-epidemic.html. [A dosage unit of hydrocodone and oxycodone is equivalent to one pill although that pill can vary in potency.]

24. U.S. Sent'g Guidelines Manual § 8 (U.S. Sentencing Comm'n 2018).

25. Controlled Substances Act, Title II of the Comprehensive Drug Abuse Prevention and Control Act of 1970, Pub. L. No. 513, 84 Stat. No. 1236 (Oct. 27, 1970), codified at 21 U.S.C. § 801, et seq.

26. Congressional Research Service, R45948, *The Controlled Substances Act (CSA): A Legal Overview for the 117th Congress,* updated February 5, 2021, 2, https://sgp.fas.org/crs/misc/R45948.pdf.

27. Chemical Diversion and Trafficking Act of 1988, Title VI, Subtitle A of the Anti-Drug Abuse Amendments Act, Pub. L. No. 100-690, 102 Stat. 4181 (Nov. 18, 1988).

28. Substance Use–Disorder Prevention that Promotes Opioid Recovery and Treatment for Patients and Communities Act, Pub. L. No. 115-271, 132 Stat. 3894 (Oct. 24, 2018).

29. Substance Use–Disorder Prevention that Promotes Opioid Recovery and Treatment for Patients and Communities Act, Pub. L. No. 115-271, 132 Stat. 3894 (Oct. 24, 2018) at §§ 3723(c) and 3292.

30. U.S. Department of Justice, Drug Enforcement Administration, "The DEA Years," accessed December 22, 2021, https://www.dea.gov/sites/default/files/2018-07/1970-1975%20p%2030-39.pdf.

31. Regulations Implementing the Comprehensive Drug Abuse Prevention and Control Act of 1970, 36 Fed. Reg. 7776 (Apr. 24, 1971) (codified at 21 C.F.R. pt. 1301).

32. U.S. Department of Justice, Drug Enforcement Administration, "The DEA Years," accessed December 22, 2021, 33-34, https://www.dea.gov/sites/default/files/2018-07/1970-1975%20p%2030-39.pdf.

33. Congressional Research Service, R45948, Controlled Substances Act (CSA): A Legal Overview for the 117th Cong., 4 (updated Feb. 5, 2021)

34. 21 U.S.C. § 812(b); "Drug Scheduling," U.S. Drug Enforcement Administration, https://www.dea.gov/drug-information/drug-scheduling.

35. U.S. Department of Justice, Drug Enforcement Agency, *96-2 Diversion Investigator's Manual,* § 5126, April 16, 1996.

36. 21 U.S.C. § 301, et seq.; Congressional Research Service, R45948, *The Controlled Substances Act (CSA): A Legal Overview for the 117th Cong.,* updated February 5, 2021, 3-4.

37. 21 U.S.C. § 812(b)(1).

38. 21 U.S.C. § 812(b)(2).

39. 21 U.S.C. § 812(b)(3).

40. 21 U.S.C. § 812(b)(4).

41. 21 U.S.C. § 802(18). *[Note: Therefore, potency is often measured in morphine equivalents.]*

42. 21 U.S.C. § 812(a).

43. 21 U.S.C. § 811(a)(1). [Congress also can always amend the statute to reclassify a drug.]

44. Congressional Research Service, R45948, *The Controlled Substances Act (CSA): A Legal Overview for the 117th Cong.,* updated February 5, 2021, 8-9.

45. Schedules of Controlled Substances: Rescheduling of Hydrocodone Combination Products from Schedule III to Schedule II, 79 Fed. Reg. 49661, 49663 (Aug. 22, 2014).

46. 21 U.S.C. § 823; 21 C.F.R. § 1301.11(a). *[Note: Online pharmacies must be separately authorized to operate over the Internet. 21 C.F.R. § 1301.11(b); Patients, the "ultimate users," are exempt from registration. 21 U.S.C. §822(c)(3) and 21 U.S.C. §802(25) (defining "ultimate user").]*

47. Electronic Prescriptions for Controlled Substances, 75 Fed. Reg. 16235, 16237 (March 31, 2010).

48. 21 U.S.C. § 822(e)(1).

49. 21 U.S.C. § 823(g).

50. "Registrant Population –Summary," U.S. Department of Justice, Drug Enforcement Administration, accessed October 31, 2021, https://apps2.deadiversion.usdoj.gov/RAPR/raprRegistrantPopulationSummary.xhtml#-no-back-button. [Mid-level practitioners include, but are not limited to, nurse practitioners, physician assistants, nurse midwives, and clinical nurse specialists that can dispense controlled substances under state law. 21 C.F.R. § 1300.01(b).]

51. "Registrant Population – Summary," U.S. Department of Justice, Drug Enforcement Administration, accessed October 31, 2021, https://apps2.deadiversion.usdoj.gov/RAPR/raprRegistrantPopulationSummary.xhtml#-no-back-button.

52. "Top U.S. Pharmacies Ranked By Prescription Drugs Market Share in 2020," Statista, July 21, 2021, https://www.statista.com/statistics/734171/pharmacies-ranked-by-rx-market-share-in-us/.

53. "Number of Stores of the Leading Drug stores in the United States in 2020," Statista, August, 19, 2021, https://www.statista.com/statistics/197848/number-of-stores-of-top-drug-stores-in-the-us/.

54. 21 U.S.C. §§ 827, 828; 21 C.F.R. pts. 1304 and 1305. *[Note: For more a more detailed discussion of these requirements see Kimberly New, "Drug Diversion," HCCA Complete Healthcare Compliance Manual.]*

55. 21 U.S.C. § 829.

56. 21 U.S.C. § 829(a).

57. 21 U.S.C. § 829(b).

58. In re: National Prescription Opiate Litigation, MDL No. 2804 (N.D. Ohio, Sep. 14, 2019), Defendants' Memorandum in Support of Motion to Disqualify Pursuant to 28 U.S.C. § 455(a) at 7.

59. 21 U.S.C. § 829.

60. U.S. v. Moore, 423 U.S. 122 (1975).

61. 21 U.S.C. § 824(a)(1) and 21 C.F.R. § 1306.04(a). *[Note: A pharmacist, who knowing fills an invalid controlled substance prescription "shall be subject to the penalties provided for violations of the provisions" of the CSA. The same applies to the prescriber issuing the prescription.]*

62. 21 C.F.R. § 1306.04(a).

63. United States v. Veal, 23 F.3d 985 (6th Cir. 1994) [Finding "[t]here was ample evidence to support a finding that the fraudulent character of the prescriptions should have been obvious to him."]

64. 21 U.S.C. §§ 823 (a)(1), (b)(1), (d)1, (e)(1).

65. 21 C.F.R. § 1301.71(a) [emphasis added].

66. Letter from Joseph Rannazzisi, DEA Deputy Assistant Administrator, Office of Diversion Control to All Registered Distributors (September 27, 2006), 2. *["All registrants—manufacturers, distributors, pharmacies, and practitioners —share responsibility for maintaining appropriate safeguards against diversion."]*

67. National Conference of Commissioners on Uniform State Laws, *Uniform Controlled Substances Act (1994)*, § 309(a), December 28, 1995, https://www.uniformlaws.org/HigherLogic/System/DownloadDocumentFile.ashx?DocumentFileKey=34039f08-ab0d-24fd-d349-b8f58e81b281.

68. Jacobellis v. Ohio, 378 U.S. 184, 197 (1964). *[Note: Stewart, J. concurring.]*

69. Letter from Joseph Rannazzisi, DEA Deputy Assistant Administrator, Office of Diversion Control to All Registered Distributors, September 27, 2006, 3. *[Note: A similar letter was sent to all registered distributors again in February 2007.]*

70. Letter from Joseph Rannazzisi, DEA Deputy Assistant Administrator, Office of Diversion Control to All Registered Distributors, September 27, 2006, 3.

71. Letter from Joseph Rannazzisi, DEA Deputy Assistant Administrator, Office of Diversion Control to All Registered Distributors, September 27, 2006, 3.

72. Letter from Joseph Rannazzisi, DEA Deputy Assistant Administrator, Office of Diversion Control to All Registered Manufacturers and Distributors, June 12, 2012, 1.

73. U.S. Drug Enforcement Administration, Pharmacist's Manual DEA-DC-046, October 8, 2020, 2, https://www.deadiversion.usdoj.gov/pubs/manuals/(DEA-DC-046)(EO-DEA154)_Pharmacist_Manual.pdf.

74. U.S. Drug Enforcement Administration, Pharmacist's Manual DEA-DC-046, Appendix D, October 8, 2020, 113–115, https://www.deadiversion.usdoj.gov/pubs/manuals/(DEA-DC-046)(EO-DEA154)_Pharmacist_Manual.pdf.

75. U.S. Drug Enforcement Administration, *Pharmacist's ManualDEA-DC-046*, October 8, 2020, 114, https://www.deadiversion.usdoj.gov/pubs/manuals/(DEA-DC-046)(EO-DEA154)_Pharmacist_Manual.pdf.

76. U.S. Drug Enforcement Administration, *Pharmacist's ManualDEA-DC-046*, October 8, 2020, 114, https://www.deadiversion.usdoj.gov/pubs/manuals/(DEA-DC-046)(EO-DEA154)_Pharmacist_Manual.pdf.

77. 21 C.F.R. § 1301.74(a), https://www.deadiversion.usdoj.gov/pubs/manuals/(DEA-DC-046)(EO-DEA154)_Pharmacist_Manual.pdf.

78. Letter from Joseph Rannazzisi, DEA Deputy Assistant Administrator, Office of Diversion Control to All Registered Distributors, February 7, 2007, 2.

79. Complaint and Demand for Jury Trial Big Bend Community Based Care Inc., et al., v. Purdue Pharma L.P., et al., Case No. 4:18-cv-00183 (N.D. Fla. Apr. 4, 2018), 6, para. 17. *[Note: Citing the Healthcare Distribution Management Association (HDMA), Industry Compliance Guidelines: Reporting Suspicious Orders and Preventing Diversion of Controlled Substances (2008). In 2016, HDMA became the Healthcare Distribution Alliance.]*

80. 21 C.F.R. § 1301.74(b).

81. 21 U.S.C. § 802(21).

82. 21 C.F.R. § 1301.74(b).

83. Substance Use–Disorder Prevention that Promotes Opioid Recovery and Treatment for Patients and Communities Act, Pub. L. No. 115-271, 132 Stat. 3894 (Oct. 24, 2018) at § 3292(b). [Codified at 21 U.S.C. § 802(57)].

84. Letter from Joseph Rannazzisi, DEA Deputy Assistant Administrator, Office of Diversion Control to All Registered Manufacturers and Distributors, December 27, 2007, 1.

85. Letter from Joseph Rannazzisi, DEA Deputy Assistant Administrator, Office of Diversion Control to All Registered Manufacturers and Distributors, June 12, 2012, 1.

86. Letter from Joseph Rannazzisi, DEA Deputy Assistant Administrator, Office of Diversion Control to All Registered Manufacturers and Distributors, June 12, 2012, 1.

87. U.S. Department of Justice, Drug Enforcement Administration, *Chemical Handler's Manual*, January 2004, https://www.justice.gov/sites/default/files/open/legacy/2014/05/09/2004-chemical-handlers-manual.pdf.

88. U.S. Department of Justice, Drug Enforcement Administration, *Chemical Handler's Manual*, Appendix E-3, January 2004, 41, https://www.justice.gov/sites/default/files/open/legacy/2014/05/09/2004-chemical-handlers-manual.pdf

89. U.S. Department of Justice, Drug Enforcement Administration, *Chemical Handler's Manual*, Appendix E-3, January 2004, 41.

90. U.S. Department of Justice, Drug Enforcement Administration, *Chemical Handler's Manual*, Appendix E-3, January 2004, 41. [emphasis added]

91. 21 C.F.R. § 1301.74(b).

92. U.S. Department of Justice, Drug Enforcement Administration, *Chemical Handler's Manual*, Appendix E-3, January 2004, 19.

93. Masters Pharmaceuticals, Inc.; Decision and Order, 80 Fed. Reg. 55418, 55478 (Sept. 15, 2015) upheld Masters Pharmaceuticals, Inc. v. DEA, No. 15-1335, (D.C. Cir. 2017).

94. Masters Pharmaceuticals, Inc.; Decision and Order, 80 Fed. Reg. 55418, 55478 (Sept. 15, 2015).

95. Masters Pharmaceuticals, Inc.; Decision and Order, 80 Fed. Reg. 55418, 55478 (Sept. 15, 2015).

96. 21 C.F.R. § 1301.74(b).

97. Substance Use–Disorder Prevention that Promotes Opioid Recovery and Treatment for Patients and Communities Act, Pub. L. No. 115-271, 132 Stat. 3894 (Oct. 24, 2018) at § 3272(b)(1). [emphasis added]

98. 21 U.S.C. §§ 823 (a)(1), (b)(1).

99. Letter from Joseph Rannazzisi, DEA Deputy Assistant Administrator, Office of Diversion Control to All Registered Manufacturers and Distributors , June 12, 2012, 2.

100. Letter from Joseph Rannazzisi, DEA Deputy Assistant Administrator, Office of Diversion Control to All Registered Manufacturers and Distributors at 2 (Dec. 27, 2007).

101. Masters Pharmaceuticals, Inc.; Decision and Order, 80 Fed. Reg. 55418, 55478 (September 15, 2015).

102. U.S. Department of Justice, Drug Enforcement Administration, Chemical Handler's Manual, January 2004, 19.

103. U.S. Department of Justice, Drug Enforcement Administration, Chemical Handler's Manual, January 2004, 19.

104. In re: National Prescription Opiate Litigation, MDL No. 2804 (N.D. Ohio, E.D.), Examination of Compliance Standards for Opioid Manufacturers and Distributors, 48-51 and 242 (Whitelaw Compliance Group, LLC., April 15, 2019). [citations omitted]

105. In re: National Prescription Opiate Litigation, MDL No. 2804 (N.D. Ohio, E.D.), Examination of Compliance Standards for Opioid Manufacturers and Distributors, 242 (Whitelaw Compliance Group, LLC., April 15, 2019). [Note: The DEA's Automation of Reports and Consolidated Orders System ("ARCOS") requires manufacturers and distributors of controlled substances to "report inventories, acquisitions, and dispositions of schedule I and II substances, and narcotic substances in schedule III as well as other selected substances such as Gamma-Hydroxybutyric Acid ("GHB")."]

106. John Gilbert and Larry Houck, "About Time: DEA Acknowledges that Long-Collected ARCOS Data is an Effective Enforcement Tool That Can Assist Manufacturers and Distributors," FDA Law Blog, February 21, 2018, http://www.fdalawblog.net/2018/02/about-time-dea-acknowledges-that-long-collected-arcos-data-is-an-effective-enforcement-tool-that-can-assist-manufacturers-and-distributors/.

107. U.S. Sent'g Guidelines Manual § 8B2.1 (U.S. Sent'g Comm'n 2018).

108. U.S. Drug Enforcement Administration, *Pharmacist's ManualDEA-DC-046*, October 8, 2020, 115.

109. U.S. Drug Enforcement Administration, *Pharmacist's ManualDEA-DC-046*, Appendix D, October 8, 2020, 113-115.

110. Don L. Bell, II, "Opioids and DEA Compliance," (Power Point presentation, National Association of Chain Drug Stores, 2019), https://regional.nacds.org/wp-content/uploads/2019-regional-conference/presentations/Opioids-and-DEA-Compliance.pdf.

111. Don L. Bell, II, "Opioids and DEA Compliance," (Power Point presentation, National Association of Chain Drug Stores, 2019), 34-37,), https://regional.nacds.org/wp-content/uploads/2019-regional-conference/presentations/Opioids-and-DEA-Compliance.pdf

112. 21 U.S.C. § 847. *["Any penalty imposed ... shall be in addition to, and not in lieu of, any civil or administrative penalty or sanction authorized by law."]*

113. 21 U.S.C. § 824(a).

114. 21 U.S.C. §§ 824(a)(1–3).

115. 21 U.S.C. §§ 824(a)(4).

116. 21 C.F.R. §§ 1301.36(d), 1301.37.

117. Andrew Hull, "What to Do When You Receive a DEA Order to Show Cause," *FDA Law Blog* (blog), November 16, 2017, http://www.fdalawblog.net/2017/11/what-to-do-when-you-receive-a-dea-order-to-show-cause/.

118. 21 C.F.R. § 1301.37.

119. Ensuring Patient Access and Effective Drug Enforcement Act of 2016, Pub. L. No. 114-145, 130 Stat. 354 (April 19, 2016).

120. Andrew Hull, "What to do When You Receive a DEA Order to Show Cause," *FDA Law Blog* (blog), November 16, 2017, http://www.fdalawblog.net/2017/11/what-to-do-when-you-receive-a-dea-order-to-show-cause/.

121. 21 U.S.C. § 824(d); 21 C.F.R. § 1301.36(e).

122. John J. Mulrooney, II and Andrew J. Hull, "Drug Diversion Administrative Revocation and Application Hearings for Medical and Pharmacy Practitioners: A Primer for Navigating Murky, Drug-Infested Waters," *Albany Law Review*, vol. 78:2 (2015): 327, 384–365, http://www.albanylawreview.org/Articles/Vol78_2/78.2.327%20Mulrooney.pdf.

123. 21 U.S.C. § 824(d)(1).

124. 21 U.S.C. § 824(d)(1); 21 C.F.R. § 1301.36(e).

125. Ensuring Patient Access and Effective Drug Enforcement Act of 2016, Pub. L. No. 114-145, 130 Stat. 354 (Apr. 19, 2016).

126. U.S. Dep't of Justice, Office of Inspector General, *Review of the Drug Enforcement's Regulatory and Enforcement Control Efforts to Control the Diversion of Opioids 19-05*, September 2019, 21, https://oig.justice.gov/reports/2019/e1905.pdf.

127. U.S. Dep't of Justice, Office of Inspector General, *Review of the Drug Enforcement's Regulatory and Enforcement Control Efforts to Control the Diversion of Opioids 19-05*, Executive Summary, September 2019, i.

128. U.S. Dep't of Justice, Office of Inspector General, *Review of the Drug Enforcement's Regulatory and Enforcement Control Efforts to Control the Diversion of Opioids 19-05*, September 2019, 22.

129. 21 U.S.C. § 842(c).

130. Natalia Mazina, "Ways to avoid DEA 's monetary penalties," *Pharmacy & Healthcare Legal Blog* (blog), July 2, 2020, https://www.pharmhealthlaw.com/single-post/2020/07/02/ways-to-avoid-deas-monetary-penalties/.

131. Federal Civil Penalties Adjustment Act, Pub. L. No. 101-410 (1990). [CMPs are adjusted for inflation.]

132. Natalia Mazina, "Ways to avoid DEA 's monetary penalties," *Pharmacy & Healthcare Legal Blog* (blog), July 2, 2020.

133. U.S. Drug Enforcement Admin., "Walgreens Agrees to Pay A Record Settlement Of $80 Million for Civil Penalties Under The Controlled Substances Act," news release, June 11, 2013, https://www.dea.gov/press-releases/2013/06/11/walgreens-agrees-pay-record-settlement-80-million-civil-penalties-under#:~:text=The%20DEA%E2%80%99s%20administrative%20actions%20demonstrated%20millions%20of%20violations,-%20V%20for%20two%20years%2C%20ending%20in%202014.

134. U.S. Drug Enforcement Admin., "Walgreens Agrees to Pay a Record Settlement Of $80 Million for Civil Penalties Under the Controlled Substances Act," news release, June 11, 2013.

135. U.S. Drug Enforcement Admin., "Two Pharmacy chains pay civil monetary penalties to resolve alleged violations of the Controlled Substance Act," news release, September, 9, 2019, https://www.dea.gov/press-releases/2019/09/09/two-pharmacy-chains-pay-civil-monetary-penalties-resolve-alleged.

136. U.S. Drug Enforcement Admin., "Two Pharmacy chains pay civil monetary penalties to resolve alleged violations of the Controlled Substance Act," news release, September, 9, 2019, https://www.dea.gov/press-releases/2019/09/09/two-pharmacy-chains-pay-civil-monetary-penalties-resolve-alleged.

137. U.S. Attorney's Office, S.D. W. Va., "Former Whitesville Pharmacy to Pay Civil Monetary Penalties to Resolve Alleged Violations of the Controlled Substances Act," news release, May 10, 2021, https://www.justice.gov/usao-sdwv/pr/former-whitesville-pharmacy-pay-civil-monetary-penalties-resolve-alleged-violations.

138. 21 U.S.C. § 846.

139. 21 U.S.C. § 841(a).

140. 21 U.S.C. § 841(b)(1)(C).

141. 21 U.S.C. § 841(b)(1)(E).

142. 21 U.S.C. §§ 841(b)(1)(C), 841(b)(1)(E)(ii).

143. 21 U.S.C. § 842(a)(1).

144. 21 U.S.C. §§ 842 (a)(2–4), 825, 829.

145. 21 U.S.C. § 842(a)(5).

146. 21 U.S.C. §§ 842 (a)(5), 842(a)(17), 842(c)(1)(B)(ii).

147. 21 U.S.C. § 842(c)(2)(A–B).

148. 21 U.S.C. § 853. [The DEA also can seize property using the general administrative and civil provisions of the U.S. Code and Code of Federal Regulations.] 18 U.S.C. § 983; 28 C.F.R. pts. 8 and 9.

149. 21 U.S.C. § 853.

150. "DEA Asset Forfeiture Statistics," U.S. Drug Enforcement Admin., September 10, 2021, https://www.dea.gov/operations/asset-forfeiture.

151. "DEA Asset Forfeiture Statistics," U.S. Drug Enforcement Admin., September 10, 2021, https://www.dea.gov/operations/asset-forfeiture.

152. Memorandum from Sally Q. Yates, Deputy Attorney Gen., U.S. Dep't of Justice, to All Component Heads and United States Attorneys, "Individual Accountability for Corporate Wrong Doing," September 9, 2015.

153. Rod J. Rosenstein, Deputy Attorney Gen., U.S. Dep't of Justice, "Keynote Address on Corporate Enforcement Policy," *American Conference Institute*, October 6, 2017, https://www.justice.gov/opa/speech/deputy-attorney-general-rod-j-rosenstein-delivers-remarks-american-conference-institute-0.

154. U.S. Dep't of Justice, "Appalachian Regional Prescription Opioid (ARPO) Strike Force Takedown Results in Charges Against 60 Individuals, Including 53 Medical Professionals," news release, April 17, 2019, https://www.justice.gov/opa/pr/appalachian-regional-prescription-opioid-arpo-strike-force-takedown-results-charges-against.

155. U.S. v. John N. Kapoor, et al., 1:16-cr-10343-ADB (D. Mass. 2019);

156. Sealed Indictment, United States of America v. Laurence F. Doud III, 19 CRIM 285 (S.D. N.Y. 2019), https://www.justice.gov/usao-sdny/press-release/file/1156386/download;

157. 18 U.S.C. § 1962(d).

158. 18 U.S.C. §§ 1341, 1343.

159. 18 U.S.C. § 1346.

160. 31 U.S.C. §§ 3729–3733.

161. 18 U.S.C. § 371.

162. 21 U.S.C. §§ 331(a), 333(a).

163. 42 U.S.C. § 1320a-7b(b).

164. U.S. Dep't of Justice, "Opioid Manufacturer Indivior's Chief Executive Officer Pleads Guilty In Connection With Drug Safety Claim," June 30, 2020, https://www.justice.gov/opa/pr/opioid-manufacturer-indivior-s-chief-executive-officer-pleads-guilty-connection-drug-safety.

165. 21 U.S.C. § 331(a).

166. 18 U.S.C. § 1347.

167. United States v. Xiulu Ruan, John Patrick Couch, Case No. 17-12653, 2-6 (11th Cir. Jul. 10, 2020).

168. 18 U.S.C. §§ 1956(h), 1957.

169. Racketeer Influenced and Corrupt Organizations, Title IX of the Organized Crime Control Act of 1970, Pub. L. No. 91-452, 84 Stat. 922 (October 15, 1970), codified at 18 U.S.C. § 1961, *et seq.*

170. "DEA Asset Forfeiture Statistics," U.S. Drug Enforcement Administration, September 10, 2021, https://www.dea.gov/operations/asset-forfeiture.

Physician Compensation

Contracts and Compensation Models

By Joe Aguilar,[1] MBA, MPH, MSN, CVA

What Are Physician Contracts and Compensation Models?

Financial arrangements between physicians and hospitals come in a variety of types; however, the majority fall under three main categories: employment agreements, foundation model agreements, and professional services agreements. With a variety of agreement types, compliance exposure risks related to physician contracts and compensation models for health systems have increased as well.

Employment Agreements

Health systems employ physicians in an effort to increase physician-hospital alignment. Under employment agreements, physicians become employees of the health system and provide professional medical/surgical services for the system. Practice assets are owned by the health system, operating costs are managed and incurred by the health system, and management of the practice staff fall under the responsibility of the health system. Each physician's compensation is determined by the specific terms within the employment agreement.

Foundation Model Agreements

Foundation models primarily occur in states that prohibit the corporate practice of medicine. Under foundation model arrangements, the health system will form a nonprofit foundation that owns the assets of the practice and manages the operations and staff. Physicians under such an arrangement will form an entity that contracts directly with the foundation for the provision of professional medical services. The medical group's compensation is determined by the foundation model agreement, and each individual physician's compensation is determined by the medical group.

Professional Services Agreements

Health systems contract with physician practices for specific professional clinical services on an hourly basis, a set fee schedule arrangement, and/or another basis. Health systems will typically assume the billing and collecting for physician services and compensate the practice out of these funds. This structure allows health systems to obtain physician services while not employing them directly. This is typically suited for health systems taking the initial steps toward physician-hospital integration or wanting less than a physician full-time equivalent. Physicians under these arrangements continue to maintain their autonomy over work hours, while reducing their administrative burden associated with billing and collecting. For more information about this kind of agreement, read "Contracts with Referral Sources: Entering into a Proper Physician Arrangement" in this chapter.

Compensation models vary within each of these agreement types, and it is within these models where the compliance risks reside.

Risk Area Governance

Physician transactions are highly regulated by federal law, a variety of state-specific fraud and abuse statutes, and government agencies. The activities and transactions of most physicians in private practice and those employed by health systems are affected by these regulations. The primary federal laws governing physician compensation include:

- Stark Law
- Anti-Kickback Statute (AKS)
- False Claims Act (FCA)

Stark Law (Physician Self-Referral Law), 42 U.S.C. § 1395nn

The Stark Law has undergone several phases to its rules, regulations, and exceptions since its introduction; however, at its core, the law "prohibits a physician from making referrals for certain designated health services payable by Medicare to an entity with which he or she (or an immediate family member) has a financial relationship, unless an exception applies; and prohibits the entity from filing claims with Medicare (or billing another individual, entity, or third party payer) for those referred services."[2]

The following are considered to be designated health services by the Centers for Medicare & Medicaid Services (CMS):

- Clinical laboratory services
- Physical therapy, occupational therapy, and outpatient speech-language pathology services
- Radiology and certain other imaging services
- Radiation therapy services and supplies
- Durable medical equipment and supplies
- Parenteral and enteral nutrients, equipment, and supplies
- Prosthetics, orthotics, and prosthetic devices and supplies
- Home health services
- Outpatient prescription drugs
- Inpatient and outpatient hospital services[3]

In limited circumstances, the Stark Law does allow for certain exceptions. All exceptions must still comply with CMS requirements, AKS, and any other applicable federal and state regulations. Exceptions are noted for specific healthcare services as well as specific healthcare entities, such as academic medical centers (AMCs), ambulatory surgery centers, (ASCs) and federally qualified health centers (FQHCs). The most notable exceptions to this law include the following:

- Employment relationships
- In-office ancillary services
- Group practice arrangements
- Fair market value exception
- Physician services
- Provider recruitment
- Risk-sharing agreements
- Equipment and space leases
- Indirect compensation arrangements
- Nonmonetary compensation
- Medical staff incidental benefits[4]

Anti-Kickback Statute, 42 U.S.C. § 1320a-7b(b)

The AKS is a federal fraud and abuse law that prohibits knowingly and willfully offering, paying, soliciting, or receiving remuneration in order to induce business payable by Medicare and/or Medicaid unless certain conditions are satisfied.[5] The AKS applies to all persons in all healthcare services, not solely physicians or hospitals. The intent of the law is to prevent overutilization of items or services through prohibiting incentive compensation to induce referrals.

In limited circumstances, the AKS does allow for certain safe harbors. All safe harbors must still comply with CMS requirements, Stark Law, and any other applicable federal and state regulations.

The most notable safe harbors to this law include the following:

- Bona fide employment relationships
- Personal services arrangements
- Group purchasing organizations
- Referral services
- Fair market value exception[6]

False Claims Act, 31 U.S.C. §§ 3729–3733

The FCA was enacted to prevent contractors and suppliers from defrauding the US government.[7][8] The FCA states that "any person who knowingly presents . . . a false or fraudulent claim for payment . . . or knowingly makes . . . a false record or statement material to a false or fraudulent claim . . . is liable to the United States government for a civil penalty."[9] Claims made against Medicare, Medicaid, and various other federal and state health insurance plans may potentially fall under the FCA.

Common fraud and abuse examples that fall under the FCA include, but are not limited to, the following:

- Kickbacks
- Services billed but not rendered
- Lack of medical necessity
- Coding irregularities (e.g., upcoding or unbundling)[10]

Antitrust Laws

From their inception with the Sherman Act in 1890, antitrust laws are aimed at preserving competition while governing the mergers and acquisitions (M&A) that occur within industry.[11] The Federal Trade Commission is tasked with overseeing the enforcement of these antitrust laws.[12] The trend has been toward increased M&A in healthcare with a focus on generating economies of scale and obtaining investment in technologies and ancillary services.[13] Even in the context of the coronavirus pandemic, healthcare transactions may have been delayed but are projected to continue and catch up to historical trends.[14]

Government Agencies

In addition to these federal laws, there are many federal and state governmental agencies that are responsible for regulatory oversight of physicians and health systems. These include CMS; accrediting agencies; Office for Civil Rights; Federal Trade Commission; Internal Revenue Service; and various state level agencies, medical boards, and courts.

2020 Final Regulations to the Stark Law and Anti-Kickback Statute

In an effort to reconcile the healthcare regulatory framework with the increasing need for coordinated care, the Department of Health & Human Services (HHS) launched an initiative in 2018, which they called a "regulatory sprint to coordinated care."[15] The primary goal was to evaluate the current regulatory framework and to remove barriers for health systems and physicians to share information—from financial arrangements to incentivize coordinated care. As a result, HHS announced on November 20, 2020, the final rule changes to the Stark Law and AKS to facilitate physicians and hospitals to coordinate care and encourage value-based arrangements. While there are regulatory differences between Stark and AKS, attempts were made to align definitions and other regulatory guidance. Specifically, definitions were consistent among the following terms that are used in value-based arrangements for the purpose of exceptions/safe harbors: value-based enterprise (VBE), VBE participant, value-based purpose, value-based activity, value-based arrangement, and target population.[16] [17] Among the other changes, these new final rules attempt to clarify the definitions of FMV and commercial reasonableness. Note that other regulatory changes are included; however, given the scope and topic for this article, those changes were not highlighted herein.

Stark Law: November 20, 2020, Final Rule Changes

Compensation Exceptions Based on Value-Based Arrangements

Three new value-based arrangement exceptions are now finalized to include:

- Arrangements under full-risk (i.e., capitated or global budget payments),[18]
- Arrangements with meaningful downside risk where physicians are liable for no less than 10% of the physician compensation if specific benchmarks are not met, and
- Value-based arrangements (regardless of risk).[19] [20]

The value-based arrangements must meet specific criteria as well as satisfy the regulatory definitions pertaining to the compensation arrangement. Criteria varies based on the level of risk. All arrangements must be commercially reasonable.

In addition, the following current regulations were amended:

- Indirect value-based arrangements:[21]
  - When an unbroken chain of financial relationships includes a value-based arrangement to which the physician (or the physician organization in whose shoes the physician stands) is a direct party, the new exceptions at 42 C.F.R. § 411.357(aa) are applicable.
  - This is in addition to the exceptions at 42 C.F.R. §§ 411.355, 411.357(n), and 411.357(p).
- Group practice rules where distribution of profits is directly attributable to a physician's participation in a value-based enterprise, notwithstanding 42 C.F.R. § 411.352 (g).[22]

AKS: November 20, 2020, Final Rule Changes

Compensation Exceptions Based on Value-Based Arrangements

Three new value-based arrangement exceptions are now finalized to include:

- Arrangements under full-risk (i.e., capitated payments)[23]
- Arrangements with substantial downside risk where financial risk is between 20%–30% of any loss subject to specific criteria[24]
- Care coordination arrangements (in-kind remuneration only)[25]
- Patient engagement and support[26]
  - Safe harbor for patient tools used to improve quality, health outcomes, and efficiency
  - In-kind items, goods, and services only
  - Direct connection to the coordination and management of care of the target patient population

The value-based arrangements must meet specific criteria as well as satisfy the regulatory definitions pertaining to the compensation arrangement. All arrangements must be commercially reasonable. Under the care coordination arrangement safe harbor, the recipient is required to pay at least 15% of the offeror's cost for the remuneration or the in-kind remuneration needs to be within fair market value.

In addition, the following current regulations were amended:

- Personal services and management contracts[27]
  - Adds flexibility with respect to part-time arrangements
- Outcomes-based payment arrangements[28]
- CMS-sponsored models safe harbor[29]
  - Reduces the need for separate and distinct fraud and abuse waivers for new CMS-sponsored models
  - Subject to specific conditions

Redefining Fundamental Terminology: FMV, Commercial Reasonableness, and the Value or Volume Standard

The final rule changes address the three key concepts that affect most of the exceptions in an effort to increase clarity and reduce the regulatory burden of moving toward value-based arrangements.

- **Fair market value (FMV)**. The final rule clarifies the definition subject to the transaction (asset acquisition, compensation arrangements, and equipment/office space rental). With each transaction type, FMV is defined to be consistent with "general market value":[30]
  - With respect to the purchase of an asset, the price that an asset would bring on the date of acquisition of the asset as the result of bona fide bargaining between a

well-informed buyer and seller that are not otherwise in a position to generate business for each other.

- With respect to compensation for services, the compensation that would be paid at the time the parties enter into the service arrangement as the result of bona fide bargaining between well-informed parties that are not otherwise in a position to generate business for each other.
- With respect to the rental of equipment or the rental of office space, the price that rental property would bring at the time the parties enter into the rental arrangement as the result of bona fide bargaining between a well-informed lessor and lessee that are not otherwise in a position to generate business for each other.

- **Commercial reasonableness**: This is defined as a "particular arrangement [that] furthers a legitimate business purpose of the parties to the arrangement and is sensible, considering the characteristics of the parties, including their size, type, scope, and specialty."[31] The new rule clarifies that commercial reasonableness is not synonymous with profitability, but it may be satisfied if the arrangement makes sense toward the accomplishment of the goals set by the parties.
- **Volume or value standard.** The definition has uncoupled fair market value with the volume or value standard and has set a mathematical equation for determining compensation meets the standard. To this end, two new rules have been created:
  - **One for compensation to a physician.** The formula used to calculate the physician's (or immediate family member's) compensation includes the physician's referrals to (or other business generated by the physician for) the entity as a variable, resulting in an increase or decrease in the physician's (or immediate family member's) compensation that positively correlates with the number or value of the physician's referrals to the entity.[32]
  - **One for compensation from a physician.** The formula used to calculate the entity's compensation includes the physician's referrals to (or other business generated by the physician for) the entity as a variable, resulting in an increase or decrease in the entity's compensation that negatively correlates with the number or value of the physician's referrals to the entity.[33]

Common Compliance Risks

Physician compensation can take the form of many financial arrangements. It is the variety of these arrangements that increases the compliance risk exposure for physicians and health systems. Various terms under different compensation models pose different potential compliance risks. These models can be found in employment agreements, foundation model arrangements, and professional services agreements. The risks described address documentation of requirements, annual base guarantees, production-based compensation, value-based compensation, stacking compensation terms, and advanced practice provider (APP) supervisory compensation.

Physician Agreements Lack Specific Requirements for Compensation

Physician agreements vary from system to system based on clarity, complexity, and level of detail when outlining requirements and compensation. To ensure compliance with respect to compensation, clarity in the subject agreement will facilitate a more accurate analysis of the arrangement. For example, here are two versions of contract terms associated with administrative services provided by a physician:

- **Option A:** Physician shall be compensated $30,000 per year for the provision of administrative services as medical director of Family Medicine Services.

- **Option B:** Physician shall provide administrative duties as medical director of Family Medicine Services and be compensated at a rate of $150 per hour, document hours by time sheets, and work up to 200 hours per year for a maximum of $30,000 per year.

The terms under Option A can theoretically be paid to the physician who only worked 30 hours in the year, resulting in an effective hourly rate of $1,000 per hour, well over FMV. This example illustrates that in the absence of a minimum number of required hours, the effective hourly rate may exceed FMV.

While in many cases there may be knowledge that a physician did in fact provide administrative services to the system, compensating physicians for undocumented services should be avoided. Subject agreements that compensate physicians a stipend for broadly defined administrative services without the explicit number of hours required are a compliance risk.

This medical directorship illustration is just one example of the risk associated with not fully documenting the necessary requirements for particular compensatory services. Adding compensation from other services without specific requirements in the subject agreement potentially places the entire compensation outside of FMV.

Annual Base Guarantee Is Not Aligned with Physician Production and Earning Streams

Many physician employment agreements include an annual base guarantee as one of the compensation terms. While it is often in the best interest of the physician to seek a higher base guarantee, the overall financial and compliance risk to the employer is reduced by minimizing the guaranteed portion of the physician's total compensation. This structure is not meant to reduce the total potential compensation to the physician, but instead ensures that a high level of compensation is only achieved when the physician's production level and/or workload is in excess of that which would support the base.

Workload can include the physician's clinical production in terms of work relative value units (wRVUs), professional collections, administrative hours, emergency room (ER) call coverage shifts, research activity, etc. A wRVU is an objective means of measuring a physician's professional work and takes into account the experience, skill, training, and intensity required to provide a given service. It is one of the three components that makes up a total relative value unit (RVU) used by Medicare to determine reimbursement by procedure (i.e., CPT code).[34] An example of a physician's total compensation package, including multiple earning streams, is illustrated in **Table 1**.

Table 1: Balance between Production and Base Guarantee

	Physician A (Low Base)	Physician B (High Base)
Proposed Base Guarantee	$500,000 per year	$1,000,000 per year
Physician wRVUs	8,000 wRVUs	8,000 wRVUs
	(~33rd percentile)	(~33rd percentile)
Call Coverage	$225,000 per year	$225,000 per year
(90 shifts per year)	($2,500 per 24-hour shift)	($2,500 per 24-hour shift)
Administrative Services	$78,000 per year	$78,000 per year
(240 hours per year)	(240 hours x $325 per hour = $78,000)	(240 hours x $325 per hour = $78,000)
Total Physician Compensation	$803,000 per year	$1,303,000 per year
	(~33rd percentile)	(~79th percentile)
Medical Group Management Association Benchmarking & Ratio Analysis		
	Physician A (Low Base)	Physician B (High Base)
Base Compensation per wRVU	$71.43 per wRVU	$125.00 per wRVU
	(~40th percentile)	(~80th percentile)
Total Compensation per wRVU	$100.37 per wRVU	$162.88 per wRVU
	(~60th percentile)	(greater than 90th percentile)

This table demonstrates how Physician B's high base guarantee carries the greatest financial risk to the employer given the physician's production at the 33rd percentile wRVU level. While total compensation for Physician B falls at the 79th percentile, the effective wRVU conversion rate of $162.88 per wRVU falls well above the 90th percentile. This is a function of the multiple earning streams coupled with the low wRVUs produced relative to the high base guarantee. The low wRVU production also translates into lower overall collections for the physician, thereby potentially creating a net loss for the employer given the discrepancy between the physician's low production level when compared to the high base guarantee.

Production-Based Models Not Considering Physician Production Levels

Production-based compensation models are typically structured around a wRVU conversion rate. While there are still employment agreements that contain compensation terms based on a percent of net professional collections, the majority reflect a wRVU conversion rate. As such, this discussion uses the wRVU conversion rate. However, the same principles apply when setting compensation terms based on a compensation-to-professional collections ratio.

The wRVU conversion rate is then multiplied by the physician's annual wRVUs to derive the physician's annual compensation. Here's an example:

Annual wRVUs		Conversion Rate		Total Compensation
10,000 wRVUs	x	$48 per wRVU	=	$480,000

While, on the surface, production-based compensation models carry less risk of exposure than base guarantee models, setting the wRVU conversion rate requires an understanding of the benchmark surveys and the inverse relationship between conversion rate and physician productivity. While compensation goes up with greater wRVU productivity, the physician's conversion rate goes down. This is counterintuitive and presents challenges in structuring compensation models for highly productive physicians.

The inclination is to set the wRVU conversion rate higher for higher-producing physicians. Upon closer review of the benchmark data, it is more complex, and on the whole, the opposite is true. The Medical Group Management Association (MGMA) has illustrated this inverse relationship across all specialties.[35]

Table 2 illustrates the MGMA survey data for total compensation, wRVUs, and compensation to wRVU ratios for family medicine physicians. It is important to note that each metric (i.e., compensation, wRVUs, and compensation to wRVU) at each quartile are not directly related to each other and do not reflect the metrics from the same physician cohort. This can be illustrated when comparing the calculated wRVU conversion rate with the survey reported conversion rate.

Table 2: MGMA Survey Data for Family Medicine Physicians

Percentiles	25th Percentile	50th Percentile	75th Percentile	90th Percentile
Compensation	$216,839	$254,665	$306,817	$376,509
Physician wRVU	4,027	4,936	5,947	7,237
Calculated Conversion Rate	$53.85	$51.59	$51.59	$52.03
Survey Conversion Rate	$46.11	$51.70	$60.58	$75.43
Variance in Rates	$7.74	($0.11)	($8.99)	($23.40)

As can be seen in Table 2, calculated conversion rates differ significantly at each quartile except for the 50th percentile. This does not reflect the appropriate rate, but only speaks to the fact that the metrics at each percentile are not related.

As a result, if compensation per wRVU is set at the 75th percentile for a physician who produces at the 75th percentile in terms of wRVUs, the total compensation would potentially be out of FMV range and, therefore, out of compliance. **Figure 1** illustrates this issue another way. Unlike Table 2, Figure 1 illustrates the compensation and wRVU conversion rate for the same physician cohort at the same wRVU production percentile. This shows the inverse relationship between production and wRVU conversion rate.

**Figure 1: MGMA 2020 Compensation and wRVU
Conversion Rate by Production Level –Family Medicine[36]**

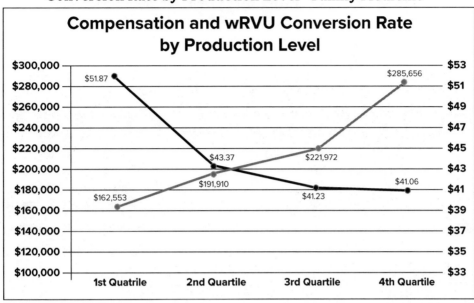

Figure 1 shows that compensation increased from $162,553 in the 1st Quartile to $285,656 in the 4th Quartile. The increase did not correspond directly to wRVU production since the compensation per wRVU ratio decreased from $51.87 to $41.06 between the quartiles. Therefore, a family physician producing at the 75th percentile should have a wRVU conversion rate closer to $41 per wRVU than the reported 75th percentile of $61 per wRVU.

Stacking Compensation Analysis Fails to Consider Each Compensatory Term in Isolation, as Well as Collectively

Stacking compensation is compensation derived from multiple earning streams that can be added to each other and ultimately paid to the physician performing each of the services. Multiple earning streams include, but are not limited to, clinical services, medical directorships, emergency call coverage, graduate medical education, research, and/or APP supervision. While it is common for physicians to provide multiple services, a potential pitfall to such an agreement that adds compensation from each service is to not evaluate each compensation term in isolation as well as collectively. For example, the value of a system-wide medical directorship is most likely valued at a different rate than for medical student preceptorship services. The opportunity cost, skill set required, and time spent can vary dramatically across these separate services and therefore impact the compensation for that specific earning stream accordingly.[37]

Many employers will look to national surveys for benchmarking purposes to provide internal support for a physician's compensation. In doing so, it is also important to understand the surveys and what exactly is being reported as compensation. For example, the MGMA *Provider Compensation* defines total compensation to include "salary, [on-call compensation,] bonus and/or incentive payments, research stipends, honoraria, and distribution of profits."[38] In this case, it would not be appropriate to compare clinical earnings only to the total compensation reported by MGMA. The more accurate comparison would be to use the sum of all forms of compensation from each of the separate earning streams.

Lastly, it is important to note that the overall compensation terms (including each earning stream) must comply with the Stark Law and take into consideration whether it falls under any exceptions and/or safe harbors.[39]

Value-Based Compensation Arrangements

Value-based compensation arrangements are becoming increasingly more popular with health systems as compensation models shift from volume to value of care. These models involve the health system sharing the financial risk and reward with physician groups based on cost control and/or quality metrics. As a result, providers are encouraged to form collaborative partnerships with other providers to ensure that quality and cost-effective care are provided. Examples of these programs included physician value-based modifiers (PVBM), merit-based incentive payment system (MIPS), hospital value-based purchasing program (HVBP), and alternative payment methods (APMs).

Compliance risks currently lie with issues surrounding utilization of services, calculation of quality metrics, potential patient inducement, and risk scores affected by coding practices. Given the shared financial risks under these compensation models, health systems need to keep an eye on appropriate utilization of services by physicians. Compensation should be reward based on standard of care and not solely on cost. Otherwise there is a compliance risk for underutilization. Second, determining the quality metrics and ensuring accurate tracking of those metrics are critical to be certain that physicians are not compensated for metrics not achieved. Third, this compensation model needs to qualify for exceptions/safe harbors under Stark and AKS. This is expected to become easier with the proposed regulatory changes. Last, risk scores for each physician will need to be monitored to ensure that they are accurately reflecting the acuity level and case mix of the patients being seen. In total, the physician compensation under these models needs to align with the actual benefit being provided by the physician services. Health systems will need to evaluate the compensation terms under a different framework than they have historically used for fee-for-service models.

Potential Undue Benefit Provided to Physician Groups by APPs as "Physician Extenders"

APPs are increasing in numbers across the US healthcare system. They work across the spectrum of healthcare settings and have found roles in nearly all medical and surgical specialties. As a result of working alongside both hospital-employed and self-employed physicians, they pose a potential compliance risk if the compensation model does not consider their impact.

APPs are most often hired by health systems in order to extend the services of a practice and/or physician. The physician compensation model should consider the extent to which the APP increases their work capacity. For example, **Table 3** illustrates two orthopaedic physicians in a health system that produce 12,000 wRVUs annually; however, one has an APP and uses that person concurrently for taking patient histories, ordering X-rays, performing procedures, and documenting visits. Under this scenario, the APP is not generating wRVUs, but instead their work product is being captured under the physician's total wRVUs. The APP is also being used for post-op follow-up visits where the total wRVUs for the surgery (inclusive of post-op visits during the global period) performed by the physician are being credited to the physician.

Table 3: Physician Compensation Impact Associated with APP Use

	Physician A	Physician B
	Orthopaedic Surgeon with 1 Full-Time Equivalent APP	Orthopaedic Surgeon
Physician wRVUs	12,000 wRVUs	12,000 wRVUs
APP wRVUs	200 wRVUs	n/a
Total Provider wRVUs	**12,200 wRVUs**	**12,000 wRVUs**
Physician compensation	$700,000 per year	$700,000 per year
APP compensation	$130,000 per year	n/a
Total Provider Compensation	**$830,000 per year**	**$700,000 per year**
Total Provider Compensation to wRVU	$68.03 per wRVU	$58.33 per wRVU
APP value differential in wRVU conversion rates = $10 per wRVU		

Side by side, each physician generates the same number of wRVUs; however, Physician A uses an APP and receives the incremental value from that person's work. The use of a hospital-employed APP's professional services to extend physician capacity and the corresponding incremental value provided to the physician or practice needs to be considered when determining the compensation term under a physician employment agreement or a practice foundation model.

Addressing Compliance Risks

Mitigating compliance risk is at the core of any health system's compliance program, and consistency and documentation are the tools to do so. First, establishing and applying protocols for physician compensation model design and contract review are required. Maintaining consistency in this process increases inter-rater as well as intra-rater reliability and thereby increases the validity of the results. Secondly, appropriate and effective documentation is critical and serves as one of the key principles in assuring compliance. The information that is recorded should be precise, factual, comprehensive, and contemporaneous to enhance the validity of the document. Documentation serves as a road map, bringing to life for the reader that which transpired or one's intent in performing an action. If the record is incomplete or inadequate, the health systems' exposure to compliance risk increases exponentially and compromises any future compliance audits. For the purposes of illustrating strategies for physician compensation models, this section addresses each of the common compliance risks identified.

Identify the Specific Requirements for Compensation in the Compensation Model

Terms within an agreement should clearly state the requirements specific to each compensatory item. In addition to stipulating the requirements, compliance teams need to maintain consistency in documentation to support fulfillment of the requirements. For example, criteria for support of hours worked may include time sheets, clinic schedules, and/or meeting minutes. Health systems should maintain a process by which they validate these documents and ensure uniform application of the process. The more assumptions used in support of compensation terms, the more systems will have to defend in the future.

Reconcile Earnings Streams against Annual Base Guarantee

An alternative to stacking multiple earning streams on top of a base guarantee would be to reconcile these earning streams against the base guarantee. Reconciling the multiple earning streams can be a way for employers to satisfy the physician's desire for a higher base guarantee while minimizing risk associated with lower-than-expected production levels. **Table 4** illustrates the two options.

Table 4: Stacked Compensation Terms Versus Reconciled Against the Base Guarantee

	Option A – Stacked		Calculation
Proposed Base Guarantee	$1,000,000 per year	A	$1,000,000
	(~56th percentile)		
Physician wRVUs Bonus	8,000 wRVUs per year	B	$0
($90 per wRVU in excess of 12,500)	~33rdpercentile)		
Call Coverage	$225,000 per year	C	$225,000
(90 shifts per year)	($2,500 per 24-hour shift)		
Administrative Services ($325 per hour)	$78,000 per year	D	$78,000
	(240 hrs x $320/hr = $78,000)		
Quality Performance	$80,000 per year	E	$80,000
Advanced Practice Provider Supervision	$18,000 per year	F	$18,000
Research Services	$40,000 per year	G	$40,000
Total Annual Physician Compensation **(A+B+C+D+E+F+G)**			**$1,441,000 (~90th percentile)**

Table 4: Stacked Compensation Terms Versus Reconciled Against the Base Guarantee (cont.)

	Option B – Reconciled		Calculation
Proposed Base Guarantee	$1,000,000 per year	A	$0
	(~56th percentile)		
Physician wRVUs Bonus	8,000 wRVUs per year	B	$720,000
($90 per wRVU)	(~33rd percentile)		
Call Coverage	$225,000 per year	C	$225,000
(90 shifts per year)	($2,500 per 24–hour shift)		
Administrative Services ($325 per hour)	$78,000 per year	D	$78,000
	(240 hrs x $320/hr = $78,000)		
Quality Performance	$80,000 per year	E	$80,000
Advanced Practice Provider Supervision	$18,000 per year	F	$18,000
Research Services	$40,000 per year	G	$40,000
Total Annual Physician Compensation (Greater of A or sum of B+C+D+E+F+G)			**$1,161,000 (~75th percentile)**

As can be seen through this analysis, the total compensation can vary significantly depending on whether additional earning streams are stacked or reconciled against the base guarantee. When reviewing the resultant total compensation ratios, the stacked version carries the greatest risk of being outside of compliance. Compensation per wRVU ratios benchmark much higher in Option A when compared to Option B where all earning streams are reconciled against the base. Under the stacking method (Option A), compliance risk decreases as wRVU production increases to the level that supports the base guarantee. In other words, the physician needs to produce enough wRVUs to support their base guarantee before they can be compensated for additional services (i.e., call compensation) in excess of the base guarantee.

Balance between "Comp: wRVU" or "Comp: Collection Ratios and Level of Production"

A one-size-fits-all approach does not work when assigning a wRVU conversion rate to physicians within their compensation models. As can be seen in Figure 1, while compensation goes up commensurate with production, there exists an inverse relationship between wRVU conversion rates and level of wRVU production. Fortunately, MGMA provides plenty of data by specialty that can help guide you in your discussions with physicians.

As a guide in determining the wRVU conversion rate for various compensation arrangements, it is recommended that compliance teams focus on establishing the appropriate total clinical compensation and not the wRVU conversion rate. The conversion rate does not drive the process but is actually a by-product of the total clinical compensation along with the level of physician production. In general, total clinical compensation will fall at a level that is 10 to 20 percentile points below where their wRVU production falls. In addition, caution should be taken when using median wRVU conversion rates for all physicians at all production levels. As illustrated in Figure 1, physicians who produce above the median will more than likely have FMV-compliant wRVU conversion rates that fall below the median.

Objectively Measure Value-Based Compensation Models

Compliance teams should focus on the following to ensure value-based compensation models are compliant:

- Value-based compensation models should focus on demonstrating that the compensation amount is within FMV, commercially reasonable, and does not take into account referrals. However, the changes to Stark and AKS reduce the regulatory hurdles associated with these arrangements.
- It is also critical for the compensation model to align with physician incentives to provide quality patient care and not to reduce medically necessary services. Safeguards need to be put in place to ensure that medical care be driven by evidenced-based practices.
- All quality metrics, along with their benchmarks, need to be separately identified and reviewed against peer physician data to appropriately measure physician performance.
- In terms of cost savings, compensation models should be based on specific cost-saving targets and administered by a third party whose compensation is not affected by the incentive compensation.
- Risk adjustments based on patient acuity mix needs to be monitored to avoid an overstatement in risk.
- Compliance risk is reduced if these programs have annual maximum compensation amounts stipulated in the agreements.
- Total compensation inclusive of all value-based compensation models needs to be within FMV and should be viewed in isolation as well as collectively with all forms of earning streams.

APP Incremental Value to Physicians and Practices Needs to be Considered

To ensure that physician compensation terms remain within FMV, health systems need to consider the incremental value created by APP professional services. Two of these options are to make an adjustment to the wRVUs credited to physicians using APPs or make an adjustment to their wRVU conversion rate. The two options discussed are meant as examples of how APP services may affect the value of physician compensation. The calculations are meant solely to illustrate an indication value for the APPs; they do not represent the complexity of the analyses needed to be performed before deriving the FMV compensation range on a specific physician's agreement.

First, the health system should estimate the incremental wRVUs associated with the APP professional services performed. For instance, if the APP extended a physician's capacity by approximately 2,000 wRVUs, then the physician's total wRVUs could be adjusted by these incremental wRVUs.

Second, determining the FMV wRVU conversion rate for each physician is complex and a function of many factors. One factor pertains to the workload generated by the physician. Health systems need to reflect the APP value differential when physicians use APPs in generating total wRVUs. If the eligible wRVUs are not being reduced, then an adjustment can be made to the wRVU conversion rate. As a result, the wRVU conversion rate for physicians using APPs may be adjusted lower to reflect the extent to which the APP increased their work capacity.

Possible Penalties

Physicians and practices enter these contracts at their own risk. For instance, the Stark Law is a strict liability statute that does not require intent by the physician or health system to result in a violation. In addition, the criminal and civil penalties under AKS and Stark, respectively, cannot be understated. Violations under Stark and AKS may result in civil monetary penalties, exclusion from federal healthcare programs, False Claims Act liability, nonpayment for services, and refunds to beneficiaries.[40] Under AKS, the violation may also result in a criminal felony subject to imprisonment.[41]

Stark Law

Penalties for violating the Stark Law can include:

- Denial of payment
- Refund of payment
- Civil monetary penalty of $15,000 per claim
- Civil monetary penalty of $100,000 for each arrangement considered to be a circumvention scheme
- Exclusion from federal healthcare programs

Anti-Kickback Statute

Penalties for violating AKS can include:

- Conviction of a felony

- Fines up to $100,000 and/or imprisonment of up to 10 years
- Civil monetary penalty of up to $100,000 for each violation
- Exclusion from federal healthcare programs

False Claims Act

Penalties for violating FCA can include:

- Civil monetary penalties per claim of between $11,665 and $23,331
- Three times the government's actual damages

Penalties can escalate and be compounded from violating each of the laws above. This can be illustrated by the case of *United States v. Rogan,* which was also upheld on appeal in 2008.[42] Referrals between two physicians resulted in violations to Stark, AKS, and FCA. The total value of the claims submitted were $16,864,677.50. Under FCA, this calculated to a penalty of $50,594,032.50, three times the actual government damages. Under civil penalties of $7,500 per claim, the total penalty amounted to $13,665,000 (1,822 claims). Total fines for this case amounted to $64,259,032.50.

Compliance Resources

Business Valuation Resources LLC

Business Valuation Resources provides resources and training for valuation professionals through market research, data analytics, and thought leadership. It provides guides, books, and training services on compensation and business valuation topics.

https://www.bvresources.com/

Centers for Medicare & Medicaid Services

Regulations & Guidance
CMS is a part of HHS and governs the Medicare and Medicaid programs as well as oversees a variety of federal programs. The CMS website includes a section for regulations and guidance pertaining to these federal programs.

https://www.cms.gov/Regulations-and-Guidance/Regulations-and-Guidance

**Frank Cohen, *RVUs: Applications for Medical Practice Success*
(Englewood: Medical Group Management Association, 2013)**

This MGMA book focuses on applying RVUs in medical practices and includes examples, calculations, and spreadsheets.

Department of Justice

Office of Public Affairs
The Department of Justice Office of Public Affairs publishes news releases on fraud and abuse cases along with Stark and AKS violations.

https://www.justice.gov/news

Department of Health & Human Services, Office of Inspector General

Compliance Resource Portal
This source of educational materials is meant to inform health systems and providers about compliance, fraud and abuse, and the various regulations that must be navigated.

https://oig.hhs.gov/compliance/compliance-resource-portal/

A Roadmap for New Physicians: Avoiding Medicare and Medicaid Fraud and Abuse
This booklet is useful for physician self-study.

https://oig.hhs.gov/compliance/physician-education/roadmap_web_version.pdf

Charles B. Oppenheim et al., *The Stark Law: Comprehensive Analysis and Practical Guide* (Washington, DC: American Health Law Association, 2014)

This book offers in-depth analysis of the Stark Law, including fair market value assessments and time-share agreements.

Risk Takeaways

Main points of interest:

- Physician compensation models are becoming more prevalent with increasing integration, and they are more complex.
- Having a firm understanding of the various models and their implications on compliance will be key to minimizing risk exposure.
- One size does not fit all when it comes to physician compensation agreements.
- Coordinated care models and value-based compensation will be more commonplace in the near future with the changes to Stark and AKS.
- The potential penalties for not establishing compliant physician compensation models are often significant.

Areas to watch:

- Changes to the Stark Law and AKS as a result of the regulatory sprint to coordinated care
- Value-based compensation arrangements
- Increasing numbers of employed physicians
- Use of APPs

Laws that apply:

- Stark Law, 42 U.S.C. § 1395nn
- Anti-Kickback Statute, 42 U.S.C. § 1320a-7b(b)
- False Claims Act, 31 U.S.C. §§ 3729-3733
- Anti-trust laws (California is proposing a law to regulate acquisitions and require state approval to avoid anti-competitive behavior)[43]
- A variety of federal and state statutes
- Government agencies (Internal Revenue Service, CMS, etc.)

Addressing compliance risks:

- Consistently apply protocols and produce consistent documentation to increase the validity of the evaluation of the models and resulting financial arrangements.
- Use compensation models with appropriate risk-mitigating terms to spread financial and compliance risk.
- Ensure appropriate utilization of benchmark survey data when determining compensation, and obtain outside legal/financial assistance when needed.

Endnotes

1. **Joe Aguilar** is partner at HMS Valuation Partners. He brings more than 25 years of extensive clinical and healthcare management experience to his practice as a healthcare valuator and nurse practitioner. As a valuator, Aguilar specializes in providing fair market valuation opinions and client advisory services for unique and complex compensation transactions to ensure compliance for various clients, including healthcare systems, hospitals, law firms, and private equity firms.

2. Medicare Program; Modernizing and Clarifying the Physician Self-Referral Regulations, 85 Fed. Reg. 77,492 (December 2, 2020).

3. "Code List for Certain Designated Health Services (DHS)," Centers for Medicare & Medicaid Services, updated February 6, 2020, https://www.cms.gov/Medicare/Fraud-and-Abuse/PhysicianSelfReferral/List_of_Codes.

4. 42 C.F.R. § 411.357.

5. 42 U.S.C. § 1320a-7b(b).

6. U.S. Department of Health & Human Services, Office of the Inspector General, "Federal Anti-Kickback Law and Regulatory Safe Harbors," fact sheet, November 1999, https://oig.hhs.gov/fraud/docs/safeharborregulations/safefs.htm.

7. U.S. Department of Justice, The False Claims Act: A Primer, accessed November 4, 2020, https://www.justice.gov/sites/default/files/civil/legacy/2011/04/22/C-FRAUDS_FCA_Primer.pdf; 31 U.S.C. §§ 3729–3733.

8. 31 U.S.C. §§ 3729–3733.

9. 31 U.S.C. § 3729(a)(1).

10. 31 U.S.C. §§ 3729–3733.

11. 15 U.S.C. §§ 1–38.

12. 15 U.S.C. § 41.

13. Jeff Lagasse, "Healthcare mergers and acquisitions continue to be active, with a positive outlook for the future," *Healthcare Finance*, February 11, 2020, https://www.healthcarefinancenews.com/news/healthcare-mergers-and-acquisitions-continue-be-active-positive-outlook-future.

14. Lydia Coutré, "After pandemic-induced delays, healthcare deals should speed up," *Modern Healthcare*, June 22, 2020, https://www.modernhealthcare.com/mergers-acquisitions/after-pandemic-induced-delays-healthcare-deals-should-speed-up.

15. U.S. Department of Health & Human Services, "HHS seeks public input on improving care coordination and reducing the regulatory burdens of the HIPAA Rules," news release, December 12, 2018, https://www.hhs.gov/about/news/2018/12/12/hhs-seeks-public-input-improving-care-coordination-and-reducing-regulatory-burdens-hipaa-rules.html.

16. 42 C.F.R. § 411.351.

17. 42 C.F.R. § 1001.952(ee)(14).

18. 42 C.F.R. § 411.357(aa)(1)

19. 42 C.F.R. § 411.357(aa)(2)

20. 42 C.F.R. § 411.357(aa)(3)

21. 42 C.F.R. § 411.354.

22. 42 C.F.R. § 411.352(i)(3).

23. 42 C.F.R. § 1001.952(gg).

24. 42 C.F.R. § 1001.952(ff).

25. 42 C.F.R. § 1001.952(ee).

26. 42 C.F.R. § 1001.952(hh).

27. 42 C.F.R. § 1001.952(d).

28. 42 C.F.R. § 1001.952(d)(2).

29. 42 C.F.R. §1001.952(ii).

30. 42 C.F.R. § 411.351.

31. 42 C.F.R. § 411.351.

32. 42 C.F.R. § 411.354(d)(5).

33. 42 C.F.R. § 411.354(d)(6).

34. "Introduction to Relative Value Units and How Medicare Reimbursement in Calculated," State of Alaska Department of Labor and Workforce Development, accessed February 19, 2021, https://labor.alaska.gov/wc/med-serv-comm/CMS_RVU_Calculations.pdf.

35. Timothy Smith, "Physician practice losses: Red ink from the misuse and abuse of physician compensation survey data," *MGMA Insight*, January 24, 2019, https://www.mgma.com/resources/financial-management/physician-practice-losses-red-ink-from-the-misuse.

36. Medical Group Management Association, *2020 MGMA DataDive Provider Compensation Survey*, 2020.

37. Timothy Smith and Mark O. Dietrich, *BVR/AHLA Guide to Valuing Physician Compensation and Healthcare Service Arrangements:Second Edition*, October 2017.

38. Medical Group Management Association, *2019 MGMA DataDive Provider Compensation*, 3, https://www.mgma.com/data/benchmarking-data/provider-compensation-data?utm_campaign=data&utm_medium=cpc&utm_source=ppc-data-providercomp-dm-ng&gclid=Cj0KCQiAst2BBhDJARIsAGo2ldXXbHJc6Uqg9oxwV8MIWPIXe8mMEZ8Cehs0Rq4KcsqajYcPCToMDq4aAqn0EALw_wcB.

39. 42 C.F.R. § 411.

40. Andrea L. Treese Berlin, "Fraud and Abuse Statutes, Administrative Authorities, and Self-Disclosures," U.S. Department of Health & Human Services Office of Inspector General, accessed February 19, 2021, https://oig.hhs.gov/reports-and-publications/featured-topics/ihs/resources/Fraud%20and%20Abuse%20Statutes,%20Administrative%20Authorities,%20and%20Self-Disclosures.pdf.

41. "Comparison of the Anti-Kickback Statute and Stark Law," U.S. Department of Health & Human Services Office of Inspector General, accessed February 19, 2021,https://oig.hhs.gov/compliance/provider-compliance-training/files/StarkandAKSChartHandout508.pdf.

42. United States of America v. Peter Rogan, 459 F. Supp. 2d 692 (2006) (517 F.3d 449 (7th Cir.)), https://www.courtlistener.com/opinion/2420537/united-states-v-rogan/.

43. Health care system consolidation: Attorney General approval and enforcement, S.B. 977 (Cali. 2020).

Managing Relationships and Conflicts of Interest

By Joe Aguilar,[1] MBA, MPH, MSN, CVA

What Are Physician Relationships and Conflicts of Interest?

Physicians establish a variety of financial relationships with their employers, health systems, ancillary services, insurance companies, medical technology firms, and other entities. These relationships can occur with employed physicians as well as with physician-owners in private practice. Some of these arrangements include direct and/or indirect compensation to the physician. Some of the direct methods may include compensation through speaking/consulting fees, supplies or services, business-related travel, meal expenses, research payments, and/or royalty agreements, while some of the indirect means occur based on the physician's position and influence to sway purchasing decisions to entities where they and/or family members have a financial interest.

While these arrangements, as well as physicians having decision-making power, are commonplace, they carry a risk for a potential conflict of interest. A conflict of interest occurs when a physician puts his/her interest, financial or otherwise, above the interest of the health system, medical staff colleagues, or patients. These conflicts arise often in the areas of daily practice, research, graduate medical education, etc. Given the numerous regulations and severe penalties for engaging in activities that result in conflicts of interest, it is critical for health systems to manage these relationships to ensure compliance.

Risk Area Governance

Physician relationships and potential conflicts of interest are highly regulated by federal law, a variety of state-specific fraud and abuse statutes, and government agencies. The activities and transactions of most physicians in private practice and those employed by health systems are impacted by these regulations. The primary laws governing physician relationships include the Physician Payments Sunshine Act (PPSA), the Stark Law, the Anti-Kickback Statute (AKS), the False Claims Act (FCA), and a variety of government agencies.

Physician Payments Sunshine Act, 42 U.S.C. § 1320a-7h

PPSA was enacted in 2010 with the Affordable Care Act and requires medical manufacturing companies to disclose to the Centers for Medicare & Medicaid (CMS) any payments or "transfer of value" made between them and physicians or academic medical systems.[2,3] The transfer of value is categorized based on the following:

- Meals, travel, or consulting fees
- Research payments
- Personal or family member ownership interest in the manufacturing company

Maximum payments allowed without reporting can be up to $10 per item or $100 per year in total.

Stark Law (Physician Self-Referral Law), 42 U.S.C. § 1395nn

The Stark Law has undergone several phases to its rules, regulations, and exceptions since its introduction; however, at its core, the law "prohibits a physician from making referrals for certain designated health services payable by Medicare to an entity with which he or she (or an immediate family member) has a financial relationship, unless an exception applies; and prohibits the entity from filing claims with Medicare (or billing another individual, entity, or third party payer) for those referred services."[4,5]

Table 1. Designated Health Service[6]
■ Clinical laboratory services
■ Physical therapy, occupational therapy, and outpatient speech-language pathology services
■ Radiology and certain other imaging services
■ Radiation therapy services and supplies
■ Durable medical equipment and supplies
■ Parenteral and enteral nutrients, equipment, and supplies
■ Prosthetics, orthotics, and prosthetic devices and supplies

Table 1. Designated Health Service[6]
▪ Home health services
▪ Outpatient prescription drugs
▪ Inpatient and outpatient hospital services

In limited circumstances, the Stark Law does allow for certain exceptions. All exceptions must still comply with CMS, the AKS, and any other applicable federal and state regulations. Exceptions are noted for specific healthcare services as well as specific healthcare entities, such as academic medical centers (AMCs), ambulatory surgery centers (ASCs), and federally qualified health centers (FQHCs). The most notable exceptions to the law include the following:

- Employment relationships
- In-office ancillary services
- Group practice arrangements
- Fair market value exception
- Physician services
- Provider recruitment
- Risk sharing agreements
- Equipment and space leases
- Indirect compensation arrangements
- Nonmonetary exception[7]

Anti-Kickback Statute, 42 U.S.C. § 1320a-7b

The AKS is a federal fraud and abuse law that prevents those who knowingly and willfully offer, pay, solicit, or receive remuneration in order to induce business payable by Medicare and Medicaid unless certain safe harbors are satisfied.[8] The AKS applies to all persons on all healthcare services, not solely physicians or hospitals. The intent of the law is to prevent over-utilization of services through prohibiting incentive compensation to induce referrals.

In limited circumstances, the AKS does allow for certain safe harbors. All safe harbors must still comply with CMS, the Stark Law, and any other applicable federal and state regulations. The most notable safe harbors to the law include the following:

- Bona fide employment relationships
- Personal services arrangements
- Group purchasing organizations
- Referral services
- Fair market value exception[9]

False Claims Act, 31 U.S.C. §§ 3729-3733

The FCA was first enacted in 1863 as a result of contractors/suppliers defrauding the US government during the US Civil War.[10] The law states that "any person who knowingly presents . . . a false or fraudulent claim for payment . . . or knowingly makes . . . a false record or statement material to a false or fraudulent claim, . . . is liable to the U.S. government for a civil penalty."[11] Claims made against Medicare, Medicaid, and various other federal and state health insurance plans may potentially fall under the FCA.

Examples of common fraud and abuse behaviors that fall under the FCA include but are not limited to the following:

- Kickbacks
- Services not rendered
- Lack of medical necessity
- Coding irregularities (upcoding or unbundling)

Government Agencies

Many federal and state government agencies provide regulatory oversight to physicians and health systems. These include the CMS, accrediting agencies, the Office of Civil Rights, the Federal Trade Commission, the Internal Revenue Service, and various state-level agencies, medical boards, and courts. In addition, health systems conducting research need to maintain compliance with respect to the funding source (i.e., National Institutes of Health (NIH)).[12]

Common Compliance Risks

Physicians and advanced practice providers (APPs) practice in the context of providing the highest-quality care to patients, securing necessary supplies and durable medical equipment, meeting the requirements of payors for reimbursement, as well as ensuring the financial viability of their practices (whether as an owner or an employee of a health system). A conflict of interest can occur at any of these intersections, as shown by these common examples.

Conflicts of Interest in Patient Care/Payors

- Disproportionately prescribing specific medications and/or utilizing specific supplies or durable medical equipment from vendors in which the provider has a financial interest or has received certain benefits.
- Medical care decision-making affected by the physician's financial interest in terms of compensation in the context of risk sharing arrangements.
- Engaging in activities for personal benefit that detracts from one's ability to perform their required duties to the health system.

Conflicts of Interest with Vendors/Health System

- Using the health system or practice resources for personal gain.
- A physician exercising any form of influence over practice or hospital purchasing decisions for equipment, technology, supplies, or services from entities that they or a family member have a financial interest.
- Disclosing private health system, practice, and/or patient information for financial gain.
- Maintaining a financial interest in an entity that does business with the health system.
- Accepting money, gifts, and/or other benefits from vendors to the health systems.

Addressing Compliance Risks

In order to address the potential compliance risk associated with the conflicts of interest that may arise out of various provider relationships, health systems will need to establish a clear policy of conflict-of-interest disclosure as well as an institutional culture of compliance. Here are some key strategies to address the compliance risks.

Establish a Culture of Compliance

- Clearly define the policy regarding conflicts of interest. The policy should be written and actively managed/updated as needed by an appointed member or committee from the compliance team.
- Health system leaders and key provider stakeholders need to embrace this culture and set the tone.
- Create a set of standards through the policy and apply procedures consistently across all providers.
- Emphasize that a successful culture of compliance is not punitive, but one centered around disclosure.
- Include contractual representation regarding conflicts of interest in physician agreements.

Provide Routine Training and Guidance to Physicians and Nonphysician Staff

- Mandatory compliance training should be provided to all incoming physicians and nonphysician staff. Annual trainings should also continue to reinforce compliance.
- Document training in employees' records.
- Guide providers in ways to foster collaboration with industry and other outside entities for research and patient care while also maintaining compliance.

Proper Documentation

- Distribute an annual disclosure questionnaire to document any potential conflicts of interest. Potential conflicts are best obtained through a questionnaire geared toward making physicians, APPs, and other key health system figures contemplate their financial relationships.
- Establish a procedure for addressing and documenting situational conflicts that may arise.
- Monitor and assess for potential prescribing patterns and/or disproportionate durable medical equipment (DME) use.

Reporting

- Establish an open-door policy for reporting potential conflicts.
- Investigate leads from different sources and evaluate each circumstance thoroughly and consistently.
- Perform routine audits and establish policies for monitoring procurements for potential conflicts of interest.
- Address disclosures at any time the need arises—not just at the annual review. These could be incidental situations, project related, or third-party disclosures.
- Establish a compliance hotline voicemail for third-party disclosures.

Possible Penalties

Physicians and practices enter into arrangements that may result in a conflict of interest at their own risk. For instance, the Stark Law is a strict liability statute that does not require intent by the physician or health system to result in a violation. In addition, the criminal and civil penalties under Stark and the AKS, respectively, cannot be understated. Violations under Stark and the AKS may result in civil monetary penalties, exclusion from programs, FCA liability, nonpayment for services, and refunds to beneficiaries.[13] Under the AKS, the violation may also result in a criminal felony subject to imprisonment.[14] The following penalties are geared more toward physician, practices, and health systems.

Stark Law

Penalties for violating the Stark Law can include the following:

- Denial of payment
- Refund of payment
- Civil monetary penalty of $15,000 per claim
- Civil monetary penalty of $100,000 for each arrangement considered to be a circumvention scheme
- Exclusion from federal healthcare programs

Anti-Kickback Statute

Penalties for violating the AKS can include the following:

- Conviction of a felony
- Fines up to $100,000 and/or imprisonment of up to 10 years
- Civil monetary penalty of up to $100,000 for each violation
- Exclusion from federal healthcare programs

False Claims Act

Penalties for violating the FCA can include the following:

- Civil monetary penalties per claim of between $10,000 and $20,000
- Three times the government's actual damages

Physician Payments Sunshine Act

The penalties under PPSA are more for medical manufactures and other purchasing/distributor companies. Penalties paid by those medical manufacturing and other entities for failing to report payments and thereby, violating PPSA can include the following:

- Unreported payments: $1,000–$10,000 per unreported payment, up to a maximum of $150,000 per year
- Deliberate failure to report payments: $10,000–$100,000 per unreported payment, up to a maximum of $1,000,000 per year

Compliance Resources

American Medical Association

- The American Medical Association (AMA) code of ethics can provide some guidance to physicians and other providers: https://www.ama-assn.org/delivering-care/ethics/code-medical-ethics-inter-professional-relationships
- A number of statements regarding the code of ethics as it pertains to patients as well as financing and delivery of care can be found here: https://www.ama-assn.org/delivering-care/ethics

Centers for Medicare & Medicaid Services

Open Payment Database

CMS maintains a database whereby the public may search payments made to health systems and physicians for research studies and nonresearch activity. In addition, the database provides information on the physician's ownership interest in the medical manufacturing, purchasing, or distribution company.

https://openpaymentsdata.cms.gov/

National Institutes of Health

Grants & Funding: Financial Conflict of Interest

The NIH funds a significant amount of medical research in the country. Medical research intersects with a wide range of health systems. In an interest to guide these systems, the NIH has established a policy for financial conflicts of interest.

https://grants.nih.gov/grants/policy/coi/index.htm

Pharmaceutical Research and Manufacturers of America

Code on Interactions with Health Care Professionals

The Pharmaceutical Research and Manufacturers of America (PhRMA) has codes and guidelines for interactions with healthcare professionals.

https://www.phrma.org/Codes-and-guidelines/
Code-on-Interactions-with-Health-Care-Professionals

U.S. Department of Health & Human Services

Office for Human Research Protections

The U.S. Department of Health & Human Services (HHS) provides some guidance with respect to conflict of interest. Specifically, the Office for Human Research Protections speaks to conflict of interest in medical research.

https://www.hhs.gov/ohrp/

Risk Takeaways

Main points of interest:
- Physicians and other providers will encounter conflicts of interest.
- Policies about reporting conflicts of interest need to be established, written, and applied consistently across the organization.
- Money is not the only source of conflict. Benefits bestowed to providers can come in many forms (i.e., receipt of gifts, free dinners, training opportunities, and/or the use of space/services/equipment).

Areas to watch:
- Relationships with pharmaceutical, DME, and other vendors within the health-care industry
- Potential conflicts of interest with value-based care arrangements

Laws that apply:
- Stark Law (Physician Self-Referral Law), 42 U.S.C. § 1395nn
- Anti-Kickback Statute, 42 U.S.C. § 1320a-7b
- False Claims Act, 31 U.S.C. §§ 3729-3733
- Physician Payments Sunshine Act, 42 U.S.C. § 1320a-7h
- Government agencies (CMS, accrediting agencies, OCR, FTC, IRS, various state-level agencies, medical boards, courts, and funding sources)

Addressing compliance risks:
- Disclosure is critical toward managing conflicts of interest.
- The growing number of health systems employing physicians and APPs is increasing the exposure risk. As a result, it is incumbent on health systems to ensure that policies are in place to manage these financial relationships and that a culture of compliance is encouraged.
- Provide routine training and guidance to physicians and nonphysician staff.
- Distribute an annual disclosure questionnaire to document any potential conflicts of interest.
- Establish an open-door policy for reporting potential conflicts.
- With gainsharing arrangements and value-based care, health systems will need to evaluate practice patterns to avoid behaviors that would limit care in an effort to reduce costs.

Endnotes

1. **Joe Aguilar** is partner at HMS Valuation Partners. He brings more than 25 years of extensive clinical and healthcare management experience to his practice as a healthcare valuator and nurse practitioner. As a valuator, Joe specializes in providing fair market valuation opinions and client advisory services for unique and complex compensation transactions to ensure compliance for various clients, including healthcare systems, hospitals, law firms, and private equity firms.

2. Transparency Reports and Reporting of Physician Ownership or Investment Interests, 78 Fed. Reg. 9458 (February 8, 2013).

3. 42 U.S.C. § 1320a-7h.

4. Medicare Program; Modernizing and Clarifying the Physician Self-Referral Regulations, 84 Fed. Reg. 55,766 (October 17, 2019).

5. 42 U.S.C. § 1395nn.

6. "Code List for Certain Designated Health Services (DHS)," Centers for Medicare & Medicaid Services, updated February 6, 2020, https://www.cms.gov/Medicare/Fraud-and-Abuse/PhysicianSelfReferral/List_of_Codes.

7. 42 C.F.R. § 411.

8. 42 U.S.C. § 1320a-7b.

9. Office of Inspector General Office of Public Affairs, "Federal Anti-Kickback Law and Regulatory Safe Harbors," fact sheet, November 1999, https://oig.hhs.gov/fraud/docs/safeharborregulations/safefs.htm.

10. 31 U.S.C. §§ 3729-3733.

11. 31 U.S.C. § 3729.

12. "Introduction to Government Ethics: Without Integrity Nothing Works," National Institutes of Health, accessed March 3, 2021, https://ethics.od.nih.gov/sites/default/files/Training/Ethics-Intro-Handout.pdf.

13. "Fraud and Abuse Statutes, Administrative Authorities, and Self-Disclosures," U.S. Department of Health & Human Services Office of Inspector General, accessed February 1, 2021, https://oig.hhs.gov/reports-and-publications/featured-topics/ihs/resources/Fraud%20and%20Abuse%20Statutes,%20Administrative%20Authorities,%20and%20Self-Disclosures.pdf.

14. "Comparison of the Anti-Kickback Statute and Stark Law," U.S. Department of Health & Human Services Office of Inspector General, accessed February 1, 2021,https://oig.hhs.gov/compliance/provider-compliance-training/files/StarkandAKSChartHandout508.pdf.

Post-Acute Care

Home Health

By Todd Selby[1]; and Elizabeth E. Hogue, Esq.[2]

What Are Home Health Agencies?

Home health agencies (HHAs) provide services in the home of a patient and are covered services under the Medicare program. Many managed care insurance products also cover home health services. State Medicaid programs cover certain types of home health services but at a much lower level of reimbursement. While the premise of providing care in the home of a patient may seem like a simple concept, the Medicare regulations and guidance governing HHAs are complex, which can lead to numerous compliance issues.

Medicare has very specific requirements on how HHAs must be organized, what qualifies as a home health service, and how a patient qualifies for the provision for HHA services. Failure to meet any of these requirements can jeopardize payments made to HHAs under the Medicare program.

Covered Home Health Services

Under Medicare, HHAs are private or public organizations that:

1. Are primarily engaged in providing skilled nursing and other therapeutic services;
2. Have policies established by a group of professional personnel, including one or more physicians and registered nurses, to govern the services provided;
3. Maintain clinical records on all patients;
4. Comply with the licensure laws of states that license HHAs;
5. Have an overall plan and budget in effect; and
6. Meet the HHA Conditions of Participation (CoPs) found at 42 C.F.R. § 484.[3]

Home Health Patient Qualifications and Homebound Status

In order to qualify for home health services under Medicare, the services or items must be provided in a patient's place of residence and be:

1. Part-time or intermittent nursing care provided by or under the supervision of a registered professional nurse
2. Physical or occupational therapy or speech-language pathology services
3. Medical social services under the direction of a physician
4. Part-time or intermittent services of a home health aide who has successfully completed an approved training program
5. Medical supplies, but not drug or other biologicals except for covered osteoporosis drugs
6. Medical services provided by an intern or resident-in-training under a teaching program of the affiliated hospital (if the HHA is affiliated with a hospital)
7. Any of the foregoing items and services that are provided on an outpatient basis, under arrangement made by the HHA, at a hospital or skilled nursing facility, or at a rehabilitation center. The items and services must involve the use of equipment that cannot readily be made available in the patient's home, or that are furnished in a facility while the patient is there to receive any such item or service involving the use of the equipment. Transportation to the facility is not a covered service.[4]

In addition to the qualifying services under Medicare, there are additional qualifications that a patient must meet. These patient qualifications require the patient be:

1. Confined to home.
2. Under the care of a physician or allowed practitioner.
3. Receiving services under a plan of care established and periodically reviewed by a physician or allowed practitioner.
4. Have a continuing need for occupational therapy.[5]

Being confined to home (also called "homebound") in order to qualify for the Medicare home health benefit is not as simple as it might sound. In order to qualify as being confined to home, the patient:

1. Must either be confined to home due to illness or injury and need the aid of supportive devices such as crutches, canes, wheelchairs, and walkers; need the use of special transportation; or need the assistance of another person in order to leave the place of residence; or
2. Have a condition that makes leaving the home medically contraindicated.[6]

If the patient meets one of these two qualifications, the patient must also meet the following two additional criteria. The first criteria is that the patient must have a normal inability to leave the home. The second criteria is that leaving the home must require considerable and taxing effort. Both of these criteria must be met in order for the patient to be considered confined to home.[7] It is also important to note that a patient is not considered confined to home if the patient is residing in a Medicare-certified skilled nursing facility. A patient is considered to be confined to home if the patient is residing in an assisted living facility. While these criteria may seem superficially simple, state and federal regulators often interpret these criteria narrowly or broadly as they see fit. Therefore, it is critical that HHAs have ironclad documentation regarding whether a patient meets the homebound criteria.

The plan of care now may be established, completed, certified, and recertified by an "allowed practitioner" in addition to a physician. Allowed practitioner includes physician assistants, nurse practitioners, or clinical nurse specialists in accordance with state law in the state where the allowed practitioner provides services.[8]

The physician or allowed practitioner must also certify that the patient qualifies for Medicare home health services. The certification must be completed when the Outcome and Assessment Information Set (OASIS) start-of-care assessment is initiated. The physician or allowed practitioner must certify that:

1. "Home health services are or were needed because the patient is or was confined to the home,"
2. "The patient needs or needed skilled nursing services on an intermittent basis . . . or physical therapy, or speech-language pathology services;"
3. "A plan of care has been established and is periodically reviewed by a physician *or allowed practitioner;*"
4. "The services are or were furnished while the patient is or was under the care of a physician *or allowed practitioner;*" and
5. A "face-to-face encounter [performed by the physician or allowed practitioner] occurred no more than 90 days prior to or within 30 days after the start of the home health care." (The face-to-face encounter may now be completed via telehealth.)[9]

The face-to-face encounter is considered a condition of payment under the Medicare program. Being a condition of payment means HHAs must pay close attention to the timing and documentation requirements for completing the face-to-face encounter. Failure to timely complete a face-to-face encounter can lead to significant paybacks for claims filed with a faulty face-to-face encounter.

Medicare reimbursement for HHAs is based on a prospective payment system (PPS). On January 1, 2020, Centers for Medicare & Medicaid Services (CMS) implemented a new PPS for HHAs called the Patient-Driven Groupings Model (PDGM). The goal of PDGM was to eliminate therapy as the driver for HHA reimbursement by creating a case-mix reimbursement methodology. Like other Medicare PPS reimbursement methodologies, another goal of PDGM was to create a value-over-volume model of reimbursement that focuses on the total condition of the patient.

One major shift with the implementation of PDGM was movement from 60-day episodes of care to 30-day periods of care. The 30-day period of care bundles all covered home health services, including medical supplies, and is paid on a reasonable-cost basis.

The care bundled in the 30-day period of care are:

1. Skilled nursing services
2. Home health aide services
3. Physical therapy
4. Speech-language pathology services
5. Occupational therapy services
6. Medical social services[10]

Services excluded from the 30-day period of care include durable medical equipment, certain injectable osteoporosis drugs, and disposable negative pressure wound devices. These services are paid pursuant to a Medicare fee schedule or are subject to consolidated billing.[11] The 30-day payment period is subject to a case-mix adjustment based on the characteristics and needs of the patient.[12]

The first step under PDGM is to establish an admission source for the patient. Under PDGM, each 30-day period is classified as a community or institutional admission source depending on the healthcare setting used by the patient in the 14 days prior to the HHA admission. The timing of the 30-day period is either considered early or late. The first 30-day period is always considered an early admission. All subsequent 30-day periods are considered late unless there is a gap of more than 60 days between the end of one 30-day period of care and the start of another.[13]

PDGM assigns patients to clinical groups based on the principal diagnosis reported for each 30-day period. There are 12 clinical groups that describe the primary reason for the home health encounter. These clinical groups are:

1. Musculoskeletal rehabilitation
2. Neuro/stroke rehabilitation
3. Wounds, post-op wound aftercare, and skin/nonsurgical wound care
4. Behavioral health care
5. Complex nursing interventions
6. Medication management, teaching, and assessment (MMTA) surgical aftercare
7. MMTA cardiac/circulatory
8. MMTA endocrine
9. MMTA infectious disease/neoplasms/blood-forming diseases
10. MMTA gastrointestinal tract and genitourinary system
11. MMTA respiratory
12. MMTA other[14]

Each 30-day period is then assigned to one of 432 case-mix groups based on the clinical groups set forth above.[15] The 30-day period also has a labor adjustment that is based on the wage index of the geographic area in which the patient resides.[16]

PDGM assigns a functional impairment level to the patient of low, medium, or high based on responses to items on the OASIS. These OASIS items include risk for hospitalization, grooming, ability to dress upper body safely, ability to dress lower body safely, bathing, toilet transferring, and ambulation and locomotion. A comorbidity adjustment of none, low, or medium is then factored in based on certain diagnoses reported on home health claims.[17]

Enforcement and Regulation

Critical focus areas for enforcement include fines, satisfying the rigorous operational and care mandates in the federal regulations, detailed billing and claims filing requirements set forth in Medicare manual guidance, and home health eligibility for Medicare beneficiaries. HHAs have also been the target of the U.S. Department of Justice (DOJ) for instances of health-care fraud.

CMS has the responsibility for ensuring compliance with the CoPs through surveys conducted by the state survey agencies. The state survey agencies conduct annual surveys of HHAs at least once every 36 months.[18] The state survey agencies also conduct abbreviated surveys of HHAs when there is a complaint allegation. Federal surveyors have the ability to conduct surveys in order to verify the state survey agencies are following federal survey protocols. Federal surveyors will sometimes assist the state survey agencies if the care at the HHA warrants their assistance.

HHAs must comply with the CoPs found at 42 C.F.R. § 484 and were most recently revised in 2017.[19] The interpretive guidelines to the CoPs are found in "Appendix B" of the CMS *State Operations Manual*.[20] The interpretive guidelines, which interpret the CoPs, are a valuable resource for HHAs. The interpretive guidelines are used by state and/or federal survey-ors when conducting surveys of HHAs. While the interpretive guidelines can be used by state and/or federal surveyors when surveying HHAs, they do not act as a substitute for the CoPs and cannot be used as the sole basis to cite an HHA.

CMS may impose civil money penalties up to $10,000 per day for violations of the CoPs.[21] Other remedies available to CMS are denials of payment for new or all admissions, installing a temporary manager, and directed plans of correction. CMS also has the authority to termi-nate HHAs from the Medicare and/or Medicaid programs in as little as 23 days for an imme-diate jeopardy violation of the CoPs.

In addition to the regulatory authority CMS has over HHAs, many states also license HHAs. States will regulate HHAs pursuant to licensure regulations separate from the CoPs. In some states, the licensure regulations defer to the CoPs or are similar to the CoPs. In other states, the licensure regulations impose requirements that have no connection to the CoPs. HHAs must pay close attention to state licensure regulations. If an HHA loses its state license, it is also automatically terminated from the Medicare and/or Medicaid program.

Recent healthcare fraud schemes involving HHAs have been announced by the DOJ. One DOJ announcement involved a healthcare fraud scheme involving more than $150 million in fraudulent claims.[22] The owner of a home health company orchestrated the fraud by certifying patients as eligible for home health that were not eligible and falsifying medical records in order to cover up the ineligibility.[23] The scheme also provided kickbacks to physicians under the guise of medical director fees to certify patients as eligible for home health.[24]

Another elaborate scheme involved an HHA that employed more than 3,000 home health and personal care aides whereby the HHA would bill for home health aide services that the home health aides claimed to have provided but in reality did not. The DOJ was able to prove that instead of providing home health aide visits, the home health aides in question "stayed home, ran personal errands, vacationed, and socialized with family and friends."[25]

While the vast majority of HHAs provide care in compliance with all state and federal laws, the nature of providing care in the home opens the industry up to healthcare fraud schemes that are not as easy to pull off in other healthcare settings.

The implementation of PDGM has created new compliance issues for HHAs. CMS has committed to closely monitor therapy service use, payment, and quality trends in the course of billing under PDGM. It is extremely important for HHAs to understand that, while therapy is not the reimbursement driver under PDGM (as it was under the prior home health PPS), HHAs are still required to provide all therapy necessary if the resident requires therapy under PDGM. CMS has warned HHAs that "[t]he need for therapy services under PDGM remains unchanged. Therapy provision should be determined by the individual needs of the patient without restriction or limitation on the types of disciplines provided or the frequency or duration of visits."[26]

Another potential compliance issue created by PDGM addresses the request for anticipated payment (RAP). Prior to PDGM, RAPs allowed HHAs to receive a portion of their payment up front. Under PDGM, even though RAPs will be totally eliminated in 2021, HHAs will still be required to file a no-pay RAP. Failure to file a no-pay RAP will result in financial penalties, so HHAs need to address this issue in their claims filing process.

Therapy use and no-pay RAPs are just examples of two of the more significant compliance issues created by PDGM. Given the complexity of PDGM, HHAs should review their entire claims filing process as part of their HHA compliance program.

Risk Area Governance

Conditions of Participation for HHAs, 42 C.F.R. §§ 484.40–484.115

The home health Conditions of Participation are the federal regulations governing HHA participation in the Medicare program.[27]

State Operations Manual, Chapter 10: Survey and Enforcement Process for Home Health Agencies

"Chapter 10" of the *State Operations Manual* sets forth how the state survey agencies carry out surveys of HHAs. This chapter also sets forth the enforcement process and the ranges of penalties that may be levied against HHAs.[28]

State Operations Manual, Appendix B: Guidance to Surveyors: Home Health Agencies

"Appendix B" contains the interpretive guidelines to the CoPs. State agency surveyors use the interpretive guidelines when conducting surveys of HHAs.[29]

Medicare Claims Processing Manual, Chapter 10: Home Health Agency Billing

"Chapter 10" of the *Medicare Claims Processing Manual* outlines the various billing requirement for HHAs to submit accurate Medicare claims under home health PPS.[30]

Medicare Benefit Policy Manual, Chapter 7: Home Health Services

"Chapter 7" of the *Medicare Benefit Policy Manual* provides an overview of HHA reimbursement, including patient eligibility for home health services, covered services, and services excluded from the Medicare home health benefit.[31]

Office of Inspector General (OIG) Work Plan

The OIG Work Plan is a valuable resource for HHAs as it identifies areas of vulnerabilities for providers. The OIG Work Plan is submitted on an annual basis and is updated throughout the year.[32]

Anti-Kickback Statute, 42 U.S.C. § 1320a–7b(b)

Prohibits requesting or receiving anything of value in exchange for referrals.[33]

Civil False Claims Act, 31 U.S.C. §§ 3729–3731

Provides for monetary penalties against those who submit false claims to the government. Damages can include treble damages and penalties of $5,500–$11,000 per false claim. False claims allegations by a whistleblower are brought in civil court. If the government elects to intervene, it becomes a criminal complaint.[34]

Criminal False Claims Acts, 18 U.S.C. § 287

Provides for actions brought by the government for the submission of false claims up to and including fines and imprisonment.[35]

HIPAA Privacy and Security Rules, 45 C.F.R. §§ 160, 164.102, 164.500

National standards for the protection of protected health information.[36]

Common Compliance Risks

Compliance with the CoPs

Failure to comply with the CoPs can lead to termination from the Medicare program as well as a whole host of other penalties. These include civil monetary penalties, denials on payments for new and all admissions, temporary management, and directed plans of correction.

Improper Contracts with Vendors

HHAs should ensure their contracts with vendors are in writing and set forth the responsibilities of the parties. The contracts should not in any way provide for compensation in return for referrals, which is prohibited by the Anti-Kickback Statute if the contract does not meet a safe harbor exception. HHAs should also be aware of their responsibility to provide education and training to their vendors under the CoPs as part of their compliance program.

Claims for Services Not Rendered or Provided as Claimed

OIG has identified common schemes whereby HHAs have falsified medical records or claims in order to bill for services not provided.

Physician or Allowed Practitioner Certifications and Recertification

HHAs should ensure that all physician or allowed practitioner certifications are obtained on a timely basis. If an HHA fails to do so, claims for services will be denied. The face-to-face encounter must occur no more than 90 days prior to the home health start of care or within 30 days of the start of home health care. Recertifications are required every 60 days after the initial 30-day period of care.

Failure to Check the OIG List of Excluded Individuals/Entities

OIG maintains a list of individuals and entities excluded from the Medicare and/or Medicaid programs.[37] Failure of an HHA to check this list could result in a payback to CMS for employing an individual excluded from Medicare and/or Medicaid. HHAs should make it a priority to routinely check the list of excluded individuals and entities and make it part of the hiring process when recruiting providers of services.

Overutilization and Underutilization of Therapy Services

With the advent of PDGM, therapy is no longer the main driver of home health reimbursement. Despite this fact, CMS has specifically stated that, while therapy is not the driver of reimbursement that it once was, HHAs are still expected to provide therapy if the patient's condition requires therapy.

CARES Act Provider Relief Funds Reporting

HHAs received financial distributions of provider relief funds under the Coronavirus Aid, Relief, and Economic Security (CARES) Act due to the COVID-19 pandemic. In order to receive these funds, HHAs were required to sign agreements with terms and conditions to attest that the money received would be used for COVID-19 purposes. HHAs were also required to report how the money was used. Failure to accurately report how CARES Act funding was used will subject HHAs to potential paybacks and audits.[38]

Use of Consulting Physicians and Medical Directors

HHAs often enter into agreements with referring physicians and medical directors for legitimate business purposes. While using consulting physicians and medical directors is a perfectly acceptable practice, it does not come without risk. HHAs should ensure the consulting physician and medical director agreements meet a safe harbor exception under the Anti-Kickback Statute or an exception under the Stark Law. The most common Anti-Kickback safe harbor used for these types of agreements is the personal services safe harbor. The most common Stark Law exception used for these types of agreements is the contractual exception. This Anti-Kickback safe harbor and Stark Law exception require the agreement to be in writing, stating payment at fair market value for services actually rendered without regard for the volume of or value of the referrals received. The Anti-Kickback Statute and Stark Law are complex, and providers should not attempt to navigate these laws, safe harbors, and exceptions without the advice of legal counsel.

Documentation of Homebound Status

Due to the vagueness of what it considered homebound status and the amount of scrutiny it receives from state and federal regulators, HHAs need to thoroughly document that patients are indeed confined to home when admitted to home health. HHAs need to document during the admission visit that the patient has been informed about the homebound criteria and that it has been shared with the patient. The HHA's Quality Assurance & Performance Improvement (QAPI) committee should routinely conduct audits to ensure this information is shared with patients. Staff should also periodically query patients to see if and why they have left the home while on service for home care. If staff have knowledge that the patient has routinely left the home, they should immediately notify HHA leadership to conduct an investigation to determine whether the patient is still homebound in order to qualify for Medicare reimbursement.

Addressing Compliance Risks

Review of Policies and Procedures

HHAs must maintain current policies and procedures in order to comply with the CoPs and Medicare billing requirements. Policies and procedures must be updated as necessary to account for regulatory and reimbursement changes.

Implementing a Compliance Program

HHAs should implement an effective compliance program. The compliance program should be designed in such a way that it is reasonably capable of reducing the prospect of criminal, civil, and administrative violations and promote quality of care. Board oversight of the compliance program is critical as the board is legally responsible for compliance program oversight.[39]

Auditing and Monitoring

HHAs should conduct auditing and monitoring that focuses on day-to-day operations including compliance with the CoPs, billing, cost reporting, contract review, and compliance with all state and federal laws and regulations governing HHAs. HHAs should consider its resources, prior compliance history, and other risk factors when assessing the degree of auditing and monitoring it performs. OIG encourages HHAs to conduct periodic compliance audits using internal or external auditors who have knowledge of federal and state laws, regulations, and other guidance.

Education and Training

Proper education and training are critical for HHAs given the myriad complex laws, regulations, and guidance that govern HHA operations. HHAs are expected to take steps to effectively communicate role-specific standards, policies, and procedures to staff, individuals providing services under contract, and volunteers. OIG expects HHAs to provide education and training on fraud and abuse laws and federal healthcare program and payer requirements. OIG also suggests that HHAs provide education and training on claims submission and development, residents' rights, and marketing practices.

QAPI Program

The CoPs require that all HHAs have a QAPI program. A robust QAPI program responds to problems when they happen and, more importantly, helps the HHA prevent problems before they happen. The CoPs require that the QAPI program must use performance indicators with the goal of improving patient outcomes focusing on high-risk, high-volume, or problem-prone areas. One aspect of QAPI that some HHAs overlook is involvement by the HHA governing body. Oversight of the QAPI program by the governing body is critical as it shows the HHA is dedicated to performance improvement. The governing body should make available all resources necessary for the QAPI program to foster its goal of performance improvement. HHAs are required by the QAPI CoPs to maintain documentary evidence that the QAPI program exists and be able to demonstrate how it functions to state and federal regulators.[40]

Emergency Preparedness

HHAs are required to have an emergency preparedness plan. The HHA must develop and maintain an emergency preparedness plan that is reviewed and updated at least every two years. The HHA must develop policies and procedures as part of its emergency preparedness plan. The policies and procedures must also be reviewed and updated every two years. The emergency preparedness plan must also implement a communication plan in the event of an emergency and conduct training and testing.[41]

Possible Penalties

Termination from the Medicare and Medicaid Programs

HHAs may be terminated from the Medicare and Medicaid programs in as little as 23 days if the deficiencies cited are considered immediate jeopardy by the state survey agency. Most HHAs avoid termination, but if terminated, readmission into the Medicare and Medicaid programs is a long and arduous process that few HHAs can survive financially.

Per-day Civil Money Penalties

The upper range for per-day civil monetary penalties in 2020 for immediate jeopardy deficiencies was $8,500–$10,000. Middle range civil monetary penalties of $1,500–$8,500 may be imposed for repeat and/or condition-level deficiencies that are not immediate jeopardy but are directly related to poor patient outcomes. Lower range civil monetary penalties of $500–$4,000 may be imposed for repeat and/or condition-level deficiencies that are not immediate jeopardy and not directly related to negative patient outcomes.[42] HHAs should be aware that these amounts are updated annually.

Per-instance Civil Money Penalties

Per-instance civil money penalties may be imposed in the amount of $1,500–$10,000 for deficiencies that are not immediate jeopardy.[43] Providers should be aware that these amounts are updated annually.

Appointment of Temporary Manager

In immediate jeopardy situations, CMS may appoint a temporary manager to operate the HHA until the HHA attains compliance. The temporary manager has wide latitude in operating the HHA, including the ability to hire and fire staff and obligate funds. The HHA will be terminated from the Medicare and Medicaid programs for failure to relinquish all management authority to the temporary manager.

Suspension of Payment for All New Admissions

An optional suspension of payment for all new admissions may be imposed when an HHA is not in substantial compliance with the CoPs. HHAs should be aware that CMS must provide adequate written notice to an HHA prior to imposing a suspension of payment for all new admissions. In immediate jeopardy situations, CMS must provide the HHA written notice two calendar before the effective date and 15 days written notice in non-immediate jeopardy situations before imposing this remedy.

Directed Plans of Correction and In-service Training

CMS, the state survey agency, or the temporary manager have the authority to dictate the terms of a plan of correction when an HHA is not in compliance with the CoPs. Mandatory in-service training may be imposed where there is a pattern of deficiencies and education is likely to correct the deficiencies.

State Licensure Penalties

In states where HHAs are licensed, states generally have the authority to revoke or place a license on probation. States may also have the authority to impose civil money penalties and appoint a temporary manager or receiver independent of CMS-imposed penalties.

Compliance Resources

The Centers for Medicare & Medicaid Services

The CMS website has invaluable information that can be used by HHAs, which includes the ROPs, *State Operations Manual*, and other Medicare manuals on billing and reimbursement issues. HHAs can also subscribe to email updates from CMS that provide the latest regulatory and reimbursement changes.

State Operations Manual
Chapter 10: Survey and Enforcement Process for Home Health Agencies

https://www.cms.gov/Regulations-and-Guidance/Guidance/Manuals/Downloads/som107c10.pdf

Appendix B: Interpretive Guidelines for Home Health Agencies

https://www.hhs.gov/guidance/sites/default/files/hhs-guidance-documents/som107ap_b_hha.pdf

Medicare Administrative Contractors

Like CMS, the various Medicare Administrative Contractors (MACs) are excellent sources of information with regard to Medicare reimbursement, enrollment, and claims filing issues. The Medicare administrative contractors also provide excellent educational resources. They include:

- **CGS Administrators**: https://www.cgsmedicare.com/
- **Palmetto GBA**: https://www.palmettogba.com/
- **National Government Services**: http://www.NGSMedicare.com
- **Novitas Solutions**: https://www.novitas-solutions.com

Program for Evaluating Payment Patterns Electronic Report (PEPPER)

PEPPER reports should be used by an HHA as it summarizes claims data that may put the HHA at risk for improper payment due to billing and coding irregularities.

https://pepper.cbrpepper.org/

National Association of Home Care & Hospice

National trade associations and their state affiliates are valuable resources to HHAs. The predominant trade association for HHAs is the National Association of Home Care & Hospice (NAHC) and its state affiliates. NAHC has robust educational programs and resources only available to members.

http://www.nahc.org

U.S. Department of Health & Human Services Office of Inspector General Enforcement and Exclusion Database

HHAs that employ individuals or contract with entities excluded from the Medicare or Medicaid programs are subject to repayment for allowing individuals or entities to provide services to residents. HHAs should regularly check and have a policy that calls for routine checks of the OIG Enforcement and Exclusion Database.

https://exclusions.oig.hhs.gov/

Risk Takeaways

Main points of interest:
- Home health agencies (HHAs) are often the target of state regulators, federal regulators, Office of Inspector General (OIG), and the U.S. Department of Justice for alleged fraudulent activity.
- HHAs are subject to a plethora of federal and state regulations on delivering quality of care and guidance on how to properly file claims for reimbursement.
- Due to the highly regulated environment in which they operate, it is critical that HHAs stay abreast of all existing regulations and program guidance governing their operations.

Areas to watch:
- Updates to guidance on Conditions of Participation enforcement and interpretive guidance on how surveys are conducted.
- U.S. Department of Justice and OIG alerts targeting HHAs.
- The Coronavirus Aid, Relief, and Economic Security Act Provider Relief Fund reporting and potential U.S. Department of Health & Human Services audits of funds received.

- Claims for services not rendered or provided as claimed.
- Implementation and surveys of compliance programs.
- Improper contractual relationships with physicians and vendors.
- Physician or allowed practitioner certifications and recertifications.
- Failure to check the OIG List of Excluded Individuals/Entities.
- Use of consulting physicians and medical directors.
- Continued focus on emergency preparedness.
- Documentation of homebound status.
- Overutilization and underutilization of therapy services.
- Possible U.S. Department of Health & Human Services proposal implementing a single reimbursement methodology for all post-acute care providers.

Laws that apply:

- Conditions of Participation for Home Health Agencies: 42 C.F.R. §§ 484.40–484.115
- Anti-Kickback Statute: 42 U.S.C. §§ 1320a-7b(b)
- Civil False Claims Act: 31 U.S.C. §§ 3729–3731
- Criminal False Claims Acts: 18 U.S.C. § 287
- HIPAA Privacy and Security rules: 45 C.F.R. §§ 160, 164.102, 164.500
- State licensure laws and regulations for states that license HHAs

Addressing compliance risks:

- Implement and update policies and procedures to account for regulatory changes.
- Continually train and educate staff on policies and procedures along with regulatory changes.
- Have a robust compliance and Quality Assurance & Performance Improvement (QAPI) program.
- Conduct auditing and monitoring of quality of care and billing areas of risk.
- Implement and update the emergency preparedness program.
- Periodically check the OIG Enforcement and Exclusions Database.

Endnotes

1. **Todd Selby** is a Shareholder at Hall Render and specializes in representing post-acute care providers. He has represented post-acute care providers for more than 30 years in all facets of legal issues, with an emphasis on regulatory compliance, reimbursement, provider enrollment, administrative litigation, and mergers and acquisitions.

2. **Elizabeth E. Hogue** is an attorney in private practice with extensive experience in healthcare. She represents clients all over the country, including professional associations, physicians, managed care providers, and institutional healthcare providers, including hospitals, long-term care facilities, home health agencies, durable medical equipment companies, private duty agencies, and hospices. Hogue has written numerous articles for trade association publications and other journals. Her books include *Informed Consent, Medicare/Medicaid Fraud and Abuse, Contracting with Managed Care Providers, Termination of Services to Patients: Use of Policies and Procedures to Avoid Liability for Abandonment,* and *Case Management: Legal Issues,* among others.

3. 42 U.S.C. § 1395x(o).

4. 42 U.S.C. § 1395x(m).

5. 42 U.S.C. § 1395f(a)(2)(C); 42 U.S.C. § 1395n(a)(2)(A).

6. Centers for Medicare & Medicaid Services, "Chapter 7: Home Health Services," § 30.1.1, *Medicare Benefit Policy Manual*, Pub. 100-02, revised November 6, 2020, https://www.cms.gov/Regulations-and-Guidance/Guidance/Manuals/Downloads/bp102c07.pdf.

7. Centers for Medicare & Medicaid Services, ""Chapter 7: Home Health Services," § 30.1.1, *Medicare Benefit Policy Manual*.

8. Centers for Medicare & Medicaid Services, "Chapter 7: Home Health Services," § 30.2.1, *Medicare Benefit Policy Manual*.

9. Centers for Medicare & Medicaid Services, "Chapter 7: Home Health Services," § 30.5.1, *Medicare Benefit Policy Manual*.

10. Centers for Medicare & Medicaid Services, "Chapter 10: Home Health Agency Billing," § 10.1 A, *Medicare Claims Processing Manual*, Pub. 100-04, revised August 7, 2020, http://www.cms.gov/Regulations-and-Guidance/Guidance/Manuals/Downloads/clm104c10.pdf.

11. Centers for Medicare & Medicaid Services, "Chapter 10: Home Health Agency Billing," § 10.1 B, *Medicare Claims Processing Manual*.

12. Centers for Medicare & Medicaid Services, "Chapter 10: Home Health Agency Billing," § 10.2 A, *Medicare Claims Processing Manual*.

13. Centers for Medicare & Medicaid Services, "Chapter 10: Home Health Agency Billing," § 10.2 A, *Medicare Claims Processing Manual*.

14. Centers for Medicare & Medicaid Services and Abt Associates, "Centers for Medicare & Medicaid Services Patient-Driven Groupings Model," accessed March 9, 2021, https://www.cms.gov/Medicare/Medicare-Fee-for-Service-Payment/HomeHealthPPS/Downloads/Overview-of-the-Patient-Driven-Groupings-Model.pdf.

15. Centers for Medicare & Medicaid Services, "Chapter 10: Home Health Agency Billing," § 10.2 A, *Medicare Claims Processing Manual*.

16. Centers for Medicare & Medicaid Services, "Chapter 10: Home Health Agency Billing," § 10.2 A, *Medicare Claims Processing Manual*.

17. Centers for Medicare & Medicaid Services, "Chapter 10: Home Health Agency Billing," § 10.2 A, *Medicare Claims Processing Manual*.

18. Centers for Medicare & Medicaid Services, "Chapter 10: Survey and Enforcement Process for Home Health Agencies," § 10007.1, *State Operations Manual*, Pub. 100-07, revised April 25, 2014, https://www.cms.gov/Regulations-and-Guidance/Guidance/Manuals/Downloads/som107c10.pdf.

19. Medicare and Medicaid Program: Conditions of Participation for Home Health Agencies, 82 Fed. Reg. 4,504 (January 13, 2017), https://www.federalregister.gov/documents/2017/01/13/2017-00283/medicare-and-medicaid-program-conditions-of-participation-for-home-health-agencies.

20. Centers for Medicare & Medicaid Services, "Appendix B: Guidance to Surveyors: Home Health Agencies," *State Operations Manual*, Pub. 100-07, revised February 21, 2020, https://www.hhs.gov/guidance/sites/default/files/hhs-guidance-documents/som107ap_b_hha.pdf.

21. Centers for Medicare & Medicaid Services, "Chapter 10: Survey and Enforcement Process for Home Health Agencies," § 10007.1, *State Operations Manual*.

22. U.S. Department of Justice, "CEO Sentenced for $150 Million Health Care Fraud and Money Laundering Scheme," news release, February 3, 2021, https://www.justice.gov/opa/pr/ceo-sentenced-150-million-health-care-fraud-and-money-laundering-scheme.

23. U.S. Department of Justice, "CEO Sentenced for $150 Million Health Care Fraud and Money Laundering Scheme," news release, February 3, 2021, https://www.justice.gov/opa/pr/ceo-sentenced-150-million-health-care-fraud-and-money-laundering-scheme.

24. U.S. Department of Justice, "CEO Sentenced for $150 Million Health Care Fraud and Money Laundering Scheme," news release, February 3, 2021, https://www.justice.gov/opa/pr/ceo-sentenced-150-million-health-care-fraud-and-money-laundering-scheme.

25. U.S. Attorney's Office for the Southern District of New York, "10 Defendants Arrested in Home-Health Aide Fraud Scheme," news release, December 16, 2020, https://www.justice.gov/usao-sdny/pr/10-defendants-arrested-home-health-aide-fraud-scheme.

26. Centers for Medicare & Medicaid Services, "The Role of Therapy under the Home Health Patient-Driven Groupings Model (PDGM)," *MLN Matters*, SE20005, February 10, 2020, https://www.cms.gov/files/document/se20005.pdf.

27. 42 C.F.R. §§ 484.40 - 484.115.

28. Centers for Medicare & Medicaid Services, "Chapter 10 – Survey and Enforcement Process for Home Health Agencies," *State Operations Manual*.

29. Centers for Medicare & Medicaid Services, "Appendix B – Guidance to Surveyors: Home Health Agencies," *State Operations Manual*.

30. Centers for Medicare & Medicaid Services, "Chapter 10 – Home Health Agency Billing," § 10.1 A, *Medicare Claims Processing Manual*.

31. Centers for Medicare & Medicaid Services, "Chapter 7: Home Health Services," § 30.1.1, *Medicare Benefit Policy Manual.*

32. "Work Plan," U.S. Department of Health & Human Services Office of Inspector General, accessed March 9, 2021, https://oig.hhs.gov/reports-and-publications/workplan/.

33. 31 U.S.C. §§ 3729–3731.

34. 31 U.S.C. §§ 3729–3731.

35. 18 U.S.C. § 287.

36. 45 C.F.R. §§ 160, 164.102, 164.500.

37. "LEIE Downloadable Databases," U.S. Department of Health & Human Services Office of Inspector General, updated February 10, 2021, https://oig.hhs.gov/exclusions/exclusions_list.asp.

38. "CARES Act Provider Relief Fund: For Providers," U.S. Department of Health & Human Services, edited February 23, 2021, https://www.hhs.gov/coronavirus/cares-act-provider-relief-fund/for-providers/index.html.

39. 42 C.F.R. § 483.85.

40. 42 C.F.R. § 484.65

41. 42 C.F.R § 484.102.

42. 42 C.F.R. § 488.845(b)(3–5).

43. 42 C.F.R. § 488.845(b)(6).

Hospices

By Cat Armato,[1] RN, CHC, CHPC; and Kimberly Olson,[2] RN, CHC, PHN, CHPN

What Is Hospice Care?

Hospice is a philosophy of care that supports patients who have a life-limiting illness (usually six months or fewer), patients' families, and patients' caregivers. Initially all volunteer, hospice became a covered Medicare Part A benefit in 1983 in Tax Equity and Fiscal Responsibility Act of 1982.[3] Since that time, most Medicaid and other commercial insurances have added a hospice benefit. Hospice focuses on palliative rather than curative care. The goal is quality compassionate care and services provided in the patient's residence, even if the patient resides in a facility.

When a patient elects the Hospice Medicare Benefit (HMB), traditional Medicare coverage ends for all things related to the terminal prognosis. Medicare pays the hospice a daily rate and from that the hospice covers all care and services related to the terminal prognosis, including medications, durable medical equipment, nursing care, physician services, medical supplies, bereavement services, and other services needed for the palliation of pain and symptoms.

Between 2000 and 2019, Medicare spending for hospice care increased from $2.9 billion[4] to $20.9 billion[5]. With the substantial increase in payments came an increase in scrutiny and multiple enforcement actions. In addition to payment scrutiny, quality of care issues have been identified.[6] In 2019, the Office of Inspector General (OIG) published a report titled "Hospice Deficiencies Pose Risks to Medicare Beneficiaries."[7] This report highlighted quality concerns and survey deficiencies that ultimately affect beneficiaries of these services. Higher payments combined with quality concerns is certainly enough to increase scrutiny.

Enforcement and Settlement Activities

Key focus areas for enforcement and settlement activity related to hospice care include patient eligibility; long lengths of stay, providing a higher level of care than appropriate; untimely documentation; inappropriate payments to non-hospice providers, and financial relationships with referral sources, including medical director reimbursement.

Patient Eligibility

To qualify for the HMB, a patient must have a prognosis of six months or fewer if the disease runs its normal course. While prognostication is not an exact science and relies on the determination of physicians, guidelines are provided for determining the patient's prognosis based on the primary terminal diagnosis. Red flags include long lengths of stay, high number of live discharges, high percentage of nursing facility and assisted living facility patients, and exceeding the Medicare aggregate cap.

In addition to this, the OIG has been focused on patients who have not had a hospitalization or emergency department visit prior to the hospice admission.[8] This type of review can be done remotely and without the hospice's knowledge that an audit is taking place.

Long Lengths of Stay

An OIG Report[9] was clear that Medicare should modify payments to prevent hospices from targeting long length of stay patients. Medicare listened and has modified payments and recommended audits of patients with long lengths of stay. As a result, hospices have seen increased audits of these patients.

Level of Care

Hospice provides four levels of care:

1. Routine home care,
2. General inpatient care,
3. Respite care, and
4. Continuous care.

The majority of care is provided at the routine level, and inpatient care is limited to 20% of the total number of Medicare patient days provided to all patients served by that provider.

Medicare has provided criteria for when each level of care may be provided.[10]Failure to meet these requirements may result in billing for a higher level of care than was necessary.

Untimely Documentation

Untimely documentation includes, among others, the written certifications, physician face-to-face visits, and records of interdisciplinary team meetings.

- **Written certifications**. The certification periods for the HMB include two 90-day benefit periods followed by an unlimited number of 60-day benefit periods. These benefit periods are based on the beneficiary, not the hospice, so if a beneficiary has received hospice services in the past, that patient may be admitted into the second or later benefit period. This is important when determining the number of days the physician is certifying and whether a face-to-face visit is required.
- **Physician face-to-face visits**. Any patient entering a third or subsequent benefit period must have a face-to-face visit with a qualified provider (physician or nurse practitioner). The results of that visit must be used when determining a terminal prognosis. The logical conclusion is that the face-to-face visit must occur prior to the written certification and both must fall within the timelines provided by the hospice regulations.
- **Records of interdisciplinary team meetings**. The plan of care must be reviewed by the interdisciplinary team, at a minimum, every 15 days.[11] It is expected that this review is documented in the clinical record. Failure to document this review results in services that are not billable. For example, if plan-of care-reviews are conducted on March 1 and April 1, the days between March 15 (15 days from the last interdisciplinary team review) and April 1 would not be billable.

Inappropriate Payments to Non-hospice Providers

In the 1983 final rule, CMS stated: "It is our general view that the [Social Security Act §1812(d)(2)(A) 'exceptional and unusual circumstances'] waiver required by the law is a broad one and that hospices are required to provide virtually all the care that is needed by terminally ill patients"[12] While this is not a new requirement, according to the OIG, Medicare paid $6.6 billion to nonhospice providers for items, services, durable medical equipment, and medications that should have been covered by the hospice per diem.[13]Medicare has clearly stated that they view virtually all care provided to the patient to be related to the terminal condition. Any variance from this requires the physician to indicate why that would not be a covered hospice benefit. Patients should also be informed when something is not covered by the hospice, and they have a right to request that information in writing.

Financial Relationships with Referral Sources

These include arrangements with another healthcare provider who the hospice knows is submitting claims for services already covered by the hospice benefit. The Medicare expectation is that hospices should be providing "virtually all care needed by the individual who has elected hospice."[14] Additionally, medical directorships may be examined closely to ensure remuneration is based on a fair market value and not based on number of referrals or an expectation of referrals. Physicians should be reimbursed based on time spent providing the hospice with services. Monthly stipends that are not based on the time spent providing hospice services are at risk.

The Anti-Kickback Statute prohibits incentives to actual or potential referral sources.[15] Closely scrutinized in this area are relationships with nursing facilities who have the potential to make patient referrals. An example of this may be a promise to provide a full-time aide for every X number of patients admitted to the hospice, or referrals to the nursing facility in exchange for referrals to the hospice.

Risk Area Governance

Anti-Kickback Statute, 42 U.S.C. § 1320a-7b(b)

Prohibits requesting or receiving anything of value in exchange for referrals.[16]

CMS State Operations Manual, Appendix M—Guidance to Surveyors: Hospice

Provides the Conditions of Participation and includes directions/advisements to surveyors. These directions help providers understand how the Conditions will be interpreted.[17]

Civil False Claims Act, 31 U.S.C. §§ 3729–3731

Provides for monetary penalties against those who submit false claims to the government. Damages can include treble damages and penalties of $5,500 - $11,000 per false claim. False claims allegations by a whistleblower are brought in civil court. If the government elects to intervene, it becomes a criminal complaint.[18]

Criminal False Claims Acts, 18 U.S.C. § 287

Provides for actions brought by the government for the submission of false claims up to and including fines and imprisonment.[19]

Health Insurance Portability and Accountability Act (HIPAA) privacy and security rules, 45 C.F.R. §§ 160, 164.102, and 164.500

National standards for the protection of protected health information.[20]

Hospice Conditions of Participation, 42 C.F.R. § 418

Defines conditions for participation in the Medicare program along with standards for meeting those conditions.[21]

Medicare Claims Processing Manual, Chapter 11: Processing Hospice Claims

Provides guidance on requirements for submitting correct claims.[22]

Medicare Program Integrity Manual, Chapter 3: Verifying Potential Errors and Taking Corrective Actions

Provides direction for government contractors on conducting pre- and post-payment reviews.[23]

Medicare Program Integrity Manual, Chapter 15: Medicare Enrollment

Provides guidance on Medicare enrollment forms, including, but not limited to, the CMS-855A applications for institutions that provide care to Medicare Part A beneficiaries.[24]

OIG Reports

OIG released six reports/studies on the topic of hospices from 2019-2022:

1. "Hospice Deficiencies Pose Risks to Medicare Beneficiaries"[25]
2. "Safeguards Must Be Strengthened to Protect Medicare Hospice Beneficiaries from Harm"[26]
3. "HHS OIG 2019 Vulnerabilities in the Medicare Hospice Program Affect Quality Care and Program Integrity: An OIG Portfolio" [27]
4. "Medicare Part D Is Still Paying Millions for Drugs Already Paid for Under the Part A Hospice Benefit"[28]
5. "Registered Nurses Did Not Always Visit Medicare Beneficiaries' Homes at Least Once Every 14 Days to Assess the Quality of Care and Services Provided by Hospice Aides"[29]
6. "Nationwide Review of Hospice Beneficiary Eligibility"[30]

The OIG's common theme of repeated concerns includes, but is not limited to, proper medication payments, home health aide supervision, quality of hospice care, and poor care planning. OIG is urging Centers for Medicare & Medicaid Services to increase its scrutiny of hospice agencies.

U.S. Department of Justice Criminal Division, Evaluation of Corporate Compliance Programs

Provides direction for the assessment of an organization's compliance program, including whether the program is designed to detect and prevent wrongdoing.[31]

U.S. Sentencing Commission's Federal Sentencing Guidelines, Chapter 8: Sentencing of Organizations

Guidelines to direct courts on remedies for harm caused, set fines, determining culpability, and directing organizations to develop programs that encourage compliant and ethical conduct.[32]

Common Compliance Risks

Insufficient Evidence of Clinical Eligibility

Patients must have a terminal prognosis of six months or less if the disease runs its normal course. Eligibility review is ongoing throughout the course of care and certified by a physician.

Failure to Provide All Care and Services Related to the Terminal Prognosis

Medicare considers virtually all care related to the terminal prognosis. The only exception is for the physician to specifically state that care or services are unrelated and why. Medicare Part D audits have revealed payments for medications that should have been covered by the hospice.

Inadequate or Late Documentation

These documents include certifications/recertifications, Notice of Election, face-to-face visits, interdisciplinary team meetings, and clinician visit notes. Each have specific requirements to be considered valid per conditions of payments in Title 42 Chapter IV Subpart B and E.[33]

Incentives to Actual or Potential Referral Sources

These violate the Anti-Kickback Statute.

Improper Nursing Facility Arrangements

These include overlap of services that a nursing home provides, improper relinquishment of core services and professional responsibility, no written contract, room and board payments that exceed what the nursing facility would have received from Medicaid, free or below fair-market-value goods to the facility to refer patients, and hospice reviewing facility patient records for purposes of recommending hospice referrals.

Inappropriate Sales Incentives

Commissions based on length of stay encourage solicitation to long length-of-stay patients.

Inadequate or Incomplete Services Rendered

Adequate assessments, care, and services sufficient to palliate pain and symptoms, improper care planning, failure to provide all levels of care, lack of physician services. [34][35]

Billing for a Higher Level of Care Than Was Necessary

This includes billing for general inpatient care or continuous care when not clinically supported.[36]

Addressing Compliance Risks

Policies and Procedures

Review program policies and procedures to ensure they support compliant day-to-day activities and follow program requirements. Employees should frequently refer back to policies to ensure that the intended behavior is the actual behavior. Management is responsible for monitoring activities based on policy requirements.

Workforce Education

After initial orientation and ongoing education, assess employee knowledge and develop compliance education based on identified gaps, audit findings, and industry updates.

Internal Auditing

Internal audits should include:

- **Clinical records**. Eligibility guidelines and technical requirements, long-length-of-stay patients, face-to-face visits, certifications/recertifications, higher levels of care and live discharges.
- **Complaint/grievance log**. Assess for quality-of-care concerns.
- **Contracts**. Fair market value, no referral incentives, professional management responsibilities.
- **Sales and marketing expenses**. Compliance with Anti-Kickback Statute.

- **HIPAA risk assessment.**
- **Mock surveys/survey readiness assessments.**

External Auditing

- Review the Program for Evaluating Payment Patterns Electronic Report (PEPPER) reports to determine any areas where your organization is an outlier.[37]
- Review any government audits to determine patterns/trends and assess charge denial rate.
- Engage external consultants to conduct an audit of clinical records.
- Review Family Evaluation of Hospice Care scores and Medicare.gov Care Compare to identify any care-related concerns.[38][39]

Prompt Response and Repayment

- Based on record reviews, initiate prompt repayment and workforce reeducation. Repayment is an area where hospices frequently fail on follow-through.
- Engage legal counsel to determine if self-disclosure is required.
- Consistently follow internal disciplinary protocols for noncompliant behavior.

Possible Penalties

Multiple fraud and abuse laws elicit a variety of administrative sanctions, including, but not limited to, the False Claims Act, Anti-Kickback Statute, civil monetary penalties law, and state laws. These penalties include:

- False claim damages can include treble damages and monetary penalties per false claim. Hospice submits claims monthly, so one patient may have multiple claims.
- Imprisonment.
- Exclusion from participation in the Medicare program.

Compliance Resources

Educational Programs

Medicare administrative contractors have each developed training modules available for their providers.

- **National Government** Services (NGS): Medicare University Courses are available on topics from basics to specific areas of concern, such as Medicare secondary payer and two-tier payments for routine home care. https://www.ngsmedicare.com/medicare-university
- **Palmetto Government Benefits Administrator (PGBA)**: Self-Paced Learning Interactive Tools and Modules offer courses from hospice eligibility to finance and accounting. https://www.palmettogba.com/palmetto/jjb.nsf/DID/AVGLBV6703
- **CGS:** Its training and education cover basics to navigating Targeted Probe and Educate. https://www.cgsmedicare.com/hhh/education/video.html

Comparative Billing Reports

Information, training, and support related to Comparative Billing Reports (CBRs).

https://cbr.cbrpepper.org/Home

National and State Association Resources

National organizations such as the National Hospice and Palliative Care Organization (NHPCO) and the National Association for Home Care & Hospice offer online resources as well as conferences, webinars, podcasts, and other resources.

- **National Hospice and Palliative Care Organization:** https://www.nhpco.org
- **National Association for Home Care & Hospice:** https://www.nahc.org
- **The Hospice Foundation of America**: State organizations are a valuable resource for education and peer-to-peer interactions. The Hospice Foundation of America has a listing of state organizations on its website. https://hospicefoundation.org/Hospice-Directory

U.S. Department of Health & Human Services Office of Inspector General

Enforcement & Exclusion Database
Identify employees, contractors, vendors, and ordering practitioners on the OIG exclusion list.

https://exclusions.oig.hhs.gov

Risk Takeaways

Main points of interest:

- Hospice is a philosophy of care that supports patients who have a life-limiting illness (usually six months or less), patients' families, and patients' caregivers.
- Between 2000 and 2019, Medicare spending for hospice care increased from $2.9 billion to $20.9 billion. This has led to a significant increase in scrutiny.

Areas to watch:

- Insufficient evidence of clinical eligibility.
- Failure to provide all care and services related to the terminal prognosis.
- Failure to cover all goods and services related to the terminal prognosis.
- Inadequate or late documentation.
- Incentives to actual or potential referral sources.
- Improper nursing facility arrangements.
- Inappropriate sales incentives.
- Inadequate or incomplete services rendered.
- Billing for a higher level of care than was necessary.

Laws that apply:

- Anti-Kickback Statute, 42 U.S.C. § 1320a-7b(b)
- Civil False Claims Act, 31 U.S.C. §§ 3729-3731
- Criminal False Claims Acts, 18 U.S.C. § 287
- HIPAA Privacy and Security rules, 45 C.F.R. §§ 160, 164.102, and 164.500
- Hospice Conditions of Participation, 42 C.F.R. § 418
- U.S. Sentencing Commission's Federal Sentencing Guidelines, Chapter 8

Addressing compliance risks:

- Policies and procedures: Review program policies and procedures to ensure they support compliant day-to-day activities and follow program requirements.
- Workforce education: After initial orientation and ongoing education, assess employee knowledge and develop education based on identified gaps, audit findings, and industry updates.
- Internal auditing, including:
  - Clinical records,
  - Complaint/grievance log,
  - Contracts,
  - Sales and marketing expenses,
  - HIPAA risk assessment, and

- Mock surveys/survey readiness assessments.
■ External auditing, including:
  - PEPPER reports,
  - Government audits,
  - External consultants, and
  - Family Evaluation of Hospice Care scores.
  - Prompt response and repayment.
■ Enforce consistent disciplinary protocols.

Endnotes

1. **Cat Armato** is Principal Consultant at Armato & Associates LLC. She specializes in home health and hospice compliance consulting, including program assessment and implementation. Armato has been in the hospice industry for more than 22 years and has served as chief compliance officer for a nationwide hospice organization. She has assisted many hospice programs during civil investigative demands, qui tams, state and federal investigations, and corporate integrity agreements.

2. **Kimberly Olson** is Chief Compliance Officer at St. Croix Hospice. She has served in the healthcare industry for more than 20 years, specializing in hospice operations and compliance for over 10 years. Olson is an advocate for hospice and palliative care utilization by serving as the co-chair of Minnesota Network of Hospice & Palliative Care's (MNHPC) Policy Committee and National Hospice and Palliative Care Organization's (NHPCO's) Legislative Affairs Committee. In 2022, she was a named a Top 50 Women Leader in Minnesota and a Top 50 Women Leader in Healthcare.

3. Centers for Medicare & Medicaid Services, "Chapter 9: Coverage of Hospice Services Under Hospital Insurance," *Medicare Benefit Policy Manual*, Pub. 100-02, revised November 6, 2020, https://www.cms.gov/Regulations-and-Guidance/Guidance/Manuals/Downloads/bp102c09.pdf.

4. Medicare Payment Advisory Commission, *Report to the Congress: Medicare Payment Policy,* March 2019, 313, https://www.medpac.gov/document/march-2019-report-to-the-congress-medicare-payment-policy/.

5. MedPAC March 2021 Report to Congress, Table 11-3, https://www.medpac.gov/document/march-2021-report-to-the-congress-medicare-payment-policy/.

6. Jim Parker, "Documentation Issues, Live Discharges, Long Lengths of Stay Drawing CMS Scrutiny," Hospice News, June 20, 2019, https://hospicenews.com/2019/06/20/documentation-issues-live-discharges-long-lengths-of-stay-drawing-cms-scrutiny/.

7. Joanne M. Chiedi, "Hospice Deficiencies Pose Risks to Medicare Beneficiaries," U.S. Department of Health & Human Services Office of Inspector General, July 2019, https://oig.hhs.gov/oei/reports/oei-02-17-00020.pdf?utm_source=summary-page&utm_medium=web&utm_campaign=OEI-02-17-00020-PDF.

8. HHS, OIG, "Nationwide Review of Hospice Beneficiary Eligibility" https://oig.hhs.gov/reports-and-publications/workplan/summary/wp-summary-0000648.asp

9. Joanne M. Chiedi, "Safeguards Must Be Strengthened to Protect Medicare Hospice Beneficiaries from Harm," U.S. Department of Health & Human Services Office of Inspector General, July 2019, https://oig.hhs.gov/oei/reports/oei-02-17-00021.pdf?utm_source=summary-page&utm_medium=web&utm_campaign=OEI-02-17-00021-PDF.

10. Centers for Medicare & Medicaid Services, "Chapter 9: Coverage of Hospice Services Under Hospital Insurance," *Medicare Benefit Policy Manual.*

11. 42 C.F.R. § 418.56(d).

12. 48 Fed. Reg. 56008, 56010–11 Dec. 16, 1983

13. HHS, OIG "Medicare Payments of $6.6 Billion to Non-hospice Providers Over 10 Years for Items and Services Provided to Hospice Beneficiaries Suggest the Need for Increased Oversight" https://oig.hhs.gov/oas/reports/region9/92003015.pdf

14. Centers for Medicare & Medicaid Services, "Hospice Payment System," *MLN Booklet*, November 2019, 6, https://www.calhospice.org/assets/docs/MLN006817_Hospice-Payment-System-Nov-2019-Interactive_Version%20%281%29.pdf.

15. 42 U.S.C. § 1320a-7b(b).

16. 42 U.S.C. § 1320a-7b(b).

17. Centers for Medicare and & Medicaid Services, *State Operations Manual*, "Appendix M - Guidance to Surveyors: Hospice," *State Operations Manual*, Pub. 100-07, revised February 21, 2020, https://www.cms.gov/Regulations-and-Guidance/Guidance/Manuals/downloads/som107ap_m_hospice.pdf..

18. 31 U.S.C. §§ 3729-3731.

19. 18 U.S.C. § 287.

20. 45 C.F.R. §§ 160, 164.102, 164.500.

21. 42 C.F.R. § 418.

22. Centers for Medicare & Medicaid Services, "Chapter 11 - Processing Hospice Claims," *Medicare Claims Processing Manual*, Pub. 100-04, revised October 30, 2020, https://www.cms.gov/Regulations-and-Guidance/Guidance/Manuals/Downloads/clm104c11.pdf.

23. Centers for Medicare & Medicaid Services, "Chapter 3 - Verifying Potential Errors and Taking Corrective Actions," *Medicare Program Integrity Manual*, Pub. 100-08, revised October 2, 2020, https://www.cms.gov/Regulations-and-Guidance/Guidance/Manuals/Downloads/pim83c03.pdf.

24. Centers for Medicare & Medicaid Services, "Chapter 15 - Medicare Enrollment," *Medicare Program Integrity Manual*, Pub. 100-08, revised October 9, 2020, https://www.cms.gov/Regulations-and-Guidance/Guidance/Manuals/Downloads/pim83c15.pdf.

25. Joanne M. Chiedi, "Hospice Deficiencies Pose Risks to Medicare Beneficiaries," U.S. Department of Health & Human Services Office of Inspector General, July 2019, https://oig.hhs.gov/oei/reports/oei-02-17-00020.pdf?utm_source=summary-page&utm_medium=web&utm_campaign=OEI-02-17-00020-PDF.

26. Joanne M. Chiedi, "Safeguards Must Be Strengthened to Protect Medicare Hospice Beneficiaries from Harm," U.S. Department of Health & Human Services Office of Inspector General, July 2019, https://oig.hhs.gov/oei/reports/oei-02-17-00021.pdf?utm_source=summary-page&utm_medium=web&utm_campaign=OEI-02-17-00021-PDF.

27. "2019: Vulnerabilities in Hospice Care," Office of Inspector General, U.S. Department of Health & Human Services, updated August 20, 2020, https://oig.hhs.gov/newsroom/media-materials/media-materials-2019-hospice/.

28. Joanne M. Chiedi, "Medicare Part D Is Still Paying Millions for Drugs Already Paid for Under the Part A Hospice Benefit," U.S. Department of Health & Human Services Office of Inspector General, August 2019, https://oig.hhs.gov/oas/reports/region6/61708004.pdf.

29. Gloria L. Jarmon, "Registered Nurses Did Not Always Visit Medicare Beneficiaries' Homes at Least Once Every 14 Days to Assess the Quality of Care and Services Provided by Hospice Aides," U.S. Department of Health & Human Services Office of Inspector General, November 2019, https://oig.hhs.gov/oas/reports/region9/91803022.pdf.

30. National Hospital and Palliative Care Organization, *Family Evaluation of Hospice Care: 2013 National Summary Report*, 2014, https://www.nhpco.org/wp-content/uploads/2019/06/2013-FEHC-National-Summary-Report-FINAL.pdf.

31. U.S. Dep't of Justice, Criminal Div., *Evaluation of Corporate Compliance Programs* (Updated June 2020), https://www.justice.gov/criminal-fraud/page/file/937501/download.

32. USSG § 8 (U.S. Sentencing Comm'n 2018), https://www.ussc.gov/guidelines/2018-guidelines-manual/annotated-2018-chapter-8.

33. "Title 42, Chapter IV, Subchapter B, Part 418," Electronic Code of Federal Regulations, Govinfo.gov, accessed November 19, 2020, https://www.ecfr.gov/cgi-bin/text-idx?tpl=/ecfrbrowse/Title42/42cfr418_main_02.tpl.

34. Joanne M. Chiedi, "Safeguards Must Be Strengthened To Protect Medicare Hospice Beneficiaries From Harm," U.S. Department of Health & Human Services Office of Inspector General, July 2019, 5, https://oig.hhs.gov/oei/reports/oei-02-17-00021.pdf?utm_source=summary-page&utm_medium=web&utm_campaign=OEI-02-17-00021-PDF.

35. Joanne M. Chiedi, "Vulnerabilities in the Medicare Hospice Program Affect Quality Care and Program Integrity: An OIG Portfolio," U.S. Department of Health & Human Services Office of Inspector General, July 2018, 4–6, https://oig.hhs.gov/oei/reports/oei-02-16-00570.pdf.

36. Daniel R. Levinson, "Hospices Inappropriately Billed Medicare Over $250 Million for General Inpatient Care," U.S. Department of Health & Human Services Office of Inspector General, March 2016, https://oig.hhs.gov/oei/reports/oei-02-10-00491.pdf.

37. "PEPPER Resources Portal," Comparative Billing Reports, accessed January 8, 2021, https://pepperfile.cbrpepper.org.

38. "Hospice Care Compare," Medicare.gov, accessed November 11, 2020, https://www.medicare.gov/hospice-compare/. .

39. National Hospital and Palliative Care Organization, *Family Evaluation of Hospice Care: 2013 National Summary Report*, 2014, https://www.nhpco.org/wp-content/uploads/2019/06/2013-FEHC-National-Summary-Report-FINAL.pdf.

Skilled Nursing Facilities

By Todd Selby[1] and Sean Fahey[2]

What Are Skilled Nursing Facilities?

Skilled nursing facilities (SNFs) offer services to Medicare beneficiaries if daily skilled care or rehabilitation services are ordered by a physician and performed by, or under the supervision of, professional or technical personnel. The services must be for an ongoing condition for which the beneficiary also received inpatient hospital services or for a new condition that arose during the SNF care for that ongoing condition.[3]

In order to qualify for SNF services, the beneficiary must have been hospitalized for at least three consecutive days (not counting the day of discharge).[4] The beneficiary must be transferred to a SNF within 30 days after discharge from the hospital, unless the condition of the beneficiary makes it medically inappropriate for admission after discharge.[5]

When these requirements are met, the beneficiary may receive up to 100 days of SNF care. The services may be provided in a Medicare-certified SNF, a distinct SNF located within a hospital, or a critical access hospital with swing bed approval.

While SNFs allow Medicare beneficiaries to access skilled long-term care services, Medicaid beneficiaries may receive skilled care in a nursing facility (NF). NFs are Medicaid-certified long-term care facilities where the beneficiary receives care under their state Medicaid program. While many of the qualifications for services are similar to a SNF, all states have income and asset requirements in order to qualify for NF skilled care. For this article, "nursing homes" refers to SNFs for Medicare and NFs for Medicaid.

Enforcement and Regulation

Critical focus areas for enforcement include fines; satisfying the rigorous operational and care mandates in the federal regulations; consistently maintaining high levels of infection control practices; billing; emergency preparedness; vendor relationships and referrals; and Coronavirus Aid, Relief, and Economic Security (CARES) Act provider relief fund use and reporting.

Nursing homes are likely the most highly regulated providers of healthcare. Nursing homes must comply with the Requirements of Participation (ROPs) found at 42 C.F.R. § 483 . The ROPs which were significantly revised in 2018 focus on patient-centered care. Most notably, the ROPs mandated that all nursing homes have a compliance program, making them the first providers of healthcare required to have a compliance program. The Centers for Medicare & Medicaid Services (CMS) is expected to issue interpretive guidance on the compliance program, which will appear as guidance to surveyors in "Appendix PP" of the CMS *State Operations Manual.*

CMS has the responsibility for ensuring compliance with the ROPs through surveys conducted by the state survey agencies. The state survey agencies conduct annual surveys of nursing homes at least once every 18 months. The state survey agencies also conduct abbreviated surveys of nursing homes when there is a complaint allegation. Federal surveyors have the ability to conduct surveys in order to verify the state survey agencies are following federal survey protocols. Federal surveyors will sometimes assist the state survey agencies if the care at the nursing home warrants their assistance.

Failure to comply with the ROPs can subject nursing homes to significant penalties, including per-day civil money penalties. Other remedies available to CMS are denials of payment for new or all admissions, installing a temporary manager, and directed plans of correction. CMS also has the authority to terminate nursing homes from the Medicare and/or Medicaid programs.

The COVID-19 pandemic caused CMS to focus on violations of the infection control ROP due to the high number of COVID-19 outbreaks in nursing homes. Nursing homes need to pay special attention to their infection control programs. CMS expects nursing homes to have an infection control program that creates "a system for preventing, identifying, reporting, investigating, and controlling infections and communicable diseases for all residents, staff, volunteers, visitors, and other individuals providing services under a contractual arrangement."[6] CMS will continue to focus on compliance with the infection control ROPs, which has led to several six-figure civil monetary penalties in recent years.

Recent healthcare fraud schemes involving nursing homes have been announced by the U.S. Department of Justice (DOJ). One DOJ announcement included an extensive healthcare fraud conspiracy involving a network of assisted living facilities and SNFs, in which the owner bribed physicians to admit patients into the facilities. The owner then cycled the patients through the facilities where they often failed to receive appropriate medical services or received medically unnecessary services billed to Medicare and Medicaid.[7]

Nursing homes are at an increased audit risk under the Patient-Driven Payment Model (PDPM) as CMS has committed to closely monitor therapy service utilization, payment, and quality trends in the course of billing under PDPM.[8] It is extremely important for providers to understand that, while therapy is not the reimbursement driver under PDPM as it was under the SNF Prospective Payment System (PPS), providers are still required to provide all therapy necessary if the resident requires therapy under the Medicare SNF benefit. Other PDPM billing-specific risk areas to consider include Interim Payment Assessment (IPA), upcoding, and care design driven by patient goals.

In 2016, CMS updated its life safety and emergency preparedness regulations to improve protections for all Medicare and Medicaid beneficiaries, including residents of nursing homes. Updates included requirements that nursing homes have expanded sprinkler systems and smoke detector coverage; an emergency preparedness plan that is reviewed, explained to staff through training, tested, and updated at least annually; and provisions for sheltering in place and evacuation. Recent Department of Health & Human Services (HHS) Office of Inspector General (OIG) reviews and surveys have found that nursing homes participating in Medicare or Medicaid programs consistently failed to comply with CMS and state requirements for life safety and emergency preparedness.

In addition to the regulatory authority CMS has over nursing homes, most states also license nursing homes. States that license nursing homes will generally refer to the nursing home as a nursing home, long-term care facility, or health facility. States will regulate nursing homes pursuant to licensure regulations separate from the ROPs. In some states, the licensure regulations defer to the ROPs or are similar to the ROPs. In other states, the licensure regulations impose requirements that have no connection to the ROPs. Nursing homes must pay close attention to state licensure regulations. If a nursing home loses its state license, it is also automatically terminated from the Medicare and/or Medicaid program.

Risk Area Governance

- **Requirements for Long Term Care Facilities, 42 C.F.R. §§ 483.1–483.95** . Also referred to as the ROPs, these are the federal regulations governing a nursing home's participation in the Medicare program.[9]
- *State Operations Manual,* **Chapter 7: Survey and Enforcement Process for Skilled Nursing Facilities and Nursing Facilities**. Chapter 7, or the *State Operations Manual,* sets forth how the state survey agencies carry out surveys of nursing homes.[10]
- *State Operations Manual,* **Appendix PP: Guidance to Surveyors for Long Term Care Facilities**. Appendix PP contains the interpretive guidelines to the ROPs. State agency surveyors use the interpretive guidelines when conducting surveys of nursing homes.[11]
- *Medicare Claims Processing Manual,* **Chapter 6: SNF Inpatient Part A Billing and SNF Consolidated Billing**. Chapter 6 of the *Medicare Claims Processing Manual* outlines the various billing requirement for SNFs to submit accurate Medicare claims under Medicare Part A and the consolidated billing requirement specific to SNFs.[12]

- ***Medicare Claims Processing Manual*, Chapter 7: SNF Part B Billing**. Chapter 7 of the *Medicare Claims Processing Manual* outlines how SNFs bill for various Medicare Part B services that are not subject to Medicare Part A payment, such as rehabilitation services, durable medical equipment, drugs, and laboratory services.[13]
- ***Medicare Benefit Policy Manual*, Chapter 8: Coverage of Extended Care (SNF) Services Under Hospital Insurance**. Chapter 8 of the *Medicare Benefit Policy Manual* provides an overview of SNF reimbursement and level of care requirements. It also outlines prior hospitalization requirements applicable to SNF beneficiaries. Physician certification requirements for SNF services are also addressed.[14]
- **OIG Work Plan**. The OIG Work Plan is a valuable resource for nursing homes as it identifies areas of vulnerabilities for providers. The OIG Work Plan is submitted on an annual basis and is updated throughout the year.[15]
- **Anti-Kickback Statute, 42 U.S.C. § 1320a–7b(b)** . Prohibits requesting or receiving anything of value in exchange for referrals.[16]
- **Civil False Claims Act, 31 U.S.C. §§ 3729–3733** . Provides for monetary penalties against those who submit false claims to the government. Damages can include treble damages and monetary penalties per false claim. False claims allegations by a whistleblower are brought in civil court. If the government elects to intervene, it becomes a criminal complaint.[17]
- **Criminal False Claims Acts, 18 U.S.C. § 287** . Provides for actions brought by the government for the submission of false claims up to and including fines and imprisonment.[18]
- **HIPAA Privacy and Security rules: 45 C.F.R. §§ 160, 164.102, 164.302, 164.500** . National standards for the protection of protected health information.[19]

Common Compliance Risks

Compliance with the ROPs

Failure to comply with the ROPs can lead to termination from the Medicare program as well as a whole host of other penalties. These include civil monetary penalties, denials on payments for new and all admissions, temporary management, and directed plans of correction.

Improper Contracts with Vendors

Nursing homes should ensure their contracts with vendors are in writing and set forth the responsibilities of the parties. The contracts should not in any way provide for compensation in return for referrals, which is prohibited by the Anti-Kickback Statute, if the contract does not meet a safe harbor. Nursing homes should also be aware of their responsibility to provide education and training to their vendors under the ROPs as part of their compliance program.

Having Exclusive Relationships with Hospices

The OIG believes there is potential for kickbacks between hospices and nursing homes.[20] The OIG is wary of nursing homes having exclusive arrangements with a particular hospice and believes the possibility of illegal remuneration is high. The OIG also cites instances where patients receiving hospice services in a nursing home receive fewer services than patients receiving hospice services in their homes.

Claims for Services not Rendered or Provided as Claimed

The OIG has identified common schemes whereby nursing homes have falsified medical records or claims in order to bill for services not provided.[21] One example the OIG identified of filing a claim for services not provided was a physician who billed for comprehensive physical examinations without seeing a single resident.

Physician Certifications and Recertifications

Nursing homes should ensure that all physician certifications are obtained on a timely basis. If a nursing home fails to do so, the resident will not qualify for skilled care. The physician certification should be obtained upon admission or as soon as is reasonable and practicable after admission. Physician recertifications are required within 14 days of admission and every 30 days thereafter.

Failure to Check the OIG List of Excluded Individuals and Entities

The OIG maintains a list of individuals and entities excluded from the Medicare and/or Medicaid programs. Failure of a nursing home to check this list could result in a payback to CMS for employing an individual excluded from Medicare and/or Medicaid. Nursing homes should make it a priority to routinely check the list of excluded individuals and entities and make it part of the hiring process when recruiting providers of services.[22]

Overutilization and Underutilization of Therapy Services

CMS has always been suspicious of nursing homes overutilizing therapy. While this was more of an issue with SNF PPS as opposed to PDPM, nursing homes should make sure they are not providing high volumes of therapy without proper documentation. Conversely, under PDPM, CMS has specifically stated the while therapy is not the driver of reimbursement that it once was, nursing homes are still expected to provide therapy if the resident's condition requires therapy.

CARES Act Provider Relief Funds Reporting

Nursing homes received general and targeted financial distributions of provider relief funds under the CARES Act due to the COVID-19 pandemic. In order to receive these funds, nursing homes were required to sign agreements with terms and conditions to attest that the money received would be used for COVID-19 purposes. Nursing homes were also required to report how the money was used. Failure to accurately report how CARES Act funding was used will subject nursing homes to potential paybacks and audits.[23]

Addressing Compliance Risks

Review of Policies and Procedures

Nursing homes must maintain current policies and procedures in order to comply with the ROPs and Medicare billing requirements. Policies and procedures must be updated as necessary to account for regulatory and reimbursement changes.

Implementing a Compliance Program

The ROPs require nursing homes to implement an effective compliance program. The ROPs require the compliance program to be designed in such a way that it is reasonably capable of reducing the prospect of criminal, civil, and administrative violations and promote quality of care. Board oversight of the compliance program is critical as the board is legally responsible for compliance program oversight.[24]

Auditing and Monitoring

Nursing homes should conduct auditing and monitoring that focuses on day-to-day operations, including compliance with the ROPs, billing, cost reporting, contract review, and compliance with all state and federal laws and regulations governing nursing homes. The nursing home should consider its resources, prior compliance history, and other risk factors when assessing the degree of auditing and monitoring it performs. The OIG encourages nursing homes to conduct periodic compliance audits using internal or external auditors who have knowledge of federal and state laws, regulations, and other guidance.

Education and Training

Proper education and training are critical for nursing homes given the complex myriad of laws, regulations, and guidance that govern nursing home operations. Nursing homes are expected to take steps to effectively communicate role-specific standards, policies, and procedures to staff, individuals providing services under contract, and volunteers. The OIG expects nursing homes to provide education and training on fraud and abuse laws and federal healthcare program and payer requirements. The OIG also suggests that nursing homes provide education and training on claims submission and development, residents' rights, and marketing practices.

Facility Assessment

Nursing homes should be integrating the information and data they collect or that arises out of their compliance programs into their Quality Assurance and Performance Improvement (QAPI) program with their required facility assessment as they develop and maintain their compliance programs.

Possible Penalties

Termination from the Medicare and Medicaid Programs

Nursing homes may be terminated from the Medicare and Medicaid programs in as little as 23 days if the deficiencies cited are considered immediate jeopardy by the state survey agency. Most nursing homes avoid termination, but if terminated, the process for readmission into the Medicare and Medicaid programs is a long and arduous process that few nursing homes can undertake financially.

Per-Day Civil Money Penalties

The upper range for per day civil monetary penalties for immediate deficiencies in 2020 was $3,050–$10,000 and $50–$3,000 for deficiencies that are not immediate jeopardy.[25] Providers should be aware that these amounts are updated annually.

Per-Instance Civil Money Penalties

Per-instance civil money penalties may be imposed in the amount of $50–$3,000 for deficiencies that are not immediate jeopardy. Providers should be aware that these amounts are updated annually.

Appointment of Temporary Manager

In immediate jeopardy situations, CMS may appoint a temporary manager to operate the facility until the nursing home attains compliance.[26] The temporary manager has wide latitude in operating the nursing home, including the ability to hire and fire staff and obligate funds. The nursing home will be terminated from the Medicare and Medicaid programs for failure to relinquish all management authority to the temporary manager.

State Monitoring

In situations where a nursing home has been cited for substandard quality of care on three consecutive standard surveys, CMS may appoint a monitor to oversee correction of the deficiencies cited in the facility. A monitor is an employee or contractor of the state survey agency, is not an employee or contractor of the monitored facility, and does not have an immediate family member who is a resident of the facility.

Required and Optional Denial of Payment for New Admissions

An optional denial of payment for new admissions may be imposed when a nursing home is not in substantial compliance with the ROPs. Denial of payment for new admissions is required if a nursing home is not in compliance for three months after being cited for non-compliance with the ROPs or has been cited for substandard quality of care on three consecutive standard surveys.

Directed Plans of Correction and In-Service Training

CMS, the state survey agency, or temporary manager have the authority to dictate the terms of a plan of correction when a nursing home is not in compliance with the ROPs. Mandatory in-service training may be imposed where there is a pattern of deficiencies and education is likely to correct the deficiencies.

State Licensure Penalties

In states where nursing homes are licensed, states generally have the authority to revoke or place a license on probation. States may also have the authority to impose civil money penalties and appoint a temporary manager or receiver independent of CMS-imposed penalties.

Compliance Resources

The Centers for Medicare & Medicaid Services

The CMS website has invaluable information that can be used by nursing homes that include the ROPs, *State Operations Manual*, and other Medicare manuals on billing and reimbursement issues. Nursing homes can also subscribe to email updates from CMS that provide the latest regulatory and reimbursement changes.

State Operations Manual
Chapter 7: Survey and Enforcement Process for Skilled Nursing Facilities and Nursing Facilities:
https://www.cms.gov/Regulations-and-Guidance/Guidance/Manuals/Downloads/som107c07pdf.pdf

Appendix PP – Guidance to Surveyors for Long Term Care Facilities:
https://www.cms.gov/medicare/provider-enrollment-and-certification/guidanceforlawsandregulations/downloads/appendix-pp-state-operations-manual.pdf

Medicare Administrative Contractors

Like CMS, the various Medicare administrative contractors are excellent sources of information with regard to Medicare reimbursement, enrollment, and claims filing issues. The Medicare administrative contractors also provide excellent educational resources. They include:

- **CGS Administrators**: https://www.cgsmedicare.com/
- **Palmetto GBA**: https://www.palmettogba.com/
- **National Government Services**: http://www.NGSMedicare.com
- **Novitas Solutions**: https://www.novitas-solutions.com

Program for Evaluating Payment Patterns Electronic Report (PEPPER)

PEPPER Reports should be used by a nursing home as it summarizes claims data that may put the nursing home at risk for improper payment due to billing and coding irregularities.

https://pepper.cbrpepper.org/

National and State Trade Associations

National trade associations and their affiliates are valuable resources to nursing homes. The predominant trade associations for nursing homes are the American Health Care Association/National Center for Assisted Living, LeadingAge, and their state affiliates. Both of these trade associations have robust educational programs and resources only available to members:

- **American Health Care Association/National Center for Assisted Living**: http://www.ahcancal.org
- **LeadingAge**: http://www.leadingage.org

**U.S. Department of Health & Human Services, Office of Inspector General
Enforcement and Exclusion Database**
Nursing homes that employ individuals or contract with entities excluded from the Medicare or Medicaid programs are subject to repayment for allowing individuals or entities to provide services to residents. Nursing homes should regularly check and have a policy that calls for routine checks of the OIG Enforcement and Exclusion Database.

https://exclusions.oig.hhs.gov/

Risk Takeaways

Main points of interest:
- Nursing homes are the most regulated providers of healthcare in the United States.
- Nursing homes are subject to a plethora of federal and state regulations on delivering quality of care and guidance on how to properly file claims for reimbursement.
- Due to the highly regulated environment in which they operate, it is critical that nursing homes stay abreast of all existing regulations and program guidance governing their operations.

Areas to watch:
- Updates to guidance on ROP enforcement and interpretive guidance on how surveys are conducted.
- Increased CMS scrutiny over infection control practices.
- CARES Act Provider Relief Fund reporting and potential HHS audits of funds received.
- Implementation and surveys of compliance programs.
- Improper contractual relationships with hospice providers.
- Continued focus on emergency preparedness.
- Education and training of contracted entities.
- A renewed CMS focus on mandatory staffing.
- Possible HHS proposal of a single reimbursement methodology for all post-acute care providers.

Laws that apply:
- Requirements for Long Term Care Facilities: 42 C.F.R. §§ 483.1–483.95
- Anti-Kickback Statute: 42 U.S.C. § 1320a–7b(b)
- Civil False Claims Act: 31 U.S.C. §§ 3729–3733
- Criminal False Claims Acts: 18 U.S.C. § 287
- HIPAA Privacy and Security rules: 45 C.F.R. §§ 160, 164.102, 164.302, 164.500

> ### Addressing compliance risks:
> - Implement and update policies and procedures to account for regulatory changes.
> - Continually train and educate staff on policies and procedures along with regulatory changes.
> - Have a robust compliance and education program.
> - Develop and update the facility assessment required by the ROPs.
> - Conduct auditing and monitoring of quality of care and billing areas of risk.
> - Implement and update the emergency preparedness program.
> - Periodically check the OIG Enforcement and Exclusions Database.

Endnotes

1. **Todd Selby** is a shareholder at Hall, Render, Killian, Heath & Lyman PC and specializes in representing post-acute care providers. Selby has represented post-acute care providers for over 30 years in all facets of legal issues with an emphasis on regulatory compliance, reimbursement, provider enrollment, administrative litigation, and mergers and acquisitions.

2. **Sean Fahey** is an attorney at Hall, Render, Killian, Heath & Lyman PC and represents the needs of skilled nursing and assisted living facilities in all areas of healthcare compliance, governance, transactions, licensure, Medicare enrollment, contracts, administrative appeals, and accounts receivable recovery.

3. 42 C.F.R. § 409.31(a).

4. 42 C.F.R. § 409.30(a)(1).

5. 42 C.F.R. § 409.30(b)(2)(i).

6. 42 C.F.R. § 483.80(a)(1).

7. Department of Justice, "South Florida Health Care Facility Owner Sentenced to 20 Years in Prison for Role in Largest Health Care Fraud Scheme Ever Charged by The Department of Justice," news release, September 12, 2019, https://www.justice.gov/opa/pr/south-florida-health-care-facility-owner-sentenced-20-years-prison-role-largest-health-care.

8. "Patient Driven Payment Model," Centers for Medicare & Medicaid Services, updated August 3, 2020, https://www.cms.gov/Medicare/Medicare-Fee-for-Service-Payment/SNFPPS/PDPM.

9. 42 C.F.R. §§ 483.1–483.95.

10. Centers for Medicare & Medicaid Services, "Chapter 7: Survey and Enforcement Process for Skilled Nursing Facilities and Nursing Facilities," *State Operations Manual*, Pub. 100-07, revised November 16, 2018, https://www.cms.gov/Regulations-and-Guidance/Guidance/Manuals/Downloads/som107c07pdf.pdf.

11. Centers for Medicare & Medicaid Services, "Appendix PP - Guidance to Surveyors for Long Term Care Facilities," *State Operations Manual*, Pub. 100-07, revised November 22, 2017, https://www.cms.gov/medicare/provider-enrollment-and-certification/guidanceforlawsandregulations/downloads/appendix-pp-state-operations-manual.pdf.

12. Centers for Medicare & Medicaid Services, "Chapter 6: SNF Inpatient Part A Billing and SNF Consolidated Billing," *Medicare Claims Processing Manual*, Pub. 100-04, revised May 15, 2020, https://www.cms.gov/Regulations-and-guidance/Guidance/Manuals/Downloads/clm104c06.pdf.

13. Centers for Medicare & Medicaid Services, "Chapter 7: SNF Part B Billing (Including Inpatient Part B and Outpatient Fee Schedule)," *Medicare Claims Processing Manual*, Pub. 100-04, revised March 18, 2016, https://www.cms.gov/regulations-and-guidance/guidance/manuals/downloads/clm104c07.pdf.

14. Centers for Medicare & Medicaid Services, "Chapter 8: Coverage of Extended Care (SNF) Services Under Hospital Insurance," *Medicare Benefit Policy Manual*, Pub. 100-02, revised October 4, 2019, https://www.cms.gov/Regulations-and-Guidance/Guidance/Manuals/Downloads/bp102c08pdf.pdf.

15. "Work Plan," U.S. Department of Health & Human Services, Office of Inspector General, accessed January 8, 2021, https://oig.hhs.gov/reports-and-publications/workplan/.

16. 42 U.S.C. §1320a-7b(b).

17. 31 U.S.C. §§ 3729–3731.

18. 18 U.S.C. § 287.

19. 45 C.F.R. §§ 160, 164.102, 164.500.

20. U.S. Department of Health & Human Services, Office of Inspector General, "Special Fraud Alert: Fraud and Abuse in Nursing Home Arrangements With Hospices," March 1998, https://oig.hhs.gov/fraud/docs/alertsandbulletins/hospice.pdf.

21. U.S. Department of Health & Human Services, Office of Inspector General, "Special Fraud Alert: Fraud and Abuse in the Provision of Services in Nursing Facilities," May 1996, https://oig.hhs.gov/fraud/docs/alertsandbulletins/SFANursingFacilities.pdf.

22. "LEIE Downloadable Databases," U.S. Department of Health & Human Services, Office of Inspector General, updated February 10, 2021, https://oig.hhs.gov/exclusions/exclusions_list.asp.

23. "CARES Act Provider Relief Fund: For Providers," U.S. Department of Health & Human Services, accessed January 7, 2021, https://www.hhs.gov/coronavirus/cares-act-provider-relief-fund/for-providers/index.html.

24. 42 C.F.R. § 483.85 .

25. 42 C.F.R. § 488.438 .

26. 42 C.F.R. § 488.408 .

Provider-Based Rules and Regulations

Provider-Based Rules and Regulations

By Ilah Naudasher,[1] BA, MA; and Shannon DeBra, Esq.[2]

What Are Provider-Based Rules and Regulations?

Hospitals and other healthcare providers often are faced with the decision of whether to treat locations or sites outside the four walls of their main provider location as part of the main provider or as freestanding entities—in other words, the decision to make them provider-based to the main provider. "Provider-based" is a Medicare payment designation established by the Social Security Act that allows facilities owned by and integrated with a healthcare provider (usually a hospital) to bill Medicare as a department of that healthcare provider, often historically resulting in these facilities receiving higher payments than they would as freestanding facilities.[3] Hospitals are the type of healthcare provider that most commonly elect to treat such locations or sites as provider-based, but other types of healthcare providers (e.g., skilled nursing facilities, federally qualified health centers, and rural health clinics) can also have locations that are considered provider-based to the main provider. This article focuses primarily on hospitals and their provider-based locations, since that is the most common use of provider-based status and that is where the Centers for Medicare & Medicaid Services (CMS) recent rulemaking efforts have focused.

Being designated as provider-based allows hospitals to treat certain departments and facilities located outside of the hospital as part of the hospital for Medicare—and, depending on state law, sometimes Medicaid and commercial payer—billing and payment purposes. Services furnished in a location meeting the applicable provider-based requirements are considered by Medicare to be hospital outpatient services, but they may not be paid under the Medicare Outpatient Prospective Payment System (OPPS), depending on the circumstances, as discussed later in this article.

A number of possible reasons exist for making a location outside the hospital provider-based to the hospital. It could be to address capacity and space issues within the hospital itself; improve patient convenience and access to hospital-level care in locations other than where the main hospital is located; for quality purposes; to permit the location to participate in hospital contracts (including payer contracts); and/or to permit the provider-based location to participate in the 340B drug discount program (as the provider-based location of the hospital will be included on the hospital's cost report and may qualify to be a child site for 340B drug discount program purposes).

When a location has provider-based status, the hospital can bill Medicare for the services provided in the location just as it would for other hospital services. Under the Medicare system, that means the hospital bills for its facility fee or technical fee, and the physician separately bills for the professional services. (The same is not true for many commercial payers that do not allow a "split bill." Payer rules will need to be consulted to determine how to bill each payer in this situation.) This ability to charge the facility fee is where the primary financial benefit of provider-based status is for hospitals. If the same services furnished in a hospital-based clinic were instead provided in a physician office, no facility fee could be billed; only the physician's professional fee, using the place of service (POS) code 11 to reflect physician office, could be billed to Medicare. The physician's reimbursement under the Medicare Physician Fee Schedule (MPFS) is higher when POS code 11 is used than when services are provided in a hospital facility location and billed using one of the applicable hospital POS codes.[4] This is because when the physician furnishes services in a hospital facility location, Medicare assumes that the physician is not incurring the same amount of overhead that the physician incurs for services provided in the physician's private office. The hospital's overhead and other expenses are reimbursed through the facility fee or technical fee that the hospital bills to Medicare for the visit. Taken together, the physician's professional fee, combined with the hospital's facility fee, usually results in a higher combined reimbursement for the service than Medicare would have paid if the services were provided in a nonhospital setting. In addition, the Medicare beneficiary who receives services from a location that is provider-based to the hospital will often have two cost-sharing liabilities—one for the hospital bill and another for the physician bill.

Historically, there has been a payment differential, known as the site differential, for services provided in hospital outpatient departments or clinics versus freestanding clinics and physician offices, but many of those payment differentials have been eliminated in recent years, especially for newer locations. Even with many of the payment differentials eliminated, there are still other advantages to being provider-based to a hospital that may make it advantageous to pursue provider-based status. Yet with those advantages there are also certain responsibilities and compliance risks.

Risk Area Governance

The Medicare regulation setting forth the requirements for provider-based status is 42 C.F.R. § 413.65—"Requirements for a determination that a facility or an organization has provider-based status" (referred to herein as the "provider-based regulation").[5] The provider-based regulation is divided into several sections, some of which have general applicability for all provider-based departments and locations, and others whose applicability only apply to hospitals or otherwise depend on particular facts and circumstances.

In addition to the specific requirements of the provider-based regulation, embedded within it are additional legal requirements with which provider-based locations of hospitals must also comply, since they are considered part of the hospital. These include the Emergency Medical Treatment and Labor Act (EMTALA) (42 U.S.C. § 1395dd) and the Medicare Conditions of Participation (COPs) for hospitals (42 C.F.R. § 482).[6][7]

Provider-Based Regulation Definitions

The provider-based regulation applies to all facilities for which provider-based status is sought. The provider-based regulation includes a number of definitions for terms used throughout the regulation. They include:[8]

- **Provider-based status**: The "relationship between a main provider and a provider-based entity or a department of a provider, remote location of a hospital, or satellite facility."
- **Freestanding facility**: An "entity that furnishes health care services to Medicare beneficiaries and that is not integrated with any other entity as a main provider, a department of a provider, remote location of a hospital, satellite facility, or a provider-based entity."
- **Main provider**: The "provider that either creates, or acquires ownership of, another entity to deliver . . . health care services under its name, ownership, and financial and administrative control."
- **Provider-based entity**: A provider of healthcare services "that is either created by, or acquired by, a main provider for the purpose of furnishing health care services of a *different* type from those of the main provider under the ownership and administrative and financial control of the main provider." (emphasis added)
- **Department of a provider**: A "facility or organization that is either created by, or acquired by, a main provider for the purpose of furnishing health care services of the *same* type as those furnished by the main provider." (emphasis added)
- **Remote location of a hospital**: A "facility or an organization that is either created by, or acquired by, a hospital that is a main provider for the purpose of furnishing inpatient hospital services under the name, ownership, and financial and administrative control of the main provider." It comprises both the physical facility that is the site of service and the personnel and equipment used to deliver the service and does not include a "satellite facility."

Provider-based entities, departments of a provider, and remote locations of a hospital include the physical facility that serves as the site of services of a type that could be claimed under the Medicare or Medicaid program *and* the personnel and equipment needed to deliver the services at that facility.

Provider-Based Determinations

The provider-based regulation makes clear that a facility or organization is not entitled to be treated as provider-based just because it believes it is provider-based. Such a facility or organization must meet all of the applicable regulatory requirements in order to be appropriately treated as provider-based. Under current CMS policy, healthcare providers may, but are not required to, seek a determination from CMS that their facilities meet the requirements of the provider-based regulation.

However, CMS will not make determinations of provider-based status for payment purposes for the following types of facilities, since such determinations would not affect either Medicare payment or Medicare beneficiary liability or scope of benefits:[9]

- Ambulatory surgery centers
- Comprehensive outpatient rehabilitation facilities
- Home health agencies
- Skilled nursing facilities (determinations are made in accordance with 42 C.F.R. § 483.5 instead)
- Hospices
- Inpatient rehabilitation units that are excluded from the inpatient prospective payment system for acute hospital services
- Independent diagnostic testing facilities furnishing only services paid under a fee schedule, facilities that furnish only clinical diagnostic tests (excluding clinical diagnostic laboratories that are parts of critical access hospitals (CAHs)), and facilities that furnish only some combination of these services
- Facilities (except those operating as part of CAHs) furnishing only physician, occupational, or speech therapy to ambulatory patients during any period when the annual payment cap for coverage of such services is suspended by legislation (see Section 1833(g)(2) of the Social Security Act for more information)
- End-stage renal disease facilities (determinations are made in accordance with 42 C.F.R. § 413.174)
- Departments of providers that perform necessary functions but do not provide services of a type for which separate payment could be claimed under Medicare or Medicaid (examples include laundry and medical records department)
- Ambulances
- Rural health clinics affiliated with hospitals with 50 or more beds

Healthcare providers that seek a determination of provider-based status must submit an attestation to CMS that documents compliance with the requirements of the provider-based regulation. The applicable requirements vary depending on whether the facility is on the campus of the main provider or not and whether the main provider is a hospital. Attestations for off-campus facilities must include documentation supporting the attestations made by the main provider as to how the facility complies with the applicable requirements of the provider-based regulation. While providers are not required to submit an attestation seeking a determination of provider-based status, the advantage to doing so is that CMS approval of the facility as provider-based eliminates the risk of retrospective recoveries should CMS later determine that the facility did not actually meet all of the requirements to be treated as provider-based.

CMS Provider-Based Requirements

The following requirements are applicable to all provider-based facilities and organizations, and all of the requirements must be met to qualify for provider-based status. These requirements expect the provider-based location to act, operate, and look like the main provider does in all that they do in order to be integral to the main provider. Any deviation in how the provider-based location operates from the main provider could jeopardize an organization's provider-based status, and thus provider-based reimbursement. To help prepare an organization, use the CMS provider-based attestation document that the applicable Medicare administrative contractor (MAC) has posted on its website as a guide to comply with these rules.[10]

Licensure

The provider-based location must do so under the same licensure of the main provider unless state law indicates differently. Not all states license hospitals, and some states require separate licensure of the provider-based entity, so it is important to verify the applicable state law regarding licensure.

Clinical Integration

Integration of clinical service means that the provider-based location handles clinical services in the same manner as the main provider by doing the following:

- All clinical staff must have the same level of medical staff privileges as those at the main provider. For example, the physicians at the provider-based location must have the same privileges as the same type of physicians at the hospital.
- The same level of monitoring and oversight must take place at the provider-based location like it does at the main provider. These locations cannot be "on an island on their own," with no supervision by the main provider.
- The medical directors of the provider-based location must report to someone at the main provider and have the same expectations (including responsibilities, supervision, and accountability) as any other main location medical director.
- Committees (such as medical director or a comparable committee) at the main provider must be responsible for the provider-based location. These committees must treat medical activities such as utilization review, quality, and coordination the same as the main provider.
- All medical records must be in the main provider's unified medical record system.

- Patients from the provider-based location must have access to all inpatient and outpatient services at the main provider.

Financial Integration

Financial operations must also be integrated with the main provider, and proof of this integration must exist. Examples of financial integration include shared income/expenses along with the costs of the provider-based location being reported on the main provider's cost report. Financial integration proof may be required when submitting a provider-based attestation via a trial balance report showing the integration truly exists.

Public Awareness

The provider-based location must present itself as a location of the main provider. When patients walk in to the provider-based location, it must be obvious that they are entering a location of the main provider and that they will receive a bill from the main provider.

In addition to entry signage, other forms of marketing and advertising, such as website information, internal wayfinding signs, patient documents (e.g., registration and letterhead), and advertisements, must include the evidence that the provider-based location is part of the main provider. In the event of submitting an attestation, proof of public awareness is required to be submitted in the form of pictures.

Public awareness and signage are also important for CMS enrollment procedures as well as provider-based rules. CMS uses a separate contractor (National Site Visit Contractor (NSCV)) to make site visits to Medicare-enrolled providers to ensure the site truly exists, that the site is capable of providing services as expressed on the enrollment documents, etc.[11] Proper and obvious signage of a provider-based location can also assist in assuring the enrollment process is seamless.

Public awareness includes how the phones are answered—do the patients know that they are calling a provider-based location? The enrollment departments of CMS also verify how the phones are answered during the enrollment process.

Lastly, patient signage is not only important in meeting the spirit of the various rules mentioned, but for the simple matter of avoiding patient confusion. If patients enter a multitenant building with more than one Medicare provider, signage simply helps patients understand where they are at, where they will receive services from, and where they will get a bill from. All it takes is one patient complaint about getting a bill from a hospital they feel they never visited to launch an inspection from CMS or a state agency.

Pay special attention to any state law on signage requirements as well—some states have specific rules on signage requirements for provider-based locations. The state of Washington, for example, has rules on signage and other requirements for provider-based facilities.[12]

Requirements Applicable to Off-Campus Hospital Outpatient Departments (HOPDs) and Hospital-Based Entities

Ownership and Control

The provider-based location must be 100% owned and operated by the main provider and have the same governing body (i.e., the hospital board).[13] This also means that the provider-based locations fall under the same rules, including human resources (HR) policies, contract approvals, and bylaws, as the main provider as further evidence that the location is truly part of the main provider.

Administrative and Supervision

All administrative operations and supervision of the provider-based location must also be performed by the main provider and its existing departments.[14] This includes the leadership of the provider-based location reporting up to someone from the main provider, in the same fashion as reporting occurs by employees of the main provider, with the same level of intensity and frequency.

All administrative operations (such as billing, human resources, medical records, finance, and supply chain) must be integrated with the main provider. This should be evidenced in the form of operations (e.g., the provider-based location should not have a separate HR department or a separate process for purchasing), and this should be documented on organizational charts. The leadership from the main provider is ultimately responsible for the operations of the provider-based location.

Location

CMS requires the provider-based location to be located within 35 miles of the main provider.[15] Measurement of the distance between the main provider and a potential provider-based location does not have to done via driving directions; the measurement can be done via a measurement of distance as the crow flies. In addition, there are exceptions to the 35-mile rule that account for whether the provider-based location is owned by a disproportionate share hospital (DSH) with an adjustment of 11.75% or greater or if at least 75% of the patients served at the provider-based location reside in the same zip code.[16] A careful analysis of the location exceptions is necessary if a facility does not meet the 35-mile rule.

Special Rules for HOPDs and Hospital-Based Entities to Qualify for Provider-Based Status

EMTALA: The Emergency Medical Treatment and Labor Act, also known as the "anti-dumping" rule, requires all patients be provided a medical screening exam and stabilization of an emergent medical condition and, if necessary, transfer to another facility, regardless of their ability to pay.[17]

Physician billing using correct POS codes:[18]

- To assure appropriate payment based on the provider-based location where the services were provided, the correct POS must be appended to the professional claim form (the CMS-1500 claim form).[19] If the location is an off-campus hospital, POS code 19 would be required, whereas POS code 22 would be used for on-campus hospital. Use of POS code 11 (office) would be inappropriate and would cause an overpayment to the physician.
- When working with independent providers in these locations, expressing this requirement in a written agreement would be advisable to assure these providers understand what type of location they are treating patients at and bill Medicare appropriately.

Provider-based locations of hospitals must comply with the hospitals' Medicare provider agreements, which incorporate the conditions of participation:[20] This includes the prohibition about sharing of clinical space and compliance with life safety code as set forth in 42 C.F.R. § 482.

Compliance with the nondiscrimination requirements must be met by all providers working in the provider-based location:[21] The main provider should already have a policy in place to assure compliance with 42 C.F.R. § 489.10, with which the provider-based location must also comply. At a high level, this condition of participation prohibits discrimination based on race, color, national origin, age, and disability.

Must treat all Medicare patients as hospital outpatients:[22] Patients treated in the provider-based locations must be treated as hospital outpatients at all times; there should not be times where some are treated as physician office and others as hospital outpatients. Remember, hospital space is hospital space 24/7, and this is the same for any type of patient.

Three-day payment window:[23] Under the three-day payment window rule, any outpatient services provided within three days of a hospital admission must be included on the inpatient claim (i.e., they will not be paid separately). When thinking about provider-based clinics of a hospital, payment for services provided in these locations would be affected by the three-day rule.

Required written notice of beneficiary coinsurance liability:[24]

- When a patient is treated at an off-campus provider-based location of a hospital, the hospital must provide a notice of coinsurance prior to the service being provided. This notice is to inform the patient that the services they are about to receive will be subject to a coinsurance from both the physician and the hospital and to advise the patient of the amount of the potential financial liability. Many patients are surprised and upset by this when they receive two bills. This is likely one of the biggest issues with provider-based billing—patients feel they are being double-billed.
- If an exact amount of the patient's potential financial liability is not known, an estimate can be given.
- If the patient is unable to receive the notice, this notice can be given to the patient's representative.

- If the services provided to the patient were in accordance with EMTALA, the notice can be given after the patient has been stabilized.

Additional Provider-Based Requirements Depending on Particular Facts

Under Arrangements

Medicare COPs require hospitals to provide certain minimum services in order to qualify as a hospital. Hospitals do not have to provide all of those services themselves though. Hospitals can arrange for some required services to be provided "under arrangements" with another entity by entering into an agreement with that entity. However, the provider-based regulation prohibits facilities and organizations from qualifying for provider-based status if all patient care services furnished at the facility or organization are furnished under arrangements.[25]

Special Rules for Joint Ventures

In order for a facility or organization operated as a joint venture to be considered provider-based, it must meet the following additional requirements:[26]

- Must "be partially owned by at least one provider" and

- Must "be located on the main campus of a provider who is a partial owner" and be provider-based to that provider.

Special Rules for Management Contracts

Off-campus facilities or organizations that wish to be treated as provider-based must meet the following additional requirements if operated under a management contract:[27]

- The main provider (or an organization that employs the staff of the main provider and is not the management company) must employ the staff who are directly involved in the delivery of patient care:
  - Exception: Management staff and staff who furnish patient care of a type that would be paid for by Medicare on a fee schedule.
  - May not use "leased" employees from the management company for the delivery of patient care (except for staff paid on a fee schedule as described above);
- "The administrative functions of the facility or organization are integrated with those of the main provider."
- "The main provider has significant control over the operations of the facility or organization."
- The management contract must be held by the main provider itself and not by a parent organization.

Medicare Payment Implications of Provider-Based Status for HOPDs and Hospital-Based Entities

As mentioned previously, Medicare payments for services furnished in provider-based clinics and departments of hospitals were historically often significantly higher than payments for the same services furnished in a freestanding facility or physician office. This payment differential was a motivation for hospitals to designate off-site locations (often physician offices) as provider-based to the hospital. But this payment differential also often resulted in higher beneficiary coinsurance liability, because two claims are submitted to Medicare—one by the hospital and one by the physician or other professional—both of which carry beneficiary coinsurance liability, which in most cases is 20% of the Medicare payment.

In light of the higher Medicare reimbursement for these services furnished in provider-based locations and the higher beneficiary costs, provider-based status has been targeted for review and reform in recent years. Dating back to 1999, the Office of Inspector General (OIG) has expressed concerns about and identified vulnerabilities associated with the provider-based status designation.[28] These include oversight challenges and increased costs to Medicare and its beneficiaries, with no documented benefits. Although CMS had taken some steps to address concerns raised by the OIG over the years, it was Section 603 of the Bipartisan Budget Act (BBA) of 2015 that truly changed the course for hospital provider-based departments.[29] Section 603 of the BBA applies to any provider-based off-campus departments that were not billing as a hospital department as of November 2, 2015 (the effective date of the 2015 BBA). As a result, effective January 1, 2017, any hospital off-campus outpatient departments that were not billing Medicare as a hospital department under the OPPS as of November 2, 2015, are subject to "site-neutral" payments, meaning that the hospital's services are not reimbursable under the OPPS and will instead be paid under another system, the Medicare physician fee schedule.[30] However, the BBA of 2015 carved out certain exceptions to this site-neutral payment rule, allowing certain off-campus hospital outpatient departments to continue to receive the higher OPPS payments. As of January 1, 2017, no off-campus hospital outpatient department may be paid under the Medicare OPPS unless (i) it is a dedicated emergency department (DED), and (ii) it is excepted.[31]

All services furnished at DEDs continue to be reimbursed under the OPPS. For purposes of the provider-based rule and OPPS reimbursement, a DED is defined by the EMTALA definition as:[32]

- Licensed by the state as an emergency room or emergency department,
- Held out to the public as a place that provides care for emergency medical conditions on an urgent basis without requiring an appointment, or
- Providing at least one-third of all of its outpatient visits for the treatment of emergency medical conditions.

The 21st Century Cures Act (Cures Act),[33] which was signed into law on December 13, 2016, revised Section 603 of the BBA of 2015 and established three new exceptions to the site-neutral payment rule established in the BBA of 2015 for off-campus hospital provider-based locations.[34][35] The first exception addressed off-campus provider-based departments that were under development but not billing as provider-based for services as of November 2, 2015 (the effective date of the BBA of 2015) and submitted a voluntary provider-based attestation to CMS before December 2, 2015.[36] This category of off-campus provider-based departments was only temporarily grandfathered and able to continue OPPS payments through 2017.

The second exception was for off-campus provider-based departments that were "mid-build" as of November 2, 2015.[37] Under the Cures Act, "mid-build" meant that the provider entered into a binding written agreement with an unrelated third party for the actual construction of an off-campus provider-based department prior to November 2, 2015. These off-campus provider-based departments were permitted to bill for services under the OPPS as of January 1, 2018, if they:[38]

- Submitted a certification to CMS from their chief executive officer or chief operating officer by February 13, 2017, certifying that the off-campus provider-based department met the definition of "mid-build."
- Submitted an attestation to CMS by February 13, 2017, stating that the off-campus provider-based department meets the requirements of being provider-based.
- Added the new off-campus provider-based department to the hospital's Medicare enrollment form.

Many hospitals took advantage of the mid-build exception and submitted the required certification and attestation and added the new off-campus provider-based department to their Medicare enrollment form. In early 2021, CMS issued determinations on whether those hospital off-campus departments qualified for the mid-build exception and were eligible to receive OPPS reimbursement.[39]

The third exception from the Cures Act added an exemption for certain cancer hospitals as long as the cancer hospital submitted an attestation to CMS within 60 days of the latter of either February 13, 2017, or the date the cancer hospital met the provider-based requirements.[40]

Excepted versus Nonexcepted Status

What does it mean to be "excepted" for purposes of the provider-based rule and OPPS reimbursement? Excepted provider-based locations are:[41]

- Off-campus HOPDs that were furnishing OPPS services prior to November 2, 2015, that have not impermissibly relocated or changed ownership;
- Off-campus HOPDs that qualify under the mid-build or cancer hospital exception; and
- HOPDs on the campus or within 250 yards of the main hospital or a remote location of a multi-campus hospital.Note: Remote locations are considered off-campus of the main hospital, but locations within the distance (i.e., within 250 yards) of a remote location are excepted.

If an excepted HOPD loses its excepted status for any reason, it will not be able to regain excepted status and will no longer be eligible for OPPS reimbursement.

Effect of Relocation on Excepted Status

As indicated previously, off-campus HOPDs that were furnishing OPPS services prior to November 2, 2015, that have not impermissibly relocated are considered excepted. The BBA of 2015 did not address whether excepted off-campus HOPDs can physically relocate and keep excepted status, but CMS (based on its belief that the intent of the BBA of 2015 was to except only off-campus HOPDs *as they existed prior to November 2, 2015*) stated in the 2017 Medicare OPPS final rule that if an excepted off-campus hospital outpatient department moved from the address on its CMS enrollment form as of November 1, 2015, to a new address, including a change of unit or suite number, the entire off-campus HOPD loses its excepted status.[42] CMS finalized a limited exception for relocation of excepted off-campus provider-based departments due to extraordinary circumstances, such as natural disasters and seismic building code requirements for public health or public safety reasons but not for business reasons such as loss of lease.[43] To use this exception, hospitals must submit a request for an extraordinary circumstances relocation request to CMS within 30 days of the date the "extraordinary circumstance" occurred.[44] The CMS Regional Offices have responsibility for approving/denying these relocation requests.[45]

Effect of Change of Ownership on Excepted Status

Changes of ownership can also affect a provider-based HOPD's excepted status. Excepted off-campus HOPDs that undergo a change in ownership will retain their excepted status and continue OPPS payments if:[46]

1. The same entity acquires the entire hospital, including the off-campus provider-based department, and
2. The new owner accepts assignment of the hospital's Medicare provider agreement.

An excepted off-campus HOPD cannot be transferred from one hospital to another and maintain excepted status. In addition, if an operator combines two certified entities under one provider number, the off-campus HOPDs of the nonretained hospital would lose excepted status.

Medicare Billing and Reimbursement for Services Provided in Excepted and Nonexcepted Provider-Based Departments of Hospitals

As noted previously, on-campus HOPDs and excepted off-campus HOPDs are paid by Medicare under the OPPS for most services. Since CMS does not maintain a list of excepted and nonexcepted HOPDs, excepted off-campus HOPDs must affix the PO modifier to their claims to indicate their excepted status, even if the particular service being billed isn't paid under the OPPS or there's no payment difference for the particular item or service.[47]

Nonexcepted off-campus hospital outpatient departments are paid at the lower rate under the Medicare Physician Fee Schedule and must add the PN modifier to their claims to indicate their nonexcepted status. CMS expects hospitals to report the PN modifier with each nonexcepted line item and service *including those for which payment will not be adjusted,* such as separately payable drugs, clinical laboratory tests, and therapy services.

The most commonly billed HOPD code under the OPPS is G0463 (hospital outpatient clinic visit for assessment and management of a patient). Historically, this code paid significantly more than the equivalent office visit codes under the Medicare Physician Fee Schedule. In November 2018, CMS released the 2019 OPPS final rule finalizing its proposal to make payments for clinic visits "site-neutral" by reducing payments for clinic visits in excepted hospital off-campus provider-based departments by 60%, which is the Medicare Physician Fee Schedule equivalent rate and the same rate it currently pays for the clinic visits furnished in nonexcepted off-campus hospital outpatient departments.[48] The payment reduction was phased in so that payments for the G0463 code were reduced by half of the total reduction in 2019 (equal to payment at 70% of the OPPS rate) and again by half of the total reduction in 2020 (equal to 40% of the OPPS rate).[49]

Options for Expanding Hospital Outpatient Services

With the inability to open new provider-based HOPDs that are reimbursed by Medicare under the OPPS since the passage of BBA of 2015, hospitals have looked for ways to provide more services in their existing provider-based locations and still be paid under the OPPS. What can hospitals do to expand their outpatient hospital services outside the four walls of the hospital?

Focus on On-campus Expansion
Because the Medicare payment cuts apply only to *off-campus* HOPDs, hospitals can add new provider-based departments on-campus (i.e., within 250 yards of any point on the main hospital buildings or a remote location of a hospital) and receive OPPS reimbursement.

Expand the Services in Existing Provider-Based Locations
CMS has twice proposed regulations (first in the 2017 OPPS proposed rule and again in the 2019 OPPS proposed rule) that would have limited hospitals' ability to expand the services provided at existing grandfathered HOPDs to what CMS referred to as the same "clinical family" of services that the hospital was providing at the location as of a specified baseline period. Under the proposed rules, if an excepted off-campus HOPD was to furnish services from any clinical family of services from which it did not previously furnish services during the baseline period, the services from the new clinical family would not be covered by Medicare as outpatient department services and would not be paid under OPPS. They would instead be paid under the Medicare Physician Fee Schedule (MPFS). However, CMS chose not to finalize the clinical family of services rule both times, instead indicating that it would continue monitoring the expansion of services in off-campus provider-based departments and that it may propose to adopt a limitation on the expansion of excepted services in the future.

Reconfigure Existing Off-Campus Provider-Based Locations

The BBA of 2015 bars hospitals from relocating most excepted off-campus HOPDs from the United States Postal Service address, including suite number, indicated on the CMS Form 855A and in the hospital's Medicare enrollment records as of January 1, 2015.[50] If an excepted HOPD impermissibly relocates, the hospital will lose OPPS reimbursement for the location. Limited reconfiguration of a suite or building may be permitted to expand the footprint of an existing post office address (e.g., adding an addition or taking over an adjacent suite and incorporating it into the existing postal address). While CMS has not commented as to the permissibility of such an expansion, it is not prohibited under the rules and guidance CMS has issued to date.

Expand the Services Furnished in Freestanding Emergency Departments

Services furnished at dedicated emergency departments (DEDs) continue to be reimbursed under the OPPS, and there is no rule that all of the services furnished in a DED have to be furnished on an emergent basis rather than on a scheduled or other nonemergent walk-in basis. In fact, under the EMTALA definition of DED, only a minimum of one-third of all of the DED's outpatient visits need to be for the treatment of emergency medical conditions to qualify as a DED.[51] That creates an opportunity for hospitals with satellite freestanding DEDs to furnish other outpatient services in those locations. CMS has noted its concerns about significant growth in the number of healthcare facilities located apart from hospitals that are devoted primarily to emergency department services and overall growth in emergency department services. As a result, CMS implemented a policy requiring that hospitals report the modifier ER on all claim lines for all outpatient hospital services (both emergency and nonemergency) furnished in an off-campus provider-based emergency department on the UB-04 form (CMS Form 1450).[52] The new modifier "ER" will allow CMS to collect data on the types of services furnished in off-campus emergency departments, which are exempt from the payment reductions affecting nonexcepted off-campus HOPDs, but currently has no effect on the rate of payment.[53]

Common Compliance Risks

Given the detailed requirements of the provider-based regulation (42 C.F.R. § 413.65), there is a number of areas where it is easy to go wrong and fall out of compliance with the requirements. Some of the compliance risks related to provider-based status follow.

Licensure

The hospital must ensure that the provider-based location is operated under the same license, unless the state requires a separate license for the department of the provider, the remote location of a hospital, or the satellite facility, or, in states where state law does not permit licensure of the provider and the prospective department of the provider, the remote location of a hospital, or the satellite facility under a single license.[54] In addition, how a state's cost review commission or rate-setting agency treats the HOPD may be an issue—if such commission or agency finds that a particular facility or organization is not part of the main provider, CMS will determine that the facility or organization does not have provider-based status.

Clinical Integration with Main Provider

Common trouble spots with this requirement include:

- Ensuring that professional staff of the HOPD have clinical privileges at the main hospital
- Ensuring that the level of monitoring and oversight of the HOPD is the same as that for other departments of the main provider
- Ensuring that the responsibilities and relationships between the medical director of the HOPD, the chief medical officer of the main provider, and the medical staff committees at the main provider are the same as far as frequency, intensity, and level of accountability as other medical directors of the hospital
- Being able to demonstrate that the medical records of patients of the HOPD are integrated into a unified retrieval system (or cross-reference) of the main provider
- Ensuring that patients treated at the HOPD who require further care have full access to all services of the main provider and are referred where appropriate to the corresponding inpatient or outpatient department or service of the main provider

Financial Integration with the Main Provider

CMS has indicated that the appropriate financial integration between the HOPD and the main provider can be shown through documentation, such as a copy of the appropriate section of the main provider's chart of accounts or trial balance that would show the location of the HOPD's revenues and expenses.

Public Awareness

This can be particularly troublesome for hospitals, especially when a HOPD was formerly a physician office. Proof that the provider-based location is held out to the public as part of the main provider can be shown via a shared name (this means the name of the hospital should be included in the provider-based location's name), patient registration forms, letterhead, advertisements, signage, and inclusion on the main provider's website. CMS has stated that advertisements that only show the facility to be part of or affiliated with the main provider's network or healthcare system (rather than being a part of the hospital itself) are insufficient in meeting the public awareness requirement.[55]

Proper Billing for Physician Services Furnished in HOPDs

Although the hospital may not have any direct control over the professional billing by physicians that furnish services in the hospital's provider-based HOPDs, CMS imputes responsibility for the proper billing by such physicians to the hospitals to ensure that Medicare does not overpay for services furnished in provider-based departments. For physicians, this means that their Medicare claims must include the appropriate POS code corresponding to the location of the provider-based department (POS code 19 for off-campus outpatient hospital or POS code 22 for on-campus outpatient hospital; not POS code 11 for office) on the CMS 1500 claim form. CMS confirmed its position that hospitals have an obligation to ensure that physicians bill these claims properly in its response to a public comment in the 2000 final OPPS rule: "We agree that physicians (or those to whom they assign their billing privileges) are responsible for appropriate billing, but note that physicians who practice in hospitals, including off-site hospital departments, do so under privileges granted by the hospital. Thus, we believe the hospital has a role in ensuring proper billing."[56] A best practice implemented by many hospitals to ensure that physicians' Medicare claims include the correct POS code is to include the requirement to use the appropriate POS code in any contract with the physician/physician practice as well as a limited right to audit a small number of claims periodically to confirm that the claims are being submitted properly.

Compliance with Hospital Provider Agreement Requirements and Applicable Hospital Health and Safety Rules

One area where compliance with the hospital conditions of participation and applicable hospital health and safety rules may be jeopardized if the hospital does not monitor for compliance is when a HOPD may be sharing space with other nonhospital healthcare providers. The Medicare COPs for hospitals permit hospitals to colocate with other hospitals or healthcare entities.[57] But, when a hospital department or facility is in the same location (campus or building) as another hospital or healthcare entity, each entity is responsible for demonstrating separate and independent compliance with the hospital COPs. What this means for provider-based locations of hospitals is that they are expected to have defined and distinct spaces of operation for which the hospital maintains control at all times. Distinct spaces would include clinical spaces designated for patient care specific to the provider-based department that protects the hospital's patients, including their right to personal privacy and to receive care in a safe environment under 42 C.F.R. §§ 482.13(c)(1) and (2), and the right to confidentiality of patient records under 42 C.F.R. § 482.13(d). In particular, CMS has expressed concerns that sharing of space with other healthcare facilities could pose a risk to the safety of a patient as the entities would have two different infection control plans and that shared clinical space could jeopardize the patient's right to personal privacy and confidentiality of their medical records. In multi-tenant buildings where a hospital's provider-based department is located among other nonhospital healthcare tenants, this requirement can be a challenge to meet, especially in open-concept buildings. In May 2019, CMS published draft guidance on space sharing that applies to provider-based locations of hospitals.[58] The draft guidance defines "shared spaces" as those "public spaces and public paths of travel that are utilized by both the hospital and the co-located healthcare entity." Examples of shared spaces include public lobbies, public restrooms, staff lounges, elevators, main corridors in a building, and waiting rooms/reception areas (with separate check-in areas and clear signage). Both entities would be individually responsible for complying with the COPs in those spaces. Under the draft guidance, travel "between separate entities utilizing a path through clinical spaces of a hospital by another entity co-located in the same building would not be considered acceptable as it could create patient privacy, security, and infection control concerns." "Clinical space" is defined as "any non-public space in which patient care occurs."

Treat all Medicare Patients as Hospital Outpatients for Billing Purposes

The provider-based location cannot treat some Medicare patients as hospital patients and others as physician office patients. This may be an issue, for example, when a patient expresses dissatisfaction with being charged a facility fee (and related coinsurance) and the treating physician requests that the hospital waive its facility fee.

Notice of Potential Coinsurance Liability

All hospital off-campus locations billing as provider-based must provide notice to Medicare beneficiaries informing them of the coinsurance liability for the service provided by the hospital and also for any physician service. This written notice must be provided to Medicare beneficiaries before the delivery of the services and must be in a format that the beneficiary can read and understand. Under the provider-based regulation, if the actual amount of the beneficiary's financial liability is not known, the hospital must provide the beneficiary with an explanation that the beneficiary will incur a coinsurance liability to the hospital that would not be incurred if the facility was not provider-based, an estimate based on typical or average charges for visits to the facility, and a statement that the patient's actual liability will depend on the actual services furnished. This requirement can be difficult to meet since the exact services to be furnished (and thus the related coinsurance amount for such services) is not always known before the services are furnished. (Note: This notice is not required if the facility furnishes only services for which the beneficiary will not incur any deductible or coinsurance liability, or services for which the beneficiary liability is the same in both the provider-based and freestanding settings (e.g., screening mammography.))

Proper Billing by Facility

In addition to ensuring that physicians who furnish services in provider-based departments of hospitals use the appropriate POS codes on their Medicare claims, hospitals also need to be sure that their own Medicare claims comply with the Medicare billing rules. This means ensuring that the appropriate modifier (PO or PN) is included on all off-campus HOPD claims to reflect the department's excepted or nonexcepted status.

Addressing Compliance Risks

Addressing compliance risks with the provider rules seems both easy and daunting at the same time. CMS is very clear in the expectations of the provider-based rules, but there are a lot of rules to make sure all of your provider-based locations (and the people at these locations) are following. In addition, it is sometimes challenging getting other leaders in the organization to understand the "why" behind the rules they need to follow. The key to success is getting organized, getting the leadership team on board, and making sure the operations team understands the CMS rules, and then conduct internal audits to assure compliance.

Master Listing of all Provider-Based Departments

One of the most important steps is to develop a master listing of all on- and off-campus provider-based locations. This is a bit time-consuming but is a critical step in the process. Take a look at the following data sources to identify all of the locations that are acting as provider-based and getting paid as provider-based (remember to include both on- and off-campus locations in the master list):

- Hospital cost report
- Department listing in the electronic medical record (EMR)
- Hospital website page of locations where services are provided
- CMS enrollment applications (form 855A)
- Hospital real estate contracts (review to identify spaces that the hospital owns/leases)
- Hospital accreditation documents (review, as most accrediting bodies will list all locations on the accreditation application)

Looking at these data sources should help the organization develop a complete list of locations that need to be audited for compliance.

Create an Audit Template

The next step is to create an audit template of the risk areas to focus on when auditing these areas. Compliance with all of the provider-based rules is mandatory, but if the organization has identified a specific risk area, breaking the audit down and focusing on that risk area may be more relevant. The sample template **Resource: Provider-Based Compliance Audit Checklist** is included after this article as a tool to use. Please note, this template is not intended to be an all-inclusive list of the required elements—it was developed as a high-level guide. Always use the CMS provider-based attestation document as a guide to what is required.

One of the best ways to audit for provider-based compliance is by conducting walk-through visits of the organization's provider-based locations. These visits are comparable to what patients see and hear when they are receiving services at the provider-based locations.

Public Awareness

Another important audit step is reviewing compliance with the public awareness requirement of the provider-based rule. CMS requires that a provider-based department is "held out to the public and other payers as part of the main provider" and that when "patients enter the provider-based facility or organization, they are aware that they are entering the main provider and are billed accordingly."[59] This means that it must be obvious to patients which hospital they are receiving services from and whom they will get a bill from. In a large network with several hospitals and numerous outpatient departments, this may be very confusing, yet a main complaint from patients is not understanding why they received a bill from a particular hospital.

The public awareness responsibilities should always include the marketing and communications team, as the marketing goals should be consistent with the public awareness requirements and be included in the overall marketing plan. Also, including the construction and facilities' management teams in this understanding is critical—as new builds and renovations take place, proper signage must be part of the plan.

Public awareness can also be problematic in multi-tenant buildings or buildings that co-locate with another provider. Shared space has been an uphill battle with providers across the country as the CMS rules make it very difficult to share space compliantly. This is also where one should analyze the CMS conditions of participation rule on colocation as well as provider-based rules. As explained previously, in 2019, CMS released draft subregulatory guidance proposing changes to the colocation rule that essentially would allow two providers to share some space, just not clinical space.[60] This draft guidance clarifies the permissibility of sharing common, nonclinical space such as entrances, waiting rooms, break rooms, and public paths of travel. While this clarification would be good news for the hospital industry, this could be an area where increased scrutiny regarding public awareness may occur as a result of the relaxation on space sharing.

The following list provides some areas to focus on regarding public awareness, matching the naming convention used by the provider-based department submitting on the CMS-855A enrollment application:

- **Media**: All brochures, advertisement, and marketing campaigns should include the main provider name (this could be different if you are marketing an entire network of hospitals).
- **Entryway signs**: It should be obvious when the patient enters a specific area of a multi-tenant building that they are entering a location of the main provider. All entrances should include the main provider's name and logo in addition to the specific facility's name to emphasize the connection to the main provider.
- **Hospital website**: Make sure the main provider's website includes in its master listing of locations all provider-based departments. In a large network of several hospitals and provider-based departments, the website should include the provider-based department along with the main provider it is tied to (e.g., "Main Street Imaging, a service of Main Hospital").

- **Patient-facing documents**: Assure documents printed and given to patients include the main provider name. This should include letterhead, emails, and appointment reminders.
- **Telephone**: Staff should answer the phone in a manner that indicates to all callers that they are calling a department of the main provider.

Space Sharing

Auditing of space sharing is interrelated to the public awareness requirements in that space sharing in the current rule is not permissible. Proper signage in buildings with more than one medical provider tenant is critical to avoid patient confusion and designate the space belonging to the provider-based facility. In buildings that include more than one provider, it is imperative that there is clear demarcation of the space and independent compliance with the CMS conditions of participation. According to CMS, all certified hospital space, departments, services, and/or locations "must be under hospital's control 24/7," "[c]annot be 'part time' part of hospital and 'part time' another hospital, ASC [ambulatory surgery center], physician office, or any other activity" and are "required to be 'the hospital' 24/7."[61]

When auditing space, looking at physical space, staff, and operations should be part of the review. Below are some tips and areas to review:

- Are there separate waiting rooms?
- Are there separate staff to register different patients presenting for hospital versus nonhospital providers?
- Can a patient obtain the services they presented for without having to walk through another provider's space? (e.g., does a patient have to walk through a physician office to get to the outpatient department?)
- Are there separate supply closets?
- Are there separate entrances using separate doors with proper signage?
- Are there suite numbers?
- Do the floorplans/blueprints show clear delineation via walls, doors, etc. of the space?

As a reminder, the space-sharing rule could be changed based on what CMS ultimately does regarding the 2019 draft guidance.

Claims Auditing

Auditing of claims is another area to focus on routinely—are claims billed with the correct main provider, and are the professional claims billed with the correct POS code? Assuring use of the correct POS code is oftentimes problematic, as the use of the correct codes affects the professional services payment. When reviewing hospital claims, proper use of the PO and PN modifiers can also be confusing if the revenue cycle team does not understand the proper usage based on the specific provider-based department. Development of a master document of all provider-based departments and the corresponding correct POS code and modifier for each would assist in an overall understanding.

Contracting with Independent Physicians

To ensure that the hospital is best positioned to ensure compliance with the provider-based regulation requirement that professional claims for services furnished in provider-based locations are submitted using the correct POS code, the hospital's legal office or other department responsible for contracting with independent physicians understands where the independent physicians will be furnishing services. Having this information is necessary to ensure that independent physicians are contractually required to use the appropriate POS code and that a limited right to audit a small number of the independent physicians' claims periodically to confirm that the claims are being submitted properly is included in the contracts. Audit the physician contract auditing process periodically to ensure these provisions are being included appropriately in physician contracts.

CMS 855 Enrollment

Provider-based departments and locations of hospitals must be included on the hospital's CMS-855A Medicare enrollment form. Using the master list of provider-based locations discussed previously, audit the list and the hospital's Medicare enrollment files against each other to ensure they match.

Policies

As a department of the main provider, provider-based locations should generally operate under the policies and procedures of the main provider in order to demonstrate the requisite level of integration. To the extent separate policies are necessary for a particular provider-based location, the provider-based location's policies should not be inconsistent with the policies of the main provider and should still demonstrate integration with the main provider. Audit any separate policies of provider-based locations to ensure such policies do not contradict policies of the main provider or create the appearance that the provider-based location operates independently rather than as part of the main provider.

Possible Penalties

If a hospital's department or location that the hospital has considered to be provider-based is determined to be out of compliance with the provider-based regulation, the primary impact will be on its reimbursement by Medicare. If a facility is found not to be provider-based to the hospital, the services of the facility will not be considered hospital services. The facility would need to be removed from the hospital's Medicare cost report, which would in turn affect the facility's ability to be a child site of the main hospital for 340B Drug Discount Program purposes. In addition, depending on the area of noncompliance, such noncompliance may result in survey findings/deficiencies as well as Medicare overpayments that would need to be refunded.

False claims and/or civil monetary penalty liability is also a possibility if the hospital acted with the requisite knowledge and intent in submitting claims for the services as outpatient hospital services when they knew or should have known they did not qualify as such. For the calendar year 2020, the penalty range under the False Claims Act[62] is up to three times the federal healthcare programs' loss plus $11,665 to $23,331 per false or fraudulent claim.[6364] OIG also has authority to impose administrative sanctions under the civil monetary penalties law (CMPL) against a healthcare provider for submitting false or fraudulent claims.[65] Per claim penalties under the CMPL for false or fraudulent claims were $20,866 in 2020.[66] In addition, the OIG has permissive exclusion authority that allows it to seek to exclude a healthcare provider from participation in federal healthcare programs for submission of false or fraudulent claims.[67]

For additional information on the history of provider-based status and further discussion on compliance risks and vulnerabilities of provider-based facilities from the OIG's and Medicare Payment Advisory Commission's (MedPAC) perspective, see the following resources.

U.S. Department of Health & Human Services Office of Inspector General

CMS is Taking Steps to Improve Oversight of Provider-based Facilities, but Vulnerabilities Remain

https://oig.hhs.gov/oei/reports/oei-04-12-00380.pdf

MedPAC

Report to the Congress: Medicare and the Health Care Delivery System
Pages 27–56 of this MedPAC report published in June 2013 discuss Medicare payment differences across ambulatory settings.

http://medpac.gov/docs/default-source/reports/jun13_entirereport.pdf

MAC Websites

Each region's Medicare administrative contractor (MAC) posts additional information and resources about provider-based status on their respective websites:

- **CGS**: https://www.cgsmedicare.com/parta/enrollment/provider_based.html
- **Noridian Healthcare Solutions**: https://med.noridianmedicare.com/web/jea/provider-types/provider-based-facilities
- **WPS Government Health Administrators**: https://www.wpsgha.com/wps/portal/mac/site/audit/guides-and-resources/provider-based-attestations-general-guidance
- **Novitas Solutions**: https://www.novitas-solutions.com/webcenter/portal/MedicareJL/pagebyid?_adf.ctrl-state=mdhl86i14_9&contentId=00004157
- **First Coast Service Options**: https://medicare.fcso.com/pard_news/0338897.asp
- **National Government Services**: https://www.ngsmedicare.com/ngs/poc/ngsmedicare?1dmy&urile=wcm%3apath%3a%2FNGSMedicareContent-NEW%2FNGSMedicareNEW%2FCost%2BReports%2FA_FQHC_HHH_MAC%2BProvider-Based%2BDesignation%2BChecklist&LOB=Part%20A&LOC=Massachusetts&ngsLOC=Massachusetts&ngsLOB=Part%20A&jurisdiction=Jurisdiction%20K

Risk Takeaways

Main points of interest:
- Key definitions in the provider-based regulation,
- Medicare payment implications of provider-based status,
- Proper billing of services furnished in provider-based hospital outpatient departments, and
- Centers for Medicare & Medicaid Services (CMS) rulemaking affecting provider-based facilities.

Areas to watch:
- Final CMS guidance on space sharing;
- Possible additional Medicare policy changes affecting reimbursement to provider-based locations, such as nonemergency services furnished in dedicated emergency departments and/or further implementation of the site-neutral payment policy;
- Will CMS eventually finalize a clinical families policy to prevent expansion of services within existing hospital outpatient departments (HOPDs)?
- Will CMS publish guidance that prohibits expansion of the footprint of an excepted HOPD?

Laws that apply:

- Requirements for a Determination That a Facility or an Organization Has Provider-Based Status, 42 C.F.R. § 413.65
- Bipartisan Budget Act of 2015, 42 U.S.C. § 1395l(t)(21)
- Definition of Excepted Items and Services, 42 C.F.R. § 419.48
- Emergency Medical Treatment and Labor Act (EMTALA), 42 U.S.C. § 1395dd
- Medicare Conditions of Participation (COPs) for Hospitals, 42 C.F.R. § 482

Addressing compliance risks:

- Keep track of the organization's provider-based locations.
- Perform periodic self-audits, including building walk-throughs, to assess compliance with provider-based regulation requirements.
- Periodically audit facility and professional claims for services furnished in provider-based locations to confirm compliance with billing rules.
- Monitor CMS rulemaking and information guidance issuances to ensure continued compliance in this changing regulatory environment.

Endnotes

1. **Ilah Naudasher** is Network Director of Compliance Operations, Corporate Integrity at Kettering Health Network. She works for a large multi-hospital network that includes several hundred employed physicians and advanced practice providers and many provider-based departments. Her responsibilities focus on developing and deploying the compliance program for the network of providers, while assuring her team of auditors creates an audit plan that focuses on auditing and monitoring of all network providers.

2. **Shannon DeBra** is an Attorney at Bricker & Eckler Law Firm, where she works in Bricker & Eckler's healthcare practice group. In addition to working in private practice as a healthcare attorney, DeBra previously worked as an attorney in the Office of Counsel to the Inspector General for the U.S. Department of Health & Human Services and for the Massachusetts Division of Medical Assistance (the state Medicaid agency) and served as chief compliance officer for an academic medical center.

3. 42 U.S.C. §§ 301–1305.

4. "Physician Fee Schedule," Centers for Medicare & Medicaid Services, updated February 3, 2021, https://www.cms.gov/Medicare/Medicare-Fee-for-Service-Payment/PhysicianFeeSched.

5. 42 C.F.R. § 413.65.

6. 42 U.S.C. § 1395dd.

7. 42 C.F.R. § 482.

8. 42 C.F.R. § 413.65.

9. 42 C.F.R. § 413.65(a)(1)(ii).

10. "Provider-Based Designation Checklist," Noridian Healthcare Solutions, accessed February 19, 2021, https://med.noridianmedicare.com/documents/10538/4310092/Provider-Based+Designation+Checklist. (A MAC provider-based attestation document example)

11. "Strengthening Provider and Supplier Enrollment Screening," fact sheet, Centers for Medicare & Medicaid Services, February 22, 2016, https://www.cms.gov/newsroom/fact-sheets/strengthening-provider-and-supplier-enrollment-screening.

12. "New Signage, Notification, and Reporting Requirements for Provider-Based Clinics," Washington State Hospital Association, December 18, 2012, https://www.wsha.org/articles/new-signage-notification-reporting-requirements-provider-based-clinics/.

13. 42 C.F.R. § 413.65(e)(1).

14. 42 C.F.R. § 413.65(e)(2).

15. 42 C.F.R. § 413.65(e)(3)(i).

16. 42 C.F.R. § 413.65(e)(3).

17. 42 C.F.R. § 413.65(g)(1).

18. 42 C.F.R. § 413.65(g)(2).

19. "CMS 1500," Centers for Medicare & Medicaid Services, accessed February 22, 2021, https://www.cms.gov/Medicare/CMS-Forms/CMS-Forms/CMS-Forms-Items/CMS1188854.

20. 42 C.F.R. § 413.65(g)(3),(8).
21. 42 C.F.R. § 413.65(g)(4).
22. 42 C.F.R. § 413.65(g)(5).
23. 42 C.F.R. § 413.65(g)(6).
24. 42 C.F.R. § 413.65(g)(7).
25. 42 C.F.R. § 413.65(i).
26. 42 C.F.R. § 413.65(f).
27. 42 C.F.R. § 413.65(h).
28. June Gibbs Brown, "Hospital Ownership of Physician Practices," OEI-05-98-00110, Office of Inspector General, U.S. Department of Health & Human Services, September 1999, https://oig.hhs.gov/oei/reports/oei-05-98-00110.pdf; June Gibbs Brown, "HCFA Management of Provider-Based Reimbursement to Hospitals," OEI-04-97-00090, Office of Inspector General, U.S. Department of Health & Human Services, August 2000, https://www.hhsoig.gov/oei/reports/oei-04-97-00090.pdf; Daniel R. Levinson, "Review of Place-of-Service Coding for Physician Services Processed by Medicare Part B Contractors During Calendar Year 2009," A-01-10-00516, Office of Inspector General, U.S. Department of Health & Human Services, September 2011, https://oig.hhs.gov/oas/reports/region10/11000516.pdf; Daniel R. Levinson, "CMS Is Taking Steps to Improve Oversight of Provider-Based Facilities, But Vulnerabilities Remain," OEI-04-12-00380, Office of Inspector General, U.S. Department of Health & Human Services, June 2016, https://oig.hhs.gov/oei/reports/oei-04-12-00380.pdf.
29. Bipartisan Budget Act of 2015, Pub. L. No. 114-74, 129 Stat. 584 (2015) (codified as amended at 42 U.S.C. § 1395l(t)(21)(A) and (B)(i)–(ii)).
30. 42 C.F.R. § 419.48(c).
31. Centers for Medicare & Medicaid Services, "CMS Finalizes Hospital Outpatient Prospective Payment Changes for 2017," news release, November 1, 2016, https://www.cms.gov/newsroom/fact-sheets/cms-finalizes-hospital-outpatient-prospective-payment-changes-2017.
32. 42 C.F.R. § 489.24(b).
33. 21st Century Cures Act, Pub. L. No. 114-255, 130 Stat. 1033 (2006).
34. 21st Century Cures Act, Pub. L. No. 114-255, 130 Stat. 1033 (2006).
35. 42 U.S.C. § 1395l(t)(21)(B)(iii)–(vi).
36. 42 U.S.C. § 1395l(t)(21)(B)(iii).
37. 42 U.S.C. § 1395l(t)(21)(B)(v).
38. 42 U.S.C. § 1395l(t)(21)(B)(iv)-(v).
39. Centers for Medicare & Medicaid Services, "Medicare Mid-Build Off-Campus Outpatient Departments Exception Audit Results," fact sheet, January 19, 2021, https://www.cms.gov/files/document/medicare-mid-build-campus-outpatient-departments-exception-audit-results.pdf.
40. 42 U.S.C. § 1395l(t)(21)(B)(vi).
41. 42 C.F.R § 419.48(b).
42. Medicare Program: Hospital Outpatient Prospective Payment and Ambulatory Surgical Center Payment Systems and Quality Reporting Programs; Organ Procurement Organization Reporting and Communication; Transplant Outcome Measures and Documentation Requirements; Electronic Health Record (EHR) Incentive Programs; Payment to Nonexcepted Off-Campus Provider-Based Department of a Hospital; Hospital Value-Based Purchasing (VBP) Program; Establishment of Payment Rates Under the Medicare Physician Fee Schedule for Nonexcepted Items and Services Furnished by an Off-Campus Provider-Based Department of a Hospital, 81 Fed. Reg. 79,562,
79,704 (November 14, 2016).
43. Medicare Program: Hospital Outpatient Prospective Payment and Ambulatory Surgical Center Payment Systems and Quality Reporting Programs; Organ Procurement Organization Reporting and Communication; Transplant Outcome Measures and Documentation Requirements; Electronic Health Record (EHR) Incentive Programs; Payment to Nonexcepted Off-Campus Provider-Based Department of a Hospital; Hospital Value-Based Purchasing (VBP) Program; Establishment of Payment Rates Under the Medicare Physician Fee Schedule for Nonexcepted Items and Services Furnished by an Off-Campus Provider-Based Department of a Hospital, 81 Fed. Reg. 79,704–705.
44. Centers for Medicare & Medicaid Services, "Extraordinary Circumstance Relocation Exception Guidance for an Off-Campus Provider-Based Department (in accordance with regulations at 42 CFR 419.22 and 419.48)," accessed February 19, 2021, https://www.cms.gov/Medicare/Medicare-Fee-for-Service-Payment/HospitalOutpatientPPS/Downloads/Subregulatory-Guidance-Section-603-Bipartisan-Budget-Act-Relocation.pdf.
45. Medicare Program: Hospital Outpatient Prospective Payment and Ambulatory Surgical Center Payment Systems and Quality Reporting Programs; Organ Procurement Organization Reporting and Communication; Transplant Outcome Measures and Documentation Requirements; Electronic Health Record (EHR) Incentive Programs; Payment to Nonexcepted Off-Campus Provider-Based Department of a Hospital; Hospital Value-Based Purchasing (VBP) Program; Establishment of Payment Rates Under the Medicare Physician Fee Schedule for Nonexcepted Items and Services Furnished by an Off-Campus Provider-Based Department of a Hospital, 81 Fed. Reg. 79,706.
46. Medicare Program: Hospital Outpatient Prospective Payment and Ambulatory Surgical Center Payment Systems and Quality Reporting Programs; Organ Procurement Organization Reporting and Communication; Transplant Outcome Measures and Documentation Requirements; Electronic Health Record (EHR) Incentive Programs; Payment to Nonexcepted Off-Campus Provider-Based Department of a Hospital; Hospital Value-Based Purchasing (VBP) Program; Establishment of Payment Rates Under the Medicare Physician Fee Schedule for Nonexcepted Items and Services Furnished by an Off-Campus Provider-Based Department of a Hospital, 81 Fed. Reg. 79,708–709.
47. Centers for Medicare & Medicaid Services, "Billing Requirements for OPPS Providers with Multiple Service Locations," *MLN Matters*, SE18002, updated May 10, 2019, https://www.cms.gov/Outreach-and-Education/Medicare-Learning-Network-MLN/MLNMattersArticles/Downloads/SE18002.pdf.
48. Medicare Program: Changes to Hospital Outpatient Prospective Payment and Ambulatory Surgical Center Payment Systems and Quality Reporting Programs, 83 Fed. Reg. 58,818 (November 21, 2018), https://www.govinfo.gov/content/pkg/FR-2018-11-21/pdf/2018-24243.pdf.
49. Medicare Program: Changes to Hospital Outpatient Prospective Payment and Ambulatory Surgical Center Payment Systems and Quality Reporting Programs, 83 Fed. Reg. 59,008–014.

50. Centers for Medicare & Medicaid Services, "CMS-855A: Medicare Enrollment Application, Institutional Providers," Centers for Medicare & Medicaid Services, accessed February 18, 2021, https://www.cms.gov/medicare/cms-forms/cms-forms/downloads/cms855a.pdf. .

51. 42 C.F.R. § 489.24(b).

52. Centers for Medicare & Medicaid Services, "Medicare Uniform Instructional Provider Bill and Supporting Regulations 42 CFR 424.5," July 19, 2019, https://www.cms.gov/Regulations-and-Guidance/Legislation/PaperworkReductionActof1995/PRA-Listing-Items/CMS-1450.

53. Centers for Medicare & Medicaid Services, "Chapter 4 – Part B Hospital (Including Inpatient Hospital Part B and OPPS)," § 20.6.18, *Medicare Claims Processing Manual*, Pub. 100-04, revised December 31, 2020, 2019, https://www.cms.gov/Regulations-and-Guidance/Guidance/Manuals/Downloads/clm104c04.pdf.

54. 42 C.F.R. § 413.65(d)(1).

55. Centers for Medicare & Medicaid Services, "Provider-based Status On or After October 1, 2002," Transmittal A-03-030, April 18, 2003.

56. Office of Inspector General; Medicare Program; Prospective Payment System for Hospital Outpatient Services, 65 Fed. Reg.18,434,18,519 (April 7, 2000), https://www.govinfo.gov/content/pkg/FR-2000-04-07/pdf/00-8215.pdf.

57. 42 C.F.R. § 482.

58. Centers for Medicare & Medicaid Services, Center for Clinical Standards and Quality/Quality, Safety & Oversight Group, "DRAFT ONLY- Guidance for Hospital Co-location with Other Hospitals or Healthcare Facilities," memorandum, May 3, 2019, https://www.cms.gov/Medicare/Provider-Enrollment-and-Certification/SurveyCertificationGenInfo/Downloads/QSO-19-13-Hospital.pdf.

59. 42 C.F.R. § 413.65(d)(4).

60. Centers for Medicare & Medicaid Services, Center for Clinical Standards and Quality/Quality, Safety & Oversight Group, "DRAFT ONLY- Guidance for Hospital Co-location with Other Hospitals or Healthcare Facilities."

61. David W. Eddinger, "Determining Independent Compliance of Hospitals That Are Co-Located," *Hospital Co-Location* webinar, American Health Lawyers Association, May 5, 2015, http://archive.healthlawyers.org/google/health_law_archive/teleconference_materials/2015_Teleconference_Recordings/050515_Hospital%20Co-Location.pdf).

62. 31 U.S.C. §§ 3729–3733.

63. 31 U.S.C. §§ 3729–-3733.

64. Civil Monetary Penalties Inflation Adjustment, 85 Fed. Reg. 37,004, 37,006 (June 19, 2020), https://www.federalregister.gov/documents/2020/06/19/2020-10905/civil-monetary-penalties-inflation-adjustment.

65. 42 U.S.C. § 1320a-7a(a)(1)(B).

66. 45 C.F.R. § 102.3.

67. 42 U.S.C. § 1320a-7(b)(7).

Resource: Provider-Based Compliance Audit Checklist

Documents Required	Provider Based Department Name/Location					
	Department/ Person Responsible	Date Requested	Documents Received Y/N	Action Items	Complete/ Final-Y/N	Comments
Provide your Annual Registration Report.						
Provide a copy of the hospital license that lists the provider-based entity's address, or a letter from the State notifying the provider that the entity is included in the hospital's license. Note: If the State does not issue a separate license for the provider-based entity, please provide documentation that the State does not require the entity to be licensed separately (i.e., letter or e-mail from the state indicating a separate license is not issued for provider-based entities or a copy of the State regulation).						
Provide a list of key personnel (i.e., table of organization) working at the provider-based facility showing job titles.						
Provide list of all clinical staff (i.e., physicians, nurses, physical therapists, radiology technicians, etc.) working at the facility or organization showing job titles and name of employer. Also include whether professional staff have clinical privileges at the main provider.						
Provide a written description of the level of monitoring and oversight of the facility by the main provider as compared to oversight for another department of the main provider.						
Provide a description of the responsibilities and relationship between the Medical Director of the provider-based facility, the Chief Medical Officer of the main provider, and the Medical Staff Committees at the main provider.						

Resource: Provider-Based Compliance Audit Checklist

Documents Required	Provider Based Department Name/Location					
	Department/ Person Responsible	Date Requested	Documents Received Y/N	Action Items	Complete/ Final-Y/N	Comments
Provide a written explanation of how inpatient and outpatient services of the facility and the main provider are integrated. Include examples of integration of services, including data on the frequency of referrals from inpatient to outpatient facilities of the provider, or vice versa.						
Provide a copy of the written policy in place that is utilized in record retrieval from both the main provider and the provider-based facility.						
Provide a copy of the appropriate section of the main provider's chart of accounts showing that the facility is integrated with the hospital's accounts and the entire trial balance that shows the location of the provider-based facility's revenues and expenses within the trial balance. Clearly identify the cost centers on the trial balance.						
Provider a copy of the filed CMS Form 2552-10 cost report indicating the provider-based facility on worksheet A, line 90.						
Provide documentation that demonstrates the facility is held out to the public as part of the main provider. Examples of documentation that could satisfy this requirement are pictures of outside signage, entrance door and interior. Mockup pictures are not acceptable. The pictures should be close enough to read the sign, yet far enough away to enable the viewer a concept of the entire environment. Include examples that show the facility is clearly identified as part of the main provider (e.g., shared name, patient registration forms, letterheads, advertisements, signage, website). Note: Advertisements that show the facility to be part of or affiliated with the main provider's network or healthcare system are not sufficient.						
Provide a copy of the detailed floor plan of the facility with the provider-based space clearly marked as well as a floor plan of the building in which the provider-based facility is located.						

Resource: Provider-Based Compliance Audit Checklist

Documents Required	Provider Based Department Name/Location					
	Department/ Person Responsible	Date Requested	Documents Received Y/N	Action Items	Complete/ Final-Y/N	Comments
Provide a copy of the main provider's EMTALA (anti-dumping) policies. Provide written policies with respect to the off-campus departments for appraisal of emergencies and referral when appropriate.						
Provide staff policy to bill the site of service.						
Provide documentation that physician services furnished at the Center are billed with the correct site-of-services so that appropriate physician and practitioner payment amounts can be determined. The Health Insurance Claim Form 1500 (OMB-0938-1197 Form 1500) is the preferred verification for site-of-service coding.						
Provide a copy of the facility's nondis-crimination policy in accordance with the non-discrimination provisions in §489.10(b) of chapter IV of Title 42."						
Provide the staff policy that all Medicare patients are billed as hospital outpatients and not as physician's office patients.						
Provide the staff policy for patients who received services at the hospital outpatient department and were admitted to the hospital as an inpatient.						
Please provide a notice of beneficiary co-insurance form with an estimated or actual co-insurance cost for services.						
Provide a copy of the policy regarding distribution of the notice of beneficiary co-insurance for the subject facility. The form and policy need to support the statement: "if beneficiary for any reason is unable to read and understand notice, the notice is provided to the patient's autho-rized representative prior to the delivery of service and in situations where emergency service is required; notice is given as soon as possible after emergency situation is stabilized."						
Provide a copy of the potential charges used to complete the beneficiary coinsur-ance financial form.						

Resource: Provider-Based Compliance Audit Checklist

Documents Required	Department/ Person Responsible	Provider Based Department Name/Location				
		Date Requested	Documents Received Y/N	Action Items	Complete/ Final-Y/N	Comments
Provide written notice to the beneficiary of potential financial liability, and policy needs to support that: if the beneficiary is unconscious, under great duress, or for any other reason unable to read a written notice and understand and act on his or her own rights, the notice must be provided, before the delivery of services, to the beneficiary's authorized representative; and in situations where emergency service is required, notice is given as soon as possible after emergency situation is stabilized.						
Provide the articles of incorporation and bylaws (aka code of regulations) for the main provider and provider-based facility if separate documents exist.						
Provide a copy of the provider-based facility lease.						
Provide a list of the key administrative staff (position/titles only) at the main provider and the provider-based facility that reflects a reporting relationship.						
Provide a copy of the organizational chart. The chart must include the main provider and the entity requesting provider-based status showing which department of the main provider the entity is included.						
Submit a written description of the facility director's reporting requirements and accountability procedures for day-to-day operation.						
Describe who has final approval for administrative decisions, contracts with outside parties, personnel policies, and medical staff appointments for the facility						
A list of various administrative functions (i.e., billing services, laundry, payroll) at the facility that are integrated with the main provider. Also, include copies of any contracts for administrative functions that are completed under arrangements for the main provider and/or facility).						
A detailed map indicating the mileage separating the provider-based facility and the Main provider to verify distance from the main provider to the entity seeking provider based status. An online service such as MapQuest may be used.						

Resource: Provider-Based Compliance Audit Checklist

Documents Required	Provider Based Department Name/Location					
	Department/ Person Responsible	Date Requested	Documents Received Y/N	Action Items	Complete/ Final-Y/N	Comments
A copy of any relevant management contracts for the facility.						
Who owns the building?						
Date department originally opened						
Does the location have separate suite numbers?						
What is the Department's Suite number?						
Need copy of most recent HFAP/TJC Accreditation document						
Need copy of original 855A that was used for original address (if moved)						
Need copy of change of location 855A for new address						
Make sure main provider organization chart shows leadership responsibility at main provider and HOPD						
Verify that all employees (nursing staff, leadership, administrative, etc.) of infusion center are employees of Grandview Medical Center (and is identified on documents such as income/expense reports).						
Proof that all expenses are rolling to main provider						
Verify that all employees are paid from main provider						
Validate if any physician services are performed AND/OR billed from the HOPD						
Specific dates of opening at new location						
Determine who should sign attestation document (typically main provider CFO-or authorized official that signs 855's)						
Written certification from CEO or COO of the main provider that the department met the mid-build exception						
Does the location have a separate phone number (and do they answer the phone as a department of main provider?)						

Contributed by Ilah Naudasher, BA, MA; and Shannon DeBra, Esq.

Revenue Cycle

3-Day Payment Rule

By Emma Trivax,[1] Stephen Shaver,[2] and Andrew B. Wachler[3]

What Is the 3-Day Payment Rule?

On June 25, 2010, the Preservation of Access to Care for Medicare Beneficiaries and Pension Relief Act of 2010 was signed into law and implemented the 3-day payment window.[4] The "3 days" refers to the three days prior to a Medicare beneficiary's admission to an inpatient hospital or a hospital's wholly owned or operated Part B entity. All diagnoses, procedures, and charges for outpatient diagnostic services and admission-related outpatient nondiagnostic services that have been furnished to the beneficiary in those three days must be billed together with a beneficiary's inpatient stay. In short, hospitals must bundle the technical component (TC) of all outpatient diagnostic services and related nondiagnostic services with the inpatient stay claim. On the other hand, if the hospital or hospital-owned entity is not paid under the Inpatient Prospective Payment System (IPPS), the required period is one day prior to the beneficiary's admission, rather than three. Thus, this rule has effectively become the 3-day or 1-day payment window rules.

This rule can be complicated to comply with when hospitals and hospitals' wholly owned or wholly operated Part B entities are compiling their billings. There are two main compliance issues with this rule: (1) understanding the differences between billing as a hospital versus a hospital's wholly owned or wholly operated Part B entity; and (2) understanding common pitfalls with interpretation of the rule, which also leads to poor billing practices. The Centers for Medicare & Medicaid Services (CMS) has released numerous policy statements to educate billers on best practices to comply with the 3-day payment window rule.

Risk Area Governance

The primary risk of failure to comply with the rule is a Medicare audit. The laws that govern the Medicare appeals process regarding an audit for an overpayment or under-payment determination are contained in the Social Security Act, as well as various provisions in the Code of Federal Regulations.[56] 42 U.S.C. § 1320a-7k is an important provision of the Social Security Act, as it discusses the Medicare and Medicaid program integrity provisions. It essentially explains the consequences of participating in federal healthcare fraud and how to respond when one has received an overpayment. Section 1320a-7k is tangentially related to 42 U.S.C. § 1395ddd, which further explains the Medicare Integrity Program. 42 U.S.C. § 1395ff is pertinent because it explains how determinations are made and the subsequent appeals process—a process many providers go through if they have received an overpayment or have otherwise billed incorrectly. The Code of Federal Regulations holds most of its relevant provisions in 42 C.F.R. § 405 et seq. This chapter of the Code contains 10 active subparts, all of which explain different terms and conditions to participating in Medicare. The last relevant provision of the Code is 42 C.F.R. § 424.535. This provision details revocation of enrollment in the Medicare program; it is considered a highly important provision that all providers who bill Medicare should be aware of.

There are also potential risks for a civil monetary penalty.[7] A civil monetary penalty can be imposed for a variety of prohibited conduct, including, but not limited to: improper drug price reporting, false and fraudulent claims to any federal healthcare program or other contract or grant, illegal kickbacks pursuant to the Anti-Kickback Statute, and violations of the Physician Self-Referral Statute (the Stark Law).

Common Compliance Risks

The 3-day and 1-day payment windows are both codified in the Code of Federal Regulations.[8] Because this rule is centered around billing procedures, it is important to understand the payment methodology that goes into the rule. As is the case normally, when Medicare billing is involved, there are several compliance risks. CMS and the Office of Inspector General (OIG) are watchful for instances of noncompliance, especially overpayments.

Wrongfully Calculating 3-Day Payment Window Services

Often, the services covered under the 3-day payment window are wrongfully calculated into the inpatient claim, which results in a double payment to the hospitals. If there is an overpayment determination, the provider that made the error must go through the lengthy appeals process. Additionally, 42 C.F.R. § 424.535 allows CMS to revoke a provider's Medicare enrollment for many reasons, including abuse of billing privileges, failure to meet documentation requirements, and noncompliance with enrollment requirements.

Other Billing Issues

There are two main billing issues that providers often find challenging. First are the slight billing differences between hospitals and hospitals' wholly owned or wholly operated Part B entities. Second, six common areas of the rule are often misunderstood by qualifying providers, also leading to incorrect billing practices. These include:

1. Understanding what clinically related services are;
2. Knowing which services are "non-diagnostic";
3. Knowing the definition of "diagnostic";
4. Understanding how critical access hospitals (CAHs) are affected;
5. Knowing when the 3-day payment window actually begins; and
6. Understanding what a "wholly owned or wholly operated entity" is.

Addressing Compliance Risks

Billing Differences between Hospitals and Hospitals' Wholly Owned or Wholly Operated Part B Entities

The billing process itself is often the most challenging aspect of the 3-day and 1-day payment window rules. Hospitals and hospitals' wholly owned or wholly operated Part B entities have different and specific billing directives. Generally, under the 3-day rule, outpatient services performed in the hospital within the three days preceding admission must be billed with the inpatient stay.

However, where outpatient services within the 3-day window are performed at a hospital's wholly owned or wholly operated Part B entity, rather than at the hospital itself, CMS requires use of the modifier "PD."[9] Where the modifier is used, CMS will pay the professional component (PC) for codes with a professional/technical component (PC/TC) split, and the facility rate for codes without such a split. For example, if a wholly owned Part B practice performed an outpatient electrocardiogram (EKG) in the three days prior to admission, the modifier PD would be appended to the Current Procedural Terminology (CPT) code for that service (CPT code 93000). The usage of this modifier would indicate that CMS pays the facility rate, because code 93000 does not have a PC/TC split.

Diagnostic services unrelated to inpatient admission are still subject to the 3-day and 1-day payment window rules as applied to the TC of the billing. However, wholly owned or wholly operated Part B entities should only bill for the PC of the diagnostic service while also appending modifiers -26 and PD to the Healthcare Common Procedure Coding System (HCPCS) code. They should not bill for the TC, because that is already included in the billing of a diagnostic service.

Hospitals have different billing instructions than wholly owned or wholly operated Part B entities when the service was furnished in the outpatient department of a hospital.[10] Outpatient services performed in the hospital within the three days preceding admission must be billed with the inpatient stay, pursuant to the 3-day rule. On the other hand, condition code 51 should be used by hospitals when billing unrelated outpatient nondiagnostic services claims.

Other Misunderstood Areas of the 3-Day Payment Window Rule

The other big obstacle for hospitals and hospitals' wholly owned or wholly operated Part B entities is understanding some very specific terms and applications of concepts—where these terms are not properly understood, billing errors may occur.

Clinically Related

The first area of confusion is what it means to be clinically related. It is common for qualifying providers to misinterpret what outpatient nondiagnostic services are clinically related to the inpatient admission. Providers should have a dedicated inpatient coder who would make the determination that the services were clinically related to the inpatient admission after the patient has been discharged and complete documentation is available. In order to have proper documentation of how the inpatient determination was made, coders should ensure that the patient's record reflects which encounters were combined, the reasons for combining them, and who was in charge of coding. These measures can significantly reduce instances of improper claims or overpayments.

Non-Diagnostic Services

The second area that if misunderstood can cause compliance issues is knowing what nondiagnostic services are. The definition of nondiagnostic services is much broader than it was prior to the codification of the 3-day payment window rule. CMS states that nondiagnostic services subject to the payment window now include "any non-diagnostic service that is clinically related to the reason for a patient's inpatient admission, regardless of whether the inpatient and outpatient diagnoses are the same."[11]

Diagnostic

The third area that that if misunderstood can cause compliance issues is what diagnostic means. The definition of diagnostic is also broad. Pursuant to chapter 6, section 20.4.1 of the *Medicare Benefit Policy Manual*, a service is diagnostic if it is "an examination or procedure to which the patient is subjected, or which is performed on materials derived from a hospital outpatient, to obtain information to aid in the assessment of a medical condition....."[1213] Furthermore, even if the diagnostic service is unrelated to the inpatient admission, the TC of each diagnostic service that falls within the 3-day window is still subject to the rule. However, a Part B entity should not separately bill for the TC of a diagnostic service subject to the payment window. This is because the modifier PD cannot apply to the TC, and the TC is considered included on the bill for the inpatient stay already.

Critical Access Hospitals

The fourth area that raises confusion for compliance is how CAHs are affected by the rule. CAHs generally are not subject to the 3-day payment window rule; however, a CAH is subject to the 3-day rule if the admitting hospital is a short-stay acute hospital paid under IPPS, or, although not paid under IPPS, a psychiatric hospital, inpatient rehabilitation hospital, long-term care hospital, children's hospital, or cancer hospital.

When the 3-Day Window Begins

The fifth area of confusion is knowing when the 3-day payment window actually begins. The 3-day payment window applies to services provided on the date of admission *and* the three days preceding the date of admission, which may cause the 3-day period to be more than 72 hours long.

Wholly Owned or Wholly Operated Entity

The sixth and last area that raises confusion is understanding what a wholly owned or wholly operated entity is. A wholly owned or wholly operated entity is one wherein a hospital is the sole owner of the entity or has exclusive responsibility for overseeing the entity.[14] Physicians and other Part B providers should use modifier PD on any HCPCS code that is thought to be subject to the payment window. It is worth noting that failure to append modifier PD to a code serves as an attestation that the hospital that wholly owns or wholly operates the physician practice believes that the nondiagnostic services were unrelated to the hospital admission.

Create a Compliance Plan

Overall, the best way to remain compliant with this rule is to create a compliance plan. Hospitals and hospitals' wholly owned or wholly operated Part B entities should work with their lawyers to create a policy that clearly explains the requirements of the rule and how to implement those requirements into their daily procedure. Once this compliance plan is in place, hospital administrators and counsel should work on educating the staff on this plan.

Conduct Internal Audits

Hospitals should regularly conduct internal audits to make sure that the staff are, in fact, complying with the compliance plan—this also ensures no surprises if your hospital is selected for an audit.

Possible Penalties

Where a provider has been overpaid on a Medicare claim, an overpayment demand is likely. If a Medicare overpayment is discovered and was not addressed by the provider, the Medicare Administrative Contractor (MAC) will begin the overpayment recovery process. If a provider disagrees with a claim denial and believes that it was not overpaid, it can initiate the five-step Medicare appeals process.

When a provider has been audited for overpayment, the provider may go through as many as five levels of appeal:

1. Redetermination by a MAC[15]
2. Reconsideration by a Qualified Independent Contractor (QIC)[16]
3. An Administrative Law Judge (ALJ) hearing[17]
4. A hearing before the Medicare Appeals Council[18]
5. Judicial review in a federal district court[19]

Though recoupment can be stayed during the first two levels of appeal, CMS may begin recouping monies during the waiting period for the ALJ hearing.[20] Recoupment is the recovery by CMS of any outstanding Medicare debt—in this instance, debt caused by overpayments to providers—by reducing Medicare payments and applying the amount withheld to the amount the provider has in debt.[21]

Aside from going through the Medicare appeals process and facing recoupment by CMS, providers who fail to comply with the 3-day payment window rule also face potential for a civil monetary penalty. The U.S. Department of Health & Human Services secretary can generally impose a civil monetary penalty of $10,000 to $50,000 per false claim or statement to any provider who knowingly presents a claim for a medical item or service that was provided but covered under another claim, not properly coded, or not supported by the medical record.[22] Furthermore, any provider whose conduct does not meet the standards set forth in 42 C.F.R. § 424.535, which could be triggered by repetitive improper billing, may be revoked from participating in the Medicare program for a period of up to 10 years.[23]

Compliance Resources

Centers for Medicare & Medicaid Services

CMS is extremely familiar with the confusion surrounding this rule. In response, CMS has published numerous documents to help clarify the rule. Although these resources were all published in 2011 and 2012, they remain relevant to this day. No great strides have been made to discuss this area ever since, nor have there been great enforcement efforts by CMS to uphold this rule. However, this should not mean that providers and hospitals should cease to remain diligent on these issues. These resources include the following.

***Medicare Claims Processing Manual,* Chapter 12: Physicians/Nonphysician Practitioners**
Change Request 7502, "Bundling of Payments for Services Provided to Outpatients Who Later Are Admitted as Inpatients: 3-Day Payment Window Policy and the Impact on Wholly Owned or Wholly Operated Physician Practices," was initially rescinded but later reissued to remove controversial instructions, finalize the CMS payment modifier, and finalize the policy. [24] This change request was later adopted as chapter 12, sections 90.7 and 90.7.1 of the *Medicare Claims Processing Manual,* Publication 100-04.

https://www.cms.gov/Regulations-and-Guidance/Guidance/Manuals/Downloads/clm104c12.pdf

MLN Matters SE 1232
Frequently Asked Questions (FAQs) on the 3-Day Payment Window for Services Provided to Outpatients Who Later Are Admitted as Inpatients
This *MLN Matters* notice explained what the 3-day payment window is, what services are considered diagnostic, what types of hospital inpatient admissions would be subject to the more allusive 1-day payment window, and so on.[25]

https://www.cms.gov/Outreach-and-Education/Medicare-Learning-Network-MLN/MLNMattersArticles/Downloads/SE1232.pdf

FAQs for Change Request 7502
This was slightly different than the *MLN Matters* notice listed previously, but it covered mostly the same information. This took the new provisions enunciated in change request 7502 and fleshed them out more so that providers and other entities could better understand the inner workings of this rule.[26]

https://www.cms.gov/medicare/medicare-fee-for-service-payment/acuteinpatientpps/downloads/cr7502-faq.pdf

Change Request 7142
Clarification of Payment Window for Outpatient Services Treated as Inpatient Services
This change request contains instructions for hospitals (as opposed to wholly owned and wholly operated Part B entities) as it relates to the 3-day and 1-day payment window rules.[27]

https://www.cms.gov/Regulations-and-Guidance/Guidance/Transmittals/downloads/R796OTN.pdf

Risk Takeaways

Main points of interest:
- Watch for tricky coding errors.
- Recall the proper time to append modifier PD, the difference between diagnostic and nondiagnostic services, and the difference between billing as a hospital and billing as a wholly operated or wholly owned Part B entity.

Areas to watch:
Medicare audits are especially common when it comes to making billing errors, which is the crux of the 3-day and 1-day payment windows. Providers should always bill properly and conduct internal audits to prevent a Medicare audit from occurring.

Laws that apply:
- Social Security Act, 42 U.S.C. § 1320a-7k, 42 U.S.C. § 1395ff, 42 C.F.R. § 405
- Civil Monetary Penalties Law, 42 U.S.C. § 1320a-7a

Addressing compliance risks:
- The biggest risk is an audit by the Centers for Medicare & Medicaid Services. Audits often lead to steep payments that can often hinder a provider's business, even leading to bankruptcy.
- Where an alleged overpayment is large enough, it may also trigger civil monetary penalties, as well as revocation of Medicare enrollment.
- Create a compliance plan.
- Understand key terms to prevent billing errors.
- Know the billing differences between hospitals and hospitals' wholly owned or wholly operated Part B entities.

Endnotes

1. **Emma Trivax** is Associate Attorney at Dickinson Wright, PLLC. Since 2018, Trivax has assisted Wachler & Associates, primarily in fraud and abuse matters; Medicare, Medicaid, and third-party payor audits; and licensing matters. Trivax began employment at Dickinson Wright PLLC in 2021, and she works in the Healthcare Law practice group. She graduated cum laude and Order of the Coif from Wayne State University Law School. Trivax has specialized experience in the Medicare audit appeals process, the backlog of appeals, and jurisdictional avenues for relief from the backlog's collateral consequences. Trivax has been published in *The Wayne Law Review*, the *Health Law Handbook*, 2020 edition, and in the *Health Care Law Section* of the State Bar of Michigan.

2. **Stephen Shaver** is Associate Attorney at Wachler & Associates PC. He represents healthcare providers and suppliers in the defense of Medicare, Medicaid, and third-party payor audits, as well as a broad range of health professional and facility licensing and regulatory compliance matters. Shaver graduated from the Washington University in St. Louis School of Law in 2015. Shaver began his career as a deputy county attorney in Phoenix, Arizona, where he prosecuted violent and gang-related crime. Prior to joining Wachler & Associates, Shaver served in the Homicide Unit of the Wayne County Prosecutor's Office. His experience includes handling high-profile prosecutions and serving as first-chair trial counsel in more than a dozen jury trials, substantially all of which resulted in convictions. Shaver is a member of the State Bar of Arizona and the State Bar of Michigan, including the Health Care Law Section.

3. **Andrew B. Wachler** is Partner at Wachler & Associates PC. He has been practicing healthcare law for more than 35 years. He counsels healthcare providers, suppliers, and organizations nationwide in a variety of healthcare legal matters. In addition, he writes and speaks nationally to professional organizations and other entities on healthcare law topics such as Medicare and third-party payor appeals, Stark Law and fraud and abuse, regulatory compliance, enrollment and revocation, and other topics. He often co-speaks with Medicare and other government officials. Wachler has met with the Centers for Medicare & Medicaid Services (CMS) policy makers on numerous occasions to effectuate changes to Medicare policy and obtain fair and equitable reimbursement for health systems. Wachler is recognized as a Fellow of State Bar of Michigan Health Care Law Section. He currently serves on the Program Planning Committee for AHLA's Institute on Medicare and Medicaid Payment Issues. He has been named as a Super Lawyer since 2006 and listed in U.S. News' "Best Lawyers in America" and DBusiness magazine's "Top Lawyers in Metro Detroit" every year since 2009. He was also one of two healthcare lawyers named as top 100 lawyers in Michigan by Super Lawyers Magazine in 2018 and 2019.

4. Preservation of Access to Care for Medicare Beneficiaries and Pension Relief Act, Pub. L. No. 111-192, § 102, 124 Stat. 1281 (2010).

5. 42 U.S.C. §§ 1320a-7k, 1395ff, and 1395ddd; 42 C.F.R. § 405, et seq.

6. 42 C.F.R. §§ 405 et seq., 424.535.

7. 42 U.S.C. § 1320a-7a.

8. 42 C.F.R. §§ 412.2(c)(5), 413.40(c)(2).

9. Centers for Medicare & Medicaid Services, "Chapter 12: Physicians/Nonphysician Practitioners," § 90.7.1, *Medicare Claims Processing Manual*, Pub. 100-04, revised September 18, 2020, https://www.cms.gov/Regulations-and-Guidance/Guidance/Manuals/Downloads/clm104c12.pdf.

10. Centers for Medicare & Medicaid Services, "Chapter 4: Part B Hospital (Including Inpatient Hospital Part B and OPPS)," § 10.12, *Medicare Claims Processing Manual*, Pub. 100-04, revised December 31, 2020, https://www.cms.gov/Regulations-and-Guidance/Guidance/Manuals/Downloads/clm104c04.pdf.

11. Centers for Medicare & Medicaid Services, "Frequently Asked Questions CR 7502 (Bundling of Payments for Services Provided to Outpatients Who Later Are Admitted as Inpatients: 3-Day Payment Window and the Impacts on Wholly Owned or Wholly Operated Physician Offices)," June 14, 2012, https://www.cms.gov/Medicare/Medicare-Fee-for-Service-Payment/AcuteInpatientPPS/Downloads/CR7502-FAQ.pdf.

12. Centers for Medicare & Medicaid Services, "Frequently Asked Questions CR 7502 (Bundling of Payments for Services Provided to Outpatients Who Later Are Admitted as Inpatients: 3-Day Payment Window and the Impacts on Wholly Owned or Wholly Operated Physician Offices)."

13. Centers for Medicare & Medicaid Services, "Chapter 6: Hospital Services Covered Under Part B," § 20.4.1, *Medicare Benefit Policy Manual*, Pub. 100-02, revised December 31, 2020, https://www.cms.gov/Regulations-and-Guidance/Guidance/Manuals/Downloads/bp102c06.pdf.

14. 42 C.F.R. § 412.2(c)(5)(i).

15. 42 U.S.C. § 1395ff(a)(3)(A) (West).

16. 42 U.S.C. § 1395ff(c), (g) (West); 42 C.F.R. § 405.904(a)(2).

17. 42 U.S.C.1395ff(d) (West); 42 C.F.R. § 405.1000(d).

18. 42 C.F.R. § 405.1100.

19. 42 U.S.C.1395ff(b)(2)(C) (West).

20. 42 U.S.C. § 1395ddd(f)(2) (West); 42 C.F.R. § 405.371(a)(3).

21. 42 C.F.R. § 405.370(a).

22. 42 U.S.C. § 1320a-7a et seq. (West).

23. 42 C.F.R. § 424.535(c)(1)(i).

24. "Bundling of Payments for Services Provided to Outpatients Who Later Are Admitted as Inpatients: 3-Day Payment Window Policy and the Impact on Wholly Owned or Wholly Operated Physician Practices," Trans. 2373, Medicare Claims Processing, Pub 100-04 (December 21, 2011), https://www.cms.gov/Regulations-and-Guidance/Guidance/Transmittals/downloads/R2373CP.pdf.

25. Centers for Medicare & Medicaid Services, "Frequently Asked Questions (FAQs) on the 3-Day Payment Window for Services Provided to Outpatients Who Later Are Admitted as Inpatients," *MLN Matters*, SE1232, accessed February 5, 2021, https://www.cms.gov/Outreach-and-Education/Medicare-Learning-Network-MLN/MLNMattersArticles/Downloads/SE1232.pdf.

26. Centers for Medicare & Medicaid Services, "Frequently Asked Questions CR 7502 (Bundling of Payments for Services Provided to Outpatients Who Later Are Admitted as Inpatients: 3-Day Payment Window and the Impacts on Wholly Owned or Wholly Operated Physician Offices)," June 14, 2012, *Supra* note 8.

27. "Clarification of Payment Window for Outpatient Services Treated as Inpatient Services," Trans. 796, One-Time Notification, Pub 100-20 (October 29, 2010), https://www.cms.gov/Regulations-and-Guidance/Guidance/Transmittals/downloads/R796OTN.pdf.

The 60-Day Rule—Medicare and Medicaid Overpayments

By David M. Glaser[1]

What Is the 60-Day Rule in the Medicare and Medicaid Overpayment and Refund Policy?

The Affordable Care Act included a provision requiring anyone who has received an overpayment from the Medicare or Medicaid program to "report and return" the overpayment while describing, in writing, the reason for the overpayment, within 60 days of the day on which the overpayment was identified.[2] While an earlier statutory provision made it a felony to conceal or fail to disclose events that affect one's initial right to payment of a federal healthcare benefit, that statute has been used very infrequently, and primarily against Medicaid beneficiaries.[3] As a result, the so-called "60-Day Rule" became the first clear requirement on healthcare organizations to refund overpayments. When it issued regulations to document this section, the Centers for Medicare & Medicaid Services (CMS) imposed an affirmative duty to search for overpayments. The regulations deem an organization to have "identified" an overpayment even when the organization does not actually know about the overpayment if it "should have through the exercise of reasonable diligence" located the overpayment.[4]

The key point is that once you are aware that you have been overpaid by the Medicare or Medicaid program, and you have determined the exact dollar amount of the overpayment, you must send the money back to Medicare or Medicaid within 60 days. Additionally, CMS believes that there is a duty to exercise reasonable diligence to review payments to locate overpayments, though the enforceability of that obligation is less clear.

Risk Area Governance

The 60-Day Rule is codified at section 1128J of the Social Security Act.[5] The statute applies to both Medicare and Medicaid, defining an overpayment as "any funds that a person receives or retains under [the Medicare or Medicaid program] to which the person, after applicable reconciliation, is not entitled under such title."[6] The overpayment must be returned by the later of (1) 60 days of its identification or (2) the date any corresponding cost report is due.[7]

The statute leaves several key terms undefined. The regulation issued February 12, 2016, offer CMS's interpretation of the statute. [8][9] The regulation states that a person has "identified" an overpayment when the person has, or should have, "determined that the person has received an overpayment and quantified the amount of the overpayment."[10] The regulation creates a six-year lookback period, requiring refund of any overpayment identified within six years of its receipt.[11]

Common Compliance Risks

While the basic principle of the 60-Day Rule is easily understandable, the definition (or lack of definition) of certain terms creates many areas for potential misunderstanding or disagreement. In some organizations, there is belief that even after a credible allegation of an overpayment there is no duty to review claims. In other organizations, a desire to "do the right thing" results in decisions to refund money where the 60-Day Rule does not require it. In essence, there are compliance risks associated with failing to refund and business risks created by unnecessarily refunding Medicare and Medicaid payments.

Failing to Search for Overpayments

The 60-day regulation imposes a duty to exercise reasonable diligence to locate overpayments. While it is possible to argue that this regulatory requirement exceeds the authority granted by the statute, an organization will likely prefer to have a program that affirmatively searches for overpayments.

The argument that the regulation exceeds the authority in the statute has merit. The statute requires an organization to refund overpayments that it has identified, making no mention of an obligation to look for an overpayment. Common sense suggests that if you are ignorant of an overpayment, that overpayment has not been identified. When issuing the regulations, CMS explains that it believes Congress intended to impose an affirmative duty to search for overpayments. Courts are increasingly hesitant to allow agencies to attempt to divine congressional intent. It is certainly possible that a court will ultimately invalidate the regulation.

Until then, however, most organizations will want to avoid running afoul of the CMS regulation. CMS explained:

> While we acknowledge that the terms 'knowing' and 'knowingly' are defined but not otherwise used in Section 1128J(d) of the Act, we believe that the Congress intended for Section 1128J(d) of the Act to apply broadly. If the requirement to report and return overpayments only applied to situations where providers or suppliers had actual knowledge of the existence of an overpayment, then these entities could easily avoid returning improperly received payments and the purpose of the section would be defeated.[12]

In the preamble, CMS made it quite clear that it expects organizations to affirmatively look for overpayments:

> We believe that undertaking no or minimal compliance activities to monitor the accuracy and appropriateness of a provider or supplier's Medicare claims would expose a provider or supplier to liability under the identified standard articulated in this rule based on the failure to exercise reasonable diligence if the provider or supplier received an overpayment. We also recognize that compliance programs are not uniform in size and scope and that compliance activities in a smaller setting, such as a solo practitioner's office, may look very different than those in larger setting, such as a multi-specialty group.[13]

The bottom line is that CMS expects organizations to conduct internal reviews looking for overpayments.

Misunderstanding When the 60 Days Start to Run

Perhaps it is the name—60-Day Rule—that causes many people to believe that an organization only has 60 days from the date it learns of an allegation of a possible overpayment until the date the check must be written. In fact, the 60-day clock only runs once the overpayment has been quantified. In the preamble to the 60-Day Rule, CMS explains that it anticipates organizations should be able to determine whether they have an overpayment within about six months: "We choose 6 months as the benchmark for timely investigation because we believe that providers and suppliers should prioritize these investigations and also to recognize that completing these investigations may require the devotion of resources and time."[14] CMS explains that it expects that most investigations should be concluded within six months of the receipt of credible information about an overpayment, absent extraordinary circumstances.[15] The timeline envisioned by CMS is that after learning of a possible problem, an entity will determine whether there is an overpayment and quantify it's size within six months. Once the overpayment is quantified, the organization has an additional 60 days to actually write the check.[16]

Misunderstanding the Six-Year Lookback Period

The regulation requires an organization to report and return an overpayment "if a person identifies the overpayment, as defined in paragraph (a)(2) of [42 C.F.R. § 401.305], within 6 years of the date the overpayment was received."[17] The conventional wisdom is that this means an organization must always go back six years. That conclusion fails to recognize an important caveat: the text only requires you to report and return an overpayment as it is defined in paragraph (a)(2). Remember that the regulation defines an overpayment as funds that were received or retained to which the person is not entitled under the Medicare program.[18] A variety of statutes and regulations limit the Medicare program's ability to recover overpayments. For example, Social Security Act § 1870 forbids Medicare from recovering an overpayment if the recovery would be contrary to equity in good conscience.[19] That statute creates a presumption that covering the overpayment would be improper if it is five years after the year in which the payment was made. Federal regulations prevent contractors from reopening claims more than four years after the date of the initial determination, unless there is fraud or similar fault.[20] This raises an important question: If Medicare is prohibited from recovering funds from an organization, is there an overpayment? The answer would seem to be "No, there is no overpayment" because if the government is not permitted to recoup the money, the organization is entitled to money. Therefore, there is an extremely strong argument that absent fraud or similar fault, an organization is only required to refund Medicare funds received within the last four years. The full six-year lookback period should apply only in the presence of fraud or similar fault.

Note that the lookback period for Medicaid is state specific. Some states have specific limits on reopening, but some states do not appear to have any temporal limits on recovery. Since the 60-day regulation only applies to Medicare, omitting Medicaid, the time period for return of Medicaid funds is more ambiguous and arguably dependent upon state law.

Private Insurance and State Law

While the 60-day statute only applies to Medicare and Medicaid, consider the issues with private insurance and state law. The 60-day statute applies to both Medicare and Medicaid claims but has no direct impact on private insurance claims. (As mentioned previously, the regulation implementing the statute only applies to Medicare claims, not referring to Medicaid.) It is important to review your contracts to determine whether they create a contractual obligation to refund. There is also the possibility that a state law could compel a refund to private insurers, though that is unlikely.

Addressing Compliance Risks

Write a Carefully Worded Refund Letter

Because the 60-Day Rule requires you to offer an explanation for the overpayment, it becomes necessary to write a letter or complete a form when refunding to the government. The wording in a disclosure can create additional risk. Carefully wording the refund letter can greatly lower the risk that your good deed is used against you. It is generally best to avoid categorical admissions of wrongdoing in the refund letter. For example, rather than stating "the services were billed incorrectly" or, worse yet, "the services were billed fraudulently," it is better to say, "We believe it would have been more appropriate to bill the services as . . . " or "We would be more comfortable defending this level of service." I would even refrain from using the term "overpayment," instead indicating that you are electing to refund the money. This makes it possible to preserve every ability to argue that the billing was proper and that the refund is voluntary. It is possible to explain a refund without categorically admitting wrongdoing. The refund letter should also refrain from disclosing any advice from legal counsel. It can be tempting to state, "Our attorney has recommended . . . ," but including such a statement runs the risk of waiving attorney–client privilege. It is also tempting to promise that the mistake will never happen again. However, mistakes happen. There is little benefit to including this promise in the letter, but including it gives the government an avenue to attack you should the mistake occur again.

Understand That You Are Only Required to Refund if It Is Agreed That There Is an Overpayment

The preamble to the 60-Day Rule explicitly addresses the question of whether you need to refund if you are audited and disagree with the auditor's decision. In the preamble's example, an organization had claims from one year audited. CMS examines whether the organization must refund for earlier years even as it disputes the findings of the initial audit. CMS explains that if "the provider appeals the contractor identified overpayment, the provider may reasonably assess that it is premature to initiate a reasonably diligent investigation into the nearly identical conduct in an additional time period until such time as the contractor identified overpayment has worked its way through the administrative appeals process."[21] The preamble recognizes that if you disagree with a finding, you are not deemed to have an overpayment until there is a final, conclusive legal finding that your position is incorrect.

It's worth emphasizing that the *Federal Register* uses the phrase "worked its way through the administrative appeals process."[22] Even if there is an initial administrative finding accepting the government's position on an overpayment, as long as further appeals are available, the 60-Day Rule is not triggered. The fact that you receive an overpayment assessment for some period of time does not trigger a duty to refund for other time periods or other locations as long as you disagree with the basis of the overpayment. One question is whether the same instruction applies if you opt not to appeal the initial audit finding because the money involved is too small to make an appeal cost effective. While the preamble doesn't address that question, there is no reason to conclude filing an appeal is required.

Understand That You Can Refund and Then Appeal

For the reasons discussed previously, if you do not believe that there is an overpayment, there is no legal obligation to submit a refund. However, in a situation where you feel more comfortable refunding, but still believe that you are entitled to the money, it is possible to voluntarily refund and submit an appeal as long as the refund is for specific, identified claims:

> Comment: Several commenters requested that CMS confirm that refunds based on statistical sampling will maintain appeal rights. Because individual claim adjustments may not be made when sampling is utilized to estimate an overpayment amount, CMS should confirm that providers and suppliers may still appeal such findings if necessary.

> Response: To the extent that the return of any self-identified overpayment results in a revised initial determination of any specific claim or claims, a person would be afforded the appeal rights that currently exist. As is currently the case under the existing voluntary refund process, there are no appeal rights associated with the self-identified overpayments that do not involve identification of individual overpaid claims and individual claim adjustments.[23]

When submitting a refund for a claim, that reopens the claim. Medicare appeal rights are tied to that reopening. Note that if a refund is based on a statistical sample, no individual claim is reopened. As a result, CMS takes the position that you may not appeal from a refund based on sampling.

Recognize That It Is Likely Appropriate to Offset Underpayments Against Any Overpayment

While CMS states in the preamble that it does not believe it is proper to offset underpayments against overpayments, that claim appears baseless. The analysis hinges on the definition of an overpayment, which is "any funds that a person receives or retains under title XVIII [Medicare] or XIX [Medicaid] to which the person, after applicable reconciliation, is not entitled under such title."[24]

The definition of overpayment includes two key terms, neither of which are defined in the statute. First, it allows "applicable reconciliation." Common sense suggests that this is a statutory answer to the question. Presumably "reconciliation" is the act of offsetting underpayments. Second, funds are "overpaid" when you are "not entitled" to them under the terms of the Medicare program. In other words, if the Medicare program would be unable to recover the money from you, it is not an "overpayment" under the provision. It is a well-accepted principle that when determining a debt, underpayments are offset against overpayments.

Perhaps the best regulatory support for the idea that you may offset underpayments is found in the reopening regulations. Those regulations permit reopening for both overpayments and underpayments. In 42 C.F.R. § 405.980(a)(1), "reopening" is defined as "a remedial action taken to change a binding determination or decision that resulted in either an overpayment or underpayment, even though the binding determination or decision may have been correct at the time it was made based on the evidence of record."[25] The timeframes for reopening contained in 42 C.F.R. §405.980(b) are 12 months for any reason, 48 months for good cause, and indefinitely for "fraud or similar fault."[26] Those time periods are not limited to overpayments; the regulations authorize a contractor to reopen a claim to address either overpayments or underpayments.

In the *Federal Register* preamble to the 60-Day Rule, CMS appears to acknowledge this point, though it did so in a backhanded manner:

> Comment: A number of commenters questioned the treatment of underpayments that providers and suppliers may identify in the course of identifying overpayments. Some commenters requested an explanation of the process by which providers and suppliers may recoup underpayments. Other comments proposed that providers and suppliers should be allowed to offset identified underpayments against identified overpayments when determining the repayment amount. Finally, several commenters suggested that the lookback period for overpaid claims should be the same as the lookback period for underpaid claims. Commenters suggested that we consider allowing providers and suppliers more than the currently allowed one year period to rebill a claim to correct an identified underpayment. Underpayment lookback periods of 3 years and 10 years (to match the proposed lookback period) were recommended by commenters.

> Response: This final rule implements section 1128J(d) of the Act, which concerns overpayments, not underpayments. Thus, underpayment issues are outside the scope of this rulemaking. Under existing policies, providers and suppliers can seek to address underpayments by requesting reopenings under § 405.980(c).[27]

It seems that CMS is asserting that providers and suppliers may *not* offset underpayments while calculating a refund, and that instead, you are supposed to refund the entire actual overpayment and then ask the contractor to reopen the claims with underpayments. But there is little logical support for the position that a healthcare organization is not permitted to perform the offset itself, particularly given that the statute specifically refers to "applicable reconciliation."[28] Reconciliation is, by definition, the act of offsetting overpayments and underpayments.

In the 60-day regulation, CMS also attempts to limit "reconciliation" to the cost report process. In a somewhat convoluted discussion on page 7668, CMS claims Congress was only referring to the cost report process when it used the term "applicable reconciliation." The flaw in CMS's position is exposed by giving some thought to this sentence from the preamble: "However, we disagree with the commenters' interpretation of the term 'applicable reconciliation' in the context of this final rule, which applies to Medicare Parts A and B."[29] There are no cost reports in Part B. If the law only applied to cost reports, it would only apply to "providers" paid under Part A, and not to "suppliers" under Part B. The law contains no such limitation.

The clear intent—and wording—of the statute is to ensure that providers and suppliers do not keep money to which they are not entitled. If you make mistakes, and some of those mistakes favor the government, and other mistakes favor the healthcare organization, the amount of money to which you are "not entitled" is the net of those errors. While CMS would assert you need to refund the money for overpayments, and then request reopening for underpayments, that assertion is inconsistent with the statute. I would feel absolutely comfortable standing in front of a judge and defending a decision to net overpayment and underpayments.

Possible Penalties

The failure to refund money as required by the 60-Day Rule creates a false claim under the False Claims Act.[30] This allows the government to seek three times the amount of the unrefunded sum, plus penalties of more than $22,000 per claim.

In addition, there is the little-used provision mentioned previously that makes it a felony to fail to disclose an event that affects the initial or continued right to a benefit under a federal healthcare program.[31]

Compliance Resources

Federal Register, Medicare Program; Reporting and Returning of Overpayments

Volume 81, Issue 29 (February 12, 2016)
The *Federal Register* preamble for the 60-Day Rule contains CMS views on a number of important issues and is quite easy to read. It also includes the text of the regulation.

https://www.govinfo.gov/app/details/FR-2016-02-12/2016-02789

Centers for Medicare & Medicaid Services

Medicare Learning Network, Medicare Overpayments
This MLN fact sheet discusses Medicare overpayments.

https://www.cms.gov/Outreach-and-Education/Medicare-Learning-Network-MLN/
MLNProducts/Downloads/OverpaymentBrochure508-09-TextOnly.pdf

Fredrikson & Byron

Avoiding Unnecessary Refunds: How to Keep Payments to Which You Are Entitled
This free webinar by David M. Glaser discusses avoiding unnecessary refunds.

https://www.youtube.com/watch?v=dK-kUb-KB-Q&feature=youtu.be

Voluntary Refunds: The 60-Day Rule and More
This free webinar by David M. Glaser discusses voluntary refunds.

https://www.youtube.com/watch?v=nBXuAzhaxkw&feature=youtu.
be&list=PLyjeM-paimEeqo2KRcc26MEHs5nAWhBn2

Risk Takeaways

Main points of interest:
- The Affordable Care Act included a provision requiring anyone who has received an overpayment from the Medicare or Medicaid program to "report and return" the overpayment while describing, in writing, the reason for the overpayment within 60 days of the day on which the overpayment was identified.
- The 60-Day Rule became the first clear requirement on healthcare organizations to refund overpayments.
- There is an affirmative duty for organizations to search for overpayments.
- Once a healthcare organization is aware that it has been overpaid by the Medicare or Medicaid program, and the organization has determined the exact dollar amount of the overpayment, it must send the money back to Medicare or Medicaid within 60 days.

Areas to watch:
- Failing to search for overpayments
- Misunderstanding when the 60 days start to run
- The issues with private insurance and state law

Laws that apply:
- Social Security Act § 1128J, 42 U.S.C. § 1320a-7k
- False Claims Act, 31 U.S.C. §§ 3729–3733

Addressing compliance risks:
- Write a carefully worded refund letter.
- Understand that an organization is only required to refund if it is agreed that there is an overpayment.
- Understand that an organization can refund and then appeal.
- Recognize that it is likely appropriate to offset underpayments against any overpayment.

Endnotes

1. **David M. Glaser** is Shareholder at Fredrikson & Byron, P.A. In his law firm's Health Law Group, Glaser assists clinics, hospitals, and other healthcare entities negotiate the maze of healthcare regulations, providing advice about risk management, reimbursement, and business planning issues. He has considerable experience in healthcare regulation and litigation, including compliance, criminal and civil fraud investigations, and reimbursement disputes. Glaser's goal is to explain the government's enforcement position, and to analyze whether this position is supported by the law or represents government overreaching.
2. 42 U.S.C. § 1320a-7k.
3. 42 U.S.C. § 1320a-7b.
4. 42 C.F.R. § 401.305(a)(2).
5. Medicare Program; Reporting and Returning of Overpayments, 81 Fed. Reg. 7,654 (February 12, 2016), https://www.govinfo.gov/content/pkg/FR-2016-02-12/pdf/2016-02789.pdf.
6. Social Security Act § 1128J(d)(4); 42 U.S.C. § 1320a-7k(d).
7. Social Security Act § 1128J.
8. Medicare Program; Reporting and Returning of Overpayments, 81 Fed. Reg. 7,654 (February 12, 2016); 42 C.F.R. §§ 401.301-401.305.
9. Medicare Program; Reporting and Returning of Overpayments, 81 Fed. Reg. 7,654; 42 C.F.R. §§ 401.301-401.305.
10. 42 C.F.R. § 401.305(a)(2).
11. 42 C.F.R. § 401.305(f).
12. Medicare Program; Reporting and Returning of Overpayments, 81 Fed. Reg. 7,660.
13. Medicare Program; Reporting and Returning of Overpayments, 81 Fed. Reg. 7,661.
14. Medicare Program; Reporting and Returning of Overpayments, 81 Fed. Reg. 7,662.
15. Medicare Program; Reporting and Returning of Overpayments, 81 Fed. Reg. 7654, 7662.
16. 42 C.F.R. § 401.305(a)(2).
17. 42 C.F.R. § 401.305(f).
18. 42 C.F.R. § 401.303.
19. 42 U.S.C. § 1395gg(c).
20. 42 C.F.R. § 405.980(b)(2),(3).
21. Medicare Program; Reporting and Returning of Overpayments, 81 Fed. Reg. 7,667.
22. Medicare Program; Reporting and Returning of Overpayments, 81 Fed. Reg. 7654, 7667.
23. Medicare Program; Reporting and Returning of Overpayments, 81 Fed. Reg. 7,668.
24. SSA § 1128J(d).
25. 42 C.F.R. § 405.980.
26. 42 C.F.R. §405.980(b).
27. Medicare Program; Reporting and Returning of Overpayments, 81 Fed. Reg. 7,658.
28. 42 U.S.C. § 1320a-7k(d)(4)(B);
29. SSA § 1128J(d).
30. Medicare Program; Reporting and Returning of Overpayments, 81 Fed. Reg. 7,668.
31. 31 U.S.C. §§ 3729–3733.
32. 42 U.S.C. § 1320a-7b.
33. SSA § 1128B.

Advance Beneficiary Notice of Noncoverage

By Ronald L. Hirsch,[1] MD, FACP, CHCQM-PHYADV, CHRI

What Is the Advance Beneficiary Notice of Noncoverage?

The Advance Beneficiary Notice of Noncoverage (ABN) is a form issued by providers (including independent laboratories, home health agencies, and hospices), physicians, practitioners, and suppliers to Original Medicare beneficiaries in situations where Medicare payment is expected to be denied and the beneficiary is expected to pay for the service. This can occur with the initiation of a service, the termination of a service, or the reduction of a service. Preparation and delivery of the ABN is complex, and each step must be followed properly or the notice is considered void and liability cannot be shifted to the beneficiary.

When an ABN is provided, the provider must indicate on the claim that there is a properly completed and signed ABN on file by attaching the -GA modifier to the claim. The -GA modifier is a code that is placed on the line item for the service when the claim is created that tells the claims processing system that the provider expects no payment from Medicare and will be charging the patient for the service. Services can be provided to Medicare beneficiaries that are not medically necessary, but the provider will not be expecting payment from Medicare. In this situation, the provider would attach modifier -GZ on the appropriate line item(s) on the claim. In this case, the -GZ tells the claim processing system that the provider expects no payment and will not be charging the patient.

ABNs are only used for Original Medicare beneficiaries. For any other payer, including Medicare Advantage (MA), the provider should contact the payer for instructions on how to shift financial liability to the patient. Furthermore, ABNs are only given to outpatients. If an inpatient is going to receive a service that is not expected to be covered, or their admission is determined by the hospital not to be medically necessary, the appropriate Hospital-Issued Notice of Noncoverage (HINN) must be used to shift financial liability to the beneficiary.[2]

Use of the ABN can be further broken down based on the location of use. Physicians may provide ABNs to Medicare beneficiaries if they are providing a service in the office to a patient that is likely to be noncovered, such as removing a benign mole, administering a tetanus vaccine without an injury, performing a cosmetic procedure such as a botulinum toxin injection, or performing an in-office lab test such as a cholesterol test prior to the approved time period. Physicians also order tests and studies that they themselves do not perform, such as laboratory tests or imaging tests, that may be medically unnecessary. In this instance, the physician may obtain the ABN for the performing entity, but it is the responsibility of the performing entity to ensure that the ABN was completed and presented properly, as outlined below. The same applies when a physician performs a procedure that is likely to be noncovered at a facility. For instance, if a surgeon is performing a cosmetic rhinoplasty at a hospital or ambulatory surgery center, the ABN can be completed by either the physician or the facility, but both are responsible for ensuring it was done properly.

Laboratories, both independent and hospital based, also commonly present ABNs to Medicare beneficiaries when a patient presents with an order for a laboratory test and the diagnosis is not covered based on the National Coverage Determination (NCD) for the test. There are 23 laboratory tests that have NCDs.[3] For example, blood counts are not covered for patients who are asymptomatic or who do not have conditions that could be expected to result in hematological abnormalities. Medicare also covers many tests as part of the preventative care benefit.[4] These often have specific frequency limitations, such as cervical cancer screening with pap tests, which cannot be performed within the 23 months after the last exam in low-risk women with no prior abnormal tests. As noted above, although the test is being ordered by the provider, it is the obligation of the entity performing the test to ensure the ABN is completed properly.

Hospital outpatient departments also perform tests and procedures that are ordered by a provider but which are not performed by the provider, such as cardiac stress testing or radiology imaging studies. For example, Positron Emission Tomography (PET) scans are approved for specific indications as outlined in their respective NCDs.[5] To add to the complexity, some Medicare Administrative Contractors (MACs) have local coverage articles specifying the billing and coding requirements to be met in order for the service to be covered. Prior to performing the service, the provider must ensure that the test is being performed for an approved diagnosis. If not, they must either contact the provider and determine if additional clinical information is available to support the coverage of the test or provide the patient an ABN. If an ABN is provided, the patient should be given the opportunity to contact their provider and discuss the situation, as it is unlikely that the person presenting the ABN at the facility will have the clinical knowledge to adequately explain to the patient why the test is likely not to be covered by Medicare.

Nursing facilities also provide ABNs to patients. They generally do so in two situations. A patient in a Medicare Part A stay whose services are ending because they are no longer medically necessary but who would like to remain in the facility would be given a Skilled Nursing Facility (SNF) ABN.[6] For a patient in a nursing facility under Medicare Part B, an ABN would be given prior to providing any services to the patient that are not medically necessary.

Although infrequent, a hospice organization may provide an ABN to a beneficiary. This would occur if a patient who is not terminally ill requests hospice services (a scenario that is hard to envision), if a hospice patient requests a service that is not medically necessary, or if the hospice patient requests a level of care that is not medically necessary. For example, if a stable hospice patient requested to be admitted to inpatient hospice, an ABN may be provided.

Other providers such as durable medical equipment and therapy providers may also issue ABNs. In the case of therapy providers, the ABN is often triggered when the patient reaches the therapy cap.

Risk Area Governance

The basis of the ABN is the Social Security Act, section 1879: Limitation on liability of beneficiary where Medicare claims are disallowed.[7] The specific guidance on the ABN is contained in the *Medicare Claims Processing Manual*, chapter 30, section 50.[8]

The requirement to provide an ABN is generally triggered at the initiation (beginning of a new patient encounter, start of a plan of care, or beginning of treatment). If the provider believes that certain otherwise-covered items or services will be noncovered (as not reasonable and necessary) at initiation, an ABN must be issued prior to the beneficiary receiving the noncovered care. In addition, an ABN is to be provided when care is reduced (frequency or duration of a service) or when care is terminated (the discontinuance of certain items or services, for example physical therapy).

The financial liability protection provisions of the Social Security Act protect beneficiaries, healthcare providers, and suppliers under certain circumstances from unexpected liability for charges associated with claims that Medicare does not pay. The provisions apply after an item or service's coverage determination is made. These provisions include the following:

- Limitation on Liability, § 1879(a)-(g)[9]
- Refund Requirements for Non-assigned Claims for Physician's Services, § 1842(l)[10]
- Refund Requirements for Assigned and Non-assigned Claims for Medical Equipment and Supplies, §§ 1834(a)(18)[11], 1834(j)(4)[12], and 1879(h)[13]

The provisions apply only when the items and/or services are denied on the basis of specific statutory or regulatory provisions and involve determinations about beneficiary and/or healthcare provider/supplier knowledge of whether Medicare was likely to deny payment for the items and/or services.

Common Compliance Risks

Improper Completion of Form

The ABN must be completed in full—there cannot be any incomplete sections. The item or service that is being provided must be indicated in blank spaces on the form. There are seven places on the ABN that this must be written. Failure to complete one of those will invalidate the form. Providers are allowed to customize the form to some extent, such as pre-populating the form for common uses. The font must be no less than 12 point for most of the form, except for the insertions in the blanks, which may be as small as 10 point.

Abbreviations Are Discouraged

In a 2014 case appealed by a beneficiary to Maximus Federal Services (a Qualified Independent Contractor (QIC)), Maximus determined that "[a]bbreviations were used without explanation," noting that, among other things, ABNs "must be written in lay terms to be understood by the beneficiary."[14] This denial is interesting in that on the Centers for Medicare & Medicaid Services (CMS) ABN page, they provide an example ABN that contains numerous abbreviations.[15]

The ABN Must Include the Estimated Cost of the Service

A good faith effort must be made to get a reasonable estimate of the charge, which should be within $100 or 25% of the actual costs. Although an estimate that exceeds the actual cost is acceptable, since the beneficiary will be charged less than expected, an estimate that underestimates the actual cost is not acceptable. If the service is covered, the claim will be paid at the Medicare fee schedule rate, but providers may use chargemaster costs when completing the ABN and may collect that amount from the beneficiary.

The ABN Must Include an Explanation of Why the Service Is Not Expected to be Covered

Although a specific explanation may be more helpful to the beneficiary, CMS allows basic explanations such as "Medicare does not pay for this test for your condition" or "Medicare does not pay for this test as often as this."[16]

Improper Delivery of Form

The form must be delivered to the beneficiary or their representative far enough in advance of delivering potentially noncovered items or services to allow sufficient time for the beneficiary to consider all available options. The beneficiary must be able to make a rational, informed decision without undue pressure. If the ABN is delivered in the emergency department, it can only be done after the patient has undergone a medical screening examination and determined to be stable.

In a case appealed by a beneficiary, an administrative law judge determined that a patient who was sent to the lab by a specialist for lab tests and who signed an ABN was not liable because the patient "was upset." The judge felt the notice was not delivered in a timely manner.[17] It is recommended that when an ABN is delivered to a patient, the time of delivery should be noted and the patient allowed sufficient time to decide on their course of action. The notifier should then return and ask the patient if they would like to sign the notice and receive the service or decline, again noting the time of that discussion.

If the Patient Is Not Competent, the ABN May be Delivered to the Patient's Authorized Representative

An individual who may make healthcare and financial decisions on a beneficiary's behalf (e.g., the beneficiary's legal guardian or someone appointed according to a properly executed "durable medical power of attorney") is an authorized representative.

The ABN Should be Signed to be Valid

CMS notes, "If the beneficiary refuses to choose an option and/or refuses to sign the ABN when required, the notifier should annotate the original copy of the ABN indicating the refusal to sign or choose an option and may list witness(es) to the refusal on the notice although this is not required. If a beneficiary refuses to sign a properly delivered ABN, the notifier should consider not furnishing the item/service, unless the consequences (health and safety of the patient, or civil liability in case of harm) are such that this is not an option."[18]

The ABN Should be Delivered in Person

If in-person delivery is not possible, it may be delivered via secure fax, mail, direct telephone call, or email. With all methods, HIPAA privacy rules must be followed. A notation should be made that delivery was not made in person and a copy of the unsigned notice kept until the signed copy is returned. If telephone contact is made, this must be followed by a hand-delivered, mailed, emailed, or faxed delivery of the form to the beneficiary or their representative.

Many services involve more than one provider, as is the case when a physician writes an order for a radiology study and instructs the patient to go to the hospital to have the test performed. In cases such as this, the ABN may be delivered by either party, but it is the obligation of the billing entity to ensure that the form was completed and delivered properly.

This is especially important in cases where a provider collected a specimen in the office and then transferred it to the laboratory for processing, such as a blood test or a pap smear. If there is no ABN completed, or the ABN is not properly completed, it is the obligation of the laboratory to ensure it is done if the laboratory is going to seek payment from Medicare. In these cases, the specimen has already been collected and the patient is under the assumption that the test will be performed. If coverage requirements are not met, the laboratory may choose to contact the patient and ask them to review and sign an ABN or perform the test and submit the claim with the -GZ modifier, indicating that they do not expect payment. In either case, the laboratory should work with the provider to develop a system to ensure that an ABN is obtained even before the specimen is collected.

Answering Questions from the Beneficiary

Unlike beneficiaries who are issued an inpatient HINN, beneficiaries who receive an ABN do not have formal immediate appeal rights. But it is expected that the notifier answer any questions from the beneficiary. If a question cannot be answered, "the notifier should direct the beneficiary to call 1-800-MEDICARE if the beneficiary has questions s/he cannot answer. If a Medicare contractor finds that the notifier refused to answer a beneficiary's inquiries or direct them to 1-800-MEDICARE, the notice delivery will be considered defective, and the notifier will be held financially liable for noncovered care."[19]

Improper Form

The ABN form is reviewed every three years by the Office of Management and Budget (OMB). Unless an extension has been issued or a transition period announced, an expired form is considered invalid and liability cannot be shifted to the beneficiary.

The ABN Should Only be Provided to Fee-For-Service Medicare Beneficiaries

MA beneficiaries may not receive an ABN, as MA patients and contracted providers have the ability to contact the plan and ask for a preservice determination of coverage. If the payer determines the service is not covered, that determination would serve as notice to the beneficiary and would outline their appeal rights.

Blanket Distribution

An ABN cannot be provided to every Medicare beneficiary undergoing a specific service or set of services "just in case" payment is denied. Issuance is appropriate only if the specific circumstances are evaluated and it is determined that the service will not be covered. For example, a lab has noted that several claims for prostate-specific antigen (PSA) tests were denied because the proper time interval had not passed since the prior test. To prevent further losses, the lab decided to issue an ABN to every patient who had a PSA test. This would not be permitted.

Generic Form Delivery

An ABN cannot be delivered that is not specific to the service being provided. For instance, indicating "lab tests" as the service would not be considered valid.

Retention Requirements

In general, it is five years from discharge/completion of delivery of care when there are no other applicable requirements under state law. Retention is required in all cases, including those cases in which the beneficiary declined the care, refused to choose an option, or refused to sign the notice. Electronic retention of the signed paper document is acceptable. Notifiers may scan the signed paper, or "wet" version of the ABN, for electronic medical record retention and, if desired, give the paper copy to the beneficiary.[20]

Addressing Compliance Risks

Compliance staff should survey and educate all departments on the proper use of ABNs. Here are some specific questions to consider and ways to educate staff on avoiding ABN compliance issues.

Ascertain How Staff Determines That an ABN is Necessary

At what point is this determination made? Is it at preregistration, check-in, arrival in department, or prior to initiation of testing? Do staff have a database of covered versus noncovered services? Is it based on Healthcare Common Procedure Coding System (HCPCS) code or a narrative description of the service? What is the source of that database? Is that database up to date? Is staff using the database correctly? If there is no database, what do they do, and is it compliant?

Review the ABN That Is Used

Is the form the current one? Is the form compliant with the proper formatting and font? If areas of the form are precompleted, is the formatting of that information correct? Are the description and cost estimate accurate?

Ask How Staff Complete the ABN

Is there a standard for how they complete the description of the service to ensure it is accurate? How do they obtain cost estimates and reasons for noncoverage? If the form is completed by hand, is the writing legible? If they use an electronic version, do they then print out a paper copy of the signed form to present to the patient?

Determine How They Deliver the Information

Do they use a script to explain the ABN? How do they handle non-English speakers? How do they deliver the ABN for beneficiaries who are not competent? Do they know who to contact if the beneficiary has questions? If they present ABNs in the emergency department, how do they ensure the patient has undergone a medical screening examination, is stabilized, and is not in distress? Do they know what to do if the patient refuses to sign the ABN but insists on receiving the service?

Ensure the Original Signed ABN is Retained and a Copy is Provided to the Patient

If the ABN is provided other than in person, were the steps taken properly documented? Was a copy of the mailed, faxed, or emailed form retained?

Educate Staff on Correct ABN Procedures

Depending on the processes in place to ensure medical necessity is met for all services provided to patients, the use of the ABN may be infrequent. As a part of ongoing education, scenarios where an ABN may be appropriate should be presented and procedures reviewed to ensure the ABN is used properly. When the form is updated, the new form and any new requirements for completion should be reviewed. If the use of the ABN is addressed in policies or procedures, those should be updated and approved as warranted.

Possible Penalties

There are no financial penalties or sanctions associated with improper use of ABNs, but the beneficiary cannot be held liable if the provider failed to give notice or deliver the notice properly. Depending on the service provided, the cost to the provider could be significant.

For example, placement of implantable cardioverter defibrillators is a constant risk area based on medical necessity. Many of these are placed electively as outpatient procedures. If requirements of the NCD are not met, the procedure is denied, and no ABN was presented, the provider would be required to refund the $30,000-plus payment. Most other services have smaller payment values, but as volume increases, the financial costs to the provider increase as well.

If services are denied and the provider did not obtain an ABN, any payments made must be refunded to the beneficiary. If the refund is not made on a timely basis, the Department of Health and Human Services Office of the Inspector General (HHS-OIG) may impose civil monetary penalties, assessments, and sanctions.[21]

Compliance Resources

Centers for Medicare & Medicaid Services

Beneficiary Notices Initiative
This website page contains links to information on all the Medicare beneficiary notices.

https://www.cms.gov/Medicare/Medicare-General-Information/BNI/index

FFS ABN
The current ABN and instructions for completion of the ABN can be found on this website page.

https://www.cms.gov/Medicare/Medicare-General-Information/BNI/ABN

Medicare Claims Processing Manual, Chapter 30: Financial Liability Protection
Starting at section 50, this manual outlines the guidelines governing the ABN.

https://www.cms.gov/manuals/downloads/clm104c30.pdf

Risk Takeaways

Main points of interest:
- The ABN is only used for fee-for-service Medicare beneficiaries when Medicare payment is expected to be denied.
- The ABN must be completed fully and accurately to be valid.

Areas to watch:
- Current form
- Legible writing
- Proper description of service
- Proper pricing of service
- Adequate description of noncoverage reason
- All blanks completed
- Delivery not under duress
- Beneficiary questions answered adequately

- Signature obtained
- Copy provided
- Proper modifier attached on claim

Laws that apply:
- Social Security Act, section 1879: Limitation on liability of beneficiary where claims are disallowed, 42 U.S.C. § 1395pp

Addressing ABN compliance risks:
- Review procedures
- Review forms
- Review retention policies

Endnotes

1. **Dr. Ronald L. Hirsch** is Vice President of R1 RCM Inc. He isa Board-certified Internal Medicine specialist with 14 years of experience as a physician advisor. He is a member of the National Advisory Boards of the American College of Physician Advisors and the National Association of Healthcare Revenue Integrity and the coauthor of The Hospital Guide to Contemporary Utilization Review, published in 2018.

2. "HINNs," Centers for Medicare & Medicaid Services, updated September 19, 2019, https://www.cms.gov/Medicare/Medicare-General-Information/BNI/HINNs.

3. "Lab National Coverage Determinations (NCDs) Alphabetical Index," Medicare Coverage Database, Centers for Medicare & Medicaid Services, accessed January 5, 2021, https://www.cms.gov/medicare-coverage-database/indexes/lab-ncd-index.aspx.

4. "Medicare Preventive Services," MLN Educational Tool, updated December 2020, https://www.cms.gov/Medicare/Prevention/PrevntionGenInfo/medicare-preventive-services/MPS-QuickReferenceChart-1.html.

5. "Medicare Coverage Database," Centers for Medicare & Medicaid Services, accessed January 5, 2021, https://www.cms.gov/medicare-coverage-database/new-search/search.aspx.

6. "FFS SNF ABN," Centers for Medicare & Medicaid Services, updated October 7, 2020, https://www.cms.gov/Medicare/Medicare-General-Information/BNI/FFS-SNF-ABN-.

7. 42 U.S.C. § 1395pp .

8. Centers for Medicare & Medicaid Services, "Chapter 30: Financial Liability Protections," § 50, *Medicare Claims Processing Manual*, Pub. 100-04, revised March 8, 2019, https://www.cms.gov/Regulations-and-Guidance/Guidance/Manuals/downloads/clm104c30.pdf.

9. 42 U.S.C. § 1395pp .

10. 42 U.S.C. § 1395u .

11. 42 U.S.C. § 1395m .

12. 42 U.S.C. § 1395m .

13. 42 U.S.C. § 1395pp .

14. Nina Youngstrom, "Hospital Loses ABN Appeal to Patient Based on Use of Acronym," *Report on Medicare Compliance* 23, no. 15 (April 28, 2014), https://assets.hcca-info.org/Portals/0/PDFs/Resources/Rpt_Medicare/2014/rmc042814.pdf.

15. "FFS ABN," Centers for Medicare & Medicaid Services, updated August 3, 2020, https://www.cms.gov/Medicare/Medicare-General-Information/BNI/ABN.

16. "Form Instructions: Advance Beneficiary Notice of Non-coverage (ABN)," Centers for Medicare & Medicaid Services, accessed January 5, 2021, https://www.cms.gov/Medicare/Medicare-General-Information/BNI/Downloads/ABN-Form-Instructions.pdf.

17. Nina Youngstrom, "ALJ Calls Beneficiary Notice Coercive, Leaves Hospital on the Hook for Labwork," *Report on Medicare Compliance* 23, no. 4 (February 3, 2014), https://assets.hcca-info.org/Portals/0/PDFs/Resources/Rpt_Medicare/2014/rmc020314.pdf.

18. Centers for Medicare & Medicaid Services, "Chapter 30: Financial Liability Protections," § 50.6.5(B), *Medicare Claims Processing Manual*, Pub. 100-04, revised March 8, 2019, https://www.cms.gov/Regulations-and-Guidance/Guidance/Manuals/downloads/clm104c30.pdf.

19. Centers for Medicare & Medicaid Services, "Chapter 30: Financial Liability Protections," § 50.7.1(A), *Medicare Claims Processing Manual*, revised March 8, 2019, https://www.cms.gov/Regulations-and-Guidance/Guidance/Manuals/downloads/clm104c30.pdf.

20. Centers for Medicare & Medicaid Services, "Chapter 30: Financial Liability Protections," § 50.6.4, *Medicare Claims Processing Manual*, Pub. 100-04, revised March 8, 2019, https://www.cms.gov/Regulations-and-Guidance/Guidance/Manuals/downloads/clm104c30.pdf.

21. Centers for Medicare & Medicaid Services, "Chapter 30: Financial Liability Protections," § 50.13.3, *Medicare Claims Processing Manual*, Pub. 100-04, revised March 8, 2019, https://www.cms.gov/Regulations-and-Guidance/Guidance/Manuals/downloads/clm104c30.pdf.

CARES Act Relief Funds

By Stephen Shaver[1]

What Are the CARES Act Relief Funds?

The Provider Relief Fund (PRF) is a $175 billion fund created by Congress to provide financial relief to healthcare providers in the wake of the COVID-19 public health emergency. Congress initially appropriated $100 billion dollars for PRF in the Coronavirus Aid, Relief, and Economic Security (CARES) Act, passed on March 27, 2020, and later appropriated an additional $75 billion in the Paycheck Protection Program and Health Care Enhancement Act, passed on April 24, 2020. [2,3]

The distribution of the PRF is administrated by the U.S. Department of Health & Human Services (HHS), which has divided the fund into a series of general allocations to eligible providers and targeted allocations directed at specific impact areas. The general allocations were divided into three phases, totaling approximately $92.5 billion.[4] The first general allocation payments were deposited directly into providers' accounts based on the amount they billed Medicare in 2019. Additional general allocation payments were available for application. In addition, HHS created several targeted allocations, totaling approximately $56 billion.[5] Targeted allocations included payments to hospitals in COVID-19 high-impact areas, rural providers, and skilled nursing facilities.

A provider that receives and accepts funds under the PRF must certify their eligibility and agree to comply with a series of requirements, including restrictions on the use of the payment and requirements to report specific information to HHS on the use of the funds. Full compliance with program requirements was material to HHS's decision to disburse the funds, thus implicating liability under the False Claims Act.[6]

In addition to HHS review of reports filed by providers, several other federal entities provide oversight of the PRF or have otherwise made pandemic-related enforcement a priority, including the Special Inspector General for Pandemic Recovery (SIGPR) within the U.S. Department of the Treasury,[7] the HHS Office of Inspector General (OIG),[8] and the Department of Justice (DOJ).[9]

Risk Area Governance

The PRF is a US federal government program created under the CARES Act and the Paycheck Protection Program and Health Care Enhancement Act of 2020.

The compliance risk areas associated with the PRF are primarily governed by the terms and conditions associated with each allocation. Each allocation has its own eligibility criteria, terms, and conditions; however, two restrictions apply to every phase of general allocation payments and a majority of the targeted allocations. They are:

1. "The Recipient certifies that it will not use the Payment to reimburse expenses or losses that have been reimbursed from other sources or that other sources are obligated to reimburse."
2. "The Recipient certifies that the Payment will only be used to prevent, prepare for, and respond to coronavirus, and that the Payment shall reimburse the Recipient only for health care related expenses or lost revenues that are attributable to coronavirus."[10]

HHS has defined "health care related expenses" broadly to include both indirect general and administrative expenses needed to operate and maintain facilities and direct patient care expenses attributable to coronavirus.[11]

Moreover, HHS views every patient as a possible case of COVID-19.[12] Recipients may choose to report their "lost revenue" by one of three methodologies outlined by HHS.[13] First, recipients may report the difference between 2019 and 2020 actual patient care revenue.[14] Second, recipients may report the difference between 2020 budgeted and 2020 actual patient care revenue.[15] Recipients who choose this method must submit their 2020 budget, which must have been in place prior to March 27, 2020.[16] Third, a recipient may use "any reasonable method of estimating revenue."[17] Recipients who use an alternate methodology must submit the methodology to HHS for approval. HHS has also indicated that recipients who use an alternate methodology face an increased likelihood of audit.[18]

In general, any provider that accepted one or more payments under the PRF totaling more than $10,000 in aggregate is required to file reports with HHS demonstrating compliance with the terms of the payment, although some of the targeted allocations are subject to separate, distinct reporting requirements..[19][20] Providers must report various data elements relating to demographic information, their expenses attributable to coronavirus not reimbursed by another source, their lost revenue attributable to coronavirus, and additional nonfinancial data.[21] Providers who accepted $500,000 or more will be required to report addition levels of detail.[22] As a practical matter, when reviewing these reports, HHS will first apply the PRF payment to healthcare expenses attributable to coronavirus not reimbursed by other sources.[23] HHS will then apply any remaining funds to lost revenue.[24]

Special Inspector General for Pandemic Recovery

The SIGPR is charged with a "duty to conduct, supervise, and coordinate audits and investigations of the making, purchase, management, and sale of loans, loan guarantees, and other investments" under programs established by the CARES Act, including the PRF.[25] SIGPR has indicated that it intends to focus on "high impact work," referring to audits and investigations of high-dollar loans or grants and high-risk areas.[26]

Common Compliance Risks

Providers face a number of compliance risks when accepting and using PRF funds. These begin when a provider first applies for a PRF payment, through their use of the funds, to later reporting on their use of the funds.

Eligibility Criteria

Providers who accept a PRF payment must certify that they meet the eligibility requirements for the allocation under which they received a payment.

Affirmative Versus Deemed Acceptance of Terms

Providers may affirmatively accept the terms and conditions of their payment through HHS's online portal—the Provider Relief Fund Application and Attestation Portal.[27] Providers who do not affirmatively attest to the terms, but who retain the payment for 90 days without contacting HHS to return it, shall be "deemed" to have accepted the terms and conditions.[28]

Transfer of Funds between Parent and Subsidiary

Generally, where a subsidiary entity received a payment under a general distribution, the parent entity may direct the use of and report on the PRF payment. A parent entity generally may not direct the use of a subsidiary's payment under a targeted distribution. However, a parent entity may transfer a targeted distribution received by a subsidiary to another subsidiary. HHS has indicated such a transfer faces an increased likelihood of audit.[29]

Change of Ownership

Generally, where an entity received a payment under a general distribution of the PRF and is subsequently sold by a purchase of stock or membership interest, the entity may retain the payment regardless of the new owner. However, if the transaction is a purchase of some or all of the recipient's assets, the payment does not transfer to the buyer.

Use of PRF Payment for Common Healthcare-Related Expenses or Lost Revenue

Providers who receive a PRF payment may only use the payment to reimburse healthcare-related expenses attributable to coronavirus and lost revenue attributable to coronavirus. HHS has defined these categories broadly, but providers should be aware of the limits.

Use of PRF Payment for Losses Reimbursed by Another Source

Providers who received a PRF payment may not use the payment to reimburse expenses or losses that have been reimbursed from other sources or that other sources are obligated to reimburse. Other sources may include loans under the Paycheck Protection Program, insurance coverage, and other federal or state relief programs.

Deadline to Use Funds

Providers who received a PRF payment must use the payment to cover coronavirus-related expenses by a certain date depending on when the payment was received. Providers who do not expend all funds received under the PRF by the given deadline may be required to return any unused funds.

Reporting Requirements

Providers who received a PRF payment must file reports with HHS regarding their use of the payment. Reports must be filed within the applicable PRF portal reporting time period depending on when payment was received. The first of these reports, covering use of funds in early 2020, was due by September 30, 2021, with a grace period for late reporting ending on November 30, 2021.[30]

Specifically, for Reporting Period 1, covering payments received from April 10, 2020 to June 30, 2020, the report must have been submitted between July 1, 2021 and September 30, 2021, with a grace period ending November 30, 2021. For Reporting Period 2, covering payments received from July 1, 2020 to December 31, 2020, the report must have been submitted between January 1, 2022 and March 31, 2022. For Reporting Period 3, covering payments received from January 1, 2021 to June 30, 2021, the report must have been submitted between July 1, 2022 and September 30, 2022. For Reporting Period 4, covering payments received from July 1, 2021 to December 31, 2021, the report must be submitted between January 1, 2023 and March 31, 2023. For Reporting Period 5, covering payments received from January 1, 2022 to June 30, 2022, the report must be submitted between July 1, 2023 and September 30, 2023. For Reporting Period 6, covering payments received from July 1, 2022 to December 31, 2022, the report must be submitted between January 1, 2024 and March 31, 2024. For Reporting Period 7, covering payments received from January 1, 2023 to June 30, 2023, the report must be submitted between July 1, 2024 and September 20, 2024.[31]

Providers who are unable to file these reports by the applicable deadline due to extenuating circumstances may have the ability to request to report late. Extenuating circumstances include things such as severe illness or death, natural disasters, or internal miscommunications or errors.

Poor Documentation or Tracking of Funds

Poor documentation or commingling of the PRF payment with other operating funds may inhibit a provider's ability to later demonstrate compliance.

Addressing Compliance Risks

Policy and Procedure Review

Understand the requirements, terms, and conditions of the specific distribution or distributions that the entity received, especially the data elements that the entity will be required to report. Implement internal policies and procedures to oversee use of the funds in a compliant manner.

Internal Controls

Create internal controls and mechanisms to track the use of PRF payments to reimburse eligible losses and expenses, as well as tracking the use of other funding sources to demonstrate that no other source reimbursed an expense that the PRF also reimbursed.

Continuous Monitoring

Monitor eligible expenses in real time to ensure the eligible expenses are adequately documented for future reporting.

Detailed Record-Keeping and Accounting

Providers must be able to demonstrate that they used the PRF payment for an appropriate purpose and show sufficient expenses and lost revenue to justify the payment received. This includes reporting revenue information from both 2019 and 2020.

Documentation of Expenses and Losses in Excess of PRF Payment Amount

HHS may disallow some of a provider's reported expenses or losses during a later review. A provider should therefore document more expenses and losses than the amount of the PRF payment to create a "buffer zone" of eligible expenses and losses.

Possible Penalties

Sanctions imposed for noncompliance with the terms, conditions, and program requirements can include:

- Recoupment of allegedly misused payments
- Civil and criminal penalties under the False Claims Act, including fines, triple damages, and imprisonment
- Other criminal penalties for fraudulent activities

Compliance Resources

U.S. Department of Health & Human Services

CARES Act Provider Relief Fund
Includes links to information, guidance, terms and conditions, and data regarding the PRF.

https://www.hrsa.gov/provider-relief

Provider Relief Fund: FAQs
Find a compilation of common questions and guidance, which are updated frequently on this site.

https://www.hrsa.gov/provider-relief/faq/general

General and Targeted Distribution: Post-Payment Notice of Reporting Requirements
Includes the reporting requirements for most general and targeted distributions.

https://www.hrsa.gov/sites/default/files/hrsa/provider-relief/provider-post-payment-notice-of-reporting-requirements-june-2021.pdf

Health Resources and Services Administration

Provider Relief Fund Reporting Portal
Providers must use this portal to report receiving one or more payments exceeding $10,000 in aggregate.

https://prfreporting.hrsa.gov/s/

Request to Report Late Due to Extenuating Circumstances
https://www.hrsa.gov/provider-relief/reporting-auditing/late-reporting-requests

Change of Ownership Fact Sheet
https://www.hrsa.gov/sites/default/files/hrsa/provider-relief/ownership-changes-fact-sheet.pdf

Special Inspector General for Pandemic Recovery

Providers can find SIGPR news and reports on this site, including information enforcement priorities. SIGPR may also post information about future investigations on this site.

https://www.sigpr.gov

Risk Takeaways

Main points of interest:
- The PRF was created by Congress to provide financial relief to healthcare providers during the COVID-19 public health emergency.
- Providers that accept payments under the PRF are required to comply with various restrictions on the use of the payment and file reports demonstrating their compliance.

Areas to watch:
- Eligibility criteria
- Affirmative vs. deemed acceptance of terms
- Transfer of funds between parent and subsidiary
- Change of ownership
- Use of PRF payment for healthcare-related expenses or lost revenue
- Use of PRF payment for losses reimbursed by another source
- Reporting requirements
- Precise timelines for use of funds and for reporting
- Poor documentation or tracking of funds

Laws that apply:
- Coronavirus Aid, Relief, and Economic Security Act, Pub. L. No. 116-136, 134 Stat. 281 (2020).
- Paycheck Protection Program and Health Care Enhancement Act, Pub. L. No. 116-139, 134 Stat. 620 (2020).

> **Addressing compliance risks:**
> - Create internal controls to track use of PRF payments and use of other funding sources
> - Maintain detailed record-keeping and accounting of PRF use
> - Document expenses and losses in excess of PRF payment amount
> - Monitor eligible expenses continuously
> - Review policies and procedures to oversee use of PRF funds

Endnotes

1. **Stephen Shaver** is an associate attorney at Wachler & Associates PC. He represents healthcare providers and suppliers in a broad range of health professional and facility licensing and regulatory compliance matters, as well as Medicare, Medicaid, and third-party payer disputes and audits. Mr. Shaver received his juris doctor from Washington University in St. Louis School of Law and his bachelor of arts from the University of Notre Dame. Mr. Shaver previously served as a prosecutor in Maricopa County, Arizona, and Wayne County, Michigan.

2. Coronavirus Aid, Relief, and Economic Security Act, Pub. L. No. 116-136, 134 Stat. 281 (2020).

3. Paycheck Protection Program and Health Care Enhancement Act, Pub. L. No. 116-139, 134 Stat. 620 (2020).

4. "CARES Act Provider Relief Fund: General Information," U.S. Department of Health & Human Services, accessed January 29, 2021, https://www.hhs.gov/coronavirus/cares-act-provider-relief-fund/general-information/index.html.

5. "CARES Act Provider Relief Fund: General Information," U.S. Department of Health & Human Services, accessed January 29, 2021, https://www.hhs.gov/coronavirus/cares-act-provider-relief-fund/general-information/index.html.

6. 31 U.S.C. §§ 3729–3733.

7. 15 U.S.C. § 9053.

8. "CARES Act Provider Relief Fund Frequently Asked Questions," U.S. Department of Health & Human Services, updated February 24, 2021, 9, https://www.hhs.gov/sites/default/files/provider-relief-fund-general-distribution-faqs.pdf.

9. Jeffrey Rosen, "Coordinated Nationwide Response to Detect, Deter, and Punish Crime Relating to the National Emergency Caused by COVID-19," memorandum, U.S. Department of Justice, March 19, 2020, https://www.justice.gov/file/1268521/download.

10. "Acceptance of Terms and Conditions," Department of Health & Human Services, accessed March 1, 2021, https://www.hhs.gov/sites/default/files/terms-and-conditions-provider-relief-30-b.pdf.

11. "General and Targeted Distribution: Post-Payment Notice of Reporting Requirements," U.S. Department of Health & Human Services, January 15, 2021, https://www.hhs.gov/sites/default/files/provider-post-payment-notice-of-reporting-requirements-january-2021.pdf.

12. "CARES Act Provider Relief Fund Frequently Asked Questions," U.S. Department of Health & Human Services, 9.

13. "General and Targeted Distribution: Post-Payment Notice of Reporting Requirements," U.S. Department of Health & Human Services, 2.

14. "General and Targeted Distribution: Post-Payment Notice of Reporting Requirements," U.S. Department of Health & Human Services, supra.

15. "General and Targeted Distribution: Post-Payment Notice of Reporting Requirements," U.S. Department of Health & Human Services, supra.

16. "General and Targeted Distribution: Post-Payment Notice of Reporting Requirements," U.S. Department of Health & Human Services, supra.

17. "General and Targeted Distribution: Post-Payment Notice of Reporting Requirements," U.S. Department of Health & Human Services, supra.

18. "General and Targeted Distribution: Post-Payment Notice of Reporting Requirements," U.S. Department of Health & Human Services, supra.

19. "General and Targeted Distribution: Post-Payment Notice of Reporting Requirements," U.S. Department of Health & Human Services, 1.

20. "General and Targeted Distribution: Post-Payment Notice of Reporting Requirements," U.S. Department of Health & Human Services, supra.

21. "General and Targeted Distribution: Post-Payment Notice of Reporting Requirements," U.S. Department of Health & Human Services, 2.

22. "General and Targeted Distribution: Post-Payment Notice of Reporting Requirements," U.S. Department of Health & Human Services, 4.

23. "General and Targeted Distribution Post-Payment Notice of Reporting Requirements, Department of Health and Human Services," supra.

24. "General and Targeted Distribution: Post-Payment Notice of Reporting Requirements," U.S. Department of Health & Human Services, 1.

25. Office of the Special Inspector General for Pandemic Recovery, *Strategic Plan: Fiscal Years 2021-2023*, December 2, 2020, 4, https://www.sigpr.gov/sites/sigpr/files/2020-12/SIGPR-Strategic-Plan-FYs-2021-23.pdf.

26. Office of the Special Inspector General for Pandemic Recovery, *Strategic Plan*, 5.

27. "Welcome to the Provider Relief Fund Application and Attestation Portal," CARES Provider Relief Fund, accessed March 1, 2021, https://cares.linkhealth.com/?#/.

28. "CARES Act Provider Relief Fund Frequently Asked Questions," U.S. Department of Health & Human Services, 32.

29. "General and Targeted Distribution: Post-Payment Notice of Reporting Requirements," U.S. Department of Health & Human Services, 7.

30. "Important Dates for Reporting," Health Resources & Services Administration, access Nov. 4, 2022, https://www.hrsa.gov/provider-relief/reporting-auditing/important-dates.

31. Id.

Credit Balances

By Darryl Rhames,[1] CFE, CHIAP, and CICA, and Symone Rosales,[2] RHIT, CHPS

What Are Credit Balances in the Revenue Cycle?

Skillfully managing the revenue cycle of a healthcare organization requires oversight of several components. Most health entities are considered creditors—organizations that offer or extend credit or services, which results in debt.[3] Each patient account may be assessed by several departments within revenue management until the debt is settled. When settling a debt, one significant risk within the healthcare revenue cycle is a "credit balance," which is defined as an excess of payment on an account. Credit balances can exist for many reasons, including, for example, failure to correct coordination of benefits (COB), improper billing, and duplicate payments. Though credit balances may occur during the normal course of business, they require consistent attention, monitoring, and ongoing resolution to prevent accumulation; overpayments not returned can result in penalties. To accurately assess the compliance risks of credit balances, an investigation of the account and payment analysis will be required. Many possible reasons exist for an account to present a negative balance; however, the most common types of credit balances are classified based on the payer source.

Patient credit balances can occur by accepting improper payments from patients. In most cases, patient overpayments result from a miscalculation of out-of-pocket costs or insurance benefits. Collection of a presumed contractual co-pay, deductible, or co-insurance without an in-depth understanding of the insurance benefits may produce a negative balance on the account after claims are processed.

Apart from patient credit balances, organizations may need to review negative account balances related to third-party payers. **Commercial-payer credit balances** may transpire in the happenstance that a private insurer makes an overpayment. These credit balances are often caused by systematic or contract issues. **Government-payer credit balances** are simply excessive or improper payments made by government entities such as Medicaid or Medicare. Overpayments from these payer sources often present the highest liability for healthcare organizations, as failure to comply with their respective guidelines may result in a violation of the False Claims Act.

Institutional providers are obligated to submit Medicare Credit Balance Reports (see CMS-838 Form), which are required under the authority of sections of the Social Security Protection Act.[45] Failure to submit this report may result in a suspension of payments under the Medicare program and may affect eligibility to participate in the Medicare program. **Clinics and individual providers** do not have to submit credit balance reports to the various federal and state agencies but are still at risk of retaining an overpayment and may potentially violate the False Claims Act[6] if they do not refund credit balances to federal payers in a timely manner and exercise due diligence in monitoring and identifying accounts.

Proper management of credit balances is essential to ensuring compliance with Medicare and Medicaid regulations, meeting contractual expectations, providing timely refunds, and reducing the risk of misappropriation of funds and False Claims Act violations.

Risk Area Governance

Ultimately, the prompt resolution of a credit balance is the most desirable outcome. Overpayments are subject to federal regulations as well as protocols further defined by states. It is recommended to review these guidelines since these entities provide specific timelines regarding how a credit balance must be handled and when the overpayment needs to be released.

State Laws

After identifying a patient credit balance, many healthcare practices hold funds with the intent to apply the credit to any future balances a patient may owe. Unfortunately, this may not always be the best course of action. Organizations may have reporting obligations to return funds to their state controller's office. States have enacted escheat or unclaimed property laws that involve an organization needing to be proactive in returning property, including credit balances, to the rightful owner. This may require written notices to the reported owner and, in the event the patient cannot be located, the credit balance may be considered unclaimed property and sent to the state controller. The time allotted for returning a patient or private-insurer overpayment to the state controller varies from jurisdiction to jurisdiction. It is recommended to review state laws to determine the designated workflow needed to properly resolve the overpayments.

Theft or Embezzlement in Connection with Health Care, 18 U.S.C. § 669

Third-party payers also have guidelines for creditors in the event of an overpayment. Commercial insurance plans are governed first by the terms of the contract and then by state statutes. While state statutes and contracts will apply, a federal statute also obligates a health-care entity to return credits to a private insurer. The "Theft or embezzlement in connection with health care" section details penalties in cases in which a person or organization "know-ingly and willfully embezzles, steals, or otherwise without authority converts to the use of any person other than the rightful owner, or intentionally misapplies any of the moneys, funds, securities, premiums, credits, property, or other assets of a health care benefit program."[7] The term "health care benefit program" is defined (in 18 U.S.C § 24) as any public or private plan.[8] In this context, it is understood that withholding overpayments from commercial insurance plans may also carry serious legal repercussions.

Fraud Enforcement and Recovery Act of 2009, Pub. Law 111–21

Overpayments made by any government payer, such as Medicaid and Medicare, must be returned under strict time limits. Prior to the Affordable Care Act (ACA), the U.S. Department of Health & Human Services (HHS) Office of Inspector General (OIG) addressed provider responsibility to return the credit balance under its *Compliance Program Guidance for Third Party Billing Companies*.[9] Ultimately, the guidance states, "failure to repay overpayments within a reasonable period of time could be interpreted as an intentional attempt to conceal the overpayment from the government, establishing an independent basis for a criminal violation."[10] In 2009, passage of the Fraud Enforcement and Recovery Act (FERA) provided further clarification on potential liability of accounts that had credit balances. This act was passed to aid in healthcare fraud enforcement and to made it clear that retention of an overpayment resulted in a liability under the False Claims Act.[11][12]

Patient Protection and Affordable Care Act, 42 U.S.C. § 1320a-7k(d)

Though prior statutes confirmed that healthcare providers are responsible for making refunds to Medicaid and Medicare in the event of an overpayment, it wasn't until passage of the Patient Protection and Affordable Care Act (ACA)[13] that specific deadlines were estab-lished. In 2010, enactment of the ACA provided Americans more access to healthcare through affordable options with third-party payers. The ACA stipulated that healthcare organizations identify overpayments received, report them, and repay the rightful owner within 60 days of identification. The act also provided an in-depth description of what it means to identify a credit balance: "[A] person has identified an overpayment when the person has, or should have, through the exercise of reasonable diligence, determined that the person has received an overpayment and quantified the amount of the overpayment. Creating this standard for identification provides needed clarity, processes, and procedures for providers and suppliers on the actions they need to take to comply with requirements for reporting and returning of self-identified overpayments."[14] The statute continues by evaluating the allotment of time a provider may need for a good faith investigation.

In the 2016, "Medicare Program; Reporting and Returning of Overpayments, Final Rule", Centers for Medicare & Medicaid Services (CMS) required "providers and suppliers receiving funds under the Medicare program to report and return overpayments by the later of the date that is 60 days after the date on which the overpayment was identified; or the date any corresponding cost report is due, if applicable".[15] The rule further clarifies that:

- A person that has received an overpayment must not only report and return the overpayment in the form and manner set forth in the rule; but also that
- A person has identified an overpayment when the person has, or should have through the exercise of reasonable diligence, determined that the person has received an overpayment and quantified the amount of the overpayment.

A person should have determined that the person received an overpayment and quantified the amount of the overpayment if the person fails to exercise reasonable diligence and the person in fact received an overpayment. Therefore, one may conclude that there is a clear expectation of applying a good faith and diligent effort to identify overpayments, i.e., by conducting compliance monitoring for overpayments. It is important that compliance officers know the time frame and parameters the Final Rule sets:

> We choose 6 months as the benchmark for timely investigation because we believe that providers and suppliers should prioritize these investigations and also to recognize that completing these investigations may require the devotion of resources and time. Receiving overpayments from Medicare is sufficiently important that providers and suppliers should devote appropriate attention to resolving these matters. A total of 8 months (6 months for timely investigation and 2 months for reporting and returning) is a reasonable amount of time, absent extraordinary circumstances affecting the provider, supplier, or their community. What constitutes extraordinary circumstances is a facts specific question. Extraordinary circumstances may include unusually complex investigations that the provider or supplier reasonably anticipates will require more than six months to investigate, such as physician self-referral law violations that are referred to the CMS Voluntary Self-Referral Disclosure Protocol (SRDP). Specific examples of other types of extraordinary circumstances include natural disasters or a state of emergency.[16]

Common Compliance Risks

Credit balances can arise in many ways. Medicare credit balances include instances where a provider is:

- Paid twice for the same service either by Medicare or by Medicare and another insurer;
- Paid for services planned but not performed or for noncovered services;

- Overpaid because of errors made in calculating beneficiary deductible and coinsurance amounts; or
- A hospital that bills and is paid for *outpatient* services included in a beneficiary's inpatient claim.[17]

While there are various ways a credit balance can occur, it is important to note as far as federal payers are concerned, no *de minimis* exception exists; even small amounts such as one dollar and five dollars need to be returned to federal payers if they are overpaid.

Though credit balances will exist within a healthcare organization's accounts, several risks are involved that may need to be resolved. The complexities of overpayments, state laws, and liability of contract terms can yield errors or increase compliance risks for the organization. Unfortunately, there are times when credit balances are left undiscovered until there is an audit. Audits by regulatory agencies may result in the high cost of remediation and increased reputational risks.

Common areas that may result in a credit balance could include errors from the payers or within internal billing teams. Internally, there could be manual- or system-posting errors present that would have an account appear to have a credit balance. For example, incorrect postings of allowable rates or adjustments may result in a negative balance on the account. This would not be a true credit but rather an error that can be resolved. Such errors could occur due to human error, but others could be a result of a computerized payment posting issue. Most organizations post utilizing Electronic Data Exchange (EDI) 835 files; however, it is possible that these files may contain a miscalculation. Another example of possible credit balances would be a true overpayment from a payer due to system errors. Payers often rely on claim systems to process payments, and there are times that the system may not be configured properly and may issue an overpayment. Timely management of credit balances would allow for an organization to promptly identify internal or external errors and correct the possible overpayment issue.

Addressing Compliance Risks

As organizations begin the daunting task of assessing compliance risks involved with credit balances, they begin to learn the depths of the regulatory issues at hand. A regular monitoring routine will make this less intimidating through modern billing systems that allow for data extraction and reports to facilitate internal monitoring. In order to sufficiently address negative account balances, organizations may consider using the following approaches.

Assess Data and Analytic Methods

Assessment involves reviewing reports and data models responsible for detailing credit balances on accounts. It is imperative that providers can first utilize their records to identify a credit balance.

Identify Payer Source

Due to different guidelines applied for each payment source, it is beneficial to stratify balances by payer. After identification, it is helpful to evaluate aging balances. The lookback period for Medicaid, commercial payers, and patients varies by state. The review period for Medicare balances is six years. However, it does not have to come to a lookback if credit balances are monitored regularly (e.g., monthly) and corrective action is taken promptly.

Perform a Root-Cause Analysis

After a data review, it would be valuable to determine if credit balances are truly the result of an overpayment. It is possible that a negative account balance may occur due to a posting or systematic error, and not necessarily from an overpayment. A root-cause analysis also assists in determining staff areas within an organization that need education, for example, if the overpayment results from over-collecting or a misunderstanding of insurance benefits.

Implement Ongoing Monitoring Efforts

To mitigate future risks, an organization may find it useful to have written policies and procedures in place to monitor credit balances. This requires an understanding of the internal controls the healthcare entity must use to perform reasonable diligence for identifying and quantifying overpayments. It also provides assurance that the provider is taking proper steps to meet state and federal guidelines and timelines. Though additional staff resources may be necessary for ongoing monitoring, it is a step that must be taken to ensure compliance. Leveraging sophisticated electronic health record (EHR) systems can aide in account reviews by creating alerts or reports.

Perform Random Audits

Aside from routine monitoring and running credit balance reports for various payers as part of the provider's business practices, the compliance department may want to conduct periodic independent audits. These can ensure that credit balances are being reviewed according to policy and procedure and, especially, that identified credit balances constituting overpayments have been returned to federal payers within 60 days. Compliance may also check that patient refunds occur consistent with internal procedures and state law. Organizations may want to review internal controls regarding credit balances. Ensuring that procedures addressing the identification process and policy on refunds will prove to be critical in determining compliance with regulations. An understanding of payment posting procedures and current claim issues may assist in identifying possible areas of risk.

Regular audits on credit balances are recommended and can easily be reviewed with the accounts receivable department. Sample selection may include credits in various stages of timelines. Reviewing credits that have been identified to be pending anywhere between 1 to

90 days could reveal weakness within internal controls that will need to be addressed to be compliant.

Provide Education and Training

Revenue cycle compliance training should include federal and state guidelines regarding credit-balance timelines. Training for the revenue team also should include payment posting reconciliation for both manual and computer-assisted posting. Since a possibility of an account incurring a credit could be a result of posting errors, staff may need to be trained to diligently watch and identify possible credit on accounts.

Compliance and billing staff need to be aware that credit balances constituting ioverpayments require timely refunding and that the 60-day rule applies for identified overpayments by federal payers. Institutional providers, such as hospitals, are quite accustomed to reviewing their credit balances, extracting data reports from their patient accounting and billing systems, and submitting their Medicare Credit Balance Reports. Smaller providers and physician practices, however, may be less familiar with the False Claims Act risk associated with lack of timely return of credit balances constituting overpayments. The compliance officer should ensure there is sufficient training and education on the matter, including deadlines and an understanding that no automatic write-offs of very small amounts are permissible either.

Possible Penalties

Not only do providers have to worry about False Claims Act lawsuits for hanging onto overpayments, they may also be fined by the OIG with a civil monetary penalty for knowingly retaining an overpayment. Once oversight agencies are aware of mishaps with account balances, they may begin to perform regular audits and impose penalties and demand refunds.

A worst-case scenario could occur if enforcement agencies pursue a corporate integrity agreement (CIA) due to False Claims Act allegations. CIAs are negotiated with providers by the OIG as part of the settlement addressing civil false claim statute violations. Entities agree to the obligations listed in a CIA and, in exchange, the OIG agrees not to seek the entities' exclusion from participation in Medicare, Medicaid, or other federal healthcare programs.

Ultimately, negative account balances require organizations to adhere to the terms of payer contracts, state regulations, and federal guidelines. Violations can carry strict penalties, such the possibility of criminal penalties, including imprisonment and criminal fines.[18] In one recent case, a healthcare organization was found to have willfully delayed repayment of more than $800,000 Medicaid overpayments. Along with the stress of the deteriorating reputation of the health system, the financial penalties totaled nearly $3 million.[19] In another case, the U.S. Department of Justice (DOJ) fined a provider more than $400,000 for failing to correct credit balances and repay overpayments to federal healthcare programs.[20]

Compliance Resources

Centers for Medicare & Medicaid Services

Medicare Credit Balance Report
https://www.cms.gov/Medicare/CMS-Forms/CMS-Forms/downloads/cms838.pdf

Federal Register

Medicare Program; Reporting and Returning of Overpayments
This final rule will provide clarification on requirements for reporting and returning overpayments.

https://www.federalregister.gov/d/2016-02789

https://www.ecfr.gov/current/title-42/chapter-IV/subchapter-A/part-401/subpart-D/section-401.305

United States Treasury

Unclaimed Assets
This publication includes resources for locating state guidelines for unclaimed property.

https://www.fiscal.treasury.gov/unclaimed-assets.html

Risk Takeaways

Main points of interest:
- Actively review and monitor accounts for credit balances and to see if they constitute overpayments.
- Identify source payer of each overpayment.
- The rules for reporting and returning an overpayment may vary per payer source.
- The 60-day rule applies to refund credit balances of federal payers.

Areas to watch:
- Review accounts for systematic or posting errors.
- Monitor accounts with overpayments for a possible training opportunities and procedure updates.

Laws that apply:

- State laws
- Theft or Embezzlement in Connection with Health Care, 18 U.S.C. § 669
- Fraud Enforcement and Recovery Act of 2009, Pub. Law 111-21
- False Claims Act, 31 U.S.C. §§ 3729–3733
- Patient Protection and Affordable Care Act, 42 U.S.C. § 1320a-7k(d)
- 42 U.S.C. §§ 1302, 1395hh ,1395w-5
- Requirements for Reporting and Returning of Overpayments, 42 C.F.R. § 401.305

Addressing credit balance compliance risks:

- Review reporting capability as most EHRs can detect a credit balance issue.
- Perform root-cause analysis on accounts to determine the direct source of overpayment.
- Implement ongoing monitoring practices.
- Perform random audits and report findings to ensure proper monitoring and corrective action.

Endnotes

1. **Darryl Rhames** is a native New Yorker who graduated from Hampton University with a B.S in Accounting and is a Certified Fraud Examiner (CFE), Certified Healthcare Internal Audit Professional (CHIAP), and a Certified Internal Controls Auditor (CICA). Rhames has been in the auditing, compliance, and accounting professions for 25 years and currently conducts various audits, fraud investigations, and internal control and compliance reviews at University Health in San Antonio, Texas. Additionally, Rhames was featured in *Compliance Today Magazine* (HCCA - October 2019) and serves on committees for the Association of Healthcare Internal Auditors, the Association of Certified Fraud Examiners, Phi Beta Sigma Fraternity, Inc., Black Nurses Rock San Antonio, Alamo City Black Chamber of Commerce, and Texas Center for Infectious Diseases, and the Multiple Sclerosis Society. He also volunteers for local youth non-profit companies to speak on leadership or offer his time to assist people in any way he can.

2. **Symone Rosales** has held a variety of roles from front line to leadership positions in Revenue Cycle management stretching over 12 years. Rosales holds a designation as a Registered Health Information Technician (RHIT) and is Certified in Healthcare Privacy and Security (CHPS) with the American Health Information Management Association. Through her roles, she has developed a strong passion for revenue cycle compliance and is motivated by the mission to help patients and employees alike as she currently serves as Compliance Auditor at University Health.

3. 15 U.S.C. § 1681m.

4. Centers for Medicare & Medicaid Services, *CMS-838 Medicare Credit Balance Report*, revised Oct 10, 2003, https://www.cms.gov/Medicare/CMS-Forms/CMS-Forms/downloads/cms838.pdf.

5. Social Security Protection Act, Pub. L. No. 108-203, §§ 1815(a), 1833(e), 1886(a)(1)(C) (2004).

6. 31 U.S.C. §§ 3729–3733.

7. 18 U.S.C § 669.

8. 18 U.S.C § 24.

9. Compliance Program Guidance for Third-Party Medical Billing Companies, 63 Fed. Reg. 70,138 (Dec. 18, 1998).

10. Compliance Program Guidance for Third-Party Medical Billing Companies, 63 Fed. Reg. 70,138, 70,144 (Dec. 18, 1998).

11. Fraud Enforcement and Recovery Act of 2009, Pub. L. No. 111-21.

12. 31 U.S.C. §§ 3729–373.

13. 42 U.S.C. § 18001 et seq.

14. Medicare Program; Reporting and Returning of Overpayments, 81 Fed. Reg. 7,654 (Feb.12, 2016).

15. Medicare Program; Reporting and Returning of Overpayments, 81 Fed. Reg. 7,654 (Feb.12, 2016).

16. Medicare Program; Reporting and Returning of Overpayments, 81 Fed. Reg. 7,654 (Feb.12, 2016).

17. Centers for Medicare & Medicaid, *CMS-838 Medicare Credit Balance Report*, revised Oct 10, 2003, https://www.cms.gov/Medicare/CMS-Forms/CMS-Forms/downloads/cms838.pdf.

18. 18 U.S.C. § 287.

19. U. S. Department of Justice, U.S. Attorney's Office for Southern District of New York, "Manhattan U.S. Attorney Announces $2.95 Million Settlement with Hospital Group for Improperly Delaying Repayment of Medicaid Funds," news release, August 24, 2016, https://www.justice.gov/usao-sdny/pr/manhattan-us-attorney-announces-295-million-settlement-hospital-group-improperly.

20. U.S. Department of Justice, U.S. Attorney's Office for the Middle District of Florida, "Jacksonville Cardiovascular Practice Agrees to Pay More Than $440,000 to Resolve False Claims Act Allegations for Failing to Reimburse Government Health Care Programs," news release, October 13, 2017,https://www.justice.gov/usao-mdfl/pr/jacksonville-cardiovascular-practice-agrees-pay-more-440000-resolve-false-claims-act.

Denials Management

By Ronald L. Hirsch,[1] MD, FACP, CHCQM-PHYADV, CHRI

What Is Denials Management?

To properly analyze the compliance risks of denials management requires stepping back and analyzing the factors that led to the denial. First, claim denials are a refusal of an insurer to pay for a patient's healthcare services at a healthcare provider. These denials can be generally classified into several types, each with a different root cause and compliance risk. Here are some of the most common types of claim denials.

Technical denials encompass those where information on the claim renders the claim unpayable. These technical factors include incomplete claim completion, submission of a claim to the wrong payer, submitting past the timely filing deadline, claims for services that have already been billed, and services not authorized.

Coding denials involve improper application of coding rules. This would include the use of invalid or nonspecific HCPCS or ICD-10 codes, improper use of modifiers, not following coding rules by unbundling services, use of codes that are not supported by the documentation, bypassing edits, and improper coding of services such as infusions or injections. Many coding denials make reference to citations such as Coding Clinics, the official guide to coding information published quarterly by the American Hospital Association. It is important to check those citations to ensure they are being interpreted correctly by the auditor and that subsequent guidance in Coding Clinics has not superseded the cited source.

Clinical validation audits, where denials state that a reported diagnosis was not clinically present, require careful analysis to determine if the diagnosis definition used by the auditor remains valid. Several conditions, such as malnutrition, have definitions that have evolved over time, and a denial based on an outdated definition should be appealed.[2] For other diagnoses, as with sepsis, the criteria for defining sepsis have evolved as the science has advanced, often leading to coding confusion and denials.[3]

Diagnosis Related Grouping (DRG) denials occur when the auditor determines that the codes entered on the claim were not valid. The audit may determine that the primary diagnosis was not correctly assigned or that a secondary diagnosis was not supported. As noted above, the audit may find a diagnosis is not clinically valid and remove it from the claim, resulting in assignment to a different DRG that is usually lower weighted. They may also determine that although the diagnosis was present, it does not meet the standard for inclusion as a secondary diagnosis as determined by the Uniform Hospital Discharge Data Set (UHDDS).[4] The UHDDS states that for reporting purposes, "the definition of 'other diagnoses' is additional conditions that affect patient care in terms of requiring clinical evaluation; or therapeutic treatment; or diagnostic procedures; or extended length of hospital stay; or increased nursing care and/or monitoring."[5]

Medical necessity denials constitute the most complex denial category. Medical necessity denials generally fall within one of two broad categories: medical necessity for the service itself and medical necessity for the level of care of the service. Medical necessity for the service itself calls into question whether the patient met the payer's guidelines to receive the service. These medical necessity guidelines may vary by payer. While some plans have an internal team that independently evaluates services to set medical necessity guidelines, others rely on the prevailing medical standard of care. This coverage can even vary within a payer. For plans that provide both commercial plans and government-sponsored plans, such as Medicare Advantage, the coverage for their commercial plans can follow internal guidelines, but the coverage for Medicare Advantage must match what is available to a fee-for-service Medicare patient.[6]

If the payer does not have a published policy for medical necessity coverage for a service, the determination of coverage often defers to the professionally recognized standard of healthcare. While defining the standard of care is difficult, the Centers for Medicare & Medicaid Services (CMS) refers to predetermined elements of healthcare developed by health professionals relying on professional expertise, prior experience, and the professional literature, with which aspects of the quality, medical necessity, and appropriateness of a healthcare service may be compared.[7] Innovation in medical practice changes rapidly and adoption of new technologies and practices varies greatly not only geographically between regions of the country, but also within organizations amongst medical staff at a single facility. As new procedures and practices are adopted, it is incumbent on the compliance team to ensure that there is a scientific basis for adopting the practice and that the service will be covered by payers.

CMS and the Medicare Administrative Contractors (MACs) publish National Coverage Determinations (NCDs) and Local Coverage Determinations (LCDs) in the Medicare Coverage Database.[8] Proposed NCDs and LCDs are published with a comment period prior to being finalized. NCDs are binding on all providers and auditors, but LCDs are not binding on appeals at the Administrative Law Judge and higher levels, although deference must be given to the policies.[9] NCDs and LCDs outline covered indications and, in many circumstances, noncovered indications. In 2015, the Department of Justice (DOJ) settled a false claims case with nearly 500 hospitals over implantation of defibrillators.[10] An analysis of that case noted that while the NCD for defibrillator placement clearly specifies when a device is covered, it does not indicate when a device is not covered, suggesting that the hospitals that settled had the opportunity to appeal each case.[11] Careful analysis of the coverage policy is necessary to determine if a denial is appropriate or should be appealed.

As noted, if an NCD is not available, a MAC may choose to develop an LCD. With multiple MACs across the country, that leads to potential confusion, especially for health systems and regional or national providers that provide services in multiple MAC jurisdictions that may then face differing medical necessity standards for the same service depending upon their location. The Office of the Inspector General (OIG) reported in 2014 that this significant variation in LCDs creates disparities in access to care for beneficiaries and is contrary to the growing practice of evidence-based medicine that eschews local variation. The OIG recommended at that time that CMS work to standardize LCDs across jurisdictions.[12]

Medical necessity denials for the level of care rest on the decision to admit the patient as an inpatient or treat the patient in the hospital as outpatient. As with medical necessity for the service, status determinations vary greatly between and within payers. It is important to note that status and medical care are not directly related. A hospitalized patient who is an outpatient should receive the same care as a hospitalized patient with the same condition who is admitted as inpatient. The difference is almost completely one of payment to the provider for the services provided. In general, inpatient admissions pay at a higher rate than the rate for the same care provided as outpatient, although this is not absolute.

Two major nonfinancial differences should be considered. For a traditional Medicare patient, if skilled rehabilitation care is needed after the hospital stay at a skilled nursing facility, the patient must be an inpatient for three or more days, not counting the day of discharge.[13] For any patient who is eligible for Medicare benefits, immediate discharge appeal rights are only available if the patient is admitted as inpatient.[14]

The status determinations for traditional Medicare beneficiaries are determined by the Two-Midnight Rule, adopted October 1, 2013.[15] This rule also applies to admissions of Medicare Advantage patients who are admitted to facilities that are not contracted with their Medicare Advantage plan. The basis of the Two-Midnight Rule is that inpatient admission is appropriate when patients are expected to have a hospital stay that crosses two midnights; the need for a surgery on the Medicare Inpatient-only list (published each year as addendum E to the Outpatient Prospective Payment System Final Rule); or a patient with a one-midnight expectation who meets one of the exceptions established by CMS.

For contracted providers providing care to a Medicare Advantage enrollee, CMS has stated that as long as the patient receives the necessary care, the determination of status and payment are a contractual issue between the provider and payer.[16] For nongovernmental payers, it is once again a contractual issue. Many payers use commercial criteria tools to aid in determining the appropriate patient status. While these tools, and internally developed guidelines, can aid in determining patient status, they are not definitive. They simply act as guides that can be overridden by a physician if clinically appropriate.

Claim denials must also be separated by payer. Denials of services provided to those insured by transitional government payers, such as Medicare and Medicaid, involve federal and state laws and regulations. Denials from commercial payers, such as employer-based plans, must be viewed on the contractual basis. If the provider is contracted with the payer, the terms of the contract apply. If the provider is noncontracted, then state laws may be applicable. Plans that are government-sponsored but provided under contract by another entity, such as Medicare Advantage or Managed Medicaid, are handled differently depending on whether the provider is contracted with the payer. Contracted providers would be bound to the provisions of the contract and noncontracted providers would use the federal or state regulations as guidance.

The proper management of denials is also crucial. While reviewing denials individually and responding appropriately is the main objective, every denial is an opportunity to collect data and improve processes. And the more granularity of data that can be collected, the more information an organization will have to prevent further denials. Each denial should be categorized by type, payer, service line, provider, coder, biller, day of the week, time of day, and so on. Accumulating this information will allow you to ascertain patterns to address in denial prevention. For example, denial for an inpatient admission that was determined to be more appropriate as outpatient with observation should be analyzed for payer; admission source (emergency department, direct admission, conversion from outpatient, surgery); admitting physician who made the admission decision; utilization review nurse who reviewed the case; physician advisor who made the second-level determination; diagnosis; day of the week; and time of day.

Who will prepare the appeal must also be determined. In the case of coding appeals, it would seem common sense to have the coding staff handle the appeal, but many coding denials are properly coded and include a clinical basis for the denial. Such would be the case in what are called "clinical validation denials," where a diagnosis is documented by a provider and coded properly onto the claim, but the payer disputes that the diagnosis actually exists. In this case, the denial must be reviewed collaboratively between the coding and clinical staff and the appeal formulated.

Denial and appeal tracking is important to ensure not only that deadlines are not missed, but also to monitor auditor behavior. CMS maintains a data warehouse that tracks the activity of all audit contractors to ensure that two auditors do not review the same case. In recent years, commercial payers have contracted with outside audit agencies to audit claims they have already paid. In some cases, this audit may be of a claim that was already audited by the payer themselves and found to be compliant. The contract should be reviewed to determine if a claim can be audited twice.

Every denial is also an opportunity to ensure that everyone is acting compliantly. While isolated denials rarely indicate intentional disregard of rules, patterns of denial types may develop, warranting a more in-depth review to ensure there is no compliance risk. While actions of individuals may not be malicious or intentionally fraudulent, the purposeful deviation from the rules should never be permitted.

The denial rate may also be subject to discussion with concerns that higher denial rates may suggest that noncompliant activities are occurring. This is not correct. A high denial rate warrants analysis, but it may be due to overaggressive denial practices by payers. Likewise, a very low denial rate is not necessarily a measure of excellent compliance, as lack of denials may suggest overly conservative practices.

Risk Area Governance

Fee-for-service Medicare denials are issued by a myriad of contractors, including:

- Medicare Administrative Contractors (MACs)
- Comprehensive Error Rate Testing Contractors (CERTs)
- Supplemental Medical Review Contractors (SMRCs)
- Quality Improvement Organizations (QIOs)
- Unified Program Integrity Contractors (UPICs)
- Recovery Audit Contractors (RACs)

Appeals of these denials follow a strict timeline established by CMS with five levels available to providers.[17][18] While there are deadlines, CMS contractors have the option to extend the deadline if good cause can be shown.[19] Likewise, parties reviewing appeals are also bound by deadlines to review and determine whether to reverse or uphold denials. Due to a large backlog of appeals, the review time at the Administrative Law Judge level for fiscal year 2021 was 1,260 days, which is substantially longer than the 90 days required by law. Chapter 3 of the *Medicare Program Integrity Manual*, "Verifying Potential Errors and Taking Corrective Actions," also describes in detail the policies and procedures required of both providers and contractors during the audit and appeal process.[20][21]

Depending on the audit topic and the auditor, the results of an audit may use statistical sampling to extrapolate the audit results to the whole universe of claims submitted for the same issue.[22] If denials are appealed and overturned, the extrapolation must be adjusted to account for the new determinations.[23] This makes the appeal process significantly more consequential and warrants careful scrutiny and appeal preparation.

For most coding denials, both the provider and payer must follow the HIPAA Code Set standard transaction rules.[24] For instance, payers may not change the sequence of codes on a claim to assign a lower-weighted principal diagnosis as adherence to the ICD-10-CM coding rules is required under HIPAA. It should be noted that this only applies to HIPAA-covered entities, including health plans, healthcare clearinghouses, certain healthcare providers, and their business associates. Certain agencies do not have to abide by HIPAA, including life insurance companies, government agencies, and workers' compensation carriers.

During the COVID-19 public health emergency, the Health Resources and Services Administration (HRSA), a division of U.S. Department of Health and Human Services, via provisions in the Coronavirus Aid, Relief, and Economic Security Act (CARES), the Families First Coronavirus Response Act (FFCRA), and the Paycheck Protection Program and Health Care Enhancement Act, established a multibillion-dollar fund for claims reimbursement to healthcare providers and facilities for testing, treatment, and vaccine administration for the uninsured.[25] One of the provisions for reimbursement for services was that the ICD-10-CM code for COVID-19 be the primary diagnosis on every claim. Claims submitted to HRSA were not required to follow the ICD-10-CM coding guidelines, so the COVID-19 diagnosis could be sequenced first even if it violated coding rules.[26]

As noted, appeals of denials issued by commercial or contracted Medicare Advantage plans are governed by the provider-payer contract. The ability to appeal may be limited to a set number of levels, and the party reviewing the appeal may be designated by the contract. Appeals that are reviewed by an external party are preferable to appeals that are handled internally.

There is a growing trend in audits by commercial payers to not only conduct audits internally, but also to contract with third parties to conduct post-payment audits of paid claims. In some cases, the payer provides prior authorization for a service but then the subcontractor reviews the claim and denies payment. It should be determined if contract language allows a denial of a previously approved service unless there is evidence of fraud.

Common Compliance Risks

Denials Indicating Potential Fraud, Waste, or Abuse

A pattern of denials for specific topics should be carefully reviewed to determine if evidence of wrongdoing exists, be it intentional or inadvertent. For example, denials for unbundling may suggest either claims preparation issues due to bypassing an edit or intentional activity to increase revenue. A pattern of denials for lack of authorization may mean the pre-procedure screening process is missing cases that require prior authorization or a provider is intentionally bypassing the process to avoid the work of having to obtain the prior authorization.

Denials of care as medically unnecessary warrant close scrutiny. While in many cases the denial may simply result from a lack of proper supporting documentation, in other cases it may indicate that care that is truly medically unnecessary is being provided. In some cases, this may be due to system issues. For example, if a hospital stay is paid per day and the payer carves out days for denial as not necessary, it may indicate a delay in care such as unavailability of advanced imaging or specialty consultation on weekends. In other cases, the care provided truly may not be medically necessary. The medical standard of care always evolves, and if physicians do not practice the standard of care, it may result in denial of payment and liability risk.[27] And while some practices may not cause harm, their overuse should nonetheless be discouraged. For example, the standard of care for cervical cancer screening has changed and is now recommended every three years, yet many physicians continue yearly screenings.[28]

Insufficient Provider Education

Every denial is an opportunity to determine the root cause and decide if further education is necessary. Status denials for traditional Medicare may suggest a provider's lack of knowledge of the main provisions of the Two-Midnight Rule. Denials for lack of adherence to a coverage determination would warrant education for providers that perform the service. This would ensure they are aware of the payer's medical necessity standards to improve their documentation or it may suggest that medical necessity was met but the information was not available in the hospital medical record for review by the auditor.

If there are denials for claims for professional evaluation and management services, it may suggest that physicians are not properly trained in code selection. The rules for selection of an evaluation and management code for office and other outpatient services were changed on January 1, 2021, and for hospital services on January 1, 2023 and now stress medical decision-making and time.[29] While the use of time for code selection is not new, during the COVID-19 public health emergency when rules were relaxed, CMS Administrator Seema Verma noted that CMS is investigating fraudulent telehealth charges, including providers that bill for "more visits than are humanly possible in a day."[30] This suggests that CMS and other payers will be using analytics to monitor for patterns of waste, fraud, and abuse in visit coding by providers.

Improper Coding or Clinical Validation

The increasing attention paid to documentation, both for clinical and financial purposes, has led to increased compliance risks. It is often said that if a doctor documented a diagnosis, it should be coded—but that is not correct. CMS described the purpose of DRG validation ensuring "that diagnostic and procedural information and the discharge status of the beneficiary, as coded and reported by the hospital on its claim, matches both the attending physician's description and the information contained in the beneficiary's medical record."[31] While coders may not have the clinical experience to validate whether a documented diagnosis is supported by the information contained in the medical record, it would be noncompliant to submit a claim with a diagnosis that is not clinically valid. Coders should have access to clinical staff, such as a nurse or physician advisor, to review cases where the clinical validity of a diagnosis is in question. The physician who documented the diagnosis should then be queried to provide further direction.

Missed Deadlines

While the timeline for appeals of traditional Medicare denials is set, the myriad of other payers may have different timelines and submission guidelines. A tracking system must be utilized to ensure deadlines are not missed.

Release of Information to Unapproved Entities

Although HIPAA regulations allow release of information necessary for processing of claims, audits performed by third parties contracted by the payer may pose risk of unauthorized disclosure. Ensuring that the auditing entity has proper authorization to obtain the records is required.

Addressing Compliance Risks

Monitor Auditor Websites for Audit Issues and Work with Audit and Appeals Team

In many institutions, compliance is not notified about denials until it is too late, such as when the DOJ arrives at the hospital's front entrance. But the compliance team should be working hand-in-hand with the audit and appeals teams to proactively review the types of claims that are being audited and the agency performing the audit. Many audits are done routinely for CMS to establish error rates, such as the CMS Comprehensive Error Rate Testing (CERT) audit program.[32] The Recovery Audit Contractor (RAC) program targets claims for specific issues where data suggests potential compliance issues that have been approved by CMS, but these audits are not targeted at specific facilities.[33] On the other hand, a Targeted Probe and Educate (TPE) audit by a MAC indicates that the data suggests that the facility's claims warrant further scrutiny.[34] Likewise, although denials from commercial payers do not carry the same consequences as audits from federal payers, the pattern of audits and denials may shed light into areas that need scrutiny.

Advise Staff to Use the Compliance Department as a Resource for Service Appropriateness Questions

Compliance staff should also be available as a resource to staff in all departments, including medical, nursing, pharmacy, case management, therapy, coding, and billing. Most compliance issues do not appear out of the blue. Every encounter in our healthcare system involves a myriad of touches and every touch should be viewed by that person as an opportunity to ask questions about the appropriateness of that service. As a physician advisor for a community hospital, I would often be asked by nurses to review a patient's care when the nurse did not understand why a patient was receiving a test or medication. In many cases the care was appropriate, but other cases led to further investigation and process change to avoid a compliance risk.

Educate Staff on HIPAA Coding and Billing Guideline Updates

Coding and billing guidelines are required to be used as mandated by HIPAA.[35] It is the responsibility of all covered entities to abide by these rules. Updates to these guidelines are published regularly and working with the coding and billing teams to ensure that the latest guidelines are followed is warranted. This may also involve a multidisciplinary approach, as when coding guideline changes affect the requirements for documentation by providers.

Review OIG Work Plan and OIG Audit Findings

OIG develops and follows a yearly "Work Plan" that indicates the areas planned for targeted auditing in that year. It develops the plan based on laws and regulations, requests made from other agencies, including Congress, and work performed by other oversight organizations. As new issues arise, OIG will update the plan and publish the new issues. The Work Plan and the results of individual provider audits can serve as a roadmap for internal audits. For example, in 2020, many of the "routine" audits of hospitals focused on inpatient rehabilitation facility admissions, coding of malnutrition, outpatient claims billed with modifiers that bypass edits (such as modifier 25), and short-stay inpatient admissions. For home health agencies, the documentation of homebound status was a common denial finding. The published audits also include the response of the audited provider and these often are written in great detail with citations to the applicable regulations and can serve as guides for all providers when facing similar denials.

Perform Random Audits

Denial prevention is always preferred over denial management so random audits to find areas of risk before the auditors find them is sensible. While the OIG Work Plan and posted audits can provide some roadmap for internal audit, internal audits should not focus only on those areas. Many of the other audit agencies, including the MACs, the SMRCs, and the RACs publish on their websites their current audit activity, and these topics should be considered for review. Providers should also consider random audits of high-volume and high-dollar services as they tend to attract auditor attention. Denial data can also guide audits to areas of risk, looking at other services performed by the same provider or department.

Possible Penalties

Denials that are accepted or not overturned on appeal result in loss of the revenue associated with that claim. That loss of revenue includes not only fixed costs, such as the salaries of the staff and the use of the room, but also variable costs including medications and most importantly implants, which can cost into the tens of thousands of dollars as with cardiac rhythm devices. When such claims are denied, these costs must be covered without any offsetting revenue. For that reason, careful scrutiny of claims denials involving high implant costs must be carefully monitored.

Denials can also lead to further action by contracted audit agencies including payment suspension, imposition of civil monetary penalties, institution of pre- or post-payment review, and additional audits.[36] A pattern of denials can also lead to extrapolation and a much larger financial cost to the institution. CMS describes the circumstances warranting extrapolation in the *Medicare Program Integrity Manual*, "Chapter 8: Administrative Actions and Sanctions and Statistical Sampling for Overpayment Estimation," noting extrapolation may be used "when it has been determined that a sustained or high level of payment error exists."[37]

As part of the TPE audit process developed by CMS, providers found to have claim problems that fail to resolve after three rounds of audits can undergo further action, including 100% prepay review, extrapolation, referral to a Recovery Auditor, or further TPE audits.[38] For the period from October 2019 to March 2020, a total of 335 providers of part A, B, durable medical equipment, and home health agencies were referred to CMS after failing three rounds of TPE audits. According to CMS, a majority of those were referred back to the MAC for a fourth round of audits rather than referred for more punitive action.[39]

In other cases, the False Claims Act calls for treble damages along with a per claim penalty that is linked to inflation, which in 2022 was set at $12,537.[40] Another risk of violating the False Claim Act is the possibility of criminal penalties, including imprisonment and criminal fines.[41]

Compliance Resources

Centers for Medicare & Medicaid Services

Medicare Coverage Database
This searchable index includes all NCDs and LCDs and all supporting documents, such as coverage analyses.

https://www.cms.gov/medicare-coverage-database/new-search/search.aspx

Medicare Fee for Service Recovery Audit Program
Links to active and proposed RAC audit targets and RAC contractor sites are on this page.

https://www.cms.gov/Research-Statistics-Data-and-Systems/Monitoring-Programs/
Medicare-FFS-Compliance-Programs/Recovery-Audit-Program

Medicare Program Integrity Manual
This manual provides an overview and chapters outlining audit contractor duties and guidelines.

https://www.cms.gov/Regulations-and-Guidance/Guidance/Manuals/
Internet-Only-Manuals-IOMs-Items/CMS019033

Parts C & D Enrollee Grievances, Organization/Coverage Determinations, and Appeals Guidance

This publication includes regulations on appeals of Medicare Advantage plan denials.

https://www.cms.gov/Medicare/Appeals-and-Grievances/MMCAG/Downloads/Parts-C-and-D-Enrollee-Grievances-Organization-Coverage-Determinations-and-Appeals-Guidance.pdf

Office of Inspector General

Compliance Resource Portal

Find access to the OIG worklist and past OIG audits to see audit targets on this site.

https://oig.hhs.gov/compliance/compliance-resource-portal/

Risk Takeaways

Main points of interest:
- Every denial is an opportunity to prevent a future denial.
- Denials expose many areas of risk, including medical necessity, documentation, coding, billing, and appeal preparation.
- The rules for appeals vary by payer, including Medicare and Medicare Advantage.
- Denials may suggest compliance issues and patterns of denials should be carefully analyzed.
- While extrapolation is generally limited to patterns of errors, OIG routinely uses extrapolation on their routine audits.

Areas to watch:
- Medical necessity of services: Does the care meet the medical necessity standard of the payer? Are procedures screened prior to performance to ensure medical necessity is met?
- Coding and billing: The coding rules change regularly. Are staff keeping up to date? Are providers educated on new guidelines?

Laws that apply:
- False Claims Act, 31 U.S.C. §§ 3729–3733
- HIPAA, 45 C.F.R. §§ 160, 162, 164

Addressing compliance risks:
- Be available to staff to discuss concerns; nothing is too small to address.
- Perform random audits.
- Monitor auditor websites for audit issues.
- Review OIG Workplan and OIG audit findings.
- Ensure feedback loop exists between provider and appeals team. Providers cannot improve if they never know their service was denied.

Endnotes

1. **Dr. Ronald L. Hirsch** is vice president of R1 RCM Inc. He is a board-certified Internal Medicine specialist with 16 years of experience as a physician advisor. He is a member of the National Advisory Boards of the American College of Physician Advisors and the National Association of Healthcare Revenue Integrity and the co-author of *The Hospital Guide to Contemporary Utilization Review*, published in 2021.

2. Nina Youngstrom, "OIG: Hospitals Overbilled $1B for Malnutrition, CMS Will Recoup; Other Audits to Resume," *Report on Medicare Compliance* 29, no. 26 (July 20, 2020), https://compliancecosmos.org/oig-hospitals-overbilled-1b-malnutrition-cms-will-recoup-other-audits-resume.

3. Mervyn Singer et al., "The Third International Consensus Definitions for Sepsis and Septic Shock (Sepsis-3)," *Journal of the American Medical Association* 315, no. 8 (February 23, 2016): 801-810, https://jamanetwork.com/journals/jama/fullarticle/2492881.

4. Health Information Policy Council: 1984 Revision of the Uniform Hospital Discharge Data Set, 50 Fed. Reg. 31,038 (July 31, 1985).

5. Nina Youngstrom, "M.D. Review of Dietician Notes May Help Prevent Malnutrition Denials," *Report on Medicare Compliance* 29, no. 6 (October 12, 2020), https://compliancecosmos.org/md-review-dietician-notes-may-help-prevent-malnutrition-denials.

6. Centers for Medicare & Medicaid Services, "Chapter 4: Benefits and Beneficiary Protections," § 10.2, *Medicare Managed Care Manual*, Pub. 100-16, revised April 22, 2016, https://www.cms.gov/Regulations-and-Guidance/Guidance/Manuals/Downloads/mc86c04.pdf.

7. 42 C.F.R. § 476.1.

8. "Medicare Coverage Database," Centers for Medicare & Medicaid Services, accessed January 5, 2021, https://www.cms.gov/medicare-coverage-database/new-search/search.aspx?redirect=Y&from=Overview.

9. 42 C.F.R. § 405.1062.

10. Department of Justice, "Nearly 500 Hospitals Pay United States More Than $250 Million to Resolve False Claims Act Allegations Related to Implantation of Cardiac Devices," news release, October 30, 2015, https://www.justice.gov/opa/pr/nearly-500-hospitals-pay-united-states-more-250-million-resolve-false-claims-act-allegations.

11. Isaac D. Buck, "Enforcement Overdose: Health Care Fraud Regulation in an Era of Overcriminalization and Overtreatment," University of Maryland Digital Commons, accessed January 5, 2021, https://digitalcommons.law.umaryland.edu/cgi/viewcontent.cgi?article=3656&context=mlr.

12. U.S. Department of Justice Office of Inspector General, *Local Coverage Determinations Create Inconsistency in Medicare Coverage*, OEI-01-11-00500, January 7, 2014, https://oig.hhs.gov/oei/reports/oei-01-11-00500.asp.

13. 42 C.F.R. § 409.30.

14. 42 C.F.R. § 405.1205.

15. 42 C.F.R. § 412.3.

16. Centers for Medicare & Medicaid Services, "Chapter 4: Benefits and Beneficiary Protections," § 10.2, *Medicare Managed Care Manual*, Pub. 100-16, revised April 22, 2016, https://www.cms.gov/Regulations-and-Guidance/Guidance/Manuals/Downloads/mc86c04.pdf.

17. "Original Medicare (Fee-for-Service) Appeals," Centers for Medicare & Medicaid Services, updated August 31, 2020, https://www.cms.gov/Medicare/Appeals-and-Grievances/OrgMedFFSAppeals.

18. Centers for Medicare & Medicaid Services, "Chapter 29: Appeals of Claims Decisions," *Medicare Claims Processing Manual*, Pub. 100-04, revised August 30, 2019, https://www.cms.gov/Regulations-and-Guidance/Guidance/Manuals/Downloads/clm104c29pdf.pdf.

19. Centers for Medicare & Medicaid Services, "Chapter 29: Appeals of Claims Decisions," § 240.1, *Medicare Claims Processing Manual*, Pub. 100-04, revised August 30, 2019, https://www.cms.gov/Regulations-and-Guidance/Guidance/Manuals/Downloads/clm104c29pdf.pdf.

20. "Average Processing Time by Fiscal Year," U.S. Department of Health & Human Services, accessed January 5, 2021, https://www.hhs.gov/about/agencies/omha/about/current-workload/average-processing-time-by-fiscal-year/index.html.

21. Centers for Medicare & Medicaid Services, "Chapter 3: Verifying Potential Errors and Taking Corrective Actions," *Medicare Program Integrity Manual*, Pub. 100-08, revised October 2, 2020, https://www.cms.gov/Regulations-and-Guidance/Guidance/Transmittals/downloads/R71PI1.pdf.

22. Centers for Medicare & Medicaid Services, "Chapter 8: Administrative Actions and Sanctions and Statistical Sampling for Overpayment Estimation," § 8.4, *Medicare Program Integrity Manual*, Pub. 100-08, revised October 9, 2020, https://www.cms.gov/Regulations-and-Guidance/Guidance/Manuals/downloads/pim83c08.pdf.

23. Centers for Medicare & Medicaid Services, "Chapter 8: Administrative Actions and Sanctions and Statistical Sampling for Overpayment Estimation," § 8.4.9, *Medicare Program Integrity Manual*, Pub. 100-08, revised October 9, 2020, https://www.cms.gov/Regulations-and-Guidance/Guidance/Manuals/downloads/pim83c08.pdf.

24. 45 C.F.R. §§ 160, 162, 164.

25. "COVID-19 Claims Reimbursement to Health Care Providers and Facilities for Testing, Treatment, and Vaccine Administration for the Uninsured," Health Resources & Services Administration, updated November 2020, https://www.hrsa.gov/CovidUninsuredClaim.

26. "FAQs for COVID-19 Claims Reimbursement to Health Care Providers and Facilities for Testing, Treatment and Vaccine Administration," Health Resources & Services Administration, accessed October 14, 2020, https://www.hrsa.gov/coviduninsuredclaim/frequently-asked-questions.

27. Peter Moffet and Gregory Moore, "The Standard of Care: Legal History and Definitions: the Bad and Good News," *Western Journal of Emergency Medicine* 12, no. 1 (2011): 109-12, https://www.ncbi.nlm.nih.gov/pmc/articles/PMC3088386/.

28. Mark Ebell et al, "Why Are We So Slow to Adopt Some Evidence-Based Practices?" *American Family Physician* 98, no. 12 (December 15, 2018): 709-710, https://www.aafp.org/afp/2018/1215/p709.html.

29. "CPT Evaluation and Management (E/M) Office or Other Outpatient (99202-99215) and Prolonged Services (99354, 99355, 99356, 99XXX) Code and Guideline Changes," American Medical Association, accessed October 20, 2020, https://www.ama-assn.org/system/files/2019-06/cpt-office-prolonged-svs-code-changes.pdf.

30. Laura Dyrda, "Telehealth providers doing 'more visits than humanly possible' in a day draw CMS scrutiny," *Becker's Hospital Review* (July 6, 2020), https://www.beckershospitalreview.com/telehealth/telehealth-providers-doing-more-visits-than-humanly-possible-in-a-day-draw-cms-scrutiny.html.

31. Centers for Medicare & Medicaid Services, "Chapter 6: Medicare Contractor Medical Review Guidelines for Specific Services," § 6.5.3, *Medicare Program Integrity Manual*, Pub. 100-08, revised October 2, 2020, https://www.cms.gov/Regulations-and-Guidance/Guidance/Manuals/downloads/pim83c06.pdf.

32. "Comprehensive Error Rate Testing (CERT)," Centers for Medicare & Medicaid Services, updated November 16, 2020, https://www.cms.gov/Research-Statistics-Data-and-Systems/Monitoring-Programs/Improper-Payment-Measurement-Programs/CERT.

33. "Medicare Fee for Service Recovery Audit Program," Centers for Medicare & Medicaid Services, updated August 10, 2020, https://www.cms.gov/Research-Statistics-Data-and-Systems/Monitoring-Programs/Medicare-FFS-Compliance-Programs/Recovery-Audit-Program.

34. "Targeted Probe and Educate," Centers for Medicare & Medicaid Services, updated November 12, 2020, https://www.cms.gov/Research-Statistics-Data-and-Systems/Monitoring-Programs/Medicare-FFS-Compliance-Programs/Medical-Review/Targeted-Probe-and-EducateTPE.

35. 45 C.F.R. § 162.1002.

36. Centers for Medicare & Medicaid Services, "Chapter 8: Administrative Actions and Sanctions and Statistical Sampling for Overpayment Estimation," § 8.4.8, *Medicare Program Integrity Manual*, Pub. 100-08, revised October 9, 2020, https://www.cms.gov/Regulations-and-Guidance/Guidance/Manuals/Downloads/pim83c08.pdf.

37. Centers for Medicare & Medicaid Services, "Chapter 8: Administrative Actions and Sanctions and Statistical Sampling for Overpayment Estimation," § 8.4.1.4, *Medicare Program Integrity Manual*, Pub. 100-08, revised October 9, https://www.cms.gov/Regulations-and-Guidance/Guidance/Manuals/Downloads/pim83c08.pdf.

38. "Targeted Probe and Educate," Centers for Medicare & Medicaid Services, updated November 12, 2020, https://www.cms.gov/Research-Statistics-Data-and-Systems/Monitoring-Programs/Medicare-FFS-Compliance-Programs/Medical-Review/Targeted-Probe-and-EducateTPE.

39. "PCG Provider Compliance Focus Group," web presentation by Dan Schwartz, October 2020.

40. 31 U.S.C. § 3729.

41. 18 U.S.C. § 287.

Government Audits

By Ghazal Irfan,[1] MBI, RHIA

What Are Government Audits?

In 2019, US healthcare spending reached a whopping $3.8 trillion, or $11,582 per person.[2] That's impressive. But what's even more impressive is the amount recovered by the government for the same year. According to the U.S. Department of Health & Human Services (HHS) and the U.S. Department of Justice (DOJ) *Health Care Fraud and Abuse Control Program Annual Report for Fiscal Year 2019*, an astounding $3.6 billion were recovered through governmental auditing and investigative activities.[3]

To ensure federal money is not wasted or lost due to fraud, the US federal government routinely conducts investigations and audits on federal programs such as Medicare and Medicaid. These audits are conducted through multiple and various agencies and programs, such as through the Recovery Audit Program and recovery audit contractors (RAC), Medicare administrative contractors (MAC), Comprehensive Error Rate Testing (CERT) program, and Targeted Probe and Educate (TPE).

RACs conduct post-payment claim reviews to ensure healthcare providers are submitting correct and appropriate claims for reimbursement. If a claim is deemed as inappropriately paid, overpayment or underpayment, the RAC refers the claim to a MAC that then adjusts the payment and recoups any overpayment. The recovered payment is transferred to the Medicare Trust Fund (MTF). MACs are responsible for reimbursing healthcare entities for Medicare and Medicaid claims but also have the added advantage of conducting prepayment audits. Through MAC's prepayment reviews, if a claim is deemed inappropriate or incorrectly billed, the MAC can deny payment to the provider. The CERT program allows the government to review fee-for-service (FFS) claims for correctness and generate an improper payment rate from the audit results. TPE is more like a review and educate program where government auditors conduct limited audits on healthcare providers and, based on the audit results, provide customized education and training. The aim of a TPE program is to help healthcare providers improve on their deficiencies to avoid future government audits.

It is important for healthcare entities to understand the different types of government audit programs currently active and the tools used to identify improper payment. The zeal and aggressive auditing approach deployed by HHS and DOJ in recent years makes it evident that if healthcare entities want to survive the ever-increasing government auditing requests, they need to have a solid and quick auditing response system in place.

CMS and OIG Audits

Healthcare entities or individual providers enrolled in Medicare and Medicaid programs may be subject to audits and investigations by the Centers for Medicare and Medicaid Services (CMS) and Office of the Inspector General (OIG). Under the False Claims Act (FCA), civil and criminal liabilities in the form of fines, imprisonment, or both can be imposed for submitting false, fraudulent, or fictitious claims to the federal government.

Healthcare fraud, waste, and abuse is a persistent costly problem for both the federal government and commercial payer. CMS works with state and federal law enforcement agencies such as the OIG to detect and deter fraudulent activity by conducting audits and investigations on Medicare and Medicaid claims. OIG either conduct audits using its internal audit resources or oversees audits done by other agencies. CMS partners with a range of contractors such as CERT, RAC, or unified program integrity contractors to help prevent, detect, and investigate potential fraud.

CERT Audits

Under the Payment Integrity Information Act of 2019 (PIIA),[4] the CERT program computes national, by contractor, by service, and by provider type improper payment rate on Medicare FFS claims submitted to Part A and B MACs and durable medical equipment MACs (DMACs). Through stratified random sampling, some 50,000 claims are selected for complex medical review to determine whether the claims were paid appropriately under Medicare's coverage, coding, and billing rules.[5] If documentation is missing or lacking, medical reviewers reach out to the provider to request additional or supporting documentation. These complex medical reviews are performed by nurses, medical doctors, and certified coders, who perform a thorough review of each claim.

Improper payment rate is calculated by the statistical contractors upon completion of complex record review. It is pertinent to note that the improper payment rate identifies overpayment as well as underpayment, meaning if a claim is deemed underpaid, it will be counted as an error. The improper payment rate is not an indication of fraud but rather an estimate of payment that didn't meet Medicare's coverage, coding, and billing policy and rules. The CERT program publishes its Medicare FFS program improper payment rate in HHS's Agency Financial Report (AFR), which comes out in November of each year.[6]

TPE Audits

In 2014–2015, MACs began reviewing hospital inpatient and home health status cases and providing education to providers on CMS chosen topic. The medical review included all providers who billed Medicare for that chosen topic under a process known as "Probe and Educate." The Probe and Educate program was a success for CMS, resulting in significant reduction in billing and denial errors. In 2017, CMS expanded to include all types of Medicare claims, and modified the Probe and Educate program to allow MACs to (i) identify the topic for probe based on CERT or other data analysis procedures, and (ii) target providers that are at higher risk of submitting noncomplaint claims or improper errors—hence the name "Targeted Probe and Educate."[7] The TPE program's goal is to help providers understand their errors and how to correct them through one-on-one education. CMS has determined that the targeted probes, education, and reviews have resulted in improved claim accuracies and reduced claim denials and appeals, ultimately reducing burden off MACs' and providers' shoulders.

Either prepayment or post-payment review, the TPE program begins with MAC selecting a topic identified through the CERT report and/or other data analysis techniques. If a provider is chosen for review, MAC will send out a notification letter stating the intent to carry out the probe on the chosen topic and the reason why the provider was selected for review. For prepayment reviews, providers will receive a Notice of Review letter, while for post-payment reviews, providers will receive an Additional Documentation Request (ADR) letter. An entire TPE program is based on three rounds of probe, review, and educate; each round consists of 20 to 40 claims and supporting medical documentation, allowing MACs to establish whether a provider represents a certain risk behavior or not. At the conclusion of the first review, if a provider is deemed compliant, then the provider is not moved to the second review and is not reviewed on that chosen topic for at least one year. If, however, some claims are denied or deemed noncompliant, the provider is invited for a one-on-one education session.[8] There is, at least, a 45-day gap before the second round of 20–40 claims reviews is performed, allowing the provider to make necessary changes and improve on its processes. If the provider is deemed compliant after the second round of reviews, it is not moved to the third round of reviews and not reviewed on the same topic for at least one year. If, however, the provider fails the second round, it is moved to the third and final round of reviews. A provider that is unable to show improvements after the third round of review is referred to CMS for further actions, which may include 100% prepayment review, referral to a recovery auditor, or extrapolation of overpayment.

MAC Audits

CMS relies on private health insurers—MACs—to process Medicare Part A & B claims and durable medical equipment (DME) claims and handle coverage or payment appeals. Each MAC spans over a defined geographic area known as a jurisdiction, where each jurisdiction includes multistate. There are 12 MACs responsible for processing Part A & B claims, four MACs processing the DME claims, and four MACs processing home health and hospice claims. Part A & B MACs process institutional providers, physicians, practitioners, and suppliers. DME MACs process durable medical equipment, prosthetics, orthotics, and supplies (DMEPOS) (see **Table 1: MAC—Medicare Part A & B, Table 2: MAC—Durable Medical Equipment**, and **Table 3: MAC—Home Health and Hospice**).[9]

Table 1: MAC—Medicare Part A & B

MAC	Jurisdiction	States
Noridian Healthcare Solutions LLC	JE, JF	**JE**: California, Hawaii, Nevada, American Samoa, Guam, Northern Mariana Islands **JF**: Alaska, Arizona, Idaho, Montana, North Dakota, Oregon, South Dakota, Utah, Washington, Wyoming
Novitas Solutions LLC	JH, JL	**JH**: Arkansas, Colorado, New Mexico, Oklahoma, Texas, Louisiana, Mississippi **JL**: Delaware, District of Columbia, Maryland, New Jersey, Pennsylvania (includes Part B for counties of Arlington and Fairfax in Virginia and the city of Alexandria in Virginia)
Palmetto GBA LLN	JJ, JM	**JJ**: Alabama, Georgia, Tennessee **JM**: North Carolina, South Carolina, Virginia, West Virginia (excludes Part B for the counties of Arlington and Fairfax in Virginia and the city of Alexandria in Virginia)
National Government Services (NGS) Inc.	J6, JK	**J6**: Illinois, Minnesota, Wisconsin **JK**: Connecticut, New York, Maine, Massachusetts, New Hampshire, Rhode Island, Vermont
First Coast Service Options (FCSO) Inc.	JN	Florida, Puerto Rico, U.S. Virgin Islands
Wisconsin Physicians Service (WPS)	J5, J8	**J5**: Iowa, Kansas, Missouri, Nebraska **J8**: Indiana, Michigan
CGS Administrators LLC	J15	Kentucky, Ohio

Table 2: MAC—Durable Medical Equipment

MAC	Jurisdiction	States
Noridian Healthcare Solutions LLC	DME A	Connecticut, Delaware, District of Columbia, Maine, Maryland, Massachusetts, New Hampshire, New Jersey, New York, Pennsylvania, Rhode Island, Vermont
	DME D	Alaska, Arizona, California, Hawaii, Idaho, Iowa, Kansas, Missouri, Montana, Nebraska, Nevada, North Dakota, Oregon, South Dakota, Utah, Washington, Wyoming, American Samoa, Guam, Northern Mariana Islands
CGS Administrators LLC	DME B	Illinois, Indiana, Kentucky, Michigan, Minnesota, Ohio, Wisconsin
	DME C	Alabama, Arkansas, Colorado, Florida, Georgia, Louisiana, Mississippi, New Mexico, North Carolina, Oklahoma, South Carolina, Tennessee, Texas, Virginia, West Virginia, Puerto Rico, U.S. Virgin Islands

Table 3: MAC—Home Health and Hospice

MAC	Jurisdiction	States
National Government Services (NGS) Inc.	J6, JK	**J6**: Alaska, American Samoa, Arizona, California, Guam, Hawaii, Idaho, Michigan, Minnesota, Nevada, New Jersey, New York, Northern Mariana Islands, Oregon, Puerto Rico, U.S. Virgin Islands, Wisconsin, Washington **JK**: Connecticut, Maine, Massachusetts, New Hampshire, Rhode Island, Vermont
CGS Administrators LLC	J15	Delaware, District of Columbia, Colorado, Iowa, Kansas, Maryland, Missouri, Montana, Nebraska, North Dakota, Pennsylvania, South Dakota, Utah, Virginia, West Virginia, Wyoming
Palmetto GBA LLN	JM	Alabama, Arkansas, Florida, Georgia, Illinois, Indiana, Kentucky, Louisiana, Mississippi, New Mexico, North Carolina, Ohio, Oklahoma, South Carolina, Tennessee, Texas

Per CMS, MACs are responsible for processing, making, and accounting for Medicare FFS claims and payments.[10] MACs work as the primary operational contact in enrolling providers in the Medicare FFS program, handling provider reimbursement services, auditing institutional provider cost reports, and redetermination requests (1st stage appeals process). MACs respond to provider inquiries, educate providers about Medicare FFS billing requirements, establish local coverage determinations (LCDs), review medical records for selected claims, and coordinate with CMS and other FFS contractors.

MACs have the ability to perform prepayment and post-payment reviews on Medicare claims.

RAC Audits

RACs are the most notoriously known government auditing agency out there that almost all healthcare facilities have dealt with. No audit or compliance meeting is complete without mentioning RAC targets and RAC activities. Starting out as a pilot program in 2005, Congress permanently expanded and implemented the RAC program nationally to review Medicare Part A & B claims. In 2010, under the Affordable Care Act (ACA), the RAC program was further expanded to also include Medicare Part C (Medicare Advantage) & D (prescription drug) programs.[11] CMS has awarded Medicare RAC contracts to four contractors (see **Table 4: Recovery Audit Contractors**).

Table 4: Recovery Audit Contractors

RAC	Region	States
Performant Recovery Inc.	1	Connecticut, Indiana, Kentucky, Maine, Massachusetts, Michigan, New Hampshire, New York, Ohio, Rhode Island, Vermont
Cotiviti LLC	2	Arkansas, Colorado, Iowa, Illinois, Kansas, Louisiana, Missouri, Minnesota, Mississippi, Nebraska, New Mexico, Oklahoma, Texas, Wisconsin
	3	Alabama, Florida, Georgia, North Carolina, South Carolina, Tennessee, Virginia, West Virginia, Puerto Rico, U.S. Virgin Islands
HMS Federal Solutions	4	Alaska, Arizona, California, District of Columbia, Delaware, Hawaii, Idaho, Maryland, Montana, North Dakota, New Jersey, Nevada, Oregon, Pennsylvania, South Dakota, Utah, Washington, Wyoming, Guam, American Samoa, Northern Marianas
Performant Recovery Inc.	5	Nationwide (all 50 states) for DMEPOS, home health, and hospice

RACs' mission is to safeguard taxpayer money and protect the Medicare Trust Fund by detecting, identifying, and correcting improper payment rate. The Medicare FFS established improper payment rate has been below 10% as established by the Improper Payments Elimination and Recovery Act of 2010.[12] RAC has been able to bring the improper payment rate down to 7.25% in 2019 as compared to 8.12% from 2018.[13] How do RACs bring the improper payment down? They conduct vigorous post-payment reviews on all types of Medicare claims, which sometimes end up a hospital's bottom line.

RACs review submitted claims data and medical record documentation against Medicare manuals, National Coverage Determination (NCD), and LCD to determine whether a claim was paid appropriately. RACs' lookback period is three years from the time the claim was paid and, just like with CERT reviews, RACs are required to employ certified coders, physicians, nurses, and therapists to conduct complex medical reviews.

Risk Area Governance

Under the following federal laws, healthcare entities or individuals committing Medicare and Medicaid fraud, waste, and abuse, face civil, criminal, and administrative penalties and corrective actions.

False Claims Act (FCA), 31 U.S.C. §§ 3729–3733

The FCA makes it a (criminal and/or civil) crime to knowingly submit fraudulent or false claims to the US government.[14] [15]

Anti-Kickback Statute (AKS), 42 U.S.C. § 1320a-7b(b)

The AKS prohibits an organization or person from offering something of value (remuneration) to a healthcare provider or a healthcare entity in exchange for referring or billing for their product or service to the federal program. An AKS example would be a pharmaceutical company offering healthcare providers deep discounts or rebates on its products in exchange for prescribing the pharmaceutical company's drug(s) to its patients regardless of efficacy, appropriateness, or effectiveness, resulting in fraud, waste, and abuse of federal money. AKS violators are subject to criminal and/or civil penalties.[16]

Physician Self-Referral Law (Stark Law), 42 U.S.C. § 1395nn

The Physician Self-Referral Law (also known as the Stark Law) prohibits a physician from referring Medicare and Medicaid patients to medical services that the physician or physician's immediate family has a financial relationship with. An example would be a physician prescribing its Medicare patient population DME and supplies from a company that the physician has a stake in. Once the patient receives DME, the physician then bills Medicare to cover the cost and receive reimbursement. Stark Law violators are subject to civil penalties only.[17]

Criminal Health Care Fraud Statute, 18 U.S.C. § 1347

The Criminal Health Care Fraud Statute is a powerful federal statute that prohibits a healthcare provider from knowingly and willfully submitting false claims to any healthcare benefit program, not just Medicare and Medicaid. An example would be a provider scheming with several other healthcare providers to submit claims for services deemed unnecessary and duplicate.[18]

Exclusion Statute, 42 U.S.C. § 1320a-7

Part of the Social Security Act, the Exclusion Statute lays out criteria under which certain individuals or entities are barred from participating in Medicare, Medicaid, and all other federal healthcare programs. Excluded providers, such as those convicted of billing fraud, cannot bill the federal healthcare programs for items or services furnished for treating a Medicare beneficiary.[19] OIG maintains an updated List of Excluded Individuals and Entities at https://oig.hhs.gov/exclusions/exclusions_list.asp.

Civil Monetary Penalties Law (CMPL), 42 U.S.C. § 1320a-7a

The CMPL empowers the OIG to impose civil monetary penalties and/or exclusion from federal healthcare program on individuals or entities who commit fraud and abuse.[20] An example would be a healthcare provider submitting a claim for 60 minutes of patient encounter when in fact the healthcare provider only spent 15 face-to-face minutes with the patient.

Common Compliance Risks

CMS and OIG

Unbundling
Billing for procedures separately when they should be bundled as a single service, or charging for services using complex codes.

Upcoding
Billing for services, diagnoses, or procedures using codes that make the service seem more expensive to increase reimbursement.

CERT Audits

No Documentation
When provider is unable to produce the requested documentation or does not have the requested documentation.

Insufficient Documentation
When documentation lacks specific elements needed to support payment for services provided, or documentation lacks a specific condition required to qualify for the payment, such as a physician signature or a physician order for the service.

Medical Necessity
Adequate documentation is provided to CERT contractors, but after review, an informed decision is made stating the claims lack medical necessity based on Medicare's coverage and payment policy and rules.

Incorrect Coding
Documentation submitted supports a different code than the one coded on the claim, or the service should not have been coded as it is part of a global package or is bundled into another Healthcare Common Procedure Coding System/Current Procedural Terminology (HCPCS/CPT) code.

Other
Documentation indicates that the service billed is a noncovered or unallowable service by Medicare.

TPE Audits

Claim Missing Provider Signature
Healthcare services need to be documented and legibly attested by the healthcare provider. If a claim is missing a provider's signature, then claim is rejected, and payment denied.

Claim Missing or Lacking Documentation to Meet Medical Necessity
For a claim to be covered by Medicare, it needs to be medically necessary and clinically supported through clear and complete provider documentation.

Claim Missing or Contains Incomplete Certification or Recertification
Any claim submitted to federal healthcare program needs to have a healthcare provider attestation or certification stating that the services were performed by the provider and the attestation needs to be signed and dated.

Claim Does Not Contain Necessary Eligibility Elements as Identified in Medicare Coverage Rule
CMS will deny a claim where the face-to-face encounter note is missing an eligibility element (e.g., a patient problem list, diagnosis, or date).

MAC Audits

MACs' prepayment reviews have the potential to deny payment to a provider if a claim is found noncompliant, leaving the provider cash strapped as the provider is unable to recover any payment for services already provided to the patient. Some of the problems uncovered by a MAC audit include:

- Claim lacking medical necessity
- Claim submitted with incorrect discharge disposition code
- Claim lacking Medicare 3-day rule to quality for a skilled nursing facility (SNF) stay
- Claims where observation stay exceeds 48 hours stay

RAC Audits

RAC reviews can be either coding- and/or billing-related or medical necessity–related. It used to be that RACs were heavily focused on inpatient (IP) claims review; however, in recent years, that focus has been shifting more toward outpatient claims review and especially toward outpatient medical necessity claims review. (See **Table 5: Top IP and OP RAC Targets for 2019 and 2020**.)

Table 5: Top IP and OP RAC Targets for 2019 and 2020

Inpatient		Outpatient	
RAC targets	**Medical necessity vs. coding**	**RAC targets**	**Medical necessity vs. coding**
Ext. OR procedure unrelated to principal diagnosis with MCC	Coding	Cataracts	Medical necessity
Periprosthetic fracture	Coding	JW modifier	Medical necessity and coding
Discharge disposition	Coding	AICD/ pacemakers	Medical necessity
Admission status	Coding	Endovenous radiofrequency ablation (EVRFA)	Medical necessity
Single MCC claims	Coding	Observation	Medical necessity and coding

Addressing Compliance Risks

Address CERT Corrective Action Items in a Timely Manner

CMS and MACs analyze the improper payment rate and develop strategies to combat improper payment by developing a corrective action plan. Some of the corrective action items included in the report are: enhancing coding and billing edits, performing risk-based provider audits, providing targeted education to providers, updating coverage policies, and generating the Program for Evaluating Payment Patterns Electronic Report (PEPPER) report. It is critical to follow and implement corrective action plans to rectify bad behaviors and to assure the government auditing agencies that past ill practices won't be repeated and accepted.

Use CERT Audit Report as a Risk Area Road Map to Reduce Improper Payments

Think of the CERT program as an audit performed by the government at a national level and its findings, the improper payment rate report, as an audit summary chock-full of information on high-risk areas where there is significant risk of improper payment. For compliance associates, the CERT report contains invaluable insights into the minds of government auditing agencies such as the OIG and RACs, who will be using the same CERT report to create their own auditing profiles for the upcoming year. Compliance associates can use the same CERT report to create risk assessment for their organizations, allowing them to assess internal processes, controls, and protocols on services with high error rates. Some of the areas included in the report are:

- Top 20 Service Types with Highest Improper Payments: Part A Hospital IPPS
- Top 20 Types of Services with Medical Necessity Errors
- Top 20 Service-Specific Overpayment Rates: Part B
- Type of Services with Upcoding Errors: Part A Excluding Hospital IPPS
- Medicare FFS Projected Improper Payments by State—Parts A & B
- Top 20 Types of Services with Insufficient Documentation Errors

Review PEPPER Reports

PEPPER summarizes provider-specific data for target areas that may be at risk for improper Medicare payments due to billing, coding, or admission necessity issues.[21] PEPPER data is published as a Microsoft Excel document on a quarterly basis, distributed by TMF Health Quality Institute under CMS's contract and direction. PEPPER reports are developed for short-term acute care hospitals, long-term acute care hospitals, critical access hospitals, inpatient psychiatric facilities, inpatient rehabilitation facilities, hospices, SNFs, and home health agencies. The PEPPER report compares a provider's performance to the aggregated national, state, and MAC jurisdiction level, making it an imperative tool for understanding a facility's billing practices over time as well as identifying potential undercoding (underpayment) or overcoding (overpayment) concerns. The report also identifies target areas where a provider may stand out as an outlier. An outlier status is established if a provider is at or above the 80th percentile (data shown in red) or at or below the 20th percentile (data shown in green) in any of the target areas.

Compliance associates should review their PEPPER reports on a quarterly basis (as that's when they are released) to evaluate their outlier status and whether they have identified an underpayment or overpayment on any of the target areas. Some of the target areas identified in a short-term acute hospital PEPPER report are: stroke intracranial hemorrhage, simple pneumonia, septicemia, unrelated operating room procedure, medical DRGs with complication or comorbidity (CC) or a major complication or comorbidity (MCC), surgical DRGs with CC or MCC, single CC or MCC, excisional debridement, emergency department evaluation and management visits, three-day SNF-qualifying admissions, 30-day readmission to same hospital and two-day stays for Medical DRGs. Since PEPPER data is based on prospective coding and billing data, it gives compliance associates an opportunity to identify any gaps and risks in their billing practices. Compliance should incorporate outlier target areas into its compliance plan and also consider conducting an internal audit and investigation on high-risk areas to help identify and prevent any improper billing errors or noncomplaint practices.

Having an understanding into the "whys" of its outlier status, compliance associates are prepared and positioned to handle and respond to any audits or denial requests more effectively and concisely. Here it's pertinent to note that being in the outlier status doesn't always necessarily translates to Medicare noncompliance. A provider may be an outlier in the stroke intracranial hemorrhage target area because it's the only specialized stroke center in its vicinity.

Ensure Your Organization is Prepared to Respond to Potential TPE Audits

Compliance associates can prepare their institutions to succinctly handle a TPE audit by ensuring complete medical records and documentation are compiled and reviewed before submitting to MAC during the ADR process. Health information management (HIM) and coding should be involved from the beginning, as they can assist with data gathering and submission. If a provider is selected for one-on-one education session, compliance needs to make sure coding, coding compliance and auditing, HIM, patient financial services (PFS), clinical documentation improvement (CDI), clinicians, care management, and utilization review professionals are in attendance. This will allow attendees to receive consistent and most updated education and training on the topic's coding, billing, and coverage requirements.

Conduct Internal Audits Based Upon TPE Audit Results

Upon TPE audit conclusion, compliance associates should conduct routine audits on the TPE topic to ensure continued compliance with Medicare rules and policies. For example, if the TPE audit topic focused on hydration services, then the healthcare provider needs to ensure that the start and stop times for hydration injection/infusion are documented in the infusion report. Provider needs to document the medical need for hydration service clearly and thoroughly by explaining the clinical need. Document loss of fluids due to excessive vomiting or diarrhea or document dried oral mucosa to indicate that the patient was suffering from dehydration and required hydration.

Follow the MAC's Quality Control Plan to Ensure Your Organization is Ready for Related CMS On-site Visits and Reviews

A MAC quality control plan identifies procedures an organization must have to comply with CMS's performance requirements. In addition, CMS may conduct on-site visits and reviews, data validation reviews, and ad hoc reviews on MACs to ensure compliance with CMS instructions.

Respond to RAC Reviews Accurately and on a Timely Basis

To succinctly handle a RAC review, providers need to ensure an effective RAC review and respond process is in place and that those responsible are fully aware of their roles and duties. These include dealing with coding and medical necessity denials.

Coding and Billing RAC Denials

If an improper payment is identified through a complex medical review, a provider is notified through a review results letter, which is followed by a demand letter (issued by the MAC) asking for the overpayment. If a provider disagrees with RAC review, an appeal can be submitted along with additional documentation during this stage. Coding-related RAC denials should be reviewed by senior coders (who have prior RAC appeals experience) and defended using the official coding resources such as the coding conventions, guidelines, or coding clinic.

The coding resources must be followed in a hierarchy to ensure correct code assignment. The hierarchy is as follows: *Coding Classification and Conventions*, followed by the "Official Guidelines for Coding and Reporting," and then the *Coding Clinics and CPT Assistant.* Coding Classification and Conventions are a set of rules outlining the structure and format of ICD-10-CM coding. These conventions are found throughout an ICD-10-CM code book. "Official Guidelines for Coding and Reporting" are annually published by the Centers for Disease Control and Prevention (CDC).[22] The ICD-10-PCS guidelines are published annually by CMS. Coding Clinic for ICD-10-CM and ICD-10-PCS are published quarterly by the American Hospital Association (AHA). *CPT Assistant* is published monthly by the American Medical Association (AMA).

RAC coding and billing denials must be defended, if appropriate, by writing a detailed appeal letter that includes clinical criteria and references to relevant documentation from the medical record. Original medical record and complete documentation should be attached with the appeal letter to help support the reinstation of original coding and billings codes and services. Compliance associates should be involved with the RAC appeal process from start to finish to keep track of any overpayments or trends identified through RAC activity, as it is not enough to just keep appealing RAC denials on a case-by-case basis, but, when needed, conduct comprehensive audits to identify root causes and actions to correct issues at their source.

Medical Necessity RAC Denials

Medical necessity RAC denials are not related to coding or billing issues but are mostly related to physician documentation or a service not meeting medical necessity as set forth by an NCD/LCD. Medical necessity RAC denial letters always state why a claim is being denied, which is almost always due to a NCD or LCD. Compliance associates need to have the physician who provided the service and site medical officer involved to start review of the RAC denial letter and medical record documentation to determine whether an appeal is warranted.

If an appeal is warranted, then the physician needs to provide the narrative for the appeal letter along with the supporting documentation to prove the billed service meets medical necessity. If, however, after review, it is determined that the RAC finding is correct, then it becomes a compliance associate's responsibility to work in collaboration with the medical officer to identify whether the finding is a one-time anomaly or a recurring theme. Based on how significant the finding is, counsel may need to be involved to guide the entity through the audit, review, and repayment process. Most of the time, the RAC finding is related to a unique provider who needs some training on documentation. Often, RAC findings are related to a new requirement of which providers aren't aware. For example, most of the automatic implantable cardioverter defibrillator (AICD) denials are due to lack of a shared decision-making (SDM) document. An SDM documents a patient and provider encounter before the AICD procedure, where the provider discusses life expectancy and quality of life with and without the device. Basically, CMS wants the patient and provider to make informed decisions in light of evidence-based literature *and* patient's preferences, health goals, and values.[23] This encounter note needs to be in the medical record before an AICD service is placed. If RAC notices that the SDM document is missing or took place after the AICD procedure, the entire payment—some $32,000—is recouped. Now multiply that by the amount of times a cardiologist performs this routine procedure, and it is apparent how important it is to ensure SDM encounters take place and are documented in the medical record before a patient is operated on.

Possible Penalties

False Claims Act

In 2020, DOJ updated the civil violations, which now range between $11,665 and $23,331 per violation.[24] Violators not only subject to jail time and monetary fines, but also risk exclusion from participating in all federal healthcare programs, including Medicare and Medicaid.

OIG has the authority to enforce the following penalties on a healthcare provider or an entity that it deems as violator(s) of the federal healthcare program:

- Impose civil monetary violations ranging between $11,665 and $23,331 per violation;
- Impose jail time;
- Enter into a corporate integrity agreement (CIA) contract with the OIG, requiring the violator to implement an effective compliance program that's based on OIG's compliance program guidance; and
- Exclude from participating in any federal healthcare program by adding the violator to the List of Excluded Individuals and Entities.

Compliance Resources

American Hospital Association

Coding Clinics

https://www.codingclinicadvisor.com/

American Medical Association

CPT Assistant

https://commerce.ama-assn.org/store/ui/catalog/
productDetail?product_id=prod270004&sku_id=sku270043

Centers for Disease Control and Prevention

ICD-10-CM Official Guidelines for Coding and Reporting FY 2021

https://www.cdc.gov/nchs/data/icd/10cmguidelines-FY2021.pdf

Centers for Medicare & Medicaid Services

Comprehensive Error Rate Testing (CERT)

https://www.cms.gov/Research-Statistics-Data-and-Systems/Monitoring-Programs/
Improper-Payment-Measurement-Programs/CERT

Medicare Fee-for-Service Recovery Audit Program

https://www.cms.gov/Research-Statistics-Data-and-Systems/Monitoring-Programs/
Medicare-FFS-Compliance-Programs/Recovery-Audit-Program

Medicare Administrative Contractor (MAC)

https://www.cms.gov/Medicare/Medicare-Contracting/
Medicare-Administrative-Contractors/What-is-a-MAC

Targeted Probe and Educate (TPE)

https://www.cms.gov/Research-Statistics-Data-and-Systems/Monitoring-Programs/
Medicare-FFS-Compliance-Programs/Medical-Review/Targeted-Probe-and-EducateTPE

**International Statistical Classification of
Diseases and Related Health Problems, 10th Revision**

Coding Conventions

https://icd.who.int/browse10/2019/en

Risk Takeaways

Main points of interest:
- Comprehensive Error Rate Testing (CERT) report allows a healthcare provider to peek inside the minds of government auditing agencies to project and anticipate the type of audits recovery audit contractor (RAC), Medicare administrative contractor (MAC), or Targeted Probe and Educate (TPE) may be undertaking in the near future.
- Program for Evaluating Payment Patterns Electronic Report (PEPPER) reports help healthcare providers identify and understand their resource usage when compared at state and national level. They also help identify whether a healthcare entity is an outlier in any of the targeted areas.
- MAC reimburses healthcare providers for Medicare and Medicaid services and conducts pre- and post-payment audits. MAC has the added advantage of conducting pre-payment reviews and denying payment if it deems appropriate.
- RAC conducts post-payment coding, billing, and medical necessity audits on Medicare and Medicaid claims. Any claim deemed inappropriately paid is referred to MAC for payment recoupment.

- Successful appeal of coding and billing audits requires a trained coding eye that spots necessary documentation and clinical indicators needed to appeal and (possibly) overturn the denial.
- Medical necessity audits are different from coding and billing audits, as the focus is on physician documentation. Successful appeal of medical necessity audits require collaboration between the compliance officer, medical officer, physician, case management, and nursing. All parties need to work in sync to ensure complete and correct documentation is collected and detailed appeal letter is penned and submitted on time for appeal's review process.

Areas to watch:
- **Outpatient:** Outpatient services and procedures such as telehealth, total knee replacement, cataract removal, implantable automatic defibrillators, cardiac pacemakers, drugs and biologicals unit, hydration infusion, and chemotherapy administration.
- **Inpatient:** Inpatient diagnosis and procedures such as severe protein calorie malnutrition, total hip arthroplasty, total knee arthroplasty, claims dropped with only either a major complication/comorbidity condition or complication/comorbidity condition code, COVID-19, and discharge disposition.

Laws that apply:
- False Claims Act: 31 U.S.C. §§ 3729–3733
- Anti-Kickback Statue: 42 U.S.C. § 1320a-7b(b)
- Physician Self-Referral Law (Stark Law): 42 U.S.C. § 1395nn
- Criminal Health Care Fraud Statute: 18 U.S.C. § 1347
- Exclusion Statute: 42 U.S.C. § 1320a-7
- Civil Monetary Penalties Law: 42 U.S.C. § 1320a-7a

Addressing compliance risks:
- Address CERT corrective action items in a timely manner.
- Use CERT audit report as a risk area road map to reduce improper payments.
- Review PEPPER reports.
- Ensure your organization is prepared to respond to potential TPE audits.
- Conduct internal audits based upon TPE audit results.
- Follow the MAC's quality control plan to ensure your organization is ready for related CMS on-site visits and reviews.
- Respond to RAC reviews accurately and on a timely basis.

Endnotes

1. **Ghazal Irfan** works as a Hospital-Coding Compliance Manager at Adventist Health-West. Irfan's key areas of expertise include coding data quality and compliance, clinical documentation improvement, medical staff documentation review, prospective payment reviews, and revenue capture. She has extensive experience in the qualitative and quantitative analysis of medical record clinical data, coding guidelines, diagnosis-related group (DRG) reimbursement, Medicare policies and regulations, and data collection.

2. "Historical," National Health Expenditure Data, Centers for Medicare & Medicaid Services, updated December 16, 2020, https://www.cms.gov/Research-Statistics-Data-and-Systems/Statistics-Trends-and-Reports/National-HealthExpendData/NationalHealthAccountsHistorical.

3. U.S. Department of Health & Human Services, U.S. Department of Justice, *Health Care Fraud and Abuse Control Program Annual Report for Fiscal Year 2019*, June 2020, https://oig.hhs.gov/publications/docs/hcfac/FY2019-hcfac.pdf.

4. Payment Integrity Information Act of 2019, Pub. L. No. 116-117, 134 Stat. 113 (2020).

5. "Background," Comprehensive Error Rate Testing (CERT), Centers for Medicare & Medicaid Services, updated July 21, 2020, https://www.cms.gov/Research-Statistics-Data-and-Systems/Monitoring-Programs/Medicare-FFS-Compliance-Programs/CERT/Background.

6. U.S. Department of Health & Human Services, *2019 Medicare Fee-for- Service Supplemental Improper Payment Data*, accessed March 2, 2021, https://www.cms.gov/files/document/2019-medicare-fee-service-supplemental-improper-payment-data.pdf.

7. Centers for Medicare & Medicaid Services, "Targeted Probe and Educate," Trans. 1919, One-Time Notification, Pub. 100-20, September 15, 2017, https://www.cms.gov/Regulations-and-Guidance/Guidance/Transmittals/2017Downloads/R1919OTN.pdf.

8. "Targeted Probe and Educate," Centers for Medicare & Medicaid Services, updated November 12, 2020, https://www.cms.gov/Research-Statistics-Data-and-Systems/Monitoring-Programs/Medicare-FFS-Compliance-Programs/Medical-Review/Targeted-Probe-and-EducateTPE.

9. Centers for Medicare & Medicaid Services, "Medicare Administrative Contractors (MACs) Provider Portals," accessed March 4, 2021, https://www.cms.gov/medicare/new-medicare-card/providers/macs-provider-portals-by-state.pdf.

10. "What is a MAC," Medicare Administrative Contractors, Centers for Medicare & Medicaid Services, edited December 18, 2020, https://www.cms.gov/Medicare/Medicare-Contracting/Medicare-Administrative-Contractors/What-is-a-MAC#WhatIsAMac.

11. "Medicare Fee for Service Recovery Audit Program," Centers for Medicare & Medicaid Services, updated August 10, 2020, https://www.cms.gov/Research-Statistics-Data-and-Systems/Monitoring-Programs/Medicare-FFS-Compliance-Programs/Recovery-Audit-Program.

12. Improper Payments Elimination and Recovery Act of 2010, Pub. L. No. 111-204.

13. Centers for Medicare & Medicaid Services, "Fiscal Year (FY) 2019 Medicare Fee-For-Service Improper Payment Rate is Lowest Since 2010 while data points to concerns with Medicaid eligibility," news release, November 19, 2019, https://www.cms.gov/newsroom/press-releases/fiscal-year-fy-2019-medicare-fee-service-improper-payment-rate-lowest-2010-while-data-points.

14. Centers for Medicare & Medicaid Services, "Medicare Fraud & Abuse: Prevent, Detect, Report," *MLN Booklet*, MLN4649244, January 2021, https://www.cms.gov/Outreach-and-Education/Medicare-Learning-Network-MLN/MLNProducts/Downloads/Fraud-Abuse-MLN4649244.pdf.

15. 31 U.S.C. §§ 3729-3733 .

16. 42 U.S.C. § 1320a-7b(b) .

17. 42 U.S.C. § 1395nn .

18. 18 U.S.C. § 1347 .

19. 42 U.S.C. § 1320a-7 .

20. 42 U.S.C. § 1320a-7a.

21. "About PEPPER," Program for Evaluating Payment Patterns Electronic Report, accessed March 5, 2021, https://pepper.cbrpepper.org/PEPPER.

22. Centers for Disease Control and Prevention, "ICD-10-CM Official Guidelines for Coding and Reporting FY 2020 (October 1, 2019 - September 30, 2020)," accessed March 5, 2021, https://www.cdc.gov/nchs/data/icd/10cmguidelines-FY2020_final.pdf.

23. Tamara Syrek Jensen et al., "National Coverage Determination for Implantable Cardioverter Defibrillators (ICDs)," CAG-00157R4, decision memo, Centers for Medicare & Medicaid Services, February 15, 2018, https://www.cms.gov/medicare-coverage-database/details/nca-decision-memo.aspx?NCAId=288.

24. Civil Monetary Penalties Inflation Adjustment, 85 Fed. Reg. 37,004, 37,006 (June 19, 2020) , https://www.federalregister.gov/documents/2020/06/19/2020-10905/civil-monetary-penalties-inflation-adjustment.

Hospital Discharge Appeal Notices

By Rose T. Dunn,[1] MBA, RHIA, CPA

What Are Hospital Discharge Appeal Notices?

Hospital discharge appeal notices serve to address initiation and termination of events. Two notices will be discussed in this chapter. The Centers for Medicare & Medicaid Services (CMS) requires that each hospitalized patient receive the Important Message from Medicare, which informs hospitalized beneficiaries of their hospital discharge appeal rights.[2] The Detailed Notice of Discharge (DND) explains the reasons for discharge and is given to a beneficiary who requests an appeal.

Each organization needs to have an effective process for notifying patients of their rights. The challenge in doing so is meeting the required deadlines, especially when lengths of stay are relatively short, and ensuring that patients understands their rights. Failure to notify patients of their hospital discharge appeals could result in extended stays and patient dissatisfaction and identify faulty processes in the organization.

For decades, The Joint Commission has encouraged early planning and alerts to patients and their families about what lies beyond a hospital stay. Early planning places special importance on this information if the patient is expected to be transferred to another care facility. The Center for Medicare Advocacy asserts "good discharge planning for patients, their families, and their healthcare providers, paves the way to successful transitions from one care setting to another. Good discharge notices and good discharge planning should go hand in hand."[3]

Today, the push for discharge planning to start at the time of admission is also emerging from the C-suite and revenue cycle. Why? With many payers paying on a case rate similar to a diagnosis related group (DRG), an extra day on the tail of the stay continues to consume resources for which the organization will not be paid. Additionally, every day that a patient unnecessarily occupies an inpatient bed is a day when an emergency department patient with an admission order cannot. The *costs* of holding the patient in the emergency department are multiple, including the safety of the patient, the impact on the patient's health outcome, and the staffing required to care for the patient as an inpatient in a holding bed. This article's focus is hospital discharge appeal notices. These notices place yet another focus on discharge planning.

The hospital discharge appeal notice is just one of nine categories of notices generated from the Beneficiary Notices Initiative (BNI).[4] The CMS website provides descriptions for the other eight notice categories (see Table 1 at the end of this article).[5] The BNI obtains its authority to mandate the use of these forms from section 1879 of the Social Security Act, which "[r]equires a provider to notify a beneficiary in advance when s/he believes that items or services will likely be denied either as not reasonable and necessary or as constituting custodial care. If such notice . . . is not given, providers may not shift financial liability to beneficiaries for these items or services if Medicare denies the claim."[6]

From a revenue cycle perspective, this authority is what drives a number of the denials for medical necessity. The use of the Advance Beneficiary Notice of Noncoverage (ABN), for example, is mandatory when the services are not reasonable and necessary, such as for certain medical equipment and/or supplies, custodial care, hospice care for a patient who is not terminally ill, and certain other services. (See the "Revenue Cycle: Advance Beneficiary Notice of Noncoverage" article in this chapter for more information.)

BNI notices are triggered by three main events:

1. Initiations:
   - Beginning of new patient encounter,
   - Start of plan of care, and
   - Beginning of treatment.
2. Reductions:
   - Decrease in a component of care.
3. Terminations:
   - Discontinuation of services or items.

Hospital discharge appeal notices serve to address initiation and termination events. Again, from a revenue cycle perspective, the process triggered by an appeal notice may result in an extended stay or possibly the conversion of a portion of the stay to self-pay (the responsibility of the patient), a situation that many revenue cycle leaders wish to avoid.

Risk Area Governance

Hospital discharge appeal notices are defined by the BNI. This initiative is overseen by CMS, specifically Medicare. Both Medicare beneficiaries and providers have certain rights and protections related to financial liability and appeals under the Fee-for-Service (FFS) Medicare and the Medicare Advantage (MA) programs. These rights are defined in the notices prescribed by BNI. These financial liability and appeal rights and protections are communicated to beneficiaries through notices given by providers.

Financial Liability Protections and Regulations

Applicable laws related to financial liability protections can be found in Title 18 (XVIII) of the Social Security Act:

- Limitation on liability: § 1879 (a)–(g); 42 C.F.R. §§ 411.400–408 (all 411 Subpart K)
- Refund requirements: §§ 1834(a)(18) and (j)(4),1842(l), and 1879(h)
- Statutory exclusions from Medicare benefits: § 1862(a)
- Expedited determination process: § 1869(b)(1)(F)
- Quality improvement organization (QIO) review of termination of services or discharge and reconsideration: Social Security Act §§ 1154, and 1155

Regulations related to expedited determinations and reconsideration are found at:

- Nonhospital process: 42 C.F.R. §§ 405.1200, 405.1202
- Hospital process: 42 C.F.R. §§ 405.1206, 405.1208
- Reconsideration process: 42 C.F.R. § 405.1204

The hospital discharge appeal notice category includes two notices:

- Important Message from Medicare (IM, Form CMS-10065)
- Detailed Notice of Discharge (DND, Form CMS-10066)[7]

Important Message from Medicare

Hospitals are required to deliver the Important Message from Medicare (IM) (formerly CMS-R-193 and now CMS-10065) to *all* Medicare hospital inpatients to inform them of their hospital discharge appeal rights. The hospital must use the standardized notice, as specified by CMS. This notice explains a patient's rights as a hospital patient, including the patient's discharge appeal rights. It is to be given at or near admission, but no longer than two calendar days following the beneficiary's admission to the hospital. See 42 C.F.R. § 405.1205 (traditional Medicare) and 42 C.F.R. § 422.620 (Medicare Advantage).[8][9]

Content of the IM Notice

The notice must include the following information:

 i. The beneficiary's rights as a hospital inpatient including the right to benefits for inpatient services and for post-hospital services in accordance with 1866(a)(1)(M) of the Act.

 ii. The beneficiary's right to request an expedited determination of the discharge decision including a description of the process under § 405.1206, and the availability of other appeals processes if the beneficiary fails to meet the deadline for an expedited determination.

 iii. The circumstances under which a beneficiary will or will not be liable for charges for continued stay in the hospital in accordance with 1866(a)(1)(M) of the Act.

 iv. A beneficiary's right to receive additional detailed information in accordance with § 405.1206(e).

 v. Any other information required by CMS.[10]

These rights are protected by the delivery timeline of the IM notice.

One of the revenue cycle challenges for healthcare facilities with the revised IM is its content for a Medicare Advantage patient. Unlike original Medicare, the IM need only include the name and telephone number for the local QIO. However, for MA, the healthcare organization must enter the appropriate toll-free number for the individual MA plan and the plan's name. The task of maintaining a current list of plan names and toll-free numbers for expedited appeal purposes will be daunting. The question remains whether the Member Services telephone number often appearing on an individual's MA plan ID card will be considered sufficient.

"The revised IM process is based on a rule that grew out of a lawsuit filed against Medicare. The lawsuit, *Weichardt v. Leavitt*, defines the intent of the settlement for notification of patients' rights. However, when the overhaul of the IM was in process, there were also some changes to the Social Security Act § 1879 that address the notification of Limitations of Liability (LOL). This concurrent revision created some confusion and resulted in the process of each becoming more difficult to understand."[11] The BNI categories helped to eliminate the confusion. Having a distinct IM sets the stage for providing guidance to patients about their rights.

More information follows about the second notice on this category, the Detailed Notice of Discharge.

Common Compliance Risks

The purpose of the hospital discharge appeal notice is to provide the beneficiary (the patient) with the right to refuse or appeal a determination. Additionally, some of the BNI notices protect the provider from liability, such as the FFS ABN, which when issued notifies the beneficiary (patient) that the charge for the service may not be covered by Medicare and that if the patient wishes to have the service, they may incur the charge for the service. Both Medicare beneficiaries and providers have certain rights and protections related to financial liability and appeals under the FFS Medicare and MA programs. These financial liability and appeal rights and protections are communicated to beneficiaries through notices given by providers, according to the BNI website.[12] The following are some common risks associated with hospital discharge appeal notices.

Timely Delivery of a BNI Notice

Evidence of delivery of any BNI notice is considered valid if the notice contains all the elements required of the notification and if:

- "The beneficiary (or the beneficiary's representative) has signed and dated the notice to indicate that he or she has received the notice and can comprehend its contents."
- "If a beneficiary refuses to sign the notice. The hospital may annotate its notice to indicate the refusal, and the date of refusal is considered the date of receipt of the notice."[13]

The key to delivery is that the patient *is* notified, not that the patient signs the notification.

Delivering the Original Copy of the IM

For the IM, two steps may be involved depending upon the discharge date and admission date. Hospitals are required to deliver *in person* the original copy of the IM at the time of or near admission but:

- not more than *seven* days pre-admission and
- not more than *two* days post-admission.[14]

Hospitals may deliver the initial copy of the notice if the beneficiary is seen during a pre-admission visit, but not more than seven calendar days prior to admission or within two calendar days after admission. Delivery includes obtaining the signature of the individual, if possible. In either case, the original copy is provided to the individual.

Documentation of the IM delivery must include:

- Date/time of receipt of notice to the representative,
- Written notice mailed on day of phone notice,
- Representative notified of planned date of discharge,
- Financial liability, and
- Beneficiary's right to appeal.

Comprehension of the IM

If the beneficiary is incapable of reading or comprehending the IM, there are several options:

1. The hospital could issue the written notice in a manner that allows the patient to comprehend the contents of the written notice. For example, when the beneficiary (or authorized representative) is unable to read the notice due to a disability (such as blindness, visual impairment, or deafness), the notification can be a verbal or electronic reading of the notice, written in Braille or large print, or other assistive technology can be used.
2. The notice can be translated. The notice is currently available in English and Spanish on the CMS website.[15] Alternatively, a translator can read the notice to the beneficiary or representative.
3. The IM could be delivered to and signed by the beneficiary's representative. However, should the hospital be unable to deliver the IM to the representative, then CMS requires the hospital to contact the representative by telephone to advise the person of the beneficiary's rights to appeal a discharge decision.

The following information should be shared with the beneficiary's representative:

- The name and telephone number of a contact at the hospital;
- The beneficiary's planned discharge date and the date when the beneficiary's liability begins;
- The beneficiary's rights as a hospital patient, including the right to appeal a discharge decision;
- How to get a copy of a detailed notice describing why the hospital and physician believe the beneficiary is ready to be discharged;
- A description of the steps for filing an appeal;
- When (by what time/date) the appeal must be filed to take advantage of the liability protections;
- The entity required to receive the appeal, including any applicable name, address, telephone number, fax number, or other method of communication the entity requires in order to receive the appeal in a timely fashion; and
- Direction to the 1-800-MEDICARE number for additional assistance to the representative in further explaining and filing the appeal.

The date the hospital conveys this information to the beneficiary or representative, whether in writing or by telephone, is the date of receipt of the notice.[16] Retain a copy in the patient's medical file. Additional information about when the representative should be used is available in CMS Transmittal 1257.[17]

Delivering the Follow-up Copy of the IM

If the beneficiary receives and signs the initial copy of the IM as part of the preadmission process and more than two days of admission, the first follow-up copy of the signed notice must be delivered within two days following admission. Although the follow-up notice may need to be delivered within two days of admission, the more common purpose of the follow-up copy is to provide the beneficiary notice of their discharge rights.

CMS Transmittal 1257, section *200.3.2-The Follow-up Copy of the Signed Important Message from Medicare*, clearly describes the requirements for delivery (see **Chart 1**). The follow-up copy must be delivered as far in advance of discharge as possible, but *no more* than two calendar days *before* the *planned* date of discharge. Thus, when discharge seems likely within one to two calendar days, hospitals should make arrangements to deliver the follow-up copy of the notice so that the beneficiary has a meaningful opportunity and reasonable time to act on it.

However, when discharge cannot be predicted in advance, the follow-up copy may be delivered as late as the day of discharge, if necessary. If the follow-up copy of the notice must be delivered on the day of discharge, hospitals must give beneficiaries who need it *at least four hours* to consider their right to request a QIO review. Beneficiaries may choose to leave during that time. However, hospitals must not pressure a beneficiary to leave during that time period.

If the hospital delivers the follow-up copy and the beneficiary's status subsequently changes so that the discharge is beyond the two-day timeframe, hospitals must deliver another copy of the signed notice again within two calendar days of the new planned discharge date. Hospitals may not develop procedures for delivery of the follow-up copy routinely on the day of discharge.

Exception to Delivery of the Follow-up Copy

The transmittal offers one exception. If delivery of the original IM is within two calendar days of the date of discharge, no follow-up notice is required under 42 C.F.R. § 405.1205(b).[18] For example, if a beneficiary is admitted on Monday, the IM is delivered on Wednesday, and the beneficiary is discharged on Friday, then no follow-up notice is required.

Chart 1: The Follow-up Notice Delivery Process Prior to Discharge

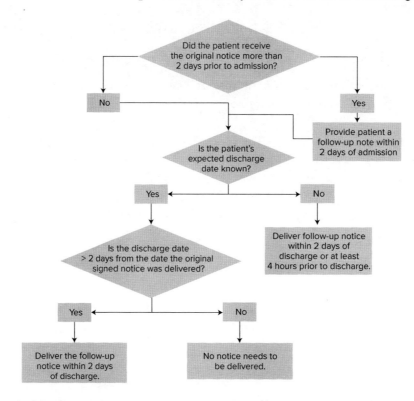

The Beneficiary's Right to Appeal

Should a beneficiary appeal the planned discharge, the beneficiary's representative is responsible for contacting the QIO no later than the planned discharge date. Identifying the QIO contact information in the IM for the beneficiary is patient friendly. Advising the beneficiary that the QIO is a group of doctors and other professionals who monitor the quality of care delivered to Medicare beneficiaries and that they are paid by the federal government and not affiliated with a hospital or health maintenance organization (HMO) is appropriate.

Attorney Charles M. Honart shared that "when a beneficiary makes a timely request for a QIO review, the beneficiary is not financially responsible for inpatient hospital services (except applicable coinsurance and deductibles) furnished before noon of the calendar day after the date the beneficiary receives notification of the expedited determination by the QIO. The QIO will render a decision on timely requests within one calendar day after all of the information is received. If the QIO does not agree with the beneficiary, liability for continued services begins at noon of the day after the QIO notifies the beneficiary that the QIO agreed with the hospital's discharge determination, or as otherwise determined by the QIO. If the QIO agrees with the beneficiary, the beneficiary is not financially responsible for continued care (other than applicable coinsurance and deductibles) until the hospital once again determines that the beneficiary no longer requires inpatient care, secures the concurrence of the physician responsible for the beneficiary's care or the QIO, and notifies the beneficiary with a follow-up copy of the IM."[19]

A beneficiary may appoint a person to file a grievance, request an organization determination, or request an appeal on the beneficiary's behalf. The "Appointment of Representative" Form CMS-1696[20] (AOR) may be used. Regardless, the patient or their representative must appeal by midnight of the day of discharge.[21] The QIO should call with its decision to the patient within 24 hours of receiving all the information it needs. If the patient is appealing to the QIO, the hospital must provide the patient with a Detailed Notice of Discharge. (See additional information in Resource 1: Detailed Notice of Discharge at the end of this article.)

"Although most QIO decisions agree with the hospital, asking for QIO review often makes sense because the process itself can often add a day or two of Medicare coverage."[22] The additional day(s) provide the patient time to prepare for their discharge but shaves or eliminates the margin on a DRG payment for the hospital.

Detailed Notice of Discharge

A DND (CMS 10066-DND) explains the specific reasons for a discharge and is given only if a patient requests an appeal or expedited review of a discharge decision.[23] (See **Resource 1: Detailed Notice of Discharge** after this article.) There are different forms for notification to a Medicare patient versus a Medicaid patient.[24] Additionally, the DND provides information about the QIO review process. Also, information about the QIO process is provided initially when the IM is provided to individuals upon admission in the IM clause:

> You can report any concerns you have about the quality of care you receive to your QIO at: {insert QIO name and toll-free number of QIO} The QIO is the independent reviewer authorized by Medicare to review the decision to discharge you.

A hospital or Medicare health plan must deliver a completed copy of the DND notice to beneficiary (or their representative) upon notice from the QIO that the beneficiary has appealed a discharge from an inpatient hospital stay. The DND must be provided no later than *noon* of the day after the QIO's notification.[25]

CMS made changes to the IM and DND forms with an effective date of April 1, 2020. The CMS forms are available in both English and Spanish. Detailed information is available on the "Hospital Discharge Appeal Notices" page of the CMS website.[26]

An early 2020 RACmonitor article quoting Ronald Hirsch referenced 79 Fed. Reg. 50,945, where CMS states that, "The crux of the medical decision is the choice to keep the beneficiary at the hospital in order to receive services or reduce risk, or discharge the beneficiary home because they may be safely treated through intermittent outpatient visits or some other care."[27] Hirsch then added, "That nicely summarizes the decision that every doctor makes every single day a patient is hospitalized, asking if they are able to safely receive care in a lesser setting. When the answer is 'yes,' then a discharge order is written."[28] A DND is provided to the beneficiary with that detailed rationale regarding the provider's decision for discharge. Oversight is provided through CMS, which monitors discharge appeals and will charge QIOs with auditing hospital processes. It is essential for hospitals to have controls in place to ensure beneficiaries are receiving the IM notices as deemed timely by CMS.

Addressing Compliance Risks

Creating a collaborative approach between access (registration), case management, and discharge planning is vital to ensuring an effective notification process. Ideally, representatives from risk management and compliance will participate in the development of the process framework.

Establish Processes for Meeting the IM and DND Timelines

Implementing processes for both the timely delivery of the IM and the DND requires coordination among the organization's staff. Organizations use different staff to accomplish the timeline requirements. For example, the pre-admission team may start the process by providing the IM for patients who actually come to the facility for pre-admission workups. Alternatively, the access (registration) staff may provide the patient or their representative with the original copy of the signed IM. The access staff may also scan a copy to the patient's file.

Although access registers every patient, some patients who should receive the IM do not. Processes need to be in place to alert case management (social work or utilization review) to follow up on those patients that did not receive or were unable to comprehend the IM at admission.

Educate Staff on IM Responsibilities

Using access staff to deliver the IM requires them to be carefully educated on the notifier's responsibilities, the content of the IM, and commonly asked questions, especially "What is the QIO and how does it get involved in my care?" Those involved in the patient's discharge plan, usually case management, utilization review, or social work, are primarily responsible for the IM and more so with the DND. These professionals interact with the patient and their physician during the patient's stay and are aware of the anticipated discharge date as well as discharge needs for the patient.

Start Discharge Communication at Time of Admission

The Center for Medicare Advocacy encourages starting the communication process with the patient from admission, which facilitates the patient and their family's expectations and understanding of next steps before discharge. Discharge day should not be a surprise—neither should the discharge destination. The center states, "Receiving oral and written notice of a proposed discharge from one care setting to another is essential. This is particularly important when the [patient may feel] that the discharge is inappropriate for any reason."[29]

Develop a Discharge Plan

The Center for Medicare Advocacy explains that discharge planning "should result in a written document, a discharge plan. The discharge plan should be a comprehensive tool and should be based on:

- "where and how a patient will get care after discharge;
- "what the patient and his or her support groups (family, friends, hired help) can do to facilitate recovery;
- "particular healthcare problems that might occur in the new care setting;
- "clarity about medications going into the new care setting;
- "arranging for necessary equipment or supplies in preparation for activities of daily living;
- "resources available to cope with and manage one's illness; and
- "resources that are available to help with costs attendant to care.

> While a good discharge plan does not necessarily have to be formal or follow a particular format, it should be clear and concise. It should be known to all relevant care givers and family members. When developed in a care setting such as a hospital, skilled nursing facility, home health agency, or hospice, the discharge plan should be included in the patient's medical record."[30]

The discharge planning function is pivotal in:

- Identifying those patients who need discharge planning services to avoid adverse health consequences upon discharge.
- Conducting timely discharge planning evaluations for all patients regardless of whether they have been identified by their physicians as needing discharge planning services.
- Establishing a comfort level for the future post-discharge by communicating the elements of the plan and discussing each element with the patient (and representatives).

Health organization leadership must assure that discharge planning evaluations and discharge plans are developed by, or under the supervision of, a registered professional nurse, social worker, or other appropriately qualified personnel.[31] The critical role of the discharge planner in developing the plan, working with the patient's provider, and ensuring ongoing communication with the patient and their representatives, facilitating awareness of the discharge date and what happens after discharge to support the IM and avoid the DND.

Possible Penalties

Possible consequences for failure to deliver the DND include the following.

Liability for Extended Stays

CMS requires the provider to comply with the timely and proper delivery of the DND to the patient. "Failure to give notice to a properly designated representative where required may result in the hospital being held liable."[32] The hospital is not permitted to bill patients for services occurring during the period that the hospital failed to comply with the notification processes and/or supplying the QIO with sufficient justification for considering the stay as no longer medically necessary. According to the QIO Discharge Appeal Rights Training Handbook,

> If the provider or MA plan does not comply with delivery of a Detailed Notice to the patient, the QIO may go forward with the appeal process, if sufficient information is otherwise obtained ... If a QIO becomes aware of a pattern of noncompliance with delivery of the Detailed Notice, this should be reported to the CMS Regional Office ... The burden of proof lies with the **hospital** (for a Medicare beneficiary) or with the **MA plan** (for an enrollee) to demonstrate that discharge is the correct decision, either on the basis of medical necessity or based on other Medicare coverage policies.[33]

Patient Rights Violation

Failure to deliver detailed notices could also result in state inspection citations for failure to provide patients with the necessary information to exercise their rights related to implemented discharge from the hospital including, but not limited to, appealing the discharge plan through the Office for Civil Rights in the applicable Department of Health & Human Services regional office. Such citations along with other patient safety or other serious citations could place the hospital at risk of losing its licensure.

Medicare Program Participation Termination

Possibly the most serious consequence for failure of a hospital to provide any of the required notices to a patient is that it could result in a deficiency for noncompliance with the Medicare conditions of participation, which may result in termination from the Medicare program.

Compliance Resources

Centers for Medicare & Medicaid Services

Medicare Claims Processing Manual, Chapter 30: Financial Liability Protections

Full instructions for the original Medicare—also known as FFS process—are available in Section 200 of Chapter 30 of the *Medicare Claims Processing Manual.*

https://www.cms.gov/Regulations-and-Guidance/Guidance/Manuals/Downloads/clm104c30.pdf

Medicare Advantage

Full instructions for Medicare health plans are available in Section 100 of the *Parts C & D Enrollee Grievances, Organization/Coverage Determinations, and Appeals Guidance*, available at https://www.cms.gov/Medicare/Appeals-and-Grievances/MMCAG/Downloads/Parts-C-and-D-Enrollee-Grievances-Organization-Coverage-Determinations-and-Appeals-Guidance.pdf.

Medicare Advantage Denial Notices

Find MA denial notices information on this site.

https://www.cms.gov/Medicare/Medicare-General-Information/BNI/MADenialNotices

Table 1: Beneficiary Notices (excluding Hospital Discharge Appeal Notices)

FFS ABN	The Advance Beneficiary Notice of Noncoverage (ABN), Form CMS-R-131, is issued by providers (including independent laboratories, home health agencies, and hospices), physicians, practitioners, and suppliers to original Medicare (fee for service (FFS)) beneficiaries in situations where Medicare payment is expected to be denied. The ABN is issued in order to transfer potential financial liability to the Medicare beneficiary in certain instances. Guidelines for issuing the ABN can be found beginning in Section 50 of "Chapter 30: Financial Liability Protections" in the Medicare Claims Processing Manual, Pub. 100-4. Note: Skilled nursing facilities (SNFs) issue the ABN to transfer potential financial liability for items/services expected to be denied under Medicare Part B only.
FFS SNF ABN	SNFs must issue a notice to original Medicare (FFS) beneficiaries in order to transfer potential financial liability before the SNF provides: ■ an item or service that is usually paid for by Medicare but that may not be paid for in this particular instance because it is not medically reasonable and necessary, or ■ custodial care. For Part A items and services: SNFs use the SNF ABN as the liability notice. For Part B items and services: SNFs use the ABN, Form CMS-R-131. The ABN and information on this notice can be found at https://www.cms.gov/medicare/medicare-general-information/bni/abn.

Table 1: Beneficiary Notices (excluding Hospital Discharge Appeal Notices) (cont.)

FFS HHCCN	Home health agencies (HHAs) are responsible for issuing the following beneficiary rights and protections notices to original Medicare (FFS) beneficiaries when notice is required: - Home Health Change of Care Notice (HHCCN) - Advance Beneficiary Notice of Noncoverage (ABN) - Notice of Medicare Noncoverage (NOMNC) - Detailed Explanation of Noncoverage (DENC) The HHCCN, Form CMS-10280, is used to notify Original Medicare beneficiaries receiving home healthcare benefits of plan of care changes. HHAs are required to provide written notification to beneficiaries before reducing or terminating an item and/or service.
HINNs	Hospitals provide Hospital-Issued Notices of Noncoverage (HINNs) to beneficiaries prior to admission, at admission, or at any point during an inpatient stay if the hospital determines that the items or services the beneficiary is receiving, or is about to receive, are not covered because they are: - Not medically necessary, - Not delivered in the most appropriate setting, or - Custodial in nature. Note: There are different HINNs: - HINN 10, also known as the Notice of Hospital Requested Review (HRR), should be issued by hospitals to beneficiaries whenever a hospital requests Quality Improvement Organization (QIO) review of a discharge decision without physician concurrence. HIINN 10 may be used for original Medicare beneficiaries or Medicare Advantage enrollees. - HINN 11, which is used for noncovered items or services provided during an otherwise covered stay. - HINN 12 should be used in association with the Hospital Discharge Appeal Notices to inform beneficiaries of their potential financial liability for a noncovered continued stay. - The Preadmission/Admission HINN, used prior to an entirely noncovered stay, is also known as HINN 1.
FFS expedited determination notices	HHAs, SNFs, hospices, and comprehensive outpatient rehabilitation facilities (CORFs) are required to provide a Notice of Medicare Noncoverage (NOMNC) to beneficiaries when their Medicare-covered service(s) are ending. The NOMNC informs beneficiaries on how to request an expedited determination from their Beneficiary and Family Centered Care Quality Improvement Organization (BFCC-QIO) and gives beneficiaries the opportunity to request an expedited determination from a BFCC-QIO. A Detailed Explanation of Noncoverage (DENC) is given only if a beneficiary requests an expedited determination. The DENC explains the specific reasons for the end of covered services.
MA denial notices	Medicare health plans are required to issue the Notice of Denial of Medical Coverage (or Payment), also known as the Integrated Denial Notice (IDN), upon denial, in whole or in part, of an enrollee's request for coverage and upon discontinuation or reduction of a previously authorized course of treatment. The IDN consolidates Medicare Advantage (MA) coverage and payment denial notices and integrates, where applicable, Medicaid appeal rights information for Medicare health plan enrollees receiving full benefits under a State Medical Assistance (Medicaid) program. Plans administering Medicaid benefits in addition to Medicare benefits are responsible for including applicable Medicaid information in the notice. Medicare health plans and Fully Integrated Dual Eligible (FIDE) plans will issue the IDN to inform enrollees of their appeal rights, as applicable, upon denial of coverage of items and services, and for discontinuation or reduction of a previously authorized course of treatment. Medicare-Medicaid Plans (MMPs) within the Financial Alignment Demonstrations also will use the IDN.

Table 1: Beneficiary Notices (excluding Hospital Discharge Appeal Notices) (cont.)

MA expedited determination notices	HHAs, SNFs, and CORFs are required to provide an NOMNC to Medicare health plan enrollees when their Medicare-covered service(s) are ending. The NOMNC informs enrollees on how to request an expedited determination from their Beneficiary and Family Centered Care Quality Improvement Organization (BFCC-QIO) and gives enrollees the opportunity to request an expedited determination from a BFCC-QIO. A DENC is given only if a beneficiary requests an expedited determination. The DENC explains the specific reasons for the end of services.
Medicare Outpatient Observation Notice (MOON)	Hospitals, including critical-access hospitals (CAHs), are required to provide a Medicare Outpatient Observation Notice (MOON) to Medicare beneficiaries (including Medicare Advantage health plan enrollees) informing them that they are outpatients receiving observation services and are not inpatients of a hospital or CAH.

Risk Takeaways

Main points of interest:
- Important Message from Medicare (IM) informs hospitalized beneficiaries of their hospital discharge appeal rights.
- Hospitals are required to deliver the IM to *all* Medicare hospital inpatients to inform them of their hospital discharge appeal rights.
- Hospital discharge appeal notices serve to address initiation and termination events. An example of a termination event would be a notice of discharge. Specific information must be included on the IM and Detailed Notice of Discharge (DND). There are prescriptive timelines for delivery of these notices.
- For Medicare Advantage (MA), the healthcare organization must enter the appropriate toll-free number for the individual MA plan and the plan's name on the IM.
- A DND explains the specific reasons for a discharge and is given only if a patient requests an appeal or expedited review of a discharge decision

Areas to watch:
- Compliance with delivery timeframe of IM and/or DND,
- Delivering the original copy of the IM,
- Patient's comprehension of the IM,
- Delivering the follow-up copy of the IM
- The beneficiary's right to appeal.

Laws that apply:
- Social Security Act:
  - Limitation on liability: § 1879 (a)–(g); 42 C.F.R. §§ 411.400–408
  - Refund Requirements: §§ 1834(a)(18) and (j)(4),1842(l), and 1879(h)
  - Statutory exclusions from Medicare benefits: §1862(a).
  - Expedited determination process: § 1869(b)(1)(F)

> - Quality improvement organization (QIO) review of termination of services or discharge and reconsideration: § 1154, §1155
> - 42 C.F.R.:
>   - Nonhospital process: 42 C.F.R. §§ 405.1200, 405.1202
>   - Hospital process: 42 C.F.R. §§ 405.1206, 405.1208
>   - Reconsideration process: 42 C.F.R. § 405.1204
>
> **Addressing compliance risks:**
> - Establish processes for meeting the IM and DND timelines
> - Educate staff on IM responsibilities
> - Start discharge communication at time of admission
> - Start developing a discharge plan at the time of admission

Endnotes

1. **Rose T. Dunn** is the chief operating officer of First Class Solutions Inc. As a revenue cycle consultant, Dunn recognizes the value of finely tuned processes that protect patient rights and avoid additional and unnecessary expenditures that further erode the net income of cash-strapped healthcare organizations. She applauds the vital role that case managers and access personnel play in the timely delivery of mandated notices.

2. "FFS & MA IM," Centers for Medicare & Medicaid Services, last modified November 17, 2020, https://www.cms.gov/Medicare/Medicare-General-Information/BNI/HospitalDischargeAppealNotices.

3. "Discharge Planning: Rights and Procedures for Medicare Beneficiaries in Various Care Settings," Center for Medicare Advocacy, accessed February 25, 2021, https://medicareadvocacy.org/medicare-info/discharge-planning/.

4. "Beneficiary Notices Initiative (BNI)," Centers for Medicare & Medicaid Services, updated August 3, 2020, https://www.cms.gov/Medicare/Medicare-General-Information/BNI.

5. "Beneficiary Notices Initiative (BNI)," Centers for Medicare & Medicaid Services, updated August 3, 2020, https://www.cms.gov/Medicare/Medicare-General-Information/BNI.

6. Centers for Medicare & Medicaid Services, "Chapter 30: Financial Liability Protections," § 50.2.1, *Medicare Claims Processing Manual*, revised February 21, 2014, https://www.cms.gov/Medicare/Medicare-General-Information/BNI/Downloads/ABN-CMS-Manual-Instructions.pdf.

7. "CMS-10065 and 10066," Centers for Medicare & Medicaid Services, accessed February 22, 2021, https://www.cms.gov/Regulations-and-Guidance/Legislation/PaperworkReductionActof1995/PRA-Listing-Items/CMS-10065-and-10066.

8. 42 C.F.R. § 405.1205.

9. 42 C.F.R. § 422.620.

10. 42 C.F.R. § 405.1205.

11. J. Birmingham "Here's what you need to know about Medicare's Important Message," Relias Media, January 1, 2008, https://www.reliasmedia.com/articles/9264-here-s-what-you-need-to-know-about-medicare-s-important-message.

12. "Beneficiary Notices Initiative (BNI)," Centers for Medicare & Medicaid Services.

13. 42 C.F.R. § 405.1205(b)(3),(4).

14. Diamond Healthcare, "Compliance Alert: Important Message from Medicare," August 4, 2017, https://www.diamondhealth.com/sites/default/files/Compliance%20Alert%20-%20Important%20Message%20from%20Medicare%20-%20080416.pdf.

15. "FFS & MA IM," Centers for Medicare & Medicaid Services.

16. Centers for Medicare & Medicaid Services, "Important Message from Medicare (IM) and Expedited Determination Procedures for Hospital Discharges," CMS Manual System Publication 100-04 Medicare Claims Processing. Transmittal 1257, May 25, 2007, https://www.cms.gov/regulations-and-guidance/guidance/transmittals/downloads/r1257cp.pdf.

17. Centers for Medicare & Medicaid Services, "Important Message from Medicare (IM) and Expedited Determination Procedures for Hospital Discharges," CMS Manual System Publication 100-04 Medicare Claims Processing. Transmittal 1257, May 25, 2007, https://www.cms.gov/regulations-and-guidance/guidance/transmittals/downloads/r1257cp.pdf.

18. Centers for Medicare & Medicaid Services, "Important Message from Medicare (IM) and Expedited Determination Procedures for Hospital Discharges," CMS Manual System Publication 100-04 Medicare Claims Processing.

Transmittal 1257, Section 200.3.2, May 25, 2007, https://www.cms.gov/regulations-and-guidance/guidance/transmittals/downloads/r1257cp.pdf.

19. Charles M. Honart, "Reminder: Effective Date for New Rules on Notification of Hospital Discharge Appeal Rights is Fast Approaching," Stevens & Lee, June 1, 2007, https://www.stevenslee.com/reminder-effective-date-for-new-rules-on-notification-of-hospital-discharge-appeal-rights-is-fast-approaching-2/.

20. Centers for Medicare & Medicaid Services, "Appointment of Representative," revised August 2018, https://www.cms.gov/Medicare/CMS-Forms/CMS-Forms/downloads/cms1696.pdf.

21. "Discharge Planning: Rights and Procedures for Medicare Beneficiaries in Various Care Settings," Center for Medicare Advocacy.

22. "How Medicare Beneficiaries Can Fight a Hospital Discharge," ElderLawAnswers, November 4, 2019, https://www.elderlawanswers.com/how-medicare-beneficiaries-can-fight-a-hospital-discharge-12218.

23. "Beneficiary Notices Initiative (BNI)," Centers for Medicare & Medicaid Services.

24. 42 C.F.R. § 405.1205.

25. "Discharge Planning: Rights and Procedures for Medicare Beneficiaries in Various Care Settings," Center for Medicare Advocacy.

26. "FFS & MA IM," Centers for Medicare & Medicaid Services.

27. Medicare Program; Hospital Inpatient Prospective Payment Systems for Acute Care Hospitals and the Long Term Care; Hospital Prospective Payment System and Fiscal Year 2014 Rates; Quality Reporting Requirements for Specific Providers; Hospital Conditions of Participation; Payment Policies Related to Patient Status, 78 Fed. Reg. 50,496, 50,945 (August 19, 2013), https://www.govinfo.gov/content/pkg/FR-2013-08-19/pdf/2013-18956.pdf.

28. Chuck Buck, "CMS Releases New MOON, Important Message from Medicare, and Detailed Notice of Discharge," RACmonitor.com, January 9, 2020, https://www.racmonitor.com/cms-releases-new-moon-important-message-from-medicare-and-detailed-notice-of-discharge#:~:text=with%20ID%3A%2010396-,CMS%20Releases%20New%20MOON%2C%20Important%20Message%20from%20Medicare,and%20Detailed%20Notice%20of%20Discharge&text=Same%20old%20New%20MOON%2C%20but,Management%20and%20Budget%20(OMB).

29. "Discharge Planning: Rights and Procedures for Medicare Beneficiaries in Various Care Settings," Center for Medicare Advocacy.

30. "Rights and Procedures for Medicare Beneficiaries in Various Care Settings," Center for Medicare Advocacy.

31. 42 U.S.C. § 1395x(ee)(2)(G); 42 C.F.R. § 482.43(a)(5).

32. TMF Health Quality Institute, *Notification of Hospital Discharge Appeal Rights QIO Handbook*, November 2007, 2, http://www.aqaf.com/perch/resources/library/dischargeappealnoticestrainingmanual.pdf.

33. TMF Health Quality Institute, *Notification of Hospital Discharge Appeal Rights QIO Handbook*, 7.

Resource 1: Detailed Notice of Discharge

[Insert contact information here]

[*Note: The name, address and telephone number of the hospital or Medicare health plan that delivers the notice must appear above the title of the form. The entity's registered logo is not required, but may be used.*]

Detailed Notice of Discharge

Date: _____

Patient name: _____

Patient number: _____

This notice gives a detailed explanation of why your hospital or Medicare health plan has determined Medicare coverage for your hospital stay should end. This notice is not the decision on your appeal. The decision on your appeal will come from your Quality Improvement Organization (QIO).

We have reviewed your case and decided that Medicare coverage of your hospital stay should end.

- The facts used to make this decision:_____
  _____
  _____

- Detailed explanation of why your hospital stay is no longer covered, and the specific Medicare coverage rules and policy used to make this decision: _____
  _____
  _____
  _____

- Plan policy, provision, or rationale used in making the decision (health plans only):
  _____
  _____
  _____

Resource 1: Detailed Notice of Discharge

If you would like a copy of the policy or coverage guidelines used to make this decision, or a copy of the documents sent to the QIO, please call us at:

[insert <u>hospital/Medicare health plan name and toll-free telephone number</u>]

According to the Paperwork Reduction Act of 1995, no persons are required to respond to a collection of information unless it displays a valid OMB control number. The valid OMB control number for this information collection is 0938-0692. The time required to complete this information collection is estimated to average 15 minutes per response, including the time to review instructions, search existing data resources, gather the data needed, and complete and review the information collection. If you have comments concerning the accuracy of the time estimate(s) or suggestions for improving this form, please write to: CMS, 7500 Security Boulevard, Attn: PRA Reports Clearance Officer, Mail Stop C4-26-05, Baltimore, Maryland 21244-1850.

Form CMS 10066-DND (Exp. 12/31/2022)

OMB approval 0938-1019

[Note: The original form can be found at https://www.cms.gov/Medicare/ Medicare-General-Information/BNI/HospitalDischargeAppealNotices.]

Resource 2: Notice of Denial of Medical Coverage

Important: This notice explains your right to appeal our decision. Read this notice carefully. If you need help, you can call one of the numbers listed on the last page under "Get help & more information."

Notice of Denial of Medical Coverage

[Note: Replace Denial of Medical Coverage with Denial of Payment, if applicable.]

Date: _____

Member number: _____

Name: _____

[Insert other identifying information, as necessary (e.g., provider name, enrollee's Medicaid number, service subject to notice, date of service)]

Your request was [insert appropriate term: *partially approved,denied***].**

We've [insert appropriate term: *denied, partially approved, stopped, reduced, suspended*] the [*payment of*] [*medical services/items or Part B drug or Medicaid drug*] listed below requested by you or your doctor [*provider*]:

_____
_____
_____
_____
_____

Resource 2: Notice of Denial of Medical Coverage

Why did we deny your request?

We [insert appropriate term: *denied, partially approved, stopped, reduced, suspended*] the [*payment of*] [*medical services/items or Part B drug or Medicaid drug*] listed above because [provide specific rationale for decision and include State or Federal law and/or Evidence of Coverage provisions to support decision]:

_____

_____

_____

_____

_____

You have the right to appeal our decision

You have the right to ask [health plan name] to review our decision by asking us for an appeal. [Insert Medicaid information explaining plan level appeal must be exhausted prior to requesting State Fair Hearing or other state external review.]

Plan Appeal: Ask [health plan name] for an appeal within **60 days** of the date of this notice. We can give you more time if you have a good reason for missing the deadline. See section titled "How to ask for an appeal with [health plan name]" for information on how to ask for a plan level appeal.

[**How to keep your services while we review your case:** If we're stopping or reducing a service, you can keep getting the service while your case is being reviewed. **If you want the service to continue, you must ask for an appealwithin 10 days** of the date of this notice or before the service is stopped or reduced, whichever is later. Your provider must agree that you should continue getting the service. If you lose your appeal, you may have to pay for these services.]

If you want someone else to act for you

You can name a relative, friend, attorney, doctor, or someone else to act as your representative. If you want someone else to act for you, call us at: [number(s)] to learn how to name your representative. TTY users call [number]. Both you and the person you want to act for you must sign and date a statement confirming this is what you want. You'll need to mail or fax this statement to us. Keep a copy for your records.

Resource 2: Notice of Denial of Medical Coverage

Important Information About Your Appeal Rights

There are 2 kinds of appeals with [health plan name]
Standard Appeal: We'll give you a written decision on a standard appeal within [insert appropriate timeframe for medical service/item or Part B drug: *30 days, 7 days*] [insert timeframe for standard internal plan Medicaid appeals, if different] after we get your appeal. Our decision might take longer if you ask for an extension, or if we need more information about your case. We'll tell you if we're taking extra time and will explain why more time is needed. If your appeal is for payment of a [medical service/item or Part B drug] you've already received, we'll give you a written decision within **60 days.**

Fast Appeal: We'll give you a decision on a fast appeal within **72 hours** [insert timeframe for expedited internal plan Medicaid appeals, if different] after we get your appeal. You can ask for a fast appeal if you or your doctor believe your health could be seriously harmed by waiting up to [insert appropriate timeframe for medical service/item or Part B drug: *30 days, 7 days*] for a decision. You cannot request an expedited appeal if you are asking us to pay you back for a [*medical service/item or Part B drug*] you've already received.

We'll automatically give you a fast appeal if a doctor asks for one for you or if your doctor supports your request. If you ask for a fast appeal without support from a doctor, we'll decide if your request requires a fast appeal. If we don't give you a fast appeal, we'll give you a decision within [insert appropriate timeframe for medical service/item or Part B drug: *30 days, 7 days*].

How to ask for an appeal with [health plan name]

Step 1
You, your representative, or your doctor [*provider*] must ask us for an appeal. Your [*written*] request must include:

- Your name
- Address
- Member number
- Reasons for appealing
- Whether you want a Standard or Fast Appeal (for a Fast Appeal, explain why you need one).
- Any evidence you want us to review, such as medical records, doctors' letters (such as a doctor's supporting statement if you request a fast appeal), or other information that explains why you need the [*medical service/item or Part B drug or Medicaid drug*]. Call your doctor if you need this information.

If you're asking for an appeal and missed the deadline, you may ask for an extension and should include your reason for being late.

Resource 2: Notice of Denial of Medical Coverage

We recommend keeping a copy of everything you send us for your records. [Insert, if applicable: *You can ask to see the medical records and other documents we used to make our decision before or during the appeal. At no cost to you, you can also ask for a copy of the guidelines we used to make our decision.*]

Step 2
Mail, fax, or deliver your appeal. [*You can also call us or submit your appeal electronically.*]

For a Standard Appeal:

Mailing Address:
[In Person Delivery Address:]
[Phone:]
[TTY Users Call:]
Fax:
[Website:]

[Insert, if applicable: *If you ask for a standard appeal by phone, we will send you a letter confirming what you told us.*]

For a Fast Appeal:

Phone:
[TTY Users Call:]
[Fax:]
[Website:]

What happens next?

If you ask for an appeal and we continue to deny your request for [*payment of*] a [*medical service/item or Part B drug or Medicaid drug*], we'll automatically send your case to an independent reviewer. **If the independent reviewer denies your request, the written decision will explain if you have additional appeal rights.**

[Insert additional State-specific Medicaid rules, as applicable.]

Resource 2: Notice of Denial of Medical Coverage

How to ask for a Medicaid State Fair Hearing

If [health plan name] denies your appeal request, you can take the steps listed below to request a State Fair Hearing. [States may also have additional language regarding other external review processes.]

Step 1: *You or your representative must ask for a State Fair Hearing [in writing] within [insert #] days of the date of the notice that denies your appeal request. You have up to [insert #] days if you have a good reason for your request being late.*

Your [written] request must include:

- Your name
- Address
- Member number
- Reasons for appealing
- Any evidence you want us to review, such as medical records, doctors' letters, or other information that explains why you need the item or service. Call your doctor if you need this information.

Step 2: *Send your request to:*

Address: _____

Phone: _____

Fax: _____

[A copy of this notice has been sent to:]

Get help & more information

- [Health Plan Name] Toll Free:
- TTY users call:
- [Insert plan hours of operation] or [plan website]
- 1-800-MEDICARE (1-800-633-4227), 24 hours, 7 days a week. TTY users call: 1-877-486-2048
- Medicare Rights Center: 1-888-HMO-9050
- Elder Care Locator: 1-800-677-1116 or www.eldercare.acl.gov to find help in your community.
- [Medicaid/State contact information]
- [State or local aging/disability resources contact information]

Resource 2: Notice of Denial of Medical Coverage

[May insert instructions for how enrollees can receive this notice in an alternate language or format from the plan.]

PRA Disclosure Statement According to the Paperwork Reduction Act of 1995, no persons are required to respond to a collection of information unless it displays a valid OMB control number. The valid OMB control number for this collection is 0938-0829. The time required to complete this information collection is estimated to average 10 minutes per response, including the time to review instructions, search existing data resources, and gather the data needed, and complete and review the information collection. If you have any comments concerning the accuracy of the time estimate(s) or suggestions for improving this form, please write to CMS, 7500 Security Boulevard, Attn: PRA Reports Clearance Officer, Baltimore, Maryland 21244-1850.

CMS does not discriminate in its programs and activities. To request this publication in an alternative format, please call 1-800-MEDICARE or email: AltFormatRequest@cms.hhs.gov

[Note: Medicare Advantage programs must follow the rules outlined in the January 1, 2020, Parts C & D Enrollee Grievances, Organization/Coverage Determinations, and Appeals Guidance.

This form can be found at https://www.cms.gov/Medicare/Medicare-General-Information/BNI/MADenialNotices.]

Incident-to Billing

By David M. Glaser[1]

What Is Incident-to Billing?

The term "incident-to billing" is a confusing shorthand for "services and supplies furnished as an incident to a physician's professional service."[2] In plain language, the term refers to the idea that Medicare permits coverage of a variety of services provided by professionals other than a physician (as long as they occur under a physician's supervision and direction), compensating the physician as if the services had been personally provided by the physician. Services billed as incident-to receive a higher rate than services billed independently by nonphysician professionals, such as nurse practitioners and physician assistants. Here's an example of an incident-to service: a nurse might take a patient's vitals when the patient visits a clinic and administer an injection or treat a wound at the doctor's direction. Under Medicare, the nurse's actions are bundled into the physician's encounter as an incidental part of the doctor's work, or incident-to expense.

Similarly, certain services furnished by a variety of medical professionals, such as physician assistants (PA), nurse practitioners (NP), and clinical nurse specialists (CNS), can be considered incident-to if the physician initiates the course of diagnosis and treatment and remains periodically involved throughout the course of care and if a few additional conditions are satisfied. For example, if a patient sees a physician and is diagnosed with pneumonia and returns for a follow-up visit a few weeks later with one of the clinic's NPs or PAs rather than the physician, the incident-to benefit allows the service to be billed by the physician even though the physician was seeing other patients while the NP or PA examined the patient. Similarly, physical, occupational, and speech therapy services can, but need not, be billed as incident-to. In addition, a variety of common procedures such as fitting a patient with a brace or delivering an injection can be billed as incident-to a physician's service as long as they meet the following conditions.

Generally speaking, a service by an auxiliary professional can be billed under the name and number of a physician as incident -to their work if:

- The service is not in a facility such as a hospital or skilled nursing facility. (Medicare's position is that the incident-to benefit cannot be used in a hospital-based clinic. Medicare does, however, permit "shared visits" in the hospital, as discussed later in this article.)
- The clinic is paying for the expense of the auxiliary professional providing the service.
- The clinic is the sole provider of medical direction.
- The physician has initiated the "course of diagnosis and treatment" for the patient and remains involved in the care, periodically seeing the patient during the course of treatment.[3] Once the physician initiates treatment, subsequent visits can be conducted solely by the nonphysician practitioner, but the physician is expected to see the patient during the initial encounter and again periodically (though no regulation specifies the frequency of follow-up). The Centers for Medicare & Medicaid Services (CMS) manuals refer to "active management and participation."[4]
- The service is something that is typically done in an office setting.
- The auxiliary professional is acting within the scope of that person's license.
- A supervising physician is present in the office suite, and the claim is submitted under the name of the supervising physician. Note that the physician supervising the service need not be the physician who initiated the course of treatment. However, the name on the claim should be the physician who was in the office suite even if that physician has never seen the patient.[5]

CMS has determined that when a service has a separate specified benefit under the Medicare program, the service may not be billed as incident-to. For example, since the Social Security Act includes a provision covering diagnostic tests, CMS asserts that diagnostic tests may not be billed incident-to a physician. Similarly, vaccines are specifically covered by a separate statutory provision.[6][7] Therefore, Medicare does not treat vaccine administration as a service incident-to a physician's services.

In many circumstances, services that are eligible to be billed incident-to a physician could also be billed independently by the professional providing the service. For example, imagine that a nurse practitioner is seeing a patient for a follow-up encounter during a patient's chemotherapy. It would be possible for the service to be billed under the nurse practitioner's name and billing number, but the reimbursement would be 85% of the amount paid if the physician bills for the service.

If services meet the incident-to requirements, the physician may bill the service and receive the full physician fee schedule reimbursement. That higher reimbursement is the primary advantage of billing incident-to the physician. Another possible benefit of billing incident-to is that under the Stark Law, a physician in a group practice may receive compensation credit for designated health services that are provided incident-to the physician's work. Stark generally prohibits physicians from receiving credit for designated health services provided by others. But in a group practice, there is an exception for designated health services that are incident-to.

Note that the incident-to benefit is created by the Medicare statute. While many state Medicaid programs and private insurers have chosen to adopt some analogous coverage, the requirements may differ from Medicare. Some payors have refused to extend any coverage for incident-to services.

Risk Area Governance

Incident-to billing is authorized by Social Security Act § 1861(s)(2)(A), which states that the program covers "services and supplies (including drugs and biologicals which are not usually self-administered by the patient) furnished as an incident to a physician's professional service, of kinds which are commonly furnished in physicians' offices and are commonly either rendered without charge or included in the physicians' bills."[8]

Most information about incident-to billing appears in the Code of Federal Regulations. In 42 C.F.R. § 410.26 are the requirements that a service must meet to qualify for coverage under Medicare (summarized in the previous section).[9] For the supervision requirements, CMS incorporates the definition of *direct supervision* found in the diagnostic test regulation, 42 C.F.R. § 410.32(b)(3)(ii):

> Direct supervision in the office setting means the physician must be present in the office suite and immediately available to furnish assistance and direction throughout the performance of the procedure. It does not mean that the physician must be present in the room when the procedure is performed.[10]

Perhaps the most important regulatory text indicates that "[s]ervices and supplies must be an integral, though incidental, part of the service of a physician (or other practitioner) in the course of **diagnosis** or treatment of an injury or illness."[11] *Diagnosis* is emphasized because many people, and even many Medicare Administrative Contractors (MACs), assert that it is impermissible for a new problem to be addressed in a visit that is billed incident-to a physician. The regulatory text, however, explicitly permits diagnosis or problems. This text establishes the principle that over the course of a patient's care, auxiliary personnel can diagnose or treat conditions without direct physician involvement.

Under the Medicare program, only statutes (United States Code), regulations (Code of Federal Regulations), and national coverage decisions are allowed to limit Medicare coverage: "No rule, requirement, or other statement of policy (other than a national coverage determination) that establishes or changes a substantive legal standard governing the scope of benefits, the payment for services, or the eligibility of individuals, entities, or organizations to furnish or receive services or benefits under this title shall take effect unless it is promulgated by the Secretary by regulation under paragraph."[12] The U.S. Supreme Court elaborated on this principle in a 2019 decision.[13] The so-called Brand memo, authored by the associated attorney general on January 25, 2018, lays out the Department of Justice's policy that Medicare manuals should not form the basis of any overpayment or False Claims Act recovery.[14] Only statutes and regulations are treated as binding.

Although the manuals are not binding in the way that a statute or regulation is, the *Medicare Benefit Policy Manual*, Chapter 15 § 60.1.B, offers insight into how CMS has instructed its contractors to implement their incident-to policy.[15] Two paragraphs are particularly enlightening, which inexplicably omit the reference to diagnosis, but confirm that care in the "course of treatment" is covered:

> Thus, where a physician supervises auxiliary personnel to assist him/her in rendering services to patients and includes the charges for their services in his/her own bills, the services of such personnel are considered incident to the physician's service [if there is a physician's service rendered to which the services of such personnel are an incidental part and there is direct supervision by the physician].
>
> This does not mean, however, that to be considered incident to, each occasion of service by auxiliary personnel (or the furnishing of a supply) need also always be the occasion of the actual rendition of a personal professional service by the physician. Such a service or supply could be considered to be incident to when furnished during a course of treatment where the physician performs an initial service and subsequent services of a frequency which reflect his/her active participation in and management of **the course of treatment**.[16]

Common Compliance Risks

The incident-to rules set out a number of potential traps; some are relatively obvious, and others much subtler. They include the following.

Billing under the Name and Number of a Physician that is Not in the Office Suite

Medicare requires that services be provided under the "direct supervision" of a physician who must be "present in the office suite" and immediately available.[17] (During a federally declared public health emergency, "immediate availability" can be met via real-time audio-visual communication.) Yet, Medicare has never defined the term "office suite." Rather than defining "office suite," the regulation merely states that any physician need not be present in the room without detailing exactly where the physician must be located. While discussing a proposed rule, CMS offered some sense of how it views the term "office suite:"

> We are not proposing that there must be any particular configuration of rooms for an office to qualify as an office "suite." However, direct supervision means that a physician must be in the office suite and immediately available to provide assistance and direction. Thus, a group of contiguous rooms should in most cases satisfy this requirement. We have been asked whether it would be possible for a

physician to directly supervise a service furnished on a different floor. We think the answer would depend upon individual circumstances that demonstrate that the physician is close at hand. The question of physician proximity for physician referral purposes, as well as for incident to purposes, is a decision that only the local carrier could make based on the layout of each group of offices. For example, a carrier might decide that in certain circumstances it is appropriate for one room of an office suite to be located on a different floor, such as when a physician practices on two floors of a townhouse.[18]

Presuming that the policy behind this requirement is a desire for the physician to be able to assist in the event of a medical emergency, it seems reasonable to assume that if the physician could reach the patient in 30 seconds to a minute, the supervision requirement has been met. Unfortunately, there is no clear authoritative source overtly confirming this advice. Moreover, various MACs have issued guidance asserting that if the physician is moving from one building to another by crossing a street or using a skyway or tunnel, they are not in the office suite. Guidance from a MAC is even less authoritative than the Medicare manuals, which are nonbinding. However, there have been instances when contractors have denied claims when a supervising physician is on a different floor of the building or across a skyway or tunnel. In those cases, it is necessary to appeal to an administrative law judge and assert that the MAC lacks authority to impose the requirement. If the skyway or tunnel is connecting different buildings, there is a much higher risk that a court might conclude that the physician is not in the office suite.

Billing under the Incorrect Physician

Note that Medicare specifically instructs clinics to bill under the name and number of the **supervising physician**. If one physician is generally overseeing the patient's care, but a different physician is physically present when the incident-to service is provided, the service should be billed under the supervising physician.[19]

Billing for Treatment Not Initiated by a Physician

Under the regulation, a physician has to be overseeing "the course of diagnosis or treatment of an injury or illness."[20] That means that there must be an initial service by the physician before other professionals can provide incident-to services. This requirement is widely misunderstood. (It is commonly understood that as long as the physician sees the patient during the initial encounter, ancillary staff may begin care before the physician enters the room.) Most people believe that if the patient has a new problem, the physician must see the patient. Contractor bulletins and articles about incident-to frequently state that the physician must address new problems. In fact, neither the regulation nor the manual contains the words "new problem." Instead, they both refer to covering anything within "the course of treatment." It is possible for a new problem to be part of a course of treatment. For example, a patient undergoing chemotherapy may develop a new infection or experience a reaction to the drug. Either event would constitute a "new problem." However, under the regulation, it is still part of the course of treatment. It is important to educate staff about the difference between a "new problem" and a new "course of treatment."

Services Provided in a Facility

Incident-to services must be provided outside a hospital or skilled nursing facility. Although Medicare has adopted a policy of permitting "shared visits" for hospital encounters, the incident-to benefit excludes services in an institution.[21] [22] Because a hospital-based clinic can seem so similar to a freestanding clinic, it can be easy to forget that the incident-to benefit is inapplicable. The "shared visit" policy is intended to help address this problem. Under the CMS shared visit policy, if a physician and a nonphysician practitioner both have an encounter with the patient on the same day, their work may be combined and billed under the physician at the full physician fee schedule rate.[23]

Addressing Compliance Risks

There are a few concrete steps that can materially lower the risk of violating the incident-to rules.

Have a Supervising Doctor of the Day

Because Medicare requires the bill to be submitted under the name of the supervising physician, it is a good risk management strategy to develop a mechanism to guarantee that the physician who appears on the bill was in the clinic when the service occurred. Because physicians may leave to perform procedures in the hospital, get lunch, or attend to administrative duties, it is advisable to have a designated physician who will be present and instruct everyone providing incident-to services to bill the service under that supervising physician. At a minimum, the professional seeing the patient should be certain that a supervising physician is present in the office suite during the encounter. Ideally, the physician's presence is documented someplace, though in a "highly organized" physician clinic, CMS has acknowledged that the presence of a supervising physician can be assumed.[24]

Understand That Billing under the Wrong Physician Does Not Require a Refund

The *Medicare Claims Processing Manual* has language indicating that an otherwise correct Medicare payment made to the wrong professional "does not constitute a program overpayment."[25] In other words, if you inadvertently bill under the wrong physician's name, you are not required to refund the payment. Under this policy, if you mistakenly bill under the physician who established the course of treatment rather than the physician present in the suite, no refund is required. It is important to try to bill under the supervising physician because

Medicare can revoke your ability to reassign claims as a penalty for billing under the wrong physician, but there is no obligation to return the payment.

Ensure the Auxiliary Professional Is Paid by the Clinic

Medicare allows a physician either to employ or lease the professionals providing services incident-to. However, the physician must bear the expense of that professional. If another organization, such as a hospital, provides the professional to the physician without charge, the physician may not bill for services provided that individual. Of course, if a hospital provides free staff to a clinic, there is a high risk of violating either Stark or the Medicare Anti-Kickback Statute as well. The bottom line is that the auxiliary person must represent an expense to the physician group.

Possible Penalties

By far the most serious potential consequences of making a billing mistake are penalties under the False Claims Act (FCA). Under the FCA, reckless disregard for a Medicare billing rule allows penalties of three times the amount billed on the claim plus a civil monetary penalty ranging from more than $11,000 to about $22,000 per claim.

The more common consequence is the assessment of an overpayment. Medicare is permitted to recoup funds for services that do not qualify for coverage. In many instances, a failure to follow the incident-to rules effectively lowers the reimbursement by 15%. For example, if the service is by an NP, a PA, or a CNS, that individual could bill independently and receive 85% of the fee schedule. In those situations, Medicare should only recoup the difference between the amount paid to the physician and the amount that was properly billable.

Compliance Resources

Centers for Medicare & Medicaid Services

Medicare Benefit Policy Manual
Chapter 15: Covered Medical and Other Health Services, § 60, Services and Supplies Furnished Incident to a Physician's/NPP's Professional Service
This section of the *Medicare Benefit Policy Manual* covers information important to incident-to billing.

https://www.cms.gov/Regulations-and-Guidance/Guidance/Manuals/downloads/bp102c15.pdf

Medicare Learning Network
"Incident to" Services
This *MLN Matters* article includes provider resources on incident-to billing.

https://www.cms.gov/Medicare/Medicare-Contracting/ContractorLearningResources/
Downloads/JA0441.pdf

Fredrikson & Byron

"Incident To," Shared Visits and Other Encounters with Non-Physician Professionals
This free webinar by David M. Glaser discusses incident-to billing.

https://youtu.be/yaIqJr3FhFE

Risk Takeaways

Main points of interest:

- Incident-to billing is done for "services and supplies furnished as an incident to a physician's professional service."
- A variety of common procedures can be billed as incident to a physician's service as long as they meet certain conditions.
- If services meet the incident-to requirements, the physician may bill the service at the higher reimbursement afforded to physician care.
- Another possible benefit of billing incident-to is that under the Stark Law, a physician in a group practice may receive compensation credit for designated health services that are provided incident to the physician's work.

Areas to watch:

- Billing for a physician that is not in the office suite
- Billing under the incorrect physician
- Billing for treatment not initiated by the physician
- Incorrect facilities

Laws that apply:

- Services and Supplies Incident to a Physician's Professional Services: Conditions, 42 C.F.R. § 410.26
- Diagnostic X-ray Tests, Diagnostic Laboratory Tests, and Other Diagnostic Tests: Conditions, 42 C.F.R. § 410.32(b)(3)(ii)
- False Claims Act, 31 U.S.C. §§ 3729-3733

Addressing compliance risks:

- Have a supervising doctor of the day.
- Understand that billing under the wrong physician does not require a refund.
- Ensure the auxiliary professional is paid by the clinic.

Endnotes

1. **David M. Glaser** is shareholder at Fredrikson & Byron PA. In his law firm's Health Law Group, he assists clinics, hospitals, and other healthcare entities with negotiating the maze of healthcare regulations, providing advice about risk management, reimbursement, and business planning issues. He has considerable experience in healthcare regulation and litigation, including compliance, criminal and civil fraud investigations, and reimbursement disputes. Glaser's goal is to explain the government's enforcement position and to analyze whether this position is supported by the law or represents government overreach.

2. Social Security Act § 1861(s)(2)(a) (omitting a parenthetical).

3. 42 C.F.R. § 410.32(b)(2) .

4. Centers for Medicare & Medicaid Services, "Chapter 15: Covered Medical and Other Health Services," § 60.1.B, footnote 9, *Medicare Benefit Policy Manual*, Pub. 100-02, revised August 7, 2020, https://www.cms.gov/Regulations-and-Guidance/Guidance/Manuals/Downloads/bp102c15.pdf.

5. 42 C.F.R. § 410.32 .

6. Social Security Act § 1861(s)(10).

7. Social Security Act § 1861(s)(3).

8. Social Security Act § 1861(s)(2)(A).

9. 42 C.F.R. § 410.26 .

10. 42 C.F.R. § 410.32(b)(3)(ii) .

11. 42 C.F.R. § 410.26(b)(2) . [emphasis added]

12. Social Security Act § 1871(a)(2).

13. Azar v. Allina Health Services, 139 S. Ct. 1804 (June 2019).

14. U.S. Department of Justice, Office of the Associate Inspector General, "Limiting Use of Agency Guidance Documents in Affirmative Civil Enforcement Cases," January 25, 2018, https://www.justice.gov/file/1028756/download.

15. Centers for Medicare & Medicaid Services, "Chapter 15: Covered Medical and Other Health Services," § 60.1.B, *Medicare Benefit Policy Manual*, Pub. 100-02, revised August 7, 2020, https://www.cms.gov/Regulations-and-Guidance/Guidance/Manuals/downloads/bp102c15.pdf.

16. Centers for Medicare & Medicaid Services, "Chapter 15: Covered Medical and Other Health Services," § 60.1.B, *Medicare Benefit Policy Manual*, Pub. 100-02, revised August 7, 2020, https://www.cms.gov/Regulations-and-Guidance/Guidance/Manuals/downloads/bp102c15.pdf. [bolded text added]

17. 42 C.F.R. § 410.32(b)(3)(ii) .

18. Medicare and Medicaid Programs; Physicians' Referrals to Health Care Entities with Which They Have Financial Relationships, 63 Fed. Reg. 1,685 (Jan. 9, 1998) . [underlined emphasis added]

19. 42 C.F.R. § 410.26(b)(5) .

20. 42 C.F.R. § 410.32(b)(2) .

21. 42 C.F.R. § 410.26(b)(1) .

22. Centers for Medicare & Medicaid Services, "Chapter 12: Physicians/Nonphysician Practitioners," § 30.6.1, *Medicare Claims Processing Manual*, Pub. 100-04, revised September 18, 2020, https://www.cms.gov/Regulations-and-Guidance/Guidance/Manuals/Downloads/clm104c12.pdf.

23. Centers for Medicare & Medicaid Services, "Chapter 12, Physicians/Nonphysician Practitioners," § 30.6.1, *Medicare Claims Processing Manual*, Pub. 100-04, revised September 18, 2020, https://www.cms.gov/Regulations-and-Guidance/Guidance/Manuals/Downloads/clm104c12.pdf.

24. Centers for Medicare & Medicaid Services, "Chapter 15: Covered Medical and Other Health Services," § 60.3, *Medicare Benefit Policy Manual*, Pub. 100-02, revised August 7, 2020, https://www.cms.gov/Regulations-and-Guidance/Guidance/Manuals/downloads/bp102c15.pdf.

25. Centers for Medicare & Medicaid Services, "Chapter 1: General Billing Requirements," § 30.2.2.1, *Medicare Claims Processing Manual*, Pub. 100-04, revised July 31, 2020, https://www.cms.gov/Regulations-and-Guidance/Guidance/Manuals/Downloads/clm104c01.pdf.

Implantable Medical Device Credit Reporting

By Michael G. Calahan,[1] PA, MBA

What Is Implantable Medical Device Credit Reporting in Relation to the Revenue Cycle?

Certain medical devices might be implanted during inpatient or outpatient procedures. Such devices may require replacement because of defects, recalls, mechanical complications, or other factors. Under certain circumstances, federal regulations require reductions in Medicare payments for inpatient, outpatient, and ambulatory surgical center (ASC) claims for replacement of implanted devices due to recalls or failures.[2] It is important for compliance officers to be aware of the requirements and determinations related to replaced medical devices and whether Medicare payments for those devices were made in accordance with Medicare requirements. The area of reporting medical device credits is subject to enforcement interest and scrutiny by the U.S. Department of Health & Human Services (HHS) Office of Inspector General (OIG), among other regulators.[3]

Since 2007, hospital providers have had to report implantable medical device credits to Medicare in relation to inpatient services; however, this particular Centers for Medicare & Medicaid Services (CMS) requirement remained a quiet niche area of compliance, hardly noticed by hospital revenue cycle staff.[4] One year later, in 2008, buoyed by this new reporting requirement's potential broad application, CMS expanded the scope of reportable device credit parameters and included implantable medical device credits related to select outpatient and ASC procedures.[5] There was a slow assimilation of this mandate industrywide.

Today, although many more healthcare networks, hospitals, outpatient departments, and ASCs are aware of and strictly follow this reporting directive, confusion and uncertainty still linger, making this issue susceptible to scrutiny from federal auditors such as the HHS OIG. The continuing confusion generally includes these standard queries: What qualifies a credit to be reported? Is there a monetary threshold, a specific type of device, or a specific associated surgical procedure? The following information answers these perennial queries.

Basis for Medical Device Credit Reporting Obligation

Undergirded by the "Prudent Buyers Principle, in *The Provider Reimbursement Manual,Part 1*, Chapter 21, Sections 2102.1 and 2103 (A & B), and enforced through 42 C.F.R. § 413.9(a)-(c), reporting replacement device credits for certain implantable medical devices has now been widely promulgated. Few know of its basis in this somewhat buried principle. As an excerpt from the Prudent Buyers Principle in the manual states: "Implicit in the intention that actual costs be paid to the extent they are reasonable is the expectation that the provider seeks to minimize its costs and that its actual costs do not exceed what a prudent and cost-conscious buyer pays for a given item or service."[6]

Further, and specific to implantable medical devices, the manual states: "Another way to minimize cost is to obtain free replacements or reduced charges under warranties for medical devices. Any alert and cost-conscious buyer seeks such advantages, and it is expected that Medicare providers of services will also seek them."[7]

This passage firmly implies that if a reduced charge or warranty is to be gained, the onus is on the provider to seek out those reductions and report them to Medicare.

Provider Obligations

As established by CMS as the baseline tenet for medical device credit reporting, the following must occur for applicable implantable medical devices undergoing *replacement*. If a healthcare provider receives a credit from a device manufacturer or vendor/supplier for a replacement device that is 50% or greater than the provider's cost for the replacement device, that credit must be reported to Medicare.[8] In essence, a healthcare provider is obliged to pass on the savings to Medicare. Further, in rare cases when a *newly implanted* device is part of an outpatient procedure and is provided to the hospital free of charge or at 100% credit (usually occurring in clinical trials), this cost savings must also be reported to Medicare.[9] Whether replacement devices or free-of-charge initially-placed devices, certain associated credits must be reported to Medicare via the (1) UB-04 hospital claim form and (2) CMS-1500 claim form for ASC claims, with the credit amount deducted from the device's line item charge.[10]

Qualifying Factors: Device-Dependent Procedures and Identifying Reportable Devices

The implantable medical device credit reporting directives pertain only to device-dependent procedures, also termed "device-intensive" procedures. This means the device would not be implanted without the surgical procedure, and/or the surgical procedure would not be performed without implanting the device. One is dependent upon the other.

In identifying reportable devices related to these device-dependent procedures, the device cost relative to the mean procedure cost (as assessed, predetermined, and published by CMS) must be "significant." The amount of the replacement-device cost relative to the predetermined total procedure cost is known as the device "offset" amount. CMS has defined this term as exceeding a device offset threshold of 30%.[11] (Note: Prior to 2019, this threshold was set at 40%). Additionally, devices must be:

- Approved by the Federal Drug Administration (FDA) for marketing and use, which includes investigational device exemption (IDE) devices classified by the FDA as a Category B device
- Considered an integral part of the service furnished
- Used for one patient only
- Used while coming into contact with human tissue
- Surgically implanted or inserted (either permanently or temporarily)[12]

Alternatively, devices must *not be*:

- Equipment, instruments, apparatus, or implements of the type for which depreciation and financing expenses are recovered as depreciable assets
- A material or supply that is furnished incident to a service (e.g., scalpel, surgical kit, sutures, or surgical clip other than a radiological site marker)[13]

For inpatients, these procedures (and their associated devices) are identified by Medicare Severity Diagnosis Related Groups (MS-DRGs) each fiscal year and made public via the Inpatient Prospective Payment System (IPPS) Final Rule, typically appearing within the rule's text in an MS-DRGs table format.[14] Device-dependent procedures and their device offset amounts for outpatient and ASC settings are published each calendar year in the Hospital Outpatient Prospective Payment System (OPPS) and ASC Payment System Final Rule, typically summarized in an addendum in Excel format (i.e., not within the rule's main text).[15] Specifically for ASC, an additional addendum identifies all procedures approved to be performed within an ASC and includes a specific "payment indicator" denoting "device-dependent procedures approved for the ASC setting." For inpatient, outpatient, and ASC settings, this annually updated information is often (but not always) republished in official CMS change request/transmittal documents for the fiscal or calendar year in question. For inpatient services, the change request/transmittal is a one-time annual release; for outpatient and ASC, the change requests/transmittals are released quarterly.

> **Inform All Surgical Specialties in Hospital & ASC Settings**
>
> Implantable medical device-dependent procedures are performed in nearly all common clinical specialties within healthcare facility settings. Whether inpatient, outpatient, or ASC, there is probably a device-credit scenario of which providers should be aware. The surgical procedures include insertion of cardiac assist devices, pacemakers, and implantable cardioverter-defibrillator (ICD) systems; orthopedic surgeries involving total joint replacements; various neurosurgical procedures involving endovascular systems and neurostimulation devices; and urological, ophthalmological, and many other surgical specialties performing device-dependent procedures. As well, clinical trials conducted in nearly all surgical specialties can have device-dependent surgeries that require device credit reporting.

Risk Area Governance

Various laws and guidance materials exist regarding implantable medical device credit reporting. The following is a short list of these laws, final rules, and guidance materials:

- 42 CFR § 413.9 Cost Related to Patient Care (i.e., Prudent Buyer's Principle)
- 42 CFR § 412.89 Payment Adjustment for Certain Replaced Devices
- Inpatient Prospective Payment System (IPPS) Final Rule: Identifies inpatient procedures and associated devices
- Medicare Hospital Outpatient Prospective Payment System (OPPS) & ASC Payment System Final Rule: Identifies device-dependent procedures with their device offset amounts for outpatient and ASC settings
- *Medicare Claims Processing Manual* 100-04 Ch. 3 §100.8 - Replaced Devices Offered Without Cost or With a Credit
- *Medicare Claims Processing Manual* 100-04 Ch. 4 § 61.1 - 61.3.6 - Billing for Devices Under the OPPS
- *Medicare Claims Processing Manual* 100-04 Ch. 14 § 40.8 - Payment When a Device is Furnished with No Cost or With Full or Partial Credit (ASC):
- *Medicare Claims Processing Manual* 100-04 Ch. 32 § 68.4 - Billing Requirements for Providers Billing Routine Costs of Clinical Trials Involving a Category B IDE

Necessity of Cross-Departmental Monitoring

Identifying, tracking, and monitoring implantable medical device credits is a cross-departmental effort within and throughout a hospital, outpatient department nexus, and/or the ASC. In essence, the facility must build a multidepartment network or team to properly address and manage reportable device credits. Here are the many departments and their functions involved in the process:

- Clinical staff members who directly deal with the device and device-intensive procedure itself, as well as communicate with the device vendor and that vendor's onsite representative who facilitates the return of the replaced device and helps facilitate device-credit claims (i.e., gaining vendor support and cooperation)
- Central Supply or Materials Management personnel considered "bridging" staff who order/store devices, assist in monitoring and tracking, and provide status updates on outstanding and/or received device credits
- Accounts Payable staff members who receive device credits, notify waiting departments of the credit's receipt, and furnish credit memo copies
- Revenue Cycle Management (billing) personnel who perform confirmatory calculations, post adjustments to patient accounts, ensure all required claim elements and adjusted line items are noted, and submit correct(ed) UB-04 and CMS-1500 claim forms
- Compliance staff members who provide process oversight, workflow guidance, educational sessions, and annual updates and who also perform due-diligence audits.

Common Compliance Risks

Reporting in Inpatient & Outpatient Settings: Common Claim Elements

The current inpatient reporting methodology has not changed much since the original CMS directive from 2007. However, the reporting strategy for outpatient services was amended in 2014 to align with the inpatient method, and consequently reportable device credits in these two settings are currently reported in the exact same way. The hospital's billing or revenue cycle department must be aware of the following information related to the device in question and its associated device credit:

1. **Replacement cost** of the device (typically found on the device purchase order or invoice)
2. **Amount of credit** (typically disclosed to the healthcare provider in a credit memo)
3. **Demonstration of the 50%-or-greater status** of the device credit using simple calculations
4. **UB-04 Claim Form** elements:

- Value Code -FD -"Credit Received from the Manufacturer for a Replaced Device" and exact dollar amount of the credit
- Condition Code (CC) -49 or -50, whichever is appropriate:
  - CC-49 Product Replacement within Product Lifecycle
  - CC-50 Product Replacement for Known Recall of a Product
- An adjusted line item charge reflecting the device-credit reduction

Reporting Example

A cardiac pacemaker is replaced at the end of the pacemaker battery lifecycle. This is covered by the manufacturer's warranty program. The healthcare provider surgically extracts the device and returns it—per manufacturer warranty program guidelines—to the manufacturer or designated vendor for device interrogation and analysis. The healthcare provider submits the required warranty claim to the manufacturer or vendor, as required. The "replacement cost" for the new device is noted on the device invoice; the amount of the device credit is noted on the "credit memo." The replacement device-credit ratio is assessed with this data and claim form elements.

Replacement Device Credit Ratio	
Replacement Cost	$10,000.00
Device Credit:	$5,500.00
Greater than 50%?	Yes, 55%
UB-04 Claim Form Elements	Value Code -FD and monetary field amount $5,500.00 Condition Code -49
Usual Device Line Item Charge	$15,000.00 (includes a hospital-applied 1.5% mark-up)
Adjusted Line Item Charge	$ 6,750.00 (reduction of credit; reflects 1.5% mark-up)

Preparing the initially correct or later-corrected inpatient or outpatient UB-04 claim with the above-noted data and claim form elements will ensure this device credit has been appropriately reported.

A current area of OIG scrutiny, listed in the OIG Annual Work Plan, is "Medical Outpatient Outlier Payments for Claims with Credits for Replaced Medical Devices."[16] This OIG target focuses specifically on hospitals receiving outpatient outlier payments (under OPPS) when device credits also are reported on the UB-04 claim forms. In the outlier calculation process, charges are compared to payments; if the total cost of the claim is artificially inflated by an unadjusted device line item (while a credit is also reported, thereby reducing the amount of reimbursement), then the outlier payment mechanism can be triggered. This results in an outlier reimbursement being wrongfully applied to the claim's reimbursement total and subsequently paid to the hospital.

The OIG has made this a focus, as stated, within its annual Work Plan. The OIG can easily electronically mine provider claims data, searching for twin claim characteristics of both device credits in the value code fields and outlier payments made to the providers.

Special Reporting for Outpatient Initially Placed Devices Given Free of Charge

CMS has carved out a special area of outpatient procedures that might involve a clinical trial sponsor providing a device free of charge to the hospital for implantation within a patient. If the clinical trial is conducted outpatient and an initially placed device is provided either free of charge or with a 100% credit issued, then the hospital must report this device credit on the UB-04 claim form, using the same methodology as typical outpatient replacement-device credit reporting procedures (previously noted). To mark this rather rare occurrence, report special condition code 53 (instead of CC-49 or CC-50) on the claim. CC-53 denotes "Initial placement of a medical device provided as part of a clinical trial or a free sample."[17] The remaining device credit-reporting steps are as previously outlined.

Ambulatory Surgery Center Reporting Methodology

Unlike the inpatient and outpatient reporting methods for replacement device credits, the billing of credited devices in the ASC setting is vastly different. The accounting and reimbursement process is modifier-triggered and "block-amount"-based, reflecting each pre-figured procedure's device-offset cost. That is, depending on which modifier is reported, a 50%-fixed-device offset amount or a 100%-fixed-device offset amount will be deducted from the final reimbursement to account for the device's credit. Since services at ASCs are billed on the CMS-1500 claim form and not the UB-04 claim form (as with hospital-based services), there is no space or claim field available for the value codes, amount of credit, or condition codes. In fact, the exact amount of the credit is never reported by the ASC. Instead, the reimbursement modifiers signal whether the device credit is 50% or greater or if the device credit is a full 100% (i.e., free of charge). These modifiers include:

- **Modifier -FB:** "Item Provided Without Cost to Provider, Supplier or Practitioner, or Full [100%] Credit Received for Replacement Device"
- **Modifier -FC:** "Partial Credit of 50% or More Received for Replaced Device"

The ASC's billing or revenue cycle department must be aware of the following information related to the device in question and its associated device credit:

1. **Replacement cost of the device** (typically found on the device purchase order or invoice)
2. **Amount of credit** (typically disclosed to the healthcare provider in a credit memo)
3. **Demonstration of the 50%-or-greater status** of the device credit via simple calculations
4. **CMS-1500 Claim Form** elements:
   - Main or "anchoring" CPT procedure code
   - HCPCS Level II device code (typically a -C code)
   - Device credit modifier (-FB or -FC, whichever is appropriate)
   - An adjusted line item charge reflecting the device-credit reduction

Reporting Example

A cardiac pacemaker is replaced at the end of the pacemaker battery's lifecycle. This is covered by the manufacturer's warranty program. The healthcare provider surgically extracts the device and returns it (per manufacturer warranty program guidelines) to the manufacturer or designated vendor for device interrogation and analysis. The healthcare provider submits the required warranty claim to the manufacturer or vendor, as required. The replacement cost for the new device is noted on the device invoice; the amount of the device credit is noted on the credit memo. The replacement device credit ratio is assessed using the following data and claim form elements.

Replacement Device Credit Ratio	
Replacement Cost	$10,000.00
Device Credit:	$ 5,500.00
Greater than 50%?	Yes, 55%
CMS-1500 Claim Form Elements	CPT code (e.g., 33228)
	Credit modifier –FC (50%-fixed-offset reduction)
	HCPCS-II device code (e.g., C1785)
Usual Device Line Item Charge	$12,500.00 (1.25% markup applied by the ASC)
Adjusted Line Item Charge	$ 5,625.00 (reduction of credit; reflects 1.25% markup)

Note, again, the actual device credit is never reported by the ASC; only the "triggering" reimbursement modifier is reported by being appended to the CPT procedure code. Importantly, note that the reimbursement modifier is not appended to the device HCPCS-II code for which the credit was received. However, the device line item charge should reflect the reduction in the device's cost.

Preparing the initially correct or later-corrected CMS-1500 claim with the above-noted data and claim form elements will ensure this device credit has been appropriately reported.

Addressing Compliance Risks

Best Practices: Staying on Top of Reportable Device Credits

The following is a list of basic recommendations and suggestions for best practices to keep the hospital and ASC staff informed, engaged, and responsible for identifying, tracking, and appropriately reporting implantable medical device credits:

- Compose, publish, and make accessible the facility's policies and procedures that specifically address identifying, monitoring, and reporting device credits.
- Hold educational sessions based on the published policies and procedures.
- Assign cross-departmental ownership for steps in the management workflow of device credits, including identification, monitoring, and reporting responsibilities.
- Create an accessible HIPAA-secure shared e-tool within the provider's system (e.g., a password-protected Excel worksheet for noting, tracking, and communicating data germane to new, pending, and completed reportable device credits.
- Provide system access to critical documents (usually scanned and electronically available) for select device-credit owners (e.g., access to posted device "credit memos" performed by accounts payable staff).
- Provide decision trees for typical device-credit workflow situations, as well as guidelines for *unusual* device-credit scenarios, which can include:
  - Device with a potential reportable credit left in situ (i.e., left in the patient) and not surgically removed to be returned per usual
  - Device not returned per vendor requirements but instead mistakenly destroyed by the pathology department
  - Replacement device obtained from one vendor with the extracted (original) device obtained from a different vendor, calling into question the availability of a credit
  - Replacement device originally implanted by one facility but replaced by a different facility, calling into question the availability of a credit
  - Device broken or damaged during the extraction surgical procedure
- Compose a contact list (names, titles, email addresses, and internal telephone numbers) for all designated device-credit workflow owners for easy communication between staff.
- Designate staff to request and receive vendor credit reports from all device vendors on a quarterly or semiannual basis. These reports should include all credits issued and can be reconciled to internal records.
- Perform timely internal audits to ensure that the facility's device-credit workflow is viable and that credits are being reported per federal compliance standards.
- Designate staff to monitor and communicate fiscal and calendar-year updates made by CMS to surgical procedures, types of devices, and device-credit reporting methodologies.

Possible Penalties

A variety of federal-level entities conduct audits of implantable medical device credit reporting. Among them are audits and focused medical reviews by Medicare Administrative Contractors (MACs); audits by Recovery Auditors (formerly known as Recovery Audit Contractors [RACs]); and audits conducted by a Quality Improvement Organization (QIO). Most of these entities, however, include implantable medical device credits reporting within the scope of a larger, more generalized effort to audit a provider's services. Examples include audits of inpatient claims with specific high-paying MS-DRGs; outpatient claims with procedures known to have high coding errors; and ASC claims associated with a specific surgeon or provider. The medical-device credit portion is simply "swept in" and, therefore, also scrutinized. Still, certain federal entities have intentionally targeted implantable-medical-device credit reporting, among them, HHS OIG.

Possible penalties for device-credit infractions uncovered by the OIG involve reimbursing CMS for each device credit that should have been reported, as well as the usual six-year retrospective audit typically leveraged by the OIG. Using an extrapolation algorithm, the OIG estimates the overpayments that result from claims with errors likely made during the specified retrospective timeframe and then assigns a monetary amount to that fiscal estimate.

In its auditing endeavors, the OIG specifically examines replacement procedures involving implantable medical devices, most notably cardiac procedures involving such devices as pacemakers and ICD systems. Prior OIG Annual Work Plan targets have included such items as "Hospitals: Payment Credits for Replaced Medical Devices That Were Implanted."[18] Another area related to device credits under current (active) audit is listed within the OIG Annual Work Plan as "Medicare Outpatient Outlier Payments for Claims with Credits for Replaced Medical Devices."[19]

Common findings emerge from various federal-level audits, particularly those performed by the OIG. They include:

- Implantable medical device credits not reported, with innumerable causes or reasons behind this finding ("credit not reported" is the most common audit finding)
- Miscalculation (i.e., under-calculation) of the 50%-or-greater reporting threshold
- Confusion around which devices are eligible for reporting and which are not
- Device line item not adjusted in relation to the credit amount
- UB-04 claim elements not reported or misreported (e.g., value code -FD inadvertently left off or device-credit dollar amount field not completed or inaccurately noted)
- ASC-only CMS-1500 claim elements not reported (e.g., reimbursement modifiers -FB or -FC)
- ASC-only reimbursement modifier appended to wrong claim line item (i.e., reported with HCPCS-II device code instead of the "anchoring" or main CPT procedure code)

With respect to the most common federal audit finding—not reporting the device credit at all—a few of the causes or reasons arise from (1) providers' uncertainty about when device credits are reported; (2) misinterpretation of the "50% or greater" threshold, particularly for replacement device credits involving systems such as pacemakers and ICDs; and quite often, (3) operational inattention or workflow laxities in monitoring and documenting received vendor credits. Relevant to the last reason, this error occurs most often when the healthcare provider has an off-campus or separated accounts payable (A/P) department, and the A/P representative processing the received device credit does not document or note the credit in the shared system as "received and processed." Thus, the device credit goes unnoticed by the hospital's device-credit workflow owners who are monitoring and reporting receipt of pending credits. The result is the processed credit is never reported.

Compliance Resources

Compliance officers should build and maintain an electronic library of all available information sources that will benefit the hospital or ASC, as well as keep assigned staff informed of yearly additions or deletions to the designated device-dependent procedures. Staying current on which devices qualify for reportable credits is crucial to staying in compliance with this mandate. If nothing else, all compliance officers should begin asking their compliance committee whether and how implantable device credits are handled and reported. That may trigger discussion, needed follow up, and corrective actions.

The electronic library assembled for implantable medical-device-credit reporting should include information about applicable laws and final rules; guidance materials; and the following reference materials:

Centers for Medicare & Medicaid Services

- *Medicare Learning Network* Fact Sheet: Cardiac Device Credits: Medicare Billing, May 2022[20] https://www.cms.gov/Outreach-and-Education/Medicare-Learning-Network-MLN/MLNProducts/Downloads/cardiacdevicecredits-ICN909368.pdf
- Annual and quarterly updates to IPPS, OPPS, and ASC published via change request/transmittal formats[21] https://www.cms.gov/Regulations-and-Guidance/Guidance/Transmittals
- Outpatient hospitals:
  - Hospital Outpatient Prospective Payment System[22] https://www.cms.gov/Medicare/Medicare-Fee-for-Service-Payment/HospitalOutpatientPPS
  - Hospital Outpatient Regulations and Notices[23] https://www.cms.gov/Medicare/Medicare-Fee-for-Service-Payment/HospitalOutpatientPPS/Hospital-Outpatient-Regulations-and-Notices
- Ambulatory surgery centers:
  - Ambulatory Surgical Centers (ASC) Center[24] https://www.cms.gov/Center/Provider-Type/Ambulatory-Surgical-Centers-ASC-Center

U.S. Department of Health & Human Services Office of Inspector General

Annual Work Plan
Review items related to credits for replaced medical devices.[25]

https://oig.hhs.gov/reports-and-publications/workplan/index.asp

"Hospitals Did Not Comply With Medicare Requirements For Reporting Cardiac Device Credits" November 2020, A-01-18-00502[26]

https://oig.hhs.gov/oas/reports/region1/11800502.asp

Risk Takeaways

Main points of interest:
- Designated implantable medical device credits, as categorized by setting (inpatient, outpatient, and ASC) must be reported to the Medicare program via the UB-04 or CMS-1500 claim forms in accordance with established reporting methodologies.
- Devices eligible for this reporting requirement are those related to "device-dependent" or "device-intensive" procedures (e.g., pacemaker insertion).
- Common denominator for reportable device credits eligible for this requirement: credit amount is 50% or greater of the replacement cost for the device.
- In rare instances, a newly placed free-of-charge or 100%-credited device implantation that is performed as an outpatient service must be reported per usual reporting protocols with CC-53.
- Identifying, tracking, monitoring, and reporting implantable device credits is a cross-departmental operational effort involving clinical staff, materials management, accounts payable personnel, billing or revenue cycle staff, and compliance representatives.
- Establish clear responsibilities for monitoring and auditing compliance requirements related to reporting implantable device credits. Document, document, document.

Areas to watch:
- Inpatient procedures involving devices identified by MS-DRGs and published annually in the IPPS Final Rule
- Outpatient procedures considered "device-dependent" identified by or published within addendums to the annual OPPS Final Rule
- ASC-approved procedures annually updated according to the same final rule as OPPS, with a special addendum listing all ASC procedures and further identified by designated "payment indicators"
- Clinical trials in the outpatient setting, especially those involving free-of-charge initially placed implantable medical devices, eligible for reporting per the Final Rule for OPPS

Laws that apply:
- Hospital Inpatient Prospective Payment System Final Rule
- Hospital Outpatient Prospective Payment System (OPPS) and the Medicare Ambulatory Surgical Center (ASC) Payment System Final Rule
- Cost Related to Patient Care (i.e., Prudent Buyer's Principle), 42 C.F.R. § 413.9
- Payment Adjustment for Certain Replaced Devices, 42 C.F.R. § 412.89

Addressing medical device credit compliance risks:

- Build a viable cross-departmental operational network or team to manage reportable device credits.
- Assign staff within that operational network to own individual segments of the device-credit identification, tracking, monitoring, and reporting workflow processes.
- Gain vendor or manufacturer support and cooperation.
- Compose a comprehensive policy-and-procedure document to address accurate, timely, and compliant device-credit reporting.
- Perform due diligence internal audits to ensure device-credit reporting compliance.
- Stay abreast of annual updates to reportable devices, device-credit thresholds, and changes in device-credit methodologies.

Endnotes

1. **Michael G. Calahan** is the vice president of HealthCare Consulting Solutions (HCS), a private healthcare consulting firm. He is a Certified Compliance Officer and performs engagements in health networks & systems, rural/critical access hospitals, and physician office arenas, as well as in the compliance sector for all "provider types" recognized by CMS (under Medicare Parts A & B). He also works in Medicare Parts C & D for Medicare Advantage and Hierarchical Condition Coding (HCC) compliance. With over 25 years' experience in healthcare, he has served in director- and administrator-level positions in both facility (hospital, health system) and physician private group practice roles, and has enjoyed a varied career in patient care and healthcare consulting. Calahan has authored numerous compliance industry books, publications, and articles for inpatient and outpatient health systems, physicians, and for federal and state healthcare compliance specialists, coders, and billers. He also performs national and jurisdictional seminars, webinars, and other public speaking events such as TV, radio, and podcast appearances for professional organizations such as AHIMA, HFMA, HCCA, state medical society and state hospital associations, and more. Holding various medical coding certifications since the early 1990s, Calahan is also an AHIMA-Approved ICD-10-CM/PCS trainer and expert.

2. 42 C.F.R. §§ 412.89, 419.45, 416.179.

3. U.S. Department of Health & Human Services Office of Inspector General, *Hospitals Did Not Comply with Medicare Requirements for Reporting Cardiac Device Credits*, November 2020, A-01-18-00502, https://oig.hhs.gov/oas/reports/region1/11800502.pdf.

4. Centers for Medicare & Medicaid Services, "Chapter 4: Part B Hospital (Including Inpatient Hospital Part B and OPPS)," Medicare Claims Processing Manual, § 20.6.9, Pub. 100-04, revised September 8, 2022, https://www.cms.gov/Regulations-and-Guidance/Guidance/Manuals/downloads/clm104c04.pdf.

5. Medicare and Medicaid Programs; Interim and Final Rule, 72 Fed. Reg. 66580 (November 27, 2007), https://www.govinfo.gov/content/pkg/FR-2007-11-27/pdf/07-5507.pdf.

6. Centers for Medicare & Medicaid Services, "Chapter 21: Costs Related to Patient Care," *The Provider Reimbursement Manual - Part 1*, Pub. 15-1, revised December 1, 2021, § 2102.1, https://www.cms.gov/Regulations-and-Guidance/Guidance/Manuals/Paper-Based-Manuals-Items/CMS021929.

7. Centers for Medicare & Medicaid Services, "Chapter 21: Costs Related to Patient Care," § 2103.A, *The Provider Reimbursement Manual - Part 1*, revised December 1, 2021, https://www.cms.gov/Regulations-and-Guidance/Guidance/Manuals/Paper-Based-Manuals-Items/CMS021929.

8. 42 C.F.R. § 419.45(a).

9. Centers for Medicare & Medicaid Services, "Chapter 4: Part B Hospital (Including Inpatient Hospital Part B and OPPS)," § 61.3.5, Medicare Claims Processing Manual, Pub. 100-04, revised September 8, 2022, https://www.cms.gov/Regulations-and-Guidance/Guidance/Manuals/downloads/clm104c04.pdf.

10. "CMS 1500," Centers for Medicare & Medicaid Services, revised February 1, 2012, https://www.cms.gov/Medicare/CMS-Forms/CMS-Forms/CMS-Forms-Items/CMS1188854.

11. Centers for Medicare & Medicaid Services, *January 2019 Update of the Hospital Outpatient Prospective Payment System (OPPS)*, MLN Matters 11099, revised January 18, 2019, https://www.cms.gov/Outreach-and-Education/Medicare-Learning-Network-MLN/MLNMattersArticles/downloads/MM11099.pdf.

12. 42 C.F.R. § 419.66(b)(1-3).

13. 42 C.F.R. § 419.66(b)(4).

14. Medicare Program; Hospital Inpatient Prospective Payment Systems for Acute Care Hospitals and the Long- Term Care Hospital Prospective Payment System and Policy Changes and Fiscal Year 2023 Rates; Quality Programs and Medicare Promoting Interoperability Program Requirements for Eligible Hospitals and Critical Access Hospitals; Costs Incurred for Qualified and Non-Qualified Deferred Compensation Plans; and Changes to Hospital and Critical Access Hospital Conditions of Participation, 87 Fed. Reg. 48780 (Aug. 10, 2022), https://www.federalregister.gov/documents/2022/08/10/2022-16472/medicare-program-hospital-inpatient-prospective-payment-systems-for-acute-care-hospitals-and-the.

15. Medicare Program: Hospital Outpatient Prospective Payment and Ambulatory Surgical Center Payment Systems and Quality Reporting Programs; Price Transparency of Hospital Standard Charges; Radiation Oncology Model, 86 Fed. Reg. 63458 (Nov. 16, 2021), https://www.federalregister.gov/documents/2021/11/16/2021-24011/medicare-program-hospital-outpatient-prospective-payment-and-ambulatory-surgical-center-payment.

16. "Medicare Outpatient Outlier Payments for Claims With Credits for Replaced Medical Devices," Centers for Medicare & Medicaid Services, accessed October 25, 2022, https://www.oig.hhs.gov/reports-and-publications/workplan/summary/wp-summary-0000340.asp .

17. Centers for Medicare & Medicaid Services, *Implementation of New National Uniform Billing Committee (NUBC) Condition Code "53" - "Initial Placement of A Medical Device Provided As Part of A Clinical Trial or A Free Sample,"* January 30, 2015, https://www.hhs.gov/guidance/document/implementation-new-national-uniform-billing-committee-nubc-condition-code-53-initial.

18. "Payment Credits for Replaced Medical Devices That Were Implanted," Work Plan, U.S. Department of Health & Human Services Office of Inspector General, accessed October 25, 2022, https://oig.hhs.gov/reports-and-publications/workplan/summary/wp-summary-0000085.asp.

19. "Medicare Outpatient Outlier Payments for Claims With Credits for Replaced Medical Devices," Centers for Medicare & Medicaid Services Office of Inspector General, accessed October 25, 2022, https://www.oig.hhs.gov/reports-and-publications/workplan/summary/wp-summary-0000340.asp.

20. Centers for Medicare & Medicaid Services, *Cardiac Device Credits: Medicare Billing*, MLN Matters Fact Sheet, May 2022, https://www.cms.gov/Outreach-and-Education/Medicare-Learning-Network-MLN/MLNProducts/Downloads/cardiacdevicecredits-ICN909368.pdf.

21. "Transmittals," Centers for Medicare & Medicaid Services, last modified December 1, 2021, https://www.cms.gov/Regulations-and-Guidance/Guidance/Transmittals.

22. "Hospital Outpatient PPS," Centers for Medicare & Medicaid Services, last modified October 14, 2022,https://www.cms.gov/Medicare/Medicare-Fee-for-Service-Payment/HospitalOutpatientPPS.

23. "Hospital Outpatient Regulations and Notices," Centers for Medicare & Medicaid Services, last modified December 1, 2021, https://www.cms.gov/Medicare/Medicare-Fee-for-Service-Payment/HospitalOutpatientPPS/Hospital-Outpatient-Regulations-and-Notices.

24. "Ambulatory Surgical Centers (ASC) Center," Centers for Medicare & Medicaid Services, last modified December 1, 2021, https://www.cms.gov/Center/Provider-Type/Ambulatory-Surgical-Centers-ASC-Center.

25. "Work Plan," U.S. Department of Health & Human Services Office of Inspector General, accessed October 25, 2022, https://oig.hhs.gov/reports-and-publications/workplan/index.asp.

26. U.S. Department of Health & Human Services Office of Inspector General, *Hospitals Did Not Comply with Medicare Requirements for Reporting Cardiac Device Credits*, A-01-18-00502, November 2020, https://oig.hhs.gov/oas/reports/region1/11800502.pdf.

Surprise Billing and the No Surprises Act

By Dan Roach[1] and Zackary Weiss[2]

What Is Surprise Billing and the No Surprises Act?

When patients see providers, they may need to pay out-of-pocket costs, even if they have health insurance. These costs may be for a co-pay, deductible, or coinsurance. If the patient visits a provider outside of their health plan's network, the patient may have to pay the entire bill. Or an out-of-network provider may bill a patient for the difference between what the plan agrees to pay and the full cost of care. These kinds of payments are expected in healthcare, but some bills far exceed a patient's expectations.

This results in surprise billing. These bills might be for services the patient thought would be covered by insurance or for uninsured patients. Another source of a surprise bill is when a patient is unexpectedly treated during an emergency situation, such as an accident or sudden illness. Surprise bills often happen when a patient has no control over their care. These surprise bills have happened to many people, too. Ultimately, if consumers have health coverage and receive care from an out-of-network provider, their health plan usually wouldn't cover the entire out-of-network cost, causing surprise billing.[3]

A 2018 University of Chicago survey found that 57% of adult Americans have received some kind of surprise bill.[4] Other studies show that surprise billing results from emergency room visits, elective surgeries, childbirth-related costs, and air-ambulance services.[5] The Peterson-KFF Health System Tracker and other studies have found this happens in about one in five emergency room visits.[6] In addition, 9%–16% of in-network hospitalizations for nonemergency care include surprise bills from out-of-network providers (i.e., anesthesiologists) not chosen by the patient.[7]

Surprise bills have long been a significant pain point for patients, and this issue has had the attention of Congress and policy makers for quite some time. While findings vary, most cited studies indicate that medical costs contribute to somewhere between one-third and two-thirds of all bankruptcies.[8] Even outside of bankruptcy, unplanned and surprise medical bills create serious financial challenges for millions of families every year. The problems seem most prevalent in the context of emergency services for uninsured patients, but also there has been extensive concern about bills of insured patients who find that one or more of their caregivers within a facility is out-of-network, even though the hospital or other provider was "in network."

On December 27, 2020, the Consolidated Appropriations Act (CAA), which includes the No Surprises Act (NSA), was enacted.[9] The NSA represents the culmination of years of bipartisan efforts to address surprise billing at the federal level, particularly for uninsured and self-pay patients and for insured patients navigating the in-network versus out-of-network challenges. The NSA directs departments to specify the information that a plan or insurer must share with a nonparticipating provider, nonparticipating emergency facility, or nonparticipating provider of air-ambulance services, as applicable, after determining the qualified payment amount (QPA).

Implementation of the law began on January 1, 2022, although enforcement of some of the law's requirements was deferred to give both payers and providers an opportunity to develop plans and processes, and to acquire the resources to comply (provided those payers and providers are engaged in good faith efforts to meet the law's requirements in the interim). The U.S. Department of Health & Human Services (HHS) has indicated that it will step up enforcement efforts in 2023.[10]

The NSA will apply to most surprise bills but focuses on three main types of services: emergency services, post-emergency stabilization services, and nonemergency services provided at in-network facilities. Surprise billing protections apply to most emergency services, including emergency departments, freestanding emergency departments, and urgent care centers that are licensed to provide emergency care. The NSA also includes post-stabilization care as emergency care until a physician determines the patient can travel safely to another in-network facility using nonmedical transport—and that the facility will accept the patient. Lastly, nonemergency services provided at in-network facilities include doctors who work in hospitals but don't work *for* the hospital. These physicians bill independently and do not necessarily participate in the same health plan networks.[11]

Risk Area Governance

The NSA is federal legislation aimed at improving healthcare cost transparency and reducing the risk that patients will be hit with unexpected medical bills.[12] The law addresses surprise medical bills for both insured and uninsured patients and adds significant protections for the consumer. It includes new obligations for both healthcare providers (including hospitals, free-standing emergency departments, surgery centers, physician offices, and air-ambulance services) and health plans (payers). Among other things, the NSA:

- Imposes coverage and payment requirements on health plans related to patients receiving emergency services at either in-network or out-of-network facilities
- Limits billing by out-of-network providers working at an in-network facility for the patient, particularly in the ancillary services context.
- Requires certain insured patients to be notified of expected charges from out-of-network-providers practicing at an in-network facility (notice and consent).
- Requires a good faith estimate to be provided to uninsured (persons without insurance) and self-pay (insured people choosing not to use their insurance) patients for scheduled services
- Limits the amount that can be billed to uninsured and self-pay patients
- Establishes two separate dispute resolution mechanisms to resolve payer-provider disputes and disputes when uninsured and self-pay patient bills vary from the good faith estimate by more than $400 (patient-provider disputes).[13]

It should also be noted that states will be the primary enforcers of the NSA, although the Center for Medicare & Medicaid Services (CMS) can take over enforcement if a state's enforcement is deemed inadequate. According to The Commonwealth Fund, nearly two-thirds of states have some type of law addressing coverage and billing of healthcare services.[14] However, these laws are inconsistent, and states are also unable to regulate self-funded health plans. The NSA closes the self-funded plan gap and creates a floor for dealing with surprise billing, while continuing to permit more restrictive state laws. Particularly for providers with a large geographic footprint, this may create implementation challenges as the standards and requirements can vary from state to state.

Common Compliance Risks

Failure to Provide Proper Notice and Consent

Prior to the NSA, if a provider or facility delivered medical services to an out-of-network patient, the common practice was to send the patient a bill for the cost of whatever services the patient's insurance would not cover. Under the NSA, insured patients seeking nonemergency services at an in-network facility are entitled to be notified of and agree to charges that may be attributable to out-of-network providers (typically physicians or other individual providers) working within the in-network facility. This notification is the "notice and consent.") Fortunately, HHS has provided templated forms for this and other required notices under the NSA that can easily be adopted for hospital or physician clinic use.[15] Out-of-network providers must provide written notice of the costs within 72 hours of the item or service being delivered and obtain consent from the patient.

At a minimum, the written notice must contain:

- Notification that the provider is out-of-network
- A good faith estimate of the charges that will be incurred for the item or service
- A list of in-network providers at the facility (if the facility is in-network)
- Information on prior authorization or other care-management requirements
- A clear statement that consent is optional and that the patient can choose an in-network provider instead, if they wish[16]

Failure to Notify Consumers by Public Disclosures

Providers and plans must also notify consumers of their surprise medical bill protections through public disclosures. Providers and facilities must post a one-page disclosure notice that summarizes NSA protections on a public website and give this disclosure to each patient for whom they provide NSA-covered services. Information in the notice should be written in plain language and include federal restrictions on providers and facilities regarding the act; any applicable state law protections against balance billing; and contact information for federal and state agencies where patients may report any violations.[17]

Billing Insured Patients for Ancillary Services in Excess of Their Applicable Cost-sharing Amount

NSA rules prohibit billing certain ancillary services in excess of the insured patient's cost-sharing amount, regardless of whether the notice and consent is provided. Furthermore, provider organizations need to adjust their billing processes so that the health plan—not the patient—is the first point of contact for an outstanding balance.[18]

Failure to Provide a Timely and Accurate Good Faith Estimate

Uninsured and self-pay patients are entitled to a good faith estimate that informs the patient of expected charges. Good faith estimates should be provided to patients seeking care who are uninsured or are opting to self-pay. [19] If the charges exceed the amount stated in the good faith estimate by more than $400, the patient has the right to use the dispute resolution process administer by HHS.[20] CMS provides a model good faith estimate form on its website for facilities and providers to use.[21]

Multiple providers may provide a single notice to patients, so long as the following requirements are met: (1) each provider's name is specifically listed on the notice document; (2) each provider includes in the notice a good faith estimate for the items and services they are furnishing, and the notice specifies which provider is providing which items and services within the good faith estimate; and (3) the individual has the option to consent to waive balance billing protections with respect to each provider separately.[22]

Addressing Compliance Risks

Addressing NSA compliance risks requires careful adherence to HHS rules, forms, and processes. HHS has provided significant guidance in the form of rules, tools, FAQs, and forms to help assist health plans with implementation. While implementing the foregoing will be challenging, perhaps the biggest challenges may be coordinating with other providers, funding additional staff necessary to provide the notice and consent or good faith estimates, and navigating the payer/provider and patient/provider dispute resolution processes.

Possible Penalties

Failing to timely and properly implement the law's requirements could have significant financial implications as well as reputational impacts on both providers and payers. States have a primary role in enforcing NSA rules against health providers, with federal enforcement as back up. These impacts include the following.

Financial Penalties

The NSA imposes civil monetary penalties of up to $10,000 per violation on providers and health plans that fail to follow the law.[23] Violations can take a variety of forms, including failing to timely provide the required notice and consent or good faith estimate, billing a patient more than is permitted for ancillary services, and holding a patient accountable for an incorrect payment amount. As of late 2022, it is too early to tell how aggressive HHS and states will be in enforcing the requirements; however, based on the very limited enforcement activities to-date, it does not appear that providers or payers can afford to ignore the requirements.

Revenue Loss

Failure to provide patients with a timely and accurate notice and consent in the case of an insured patient (who may receive services from an out-of-network provider) or a timely and accurate good faith estimate (in the case of the uninsured/self-pay patient) may limit the provider's ability to collect on its bills.

Reputational Damage

Fines for noncompliance with NSA requirements will be public, as will the results from audits or investigations conducted by states or CMS. Any failure to adhere to NSA requirements will likely result in negative press for the health plan and/or the provider.

Compliance Resources

Centers for Medicare & Medicaid Services

Ending Surprise Medical Bills
On this site are resources for consumers and providers about the No Surprises Act, resolving out-of-network payment disputes, and policies and fact sheets about the act.

https://www.cms.gov/nosurprises

Standard Notice and Consent Documents Under the No Surprises Act
These standard NSA notice and consent forms were developed by HHS. Two versions are included—one for use only in 2022 and another for use in 2022 and beyond.

https://www.cms.gov/files/document/standard-notice-consent-forms-nonparticipating-providers-emergency-facilities-regarding-consumer.pdf

---

Risk Takeaways

Main points of interest:
- The No Surprises Act was signed into law in 2020 and represents the culmination of years of bipartisan efforts to address surprise billing at the federal level, particularly for uninsured and self-pay patients and for insured patients navigating the in-network versus out-of-network challenges.
- The law applies to healthcare facilities, providers, group health plans, or health insurance issuers and is designed to protect consumers from certain out-of-network charges relating to services obtained at an in-network facility and excessive bills for uninsured and self-pay patients seeking scheduled services.

Areas to watch:
- Failure to provide proper notice and consent
- Failure to notify consumers by public disclosures

- Billing an insured patient for ancillary services in excess of the patient's applicable cost sharing amount
- Failure to provide a timely and accurate good faith estimate

Laws that apply:
- No Surprises Act, Public Law No. 116-260, 134 Stat. 1182, Division BB, § 109. Applicable regulations are found in 45 C.F.R. § 149.
- Various state laws: Many states, including California and Colorado, for example, have laws that address the topic of surprise bills. Understanding the interplay between the NSA and state law can be challenging and may require input from competent legal counsel.

Addressing compliance risks:
- The law and rules are too new to have been the subject of many enforcement actions. At this point, activities aimed at mitigating compliance risks need to focus on creating provider or payer processes to effectively implement the rules, monitoring HHS pronouncements as it issues new or revised rules, and monitoring enforcement activity for clues on where HHS and/or states will direct enforcement resources.

Endnotes

1. Dan Roach is a compliance officer and attorney with 38 years of healthcare provider experience as an attorney, general counsel, compliance officer, and in other roles that no one wanted. He is also a past HCCA president and board member.
2. Zackary Weiss is a litigation associate at Nelson Mullins Riley and Scarborough. Zack's practice focusses on business and healthcare litigation. He is a previous author of the Complete Healthcare Compliance Manual 2022.
3. "Surprise Billing & Protecting Consumers," Centers for Medicare & Medicaid Services, last modified January 14, 2022, https://www.cms.gov/nosurprises/Ending-Surprise-Medical-Bills.
4. NORC at the University of Chicago, *NORC AmeriSpeak Omnibus Survey: Surprise Medical Bills*, NORC, August 16, 2018, https://www.norc.org/PDFs/Health%20 Care%20Surveys/Surprise%20Bills%20Survey%20 August%202018%20Topline.pdf.
5. U.S. Department of Health & Human Services, Assistant Secretary for Planning and Evaluation, Office of Health Policy, *Evidence of Surprise Billing: Protecting Consumers with the No Surprise Act*, HP-2021-24, November 22, 2021, https://aspe.hhs.gov/sites/default/ files/documents/acfa063998d25b3b4eb82ae159163575/ no-surprises-act-brief.pdf.
6. Karen Pollitz, *No Surprises Act Implementation: What to Expect in 2022*, Kaiser Family Foundation, Issue Brief, December 10, 2021, https://www.kff.org/health-reform/ issue-brief/no-surprises-act-implementation-what-to-expect-in-2022/.
7. Pollitz, *No Surprises Act Implementation*.
8. David U. Himmelstein, Robert M. Lawless, Deborah Thorne, et al., Medical Bankruptcy: Still Common Despite the Affordable Care Act, *American Journal of Public Health* 109, no. 3, (March 2019): 431, https://www. ncbi.nlm.nih.gov/pmc/articles/PMC6366487/.
9. No Surprises Act, Pub. L. No. 116-260, 134 Stat. 1182, Division BB, § 109.
10. Pollitz, *No Surprises Act Implementation*.
11. Pollitz, *No Surprises Act Implementation*.
12. No Surprises Act, Pub. L. No. 116-260, 134 Stat. 1182, Division BB, § 109,
13. "Overview of rules & fact sheets," Centers for Medicare & Medicaid Services, last modified December 13, 2022, https://www.cms.gov/nosurprises/policies-and-resources/overview-of-rules-fact-sheets.
14. Madeline O'Brian, "Map: No Surprises Act Enforcement," The Commonwealth Fund, updated September 6, 2022, https://www.commonwealthfund. org/publications/maps-and-interactives/2022/feb/map-no-surprises-act.

15. U.S. Centers for Medicare & Medicaid Services, *Standard Notice and Consent Documents Under the No Surprises Act,* OMB Control Number: 0938-1401, accessed December 15, 2022, https://www.cms.gov/files/document/standard-notice-consent-forms-nonparticipating-providers-emergency-facilities-regarding-consumer.pdf.

16. U.S. Centers for Medicare & Medicaid Services, *Standard Notice and Consent Documents Under the No Surprises Act,* OMB Control Number: 0938-1401, accessed December 15, 2022, https://www.cms.gov/files/document/standard-notice-consent-forms-nonparticipating-providers-emergency-facilities-regarding-consumer.pdf.

17. 45 C.F.R. § 149.430.

18. "What Does the No Surprises Act Mean for Providers?," *Symplr* (blog), December 23, 2021, https://www.symplr.com/blog/no-surprises-act-for-providers.

19. 45 C.F.R. § 149.610.

20. Centers for Medicare & Medicaid, Center for Consumer Information & Insurance Oversight, *The No Surprises Act's Good Faith Estimates and Patient-Provider Dispute Resolution Requirements,* CMS, April 24, 2022, https://www.cms.gov/files/document/gfe-and-ppdr-requirements-slides.pdf.

21. Centers for Medicare & Medicaid Services, *Standard Form: "Good Faith Estimate for Health Care Items and Services" Under the No Surprises Act,* OMB Control Number: 0938-NEW, October 7, 2021, https://www.cms.gov/files/document/good-faith-estimate-example.pdf.

22. Requirements Related to Surprise Billing; Part I, 86 Fed. Reg. 36,872 (July 13, 2021).

23. Requirements Related to Air Ambulance Services, Agent and Broker Disclosures, and Provider Enforcement, 86 Fed. Reg. 51730, (Sept. 16, 2021).

Vendor Management

Monitoring Contractor Performance and Proactive Risk Management

By Jiajia Veronica Xu,[1] Esq., CHC, CHPC, CCEP

Why Is it Necessary to Monitor Performance and Manage Risks with Vendors?

Regardless of an organization's line of business, it most likely has vendors that render services or supply goods to support an organization's operations. Vendors, who are generally bound by regulatory requirements and contractual terms and conditions, are essentially the business partners of the organization. To err is human, and vendors are no exception. Although vendors are separate legal entities, their mistakes and errors (including their accidents, incidents, or system breakdowns) can cause significant disruptions and catastrophic damages (i.e., financial, legal, reputational) to an organization's business operations and performance, not to mention the impacts on customers and clients. Debt collection agency Professional Finance Company, Inc., for example, reported in July 2022 that its data breach affected 657 clients (healthcare providers) and involved almost 2 million patients' records.[23]

Maintaining proper vendor contracts and knowing the legal obligations are of paramount importance, especially in the event of an incident, so that organizations can ensure regulatory requirements are met, patients protected, and damage mitigated. Business associates are individuals or entities who are not employed by the covered entity but who are given access to protected health information (PHI) to perform certain functions on behalf of the covered entity. If their work includes creating, receiving, maintaining, or transmitting PHI, they are required to sign a business associate agreement (BAA).[4] Although contracts generally are written based on contracting parties' particular needs and circumstances, BAAs have specific legal provisions that must be included. Among these are the scope of the business associate's use and disclosure of the PHI; the appropriate safeguard measures that the business associate implements to protect the PHI; and the business associate's obligation to report any breaches.[5] Given the amount of scrutiny from oversight agencies and the statutory mandates, properly managed vendor contracts are crucial to any organization's compliance with laws and regulations.

Not only will having a comprehensive vendor management program help organizations meet certain legal requirements, it also but will reduce risk exposure, save time by allowing organizations to address issues in a timely fashion, and mitigate any potential damages.

Risk Area Governance

In the healthcare sector, laws and regulations that govern an organization's operations and practices would generally extend to vendors who provide services or goods on behalf of or to the organization, such as exclusion screening, patient privacy and information security, conflicts of interest, and the quality of goods or services. Several laws affect different aspects of vendor management, including exclusion screening, patient privacy and information security, conflicts of interest, and the quality of goods or services.

The Exclusion Statute, 42 U.S.C. § 1320a-7 and 42 U.S.C. § 1320c-5

This federal law prohibits excluded individuals or entities from participating in any federal healthcare program. Failure to comply with the law may lead to the imposition of civil monetary penalties on healthcare providers that employ or contract with excluded individuals or entities for items or services provided to federal program beneficiaries.[6] Penalties can equal up to $10,000 for each item or service furnished by the excluded individual or entity, as well as an assessment of up to three times the amount claimed.[7]

Health Insurance Portability and Accountability Act, Pub. L. No. 104–191

Although the scope of services and transactions are usually governed by legal contracts between the parties, not all vendors are created equal. Depending on the services and supplies rendered, there are different types of vendors who may not be subject to the same standards, rules and laws. For example, a landscaper or a plumber hired by an organization is not facing the same legal requirements as the organization's radiologist or pharmacist. Various laws and regulations may apply. For example, if a vendor performs work involving the use, transmission, and disclosure of patient PHI on behalf of a healthcare organization, the vendor is likely considered a business associate of the organization. Under the Health Insurance Portability and Accountability Act (HIPAA) Privacy Rule, healthcare organizations (often referred to as covered entities) are required to "enter into written contracts ... with business associates which *protect the privacy of protected health information*" and the healthcare organization can only disclose PHI to a business associate if the appropriate business associate agreement is duly executed.[89] Generally, healthcare organizations are not liable for their vendors' conduct. However, if a covered entity is aware of its business associate's material breach or violation of the contract, "it must take reasonable steps to cure the breach or end the violation, and, if unsuccessful, terminate the contract with the business associate."[10] When termination is not feasible, "the covered entity must report the problem to the Department of Health and Human Services [HHS] Office for Civil Rights."[11] In addition, the Health Information Technology for Economic and Clinical Health Act (HITECH) and the Omnibus Rule also extended HIPAA's privacy and security rules by imposing liabilities and penalties on business associates.

Anti-Kickback Statute, 42 U.S.C. § 1320a–7b(b), and the Physician Self-Referral Law, 42 U.S.C. § 1395nn

In the process of rendering care to patients, healthcare organizations may interact with various types of vendors, which may include other physician practice groups, pharmaceutical companies, and medical device suppliers. Those vendor relations can become problematic if not handled properly; they could involve questionable practices or even illegal activities. Federal laws govern the issue of conflicts of interest. Specifically, the federal Anti-Kickback Statute prohibits the payment or receipt of any remuneration intended to "induce or reward patient referrals or the generation of business involving any item or service payable by the federal healthcare programs."[12] Recently, a distributor of spinal implant devices agreed to pay $1 million to resolve a lawsuit against them. The U.S. Department of Justice Department (DOJ) alleged that the distributor paid physicians to use the medical devices and that the physician-owned distributorships were allegedly vehicles for the payment of kickbacks to induce physicians to use the medical devices in their surgeries. The Anti-Kickback Statute prohibits offering or paying anything of value to encourage the referral of items or services covered by federal healthcare programs.[13] In addition, the Physician Self-Referral Law (Stark Law) prohibits healthcare providers from making referrals to other organizations in which the provider has a financial interest.[14]

False Claims Act, 31 U.S.C. §§ 3729-3733

This federal law may be applied in cases where claims submitted to Medicare or Medicaid for payment are false or fraudulent. The claims can include goods and services. Under this law, no specific intent is required. The standard the law sets is whether the healthcare organization knows or should have known the falsity or fraudulent nature of the claims. If the organization possessed the actual knowledge of the falsity of the claims or acted in deliberate ignorance or reckless disregard of the truth of the claims, then the organization will be held liable.[15] In other words, if an organization is aware that goods or services rendered by its vendor are substandard and the organization fails to rectify the situation, penalties may be imposed on the organization.

Common Compliance Risks

Lack of Policies and Procedures

Having policies and procedures is the first key element of an effective compliance program; they establish a framework and set expectations for teams to follow, as well as provide guidance and ensure consistent practices. When an organization lacks policies or procedures governing vendor management (i.e., vendor screening, criminal background checks, onboarding, contract review, training, etc.), a huge potential exists for inconsistent processes, incomplete vendor information, and missing essential documentation, among other issues.

Lack of Effective Contract Management

Because of the nature of the industry, healthcare organizations must adhere to stringent rules and regulations. As a result, healthcare providers are under an enormous amount of scrutiny from oversight agencies. Contracting is a crucial part of vendor management; it outlines legal obligations and contractual responsibilities by which both parties must abide. Some common issues with vendor management include:

- **Lack of contracts**: Treating and caring for people seems to be in the DNA of healthcare providers, but managing contracts may not be their forte. One area of weakness is the lack of fully executed contracts between healthcare organizations and their vendors. When medical services and supplies are urgently needed, signing contracts is not always the first thing on providers' minds. Ensuring they have a gatekeeper designated to oversee contract execution can be easily overlooked.
- **Lack of critical contractual provisions**: Oftentimes, contracts fail to include key provisions pertaining to vendors' reporting obligations, including reporting to governmental authorities or the organization. For example, if a vendor identifies a system security breach leading to patient information being compromised, the vendor should be required to promptly notify the organization of the breach upon discovery. Missing such a requirement could cause the organization to lose valuable time to double-check its system, as well as implement necessary measures to safeguard its data and prevent further systematic issues.
- **Disorganized contracts**: Having fully executed contracts is not the answer to all the issues—having disorganized contracts with no process or system to manage them can be just as disastrous as not having contracts at all. Organizations can either implement a process internally or deploy an external software-based platform to monitor, maintain contracts, accurately and effectively capture data, and provide real-time information to the organizations when needed. Regardless of whether developed in-house or outsourced, contracts and their duration should be tracked on a continuous basis. Types of contracts include service agreements, confidentiality and non-disclosure agreements, and business associate agreements.

Lack of Process and Ongoing Monitoring

It is not uncommon to see organizations struggle to accurately locate vendor information or pull contract history. At issue is a lack of a holistic and comprehensive process for system integration. From vendor screening and criminal background checks to the ongoing monitoring of vendors' exclusion status, among other things, an integrated system and proper measures should exist to ensure all the boxes are checked. In addition, monitoring the quality of the work that vendors perform is another vital piece that should not be overlooked. Whether a vendor is providing billing, coding, or staffing services, the healthcare organization should establish processes to monitor and audit the work completed by vendors to ensure quality and compliance. After all, vendor management is a process that involves many moving parts, all of which are critical to the health and success of an organization's long-term growth and business development.

Lack of Vendor Training

For many healthcare providers, signing a contract with a vendor seems to be the end of the vendor management process. In fact, it is just the beginning of a business partnership. Engaging a vendor is not a one-and-done task. Instead, it is an ongoing collaboration that requires continual attention and effective communication. Training, including orientation, is a form of communication through which organizations share and reiterate their expectations, legal requirements, company values, mission, and the compliance program to vendors—which creates a foundation for better mutual understanding and level of compliance. With the ever-evolving regulatory environment, providing periodic vendor training is an effective way to update vendors on legal and regulatory changes, as well as refresh their knowledge about the organization's commitment to compliance.

Addressing Compliance Risks

Policies and Procedures

Establishing comprehensive policies and procedures builds a solid foundation for managing vendors and the risks associated with vendor business dealings. Having standardized steps and consistent guidance will make it easier for frontline teams to remain compliant and will also facilitate the compliance team's continuing review, evaluation, and improvement of overall processes.

Designated Personnel

Without clear designation of duties, it is tremendously difficult to ascertain systematic breakdowns or hold anyone accountable for those breakdowns. Thus, it is imperative that the organization designate appropriate personnel with adequate authority, knowledge, and experience to oversee and manage vendor management process, including but not limited to, vendor information intake, screening, contracting, and training.

Cross-Functional Collaboration

Vendor management is never a one-department or one-person job. Rather, it is a complex project with multiple facets of operational functions, such as accounts payable, purchasing, legal, and contracting. Collaboration among teams and departments (i.e., accounting, legal, purchasing, and procurement) intimately involved in vendor communications and interactions plays a vital role in the long-lasting success of an organization's vendor management process.

Vendor Onboarding, Orientation, and Periodic Training

As a third party, vendors are not necessarily familiar with a healthcare organization's legal obligations, internal controls, expectations, or compliance program. Incorporating orientation and training into vendor onboarding is an effective way to communicate the organization's requirements and expectations. Ensuring vendor understanding of the organization's culture builds a stronger foundation for a mutually beneficial and long-term partnership. Periodic training (at least on an annual basis) is equally important. A yearly refresher can help reinforce a vendor's knowledge of the healthcare organization's commitment to compliance and reiterate the importance of meeting certain legal requirements.

Documentation of Vendor Screening and Training

Documenting vendor screening—including exclusion status and criminal background checks—serves as evidence of a healthcare organization's adherence to laws, regulations, and internal policies. Moreover, vendor completion of any training (i.e., on the compliance program, Physician Self-Referral Law [Stark Law], or Anti-Kickback Statute) provided by the healthcare organization should also be captured and documented—whether on paper or in an electronic format. Failure to maintain documentation will hinder an organization's ability to demonstrate compliance.

Vendor Risk Assessment

Conduct risk assessments on all vendors. Having all vendors undergo this routine exercise will enable healthcare organizations to stay abreast of the risks that their vendors could potentially pose to the organization, including conflicts of interest, patient referrals, and system security measures. In addition, completing vendor risk assessments demonstrates that the healthcare organization exercised due diligence by performing vendor oversight activities.

Periodic Audits

Auditing is one of the primary responsibilities of a compliance team. Because each organization's operational and management structures vary, different teams may be involved in and responsible for the audit process. When it comes to vendor management, several areas should be reviewed and audited, including but not limited to whether the following are in place:

1. Vendor information (i.e., its legal name, mailing address, or tax identification number) is complete in the system;
2. Documentation shows that criminal background checks and exclusion screenings were conducted prior to engaging the vendor to perform work;
3. Required vendor credentials, certifications, and qualifications are kept on file;
4. Necessary legal documents (i.e., service agreement, business associate agreement, or confidentiality and nondisclosure agreement) have been duly signed by authorized representatives;
5. The vendor completed the onboarding process and orientation;
6. Active vendors have completed periodic training assigned by the healthcare organization;
7. The vendor is performing the services in accordance with applicable federal and state laws, regulations, and the healthcare organization's policies; and
8. The vendor completes the job in a timely fashion and the quality of work meets the healthcare organization's expectations and industry standards.

Possible Penalties

Vendor noncompliance can lead to serious consequences and various penalties, including stiff fines, program exclusions, and criminal prosecution. Therefore, it is essential that compliance officers monitor vendor risks related to exclusion, fraudulent claims, physician kickbacks, incorrect billing, and patient privacy and security.

Exclusion-Related Penalties

Pursuant to sections 1128 and 1156 of the Social Security Act, the HHS Office of Inspector General (OIG) is given the authority to exclude individuals and entities from participating in federal healthcare programs.[16] Violation of OIG exclusion may lead to stiff penalties. According to section 1128A(a)(1)(D) of the Social Security Act, an excluded individual or entity that submits a claim for reimbursement to a federal healthcare program, or causes such a claim to be submitted, may be subject to a civil monetary penalty of $10,000 for each item or service furnished during the period that the person or entity was excluded.[17] The individual or entity may also be subject to treble damages for the amount claimed for each item or service.[18] In addition, program exclusion may also be imposed.[19]

Physician Self-Referral Law (Stark Law) Penalties

Because the Physician Self-Referral Law (Stark Law) is a strict liability statute, proof of specific intent to violate the law is not required. The law prohibits the submission, or causing the submission, of claims in violation of the law's restrictions on referrals. Penalties for physicians who violate this law include fines as well as exclusion from participating in federal healthcare programs.

Anti-Kickback Statute Penalties

The Anti-Kickback Statute includes both criminal penalties and administrative sanctions for violations, including fines, jail terms, and exclusion from participating in federal healthcare programs.[20] Under the Civil Monetary Penalties Law, physicians who pay or accept kickbacks also face penalties of up to $50,000 per kickback plus three times the amount of the remuneration.[21]

False Claims Act Penalties

Under the civil False Claims Act, each instance of an item or a service billed to Medicare or Medicaid counts as a claim. Filing false claims may result in "fines of up to three times the programs' loss plus $5,000 to $10,000 per claim filed."[22] Furthermore, under the criminal False Claims Act, criminal penalties for submitting false claims include imprisonment and criminal fines.[23] OIG can also impose administrative civil monetary penalties for false or fraudulent claims.[24]

HIPAA Penalties

For non-compliant organizations and their business associates, the HHS Office for Civil Rights may impose fines for HIPAA violations.[25] These penalties may include a corrective action plan, settlement agreement, and governmental monitoring for a set period of time. In addition, HIPAA also contains criminal provisions, which means an individual or entity can be prosecuted under the law for their criminal conduct.

Compliance Resources

U.S. Department of Health & Human Services Office of Inspector General

Exclusions Database
OIG maintains and publishes the List of Excluded Individuals/Entities (LEIE), which names individuals and entities prohibited from participating in federal healthcare programs. Healthcare providers should check vendors against the LEIE prior to hiring them.

https://exclusions.oig.hhs.gov/

Exclusion FAQs
The site lists answers to commonly asked questions pertaining to exclusions.

https://oig.hhs.gov/faqs/exclusions-faq.asp

Federal Register
This government publication outlines and explains regulatory requirements and expectations.

https://oig.hhs.gov/documents/compliance-guidance/793/nhg_fr.pdf

Fraud & Abuse Laws
OIG provides a brief overview of the fraud and abuse laws, including the False Claims Act, the Anti-Kickback Statute, the Physician Self-Referral Law, the Exclusion Authorities, and the Civil Monetary Penalties Law.

https://oig.hhs.gov/compliance/physician-education/fraud-abuse-laws/

Physician Self-Referral Guidance

The Centers for Medicare and Medicaid Services issued guidance on the scope and application of the Physician Self-Referral Law (Stark Law).

https://www.hhs.gov/guidance/document/physician-self-referral

General Services Administration's System for Award Management

System for Award Management Exclusion Database
Healthcare providers can use this search exclusions on this site to ensure that vendors they engage are not excluded by this agency.

https://sam.gov/content/exclusions/federal

Risk Takeaways

Main points of interest:
- Vendor management is a complex process that involves and directly affects multiple aspects of business operations.
- Without proper measures or systems in place, vendors may pose enormous risks that could cause significant operational disruptions and lead to irreparable damages to healthcare organizations.
- An integrated and holistic approach to managing vendors will help reduce and minimize healthcare organizations' exposure to legal, financial, and ethical liabilities.

Areas to watch:
- Vendor screening, including criminal background checks and exclusion screening
- Vendor intake process and onboarding
- Safeguard measures implemented by vendors to protect patient privacy and information security
- Conflicts of interest
- Quality of goods and services provided by vendors
- Contracting
- Vendor training

Laws that apply:
- The Exclusion Statute, 42 U.S.C. § 1320a-7 and 42 U.S.C. § 1320c-5
- Physician Self-Referral Law, 42 U.S.C. § 1395nn
- Anti-Kickback Statute, 42 U.S.C. § 1320a-7b
- False Claims Act, 31 U.S.C. §§ 3729-3733
- Health Insurance Portability and Accountability Act, Pub. L. 104-191

Addressing vendor management compliance risks:
- Establish comprehensive policies and procedures regarding vendor management.
- Designate appropriate personnel to manage and oversee the vendor management process.
- Collaborate with teams and departments that interact, communicate and work with vendors.
- Provide vendor onboarding, orientation and periodic training and maintain documentation.
- Complete vendor screening and vendor risk assessments.
- Conduct periodic audits.

Endnotes

1. Jiajia Veronica Xu, Esq., CHC, CHPC, CCEP, is the Chief Compliance Officer for Saber Healthcare Group headquartered in Cleveland, Ohio. Veronica manages the organization's compliance program and oversees the compliance performance of 115+ long-term care facilities across seven states. As an active member of healthcare associations and the compliance community, Veronica is a voluminous author of many articles regarding various regulatory requirements, and she has also been frequently invited by different organizations to provide insights on a wide range of compliance topics.

2. Heather Landi, "More than 600 Providers Impacted By Ransomware Attack on Payment Vendor,"*Fierce Health Tech*, July 8, 2022, https://www.fiercehealthcare.com/health-tech/more-600-providers-impacted-ransomware-attack-payment-vendor.

3. Rebecca Pifer, "Data Breach at Debt Collector Affects Almost 2M Healthcare Patients," *Cybersecurity Dive*, July 19, 2022, https://www.cybersecuritydive.com/news/healthcare-data-breach-professional-finance-company-PFC/627508/.

4. 45 C.F.R. § 160.103.

5. 45 C.F.R. § 164.504.

6. 42 C.F.R. § 1003.100.

7. U.S. Department of Health & Human Services, Office of Inspector General, *Updated Special Advisory Bulletin on the Effect of Exclusion from Participation in Federal Health Care Programs*, May 8, 2013, https://oig.hhs.gov/exclusions/files/sab-05092013.pdf

8. U.S. Department of Health & Human Services, *Is A Covered Entity Liable for, or Required to Monitor, the Actions of Its Business Associates?*, last reviewed July 26, 2013, https://www.hhs.gov/hipaa/for-professionals/faq/236/covered-entity-liable-for-action/index.html.

9. "Business Associates," U.S. Department of Health & Human Services Office for Civil Rights, last reviewed May 24, 2019, https://www.hhs.gov/hipaa/for-professionals/privacy/guidance/business-associates/index.html. (*Emphasis added*)

10. U.S. Department of Health & Human Services, *Is A Covered Entity Liable for, or Required to Monitor, the Actions of Its Business Associates?*, last reviewed July 26, 2013, https://www.hhs.gov/hipaa/for-professionals/faq/236/covered-entity-liable-for-action/index.html.

11. U.S. Department of Health & Human Services, *Is A Covered Entity Liable for, or Required to Monitor, the Actions of Its Business Associates?*, last reviewed July 26, 2013, https://www.hhs.gov/hipaa/for-professionals/faq/236/covered-entity-liable-for-action/index.html.

12. 42 U.S.C. § 1320a-7b.

13. U.S. Department of Justice, "Department of Justice Settles Lawsuit Against Spine Device Distributor and its Owners Alleging Illegal Kickbacks to Physicians," news release, July 1, 2022, https://www.justice.gov/opa/pr/department-justice-settles-lawsuit-against-spine-device-distributor-and-its-owners-alleging.

14. 42 U.S.C. § 1395nn.

15. Centers for Medicare & Medicaid Services, *Current Law and Regulations*, last modified December 1, 2021,https://oig.hhs.gov/compliance/physician-education/fraud-abuse-laws/.

16. "Exclusion Authorities," U.S. Department of Health & Human Services, Office of Inspector General, last accessed December 5, 2022, https://oig.hhs.gov/exclusions/authorities.asp.

17. 42 U.S.C. § 1320a-7b(b).

18. https://oig.hhs.gov/exclusions/effects_of_exclusion.asp

19. U.S. Department of Health & Human Services, Office of Inspector General, "Updated Special Advisory Bulletin on the Effect of Exclusion from Participation in Federal Health Care Programs, Special Advisory Bulletin | May 8, 2013," https://oig.hhs.gov/exclusions/files/sab-05092013.pdf.

20. "Fraud and Abuse Laws," U.S. Department of Health & Human Services, Office of Inspector General, last accessed December 5, 2022, https://oig.hhs.gov/compliance/physician-education/fraud-abuse-laws/.

21. 42 U.S.C. § 1320a-7a.

22. 31 U.S.C. §§ 3729-3733.

23. 18 U.S.C. § 287.

24. "Fraud and Abuse Laws," U.S. Department of Health & Human Services Office of Inspector General, last accessed December 5, 2022, https://oig.hhs.gov/compliance/physician-education/fraud-abuse-laws/.https://oig.hhs.gov/compliance/physician-education/fraud-abuse-laws/.

25. 45 C.F.R. §§ 160.402, 160.404, 160.408, and 160.418.

Whistleblowers

Federal and State False Claims Acts

By Denise Atwood,[1] RN, JD, CPHRM

What Are Federal and State False Claims Acts in Relation to Whistleblowers?

The federal False Claims Act (FCA) prohibits healthcare providers from submitting claims for payment to the federal government that are fraudulent or false.[2] The U.S. Department of Health & Human Services (HHS) Office of the Inspector General (OIG), in consultation with the U.S. Department of Justice (DOJ) Office of the Attorney General (AG), reviews and determines whether state false claims laws can qualify for a federal incentive under section 1909 of the Social Security Act (SSA).[3] Those states with deemed or approved laws receive a 10% increase in the share of FCA amounts recovered under the law.

Once approved, the OIG sends a letter to the state attorney general saying it received, reviewed, and approved the state's request; under the requirements of section 1909 of the SSA, this provides financial incentive for the state to enact a law relating to the submission of fraudulent or false claims to the state Medicaid program. To date, 22 states have false claims laws that have been reviewed and approved, seven states have false claims laws and supplemental submissions that have not been approved, and 21 states have not submitted state false claims laws for OIG/AG review.

Qui Tam Relators/Whistleblowers

Under federal and state false claims acts, a qui tam relator is a private party or person who brings an action or lawsuit on the government's behalf. Here, the person and not the government is considered the plaintiff. A qui tam relator may also be known as a whistleblower under the FCA. Whistleblowers are typically private, public, or government employees who discover fraudulent activities during their employment. Examples of fraudulent business activities commonly reported by whistleblowers in healthcare may include knowingly over-billing the Medicaid program for a surgical service, knowingly including false documentation in medical records to decrease an obligation to pay money to the federal government, conspiring with others to get a false claim paid by Medicare for services that were not rendered, or avoiding the obligation to repay identified overpayments.

A private citizen whistleblower may choose this course of action (to bring a lawsuit) because of concerns that were presented to the healthcare organization that were not adequately addressed, remediated, or resolved by the organization. Similarly, an employee whistleblower may take this path for several reasons, including:

- Lack of a confidential internal reporting process;
- Fear of retaliation by the organization or job loss;
- Desire to improve billing services and charges to patients, expose the wrongdoing to protect the public, and improve the organization; or
- An internal report was made but not addressed, remediated, or resolved by the organization.

If the government prevails and the defendant is found to have defrauded a government program such as Medicare or Medicaid, then the plaintiff (the qui tam relater or whistleblower) receives a portion of the recovery from the defendant. If the whistleblower lives in a state where the OIG has approved the state law and the defendant is found guilty of defrauding the state Medicaid program, then the whistleblower is entitled to a 10% larger award from the defendant.

State False Claims Laws

As a compliance professional it is essential to familiarize yourself not only with the federal FCA laws but also with the state false claims laws that govern your healthcare organization and whistleblower claims. **Table 1. State False Claims Laws Reviewed and Approved by the OIG** lists states with federally approved false claims laws that would permit a 10% state recovery increase, and **Table 2. State False Claims Laws Reviewed and Not Approved by the OIG** lists states that have not received approval.[4]

Table 1. State False Claims Laws Reviewed and Approved by the OIG

State and Date Enacted	Link to Approval Letter
California (1/25/19)	https://oig.hhs.gov/documents/false-claims-act/277/California.pdf
Colorado (12/28/16)	https://oig.hhs.gov/documents/false-claims-act/278/Colorado.pdf
Connecticut (12/30/16)	https://oig.hhs.gov/documents/false-claims-act/279/Connecticut.pdf
Delaware (1/25/19)	https://oig.hhs.gov/documents/false-claims-act/280/Delaware.pdf
Georgia (1/25/19)	https://oig.hhs.gov/documents/false-claims-act/284/Georgia.pdf
Hawaii (10/1/19)	https://oig.hhs.gov/documents/false-claims-act/286/Hawaii.pdf
Illinois (12/5/17)	https://oig.hhs.gov/documents/false-claims-act/287/Illinois.pdf
Indiana (12/28/16)	https://oig.hhs.gov/documents/false-claims-act/252/Indiana.pdf
Iowa (12/28/16)	https://oig.hhs.gov/documents/false-claims-act/253/Iowa.pdf
Massachusetts (12/28/16)	https://oig.hhs.gov/documents/false-claims-act/255/Massachusetts.pdf
Minnesota (5/27/21)	https://oig.hhs.gov/documents/false-claims-act/369/Minnesota_False_Claims_Act_Letter_05272021.pdf
Montana (10/4/21)	https://oig.hhs.gov/documents/false-claims-act/1003/montana2021.pdf
Nevada (12/28/16)	https://oig.hhs.gov/documents/false-claims-act/261/Nevada.pdf
New York (1/25/19)	https://oig.hhs.gov/documents/false-claims-act/266/NewYork.pdf
North Carolina (10/26/18)	https://oig.hhs.gov/documents/false-claims-act/267/NorthCarolina.pdf
Oklahoma (6/6/17)	https://oig.hhs.gov/documents/false-claims-act/268/Oklahoma.pdf
Rhode Island (1/25/19)	https://oig.hhs.gov/documents/false-claims-act/269/RhodeIsland.pdf
Tennessee (12/28/16)	https://oig.hhs.gov/documents/false-claims-act/270/Tennessee.pdf
Texas (12/28/16)	https://oig.hhs.gov/documents/false-claims-act/271/Texas.pdf
Vermont (12/28/16)	https://oig.hhs.gov/documents/false-claims-act/272/Vermont.pdf
Virginia (8/14/18)	https://oig.hhs.gov/documents/false-claims-act/273/Virginia.pdf
Washington (8/14/18)	https://oig.hhs.gov/documents/false-claims-act/274/Washington.pdf

Table 2. State False Claims Laws Reviewed and Not Approved by the OIG

State and Date of Opinion	Link to Opinion Letter
Florida (3/21/11)	▪ https://oig.hhs.gov/documents/false-claims-act/281/Florida.pdf
Supplement (8/31/11)	▪ https://oig.hhs.gov/documents/false-claims-act/282/florida-supplement.pdf
Supplement 2 (12/28/16)	▪ https://oig.hhs.gov/documents/false-claims-act/283/florida-supplement2.pdf
Louisiana (11/15/11)	▪ https://oig.hhs.gov/documents/false-claims-act/254/Louisiana.pdf
Michigan (3/21/11)	▪ https://oig.hhs.gov/documents/false-claims-act/256/Michigan.pdf
Supplement (8/31/11)	▪ https://oig.hhs.gov/documents/false-claims-act/257/Michigan-supplement.pdf
Supplement 2 (12/28/16)	▪ https://oig.hhs.gov/documents/false-claims-act/258/Michigan-supplement2.pdf
New Hampshire (7/24/08)	▪ https://oig.hhs.gov/documents/false-claims-act/262/NewHampshire.pdf
Supplement (12/28/16)	▪ https://oig.hhs.gov/documents/false-claims-act/263/NewHampshire-supplement.pdf
New Jersey (3/21/11)	▪ https://oig.hhs.gov/documents/false-claims-act/264/NewJersey.pdf
New Mexico (7/27/08)	▪ https://oig.hhs.gov/documents/false-claims-act/265/NewMexico.pdf
Wisconsin (3/21/11)	▪ https://oig.hhs.gov/documents/false-claims-act/275/Wisconsin.pdf
Supplement (12/28/16)	▪ https://oig.hhs.gov/documents/false-claims-act/276/Wisconsin-supplement.pdf

The following is a list of states that have not submitted state laws for review and where there would be no additional recovery percentage under federal or state law. States without submissions for OIG review are:

- Alabama
- Alaska
- Arizona
- Arkansas
- Idaho
- Kansas
- Kentucky
- Maine
- Maryland
- Mississippi

- Missouri
- Nebraska
- North Dakota
- Ohio
- Oregon
- Pennsylvania

- South Carolina
- South Dakota
- Utah
- West Virginia
- Wyoming

Risk Area Governance

Public policy supports that persons who are aware of fraud against the government should report the fraud without fear of retaliation from the fraudulent actor, namely their employer. The FCA has been amended a few times since enactment of section 1909 of the SSA to help decrease retaliation. Combined, these acts amended bases for liability under the FCA and expanded certain rights of qui tam relators.

Fraud Enforcement and Recovery Act of 2009, Public Law 111–21

This law confirmed that in addition to bills submitted directly to the federal government for payment, the FCA applies to bills submitted to the government via a fiscal intermediary. The Fraud Enforcement and Recovery Act also expanded a whistleblower's right to bring an action against an organization for overpayment retention and the government's right to repayment.

Patient Protection and Affordable Care Act, Public Law 111–148

The Patient Protection and Affordable Care Act aligns with the FCA to protect employees from discrimination and retaliation for good faith reporting of potential violations of the act.

Dodd-Frank Wall Street Reform and Consumer Protection Act, Public Law 111–203

This law expanded protections for employee whistleblowers and prohibitions of retaliation against the employee, creating the right of an employee to file a retaliation complaint in federal court against an employer if the employee believes they were retaliated against.[5]

Deficit Reduction Act of 2005, Public Law 109–171

In addition to these federal FCA amendments, the Deficit Reduction Act includes relator protections for FCA violations and, as a condition of payment, requires organizations that make or receive $5 million or more annually in Medicaid payments to establish and implement written policies addressing FCA and other laws aimed at detecting or preventing fraud and abuse. Additionally, Section 6032(c) states that if an employer maintains an employee handbook, then it must include FCA information, including rights of employees to be protected as whistleblowers and the organization's policies for detecting or preventing fraud, waste, and abuse.[6]

Section of the DRA of 2005 (as of 02/28/2006)	CMS Implementing Document	Subject	Effective Date
6032	State Medicaid Director Letter and State Plan Amendment	Employee education about false claims recovery. Requires any entity (i.e., those that receive or make annual Medicaid payments under the state plan of at least $5 million) to provide federal False Claims Act education to their employees.	01/1/07

Recent Changes

In October 2021, the DOJ, as part of the increased focus on FCA enforcement, announced it is launching the Civil Cyber-Fraud Initiative. This initiative makes FCA whistleblowers and relators critical parts of the government's cybersecurity strategy as it is encouraging cyber fraud. This includes such things as failing to report cybersecurity breaches, failing to conduct due diligence to ensure business associates implement sufficient and sound cyber practices, or claims by an organization that they provide cybersecurity services when they do not.

According to the *National Law Review*, "Centering the DOJ's Civil Cyber-Fraud Initiative around the False Claims Act highlights the importance of whistleblowers in bringing malfeasance to the government's attention. For reporting fraud, whistleblowers can receive 15–25% of the government's recovery."[7] This recent change shows the importance the DOJ is placing on fraud reports and government enforcement in tandem with whistleblowers and relators.

In fiscal year 2020, the DOJ recovered more than $2.2 billion from FCA cases.[8] As private citizens we applaud relators and the government for these large recoveries. However, as compliance professionals, it bears mentioning that whistleblower actions have become a cottage industry. To mitigate organizational risk, it is imperative to have a well-developed compliance program that supports a culture of open reporting and nonretaliation. The goal of open communication channels is to allow employees to report potential FCA matters and for the organization to have the opportunity to correct potential fraud, waste, abuse, and overpayments internally, instead of externally via a lawsuit.

Common Compliance Risks

Lack of Employee Trust in Internal Reporting Systems or Processes

Employees may not feel comfortable coming forward to disclose or discuss potentially fraudulent business activities, because they do not trust their employer's reporting system or the process. They may fear that the systems/processes will not protect their identities and that they will be exposed within the organization. It is also possible that employees will become relators that report outside of the organization if they found internal reporting channels ineffective or unsatisfactory. Consequently, an effective hotline that is periodically tested as part of internal auditing and monitoring is an important feature of an effective compliance program.

Fear of Retaliation or Job Loss

While the employee may not want to participate or further the fraudulent or illegal activities, they may not feel comfortable reporting the activities either due to fear of retaliation or fear of job loss. Compliance programs should include thorough policies written in everyday language, not legal jargon, on how to report questionable activities without fear of retaliation. Some organizations may also choose to include nonretaliation policies under the human resources department, because the employee may feel they are more protected from retaliation if human resources staff, in addition to compliance staff, are involved. Moreover, the compliance and human resources policies and related employee education should include the compliance hotline number and employee confidentiality when reporting, in addition to the organization's nonretaliation policy and practice.

Fear of Exposure or Lack of Government Action

The government may not intervene or the identity of the whistleblower may be disclosed. If the whistleblower/relator files a lawsuit, the DOJ will investigate the claim. During the investigation, the whistleblower's employer is unaware of the investigation and the whistleblower's identity. If the government decides it will intervene in the lawsuit, the government takes over the case, including the cost of trying the case. In some cases, if the government wants to try to reach a settlement, the identity of the whistleblower may be disclosed. However, government intervention happens in a small percentage of qui tam cases.[9] If the government does not intervene, the relator must pay for the legal costs. This means the organization is still exposed and at risk because the relator may continue with the lawsuit against the organization independent of the government. Prevention is the best way to mitigate organizational risks—with a comprehensive compliance program and educating staff on the program, the policies, and the reporting process. The goal is to address employee concerns internally before the employee feels the need to report the concerns externally.

Addressing Compliance Risks

As a compliance professional, it is important to develop a compliance program that includes staff education on the FCA, how to report concerns about noncompliance, the organization's nonretaliation policies, and the anonymous reporting mechanism (such as a hotline). The compliance program must be engaging and evolving, and not simply one that exists on paper or online. It is important for staff to genuinely feel comfortable that the organization embraces an environment of open reporting and nonretaliation.

During any investigation, a compliance professional must also ensure that the identity of staff involved remains confidential. It is important to demonstrate to the healthcare organization's staff if they report a concern or complaint that it will be promptly addressed, and they will remain anonymous. The same is true if you work for an organization and become aware of a qui tam action. As a compliance professional, do your best to ensure the whistleblower remains anonymous.

According to the American Bar Association (ABA), you can ask that the whistleblower's identity be kept anonymous for the protection of the person and their family: "Lawmakers and media have generally honored that request. But in terms of federal law, as the ABA Legal Fact Check points out, the whistleblower has more assurance that his or her job, rather than identity, will be protected."[10] If the identity of the whistleblower becomes known, as a compliance professional, work with the healthcare organization's human resources department to ensure there is no retaliation against the whistleblower/employee. No retaliation includes no discrimination, no harassment, and no termination.

Possible Penalties

Originally, the FCA provided any person who knowingly submitted false or fraudulent claims to the government was liable for double the government's damages plus a penalty. The FCA has been amended several times, and now providers in violation of the FCA are liable for treble (or up to three times) actual damages plus a penalty that is linked to inflation.[11]

Finally, courts have begun to weaken the whistleblower protection provision of the FCA by construing it to prohibit only retaliatory acts that occur during employment, leaving those who report potential actions post-employment vulnerable to retaliation. For example, in *Potts v. Ctr. for Excellence in Higher Educ., Inc.*, the Tenth Circuit held that the FCA's antiretaliation provision excluded relief for retaliatory acts that occurred after the employee left employment.[12]

However, in United States ex rel. Felten v. William Beaumont Hospital, the Sixth Circuit rejected *Potts* with an opinion that upholds the purpose of the FCA's whistleblower protection provision and supports FCA protection of former employees alleging post-termination retaliation.[13]

As noted previously, the Dodd-Frank Wall Street Reform and Consumer Protection Act expanded whistleblower protections included broadened prohibitions against retaliation. Following the passage of the act, the Securities and Exchange Commission (SEC) implemented rules that enabled the SEC to take legal action against employers who retaliate against whistleblowers. According to the SEC, "This generally means employers may not discharge, demote, suspend, harass, or in any way discriminate against an employee in the terms and conditions of employment who has reported conduct to the SEC that the employee reasonably believed violated the federal securities laws."[14]

The takeaway for compliance professionals is the law is either divided or developing around whistleblower protections and penalties. Currently there appears to be more protections available for federal employees than private employees. It would be prudent to understand if and how wrongful termination laws in your state protect FCA whistleblowers.

Compliance Resources

U.S. Department of Health & Human Services, Office of the Inspector General

Consumer Alerts
This resource allows citizens to remain aware of and report a variety of scams in which fraudsters use technology to impersonate official government personnel from HHS or OIG.

https://oig.hhs.gov/fraud/consumer-alerts/

State False Claims Act Reviews
In addition to addressing which states have been approved for incentives, this resource provides information on how states can qualify for an incentive under section 1909 of the Social Security Act.

https://oig.hhs.gov/fraud/state-false-claims-act-reviews/

Whistleblower Protection Coordinator
This resource addresses the Whistleblower Protection Enhancement Act of 2012 and established a whistleblower ombudsman in the OIG to educate department employees about prohibitions on retaliation for whistleblowing, as well as employees' rights and remedies if anyone retaliates against them for making a protected disclosure (i.e., whistleblowing).

https://oig.hhs.gov/fraud/whistleblower/

U.S. Department of Justice

The False Claims Act

This resource provides an overview and links to FCA recovery statistics, reporting guidance, and contact information.

https://www.justice.gov/civil/false-claims-act

Risk Takeaways

Main points of interest:

- Impact of federal and state false claims laws on whistleblowers
- Whistleblowers often fear retaliation and do not feel comfortable reporting non-compliance internally
- Whistleblowers can potentially receive large monetary awards for reporting non-compliance to the government

Areas to watch:

- Developing area of law with regard to whistleblower protections for current and former employees
- Compliance reporting systems
- Organizational culture related to retaliation

Laws that apply:

- False Claims Act (FCA), 31 U.S.C. §§ 3729–3733
- State false claims laws
- Deficit Reduction Act of 2005, Public Law 109-171
- Fraud Enforcement and Recovery Act of 2009 (FERA), Public Law 111-21
- Patient Protection and Affordable Care Act (ACA), Public Law 111–148
- Dodd-Frank Wall Street Reform and Consumer Protection Act, Public Law 111–203

Addressing compliance risks:

- Have a clear and accessible nonretaliation policy
- Have an anonymous reporting system that employees are aware of
- Educate staff on the organization's stance of nonretaliation

Endnotes

1. **Denise Atwood** is the chief risk officer for District Medical Group Inc. and vice president of the District Medical Group Insurance Company both in Phoenix, Arizona. She is also the owner of Denise Atwood PLLC, where she provides compliance, risk, ethics, and medical-legal consulting, writing, and public speaking.

2. U.S. Department of Justice, "The False Claims Act: A Primer," accessed December 7, 2021, https://www.justice.gov/sites/default/files/civil/legacy/2011/04/22/C-FRAUDS_FCA_Primer.pdf.

3. "State False Claims Act Reviews," U.S. Department of Health & Human Services Office of Inspector General, accessed December 7, 2021, https://oig.hhs.gov/fraud/state-false-claims-act-reviews/.

4. "State False Claims Act Reviews," U.S. Department of Health & Human Services Office of Inspector General.

5. "State False Claims Act Reviews," U.S. Department of Health & Human Services Office of Inspector General.

6. Centers for Medicare & Medicaid Services, "Deficit Reduction Act of 2005 All CMS Provisions as of February 28, 2006," accessed December 7, 2021, https://www.cms.gov/Regulations-and-Guidance/Legislation/LegislativeUpdate/Downloads/DRA0307pdf.

7. Tycko & Zavareei LLP, "Calling all Cybersecurity Whistleblowers: DOJ Wants You to Report Cyber Fraud," *National Law Review* XI, no. 286 (October 13, 2021), https://www.natlawreview.com/article/calling-all-cybersecurity-whistleblowers-doj-wants-you-to-report-cyber-fraud.

8. U.S. Department of Justice, "Justice Department Recovers Over $2.2 Billion from False Claims Act Cases in Fiscal Year 2020," news release, January 14, 2021, https://www.justice.gov/opa/pr/justice-department-recovers-over-22-billion-false-claims-act-cases-fiscal-year-2020.

9. "Qui Tam Lawsuits and Whistleblower Rights," Justia, last reviewed October 2021, https://www.justia.com/employment/retaliation/qui-tam-whistleblower/.

10. American Bar Association, "With White House whistleblower, protection only goes so far," ABA News, December 23, 2019, https://www.americanbar.org/news/abanews/aba-news-archives/2019/12/whistleblower-laws-fact-check/.

11. "The False Claims Act," U.S. Department of Justice, updated January 14, 2021, https://www.justice.gov/civil/false-claims-act.

12. *Potts v. Ctr. for Excellence in Higher Educ., Inc.,* 908 F.3d 610, 618 (10th Cir. 2018).

13. *United States ex rel. Felten v. William Beaumont Hospital,* No. 20-1002, 2021 WL 1204981 (6th Cir. Mar. 31, 2021).

14. "Office of the Whistleblower, Whistleblower Protections," U.S. Securities and Exchange Commission, modified July 21, 2021, https://www.sec.gov/whistleblower/retaliation.

Healthcare Compliance Glossary

accountable care organization (ACO): Groups of doctors, hospitals, and other healthcare providers that voluntarily come together to provide coordinated high-quality care to their Medicare patients.

additional documentation request (ADR): If a claim is selected for review or needs additional documentation, an ADR letter is sent to the provider requesting that documentation and/or medical records be submitted. The response must be submitted within a specific time frame to the requesting Medicare contractor identified on the letter for review and payment determination.

adjusted average per capita cost (AAPCC): Centers for Medicare & Medicaid Services' best estimate for the amount of money it costs to care for Medicare recipients in a year under fee-for-service Medicare in a given area.

adjusted community rating: Under the Affordable Care Act (ACA), insurers can't raise premiums based on health status, medical claims, gender, or most of the other factors that they had previously used to determine rates prior to ACA implementation.

Advance beneficiary notice of noncoverage (ABN): The ABN (Form CMS-R-131) is issued by providers (including independent laboratories, home health agencies, and hospices), physicians, practitioners, and suppliers to Original Medicare (fee-for-service) beneficiaries when Medicare payment is expected to be denied. In certain situations, the ABN transfers potential financial liability to the Medicare beneficiary.

advisory opinion (of the OIG): A legal opinion issued by the Office of Inspector General (OIG) to one or more requesting parties about the application of the OIG's fraud and abuse authorities to the party's existing or proposed business arrangement. An OIG advisory opinion is legally binding on the Department of Health & Human Services and the requesting party or parties. It is not binding on any other government department or agency.

affiliated covered entity (ACE): Under the Health Insurance Portability and Accountability Act, legally separate covered entities under common ownership or control have an option to be treated as a single legal entity by choosing to designate as ACE. This enables the entities to share information in a way that would otherwise be impermissible (use vs. disclosure).

Agency for Healthcare Research and Quality: Agency within the Department of Health & Human Services (HHS) whose mission is to produce evidence to make healthcare safer, higher quality, more accessible, equitable, and affordable and to work with HHS and other partners to make sure that the evidence is understood and used.

Anti-Kickback Statute (AKS): Federal criminal statute that prohibits the exchange (or offer to exchange) of anything of value in an effort to induce (or reward) the referral of federal healthcare program business.

attestation: The affirmation by signature, usually on a printed form, that the action outlined has been accomplished by the individual signing (e.g., the individual has read the code of conduct and agreed to adhere to its principles).

attorney–client privilege: A legally accepted policy that communication between a client and attorney is confidential in the course of the professional relationship and that such communication cannot be disclosed without the consent of the client. Its purpose is to encourage full and frank communication between attorneys and their clients.

audit, baseline: A systematic inspection of records, policies, and procedures with the goal to establish a set of benchmarks for comparison for future inspections.

audit, concurrent: An inspection of records, policies, and procedures at a given point in time in which identified potential problems are audited as they arise (e.g., documentation reviewed and codes substantiated prior to dropping a bill).

audit, retrospective: An audit of historical events (e.g., paid claims audits, executed contracts, etc.). How far back it goes can be determined by specific milestones or a legal statute (e.g., new or revised laws, new departments, new system, etc.).

Balanced Budget Act of 1997: Legislation containing major reform of the Medicare and Medicaid programs, especially in the areas of home health and patient transfers. It also mandated permanent exclusion from participation in federally funded healthcare programs of those convicted of three healthcare-related crimes.

bankruptcy: Legal status of person or entity that cannot repay the debts it owes to creditors.

benchmarking: The measurement of performance against best-practice standards.

best practices: Generally recognized superior performance by organizations in operational and/or financial processes.

business associate: A business associate is a person or entity that performs certain functions or activities that involve the use or disclosure of protected health information (PHI) on behalf of, or provides services to, a covered entity. A member of the covered entity's workforce is not a business associate. A covered healthcare provider, health plan, or healthcare clearinghouse can be a business associate of another covered entity. The Privacy Rule lists some of the functions or activities, as well as the particular services, that make a person or entity a business associate if the activity or service involves the use or disclosure of PHI. The types of functions or activities that may make a person or entity a business associate include payment or healthcare operations activities, as well as other functions or activities regulated by the Administrative Simplification Rules. Business associate functions and activities include claims processing or administration; data analysis, processing, or administration; utilization review; quality assurance; billing; benefit management; practice management; and repricing. Business associate services are legal, actuarial, accounting, consulting, data aggregation, management, administrative, accreditation, and financial. See the definition of "business associate" at 45 C.F.R. § 160.103 .

business associate agreement (BAA): The Health Insurance Portability and Accountability Act (HIPAA) Privacy Rule requires that, before protected health information (PHI) can be shared between a covered entity and a business associate, the business associate must sign a written agreement that gives satisfactory assurances that it will not use or disclose PHI in a manner that contradicts the Privacy Rule requirements. HIPAA also requires a business associate agreement to define the function of the business associate and the limitations on their uses and disclosures of PHI. The business associate agreement must also define what will happen to the PHI held by the business associate upon termination of the agreement.

Caremark International derivative litigation: The 1996 U.S. civil settlement of Caremark International Inc. in which an imposed corporate integrity agreement precluded Caremark from providing healthcare in certain forms for a period of five years. Also suggests that the failure of a corporate director to attempt in good faith to institute a compliance and ethics program in certain situations may be a breach of a director's fiduciary obligation.

Centers for Medicare & Medicaid Services (CMS): Previously known as the Health Care Financing Administration, the agency that administers the Medicare, Medicaid, and state Children's Health Insurance programs within the Department of Health & Human Services.

Certified Professional Coder (CPC): A coder who has satisfied certification requirements as established by the American Academy of Professional Coders.

Civil Monetary Penalties Law (CMPL): Regulations that apply to any claim for an item or service that was not provided as claimed or that was knowingly submitted as false and that provide guidelines for the levying of fines for such offences.

Civilian Health and Medical Program of the Uniformed Services: A federal program providing healthcare coverage to families of military personnel and others.

Clinical Laboratory Improvement amendments: Federal regulations that include federal standards applicable to all US facilities or sites that test human specimens for health assessment or to diagnose, prevent, or treat disease.

Committee of Sponsoring Organizations of the Treadway Commission (COSO): A joint initiative of five private-sector organizations that are dedicated to providing thought leadership through the development of frameworks and guidance on enterprise risk management, internal control, and fraud deterrence.

compliance: Adherence to the laws and regulations passed by official regulating bodies as well as general principles of ethical conduct. In the United States, such regulating bodies include the U.S. Congress, federal executive departments and federal agencies and commissions, and corresponding state-level entities.

conflict of interest: A conflict of interest occurs when an individual's private interest interferes in any way—or even appears to interfere—with the interests of the corporation as a whole. A conflict situation can arise when an employee, officer, or director takes action or has interests that may make it difficult to perform their company work objectively and effectively.

Consolidated Omnibus Budget Reconciliation Act (COBRA): Continuation health coverage legislation that gives employees and families who lose health benefits the right to choose to continue group health benefits provided by their group health plan for limited periods of time under certain circumstances.

Consumer Assessment of Healthcare Providers & Systems: An initiative by the federal government for Medicare & Medicaid the aim of which is to develop a set of satisfaction surveys built off of a core of standardized items and supplemented by additional targeted elements to make the surveys both adaptable to different subpopulation and suitable for making some cross-group comparisons.

corporate integrity agreement (CIA): A negotiated settlement between an organization and the government in which the provider accepts no liability but must agree to implement a strict plan of government-supervised corrective action.

covered entities: Health plans, healthcare clearinghouses, and healthcare providers that electronically transmit health information connected with transactions (generally regarding billing and payment for services or insurance coverage) that are guided by the U.S. Department of Health & Human Services standards.

culpability score: Part of the U.S. Sentencing Commission guidelines for the sentencing of organizations, a system that adds points for aggravating factors and subtracts points for mitigating factors in the determination of fines imposed for fraud or abuse.

Current Procedural Terminology (CPT®): A publication of the American Medical Association that lists and assigns codes to procedures and services performed by physicians.

de-identified information: Health information from a patient's health record that has been stripped of information that could be used to identify the patient, such as Social Security number, name, and email addresses, among other items, as defined in the Health Insurance Portability and Accountability Act.

Department of Health & Human Services (HHS): The department of the executive branch of the US government with healthcare accountabilities, including responsibility for the Public Health Service, the Centers for Medicare & Medicaid Services, and the Social Security Administration.

Department of Justice (DOJ): The Department of Justice works to enforce federal law, to seek just punishment for the guilty, and to ensure the fair and impartial administration of justice. It accomplishes this with various agencies under its umbrella.

Department of Labor (DOL): This federal agency administers and enforces laws and regulations that govern workplace activities, including wages and overtime pay (through the Wage and Hour Division), workers' compensation, workplace safety and health (through the Occupational Safety and Health Administration), employee benefits, certain nonimmigrant visa programs, etc.

designated health services: Under Stark Law, the services covered are:

(i) Clinical laboratory services. (ii) Physical therapy, occupational therapy, and outpatient speech-language pathology services. (iii) Radiology and certain other imaging services. (iv) Radiation therapy services and supplies. (v) Durable medical equipment and supplies. (vi) Parenteral and enteral nutrients, equipment, and supplies. (vii) Prosthetics, orthotics, and prosthetic devices and supplies. (viii) Home health services. (ix) Outpatient prescription drugs

(x) Inpatient and outpatient hospital services.

(2) Except as otherwise noted in this subpart, the term "designated health services" or DHS means only DHS payable, in whole or in part, by Medicare. DHS do not include services that are paid by Medicare as part of a composite rate (for example, SNF Part A payments or ASC services identified at § 416.164(a)), except to the extent that services listed in paragraphs (1)(i) through (1)(x) of this definition are themselves payable under a composite rate (for example, all services provided as home health services or inpatient and outpatient hospital services are DHS).

Designated record set:

1. A group of records maintained by or for a covered entity that is:
   i. The medical records and billing records about individuals maintained by or for a covered health care provider;
   ii. The enrollment, payment, claims adjudication, and case or medical management record systems maintained by or for a health plan; or
   iii. Used, in whole or in part, by or for the covered entity to make decisions about individuals
2. For purposes of this paragraph, the term record means any item, collection, or grouping of information that includes protected health information and is maintained, collected, used, or disseminated by or for a covered entity.

diagnosis-related groups (DRG): Classifications of diagnoses determined by the average cost of treating a particular condition, regardless of the number of services rendered or the length of patient stay. Medicare reimbursement is assigned by DRG.

disclosure: The release, transfer, provision of, access to, or divulging in any other manner of information outside the entity holding the information.

Drug Supply Chain Security Act: Outlines critical steps to build an electronic, interoperable system to identify and trace certain prescription drugs as they are distributed in the United States, identify illegitimate drugs, and facilitate recalls.

durable medical equipment (DME): Owned or rented medical equipment that is placed in the home of an insured person to facilitate treatment and/or rehabilitation. DME generally consists of items that can withstand repeated use. DME is primarily and customarily used to service a medical purpose and is usually not useful to a person in absence of illness or injury.

durable medical equipment, prosthetics, orthotics, and supplies (DMEPOS): An industry that sells or rents certain medical equipment that is closely controlled by the Centers for Medicare & Medicaid Services.

electronic health record (EHR): A digital version of a patient's health record.

electronic protected health information (ePHI): Health Insurance Portability and Accountability Act covered entities are required to protect ePHI from data breach or loss and improper use or disclosure. See also: *protected health information (PHI)*.

Emergency Medical Treatment and Labor Act (EMTALA): Federal law ensuring public access to emergency services regardless of ability to pay. Medicare-participating hospitals that offer emergency services must provide a medical screening examination (MSE) when a request is made for examination or treatment for an emergency medical condition (EMC), including active labor, regardless of an individual's ability to pay. Hospitals must provide stabilizing treatment for patients with EMCs.

Employee Retirement Income Security Act (ERISA): Established in 1974, ERISA set up plan design, funding, and administration requirements for employee pension plans to protect the rights of plan participants and beneficiaries, preempting certain state laws relating to employee benefit plans, including medical plans self-insured by employers.

enterprise risk management (ERM): A risk-based approach to managing an enterprise; a framework to identify, assess, mitigate, and communicate risk in an integrated approach to help influence decision-making and strategic development.

Equal Employment Opportunity Commission (EEOC): US agency created in 1964 to end discrimination based on race, religion, sex, or national origin in employment. The commission reviews and investigates charges of discrimination and, if found to be true, attempts remedy through conciliation or legal means.

False Claims Act (FCA): Originally adopted by the U.S. Congress in 1863 during the Civil War to discourage suppliers from overcharging the federal government, legislation that prohibits anyone from knowingly submitting or causing to be submitted a false or fraudulent claim.

Family Educational Rights and Privacy Act (FERPA): The federal act that provides for the protection of student educational records for both K-12 students and secondary education students.

Federal Drug Administration (FDA): A federal agency of the Department of Health & Human Services that is responsible for protecting the public health by ensuring the safety, efficacy, and security of human and veterinary drugs, biological products, and medical devices; ensuring the safety of our nation's food supply, cosmetics, and products that emit radiation; and regulating the manufacturing, marketing, and distribution of tobacco products to protect the public health and to reduce tobacco use by minors.

Federal Sentencing Guidelines for Organizations (FSGO): Enacted November 1, 1991, by the U.S. Sentencing Commission. Organizations with compliance and ethics programs meeting defined standards earn credit toward reduced penalties if employees engage in wrongdoing.

financial assistance policy: A requirement for 501(c)(3) hospitals to maintain tax-exempt status by establishing a written financial assistance policy governing billing and collection of certain eligible individuals.

fiscal intermediary/fiduciary intermediary: A person or organization that, under agreement with the Department of Health & Human Services under part A of Medicare, processes claims, provides services, and issues payments on behalf of private, federal, and state health benefit programs or other insurance organizations.

Fraud Enforcement and Recovery Act (FERA): A federal law enacted in 2009 that expands the reach of the False Claims Act that prohibits defrauding the government, including Medicare and Medicaid payments.

General Services Administration (GSA): The federal agency that manages the federal government's property and records, including the construction and operation of buildings and procurement and distribution of supplies, among other functions.

good clinical practice (GCP): Food and Drug Administration regulations governing the conduct of clinical trials describe GCPs for studies with both human and nonhuman animal subjects.

good laboratory practice (GLP): Rules for conducting nonclinical laboratory studies that support or are intended to support applications for research or marketing permits for products regulated by the Food and Drug Administration. May also apply to conducting studies related to health effects, environmental effects, and chemical fate testing to ensure the quality of data for the Toxic Substances Control Act (TSCA).

healthcare: Care, services, or supplies related to the health of an individual, including but not limited to: (1) Preventive, diagnostic, rehabilitative, maintenance, or palliative care, counseling, service, assessment, or procedure with respect to a physical or mental condition or functional status of an individual or that affects the structure or function of the body; and (2) Sale or dispensing of a drug, device, equipment, or other item pursuant to a prescription.

healthcare clearinghouse: A public or private entity, including a billing service, repricing company, community health management information system or community health information system, and 'value-added' networks and switches, that does either of the following functions:

1. Processes or facilitates the processing of health information received from another entity in a nonstandard format or containing nonstandard data content into standard data elements or a standard transaction;
2. Receives a standard transaction from another entity and processes or facilitates the processing of health information into nonstandard format or nonstandard data content for the receiving entity.

Healthcare Common Procedure Coding System (HCPCS): A set of codes used by Medicare that describes services and procedures; HCPCS Level 1 codes are Current Procedural Terminology (CPT) codes, Level II codes are for suppliers and non-CPT codes, and Level III are locally set codes.

Health Care Financing Administration (HCFA): Created in 1977 to combine under one administration the oversight of the Medicare program, the federal portion of the Medicaid program, and related quality assurance activities. HCFA was renamed the Centers for Medicare & Medicaid Services in July 2001.

Health Care Fraud Prevention and Enforcement Action Team (HEAT): Auditing team focused on preventing fraud and abuse in the Medicare and Medicaid programs by identifying fraud perpetrators and those abusing the system.

healthcare operations: Any of the following activities of the covered entity to the extent that the activities relate to covered functions:

1. Conducting quality assessment and improvement activities, including outcomes evaluation and development of clinical guidelines, provided that the obtaining of generalizable knowledge is not the primary purpose of any studies resulting from such activities; population-based activities relating to improving health or reducing healthcare costs, protocol development, case management, and care coordination; contacting of healthcare providers and patients with information about treatment alternatives; and related functions that do not include treatment;
2. Reviewing the competence or qualifications of healthcare professionals; evaluating practitioner and provider performance; health plan performance; conducting training programs in which students, trainees, or practitioners in areas of healthcare learn under supervision to practice or improve their skills as healthcare providers;

training of nonhealthcare professionals; accreditation, certification, licensing, or credentialing activities;

3. Underwriting, premium rating, and other activities relating to the creation, renewal, or replacement of a contract of health insurance or health benefits and ceding, securing, or placing a contract for reinsurance of risk relating to claims for healthcare (including stop-loss insurance and excess of loss insurance), provided that the requirements of 45 C.F.R. § 164.514(g) are met, if applicable;

4. Conducting or arranging for medical review, legal services, and auditing functions, including fraud and abuse detection and compliance programs;

5. Business planning and development, such as conducting cost management– and planning-related analyses related to managing and operating the entity, including formulary development and administration, development or improvement of methods of payment or coverage policies; and

6. Business management and general administrative activities of the entity, including, but not limited to:

   a. Management activities relating to implementation of and compliance with the requirements of this subchapter;

   b. Customer service, including the provision of data analyses for policy holders, plan sponsors, or other customers, provided that protected health information is not disclosed to such policy holder, plan sponsor, or customer;

   c. Resolution of internal grievances;

   d. The sale, transfer, merger, or consolidation of all or part of the covered entity with another covered entity, or an entity that, following such activity, will become a covered entity, and due diligence related to such activity; and

   e. Consistent with the applicable requirements of 45 C.F.R. § 164.514 , creating de-identified health information or a limited data set, and fundraising.

healthcare provider: A provider of services (as defined in section 1861(u) of the Social Security Act, 42 U.S.C. § 1395x(u)), a provider of medical or health services (as defined in section 1861(s) of the Social Security Act, 42 U.S.C. § 1395x(s)), and any other person or organization who furnishes, bills, or is paid for healthcare services or supplies in the normal course of business.

health information: Any information, oral or recorded, in any form or medium, that:

1. Is created or received by a health care provider, health plan, public health authority, employer, life insurer, school or university, or health care clearinghouse; and

2. Relates to the past, present, or future physical or mental health or condition of an individual; the provision of health care to an individual; or the past, present, or future payment for the provision of health care to an individual.

health information management (HIM): HIM professionals work in a various settings and job titles in the healthcare industry. They often serve in roles connecting clinical, operational, and administrative functions.

Health Information Technology for Economic and Clinical Health (HITECH) Act: Part of the American Recovery and Reinvestment Act of 2009. HITECH Act is designed to encourage healthcare providers to adopt health information technology that establishes electronic health records in a standardized manner that protects patients' private health information. In addition, it requires the Department of Health & Human Services to modify the Health Insurance Portability and Accountability Act Privacy, Security, and Enforcement rules to strengthen health information privacy and security protections.

Health Information Trust Alliance (HITRUST): Organization that established a Common Security Framework that can be used by all organizations that create, access, store, or exchange sensitive and/or regulated data.

Health Insurance Portability and Accountability Act (HIPAA) of 1996: A federal law stating that a covered entity may not use or disclose protected health information, except as permitted or required.

health maintenance organization (HMO): A managed care organization that aims to lower healthcare costs by contracting with a network of providers to provide services for reduced cost. Through contracts with providers, the HMO can predict costs by shifting risk to the provider for services used by members. The HMO manages costs by limiting members to seeing approved providers and controlling access to specialty services.

health plan: Per 45 C.F.R. § 160.103 , an individual or group plan that provides, or pays the cost of, medical care (as defined in section 2791(a)(2) of the Public Health Service Act, 42 U.S.C. § 300gg-91(a)(2)) of the Act:

1. A health plan includes the following, singly or in combination:
    i.   A group health plan, as defined in this section.
    ii. A health insurance issuer, as defined in this section.
    iii. A health maintenance organization, as defined in this section.
    iv. Part A and B of the Medicare program under title XVIII of the Act.
    v.   The Medicaid program under title XIX of the Act.
    vi. An issuer of a Medicare supplemental policy.
    vii. An issuer of a long-term care policy, excluding a nursing home fixed indemnity policy.
    viii. An employee welfare benefit plan or any other arrangement that is established or maintained for the purpose of offering or providing health benefits to the employees of two or more employers.
    ix. The healthcare program for active military personnel under title 10 of the United States Code.
    x.   The veterans' healthcare program under 38 U.S.C. § 17 .
    xi. The Indian Health Services program.
    xii. The Federal Employees Health Benefits Program.
    xiii. An approved state child health plan under title XXI of the Act.
    xiv. A high-risk pool established under state law to provide health insurance coverage or comparable coverage to eligible individuals.
    xv. Any other individual or group plan, or combination of individual or group plans, that provides or pays for the costs of medical care.

2. A health plan excludes:
   i. Any policy, plan, or program to the extent that it provides, or pays for the cost of, excepted benefits that are listed in section 2791(c)(1) of the Public Health Service Act, 42 U.S.C. § 300gg-91(c)(1) ; and
   ii. A government-funded program (other than one listed in paragraph (1) (i)-(xvi) of this definition);

      A. Whose principal purpose is other than providing, or paying the cost of, healthcare; or
      B. Whose principal activity is:
         i. The direct provision of healthcare to persons; or
         ii. The making of grants to fund the direct provision of healthcare to persons.

Health Plan Management System (HPMS): Centers for Medicare & Medicaid Services' web-enabled information system that serves a critical role in the operations of the Medicare Advantage, Part D, and accountable care organization programs.

Health Resources and Services Administration (HRSA): Agency within the Department of Health & Human Services. Is the primary federal agency for improving access to healthcare by strengthening the healthcare workforce, building health communities, and achieving health equity. HRSA's programs provide healthcare to people who are geographically isolated and/or economically or medically vulnerable.

home health agency (HHA): An organization primarily engaged in providing skilled nursing services and other therapeutic services; has policies established by a group of professionals (associated with the agency or organization), including one or more physicians and one or more registered professional nurses, to govern the services it provides. For purposes of Part A home health services under Title XVIII of the Social Security Act, the term "home health agency" does not include any agency or organization that is primarily for the care and treatment of mental diseases.

hospice: According to the Social Security Act, Title 18, § 1861(dd), "items and services provided to a terminally ill individual by, or by others under arrangements made by, a hospice program under a written plan (for providing such care to such individual) established and periodically reviewed by the individual's attending physician and by the medical director (and by the interdisciplinary group described in paragraph (2)(B)) of the program."

hospital payment monitoring system: A Centers for Medicare & Medicaid Services requirement that involves monitoring and detecting unacceptable reimbursement claims and ensuring accuracy of claims.

hybrid covered entity: A covered entity that does both covered and noncovered functions under the Health Insurance Portability and Accountability Act Privacy Rule has the option to restrict the application of the Privacy Rule to certain parts of its organization by designating healthcare components.

Immediate Corrective Action Required: A Centers for Medicare & Medicaid Services audit finding; the result of noncompliance with specific requirements that has the potential to cause significant beneficiary harm.

independent review organization (IRO): Part of corporate integrity agreements; provide objective, unbiased determinations on what the root cause of a particular treatment was, or whether there was a medical necessity for a treatment.

individually identifiable health information (IIHI): Information that is a subset of health information, including demographic information collected from an individual, and:

1. Is created or received by a healthcare provider, health plan, employer, healthcare clearinghouse; and
2. Related to the past, present, or future physical or mental health or condition of an individual; the provision of healthcare to an individual; or the past, present, or future payment for the provision of healthcare to an individual; and
    i. That identifies the individual; or
    ii. With respect to which there is a reasonable basis to believe that the information can be used to identify the individual.

International Classification of Diseases, 10th Revision (ICD-10): A coding of diseases, signs and symptoms, abnormal findings, complaints, social circumstances, and external causes of injury or diseases, as classified by the World Health Organization

International Classification of Diseases, 10th Revision, Clinical Modification (ICD-10-CM): A two-part classification system in current use for coding patient medical information and for classifying patients into diagnosis-related groups (DRGs) for Medicare and other third-party payers. The first part provides a comprehensive list of diseases with corresponding codes compatible with the World Health Organization's list of disease codes. The second part contains procedure codes independent of the disease codes. Published by the Commission on Professional and Hospital Activities (CPHA) and by the federal government.

International Classification of Functioning, Disability and Health: An international classification system that describes and measures health and disability and includes environmental factors.

The Joint Commission: An independent, nongovernmental nonprofit organization that certifies and accredits healthcare organizations for quality.

low probability of compromise (LoProCo): In Health Insurance Portability and Accountability Act, "low probability" is based on 4 factors:

1. What was the nature and extent of the protected health information (PHI) involved, including the types of identifiers in the information and the likelihood of reidentification?
2. To whom was the unauthorized information disclosed?

3. Was the PHI actually acquired or viewed?
4. What was the extent to which the risk to PHI has been mitigated?

managed care: Provides for the delivery of Medicaid health benefits and additional services through contracted arrangements between state Medicaid agencies and MCOs that accept a set per-member per-month payment for these services.

managed care organization (MCO): An organization that combines the functions of health insurance, delivery of care, and administration. An umbrella term for health plans that provide healthcare in return for a predetermined monthly fee and coordinate care through a defined network of physicians and hospitals. Examples: health maintenance organization, point of service, preferred provider organization.

Medicaid: A program under the Department of Health & Human Services that provides low- or no-cost basic health coverage for low-income adults and children.

Medicaid Fraud Control Unit (MFCU): Single entity of state government annually certified by the secretary of the Department of Health & Human Services responsible for conducting a state initiative aimed at investigating and prosecuting providers that defraud the Medicaid program.

Medicaid Integrity Program (MIP): Created by the Deficit Reduction Act of 2005 as the first comprehensive federal strategy to prevent and reduce provider fraud, waste, and abuse in the Medicaid program. The program has two responsibilities: hire contractors to review provider activities and support states in their efforts to combat fraud and abuse.

Medicare: A health insurance program administered by the Centers for Medicare & Medicaid Services under the Department of Health & Human Services. Medicare is comprised of several parts, including hospital insurance; medical insurance; and prescription drug insurance for people over 65, people under 65 with disabilities, and people of all ages with end-stage renal disease.

monitoring: Monitoring is a quality control tool for determining whether study activities are being carried out as planned so that deficiencies can be identified and corrected.

National Uniform Billing Committee (NUBC): Brought together by the American Hospital Association (AHA) in 1975, NUBC includes the participation of all the major national provider and payer organizations. The NUBC was formed to create a uniform billing form and standard data set for institutional providers and payers to use for handling healthcare claims.

Occupational Safety And Health Administration (OSHA): A component of the Department of Labor that develops and administers standards relating to the well-being of workers at the job site, develops and issues regulations in this area, conducts investigations and inspections to determine status of compliance with safety and health standards and regulations, and issues citations and proposes penalties for noncompliance.

Office for Civil Rights (OCR): An agency within in the Department of Health & Human Services that enforces civil rights claims and the Health Insurance Portability and Accountability Act Privacy and Security rules.

Office for Human Research Protections (OHRP): Provides leadership in the protection of the rights, welfare, and well-being of subjects involved in research conducted or supported by the Department of Health & Human Services.

Office of Inspector General (OIG): The Office of Inspector General of the Department of Health & Human Services (HHS) fights waste, fraud, and abuse in Medicare, Medicaid, and more than 300 other HHS programs.

Office of Inspector General (OIG) Compliance Program Guidance: Guidelines issued by the Office of Inspector General for the suggested development of compliance programs. Compliance program guidances have been issued for hospitals; home health agencies; clinical laboratories; third-party billers; the durable medical equipment, prosthetics, orthotics, and supplies industry; hospice providers; physician practices; research (draft); skilled nursing; and Medicare+Choice organizations.

Office of the Medicaid Inspector General: Independent agencies within individual state departments of health tasked with improving the integrity of state Medicaid programs by coordinating the fraud and abuse activities for multiple state agencies that provide Medicaid-funded services.

organized healthcare arrangements (OHCA): (1) A clinically integrated setting in which individuals typically receive healthcare from more than one healthcare provider; (2) an organized system of healthcare in which more than one covered entity participates and in which the participating covered entities hold themselves out to the public as participating in a joint arrangement and participate in joint activities; (3) a group health plan and a health insurance issuer or health maintenance organization (HMO) with respect to such group health plan, but only with respect to protected health information created or received by such health insurance issuer or HMO that relates to individuals who are or who have been participants or beneficiaries in such group health plan; (4) a group health plan and one or more other group health plans each of which are maintained by the same plan sponsor; or (5) the group plans described in (4) and health insurance issuers or HMOs with respect to such group health plans, but only with respect to protected health information created or received by such health insurance issuers or HMOs that relates to individuals who are or have been participants or beneficiaries in any such group health plans.

Patient Protection and Affordable Care Act (PPACA or ACA): Commonly referred to as the Affordable Care Act or Obamacare. Enacted to increase the affordability and quality of health insurance, lower the uninsured rate by expanding public and private insurance coverage, and reduce the cost of healthcare for individuals and the government. The law requires insurance companies to cover all applicants within minimum standards and offer the same rates regardless of preexisting conditions or sex.

Patient Safety and Quality Improvement Act: Law enacted in 2005 that created patient safety organizations to collect, aggregate, and analyze confidential information reported by healthcare providers in order to identify patterns of failures and propose measures to eliminate patient safety risks and hazards.

payment:

1. The activities undertaken by:
    i. [A] health plan to obtain premiums or to determine or fulfill its responsibility for coverage and provision of benefits under the health plan; or
    ii. A health care provider or health plan to obtain or provide reimbursement for the provision of health care; and
2. The activities in paragraph (1) of this definition relate to the individual to whom health care is provided and include, but are not limited to:
    i. Determinations of eligibility or coverage (including coordination of benefits or the determination of cost sharing amounts), and adjudication or subrogation of health benefit claims;
    ii. Risk adjusting amounts due based on enrollee health status and demographic characteristics;
    iii. Billing, claims management, collection activities, obtaining payment under a contract for reinsurance (including stop-loss insurance and excess of loss insurance), and related health care data processing;
    iv. Review of health care services with respect to medical necessity, coverage under a health plan, appropriateness of care, or justification of charges
    v. Utilization review activities, including precertification and preauthorization of services, concurrent and retrospective review of services; and
    vi. Disclosure to consumer reporting agencies of any of the following protected health information relating to collection of premiums or reimbursement:
        a. Name and address;
        b. Date of birth;
        c. Social security number;
        d. Payment history;
        e. Account number; and
        f. Name and address of the health care provider and/or health plan.

physician: Under the Stark Law, a doctor of medicine or osteopathy, a doctor of dental surgery or dental medicine, a doctor of podiatric medicine, a doctor of optometry, or a chiropractor, as defined in section 1861 of the Act. A physician and the professional corporation of which they are a sole owner are the same for purposes of this subpart.

Physicians at Teaching Hospitals (PATH): A Department of Health & Human Services/ Office of Inspector General nationwide review of compliance with rules governing physicians at teaching hospitals. Records were reviewed to determine adequate physician involvement in patient care according to IL373, the Medicare rule that dictates that an attending physician must be present when supervising an intern or resident in order to bill for the care provided by the intern or the resident.

Physician Payments Sunshine Act (PPSA): Part of the Affordable Care Act that requires manufacturers of drugs, medical devices, and biologicals that participate in the federal healthcare programs to report certain payments and items of value given to physicians and teaching hospitals. Centers for Medicare & Medicaid Services implements the program and calls it the Open Payments Program.

Physician Quality Reporting System (PQRS): A Centers for Medicare & Medicaid Services reporting tool that provides incentives and penalties to eligible professionals for reporting quality information.

Physician Self-Referral Law (Stark Law): The Omnibus Budget Reconciliation Act (OBRA) of 1989 bans physicians from referring lab specimens to any entity with which the physician has a financial relationship. Amended by OBRA '90 to exclude financial relationships between hospitals and physicians unrelated to clinical laboratory services. OBRA '93 (Stark II) expanded to include 10 other designated healthcare services.

Program for Evaluating Payment Patterns Electronic Report (PEPPER): A comparative data report that summarizes one provider's Medicare claims data statistics for services vulnerable to improper Medicare payments.

Prospective Payment System (PPS): The system for paying for services for Medicare patients (see *DRGs*) whereby patients are classified into categories for which prices are negotiated or determined in advance.

protected health information (PHI): Individually identifiable health information:

1. Except as provided in paragraph (2) of this definition, that is:
   i. Transmitted by electronic media;
   ii. Maintained in any medium described in the definition of electronic media at § 162.103 of this
   iii. subchapter; or
   iv. Transmitted or maintained in any other form or media.
2. Protected health information excludes individually identifiable health information in:
   i. Education records covered by FERPA;
   ii. Records described at 20 U.S.C. § 1232g(a)(4)(B)(iv) ; and
   iii. Employment records held by a covered entity in this role as an employer.
3. That is or has been electronically maintained or electronically transmitted by a covered entity, or transmitted or maintained in any other form or media.

Provider Statistical & Reimbursement Report (PS&R): Centers for Medicare & Medicaid Services' system-generated reports of statistical and reimbursement data applicable to the processed and finalized Medicare Part A claims.

qui tam: Legal term for the mechanism in the federal False Claims Act (FCA) that allows persons and entities with evidence of fraud against federal programs or contracts to sue the wrongdoer on behalf of the government. A qui tam action is one brought under the FCA by a private plaintiff (relator) on behalf of the federal government (rather than by the government itself).

recovery audit contractors (RAC): The contractors that carry out Recovery Audit Program activities.

relator: The legal term for a person who is the whistleblower in a qui tam lawsuit brought under the False Claims Act.

remuneration: In the Anti-Kickback Statute, the transfer of anything of value, directly or indirectly, overtly or covertly, in cash or in kind.

Risk Adjustment Data Validation (RADV): The process of verifying that diagnosis codes submitted for payment by a Medicare Advantage organization are supported by medical record documentation for an enrollee.

risk assessment: A systematic process for identifying and assessing the risks involved with doing business that may cause harm to an organization that results in noncompliance with a regulation.

risk-based monitoring: A mix of centralized monitoring and on-site monitoring. Monitoring activities should focus on preventing or mitigating important and likely sources of error in conduct, collection, and reporting of critical data and processes necessary for human subject protection and study data integrity.

safe harbors: Explicit regulatory exceptions to otherwise legally prohibited conduct. Federal safe harbor regulations specify certain joint ventures and other arrangements concerning hospitals and/or physicians that do not violate Medicare fraud and abuse laws.

self-reporting: Having identified actual wrongdoing, the organization informs the government. Although not protected from civil or criminal action under the False Claims Act, providers disclosing fraud are advised in the government self-disclosure protocol that timely self-reporting of wrongdoing may offer mitigating factors in potential penalties and/or fines.

skilled nursing facility (SNF): An institution or a distinct part of an institution, such as a skilled nursing home or rehabilitation center, that has a transfer agreement in effect with one or more participating hospitals and that:

A. Is primarily engaged in providing skilled nursing care and related services for residents who require medical or nursing care, or rehabilitation services for the rehabilitation of injured, disabled, or sick persons, and

B. Meets the requirements for participation in section 1819 of the Social Security Act and in regulations in 42 C.F.R. §§ 483.1–483.95 .

treatment: The provision, coordination, or management of healthcare and related services by one or more healthcare providers, including the coordination or management of healthcare by a healthcare provider with a third party; consultations between healthcare providers relating to a patient; or the referral of a patient for healthcare from one healthcare provider to another.

treatment, payment, and healthcare operations (TPO): The primary areas where healthcare workers have a need to use patients' protected health information.

upcoding: Coding for a higher level than the documentation warrants.

use: With respect to individually identifiable health information, the sharing, employment, application, use, examination, or analysis of such information within an entity that maintains such information.

workforce: Employees, volunteers, trainees, and other persons whose conduct, in the performance of work for the covered entity, is under the direct control of such entity, whether or not they are paid by the covered entity.

Healthcare Compliance and CMS Acronyms

Acronym	Term
A&R	Audit & Reimbursement
AAFP	American Academy of Family Physicians
AAHA	American Association of Homes for the Aging
AAHP	American Association of Health Plans
AAMC	Association of American Medical Colleges
AAO	American Academy of Ophthalmology
AAP	American Academy of Pediatrics
AAPC	American Association of Professional Coders
AAPCC	Adjusted Average Per Capita Cost
ABA	American Bar Association
ABN	Advanced Beneficiary Notice
ABR	American Board of Radiology
ABS	Annual Beneficiary Summary
AC	Actual Charge
ACA	Patient Protection & Affordable Care Act (also PPACA)
ACC	Automated Change Control
ACE	Affiliated Covered Entity
ACE	(Carrier) Automated Claims Examination
ACER	Annual Contractor Evaluation Report
ACMP	Audit/Civil Monetary Penalties
ACMS	Advanced Cost Management Systems
ACO	Accountable Care Organization
ACR	Adjusted Community Rate
AD	Admitting Diagnosis
ADA	American Dental Association
ADA	American Dietetic Association
ADA	Americans with Disabilities Act of 1990
ADAMHA	Alcohol, Drug Abuse & Mental Health Administration
ADG	Ambulatory Diagnostic Group

Acronym	Term
ADG-HOSDOM	Ambulatory Diagnostic Group Hospital Dominant
ADHA	American Dental & Hygienists Association
ADJ	Adjusted Claim
ADMC	Advance Determination of Medicare Coverage
ADT	Admission/Discharge Transfer
AFEHCT	American Federation of Electronic Health Care Transactions
AFEHCT	Association for Electronic Health Care Transactions
AFHHA	American Federation of Home Health Agencies
AHA	American Hospital Association
AHCA	American Health Care Association
AHIMA	American Health Information Management Association
AHRQ	Agency for Healthcare Research and Quality
AIC	Amount In Controversy
AKS	Anti-Kickback Statute
ALBN	Amount of Last Billing Notice
ALC	Alternate Level of Care
ALOS	Average Length of Stay
ALT	Average Length of Treatment
AMA	American Medical Association
AMASDS	Asset Management & Automated Software Distribution System
AMCS	Automated Medical Coding System
AMRA	American Medical Records Association
AN	Account Number (also A/N)
ANA	American Nurses Association
AOPA	American Orthotic & Prosthetic Association
APA	American Pharmaceutical Association
APA	American Psychiatric Association
APACHE	Acute Physiology & Chronic Health Evaluation
APC	Ambulatory Payment Class
APG	Ambulatory Patient Group
APG	Ambulatory Payment Group
APM	Admission Pattern Monitoring
APM	Audit Priority Matrix
APMA	American Podiatric Medical Association
APME	Advisory Panel on Medicare Education
APR - DRG	all payer refined - diagnosis related groups
APS	Acquisition Planning Schedule

Acronym	Term
AQI	Audit Quality Initiative
AQL	Acceptable Quality Level
AQRP	Audit Quality Review Program
AR	Accounts Receivable
ASCA	Administrative Simplification Compliance Act
ASCII	American Standard Code for Information Interchange (see ANSCII)
ASCW	Audit Selection Criteria Worksheet
ASH	Assistant Secretary for Health
ASHP	American Society of Health Systems Pharmacists
ASHP	American Society of Hospital Pharmacists
ASHRM	American Society of Healthcare Risk Management
ASIM	American Society of Internal Medicine
ASTER	Automated System for Transaction Exception Resolution
ATARS	Audits Tracking & Reporting System
BA	Business Associate
BAC	Billing Action Code
BMACS	Part B Medicare Automated Claims Systems
BOME	Bureau of Medical Examiners
BP	Business Partner
BPST	Bill Processing System Test
BQAS	Part B Quality Assurance System
BSR	(Part B) Bill Summary Records
BUR	Billing Update Record
CA	Claims Analyst
CAH	Critical Access Hospital
CAHPS	Consumer Assessment of Health Plan Survey
CAP	Corrective Action Plan
CAPS	Claims Automated Processing System (SSA MBR)
CAR	Corrective Action Review
CB	Consolidated Billing
CB	Cost Benefit
CBA	Cost/Benefit Analysis
CBR	Cost Based Reimbursement
CBSS	Customer Billing Services System
CC	Claims Control
CCI	Correct Coding Initiative
CCP	Comprehensive Compliance Program

Acronym	Term
CCP	Coordinated Care Plans
CCR	Coverage Compliance Reviews
CDC	Center for Disease Control
CDM	(Hospital) Charge Description Master (Files)
CDOC	Covered Days of Care
CDRG	Children's Diagnosis Related Groups
CE	Covered Entity
CERT	Comprehensive Error Rate Testing
CHAMPUS	Civilian Health and Medical Program of the Uniformed Services
CHC	Community Health Center
CHC	Comprehensive Health Center
CHC	Continuous Home Care
CHCC	Center for Hospital & Community Care
CHCL	Center for Health Care Law
CHDS	(National) Charge Distribution System
CHHA	Certified Home Health Agency
CHHC	Continuous Home Health Care
CHIM	Center for Healthcare Information Management
CHIME	College of Healthcare Information Management Executives
CHIP	Child Health Insurance Program
CHO	Community Health Organization
CIN	Common Identification Number
CIP	Claims In Process
CLCCP	Comprehensive Limiting Charge Compliance Program
CLFS	Clinical Laboratory Fee Schedule
CLIA	Clinical Laboratory Improvement Act (of 1965) (Amendments 1988)
CLIA	Clinical Laboratory Interstate Act (or Amendments)
CLOE	(Carrier) Claims Only Entry System
CLT	Certified Lab Technician
CMHC	Community Mental Health Center (or Clinic)
CMN	Certified Medical Necessity
CMP	Civil Monetary Penalty
CMPL	Civil Monetary Penalty Law
CMPL	Civil Monetary Penalty Liability
CMPTS	Civil Monitory Penalty Tracking System
CMS	Centers for Medicare & Medicaid Services
CN	Claim Number (also C/N)

Acronym	Term
CNH	Community Nursing Home
CO	Change Order
COBRA	Consolidated Omnibus Budget Reconciliation Act (of 1985)
COI	Conflict of Interest
COP	Conditions of Participation
CORF	Comprehensive Outpatient Rehabilitation Facility
CORTS	Calculation of Overpayment Recovery Timeliness System
COSO	Commission of Sponsoring Organizations
CP	Claims Processing
CPAP	Common Provider Audit Program
CPAS	Claims Processing Assessment System
CPM	Claims Processing Manual
CPT	Common Procedural Terminology
CPT	Current Procedural Terminology
CPT-4	Current Procedural Terminology, Version 4
CQI	Continuous Quality Improvement
CR	Change Request
CR	Cost Report
CRAG	Contractor Risk Assessment Guide
CREP	Cost Report Evaluation Program
CRF	Change Request Form
CS	Claims Services
DATAMED	Medicaid Quality Control System
DEA	Drug Enforcement Administration (or Agency)
DEFRA	Deficit Reduction Act of 1984
DHS	Designated Health Services (Stark Law)
DME	Durable Medical Equipment
DME MAC	Durable Medical Equipment Medicare Administrative Contractor
DMEFS	Durable Medical Equipment Fee Schedule
DMEPOS	Durable Medical Equipment Prosthetic, Orthotics, and Supplies
DMERC	Durable Medical Equipment Regional Carrier
DOD	Department of Defense
DOJ	Department of Justice
DRG	Diagnostic Related Group (patients with similar illness)
DSCSA	Drug Supply Chain Security Act
DSH	Disproportionate Share Hospital
DSM	Diagnostic & Statistical Manual

Acronym	Term
DSM–IV	Diagnostic & Statistical Manual of Mental Disorders, 4th Edition
EACH	Essential Access Community Hospital
ED	Emergency Department
EFT	Electronic Funds Transfer
EFTS	Electronic File Transfer System (GHP large volume transfer to HDC)
EFTS	Electronic Funds Transfer System
EH	Emergency Hospital
EMB	Eligible Medicare Beneficiary
EMEVS	Electronic Medicaid Eligibility Verification System
EMT	Emergency Medical Technician
EMTALA	Emergency Medical Treatment and Active Labor Act or Emergency Medical Treatment and Labor Act
EOB	Explanation of Benefits
EOC	Episode of Care
EOMB	Explanation of Medical Benefits
ePHI	Electronic Protected Health Information
ERISA	Employee Retirement Income Security Act
ERM	Enterprise Risk Management
EVS	Eligibility Verification System
EWU	Equivalent Work Unit
F&A	Fraud & Abuse
FAH	Federation of American Hospitals
FAHS	Federation of American Health Systems
FAP	Financial Assistance Policy
FBI	Federal Bureau of Investigation
FCA	False Claims Act
FDA	Food & Drug Administration
FERA	Fraud Enforcement Recovery Act
FERPA	Family Education Privacy Rights Act
FFS	Fee for Service
FMV	Fair Market Value
FOIA	Freedom of Information Act
FQHC	Federally Qualified Health Center
FSGO	Federal Sentencing Guidelines for Organizations
FTC	Federal Trade Commission
FTP	File Transfer Protocol
GAO	Government Accounting Office
GCP	Good Clinical Practice

Acronym	Term
GHP	Group Health Plan
GHPPS	Group Health Plan Payment System
GLP	Good Laboratory Practice
GPO	Group Purchasing Organization
GSA	General Services Administration
HAASC	Hospital Affiliated Ambulatory Surgical Center
HBP	Hospital Based Physician
HCE	Hybrid Covered Entity
HCFA	Health Care Financing Administration
HCPC	HCFA Common Procedure Code
HCPCS	Healthcare Common Procedure Coding System
HCQII	Health Care Quality Improvement Initiative
HCQIP	Health Care Quality Improvement Program
HEAT	Health Care Fraud Prevention and Enforcement Action Team
HFMA	Healthcare Financial Management Association
HHA	Home Health Agency
HHABN	Home Health Advanced Beneficiary Notice
HHC	Home Health Care
HHQI	Home Health Quality Initiative
HHS	Department of Health and Human Services
HHS	Home Health Services
HIM	Health Information Management
HIPAA	Health Insurance Portability & Accountability Act of 1996
HPMP	Hospital Payment Monitoring Program
HPMS	Health Plan Management System
HIPPS	Health Insurance Prospective Payment System, a CMS payment code system
HITECH	Health Information Technology for Economic and Clinical Health Act
HITRUST	Health Information Trust Alliance
HMO	Health Maintenance Organization
HMO/CMP	HMO Competitive Medical Plan
HMODR	CMS Medicare Outpatient Data Review
HRSA	Health Resources and Services Administration
ICAR	Immediate Corrective Action Required
ICD	International Classification of Diseases
ICD-10-CM	International Classification of Diseases, Tenth Revision, Clinical Modification

Acronym	Term
ICD-10-PCS	International Classification of Diseases, 10th Revision, Procedure Coding System
ICF	International Classification of Functioning, Disability and Health
ICR	Incomplete Claims Reject
IP/SNF	Inpatient SNF
IRB	Institutional Review Board
IRF	Inpatient Rehabilitation Facility
IRO	Independent Review Organization
IRP	Incentive Reward Program
JAMA	Journal of the American Medical Association
JC/JCAHO	Joint Commission or Joint Commission on Accreditation of Healthcare Organizations
L-H	Labor Hour
LCD	Local Coverage Determination
LEIE	List of Excluded Individuals & Entities
LoProCo	Low Probability of Compromise (in HIPAA)
LTC	Long Term Care
LTCF	Long Term Care Facility
LTCU	Long Term Care Unit
M&M	Medicare & Medicaid
M+C	Medicare + Choice
M+C NSF	Medicare + Choice National Standard Format
M+CO	Medicare + Choice Organization
MA	Medicaid Agency
MA	Medicare Advantage (formerly Medicare+Choice)
MA BSF	Medicare Advantage Benefit Stabilization Fund
MA-PD	Medicare Advantage Prescription Drug Plans
MAC	Medicare Administrative Contractor
MAO	Medicare Advantage Organization
MAPD	Medicare Advantage Prescription Drug
MBD	Medicaid Beneficiary Database
MBN	Medicare Benefit Notice
MCE	Medicare Code Editor
MCM	Medicare Carrier Manual
MC	Medicare
MCO	Managed Care Organization
MCPS	Medicare (Part A) Claims Processing System (Veritus)

Acronym	Term
MCS	Mandatory Claim Submission System
MDC	Major Diagnosis Category
MDH	Medicare Dependent Hospital
MDSRH	Medicare Dependent Small Rural Hospital
MED-ED	Medical Education
MEDB	Medicare Part B
MEDPAC	Medicare Payment Advisory Commission
MFCU	Medicaid Fraud Control Unit
MFS	Medicare Fee Schedule
MFSDB	Medicare Fee Schedule Database
MHB	Maximum Hospital Benefit
MIP	Medicare Integrity Program
MMCQI	Medicare Managed Care Quality Improvement
MN	Medical Necessity
MPD	Medicare Provider Database
MPDB	Medicare Prescription Drug Beneficiaries
MPFS	Medicare Physician Fee Schedule
MQA	Medicare Quality Assurance (CWF data validation)
MQAG	Medicare Quality Advisory Group
MQC	Medicaid Quality Control
MQM	Medicare Quality Monitor
MR/UR	Medical Review / Utilization Review
MRRS	Medicaid Retrospective Reimbursement System
MSHIP	Medicare Supplemental Health Insurance Programs
MTAG	Medicare Technical Advisory Group
MTOP	Multiple Type of Provider
NAATP	National Association of Addiction Treatment Providers
NACHC	National Association of Community Health Centers
NACHRI	National Association of Children's Hospitals & Related Institutions
NAHC	National Association for Home Care
NAHDO	National Association of Health Data Organizations
NAMES	National Association of Medical Equipment Suppliers
NAPH	National Association of Public Hospitals
NAPHS	National Association of Psychiatric Health Systems
NARA	National Association of Rehabilitation Agencies
NARF	National Association of Rehabilitation Facilities
NAS	National Academy of Sciences
NASMD	National Association of State Medicaid Directors

Acronym	Term
NCCLS	National Council of Clinical Laboratory Services
NCD	National Coverage Determination
NCHS	National Center for Health Statistics
NCQA	National Committee for Quality Assurance
NCQHC	National Committee for Quality Health Care
NDC	National Drug Code
NDPS	National Drug Pricing System
NH	Nursing Home
NHA	Nursing Home Administrator
NHB	National Health Board
NHO	National Hospice Organization
NIA	National Institute on Aging
NIAID	National Institute of Allergies & Infectious Diseases
NIAMSD	National Institute of Arthritis & Musculoskeletal & Skin Diseases
NIDA	National Institute on Drug Abuse
NIDDKD	National Institute of Diabetes, Digestive & Kidney Diseases
NIDR	National Institute of Dental Research
NIH	National Institutes of Health
NIMBE	Not Including Medicare Benefits Exhausted
NIMH	National Institute of Mental Health
NIMMS	National Integrated Medicaid Management System
NINDS	National Institute of Neurological Disorders & Stroke
NIOSH	National Institute for Occupational Safety & Health
NIST	National Institute of Standards & Technology
NLN	National League of Nursing
NMC	National Maintenance Contractor
NME	National Medical Enterprises
NMEP	National Medicare Education Program
NMFA	National Medicare Fraud Alert
NMFAI	National Medicaid Fraud & Abuse Institute
NMUD	National Medicare Utilization Database
NODMAR	Notice of Discharge & Medicare Appeal Rights
NOU	Notice of Utilization
NP	Nurse Practitioner
NP/PA	Nurse Practitioners / Physician Assistants
NPF	National Provider File
NPI	National Provider Identifier

Acronym	Term
NPRM	National Provider Reimbursement Manual
NRC	National Research Council
NTH	NonTransplant Hospital
NUBC	National Uniform Billing Committee
OAC	OASIS Automation Coordinator
OASIS	Outcome & Assessment Information Set
OBQI	Outcome Based Quality Improvement
OBQIM	Outcome Based Quality Improvement Management
OBQM	Outcome Based Quality Monitoring
OBRA	Omnibus Budget Reconciliation Act
OCE	Outpatient Code Editor (System)
OCESAA	Omnibus Consolidated & Emergency Supplemental Appropriations Act for FY 1999
OCFAA	Office of Civil Fraud & Administrative Adjudication
OCR	Office for Civil Rights
ODL	Outpatient Diagnostic Laboratory
OEP	Open Enrollment Period
OFCCP	Office of Federal Contract Compliance Programs
OGE	Office of Government Ethics
OHCA	Organized Health Care Arrangements
OHRP	Office for Human Research Protections
OIG	Office of the Inspector General
OLTC	Other Long Term Care
OMIG	Office of the Medicaid Inspector General
OP	Outpatient
OP	Overpayment
OPAC	Online Payment & Accounting Collection (System) (Treasury)
OPD	OutPatient Department
OPDIV	OPerating DIVision
ORF	Outpatient Rehabilitation Facility
P&E	Parenteral & Enteral
P&T	Pharmaceutical and Therapeutic
P/B	Provider / Beneficiary
PARD	Provider Audit & Reimbursement Department
PARL	Physician/Supplier Assignment Rate List
PART A	Medicare Hospital Insurance
PART B	Medicare Supplementary Medical Insurance

Acronym	Term
PAYERID	Payer Identification (national provider identifier initiative)
PBC	Premium Billing Code
PBGC	Pension Benefit Guaranty Corp.
PBIS	PerformanceBased Incentive System
PBP	Provider Based Physician
PCH	Primary Care Hospital
PCP	Primary Care Physician (or Provider)
PCPR	Provider Claims Processing Requirements
PDMA	Prescription Drug Marketing Act of 1988
PDP	Prescription Drug Plan
PEBTAG	Provider Electronic Billing Technical Advisory Group
PEPPER	Program for Evaluating Payment Patterns Electronic Report
PFCRA	Program Fraud Civil Remedies Act
PHI	Protected Health Information
PHRMA	Pharmaceutical Manufacturers and Researchers of America
PHY/SUP	Physician/Supplier
PIG	Program Integrity Group, OFM, CMS
PIM	Medicare Program Integrity Manual
PIPDCG	Principal Inpatient Diagnostic Cost Group
POC	Plan of Care
POL	Physician Office Laboratories
POMS	Program Operations Manual System (SSA) (formerly Claims Manual CM)
POR	Provider Overpayment Recovery
POR	Provider Overpayment Report
PORS	Provider Overpayment Recovery System
PORS	Provider Overpayment Reporting System
POT	Plan of Treatment
PPACA	Patient Protection & Affordable Care Act (also ACA)
PPC	Processing Payment Cycle
PPG	Primary Care Physician Groups
PPS	Prospective Payment System (Medicare Part A)
PPSA	Physician Payment Sunshine Act
PQRS	Physician Quality Reporting System
PRM	Provider Reimbursement Manual
PRMDS	Provider Minimum Data Set
PRS	Payment Reconciliation System
PS&RR	Provider Statistical & Reimbursement Report

Acronym	Term
PSPRICE	Physician Fee Schedule System
PTA	Part A (of Medicare)
PTAMUS	Part A Medicare Utilization System
PTB	Part B (of Medicare)
QMB	Qualified Medicare Beneficiaries
RA	Risk Assessment
RAAC	Risk Adjustment Advisory Committee
RAC	Reimbursement Advisory Committee
RADV	Risk Adjustment Data Validation
RAPS	Risk Adjustment Processing System
RAPS	Risk Adjustment Processing System
RAS	Risk Adjustment System
RCL	Routine Cost Limit
RCP	Reasonable Charge Pricing
RCT	Randomized Clinical Trials
RH	Rural Hospital
RHC	Rural Health Center
RHC	Rural Health Claim
RHC	Rural Health Clinic
RHP	Rebundling of Hospital Payment
RMFA	Restricted Medicare Fraud Alert
ROAR	Recovery of Overpayments Accounting & Reporting System (SSA)
ROAR	Regional Office Automating Representatives for Managed Care Operations (ROAR for MCO)
RPCH	Regional Primary Care Hospital
RPCH	Rural Primary Care Hospital
RTP	Return To Provider (or Plan)
SA	Settlement Agreement
SMG	State Medicaid Group
SMM	State Medicaid Manual
SNC	Skilled Nursing Care
SNF	Skilled Nursing Facility
SOM	State Operations Manual
SRA	Significant Regulatory Actions
SSA	Social Security Act
SSA	Social Security Administration
SSA	State Survey Agency

Acronym	Term
SSH	Short Stay Hospital
T18	Title XVIII of the Social Security Act (Medicare)
T19	Title XIX of the Social Security Act (MAA (Medicaid))
UPL	Upper Payment Limit (Medicaid)
UR	Utilization Review
URAC	Utilization Review Accreditation Commission
WHO	World Health Organization
WPA	Whistleblower Protection Act

Index

[Note: Page numbers followed by an *f* or *s* indicate a figure or sample resource, respectively.]

E

ABOUT THE

HEALTH CARE
COMPLIANCE ASSOCIATION

Established in 1996, Health Care Compliance Association (HCCA) is a member-based association for healthcare compliance professionals. Serving more than 12,000 members across the country, we are dedicated to enabling the lasting success and integrity of those working in or supporting healthcare organizations.

In 2004, we created Society of Corporate Compliance and Ethics (SCCE) to serve cross-industry compliance and ethics needs. The associations incorporated in 2011 as Society of Corporate Compliance and Ethics & Health Care Compliance Association (SCCE & HCCA).

——SCCE & HCCA MAJOR FUNCTIONS——

- To promote the highest standards in compliance programs—from their introduction and development to continuing maintenance
- To create high-quality educational training events and resources to support individual professional growth
- To provide a forum for interaction and information exchange for the compliance community